ETHICS IN PSYCHOLOGY
AND THE MENTAL HEALTH PROFESSIONS

ETHICS IN PSYCHOLOGY AND THE MENTAL HEALTH PROFESSIONS

Standards and Cases

Third Edition

GERALD P. KOOCHER
Dean, Health Studies, Simmons College

PATRICIA KEITH-SPIEGEL
Voran Honors Distinguished Professor of Social
and Behavioral Sciences (Emerita), Ball State University

OXFORD
UNIVERSITY PRESS

2008

OXFORD
UNIVERSITY PRESS

Oxford University Press, Inc., publishes works that further
Oxford University's objective of excellence
in research, scholarship, and education.

Oxford   New York
Auckland   Cape Town   Dar es Salaam   Hong Kong   Karachi
Kuala Lumpur   Madrid   Melbourne   Mexico City   Nairobi
New Delhi   Shanghai   Taipei   Toronto

With offices in
Argentina   Austria   Brazil   Chile   Czech Republic   France   Greece
Guatemala   Hungary   Italy   Japan   Poland   Portugal   Singapore
South Korea   Switzerland   Thailand   Turkey   Ukraine   Vietnam

Published by Oxford University Press, Inc.
198 Madison Avenue, New York, New York 10016

www.oup.com

Oxford is a registered trademark of Oxford University Press

Library of Congress Cataloging-in-Publication Data
Koocher, Gerald P.
   Ethics in psychology and the mental health professions : standards and
cases / Gerald P. Koocher, Patricia Keith-Spiegel.—3rd ed.
        p. cm.
   Includes bibliographical references and index.
   ISBN-13: 978-0-19-514911-1 (cloth : alk. paper)
   ISBN-10: 0-19-509201-5 (cloth : alk. paper)
   1. Psychologists—Professional ethics.   2. Psychology—Research—Moral and ethical aspects.
3. Psychology—Study and teaching—Moral and ethical aspects.   4. Psychology—Standards.
I. Keith-Spiegel, Patricia.   II. Title.
   BF76.4.K46 2008
   174'.915—dc22   2007027873

15 14 13 12 11

Printed in the United States of America
on acid-free paper

Dedicated to our colleagues who demonstrate the courage to act with integrity.

Preface

To be good is noble, but to teach others to be good
is nobler and less trouble.

Mark Twain

China executed the former head of its State Food and Drug Administration for taking $800,000 in bribes to approve the export of tainted and untested products.

After 4 years of stonewalling and legalistic warfare, the Los Angeles Catholic diocese paid $660 million to over 500 victims of sexual abuse by clergy members.

Despite being well aware that Pat Tillman, football star turned soldier, had died as the result of "friendly fire," Army generals approved awarding him two medals for heroism based on a detailed account of a supposed battle—which the generals knew had never taken place—to cover up the embarrassment of the incident.

A man infected with a resistant strain of tuberculosis set off on a European honeymoon, putting other airline passengers at risk of infection, and justified his actions in part by noting that no one told him he posed a risk to others.

"Family values" congressman admits to visiting brothels.

Former surgeon general testifies to pressure to put politics over science that interfered with his public health mission.

President of World Bank steps down after scandal involving playing favorites with his girlfriend's employment.

County auditor convicted of first-degree grand larceny for stealing over $1 million from the state.

These are but a few of the thousands of scandals taken from headlines as we complete writing our third edition of this book. It certainly feels that our Western society has taken a spin for the worse since our first two editions (mid-1980s and late 1990s). Whether it was 9/11, the ever-breaking revelations that some corporate, political, and religious leaders placed far more value in servicing their own needs than the health and welfare of the people they are supposed to be serving, the erosion of personal privacy and other rights we all presumed could never be diminished, an unpopular war that is killing too many people while seemingly going nowhere as it rapidly depletes our treasury, or myriad other factors in a world shrunk by communication technologies and a global economy, we have become more afraid and less trusting.

Perhaps concern for the everyday behavior of those in the mental health professions seems trivial in comparison to the larger and very serious national and international problems we face now. But, we all have to start making a positive mark somewhere, and clinging to the highest standards in our professions, even while the values around us often appear to be tumbling, is an honorable personal goal that does have impact, even if just on one person at a time.

The contents of this revised volume reflect the changing scope of what mental health professionals do on the job. They continue to fill their traditional roles as teachers, researchers, diagnosticians, psychotherapists and counselors, measurement consultants, curriculum designers, and so forth. However, increasing numbers of mental health professionals work as managers, organizational and agency consultants, elected officials, public policymakers, foundation heads, and university administrators as well as in a host of new niche practice areas.

When we published our first edition in 1985, microcomputer technology remained an expensive novelty, no one had heard of the Internet, and newly licensed practitioners seemed eager to enter the private practice of long-term psychotherapy. Deinstitutionalization had become a buzzword; people rarely sued mental health professionals; few people connected physical health with mental well-being; managed care and "telemedicine" had not yet appeared on our event horizon; and no one spoke of "evidence-based practice." The "hot" ethical controversies of the day focused on issues such as therapists giving advice in the broadcast media and on professional advertising. Few openly questioned the notion that sexual intimacies between clients and psychotherapists should be prohibited for life.

Notwithstanding the changes in the size and shape of the mental health professions, our colleagues have insisted on maintaining and enforcing codes of ethics; this is especially true of those who belong to the major associations,

such as the American Psychological Association, Canadian Psychological Association, National Association of Social Workers, American Counseling Association, American Association for Marriage and Family Therapists, or American Psychiatric Association or those who hold licenses to practice from state, provincial, or territorial licensing boards. Each of the major professional associations has an ethics code, and most are relatively brief and easy to read. Even so, the actual application of these codes in specific situations often becomes extremely difficult. No set of rules can cover all possible situations or anticipate new developments in society and technology. Thus, many of the implicit and complex ethical dilemmas remain left for individuals to resolve on their own.

PURPOSE AND GOALS OF THE BOOK

We seek to present the full range of contemporary ethical issues in the mental health professions, not only as relevant and intriguing but also as integral and unavoidable aspects of the our complex professional roles and social responsibilities. Regardless of one's training specialty or the work setting, critical dilemmas will arise— probably with some regularity—and we will often need to make challenging decisions or take intervention steps, sometimes right on the spot. By providing an awareness of the ethical expectations of mental health professionals and by revealing how they apply in specific situations, we hope to achieve a useful and practical guide for education and for decision making.

After serving for many years on ethics committees and credentialing bodies, we began to realize that numerous people already functioning as fully trained clinicians do not have well-tuned expectations for ethical conduct or accurate understanding of how the mental health professions monitor themselves. We also observed that inquiries to ethics committees or calls for consultation on ethical matters are often late in the game or arrive after the fact. Often, the resolution of the problem then becomes primarily reactive or remedial rather than preventive. Mental health services have won greater public acceptance and have become less stigmatizing, meaning that consumers of our services have become more likely to step forward and file complaints when they feel aggrieved. As a result, mental health professionals now have a far greater likelihood of facing a licensing board complaint, and losing their ability to practice, than a lawsuit. Consequently, this book aims to sensitize readers to the monitoring and redress mechanisms available when ethical violations occur and to provide information and decision-making strategies to assist in avoiding or preventing ethical misconduct.

Nonetheless, we cannot provide solutions to every conceivable ethical problem that might arise in psychotherapy practice, assessment, research, or teaching. Many specific situations become so complicated that no ethics code, policy guideline, or law can deftly point the way to a satisfactory and ethically correct resolution. In some situations, for example, one ethical principle may seem pitted against another. Or, upholding an ethical principle may seem at variance with a legal requirement, leaving the therapist stuck somewhere in the middle. Moreover, the mental health professions as well as our society in general constantly evolve, causing profound ethical dilemmas that neither the ethics codes nor the professions can fully prepare to handle. We do assume, however, that more information and sensitization to issues will lead to better professional practice. We aim to help both trainees and senior colleagues sort out even the most complex ethical problems in order to make the best possible judgments and outcomes.

SOME SPECIFIC FEATURES OF THIS BOOK

In recognition of the wide range of professionals currently providing behavioral health and mental health services, we have broadened the scope of our book beyond psychology (the focus of our first two editions) to include all of the relevant professional groups. Readers will note that the cases include physicians, counselors, social workers, and family therapists as well as psychologists. In addition, the appendices include the ethics codes of all the major membership-based professional associations addressing behavioral and mental health.

We have annotated the text of the book with reference to the 2002 American Psychological Association's ethics code throughout. When relevant, we cite the portions of the code that are aspirational (i.e., the Ethical Principles of Psychologists, denoted by letters of the alphabet) with parenthetical notations to the relevant principle, thus: (APA 02: A) cites Ethical Principle A. When referring to the enforceable standards of the code (i.e., the Code of Conduct, denoted in Arabic numerals), we use the parenthetical notation (APA 02) followed by the specific numerical location to identify the relevant ethical standard. We hope that this will make it easy for the reader to look up the exact wording of the code in Appendix A as relevant to the text discussion.

Because ethical problems often overlap or cluster around several principles, it proved challenging to create neat piles of material from which to develop discrete chapters. Whereas each chapter has a specific focus, we use substantial cross-referencing to alert readers where additional information may be found. Although we have strived for comprehensiveness, we certainly could not possibly cover, in a single volume, every conceivable ethical situation that behavioral health and mental health clinicians might face. The readers should not regard the omission of specific topics as suggesting that we think them unimportant or assume the neglect of some forms of questionable conduct means that such behaviors are implicitly condoned.

We use brief case vignettes to illustrate ethical problems. We adapted our case examples from ethics committee case files, licensing board decisions, news accounts, case law, public records, and actual incidents known to us. Except for public information (e.g., news stories and case law with the actual source cited in the text), we have disguised the material in a variety of ways, such as through combining the details of one case with another, switching the sex of one or more principals, changing the relevant degree or licensing status, or altering contexts in which the activity occurred. Please also note that we have often "trimmed" cases by focusing on only one key element of the ethical charge or violation. In fact, most cases brought to the attention of ethics committees involve charges of violating two or more ethical principles.

As in our two previous editions, we continue to avoid routine naming methods (e.g., Dr. A. or "the client") for designating the principal characters in our case material. We also aim to reduce the risk of using bogus names that might correspond to those of real people. Hence, most of our pseudonyms are highly contrived. Students reported that this technique makes the content both more readable and memorable. In using clearly bogus names, it is *never* our intent to trivialize the seriousness of the content under discussion but rather to enhance interest and aid recall of specific cases. Any resulting resemblance between the names of our characters and those of actual people with similar names is purely coincidental. We took care to ensure that the names used in particular cases do not even remotely resemble the names of the actual people involved. When we do use actual names of the principals, the case material includes citation in the text of the relevant legal case or other public source.

For the sake of simplicity, we also adopted a set of degree labeling conventions limiting ourselves to Ph.D., Psy.D., or Ed.D. for psychologists; M.D. for psychiatrists; D.S.W. or M.S.W. for social workers; L.M.F.T. for licensed marriage and family therapists; and L.M.H.C. for licensed mental health counselors. We know that some psychiatrists have D.O. or European medical degree designations; that some social workers use L.C.S.W. or L.I.C.S.W. designations; and that many different types of master's degrees qualify professional licenses with letter designations that vary widely from state to state. We intend no disrespect if we have omitted your particular degree, board certification, or other hard-earned professional credential. In addition, we randomly distributed the professional designations and degrees of the professionals portrayed, except when the case circumstances specifically called for a particular profession (e.g., a psychologist in the case of neuropsychological assessment).

We would like to extend warm thanks to Joan Bossert, the vice president/publisher and our editorial director at Oxford University Press. Her wisdom, patience, and good humor have been part of our professional lives for over two decades. We also thank Abby Gross, associate editor at Oxford, for her support and very helpful assistance throughout the revision process. Finally, we thank Jean Blackburu and Kathleen Brown for their heroic efforts in preparing the manuscript for publication.

Boston, Massachusetts   G. P. K.
Aptos, California   P. K.-S.
July 2007

Contents

ETHICS IN PSYCHOLOGY
AND THE MENTAL HEALTH PROFESSIONS

1

On Being Ethical

Always do right; this will gratify some people and astonish the rest.

Mark Twain

Contents

NOWHERE TO HIDE

If you are already a mental health professional and have been at it for a while, you have almost certainly come in contact with at least one ethical dilemma that either involved you directly or involved a colleague you know personally. If you are still in training, we guarantee that you will confront multiple ethical dilemmas in the course of your professional career and

3

probably at least one before you complete your internship. You will have to make a decision about either your own conduct or that of another. Early recognition and a little lead time can prevent many potential ethical problems from escalating to the point of causing harm. Every now and again, however, a whopper will surface and affect you directly in some way. You may not have created the problem, but you may have no choice but to respond. How you react could have significant implications for your reputation and your career.

Whether through delivering psychotherapy or counseling services, teaching, or conducting social-behavioral research, most of us chose our careers because we want to do our part to improve the quality of people's lives. Whenever we facilitate the mending of emotional pain or teach a new coping skill, we are also fulfilling our personal goals. As such, we would never intentionally harm those with whom we work. Alas, *ethical perfection* lies beyond reach for virtually all of us humans, even if we could completely agree on the ethically correct response in every situation. And, unfortunately, good intentions will prove insufficient to ensure that wrongs will not occur.

Sometimes, we will have no choice but to make decisions with ethical implications under ambiguous circumstances. Confusion, pressure, frustrations, anxiety, conflicting loyalties, insufficient information, and the tendency to rationalize are common responses to ethical challenges. Such reactions complicate the matter and greatly elevate the chances of errors in decision making.

Ethical dilemmas also have a way of popping up when not expected. How would you react to the following scenarios?

An exuberant client, having just won the blue ribbon at the county fair for "Best Chili," spots you in the crowd and bounces toward you with wide, outstretched arms and puckered lips.

You have tried hard to remain objective and compassionate, but your client's obnoxious personality and foul body odor have become increasingly difficult to ignore. You dread the approach of this client's regular appointment day.

Your client's mental state has worsened over the last couple of months. Nothing you have attempted seems to help. You inform the client that you would like to refer him to someone else, but he insists that he wants to stay with you.

You arrive at your office to meet the new bookkeeper your partner hired while you were on vacation. At the desk sits a person who you treated in intensive therapy for 4 years before she unexpectedly dropped you for a new therapist.

Couples counseling has resulted in a decision by your clients to dissolve their marriage. They also decide to quit counseling. The wife calls you a week later and asks that you to serve as a witness on her behalf in a child custody dispute.

Your brother's wife drinks way too much. He begs you to take her on as a therapy client because she adamantly refuses to talk to anyone except you.

After venting frustration toward his spouse for nearly the entire session, your client has a wild look in his eyes as he abruptly leaps from his chair, races for the door, then turns around and growls, "She's messed up her last man," and heads out of the building. You are pretty sure he owns a gun.

Mental health professionals must often think fast to react appropriately. An effective response requires developed skills, planned resources, the right information, and a preestablished ethical awareness. The scenarios above could play out with relatively benign or quite serious repercussions, depending largely on the response to each. Our book aims to provide insights and ideas that will help you recognize, constructively approach, and reconcile ethical predicaments, while at the same time remaining compassionate and attuned to the well-being of those with whom you work.

WHAT IS ETHICAL?

Ethics is traditionally a branch of philosophy dealing with moral problems and moral judgments. White (1988) defined ethics as the evaluation of human actions. In doing so, we assign judgments to behavior as "right" or "wrong" and "good" or "bad" according to the perspective of a moral principle or ethical guideline. You will find our approach to professional ethics and standards very practical, applying core ethical principles to situations presented in the course of the work that mental health professionals, educators, and social-behavioral scientists do. Although we may all strive to be responsible and good, there is often a gap between the ideal outcome and what can realistically be accomplished. Situations do not always sort into clear black-and-white choices; when dealing with actual incidents, we must often deal with shades of gray.

The most practical way for us to talk about professional ethics is to ground our discussions in the ethics codes of professional associations that represent mental health fields. We have selected as our model the most recent ethics code of the American Psychological Association (APA) (2002) because of its applicability to most mental health professions and its close similarity to the provisions in most other codes. We cite a specific principle of the 2002 APA Ethics Code (designated by the initials for the organization and the year the code was issued, followed by the appropriate number designations, e.g., APA 02: 3.01.). See Appendix A for the full text of the ethics codes for the American Psychological Association (2002).

It is imperative for all mental health professionals to stay well informed about the most relevant ethics code representing their profession. However, it is also wise to keep aware of the provisions of the codes promulgated by their sister professions because of the high probability of interacting with colleagues with different training backgrounds. Despite the focus on psychology, our book is also highly relevant for marriage and family therapists, social workers, counselors, and psychiatrists. See Appendix B for the entire ethics code of the Canadian Psychological Association (2000); Appendix C for the American Counseling Association (2005); Appendix D for the National Association of Social Workers (1999); Appendix E for the American Association for Marriage and Family Therapy (2001); and Appendix F for the American Psychiatric Association (2006).

Practicing Defensive Ethics: Risk Management

A risk management approach to ethics probably provides the most practical way to avoid ethical dilemmas, although it has some ethical and personal liabilities of its own, which we present below. The key to effective risk management is to scrupulously uphold the tenets of relevant laws, policies, professional standards, and ethics codes, taking as many steps as possible to avoid ever being placed in precarious ethical or legal circumstances. The central focus, then, is on assisting in self-protection against the legal and other hazards of modern-day professional services (Baerger, 2001; Bennett, Bryant, VandenBos, & Greenwood, 1990; Gottlieb, 1994; Montgomery, 1999; Stromberg et al., 1988; VandeCreek & Knapp, 2000; Walker, 1999).

Many strategies to manage risks consist simply of the elements of good practice, such as refraining from having sexual contacts with clients, keeping careful notes, reviewing client files often, recording reasons for termination, and consulting with colleagues or appropriate others about difficult clients and documenting such meetings (Kennedy, Vandehey, Norman, & Diekhoff, 2003). One concern with an overly strict adherence to risk management, however, is that clients who urgently need help can be shut out. Risk-aversive therapists might choose to avoid high-risk clients, even when trained to competently treat them. Individuals with borderline personalities (especially if accompanied by hysteroid or paranoid features) or who have a history of dangerousness or suicide attempts would have a difficult time finding appropriate help should all therapists ascribe to a rigid risk management style. Clients who develop rapid and intense transferences may be referred elsewhere or terminated, not based on sound clinical judgment but on fear of ethical entanglements.

Therapists who approach their work from a risk management perspective might also avoid high-risk practice areas such as child custody and other forensic work or practice venues in which scrutiny will be intense. Yet, many people desperately need these services. We know a therapist who receives more referrals than she can handle for adolescent clients from colleagues who openly admit that they want to avoid possible harassment or legal action brought against them by discontented parents.

Pamela Birrell (2006) offered an exceptionally thought-provoking perspective:

> I am sure that I am not alone in being daunted by what ethics actually means, apart from ethical codes and legal management. But in this avoidance of what it means to be with another human being, what it means to be a healing presence, what it means to be truly ethical, we run the risk of conflating ethics with risk management, mistaking rules for relationships, and damaging those very people we so desperately want to help. (p. 95)

Of course, mental health professionals should pay attention when a client's behavior suggests that resistances have been mismanaged or that the therapy is at an impasse or is deteriorating, as evidenced by many missed sessions, nonpayment or late fee payments, overt or covert expressions of dissatisfaction with therapy, or the desire to see another therapist (Korner, 1995). Nevertheless, therapists can become overly obsessed, such as viewing articulate clients with suspicion because if things go badly they can make a cogent complaint or by putting up extra walls whenever a client discloses a complaint about a previous therapist. Although the scrupulous practice of defensive ethics is understandable in a litigious society, a mind-set that views every client as a potential landmine may also become insidiously instilled. Harboring constant apprehension and distrust toward those we were trained to help hardly constitutes a healthy foundation for an authentic therapeutic alliance.

Practicing Vigilant Ethics: A More Positive Attitude

We take the position that the primary rationale for being an ethically aware and sensitive therapist is *not* for self-protection. There is another more positive reason. Reaching for the highest standards emboldens us in the face of ethical uncertainty. We respect ourselves and what we do if we feel confident that we are practicing appropriately and within our boundaries of competence, which in turn enhances the quality of our services. Maintaining high standards allows us to act with benevolence and courage rather than donning protective armor and remaining constantly on the lookout for escape hatches.

Aristotle spoke of the ethical life as a happy life. This makes sense in our context. Maintaining high ethical standards may well be the prerequisite to a personally gratifying career. The old saw, "Virtue as its own reward" veils the fact that being a decent, responsible, honest human being elevates both self-respect as well as respect from others.

Perhaps the most agonizing moral dilemma that we face as mental health professionals occurs when doing what is best for the client constitutes unethical behavior (as defined by their professional ethics codes), disobeys a law, or is even fraud (Maesen, 1991). We do not advocate defying ethical code provisions or breaking the law to serve clients' needs, but we do hold that mental health professionals should always vigorously attempt to resolve such dilemmas in a way that protects client welfare to the greatest extent possible. This often takes some extra time and effort, but the results can be well worth it, as we discuss in the next chapter.

ETHICAL PRINCIPLES AND VIRTUES

We see overarching descriptions of "the ethical person" reflected in professional ethics codes. We adapt from the core ethical principles that we believe should serve as an overall guide for the behavior of those in a mental health field from several classic sources (Beauchamp & Childress, 1989; Frankena, 1973; Gilligan, 1982; Kitchener, 1985; Ross, 1930).

- *Do no harm* (nonmaleficence). Mental health professionals must strive to benefit those with whom we work, while at the same time taking care to ensure that the potential for damage is eliminated or minimized to the greatest extent possible. Whereas we may not be able to help every client, the duty to cause no harm is paramount.
- *Respect autonomy*. Individuals have the right to decide how to live their lives as long as

their actions do not interfere with the rights and welfare of others. Respect for autonomy is accepted by mental health professionals because the underlying goal of psychotherapy and counseling is often to move those with whom we work toward greater self-reliance and self-determination.

- *Be just.* The actions of mental health professionals should be fair and equitable. Others should be treated as we would want to be treated under similar circumstances.
- *Be faithful.* Issues of fidelity, loyalty, truthfulness, and promise keeping toward those with whom we work converge to form the delicate balance of standards required in fiduciary relationships. The therapy or counseling relationship should allow clients to feel safe and as free as possible from irrelevant and extraneous variables.
- *Accord dignity.* Mental health professionals should view those with whom we work as worthy of respect. We must strive to understand cultural and other ways that people differ from ourselves and to eliminate biases that might have an impact on the quality of our work.
- *Treat others with caring and compassion.* The mental health field is almost defined by kindness and consideration toward those with whom we work and simultaneously maintaining appropriate professional roles.
- *Pursue excellence.* Maintaining competence, doing our best, and taking pride in our work form the bases of quality mental health services.
- *Be accountable.* When errors have been made, mental health professionals consider possible consequences, accept responsibility for actions and inactions, and avoid shifting blame or making excuses.
- *Be courageous.* We do not see courage mentioned often enough in the professional ethics literature. But, the truth is that it often takes backbone to actively uphold ethical principles, especially when one observes unethical actions perpetrated by others. Does one avert one's eyes from ethical matters because of fear of retaliation? Does one follow unethical orders? Or, does one take principled action? Those with courage have an advantage in that courage itself emboldens us to do the right thing. In fact, we may

ask if it is even possible to be an ethical practitioner without the strength to act on moral convictions.

What may strike you about these core ethical principles is that they are unlikely to be practiced unless they are already embedded in the fabric of a person's character. Is it even possible for someone to *act* with caring and compassion if such characteristics are not already an integral part of that person's identity? Ideally, mental health professionals behave ethically because they are also virtuous people, but it can be difficult to apply the concept of virtue to professional ethical standards and behavior.

Universal virtuous characteristics include such traits as wisdom, creativity, curiosity, caring for humanity, fairness, forgiveness, appreciation of beauty and excellence, prudence, integrity, respectfulness, and benevolence (Meara, Schmidt, & Day, 1996; Peterson & Seligman, 2004). As Bersoff (1996) has pointed out, however, virtue ethics are difficult to apply to upholding or transgressing specific ethical principles of a profession. They often become irrelevant or confusing in such analyses, and virtues are probably impossible to teach. For example, can we teach wisdom? How easily can we apply the concept of wisdom to everyday ethical practice? Virtues can even be misapplied in specific instances. For example, the therapist who possesses creativity might attempt a technique that colleagues would consider too risky or far outside the traditional standards of care. The therapist who possesses curiosity may delve into subject matters with clients that are irrelevant or inappropriate to the therapeutic goals.

When it comes to proactively dealing with what most of us would agree to be inexcusable actions, virtue ethics are difficult to enforce. What would you think if a therapist said to a client who recently underwent brain surgery, "Why don't you just go shoot your brains out to get rid of the pain?" Or, to an overweight client, "Let's face it, if your husband were to die tomorrow, who would want you?" Such callous statements violate the dignity that should be accorded clients who seek our services, but whether anything can be done to rein in a therapist who is complained about for being insulting is uncertain. In the actual case on which these two examples were adapted, the caregiver was a physician. Attempts to hold him responsible for these and other incredibly crass remarks to his patients were unsuccessful. In fact, he vowed to sue those who tried to hold him accountable (Tirrell-Wysocki, 2006).

In this book, we primarily apply *principle ethics*, reflected in the nine core ethical principles we presented above and refined for decision-making purposes in professional ethics codes. Virtues and ethical principles overlap, and virtuous people would likely act on ethical principles because they are predisposed to do the right thing (Kitchener, 1996). However, principles are usually more specific and easier to translate into proscribed, observable obligations acted out in a professional context. Thus, virtue ethics are about "Who shall I be?" whereas principle ethics are about "What shall I do?" (Jordan & Meara, 1990).

Applying principle ethics allows for the curious possibility that upstanding ethical behavior can occur solely as the result of professional obligation and deliberate adherence to rules rather than as a reflection of one's personally held values. For example, a bright but an otherwise selfish and imprudent individual might be able, by dint of focus and constant self-monitoring, to follow all of the rules. However, we doubt that those with character defects would be capable of maintaining satisfactory ethical performances throughout their professional careers. They will stumble sooner or later. We recall a young counselor mandated to take our ethics class as part of a sanction for his unethical conduct. This student's exam scores were the highest in the class, and he could clearly articulate appropriate professional ethical responsibilities during class discussions. And yet, less than a year after completing the class this same individual was in serious trouble again with a state licensing board.

WHO ARE THE UNETHICAL MENTAL HEALTH PROFESSIONALS?

The stereotype of the "unethical mental health professional" is outright unsavory. "Greedy,"

"stupid," "psychopathic," "devious," and "immoral" are among the common descriptors according to our own informal polling of colleagues. At times, some therapists willfully, even maliciously, engage in acts they know to be in violation of ethical and legal standards. How avarice, expediency, and other self-serving motives can blur judgments is illustrated throughout this book.

The cases below illustrate the lurid, extreme range of unacceptable acts by mental health professionals. These stories may seem so bizarre that you might think them fictitious, but we assure you that each is adapted from actual headlines.

Case 1–1: A client complained to a licensing board that a psychologist talked about himself and his own problems most of the time, constantly interrupted the session by taking and making non-emergency phone calls, cut sessions short while still charging the full fee, and finally, literally kicked the client out of the office. The client suffered bruises on his legs and one thigh that required medical attention. The psychologist was arrested for assault. When a reporter of a local paper wrote a story, several other ex-clients came forward to verify the psychologist's outrageous behavior.

Case 1–2: A clinical social worker abruptly terminated a client who was still struggling with depression and alcohol dependence. He called his just-terminated client the following day and invited her to his apartment to see a movie. The social worker served popcorn and wine and, during the movie, sexually assaulted her. The client told her minister about the incident who contacted the social worker for an explanation. The social worker offered the minister a new computer for the church office if he could talk the client out of calling the authorities.

Case 1–3. A marriage and family therapist convinced a client who could not afford therapy to commit an act of abuse on her minor child in order to qualify for funds for mental health treatment. The mother and the therapist were both arrested and found guilty of a misdemeanor.

Case 1–4: A licensed mental health counselor plotted against a former client who had accused him of overbilling and was threatening to take the counselor to small claims court. The counselor hired a man to burglarize a business and place the stolen items in the ex-client's home. The hired burglar then was supposed to call the police with a tip that a person fitting the client's description was observed leaving the business in a car with the ex-client's license number. Fortunately for the ex-client, the hired burglar repeated the story to others while drinking heavily in a bar, leading to his quick arrest and disclosure of the counselor's plot.

Case 1–5: A judge found in favor of the client of a psychiatrist and awarded her a large monetary sum after the client made a compelling case that he had sex with her regularly over a 10-year period while she was his client. In addition, the psychiatrist had rented a home for her and employed her as his family's housekeeper. The defendant claimed that his conduct should be excused because the "the sex was good for both of them" and the client was no more disabled currently than when she entered his care. His attempt to escape liability was not persuasive to the court.

Case 1–6: A psychotherapist solicited one of his own clients to kill six people and dump the bodies in the ocean. The client was also instructed to purchase a gun with a silencer, rent a sturdy vehicle that could hold 500 pounds of body weight, arrange a boat rental, buy bait, and locate shark-infested waters. The client reported this bizarre offer to the police.

Are such drastic behaviors typical of mental health professionals who violate ethical standards? Thankfully, *absolutely not*. However, the "bad apple" argument that attributes all unethical behavior to a few sleazy characters within a profession is not correct either. In our experience, the prevailing portrait of those crossing over the line is muted and complex and includes people of decency, intelligence, and emotional fitness caught up in circumstances that they did not evaluate or respond to appropriately.

Although rarely mutually exclusive, characteristics of most mental health professionals who engage in questionable, unethical, or unprofessional behavior could be described as having one or more underlying characteristics:

- are ignorant or misinformed regarding the ethical standards of their profession
- practice outside their realm of competence and expertise, with or without awareness
- show insensitivity to the needs of those with whom they work or to situational dynamics
- exploit clients by putting their own needs (usually sexual or financial) first
- behave irresponsibly due to laziness, stress, lack of awareness, or other reasons that take their attention away from their professional responsibilities
- seek vengeance against perceived harms to themselves by clients or others with whom they work
- suffer from burnout or other emotional impairment
- have no concept or have distorted views of interpersonal boundaries
- rationalize actions that are often unrecognized as self-serving
- usually behave competently, ethically, and with good awareness, but "slip" by losing sight of a goal or becoming momentarily distracted

Each category is described and illustrated more fully below.

The Ignorant or Misinformed

A substantial number of violators appear to be either naive or uneducated about the standards of their profession and how they are expected to behave. Offenses of ignorance can often be minor and, fortunately, cause no real harm, as the next case illustrates.

Case 1–7: Recently licensed Newt Unworldly,[1] Ph.D., accepted the offer of Trendy Cool, his brother-in-law and marketing specialist, to promote

---

1. All of the cases presented in this book, with one clearly noted exception, are adapted from actual incidents. We use improbable names throughout to enhance interest and ensure that identities of all parties are not discernible. It is not our intention to trivialize the seriousness of the issues. When we do use actual names, our adaptations reflect information in the public domain. As part of our disguising process, we also randomly assign various professional designations and earned degrees or licensure status.

his fledgling private practice. A flashy advertisement in the local paper gave a misleading description of Unworldly's professional experience. For example, "interned at Memorial Hospital" referred to a summer of volunteer work that Unworldly performed as a high school senior. Another counselor in the agency pointed out that Unworldly himself retained responsibility for such statements and was lax in allowing his advertising agent to run loose around the truth. Unworldy quickly retracted the ad.

For more minor violators in this category, educative approaches typically prove sufficient to ensure that the behavior will not recur. Often inexperienced, these therapists are usually embarrassed on being informed of their obliviousness or short-sightedness. Sadly, they also frequently insist that such matters never came up for discussion during their formal training.

Sometimes, mental health professionals operate under the belief that they are aware of an ethical provision when, in fact, no such provision exists. Or, they misinterpret the actual ethics code of their profession.

Case 1–8: When questioned by an ethics committee about a sexual affair that went awry with a client he had terminated only a month earlier, Romeo Quickie, Psy.D., replied that the ethics code of the American Psychological Association specifically states that sex with ex-clients is perfectly acceptable.

Response of the APA to the acceptability of sexual relationships with former clients is discussed fully in Chapter 12. We note here that Dr. Quickie's understanding seemed conveniently confused and inaccurate. Not uncommonly, therapists attempt to defend unethical acts with a claim that they were unaware of the relevant content of the ethics code. Ignorance will not let Dr. Quickie off the hook. A thorough familiarity with and a commitment to uphold high standards of conduct provide hedges against engaging in ethical misconduct.

For ignorant or misinformed violators who are more experienced but who have lost touch with their professional identity and commitment, remediation can be more difficult.

Case 1–9: Hy Upper, Ph.D., was contacted by an ethics panel regarding his alleged distribution of amphetamines during group therapy sessions. He responded that he was "under the distinct impression that psychologists in his state had the same rights to pass out drugs as do physicians." He claimed to "have read about it somewhere."

Occasionally, those who you think would hold special competencies because of their considerable experience come to see themselves as beyond learning anything new or above the law. In the actual incident, "Dr. Upper" had been in practice for over 25 years. However, he had clearly drifted far from an awareness of relevant law and professional standards.

The Incompetent

The misconduct of mental health professionals in the category of incompetence arises from an incapacity to perform the services rendered. Sometimes, emotional disturbance or substance abuse can blunt the ability to perform satisfactory work, even if the therapist has been properly trained. But, more often, inadequate training and experience are at issue. Many therapists who come to the attention of ethics committees, licensing boards, or the courts have vastly miscalculated the level of their overall skills or of their ability to apply specific techniques or services, such as a neuropsychological assessment or expert forensic testimony.

Case 1–10: A clinic supervisor recognized that many clients seemed to acquire misdiagnoses or inappropriate treatment plans based on the reports of Remi Partway, Ed.D. When the supervisor asked Dr. Partway to detail her training and experience, Partway admitted she had virtually no training or experience in these specific assessments but believed she was "picking up speed" as she went along.

Dr. Partway's circumstance unfortunately occurs all too commonly. Typical training programs can not teach every skill that a particular employer or client may require. We have run across cases in which employers insist that therapists provide services despite having full knowledge that requisite training and experience are lacking. (Chapter 4 is devoted to fully exploring the ethical ramifications of incompetence.)

The Insensitive

Although an elusive category, mental health professionals often exceed the bounds of ethical propriety because of insufficient regard for the needs and feelings, and sometimes the rights and welfare, of those with whom they work. Reasons for this vary and include lack of empathy, a need to exercise control, overzealousness regarding a specific approach, self-absorption, and prejudicial attitudes toward certain groups of people. Often, such insensitivities preclude the recognition that an ethical issue even exists.

Case 1–11: Justin Tyme, L.M.H.C., was often late for therapy sessions. When a single mother of four complained that she didn't like waiting for up to a half hour because it threw off her schedule, he responded, "You don't have a job, so what difference does it make?"

Case 1–12: After taking continuing education classes in hypnosis, Lila Spellbinder, M.S.W., wanted to use her newly acquired skill on every client regardless of their reasons for consulting her. When a client expressed reticence, she told him that he was being silly and stupid, and if he really wanted to improve he would do things her way.

Case 1–13: Fred Narrow, Ph.D., informed the international interns who attempted to introduce information about their cultures during supervisory sessions that their perspectives were not germane to our society. Soon, these supervisees no longer participated in discussions. Narrow then faulted them for their seeming disinterest and remarked, "You are here to learn our ways, and you can't do that by just sitting there like lumps."

Empathy and cultural sensitivities are among the hallmarks of being an effective and ethical therapist. Deficits in either area are likely to lead to ethical lapses.

The Exploitative

Exploitation occurs when mental health professionals take advantage of consumers by abusing their positions of trust, expertise, or authority. Therapists who allow their own needs to take precedence over those of clients they serve, or who put the lure of financial gain above client welfare, best fit the common stereotype of the unethical professional. Therapists who themselves have character disorders seem most likely to fall in this category.

Engaging in sexual activity with current clients constitutes the most commonly discussed form of exploitation, and sexual misconduct is what usually comes to mind when we think about exploitation. However, most therapists do not have sex with their clients. Yet, a great many other circumstances present themselves in the context of psychotherapy that allow for exploitation, abuse, and harm to clients (Pope, Sonne, & Greene, 2006). Many of these situations, especially activities entered into for the purpose of giving the therapist some advantage or personal gratification, are discussed throughout this book. Here, we illustrate how such exploitation can occur in subtle and largely undetectable ways.

Case 1–14: Tom Stare, D.S.W., created a seating plan in his group therapy that purposely placed Minny Monroe directly across from his seat in the circle. He confided to a colleague that the entire seating scheme was done to position himself to look at an "adorable chick who wears short skirts and doesn't always pay attention to what her legs are doing." When the colleague suggested that his behavior was questionable, Stare countered that the colleague had no sense of humor and was obviously getting old.

Dr. Stare's attitude is typical of exploitative professionals. He clearly has no insight into how his notion of harmless gratification probably influences the level of the care and genuineness accompanying his services, especially regarding the client he objectifies as an "adorable chick." He also takes advantage of a client to whom he owes a professional responsibility, even though she may remain unaware of it.

The percentage of exploitative therapists who could be described as avaricious and who place financial considerations ahead of professional obligations is probably low, even though they represent a high percentage of cases brought before adjudicating bodies. We sometimes refer to inexperienced or novice therapists in a hurry to become wealthy or successful as "green menaces." They often try a misguided gimmick or overrate their services. Occasionally, as illustrated in the next case, someone calls them on it.

Case 1–15: Jacob Ladder, L.M.H.C., attempted to convince his client, who was a supporting actor in a long-running television series, to pass out Ladder's business cards on the set and to attest to his "magical skills" as a therapist. When the client expressed discomfort with the request, Ladder expressed considerable anger toward the client, calling him ungrateful and selfish.

Some exploitative therapists are recalcitrant and difficult to educate. Their infractions can be serious, such as defrauding insurance companies, accepting kickbacks, using elaborate bait-and-switch techniques or making highly misleading claims about the effectiveness of their services. The next case describes an outrageous swindle. Incidents of this sort are, thankfully, extremely rare.

Case 1–16: Buck Scam, Ph.D., prevailed on the husband of a couple he was treating for an unsecured loan of $150,000 from the husband's pension fund. The wife was not informed in advance and threatened exposure when she discovered the transaction several months later. The therapist promised to repay what he owed if the wife would agree, in writing, never to contact an ethics committee or licensing board. On signing this promise, the therapist presented her with a bill for $120,000 for extra sessions for which the therapist alleged the couple had never paid.

This contemptible case clearly reveals how communication breakdowns in a marriage can wreak considerable havoc. However, that the therapist to whom they came for help is responsible for causing it is unconscionable. In this actual case, the couple did complain to a licensing board, and the therapist lost his license to practice.

The Irresponsible

Ethical infractions based on irresponsible behavior arise in several forms, including unreliable execution of professional duties, shoddy or superficial professional work, and attempts to blame others, cover up, or make excuses for one's own mistakes and inadequacies.

Case 1–17: Janet Turtle, Ph.D., agreed to support her supervisee, Job Hunter, in his quest for employment. However, Mr. Hunter learned that Dr. Turtle failed to return prospective employers' calls and that the promised letters of recommendation were never written. When Hunter expressed disappointment to Dr. Turtle, she apologized, explaining that she had gotten so busy that she could not even handle her own priorities. In the meantime, the prospective employers offered the positions to others.

Abandonment is a form of irresponsibility and occurs when therapists fail to follow through with their duties in a way that then causes clients to become vulnerable, to feel discarded or rejected, or to suffer some other foreseeable harm. Many complaints from therapy clients echo themes of abandonment, such as illustrated in our next case.

Case 1–18: As Dee Compensating became increasingly ill, Lucia Panicky, Ph.D., did not feel comfortable treating her. Dr. Panicky informed Dee that she could no longer see her and told her to find another therapist. When Dee asked for an explanation, Panicky only replied, "I have my reasons."

All therapists have probably found themselves in situations from which they wished to extricate themselves. In many such instances, they probably should disengage. Dr. Panicky may well have lacked the competence to continue treating her client and appropriately recognized this.

However, termination of services requires sensitivity and due regard for consumers' needs and welfare, as is discussed more fully in Chapter 5. Dr. Panicky failed in these regards, leaving her client bewildered and adrift.

In the next chapter, we discuss the responsibility of mental health professionals to assist in upholding the ethics of their profession. To fail to do so constitutes irresponsibility.

Case 1–19: Lila Witness, M.S.W., caught a glimpse in the hallway of her office partner Hulk Scary, D.S.W., as he was buttoning his pants while a female client scurried out the door. Ms. Witness had suspected misbehavior but never confronted Scary because she found him intimidating. Several months later, the client contacted Dr. Witness. The client had noticed Witness observing her departure from Scary's office and asked if she would testify to what she saw in a civil trial. Dr. Witness denied seeing anything and suggested that the client drop the case.

Dr. Witness had no active accomplice role, and she did not owe the woman the same duty she would owe someone in her care. But, Scary was her colleague, and she chose to lie to protect him, tainting herself ethically.

The Vengeful

Mental health professionals who seek revenge on a colleague, client, or others who they perceive as having done them wrong are not commonly seen by ethics committees or in the courts. However, some outraged mental health professionals have allowed their emotions to supersede professional judgment. Usually, the infraction involves an impulsive act, as opposed to a premeditated plot to retaliate against an antagonist. The behavior often has a childish quality.

Case 1–20: Alotta Deduce, Ph.D., became increasingly resentful of a client who often disagreed with her interpretations of the relevance of past events in the client's life. Once after the client doubted whether the loss of a puppy at age 10 had anything to do with his current emotional pain, Dr.

Deduce shook her finger and roared, "You are without a doubt the most thick-headed prick on the planet," and, "I must be crazy myself to agree to keep seeing you."

Impulsively vengeful therapists often feel remorseful and foolish later and frequently apologize for their loss of control. Unfortunately, permanent damage may already have occurred because the impact of such outbursts can not always be fully rectified. Rarely, acts of vengeance can prove perilous, as illustrated in the next case.

Case 1–21: After Vinny Dictive, L.M.H.C., was laid off from his job at a mental health clinic, he waited with a handgun in the parking lot and fired a shot at the medical director as she entered her car, wounding her in the neck.

One of the strangest cases ever to come to our attention involves a spurned supervisor who was so obsessed with his supervisee that he willfully jeopardized his own reputation in an attempt to ruin hers.

Case 1–22: Harry Karry, Ph.D., went overboard for Erica Gimme, his supervisee. He helped her with her clinical notes, adjusted his schedule to fit hers, drove her anywhere she wanted to go, made himself available to her by telephone at any time, brought snacks and soft drinks to each of their frequent meetings, and even wrote a course paper for Ms. Gimme when she ran short of time. Although, according to Dr. Karry, the two did not engage in any romantic behavior, Gimme told him that his accommodations had begun to feel more burdensome than helpful and asked for a transfer to another supervisor. A crestfallen and fuming Karry wrote to an ethics committee reporting that Gimme was guilty of plagiarism. Dr. Karry divulged that he knew for certain Ms. Gimme cheated because he was the one who wrote the paper for her.

The ethics committee informed Dr. Karry that he should pursue the matter within the institution. Yet, privately, the committee members worried about Kerry's mental stability.

The Burned Out and Those With Other Impairments

Therapists suffering from their own emotional and physical challenges, burnout, marital problems, and other stressors reveal themselves in a substantial number of cases involving professional misconduct (Katsavdakis, Gabbard, & Athey, 2004). Such problems often lead to poor professional judgment and incompetent performances. Although some who fall in this category may elicit sympathy, they can also cause considerable harm to vulnerable consumers.

Case 1–23: Cecila Pow, L.M.F.C., had become increasingly frustrated with the lack of progress in all of her clients. She quit taking any notes, resulting in an inability to keep track of what transpired during previous sessions and mixing up clients' issues. At home, she was caring for her ailing mother while attempting to keep her two rebellious teenagers from getting into trouble.

Case 1–24: Colleagues reported to the clinic manager that Mordred Gloom, Psy.D., failed to keep many of his appointments and did not call to cancel them. It took some of his clients almost an hour by bus to get to the clinic. A few quit coming at all, complaining to the receptionist that their therapist did not even care enough about them to show up. It was then discovered that Gloom had become so depressed over the recent breakup with his wife that he could not always pull himself out of bed in the morning.

Case 1–25: Ed Bellevue, Ph.D., physically attacked a client with an umbrella, claiming that she was an agent of Zormont, the charged ion force that dwells on the dark side of Pluto.

Case 1–26: As a sufferer of Crohn's disease, abdominal pain and diarrhea would cause Sam Sick, L.M.H.C., to frequently excuse himself in the middle of therapy sessions. One client claimed that she resented paying for partial sessions, some of which lasted only 10 minutes, and pressed ethics charges.

Mental health professionals are not immune to emotional disorders, including serious psychopathology. Dr. Pow may have reason to be disappointed in some of her clients, but she seems noticeably affected by burnout and must take immediate steps to refresh herself before her career unravels. She has already committed ethical errors by showing disrespect for her clients and their welfare. Obviously, the actual people we call Drs. Gloom and Bellevue were in need of intensive treatment themselves. Mr. Sick may be viewed as the most sympathetic of the lot because people generally have more compassion and forgiveness for those with physical illnesses as compared to those inflicted with mental conditions. However, the client who protested was not being well served. Mr. Sick should not attempt to treat clients until his condition has stabilized sufficiently for him to give clients the full attention they deserve. (See more about the distressed and mentally unfit therapists in Chapter 4.)

Those With No Boundaries

This book contains three chapters on boundary issues, and for good reason. A great many ethical infractions involve some form of blending the professional role with another that ultimately harms clients and often enough hurts the therapists themselves. While recognizing that it is impossible to avoid all boundary crossings and that not all role-mixings are unethical or harmful, we show how unaware, rationalizing, and malintentioned therapists can do considerable damage to those with whom they work. The chapters devoted to this topic describe boundary violations using discrete categories (e.g., accepting former lover as a therapy client or going into business with a client). However, sometimes cases reveal therapists who are *totally* fluid in their professional interactions with clients, imposing no restrictions whatsoever on how they tangle their own lives with those of their clients. Whether this is from ignorance, self-absorption, avarice, neediness, or a mental condition is not always clear. The next actual case illustrates a "boundary-free" therapist.

Case 1–27: Twofer Junk, L.M.F.T., had her lower-paying clients schedule appointments on Saturdays in front of her home, where she also held weekly yard sales, consisting of items she would barter in exchange for therapy sessions with other clients and then sell for a profit. When a customer drove up, the therapy was interrupted, and the clients were expected to assist with selling items until another lull occurred, at which time therapy would resume. Ms. Junk also hired clients to clean her house, run errands, drive her around, and do her accounting. She also rented an extra bedroom to a client who babysat during the week and while she was running her yard sale/therapy sessions on Saturdays.

Those Who Rationalize

Self-awareness is an agreed-on hallmark of a well-functioning mental health professional (Schwebel & Coster, 1998). Lack of self-awareness forms the basis of many unethical actions (Bazerman & Banaji, 2004). As Moore (2004) pointed out, self-interest functions in an automatic, compelling, and often unconscious manner. Self-deception allows one to engage in an "internal con game," to act out of self-interest while believing that one has acted morally (Tenbrunsel & Messick, 2004).

Over the years, we have found ourselves continually dazzled by the array of defenses therapists use to justify behaviors that objective observers would judge as highly questionable. We offer five examples, the first three being outrageous (including an attempt to blame the victim) and two more that are more representative of what well-meaning therapists get themselves into without fully thinking a matter through.

Case 1–28: When asked why he admitted to having had sex with 17 clients even though he knew it was prohibited, Cloudy Thot, Ph.D., replied, "It was my way of giving generously of myself to women who desperately needed love."

Case 1–29: Bucks Allgone sued his counselor for pressuring him to invest in his counselor's high-risk startup vitamin supplement company. The company went bust, causing Allgone to lose over a half million dollars. The counselor attempted to defend himself by saying that he only wanted to cut his client in on a deal that should have made them both millions.

Case 1–30: Taken Keepit, M.S.W., refused a recently terminated client's husband's demand to give back the client's mother's extremely valuable collection of antique crystal figurines. The husband took Keepit to small claims court and argued that his wife was distraught and vulnerable and was not capable of making competent decisions. Mr. Keepit asserted that he was under no obligation to return a client's gift, and that if the husband wanted redress he should sue his own wife.

The first two cases resulted in successful legal action against the therapists, However, Mr. Keepit got away with his ill-gained booty.

The next case illustrates a therapist who was trying to do something positive, but her actions were ultimately not helpful to the client and caused her considerable grief.

Case 1–31: Joy Ride, Ph.D., offered to take Royce Turbo, her car-obsessed client, for a spin in her brand new sports car. She could envision no consequences and thought a little outing just this one time would strengthen the therapeutic alliance. The brief experience confused Mr. Turbo, who asked if they could drive all the way to the beach next time. When Dr. Ride pulled back, Turbo terminated therapy and accused Dr. Ride of wanting only his money so that she could pay for her expensive new car.

This incident was never reported to an ethics committee, but Dr. Ride learned a lesson the hard way. The next case, however, represents the commission of insurance fraud in an ostensible effort to help a patient.

Case 1–32: Tryin Tohelp, Ph.D., wanted to assist his financially shaky client, who had a troubled marriage and characteristics of an antisocial personality disorder. He decided not to disclose the *Diagnostic and Statistical Manual's* Axis II diagnosis or the diagnosis of a personality disorder "V code" of marital problems because the client's insurance carrier frequently declined to pay for treatment for these conditions.

Rationalization often operates under subtle and seemingly harmless circumstances, sometimes to justify inaction or convenience.

Sometimes, the "tipping point," the act that spilled over into unethical territory, takes a while in coming as the therapist slowly slides down a slippery slope. For example, and as we show in Chapter 12, sexual exploitation of a client is often the culmination of seemingly innocent flirtations. Therapists need to remain alert because we can all fall prey to talking ourselves in or out of doing something based on reasoning that is other than honest and clearheaded. Beware whenever you hear yourself thinking, "It's just a minor thing," "This time it's different," "Everyone does it," "No one will get hurt," "I can still be objective," "Nobody else will care," and "Just this one time." Pope and Vasquez (2005) added more alerts, if you have such thoughts such as, "It's not unethical as long as no one can prove your did it," "It's not unethical if your client wanted you to do it," and "It's not unethical if none of your clients has ever complained about it." Denial or perceptual distortion, prejudice, bias, and other rigid mental sets can have the same effect as rationalization. These processes also preclude objective judgment, which in turn greatly elevates the chances of making poor judgments.

Those Who Slip

A fairly substantial percentage of ethics violators appear to be mental health professionals who usually conduct themselves in an ethical and competent manner and who, under normal circumstances, show sensitivity to ethical dilemmas. However, circumstances converge to displace usual awareness, perhaps due to inconvenience or distraction. Often based on immediate situational demands, therapists commit acts that have unintended consequences.

Case 1–33: Skid Greenspace, M.S.W., prided himself on using anything that had remaining function before recycling it. Mr. Greenspace was chagrined when a client pointed out that the scratch paper he left in the waiting room for children to draw on had confidential client treatment notes on the back.

Case 1–34: Broma Seltzer, a fragile client, made a frantic call asking to see her therapist, Delta Flyaway, L.M.H.C., right away. Ms. Flyaway was already running late to catch a plane for a long-anticipated trip to Europe. She told Ms. Seltzer that she would have her backup therapist make contact immediately. Ms. Flyaway became distracted by yet another call and left for the airport without contacting her backup. A week later, while skiing in the Swiss Alps, Ms. Flyaway suddenly remembered the call to backup that she had failed to make.

We leave this section by illustrating how slips sometimes occur when whatever pushes the therapist's "buttons" results in an uncustomary emotional response, leading to disastrous consequences.

Case 1–35: As Jumbo Smack, M.A., was walking past the Republican Party headquarters in his local mall on his way to the fast food chicken counter, he hit the face of a President Bush cardboard stand-up, knocking it over. Vic, an office staffer, ran out, and an argument ensued. The squabble got physical, and Smack knocked Vic to the ground, breaking Vic's nose.

Jumbo was arrested for and found guilty of assault, he lost a civil suit for damages, and his private practice bottomed out. Every mental health professional is vulnerable to membership in this "Oops!" category, and it is the most difficult type of infraction to predict or prevent. Thus, it is fitting that we turn now to a discussion of how any of us can find ourselves in an ethical predicament.

RISKY CONDITIONS

Carelessness, lack of awareness, inadequate knowledge or training, self-delusion, or some deficit in the therapist's character are not the only conditions spawning ethically questionable actions. Alert, well-meaning, sensitive, mature, and adequately trained therapists functioning within their bounds of competence will also encounter ethical dilemmas that can result in vulnerability to charges of misconduct. Several common conditions that result in confronting an ethical situation are adapted from Sieber's (1982) scheme.

Unforeseen Dilemmas

Sometimes, an ethical issue is simply not predictable. For example, suppose that a conflict of interest does not become known until some time after taking on a client. The client may turn out to be the therapist's mother's boss. An agitated client could discover a therapist's home address and unexpectedly show up at the front door, opened by the therapist's 9-year-old daughter. Crisis situations may present ethical challenges, and these also often crop up unforeseen.

Inadequate Anticipation

A therapist may understand an ethical problem but not expect it to arise. Or, a therapist might underestimate the magnitude of the problem or decide that taking safeguards would prove unnecessary or too costly. For example, a therapist treating a couple may not attend sufficiently to the possible confidentiality dilemmas that could develop if a divorce occurs and one parent later attempts to subpoena the treatment records for use in a custody dispute. Potential ethical problems may never materialize, but if they do, the therapist will remain responsible for not taking reasonable precautions.

Unavoidable Dilemmas

Even when foreseeing a potential ethical problem, there may be no apparent way to avoid it. In some circumstances, at least one party will become upset or feel betrayed, but no feasible options exist to prevent the distress. For example, to protect the welfare of a client, a therapist may recognize no other course of action except to share with others information obtained in confidence. Or, when a therapist intervenes on behalf of a client who claims to have experienced abuse, other family members may become distraught and feel wronged. If there is a complaint, ethics committees and licensing boards (as illustrated in Chapter 3) may judge the therapist's actions after the fact regarding whether the problem could have been avoided.

Unclear Dilemmas

In a variation of the inadequately anticipated dilemma, a problem could be seen as possibly arising, but ambiguous features may cloud the choice of what action to take. We can not always predict the consequences of available alternatives as we attempt to make a decision about how best to confront an ethical problem. The use of some innovative or controversial research or therapeutic techniques, for example, becomes problematic because the risks, if any, are simply unknown.

Inadequate Sources of Guidance

An ethical problem may arise whenever relevant guidelines or laws prove inadequate, nonexistent, ambiguous, or contradictory. The general or nonspecific nature of ethics codes and other regulations can create considerable confusion. Revision of ethics codes is a long and arduous process. In the meantime, new issues arise, such as emerging technology and its potential for ethical pitfalls. Furthermore, most ethics codes provide some latitude for interpretation because of vagueness and ambiguity (Bersoff, 1994; Keith-Spiegel, 1994). Ethics codes often do not deal adequately with many contradictions that can arise. For example, although most codes stress client welfare, not uncommonly a circumstance will arise in which protecting a client or other consumer of our professional services may simultaneously place another person, group, or even the general community at risk.

Loyalty Conflicts

An ethical problem may present itself whenever discrepancies exist among the demands of a law, governmental policy, employer, or ethical principle that simultaneously jeopardizes the welfare of client. In individual situations, therapists may feel torn among those who pay for their services or to whom they owe a favor, taxpayers or other third-party payers, colleagues, employers, or employees. These thorny dilemmas cause considerable distress because a single choice must often be made from among several legitimate loyalties. Someone or some entity may not feel well served as a result, no matter what the choice. It often becomes difficult, if not impossible, to protect the rights and fulfill the legitimate needs of all constituencies simultaneously.

Conflicting Ethical Principles

When making ethical decisions, a thorny dilemma arises when one moral principle conflicts with another. Which one takes precedence? The application of principle ethics, as we presented at the beginning of this chapter, does not rank them in order of importance. And, ethical principle clashes occur more regularly than you might think. For example, you might consider holding back a truthful response because the client would likely be upset or harmed by it. Or, divulging information to help one person can involve breaking another's confidence.

Fortunately, mental health professionals have resources that will greatly assist in the resolution of ethical dilemmas. In the next chapter, we present ways to define ethical dilemmas so that they can be approached responsibly, how to make decisions, and how to intervene when colleagues behave unethically.

References

American Association for Marriage and Family Therapy. (2001). *AAMFT code of ethics.* Alexandria, VA: Author. Retrieved May 29, 2006, from http://www.aamft.org/Resources/lrmplan/Ethics/ethicscode2001.asp

American Counseling Association. (2005). *ACA code of ethics.* Alexandria, VA: Author. Retrieved May 19, 2006, from http://www.counseling.org/AboutUs/

American Psychiatric Association. (2006). *The principles of medical ethics with annotations especially applicable to psychiatry.* Arlington, VA: Author. Retrieved May 19, 2005, from http://www.psych.org/psych_pract/ethics/ppaethics.cfm

American Psychological Association. (2002). *The ethical principles of psychologists and code of conduct.* Washington, DC: Author. Retrieved May 20, 2006, from http://www.apa.org/ethics/code2002.html

Baerger, D. R. (2001). Risk management with the suicidal patient: Lessons from case law. *Professional Psychology, 32,* 359–366.

Bazerman, M. H., & Banaji, M. R. (2004). The social psychology of ordinary ethical failures. *Social Justice Research, 17,* 111–115.

Beauchamp, T. L., & Childress, J. F. (1989). *Principles of biomedical ethics.* New York: Oxford University Press.

Bennett, B. E., Bryant, B. K., VandenBos, G. R., & Greenwood, A. (1990). *Professional liability and risk management.* Washington, DC: American Psychological Association.

Bersoff, D. N. (1994). Explicit ambiguity: The 1992 ethics code as oxymoron. *Professional Psychology, 25,* 382–387.

Bersoff, D. N. (1996). The virtue of principle ethics. *Counseling Psychologist, 24,* 86–91.

Birrell, P. J. (2006). An ethic of possibility: Relationship, risk, and presence. *Ethics & Behavior, 16,* 95–115.

Canadian Psychological Association. (2000). *Canadian code of ethics for psychologists* (3rd ed.). Ottawa, Ontario: Author. Retrieved May 16, 2007, from http://www.cpa.ca/cpasite/userfiles/Documents/Canadian%20Code%20of%20Ethics%20for%20Psycho.pdf

Frankena, W. K. (1973). *Ethics.* Englewood Cliffs, NJ: Prentice-Hall.

Gilligan, C. (1982). *In a different voice: Psychological theory and women's development.* Cambridge, MA: Harvard University Press.

Gottlieb, M. C. (1994). Ethical decision making, boundaries, and treatment effectiveness: A reprise. *Ethics & Behavior, 4,* 287–293.

Jordan, A. E., & Meara, N. M. (1990). Ethics and the professional practice of psychologists: The role of virtues and principles. *Professional Psychology, 21,* 107–114.

Katsavdakis, K., Gabbard, G. O., & Athey, G. I. (2004). Profiles of impaired health professionals. *Bulletin of the Menninger Clinic, 68,* 60–72.

Keith-Spiegel, P. (1994). The 1992 ethics code: boon or bane? *Professional Psychology, 25,* 315–316.

Kennedy, P. F., Vandehey, M., Norman, W. B., & Diekhoff, G. M. (2003). Recommendations for risk-management practices. *Professional Psychology, 34,* 309–311.

Kitchener, K. S. (1985). Ethical principles and ethical decisions in student affairs. In H. J. Canon

& R. D. Brown (Eds.), *Applied ethics in student services* (pp. 17–29). San Francisco: Jossey-Bass.

Kitchener, K. S. (1996). There is more to ethics than principles. *Counseling Psychologist, 24*, 92–97.

Korner, S. (1995). Risk management and the resolution of treatment destructive resistances or consulting with patients to prevent malpractice. *Psychotherapy, 13*, 33–48.

Maesen, W. A. (1991). Fraud in mental health practice: A risk management perspective. *Administration and Policy in Mental Health, 18*, 421–432.

Meara, N. M., Schmidt. L. D., & Day, J. D. (1996). Principles and virtues: A foundation for ethical decisions, policies, and character, *Counseling Psychologist, 24*, 4–77.

Montgomery, L. M. (1999). Complaints, malpractice, and risk management: Professional issues and personal experiences. *Professional Psychology, 30*, 402–410.

Moore, D. A. (2004). Self-interest, automaticity, and the psychology of conflict of interest. *Social Justice Research, 17*, 189–202.

National Association of Social Workers. (1999). *Code of ethics*. Washington, DC: Author. Retrieved May 26, 2006, from http://www.socialworkers.org/pubs/code/code.asp

Peterson, C., & Seligman, M. E. P. (2004). *Character strengths and virtues: A handbook and classification*. Washington, DC: American Psychological Association.

Pope, K. S., Sonne, J. L., & Greene, B. (2006). *What therapists don't talk about and why*. Washington, DC: American Psychological Association.

Pope, K. S., & Vasquez, M. T. (2005). *How to survive and thrive as a therapist*. Washington, DC: American Psychological Association.

Ross, W. D. (1930). *The right and the good*. Oxford, England: Clarendon Press.

Schwebel, M., & Coster, J. (1998). Well-functioning professional psychologists: As program heads see it. *Professional Psychology, 29*, 284–292.

Sieber, J. E. (1982). Ethical dilemmas in social research. In J. E. Sieber (Ed.), *The ethics of social research: Surveys and experiments* (pp. 1–29). New York: Springer-Verlag.

Stromberg, C. D., Haggarty, D. J., Liebenluft, R. F., McMillan, M. M., Mishkin, B., Rubin, B. L., et al. (1988). *The psychologist's legal handbook*. Washington, DC: Council for the National Register of Health Service Providers in Psychology.

Tenbrunsel, A. E., & Messick, D. M. (2004). Ethical fading: The role of self-deception in unethical behavior. *Social Justice Research, 17*, 223–236.

Tirrell-Wysocki, D. (2006). Court says stop case against rude doctor. Retrieved September 18, 2006, from http://www.washingtonpost.com/wp-dyn/content/article/2006/07/06/AR2006070601728.html

VandeCreek, L. & Knapp, S. (2000). Risk management and life-threatening patient behaviors. *Journal of Clinical Psychology, 56*, 1335–1351.

Walker, R. (1999). Heading off boundary problems: Clinical supervision as risk management. *Psychiatric Services, 50*, 1435–1439.

White, T. I. (1988). *Right and wrong: A brief guide to understanding ethics*. Englewood Cliffs, NJ: Prentice-Hall.

2

Making Ethical Decisions and Taking Action

All that is necessary for evil to triumph is for good men to do nothing.

Edmund Burke

Contents

When ethical conflicts arise, the best possible outcome becomes far more likely if several other conditions pertain. These include the following (adapted from Babad and Salomon 1978):

- sufficient time available for the systematic collection of all pertinent information necessary to consider strategies, consultation, intervention, and follow-up

- proper identification of the person or entity to whom one owes primary allegiance
- an opportunity to involve all relevant parties
- operating under low stress and a mind-set that maximizes objectivity
- the maintenance of an ongoing evaluation that allows for midcourse corrections or other changes to satisfactorily resolve the dilemma

Fortunately, most of the time one does not need to rush into a decision before meeting the conditions listed. Either nothing will happen until these conditions can be satisfied or the problematic act has already occurred but incremental damage seems unlikely in the immediate future.

Do professional ethics codes readily tell us how to actually deal with ethical conflicts and dilemmas? Unfortunately not. A thorough knowledge of relevant codes accompanied by a sincere motivation to follow them does not completely insulate therapists from questionable conduct. Why? This is so because professional ethics codes consist primarily of general, prescriptive guideposts with inherent gaps when it comes to deciding what *specific* action to take (Bersoff, 1994; Keith-Spiegel & Whitley, 1994; Kitchener, 1984). Indeed, ethics codes were never intended to cover every conceivable act. Furthermore, it seems unlikely that the creation of a comprehensive guideline is even possible, leaving it to ethics boards to determine the appropriateness of any given action in a specific context. Therefore, all mental health professionals should internalize a *decision-making strategy* to assist in coping with every ethical matter as it arises. We expect that such a process will maximize the chances of an ethically sound result, although we also readily acknowledge that this does not always happen. Some outcomes will remain problematical no matter how hard one tries to resolve them. However, those who can document a sustained, reasoned effort to deal with the dilemma will have a distinct advantage should their decisions and actions ever be challenged.

We must stress at the outset that the application of ethical decision-making strategies does not actually *make* a decision. However, a systematic examination of the situation will likely have a powerful influence on a final decision.

A SUGGESTED ETHICAL DECISION-MAKING STRATEGY

People differ in their ability to perceive that something they might do, or are already doing, could directly or indirectly affect the welfare of others (Rest, 1982). As noted in Chapter 1, many violators of ethics codes did not judge a situation accurately, for reasons such as ignorance or denial, and thus failed to undertake any decision-making process before acting.

Even when one perceives an incident to have ethical ramifications, a knee-jerk reaction will probably not lead to the best response. Taking the time to document, reflect, and consult is far more likely to produce a better result. Whereas one should undertake decision making deliberately, the actual process can range from a few minutes to days or weeks. (We discuss necessity to make swift decisions under emergency or other urgent conditions in the next section.) Our suggested model, partially adapted from other sources (Haas and Malouf, 1989; Hansen & Goldberg, 1999; Tymchuk, 1981) follows.

1. *Determine whether the matter truly involves ethics.* First, the situation must involve an ethical issue as described in our first chapter. The distinction between the merely unorthodox or poor professional etiquette and unethical behavior may become clouded, especially if one feels emotionally involved or under attack. Sometimes, a claim of, "That's unethical!" more accurately translates as, "I'm so upset by your behavior that it must violate some rule!"

A helpful starting point focuses on identifying the general moral or ethical principle applicable to the situation at hand. As we have already noted, overarching ethical principles such as respect for autonomy, nonmaleficence (doing no harm), justice, and according dignity and caring toward others rank among those often cited as crucial for the evaluation of ethical concerns. Readers will find elements of these principles reflected in most ethics codes, although sometimes one will take precedence over another. For example, autonomy ranks below responsibility if a client threatens to harm another party or talks seriously about suicide. The ethical matter in question can often link to a specific element of a relevant ethics code, policy, or law, which makes this phase easier to complete.

2. *Consult guidelines already available that might apply as a possible mechanism for resolution.* Be prepared to do some homework by finding the resources that represent the moral responsibilities of mental health providers. Ethics codes and policy statements from

relevant professional associations, federal law, or local and state laws (including those regulating the profession), research evidence (including case studies that may apply to the particular situation), and general ethics writings are among the materials that one might consult. As examples, Fisher's (2003) *Decoding the Ethics Code* provides illustrations and interpretation for members of the American Psychological Association (APA). The American Association for Marriage and Family Therapy's (2001) *User's Guide to the AAMFT Code of Ethics* provides the same kind of assistance for its members. One can also find considerable relevant material available on the Internet. Most mental health professional associations post their ethics codes and related information on their Web sites.

The solution does not necessarily become clear at this point, and contradictions may crop up that cause more confusion than before this decision-making process started. Nevertheless, collecting relevant information constitutes a critical step to take conscientiously. A disregard for extant policy or relevant ethical obligations may result in unwanted consequences.

Early in the process, you should also collect information from all relevant parties involved. Sometimes, this step reveals that a simple misunderstanding led to an improper interpretation, or the new data may reveal the matter as far more grave than first suspected. Confidentiality rights must be assessed and, if relevant, protected throughout the process. In some cases, confidentiality issues may preclude taking any further steps.

3. *Pause to consider, as best as possible, all factors that might influence the decision you will make.* An extremely common reason for poor ethical decisions arises from the inability to see the situation objectively because of prejudices, biases, or personal needs that distort the perception of the dilemma. We recommend pausing to introspect and gain an awareness of any rigid mind-sets that could be affecting your judgment. Avoid undue influence by irrelevant variables, such as an individual's personal appearance, political affiliation, or social status. We also recommend searching out any financial ramifications (or other factors that work to

your personal advantage), seeking to ensure that these do not blur anyone's vision, including your own.

Except in those instances when the issues appear clear-cut, salient, and specifically defined by established guidelines, mental health professionals may well have differing opinions regarding the *best* decision. Personality styles and primary guiding moral or religious principles can significantly influence the ethical decision-making process. Other personal characteristics that influence decisions include criteria used to assign innocence, blame, and responsibility; personal goals (including level of emotional involvement); a need to avoid censure; a need to control or for power; and the level of risk one is willing to undertake to get involved. Divergent decisions could also be reflected in judgments about the reprehensibility of a particular act. For example, no bright line demarcates the appropriate level of personal involvement with a client, as we illustrate many times in the chapters on multiple-role relationships. Indeed, we have observed marked discrepancies about the seriousness of an alleged violation during actual ethics committee deliberations! Such lively debates have included differences in the perceived degree of harm or potential for harm, the presumed motivations of the accused therapist, and estimates of the likelihood that the act will reoccur.

Finally, consideration of any culturally relevant variables becomes important (American Psychological Association, 1993; Hansen & Goldberg, 1999). If such factors as the degree of expected confidentiality, gift-giving traditions, bartering practices, geographic locale, placement of professional boundaries, gender, age, ethnicity, or culturally based expressive behaviors exhibited during therapy sessions play a part in an ethical matter, an inappropriate decision might result if culturally based variables are not considered in the mix. Many proscribed acts are unethical no matter what the culturally relevant variables, but other instances can be influenced one way or the other depending on the cultural context.

4. *Consult with a trusted colleague.* Because ethical decision making involves a complicated process influenced by our own perceptions and

values, we can usually benefit by seeking input from others. We suggest choosing consultants known in advance to have a strong commitment to the profession and a keen sensitivity to ethical matters. Choose a confidant with a forthright manner, not an individual over whom you have advantaged status; otherwise, you may hear only what he or she thinks you want to hear.

We have heard of confidants who gave flawed advice, even causing the person seeking it to commit an ethical infraction. For example, a therapist asked a colleague whether he should agree to treat a rape victim, given that he had no relevant experience or training related to victims of sexual violence. They colleague allegedly replied, "Sure, how else are you going to learn?" In another incident, a poorly selected consultant advised a newly licensed counselor to simply "trust his gut" when it came to intermingling with clients outside the office. His barely begun career came to an abrupt halt when, shortly thereafter, his status as a business partner of his sociopathic client became public. This client, a convicted con artist many times over, left the counselor open to prosecution. The counselor's pleas of ignorance persuaded neither the court nor the licensing board. Bottom line: If you doubt a confidant's advice, seek a second opinion.

5. *Evaluate the rights, responsibilities, and vulnerability of all affected parties,* including, if relevant, an institution and the general public. All too frequently a flawed decision results from failing to take into account a stakeholder's right to confidentiality, informed consent, or evaluative feedback.

6. *Generate alternative decisions.* This process should take place without focusing on the feasibility of each option and may even include alternatives otherwise considered too risky, too expensive, or even inappropriate. The alternative of not making a decision at this time and the decision to do nothing at all should also be considered. Establishing an array of options allows the occasional finding that an alternative initially considered less attractive may be the best and most feasible choice after all.

7. *Enumerate the consequences of making each decision.* Whenever relevant, attempt to identify the potential consequences of a decision. These include psychological and social

costs; short-term, ongoing, and long-term effects; the time and effort necessary to implement the decision; any resource limitations; any other risks, including the violation of individual rights; and any benefits. Consider any evidence that the various consequences or benefits resulting from each decision will actually occur. The ability to document this phase may also prove useful should others later question the rationale for your final decision and corresponding action.

8. *Make the decision.* Rachels (1980) has observed that the right action is the one backed by the best reasons. If the above phases have been completed conscientiously, perhaps with the ongoing support of a consultant, a full informational display should now be available. Happily, a decision that also feels like the right thing to do may well become obvious at this point. Even so, many moral and just decisions do not always protect every involved person from some form of injury. Therefore, if anyone could suffer harm, pause to consider any steps that could minimize the damage. For example, if a therapist suspects that an out-of-control adult client might harm his child, the therapist may have to file a report with the state's child protection agency. Sometimes, a more positive outcome can occur with parental engagement rather than alienation, as could happen in the next case.

Case 2–1: Robyn Resque, M.S.W., had treated Betty Boozer, an alcoholic single mother of two, for 18 months. Boozer had remained sober for more than a year and had made sincere efforts to attend effectively to her children, now ages 6 and 8. One day, she appeared for a therapy session intoxicated. She had just learned that she faced a layoff from her job at a local business that had filed for bankruptcy. She felt embarrassed and depressed that she had broken her sobriety and mentioned that she had lost her temper and beaten the children with a belt before coming to therapy.

In most states, Ms. Resque would be obligated to breach Ms. Boozer's confidentiality by filing a report of suspected child abuse with child protection authorities. Doing so would protect the children, conform to state law, and constitute ethically acceptable behavior.

Ms. Resque could, however, also go a step further by attempting to engage Ms. Boozer in collaborating with filing the report and by attempting to engage the authorities in assisting the family while Ms. Boozer strives to restore her sobriety and find alternative employment. The first course of action addresses ethical necessity. The second alternative involves considerably more effort and advocacy but also could yield a better outcome all around.

Ideally, information about the decision should be shared with all affected parties or at least with some subset of representatives if a larger population is involved. Sometimes these parties can not be contacted, are unable to participate, or can not give consent due either to age or to physical, mental, or other limitations. In such cases, additional responsibilities to protect their welfare apply. Special advocates or other safeguards may become necessary in complex situations.

In some cases, your role will extend only to presenting the assembled information because those affected have the right to make the final decision themselves. Sometimes when this happens, professionals experience a personal dilemma. Whereas we are morally obligated to make decisions in the best interests of those with whom we work, clients may choose to make decisions we would not have made on their behalf. Some potential decision options can be quickly dismissed because they involve flagrant violations of respectable governing policies or someone's rights or because the risks far outweigh the potential benefits. Sometimes, several decisions appear equally feasible or correct. Alternatively, the best decision may not be feasible due to various factors, such as resource limitations, requiring a consideration of a less preferable option. However, in our experience the right decision usually clearly presents itself, and it is time to proceed to the next, and perhaps most difficult, step.

9. *Implement the decision.* Mental health professions will remain strong and respected only to the extent that their members willingly take appropriate actions in response to ethical dilemmas. This often demands moral backbone and courage. So, it is at this point that the decision-making process comes to fruition, and the decision maker must actually *do* something. This becomes the most difficult step, even if the decision and course of action seem perfectly clear. According to Rest (1982), "executing and implementing a plan of action involves figuring out the sequence of concrete actions, working around impediments and unexpected difficulties, overcoming fatigue and frustration, resisting distractions and other allurements, and keeping sight of the eventual goal" (p. 34).

The ideal resolution results when a decision can be made *prior* to the commission of an ethical infraction that would otherwise have untoward consequences. But, often enough, the decision occurs in response to an ongoing, problematic situation. Sometimes, the appropriate action involves simply ceasing and desisting from a practice that, after a careful decision-making analysis, seems ethically risky even if no harm has yet occurred. Sometimes, the best course of action is the recognition that a therapist lacks competence, and that continuing education or additional supervision is required. Often, the implementation will involve the need to do something differently from now on and an attempt to ameliorate any damage. Remediation attempts can range from making an apology to an additional intervention or the provision of services or resources to those who were wronged. Sometimes, the implementation will involve contacting an ethics committee or a licensing board to determine the appropriate resolution.

Unfortunately, the implementation phase also becomes a point at which this entire process can derail. Research tells us that most therapists can formulate what they *should* do. However, they will more likely respond to their own values and practicalities when determining what they would *actually do*, which is *less* than they know they should do (Bernard & Jara, 1986; Bernard, Murphy, & Little, 1987; Wilkins, McGuire, Abbott, & Blau, 1990). Tenbrunsel and Messick (2004) used the term *ethical fading* to describe the tendency to move the ethical or moral implications of implementing a decision into the background. Ethical fading is enabled by such factors as language euphemisms (assigning a label to an act that is less serious or benign) and errors in perceptual causation (letting the offender off the hook, perhaps by blaming the victim).

An alarmingly high percentage of scientists and advanced students confide that they know of scientific misconduct committed by their peers, but most do nothing about it. Relatively few cases of scientific misconduct ultimately get reported to the appropriate agencies (Eastwood, Derish, Leash, & Ordway, 1996; Glick, 1989; Steneck, 1999; Swazey, Anderson, & Lewis, 1993; Tagney, 1987; Zweibel & Goldstein, 2001). Dracy and Yutrzenka's (1997) sample of paraprofessional mental health workers said they would confront or report to their supervisors serious violations but were less likely to report less serious violations. Other surveys have revealed, discouragingly, that respondents most often reported a willingness to implement less direct and less restrictive decisions that are less consistent with ethical guidelines, often acting instead from expedience and opportunism (Smith, McGuire, Abbott, & Blau, 1991).

We understand that confronting another person for an uncomfortable reason raises a range of emotions: anxiety, fear of an unknown response and outcome, concerns about retaliation and longer-term consequences, loss of an established relationship, and so on. In their "risk-as-feelings" hypothesis, Lowenstein and his colleagues proposed that emotional reactions to risky situations can overpower cognitive assessments and drive the ultimate decision (Loewenstein, Weber, Hsee, & Welch, 2001). Unfortunately, that decision may be to do nothing or very little as a way of avoiding the overwhelming negative emotions associated with taking more responsible action.

We must also note that the organizational culture in which one works plays a significant role when ethical decisions must be followed by an action. Conflicts are unlikely to arise when the integrity of the employer parallels more general ethical guidelines and employees feel confident that their decisions will be supported up the line. Dilemmas can prove problematic,

however, when an employer's policy does not support or seems contradictory to general moral principles, professional ethics codes, and one's own moral commitments.

Case 2–2: A counselor in a community agency complained to the agency manager that Lucy Lips, Ph.D., often talked in intimate detail about her clients, using their real names, in the coffee lounge. The manager replied, "Don't be so critical. We all work here, and these people don't really care if we talk about them among ourselves."

The "bad barrels" argument holds that characteristics of an organization's culture can inhibit ethical behavior, even among individuals with otherwise high moral standards (Trevino & Youngblood, 1990). Such characteristics include support for and encouragement of unethical behavior by management, widespread and unchecked unethical actions by colleagues, unjust organizational policies, and intense pressure to perform. Such characteristics cause painful conflicts for ethical mental health professionals.

So, here is a hard question. Is it *unethical* to stay on the job when an employer's actions or policies are contrary to the professional's ethical guidelines? The APA ethics code mandates that its members should clarify any conflicts with organizations with which they affiliate, declare their commitment to the APA ethics code, and if feasible attempt to resolve the matter in ways that uphold the disputed provision in the ethics code. The code does not, however, impose any penalty should the matter remain unresolved. We do know of colleagues who have voluntarily terminated their employment rather than remain associated with dishonorable employing institutions. Unfortunately this solution is not practical for most employed mental health professionals.

When requirements in the ethics code clash with laws, regulations, or other governing legal authorities and reasonable attempts to resolve the matter fail, psychologists are released from the demands of the code if they so choose (APA 02: 1.02) in order to obey the legitimate lawful authority.

ETHICAL DECISION MAKING UNDER CRISIS CONDITIONS

Frantic phone calls from clients or their families, clients' threats to harm themselves or someone else, unexpected client behavior or demands, and alarming revelations during a therapy session are not rare occurrences. As a result, ethical dilemmas demanding an immediate response can and do unexpectedly arise. With no time to prepare a carefully reasoned decision using a procedure such as the one we have just presented, therapists may rightly feel anxious and become prone to react less than satisfactorily.

Mental health providers rank high among the professions vulnerable to ethical and legal requirements when making decisions and acting under crisis conditions (Hanson, Kerkhoff, & Bush, 2005). We can even find ourselves called on when not directly involved in the emergency itself. Rubin (1975) vividly describes an instance in which he was summoned by the administrators of his university to manage a threatening and armed student. Time was of the essence. Even the determination of "client" could not be carefully pondered. Was it the violent student? The people he was menacing? The university? The public? This psychologist could hardly maintain an objective stance because his own life was put in danger. Although this was an extreme case, most therapists will face at some point a serious situation requiring ethical decision making and action during less-than-optimal conditions.

The next case grouping involves instances when something terrible is or appears to be in progress.

Case 2–3: A client expressed considerable anger toward a boss who had recently threatened to fire him. During a psychological assessment, the client described his boss to the therapist as "an exploiter of the working class who deserved to be exterminated." The client detailed a clear plan to perform the "execution" himself with a hunting knife he kept in the trunk of his car.

Case 2–4: A mother brought her 10-year-old daughter to therapy because she was becoming unusually reserved and withdrawn. The mother could offer no explanation for this abrupt change in her daughter's demeanor. When the mother left the room, the child revealed that for the past 3 months her stepfather had entered her room after everyone else went to sleep. He touched her body and requested that she fondle his genitals. The stepfather had warned the girl not to tell her mother or brothers because, if she did, the police would break up the family because of her tattling.

Case 2–5: Halfway through a therapy session an angry husband pulled a gun from his jacket and shot at his wife, who promptly pulled a gun from her purse and shot back.

Involving the appropriate authorities would be acceptable in all of the above cases despite the fact that reporting might violate a confidence in the process (see Chapter 8). The client's boss appears to be in danger of bodily harm or even death, and a child may be experiencing ongoing harm. In the last case—and we swear this incident actually occurred—the warring spouses remained alive. So, the therapist found himself in a potentially perilous situation in the presence of two clients who were enraged, wounded, *and* armed.

Sometimes crises do not involve immediate danger, but they do necessitate immediate action.

Case 2–6: A marriage and family counselor took a call from the 13-year-old daughter of a couple he was seeing. The girl sobbed, "I just called to say goodbye because I am running away from home," and hung up.

Because the child is a legal minor, the therapist should inform the parents immediately, and the authorities might become involved if the child proves difficult to locate in short order.

Despite many warning signs, a crisis may not clearly exist. The next cases illustrate ambiguous situations. The therapists' suspicions could prove unfounded, and yet ignoring them could lead to disastrous consequences. How would you react to the next three situations?

Case 2–7: A client who had expressed suicidal ideation in the past showed uncommonly flat affect during a therapy session. The therapist knew that the client had experienced stressors recently and became concerned that his apathy and apparent peacefulness might indicate a resolve to kill himself rather than a sign of improvement. The client vehemently denied any intent regarding self-harm. Fifteen minutes before the scheduled end of the session, the client stood up and calmly stated that he had to be somewhere else.

Case 2–8: A therapist was awakened in her home at midnight by a loud pounding on her front door and someone yelling her name. She recognized the voice of one of her clients.

Case 2–9: A therapist knows that tensions exist in the home of his elderly client who lives with her son and his wife, but becomes particularly concerned because the client has been rapidly losing weight. He asks the client about a bruise on her arm, and after fumbling with her words, the client claims she fell in the shower. The therapist doubts the bruise could have occurred in that way, but the client insists that her living arrangement has improved and promises to see a physician about her weight loss.

As each of the above cases illustrates, crises requiring some decision that is bound to have ethical implications occur most often when an element of ongoing harm or immediate danger appears to be present. As seasoned clinicians know, uncommonly flat affect in clients at risk for suicide could indicate that the client has made a decision to resolve personal pain by exercising the "ultimate solution." Clients who stalk their therapists are not uncommon, and estimates of the risk of such stalkers becoming aggressive are as high as 25% (Kaplan, 2006). Elder abuse is not rare, and the vulnerable victims may be too intimidated to report it. Yet, none of these cases is clear-cut.

Regardless of the nature of the actual or impending crisis, therapists are in the unenviable position of having to make a number of delicate decisions at a time they, themselves, may feel anxious. Do both ethical and legal perspectives require maintaining confidentiality? If a disclosure appears warranted or mandated, who should be drawn into the matter? A client's family? A state agency or emergency response team? The police? What details can one appropriately dis-

close? What is an acceptable alteration in the degree of acceptable involvement with a client during a crisis? We argue consistently throughout this book that therapists almost always serve the consumers of their services best when they hold to appropriate professional roles, and we offer many examples of boundary violations that have substantially harmed others. However, crises may call for temporary exceptions to our usual advice. The most ethical response under conditions of possible calamity—especially those involving matters of life and death—might conceivably involve ministering to distraught family members, breaking a confidence that would have remained secure under usual circumstances, showing more patience or engaging in more than the usual nonerotic touching, or even actively searching for the whereabouts of clients or their significant others. For example, Case 2–6 presents one of those rare occasions when the therapist might consider jumping in his car and driving to the family home in the hopes of finding that the minor child has not yet run away.

Because of their very general nature, ethics codes will often offer little help in such crises. The APA ethics code, for example, allows divulging information shared in confidence only as mandated or permitted by law (APA 02: 4.05.b). Statutes, regulations, or case law in many states allow disclosure when a client or others require protection from harm. Yet, if a client says, "I get so mad at my mother that I feel like wringing her neck," has the remark crossed a sufficient threat threshold? Prediction of the actual level of immediate danger is not an exact science, but mental health professionals can be held accountable for their inaction and misjudgments. (See Chapter 8 for a more detailed discussion of disclosure obligations.)

Mental health professionals are, on occasion, themselves the target of a potential crisis. Fortunately it is rare for a therapist to be harmed or killed by a client, but it does happen on occasion. In one instance, an entire ethics committee appeared to be targeted for "elimination."

Case 2–10: Wyde Awake, Ph.D., was referred to an ethics committee by an insurance carrier. The company's audit revealed that Dr. Awake billed for 100 hours of psychotherapy during a 5-day period, for an average of 20 hours a day. Although Dr. Awake's clients failed to substantiate that these sessions actually took place, Awake insisted that his patients' recollections were in error, and that he did not require much sleep. When Awake was asked by an ethics committee to better explain his hours, he threatened to hire the Mafia to kill all of its members unless the charges against him were dropped immediately.

Dr. Awake proved to be mentally ill, and the death threats proved hollow. More commonly, therapists may experience stalking by their clients, as already noted. According to a survey conducted by Purcell, Powell, and Mullen (2005), about one fifth of the stalking clients were believed to be acting from infatuation, and almost half were regarded as resentful. Most of the victims were women. Such incidents pose difficult ethical issues in that the therapists must decide whether to violate confidentiality by reporting their clients in the absence (usually) of any direct threat of bodily harm.

Clients at Special Risk for Crises

Some clients wait until their situation reaches urgent proportions before consulting a mental health professional. In such instances, therapists may have to make critical judgments with potentially significant consequences about people with whom they have not yet formed a professional relationship or gathered sufficient information. The next case illustrates this predicament.

Case 2–11: During the first 5 minutes of the initial therapy session, a highly agitated man claimed that a neighbor was abusing his 26-year-old daughter by forcing her into "sexual slavery." He rambled on, alleging bizarre sex acts that the neighbor regularly perpetrated on his daughter. He restated several times his conviction that the neighbor posed an immediate threat to his daughter's life.

Does the father's story seem credible? After all, the therapist does not yet know this person. Does his agitation arise from actual events or perhaps from a misunderstanding of consenting adults' particular sexual proclivities? Could the father's concerns reflect a delusional state of mind? Why has he not brought his daughter with him? Where is she now? Without answers to these questions, an optimal course of action is difficult to discern. The careful therapist can obviously listen with an empathic diagnostic ear but can not rush to judgment. (For an example of how such a situation played out in court, see Case 8–16.)

Assessing and responding to a client who may pose a risk of suicide carries a heavy and stress-provoking responsibility. Becoming well versed in the clues that suggest a risk of suicide should be an essential part of all psychotherapists' training. These include a verbal statement of intent, suicidal ideation, a history of past attempts, a precipitating event, deterioration in social or vocational functioning, a plan of action, intense affect, and expressed feelings of hopelessness and despair (Bongar, 1992; Hendin, Maltsberger, Haas, Szanto, & Rabinowicz, 2004; Hendin, Maltsberger, Lipschitz, Pollinger-Haas, & Kyle, 2001; Pope & Vasquez, 2005). Depending on the situation, some therapists may struggle with the ethics of suicide itself, as when a client has a terminal illness and experiences constant and severe pain (Curry, Schwartz, Gruman, & Blank, 2000; Peruzzi, Canapary, & Bongar, 1996; Werth, 1999a, 1999b).

According to several surveys, nearly one quarter to one half of therapists sampled lost a client through suicide (e.g., Brown, 1987; Chemtob, Bauer, Hamada, Pelowski, & Muraoka, 1989; Chemtob, Hamada, Bauer, Torigoe, & Kinney, 1988). Legal analyses of actions by suicide patients' families reveal no agreed-on, clear-cut course of action when clients threaten to harm themselves (Berman & Cohen-Sandler, 1983; Fine & Sansone, 1990; Litman, 1991; Slawson, Flinn, & Schwartz, 1974). An important step therapists should take in such cases involves carefully documenting concerns and decisions when working with potentially suicidal clients. Such records will prove critical to a later defense should a therapist be sued, and the quality of such documentation may determine whether a defense attorney will take the case (Simpson & Stacey, 2004). Lawsuits against mental health professionals remain fairly rare (although on the rise), yet client suicide accounts for a significant proportion of them. The wise therapists will become well versed in the legal aspects of suicide in advance of being forced to learn them (see Baerger, 2001; Feldman, Moritz, Benjamin, & Andrew, 2005; Gross, 2005; Gutheil, 2004; Packman, Pennuto, Bongar, & Orthwein, 2004; Remley, 2004; VandeCreek & Knapp, 2000; Weiner, 2005).

Clients with certain diagnoses, such as borderline personality disorder, seem exceptionally prone to crises (Shinefield & Kalafat, 1996) because of emotional lability, impulsivity, and tenuous relationship histories. The high incidence of child abuse in our society suggests that most therapists will also have to deal with challenging family crisis and the associated legal reporting mandates. Preparing for what to expect and what to do in such circumstances alleviates the tension to some extent and maximizes the chances for the best outcome (Committee on Professional Practice and Standards, 1995; Kalichman, 1999; Zellman & Fair, 2002). Chapter 5 addresses high-risk clients in greater detail.

Preparing for Crises in Advance

Although crisis management techniques are well beyond the scope of this book, we conclude this section by offering suggestions for preventive action if you are ever forced to make decisions under conditions of an intense time constraint or emergency conditions.

1. *Know the emergency resources available in your community.* Keep the names, numbers, and descriptions of community services in your area in an easy-to-access location. The prudent therapist will also check the quality of the resources Sometimes, promotional materials promise more than agencies actually deliver. Some are known to be slow or disorganized, ineffective, or even inhumane in actual crisis situations. This list should be updated at least once every year because well-meaning and enthusiastic community support services are sometimes short-lived.

Some lose their funding and disband, new ones are established, and others undergo reorganizations that improve or downgrade the quality of services. If such emergency resources are used during a crisis, follow up on the quality of their performance and carefully monitor the client's progress.

2. *Form or join an alliance of colleagues in your community; each person agrees to be available for consultation when emergencies arise.* Ideally, a mental health professional with experience in crisis care should be included. Keep these names and numbers in your easy-access emergency resource file.

3. *Know the laws and policies in your state or locale relating to matters that are likely to accompany crisis events.* These include mandated reporting statutes (specifying the conditions under which information obtained in confidence must be reported to authorities) and commitment procedures. Seek clarification on any sections of the law or policies that seem unclear before responding becomes necessary. Frantic searches through files or frenetic phone calls to colleagues or attorneys are poor substitutes for preexisting knowledge.

4. *Locate an attorney in your community who is knowledgeable about matters that have legal implications relevant to your practice.* Keep that phone number in your emergency resource file.

5. *Actively seek out learning experiences that will sharpen your knowledge about the kinds of crises that may arise in your professional practice.* Take a continuing education class in crisis counseling if your formal training was deficient in this area. Courses in first aid and cardiopulmonary resuscitation are also a good idea, just in case.

6. *Conscientiously define your own areas of competence, then practice only within these confines.* Although competence is an ethical issue in and of itself (see Chapter 4), practicing within your competence bounds provides an additional advantage during emergencies. The ability to function admirably during crises is often related to the level of expertise and experience with a particular clientele population or diagnostic group. Early on, refer clients who exceed your training and expertise to appropriate other practitioners.

7. *Carefully monitor the relationship between yourself and those with whom a close and trusting alliance has been built.* Therapeutic miscalculations can result in intense client–therapist dynamics that lead to unanticipated outcomes. The mishandling of transference by therapists has been traced as the cause of client crises, including completed suicides (Skodol, Kass, & Charles, 1979; Stone, 1971). Gaining information about clients' spiritual beliefs early on is also advised. Those undergoing a severe loss or other difficult life situation may also experience a spiritual crisis, and the therapist who understands a deeper meaning of a client's despair is in a better position to respond effectively (Cunningham, 2000).

8. *Never rely solely on your memory.* Carefully document any crisis event, including the decisions you made and your rationale for making them. Careful records will greatly assist you, and possibly others, should the event later require a formal review.

Crises in the Therapist's Life

We have discussed crises and emergencies as they happen to clients and their families. However, therapists can also experience calamities with little time to make adjustments for their clients and other professional commitments. The therapist who, for example, falls acutely ill must deal with revised session scheduling, how much to disclose to clients, and how they should refer their clients if it becomes necessary to interrupt services (Kahn, 2003). Juggling these unwelcome adjustments becomes even more difficult because of the reason for making them.

Case 2–12: The client felt increasingly irritated as her counselor, Di Verted, L.M.H.C., became unresponsive and distracted during the session. The client finally snorted, "I feel like you are not paying any attention to what I am trying to tell you, and it upsets me because my husband forgot my birthday again, and you don't seem to care." Ms. Diverted apologized and haltingly disclosed that her 3-year-old granddaughter had drowned in the family swimming pool a few days ago. The stunned client expressed sympathy, got up, and left.

The counselor did not handle her understandable personal grief as it affects her clients well. A client felt ignored and then was forced to deal with mixed feelings about being embarrassed about complaining about what was, by contrast, a trivial matter. The client was also perhaps more drawn into her therapist's personal life than felt comfortable to her. Ms. Di verted needed more time before commencing her practice. She might have considered canceling appointments or referring urgent cases to a backup therapist, explaining to her clients that she needed some time to deal with "a pressing family matter." In the situation described, Ms. Di Verted might consider sending the client a note apologizing for not recognizing her need for more personal time and for any discomfort the situation caused.

INFORMAL PEER MONITORING

This book is mostly about the ethical obligations of mental health professionals in their own work with clients. However, we also have some responsibility to watch out for each other. Unethical activity often persists, totally unchecked, unless someone takes notice and intervenes. Observing or learning of an ethically questionable act constitutes the front-line opportunity for a corrective intervention. Action can be taken directly by confronting the colleague or indirectly in the form of advising clients or others on how to proceed with concerns about another mental health professional's actions.

What should you do when you observe an ethical violation or hear about an alleged unethical act committed by a colleague? Should you infer that it is a one-time-only mistake and forget about it? Believe that others will take care of it, letting you off the hook? Trust that what goes around comes around, and that somehow the matter will take care of itself? Convince yourself that no one will be harmed, even if this pattern of behavior continues? Oddly, how to respond to the unethical behavior of others is rarely discussed in any detail in the professional literature. However, we believe that this matter is extremely important and deserves a thorough airing.

Ironically, therapists frequently divulge their ethical infractions to one of their peers, sometimes without any awareness of doing so.

Case 2–13: During a casual, private conversation at a professional meeting about unconventional therapy techniques, Spanky Noclue, Ph.D., described an adult female client whom he would take across his knee and slap gently on the buttocks. He claimed that the technique was extremely useful in "facilitating transference in histrionic women" and, in an apparent gesture of helpfulness, encouraged the listener to try it.

The stunned listener did not comment on Dr. Noclue's unconventional paddling at the time, but the talk lingered in the listener's mind, and he struggled with what, if anything, to do about it. He did not know Dr. Noclue very well, and they lived a thousand miles apart. In the actual incident, the listener believed he did the best he could when, after making a telephone call resulting in a long conversation, Noclue agreed that his technique was not appropriate and stated that he would discontinue it.

More commonly, colleagues come for advice before a contemplated action occurs. More often than not, gaining your approval of the contemplated act is the primary motive for soliciting you as a confidant. In such situations, you have been presented with an exceptional opportunity to be a part of upholding the integrity of the profession by setting your colleague straight.

Case 2–14: Spot Lite, Psy.D., had treated a recently convicted murderer for a few months. Details about the gruesome crime ran as the lead story on local TV news every night. Lite asked a colleague if she thought it would be OK to contact the media with interesting tidbits about the murderer's childhood and other revelations made during counseling. Mr. Lite defended his plan as an opportunity to educate the public. He also figured it was a way to get his name and face out to the community, and it could not cause a convicted murderer any further harm. The colleague quickly advised Lite that this would be totally inappropriate and why.

Mr. Lite hoped that his colleague would validate his self-serving brainchild. But Lite at some level probably knew better himself, making the task of assisting in the prevention of a contemplated confidentiality violation easier.

When an Informal Resolution May Fail

Sometimes, attempting an informal resolution with a colleague may not be a sound option. Possible indicators include the following:

- The colleague's contentious or abrasive personality would likely cause an informal approach to fail.
- The possible infraction is so serious that it should not be dealt with informally.
- The colleague is addicted to drugs of alcohol.
- The colleague is acutely stressed, emotionally disturbed, or mentally ill.
- A great deal is at stake, such as the welfare of many clients or the reputation of the institution.
- Preexisting bad feelings already exist toward the suspected colleague, making an informal approach more likely to be confrontational and unbeneficial.
- A status or power differential vis-à-vis the suspected violator is not in your favor.
- Overall incompetence is at issue.
- Others, significant to validating or resolving the incident, will not allow their identities to be known.

We know of rare instances of threatened physical harm, retaliation, or legal action for harassment and slander against therapists who attempted to deal directly with the ethical misconduct of their colleagues. The next case illustrates this difficult circumstance.

Case 2–15: Melba Goodtry, Psy.D., received complaints from several clients and other therapists about the "whiskey breath" of Groggy Sot, M.S.W., one of the counselors in her group office practice. She approached him with her concerns. Mr. Sot yelled at Dr. Goodtry, accused her of being jealous of his wife, and threatened to sue her if she repeated these "vicious allegations" to anyone else. Dr. Goodtry felt helpless and afraid. However, she had also detected a strong stench of liquor on Sot's breath.

We would advise Dr. Goodtry to request a formal investigation. Fortunately, she knows others who may join with her in doing so. Whereas Mr. Sot proved a poor candidate for informal collegial intervention, some impaired therapists with more temperate and likable personalities may respond well to a supportive colleague's honesty and concern.

Currently, and partially because of reported incidents of harassment and intimidation, the APA ethics code gives its members the option of deciding the appropriateness of dealing with the matter directly (APA: 02: 1.04). If an informal solution seems unlikely (for reasons left un-elaborated), and substantial harm has already occurred (or is likely to occur), psychologists should take formal action—such as contacting a licensing board or ethics committee—as long as any client confidentiality rights or other conflicts do not preclude reporting (APA 02: 1.05).

Ethical violations often involve colleagues whose conduct and professional judgment are affected by addiction, physical, or more often, emotional problems, and marital discord (Katsavdakis, Gabbard, & Athey, 2004). According to a survey undertaken by the APA Task Force on Distressed Psychologists, almost 70% of the sample personally knew of therapists experiencing serious emotional difficulties. However, only about a third were believed to have made substantive attempts to help themselves (reported in VandenBos & Duthie, 1986). We estimate, from our own experiences sitting on ethics committees, that about half of the therapists with sustained complaints appear to have some personal turmoil or emotional condition that very likely contributed to the commission of an ethical violation.

If a colleague appears generally incompetent, informal intervention will not resolve the problem. Such individuals rarely have insight into their shortcomings and could cause considerable harm to clients. However, if the incompetence seems restricted to a single technique or application that could benefit from either remediation or discontinuation, informal intervention remains a viable option.

Mental health professionals may be requested by another colleague or a client to assist in confronting an alleged violator, but the requester also insists on concealing his or her identity. Often, such people fear reprisal or feel inadequate to defend themselves. Occasionally, a third person critical to pursuing the matter is unavailable or unwilling to become involved or to be identified. These situations pose extremely frustrating predicaments. Approaching colleagues with charges issued by unseen accusers violates the essence of due process. Furthermore, alleged violators often know (or think they know) their accusers' identities anyway.

When the alleged unethical behaviors are extremely serious, possibly putting yet others in harm's way, and when the fearful but otherwise credible individuals making the charges adamantly insist on remaining anonymous, therapists may not feel comfortable ignoring the situation altogether. However, there may be nothing else that can be done. Sometimes, the option to do nothing may not exist, as with adherence to a state's mandatory reporting laws (Canter, Bennett, Jones, & Nagy, 1994). However, for other reporting situations not required by law, the current APA code leaves psychologists no options if confidentiality issues can not be resolved.

Case 2–16: A new client told Ima Current, Ph.D., that he had adverse experiences with his previous therapist. He claimed that Dr. Weary Brusque would sit for most of the hour saying nothing or browsing through a magazine or doing paperwork while the client spoke. When Brusque did occasionally respond, the client claimed he simply barked quick orders, such as, "Just cut off that relationship." Dr. Current was acquainted with Dr. Brusque and thought him extremely odd. She wanted to attempt to discuss the matter with Dr. Brusque, but when she offered to intervene, the client became frantic and remained resolute in his refusal to be identified.

Dr. Current is stuck. She can not completely discount the remote possibility that Dr. Brusque had attempted to apply some strategic or paradoxical principles with this particular client. She can, however, certainly educate the client about behavior expected of professionals and possibly help him gain strength to later follow through with a complaint, if that should become the client's wish.

Your Relationship to the Potential Ethics Violator

Those who observe or hear about the possible unethical actions by other mental health professionals often know the alleged offenders personally. How you get along with a suspected colleague will affect both your interpretation of the situation and the approach taken. The colleague could be a good friend or an intensely disliked adversary. He or she could be a subordinate or a supervisor. Reactions, depending on the relationship with someone suspected of ethics violations, have ramifications for how to deal with them. Taking direct action sometimes proves easier with a subordinate (not so threatening) or when one dislikes the suspected colleague. Anger is a powerful motivator to get involved. One should never attempt such an intervention, however, when one's own rage or other strong emotion might get in the way.

If the colleague is a friend or acquaintance with whom no previous problematic interactions have occurred, a confrontation can go very well. You can express to your friend that your interest and involvement arise out of caring and concern for his or her professional standing. The danger, of course, lies in risking disruption of an established, positive relationship. If you can effectively educate your friend, however, you may well have protected this individual from embarrassment or more public forms of censure. Discomfort, to the extent that it ensues, may well prove temporary. Similarly, should someone ever approach you with a concern about your own conduct, treat this as a professional gift and carefully consider the opinion offered. If one person dares to speak with you about the matter, many others might already be aware of the possible problem as well.

If you do not know the colleague personally, the confrontation will feel, by definition, more reserved. An expression of concern and a willingness to work through the problem cooperatively may still prove quite effective.

If you dislike a colleague or feel upset by this person's behavior, courage to act may come more from the thrill of revenge than from genuine bravery and conviction. Proceed more cautiously in such instances. If others know the same information (or if it can be appropriately shared with others), you might consider asking someone who has a better relationship with the individual to intercede or to accompany you. If that proves not feasible, and a careful assessment of your own motivations reveals that the possible misconduct clearly requires intervention on its own merits, then you should take some form of action. It may still prove possible to approach this individual yourself, and if you maintain a professional attitude, it may work. We know of one therapist who approached his long-standing nemesis with concern about her ethical conduct. The two eventually became friends as a result of working through the matter together!

Is There a Moral Obligation to Intervene?

Because less serious forms of reported unethical behavior may not be pursued in formal venues (see Chapter 3), informal peer monitoring creates the best chance to intervene and correct the questionable behavior of colleagues for three reasons:

1. Colleagues have specialized knowledge about expectations of members in the field.
2. Colleagues are in an advantageous position to observe or hear about unethical behaviors among peers.
3. Colleagues may be able to prevent ethical infractions from ever materializing.

By applying Whitley's theory of proximate causes of academic dishonesty (Whitley, 1998; Whitley & Keith-Spiegel, 2002), we see how colleagues may often constitute the *only* source for preventing or confronting unethical behavior. Whitley holds that intent to engage in unethical behavior rests on three factors:

1. The colleague's moral attitudes toward committing an unethical act and what the colleague perceives as the norms regarding the act.
2. The benefits that the individual expects from acting unethically.
3. The perceived risk of getting caught.

As this model indicates, any thought of purposely engaging in unethical acts are quickly reversed if the person realizes that his or her own values and commitment to professional ethical standards preclude engaging in such an act. Or, even if a colleague talks him- or herself into the acceptability of a questionable act, the perceived benefits may rank lower than the perceived risks of exposure. However, when a colleague rationalizes a need to commit an unethical act, anticipates benefit from doing so, and perceives a negligible risk of getting caught, the factors align to form a strong intent to carry through with it. At that point, using Whitley's model, there remains only one source of intervention, a *situational constraint*. Colleagues at the site or with inside knowledge may constitute the *only* source of situational constraint.

What about acts committed without awareness or due to ignorance or emotional distress that clouds judgment? The impact can prove just as harmful as if committed by those who know with certainty that they are acting inappropriately. Again, peer colleagues stand in the best position to intervene, to attempt to minimize any harms, and to help ensure that the act will not likely recur.

When a colleague has already committed a questionable act, and the colleague willfully engages in professionally irresponsible or unethical behavior, intervention becomes more demanding, uncomfortable, and worrisome. This takes personal courage, and we attempt to assist you with the process at the end of this chapter.

Sources of Resistance to Getting Involved

The urge to flee from such responsibility is, sadly, also understandable. In group practice, treatment centers, or research settings, one might feel reluctant to appear disloyal by complaining about a colleague. Conflicting feelings between a perceived duty to take some action and wanting to maintain a protective stance toward a colleague comprise a common source of reticence to get involved. It is also tempting to rationalize that someone else will deal with it ("bystander apathy") or that the matter is not serious enough for concern. It is all too easy to procrastinate until the matter no longer seems relevant, especially if the evidence seems the least bit ambiguous, as it often is.

Another source of resistance is a fear of retaliation, especially if the individual already seems menacing or is of higher professional status. Knowledge of the often-publicized fate of whistle-blowers ending up as targeted themselves may explain why observers choose to remain silent (e.g., Rothchild & Meithe, 1999; Sprague, 1993, 1998). (See a more detailed discussion of whistle-blowing in Chapter 15.) However, most cases receiving media attention involve high-profile reporting to outside agencies. We know less about the gentler, behind-the-scenes interventions that mental health colleagues might undertake to play their part in maintaining the public's trust in their professions. One of the very attractive features of informal peer monitoring is that when it works out well, two goals can be met simultaneously: A problem is solved, and a colleague may have been saved from scrutiny by a more formal (and onerous) correctional forum.

The High Price of Turning Away

We suspect that those who know of ethical violations, especially when the breaches could harm vulnerable clients but they still can not muster the courage to intervene, pay a price anyway. "Moral distress" can result when one knows better but does nothing (Austin, Rankel, Kagan, Bergum, & Lemermeyer, 2005). Furthermore, the misconduct of others, left unabated, can become *your* problem. An unethical office mate or collaborator may taint your own work. An organization discovered to have shamelessly treated its clients pollutes your own association with it. For example, what comes to mind if someone tells you that they used to work for Enron? The national accounting firm acting as Enron's auditors went out of business months after Enron's stock collapsed despite the fact that only a small number of people in one of the audit firm's regional offices overlooked shoddy financial practices. In short, the sins of your associations may rub off on you despite your innocence (Biaggio, Duffy, & Staffelbach, 1998).

Failure to get involved can also dampen our professional self-esteem and perhaps even how we judge ourselves as human beings. Austin and her colleagues (2005) offered a literary example from Camus' novel *The Fall*. The narrator, Clamence, recounts seeing a young woman on a bridge over the Seine one late night, followed by a splashing sound and pitiful cries. An "irresistible weakness" swept over him, and he did not act. For many years thereafter, Clamence was haunted by the desire to go back in time so he could try to save her and, by doing so, save himself.

Case 2–17: A colleague confided to us that she once knew that a therapist in her office complex had become sexually involved with several female clients on a regular basis. She would see her colleague and various clients together, outside of therapy, having dinner in candlelit cafes, walking hand in hand in the park, and embracing in the parking lot. "You can just tell something is going on," she told us, but she never said a word to anyone. The offending therapist is since long deceased, yet she still berates herself for not doing something to call him on the carpet back then.

Case 2–18: Another colleague confided to us that he had discovered that a student lied about supervisory hours and cheated on exams. Because of the attraction he felt toward her, he did nothing. This colleague censures himself for letting down his life-chosen profession as well as himself. When he learned that the woman, now a practicing counselor, was being sued for harming a client due to extreme incompetence, he felt partially responsible.

Perceptions of oneself as shirking a duty and as a result feeling somehow complicit in the unethical actions of another do not sit well over time. So, next we present how to confront a colleague suspected of engaging in unethical conduct and how to deal with the resistances that can get in the way.

Hints for Engaging in Informal Peer Confrontation

1. *Before going ahead, make sure that you identify the relevant ethical principle or law that applies to the suspected breach of professional ethics.* If no violation of law, relevant policy, or ethical responsibility has occurred, then the matter may lie outside the domain of ethics. Perhaps the colleague has an offensive personal style that feels unpleasant but does not rise to the level of ethical misconduct. Perhaps the colleague holds personal views that seem generally unpopular or widely divergent from your own. In such instances, you have the right, of course, to express your feelings to your colleague but should not construe doing so as engaging in a professional duty.

2. *Assess the strength of the evidence that an ethical violation has occurred.* Ethical infractions, particularly the most serious ones, seldom involve acts committed openly before a host of dispassionate witnesses. With few exceptions, such as plagiarism or inappropriate advertising of professional services, no tangible exhibits corroborate that an unethical event ever occurred.

A starting point involves categorizing the source of your information into one of five categories:

- Direct observation of a colleague engaging in unethical behavior.
- Knowing or unknowing direct disclosure by a colleague that he or she has committed (or is about to commit) an ethical violation.
- Direct observation of a colleague's suspicious, but not clearly interpretable, behavior.
- Receipt of a credible secondhand report of unethical conduct.
- Casual gossip about a colleague's unethical behavior.

If you observed ethical behavior, have clear evidence, or the colleague disclosed an unethical act, you have a professional responsibility to proceed in some way. Having a suspicion of unethical behavior without clear-cut evidence, however, will probably occur more often. Proceeding may take more tact and feel more precarious, but if you have good communication with the colleague we suggest carefully moving forward.

If you do not have direct knowledge, ask yourself about the credibility of your source of information. Reports by clients about previous treatment relationships can be difficult to evaluate, requiring clinical skills to assess the likelihood of accuracy based on factors such as the degree of psychopathology (Overstreet, 2001). If the information came by casual gossip, proceed with considerable caution. The motivations of those passing on the story, coupled with the exaggeration and distortion that always hangs heavy on "grapevines," could cause a colleague unfair damage. If no way exists to obtain any substantial, verifiable facts, you may choose to ignore the information or, as a professional courtesy, inform your colleague of the scuttlebutt. If the colleague is guilty of what the idle hearsay suggests, you may have a salutary effect. However, we recognize that this constitutes risky business and may prove effective only if you feel reasonably confident that you can anticipate the colleague's reactions.

If you find yourself approached by a credible person who claims firsthand knowledge and seeks assistance to pursue the matter, we suggest providing as much help as you can. Because we will often advise you to consult with colleagues before taking any action, it seems only fitting that you should react receptively when others approach you. You will likely be able to assist the person with a plan of action that will not include your direct involvement. Or, you might offer a referral if you feel that you can not comment confidently about the dilemma. If you do agree to become actively engaged, make certain that you have proper permission to reveal any relevant identities and that your information is as complete as possible.

3. *Get in close touch with your own motivations to engage in (or to avoid) a confrontation with a colleague.* If you are (or perceive yourself to be) directly victimized by the conduct of a colleague, you will probably feel more disposed to getting involved. In addition to any fears, anger, biases, or other emotional reactions, do you perceive that the colleague's alleged conduct—either as it stands or if it continues—could undermine the integrity of the profession or harm one or more of the consumers served by the colleague? If your answer is affirmative, then some form of proactive stance is warranted. However, if you recognize that your emotional involvement or vulnerability (e.g., the colleague is your supervisor) creates an extreme hazard that will likely preclude a satisfactory outcome, you may wish to consider passing the intervention task to another party. In such cases, first settle any confidentiality issues.

4. *We strongly recommend consultation with a trusted colleague who has demonstrated sensitivity to ethical issues, even if only to assure yourself that you are on the right track.* "Fresh eyes" have a way of clarifying ambiguities and ensuring coverage of all of the bases. Caudill (2002) asserted that a failure to maintain regular peer consultation creates the potential for poor clinical judgments, whereas ongoing consultations may prove the best way to avoid ethical pitfalls.

5. *Avoid the easy outs.* You may well find yourself tempted to engage in one of two covert acts as alternatives to confronting a colleague directly. The first involves casually passing the information along to others in an effort to warn them. Although informing others may provide a sense that duty has been fulfilled, this step will more likely only serve to diffuse responsibility. Idle talk certainly can not guarantee that an offending colleague will shape up or that the improved public protection will follow.

The second temptation involves engaging in more direct, but anonymous, action, such as sending an unsigned note or relevant document (e.g., a copy of an ethics code with one or more sections circled in red). This approach also does not guarantee constructive results. The reaction to an anonymous charge may prove counterproductive, only assisting an offender in perfecting nondetection. A certain amount of paranoia may result, adding suspiciousness to the colleague's character.

Another problem with both of these surreptitious approaches is that you might have gotten it wrong. The presumed violator may have been misjudged. To gossip or become a "mystery accuser" that an innocent individual can not identify imposes unfair stress and harm to the reputation of a colleague. Such tactics, if unwarranted, would constitute a moral failure on your part.

6. *If you decide to go ahead with a direct meeting, schedule it in advance, although not in a menacing manner.* For example, do *not* say, "A matter has come to my attention about you that causes me grave concern. What are you doing a week from next Thursday?" Rather, indicate to your colleague that you would like to speak privately and schedule a face-to-face

meeting at your colleague's earliest convenience. An office setting would normally be more appropriate than a home or restaurant, even if the colleague feels like a friend. We do not recommend attempting to handle such matters on the phone unless geographical barriers preclude a direct meeting. Letters create a record but do not allow for back-and-forth interaction and observation of body language and contemporaneous emotion, which we believe conducive to a constructive exchange in matters of this sort. We do not recommend e-mail for the same reasons, as well as the additional concern that electronic communications may allow unauthorized others to gain access.

7. *Set the tone for a constructive and educative session.* Do not take on the role of accuser, judge, jury, and penance dispenser. The session will probably progress best if you view yourself as having an alliance with the colleague. Such a partnership would not proceed in the usual sense of consensus and loyalty but rather as a collaborative effort between colleagues attempting to solve a problem together.

8. *When entering the confrontation phase, remain calm and self-confident.* The colleague may display considerable emotion. Remain as nonthreatening as possible. Even though it may feel like a safe shield, avoid a rigidly moralistic demeanor. Most people find righteous indignation obnoxious. We suggest soothing language, such as expressing confusion and seeking clarification. It might go something like this: "I met a young woman who, on learning that I was a therapist, told me that she was your client, and that the two of you were going to start dating. I thought we should talk about it." Things are not always as they seem. Social comparison research has shown that people tend to view others as less ethical than themselves and judge themselves to be less ethical than they actually are (Halbesleben, Buckley, & Sauer, 2004). It will always prove wise at the onset to allow an explanation rather than provoking anxiety. For example, you may learn that the young woman was a client of your colleague, but only briefly and several years earlier. Such responses may not render the matter entirely moot, but the discussion would likely proceed far differently than if had you stormed into the meeting spouting accusations with only one side of the story.

9. *Describe your ethical obligation, noting the relevant moral or ethics code principles that prompted your intervention.* Do not play detective by attempting to trap your colleague through leading questions or withholding any relevant information that you are authorized to share. Such tactics lead only to defensiveness and resentment, thus diminishing the possibility of a favorable outcome.

10. *Allow the colleague ample time to explain and defend his or her position in as much detail as required.* The colleague may become flustered and repetitive. Be patient.

11. *If you are intervening on behalf of another, you will first have to disclose why you are there and offer any other caveats.* You might say something like, "I, myself, have no direct knowledge of what I want to discuss with you, but I have agreed to speak with you on behalf of two of your supervisees." Your role in such instances may involve arranging another meeting with all of the parties present and possibly serving as mediator during such a meeting.

12. *If the colleague becomes abusive or threatening, attempt to steer the person to a more constructive state.* Although many people need a chance to vent feelings, they may settle down if the confronting person remains steady and refrains from becoming offensive in return. If a negative reaction continues, it may be appropriate to say something calming, such as, "I see you are very upset right now. I would like you to think about what I have presented and, if you would reconsider talking more about it, please contact me within a week." If a return call does not follow, consider other forms of action. This could involve including another appropriate person or pressing formal charges. It would probably prove wise to have another consultation with a trusted colleague at this point. You should inform the suspected offender, in person or in a formal note, of your next step if you plan to take more formal action.

The next chapter examines ethics codes in more detail and discusses what happens when alleged ethics violations are taken to a formal level of review.

References

American Association for Marriage and Family Therapy. (2001). *User's guide to the AAMFT code of ethics.* Washington, DC: Author.

American Psychological Association. (1993). Guidelines for providers of psychological services to ethnic, linguistic, and culturally diverse populations. *American Psychologist, 48,* 45–48.

Austin, W., Rankel, M., Kagan, L., Bergum, V., & Lemermeyer, G. (2005). To stay or to go, to speak or stay silent, to act or not to act: Moral distress as experienced by psychologists. *Ethics & Behavior, 15,* 197–212.

Babad, E. Y., & Salomon, G. (1978). Professional dilemmas of the psychologist in an organizational emergency. *American Psychologist, 33,* 840–846.

Baerger, D. R. (2001). Risk management with the suicidal patient: lessons from case law. *Professional Psychology, 32,* 359–366.

Berman, A. L., & Cohen-Sandler, R. (1983). Suicide and malpractice: Expert testimony and the standard of care. *Professional Psychology, 14,* 6–19.

Bernard, J. L., & Jara, C. S. (1986). The failure of clinical psychology graduate students to apply understood ethical principles. *Professional Psychology, 17,* 313–315.

Bernard, J. L., Murphy, M., & Little, M. (1987). The failure of clinical psychologists to apply understood ethical principles. *Professional Psychology, 18,* 489–491.

Bersoff, D. N. (1994). Explicit ambiguity: The 1992 Ethics code as oxymoron. *Professional Psychology, 25,* 382–387.

Biaggio, M., Duffy, R., & Staffelbach, D. F. (1998). Obstacles to addressing professional misconduct. *Clinical Psychology Review, 18,* 273–285.

Bongar, B. M. (Ed.). (1992). *Suicide: Guidelines for assessment, management, and treatment.* New York: Oxford University Press.

Brown, H. N. (1987). Patient suicide during residency training: Incidence, implications, and program response. *Journal of Psychiatric Education, 11,* 201–216.

Canter, M. B., Bennett, B. E., Jones, S. E., & Nagy, T. F. (1994). *Ethics for psychologists: A commentary on the APA ethics code.* Washington, DC: American Psychological Association.

Caudill, B. (2002). Risk management for psychotherapists: Avoiding the pitfalls. In L. VandeCreek and T. L. Jackson (Eds.), *Innovations in clinical practice: A source book* (Vol. 20 pp. 307–323). Sarasota, FL: Professional Resource Press.

Chemtob, C. M., Bauer, G. B., Hamada, R. S., Pelowski, S. R., & Muraoka, M. Y. (1989). Patient suicide: Occupational hazard for psychologists and psychiatrists. *Professional Psychology, 20,* 294–300.

Chemtob, C. M., Hamada, R. S., Bauer, G., Torigoe, R. Y., & Kinney, B. (1988). Patient suicide: Frequency and impact on psychologists. *Professional Psychology, 19,* 416–420.

Committee on Professional Practice and Standards, APA Board of Professional Affairs. (1995). Twenty-four questions (and answers) about professional practice in the area of child abuse. *Professional Psychology, 26,* 377–385.

Cunningham, M. (2000). Spirituality, cultural diversity and crisis intervention. *Crisis Intervention and Time-Limited Treatment, 6,* 65–77.

Curry, L, Schwartz, H. I., Gruman, C., & Blank, K. (2000). Physicians' voices on physician-assisted suicide: Looking beyond the numbers. *Ethics & Behavior, 10,* 337–361.

Dracy, D. L., & Yutrzenka, B. A. (1997). Responses of direct-care paraprofessional mental health staff to hypothetical ethics violations. *Psychiatric Services, 48,* 1160–1163.

Eastwood, S., Derish, P., Leash, E., Ordway, S, (1996). Ethical issues in biomedical research: Perceptions and practices of postdoctoral research fellows responding to a survey. *Scientific and Engineering Ethics, 2,* 89–114.

Feldman, S. R., Moritz, S. H., Benjamin, G., & Andrew, H. (2005). Suicide and the law: A practical overview for mental health professionals. *Women & Therapy, 28,* 95–103.

Fine, M. A., & Sansone, R. A. (1990). Dilemmas in the management of suicidal behavior in individuals with borderline personality disorder. *American Journal of Psychotherapy, 44,* 160–171.

Fisher, C. B. (2003). *Decoding the ethics code: A practical guide for psychologists.* Thousand Oaks, CA: Sage.

Glick, J. (1989). On the potential cost effectiveness of scientific audits. *Accountability in Research, 1,* 77–83.

Gross, B. (2005). Death throes: Professional liability after client suicide. *Annals of the American Psychotherapy Association, 8,* 34–35.

Gutheil, T. G. (2004). Suicide, suicide litigation, and borderline personality disorder. *Journal of Personality Disorders, 18,* 248–256.

Haas, L. J., & Malouf, J. L. (1989). *Keeping up the good work: A practitioner's guide to mental health ethics.* Sarasota, FL: Professional Resource Exchange.

Halbesleben, J. R. B., Buckley, M. R., & Sauer, N. D. (2004). The role of pluralistic ignorance in perceptions of unethical behavior: An investigation of attorneys' and students' perception of ethical behavior. *Ethics & Behavior, 14,* 17–30.

Hansen, N. D., & Goldberg, S. G. (1999). Navigating the nuances: A matrix of considerations for ethical-legal dilemmas. *Professional Psychology, 30,* 495–503.

Hanson, S. L., Kerkhoff, T. R., & Bush, S. S. (2005). *Crisis and emergency care: Health care ethics for psychologists.* Washington, DC: American Psychological Association.

Hendin, H., Maltsberger, J. T., Haas, A. P., Szanto, K., & Rabinowicz, H. (2004). Desperation and other affective states in suicidal patients, *Suicide and Life-Threatening Behavior, 34,* 386–394.

Hendin, H., Maltsberger, J. T., Lipschitz, Pollinger-Haas, A., & Kyle, J. (2001). Recognizing and responding to a suicide crisis. *Suicide and Life-Threatening Behavior, 31,* 115–128.

Kahn, N. E. (2003). Self-disclosure of serious illness: The impact of boundary disruptions for patient and analyst. *Contemporary Psychoanalysis, 39,* 51–74.

Kalichman, S. C. (1999). *Mandated reporting of suspected child abuse: Ethics, law, and policy* (2nd ed.). Washington, DC: American Psychological Association.

Kaplan, A. (2006). Being stalked—An occupational hazard? *Psychiatric Times.* Retrieved October 18, 2006, from http://www.psychiatrictimes.com/Workplace/showArticle.jhtml?articleID=190900641

Katsavdakis, K., Gabbard, G. O., & Athey, G. I., Jr. (2004). Profiles of impaired health professionals. *Bulletin of the Menninger Clinic. 68,* 60–72.

Keith-Spiegel, P., & Whitley, B. E. (1994). The 1992 ethics code: Boon or bane? *Professional Psychology, 25,* 315–316.

Kitchener, K. S. (1984) Intuition, critical evaluation and ethical principles: The foundation for ethical decisions in counseling psychology. *Counseling Psychologist, 12,* 43–55.

Litman, R. E. (1991). Predicting and preventing hospital and clinic suicides. *Suicide and Life Threatening Behavior, 21,* 56–73.

Loewenstein, G. F., Weber, E. U., Hsee, C. K., & Welch, N. (2001). Risk as feelings. *Psychological Bulletin, 127,* 267–286.

Overstreet, M. M. (2001). Duty to report colleagues who engage in fraud or deception. In APA Ethics Committee (Eds.), *Ethics primer of the American Psychiatric Association* (pp. 51–55). Washington, DC: American Psychiatric Association.

Packman, W. L., Pennuto, T. O., Bongar, B., & Orthwein, J. (2004). Legal issues of professional negligence in suicide cases. *Behavioral Sciences & the Law, 22,* 697–713.

Peruzzi, N., Canapary, A., & Bongar, B. (1996). Physician-assisted suicide: The role of mental health professionals. *Ethics & Behavior, 6,* 353–366.

Pope, K. S., & Vasquez, M. J. T. (2005). Assessment of suicidal risk. In G. P. Koocher, J. C. Norcross, & S. S. Hill (Eds.), *Psychologists' desk reference* (2nd ed., pp. 63–66). New York: Oxford University Press.

Purcell, R., Powell, M. B., & Mullen, P. E. (2005). Clients who stalk psychologists: Prevalence, methods, and motives. *Professional Psychology, 35,* 537–543.

Rachels, J. (1980). Can ethics provide the answers? *Hastings Center Report, 10,* 32–41.

Remley, T. P. (2004). Suicide and the law. In D. Capuzzi (Ed.), *Suicide across the life span: Implications for counselors* (pp 185–208). Alexandria, VA: American Counseling Association.

Rest, J. R. (1982). A psychologist looks at the teaching of ethics. *Hastings Center Report, 12,* 29–36.

Rothchild, J., & Meithe, T. D. (1999). Whistleblower disclosures and management retaliation: The battle to control information about organization corruption. *Work and Occupations, 26,* 107–128.

Rubin, J. (1975). A psychologists dilemma: A real case of danger. *Professional Psychology, 6,* 363–366.

Shinefield, W., & Kalafat, J. (1996). Effective management of borderline individuals in crisis.

Crisis Intervention and Time-Limited Treatment, 2, 267–282.

Simpson, S., & Stacey, M. (2004). Avoiding the malpractice snare: Documenting suicide risk assessment. *Journal of Psychiatric Practice, 10,* 185–189.

Skodol, A. F., Kass, F., & Charles, E. S. (1979). Crisis in psychotherapy: Principles of emergency consultation and intervention. *American Journal of Orthopsychiatry, 49,* 585–597.

Slawson, P. F., Flinn, D. E., & Schwartz, D. A. (1974). Legal responsibility for suicide. *Psychiatric Quarterly, 48,* 50–64.

Smith, T. S., McGuire, J. M., Abbott, D. W., & Blau, B. I. (1991). Clinical ethical decision making: An investigation of the rationales used to justify doing less than one believes one should. *Professional Psychology, 22,* 235–239.

Sprague, R. L. (1993). Whistleblowing: A very unpleasant avocation. *Ethics & Behavior, 3,* 103–133.

Sprague, R. L. (1998). The voice of experience. *Science and Engineering Ethics, 4,* 33–44.

Steneck, N. H. (1999). Confronting misconduct in the 1980s and 1990s: What has and has not been accomplished? *Science and Engineering Ethics, 5,* 161–176.

Stone, A. (1971). Suicide precipitated by psychotherapy: A clinical contribution. *American Journal of Psychotherapy, 25,* 18–26.

Swazey, J. P., Anderson, M. S., & Lewis, K. S. (1993). Ethical problems in academic research. *American Scientist, 81,* 542–554.

Tagney, J. P. (1987). Fraud will out—Or will not? *New Scientist, 115,* 62–63.

Tenbrunsel, A. E., & Messick, D. M. (2004). Ethical fading: The role of self-deception in unethical behavior. *Social Justice Research, 17,* 223–236.

Trevino, L. K., & Youngblood, S. A. (1990). Bad apples in bad barrels: A causal analysis of ethical decision-making behavior. *Journal of Applied Psychology, 75,* 378–385.

Tymchuk, A. J. (1981). Ethical decision making and psychological treatment. *Journal of Psychiatric Treatment and Evaluation, 3,* 507–513.

VandeCreek, L., & Knapp, S. (2000). Risk management and life-threatening patient behaviors. *Journal of Clinical Psychology, 56,* 1335–1351.

VandenBos, G. R., & Duthie, R. F. (1986). Confronting and supporting colleagues in distress. In R. R. Kilburg, P. E. Nathan, & R. W. Thorenson (Eds.), *Professionals in distress* (pp. 211–231). Washington, DC: American Psychological Association.

Weiner, K. M. (2005). *Therapeutic and legal issues for therapists who have survived a client suicide: Breaking the silence.* New York: Haworth Press.

Werth, J. L. (1999a). When is a mental health professional competent to assess a person's decision to hasten death? *Ethics & Behavior, 9,* 141–157.

Werth, J. L. (1999b). Mental health professionals and assisted death: Perceived ethical obligations and proposed guidelines for practice. *Ethics & Behavior, 9,* 159–183.

Whitley, B. E. (1998). *Principles of research in behavioral science* (2nd ed.) New York: McGraw-Hill.

Whitley, B. E., & Keith-Spiegel, P. (2002). *Academic dishonesty: An educator's guide.* Mahwah, NJ: Erlbaum.

Wilkins, M., McGuire, J., Abbott, D., & Blau, B. (1990). Willingness to apply understood ethical principles. *Journal of Clinical Psychology, 46,* 539–547.

Zellman, G. L., & Fair, C. C. (2002). Preventing and reporting abuse. In J. E. B. Myers, L. Berliner, J. Briere, T. C. Hendrix, & J. Carole (Eds.), *The APSAC handbook on child maltreatment* (2nd ed., pp. 449–475). Thousand Oaks, CA: Sage.

Zweibel, E. B., & Goldstein, R. (2001). Conflict resolution at the University of Ottawa Faculty of Medicine: The pelican and the sign of the triangle. *Academic Medicine, 76,* 337–344.

3

Enforcement of Ethical Conduct

One cool judgment is worth a thousand hasty
councils.

Thomas Woodrow Wilson

Contents

It is to every mental health practitioner's *personal* best interest to judiciously uphold the guiding ethical principles of his or her profession. Why? For a profession to thrive, the public must have faith in those who practice within it. That trust is ultimately determined by its members' collective commitment to integrity and competence. Unfortunately, self-monitoring and informal peer monitoring have not proven sufficient to fully protect consumers of mental health services from unethical practitioners. Other formalized rules and adjudication venues have been put in place to educate both therapists and the public about ethical practice, to investigate complaints, and to impose penalties on those who have violated professional and ethical standards.

This chapter purposely provides substantial detail because we sincerely believe that a thorough understanding of the role of ethics codes and formal mechanisms for monitoring, processing, and dealing with ethical complaints will assist our readers in avoiding future entanglements.

ETHICS CODES OF PROFESSIONAL ORGANIZATIONS

The Many Faces of Ethics Codes

Ethics codes are almost as old as recorded history. The first profession-generated ethics code is the Hippocratic oath, written in around 400 B.C.E. (Sinclair, Simon, & Pettifor, 1996). This fascinating guide for physicians of that day contains anachronistic directives, such as forbidding the removal of kidney stones. Yet, it also echoes themes that remain in today's professional codes, such as upholding confidentiality and forbidding sexual relations with patients (specifying, interestingly, patients of both sexes and slaves).

As professions emerged, the public expected their providers to be trustworthy and competent. Most professions can be characterized as having a formal organization that speaks for its members, a systematic program of required training, a body of knowledge to teach, a means of regulating or influencing the members who provide the service, and an ethics code (Pryzwansky & Wendt, 1999). A code of ethical standards is one of the major features of a profession because it creates an implied social contract that purports to balance professional privilege with responsibility and a commitment to consumer welfare (Sinclair et al., 1996; Weinberger, 1988; Wilensky, 1964). Despite variations in length and specificity, most of today's professional ethics codes echo similar themes:

- promotion of the welfare of consumers served
- maintaining and practicing within the bounds of one's competence

- doing no harm
- protecting clients' confidentiality and privacy
- acting responsibly
- avoiding exploitation
- upholding the integrity of the profession through exemplary conduct

Besides serving as a pledge to the public, ethics codes of professional organizations attempt to perform many other functions, probably too many. At once, ethics codes

- are impressive public relations documents leading to the enhancement of public confidence in the profession
- clarify a critical mission of the organization
- spell out which principles morally responsible members are expected to follow
- attempt to clarify the proper use and misuse of skills and expertise
- provide general guides to decision making
- assist in educating the next generation of professionals
- spell out the rules for judging those whose actions have been called into question by ethics committees and other regulating agencies
- form the basis for weeding out unethical members

It is easy to see how ethics codes may create conceptual confusion in their attempt to be and do so much for so many. As a further complication, not every organization with an ethics code, especially smaller and state-level organizations, has a mechanism for actually handling complaints or for enforcing the code. Therefore, some may view ethics codes with no mechanism to back them up as mere window dressing or perhaps even deceptive. However, codes alone still serve important purposes: They set aspirations and expectations for members, reduce internal bickering about what is and is not proper conduct, and serve as tools for licensure boards, civil litigants, and other formal mechanisms of redress to cite in sanctioning and defending professional conduct.

Ethics codes also serve to safeguard the profession itself. Because they may forestall outside regulation by attempting to preclude the necessity for it, consumers may perceive ethics codes as protective of the profession, perhaps by watering down or even leaving out some ethical issues altogether (Kitchener, 1984). Ethics codes represent the collective experiences of those within the organization empowered to make decisions about ethical matters. Therefore, ethics codes invariably become the product of both expertise and political compromise (Bersoff & Koeppl, 1993).

Finally, the creators of ethics codes understand that mental health professionals can not avoid or prevent every possible harm or ethics-related incident. Practitioners can not be expected to come up with perfect solutions to every dilemma that comes their way, even when they do everything that we would expect of them. Also, codes can not speak to every context in which an incident occurs. Thus, a degree of generality and flexible language (e.g., "attempts to," "takes reasonable precautions," and "whenever feasible") sometimes become necessary. The effect, unfortunately, could also be to narrow liability by creating enough ambiguity and loopholes to wriggle out of charges of unethical misconduct (Bersoff, 1994; Keith-Spiegel, 1994; Koocher, 1994). For example, the APA (American Psychological Association) code states, in part, "Psychologists *do not knowingly* engage in behavior that is harassing or demeaning to persons with whom they interact" (emphasis added) (APA 02: 3.03). So, what do you think about this next case?

Case 3–1: Jenny Curvy complained to her new therapist that Buster Clueless, Ph.D., always focused his eyes on her breasts instead of making eye contact during therapy and often made comments about her "incredible body." She became so self-conscious that she stopped going to therapy. With Jenny's permission, her new therapist called Dr. Clueless to inform him of his offensive behavior. Rather than deny it, Clueless said, "Since when is admiring a client unethical?"

It appears that Dr. Clueless meant no harm in his own mind; in fact, he actually thought he was paying his client compliments. So can he, according to the APA code, be held responsible for this insensitivity and resulting inappropriate behavior? We can hope that Ms. Curvy's new therapist educated him to recognize the problem.

An Overview of Selected Ethics Codes of Mental Health Professionals

Although we refer primarily to the ethics code of the APA (2002) throughout this book, we also briefly describe the ethics codes of six other professional organizations closely related to the practice of psychology. The major sections of each code are listed below, along with some examples whenever the title of the main section does not fully describe which topics are included.

American Psychological Association's Ethical Principles of Psychologists and Code of Conduct

In 1939, APA established an ethics committee to hear cases informally but did not have a formalized code until 1952. Since then, it has undergone a number of major and minor revisions. The most recent APA ethics code was adopted in 2002 and consists of two major sections: *aspirational* principles and *enforceable* standards. The aspirational principles are noble statements, similar to the virtues described in Chapter 1, expressing ideal moral behaviors to which all psychologists should aspire. Included are respecting people's rights and dignity, doing no harm, acting responsibly and maintaining the trust of those with whom we work, acting with integrity, and being just and fair.

The bulk of the 2002 APA code consists of 89 enforceable standards, intended to be specific enough to use as compelling rules that result in sanctions should they be broken. The 10 section headings are: "Resolving Ethical Issues" (including conflicts among ethics and the law and other organizational demands and how to deal with and report ethics violations); "Competence" (including maintenance, providing emergency services, delegation of work to others, and personal problems); "Human Relations" (including principles relating to sexual harassment, informed consent, and multiple role relationships); "Privacy and Confidentiality" (including disclosure and the limits of confidentiality); "Advertising and Other Public Statements"; "Record Keeping and Fees"; "Education and Training"; "Research and Publication";

"Assessment"; and "Therapy" (including informed consent, couple and family relationships, issues surrounding sexual intimacies with current and former clients, and termination of services). The ethics code of the American Psychological Association can be viewed in its entirety as Appendix A.

The APA ethics code is not the sole publication concerned with ethical matters within the APA, although it is the only standard enforceable by the APA's ethics committee. The APA issues two types of guidelines. *Treatment guidelines* provide specific recommendations for therapy interventions; *practice guidelines* deal with conduct regarding particular aspects of practice (Reed, McLaughlin, & Newman, 2002). Examples of APA guidelines dealing, at least in part, with ethical matters include the *General Standards for Providers of Psychological Services* (APA, 1987), *Record Keeping Guidelines* (APA, 2007), and *Standards for Educational and Psychological Testing* (American Educational Research Association, American Psychological Association, & National Council on Measurement in Education, 1999).

Canadian Psychological Association's
Canadian Code of Ethics for Psychologists

The Canadian code (Canadian Psychological Association, 2000) revolves around four major principles: respect for dignity of persons (including fair treatment, dignity for persons, informed consent, privacy and confidentiality, protections of vulnerable persons); responsible caring (including risk–benefit analysis, competence and self-knowledge, care of animals); integrity in relationships (including accuracy and honesty, objectivity and lack of bias, conflict of interest); and responsibility to society (beneficial activities, respect and development of society). A preamble presents helpful information such as the uses of the code, ethical decision making, and general advice about what to do when ethical principles conflict. The most unusual feature of the Canadian code is an attempt to order ethical principles, values, and standards in terms of significance should conflicts arise. Thus, respect for the individuals with whom psychologists work is primary, whereas respon-

sibility to society is placed last. The creators of the code are quick to point out that this ranking will not always prove appropriate. In some situations, for example, the welfare of society takes precedence over respect for an individual. (For a discussion of how the principles of the Canadian code were ranked, see Hadjistavropoulos & Malloy, 1999.) The ethics code of the Canadian Psychological Association appears in its entirety as Appendix B.

American Counseling Association's
Code of Ethics

The American Counseling Association (ACA) code (ACA, 2005) is exceptionally detailed and, like the others, spells out overarching values that should guide counselors. These include a dedication to enhancing human development throughout the life span and embracing a cross-cultural approach in support of the dignity and uniqueness of people. The ACA code is divided into eight sections: "The Counseling Relationship" (including client welfare, informed consent, multiple clients and group work, fees, terminology, and the use of technology); "Confidentiality, Privileged Communication, and Privacy"; "Professional Responsibility" (including competence, impairment, advertising, nondiscrimination, and public statements); "Relationships With Other Professionals"; "Evaluation, Assessment, and Interpretation"; "Supervision, Training, and Teaching"; "Research and Publication"; and "Resolving Ethical Issues." The ethics code of the American Counseling Association appears in its entirety as Appendix C.

National Association of Social Workers'
Code of Ethics

The National Association of Social Workers (NASW) code (NASW, 1999) in its preamble promotes the enhancement of human well-being. It also offers several broad ethical principles to which social workers should aspire that reflect the virtues similar to those discussed in Chapter 1. These include service, social justice, dignity and the worth of persons, the importance of human relationships, integrity, and competence. This detailed code consists of expectations of social workers in the following six areas: "Ethical Responsibilities to Clients" (including competence, conflict of interest, confidentiality, access to records, physical contact, payment for services); "Ethical Responsibilities to Colleagues" (including respect, interdisciplinary collaboration, consultation, collegial disputes, referrals, and dealing with incompetent and unethical colleagues); "Ethical Responsibilities in Practice Settings" (including supervision, education and training, performance evaluation, client records and transfer, billing, administration, continuing education, and commitments to employers); "Ethical Responsibilities as Professionals" (including competence, discrimination, private conduct, impairment, misrepresentation, client solicitation, and giving credit); "Ethical Responsibilities to the Social Work Profession" (including promoting integrity and evaluation and research); and "Ethical Responsibilities to the Broader Society" (including social welfare, public participation, public emergencies, social and political action). The ethics code of the National Association of Social Workers appears in its entirety as Appendix D.

American Association for Marriage and Family Therapy's Code of Ethics

The American Association of Marriage and Family Therapists (AAMFT) members are guided by a code (AAMFT, 2001) with the following eight major principles: "Responsibility to Clients" (including nondiscrimination, informed consent to therapy, avoiding exploitation, and working with clients at the request of a third party); "Confidentiality"; "Professional Competence and Integrity" (including emotional fitness, avoiding conflict of interest, avoiding undue influence, and a list of conditions under which a member can be sanctioned, such as being convicted of any felony); "Responsibility to Students and Supervisees"; "Responsibility to Research Participants"; "Responsibility to the Profession" (including accountability, authorship credit assignment); "Financial Arrangements"; and "Advertising" of services and qualifications. The ethics code of AAMFT appears in its entirety as Appendix E.

American Psychiatric Association's Principles of Medical Ethics With Annotations Especially Applicable to Psychiatry

Because psychiatrists have medical degrees, their primary code is that of the American Medical Association (2001). The AMA code is short, consisting of only 11 sentences (although it is accompanied by an extensive series of "opinions" that offer more specific guidance to its members). The American Psychiatric Association takes from the basic AMA code and offers annotations that fill in the expectations for ethical behavior of its members (American Psychiatric Association, 2006). Their nine principles are competence and compassion (including the avoidance of exploitation, nondiscrimination); standards of professionalism (including the requirement to report other physicians deficient in character or competence, avoiding misuse of power, practicing within competence boundaries, ensuring that clients understand the therapeutic arrangement, avoiding fee splitting); respect for the law (including right to protest social injustices); respect for the rights of patients and colleagues (including such matters as safeguarding confidentiality, human research guidelines, admonition against sexual involvement with students and trainees); maintenance of competence (including continuing education, collaboration with other professionals); right to choose with whom to work; responsibility to contribute to the community; paramount responsibility is to the patient; and support for access to care for all people. The ethics code of the American Psychiatric Association appears in its entirety as Appendix F.

The underlying themes, issues, and directives among these five codes are far more similar than different, although the topics are shuffled into different categories. Also, emphases vary from code to code, usually based on the context in which members of each profession works. Examples here include the amount of space dedicated to relationships with members of other professions and supervision of interns. Unique differences are less common, but when they occur they are quite interesting. For example, the code for social workers includes a prohibition against the use of derogatory language while performing in a professional role. The psychiatrists' code specifically forbids its members from participating in legally authorized executions or torture and admonishes its members to conduct themselves with propriety in all life actions, not only while operating in a professional role. (This differs from the American psychologists' code, which focuses, in most cases, only on questionable acts taking place when performing a professional activity.) The counseling association code is unique in covering specifics when working with terminally ill patients.

ENFORCEMENT OPTIONS

Various formal mechanisms have been established by law and within professions themselves to protect the public from unlawful, incompetent, and unethical actions perpetrated by mental health providers. These include

- criminal and civil laws applicable to all citizens, including members of any profession
- ethics committees of professional associations that investigate and adjudicate complaints
- profession-specific legal controls that emanate from state laws via licensing boards
- professional review committees associated with third-party payers and institutions or employers
- civil litigation involving claims of malpractice or other professional liability
- federal and state laws and regulations, such as policies issued on the protection of human participants in social and behavioral science research, confidentiality of records, civil rights violations, or prescribing medication

The existence of several venues set up to protect the public from unethical practitioners has both advantages and drawbacks. The primary asset is that each source has its own focus, which ideally allows an incident to have a most fitting forum for a hearing and resolution. For example, if a therapist extorts money from a client, adjudication by criminal law would probably result in the most appropriate outcome. When a therapist poses a hazard to the public, licensing boards may constitute the most suitable contact because they have the power to revoke a license to practice. If an insurance company questions treatment applicability or claims, a peer standards review committee would seem particularly well-suited forums for evaluation. (Reviews undertaken by managed care organizations are unfortunately too often driven chiefly by economic concerns and therefore are not necessarily favorably disposed toward the consumer, as is discussed more fully in Chapter 7.)

Despite these other resources, it is fairly easy to generate a list of reprehensible, objectionable, and blatantly unethical acts that are neither illegal nor in violation of any policy *except* the ethics codes of professional organizations. In such cases, ethics committees may be the sole source of consumer redress, assuming that the alleged violator is a member of the organization. Membership in these organizations is voluntary, and as we explain in more detail, professional organizations have no jurisdiction over nonmembers.

Sometimes, more than one enforcement option has jurisdiction over a single incident. For example, an ethics committee of a professional association would probably want to investigate a sustained complaint of criminal conduct against a member. In fact, it is theoretically possible for a single case to ultimately play out in all six venues noted above. Herein lies a significant drawback associated with the existence of many avenues consumer redress. Efforts may be duplicated, resulting in unnecessary expense and confusion. Moreover, investigators within each source may expect that another arena has primary control over the matter, resulting in diffusion of responsibility and an inadequate examination of the matter. Territoriality, the need for confidentiality, and poor communication channels among sources of control can cause obfuscation and confusion. None of these arenas is known for its swiftness in responding to, investigating, and deciding cases. It takes several months to years to resolve complaints, much to the consternation of *complainants* (the individual making the complaint) and *respondents* (those against whom the compliant is lodged).

Finally, an exemplary enforcement operation is costly. The APA maintains a full-time ethics director (who holds both a law degree and psychology doctorate), associate director, and a small support staff. The office consults regularly with legal counsel, creates educational materials, manages considerable correspondence and other paperwork, and works with the ethics committee and various consultants during deliberations and appeals. Despite the fact that as much business as possible is conducted by mail, in 2006 the APA spent almost $700,000 to administer its ethics program.

The Relationship Between Law and Ethics

General criminal and civil law do not adequately protect consumers from unethical conduct by mental health professionals. Morality is external to law despite the apparent overlap. Morals and laws usually have similar purposes, which is to specify conduct that facilitates harmonious living and respect for each other's rights, property, and physical safety. But, some laws have been criticized and even overturned because they were deemed immoral and unjust. Furthermore, a great many matters of morality and ethics can not be enforced by laws. We can not, for example, legally force people to be thoughtful and kind to each other. The result is that the correspondence between "legal" and "ethical" as well as between "illegal" and "unethical" is often complicated and sometimes incongruent.

Conduct specified as unethical in professional ethics codes often also qualifies as civilly or criminally actionable. Mental health professionals usually lose their license to practice and face expulsion from their professional associations simply as a result of being found guilty of a felony. However, conviction on a misdemeanor will not usually be handled in the same manner by ethics committees unless the offense also involved the violation of an ethical principle. Thus, a therapist fined for unpaid parking tickets, nude sunbathing, or trespassing at an antiwar demonstration would probably not be deemed professionally unethical even though the behavior carries legal sanctions. Differences among state legal statutes allow discrepancies in these cases. For example, engaging in sexual intimacies with psychotherapy clients is a criminal offense in some jurisdictions but not in others.

The more striking disparity between ethics and the law can be found in the many instances of fully legal conduct (or, perhaps stated more correctly, conduct that ordinarily would not be in violation of any criminal or civil law) that are unethical according to the profession's ethics code. Consider this case:

Case 3–2: Cruella Snile, Ph.D., had her own downturns in life. She and her only surviving parent were estranged, a recent divorce left her bitter, and she was drinking too much at night. She was increasingly short-tempered with her clients and forgot or mixed up their case narratives from one week to the next.

Dr. Snile is not breaking any law; she also is not providing competent, ethical services. As individuals, we may sympathize with her personal troubles, but ethical standards are unforgiving. If one of her clients complains about her, an ethics committee may show lenience if she has no previous violations and is committed to taking concrete steps to solve her own problems. But, she would likely also receive a letter of reprimand.

Finally, mental health professionals may occasionally find themselves placed in a most challenging dilemma. They might believe that it is in a client's best interest to resist responding to a legal reporting mandate or to openly defy some law they view as irrelevant or harmful to a client's particular situation. For example, a therapist may not report child or elder abuse in the sincere belief that continued psychotherapy would better restore the family than turning the families over to legal authorities or public agencies. Or, reporting information about clients as required by state or government institutional regulations may be viewed by some therapists as violating their clients' rights to privacy. Ansell and Ross (1990) suggested that because laws are not framed by therapists and sometimes require impossible skills (e.g., accurate predictions of future violence), it is not surprising that the behavior of scrupulously ethical psychologists is not always consistent with the law.

Defying the law can sometimes be a matter of personal conscience. This dilemma is illustrated in the next case.

Case 3–3: After many attempts at negotiation, a group of therapists agreed to participate in a sit-in in the administrative office of Bozo Managed Care, Incorporated. The therapists contended that the company misled patients and encouraged incompetent treatment. The management at Bozo allegedly told the therapists earlier that if they continued criticizing the organization they would all face termination as providers. Those who participated in the sit-in felt so strongly about their concerns that they were willing to lose their provider status despite the fact that Bozo threatened to call the police and have them all arrested for trespassing. The therapists stayed put, and the police came. The therapists were arrested when they refused to leave.

We are not in a position to encourage or dissuade colleagues from acting according to their conscience or engaging in nonviolent civil disobedience. This takes courage, commitment, and an understanding of consequences and is not always well advised. In Chapter 15, we present more about "ethical resistance" and "whistle blowing" and offer guidelines for decision making whenever these soul-searching matters arise.

Licensing Boards

State licensing laws establish the scope of practice of practitioners and how these laws are to be enforced by licensing boards. Licensing boards evaluate the entry-level qualifications required to offer mental health services to the public under protected titles, such as "psychologist," "physician/psychiatrist," or "marriage and family therapist." The relevance to the ethical principles of a professional organization is that well-functioning licensing boards stand in a position to help ensure competence through the setting of regulatory standards (see also Chapter 4). State licensing boards are also charged with monitoring the conduct of the professionals they have already licensed. In general, state boards often adopt some or all of provisions of the profession's ethics code. This means that the same misconduct may qualify for sanctioning at both the statutory state and ethical organizational levels, although reasons specified for denial, revocation, or suspension of licensure can vary significantly among the states. It has been estimated that as many as 11% of psychologists will have to respond to a licensing board complaint during the course of their careers (Schoenfeld, Hatch, & Gonzales, 2001). At present, mental health professionals are more likely to face a licensing board complaint than a lawsuit (Bennett et al., 2007).

Most state licensing boards are comprised of licensed members of the profession and public members appointed by the governor or other executive branch official. In some states, each profession has its own board, while in others many professions may be clustered under an omnibus-style board. For example, the New Hampshire Board of Mental Health Practice has three public members, one psychologist, one mental health counselor, one marriage and family therapist, one social worker, and one pastoral psychotherapist, thus regulating five professions. Psychiatrists in New Hampshire are licensed with all other medical specialties under a single medical board.

Licensing boards are not without their detractors. Some have come under attack for abuse of power, failure to provide due process for the accused, and unfair or improper investigative procedures (Peterson, 2001; Williams, 2001). Often enough, complaints about state licensing boards are little more than self-righteous whining, but cases of well-documented abuses are on record. Consider these examples:

Case 3– 4: A licensing board of Largely Rural State relied on a system that involved deputizing local psychologists to conduct investigations of cases far from the board's headquarters. In one situation, the ex-wife of a client treated by Ima Sucker, Psy.D., complained that the individual psychotherapy her former husband had received led to their divorce. The woman was never Dr. Sucker's client, and her ex-husband never signed a release of information to the licensing board. Nonetheless, the board asked a local psychologist to investigate. Not knowing any better, the local psychologist contacted Dr. Sucker. In an effort to cooperate fully, Dr. Sucker gave information without asking for a release from the former husband.

Case 3–5: Mary Tripped-Up, Ph.D., was asked to undertake a child sexual abuse evaluation by a woman who was seeking a divorce because of domestic violence. Dr. Tripped-Up evaluated the child and found no signs of abuse. Nonetheless, she was subpoenaed to court by both parties in the divorce. In an informal meeting with both parties and their lawyers outside court, she was asked for "informal advice" on a child custody settlement. She made a variety of properly qualified recommendations, which were readily accepted by all concerned, and a court hearing was avoided. Months later, however, the settlement agreement broke down, and the father filed a licensing board complaint. The board, in a hurry to resolve cases, did not do a careful investigation and offered Dr. Tripped-Up a consent decree by which, if she admitted giving improper advice, they would simply issue a reprimand. Tripped-Up's lawyer, who was unfamiliar with the issues and potential consequences, urged her to take the offer without seeking any expert advice. She accepted and was promptly sued by the father, who cited the consent agreement as evidence.

Dr. Sucker's case soon became a major embarrassment for the licensing board when it realized that it had unintentionally led Dr. Sucker to breach the man's confidence. Dr. Tripped-Up was dropped from two managed care panels because of disciplinary sanctions by the board. Ironically, Dr. Tripped-Up had done nothing wrong except to obtain and accept poor legal advice.

Licensing boards have also been criticized for doing less to protect the public than to shield professions from competition. In his historical analysis, Gross (1979) described licensing as "a mystifying arrangement that promises protection of the public but that actually institutionalizes a lack of accountability to the public" (p. 1009). Gross asserted that passing an exam may provide little more than an illusion of competence, restrict competition, and set prices. Further, he declared that licensing only provides a loosely woven safety net because licensing boards, with their few resources and low budgets, do an incompetent job of ejecting incompetents.

The quality of licensing exams and statutes have also been called into question (e.g., Herbsled, Sales, & Overcast, 1985; Koocher, 1979, 1989). However, in all fairness, licensing boards are placed in an impossible position when it comes to an expectation that they will license *only* those who are competent and morally fit and then later weed out any who slip through. Perhaps more responsibility for culling those of poor character should be placed on training institutions. But, that notion raises yet other difficult issues, such as using other-than-academic criteria for evaluation, differing views on what exactly constitutes sufficiently poor character, and concerns about violating Title II of the Americans with Disabilities Act (Johnson, Porter, Campbell, & Kupko, 2005).

Unlike ethics committees, licensing boards can prevent an unscrupulous and harmful individual from operating with a protected title in the state in which they are licensed. This is a tremendous power when one realizes that even successful criminal or civil litigation may not prevent a mental health professional from continuing to practice. In balance, the public is well served when a licensing body is functioning effectively and is focused on its primary function of protecting the public from unqualified and unethical practitioners.

Ethics Committees

State regulatory boards rarely have sufficient access to the resources or even the inclination to deal with more minor violations of ethics codes. They are not typically interested in behaviors that may be extremely offensive to professional sensibilities, but not necessarily harmful to the public, such as a dispute over a publication credit or a spat between two practitioners that interferes with the work of others in a group practice setting. It is in such contexts that the ethics committees of professional associations can fill the gap.

Ethics committees consist of members of the profession—typically experienced and well regarded for their sensitivity to ethical matters—elected or appointed by the governing body of the professional association. Some committees include public members. Committee members serve without pay and, at the state and local levels, often without reimbursement for expenses. Serving on an ethics committee is not an easy duty. The dilemmas committee members face are often extremely difficult because the issues are intricate, the parties to the action are distressed, and the facts of the case are not always clear. The time commitment can be extensive, and the experience itself is often both agonizing and exhausting.

Although most state professional associations have ethics committees, most currently function solely as educative bodies and cheerleaders for encouraging members to uphold the ethical standards of the profession. There are reasons why most states no longer investigate and adjudicate complaints. As complaints became more diverse and complex, the conclusions reached by ethics committees have increasingly been appealed or challenged. Whereas ethics committees were originally intended to serve as the hallmark of a profession—namely, fulfilling an autonomous, monitoring function—accused mental health professionals today more often view the process as adversarial rather than collegial. Legal assistance, outside consultants, liability insurance, and associated clerical and duplicating services quickly drain the already-modest budgets of most state and other smaller organizations.

Some state associations drop members who have been adjudicated for serious infractions by another legitimate authority. For example, APA will normally notify any other professional associations and licensing boards that may have jurisdiction whenever it expels a member. Some of those groups may then open an investigation or take action based on the prior adjudication. However, if a complaint is received about a member who has been convicted of a felony, found by a court of competent authority to have committed malpractice, has lost a license, and a few other findings of ethical failings as adjudicated by another body, the committee will accept such findings as prima facie evidence and take action. Thus, the burden of ethics monitoring currently falls largely on national professional organizations, licensing boards, and the courts.

The Effectiveness of Ethics Committees

Although ethics committees of professional associations seem uniquely able to pick up some of the slack that other levels of control may be unwilling or unable to handle, whether they always exert a constructive and efficient means of peer control and public protection has been called into question. Specific criticisms of ethics committees include the following:

- conflict of interest or bias among committee members
- lack of training and experience of members to function adequately in a quasi-judicial capacity
- excessive time taken to adjudicate cases, resulting in possible harm to the public in the interim
- insufficient investigatory and other resources to do the job properly
- failure to follow due process
- timid procedures from fear of lawsuits
- reactive rather than proactive procedures
- the tendency to protect guild interests and due process rights of respondents over the welfare of the complainants
- (conversely) the tendency to take the complainants' sides while depriving the respondents of due process and an unbiased tribunal

Frustrated complainants are increasingly contacting lawyers or the media when sources of redress are inefficient or reach unwelcome conclusions.

Case 3–6: Upsetta Grandee became impatient with the lengthy delay and interminable paperwork involved in submitting a complaint to an ethics committee. She had some incriminating notes handwritten by her therapist and took her evidence to the local newspaper. The paper carried a front-page story that attracted the interest of the local television station. A camera crew showed up, unannounced, at the counselor's home. He yelled at them, charging harassment because he had not yet had an opportunity to defend himself. This outburst caught the attention of a popular tabloid television show producer, who ran the story on national, syndicated television.

As a result of the media coverage, the therapist's practice and reputation diminished considerably, and the complainant, whose fragile private life was also exposed, felt humiliated. Two of the charges against this therapist—both involving poor judgment in treating this particular client—were eventually sustained, but we can only speculate whether the therapist and the complainant would have been better served had the ethics committee been able to process the complaint more expeditiously.

Without denying that criticisms of ethics committees sometimes have merit, we sustain a far more positive view of them and their potential effectiveness. Having to respond to an ethics committee can have a salutary effect by encouraging the respondent to be more careful in the future. And, although respondents may not always appreciate it, there are advantages to well-functioning, readily available ethics committees who handle complaints discreetly and take care to protect the rights of the accused as well as the accuser. The existence of ethics committees with disciplinary powers may even offer financial advantages to all mental health practitioners. Should professional association ethics committees undergo significant downshifting or go out of business altogether, the onus of monitoring would fall on licensing boards and malpractice litigation, thus substantially raising the cost of malpractice insurance.

When ethics committees function well, they have some significant advantages over other monitoring methods. The flexibility of ethics committee proceedings, compared with legal and administrative procedures, permits a wider range of data-gathering methods without forcing stringent evidence and examination re-

quirements. Because many matters can be handled without an adversarial process, ethics committees can simultaneously serve both the consumer and the profession. An investment in protecting the profession does not eliminate a concern for the welfare of consumers and society because the reputation of a profession is based primarily on the public's image of it. Thus, it is in the professions' best interests to maintain high ethical standards and to effectively police themselves.

The next case illustrates how ethics committees can uniquely serve the needs of distraught clients in a way that has positive results for everyone concerned.

Case 3–7: Virgil Zinger complained to an ethics committee that Seymour Straighttalk, Ph.D., suggested that Zinger might explore the possibility that he resented his mother as opposed to his melodramatic declarations of undying love for her. He explained the concept of "reaction formation" and how it might be relevant to his troubled relationship with his mother. Zinger flew into a rage and never returned, despite Dr. Straighttalk's several attempts to reach him. In the meantime, Mr. Zinger contacted an ethics committee claming that he was being harassed and demeaned by his therapist.

Whereas interpretations that annoy or upset clients are usually resolved within the therapy setting, in this case an ethics committee was able to serve as an intermediary. Dr. Straighttalk was asked to write Zinger a note inviting him to get together, and the committee chair also wrote Zinger directly, urging him to accept the therapist's forthcoming invitation. A follow-up confirmed that the meeting was productive, and that therapy was continuing.

Finally, one might ask the question, "Besides inconvenience and emotional distress, does a guilty finding by an ethics committee have any real impact on the violator?" After all, as we describe later in the chapter, the penalties often do not involve expulsion or any public exposure. However, malpractice insurance applications, license renewal forms, insurance provider applications, and hospital staff membership applications ask whether any disciplinary actions have ever been sustained against the applicant. Thus, even a reprimand would have to be reported and explained, with an attendant risk of nonrenewal or exclusion. In addition, professional job applications may require disclosure of any discipline for professional misconduct, which means that hospital or managed care organization (MCO) privileges could be denied, even for sustained minor infractions. (See Chapter 17 for more about malpractice.)

Ethics Complaints Not Pursued

Ethics committees can not pursue every complaint that they receive. The seven most common reasons for declining to pursue formal charges are as follows:

1. *No Provision in the Code.* An ethics code can not cover every conceivable unethical act or poor judgment that mental health professionals might make. Indeed, the creators of ethics codes are faced with a dilemma. If they make the code very specific and detailed, then loopholes abound. But, if codes are composed of very general statements, then complainants can always claim that their contentious act was not clearly addressed. Seeking a proper balance between specificity and generality is an ongoing challenge.

Case 3–8: Tim Nopenny, a graduate student, complained that Don Staunch, Ph.D., director of a clinical internship program, discriminated against him and any other applicants with limited financial resources living some distance from the facility. The program required applicants to appear for a personal interview. Tim claimed that he did not have the funds to make the trip and requested a telephone interview. Dr. Staunch explained that the entire staff was involved with the evaluation process, and on-site applicant visits were critical to the determination of suitability for training.

Although an ethics committee sympathized with Tim Nopenny's predicament, nothing in the ethics code prohibits an agent for an internship program from administering reasonably justifiable selection policies.

2. *When an Ethics Committee Is Not the Appropriate Mediator.* Sometimes, an ethics committee refuses to process complaints when it becomes clear that the committee will be unable to make any reasonable contribution to a solution. This occurs most often under the following circumstances:

- when two or more therapists are involved in an intense interpersonal conflict that bubbles over into their professional relationship with each other
- when the infraction involved an act that might conceivably be unethical but is virtually impossible for ethics committees to evaluate or investigate
- when the issues are related to other than ethical aspects regarding standards of practice or interprofessional political disputes
- when other sources of redress are clearly more appropriate

Case 3–9: Edgar Potshot, Ed.D., had a long-standing and intense dislike for his colleague, Nick Nitpick, Ph.D. Potshot complained that Nitpick engaged in unprofessional conduct when he told the counseling center receptionist that Potshot had "crap for brains." When the committee asked Nitpick about the incident, he countercharged that Potshot had been making horrendous remarks to their colleagues about him for years.

An ethics committee realized that it was not going to resolve the ethical issues or the intense and ingrained interpersonal difficulties between these wrangling colleagues. A duplicate letter informed both men that the committee would not be accepting the case and pointed out that this was a no-win situation for all concerned. The letter stressed the professional responsibilities of both parties and urged them to embark on some course of action that would lead to neutralization of the destructive nature of their working relationship.

Case 3–10: A student complained that a counseling psychology professor gave her a B in a course when she believed she deserved an A.

Some complaints, including most involving performance evaluation disputes, are virtually impossible for ethics committees to assess adequately. The student in Case 3–10 was encouraged to speak with the professor about the matter and, if she was not satisfied, to seek appropriate redress within her university. Some matters are far better handled through established channels closer to the source.

Other complaints reaching ethics committees involve disputes over acceptable standards of practice or intraprofessional disagreements.

Case 3–11: A Ph.D. psychologist complained that the clinic director hired a master's-level person as an agency counselor. The Ph.D.-level psychologist had applied for the job and felt that he should have gotten it because of his more advanced degree.

Degree status, per se, can not be conclusively designated as the marker of competency or fitness for a particular job. Unless a prospective employee could demonstrate that he or she was the victim of discriminatory hiring practices, an ethics committee would have no place in evaluating the matter. And, even if hiring practices were potentially discriminatory, other agencies (e.g., the Equal Employment Opportunity Commission) would be more likely to remedy the problem. So, unless incompetence or malicious intent is clearly involved, ethics committees would typically send the parties back to try to resolve the matters between themselves.

Ethics committees may inform complainants that other sources of redress are more appropriate and suggest that these be pursued. In such instances, the committee takes the role of facilitator by serving as a resource or referral agent.

Case 3–12: An ethics committee received a charge alleging that Rob Filch, L.M.H.C., had bilked the complainant's niece out of most of her father's inheritance when Filch was a staff counselor at a psychiatric facility in which the young woman was being treated. Mr. Filch allegedly told the young woman's uncle that she begged him to take the money because she hated her now-deceased father and didn't want anything to do with anything about him. He added that he was happy to help her out. The uncle insisted that Filch was capitalizing on his niece's mental condition.

Ethics committees do not have the necessary resources to fully explore such a complaint or the authority to make appropriate restitution should that be warranted. The complainant was advised to seek legal counsel.

3. *When Respondents Are Not Members of the Professional Organization.* Professional associations are voluntary membership organizations, and the jurisdiction of their ethics committees extends only to current members. It is not uncommon for complaints to be filed against licensed mental health professionals who are not members of the association to which the complaint is sent. These can not be processed, although information can be offered to the complainant about alternative sources of redress with jurisdiction. Complaints against licensed practitioners can be referred to state boards, many of which adopt or follow the ethics code. However, as we noted, there is considerable variability in the responsiveness of many of these regulating bodies, except in those fairly rare instances when the alleged infraction poses imminent harm to the public. The next case illustrates how an ethics committee can not be of assistance if the respondent is not a member.

Case 3–13: After numerous attempts to make contact, Lostmi Numbers, Ph.D., brought a complaint to an ethics committee against Holden Stats, L.M.H.C. Despite many attempts to contact him, Mr. Stats had refused to return research data owned by Dr. Numbers after Stats had originally volunteered to help analyze it. Dr. Numbers was quickly informed that Stats was not a member of the association, and that she should contact a licensing board. After 2 years of inaction, a member of the licensing board finally informed Dr. Numbers that, "The case is so low on the priority list that it is unlikely to ever surface." As a result, Dr. Number's research project, which had already taken over a year of work on her part, had to be scuttled.

Dr. Numbers's dilemma proves again that backing up valuable information should be routine practice. Nevertheless, Mr. Stats acted irresponsibly and unprofessionally and got away with it.

Case 3–14: A group of students presented evidence from their own "sting operation" to support the allegation that Sammy Scam, Psy.D., owner of a consulting firm, would supply letters of reference for a $100 dollar fee to students he had never even met in support of their applications to graduate school or for employment.

Dr. Scam was neither a member of any professional association or licensed. Scam is especially difficult to restrain because, despite the impropriety of the service he performs, its illegality is not clear-cut.

Case 3–15: A client and her attorney gathered considerable evidence to substantiate that Ransom Fleece, "Ph.D." (later identified as unlicensed and holding a "doctorate" supplied by a mail-order diploma mill), was extorting large sums of money to buy his silence. Fleece told the woman that he would inform her influential and wealthy husband of her many affairs and follies as revealed to him during the course of "psychotherapy" unless she complied with his demands for monthly payment.

"Dr." Fleece's actions are clearly illegal and could be pursued in a court of law if the client so desired.

Finally, we must note that membership in a professional association does not guarantee competence or virtuous qualities, and lack of membership in a professional organization does not suggest incompetence or impoverished character. However, consumers have additional protection when the therapists providing services for them have voluntarily agreed to ethical scrutiny by virtue of their membership in organizations with peer control mechanisms.

4. *When Complaints Are Against Groups, Agencies, Corporations, or Institutions.* Whereas a complainant can name more than one person in a single complaint, each respondent must be known to the ethics committee by name, and the involvement of each in the dispute must be specified. Ethics committee mechanisms are not set up to deal with an organization or a corporation, as is possible in the courts. Even a cursory reading of ethics codes reveals a focus on the ethical responsibilities of *individuals*. Thus, when complaints are received against a government

agency, a state examining committee, an academic department, or a mental health clinic, the material is returned to the complainant.

5. *When Complaints Are Anonymous.* Occasionally, an ethics committee receives an unsigned complaint. Usually, the reason for anonymity is noted, and it is typically fear of retribution. Ethics committees are often concerned, especially when a letter is well documented and the alleged infraction is grievous. But, the rules and procedures of ethics committees allow the respondent the right to know his or her accuser and to due process. Thus, unless the complaint contains information that can be substantiated in some other way (e.g., all the necessary information to move forward is available through public sources), the committee can not pursue the case.

Related to the anonymous complainant are those who reveal their identity but insist that the committee not disclose it to the respondents. In such cases, the committee is able to explain the procedures—including which safeguards the committee is able to extend—and defend the requirement for making identities known to respondents. Some then agree to pursue the case according to the necessary procedures, while others choose to withdraw their complaints.

6. *When the Complaints Are Improper.* Occasionally, ethics committees receive complaints that, based on the available evidence, are judged frivolous and intended to harm or harass someone rather than to protect the public. In such cases, formal ethics committee inquiries may be unwarranted. When the complainant is not a member of the professional association, an allegation that appears to be harassing, speculative, or internally inconsistent will usually be disregarded, as illustrated in the next case.

Case 3–16: Nute Rankled, M.D., wrote to an ethics committee complaining that Charlton Rebuff, Ph.D., an APA member, had promised to refer clients to him. However, Rebuff failed to follow through with his offer.

Dr. Rankled may find himself disappointed that Dr. Rebuff did not measure up to expectations, and Rebuff may not be a steadfast individual, but there is nothing in this scenario that should involve an ethics committee. It appears that Rankled is attempting to use an ethics committee to aggravate Rebuff.

If the complainant *is* a member of the APA and the committee decides that the charge was frivolous and intended to harm the respondent, then he or she may receive an unwelcome surprise. It is an ethics violation *in and of itself* for other APA members to issue complaints against members who have a reckless disregard for the facts (APA 02: 1.07) or who appear to abuse the ethics committee process (APA, 2001). In the next case, both parties are APA members.

Case 3–17: At the holiday office party of the 72nd Street Counseling Center, Johnny Sot, Ph.D., had too much to drink. He got into an argument about the future direction of the center with Tilly Sober, Psy.D., and shoved her against the food table, knocking over platters of appetizers. Sober was basically unharmed, but her silk dress was ruined. Dr. Sober sued Dr. Sot in small claims court for the cost of her dress. In return, Sot contacted an ethics committee and attempted to press charges of fraud against Sober for "bilking him out of $75 by telling the court that her ugly dress cost $200 when he saw the same one in a shop window for $125."

An ethics committee would have had difficulties had Sober pressed a charge against Sot because his abusive act was committed in a professional workspace (a counseling center) but not in a professional context (off-hours social party). However, the committee was confident in tagging Sot for a frivolous and likely vengeful motivation in his charges against Sober.

7. *When Complaints Arrive Beyond the Statute of Limitations.* Ethics committees expect that complaints should be filed within specified periods of time after the alleged violation occurred or came to the complainant's attention. With a few narrow exceptions, the APA rules and procedures allow an elapsed time of 3 years when the complaint is issued by an APA member. For nonmembers and student affiliates, the time is extended to 5 years. The reason for the discrepancy favoring the nonmember is that members are expected to be more aware of the ethics code and redress procedures and to

act promptly. Nonmembers, on the other hand, usually do not possess such knowledge, and it may not become available to them for some period of time. In addition, other factors could interfere with punctual reporting. In some cases, the nonmembers suffered emotionally in ways that were immobilizing for an extended period, and they were incapable of pursuing their complaints until the trauma had been worked through or had dissipated. Students may wish to wait until after graduation before pressing charges against one of their educators. Under certain conditions involving more serious situations, these limits can be extended further (APA, 2001).

The next case was heard by an ethics committee, under the special provisions, even though 8 years had passed since the alarming episode occurred.

Case 3–18: Arthur Stunned agreed, as requested, to disrobe and turn his back to Frank Bigshot, Ph.D. Mr. Stunned charged that Bigshock then, without warning, shoved his thumb into Stunned's anus. Bigshock then declared that Stunned would now never feel fear again because he had been "set free." Stunned was so traumatized by this "therapy" technique that he left treatment and did not confide to anyone about his ordeal for 7 years. He did eventually correspond with Dr. Bigshock and saved the response letter from Bigshock describing the technique and why it was designed to be beneficial.

Mr. Stunned, with the support of his new therapist, requested that the APA hear the case. The ethics committee agreed to do so. Dr. Bigshot was expelled from the organization, and a report was sent to the state licensing board in which he practiced.

8. *Infractions Not Committed in the Course of Professional Work.* Maintaining a distinction between professional and personal behavior is rooted in our nation's cultural value that emphasizes every citizen's right to a private life (Pipes, Holstein, & Aguirre, 2005). When people are unhappy with a mental health practitioner's private behavior, they may try to involve an ethics committee. Strictly private behavior, however, does not fall under the APA ethics

code and is specifically marked as off limits for adjudication unless the psychologist commits a felony (APA, 2001). However, given the erosion into our privacy, whether from post-9/11 statues or invasive technology and media, the line between private and pubic behavior is increasingly blurred, making it difficult to sort acts into two distinct piles.

A public relations problem occurs when the private actions of a therapist are dishonorable and made public. For example, a therapist who is a racist, a scoundrel, and an exploiter is untouchable by an ethics committee as long as the display of these undesirable traits do not amount to a felony or spill into his or her professional work. This individual will not be scrutinized by most professional ethics committees despite the fact that most of us would not want to embrace this person as a colleague and would doubt the quality of services provided. After all, if one is morally impaired in the personal realm, how likely is it that their professional services are unaffected? What do you think about the next actual case gleaned from a local paper's headlines?

Case 3–19: Lush Juiced, Psy.D., was found passed out on the sidewalk, unable to stand. He pled guilty to a misdemeanor and admitted to the court that he has a "sometimes drinking problem" and promised to seek help. The judge fined Dr. Juiced $500 and accepted his word that he would voluntarily seek treatment.

Dr. Juiced presents an interesting dilemma. We can probably assume that alcoholism likely interferes with the quality of the counseling services he performs and would like to see him mandated to treatment. However, a client has not complained, and he was convicted of a misdemeanor, not a felony. In another instance, a counselor was stopped for speeding, and the police found a small amount of cocaine on his person. This counselor's license was quickly revoked. Thus, which behavior can lead to sanctions depends on how it is legally classified, and this differs among the states.

Even individuals who serve on ethics committees do not always agree that charges of unethical conduct should be rejected when therapists were acting strictly as private citizens or in some other nonprofessional role, especially if the misconduct was menacing or bizarre or becomes an embarrassing media story. When that individual's profession is prominently noted, the public trust of all practitioners in the field is tarnished, at least temporarily. One of our friends showed us an article in his local paper describing a psychotherapist whose wife divorced him because he insisted that the entire family sleep in a plastic pyramid, believing that this would increase their longevity. Our friend then said, "That's why I would never go to a shrink. They are crazier than I will ever be."

The conceptual distinction between public and private behavior also breaks down *within* the APA ethics code itself (Pipes et al., 2005). For example, psychologists are admonished to refrain from practice if their personal problems reduce their professional competence (APA 02: 2.06). But, aren't personal problems private matters? The ethics code also states that comments made in public, including to the media, are to be truthful and based on professional knowledge (APA 02: 5.01; 5.04). But, are comments made to the media necessarily done as a professional? Finally, the admonition against multiple role relationships could be said to be logically inconsistent when the roles imposed on the therapy relationship are about private matters rather than professionally related.

Of course, in many instances, similar to the debacle at the 72nd Street Counseling Center (Case 3–17), ethics committees would not be the appropriate recourse for mediation of strictly private disputes. The next case is illustrative.

Case 3–20: Bucky Newoff, a recently divorced man who worked as an accountant in the same office building with Stan Onenite, Ph.D., complained to an ethics committee that the psychologist had exploited him and was responsible for his current high-anxiety state. The two had started seeing each other socially and had spent the night together on one occasion. Then, he claimed, Dr. Onenite abruptly broke off the relationship without explanation.

After clarifying with the complainant that he was not now and never had been a psychotherapy client of Dr. Onenite, the ethics committee informed Mr. Newoff that it would not intervene in relationship failures between consenting adults functioning in their roles as private citizens.

Stromberg (1990) contended that it is often difficult to prove that the consumers were, in fact, harmed by therapists' private actions. He believed that ethics committees should, however, be empowered to consider any conduct that seems reasonably likely to impair professional functioning or violates the values that the profession is sworn to uphold. The Canadian ethics code (2000; see Appendix B), echoes Stromberg's thinking in that the Canadian Psychological Association upholds the right to a private life, but cautions that a member's behavior that undermines the public trust of the discipline or raises questions about the member's ability to function responsibly as a professional will constitute a valid concern.

There are conditions in which the APA's Ethics Committee can act even when the behavior involved was strictly in the private realm. The APA procedures allow accelerated action when a member has been found guilty of a felony, regardless of the direct relevance of the crime to that person's professional activities. A "show cause" proceeding offers a short period of time for the psychologist/felon to explain why the APA should not expel him or her from the organization. The next two cases are illustrative.

Case 3–21: Mat Carpet, Ph.D., paid a heavy fine and was convicted on one count of attempted larceny for claiming that his valuable Oriental rug was damaged during a heavy storm. An insurance investigator discovered that Dr. Carpet purchased the water-damaged rug from a local store several days after the storm and placed it in his home for the adjuster to see. After the adjustor left, Dr. Carpet took the damaged rug back to the store for a refund.

Case 3–22: Andrew Bumpoff, Ph.D., was convicted of the attempted murder of his wife when the young man he hired to do the killing confessed after questioning by the police. The man claimed that Dr. Bumpoff had taken out a large insurance policy on his wife's life and promised the man one quarter of

the payoff if he would break into the house on a particular evening when Dr. Bumpoff was seeing clients, shoot the wife, and take a few expensive items to make it look like a robbery. The trial was widely publicized, and Dr. Bumpoff's profession was prominently woven into every story.

Dr. Bumpoff's behavior was so extreme that his unfitness as a therapist seems beyond debate. Compared to Bumpoff, Dr. Carpet's act seems more like a foolish indiscretion. Or is it? One would be hard pressed to make a connection between delivering counseling services at the local community agency and his attempted scam. But, questions of Dr. Carpet's character are obvious, especially since the fraud was premeditated and rather complicated, requiring him to traipse around town with a large rug.

Other actual cases of private misconduct resulting in expulsions using a show cause procedure include those involving a clinical psychologist who strangled his housekeeper to death and another who abused drugs with clients in group therapy sessions. One psychology professor purposely set the university administration building on fire, and another professor was found spying for Cuba. The same show cause process can be used for members who have had their licenses revoked or suspended by a state board or have been expelled or suspended by a state or local association (APA, 2001).

WHO COMPLAINS TO ETHICS COMMITTEES?

As psychologists who served for many years on ethics committees, we have arrived at some solid impressions about the characteristics of people who press complaints. A majority of complaints, at least 60% in our estimation, come from persons who are (or were) psychotherapy clients or family members of psychotherapy clients and who were dissatisfied with the conduct, therapy techniques, competence, or payment policies of their psychotherapists. Therapists' professional involvement in child custody cases is currently an especially high-risk area of practice. A substantial minority of complaints, perhaps 25%, comes from other psychologists or closely allied professionals concerned about the conduct of a colleague. The small remainder is divided almost equally among students, supervisees, and other private citizens dissatisfied with psychologists' nontherapeutic services, such as teaching methods and performance evaluations, business consultations, or research procedures.

The majority of complainants have had direct, personal interactions with the psychologists against whom they are charging ethical misconduct. However, a minority of the cases (perhaps 10%) are complaints about persons the complainants do not know personally. In such instances, the complainants are usually other mental health professionals. For example, therapists may mail in newspaper accounts of misconduct or lawbreaking by other therapists and suggest that the ethics committee undertake an investigation if they have not already done so. Most cases involving plagiarism, for example, are discovered by other academics or by students in the course of their literature searches. Sometimes, therapists will assist a client in pressing charges against the client's previous therapist, teacher, or employer.

People who complain to ethics committees appear to share several common characteristics. They tend to be knowledgeable about redress procedures, capable of clearly describing the situation as they see it, and sufficiently motivated to sustain themselves through the various, and sometimes arduous, stages of the ethics inquiry process. Anger is often evident among complainants who were personally involved with the accused therapists. Often, the antagonism is explicitly described (e.g., "I have never felt such intense rage"), while at other times it is easily inferred (e.g., "Dr. Slovenly is a lame excuse for a human being").

Ethics committees, then, tend to hear from complainants who are resourceful, articulate, rankled, and persevering. They may well comprise a highly selective group. Consumers who may have legitimate grievances against their therapists but who are frightened, debilitated by hurt, unassertive, unresourceful, inarticulate, overwhelmed, or lack knowledge about how to pursue a grievance may never come to the attention of ethics committees or any other redress mechanism.

We note here, as an interesting aside, that we know of instances when ethics complaints were considered but never pressed because the therapist apologized to the client for whatever it was that was of concern and made it right. Apologies can avert lawsuits (Robbennolt, 2003). Of course, an apology is also tantamount to an admission of guilt, so we are not making a blanket recommendation. However, every one of us has experienced the healing power of the words, "I'm really sorry."

We are often questioned about the prevalence of complaints from people who are deeply troubled or delusional, assuming the rate to be quite high. After all, people who consult therapists have emotional issues. In fact, few complainants could be characterized, solely on the basis of the correspondence, as seriously impaired. When committees receive complaints such as the ones illustrated next, the most common recourse is to ask for more specific details and evidence or to contact the respondents for their impressions of what took place.

Case 3–23: A woman complained that her social worker had claimed the souls of her cat, two dogs, and the canary.

Case 3–24: A retired military officer charged two Veterans Affairs psychologists with attempting to brainwash him into killing small boys, overthrowing the Saudi royal family, and bombing Los Angeles.

Case 3–25: An office worker wrote a long and rambling letter charging her therapist with following her everywhere she went, tapping into her home telephone, stealing small items from her apartment, and hiring someone to drive by her apartment on a motorcycle at all hours of the day and night.

Ethics committees should not simply dismiss such complaints without some further exploration. At the very least, an attempt is made to ensure that the therapists did their utmost to protect the welfare of these individuals.

Occasionally, ethics committees press charges *sua sponte*. That is, based on information in the public domain (e.g., newspaper articles, local television news stories, service advertisements, or court records), the committee initiates the investigation on its own.

Case 3–26: A large envelope was sent to an ethics office with no identifying information about the sender. The contents consisted of a 1995 monograph describing the results of a survey on teenage runaways and a copy of a 2006 doctoral dissertation, authored by someone else, containing the same data and most of the text as it appeared in the earlier monograph.

Although ethics committees do not normally pursue anonymous complaints, this case became an exception because the evidence was objective and publicly available. The committee charged the therapist with a plagiarism violation.

Case 3–27: Five students charged a counselor at the local college mental health center with sexual misconduct, and the matter went to trial. The evening news carried a story about the guilty verdict. Another therapist who viewed the news report wrote down the information and informed an ethics committee of the incident.

The viewer did not have to put herself in the position of being an identified complainant. The story was in the public domain, allowing the ethics committee to make its own inquiry if it chose to do so.

The Perils of Being a Complainant

The Internet makes it much easier for a person seeking to complain and to learn about the ethics operations of professional mental health organizations. Each organization offers its ethics code, information about how the ethics committee does its work, and how to make a complaint. However, there are requirements—many related to maintaining due process for the respondent— by which complainants must abide, and these can cause discomfort. Complainants must be willing to have their identities and the nature of their complaint shared with the accused therapist. They must also sign a waiver allowing the respondent to share information relevant to the case. Often, this material was originally shared

in confidence (i.e., therapy notes, diagnoses, or psychological assessment records) but will now be shared with complete strangers (i.e., ethics committee members). Complainants may feel especially distressed because their earlier disclosures to their therapists might now be used as a defense against the charges. Unfortunately, at this point some sincere complainants may decide that they are unwilling to endure the process. Those who persist, as most who start the process do, have agreed to have their identities known to the respondent and relevant matters about themselves shared with the committee from the perspective of the respondent.

Case 3–28: On receiving an inquiry letter from an ethics committee, Sanford Assail, Ph.D., responded, "This woman is totally bonkers. You can not believe anything she says."

Ethics committee members will not dismiss a complaint simply because a respondent claims that the complainant is not credible. They respect the vulnerability of complainants and will look further into the matter before making a final decision. Dr. Assail made a poor impression on the committee because of his offhanded and unprofessional description of his client.

Sometimes, the respondent does not offer a defense and agrees that the ethical violation occurred as the complainant described it, making it straightforward for the committee to proceed. Occasionally, in an attempt to create a defense, the respondent will, unwittingly, offer additional incriminating data.

Case 3–29: Footin Mouth, Psy.D., told an ethics committee that the reason she sat in her client's lap and allowed him to stroke her hair during their therapy sessions was because the client insisted on it. She wrote, "I pride myself in responding to the needs of all of my clients, whatever those needs might be."

Complainants may be asked for additional information as the committee assembles relevant materials. Then, they wait. Cases can sometimes take more than a year to adjudicate. This may be distressing to the complainant (and the respondent as well) because the act of pressing a charge, as well as being on the receiving end of one, sets up a persistent, uncomfortable anticipation while awaiting resolution. When the investigation is complete and the decision has been reached, the complainant will be informed. But, feedback about the details is likely to be scanty compared with what most complainants would like to know. If the charges proved valid, complainants may have to settle for feeling satisfied that they helped a profession help itself.

Countercharges

When the complainant is also a mental health professional, occasionally the respondent files a countercomplaint. Sometimes, both appear to have a legitimate complaint against each other. The APA Ethics Committee attempts to ascertain what led to the first complaint but will not normally act on the second complaint until the first one is resolved. However, with a two-thirds vote of the ethics committee, simultaneous charges can be reviewed.

Countercharges can also be for no purpose other than to harass the one making the original charge, a ploy that APA does not condone.

Case 3–30: Terry Pushy, Psy.D., complained to an ethics committee that Hunker Downe, Ph.D., had refused, after three requests, to supply information about an ex-client who Pushy was currently seeing. Downe issued a countercomplaint, insisting that that Dr. Pushy was rude and therefore "an unworthy recipient of a professional courtesy."

Committees become uneasy when thrust into the role of "weapon" and attempt to minimize being used for this purpose (APA, 2001; APA 02: 1.07). Dr. Hunker should have released the information that the client and the new therapist requested shortly after receiving the initial request. Even if Dr. Pushy had a rude manner (which might be understandable after multiple requests for information), that does not absolve Dr. Downe from failing to fulfill a professional responsibility. Downe's countercomplaint appears to be an attempt to evade responsibility and shift blame to Pushy.

The Perils of Being a Respondent and How to Respond If Charged

On receiving the charge letter from an ethics committee, some respondents express outrage that anyone would dare question their judgment or their method of practice. Sometimes, they refuse to interact with the committee at all, although they may come around on learning that failure to respond is, in itself, an ethics violation (APA, 2001; APA 02: 1.06). Some respondents are so stressed and upset that they appear to jeopardize their own health. Many are able to retain a dignified approach to the charge but can not escape underlying anxiety. No matter what the reaction to being charged, every respondent wants the matter resolved as quickly as possible.

Others see a charge as a game of wills and attempt to outmaneuver the committee, perhaps with the aid of an attorney. What mental health professionals who are charged with an ethical infraction must keep foremost in mind is that "beating the system" is *not* the appropriate goal. Those who join professional mental health associations with ethics committees have agreed—voluntarily and with full consent—to be on the inside of a profession that has obligated itself to formal peer monitoring. All of us, as well as the public, receive advantages from this system. Were all ethics committees to be discontinued, the professions would be at the total mercy of outside control.

Here is our best advice on how to respond if you are ever a complainant.

1. Know who you are dealing with and understand the nature of the complaint and the potential consequences before responding.
   • Are you dealing with a statutory licensing authority or a professional association?
   • Are you dealing with nonclinician investigators or professional colleagues?
   • Is the contact an informal inquiry or a formal charge? (Sometimes licensing boards and ethics committees approach less serious allegations by asking the therapist to respond before they decide to make formal charges. In such instances, however, "informal" does not mean the

same as "casual." Rather, such inquiries may be a sign that the panel has not yet concluded that the alleged conduct was serious enough to warrant drastic action or meets their definition for issuing a formal charge. The correct response should be thoughtful and cautious.)

- Do you have a detailed and comprehensible rendition of the complaint made against you, including a list of the specific alleged infractions or sections of the code that were allegedly violated by you?
- Do you have copies of the rules, procedures, or policies under which the panel operates?

2. Do not do anything impulsive. Knee-jerk actions are more likely than not to be counterproductive.

3. Do not contact the complainant directly or indirectly. The matter is no longer subject to informal resolution. Any contact initiated by you may be viewed as coercion or harassment.

4. If appropriate, confide in a colleague who will be emotionally supportive through the process. We strongly advise, however, that you refrain from discussing the charges against you with lots of other people. As described in Chapter 17, this can backfire if you are later sued and the colleague you spoke to is subpoenaed. Spreading your story, even spinning it in your own defense, will likely produce an adverse impact as more and more individuals become aware of your situation and indiscriminantly pass the story along. This may even raise additional problems regarding confidentiality. In no instance should you identify the complainant to others, aside from the board making the inquiry.

5. If the complainant is a client, be sure that the authorities have obtained and provided you with a signed waiver authorizing you to disclose confidential information *before* responding to the charges. We know of instances of licensing boards asking recipients of complaints to obtain consent from their own clients. Such requests are inappropriate because they put the mental health professional in the uncomfortable and awkward position of asking a complainant to surrender his or her confiden-

tiality to serve the needs of the person charged with misconduct.

6. Assess the credibility of the charge. Compile and organize your records and the relevant chronology of events. (This is when you will be grateful that you keep careful records.) Respectfully respond fully to the committee's questions within the allotted time frame. Limit the scope of your response to the content areas and issues that directly relate to the complaint. If you need more time, ask for it. Be sure to retain copies of everything you send.

7. Do not take the position that the best defense is a thundering offense. This will polarize the proceedings and lower the chances for a collegial solution.

8. If you believe that you have been wrongly charged, state your case clearly and provide any appropriate documentation.

9. If the complaint accurately represents the events but does not accurately interpret them, provide your account with as much documentation as you can.

10. If you have committed the offense, document the events and start appropriate remediation actions immediately. Present any mitigating circumstances and any corrective steps taken.

11. Be patient. It is likely that you will have to wait for what will seem like a long while before the matter is resolved.

12. Take active, constructive steps to minimize your own anxiety and stress levels. If this matter is interfering with your ability to function professionally, you might benefit from a professional counseling relationship in a privileged context (see Pope & Vasquez, 2005; Thomas, 2005).

13. Consultation with a lawyer is advised if the matter involves an alleged legal offense, if the ethics committee is not following the rules and procedures you consented to follow by virtue of your membership in the organization, or if the action might lead to public disciplinary action. The professional staff of the organization may be available to discuss questions about procedure. However, except for expulsion hearings or formal license revocation, respondents are typically expected to respond personally to the inquiry. A letter from an attorney is not

sufficient and will probably also be regarded as inappropriate. If a charge is sustained and you are asked to accept disciplinary measures without a formal hearing, then you may want to consider reviewing the potential consequences of the measures with an attorney before making your decision.

14. Know your rights of appeal.

DISPOSITIONS AND LEVELS OF SANCTIONS

We use the procedures of the APA to explore how ethics committees work from the inside. Each association has its own method, but their purposes are similar. All ethics committees aspire to educating all of their members (including those who have been charged with ethical misconduct), assessing the validity of complaints by uncovering the accurate nature of the events leading up to them, using the ethics code as the guide for deciding whether the complaints fall within their purview, and judging whether the members were at fault and, if so, exacting appropriate corrections and penalties.

Our brief discussion of ethics committee deliberations is based on the 2001 version of the APA Rules and Procedures (R&P). This document will change in the face of new challenges. Indeed, the ethics committee members of 25 or so years ago would likely be stunned by how detailed and legalistic the complaint and decision process has become. We refer here to the R&P in general terms, but this complicated, extensive document requires careful scrutiny in its own right to fully appreciate the ethics committee procedures.[1]

When a complaint of alleged unethical conduct is received by the APA, it is evaluated to determine its appropriateness before being presented to the full committee. Some complaints are dismissed for reasons presented in this chapter in the descriptions of those that are not pursued. Membership can also be voided if it was obtained by false or fraudulent means. For example, if an individual listed an academic degree that was, in fact, proven to be unearned, that individual will be dropped.

In a recently instituted alternative provision, before opening a case APA allows respondents to resign from the association, and about one in five choose to do so (APA Ethics Office, personal communication, February 21, 2007). Before 2001, this was not possible. The accused could not escape the ethics committee's review by resigning or by not paying dues. The new provision, however, is not exactly a clean getaway. The formal record will read, "resigned while under ethics investigation," and such information will be reported to the complainant, the membership, and anyone else who requests the information. Such a designation becomes publicly available and is probably perceived by others—correctly or not—as pleading guilty to whatever they were charged with doing. Otherwise, it would seem that they would have stuck out the process to defend themselves. Although this provision has substantially reduced the previously escalating cost of running the APA Ethics Office, complainants may not be at all happy on learning that the individual about whom they complained will not be held directly accountable.

If a case is opened, the respondent receives a charge letter, and a formal mechanism is set into motion. Here, we briefly describe and illustrate the various dispositions available to the APA Ethics Committee.

Dismissal of Charges

No Violation

When no evidence of wrongdoing as charged is revealed, the respondent and complainant are so informed, and the case is closed. In such instances, the complainant often misunderstood

---

1. This document can be accessed at http://www.apa.org/ethics/rules.html. The rules and procedures for the National Association of Social Work can be accessed at http://www.socialworkers.org/nasw/ethics/procedures.pdf; American Association for Marriage and Family Therapists at http://www.aamft.org/Resources/lrmplan/Ethics/eth_PROCEDURES.asp; American Counseling Association at http://www.counseling.org/Resources/CodeOfEthics/TP/Home/CT2.aspx; and the American Psychiatric Association at http://www.psych.org/psych_pract/ethics/ethics.cfm.

the psychologist's conduct or did not understand the psychologist's responsibilities in certain difficult situations. At other times, the psychologist's conduct (and often that of the complainant as well) could hardly be characterized as exemplary but was judged to be inside the arena of tolerable expression of emotion or behavior given the situational context. Three cases illustrate appropriate dismissal of charges.

Case 3–31: Mazy Pickle complained that she was tricked into committing herself to expensive psychotherapy through a bait-and-switch technique. She claimed that she was seeing a therapist at no charge because her company agreed to pay for her sessions, but during the 10th session the therapist announced that the fee would now be $50 per session. Mazy suspected that he was collecting from both the company and from her and quickly contacted the ethics committee.

The therapist explained, and the company's personnel director corroborated, that he was part of an employee assistance referral network for the company that agreed to pay for the first 10 sessions. Afterward, if the client wished to continue, fees would be charged based on the employee's ability to pay. The company's benefits brochure fully described this arrangement, and according to the therapist, he discussed it briefly during the initial session. On further inquiry, the client remained confused but did vaguely remember something about 10 sessions.

Case 3–32: Mia Frantic complained that her psychologist, Leslie Concerned, Ph.D., called the paramedics and the police and told them she was suicidal when she claimed she was, in fact, only a little agitated and only wanted to get her therapist's attention. Ms. Frantic claimed she suffered embarrassment, and that her landlord asked that she move because of the commotion. She also complained that the psychologist violated his duty to keep information shared between them confidential.

Dr. Concerned responded that his answering service called him at 3:00 A.M., informing him that Ms. Frantic claimed to have taken "lots of pills," and that he should go over to her place right away. Because he feared for her safety and

did not know what kind of pills or how many were ingested, he decided that other forms of assistance should also be marshaled. When he arrived, the police (called by the paramedics) were already there, and the client was throwing books at them before being restrained. A hospital report indicated that the woman had not taken any pills. The psychologist's account of the evening and some of the other dynamics between the two persuaded the committee that he exercised appropriate professional judgment given the apparent emergency.

Case 3–33: Billy Blunt, an employee at a state mental facility, complained that a staff psychologist had called him "an inept boob" in front of patients and other staff, thus jeopardizing his employment status.

The psychologist admitted that she was extremely angry at the employee, but that his behavior deserved a sharp reaction. She was able to document that Mr. Blunt had just struck a severely regressed schizophrenic in the face because the man had ignored his orders to go to the dayroom.

A Violation Would Not Warrant Further Action

A complaint can be dismissed up front if the charge is true but only a minor or technical violation occurred, if the problem had already been adequately addressed in another way, or if a minor error is likely to be corrected.

These circumstances are illustrated in the next case.

Case 3–34: A therapist was distressed to see a splashy brochure on the supermarket public board sporting goofy-looking cartoons with text bubbles saying things like, "I'm nuts, but Dr. Cureall will make me all better," and "Goodbye to psychosis. Hello to Dr. Cureall!" The therapist pulled the brochure off the board and sent it to an ethics committee along with a copy to Dr. Cureall expressing disapproval.

Dr. Cureall explained that she had hired a small local company to create a promotional brochure, and it had gone ahead and posted the brochures without ever showing them to her. She reported feeling highly embarrassed and actively attempted to reclaim and destroy the already distributed brochures. Even though Dr. Cureall technically violated APA 02: 5.02 (a), which holds psychologists responsible for promotional materials created by others, the respondent appeared to be sincere, and the problem had been addressed. Bringing in the full force of ethics committee time and resources was unnecessary.

Insufficient Evidence

When it is decided that a complaint, if valid, would constitute a breach of ethics, the ethics committee may still be unable to move to a cause for action (i.e., open a formal case) when sufficient evidence can not be gathered during a preliminary investigation. So, unless additional credible witnesses or supporting documents can be produced, it usually becomes the complainant's word against that of the respondent. Impressions of credibility do factor in but are not always persuasive one way or the other. Both the complainant and respondent may be informed that definitive evidence is lacking, and that any additional evidence or information that either may possess should be shared with the committee. But, alleged infractions often occur in private, and no evidence beyond hearsay or opinion is available to either party or the ethics committee.

Closing the matter without further action is frustrating, both to an individual who made a valid complaint or to an innocent psychologist who was complained against. The complainant who was indeed wronged by the respondent no doubt experiences further stress when an ethics committee is unable to substantiate the charge. In these unfortunate cases, complainants suffer an additional insult when the profession seemingly lets offenders off the hook. This perception on the part of complainants is understandable, although not entirely accurate. The records are not destroyed for a long period of time and should similar complaints arise against those same psychologists in the future, the initial complaints may be retrieved and reviewed.

In addition, ethics committee members are hopeful that the investigation process had a salutary effect on psychologists who were, in fact, guilty of an ethical violation. Even though lack of evidence may have allowed escape this time, sensitization to the issues and the noxious experience of undergoing an ethics inquiry by their peers may preclude a reoccurrence of such infractions.

As for the unjustly accused psychologist who could not prove his or her innocence, a lingering feeling of unrest may persist despite the fact that no violation was substantiated. It is unfortunate that an innocent therapist would have to undergo an inquiry by peers who close the case in doubt. Certainly, ethics committee members themselves are also disappointed when cases are shut due to insufficient evidence. They know that someone was not served well, but they could not determine who that someone was.

Educative Letters

Ethics committees take every opportunity to educate those who appear before them. Even when the charges are dismissed, the respondent may receive an educative letter. For example, Mazy Pickle's therapist (Case 3–31 above) was found innocent of perpetrating bait-and-switch fee setting. However, the letter from the ethics office closing the matter offered him some ideas for ensuring that no such misunderstandings resurfaced in the future.

For minor violations, when it seems clear that they resulted in no real harm and when the psychologist seems amendable to understanding what needs to be done differently, an educative letter may also be issued.

Sustained Charges, Sanctions, and Directives

Psychologists who have been found to have violated the ethics code may receive an educative letter along with one of several other sanctions and directives. It is generally useful to consider the degree of seriousness of an infraction as a criterion for determination of any penalties, although as we illustrate next, other factors may mitigate or aggravate the determination of penalty ultimately imposed.

Box 3–1 Levels of Ethical Violations and Possible Directives or Sanctions

Level I-A. A finding that a therapist's behavior or practice was not clearly unethical but in poor taste or insufficiently cautious.

Level I-B. A finding that a minor infraction occurred, but the potential for harm was unlikely. The therapist may have been insufficiently cautious, though not necessarily intentionally.

Level II-A. A finding of clearly unethical misconduct although unlikely to harm the public or profession substantially.

Level II-B. Deliberate or persistent behavior that could potentially lead to substantial harm to the client or public, although little harm may have actually occurred.

Level III-A. Continuing or dramatic misconduct producing a genuine hazard to clients, the public, and the profession.

Level III-B. Individual clients or others with whom the therapist worked are substantially injured, and there are serious questions about the potential rehabilitation of the therapist.

As is clear on even a cursory reading of the APA or any other professional ethics code, violating some principles causes far more harm than violating others. A scheme to aid in understanding the seriousness of infractions is presented in Box 3–1 (adapted from Koocher, Keith-Spiegel, & Klebanoff, 1981) and remains in general agreement with rules and procedures used today. This scheme allows a consideration of the appropriateness of sanctions and other mediating factors.

Level I deals essentially with *malum prohibitum* offenses, that is, behavior that is wrong primarily because it is proscribed in a code of ethics in contrast to behavior that is inherently immoral. No malicious intent can be ascribed to the therapist in question, and an ethics committee could respond by educating the individual or suggesting better ways of handling such matters in the future.

Level I-B carries I-A a step further, addressing behavior that is unquestionably inappropriate and somewhat offensive. Still, the committee may have the sense that the violation is a relatively minor one, that the individual in question did not fully realize the nature of the problem, and that an educative stance rather than a punitive one would be most effective. Such cases might include advertising infractions, inappropriate public statements, or mild

lack of collegiality. An ethics committee may request that the therapist cease and desist from engaging in the activity or behavior, noting that a more serious finding could result if the practice continued.

Level II (and Level III) involves *malum in se* offenses, that is, behavior that is unethical in itself in the view of the professional/scientific community. This category is reached when an ethics committee finds that a substantive violation did indeed occur. For Level II offenses, the therapist clearly should have known better, although the action or inaction did not result in any harm beyond remedy. The appropriate sanction may be a letter of reprimand.

When it has been determined by an ethics committee that a violation of the ethics code has occurred but that a recommendation of loss of membership does not appear warranted because the violation itself was unlikely to cause harm to another or to substantially tarnish the profession, the respondent may receive a letter of reprimand. If the violation was more likely to cause harm, but not gravely serious harm, to another or to the profession, the member may be censured.

Remedial directives assigned by an ethics committee might include mandated supervision or psychotherapy, enrollment in a continuing education course or tutorial, or other appropriate corrective action. Monitored probation can be imposed to ensure that the psychologist is in compliance with other directives. Ethics committees can not order monetary payments to complainants or any other entity, but occasionally respondents themselves offer to return fees to dissatisfied clients or consumers on their own as part of a good faith effort to resolve the problem.

Level III is reached when substantial harm accrues to others or to the profession as a result of the respondent's unethical behavior. The respondent may seem resistant to or ill-suited for rehabilitation and poses a threat to the public. Motivation to change or to demonstrate concern for the behavior is unclear. In some cases, resignations with stipulations are permitted, while in other cases ethics committees recommend expulsion from the organization, and the relevant state licensing board is informed. Expulsion is, of course, the most severe sanction and represents banishment from one's profession. The process is an extended one, involving formal hearings and board of directors' approval, too detailed to be adequately described here. The next two cases illustrate expulsion offenses.

Case 3–35: Seymour Fraud, Ph.D., who was found guilty of cheating insurance companies out of thousands of dollars, was being investigated by a state regulatory agency and an ethics committee. During the period when both investigations were actively open, an insurance company charged that Dr. Fraud had billed for over 50 additional client sessions that had never taken place.

Case 3–36: Harley Stud, Ph.D., was charged by several women with sexual exploitation. Dr. Stud admitted engaging in sexual relations with them but denied that it was exploitative. He claimed that they all needed special types of sexual activity in order to function as effective women. The only issue on which he would agree was that his form of therapy "did not work on these four women, but," he added, "it has worked beautifully on scores of others."

Both psychologists appeared to be unsuitable candidates for rehabilitation because neither revealed any insight into the problematic nature of their behavior or any indication that their views and practices would change.

Stipulated resignations, a less formidable sanction, can be offered by the committee contingent on the approval of the board of directors. The agreement may include various provisos. This sanction is most likely to be offered when respondents admit to an ethical violation or the act that prompted a show cause action. The violator is offered an opportunity to resign from the association for a negotiated period of time. At the end of this period, the violator may reapply. The committee will reexamine the case to see if the psychologist can demonstrate that major steps, either those stipulated or those taken on their initiative, have been taken to ensure that the nature of the difficulties have been ameliorated and are unlikely to resurface. At its option, the committee can act to restore the psychologist to membership in good standing. This sanction is not reported to the membership or to others.

What if a member is unhappy with the decision reached by the ethics committee? There are additional possibilities for review before the ethics process is finalized. Failure of the ethics committee to follow their own rules would be grounds for reconsideration. Other options, such as a request for independent adjudication or a formal hearing, are also available for certain sanctions.

Mitigating Factors and Exposure

The system we described provides a helpful framework to assist in curbing capricious punishment or excessive leniency relative to the specific violation. It must be recognized, however, that violations that appear identical may be decided somewhat differently. Common mitigating factors that might lead to different sanctions or directives for similar violations include

- the motivation or intent of the respondent
- the number of prior complaints against the respondent
- years of experience in the field
- the willingness of the respondent to accept responsibility for his or her actions
- the respondent's self-initiated attempts at remediation

So, an ethics committees may show lenience (e.g., apply an educative approach) to a first offender who committed a relatively minor offense due to inexperience. If the same offense were committed by a recalcitrant, experienced psychologist, however, a more severe sanction would be considered.

Sanctions have an immediate impact to the extent that the respondents have been educated, sensitized, embarrassed, or shamed into shaping up their practices. Other more tangible consequences may also accrue as noted. However, the APA can not, on its own, take away a psychologist's license. It can, however, inform licensing and certification boards when an APA member is expelled. The board receiving the information may then take some action. At its discretion, the APA may also inform other parties if it is determined that additional sharing of information would be in the best interests of the public or the profession. The APA members learn the identity and the general nature of the standards violated as a part of the annual membership dues statement package. The APA Ethics Office may inform any person who inquires in writing that a former member lost APA membership because of a sustained ethics charge or show cause action if the process occurred after June 1, 1996, or if the individual resigned while under ethics investigation. (Stipulated resignations are excluded unless such disclosure was part of the stipulation.)

The APA has not yet proactively disclosed serious violators to the public at large through easily located venues. Some other associations have more actively publicized disciplined mental health professionals. The California chapter of the professional association representing marriage and family counselors, for example, describes in its bimonthly magazine sustained charges that led to licensure revocation or suspension of marriage and family counselors as well as psychologists and social workers. Identities and location of practice are disclosed. These descriptions are in such detail that we have been able to adapt a number of our cases from them. In addition, technological innovations have provided easier access to disciplinary actions (Van Horn, 2004). The NASW, for example, posts the names (and adjudicating

chapter location) of those social workers with sanctions still in force for the past 10 years on its public Web site.

WHO TUMBLES THROUGH THE CRACKS?

As we stated, licensure and professional association membership do not ensure that a given therapist is competent and ethical. However, consumers are afforded more protection and redress channels when their service providers voluntarily agree to ethical scrutiny by virtue of their membership in organizations with peer control mechanisms. Even those members who decide to resign rather than face an ethics inquiry are forever labeled in a way that suggests, fairly or not, that they chose to escape rather endure an inquiry that might have exonerated them or resulted in a penalty that would not be discoverable by the public. Mental health practitioners who have earned credentials that qualify them for licensure or membership in a professional association with a monitoring mechanism but who seek neither are subject only to criminal or civil law or, if not self-employed, to the quality control mechanisms at their place of employment.

Most medium- to large-size communities have several individuals who offer services that appear to strongly resemble those of regulated professionals, but these individuals have neither suitable formal training nor the credentials to qualify them for licensure or membership in a professional association. Some of these individuals have purchased impressive-looking credentials from "diploma mills" to hang on their walls. Except for the most blatant transgressors, most stay away from using the protected titles that only state-licensed mental health professionals can use legally to identify their practice to the public. Instead, they devise unprotected titles that sound legitimate, such as "personal counselor" or "relationship expert."

Bogus therapists often become slippery when pursued because whenever a complaint appears imminent, they usually pick up stakes and relocate. In some states, a complaint can be investigated by authorities if an unwary complainant was reasonably led to believe that the individual was a licensed mental health professional. But, generally speaking, the public does not have adequate protection from these counterfeit practitioners.

References

American Counseling Association. (2005). *ACA code of ethics*. Alexandria, VA: Author. Available at http://www.counseling.org/ethics

American Educational Research Association, American Psychological Association, & National Council on Measurement in Education. (1999). *Standards for educational and psychological testing*. Washington, DC: AERA Publication Sales.

American Medical Association. (2001). *Principles of medical ethics*. Washington, DC: Author. Available at http://www.ama-assn.org/ama/pub/category/2498.html

American Psychiatric Association. (2006). *The principles of medical ethics with annotations especially applicable to psychiatry*. Arlington, VA: Author. Available at http://www.psych.org/psych_pract/ethics/ppaethics.cfm

American Psychological Association. (1987). *General guidelines for providers of psychological services*. Washington, DC: Author.

American Psychological Association. (2001). *Rules and procedures*. Washington, DC: Author.

American Psychological Association. (2002). *Ethical principles of psychologists and code of conduct*. Washington, DC: Author. Available at http://www.apa.org/ethics

American Psychological Association. (2007). *Record keeping guidelines*. Washington, DC: Author. Retrieved June 19, 2007, from http://www.apa.org/practice/recordkeeping.html

Ansell, C., & Ross, H. L. (1990). When laws and values conflict: A reply to Pope and Bajt. *American Psychologist, 45*, 399.

Bennett, B. E., Bricklin, P. M., Harris, E. A., Knapp, S., VandeCreek, L., & Younggren, J. N. (2007). *Assessing and managing risk in psychological practice: An individualized approach*. Rockville, MD: APA Insurance Trust.

Bersoff, D. N. (1994). Explicit ambiguity: The 1992 ethics code as oxymoron. *Professional Psychology, 25*, 382–387.

Bersoff, D. N., & Koeppl, P. M. (1993). The relation between ethical codes and moral principles. *Ethics & Behavior, 3*, 345–357.

Canadian Psychological Association. (2000). *Canadian code of ethics for psychologists*. Retrieved on October 25, 2005, from http://www.cpa.ca/cpasite/userfiles/Documents/Canadian%20Code%20of%20Ethics%20for%20Psycho.pdf

Gross, S. (1979). The myth of professional licensing. *American Psychologist, 33*, 1009–1016.

Hadjistavropoulos, T., & Malloy, D. C. (1999). Ethical principles of the American Psychological Association: An argument for philosophical and practical ranking. *Ethics & Behavior, 9*, 127–140.

Herbsled, J. D., Sales, B. D., & Overcast, T. D. (1985). Challenging licensure and certification. *American Psychologist, 40*, 1165–1178.

Johnson, W. B., Porter, K., Campbell, C. D., & Kupko, E. N. (2005). Character and fitness requirements for professional psychologists: An examination of state licensing application forms. *Professional Psychology, 36*, 654–662.

Keith-Spiegel, P. (Ed.). (1994). Special section. The 1992 ethics code: Boon or bane? *Professional Psychology, 25*, 315–387.

Kitchener, K. S. (1984). Intuition, critical evaluation and ethical principles: The foundation for ethical decisions in counseling psychology. *Counseling Psychologist, 12*, 43–55.

Koocher, G. P. (1979). Credentialing in psychology: Close encounters with competence? *American Psychologist, 34*, 696–702.

Koocher, G. P. (1989). Screening licensing exams for accuracy. *Professional Psychology, 20*, 269–271.

Koocher, G. P. (1994). The commerce of professional psychology and the new ethics code. *Professional Psychology, 25*, 315–387.

Koocher, G. P., Keith-Spiegel, P., & Klebanoff, L. (1981). Levels and sanctions. Unpublished report of the APA Task Force on Ethics System Procedures.

National Association of Social Workers. (1999). *Code of ethics*. Washington, DC: Author. Available at http://www.naswdc.org/pubs/code/code.asp

Peterson, M. B. (2001). Recognizing concerns about how some licensing boards are treating psychologists. *Professional Psychology, 32*, 339–340.

Pipes, R. B., Holstein, J. E., & Aguirre, M. G. (2005). Examining the personal-professional distinction: Ethics codes and the difficulty of drawing a boundary. *American Psychologist, 60,* 325–334.

Pope, K. S. & Vasquez, M. J. T. (2005). *How to survive and thrive as a therapist.* Washington, DC: American Psychological Association.

Pryzwansky. W. B., & Wendt, R. N. (1999). *Professional and ethical issues in psychology.* New York: Norton.

Reed, G. M., McLaughlin, C. J., & Newman, R. (2002). The development and evaluation of guidelines for professional practice. *American Psychologist, 57,* 1041–1047.

Robbennolt, J. (2003). Apologies and legal settlement: An empirical examination. *Michigan Law Review, 102,* 460–516.

Schoenfeld, L. S., Hatch, J. P., & Gonzales, J. M. (2001). Responses of psychologists to complaints filed against them with a state licensing board. *Professional Psychology, 32,* 491–495.

Sinclair, C., Simon, N. P., & Pettifor, J. L. (1996). The history of ethical codes and licensure. In L. J. Bass, D. T. DeMers, J. R. Ogloff, C. Peterson, J. L. Pettifor, R. P. Reaves, et al. (Eds.), *Professional conduct and discipline in psycholo-gy* (pp. 17–38). Washington, DC: American Psychological Association and Montgomery, AL: Association of State and Provincial Psychology Boards.

Stromberg, C. D. (1990). Key legal issues in professional ethics. In *Reflections on ethics: A compilation of articles inspired by the May, 1990 ASHA Ethics Colloquium* (pp. 15–38). Rockville, MD: American Speech–Language–Hearing Association.

Thomas, J. T. (2005). Licensing board complaints: Minimizing the impact on the psychologists' defense and clinical practice. *Professional Psychology, 36,* 426–433.

Van Horn, B. A. (2004). Psychology licensing board disciplinary actions: The realities. *Professional Psychology, 35,* 170–178.

Weinberger, A. (1988). Ethics: Code value and application. *Canadian Psychology, 29,* 77–85.

Wilensky, H. L. (1964). The professionalization of everyone? *American Journal of Sociology, 70,* 137–158.

Williams, M. H. (2001). The question of psychologists' maltreatment by state licensing boards: Overcoming denial and seeking remedies. *Professional Psychology, 32,* 341–344.

4

Knowing Thyself

Understanding Competence and Credentials

There is nothing more dangerous than ignorance
in action.

Johann Wolfgang von Goethe

Contents

The quotation from Faust stands as a warning to colleagues who believe that they have mastered all there is to know about their specialized field. Truly competent professionals recognize their limitations and weaknesses as well as their strengths and skills. When we become blind to our areas of inadequacy, clients may be hurt and the public put at risk. The ability to explore one's motives and relationships insightfully is not easily taught and never perfected, yet these skills count among the most critical to functioning as an ethical mental health professional.

It will become evident that competence-related issues pervade many chapters in this book. Competence issues related to psychodiagnostic assessment and testing are specifically addressed in Chapter 9. Similarly, issues related to competence as a psychotherapist are implied in the details of Chapters 5 and 6. The focus of this chapter is on matters of general competence and weakness and relates chiefly to the personal development and professional behavior of the mental health clinician, educator, or researcher.

Before exploring the problems of incompetent or troubled mental health professionals, it is important to understand basic ethical problems associated with training, credentialing, and maintaining competence at the postgraduate level, as well as recognizing problem relationships when they develop. Differing opinions on the standards and credentials necessary for competent practice exist both within and across professions. However, no one can argue against the critical importance of recognizing the boundaries of one's competence and the limitations of one's techniques (Clark & Abeles, 1994).

CONCEPTUAL ISSUES

High-quality professional practice demands two very different types of competencies: *intellectual competence* and *emotional competence* (Pope & Brown, 1996). Intellectual competence refers to the acquisition of knowledge based on empirical research and sound clinical scholarship regarding practice with a particular client population. Intellectual competence may also refer to a general ability to assess, conceptualize, and plan appropriate treatment for a particular client or problem. Most important, possessing intellectual competence means recognizing what one does not know. For example, vast experience in treating middle-class American Caucasian clients does not necessarily translate into the special competence needed to treat clients with other cultural or racial identities (e.g., see the discussion of race, ethnicity, and psychotherapy in

Chapter 5). This does not mean that therapists should only assess or treat members of their own racial or ethnic groups, but rather that they must strive to recognize all relevant individual differences and seek to acquire any incremental knowledge needed to treat such clients effectively or make appropriate referrals.

Emotional competence refers to therapists' ability to emotionally contain and tolerate the clinical material that emerges in treatment, their willingness and skill at detecting the intrusion of personal biases into their work, and their capacity for self-care in the context of the difficult work that is psychotherapy (Pope, Sonne, & Greene, 2006; Welfel, 2006). A wide range of scholarly articles illustrates that not all therapists can competently work with every type of client or with all kinds of problems (Brenner, 2006; Haldeman, 2006; N. D. Hansen et al., 2006; Koocher, 2003; Maxie, Arnold, & Stephenson, 2006; Sue, 1998). Recognizing and acknowledging this fact does not constitute a sign of weakness. Quite the contrary. But, unfortunately, many mental health professionals may feel financial, personal, or social pressures to see whoever comes to their office.

Many organizations of mental health professionals have long struggled with the problem of defining professional competence and remedies for incompetence. These efforts, some of which were described in Chapter 3, have taken many forms. They include the development of ethics codes, standards of practice or practice guidelines, third-party-payer quality assurance programs, state licensing or certification boards (Packard, Simon, & Vaughn, 2006), and other types of credentialing bodies. Despite these efforts, however, none of the extant structures have yet proved able to effectively detect and then act in response to incompetent professional behavior or even to routinely enforce sanctions against those deemed incompetent.

The most egregious instances of incompetence, those that lead to filing formal complaints, are often the only ones that come to the attention of licensing boards and ethics committees. Part of the difficulty relates to a general presumption of competence, much akin to the dictum that one is "innocent until proven guilty." Obtaining a consensus on a definition of competence also has been elusive both within and across health and mental health disciplines (Claiborn, 1982; Epstein & Hundert, 2002; Kaslow, 2004). In addition, incompetence is often difficult to prove, especially when investigators must function under the constraints of due process and the need to accumulate substantial evidence.

Standards of Practice

From the perspective of professional competence, we recognize that perfection is not the standard. Rather, we expect each practitioner to function as a "good enough therapist," as judged by peers who understand the standards of care expected in the context of each case. The American Psychological Association (APA) and many other professional groups have promulgated documents that represent significant and comprehensive attempts to codify both general standards of practice and guidance in specialty areas. These range from conducting psychotherapy or assessment with special populations (e.g., by gender, ethnicity, or sexual preference); in special contexts (e.g., child custody or other forensic activities); or with respect to particular activities (e.g., record keeping or obtaining consent). In general, such documents help to define minimum levels of competent professional practices and procedures, both generally and within specific specialty areas. Although worthy efforts, these documents often do not carry specific enforcement weight unless some type of formal complaint or lawsuit ensues. Nevertheless, we recommend actively seeking out whatever guidelines or standards apply to your work and becoming familiar with them as a best practice for ensuring professional competence and reducing liability risks (Bennett et al., 2007). (Professional liability and malpractice from the perspective of professional negligence are discussed in Chapter 17.)

One illustration of confusion regarding determination of competence involves controversy about what constitutes a specialty, subspecialty, proficiency, or particular area of expertise in the practice of psychology or related field. Clinical, counseling, industrial/organizational, and school psychology have traditionally been rec-

ognized as specialties, but there are certainly many special areas of expertise within each of these headings. For example, an industrial psychologist competent in human-factors engineering may not be qualified to consult on personnel selection. A clinical psychologist well trained in psychotherapy and assessment may lack the forensic knowledge to evaluate a defendant's competence to stand trial. And, a counseling psychologist with many years of experience as a psychotherapist to adults may be untrained in work with children. What constitutes the basic qualification needed to practice personnel consultation, forensic evaluations, or child psychotherapy? Are these specialties or subspecialties or simply special types of competence, proficiencies, or skills? The mental health professions have often lacked clear consensus on these matters. Consider the following examples:

Case 4–1: Charlotte Hasty, M.S.W., had practiced individual psychoanalytically oriented psychotherapy with adult clients for 10 years. After attending a half-day continuing education workshop on family therapy, Ms. Hasty began to conduct family therapy sessions for some of her clients, while reading books in the field during her spare time.

Case 4–2: Carl Klutzkind, Psy.D., treated a woman with many adjustment problems in the wake of a separation and impending divorce. After Dr. Klutzkind had worked with the client for 6 months, her attorney asked whether he would testify in support of her having custody of her 7-year-old child. Despite having no forensic training or experience, Dr. Klutzkind agreed and from the witness stand offered many opinions about the adjustment of the woman and her child. The client's husband filed an ethical complaint against Klutzkind, noting that he lacked any training in child work, he never actually interviewed the child, and he was therefore negligent in offering an opinion. It seems that the child had been in treatment with another psychologist, and Klutzkind never sought information from that colleague or the child's father.

Case 4–3: Sarah Bellum, Ed.D., completed her graduate training in the 1970s, before clinical neuropsychology evolved as a clinical specialty. She was trained to "assess organicity" using the first edition of the Wechsler Adult Intelligence Scale (WAIS), House–Tree–Person drawings, and the Bender Motor Gestalt Test. She has never studied neuroanatomy and has no knowledge of newer assessment tools designed for use in neuropsychological assessment. Her current practice focuses chiefly on psychotherapy. An attorney contacted Dr. Bellum about assessing a client who had suffered a closed head injury and was experiencing language, memory, and perceptual sequellae. She accepted the referral and tested the client using the "tried-and-true" techniques she learned decades earlier.

In these three cases, the practitioners have failed to recognize the boundaries of their respective formal training. While we acknowledge that no uniform professional standards now exist to define expertise in family therapy or forensic practice across professions and jurisdictions, Dr. Klutzkind and Ms. Hasty lacked even the minimum levels of competence one should reasonably possess. Dr. Klutzkind's lack of knowledge about forensic practice and failure to recognize the deficiency led him ethically astray. Perhaps his concern for his client, his desire to expound his views in court, or simple ignorance led him into trouble. His behavior clearly had a potentially hurtful impact on all the parties in the case and clearly violates both the APA's ethics code (APA 02: 9.01) and other extant professional standards of which he seems unaware. In Hasty's case, we can not say for certain whether she actually hurt or helped anyone. No one would necessarily discover her lack of training under normal circumstances (i.e., unless a formal complaint were filed). Ms. Hasty does not see anything wrong with applying this new technique because she regards herself as an "experienced psychotherapist."

Dr. Bellum, who trained in an era that predated most of what we now consider current neuropsychological assessment science, has made no effort to keep current with that part of her training. She made no ethical errors until she agreed to take on a case for which her skills were no longer current or adequate. We can not tell whether Dr. Bellum even has a clue regarding of the evolution in the field since completing her doctoral training some 40 years ago. Both Drs.

Bellum and Klutzkind also appear ignorant of ethical constraints on functioning as expert witnesses. (See Chapter 17 for a full discussion.)

If no formal standards exist for many specific types of practice or techniques, therapists should exercise prudence and take a conservative stance in assessing whether they require additional education or training prior to beginning the work. In such circumstances, we recommend seeking guidance from colleagues widely regarded as experts on the particular matters at hand. These colleagues can offer wise guidance regarding adequacy of training or of current practice standards. An important trend in professional education involves focusing training and accreditation standards on development of particular competencies. The Association of Psychology Postdoctoral and Internship Centers (APPIC) has led the field in these initiatives, and their Web site (http://www.appic.org/) provides many useful reports that have broad generalizable utility across many different mental health professions.

At the Competencies Conference: Future Directions in Education and Credentialing in Professional Psychology (APPIC, 2002), considerable discussion focused on the concept of professional development, which is a broad and vaguely defined construct that seems to underlie much of the training of mental health professionals. Attendees at the conference discussed professional development as intrinsic to professional functioning, or professionalism, throughout one's career, and three of them proposed a definition of professional development that focused on two elements: *interpersonal functioning* and *thinking like a psychologist* (Elman, Illfelder-Kaye, & Robiner, 2005). Such skills develop most strongly in vivo, that is, as a function of close and continually ongoing interaction with mentors and peers over time. This approach generalizes across the mental health professions and carries implications for both training and lifelong practices of therapists. Many clinical educators worry that distance learning or external degree programs do not teach such skills effectively.

A related recommendation involves training for ethics competency by using integrity checks in all course work (e.g., for plagiarism, data falsification, and misrepresentation); clinical competence (e.g., for confidentiality, boundary violations, client welfare, procedural breaches); 360° evaluations in which everyone in the training environment evaluates each other; and assessing responses to actual ethical dilemmas (de las Fuentes, Wilmuth, & Yarrow, 2005). Such a model would teach professionalism by example.

Detecting Incompetence

Ethics codes enjoin us to avoid practicing beyond our areas of competence; however, such codes necessarily will have a very general nature and give too few specifics to permit us to easily identify incompetent practice. Detection of incompetence must rely on observation and, ultimately, complaints by someone. As we saw in Chapter 3, expulsion from a professional organization will not necessarily interrupt the practice of the offender. They may simply practice without joining a professional association. If a licensing board revokes the practitioner's license, then the individual may often continue to practice under an unregulated title such as "psychotherapist" or "counselor." Incompetence can become a basis for malpractice litigation; however, one must first establish that damages have occurred (as discussed in Chapter 17).

Can incompetence be detected early? A particularly interesting study by Peterson and Bry (1980) examined competence by reviewing appraisals of 126 doctor of psychology students by 102 faculty and field supervisors. After rating students with whom they had worked, faculty and supervisors were asked to describe the dominant characteristics of both "outstanding" and "incompetent" trainees. The quality most frequently mentioned for outstanding students was "high intelligence," while the most common characteristic for incompetent trainees was "lack of knowledge." When supervisors used a rating scale composed of the 28 most commonly used terms to evaluate students the subsequent year, four factors emerged as central to the conceptualization of competence:

- professional responsibility
- interpersonal warmth
- intelligence
- experience

The data also suggested that behaviorally oriented supervisors gave somewhat less weight to warmth in evaluating competence than did eclectic or psychodynamically oriented supervisors.

Another problem to keep in mind when considering the conceptualization and detection of incompetence involves understanding the range or variability of skill among mental health professionals, whether they work as practitioners, academics, or consultants to industry. Daniel Hogan made the point well in his four-volume work on the regulation of psychotherapists; he noted the substantial discrepancy between *adequate* and *superior* competence. Within each pool of licensed mental health professionals, there will be some who just barely passed the admission criteria and are, hopefully, unlikely to cause anyone harm. Many others will fall somewhere in the middle, and some will "top the pool" (Hogan, 1977). Except in Garrison Keillor's fictional Lake Woebegone (Altman, 2006), not everyone can be "above average." While exceptional competence is certainly desirable, it is not unethical to practice in an area in which one's competence is simply "adequate," assuming we know what adequate means (APA: 2.01–2.06) and have correctly established that threshold.

TRAINING ISSUES

A variety of controversies surround the training of mental health practitioners. These controversies involve questions about just how they ought to be educated and how behavioral scientists, physicians, or other professionals not trained as mental health practitioners ought to undertake retraining or acquire new skills should they wish to become human service providers. A variety of conferences addressing such issues for psychology as a field have occurred, often referred to by the meeting's geographic site, yielding the Boulder or Vail (Colorado) training models or the Virginia Beach recommendations. We do not intend to explore the question of whether a scientist–practitioner training model constitutes the ideal or whether a professional school program will prove most appropriate for modern practitioners.

Rather, we are concerned about ethical issues in the conduct of training. Are practitioners adequately trained for the jobs they intend to perform? Are the techniques used to train them ethically defensible? Are students evaluated in an ethically appropriate manner? Is the institution providing the training competent to do so? These comprise the substantive ethical problems linked to the training of all mental health professionals.

Competence by Degrees?

In the fields of law and medicine, the entry-level practice degrees in the United States are recognizable (i.e., as the J.D. and M.D., respectively). Using psychology as our example, we find more historical diversity. In addition to the Ph.D., Ed.D., Psy.D., M.A., and M.S. degrees, psychologists have historically listed a number of other earned degrees in reporting their qualifications for recognition as psychological health service providers (Wellner, 1978), including C.A.G.S. (Certificate of Advanced Graduate Study); D.Sc. (Doctor of Science); Ed.S. (Educational Specialist); D.M.H. (Doctor of Mental Health); Th.D. (Doctor of Theology); D.Min. (Doctor of Ministry); M.Ed. (Master of Education); and M.S.S.S. (Master of Science in Social Services). Not only have the degree designations varied historically, but in addition to departments of psychology, the following academic departments were listed by applicants as granting "closely related degrees" as they sought recognition as psychologists (Wellner, 1978): American civilization, anthropology, child study, divinity, education, educational research and measurement, general studies, guidance counseling, health and physical education, home and family life, law, philosophy, political science, rehabilitation, religion, social and human relations, special education, and speech pathology.

To complicate matters even further, the major fields within these departments in which degrees were granted are even more diverse. In part, this variety sprang from the fact that many state laws at one time recognized degrees in psychology "or a closely related field" as a qualification for psychology licensing. Since the 1990s, highly successful efforts on a state-by-

state level have resulted in elimination of the closely related field options for would-be psychologists. Many who were accepted for licensing up to the mid-1980s, however, were approved on the basis of their seniority at the time legislation was passed. Such regulations are often termed *grandparenting provisions*. By definition, these professional "grandparents" can retain their license for life, even though they could not qualify under the updated criteria.

Medicine also has some interesting distinctions in degrees and training subtleties that raise competence issues. For example, most people will recognize the Doctor of Medicine (M.D.) but not know that many licensed physicians hold Doctor of Osteopathy (D.O.) degrees. In the United Kingdom, students typically begin medical studies at the age of 18 or 19, in contrast with the U.S. system, in which medical schools require a bachelor's degree. British medical courses typically last 5 years and lead to a Bachelor of Medicine and Surgery, usually abbreviated as M.B.Ch.B. or sometimes as B.M. for Bachelor of Medicine. No medical degree, however, involves significant training in psychopathology or psychotherapy.

The relationship between a medical degree and competence to perform counseling and psychotherapy services has recently become increasingly challenging. State laws do not typically regulate the practice of "counseling" by physicians in general. A former president of the American Psychiatric Association estimated that general physicians, not psychiatrists, write more than 75% of all prescriptions for psychiatric medications in the United States (Sharfstein, 2006). In addition, typical medical students have had only six to eight weeks of training in psychiatry at graduation, and essentially get on-the-job training when they enter a psychiatric residency. Because of economic factors, such as low insurance reimbursement rates for 50-minute verbal psychotherapy sessions, in contrast to fees received for much briefer medication visits, fewer psychiatrists find steady employment or fill their practices by conducting traditional psychotherapy. Instead, many focus on a more remunerative psychopharmacology practice, and psychiatric residency training programs are placing less emphasis on teaching verbal psychotherapy (Koocher, 2007). These factors may well contribute to the decline in U.S. medical school graduates entering psychiatric residencies (Moran, 2006).

The Doctoral Versus Master's Degree

The doctoral degree has been well established as the entry-level practice credential in psychology (Fox, 1994; Robiner, Arbisi, & Edwall, 1994), although approximately 8,000 master's degrees are awarded each year in psychology, leading to long-recognized potential identity crises for those who do not continue study to the doctoral level (Moses, 1990). Unlike doctoral programs, the APA does not accredit master's programs. An examination of course content, curriculum, and duration also substantiates that master's and doctoral training in psychology are not equivalent (Robiner et al., 1994). In states where master's-level psychologists may sit for the national licensing exam administered under the auspices of the Association of State and Provincial Psychology Boards (i.e., the Examination for the Professional Practice of Psychology, EPPP), doctoral-level licensing candidates consistently outscore them (Robiner et al., 1994).

Does all this mean that holders of doctoral degrees are always more competent at specific professional tasks than holders of master's degrees? Of course, it does not. Rather, the data suggest that, on the whole, a person trained at the doctoral level will often have acquired a more substantial foundation in terms of both required course work and supervised experience. All of the U.S. states license social workers and nurses at various levels (i.e., from career entry to advanced practice), and many states also license mental health, rehabilitation, or marriage and family therapists or counselors. A number of professions do recognize a master's degree as the entry-level credential for independent (i.e., unsupervised) professional practice, including mental health counseling (i.e., Licensed Mental Health Counselor credential); marriage and family therapy (i.e., Licensed Marriage and Family Counselor credential); social work (i.e., Licensed Clinical Social Worker or Licensed Independent Clin-

ical Social Worker); and advance practice nursing (Master of Science in Nursing or Clinical Specialist).

From an ethical perspective, three key issues independent of degree or training program apply:

- accurately representing one's training and credentials
- practicing within the scope of such training
- adhering to the ethics, laws, and regulations applicable to similarly licensed professionals in one's practice jurisdiction (e.g., not holding oneself out as a psychologist, social worker, or physician in a state where one's degree and experience do not qualify for use of that title)

Psy.D. Versus Ph.D.

The Psy.D. degree first began in response to a perceived need to offer specialized doctoral training for practitioners not seeking research careers (Peterson, 1976). Some psychologists subsequently argued that a Ph.D. degree was too generic a scholarly credential for determination of who ought to be recognized as a health service provider in psychology (Shapiro & Wiggins, 1994). They suggested that a Doctor of Psychology (or Psy.D. degree) should identify the doctoral-level health service provider in psychology and went so far as to recommend that Psy.D. degrees be awarded retroactively, in much the same manner as the J.D. degree was awarded to attorneys who had earned L.L.B. degrees prior to the mid-1960s. The APA Council of Representatives was not receptive to such arguments, leading to abandonment of the effort in 1996.

Many professions that once considered the master's degree as the top clinical practice credential in their field have begun to imitate the Psy.D. degree. Physical therapy has encouraged a move from the master's degree to the Doctor of Physical Therapy (D.P.T.) degree by 2020. Graduate nursing programs have begun to establish the Doctor of Nursing Practice (D.N.P.) degree. Such credentials recognize advanced practice skills without the heavy research career training components typically a part of Ph.D. curricula.

In psychology, a large number of professional schools have evolved, some offering both Psy.D. and Ph.D. options. While some professional schools of psychology exist within university systems, other are free-standing entities, and some are proprietary (e.g., owned by investors, as opposed to standing as nonprofit educational institutions). Information on schools offering the Psy.D. degree can be found at the Web site for the National Council of Schools and Programs of Professional Psychology (http://www.ncspp.info/). The key to identifying a quality program in psychology or any other mental health field lies in checking sites of respected accrediting bodies for each profession that have earned recognition by the U.S. Department of Education through its Council on Higher Education Accreditation (http://www.chea.org). For psychology, this would be the APA's Office of Program Consultation and Accreditation (http://www.apa.org/ed/accreditation/). Other useful data sites for psychology include http://www.appic.org and http://www.asppb.org to seek internship placement rates and licensing examination scores, respectively.

Any professional degree program in any of the mental health fields should readily advise applicants of important data relevant to accreditation, graduation rates, internship and job placement rates, licensing exam pass rates for first-time attempters, and similar data. While no single datum affords an absolute assurance of competence, the types of information noted here do offer an indication of the degree to which any given program produces graduates who succeed in the early stages of their careers.

Ingredients of the Psychology Human Services Graduate Program

Psychology provides a useful example regarding how a training program is configured at the doctoral level. Recognizing that psychologists who act as human service practitioners take on great responsibilities, the APA has developed a thoughtful and detailed accreditation system (http://www.apa.org/ed/accreditation/) that provides a means for evaluating academic and internship programs purporting to train psy-

chological practitioners. Curricula *must* address the following:

- biological, cognitive–affective, and social bases of behavior
- history and systems of psychology
- psychological measurement and research methods
- techniques of data analysis
- scientific foundations of practice
- assessment and diagnosis
- cultural and individual diversity

Considerable latitude is permitted within categories, however. For example, a student can graduate from a fully approved clinical psychology doctoral program without ever treating a child, working with a geriatric client, or learning to administer projective personality tests. Some programs send students out on internship following experience in several practicum placements and with dozens of client assessments behind them. Other program faculty believe that students who may have seen fewer than a dozen assessment and treatment cases are "good to go" on their internship.

Different professions will similarly have differing treatment models and a range of accrediting bodies. Although we use psychology as our primary illustrative model, other professions encounter similar variability. In social work, for example, people with bachelor's degrees (i.e., B.S.W.) may qualify for some jobs and credentials, while an M.S.W. plus years of experience may stand as the prerequisite for an independent practice license. In addition, some social workers may train primarily for administration, community organization, or child protective services work and not as psychotherapists, while others may focus heavily on psychotherapeutic practice techniques or specialize in treating particular populations or disorders.

Variability in educational program emphasis across different programs within any profession is not necessarily bad as long as graduates remain aware of their competence and limitations. The recent graduate of a doctoral program who recognizes a training inadequacy for a particular career goal can remedy it in many ways, including postgraduate fellowships, continuing education (CE) programs, and proficiency development programs. More substantial difficulties face the psychologist who aspires to change specialties, such as a social, experimental, or developmental psychology graduate who wishes to become a health services provider. Such shifts are occasionally permitted by generic state licensing laws, as discussed in the following section.

Postgraduate Transformations

The APA policy adopted by its Council of Representatives holds that simply completing internship or applied training as such is insufficient for the professional "retread," as those who wish to convert to clinical work are sometimes called. The policy holds that such individuals must also complete course work that would be equivalent to the desired degree but is missing from their academic records. It is preferable that this course work be taken in a programmatic, sequential, and carefully monitored program, as opposed to a loose collection of casually collected courses. Some universities offer special 1- or 2-year programs aimed at retraining such individuals. Psychologists sometimes choose a "backdoor" route, seeking internships or training in applied settings without accompanying course work. Licensing or credentialing bodies do not look kindly at such candidates. Consider these examples that describe specialized services to children:

Case 4–4: George Grownup, Ph.D., completed a degree in clinical psychology from a program fully accredited by the APA. He took all of his practica, field work, and internship training at settings treating adults (i.e., a college counseling center and Veterans Administration Hospital). Although he has not taken courses in child development or child psychopathology, he now wants to do clinical work with children. He begins to add child clients to his practice after reading a half dozen books about developmental psychology and child treatment.

Dr. Grownup is a well-trained adult clinician whose attempt to prepare himself to work with children is glaringly superficial. His approach certainly exceeds his trained competencies, although he does not seem to realize it. Although a regulatory board may never catch him unless someone files a complaint, his conduct remains ethically inappropriate.

Case 4–5: Dee Vella Pmental, Ph.D., completed her degree in human development within a psychology department. She then worked for 2 years as a researcher interviewing victims of family violence and assessing the cognitive development of infants with Down syndrome. She has decided that she would like to be able to do more clinical forms of work, including personality assessment and psychotherapy, with the types of patients she has been studying. Dr. Pmental volunteers more than a dozen hours per week for 3 years at a local teaching hospital with an APA-approved internship program. She sees patients under close supervision while also attending didactic seminars and taking courses in personality assessment at a local university.

Dr. Pmental has better training to work with children than does Dr. Grownup, but technically she has not sought formal retreading. She has gone further and seems considerably more cautious than Dr. Grownup in attempting to ensure her competence in the activities she hopes to practice. Although her behavior may technically violate an APA policy or professional standard, it is not necessarily unethical. As long as she limits her practice to the areas in which she is well trained, her behavior would be considered ethically appropriate.

The following case illustrates similar issues in the context of a master's-prepared licensed clinician from another profession.

Case 4–6: Meta Morphosis, M.S.W., completed her field placements as a medical social worker at a large general hospital. She became experienced in assisting families cope with serious illness, locating community resources, and discharge planning. A few years following her graduation, Ms. Morphosis developed an interest in practicing psychotherapy. So, she sought out a social work fellowship program offering clinical supervision in psychotherapeutic practice from well-credentialed senior colleagues as part of the training program.

Ms. Morphosis recognized that her education and training had not prepared her for a new area of practice she hoped to enter. She sought out an appropriate training opportunity that will allow her to develop the skills she seeks within a pathway recognized by her profession and licensing authority.

The Student in Transition

Students in psychology are obligated to abide by ethical principles, just as are other psychologists. At times, however, some advanced students or individuals seeking a shift in professional identity find themselves caught in a perplexing bind as they attempt a professional transition. Consider the following case example:

Case 4–7: Karen Quandary, M.S.W., has 4 years of experience as a clinical social worker and is licensed as an "independent clinical social worker" in her state. She decides to enter a fully accredited and approved program in clinical psychology offered by the Applied Institute of Professional Psychology. Ms. Quandary acknowledges that she does not hold a psychology license, although she is a "psychology graduate student" and has identified with the profession by becoming a student member of APA. At the same time, she trained in psychotherapy through her social work degree program. She holds a license to practice as a social worker. While she does not qualify for licensing as a psychologist, and thus can not practice as a psychologist (e.g., undertake psychodiagnostic testing without supervision), one must presume she can competently practice within the scope of her license as a social worker.

A person with two valid professional identities has no obligation to surrender one while developing the second. As long as Ms. Quandary does not lead the public or her clients to believe that she is a psychologist, and as long as she practices within her areas of social work competency, she has not behaved unethically. Technically, Ms. Quandary can not consider herself to be a psychologist or announce herself as one to the public until she meets appropriate professional and statutory standards for that profession. One must, however, discriminate between profes-

sional titles and professional functions for which one has appropriate training. To the extent that social work ethics and psychology ethics differ in specificity, Ms. Quandary should always hold herself to the more stringent standard. In addition, she would be wise to check with her faculty about any special rules imposed on her as a student in her particular degree program. Some programs places practice limitations on their students more stringent than the requirements of the ethics code.

Student Evaluations

The APA's *Guidelines and Principles for Accreditation of Programs in Professional Psychology* (American Psychological Association Office of Program Consultation and Accreditation, 2000) points out the special responsibility of faculty to assess the progress of each student and to keep the students advised of these assessments. Students who exhibit long-term serious problems or who do not function effectively in academic or interpersonal spheres should be counseled early. If necessary, they should be made aware of career alternatives or, after appropriate due process procedures, dropped from the program. Each program should have specific procedures to routinely assess the progress and competence of students, advise them of the outcome, and delineate appropriate sequences of action and alternative outcomes. These procedures should be explicit, written, and available to all students and faculty. Graduate students terminated from degree programs represent an occasional source of ethics complaints against faculty, which raises competence issues.

Case 4–8: Michael Mello left his urban West Coast home to attend graduate school at a rural Midwestern university. At the end of his third semester, he received a written notice that he was being terminated as "personally unsuited" to continue in the school's counseling program. Mello filed ethics complaints against the director of training and department chair. He complained that he had never previously been advised of problems. Furthermore, his grades were excellent, and he had been denied due process.

Case 4–9: Liz Militant also traveled across the country to attend graduate school in psychology. After 3 years in the program with satisfactory grades, she took her comprehensive examinations and failed. In a hurry to take an internship for which she had been accepted, Ms. Militant again attempted the exams and failed. As a result of failing twice, she was terminated as a degree candidate in accordance with department regulations. Ms. Militant filed an ethics complaint against several faculty members, noting that the grading of the exams she failed was highly subjective, and other psychologists to whom she had shown her answers thought they were well done. She went on to claim that her strong feminist views and ethnic heritage had been a source of friction between herself and some faculty for her 3 years at the school. She attributed her failures to contamination by these factors in the subjective grading of her exams.

These two cases had several elements in common when they came before an ethics committee at approximately the same time. They involved students with cultural values different from the majority of the faculty and community within which they were training. On inquiry by the ethics committee, it became clear that both schools lacked formal procedures for student grievances, and that both students were "surprised" by the efforts to dismiss them. Mello claimed to have had no warning that the program deemed him to have serious problems prior to the written notice. Although he received a variety of ambiguous messages, he had never had clear counseling or warning that dismissal loomed within the realm of possibility. Militant had sensed friction with some faculty members but had received good evaluations from her field placement supervisors and satisfactory or better grades in all courses. While she had known about the rule that two failures terminated candidacy, she had expected to pass and felt, in any case, entitled to an appeal.

While the universities and students involved each had valid reasons for criticizing the other's behavior, the students clearly were the more vulnerable parties and had been, at the very least, subjected to poor communications. Mediation by the ethics committee led to Mello's being awarded a master's degree for work completed, and he transferred to another university. Militant's university agreed to ask a panel of psychologists, suggested by the ethics committee, from universities in neighboring states to evaluate her exam answers independently and to take guidance from their judgment. In the end, her university restored her status, and she successfully completed her degree. Much of the acrimony generated in these episodes might have been prevented had the universities involved developed more specific procedures for monitoring the progress of students and given them timely feedback about their perceived competence problems.

We address the problem of the impaired psychologist or "sick doctor" at the end of this chapter. Many of the issues discussed under that heading can also apply to students, and it seems appropriate to highlight the impaired student at this point. The students mentioned in Cases 4–8 and 4–9 did not have clear signs of any medical or psychological impairment. Consider the following cases from psychology and medical graduate schools:

Case 4–10: In 1975, Jane Doe entered New York University's Medical School. Prior to her admission, she had a long history of emotional problems, including numerous involuntary hospitalizations, which she never revealed to the school. During her first year, the emotional problems "flared up" again, and she began behaving in a "bizarre and self-destructive manner," including at least one alleged suicide attempt in a laboratory on campus. The school encouraged her to take a leave of absence; she sought voluntary hospitalization and was released with a "guarded" prognosis. The medical school later denied her readmission after an examining psychiatrist deemed her emotionally "unfit to resume her medical education" (*Doe v. New York University*, 1981).

As the citations indicate, the Jane Doe case is drawn directly from case law. A federal court in New York issued a preliminary injunction ordering the medical school to readmit Ms. Doe as an "otherwise qualified" person under federal antidiscrimination legislation. The court found that she would "more likely than not" be able to complete her education, despite her psychiatric history, based in part on the fact that she had earned a master's degree in public health at Harvard and had held down a stressful job without deterioration during the years of litigation.

Case 4–11: Irwin Flamer was enrolled as a graduate student in social work at Middle State University. After a series of 12 arson fires in the psychology building, Flamer was discovered as the culprit and sentenced to a term in prison. Following his parole, he reapplied to complete his degree. He had earned straight A grades and nearly completed a master's degree prior to his arrest.

Case 4–12: Emma Petuous had enrolled as a graduate student at the Manhattan School of Professional Psychology, where she earned respectable, but not outstanding, grades. Some of the practica supervisors noted that she tended to be "impulsive and somewhat emotionally immature," although she seemed able to function quite well in a number of professional circumstances. After receiving an unsatisfactory C grade in her statistics course, Ms. Petuous prepared a batch of handbills characterizing the instructor as "sexist and idiotic, with an anal personality and a perverse intellectual style" and a variety of other unflattering terms. She placed the handbills on bulletin boards around the school building and inserted them in student and faculty mailboxes.

Mr. Flamer and Ms. Petuous represent disguised cases of variable pathology. They presented focal symptoms that demand consideration in light of the emotional context, their other behavior, and their professional goals. One can not say without more information whether the behavior cited constitutes grounds for termination from the program, as opposed to some less drastic and more rehabilitative approach. The most difficult cases involve students who seem personally unsuited to the field in which they are seeking a degree or credential, but whose problems are more diffuse and less easily documented.

Case 4–13: Arroganto Obnoxia performed well in class but earned the disdain of his educators and fellow students alike. He seemed to enjoy showing off with what he self-assuredly assumed to be his superior knowledge. He often provoked arguments and then seemed to relish in the ensuing verbal skirmish. The faculty worried that Mr. Obnoxia not only would become a risky mental health professional but also would reflect poorly on the department and institution.

Mr. Obnoxia presents a particularly difficult case because his annoying personality style, rather than his academic ability, leads to the problematic behavior. Readers may also want to review issues related to writing reference letters for this sort of person or dealing with such individuals as colleagues (see Chapter 13). The ability to engage in and maintain good collegial relationships can form the basis of valid performance criterion and reason for dismissing a person from the workplace, described by a Stanford professor as "the no asshole rule" (Sutton, 2007). However, educational and professional training programs have the obligation to tie dismissal to bona fide criteria, objectively applied, with appropriate warning, and efforts at remediation, when appropriate. Student handbooks or codes of conduct that delineate expectations and potential penalties provide good approaches to dealing with such problems.

The key point is that mental health professionals who operate training programs hold a dual responsibility, one focused on the public and potential clients and the other on the student. Considerable time and careful due process are required to advise students of any perceived difficulties, to suggest remedies, to monitor their progress, and possibly to assist them in exploring other alternatives. Nonetheless, these responsibilities must be assumed by mental health professionals who direct academic and field training programs. The consequences for programs and faculty who default on their ethical obligations can be both serious and expensive, as illustrated in the following case:

Case 4–14: In 1992, Susan A. Stepakoff was expelled from the clinical–community doctoral psychology program at the University of Maryland. Stepakoff had complained within the psychology department about racist and sexist remarks made by faculty members and about other alleged faculty misconduct. In one of many examples provided to the court, Stepakoff alleged that during one class, when students watched a group therapy session through a one-way window, a professor remarked that he was "imagining the clients naked." He reportedly added that he found the thought of viewing one large woman naked "really disgusting" (Shen, 1996). Stepakoff also complained that some professors were having sex with students. Department and university officials failed to respond to her requests for action. Instead, some faculty made a variety of allegations about Ms. Stepakoff and succeeded in having her expelled after she had been admitted to doctoral candidacy. These were not, however, sufficient allegations to convince a court of law. In June 1996, a Prince Georges County jury found that Stepakoff's free speech rights had been violated and awarded her $600,000 in compensatory and punitive damages (*Susan A. Stepakoff v. University of Maryland at College Park, Robert Brown, Robert Dies, Raymond Lorion, and Barry Smith, 1996*). In November 1996, the state settled with Stepakoff for $550,000 rather than appeal the case ("State agrees to pay," 1996).

One of the authors of this book (G. P. K.) served as an expert witness for Ms. Stepakoff. All facts reported here, however, are drawn solely from public sources, as cited.

The Incompetent Institution

While many people are aware that it is possible to purchase phony diplomas by mail or online, few realize that the diploma mill industry flourishes in this country and abroad. Certificates or transcripts based on flimsy correspondence courses or no course work at all can easily be used to mislead and defraud the uninformed consumer. Often, such incompetent institutions provide larger and more impressively decorated diplomas than those from accredited schools. Some institutions attempt to cover any liability by describing the diplomas as "novelty items" in their advertisements. But, in recent years, those running these useless degree programs have become much bolder by omitting any disclaimers and even promising that these degrees are legitimate, fully accredited, and will benefit one's career status. Most of these so-called degrees are advertised over the Internet,

and the "educational institution" is a post office box in a foreign country.

The names of these diploma mills—and they go in and out of business regularly—can sound quite impressive (e.g., Lawford State University, the Royal Academy of Science and Art, Sussex College of Technology, Atlantic Southern University, Oxford Institute for Applied Research, the Carnegie Institute of Engineering, and Brownell University). Sometimes, the names of legitimate institutions of higher learning or close to it (e.g., Stamford University, Dartmuth College) are used as well.

Many of these bogus outfits attempt to give the illusion of a criterion to "earn" the degree, namely, "life experience." The definition is broad, generally amounting to the fact that one has remained alive and can come up with price of the product. A number of these enterprises offer services that will further assist the "grantee" in perpetuating an intentional fraud. For an extra payment, one can purchase transcripts (some charge extra for all A's), and so-called verification services in case an employer wants to make sure that the degree was actually "earned." Back when these degrees were mere novelty items (and marketed as such), the cost was low, less than $100. Today, the charge can be well over $1,000 depending on how many extras are purchased.

Case 4–15: The outgoing and superficially charming Shammy Fake opened up a practice sporting five advanced degrees from fancy-sounding institutions, none of which involved any academic work or supervised experience. He called himself a "personal counselor" and ran splashy advertisements in the local underground paper bragging about his vast experience and educational accomplishments. His practice always had a waiting list until one client complained to her psychologist friend that for $200 an hour she should be doing better. The friend became suspicious and took a closer look. She reported Mr. Fake to the licensing board, but because he was not licensed or a member of any legitimate organization, they could not readily proceed against him.

Such individuals are around and cause legitimate mental health professionals concern for the public welfare. Mr. Fake will be difficult to stop unless the licensing board in his state has a clause that allows intervention if a complaining client was reasonably led to believe that the individual was a genuine mental health care provider.

The rules and regulations relative to awarding degrees vary from state to state, and there are few regulations with any impact on the sale of such "credentials" via the Internet. Thus, many opportunities for deception exist, and consumers can be misled at best and harmed at worst. No uniform national standards exist for accreditation of degrees in general, and a school that may hold state accreditation in California might not be recognized in New York. The watchword in determining a degree's professional validity is regional accreditation.

The following commonly used terms do *not* equal accreditation: licensed, recognized, authorized, approved, or chartered. These terms may differ in legal meaning from state to state and may have no relevant meaning at all. Many poor-quality schools or bogus degree programs will claim accreditation, but often by a spurious or unrecognized body. We identified over 70 so-called accreditation agencies that phony degree outfits claim in an attempt to substantiate legitimacy. One such outfit is so audacious as to compare itself favorably to "those phony diploma mills." The U.S. Department of Education and its Council on Higher Education Accreditation (CHEA) are the bodies that recognize accrediting associations; for colleges or universities, there are only six regional accrediting associations, the Middle States, North Central, Northwest, Southeastern, Western, and New England Association of Schools and Colleges. The CHEA posts considerable helpful information and articles about degree mills and accreditation mills on its Web site (see, e.g., http://www.chea.org/degreemills/frmPaper.htm).

One must also take care to differentiate between diploma granting certification boards and bogus or so-called vanity boards. For example the member boards of the American Board of Medical Specialties (http://www.abms.org/) and the American Board of Professional Psychology (http://www.abpp.org/) require careful documenting of primary credentials and passing a rigorous examination process before awarding "board certification." On the other hand, a

number of other organizations, including one run out of a private home (M. Hansen, 2000), appear to offer "sheepskins for sale" (S. L. Golding, 1999). When in doubt, consumers and professionals alike should look to their professional associations for guidance and eschew credentials that require no solid documentation of clinical competence.

Only earned degrees from regionally accredited universities and colleges may be cited by APA members when discussing their credentials (APA 02: 5.01c), and similar requirements exist for other mental health professionals. While not intrinsically unethical to purchase or hold a phony degree, any misleading or deceptive use of such a degree to imply competence would be unethical. This includes hanging or posting the degree in a location where a client or member of the public might be mistakenly influenced by it.

CREDENTIALING ISSUES

Credentials presumably exist as a tangible indicator of accomplishment in a given field, with implications for gauging the competence of the holder. In psychology, there are at least three levels of credentials, distinguished by their intrinsic characteristics and the data on the basis of which they are awarded. These have been referred to as primary, secondary, and tertiary credentials (Koocher, 1979). As one moves from the primary toward the tertiary level, one moves further and further away from the data most relevant for predicting potential competence. The need to develop valid measures of entry-level and continued professional competence is widely acknowledged, but the predictive validity of current levels of credentials is highly variable.

Primary Credentials

Primary credentials are those earned over time by direct contact with trained instructors. They are based on longitudinal samples of the practitioner's behavior, with person-to-person supervision and direct observation by senior colleagues. Objective and subjective evaluations of progress are made by multiple evaluators as training progresses in a stepwise fashion. Examples of such credentials include course work, graduate training programs, supervised practica, internships, and specialized postdoctoral training. Such credentials are not generic but rather reflect expertise in the particular matters and activities studied. The outcome measures may include transcripts of grades, degrees, certificates of completion, or evaluative letters from supervisors or instructors. Typically, the costs of a primary credential (i.e., tuition and time spent in training) are paid before the credential is awarded, and no charges are assessed after completion.

Secondary Credentials

Secondary credentials use primary credentials as prerequisites but also incorporate other elements in determining qualifications. Such credentials include statutory licensing and certification, as well as recognition by specialized certification boards (e.g., American Boards of Professional Psychology). One must first complete the appropriate training and degree programs (i.e., have the appropriate primary credentials) to be considered for a secondary-level credential. Next, some sample of the practitioner's professional behavior is sought. The sample is usually cross-sectional in nature and may consist of a multiple-choice, essay, or oral examination; submission of a work sample; direct observation of a session with a client; or a combination of these. Secondary credentials typically require payment of an application fee, followed by regular renewal charges. Some secondary credentials (e.g., practice licenses in some states) require periodic completion and documentation of continuing professional education at renewal intervals, but many do not.

Some of the examination models used may be extensive and well representative of the practice domain the practitioner intends to enter, but others have historically demonstrated notorious inappropriateness (Carsten, 1978; Greenberg, 1978). An example of the inappropriate type would include using a multiple-choice pencil-and-paper instrument to predict competence in delivery of psychotherapy, even though no

validity data exist to justify such predictions. Another example involved an attempt by the Association of State and Provincial Psychology Boards (ASPPB) to ignore errors in the EPPP and then to block public revelation of their behavior (Koocher, 1989a, 1989b). The ASPPB now provides substantial information on the development of the instrument (see, e.g., the publication tab at http://www.asppb.org) but, like most owners of credentialing tests, allows no independent oversight. Most early career psychologists have come to view the process of passing the test as a kind of traumatic rite of passage (Ryan & Chan, 1999), and that phenomenon is most likely shared by early career professionals in other mental health fields.

In the absence of detailed knowledge of the candidate's background and behavior over time, the grantors of secondary credentials usually require the approval or endorsement by colleagues chosen by the candidate. In general, secondary credentials place heavy reliance on the honor system, and the credential granted is often generic in nature. This principle holds true across nearly all regulated professions since routine attempts to evaluate and reevaluate professional competence would prove time consuming and costly. Mental health professionals are supposed to recognize, acknowledge, and abide by their limitations (Hogan, 1977; Koocher, 1979) and should not inadvertently perpetuate images of competence in undeserving individuals.

Tertiary Credentials

Tertiary credentials are distinguished from the other two types by virtue of requiring no behavioral sample, first-person contact, or substantial individual scrutiny intrinsic to the credential itself. Rather, they are based solely on evidence that primary and secondary credentials have been obtained. In a sense, they simply attest to the fact that the professional holds primary and secondary credentials. Membership in certain APA divisions, state or local professional associations, or listing in the *National Register of Health Service Providers in Psychology* are examples of tertiary credentials.

In Chapter 14, we discuss the listing of various credentials in advertising or presentations of oneself in a professional manner to the public. We also suggest that the public may not necessarily understand the meaning or underpinnings of certain credentials, and that these credentials may sound more impressive than is justified. Certainly, in terms of content validity, criterion-related validity, or predictive validity for which professional competence is at issue, tertiary credentials are relatively worthless, and secondary credentials may be suspect for reasons discussed in the following pages. Primary credentials are the most likely to provide predictive validity regarding a practitioner's competence as long as they are accurately represented and understood by the holder. How does this become an ethics issue? Consider the following case:

Case 4–16: Narcissa Schmit, Psy.D., served as a field placement supervisor for the Central States School of Professional Psychology and, as such, was appointed an adjunct assistant professor at the school. Her role consisted of volunteering 2 hours per week of supervision. She was also listed in the National Register of Health Service Providers in Psychology by virtue of her degree, state license, and 2 years experience working in a health care setting. Next to her diplomas and licenses in her waiting room were framed copies of a letter confirming her "faculty" status and a "certificate of inclusion" in the register. She also chose to list those credentials in a published announcement of her practice and on her office letterhead.

Dr. Schmit's behavior falls in that gray area between the unethical and the acceptable in professional behavior. The uninformed member of the general public has no idea what the *Register* listing signifies and could misinterpret these as constituting an some incremental credential or testimony to Dr. Schmidt's competence. The reference to faculty status could also be misleading and represent a deceptive attempt to boost her prestige by implication of a university affiliation that has little or no bearing on her practice. Depending on how these affiliations are presented, Schmit could be behaving unethically should the misrepresentation be deemed substantive. It would be better not to present these accomplishments and affiliations as if they are credentials because they are not.

Licensing

In most states, the psychology license is a generic one. That is, one is licensed as a psychologist—period. In the application, the candidate may have been asked to specify and document areas of expertise (e.g., clinical psychology, school psychology, industrial consultation, etc.), but there is seldom any monitoring of this specialization after licensing unless a complaint is filed or suspicions are aroused. Some states designated some psychologists as health service providers during the licensing process as a way of identifying those who may bill third parties for mental health services. Similarly, social workers and counselors who hold state licenses will typically have no special qualifications listed, although subcategories may exist as independent practice requirements. Psychiatrists hold licenses to practice medicine as physicians in general but no special license in mental health practice per se. The range of professions engaged in mental health care, along with the range of degrees and generic licensure, creates a public information problem because many people do not fully grasp the educational or practice differences among the mental health professions. All of the professions expect their members to recognize their own limitations and refer clients they lack the competence to treat. Clearly, this does not always happen.

Licensing of the professions has rarely originated as a result of public outcry. More often, licensing professionals have sought licensing as a legal means to obtain recognition by the state, although protection of the public has historically been cited as the paramount rationale. The relationship between licensing and the competence of practitioners is at best speculative and is based on unverified assumptions. In fact, some commentators attempt to refute the claim that licensing protects the public and suggests it may even have some potential adverse effects by limiting access to therapists with nontraditional credentials (Danish & Smyer, 1981; Gross, 1978; Hogan, 1977).

Aside from questions of the validity of the examinations on which licensure is based, as noted above, Hogan's (1977) classic treatise demonstrating how, in the case of psychotherapy, licensure has failed to protect the public adequately has gone effectively unchallenged. Except for the most populous states, licensing boards are often so overworked and underfunded that disciplinary enforcement is nearly impossible except in the most flagrant cases of abuse or misconduct, as was discussed in Chapter 3.

Given the time-consuming task of investigating complaints with due process for the accused while also screening applications, conducting examinations, drafting regulations, and attending to the other duties of the board, little time remains to worry about such idealistic matters as checking the competence of practitioners about whom no complaints have been received. One study examined applications for psychology licensing from all 50 states and the District of Columbia in an effort to determine how boards approached screening applicants and found marked heterogeneity with respect to explicit screening for character and fitness indicators (Johnson, Porter, Campbell, & Kupko, 2005). The investigators found little consensus on which characteristics of applicants should be scrutinized prior to licensure. They recommended a national application for licensing with agreed-on screening questions aimed at differentiating among character and fitness (foundational characteristics) as distinct from impairment and competence. Such questions would typically involve asking about an applicant's current or previous licensure, criminal history, prior complaints or investigations, history of mental health problems, and concerns related to education and training.

Mobility

Perhaps the greatest single problem with licensing statutes for psychology and some other mental health professions is their variability from state to state (DeLeon & Hinnefeld, 2006; Kim & VandeCreek, 2003; Rehm & DeMers, 2006; Vaughn, 2006). Even states that use the same examination procedure may employ different cutoff scores or have special educational requirements. An individual who is deemed qualified to sit for the licensing examination in one state may be denied entry to the examination in a neighboring state (Vaughn,

2006). In general, physicians and nurses can move across state lines easily, although states do vary in the functions allowed to advance practice nurses. The privileges afforded psychologists, social workers, and other master's-level practitioners will vary widely from state to state with respect to qualifications, titles, access to insurance reimbursement, and level of independent practice. The ASPPB has taken steps to improve the situation for psychologists by creating the Certificate of Professional Qualifications or CPQ (see DeMers & Jonason, 2006; Hall & Lunt, 2005; Jonason, DeMers, Vaughn, & Reaves, 2003). The CPQ serves as a tertiary credential that documents other credentials held and makes it easier for psychologists who qualify to obtain licensing in new jurisdictions.

The importance of understanding mobility as an ethics issue relates to the legality of performing services in a jurisdiction not covered by one's license. Although a licensed practitioner may have the competence necessary to perform a particular service, differing licensing criteria and statutes may preclude performing that service in a different jurisdiction. This set of circumstances illustrates a classic "law-versus-ethics" dilemma. Ethically, you may have the education and skill necessary to competently perform clinical duties or render a professional service. Yet, if you lack a valid license (i.e., legal authorization) to provide such services in a given jurisdiction, doing so violates law. Psychologists must ethically obey the law unless a specific ethical obligation runs counter to the law (APA 02: 1.02).

MAINTAINING PERSONAL COMPETENCE

Using the analogy of radioactive decay, one psychologist estimated the half-life of the knowledge acquired by earning a doctoral degree in psychology at about 10 to 12 years (Dubin, 1972). That is, after a decade or so, half of what was learned in graduate school is now outdated. Mental health professionals function in the worlds of behavioral science, medicine, and law. As science advances and case law evolves, the pressure builds for us to keep up. In some fields, one must not only keep pace with the march of new knowledge, but also actually strive to stay several steps ahead. For example, one estimate put the half-life of an undergraduate engineering degree at 4 to 5 years (Eriksen, 1998). Even if we agree on a decade-long half-life for mental health practice, how can one retain any modicum of professional competence over a career that spans more than 30 years (Jensen, 1979)?

A variety of strategies have been advanced to ensure that professionals strive to maintain competence. These include mandated CE, recertification requirements, and professional development models. Most states now require practitioners to complete certain amounts and types of CE course work to maintain a professional license, but many do not. No states or certifying bodies, however, have yet deemed it appropriate to require formal reexamination or recertification of license holders or diploma holders.

Part of the difficulty in implementing plans to monitor practitioner competence over time originates with a definitional problem. What constitutes a meritorious step toward maintaining one's competence? Is attending a workshop commensurate with teaching one? Is writing an article for a refereed journal a sign of continuing competence? Will taking or retaking a multiple-choice examination prove anything? Before we can address a means of maintaining professional capabilities, we must arrive at criteria that are linked to continuing competence (Jensen, 1979). Professional skills, competently executed on a daily basis, will certainly enhance competence. But, experience per se does not immunize one against error. It seems unlikely that a comprehensive solution to the problem of maintaining competence over time will be found in the near term. The most appropriate course of action for a mental health professionals is to strive for a constant awareness of their limitations, recognize that these can increase over time after formal training has ended, and seek constructive remedies by both formal and informal means to keep skills current.

Case 4–17: Nardell Slo, Ed.D., conducted a cognitive evaluation of an adult client using the Wechsler Adult Intelligence Scale–Revised (WAIS-R) a full 4 years after the revised form

(WAIS-III) had been published. When questioned on this point, he noted, "They're about the same, and the new kit is too expensive."

Case 4–18: I. P. Freely, L.M.F.T., continued to recommend long-term individual psychotherapy for child clients with secondary reactive enuresis despite substantial evidence that certain behavioral treatments for this problem can be highly effective in a relatively brief time. When this was called to his attention, he seemed surprised and sought information in the professional literature.

Dr. Slo and Mr. Freely are in the same category as the college professor who has not bothered to update course notes in several years. Both are delivering substandard service to their clients. Dr. Slo does so with some disturbing and inaccurate rationalizations, while Mr. Freely simply seems ignorant of proven, more effective treatments. At least Freely seemed willing to attempt to find out about his area of ignorance, although the apparent apathy (implied by the fact that he did not do so sooner) is worrisome. Dr. Slo's resistance suggests a more serious problem, blending ignorance with arrogance. Clients who rely on the expertise of these practitioners will not receive the most efficient and effective treatments. Even if some new technique (e.g., the behavioral treatment for enuresis) presents problems from Freely's professional and theoretical perspective, he has a responsibility to remain aware of the development and to advise clients of alternative treatments and choices when discussing his recommendations with them.

Continuing Professional Education

As noted, many (but not all) professional organizations and licensing require clinicians to participate in CE, both as a means of keeping up to date and as a means of focusing attention on important issues. For example, some states have required all licensees to complete course work related to ethics, domestic violence, multicultural competence, or other important public interest topics. Most CE focuses on helping practitioners keep pace with emerging issues and technologies. Other goals include helping to maintain, develop, and increase professional competencies as a means to improve services (L. Golding & Gray, 2006). Evaluation usually involves an immediate assessment of participants' degree of satisfaction that the program met the stated goals, chiefly in terms of content (Jameson, Stadter, & Poulton, 2007).

One survey, limited to psychologists in the Commonwealth of Pennsylvania, found that although 75% of respondents favored mandatory CE, far fewer would participate if CE credits were not mandatory. Forty-five percent of respondents believed that attendance at CE programs often increases their clinical effectiveness, while 41% reported this as occurring sometimes, and 11% as only rarely (Sharkin & Plageman, 2003). Some might challenge the effectiveness beliefs expressed in the survey, noting that a wide gap can occur between mostly brief didactic presentations and clinical implementation.

Accreditation of CE has raised many concerns as the different mental health professions vary widely with respect to the rigor imposed on CE sponsors. The APA, as one example, has established standards (APA, 2005) that have been applied to reject awarding credit for some proposed sponsors and on some topics deemed insufficiently rigorous or unrelated to professional competencies in the field. Other good standards and best practices exist (e.g., see L. Golding & Gray, 2006), but not all those offering approved CE across professions do a good job. Many opportunities exist to do "CE lite," as with online courses that end with a perfunctory open-book quiz on the content.

The bottom line seems to tell us that CE is probably better than doing nothing as a way to encourage maintaining professional competence. At the same time, no research yet reports on the effects of CE on the participants' understanding of the content or their application of it (Jameson et al., 2007).

NEW PRACTICE DOMAINS

Beyond Competence

At times, it may seem reasonable for mental health professionals to stretch in extending their areas of competence, even if doing so demands special arrangements and breaking down old taboos. One such occasion might be termed the *compassionate exemption*, a term occasionally used in drug trials when treatment with an experimental protocol is authorized for a patient in extreme or unique need. Clinicians in rural areas know this problem well (Hargrove, 1986).

Case 4–19: Frederick Focus, Ph.D., was trained primarily in short-term treatment models. When he and his family moved to a small town in a mountain community, one they found very much suited to their ideal lifestyle, Dr. Focus was not prepared for the severity of problems that a few of his clients presented. Some of these people could clearly benefit from longer-term psychotherapy, but the nearest practitioners trained in such models lived almost 200 miles away.

Will counseling from a therapist who lacks sufficient background in treating certain problems prove better than no treatment at all? No single correct answer covers all such possible cases, but the undisputed facts are that not all people are helped by therapy, and that some may actually experience harm as a result. Dr. Focus must strive to ensure that he causes no harm. One strategy might involve engaging in a three-step process. First, Dr. Focus must ensure that he fully understands every possible referral resource available in his community. If no appropriate resources exist, Dr. Focus might consider a second step: treating particular clients with ongoing, supportive consultation from a distance with a colleague who does have the proper competencies. We would quickly underscore that mental health professionals should not stretch too far using this second step, and the consulting colleague can help determine the reasonableness of the approach. Finally, if the discrepancy between the client's needs and the therapist's competence is too disparate, then the therapist risks causing more harm than good and should not undertake treatment. In the most recent iteration of its ethics code, the APA recognized this problem and offered specific guidance for practitioners who feel inclined to stretch their competence in emergency or other challenging situations (APA 02: 2.01–2.02).

Prescription Privileges: Psychology Versus Psychiatry

Perhaps no single issue has stirred more controversy among psychologists and psychiatrists since the 1990s than the notion of granting some psychologists prescription privileges. Arguments reported in favor of the practice include the following:

- The majority of psychiatric drug prescribing already originates with nonpsychiatrist providers, such as primary care physicians (Sharfstein, 2006).
- Psychologists practice in many communities lacking psychiatrists.
- Improved care of elderly overmedicated patients in nursing homes would become possible.
- Psychologists already have much of the knowledge and skills necessary to assess behavioral and cognitive changes in a scientific manner.
- Some other categories of nonphysician providers, such as optometrists, podiatrists, nurse practitioners, and even pharmacists, already have prescription privileges.
- Psychologists typically have better training in human psychopathology and psychotherapy at initial licensing than do most psychiatry residents.

Social necessity has proved the most compelling arguments in favor of psychologists' entry into this new practice domain, followed by effective demonstration projects conduced under military auspices (DeLeon, Sammons, & Sexton, 1995; Sammons, Paige, & Levant, 2003). On the basis of these arguments, the prescription privileges movement by psychologists has advanced significantly. The U.S. territory of Guam legalized prescription privileges for psychologists (under the supervision of physicians), prescriptive authority bills have been introduced in nearly a score of state legislatures, and by 2002 at least 39 states had prescription privileges task forces directed by state psychological associations and at least 12 programs now

in existence to train civilian-sector psychologists (Fagan et al., 2004). In March 2002, New Mexico became the first state to provide statutory recognition of prescriptive authority for psychologists, followed by Louisiana in May 2004.

Opponents of prescription authority within the profession of psychology have asserted that granting prescriptive authority to psychologists would medicalize the discipline at the expense of the more traditional psychotherapies that target the social causes of mental disorders (Albee, 2002). In addition, they have pointed to the need for more science-based course work than is currently taught to psychology students if they are to gain competence in psychopharmacology and have suggested that adding this training to current graduate programs would require dramatic changes in the training model currently in use (Sechrest & Coan, 2002). Finally, added training time and costs have been raised and used as an argument against prescription privileges (Fagan et al., 2004; Olvey, Hogg, & Counts, 2002; Wagner, 2002). Those who oppose prescription privileges have also expressed concern that psychologists who prescribe may experience atrophy of psychotherapy skills or experience incidences of prescription drug abuse similar to physicians and nurses (Koocher, 2007).

Arguments from the American Psychiatric Association have asserted that psychiatrists use all their training to function as a physician for the whole patient, and psychologists would need full medical school training to do so, adding that the nonphysician providers who currently do prescribe at least have medical backgrounds. Such assertions seem hollow considering two facts. First, declining numbers of young American physicians choose psychiatric residencies. Second, those who do enter psychiatry focus on psychopharmacology to the relative exclusion of psychotherapy training (Gabbard, 2005; Koocher, 2007; Sharfstein, 2006) Very real concerns exist about the potential economic collapse of psychiatry as a medical specialty.

As with any area of practice, mental health professionals with established competence based on education and training can ethically practice any techniques or treatments legally authorized under their licenses. As new areas of practice emerge, the ethical practitioner will want to move forward with caution, informed by and avoiding the errors of others who have entered the domain before.

THE SICK DOCTOR

When personal problems begin to interfere with professional activities, mental health professionals become a serious danger to clients. Much more has been written about the impaired physician than the impaired psychotherapist, but perhaps that is because physicians' access to drugs makes them more visible foci of concern. There are many facets to the problem of the sick doctor, including consideration of some types of psychological practice as "high-risk" or "burnout-prone" occupations (Freudenberger & Robbins, 1979; Jenkins & Maslach, 1994; Koocher, 1980; Maslach, 1993). Another facet is a therapist's failure to recognize when a client is not improving or is deteriorating while in the therapist's care. Most dramatic, however, are the instances when the therapist, by virtue of addiction, emotional disturbance, or other problem-induced inadequacy, begins to harm clients and presents a danger to the public.

Although physicians have long had programs to assist and monitor impaired colleagues (Green, Carroll, & Buxton, 1976; Katsavdakis, Gabbard, & Athey, 2004), formal rehabilitation programs for impaired psychologists and other mental health professionals are rare, although not unheard of (Barnett & Hillard, 2001; Igartua, 2000; Laliotis & Grayson, 1985; Larson, 1981). However, increasing attention is being devoted to this problem across the professions (Enochs & Etzbach, 2004; Farber et al., 2005; Hurst et al., 2007; Mearns & Allen, 1991; Sadoff & Sadoff, 1994). Annas (1978) did an excellent job of summarizing the difficulty in handling impaired practitioners. He noted that a conference of physicians agreed that an emotionally impaired airline pilot should be grounded immediately and, before being permitted to fly again, required to submit to carefully monitored treatment until benefi-

cial results are documented. Not surprisingly, a group of pilots believed that impaired physicians should immediately cease practicing and abstain from practicing permanently unless successfully treated and rehabilitated. Some pilots argued that at least they have copilots present in the cockpit. Needless to say, some physicians find this sort of turnabout unfair play.

Burnout

Burnout is described as a kind of emotional exhaustion resulting from excessive demands on energy, strength, and personal resources in the work setting (Baker, 2003; Maslach, Schaufeli, & Leiter, 2001; Shirom, 2006). Job-related burnout has long been recognized as a factor in the work of mental health professionals (Freudenberger, 1975). Neglecting self-care can result in corrosive consequences for therapists, such as making poor decisions and disrespecting one's clients (Pope & Vasquez, 2005). It may involve a loss of concern for the people one works alongside, as well as a loss of positive feelings, sympathy, and respect for one's clients (Maslach, 1993). Important client factors related to staff burnout include the client's prognosis, the degree of personal relevance the client's problems have for the therapist, and the client's reactions to the therapist (Maslach, 1993). Burnout is also especially likely when therapists have little control over work activities, are working too many hours, and are overburdened with administrative tasks (Rupert & Morgan, 2005).

Feelings of powerlessness and emotional loss have long been recognized as causal components of depression (Seligman, 1975) and as powerful components of countertransference stress (Adler & Buie, 1972; Maltsberger & Buie, 1974). These stresses can arouse substantial anger in the therapist. The anger appears to have two distinct components: *aversion* and *malice*. Societal and professional values mediate against direct expressions of malice or sadism toward one's clients. The aversion component of countertransference stress may prove more subtle and, as a result, more insidious. The therapist may experience aversion in relation to the client both directly and unconsciously. A schedule suddenly becomes "too crowded for an appointment this week." A troubled client who gripes, "I don't need any help," is permitted to withdraw emotionally instead of being engaged in dialogue.

Expressions of burnout are especially likely when the therapist feels helpless with guilt because the client has not made satisfactory progress or continues to manifest signs of difficulty (e.g., suicidal ideation, addiction problems, or coping emotionally with a life-threatening illness). If a therapist's efforts to assert control over his or her own emotional issues and a client's distress fail, perceived helplessness may result (Baker, 2003; Seligman, 1975). Therapists experiencing this reaction no longer believe that their actions have any effect on the outcomes. Both client and therapist may come to feel that they will suffer regardless of their behavior. In such circumstances, a therapist may defend against experiencing strong emotion by becoming detached (Maslach, 1993; Maslach et al., 2001). While some in medicine have traditionally suggested that a style of "detached concern" constitutes an appropriate means of relating to clients (Lief & Fox, 1963), clear dangers are inherent in this type of response. Clients may experience such detachment as a lack of caring or unresponsiveness, with resulting failure to adhere to treatment (Baker, 2003; Koocher, McGrath, & Gudas, 1990).

Case 4–20: George Sarcoma, M.S.W., worked as a social worker and psychotherapist at a cancer treatment facility. He had worked at this full-time job for several years and, as a caring and sensitive clinician, made himself available "on call" for extended service hours. Following both the death of a client with whom he felt particularly close and a disruption in his marriage, Mr. Sarcoma's performance began to fall off. He failed to respond to messages from colleagues and clients, occasionally missed appointments without notice, and became somewhat distanced from his clients. Ultimately, he was fired from his job but went on to perform well at another setting.

Case 4–21: Susan Skipper, Ed.D., worked as an educational psychologist in a large urban public school system. She felt overworked and unappre-

ciated by clients and administrators, who often made unreasonable demands on her time. Dr. Skipper could not set limits on her work situation and began to dread going to work each day. She applied for and got a job in another part of the country and resigned her current position, giving less-than-adequate notice and leaving behind several uncompleted student evaluations.

Mr. Sarcoma and Dr. Skipper both experienced burnout. This occurred as a result of an interaction of their jobs, personal life events, the stressful client problems they dealt with regularly, and a variety of other factors. Any mental health professional who spends most of his or her day listening to the problems of others is a potential victim. Both Sarcoma and Skipper suffer from learned helplessness and depression, and both hurt their clients as a result. Sarcoma's avoidance and detachment may not have yielded identifiable injury to clients; however, it is likely that some suffered as a result. While Dr. Skipper's abrupt departure has elements of vengeful retaliation against her ungrateful employer, it also doubtlessly disadvantaged a number of students.

As with many potential ethical problems, the best way to deal with burnout is through prevention (Leiter & Maslach, 2005). Employers need to be aware of impending problems among their employees, and mental health professionals who begin to see symptoms of burnout in colleagues or sense it in themselves should take steps toward early intervention (Koocher, 1980). Warning signs of burnout include

- uncharacteristic angry outbursts
- apathy
- chronic frustration
- a sense of depersonalization
- depression
- emotional and physical exhaustion
- hostility
- feelings of malice or aversion toward patients
- reduced productivity or lowered effectiveness at work

A substantial body of research (Dupree & Day, 1995; Jenkins & Maslach, 1994; Koeske & Kelly, 1995; Koocher, 1980; Lee & Ashforth,

1996; Maslach, 1993; Maslach et al., 2001; McKnight & Glass, 1995; Shirom, 2006) has identified many factors that can predispose a person to professional burnout, including

- role ambiguity at work, including vague or inconsistent demands and expectations
- conflict and tension in the workplace
- a high level of discrepancy between ideal and real job functions
- unrealistic preemployment expectations
- lack of social support at work
- a perfectionist personality with a strong sense of being externally controlled
- losses through death or divorce in the family
- chronic helplessness
- permeable emotional boundaries
- substance abuse
- overly high expectations for oneself, such as a "savior complex"

Conversely, factors that can help insulate a person from burnout include

- role clarity
- positive feedback
- an enhanced sense of autonomy at work
- opportunities for rehabilitation from stress at work
- social support in the workplace
- personal accomplishment
- realistic criteria for client outcome
- an accurate awareness of personal strengths and weaknesses along with a good sense of internal control

The Troubled Mental Health Professional

Whether the troubled therapist works in research, teaching, or psychotherapy does not seem to matter so far as incidence of pathology is concerned. While the variety of resulting ethical infractions seems endless, many people, including the mental health professional involved, are hurt in the end. Consider these examples:

Case 4–22: An ethics complaint charged Martha Ottenbee, L.M.H.C., with overbilling clients. She proved to be an extremely disorganized, absent-minded mental health counselor, whose case notes and financial records were often incomprehensible. She appeared totally inept at managing

her practice, although she seemed basically good hearted. She responded in a slightly frantic and easily distracted manner when asked to explain her behavior to the ethics committee.

Case 4–23: Kurt Mores, L.M.F.C., was convicted in state court of "fornication" after a female client complained that she had been emotionally harmed as a result of having sex with him. At an ethics committee hearing, Mr. Mores admitted having had sexual intercourse with many of his female clients over the past few years. He added that extreme pressure within his marriage had caused considerable anxiety, loss of self-esteem, and feelings of sexual inadequacy. He told the committee, referring to his sexual activity with clients, "I didn't charge them for that part of the session." He also expressed the belief that, "It's okay to ignore the ethical code as long as you think about it carefully first and talk it over with clients."

Case 4–24: Paul Pious, Ph.D., nationally known as a psychologist and author in the field of moral development, had developed a major teaching program for application in public schools when his life began to come unglued. He was involved in a stressful divorce and publicly listed in a newspaper as a "tax delinquent." He found himself becoming increasingly suspicious about the motives of people with which he worked. When a schoolteacher raised objections to his teaching program, Dr. Pious called the school superintendent and reported that the teacher, an openly gay man, had engaged in sexual relationships with high school students. An investigation revealed no support for the allegations, and Dr. Pious acknowledged lying to protect his project. He subsequently sought admission to a mental hospital for treatment.

Case 4–25: Lester Lapse, Ed.D., came before an ethics committee following a complaint that he had plagiarized an entire article from a professional journal and submitted it to another journal, listing himself as the sole author. At the committee hearing, Dr. Lapse appeared despondent. He described many pressures in his life and admitted that he must have plagiarized the article, although he had no conscious memory of having done so. He actually believed that he had conducted the study himself, even though there was no evidence that he had done so, and the article he submitted was identical, down to four decimal places in the tabular data reported, to the prior publication by another researcher.

Ms. Ottenby's incompetence in the business end of her practice causes one to wonder what she is like as a therapist. Mr. Mores seemed to have a unique moral outlook, with minimum insight into problems caused by his conduct and few, if any, regrets. Dr. Pious found himself in a desperate situation and adopted a distorted moral standard that permitted him to lie and nearly ruin the career of an innocent party. Dr. Lapse, like Dr. Pious, seems to have a mental illness defense for his admittedly unethical conduct. Will Mr. Mores' arrogant attitude justify a harsher sanction than dealt to Drs. Lapse and Pious, who each acknowledge their weaknesses? Should the committee investigating Ms. Ottenby's slipshod business practices seek to investigate her clinical skills, even though they have not been specifically addressed in the complaint?

Case 4–26: Two clients had almost died while in treatment with Flip Grando, Ph.D. At an ethics hearing looking into the case, Dr. Grando explained these unfortunate occurrences as the result of "insufficient faith" on the part of the clients. Dr. Grando's therapy technique involved locking the client in an airtight box for an extended period of time because, Grando explained, he had been given the special power to convert the client's own carbon dioxide into a healing force for all emotional and physical ailments. Dr. Grando's whole demeanor suggested a serious emotional disorder.

Case 4–27: Willis C. Driscoll, Ph.D., worked as a well-regarded psychologist in central Ohio. One day in 1991, he left Columbus in a hurry, never returning from lunch to retrieve files or say goodbye. He left behind two daughters and three sons, relocating to his mother's home in North Carolina. In May 1996, his sister telephoned local North Carolina police from her home in Florida. She was concerned that Dr. Driscoll would not allow her to talk to her mother on the telephone. After obtaining a search warrant, police located the skeletal remains of 96-year-old Mrs. Driscoll behind

her locked bedroom door, on the floor, surrounded by trash. Dr. Driscoll was sent to the Dorothea Dix Hospital in Raleigh for evaluation (Stephens & Somerson, 1996).

Case 4–28: Holli L. Bodner, Ph.D., who had performed competency exams for the court system in two Florida counties, lied about neighbor Jean Pierre Villar's mental health in court documents to convince a judge to commit him to a mental health facility for evaluation. Bodner and Villar had allegedly feuded for a year over issues including dog droppings and street lights. Local police were well aware of the dispute. Bodner allegedly told an officer that Villar "was missing the frontal lobes of his brain, had a low IQ, was mixing alcohol with his pain medication . . . [and] was abusing his wife and daughter."

Two deputies armed with a judge's order to take Villar into custody arrived at his home. Villar, wearing a back brace as he was rehabilitating from a spinal surgery following an injury suffered while doing construction work, answered the door. He allegedly suffered injuries when the deputies grabbed his arms and bent him over after he refused to get in the car, while screaming and crying.

Bodner pleaded no contest to perjury for lying on the commitment papers. She was sentenced to 10 weekends in jail and 6 months probation. The Florida Board of Psychology disciplined Bodner, leaving her license active on probationary status. She paid a $150,000 settlement to Villar as compensation for pain, mental anguish, and humiliation (Scarella, 2006).

Will Dr. Grando eventually cause a person's death? If Dr. Driscoll ever resumes practice, will clients who know his history feel comfortable with him? What drove Dr. Bodner to feel entitled to misuse her professional authority to attempt incarceration of an annoying neighbor? Certainly, no single remedy or rehabilitation plan will apply across all of these cases. Ask yourself, "Should one even bother to try to rehabilitate the professionals mentioned?" Or, "Is mental illness a proper defense against a charge of ethical misconduct?"

These complex questions demand additional data before we can frame an adequate answer, but such complexities lie at the very nature of these complaints. In general, we would agree that rehabilitation ought to be the paramount goal, except when the behavior itself is sufficiently objectionable to warrant more strictly punitive action. Mental illness is certainly an issue that mental health ethics experts will want to consider, but it does not justify ethical misconduct. Many mental health professionals with serious emotional problems are able to seek treatment without committing ethical misconduct. An interesting paper on the claim of mental illness as a defense by lawyers, brought before the bar association on charges of misconduct, suggests similar reasoning. The authors concluded that, while bar association discipline committees and courts will consider mental illness as a mitigating factor, it will seldom be a fully adequate protection (Skoler & Klein, 1979).

We have observed that the impaired mental health practitioner is most typically a professionally isolated individual. This fact suggests that those mental health professionals who strive to maintain regular professional interactions with colleagues may prove less susceptible to burnout and decompensation or may simply have such problems called to their attention constructively prior to committing serious ethical infractions (APA 02: 2.06). Of course, it is also possible that some therapists become marginalized or rejected by their colleagues because they are emotionally impaired, thus forcing them into professional isolation.

Mental health professionals who recognize problems with their behavior and who seem committed to addressing them constructively certainly will be more likely to rehabilitate successfully than those who do not. At the same time, one must exercise caution when broadening an ethics inquiry to include aspects of therapists' lives not in question.

Case 4–29: A licensing board received a complaint against Knotty C. Kret, M.D., from a former client, who accused Dr. Kret of improper billing practices. In the complaint document, the client added a comment that he had witnessed Dr. Kret from a distance cavorting at a local club where like-minded people gather for anonymous sexual encounters.

In this instance, the licensing board investigated the billing complaint, while appropriately ignoring the allegation regarding aspects of Dr. Kret's life, unrelated to any complaint of professional misconduct. However, if an ethics inquiry uncovers signs of personal impairment or mental illness, a broadened inquiry may prove necessary in the public interest. This becomes particularly important if the therapist asserts emotional problems as a defense. Such a claim might imply the presence of impairments that could adversely affect other clients.

It is not often that therapists will spontaneously recognize the fact that personal distresses have impaired their judgments. It is still more infrequent that therapists will be willing to make these judgment errors public. A rare and sensitive paper by Kovacs (1974) traced such events and their consequences for him and one particular client. It is certainly worth reading for anyone who would like to see the subtle encroachments of poor judgment in eroding a therapeutic relationship (see also Chapter 10).

An important potential remedy for the troubled colleague might involve the formation of support networks through professional associations at the state and local levels. Such groups might offer consultation and referral to colleagues willing to treat disturbed peers. Mutual support groups for mental health professionals working in particularly stressful settings are another possibility, as are the checklists or guides to the warning signs of professional burnout presented in this chapter.

THE CLIENT WHO DOES NOT IMPROVE

The APA ethical code clearly indicates that a psychologist should seek to terminate a relationship with a client when it is evident that the client no longer needs services or has ceased to benefit (APA 02: 10.10a). This may involve transferring the client to another practitioner, who may be able to treat the client more effectively, or it may mean simply advising the client that services are no longer needed. Consider the following cases:

Case 4–30: Ida Demeaner had been in psychotherapy with Manny Continua, Psy.D., every week for 6 years. Ida had successfully dealt with the issues that first brought her to treatment but had become very dependent on her sessions with Dr. Continua. While there had been no real change in Ms. Demeaner's emotional status for at least 4 years (aside from the increasing attachment to him), Dr. Continua made little effort to move toward termination. His philosophy is, "If the client thinks she needs to see me, then she does."

Dr. Continua has a conceptualization of treatment that suggests the potential for endless psychotherapy. While it is not possible to state categorically that diminishing returns begin at a certain point or that all treatment beyond X number of sessions is useless, Continua may well be mistreating his client. He may have fostered her dependency and actually perpetuated her "need" for treatment. Ideally, he should evaluate his work with her critically from time to time and refer her for a consultation with another therapist if he has doubts about the necessity for continued treatment. This assumes that he does not have an emotional (or financial) blind spot that prevents him from recognizing her situation.

Case 4–31: Nemo Creep initially entered psychotherapy with Harold Narrow, L.M.H.C., for treatment of his growing anger at his employer. It became evident to Mr. Narrow that Mr. Creep was becoming increasingly paranoid and troubled. Narrow tried to suggest hospitalization to Creep several times, but each time Creep refused to consider the idea. Narrow continued to treat him and ultimately became the object of Creep's paranoid anger.

Mr. Narrow has failed to recognize that a case is beyond his capability to treat. When it became clear that Mr. Creep needed more intensive (i.e., inpatient) treatment, but was refusing to consider it, Mr. Narrow could have taken a number of steps to help Creep. One such step would have been to decline to further treat Creep unless he would seek appropriate care for himself. If Creep's behavior presented a danger or warranted a commitment for involuntary hospitalization, Mr. Narrow would be responsible for considering those options.

Case 4–32: Ivan Snidely, Ph.D., is an industrial/organizational psychologist hired to assist a major corporation improve employee morale and reduce product defects in a large factory. According to effectiveness data Snidely collected himself, it was evident that his efforts were not meeting with success. Nonetheless, he chose to ignore the data, tell the company that a longer trial period was needed, and continued to supply the ineffective services at a high fee for several additional months before the company canceled its contract with him.

Dr. Snidely may be greedy or simply blind to his own inadequacy for the task at hand, but there is no excuse for his ignoring the data. If he had no alternative plan, he should not have continued to provide services that he knew to be ineffective. The failure to reassess treatment plans in the face of continued client problems and the failure of the intervention are inexcusable.

MENTAL HEALTH PROFESSIONALS AS TEACHERS AND RESEARCHERS

The focus of this chapter has been on mental health professionals who perform clinical and related services. This is because the discipline has almost exclusively confined its attention to competence evaluation in these areas. State laws do not require specific training or licensing for teaching psychology, social work, medicine, or counseling or for conducting research, despite the fact that most who engage in such work have usually earned advanced degrees or are in the process of earning them. Our relative neglect of the competence issues surrounding teaching and research activities does not imply that profound ethical problems are irrelevant or rare. In Chapters 16 and 19, many of the case examples involve competency deficits that have harmed students and research participants.

SUMMARY GUIDELINES

1. Official documents by professional associations describing standards of practice or guidelines of various sorts do not carry the weight or enforcement mandate of the ethics code, but they can be useful in guiding competent practice behaviors. It is important to be aware of such documents as they may be cited as indices of failure to follow professional standards should an ethics complaint or malpractice lawsuit arise.

2. Many subareas, specialty interests, or unusual techniques require expertise for which no generally accepted practice criteria exist. In those situations, therapists should consult with experienced practitioners in that subarea, specialty, or technique to assess appropriate levels of training before using such interventions.

3. There is no comprehensive consensus on course work or training ingredients for all types of degrees in psychology and other mental health disciplines. The holders of many types of psychology degrees (i.e., Ph.D., Ed.D., or Psy.D.) may be equally well qualified to perform certain tasks. Ultimately, however, it is each mental health professional's personal responsibility to ensure that he or she is practicing within the range of activity appropriate to personal training. All practitioners should base their practices on conservatively assessed indicia of competence and legally authorized practice domains.

4. Those administering training programs should recognize and balance dual sets of responsibilities, one set of duties to their students and another set to the public who will be studied, counseled, or otherwise served by their graduates.

5. Students in mental health training programs should expect timely evaluations of their developing competence and status. Each program should have a formal evaluation system with routine means of feedback, progress assessment, and appeal.

6. Many institutions or organizations exist that grant degrees of a questionable or totally bogus nature. Ethical professionals should not associate themselves with such institutions and should not behave in any way that implies that the credentials granted by such programs suggest competence in the field.

7. Generic licensing laws and the variety of valid earned degrees held by people licensed as mental health practitioners in various states present the potential for considerable ambiguity. Ethical professionals should behave in ways that make the nature of their training and credentials explicit, recognizing that some credentials have little relationship to competence or present an ambiguous meaning to the public at large. Consumer questions should be answered frankly, honestly, and with appropriate factual information.

8. Students or practitioners with limited licenses may well have the competence to perform a number of sophisticated professional functions, but they must abide by all appropriate statutes and professional standards.

9. Therapists should be mindful of the potential for burnout or exhaustion in certain types of job settings. They should counsel colleagues who are distressed or seek help themselves as needed to avoid causing distress, inconvenience, or harm to the clients they serve.

10. When a client does not show progress or seems to be worsening despite a practitioner's interventions, consultation or appropriate means to terminate the ineffective relationship should be sought.

11. Distressed or impaired therapists should refrain from practicing to the extent that their impairments bear on ability to perform work with competence and responsibility. If in doubt, professionals should consult with colleagues familiar with their skills and problems.

References

Adler, G., & Buie, D. H. (1972). The misuses of confrontation with borderline patients. *International Journal of Psychoanalytic Psychotherapy, 1*, 109–120.

Albee, G. W. (2002). Just say no to psychotropic drugs! *Journal of Clinical Psychology, 58*, 635–648.

Altman, R. (Director). (2006). *A prairie home companion* [Motion picture]. New York: GreeneStreet Films and Prairie Home Productions

American Psychological Association. (2005). *Standards and criteria for approval of sponsors of continuing education for psychologists* Retrieved May 12, 2007, from http://www.apa.org/ce/scman_05 .pdf

American Psychological Association Office of Program Consultation and Accreditation. (2000). *Guidelines and principles for accreditation of programs in professional psychology.* Washington, DC: American Psychological Association.

Annas, G. J. (1978). Law and the life sciences: Who to call when the doctor is sick. *The Hastings Center Report, 8,* 18–20.

Association of Psychology Postdoctoral and Internship Centers (APPIC). (2002). *Competencies Conference: Future Directions in Education and Credentialing in Professional Psychology.* Retrieved May 12, 2007, from http:// www. appic.org/news/3_1_news_Competencies.htm

Baker, E. K. (2003). *Caring for ourselves: A therapist's guide to personal and professional well-being.* Washington, DC: American Psychological Association.

Barnett, J. E., & Hillard, D. (2001). Psychologist distress and impairment: The availability, nature, and use of colleague assistance programs for psychologists. *Professional Psychology, 32,* 205–210.

Bennett, B. E., Bricklin, P. M., Harris, E. A., Knapp, S., VandeCreek, L., & Younggren, J. N. (2007). *Assessing and managing risk in psychological practice: An individualized approach.* Rockville, M.D: American Psychological Association Insurance Trust.

Brenner, A. M. (2006). The role of personal psychodynamic psychotherapy in becoming a competent psychiatrist. *Harvard Review of Psychiatry, 14,* 268–272.

Carsten, A. (1978). A public perspective on scoring the licensing exam. *Professional Psychology, 9,* 531–532.

Claiborn, W. L. (1982). The problem of professional incompetence. *Professional Psychology, 13,* 153–158.

Clark, B. J., & Abeles, N. (1994). Ethical issues and dilemmas in the mental health organization. *Administration and Policy in Mental Health, 22,* 7–17.

Danish, S. J., & Smyer, M. A. (1981). Unintended consequences of requiring a license to help. *American Psychologist, 36,* 13–21.

de las Fuentes, C., Wilmuth, M. E., & Yarrow, C. (2005). Competency training in ethics education and practice. *Professional Psychology, 36,* 362–366.

DeLeon, P. H., & Hinnefeld, B. J. (2006). Licensure mobility. In T. J. Vaughn (Ed.), *Psychology licensure and certification: What students need to know* (pp. 97–105.). Washington, DC: American Psychological Association.

DeLeon, P. H., Sammons, M. T., & Sexton, J. L. (1995). Focusing on society's real needs: Responsibility and prescription privileges? *American Psychologist, 50,* 1022–1032.

DeMers, S. T., & Jonason, K. R. (2006). The ASPPB Credentials bank and the certificate of professional qualification in psychology: Comprehensive solutions to mobility obstacles. In T. J. Vaughn (Ed.), *Psychology licensure and certification: What students need to know* (pp. 107–115.). Washington, DC: American Psychological Association.

Doe v. New York University, Civ. 6285 No. 77 (S.D. N.Y. 1981).

Dubin, S. S. (1972). Obsolescence or lifelong education: A choice for the professional. *American Psychologist, 27,* 486–498.

Dupree, P. I., & Day, H. D. (1995). Psychotherapists' job satisfaction and job burnout as a function of work setting and percentage of managed care clients. *Psychotherapy in Private Practice, 14,* 77–93.

Elman, N. S., Illfelder-Kaye, J., & Robiner, W. N. (2005). Professional development: Training for professionalism as a foundation for competent practice in psychology. *Professional Psychology, 34,* 367–375.

Enochs, W. K., & Etzbach, C. A. (2004). Impaired student counselors: Ethical and legal considerations for the family. *Family Journal: Counseling and Therapy for Couples and Families, 12,* 396–400.

Epstein, R. M., & Hundert, E. M. (2002). Defining and assessing professional competence. *Journal of the American Medical Association, 287,* 226–235.

Eriksen, A. B. (1998). *Wired to learn*. Retrieved March 30, 2007, from http://www.graduating engineer.com/articles/feature/07.27.98.html

Fagan, T. J., Ax, R. K., Resnick, R. J., Liss, M., Johnson, R. T., & Forbes, M. R. (2004). Attitudes among interns and directors of training: Who wants to prescribe, who doesn't, and why. *Professional Psychology, 35*, 345–356.

Farber, N. J., Gilibert, S. G., Aboff, B. M., Collier, V. U., Weiner, J., & Boyer, E. G. (2005). Physicians' willingness to report impaired colleagues. *Social Science & Medicine, 61*, 1772–1775.

Fox, R. E. (1994). Training professional psychologists for the 21st century. *American Psychologist, 49*, 200–2006.

Freudenberger, H. J. (1975). The staff burnout syndrome in alternative institutions. *Psychotherapy: Theory, Research, and Practice, 12*, 73–81.

Freudenberger, H. J., & Robbins, A. (1979). The hazards of being a psychoanalyst. *Psychoanalytic Review, 66*, 275–300.

Gabbard, G. O. (2005). How not to teach psychotherapy. *Academic Psychiatry, 29*, 332–338.

Golding, S. L. (1999, August 22). *The voir dire of forensic experts: Issues of qualifications and training.* Paper presented at the American Psychological Association Convention, Boston, MA.

Golding, L., & Gray, I. (2006). *Continuing professional development for clinical psychologist: A practical handbook.* Leicester, England: British Psychological Society.

Green, R. C., Carroll, G. J., & Buxton, W. D. (1976). Drug addiction among physicians: The Virginia experience. *Journal of the American Medical Association, 236*, 1372–1375.

Greenberg, M. D. (1978). The Examination of Professional Practice in Psychology (EPPP). *American Psychologist, 33*, 88–89.

Gross, S. J. (1978). The myth of professional licensing. *American Psychologist, 33*, 1009–1016.

Haldeman, D. E. (2006). Queer eye on the straight guy: A case of male heterophobia. In M. Englar-Carlson & M. A. Stevens (Eds.), *In the room with men: A casebook of therapeutic change* (pp. 301–317). Washington, DC: American Psychological Association.

Hall, J. E., & Lunt, I. (2005). Global mobility for psychologists: The role of psychology organizations in the United States, Canada, Europe, and other regions. *American Psychologist, 60*, 712–726.

Hansen, M. (2000). *Expertise to go*. Retrieved May 12, 2007, from http://www.abanet.org/journal/may00/02fpert.html

Hansen, N. D., Randazzo, K. V., Schwartz, A., Marshall, M., Kalis, D., Frazier, D., et al. (2006). Do we practice what we preach? An exploratory survey of multicultural psychotherapy competencies. *Professional Psychology, 37*, 66–74.

Hargrove, D. S. (1986). Ethical issues in rural mental health practice. *Professional Psychology: Research and Practice, 17*, 20–23.

Hogan, D. B. (1977). *The regulation of psychotherapists* (Vols. 1–4). Cambridge, MA: Ballinger.

Hurst, S. A., Perrier, A., Pegoraro, R., Reiter-Theil, S., Forde, R., Slowther, A. M., et al. (2007). Ethical difficulties in clinical practice: Experiences of European doctors. *Journal of Medical Ethics, 33*, 51–57.

Igartua, K. J. (2000). The impact of impaired supervisors on residents. *Academic Psychiatry, 24*, 188–194.

Jameson, P., Stadter, M., & Poulton, J. (2007). Sustained and sustaining continuing education for therapists. *Psychotherapy: Theory, Research, Practice, Training, 44*, 110–114.

Jenkins, S. R., & Maslach, C. (1994). Psychological health and involvement in interpersonally demanding occupations: A longitudinal perspective. *Journal of Organizational Behavior, 15*, 101–127.

Jensen, R. E. (1979). Competent professional service in psychology: The real issue behind continuing education. *Professional Psychology, 10*, 381–389.

Johnson, W. B., Porter, K., Campbell, C. D., & Kupko, E. N. (2005). Character and fitness requirements for professional psychologists: an examination of state licensing application forms. *Professional Psychology, 36*, 654–662.

Jonason, K. R., DeMers, S. T., Vaughn, T. J., & Reaves, R. P. (2003). Professional mobility for psychologists is rapidly becoming a reality. *Professional Psychology, 34*, 468–473.

Kaslow, N. J. (Ed.). (2004). Competencies conference—Future directions in education and credentialing in professional psychology [Special issue]. *Journal of Clinical Psychology, 60*.

Katsavdakis, K., Gabbard, G. O., & Athey, G. I. (2004). Profiles of impaired health professionals. *Bulletin of the Menninger Clinic, 68*, 60–72.

Kim, E., & VandeCreek, L. (2003). Facilitating mobility for psychologists: Comparisons with and lessons from other health care professions. *Professional Psychology, 34*, 476–479.

Koeske, G. F., & Kelly, T. (1995). The impact of overinvolvement on burnout and job satisfaction. *American Journal of Orthopsychiatry, 65*, 282–292.

Koocher, G. P. (1979). Credentialing in psychology: Close encounters with competence? *American Psychologist, 34*, 696–702.

Koocher, G. P. (1980). Pediatric cancer: Psychosocial problems and the high costs of helping. *Journal of Clinical Child Psychology, 9*, 2–5.

Koocher, G. P. (1989a). Confirming content validity in the dark. *Professional Psychology, 20*, 275.

Koocher, G. P. (1989b). Screening licensing examinations for accuracy. *Professional Psychology, 20*, 269–271.

Koocher, G. P. (2003). Ethical issues in psychotherapy with adolescents. *Journal of Clinical Psychology, 59*, 1247–1256.

Koocher, G. P. (2007). Twenty-first century ethical challenges for psychology. *American Psychologist, 62*, 373–384.

Koocher, G. P., McGrath, M. L., & Gudas, L. J. (1990). Typologies of nonadherence in cystic fibrosis. *Journal of Developmental and Behavioral Pediatrics, 11*, 353–358.

Kovacs, A.L. (1975). The valley of the shadow. *Psychotherapy Theory, Research and Practice, 11*, 376–382.

Laliotis, D. A., & Grayson, J. H. (1985). Psychologist heal thyself: What is available for the impaired psychologist? *American Psychologist, 40*, 84–96.

Larson, C. (1981). Media psychology: New roles and new responsibilities. *Monitor on Psychology, 12*, 3.

Lee, R. T., & Ashforth, B. E. (1996). A meta-analytic examination of the correlates of the three dimensions of job burnout. *Journal of Applied Psychology, 81*, 123–133.

Leiter, M. P., & Maslach, C. (2005). *Banishing burnout: Six strategies for improving your relationship with work*. San Francisco: Jossey-Bass.

Lief, H. I., & Fox, R. C. (1963). Training for detached concern in medical students. In H. I. Lief (Ed.), *The psychological basis of medical practice* (pp. 12–35). New York: Hoeber Medical Division, Harper and Row.

Maltsberger, J. T., & Buie, D. H. (1974). Countertransference hate in the treatment of suicidal patients. *Archives of General Psychiatry, 30*, 625–633.

Maslach, C. (1993). Burnout: A multidimensional perspective. In W. B. Schaufeli, C. Maslach, & T. Marek (Eds.), *Professional burnout: Recent developments in theory and research.* (pp. 19–32). Philadelphia: Taylor & Francis.

Maslach, C., Schaufeli, W. B., & Leiter, M. P. (2001). Job burnout. *Annual Review of Psychology, 52*, 397–422.

Maxie, A. C., Arnold, D. H., & Stephenson, M. (2006). Do therapists address ethnic and racial differences in cross-cultural psychotherapy? *Psychotherapy: Theory, Research, Practice, Training, 43*, 85–98.

McKnight, J. D., & Glass, D. C. (1995). Perceptions of control, burnout, and depressive symptomatology: A replication and extension. *Journal of Consulting and Clinical Psychology, 63*, 490–494.

Mearns, J., & Allen, G. J. (1991). Graduate students' experiences in dealing with impaired peers, compared with faculty predictions: An exploratory study. *Ethics & Behavior, 1*, 191–202.

Moran, M. (2006). Psychiatry match numbers drop slightly after 5 years of increase. *Psychiatric News, 41*, 1.

Moses, S. (1990). Education: Master's graduates suffer identity crisis. *Monitor on Psychology, 21*, 8.

Olvey, C. D. V., Hogg, A., & Counts, W. (2002). Licensure requirements: Have we raised the bar too far? *Professional Psychology, 33*, 323–329.

Packard, T., Simon, N. P., & Vaughn, T. J. (2006). Board certification by the American Board of Professional Psychology. In T. J. Vaughn (Ed.), *Psychology licensure and certification: What students need to know* (pp. 117–126). Washington, DC: American Psychological Association.

Peterson, D. R. (1976). The need for the doctor of psychology degree in professional psychology. *American Psychologist, 31*, 756–764.

Peterson, D. R., & Bry, B. H. (1980). Dimensions of perceived competence in professional psychology. *Professional Psychology, 11*, 965–971.

Pope, K. S., & Brown, L. S. (1996). *Recovered memories of abuse: Assessment, therapy, forensics.* Washington, DC: American Psychological Association.

Pope, K. S., Sonne, J. L., & Greene, B. (2006). *What therapists don't talk about and why: Understanding taboos that hurt us and our clients.* Washington, DC: American Psychological Association.

Pope, K. S., & Vasquez, M. J. T. (2005). *How to survive and thrive as a therapist: Information, ideas, and resources for psychologists.* Washington, DC: American Psychological Association, 2005.

Rehm, L., & DeMers, S. T. (2006). Licensure. *Clinical Psychology: Science and Practice, 13,* 249–253.

Robiner, W. N., Arbisi, P., & Edwall, G. E. (1994). The basis of the doctoral degree for psychology licensure. *Clinical Psychology Review, 14,* 227–254.

Rupert, P. A., & Morgan, D. J. (2005). Work setting and burnout among professional psychologists. *Professional Psychology, 36,* 544–550.

Ryan, A. M., & Chan, D. (1999). Perceptions of the EPPP: How do licensure candidates view the process? *Professional Psychology, 30,* 519–530.

Sadoff, R. L., & Sadoff, J. B. (1994). The impaired health professional: Legal and ethical issues. In H. Bluestone, S. Travin, & D. B. Marlowe (Eds.), *Psychiatric-legal decision making by the mental health practitioner: The clinician as de facto magistrate.* (pp. 250–268). New York: Wiley.

Sammons, M. T., Paige, R. U., & Levant, R. F. (Eds.). (2003). *Prescriptive authority for psychologists: A history and guide.* Washington, DC: American Psychological Association.

Scarella, M. A. (2006, December 23). Psychologist settles federal suit: The $150,000 settlement is compensation for pain and mental anguish in a 2003 Baker Act case. *Herald Tribune* Retrieved January 23, 2006, from http://www.heraldtribune.com/apps/pbcs.dll/article?AID=/20060123/NEWS/601230339/1029

Sechrest, L., & Coan, J. A. (2002). Preparing psychologists to prescribe. *Journal of Clinical Psychology, 58,* 649–658.

Seligman, M. E. P. (1975). *Helplessness: On depression, development, and death.* New York: W. H. Freeman.

Shapiro, A. E., & Wiggins, J. G. (1994). A PsyD degrees for every practitioner: Truth in labeling. *American Psychologist, 49,* 207–210.

Sharfstein, S. (2006). How will psychologists practicing medicine affect psychiatry? *Psychiatric News, 41,* 3.

Sharkin, B. S., & Plageman, P. M. (2003). What do psychologists think about mandatory continuing education? A survey of Pennsylvania practitioners. *Professional Psychology, 34,* 318–323.

Shen, F. (1996, June 8). Woman awarded $600,000 by jury: Expelled student objected to U M.D. *Washington Post,* p. B1.

Shirom, A. (2006). Job-related burnout: A review. In J. C. Quick & L. E. Tetrick (Eds.), *Handbook of occupational health psychology* (pp. 245–264). Washington, DC: American Psychological Association.

Skoler, D. L., & Klein, J. (1979). Mental disability in lawyer discipline. *John Marshall Journal of Practice and Procedure, 12,* 227–252.

Stephens, S., & Somerson, M. D. (1996, May 21). Police say psychologist lived with dead mom. *Columbus Dispatch,* p.1

Sue, S. (1998). In search of cultural competence in psychotherapy and counseling. *American Psychologist, 53,* 440–448.

Susan A. Stepakoff v. University of Maryland at College Park, Robert Brown, Robert Dies, Raymond Lorion, and Barry Smith. Cal. 92 17117 (Cir. Prince Georges County 1996).

Sutton, R. I. (2007). *The no asshole rule: Building a civilized workplace and surviving one that isn't.* New York: Warner Books.

Vaughn, T. J. (Ed.). (2006). *Psychology licensure and certification: What students need to know.* Washington, DC: American Psychological Association.

Wagner, M. K. (2002). The high cost of prescription privileges. *Journal of Clinical Psychology, 58,* 677–680.

Welfel, E. R. (2006). *Ethics in counseling and psychotherapy: Standards, research, and emerging issues* (3rd ed.). Belmont, CA: Thompson/Brooks-Cole.

Wellner, A. M. (1978). *Education and credentialing in psychology.* Washington, DC: American Psychological Association.

5

Psychotherapy Part I
Ethical Obligations of Psychotherapists

Neurotic means he is not as sensible as I am, and
psychotic means that he is even worse than my
brother-in-law.

Karl Menninger

Contents

WHAT IS PSYCHOTHERAPY
AND HOW DOES IT WORK?

Ask any mental health professional about the
ethics of their work, and they tend to become
philosophers. Writing on the ethics of their craft,
psychotherapists have referred to the practice of
therapy as a science (Karasu, 1980); an art (Bugenthal, 1987); a source of honest and nonjudg-
mental feedback (Kaschak, 1978); the systematic

use of a human relationship for therapeutic purposes (Bugenthal, 1987); and a means of exploring one's "ultimate values" (Kanoti, 1971). Less
flattering descriptions from within the profession
include "a house of cards" (Dawes, 1994); the
purchase of friendship (Schofield, 1964); a
means of social control (Hook, 2003; Hurvitz,
1973); tradecraft (Blau, 1987); and even as
"a potentially difficult, embarrassing, and overall risky enterprise...[that can] induce fear

101

and avoidance in some individuals" (Kushner & Sher, 1989, p. 256). Our personal favorite definition of psychotherapy came from the secretary for the proceedings of the historic Boulder conference on the training of psychologists, who satirically noted: "We have left therapy as an undefined technique which is applied to unspecified problems with a nonpredictable outcome. For this technique we recommend rigorous training" (Lehner, 1952, p. 547).

Debate about the worth of psychotherapy or the need to use trained experts to provide it has spanned more than five decades in the scientific literature (Eysenck, 1952; Freedheim, 1992; Garfield, 1981; Marshall, 1980; Norcross, Beutler, & Levant, 2005). Challenges to the objective assessment of the worth of psychotherapy began with Freud's assertion that psychoanalysis ought to be exempt from systematic study (Strupp, 1992). As Garfield (1992) noted in reviewing 100 years of development, "Carrying out research on psychotherapy is a complex, difficult, and even controversial activity" (p. 354). Despite some controversy, however, the majority of clients apparently benefit from psychotherapy (Seligman, 1995).

Public perceptions of the effectiveness of psychotherapy vary widely. One national poll (Goode & Wagner, 1993) revealed that 81% of Americans think that therapy for personal problems would be helpful "sometimes" or "all of the time." The same article suggested that more than 16 million Americans sought mental health treatment that year. However, a national poll in Australia (Jorm et al., 1997) reflected a belief that general medical practitioners (83%) would likely prove more helpful in addressing concerns such as depression than psychiatrists (51%) or psychologists (49%). Respondents to that same study believed many standard psychiatric treatments (e.g., antidepressant and antipsychotic medications, electroconvulsive therapy, admission to a psychiatric ward) could prove more often harmful than helpful, while also believing that some nonstandard treatments (e.g., increased physical or social activity, relaxation and stress management, vitamins, and special diets) would prove more helpful than medication. A poll of *Consumer Reports*

readers confirmed the benefits of psychotherapy in the eyes of the public and ascribed increased benefits to a longer duration of treatment and greater experience of the therapist (Seligman, 1995). More recent polls suggested that nearly 20% of Americans have seen a psychotherapist for treatment, and an equal number have taken medication for depression (Adler, 2006).

Research has also taught us that a powerful placebo effect exists with respect to psychotherapy, meaning that good evidence demonstrates that seemingly inert "agents" or "treatments" may prove to have psychotherapeutic effects (Baskin, Tierney, Minami, & Wampold, 2003; Geers, Weiland, Kosbab, Landry, & Helfer, 2005; O'Leary & Borkovec, 1978; Shapiro & Struening, 1973). Aside from the general practice of psychotherapy, we must also consider placebo effects when considering child therapy (Weisz, McCarty, & Valeri, 2006) and so-called positive psychology interventions (Seligman, Steen, Park, & Peterson, 2005). In addition to a general placebo effect, expectations, anticipated outcomes, and fears related to self-disclosure also play a powerful role in predicting results (Vogel, Wester, Wei, & Boysen, 2005).

From the client's viewpoint, it may matter little whether positive changes or perceived improvements result from newly acquired insights, a caring relationship, restructured cognitions, modified behaviors, abandoned irrational beliefs, expectancies, *or* a placebo effect. From the ethical standpoint, the central issue remains *client benefit*. If the client improves as a result of the therapist's placebo value, so much the better. If, however, the client fails to improve or his or her condition worsens while under care, the therapist has an ethical obligation to take corrective action (American Psychological Association [APA] 02: 10.10a). When the client seems to be deteriorating clinically, consultation with more experienced colleagues in an effort to find alternative treatment approaches becomes more urgent. Should a client fail to or cease to benefit from treatment, termination of the relationship and an offer to help the client locate alternative sources of assistance would likely be the best course of action.

Considering the therapist's ethical obligations, recognition of a problem in the therapeutic relationship can prove difficult. Once detected, dealing with a sensitive problem can pose many difficulties. *Recognizing, preventing, and remediating problems in the client–therapist relationship form the crux of ethical concern for client welfare in psychotherapy.*

ETHICAL OBLIGATIONS OF PSYCHOTHERAPISTS

In this chapter, we discuss the nature of the treatment contract and the special obligations of the psychotherapist. In Chapter 6, we discuss technique-oriented ethical problems, such as the special difficulties of multiple-client treatment (i.e., group, marital, and family therapy), sex therapy, hypnosis, behavioral approaches, and unproven or fringe therapies.

In a rather angry and overly one-sided volume about the practice of psychotherapy, which even the most favorable reviewers described as showing questionable scholarship "owing to lack of completeness" (Miller, 1995, p. 132) and "occasionally offering firmer negative conclusions than the data warrant" (p. 131), Robin Dawes (1994) claimed that we (G. P. K. and P. K. S.) have previously viewed the psychologist–client relationship as analogous to that of parent and child. Dawes contended that this results in adhering to a "paternalistic ethic" that allegedly "not only resolves problems raised by the professionals' ambivalent feelings toward their clients but advances the profession" (p. 256).

Our actual view of the ethical obligations of mental health professionals does not arise from any sense of paternalism. Rather, it flows from premises of trust and knowledge of intimate secrets. We do not, as Dawes apparently concluded, espouse the view that psychotherapists position themselves "one up" on their clients as a matter of course. Rather, we believe that clients invest us with a significant degree of confidence when they come seeking help with their most personal concerns. This reliance demands particular safeguards. An airline pilot who takes people where they want to fly, an architect who designs a safe and attractive new home, and the plumber who installs a new toilet in conformity with sanitary codes all exercise a degree of professional expertise to take care of our needs. We rely on these people and trust them to work on our behalf as professionals with special skills. Because the competent psychotherapist has special knowledge and expertise related to understanding human distress, psychopathology, and intervention strategies, a degree of authority accrues, and we must exercise it thoughtfully and collaboratively with the client. We assert that therapists have an *exceptional* responsibility to respect the rights of all clients and to advance their well-being as professional consultants or advisors in partnership with them. This stance should become enabling in every respect, not paternalistic.

The Therapeutic Contract

If a client and therapist expect to form a therapeutic alliance, they must share some basic goals and understandings about their work together. Strupp (1975) noted that clients have a right to know what they are buying, and therapists have a responsibility to address this issue explicitly (p. 39). In warning psychotherapists about how not to fail their clients, Strupp noted three major functions of the psychotherapist.

1. The healing function or the alleviation of emotional suffering through understanding, support, and reassurance.
2. An educational function, including promoting growth, insight, and maturation.
3. A technological function, by which we may apply various techniques to change or modify behavior.

The notion of a client–therapist contract is not new, although attempts to define the parameters of such contracts did not begin until the late 1970s (Everstein et al., 1980; Hare-Mustin, Marecek, Kaplan, & Liss-Levenson, 1979; Harris & Bennett, 2005; Liss-Levenson, Hare-Mustin, Marecek, & Kaplan, 1980). The ethics codes of professional associations and a number of state and federal laws now make it clear that the therapist must inform clients of a number of aspects of the professional relationship at the outset of their work together by addressing informed consent (APA 02: 3.10), the limits of confidentiality (APA 02: 4.02); *Health Insurance Portability and Accountability Act*, (1996), relationships with thirds parties (APA 02: 3.07), and the like.

In general, the notion of contracting dictates that the therapist should assume responsibility to provide clients with the information they need to make their own decisions about therapy. The therapist should be willing to treat the client as any consumer of services has a right to expect. This may include responding to clients' questions about training and experience, attempting to resolve clients' complaints, and even using formal written contracts when indicated (Bennett et al., 2007). Although many therapists do not use written contracts, some therapists and clients do agree to highly structured written documents outlining their relationship in great detail, particularly in certain legal (e.g., court-ordered therapy) or treatment contexts (e.g., work with substance-abusing or suicidal clients). We summarize the essential elements of any client–therapist treatment agreement in Box 5–1 from the perspective of the questions clients may have in mind.

Some state laws have mandated various types of consent to treatment procedures as part of a therapeutic contract. In one attempt to assess the impact of such a law, Handelsman and his colleagues (Handelsman, Martinez, Geisendorfer, & Jordan, 1995) found that psychotherapists in Colorado obeyed the law but did not necessarily provide ethically desirable information in a form that clients could readily use. For example, the average readability of the consent forms they reviewed fell at a grade level of 15.7 (i.e., upper-level college), whereas 64% of the forms reached a readability grade of 17 plus. Some states have placed limits on some psychotherapeutic techniques. For example, on April 17, 2001, then Colorado Governor Bill Owens signed a bill into law that specifically prohibits the use of "rebirthing" techniques by mental health professionals (Colorado Revised Statutes Section 2., 12-43-222). This action occurred 1 year after a 10-year-old girl died while undergoing such therapy. (A more detailed discussion of such unorthodox techniques appears in Chapter 6.)

The Client's Frame of Reference and the Quest for Empiricism

The key assumption implicit in the contracting process requires the therapist to take account of the client's unique frame of reference and personal psychosocial ecology when deciding whether and how to organize treatment. Therapists unfamiliar with the social, economic, and cultural pressures confronting women, minority group members, and the poor may fail to recognize the contribution of such stresses in creating or exacerbating psychological problems. Conventional psychotherapy training historically emphasizes clients' contributions to their problems, at times neglecting to adequately consider the external forces that help to shape the client's behavior.

Beginning in the late 1990s, a zeitgeist focusing on the use of empirical data to validate psychotherapeutic approaches became increasingly prominent. Advocates of this perspective demanded basing clinical practice on robust, primarily research-based evidence. This movement has used various terminology, such as empirically supported treatments (EST), empirically supported relationships (ESR), evidence-based practices (EBPs), and called for the approval of assorted practice guidelines that are focused on diagnostic categories or behavioral symptoms. As several fine collected works have noted (e.g., Castonguay & Beutler, 2006; Norcross et al., 2005; Spirito & Kazak, 2006), some well-researched treatment approaches have proven highly effective in the treatment of some conditions, but many questions remain open, and many challenges continue. Such questions include the following:

- What qualifies as an EBP (e.g., clinical expertise, scientific research, or patient values and preferences)?
- What qualifies as research on which to judge effective practice (e.g., case studies, single-participant design research, qualitative research, effectiveness research, or only randomized clinical trials)?

Box 5–1 Key Elements of a Therapeutic Contract

Setting the goals of treatment
  Who is my client (e.g., an individual, a family, a group)?
  What will we be working toward?
  How will the process of therapy go forward?
  How will we work together?
  When and how often will we meet?
  How can we remain in contact between sessions, when necessary?
  What are the client's rights and responsibilities?
  What are the therapist's rights and responsibilities?
  How does the client's legal status bear on the work (e.g., minor status, mandated treatment, etc.)?

What should both of us expect regarding . . .
  The process of therapy?
  What risks may accompany treatment?
  Fees, methods of payment, and services covered by third-party payments (or not)?
  Treatment techniques to be used?
  Therapist availability and communication modes (e.g., access by telephone or Internet, emergencies, etc.)?
  What are the limits of confidentiality?
  What professional records do I keep?
  What state or federal laws govern access to my records?
  What are my personal policies within the statutory options?
  How does this bear on minors or incompetent clients?

- Which treatment goals or outcome measures should we use to establish EBP (e.g., self-report measures, objective behavioral indices, therapist judgment, external society decisions)?
- Does the use of treatment manuals improve therapy outcomes, and if so, how often (i.e., rarely, sometimes, frequently)?
- How often do research participants and clinical trials adequately represent actual real-world practice?
- What should we actually attempt to validate (e.g., treatment methods, therapists' behavior, therapy relationships, or other variables)?
- Which factors should influence publication, thereby qualifying it as published evidence (e.g., theoretical allegiance, funding source, conventional wisdom, pure-form therapies)?
- Do EBTs produce outcomes superior to non-EBT therapies, and if so, how often?

- How well do EBPs address various dimensions of diversity (e.g., ethnic minority, gender, sexual orientation, disability status)?
- Do efficacious lab-validated treatments readily generalize to clinical practice, and if so, how often?

Consider the following cases:

Case 5–1: Sammy Soggy, age 6, completed toilet training at age 2 but still has occasional bed-wetting "accidents" at night. This nocturnal enuresis seems to have increased in frequency since the birth of a sibling a few months ago. Sammy's parents have consulted child psychiatrist Seymour Toodoo, M.D. Dr. Toodoo has many years experience as a child psychoanalyst and advises the parents that the enuresis most likely represents displaced aggression tied to sibling rivalry. He recommends psychodynamic therapy three times a week to assist Sammy in addressing his tensions related to the new baby.

Dr. Toodoo seems woefully unaware of the significant body of literature documenting the highly beneficial results in treating nocturnal enuresis with brief behavioral interventions (Mellon & McGrath, 2000). Alternatively, he may have theoretical blinders that preclude his recognizing the viability of interventions outside his primary frame of reference. Whatever the reason, failure to attempt state-of-the-art intervention with well-proven efficacy or, at the very least, failure to acknowledge it as a viable alternative to his proposed course of action creates a serious ethical problem.

Case 5–2: Troubled by residual anxiety, sexual assault victim Connie Sensus sought treatment at the Comprehensive Rape Anxiety Program. A newspaper advertisement described the program as having "well-established high success rates." The counselor told Connie about their special 10-session program with "guaranteed results" and explained that the program's founder had developed a validated manual-based treatment approach. Connie agreed to try the program. At the end of each session, the counselor asked her to rate her PLD (personal level of distress) on a 10-point scale of intensity, explaining that she could remain in the treatment program as long as necessary after the 10 sessions ended, free of charge, until her PLD declined to zero as the program's guarantee. Connie did not find the sessions helpful, but felt too unassertive to tell this to the enthusiastic, confidence-exuding counselor. After three sessions with no change and no sense of emotional connection to the counselor, Connie lied. She reported that her PLD had fallen to zero, and that she was done with the treatment.

Connie Sensus has a very unsatisfying treatment experience at the hands of a clinician who seemed bent on applying a formulaic approach to her problems. The difficulty may lie in an attempt to apply a manualized treatment by rote without first investigating the specific needs, desires, and inclinations of the client. Interestingly, Connie's response to the demand characteristics of the situation led her to exit non-

confrontationally by saying she had improved. The counselor probably chalked her response up as yet another successful outcome.

Another element of ethical practice relative to clients' frames of reference involves counseling clients from diverse backgrounds by therapists not trained to work with such groups. Factors associated with age, sex, gender identity, race, ethnicity, culture, national origin, religion, sexual orientation, disability, language, or socioeconomic status all have significant implications for psychotherapeutic work. Many subgroups of society, including women, children, the elderly, people living in institutional care, and some racial or ethnic groups, experience social forces in a manner that may accustom them to having their individual rights to self-determination denied (Liss-Levinson et al., 1980). As just one illustration of the degree to which society inculcates troubling and enduring prejudices, Sue (D. W. Sue, 2003; S. Sue, 1998) invited us to consider "Who owns history?" He noted that traditional instruction in American history and even some IQ tests have suggested that "Columbus discovered America," when the simple fact is that Columbus was lost when he reached the "New World," thinking at first that he had found India.

Another concrete example of the critical need for cultural competence in psychotherapy involves the clinical problem posed by suicidal clients. A series of articles in *Science* (Miller, 2006a, 2006b, 2006c; Zonana, 2003) documented the very different ways that depression and suicide risk become manifest in non-Western populations. For example, some Asian and South American groups may express depressive symptoms more frequently as somatic than emotional. In the Chinese language, for example, the tendency to express emotion in terms of physical distress is clearly demonstrated by use of the word for heart in describing symptoms of depression. These commonly include xinhuang (heart panic), xinfan (heart vexed), and xintong (heart pain). Miller also noted that some Asian populations have no religious or moral taboo against suicide, with the net result that it becomes entertained more frequently as a legitimate option. In Western societies, women attempt suicide more often than men, but men succeed more often. In China, successful suicides by women (particularly in rural areas) outnumber those by men. One study reported data suggesting that for 45% of suicides in China, the contemplation time prior to a suicide attempt was 10 minutes or less (Miller, 2006a).

Therapists must remain sensitive to cultural competence issues and to the general reluctance that an emotionally troubled client may have in asking important questions or raising certain needs or concerns. In such cases, the therapist must assess the client's circumstances carefully and elicit basic information needed to forge a meaningful treatment contract.

Brown (1994) introduced the notion of "empowered consent" as a means of framing what would constitute a genuine and competent informed consent process essential to a therapeutic contract. To provide empowered consent (as opposed to simply informed consent), the therapist considers the quality of information and the manner in which it is presented to maximize the client's optimal capacity to consent freely and knowingly to all aspects of the therapy relationship without feeling in any way coerced. The goal of such a process is to reduce the risk that a therapist might unilaterally impose a risky or unwanted intervention on an unwitting client. Consider these illustrations:

Case 5–3: Marsha Young, a recent business school graduate, won a job at a prestigious advertising agency. The office was highly competitive, and she soon developed anxiety attacks and insomnia. At times, she felt as though she were the "token woman" in the organization, and she feared that her work was being scrutinized far more critically than that of recently hired males. She sought a consultation with Jack Chauvinist, Ph.D. Dr. Chauvinist soon concluded that Ms. Young suffered from "penis envy" and was afraid of heterosexual intimacy. He advised her that it was critical for her to address these matters in therapy if she ever hoped to be able to be married and bear a child, thus fulfilling herself as a woman.

Case 5–4: Yochi Tanaka was the eldest son of a proud Japanese family; he was sent off to attend college in the United States at age 17. He had some difficulty adjusting at the large state university and failed midterm exams in three subjects. Mr. Tanaka sought help at the college counseling center and was seen by Hasty Focus, M.A., an intern. Mr. Focus became misled by Tanaka's excellent command of English, Western-style fashion consciousness, and tendency to nod in seeming assent whenever Focus offered a suggestion or interpretation. Focus failed to recognize the subtle, but stressful, acculturation problems or to detect the growing sense of depression and failure Tanaka was experiencing. Tanaka was apparently unwilling to assert his concerns over the interpretations of the "expert" in an impolite or unseemly fashion. After five sessions and 6 weeks, fearing failure on his final exams and disgrace in the eyes of his family, Tanaka committed suicide.

Case 5–5: Inda Closet had always felt attracted to other women but had dated men from time to time because it was what her parents and society seemed to expect of her. Concerned about sexuality, fearful of social rejection, and wondering about how to explore her sexual feelings, Ms. Closet built up the courage to consult a psychotherapist and made an appointment with Heda Knowsitall, Ph.D. After taking a brief history, Dr. Knowsitall informed Ms. Closet that she was "definitely heterosexual" because "she had a history of dating men and therefore had instinctual drives toward heterosexuality." Closet was advised to enter behavior therapy to "unlearn" her attraction to women.

All three of these cases suggest degrees of incompetence on the part of the therapist, but our intent here is to show that a more central problem was the ultimate failure to adequately detect and incorporate the client's psychosocial needs into the treatment plan. Dr. Chauvinist seems to have ignored some very real life stresses in Ms. Young's psychological and social ecology. He had little sense of her possible career goals, professional interests, or the pressures she might be feeling. Instead, Chauvinist seemed to be relying on a stereotypic interpretation of her complaint, which may have little relevance to her immediate needs or symptoms. Likewise, Mr. Focus was unaware of the cultural pressures his client felt and the impact of these with respect to the current problem. Focus was deceived in part by Tanaka's head nodding, a cultural response intended as a common courtesy, interpreted by Focus as license to pursue irrelevant goals. Dr. Knowsitall manifested little understanding of lesbian sexuality and was far too glib in offering her unfounded opinions as the primary basis for directing therapy. None of these therapists showed much interest in eliciting specific goals or therapeutic direction from the client, although all would probably claim to have done so.

Another sort of dilemma tied to the client's frame of reference and goals involves a tactic described as the "bait and switch" in psychotherapy (Williams, 1985). This term refers to the unethical tactic sometimes used in retail sales. A department store may advertise a product at substantial savings to lure customers into the store. Once on the scene, a salesperson will attempt to make the specific item on sale seem inferior and encourage the client to purchase a more expensive model. Williams drew the analogy between this practice and certain types of long-term psychotherapy. He presented the following comments from one of his clients, describing a previous therapist:

> My physician was concerned that there might be a psychological cause for my high blood pressure, so he sent me to see a psychotherapist. I was eager to go because I had become desperate for some kind of relief, and the medicine I took had too many bad side effects. Psychotherapy was an approach I hadn't even considered. I walked into the therapist's office for my first session. He greeted me and asked me to sit down, and we sat there looking at each other for a while. Finally, he asked me about my sex life, which I said was fine. We looked at each other some more, then he told me that the time was up. He expected to see me the following week, but I never went back (p. 112).

In this case, the client had consulted a therapist for help in managing hypertension. The next thing he knew, the topic of discussion was his sex life. In the client's view, the therapist had a certain agenda different from his own and expected the client to buy it without serious questions. If the client explicitly chose to discuss his sex life or any other issues on his own, or if the therapist indicated some connection might exist between the topic and the presenting symptom, there would have been no "switch" and therefore no ethical problem. If the client decided to seek personal growth and exploration through treatment, there would also be no ethical problem. Instead, however, the story implies that the pursuit of this other issue was a unilateral and never-discussed decision of the therapist, possibly intended to extend the duration of contact with the client. Perhaps this particular approach was therapeutically indicated and perhaps not. Regardless, the rationale should have been discussed openly with the client.

Williams (1985) noted that diverse psychotherapy systems, including psychoanalysis and Gestalt therapy, incorporate rationales for such bait-and-switch tactics (e.g., "the problem is really unconscious, and the patient is unaware of the real meanings," or "anybody who goes to a therapist has something up his sleeve"). However, a theoretical rationale does not make use of the technique ethical. It is clearly possible to retain one's theoretical integrity in any psychotherapy system and still call on the client for active participation in setting goals and doing the work of treatment.

Case 5–6: Mary Slick, Psy.D., advertised a special "assessment package" and low-cost "short-term treatment option" for children with behavior problems at a relatively inexpensive rate. One consumer complained that when she took her child for the appointment she was encouraged to purchase the more expensive "complete assessment battery" rather than the less-costly one advertised.

Dr. Slick's behavior in this case seems more obviously unethical than the situation described by Williams (1985). Dr. Slick advertised an attractive price and then attempted to switch the client to a more expensive arrangement after she arrived at the office. Slick's inclusion of a treatment option as part of an assessment package also sounds suspiciously as though she has preordained the existence of a problem requiring such intervention.

Conflicting Values in Psychotherapy

What about the situation in which the goals and values of the client and therapist are at variance or the result of treatment may be more than the client bargained for? One of the most fundamental dilemmas related to therapy goals is whether to encourage a client to rebel against a repressive environment or attempt to adjust to it (Karasu, 1980). Issues related to abortion choice, sexual preference, religion, and family values are among the potential conflict areas. The therapist must assume responsibility for avoiding the imposition of personal values on the client.

Case 5–7: Arnold Polite, age 14, is referred to Frank Facilit, Psy.D., out of concern that he is becoming increasingly depressed and socially withdrawn. Dr. Facilit finds Arnold to be somewhat inhibited by the close, and at times intrusive, ministrations of his parents while Arnold struggles to develop a sense of adolescent autonomy. Over several months, Facilit sees good progress in his work with Arnold, but then he begins to get telephone calls from Mr. and Mrs. Polite, who express concern that Arnold is becoming too assertive and too interested in people and activities apart from the family. They express the fear that Facilit's work with Arnold will alienate him from the family.

In this instance, the progress of the client toward more developmentally appropriate behavior alters his relationship with his parents, and they may not care for the new behavior. As we discuss in this section, the best interests of one client may well be antithetical to the best interests of a co-client or close family members. Perhaps Dr. Facilit can work toward some accommodation by means of a family conference or similar approach, but the possibility exists that this will not prove satisfactory.

Case 5–8: Sam Escape, age 23, moved from Boston to Chicago and entered psychotherapy with Sidney Silento, Ph.D. Shortly thereafter, Mr. Escape terminated contact with his family in Boston. His parents and an uncle, a psychiatrist, contacted an ethics committee to complain that Dr. Silento would not respond to inquiries about the location or

welfare of the young man. Because Mr. Escape was an adult, the committee was reluctant to become involved; however, it seemed to the committee members that the family was at least entitled to a response to their unanswered letters and phone calls. Dr. Silento ignored three letters from the committee and was then sent a letter from the committee's legal counsel threatening him with sanctions for failure to respond to a duly constituted ethics panel. At that point, Dr. Silento replied apologetically, noting that he was preoccupied with his day-to-day therapeutic efforts and had a poor correspondence filing system. He reported that Mr. Escape sought to establish himself as an autonomous adult in Chicago and did not wish to contact his family or to authorize contacts by Dr. Silento.

In this situation, Dr. Silento had not behaved unethically for failing to give information to the family, although he certainly could have responded to them with that fact rather than simply ignoring their calls and letters. His excuse for failing to respond to the ethics committee over several months constituted another matter. His procrastination only dragged out the case and exacerbated the family's considerable anxiety, while costing the professional association a substantial sum in staff time and legal fees needed to evoke a simple explanation. The extent to which treatment with Dr. Silento contributed to Escape's decision to avoid family contacts remained unclear, although Escape stood well within his rights to do so. Dr. Silento did have a legitimate obligation to respect that decision, even if he felt sympathy for the family.

Case 5–9: Helena Sistine, M.D., a psychiatrist and a conservative Christian, holds deep traditional values. She works in the counseling center of a state university. Carl Quandary came in for an initial appointment and wanted to discuss the anxiety he has experienced over several homosexual contacts he had during the prior 6 months. Mr. Quandary reported, "I don't know what I'm supposed to be. I want to try and figure it out." Dr. Sistine realized that her own feelings of opposition to homosexuality would make it difficult for her to work with Quandary objectively, especially if he should decide to continue having sexual relationships with other men. She listened carefully to his concerns and explained that she planned to refer him to a colleague at the counseling service who had particular experience helping clients with similar issues.

Dr. Sistine recognized her potential value conflict with Quandary's need to make important life decisions according to his own values. In addition, she realized that she lacked familiarity with the life experiences and issues with which he struggled. She also recognized Quandary's highly vulnerable emotional state, so she did not expose her value system to him and did not attempt to engage him in a therapeutic dialogue. Instead, she collected the information needed to make an appropriate referral and presented the referral to the client in a positive manner to minimize the risk of his feeling rejected or abandoned. (In Chapter 6, we address controversies associated with so-called reparative psychotherapies as these might apply in Cases 5–5 and 5–9.)

The key to an ethical response in any treatment involving matters laden with social, political, or religious significance includes conducting a careful assessment and offering an intervention that has proven efficacy and meets the preferences and needs of the client, apart from any preordained biases of the therapist.

Ethnic and Cultural Diversity

More than a decade ago, Hays (1995) noted that clinical literature on multiculturalism mental health tended to focus almost entirely on race and ethnicity. Whatever the reason, that state of affairs ignores many minority populations facing special cultural issues and related needs, for example, elderly people, urban teenagers, gay men, lesbians, religious minorities, people with sensory or mobility disabilities, and people with a serious illness such as AIDS. Hays suggested a model to conceptualize individual differences; she has assigned the model the acronym ADDRESSING, meaning

- age
- disabilities, acquired
- disabilities, developmental
- religion
- ethnicity
- social status
- sexual orientation
- indigenous heritage
- nationality
- gender

Despite the egalitarian appeal of the ADDRESSING concept, we must not lose sight of how critical race and ethnicity are in the United States. Given that the percentages of people of color credentialed as psychotherapists in the United States sits in the single digits, most individuals of color who seek psychotherapy will of necessity get treatment from European Americans. Although all accredited programs must incorporate teaching on matters of diversity, accomplishing this in a sensitive and effective manner is extremely difficult. Tatum (1972, 1997) illustrated the problems inherent in teaching about racism quite effectively by describing and delineating the extent of guilt, anger, and distress involved in confronting issues of racism, even in a supportive setting. Despite frequent encouragement for therapists to become multiculturally competent, we often do not intervene in multiculturally responsive ways. One survey of 149 psychologists regarding their practices and beliefs reported that on 86% of the individual items explored, participants did not practice what they preached. For example, 42% of the respondents rarely or never implemented a professional development plan to improve their multicultural competence, 39% rarely or never sought culture-specific case consultation, and 27% rarely or never referred a client to a more culturally qualified provider (Hansen et al., 2006).

A number of investigators have documented the importance of the therapeutic alliance in the multicultural therapeutic relationship, using the term *culture* in the broadest sense to include ethnicity, race, gender, age, sexual orientation, social class, physical ability, religion and spirituality, nationality, language, immigration and refugee status, and generational level and the interactions among these characteristics (Comaz-Diaz, 2006; Moodley & Palmer, 2006). Box 5–2 provides a list of 10

Box 5–2 Key Considerations on Addressing Cultural Issues in Psychotherapy

1. Recognize that cultural differences are subjective, complex, and dynamic.
2. Understand that forming a good therapeutic alliance requires addressing the most salient cultural differences first.
3. Addressing similarities can form a good prelude to discussion of cultural differences.
4. Recognize that the client's level of distress and presenting problem will influence appropriate timing for discussion of cultural differences in psychotherapy.
5. Consider cultural differences as assets that can advance the therapeutic process.
6. Understanding the client's cultural history and racial identity development is critical to assessing how best to conceptualize presenting problems and achieve treatment goals.
7. The meanings and salience of cultural differences are influenced by ongoing issues within the psychotherapeutic relationship.
8. The psychotherapeutic relationship exists embedded within the broader cultural context, which in turn affects the relationship.
9. The therapist's cultural competence will have an impact on the way differences are addressed.
10. Dialogues about cultural differences can have an effect on the client's cultural context.

Source: Adapted from La Roche and Maxie (2003).

---

critical considerations about which therapists should remain mindful as they attempt to function effectively in a multicultural clinical context (La Roche & Maxie, 2003).

We have adapted the next set of case vignettes from reports about a prior therapist made by clients to a subsequent therapist, who shared them with us for teaching purposes (J. Daniel, personal communication, December 1995).

Case 5–10: During her first session with Nan Turner, a 28-year-old African-American woman, Darla Dense, M.D., asked about which part of the urban ghetto Turner had grown up. Turner explained that she grew up in the same suburban community as Dr. Dense, but the psychiatrist could not believe some of the experiences Turner reported. Dr. Dense's perceptions of the town were quite different from Ms. Turner's, and Dense could not recognize the possibility of such things happening, so she concluded that Turner was either misrepresenting her past due to shame or had poor reality testing abilities.

Case 5–11: When Henry Tower, an African-American college student over 6 feet tall, went to the University Counseling Center for help in dealing with difficulties he was experiencing on cam-

pus, he was assigned to Biff Jerko, Psy.D. In an effort to "forge an early alliance," Dr. Jerko attempted to greet Mr. Jackson with a "high five" instead of a more traditional handshake. During the course of the session, Dr. Jerko continued his "attempt to connect" by using profanity and slang that he regarded as emulating "ghetto talk." Mr. Jackson wanted to talk about the fact that his imposing stature and dark skin seemed to make people uncomfortable. Dr. Jerko quickly attempted to reassure Mr. Jackson that he would be judged only by his character and studies on campus and resisted exploring the impact of prejudice that may accrue to tall black males. Neither the hand greeting nor slang use were a part of Mr. Jackson's background, and both were perceived as alienating. Adding insult to injury, Dr. Jerko asked Mr. Jackson whether he planned to try out for the college basketball team. Jackson did not have the energy or assertiveness to attempt reeducation of the therapist, and he never returned for another appointment.

Case 5–12: Carlotta Familia, a Latino woman in her early 20s, was struggling with issues involving her relationship with her mother when she sought consultation with Carl Cutter, M.S.W. Ms. Hernandez was the first college-educated person in her extended family and was torn between traditional obligations to family and her newly experienced social mobility. Mr. Cutter praised her academic achievement and encouraged her to sever or at least minimize contact with her family, which continued to reside in a poor inner-city neighborhood. He did not understand the importance of balancing family connections with individual achievement manifested in many Latino cultures. Ms. Hernandez needed to pursue options of how to stay connected in an emotionally healthy way. The more Mr. Cutter pressed her to disconnect, the more depressed she became.

Case 5–13: Pam Passer, a very fair-skinned African American, was concerned about just how "Black" she was given that she could "pass" as White. Robert Blinders, L.M.H.C., her therapist, dismissed such concerns, stating that she should just see herself "as an American." Passing for White might give her greater social and professional mobility, but the price would be disconnection from her family and the community in which she was raised. Dr. Blinders could not hear the implications of the disconnections for her as these were not his values.

These case examples illustrate a range of inappropriate behaviors with a common theme: insensitivity or inadequate attention to the individualized needs of clients who are different because of race or social class. Dr. Dense made damaging assumptions regarding her client and could not entertain the concept that the client's reality of living in the same town might be different from her own. Dr. Jerko based his feeble attempt at establishing rapport on caricature stereotypes and could not recognize or acknowledge the impact of being a large Black man on Mr. Jackson's day-to-day existence in a biased society. Mr. Cutter and Dr. Blinders could not grasp the struggle for acceptance and accomplishment balanced with the need to value family connections that is very much a part of life for many ethnic minorities. Being uninformed, unwilling to learn, unable to hear, and relying on stereotypes as reality remain major ethical problems to which too many mental health professionals are inadequately attentive.

Just as one can not reasonably expect that any given therapist will have the ability to adequately meet the treatment needs of every client, it is also unreasonable to expect that the ideal therapist (i.e., in terms of ethnicity, culture, etc.) for any given client will be readily available in every community. In recognition of this reality, the APA has assembled a series of guidelines to assist therapists in enhancing their sensitivity and understanding of diverse client needs. These APA guidelines have addressed sex bias (1975); psychotherapy with women and girls (1978, 2006); work with gay or lesbian clients (1991); intervention with ethnically, culturally, or linguistically diverse client populations (1990); and multicultural education, training, research, practice, and organizational change (2005).

In unusual situations, one can often learn much simply by asking direct questions.

Case 5–14: Annie Pueblo was a 5-year-old Native American who had been relocated along with her mother from her home on a reservation to a major urban center by the Federal Indian Health Service. Annie was in critical need of an organ transplant and was "on standby" at a large medical center. A nurse became concerned after overhearing a partial conversation in which Annie and her mother were talking about communicating with the dead. The nurse expressed her concern to the consulting psychologist on the organ transplant team: "Conversations about such things are certain to depress the child." The psychologist met with the child, who told him of a dream: "Dead people are trying to give me food, but I'm not gonna take it!" The child's mental status and behavior were normal aside from these unusual remarks, so the psychologist sought out the child's mother and asked for her help by noting, "I'm not familiar with the ways of your people. Do you have any ideas about why Annie is saying this?" The mother laughed and explained that Annie had reported dreaming of an old woman in distinctive costume who offered her food. The mother explained that she did not know who it could be, so she telephoned her own mother on the reservation. Annie's grandmother listened to the report of the dream and immediately recognized the spirit of her own mother. The dream spirit was Annie's long-deceased great-

great-grandmother coming to watch over her. This was a good and protective omen; however, it is also very important that one not accept food from spirits of the dead. Doing so requires that you join them. It was important that Annie know how to accept the protection but decline the food (e.g., pretend you don't hear the offer or politely say, "Thank you, but I'm not hungry").

By seeking information, the psychologist picked up valuable data that could be used to assure the nursing staff that Annie was in no way depressed or being put at risk. In fact, Annie had been given culturally appropriate information that helped her to feel cross-generational social support in a way that the local health care team could not provide. By recognizing that this family was culturally different, and by respectfully seeking information about those differences, the psychologist was able to defuse misunderstandings and educate others on the hospital staff. (For an excellent commentary on cultural diversity issues in the treatment of children, readers are directed to Tharp, 1991.)

Consent for Treatment

We discuss matters of informed consent and the right to refuse participation at many points in this book, especially in relation to confidentiality (Chapter 8) and participation in research (Chapter 19). From the client's frame of reference, however, consent issues in the context of psychotherapy may feel quite different. Psychotherapy unavoidably affects important belief systems and social relationships. Consider, for example, the case study of Mary, a Christian Scientist with a socially reinforced obsessive disorder (Cohen & Smith, 1976). In a discussion of the ethics of informed consent in this case, Mary clearly experienced some sense of divided loyalties about her religious practices as a result of psychotherapy. Coyne (1976) noted "even the simplest intervention may have important repercussions for the client's belief system and social relationships" (p. 1015).

The consent-getting process for mental health professionals should generally involve a discussion with clients of goals, expectations, procedures, and potential risks (Becker-Blease & Freyd, 2006; Bennett et al., 2007; Everstein et al., 1980; Hare-Mustin et al., 1979; Vogel & Wester, 2003). (The need to disclose the limits of confidentiality in particular is discussed in Chapter 8.) Clients might also reasonably expect warning about other foreseeable as well as unforeseen effects of treatment. Obviously, no therapist can anticipate every potential indirect effect, but a client who presents with marital complaints, for example, might change behavior or make decisions that could drastically alter the dynamics of the relationship for better or worse. Likewise, a client who presents with job-related complaints might choose to change employment as a result of therapy. Such cautions seem particularly warranted when the client has many inadequately addressed issues and the therapist suspects that uncovering these concerns (e.g., long-repressed anger) might lead to distressing feelings.

Consider the married adult who enters individual psychotherapy hoping to overcome individual and interpersonal problems and to enhance the marriage. What if the result leads to a decision by one partner to dissolve the marriage?

Case 5–15: Tanya Wifely enters psychotherapy with Nina Peutic, L.M.F.C., complaining of depression, feelings of inadequacy, and an unsatisfactory sexual relationship with her spouse. As treatment progresses, Ms. Wifely becomes more self-assured, less depressed, and more active in initiating sexual activity at home. Her husband feels ambivalent regarding the changes and the increased sense of autonomy he sees in his wife. He begins to believe that she is observing and evaluating him during sexual relations, which leads him to become uncomfortable and increasingly frustrated. He begins to pressure his wife to terminate therapy and complains to an ethics committee when she instead decides to separate from him.

We certainly do not have sufficient information to elucidate all of the psychodynamics operating in this couple's relationship, but treatment did change it. Perhaps Ms. Wifely experiences the change as one for the better. She certainly has the right to choose to separate from her spouse and continue in treatment. On the basis of these facts, we can not conclude that Ms. Peutic did anything unethical. However, we do not know whether Ms. Peutic ever informed Ms. Wifely that her obligation as a therapist was to Wifely's mental and emotional health, not to the marriage. We must wonder whether the outcome might have been different had Ms. Peutic warned Ms. Wifely that changes could occur in the marriage as a result of her individual therapy.

The Right to Refuse Treatment

A client who does not like the specifications and risk–benefit statement offered by the therapist can generally decide not to seek treatment or to seek alternative care. Some clients do not have such a choice. These clients may include patients confined in mental hospitals and minors brought for treatment by their parents or guardians. We discuss some ethical issues related to special work settings (e.g., schools, the military, and correctional institutions) in Chapter 18. However, therapists should take pains to recognize and respect the rights and preferences of clients regarding the conduct and goals of psychotherapy, particularly when the client has particular vulnerabilities (e.g., those associated with institutional confinement).

In the landmark case *O'Connor v. Donaldson* (1975), the U.S. Supreme Court recognized for the first time a constitutional basis for a "right to treatment" for the nondangerous mentally ill patient. Mr. Donaldson suffered from schizophrenia, and his father sought to have him committed for psychiatric care. Once in the hospital, Mr. Donaldson declined somatic treatments based on his Christian Science religious beliefs. He remained confined for refusing medication, despite the fact that he posed no danger to himself or others. No verbal or behavioral therapies were offered. This ruling essentially said that the state could not confine such patients unless treatment was provided. Yet, what if the patient does not want the treatment? A host of lawsuits asserting the right of mental patients to refuse treatment, especially

those that involve physical interventions (e.g., drugs, psychosurgery, and electroconvulsive shock therapy), have highlighted special ethical problems (Appelbaum & Gutheil, 1980; White & White, 1981). In particular, the right of the patient to refuse medication has been described ironically as the "psychiatrist's double bind" (Ford, 1980) and dramatically as the "right to rot" (Appelbaum & Gutheil, 1980).

Until recently, nonphysician psychotherapists historically have not had legal authorization to employ somatic psychotherapeutic tools (e.g., medication, psychosurgery, and shock therapies) and have therefore not yet become the object of such suits. Nurse practitioners practicing psychotherapy and psychopharmacology and psychologists authorized to prescribe (as discussed in Chapter 4) may soon find themselves the focus of litigation by clients wishing to refuse medications, as happened to Dr. O'Connor, the psychiatrist in *O'Connor v. Donaldson*. However, a pair of more recent federal court cases provides an intricately complex set of legal and ethical issues.

Case 5–16: Charles Sell, D.D.S., practiced as a dentist in Missouri and had a troubled emotional history. In September 1982, after telling doctors that the gold he used for fillings had been contaminated by communists, Sell was hospitalized, treated with antipsychotic medication, and discharged.

- In June 1984, he called the police to report a leopard was outside his office boarding a bus, and he then asked the police to shoot him (i.e., Dr. Sell). On other occasions, he complained that public officials, a state governor and the police chief, were trying to kill him.

- In April 1997, he told law enforcement personnel that he "spoke to God last night," and that "God told me every person I kill, a soul will be saved."

- In May, 1997, the U.S. government charged Sell with Medicaid, insurance, and mail fraud, alleging he had submitted multiple false claims. A judge ordered a psychiatric examination and found Sell "currently competent" but noted that Sell might experience "a psychotic episode" in the future. The judge released Sell on bail. A grand jury later indicted Sell and his wife on numerous counts of mail fraud, Medicaid fraud, and money laundering.

- In early 1998, the government claimed that Sell had sought to intimidate a witness. During a bail revocation hearing, Sell's behavior at his initial appearance was, in the judge's words, "totally out of control," involving "screaming and shouting," the use of "personal insults" and "racial epithets," and spitting "in the judge's face." The judge revoked Sell's bail.
- In April 1998, the grand jury issued a new indictment charging Sell with attempting to murder the agent from the Federal Bureau of Investigation who had arrested him and a former employee who planned to testify against him in the fraud case.
- In early 1999, the court sent Sell to the U.S. Medical Center for Federal Prisoners at Springfield, Missouri, for examination. Subsequently, the judge found that Sell was "mentally incompetent to stand trial." He ordered Sell "hospitalized for treatment" at the Medical Center for up to 4 months "to determine whether there was a substantial probability that [Sell] would attain the capacity to allow his trial to proceed."
- Two months later, medical center staff recommended that Sell take antipsychotic medication. Sell refused to do so. The staff sought permission to administer the medication against Sell's will.

The U.S. Supreme Court ruled by a 6–3 majority that the government may involuntarily administer antipsychotic medications to a mentally ill defendant to render the defendant competent to stand trial, "but only if the treatment is medically appropriate, is substantially unlikely to have side effects that may undermine the fairness of the trial and, taking account of less intrusive alternatives, is necessary significantly to further important governmental trial-related interests." The Court clarified that (1) in determining whether the government has an important interest in bringing a defendant to trial, a trial court must consider whether the defendant will be civilly committed or has already been detained for a lengthy period; (2) the government must show that the medication is substantially likely to render the defendant competent to stand trial; (3) the court must find that no alternative, less intrusive approach is likely to achieve substantially the same result of restoring a defendant to competency; and (4) the particular medication must be in the patient's best interest, taking into account both efficaciousness and side effects (*Sell v. United States*, 2003). Based on this ruling, mental health professionals will want to give careful consideration to the role that forced medication may play in the lives of very troubled clients who become involved with the legal system (Heilbrun & Kramer, 2005).

Case 5–17: Nancy Hargrave had a long history of paranoid schizophrenia and multiple admissions to the Vermont State Hospital. During a period of emotional stability, when not hospitalized, Ms. Hargrave completed an advance directive in the form of a durable power of attorney (DPOA) for health care. The document designated a substitute decision maker in case she again became psychotic and incompetent by reason of psychosis. The DPOA specified that she wished to refuse "any and all anti-psychotic, neuroleptic, psychotropic, or psychoactive medications" should she ever again be involuntarily committed.

The state legislature subsequently passed Act 114, a 1998 Vermont statute that attempted to address a dilemma inherent in such psychiatric advance directives. Although intended to facilitate patients' participation in treatment decisions, such DPOAs have the potential to prevent all treatment, even of patients who are ill enough to qualify for civil commitment under dangerousness standards. The statute allowed hospital (or prison) personnel to seek court permission to treat incompetent involuntarily committed patients, notwithstanding any advance directives to the contrary. Ms. Hargrave believed that the new law violated her rights under the Americans With Disabilities Act.

The U.S. District Court and the Second Circuit Court of Appeals agreed, failing to find any of these state's contentions persuasive.

With regard to claims that Hargrave and other involuntarily committed patients constitute a direct threat, the three-judge panel noted that not all committed patients would pose a threat to others, as required under the Americans With Disabilities Act, because many became hospitalized only for danger to themselves. Even people found to be dangerous to others at the time of commitment, the court held, could not still be presumed dangerous when seeking to override their advance directives. Hence, the court concluded that the statute violated the Americans With Disabilities Act and enjoined its enforcement (Appelbaum, 2004).

One predictable development on the basis of cases finding a right to refuse medication and other somatic treatments is an increased demand for nonmedical approaches to the treatment of psychological disorders. There are instances in which institutionalized clients have asserted a right to refuse psychological treatment not involving somatic approaches, but these have generally been technique related (e.g., behavior modification and aversive therapies) and are discussed in Chapter 6.

Obtaining consent for treatment from a minor presents another set of issues (Koocher & Keith-Spiegel, 1990; Melton, Koocher, & Saks, 1983; Molin & Palmer, 2005; Parekh, 2007; Pinnock & Crosthwaite, 2005; Potter, 2004). Although a small number of states (e.g., the Commonwealth of Virginia) permit minors to consent to psychotherapy independently of their parents, such authority represents an exception to the norm. In some states, such services could conceivably be provided as adjuncts to a minor's right to seek, without parental consent, birth control or treatment for sexually transmitted diseases or substance abuse. Usually, however, a parent's permission would be needed to undertake psychotherapy with a minor client (Koocher, 1995, 2003). If a child wishes to refuse treatment authorized by a parent, there will most likely be no legal recourse, even if the proposed treatment involves inpatient confinement (Koocher, 2003; Melton et al., 1983; Weithorn, 1987, 2006). The courts have tended to assume that the mental health professional called on to hospitalize or treat the child at the parent's behest is an unbiased third party who can adequately assess what is best for the child (J. L. v. Parham, 1976; Parham v. J. R., 1979). Some mental health professionals have argued that the best interests of parents are not necessarily those of children, and that mental health professionals are not always able to function in the idealized unbiased third-party role imagined by the court (Koocher, 1983; Melton et al., 1983; Weithorn, 1987, 2006).

Case 5–18: Jackie Fled, age 13, walks into the Downtown Mental Health Center and asks to talk to someone. Jackie is seen by Amos Goodheart, Ph.D., and tells him of many personal and family problems, including severe physical abuse at home. Jackie asks Dr. Goodheart not to discuss the case with "anyone, especially my folks." Dr. Goodheart discusses his options with Jackie, explaining that he can not offer treatment to anyone under 18 years of age without parental consent. Goodheart also discusses his duty to report suspected child abuse to the state's Department of Child Welfare. Jackie feels betrayed.

Some decisions are too difficult or complex for children to make independently (Koocher, 2003). While it is clear that some children under age 18 may be competent to consent to treatment in the intellectual and emotional sense, it is also evident that many are not (Grisso & Vierling, 1978). Dr. Goodheart recognized two important legal obligations and an additional ethical obligation. First, he recognized that he could not legally accept Jackie's request as a competent informed consent for treatment with all that it implies (including responsibility to pay for services), although it did not occur to him to provide Jackie with a careful explanation about the limits of confidentiality from the start of their session, as required under HIPAA (Health Insurance Portability and Accountability Act, 1996). Second, he recognized his obligation to report the case to authorities duly constituted to handle child abuse complaints. This is a statutory obligation in all states, although it certainly would have been less than professionally responsible had he sent Jackie home to additional potential abuse and done nothing. Finally, he recognized Jackie's rights as a person and a client, taking the time to discuss his intended course of action with Jackie, thereby showing considerable respect for the child.

SPECIAL OBLIGATIONS OF THE THERAPIST

At this point, it may seem that we have already discussed many obligations of mental health professionals to their clients. However, there are three special types of obligation that deserve highlighting: respect for the client, even the difficult or obnoxious client; duties owed to clients who make threats; and the obligation to terminate a relationship when it is clear that the client is not benefiting. These are common factors related to ethical complaints. That is, few clients complain to ethics committees about a psychologist's failure to obtain treatment consent or adequately consider their cultural value system. However, many complaints grow out of cases related to particularly difficult clients or the failure to terminate a nonbeneficial relationship or treatment that has "gone wrong" (APA 02: 10.10).

The Exceptionally Difficult Client

The definition of the exceptionally difficult type of client is a relative one because the client who may prove difficult for one therapist could be another's forte. However, some types of clients would be considered difficult by virtually any therapist. These include the client who makes frequent suicidal threats, who is intimidating or dangerous, who fails to show for appointments or fails to pay bills, who is actively decompensating and acting out, who is overly dependent and telephones with urgent concerns at all hours of the day and night, or who harasses the therapist's family.

Case 5–19: Robert Bumble, L.M.H.C., began treating a troubled young woman in an office at his home. Mr. Bumble failed to recognize signs of increasing paranoid decompensation in his client until she began to act out destructively in his office. At that point, he attempted to refer her elsewhere, but she reacted with increased paranoia and rage.

Mr. Bumble terminated the relationship, or so he thought. The ex-client took an apartment across the street from his home to spy on him, telephoned him at all hours of the day and night with an assortment of complaints and explicit threats, and filed several ethical complaints against him.

Mr. Bumble failed to realize that his client was beyond his ability to treat until matters had seriously deteriorated. When he finally recognized that the case had gone awry, there was little he could do. Although many of the client's bizarre accusations proved unfounded, it was evident to the committee that Bumble had been practicing beyond his level of competence and, as a result, had contributed to the client's problems. Bumble ultimately had to seek police protection and obtain a court restraining order in an effort to stop his ex-client's intrusive harassment. Bumble also learned a lesson about a potential downside to using an office in one's home.

Case 5–20: An ethics committee received a long, handwritten letter from Anna Crock, an anguished client of a public agency, complaining that Ira Brash, Ph.D., the supervisor of her therapist, had treated her in an unprofessional manner, creating considerable stress and depression. The therapist was a psychology intern who was apparently having severe difficulties with Ms. Crock and had asked her to attend a joint meeting with Dr. Brash. Crock had seen the intern for 14 sessions but had never met the supervisor. She complained that during the joint session Dr. Brash was extremely confrontational. The committee wrote to Dr. Brash asking for his account of these events. Brash gave a clinical description of Ms. Crock's "negative transference" to the intern. Ms. Crock allegedly treated the intern in a hostile manner, calling him "stupid" and "a know-nothing." He indicated that the joint meeting was an attempt to "work through" the problem. He stated that the use of confrontational tactics was an effort to get Ms. Crock to release some feelings. He stated that he had to leave the joint meeting early and alleged that after his departure the intern berated Ms. Crock for her abusive behavior during the joint meeting and abruptly terminated her. Dr. Brash attempted to remedy this later in another meeting with Ms. Crock, in which, by her account, "He was a completely different person." However, she was still quite angry.

The case of Ms. Crock, Dr. Brash, and the intern has a number of troubling elements. To begin, Ms. Crock thought that treatment had gone well for 14 weeks, whereas the intern and his supervisor believed that treatment was progressing poorly. Brash's attempt to handle a complicated clinical problem in a single session, which he had to leave prematurely, showed questionable judgment. His use of a confrontational style with Crock in the absence of a therapeutic contract, alliance, or even minimal rapport also seemed questionable in the ethics committee's view. The committee also chastised Dr. Brash for attempting to shift some of the responsibility for the premature termination to the intern. As the supervisor, Brash could not escape ultimate responsibility. Poor communication, a difficult client, an attempt to move too quickly in therapy, and a botched termination all combined in a manner that left the client feeling angry and hurt.

In working with challenging clients, it is essential that therapists remain cognizant of their professional and personal limitations. This means knowing enough not to take on clients that one is not adequately prepared to treat or knowing enough to help clients in need of different services to find these services early in the relationship rather than waiting until problems develop. Some types of clients seem especially likely to evoke troubling feelings therapists. The client who is verbally abusive or sarcastic or does not speak very much during the session can certainly generate a number of unpleasant feelings on the therapist's part. Also, remember that therapists have no obligation to take on all comers. Habitual substance abusers, pedophiles, individuals with borderline personality disorders, people involved with legal proceedings, and individuals with histories of violence can easily demand levels of special expertise that many therapists may not possess. When a therapist feels personally or professionally unprepared to take on a client, a prompt referral elsewhere will usually prove the best course of action.

There is nothing unethical about refusing to treat a client who stirs up troubling feelings or anger in the therapist. In fact, it is probably more appropriate to refer such clients than to try to treat them while struggling with strong countertransference. On the other hand, it is important to minimize the risk and discomfort to all clients. One should therefore learn to identify those sorts of clients one can not or should not work with and refer them appropriately and quickly without causing them personal uneasiness or stress.

Case 5–21: Jack Fury was an angry 15-year-old referred to Harold Packing, M.D., for displaying antisocial behavior, including school vandalism. After the fourth session, while Dr. Packing was in an appointment with the next client, they smelled smoke and discovered that a fire had been set in the waiting room. The fire was put out, and Dr. Packing called Jack and his parents in for a meeting. Jack acknowledged setting the fire. When Packing expressed concern that he could have been killed in the blaze, Jack replied, "Everybody's got to go sometime."

Dr. Packing felt so angry at Jack Fury's fire setting and subsequent indifference that he was unwilling to continue treating him. Whereas some therapists might have agreed to continue working with Jack, Dr. Packing was not. Presumably, he would be willing to refer the family elsewhere, giving the new therapist an appropriate warning about Jack's behavior. Packing recognized these feelings and dealt with them promptly. Psychotherapists have no ethical obligation to continue treating clients when threatened or otherwise endangered by that client or another person with whom the client has a relationship (APA 02: 10.10b). After all, one can hardly devote full professional attention to such clients with threats or danger looming.

Case 5–22: Serena Still contacted Patience McGraw, M.S.W., seeking psychotherapy as a means to overcome her shyness and difficulty in establishing new relationships. The sessions were characterized by long periods of silence. Ms. McGraw found herself unable to draw Ms. Still into conversation aside from the most superficial pleasantries. She tried several different approaches, including asking Ms. Still to write down her thoughts about events between sessions, but Ms. Still remained taciturn and uncommunicative. After four such sessions, Ms. McGraw suggested that perhaps she should attempt to help Ms. Still find a therapist with whom she could communicate better, or that they should discontinue sessions until Ms. Still had some issues she wished to discuss.

Ms. McGraw had a somewhat different problem. Her client's stated problem was shyness, and this seems the manifest symptom the client has not felt able to address in treatment sessions. Ms. McGraw's best efforts to engage the client have been fruitless, and she feels somewhat frustrated. Certainly, she should raise the problem directly with Ms. Still and explore alternatives (e.g., a different therapist or a break in the treatment program), but she should do this as gently as possible given the likelihood that this is a source of probable anxiety for the client. We address the matter of the client who is not benefiting from treatment in a separate section. We raise the problem of Ms. Still to underscore therapists' common tendency to become angry by a client's lack of participation, resulting in a failure to be fully sensitive to the client's fears.

Yet another type of difficult client is the one whose behavior or problems tend to interact with the psychological conflicts of the therapist to cause special countertransference situations.

Case 5–23: Barbara Storm sought a consultation from Michael Splitz, Psy.D., shortly following her divorce. Splitz was also recently divorced, although he did not mention this to Ms. Storm. Her presenting complaint was that she had difficulty controlling her rage toward her ex-spouse. As Dr. Splitz listened to her vindictive attacks on her ex-husband, he found himself tensing considerably and continually biting his lip. Minutes later, Ms. Storm screamed and fled out of the office. She wrote to an ethics committee, complaining that Dr. Splitz was a vampire. The committee feared that they were dealing with a very disturbed complainant, but contacted Dr. Splitz, asking if he could provide any explanation for her perception.

Dr. Splitz recounted essentially the same story, noting he had unconsciously bitten his lip

to the point that it began to bleed. He had not realized it until after Ms. Storm had left, when he looked in a mirror and saw the trickle of blood that ran from his lip to his shirt collar.

Aside from the unfortunate stress the incident caused Ms. Storm, the scene might have been laughable. The point here is that therapists must strive for sufficient self-awareness to recognize their anger toward clients and make every effort to avoid acting out or otherwise harming the client unnecessarily. There are many appropriate ways to handle anger toward a client, ranging from direct overt expression (e.g., "I am annoyed that you kicked that hole in my office wall and am going to charge you the cost of repairing it") to silent self-exploration (e.g., the client who stirs up countertransference feelings because of similarities to some "significant other" in the therapist's life). The therapist should always consider the client vulnerable to harm and avoid using the power position inherent in the therapist role to the client's detriment. When such problems occur more than rarely in a therapist's career, it is likely that one is practicing beyond the scope of personal competence or has a personal problem that needs attention.

The most difficult sort of client a psychotherapist can encounter is one who not only presents a clinical challenge but also presents issues that resonate heavily with personal concerns of the therapist.

Case 5–24: Ralph Redneck, a 15-year-old high school sophomore, has sought treatment in response to feelings of inadequacy and embarrassment about his lack of athletic ability and late pubertal development. A good therapeutic alliance has formed, and Ralph is working effectively on these sensitive issues. As he has felt more comfortable in therapy, Ralph has begun to evidence a considerable amount of racial and ethnic prejudice. He often criticizes some of his classmates as "niggers" or "Jew bastards." Ralph is unaware that his "White" therapist is Jewish and married to a person of color.

The case of Ralph Redneck focuses clearly on the clash of client and therapist values. Should the therapist offer self-disclosure in an effort to provoke some enlightened attitude change on Ralph's part? After all, Ralph clearly did not seek psychotherapy to improve his racial sensitivity. In such cases, the therapist should make every effort to maintain clear personal boundaries and focus treatment on the issues raised by the client. Should Ralph discover that his prejudices apply to the therapist, it would then be appropriate to discuss them as one would any aspect of the therapeutic relationship. Self-disclosure and initiation of such a discussion by the therapist, however, would constitute an inappropriate intrusion into Ralph's ongoing treatment because Ralph does not (at least initially) experience his biases as problems. Attempting to call his attention to these prejudices could place additional emotional stress on Ralph while not addressing the problems he presented in requesting help.

A more difficult question is whether Ralph's therapist can maintain an adequately empathic relationship or whether negative countertransference and conscious anger will begin to compromise treatment. This is a question that therapists must ask themselves frequently when clients present values conflicting with those of the therapist, but unrelated to the foci of treatment. In such circumstances, the most appropriate course of action for the therapist would involve seeking guidance or perhaps therapeutic consultation from a colleague to assess the legitimate therapeutic needs of the client as distinct from their own. The therapist's issues should never become the client's problems.

Case 5–25: Two weeks prior to his scheduled appearance before the state parole board, Mickey Malevolent telephoned Charlene Choice, M.S.W., from prison. Mr. Malevolent explained that he was in the 8th year of a 20-year criminal sentence for child rape and ritualized sexual abuse of children and was now eligible to apply for an early release from prison. He explained that his case before the parole board would be helped if he could line up a psychotherapist to work with him after release. Mr. Malevolent noted that he was innocent of all wrongdoing, despite his conviction, but had been "framed" and "railroaded" by the parents of several "oversexed kids" and a legal system biased against his satanic religious beliefs. He went on to say that he really did not need therapy but just

wanted to show the authorities that he knew "how to play their game." When Ms. Choice declined to take him as a client, Mr. Malevolent filed an ethics complaint, claiming that Ms. Choice had unreasonably discriminated against him by not accepting him as a potential client or offering him a referral to another practitioner.

Ms. Choice found herself confronted with a self-referral from an individual whose conduct and belief system she found despicable. She has no ethical obligation to take any particular new client who calls for an appointment. She is free to turn down any such referral without giving a reason. In addition, she has ample reason to believe that Mr. Malevolent is not truly seeking treatment but rather is seeking to manipulate the parole system. By his own statements, Mr. Malevolent presents himself as an individual unlikely to make appropriate use of psychotherapy and who may be at high risk to offend again. In addition, she has no ethical or professional obligation to Mr. Malevolent and need not assist him locating another therapist. In fact, she might be doing a disservice to colleagues were she to pass their names on to Mr. Malevolent, who might mistakenly assume that her referral was a recommendation that they agree to work with him.

When a Client Threatens

The worst thing the therapist can do when a client becomes threatening is nothing. Do not assume that the threats will stop or go away spontaneously. All threats or acts of violence by clients should be taken seriously. Such threats should trigger a reassessment of the patient, the diagnosis, and the treatment plan. Violence may escalate over time, and verbal threats may progress to actions. Pay special attention to the client's history with respect to violence or acting out. But remember, although prior violence may be a predictor of future violence, there was always a first time. Make it clear to patients who verbally abuse or threaten that such behavior is unacceptable and could lead to termination of the relationship. Document all threats, your responses, and the rationales for your responses in your clinical record (Bongar, 2002; Vande-

Creek, 2005; VandeCreek & Knapp, 2000). Duties to warn and protect third parties are discussed in Chapter 8, but the same action principles apply whether the threat is made to the therapist or to others.

Clients who threaten are often overwhelmed by personal or family distress. Many have serious mental illness in addition to difficulty with impulse control, problems with anger control, or a history of antisocial behavior (Deffenbacher, 1994). Be mindful of the potential danger when taking on such clients and be certain you are reasonably qualified to handle what may come up (Blau, 1987; Botkin & Nietzel, 1987). When conducting intake interviews with new or prospective clients, be sure to ask about difficulties in these areas (Bennett et al., 2007; Knapp & VandeCreek, 2000). Consider asking, "What is the most violent or destructive thing you have ever done?"

When threats occur, obtain consultation on the case as soon as practical from your attorney and senior colleagues. Do not wait until an event occurs to hunt for such consultants. Draw up a list of names and telephone numbers of potential consultants and keep it available. State psychological associations will often prove especially helpful in referring colleagues to attorneys in their geographic area who are familiar with psychological practice issues. Review your treatment plan and revise it to take into account the new developments. Consider a hierarchy of responses from least intrusive to more confrontational, keeping the safety of yourself and others in mind. Be certain that you are not alone in the office area or at a remote location when meeting with the potentially violent client. If working in an institution, notify security personnel. When threats or actions occur outside the office, contact the police. If work with the client is to continue, set clear rules regarding threatening behavior and consider increasing the frequency of sessions with a focus on rage and fear themes (Blau, 1987; VandeCreek, 2005; VandeCreek & Knapp, 2000). Clinical competence, good diagnostic skills, an understanding of the confidentiality issues involved (see Chapter 8), and careful advance planning are the best preventive measures.

Sometimes, there is simply not much that a therapist can do to avoid becoming the victim of an angry client:

Case 5–26: Bertha Blitz had intermittently failed to keep or cancel several appointments with her psychotherapist, Vic Tem, Psy.D. After several warnings, Dr. Tem informed Ms. Blitz that he would have to begin charging a fee for missed sessions not properly canceled in advance, as specified in the written billing policies she had received at the start of therapy. Blitz missed the next session without canceling, and during the subsequent kept appointment Dr. Tem reminded her that there would be a fee for the missed appointment. Ms. Blitz said that she had used the time to go to a smoking cessation group as Dr. Tem had urged her to do. Dr. Tem replied that he approved of her participation in the group but that did not make up for her failure to cancel their appointment. Ms. Blitz became angry, asked how much she owed for the missed session, wrote out a check, slammed it on the therapist's desk, and stormed out of the office. When Dr. Tem left the office 2 hours later, he found over 100 hammer dents in the hood and roof of his car. He had no proof that Ms. Blitz was responsible but was strongly suspicious.

In this instance, Dr. Tem can do nothing without evidence. At the same time, however, it appears that he may have missed an opportunity to deal with Ms. Blitz's anger in the office. We will never know whether direct efforts to engage her in conversation about her feelings of not being treated fairly might have prevented the mysterious automobile damage.

Failure to Terminate a Client Who Is Not Benefiting

Termination when treatment is no longer beneficial was discussed in Chapter 4 but warrants additional comment with respect to psychotherapy (APA 02: 10.10). Ethical problems related to the duration of treatment fall in this category. In the previous case examples, we discussed premature termination. But, what of the client who, by virtue of fostered dependency or other means, is encouraged to remain "in treatment" past the point of actual benefit? Such judgments are complicated by varying theoretical orientations. Some therapists would argue, "If you think you need therapy, then you probably do." Others might argue, "If you are sure you don't need it, then you definitely do."

We recognize such biases in many of our colleagues and could choose two of them on opposite ends of the continuum for a test. A person might be selected at random and sent to each for a consultation. One would predictably find the person basically well adjusted, whereas the other would probably find the same person in need of treatment. A casual observer might presume that one or the other is unethical, either for suggesting treatment when none is needed or for dismissing a person prematurely who is in need of help, but neither situation is necessarily the case. If the therapist presents the client with the reasons why treatment is or is not needed and proposes a specific goal-directed plan (Hare-Mustin et al., 1979), the client is in a position to make an informed choice. The therapist who sees emotional health may do so in the absence of symptoms, while the therapist recommending treatment may sense some unconscious issues or potential for improved functioning. These views can and ought to be shared with the client.

Ethical problems arise if the therapist attempts to play on the client's fears, insecurities, or dependencies as a basis for initiating or continuing unnecessary treatment. Consider these examples:

Case 5–27: Justin Funk has been quarreling with his spouse about relationships with in-laws and decides to consult a psychotherapist, Tyrone Mull, L.M.H.C. A half-dozen sessions later, Mr. Funk believes that he has acquired some new insights into matters that upset him and some new ways of handling them. He is arguing less with his wife, thanks to Mr. Mull, and states his intent to terminate treatment. Mull acknowledges that progress has been made but reminds Funk of many sources of stress in his past that have "not been fully worked through," hinting darkly that problems may recur.

Mr. Funk believes that he has gotten something out of psychotherapy, but Mr. Mull's remark suddenly leaves him feeling somewhat anxious. Has he really made progress? Will he experience a "pathological regression" if he drops treatment now? Will his marriage deteriorate? Mr. Mull seems to be using his powerful position (i.e., as an expert) to hint that additional treatment is needed. This seems at variance with Funk's desires, but instead of outlining the basis of his impression and suggesting an alternative contract, Mull stirs Funk's insecurities in a diffuse and unethical manner.

Case 5–28: Brenda Schmooze has been in psychotherapy with Vivian Vain, Psy.D., for nearly 5 years. At the beginning of treatment, Ms. Schmooze was very unhappy with the hostile–dependent relationship she had developed with her intrusive mother. Schmooze had long since resolved those problems and was living independently, working in an office, and coping well in a general sense, although she remained an emotionally needy and lonely person. Her therapy sessions with Dr. Vain have generally entailed discussions of her activities, mixed with praise for Dr. Vain's help. There has been little change in Schmooze's social or emotional status for nearly 2 years.

Ms. Schmooze and Dr. Vain seem to have established a symbiotic relationship. Schmooze has acquired an attentive ear and Vain an admiring client. Some might say, "What's wrong with that if it's what Schmooze wants? She's an adult and free to make her own choice." Unfortunately, it seems that Dr. Vain may have replaced Ms. Schmooze's mother as a dependency object. Schmooze may not be able to recognize this, but Dr. Vain ought to recognize what is going on. It might be that the intense relationship with Dr. Vain is preventing Ms. Schmooze from forming more adaptive friendships outside treatment, for which she would not be paying a fee. If Vain does not find treatment issues to raise and work on with Ms. Schmooze, she is ethically obligated to help the client work toward termination.

From time to time, legitimate doubts will arise regarding a client's therapeutic needs. When this occurs, the client and therapist should discuss the issues, and the client should probably be referred for a consultation with another mental health professional. This procedure is also often useful when a client and therapist disagree on other major treatment issues.

Case 5–29: Ernest Angst had been in treatment with Donald Duration, M.D., intermittently over a 3-year period. Angst had many long-standing neurotic conflicts with which he struggled ambivalently. He began to wonder aloud in his sessions with Dr. Duration if therapy was doing him any good at all. Angst acknowledged that he wanted to work on his conflicts but had mixed feelings about them. He expressed the thought that perhaps someone else could be of more help to him. Dr. Duration interpreted these comments as a means of avoiding other issues in treatment but suggested that Angst should get a second opinion. He provided Angst with the names of several well-trained professionals in the community. Angst selected one and saw him for two sessions. Both client and consultant decided that Angst should continue trying to address the difficult conflicts he felt with Dr. Duration, who knew him well and could help focus the work better than could a new therapist.

In this case, the client raised a legitimate issue, and the therapist had a contrary opinion. The therapist suggested a consultation in a nondefensive manner and assisted the client in obtaining it. In the end, the client returned to treatment with renewed motivation and reassured trust in his therapist. Just as with the other cases in this chapter, the focus rests on the ethical fundamentals of the therapeutic relationship and the role of the therapist. The next chapter explores how specific strategies and tactics interact with professional ethics.

SUMMARY GUIDELINES

1. Mental health professionals should strive to reach explicit understandings with their clients regarding the terms of the treatment contract, whether formal or informal. This includes some mutual discussion about the goals of treatment and the means to achieve these goals.
2. Therapists are obliged to consider carefully the unique needs and perspective of each client in formulating therapeutic plans. This includes special attention to issues of diversity, particularly race and social class issues relevant to the client.
3. Therapists' personal beliefs, values, and attributes may limit their ability to treat certain types of clients. They should strive for awareness of such characteristics and limit their practices appropriately.
4. In certain circumstances, clients have specific legal rights either to receive or to refuse treatment. Therapists should remain aware of these rights and respect the underlying principles, even when no specific laws are in force.
5. Therapists have no obligation to treat any and all clients who walk through their doors. If practitioners do not feel competent to treat the client, or have biases or concerns that might compromise care, they should refer the potential client elsewhere in a respectful professional manner.
6. Therapists should strive to recognize their feelings with respect to each client as well as the degree to which these feelings may interfere with therapy.
7. When the client does not seem to be benefiting or the client's behavior is threatening or provocative, the therapist should promptly consider alternative courses of action.

References

Adler, J. (2006, March 27). Freud in our midst. *Newsweek, 147*, 43–49.

American Psychological Association. (1975). Report of the task force on sex bias and sex role stereotyping in psychotherapeutic practice. *American Psychologist, 30*, 1169–1175.

American Psychological Association. (1978). Guidelines for therapy with women. *American Psychologist, 33*, 1222–1223.

American Psychological Association. (1990). Guidelines for providers of psychological services to ethnic, linguistic, and culturally diverse populations. *American Psychologist, 48*, 45–48.

American Psychological Association. (1991). *APA policy statements on lesbian and gay issues.* Washington, DC: Author.

American Psychological Association. (2005). *Guidelines on multicultural education, training, research, practice, and organizational change.* Washington, DC: Author.

American Psychological Association. (2006). *Guidelines for psychological practice with girls and women*. Washington, DC: Author.

Appelbaum, P. S. (2004). Law and psychiatry: Psychiatric advance directives and the treatment of committed patients. *Psychiatric Services, 55,* 751–763.

Appelbaum, P. S., & Gutheil, T. G. (1980). Drug refusal: A study of psychiatric inpatients. *American Journal of Psychiatry, 137,* 340–345.

Baskin, T. W., Tierney, S. C., Minami, T., & Wampold, B. E. (2003). Establishing specificity in psychotherapy: A meta-analysis of structural equivalence of placebo controls. *Journal of Consulting and Clinical Psychology, 71,* 973–979.

Becker-Blease, K. A., & Freyd, J. J. (2006). Research participants telling the truth about their lives: The ethics of asking and not asking about abuse. *American Psychologist, 61,* 218–226.

Bennett, B. E., Bricklin, P. M., Harris, E. A., Knapp, S., VandeCreek, L., & Younggren, J. N. (2007). *Assessing and managing risk in psychological practice: An individualized approach*. Rockville, MD: American Psychological Association Insurance Trust.

Blau, T. H. (1987). *Psychotherapy tradecraft*. New York: Bruner/Mazel.

Bongar, B. (2002). *The suicidal patient: Clinical and legal standards of care* (2nd ed.). Washington, DC: American Psychological Association.

Botkin, D., & Nietzel, M. (1987). How therapists manage potentially dangerous clients. *Professional Psychology, 18,* 84–86.

Brown, L. S. (1994). *Subversive dialogues: Theory in feminist therapy*. New York: Basic Books.

Bugenthal, J. F. T. (1987). *The art of the psychotherapist*. New York: Norton.

Castonguay, L. G., & Beutler, L. E. (2006). *Principles of therapeutic change that work*. New York: Oxford University Press.

Cohen, R. J., & Smith, F. J. (1976). Socially reinforced obsessing: Etiology of a disorder in a Christian Scientist. *Journal of Consulting and Clinical Psychology, 44,* 142–144.

Comaz-Diaz, L. (2006). Cultural variation in the therapeutic relationship. In C. D. Goodheart, A. E. Kazdin, & R. J. Sternberg (Eds.), *Evidence-based psychotherapy: Where practice and research meet* (pp. 81–105). Washington, DC: American Psychological Association.

Coyne, J. C. (1976). The place of informed consent in ethical dilemmas. *Journal of Consulting and Clinical Psychology, 44,* 1015–1017.

Dawes, R. M. (1994). *House of cards: Psychology and psychotherapy based on myth*. New York: Free Press.

Deffenbacher, J. (1994). Anger reduction: Issues, assessment, and intervention strategies. In A. Siegman & T. Smith (Eds.), *Anger, hostility, and the heart* (pp. 223–269). Mahwah, NJ: Erlbaum.

Everstein, L., Everstein, D. S., Heymann, G. M., True, R. H., Frey, D. H., Johnson, H. G., et al. (1980). Privacy and confidentiality in psychotherapy. *American Psychologist, 35,* 828–840.

Eysenck, H. J. (1952). The effects of psychotherapy: An evaluation. *Journal of Consulting Psychology, 16,* 319–324.

Ford, M. D. (1980). The psychiatrist's double bind: The right to refuse medication. *American Journal of Psychiatry, 137,* 332–339.

Freedheim, D. K. (1992). *History of psychotherapy: A century of change*. Washington, DC: American Psychological Association.

Garfield, S. L. (1981). Psychotherapy: A 40 year appraisal. *American Psychologist, 36,* 174–183.

Garfield, S. L. (1992). Major issues in psychotherapy research. In D. K. Freedheim, H. J. Freudenberger, J. W. Kessler, S. B. Messer, & D. R. Peterson (Eds.), *History of psychotherapy: A century of change* (pp. 335–359). Washington, DC: American Psychological Association.

Geers, A. L., Weiland, P. E., Kosbab, K., Landry, S. J., & Helfer, S. G. (2005). Goal activation, expectations, and the placebo effect. *Journal of Personality and Social Psychology, 89,* 143–159.

Goode, E. E., & Wagner, B. (1993, May 24). Psychotherapy. *U.S. News & World Report,* 56–65.

Grisso, T. J., & Vierling, L. (1978). Minors' consent to treatment: A developmental perspective. *Professional Psychology, 9,* 412–427.

Handelsman, M. M., Martinez, A., Geisendorfer, S., & Jordan, L. (1995). Does legally mandated consent to psychotherapy ensure ethical appropriateness? The Colorado experience. *Ethics & Behavior, 5,* 119–129.

Hansen, N. D., Randazzo, K. V., Schwartz, A., Marshall, M., Kalis, D., Frazier, D., et al. (2006). Do we practice what we preach? An exploratory survey of multicultural psychotherapy competencies. *Professional Psychology, 37,* 66–74.

Hare-Mustin, R. T., Marecek, J., Kaplan, A. G., & Liss-Levenson, N. (1979). Rights of clients, responsibilities of therapists. *American Psychologist, 34,* 3–16.

Harris, E. A., & Bennett, B. E. (2005). Sample psychotherapist–patient contract. In G. P. Koocher, J. C. Norcross, & S. S. Hill (Eds.), *Psychologists' desk reference* (pp. 635–639). New York: Oxford University Press.

Hays, P. A. (1995). Multicultural applications of cognitive behavior therapy. *Professional Psychology, 26,* 309–315.

Health Insurance Portability and Accountability Act, Pub. L. No. 104–191 (1996).

Heilbrun, K., & Kramer, G. M. (2005). Involuntary medication, trial competence, and clinical dilemmas: Implications of Sell v. United States for psychological practice. *Professional Psychology, 36,* 459–466.

Hook, D. (2003). Psychotherapy and "ethical sensibility": Towards a history of criticism. *International Journal of Psychotherapy, 8,* 195.

Hurvitz, N. (1973). Psychotherapy as a means of social control. *Journal of Consulting and Clinical Psychology, 40,* 232–239.

J. L. v. Parham, 412 112 (M.D. Ga. 1976).

Jorm, A. F., Korten, A. E., Jacomb, P. A., Christensen, H., Rodgers, B., & Pollitt, P. (1997). "Mental health literacy": A survey of the public's ability to recognize mental disorders and their beliefs about the effectiveness of treatment. *Medical Journal of Australia, 166,* 182–186.

Kanoti, G. A. (1971). Ethical implications in psychotherapy. *Journal of Religion and Health, 10,* 180–191.

Karasu, T. B. (1980). The ethics of psychotherapy. *American Journal of Psychiatry, 137,* 1502–1512.

Kaschak. (1978). Therapist and client: Two views of the process and outcome of psychotherapy. *Professional Psychology, 9,* 271–278.

Knapp, S., & VandeCreek, L. (2000). Real-life vignettes involving the duty to protect *Journal of Psychotherapy in Independent Practice, 1,* 83–88.

Koocher, G. P. (1983). Consent to psychotherapy. In G. B. Melton, G. P. Koocher, & M. Saks (Eds.), *Children's competence to consent* (pp. 78–93). New York: Plenum.

Koocher, G. P. (1995). Ethics in child psychotherapy. *Child and Adolescent Psychiatric Clinics of North America, 4,* 779–791.

Koocher, G. P. (2003). Ethical issues in psychotherapy with adolescents. *Journal of Clinical Psychology, 59,* 1247–1256.

Koocher, G. P., & Keith-Spiegel, P. C. (1990). *Children, ethics, and the law: Professional issues and cases.* Lincoln: University of Nebraska Press.

Kushner, M. G., & Sher, K. J. (1989). Fears of psychological treatment and its relation to mental health service avoidance. *Professional Psychology, 20,* 251–257.

La Roche, M. J., & Maxie, A. (2003). Ten considerations in addressing cultural differences in psychotherapy. *Professional Psychology, 34,* 180–186.

Lehner, G. F. J. (1952). Defining psychotherapy. *American Psychologist, 7,* 547.

Liss-Levenson, N., Hare-Mustin, R. T., Marecek, J., & Kaplan, A. G. (1980, March). The therapist's role in assuring client rights. *Advocacy Now,* pp. 16–20.

Marshall, E. (1980). Psychotherapy faces test of worth. *Science, 207,* 35–36.

Mellon, M. W., & McGrath, M. (2000). Empirically supported treatments in pediatric psychology: Nocturnal enuresis. *Journal of Pediatric psychology, 25,* 193–214.

Melton, G. B., Koocher, G. P., & Saks, M. J. (1983). *Children's competence to consent.* New York: Plenum Press.

Miller, G. (1995). Strong medicine. *Psychological Science, 6,* 129–132.

Miller, G. (2006a, January 27). China: Healing the metaphorical heart. *Science, 311,* 462–463.

Miller, G. (2006b, January 27). A spoonful of medicine—And a steady diet of normality. *Science, 311,* 464–465.

Miller, G. (2006c, January 27). The unseen: Mental illness's global toll. *Science, 311,* 458–461.

Molin, R., & Palmer, S. (2005). Consent and participation: Ethical issues in the treatment of children in out-of-home care. *American Journal of Orthopsychiatry, 75,* 152–157.

Moodley, R., & Palmer, S. (Eds.). (2006). *Race, culture and psychotherapy: Critical perspectives in multicultural practice.* New York: Routeledge.

Norcross, J. C., Beutler, L. E., & Levant, R. F. (Eds.). (2005). *Evidence-based practices in mental health: Debate and dialogue on the fundamental questions.* Washington, DC: American Psychological Association.

O'Connor v. Donaldson, 575 (422 U.S. 1975).

O'Leary, K. D., & Borkovec, T. D. (1978). Conceptual, methodological, and ethical problems of placebo groups in psychotherapy research. *American Psychologist, 33,* 821–830.

Parekh, S. A. (2007). Child consent and the law: An insight and discussion into the law relating to consent and competence. *Child: Care, Health and Development, 33,* 78–82.

Parham v. J. R., 442 U.S. 584 (S. Ct. 1979).

Pinnock, R., & Crosthwaite, J. (2005). When parents refuse consent to treatment for children and young persons. *Journal of Paediatrics and Child Health, 41,* 369–373.

Potter, R. (2004). Consent quiz: How well would you do? A survey of the knowledge of CAMHS workers of the law relating to consent to treatment in children. *Psychiatric Bulletin, 28,* 91–93.

Schofield, W. (1964). *Psychotherapy: The purchase of friendship.* Englewood Cliffs, NJ: Prentice-Hall.

Seligman, M. E. P. (1995). The effectiveness of psychotherapy: The *Consumer Reports* study. *American Psychologist, 50,* 965–974.

Seligman, M. E. P., Steen, T. A., Park, N., & Peterson, C. (2005). Positive psychology progress: Empirical validation of interventions. *American Psychology Law Society News, 60,* 410–421.

Sell v. United States, 539 (U. S. 166 2003).

Shapiro, A. K., & Struening, E. L. (1973). The use of placebos: A study of ethics and physicians' attitudes. *Psychiatry in Medicine, 4,* 17–29.

Spirito, A., & Kazak, A. E. (2006). *Effective and emerging treatments in pediatric psychology.* New York: Oxford University Press.

Strupp, H. H. (1975). On failing one's patient. *Psychotherapy: Theory, Research and Practice, 12,* 39–41.

Strupp, H. H. (1992). Overview: Psychotherapy research. In D. K. Freedheim (Ed.), *History of psychotherapy: A century of change* (pp. 309–310). Washington, DC: American Psychological Association.

Sue, D. W. (2003). *Overcoming our racism: The journey to liberation.* San Francisco: Jossey-Bass.

Sue, S. (1998). In search of cultural competence in psychotherapy and counseling. *American Psychologist, 53,* 440–448.

Tatum, B. D. (1972). Talking about race, learning about racism: The application of racial identity development theory in the classroom. *Harvard Educational Review, 62,* 1–24.

Tatum, B. D. (1997). *Why are all the Black kids sitting together in the cafeteria? and other conversations about race.* New York: Basic Books.

Tharp, R. G. (1991). Cultural diversity and treatment of children. *Journal of Consulting and Clinical Psychology, 59,* 799–812.

VandeCreek, L. (2005). A model for clinical decision making with dangerous patients. In G. P. Koocher, J. C. Norcross, & S. S. Hill (Eds.), *Psychologists' desk reference* (2nd ed., pp. 612–614). New York: Oxford University Press.

VandeCreek, L., & Knapp, S. (2000). Risk management and life-threatening patient behaviors. *Journal of Clinical Psychology, 56,* 1335–1351.

Vogel, D. L., & Wester, S. R. (2003). To seek help or not to seek help: The risks of self-disclosure. *Journal of Counseling Psychology, 50,* 351–361.

Vogel, D. L., Wester, S. R., Wei, M., & Boysen, G. A. (2005). The role of outcome expectations and attitudes on decisions to seek professional help. *Journal of Counseling Psychology, 52,* 459–470.

Weisz, J. R., McCarty, C. A., & Valeri, S. M. (2006). Effects of psychotherapy for depression in children and adolescents: A meta-analysis. *Psychological Bulletin, 132,* 132–149.

Weithorn, L. A. (Ed.). (1987). *Psychology and child custody determinations: Knowledge, roles, and expertise.* Lincoln, NE: University of Nebraska Press.

Weithorn, L. A., (2006). The legal contexts of forensic assessment of children and families. In S. N. Sparta & G. P. Koocher (Eds.), *Forensic mental health assessment of children and adolescents* (pp. 11–29). New York: Oxford University Press.

White, M. D., & White, C. A. (1981). Involuntarily committed patients' constitutional right to refuse treatment: A challenge to psychology. *American Psychologist, 36,* 962–963.

Williams, M. H. (1985). The bait-and-switch tactic in psychotherapy. *Psychotherapy: Theory, Research, Practice, Training, 22,* 110–113.

Zonana, H. V. (2003). Competency to be executed and forced medication: Singleton v. Norris. *Journal of the American Academy of Psychiatry and the Law, 31,* 372–376.

6

Psychotherapy Part II
Techniques and Controversies

Preliminary investigations further established that the group, like most of the dominant religions on the planet from the same time period, was monotheistic, confining worship to the deity "Talk."

Miller and Hubble

Contents

The quotation used to introduce this chapter comes from an article reporting the history of the field we know as "psychotherapy" from the perspective of an extraterrestrial archeological survey team (Miller & Hubble, 2004). At the time of the team's visit to Earth in the distant future, a collision with a comet had long since wiped out the Earth's population. The group discovers, however, that the apparent religion known as "Therapy" died out long before the cataclysmic collision.

THE MOVEMENT TOWARD EVIDENCE-BASED TREATMENTS

Just as Chapter 5 focused on the basic obligations of psychotherapists to all clients, this chapter addresses technique-oriented issues in psychotherapeutic practice. In some sense, this moves us from a consideration of the definition of psychotherapy to a consideration of what sorts of relationships and activities may have psychotherapeutic effects. The strategies and tactics of therapists differ widely across a range of psychological problems and client populations. Some approaches to psychological treatment demand highly specialized training along with competencies and ethical considerations beyond the basic skills required for entry to practice. Certain special client circumstances may also require modification of a therapist's standard operating procedures. Thinking through the ethical dilemmas posed by such variations requires thoughtful planning, creativity, and ethical sensitivity.

As discussed in the Chapter 5, the 1990s saw considerable interest in basing medical and mental health practice on a firm evidentiary footing (Institute of Medicine, 2001). As a result, so many different groups began work on assorted treatment guidelines that the American Psychological Association (APA) issued model criteria for evaluating them (APA, 2002). Research and scholarly debate led the APA Division of Clinical Psychology to sponsor a book on empirically supported treatments, *A Guide to Treatments That Work* (Nathan & Gorman, 1998, 2007). A burgeoning literature on so-called empirically supported or empirically based therapy and empirically supported relationships led to the creation of an APA presidential task force (Bohart, 2005; Messer, 2004; Norcross, Beutler, & Levant, 2005; Presidential Task Force on Evidence-Based Practice, 2006; Safren, 2005; Spirito & Kazak, 2006). APA's formal reports and policies appear online at http://www.apa.org/practice/ebp.html. Other therapists have responded by seeking to focus attention on discredited or so-called psychoquackery (Jacobson, Foxx, & Mulick, 2005; Norcross, Koocher, & Garofalo, 2006).

THERAPIES INVOLVING MULTIPLE CLIENTS

In marital, family, and group therapies, the therapist has more than one client in the session simultaneously. It seems most unlikely that the goals or best interests of every client in the treatment room will fully coincide with those of the others. Especially in marital and family work, the needs or wishes of one member will often prove quite different and at times in direct opposition to those of another (Lakin, 1994; Snyder & Doss, 2005; Southern, 2006; Southern, Smith, & Oliver, 2005). Competence needed to conduct couples or group therapies successfully also requires different techniques and training than typically required for individual psychotherapies. Such multiple therapies raise a host of other ethical issues, including matters of confidentiality and social coercion (Lasky & Riva, 2006). In this section, we attempt to highlight some of the most common ethical dilemmas associated with multiple-client therapies.

Marital and Family Therapy

Ethical guidelines dealing with a therapist's responsibility to clients, confidentiality, informed consent, and client rights are certainly ambiguous at times, even when considering the interaction between one therapist and one client (Bass & Quimby, 2006; Gladding & Coombs, 2005; Southern, 2006; Southern et al., 2005). When treatment involves a couple or multiple family members, matters become more complicated. Treatment will often involve a therapeutic obligation to several individuals with conflicting needs (Bass & Quimby, 2006; Gladding & Coombs, 2005; Hare-Mustin, 1979, 1980; Hines & Hare-Mustin, 1978, 1980; Margolin, 1982). Margolin (1982) cited several illustrations of such conflicts. She described the mother who seeks treatment for her child so that he will behave better, which may ease pressure on the mother while not necessarily helping her child. Margolin also cited the case of the wife who seeks to surmount fears of terminating her marriage, whereas her husband's goal focuses on maintaining the status quo. A therapist in such situations must strive to ensure that improvement in the status of one family member does not occur at the expense of another. When such an outcome may be unavoidable (e.g., in the case of the couple whose treatment may result in the decision of one or both partners to seek a divorce), the therapist should advise the couple of that potential outcome early in the course of treatment as part of the consent process (discussed in Chapter 5). In this type of situation, the therapist's personal values and theoretical orientation are of critical importance (Hare-Mustin, 1979, 1980; Hines & Hare-Mustin, 1980).

Case 6–1: Hugo Home, Psy.D., likes to consider himself a "gentleman of the old school" who holds the door open for women, tips his hat when passing them on the street, and generally behaves quite genially to the "fair sex." In conducting family therapy, however, Dr. Home has a clear bias, favoring the view of women cast in the wife–mother role. He believes that mothers of children under 12 should not work outside the home and frequently asks his female clients who seem depressed or irritable whether it is their "time of the month again." Dr. Home does not recognize how these biases might adversely affect the female partner in marital counseling.

Case 6–2: Ramona Church, L.M.F.T., is a family therapist and devout member of a religious group that eschews divorce under any circumstances. She continues to encourage her clients in marital therapy to work with her, "grow up," and "cease acting out immature fantasies," even when both partners express a serious consideration of divorce. She will often tell clients who have worked with her for several months that they will have failed in treatment and that she will have no more to do with them if they choose divorce.

Both Dr. Home and Ms. Church have clear biases and seem either oblivious to their impact or self-righteously assertive of them. They fail to recognize the power and influence they wield as psychotherapists and their accompanying responsibility to clients. Neither should treat couples in marital therapy, at least not without a clear warning from the outset about their biases.

Ms. Church's threat to abandon any of her clients who stray from the personal values she prescribes holds particular danger. The vulnerable and insecure client may experience harm at the hands of such therapists. In addition, Ms. Church's stance essentially threatens client abandonment. Hines and Hare-Mustin (1978) highlighted the "myth of valueless thinking" and enjoined therapists to carefully assess the impact that their own values and stereotypes may have on their work.

More than three decades ago, the APA Task Force on Sex Bias and Sex-Role Stereotyping (APA, 1975) noted that family therapists surveyed at that time had particular vulnerability to certain biases. These included the assumption that remaining in a marriage represents the better adjustment for a woman and a tendency to defer to the husband's needs over those of the wife. The same report noted the tendency to demonstrate less interest in or sensitivity to a woman's career as opposed to a man's and the perpetuation of the belief that child rearing and children's problems fall primarily in the woman's domain. The report also noted that therapists tended to hold a double standard in response to the extramarital affairs of a wife compared to those of a husband. Although we believe societal and training changes have significantly improved the situation, we must remain aware of the historical problem as an illustration and continually maintain sensitivity to such issues.

Several authors have noted that the prevailing "therapeutic ideology" holds that all persons can and should benefit from therapy (Hines & Hare-Mustin, 1978). Some family therapists also insist that all members of the family must participate in treatment (Hare-Mustin, 1979, 1980; Margolin et al., 2005; Southern, 2006; Southern et al., 2005). What does this do to a person's right to decline treatment? Must the reluctant adolescent or adult be pressured into attending sessions at the behest of the psychotherapist? Data suggest children as young as 14 are as competent as adults in making decisions about treatment (Grisso & Vierling, 1978; Koocher, 2003), yet it remains unclear how often young family members have a truly voluntary choice.

Case 6–3: Ronald McRigid, M.S.W., a family therapist, was consulted by Harold and Anita Hassol. The Hassols have three children ranging in age from 12 to 18. The youngest child had engaged in considerable acting out, including a recent arrest for destroying school property. The juvenile court judge recommended family counseling. The Hassol's oldest child had no interest in participating, but both parents and the two younger children (including the identified client) did express a willingness to attend sessions. Mr. McRigid informed the Hassols that he would not treat them unless everyone attended every session.

While Mr. McRigid may have good clinical or theoretical reasons for his stance, we can not condone coercion of any reluctant family member to participate in treatment. This does not preclude a therapist's urging that the resistant family member attend at least one trial session or attempting to address the underlying reasons for the refusal. The therapist who strongly believes that the whole family must participate should not use coercion to drag in the reluctant member or permit that reluctant member's refusal to deny treatment to the rest of the family who wish to have it. In such cases, the therapist should at the very least provide the names of other professionals in the community who might willingly treat the subgroup desiring treatment. When the client in question is a minor child, the therapist has a special duty to consider that client's needs as distinct from those of the parents (Koocher, 1976, 2003; Koocher & Keith-Spiegel, 1990; Melton, Koocher, & Saks, 1983).

Confidentiality constitutes yet another issue that complicates marital and family therapy. Should a therapist tolerate secret keeping or participate in it? Should parents be able to sign away a child's right to confidentiality? The concept and conditions of confidentiality are somewhat different in the family context than as discussed in Chapter 8. Often, couples may have difficulty in establishing boundaries and privacy with respect to their own lives and those of their children (Bartlett, 1996; Dishion & Stormshak, 2007; Koocher & Keith-Spiegel, 1990). Adult clients can, and should, have the ability to assert some privacy with respect to their marriage and to avoid burdening their

children with information that may prove frightening, provocative, or simply beyond their ability to comprehend adequately. On the other hand, many attempts to maintain secrets have a manipulative purpose and do not serve the general goals of treatment.

The most reasonable way to handle this matter ethically would involve formulating a policy based on therapeutic goals and defining that policy to all concerned at the outset of treatment. Some therapists may state at the beginning of therapy that they will keep no secrets. Others may express some willingness to accept information shared in confidence to help the person offering it determine whether it is appropriate for discussion in the whole group. Still another option would involve discussing the resistance to sharing the information with the member in question. That approach might help the person to share the information with the family, if indicated. Secret keeping presents the added burden of recalling which secret came from whom, not to mention the need to recall what was supposed to be kept "secret" and what was not. The therapist who fails to consider and discuss these matters in advance with family clients may make accidental disclosures within a very short time that could have serious ethical fallout.

Group Therapy

Mental health professionals may treat unrelated clients in groups for a variety of reasons, ranging from simple economy to specialized treatment plans. For example, a group may consist of people with similar problems, such as recently hospitalized mental patients, divorced males, women with eating disorders, bereaved parents, or children with handicaps. In such groups, the identified clients gather to address similar emotional or social problems in a common supportive context. Other groups may focus on enhancing personal growth or self-awareness, as opposed to addressing personal psychodynamics or psychopathology (Coleman, 2005; Klontz, 2004; Nagy, 2005; Page, DeLucia-Waack, Gerrity, Kalodner, & Riva, 2004; Tkachuk & Martin, 1999). In his classic book on the subject, Carl Rogers (1970) offered a sample listing of group types, including so called "T-groups," encounter groups, sensitivity groups, task-oriented groups, sensory awareness or body awareness groups, organizational development groups, team-building groups, victim groups, perpetrator groups, and Gestalt groups.

Group treatment has considerable potential for both good and harm. The influence and support of peers in the treatment process may facilitate gains that would be slow or unlikely in individual treatment. The group may also become a special therapeutic ecology within which special insights and awareness may develop. At the same time, significant hazards to group members exist when the group leader lacks proper training or the ability to adequately monitor the experience for all members (American Group Psychotherapy Association [AGPA], 2002). Pressures toward cohesion and emotional expressiveness common in group therapy can be inappropriate for some clients (Lakin, 1994). The group therapist has much less control over the content and direction of the session than does an individual therapist. As a result, a greater potential exists for individuals in the group to have unfavorable or adverse experiences. Problems might include stresses resulting from confrontation, criticism, threats to confidentiality, or even development of dependency on the group (American Group Psychotherapy Association, 2002; Lasky & Riva, 2006). In many ways, then, the risk of harm to individual clients is greater in group than in individual therapies (Corey, Williams, & Moline, 1995).

Our discussion here focuses on two sets of related issues, the first regarding groups intended as psychotherapy experiences and then on that subset of group programs intended as growth experiences. The term *growth experiences* refers to short-term group programs focusing on individual development or growth rather than psychotherapy or treatment of psychopathology. We use the term *group therapy* to generally discuss treatment for people seeking help in response to specific emotional or psychological symptoms; such treatment usually occurs over a period of months or years rather than days or weeks as in the growth experience programs.

In the 1960s, a plethora of growth-oriented interventions bloomed, and APA issued a one-page "Guidelines for Psychologists Conducting Growth Groups" (APA, 1973), making several important points as mandates for the clinician leader to provide informed consent, ensure that participation is fully voluntary, conduct proper screening of participants, and carefully differentiate roles based on whether the group is intended as therapeutic or educational. These guidelines make it evident that the responsibility for these obligations rests on the therapist leading the group. The more modern AGPA standards (available online at http://www.agpa.org/group/ethicalguide.html) address similar responsibilities of the psychotherapist (American Group Psychotherapy Association, 2002).

The following three cases suggest inadequacies in preparation, screening, orientation, and follow-through by the therapists in question:

Case 6–4: The president of a small manufacturing company became so excited about the insights he acquired in a weekend marathon therapy session conducted by Grover Grouper, Ed.D., that he hired Grouper to run such a session for his executive staff and ordered them all to participate.

Dr. Grouper, in agreeing to conduct the sessions, seems to have overlooked the coercion involved in demanding that the staff attend. Both the nature and the goals of the group remain unclear. If intended as therapy, the failure to screen potential participants for appropriateness and the enforced participation (or even voluntary participation) of people who work together raises serious questions regarding individual privacy and therapeutic merit. If the goals of the group focus on growth or team building, it still behooved Grouper to screen participants carefully and ensure that no coercion, however subtle, played a role in their decisions.

Case 6–5: Lena Lonely was a socially isolated freshman at a large state college. She joined an 8-week "encounter group" run by intern Vivian Speedo, M.A., at the college counseling center. Ms. Lonely hoped that the group experience would help to remedy her social isolation. When the group sessions ended 8 weeks later, Lonely felt disillusioned by her lack of accomplishment and despaired over what she perceived as her inadequacies. She dropped out of school.

One must wonder whether Ms. Speedo adequately screened candidates for the group to assess the appropriateness of the program for Ms. Lonely. Even if the referral to the group seemed appropriate, Ms. Lonely clearly did not benefit from participating. Speedo should have monitored the status of participants sufficiently to identify any group members whose condition seemed to worsen or whose needs went beyond what the group offered. Had Ms. Speedo done so, she might have identified Ms. Lonely's continuing problems and assisted with a fresh referral.

Case 6–6: Fernando Frank, L.M.H.C., describes himself as a strong proponent of the "get real and tell it like it is" school of therapy. In the first meeting of a new group, Mr. Frank focused attention on Jack Small, encouraging Small to reveal some intimate detail of his life to the group. Mr. Small shared such a detail, only to have Frank and the other group members focus on it and highlight the personal inadequacies it implied. Small never returned to the group, and 2 weeks later sought admission to a mental hospital, experiencing severe depression.

As in the previous case, it appears that Mr. Frank may have not adequately screened candidates for appropriateness. In addition, Mr. Frank apparently did not recognize the potential emotional damage to Mr. Small. Had he done so, Mr. Frank could have attempted to mitigate any emotional harm during the session or reached out to Mr. Small on an individual basis following the session.

During the 1960s and 1970s, some proponents of growth groups essentially argued that participants owned responsibility for whatever happened in the sessions. As one example, Parker (1976) reported the exuberantly radical views of Schultz (1971) that each person in the group is solely responsible for him- or herself. Parker quoted Schultz as writing, "You have your choice. If you want to bow to pressure or resist it, go crazy, get physically injured, stay or leave or whatever, it's up to you." Parker rightly

recognized that philosophy as one that leads to high-risk groups and a dangerous laissez-faire leadership style. However trendy or attractive this may seem at the time, it is dangerous and presents the potential of serious harm to clients.

Yalom and his colleagues (Vinogradov, Yalom, Hales, Yudofsky, & Talbott, 1994; Yalom, 1995) identified many participant vulnerability factors therapists should consider in constructing and conducting groups. These include the following:

- vulnerability to aggression
- fragile self-esteem
- excessive dependency needs
- intense fears of rejection
- history of withdrawal
- transference to the group leader
- internal conflicts aroused by group discussions
- unrealistic expectations
- guardedness

The matters of confidentiality and privileged communication in group psychotherapy also differ significantly from individual therapy in important ways. Although we generally discussed these in Chapter 8, the group context adds new variables to the equation since, by definition, more than two people stand in a position to disclose a confidence learned in the session (i.e., the therapist and at least one other client). After reviewing Chapter 8, readers will recognize the differences between privilege and confidentiality. In most jurisdictions, no statutory privilege extends to material disclosed in group sessions to client members of the group (Behr, 2006; Coleman, 2005; Hawkins, Schermer, Motherwell, & Shay, 2005; Lasky & Riva, 2006). The therapist should therefore advise clients in two ways early in the group treatment process. First, the clients must be cautioned about the lack of legal protections (i.e., privilege) regarding information disclosed. Second, the therapist should encourage recognition of the importance to all group members of a mutually respectful duty of confidentiality regarding what each member says in the course of treatment.

Therapists tend to express far more concern about issues of confidentiality than members of groups (Slovenko, 1977). One wonders whether clients in group treatment should automatically recognize that gossip about sensitive material revealed in sessions may be communicated to others outside the group by their peers. As a result, clients might normally self-censor particularly sensitive revelations or material. Even so, not everyone has sound judgment, and the pressures toward self-disclosure in group therapy or even experiential growth programs may prove very intense. Therapists should have these issues in mind as the group sessions proceed.

SPECIAL TECHNIQUES AND ISSUES

Under the general practice of psychotherapy, a number of special issues or techniques have attracted sufficient numbers of ethics inquiries over time to warrant specific discussion. These include the issue of triage and intake procedures, as well as techniques associated with sex therapy, behavior modification, the use of psychological devices, so-called coercive treatment techniques, and electronic media. Some therapy techniques that attract special ethical concerns originate in part as a function of the sensational nature of the context within which they are applied and in part as a function of the special social concerns associated with the treatment issue. Examples include sexual practices and sex therapy and the civil rights issues associated with coercive treatment programs.

Triage and Intake

The concept of triage applies in medical emergency situations, referring to a priority assignment for certain patients waiting in a queue. For example, a patient who has stopped breathing or who is hemorrhaging will be seen immediately, even if other less severely injured patients must wait for an extended period in pain and discomfort. Likewise, a clinic with a long psychotherapy waiting list might move a suicidal client to the head of the line for treatment because of the urgent nature of the problem. At times, however, clients remain uninformed of such priorities, even if reasonable, with the result that

the client may suffer needless delay rather than seeking an alternative treatment. In some instances, the system of priorities and intake procedures themselves raise ethical questions.

Case 6–7: Midtown Psychotherapy Associates, Incorporated, is a private group practice consisting of several licensed therapists. To keep all available appointment times filled, the administrative assistant keeps a waiting list of at least 8 to 10 clients. She informs potential clients seeking an intake appointment that she has put them on a short waiting list and will call them for an appointment soon, even when the practice has no openings in the foreseeable future.

Case 6–8: The Capitol Mental Health Center (CMHC) had a 6-week backlog for intake assessments and a policy that only emergency cases could be taken out of order. Nicholas Bluster, the mayor of Capitol City, telephoned the therapist who directed the CMHC seeking an immediate appointment for his adolescent son, who had been "mouthing off at home." The therapist in charge placed Junior Bluster at the head of the list.

Both of these cases demonstrate unethical priority setting in a manner that was detrimental to some clients. In the case of Midtown Psychotherapy Associates, the people waiting for appointments should more appropriately be advised of the potential duration of their wait and offered the opportunity for a referral elsewhere. An indefinite hold on the waiting list could be reasonable if the potential client, advised of the details, chooses to wait (i.e., based on convenience, cost, or perceived quality), but the situation described at Midtown misleads callers. The director of the CMHC was clearly responding to political expedience. Perhaps Junior Bluster does need services and qualifies to receive them at the center; however, moving him ahead of others on the list provides an unfair priority unless an emergency intervention is required. The director could have met the political social demands of the situation in many appropriate ways, such as offering a referral elsewhere or making time available personally to assist the Blusters, while not delaying services to others in need.

Sex Therapy

The very word *sex* immediately captures the attention of an adult audience, and when using the term *sex therapy*, most mental health professionals think only of the most common presenting symptoms, such as erectile dysfunction, premature ejaculation, anorgasmia, dyspareunia, vaginismus, and loss of interest in sexual activity (LoPiccolo & Van Male, 2005a, 2005b). However, a variety of other problems might become the focus of sex therapy. These include hysterical conversion reactions with a sexual focus; paraphilias (e.g., exhibitionism, pedophilia, and voyeurism); gender dysphoria syndromes (e.g., transsexualism); physical developmental disorders (e.g., hypospadias); disease-related disorders; and problems resulting from medical side effects, surgery, or traumatic injury to the sex organs (Aloni & Katz, 2003; Rosen & Leiblum, 1995a, 1995b; Southern, 1999). Significant numbers of clients may also present with varying degrees of concern about sexual functioning, gender preference, or homosexuality. Considerable guidance for treating such clients exists (APA, 2000; Drescher, 2002; Safren, 2005). In the next section, we discuss some of the ethical issues that accompany various sexually related therapies.

The American Association of Sexuality Educators, Counselors, and Therapists (2004) published a code of ethics and training guidelines for individuals practicing in this specialized field. These guides and other writings on sex therapies highlight the complexity of the social, psychological, anatomic, and physiological factors that may become involved in sexual problems (Leiblum & Rosen, 2000; LoPiccolo, 2002). As these complexities illustrate, this field of practice demands special skills and ethical sensitivities. Often, the style and substance of clinically appropriate sex therapy will differ dramatically from other therapeutic activities and become laden with personal and societal values. For example, more than three decades ago one set of authors (Lowery & Lowery, 1975) asserted that the most ethical sex therapy is that "which cures the symptom and improves the marital relationship in the briefest time and at the least cost" (p. 229). They also specified that

neither insight-oriented treatment nor therapist–client sexual activity satisfy these criteria.

Emotional reactions linked treating sexual problems (e.g., feelings associated with personal insecurities, embarrassment, or compromised quality of life) are not limited to the general public. A fascinating debate began in the professional literature with the publication of a study describing highly specific behaviorally oriented masturbation procedures for anorgasmic women (Zeiss, Rosen, & Zeiss, 1977). This was followed by a critique entitled "Psychotherapy or Massage Parlor Technology?" (K. G. Bailey, 1978), which invoked ethical, moral, and philosophical (as well as social psychological) reasoning. This was followed by one comment describing Bailey's critique as "antiscientific" (Wagner, 1978), and another well-reasoned critique noting that value-free therapy does not exist and that the client should be fully engaged in goal setting while conducting the least intrusive treatment (Wilson, 1978).

Therapists may also find themselves caught between members of an intimate dyad with very different sexual preferences, goals, and expectations. For example, consider the therapists confronting the ethical problems that arose when a couple presented for sex therapy to address the wife's sexual reluctance, particularly in relation to conflicts over the husband's demands for anal sex (Wylie, Crowe, & Boddington, 1995). Should the therapeutic goal in such circumstances focus on helping the husband to respect and accept his wife's reluctance or on encouraging the wife to consider acceptance of her husband's wishes?

Sexual Surrogates

Perhaps the most dramatic focus of concern in the evolution of practice in sex therapy involves the use of sexual surrogates—sexual partners used by some mental health professionals to assist certain clients by engaging in a variety of social and sexual activities for a fee. Surrogate use, initially employed by Masters and Johnson (1976) with some single clients and discussed in the 1970s as more than a prescription for prostitution (Jacobs, Thompson, & Truxaw, 1975), is rarely reported in professional circles today.

More attention is paid to a host of other issues and techniques, for example, biomedical treatments, cognitive and behavioral approaches, psychoeducational interventions, and approaches combining multiple techniques (Leiblum & Rosen, 2000; LoPiccolo, 2002; LoPiccolo & Van Male, 2005a, 2005b; Rosen & Leiblum, 1995a). Still, some psychotherapists may find themselves tempted to use surrogates from time to time (i.e., with medically disabled clients), although this may lead to substantial ethical and legal complications (Aloni & Katz, 2003; Balon, 2005; Gianotten, 1997; Poelzl, 2001).

In some states, a mental health professional who refers a client to a sex surrogate may become liable for criminal prosecution. Some state laws could lead to prosecution under procurement, prostitution, and antifornication laws, or even rape charges, should some aspect of the relationship go wrong or come to the attention of a zealous district attorney. A variety of potential civil liabilities or tort actions are possible if one spouse objects to the other's use of a surrogate or if the client contracts a sexually transmitted disease from (or transmits one to) the surrogate. In the case of HIV or hepatitis viral transmission, the costs can prove especially high. In such cases, the referring therapist may have a vicarious liability and will generally find his or her liability insurer unwilling to cover a resulting claim.

These dramatic cases illustrate some of the complex problems, including the blurring of roles and values, that often seem to occur when sexual surrogates come into play.

Case 6–9: Lorna Loose worked as a receptionist and secretary to Cecil Thud, Ph.D. Dr. Thud approached her about acting as a sexual surrogate for some of his male clients. Ms. Loose agreed and allegedly enjoyed the work so sufficiently that she began to offer such services on a freelance basis in addition to her work with Thud's clients. Subsequently, her ex-spouse sued for custody of their two children, citing her work as "a prostitute" in court. Loose allegedly sought emotional and documentary support from Thud and later claimed that he seduced her.

Dr. Thud denied ever having had sex with Ms. Loose, although he did acknowledge recruiting her as a sex surrogate and admitted that this role later caused her considerable personal difficulty. In the actual incident on which our case is based, the therapist was sued by his employee and won a substantial award in a highly publicized trial.

Case 6–10: George Trotter, L.M.F.T., employed one male and three female assistants with master's degrees in counseling fields to work in his clinic specializing in sex therapy. He would occasionally refer some of his clients to one of the assistants, who would act as a sexual surrogate. Trotter reasoned that he was practicing appropriately since the surrogates had all obtained counseling training and were not the therapists of the specific clients in question. Ultimately, Dr. Trotter faced prosecution on prostitution charges and on fraud charges filed by an insurance company, claiming that Trotter had billed the sex sessions with his assistants as psychotherapy.

Mr. Trotter was at best ethically insensitive and careless in his conclusion that the use of his assistants, however willing, did not create a conflict-ridden situation. His decision to bill these visits as insured services, when he had clear information that they were not covered by the insurance company, constituted strong evidence of fraud. Although the prostitution charges were ultimately dropped, a substantial amount of harmful publicity deeply troubled the more appropriate and conservative sex therapists in the community.

Case 6–11: Nova Gyna sought treatment for depression and marital dissatisfaction involving a number of life issues by her therapist, Oopsie Daisy, M.S.W. One important issue to Ms. Gyna involved her ability to have orgasms when masturbating but never with her highly critical husband of 5 years. Her family physician had prescribed an antidepressant medication. Ms. Daisy recommended couples therapy, but Mr. Gyna refused. She attempted to refer the couple to a sex therapist, but again Mr. Gyna declined to participate. Ms. Daisy suggested some self-help books that Ms. Gyna might use to encourage her spouse in different approaches to lovemaking, but her client could not work up the courage to ask her husband to do anything differently from his routine. Feeling at the end of her ideas, Ms. Daisy suggested that Ms. Gyna pay a visit to an adult sex club in a neighboring city, where she might find an anonymous willing partner for "practice purposes, using safe sex," of course. Ms. Gyna ultimately contracted an HIV infection and passed the virus on to her spouse, who filed for divorce.

We do not know whether Ms. Daisy had any competence as a sex therapist, and we recognize that Mr. Gyna's refusal to participate complicated best practice approaches for treating his wife's marital anorgasmia. If Ms. Daisy had sought consultation from a colleague more experienced with this condition, she might have come up with better and less risky suggestions, including investigation of the influence of some antidepressant medication (Ashton, 1999; Brown University, 2002; Kuriansky, Sharpe, & O'Connor, 1982; LoPiccolo and Van Male, 2005a).

Sexual behavior is an emotionally charged, value-laden aspect of human life, and therapists working actively at altering such behaviors must take appropriately cautious and sensitive approaches to both community and professional standards. Sexual practices also pose significant potential for transmission of a range of serious diseases. In such areas of practice, haphazard ethical practices and indiscretions will prove much more likely to lead to major problems for the client and practitioner than in almost any other realm.

Sexual Orientation Conversion or Reparative Therapy

Sexual orientation conversion therapies, once considered the treatment of choice in the era when homosexuality was considered an illness or form of psychopathology, raise a number of ethical challenges. For over a century, medical, psychotherapeutic, and religious practitioners sought to reverse unwanted same-sex attraction or homosexual orientation through a variety of methods, including psychoanalysis, prayer, electric shock, nausea-inducing drugs, hormone therapy, surgery, and a variety of behavioral treatments, including masturbatory reconditioning, visits to prostitutes, and even excessive bicycle riding (Murphy, 1992). The American Psychiatric Association's 1973 decision to remove homosexuality from its *Diagnostic and Statistical Manual of Mental Disorders* marked the official passing of the illness model of homosexuality (Spiegel, 2002). Despite this now-complete official "depathologizing" of homosexuality, efforts by both mental health professionals and pastoral care providers to convert lesbians and gay men to heterosexuality have persisted (Greene, Bieschke, Perez, & DeBord, 2007; Haldeman, 1991, 1994; M. S. Schneider, Brown, & Glassgold, 2002).

Such efforts variously described as conversion therapy, reparative therapy, or therapy to eliminate same-sex attraction, span a variety of treatment modalities. So-called reparative therapy emerged in the early 1980s as a "new method of curing" homosexuals. Elizabeth Moberly, a conservative British Christian theologian with a Ph.D. degree in experimental psychology, became a key proponent of the approach in 1983 after publishing her theory "that the homosexual . . . whether man or woman . . . has suffered from some deficit in the relationship with the parent of the same sex; and that there is a corresponding drive to make good this deficit . . . through the medium of same-sex, or 'homosexual,' relationships" (p. 2). Organizations currently promoting psychotherapeutic care for individuals with same-sex attraction often have moralistic or religious underpinnings and include the National Association for Research and Therapy of Homosexuality (NARTH) and Jews Offering New Alternatives to Homosexuality (JONAH).

As noted in Chapter 5, the concepts of taking guidance from clients and engaging clients in goal setting stand at the center of the psychotherapeutic enterprise. Clients may well present themselves for treatment and describe emotional problems associated with same-sex attraction. In such circumstances, the therapist has an obligation to carefully explore how patients arrive at the choices they wish to make. At times, motives may result from social pressures or experiences with homophobic environments. No type or amount of individual psychotherapy will modify social prejudices. In addition, as part of informed consent to treatment, clients must understand the potential consequences of any treatment, including those intended to modify sexual orientation. Clients must understand that reparative treatments lack any validated scientific foundation and may prove harmful. Finally, our clients ought to know from the outset that organizations representing the mental health professions do not consider homosexuality a mental disorder (see http://www.apa.org/pi/lgbc/policy/0806koocher.pdf).

Two major ethical concerns accompany so-called reparative treatments. First, to what extent does offering such treatments comport with the issues of therapist responsibility and consumer welfare? Second, given that rigorous empirical studies fail to show that conversion therapies work, do therapists offering such interventions without clear disclaimers and cautions mislead clients (Greene et al., 2007; Haldeman, 1994; Morrow, 2000; M. S. Schneider et al., 2002; Spiegel, 2002)? The APA addressed these issues with a "Resolution on Appropriate Therapeutic Responses to Sexual Orientation" (APA, 1998), and similar positions have emanated from other professional groups (American Psychiatric Association, 1998, 2000; National Association of Social Workers, 2000). These standards essentially allow therapists to address the stated needs of clients as long as they fully inform clients regarding known limitations.

Why do gay, lesbian, and bisexual people seek such treatments? In one study, investigators interviewed 202 consumers of sexual orientation conversion interventions and asked two basic questions: What motivates people to pursue conversion therapy and ex-gay groups? How do they perceive its harmfulness and helpfulness? The results indicated that a majority failed to change sexual orientation, and many reported that they experienced harm as part of conversion interventions. A minority reported feeling helped, although not necessarily with their original goal of changing sexual orientation (Shidlo & Schroeder, 2002).

Case 6–12: At age 30, Frank Faithful, who had self-identified as gay since his late teens, sought treatment. He had never felt entirely comfortable with being gay, in part because of his upbringing in a Pentecostal faith that strongly condemned ho-

mosexuality. He had struggled to find a common ground between his strong Christian religious beliefs and his clear lack of sexual or romantic attraction to women. He had many female friends, whose company he enjoyed because he felt no sexual pressure in those relationships. He sought treatment from pastoral counselor Ida Knoway, M.Div., who informed Frank that he was "not really gay," and that his same-sex desires were the result of having been abandoned by his father as a child. For many months, Frank worked with the therapist on reorienting his sexuality using cognitive, behavioral, and imaginal techniques. He followed her instructions to withdraw from contact with gay male friends and stayed away from gay male communities where he had previously socialized. He prayed and attended church even more frequently than in the past. At the end of this time, Frank found himself feeling depressed, despondent, and a failure because, despite his best efforts, he continued to feel no sexual or romantic attraction toward women. His previously good friendships with women became so fraught with tension as he sought to achieve heterosexuality that he became more socially isolated. He reported feeling spiritually bereft as well, as if "God was not listening to my pleas."

We adapted this case from one of the excellent vignettes presented for discussion by Schneider and her colleagues (M. S. Schneider et al., 2002). One hopes that Ms. Knoway's training program in pastoral counseling included substantive content on psychodiagnostics, psychopathology, and psychotherapeutics, even though her behaviors do not reflect competence in those arenas. The data suggest she may have leapt to diagnostic conclusions without foundation and had an ideological predisposition to do so. She has overlooked the need to first "do no harm." (Morrow, 2000). In the end, she has left Frank in significantly worse condition than before he sought counseling.

Case 6–13: Connie Fused had dated boys in high school because it seemed expected in her community and social group. Although she actually felt more sexual and romantic attraction toward some female friends, she never felt comfortable expressing those feelings. When Connie left home to attend college in another state, the new environment gave her a sense of freedom to explore. She developed an intimate relationship with another young woman. During the semester break she "came out" to her parents, who became alarmed and insisted on enrolling her at the Healing Eternal Love Lodge, a residential program designed to literally straighten out people who had "homosexual leanings." Wanting to please her parents and feeling unsure of her own identity, Connie entered the program. A few weeks later, she finished the program, moved back to her parents' home, and transferred to a nearby college. The Healing Eternal Love Lodge kept in touch with Connie by phone on a weekly basis at first and then monthly. If she reported any "backsliding," the staff at the Lodge promised to send a treatment team to her home to provide "booster sessions." Connie reported that the program had worked, dated a few young men, and moved away from her home community after college. She realized that she still felt greater attraction to women but kept these feelings and her relationships with women secret from her family. The follow-up calls from the Healing Eternal Love Lodge still come in every few months, and she still tells them that the treatment worked so that they will leave her alone.

The situation experienced by Connie illustrates the familial and social pressures that can affect clients' decision making in such cases. We have no information on the competence or credentials of the counseling staff at the Healing Eternal Love Lodge. They probably think that they collect great follow-up data and consider Connie's case a successful outcome because of what they hear when they follow up with her. Connie just wants the pressure off and finds it easier to keep important aspects of her life private.

The key to an ethical response in any treatment involving matters laden with social, political, or religious significance includes conducting a careful assessment and offering an intervention that has proven efficacy and meets the preferences and needs of the client apart from preordained biases of the therapist. We can not avoid the influence of societal and professional beliefs and biases concerning gay, lesbian, and bisexual people, and too often education and training programs devote inade-

quate attention to such issues (Biaggio, Orchard, Larson, Petrino, & Mihara, 2003; Greene et al., 2007; Lasser & Gottlieb, 2004).

Behavioral Techniques

As in the case of sex therapy, the application of behavioral techniques such as operant conditioning, classical conditioning, aversive therapies, and other types of physical interventions (e.g., physiological monitoring, biofeedback, stress management, etc.) require specialized training of an interdisciplinary nature (Farmer & Nelson-Gray, 2005; Martin & Pear, 1996). This may include training in anatomy and physiology as well as the analysis of behavior and application of learning theory. In addition, one must also maintain a keen awareness of special caveats, such as knowing when a medical consultation is indicated or when a certain instrumental procedure may edge toward the violation of a client's rights. Although many behavioral and cognitive interventions originated as the work of psychologists, many types of therapists have access to training in the use of complex approaches involving an assortment of cognitive and behavior therapies in ways unimaginable to the earliest practitioners of these approaches (Farmer & Nelson-Gray, 2005; Reamer, 2006). The depth and breadth of training across therapists from different professions vary widely.

The application of behavioral techniques usually involves the assumption of a substantial degree of control over the client's environment. Generally, this takes place with the active involvement and consent of the client (J. S. Bailey & Burch, 2006; Martin & Pear, 1996). In some instances, however, the client may be technically or literally incompetent to consent, as in the case of mentally retarded or severely psychotic clients. When the client is incompetent to fully consent and powerful environmental controls are enforced, special substituted judgment procedures using independent advocates may be warranted (Bregman et al., 2005; Koocher, 1976, 1983).

From time to time, there have been outcries in the mass media about the application of behavioral techniques in schools, prisons, and other settings. For example, consider the issue of behavior therapy in correctional settings in the context of the popular political mantra of "getting tough on crime." Many behavioral techniques (e.g., increased privilege levels as rewards for good behavior) have long found use in such institutions. Privately operated correctional systems now frequently contract with state and local government to manage facilities. Should behavior therapists develop a niche of their own within the private incarceration industry? Expanding work with a private or for-profit prison system may lead to ignoring ethical, theoretical, and scientific principles (Wong & Wong, 2003).

Many have historically called for, produced, or rebutted the need for specialized guidelines to be used in applying behavioral techniques (Bregman et al., 2005; Davidson & Stuart, 1975; Stolz, 1977; Thaw, Thorne, & Benjamin, 1978; Turkat & Forehand, 1980). We find that behavioral therapies are no more or less in need of regulation per se than other forms of treatment also subject to abuse. As Stolz noted, behavioral clinicians, like other therapists, should follow the ethics code of their professions; also, the ethics of all intervention programs should undergo evaluation in terms of existing ethics codes.

Specific complaints regarding behavior therapies commonly encountered by ethics committees are illustrated in the following several cases:

Case 6–14: Gordon Convert, M.D., agreed to treat Billy Prissy, age 5, whose parents were concerned about his "effeminate" behaviors. Dr. Convert devised a behavioral program for implementation in the office and at home involving the differential reinforcement of toy choice, dress-up play, and a variety of other activities of a stereotyped sex-role nature. When reports of this project appeared in professional journals, a storm of protest resulted.

The case of Dr. Convert is typical of those complaints that revolve around the matter of client choice and goal setting in therapy. It is not possible to tell from the brief information we have given here just how appropriate or inappropriate the program was. The context and nature of decision making and treatment goal setting are critical (Bregman et al., 2005; Stolz, 1978). In this case, Billy's viewpoint demands just as much consideration as the preferences expressed by his parents. In addition, many of the criticisms of conversion therapies that focused on gay men, as described in this chapter, may also apply here.

These issues were well illustrated historically in a series of comments to a manuscript on alternatives to pain medication (Cook, 1975; Goodstein, 1975; Karoly, 1975). The original report focused on a 65-year-old man admitted to a psychiatric ward with symptoms of chronic abdominal pain and a self-induced drug habit to control the pain (Levendusky & Pankratz, 1975). He was successfully withdrawn from the drug using a treatment procedure that involved some deception and lacked fully informed consent. The ethical dilemma here is the matter of client involvement in making choices rather than the technique itself.

Case 6–15: Seymour Diversion, Ph.D., worked in a state hospital for children with emotional problems. He designed a specialized program that applied aversive stimulation (e.g., brief application of an electric shock rod) to interrupt self-injurious behavior in a head-banging child. The child had caused permanent damage to one eye and was in danger of losing the other as well. Less drastic means of interrupting the behavior had failed. A nurse at the hospital was outraged and informed local newspapers of how Dr. Diversion was "torturing" the child.

An ethics committee asked Dr. Diversion to respond to the complaint, and he did so with openness and in detail. Several less-invasive attempts to prevent the child from destroying his remaining eye by head banging had been unsuccessful. A special panel had been asked to review the case and approve the trial of aversive techniques independently of Dr. Diversion and the hospital. Diversion managed the program personally and noted that he had been prepared to discontinue the use of aversive stimuli promptly if no benefit resulted for the child. The committee agreed that every appropriate precaution had been taken, and that

Diversion had behaved appropriately, given the severe nature of the child's self-injury.

Case 6–16: Thelma Splatter, L.M.H.C., designed an aversive treatment program to deal with severely retarded residents of a state facility, who were toileting in public on the grounds of the school and in the corridors. The program involved an operant reward system as well as a spray of ice water in the face, administered from a small squirting bottle. Some of the attendants were inadequately trained in the rationale and application of the technique. One evening, an attendant caught a male resident of the school smearing feces and pushed the man's face into a toilet bowl while flushing it several times. He reported that he did not have the spray bottle with him.

Ms. Splatter's program may have been adequately conceptualized, but it was poorly implemented. The attendant clearly did not discriminate between the intended shock value of the ice-water spray and the sadistic and punitive act of holding a person's face in the toilet. The unethical behavior here was chiefly Splatter's failure to adequately supervise the people charged with executing her treatment program. If she were unable to adequately supervise all of those participating in the program she designed, then she should have carefully limited the scope of the program to those she could adequately supervise. Although the attendant remained responsible for his own behavior, Dr. Splatter may have inadvertently provided a context within which the act seemed appropriate to him.

During a conversation hour at an APA convention many years ago, the late B. F. Skinner told bemusedly about the controversy that seemed to focus on labels as opposed to practice. He noted that a school board had promulgated a threat to fire any personnel who used behavior modification. Skinner then wondered aloud what would happen the next payday when "reinforcements" were handed out in the form of paychecks. This illustrates again that it is not the technique itself that presents ethical problems but the manner in which it is applied and labeled.

Unfortunately, not all therapists who attempt to employ behavioral techniques are well trained in underlying learning theory. Confusion on the distinction between the concepts of "punishment" and "negative reinforcement" constitutes one prime example of a common problem. In other instances, aversive treatment protocols have occasionally been introduced without first trying less restrictive techniques.

It is especially important that therapists show careful concern for ethical problems inherent in the use of aversive stimuli with relatively powerless clients. This would include, for example, institutionalized, incarcerated, or incompetent individuals, as well as children or other people not fully able to assert their rights.

Case 6–17: Marquis deSique, Ph.D., operated a private residential facility for emotionally disturbed and delinquent children. The parents of a 10-year-old boy filed ethics charges when they discovered multiple bruises and lacerations all over their son's body during a visit. Dr. deSique explained that the boy required several beating sessions each week to "break his strong will" and permit more appropriate behavior to emerge. It was later discovered that all of the residents were routinely subjected to such sessions, conducted in a specially equipped punishment room. In addition, Dr. deSique would also take nude photographs of them following the beatings.

This sort of case causes sensitive, objective, and competent behavioral clinicians considerable outrage because Dr. deSique's "treatments" do not conform to standards of professional practice or ethics. The practices also have no basis in empirical data or learning theory. It seems more likely that deSique was satisfying some peculiar needs of his own at the expense of his vulnerable wards.

Psychotherapeutic Devices

The report of the APA Task Force on Psychologists' Use of Physical Interventions (APA, 1981) listed more than a score of instruments and devices used for clinical assessment and psychotherapy at the time. These included a variety of electrodes and monitors used in biofeedback training, as well as an assortment of color vision testers, dynamometers, audiometers, restraints, and even vibrators. In the years since that report came forth, the number devices used in psychotherapeutic treatments (Barlow, 2004) or in psychodiagnostic assessment with proven efficacy (i.e., excluding quackery) has grown exponentially.

Case 6–18: Reeka Sniff, Psy.D., offers her clients a "new form of adjunct therapy" designed to substantially reduce stress and other emotional disturbances. She also informs her clients that alternative therapies are now recognized by the National Institutes of Health (NIH). She has purchased an "Aromatherapy Decoder Wheel" that assists her in mixing just the right blend of some 100 different fragrant oils. She places the mix in a container warmed by a small candle to help disperse the fragrance on a small table between herself and the client. They then continue the counseling sessions as usual.

On the one hand, Dr. Sniff's use of fragrance probably causes no harm, assuming that the client has no allergic reactions. If the client likes the aromas, they may even offer a placebo benefit. However, Dr. Sniff has engaged in some elements of misdirection. The comment about NIH appears intended to legitimize her use of the technique. One can find aromatherapy wheels and scents sold commercially, but these have not been validated as medical or psychological treatments. In addition, if Dr. Sniff sells such supplies to clients, she will have crossed a critical multiple-role boundary involving an unproven or quack product.

Psychiatrists have seen a resurgence of interest in electroconvulsive therapy (ETC) for the treatment of severe refractory depression (Dukakis & Tye, 2006), and some have worked with neurosurgeons to explore the viability of deep brain stimulation (DBS) in severe cases (Carpenter, 2006; Fitzgerald, 2006; Glannon, 2006). Some of these devices that involve connection to or insertion in the human body are regulated by the U.S. Food and Drug Administration, and most require specialized training for proper use.

Biofeedback devices, ranging from skin temperature to plethysmographic monitors, have seen enormous growth (Ackerman & Banks,

1990; Paul, Cassisi, & Larson, 1996; Percival & Striefel, 1994). Despite considerable controversy, the use of lie detectors or deception involving the alleged ability to detect lying still abound (Aguinis & Handelsman, 1997; Candilis, 1998). Virtual reality devices and a burgeoning market full of other devices and computer applications with varying levels of proven efficacy appear regularly in publications aimed at mental health professionals (Newman, 2004; Rizzo, Strickland, & Bouchard, 2004; Sampson, 1983; Wiederhold & Wiederhold, 2005). One particularly interesting approach involves the development of virtual reality programs that engage all of the senses in an effort to apply realistic exposure interventions to help reduce posttraumatic stress among military personnel returning from combat (Jardin, 2005; Rizzo et al., 2004). The use of technology in the future of psychotherapy seems likely to increase and along with it ethical complaints of a related nature. Skip ahead to the case of Dr. Anna Sthesia (Case 17–20) to see an example of technology-related negligence.

The basic caveat is as follows: All psychotherapists should recognize the boundaries of their competence, especially when attempting to make use of new technologies (Newman, 2004; Wiederhold & Wiederhold, 2005). They must avoid using unsafe or unproven devices, not to mention those that might prove dangerous to clients through electric shock or other hazards. Therapists must also remain mindful that they should never attempt treatment of problems with possible organic causes without a collaborative relationship with a qualified physician. This mandate applies equally to psychiatrists and psychiatric nurse practitioners, whose internal medicine expertise may be quite limited. In addition, federal law may govern the licensing and use of some instruments, and practitioners have an obligation to keep themselves abreast of these statutes and resulting duties.

Coercive Therapies

As noted in Chapter 5, psychotherapy has sometimes been considered a means of social control (Hurvitz, 1973) and compared in some ways with brainwashing (Dolliver, 1971; Gaylin,

1974). The use of "coercive persuasion," "deprogramming," and hypnotic suggestion techniques (Fromm, 1980; Kline, 1976) have all been discussed from the viewpoint of client manipulation. Many other types of coercive practices have become central to some psychotherapeutic approaches with strong public approval. These include court-ordered therapy for a range of conditions (e.g., anger management, driving while intoxicated, sexual acting out); restrictions placed on nonincarcerated sex offenders (Schopp, 2003); restrictions in educational settings (Sidman, 1999); and coercive restraint or forced holding therapies for children (Mercer, 2003). To what extent do certain psychological techniques permit the psychotherapist to manipulate or control the client by force or threat? In Chapter 5, we also discussed the right to refuse treatment, and we cite these issues here as examples of techniques that from time to time have been the object of complaints. More recent concerns have included the possible role of therapists in dealing with alleged terrorist detainees held by military authorities. However, those roles do not involve psychotherapy and are addressed in Chapter 18.

Case 6–19: Thinny Asarail, age 16, has "felt fat" for many years and, despite the fact that her 5 foot 4 inch tall body weighs a mere 75 pounds, she still believes she must restrict her food intake. Her battle with anorexia nervosa has left her with significant health problems and often unstable vital signs, prompting her parents to send her to a residential treatment program. Still, she refuses many meals. When she will not eat, a nurse and hospital attendant restrain Thinny as a physician passes a nasogastric (NG) tube through her nostril and into her stomach to deliver a nutritional supplement. After removal of the NG tube, Thinny must sit in view of the staff for at least 90 minutes to ensure that she does not attempt to vomit the feeding.

Thinny's medical condition demands such care to ensure her survival, even though she does not agree. Her parents and the medical team have authorized this treatment over her objections. When Thinny reaches the age of majority, she can no longer be coerced into such treatment unless a court rules her mentally incom-

petent. It is hoped that psychotherapeutic intervention and nutritional support will help effect a cure and avoid the need for prolonged coercive intervention.

In general, it is unethical for a psychotherapist to coerce a client into treatment or to force certain goals or outcomes against the client's wishes. In Chapter 18, we discuss some special problem situations along these lines (e.g., clients who are in the military or are involuntarily confined in institutions such as prisons). It is most difficult to be sensitive to the more subtle aspects of coercion: group pressure, guilt induction, introduction of cognitive dissonance, attempts at total environmental control, and the establishment of a trusting relationship with the goal of effecting change in another person (Dolliver, 1971). It is critical that the therapist attempt to remain aware of potentially coercive influences and avoid any that do not offer full participation, discussion, and choice by the client. The constant critical reexamination of the strategies and goals of treatment involving both client and therapist is the best means to this end.

Teletherapy

Rapid advances in microelectronics have made portable communication, data, image, sound storage, and transmission devices affordable and readily available in much of the world. A broad array of personal communications and business transactions now occur in the realm of cyberspace. We must expect that mental health practitioners will increasingly face expectations by our clients to provide services in the context of their preferred modes of communication. As we move away from the traditional context of sitting face to face with our client across a room, the Greek prefix *tele*, meaning from a distance, leads naturally to considering the ethics of teletherapy. Many colleagues have used *telehealth* as a term in medicine and mental health for a variety of models for providing professional services via telephone and other electronic means (Barnett & Scheetz, 2003; C. B. Fisher & Fried, 2003; Jerome & Zaylor, 2000; Maheu, Whitten, & Allen, 2001; Nickelson, 1998; VandenBos & Williams, 2000). Radiology and cardiology are just two of many medical specialties that have regularly used these techniques for consultation among professionals. What we have traditionally agreed to in forming alliances and contracts with individual clients and professional standards will certainly require rethinking.

From the perspective of professional ethics, consider the four Cs: contracting, competence, confidentiality, and control (Koocher, 2007). In the context of teletherapy, these questions arise:

- What contracts or agreements for providing distance services will we make with our clients?
- What competencies will we need to offer services remotely?
- What new factors will constrain confidentiality protections?
- Who will control the practice of teletherapy (i.e., the regulation of practice and data access)?

When we agree to work with clients via telemetry, the nature and terms of how we relate will change. We will need to reach accords on new contracts or agreements regarding the nature of psychological services and manner of providing them. For example, we will have to obtain and document clients' informed consent to communicate with them electronically (APA 02: 2.10a). Such consent will doubtless require many changes, such as requiring us to establish reasonable security and encryption precautions and to provide precise instructions regarding the nature of the services, access, and emergency coverage (APA 02: 4.02c). Still other questions must be answered:

- Will we contract to correspond electronically only with existing therapy clients, or will we readily accept new referrals of people we have never met for any or all of our professional services?
- Will we agree to conduct all assessment, consultation, or therapy relationships entirely via telemetry or only a limited range of services?
- Will we promise real-time electronic access 24/7/365? (See APA 02: 501a.)
- How will record keeping change given the ease with which we can record, store, and alter such communications?

- Will our fees and reimbursement policies differ from office-based services?
- Will we offer emergency coverage? If so, what backup must we organize for clients who live hundreds or thousands of miles away?

New standards of care and professional competencies will apply when we offer direct services remotely. The APA has not chosen to address teletherapy directly in its ethics code (APA Ethics Committee, 1997) and by this intentional omission has created no rules prohibiting such services. The committee has consistently stated a willingness to address any complaints regarding such matters on a case-by-case basis, while directing us to apply the same standards used in "emerging areas in which generally recognized standards for preparatory training do not yet exist" by taking "reasonable steps to ensure the competence of their work and to protect patients, clients, students, research participants, and others from harm" (APA 02: 2.01e). Aside from another general caution about reviewing "the characteristics of the services, the service delivery method, the provisions for confidentiality, and licensure board rules," no clear professional consensus or detailed ethical guidelines currently exist. The committee noted that telephone contact can offer an important and beneficial tool, citing the well-established success of suicide hot lines, brief crisis and referral services, or provision of educational messages by telephone (APA Ethics Committee, 1997).

At present, a substantial and growing body of literature, including whole journal special issues (Newman, 2004), has documented the process of combining technological advances with established methods for the provision of mental health services (Barnett, 2005; C. B. Fisher & Fried, 2003; Maheu, 2003; Ragusea & VandeCreek, 2003). Psychotherapists have long used electronic means to keep in touch with traditionally established clients during vacations, relocations, and emergencies. A growing body of research has also demonstrated the potential benefits of delivering psychological interventions by telephone (Bastien, Morin, Ouellet, Blais, & Bouchard, 2004; Heckman et al., 2004; McKay et al., 2004; Mermelstein, Hedeker, &

Wong, 2003; Sandgren & McCaul, 2003). The practical value of electronically mediated health and mental health care delivery (Jerome & Zaylor, 2000; Maheu & Gordon, 2000) as well as clinical supervision (Wood, Miller, & Hargrove, 2005) has been well documented. Not surprisingly, however, some research has shown ratings of therapeutic alliances formed via videoconferencing to fall significantly below similar ratings of interactions under face-to-face conditions (Rees & Stone, 2005). We actually know very little about which specific competencies of individual psychotherapists translate into which types of alliances (effectively or ineffectively) for particular clients. Some types of therapeutic intervention will not easily translate into electronic activities (e.g., play therapy with young children or interventions involving therapeutic touch). This challenging domain remains one of the most rapidly evolving areas of professional practice and the ripest areas for clinical research.

We must also not overlook the obvious potential for mischief. Both those offering to provide services and those seeking to obtain them may more easily engage in misrepresentation. How can one be certain that the person on the other end of the phone line or computer terminal is the person he or she claims to be? How accurate are the claims of teletherapy practitioners regarding their credentials, skills, and success rates with remote interventions? How will you feel when someone intent on a modern-day replay of Rosenhan's famous study (Rosenhan, 1973) or an angry former client posts edited excerpts of their "sessions" with you on youtube.com or stupidvideos.com? Will teletherapy lead to greater caution and reduced liability (e.g., by reducing the risk of client–therapist sexual intimacy) or greater risk (e.g., reduced ability to respond across distances with suicidal clients)? We will probably have more answers to such intriguing questions in the not-so-distant future.

Questions about the control or regulation of teletherapy practice remain highly fluid. One survey (Koocher & Morray, 2000) documented considerable variability across licensing jurisdictions in the United States with respect to electronic practice across state lines. With state, provincial, and territorial governments regulat-

ing professional practice within U.S. and Canadian jurisdictions, the Association of State and Provincial Psychology Boards (ASPPB) has taken the lead in attempting to foster interstate practice and mobility credentials for psychologists in North America. However, little agreement exists regarding standards for interstate or international telepractice. The fundamental concepts involved will prove challenging to resolve. When a client in Boston enters teletherapy with a psychotherapist in Los Angeles, Toronto, or Hyderabad, who regulates the practice? Does the treatment take place where the client sits, where the therapist sits, or in cyberspace? If something goes wrong, to whom can one complain? Will a domestic licensing board even open a complaint against one of its licensees who has treated a client residing outside their geographic jurisdiction? If they do, will the state government's enforcement branch authorize prosecution, and will the courts recognize jurisdiction? Will telepractice qualify as interstate (or international) commerce exempt from state licensing authorities? We simply do not know the answers at this time.

We do have some specific suggestions for colleagues who choose to communicate with clients using electronic mail; these are compiled in Box 6–1.

Use of Emerging Technologies

Apart from teletherapy as a *specific* practice, novel or emerging technologies will continually create new ethical issues. Ethical standards related to competence (APA 02: 2.01e) apply when clinicians wish to develop or implement new practice techniques for which generally agreed-on scientific or professional qualifications do not yet exist. For example, therapists using e-mail or chat rooms to provide behavioral health services to clients at a distance are venturing into relatively uncharted territories. In addition, traditional assessment and psychotherapy techniques based on oral and nonverbal cues may not transfer to communications via written text (Maheu & Gordon, 2000; Nickelson, 1998; VandenBos & Williams, 2000). Harm to Internet clients may occur when therapists inappropriately diagnose a disorder, fail to

> **Box 6–1 Special Considerations When Using E-mail or the Internet to Communicate With Clients**
>
> - Consider carefully and in advance which services and types of communication you want to provide electronically (e.g., appointment scheduling, impromptu requests, clinical updates, or emergency messages).
> - Discuss with clients those topics that you are willing to discuss via e-mail, as well as the potential benefits, risks, and limitations involved with e-mail communication (e.g., including the potential access by others to unencrypted e-mail).
> - Emphasize limitations and constraints on access to you via e-mail (e.g., do you plan to offer 24/7/365 coverage? Can a client expect a response within a particular time frame?).
> - Obtain and document (via a personally or electronically signed document) patients' informed consent to communicate with them in this manner.
> - Establish security and encryption precautions prior to using e-mail with patients.
> - Make sure that any information posted on your practice's Web site is up to date and accurate.
> - Monitor online scheduling programs or access by others to your account carefully to ensure that confidentiality is preserved.
> - Check e-mail frequently.
> - Print or otherwise preserve all e-mail exchanges with patients and keep them with patients' treatment records.

identify suicidal or homicidal ideation, or reinforce maladaptive behavior, for example, social phobia (see APA 02: 3.04). Steps that therapists using Internet-mediated assessment or therapeutic services might take to ensure the competence of their work and to protect clients from harm include staying abreast of advances in the field; requiring an in-person initial consultation; and identifying professionals and health and social service agencies that are in the area in which the client/patient lives that can be called in crisis situations (Maheu et al., 2001).

Consider some cases involving novel treatments for which generally recognized techniques and procedures have not been established:

Case 6–20: Neuro Transmitter, Psy.D., works in Paramus, New Jersey, and provides services through a service known as 1-900-SHRINK-ME of Dallas, Texas. One afternoon, he is connected by phone with a new caller to the service, Ann Hedonia of Simi Valley, California. After 20 minutes of the session, Dr. Transmitter recognizes that Ms. Hedonia is seriously depressed with suicidal ideation and is feeling at the edge of her ability to cope. He gently suggests that perhaps she ought to think about hospitalization near her home. Ms. Hedonia replies, "Even you don't care about me! That's it. I'm going to do it!" and slams down the telephone receiver.

How does one conduct an adequate suicide risk assessment of a brand new client over the telephone to enable formulation of an adequate treatment plan? How does one intervene in the event of suicidal or homicidal ideation? How does one ensure privacy from electronic eavesdropping or simple monitoring by someone over an extension phone? Suppose Ms. Hedonia has a complaint about Dr. Transmitter. From whom can she seek a remedy? Which state's law applies for professional practice, confidentiality, or licensing qualifications? Must Dr. Transmitter even have a state license to offer this service? Arguably, such therapy constitutes interstate commerce, so no single state's laws (and licensing board) may have clear authority. What remedies does an aggrieved client have?

Similar issues apply to a plethora of new assessment and treatment services offered on the World Wide Web. One service invited people to submit questions that will be answered privately within 48 hours "by a person with at least a master's degree in counseling." That service charges according to the byte size of the reply, possibly inviting the longest replies the consultant can generate. Another service offers to answer individual questions for a flat $50 fee and provides a listing of half a dozen doctoral-level clinicians who will field the items submitted. Still a third service invites participants to a private real-time dialogue with a therapist via a computerized chat service. All require payment in advance by credit card, and all raise the same questions as the pay-per-minute telephone service, plus a few more.

Case 6–21: Dr. Transmitter checked in with Psych-Autix Ltd., an international electronic mail network for mental health practitioners. He finds a private posting from one of his clients, Art Tonomy, who sent the message by Internet from his workstation at the accounting firm of Dewey, Cheatem, and How, LLC. Mr. Tonomy feels somewhat guilty about a secret extramarital affair he has begun with the wife of one of the firm's senior partners. He seeks some confidential help. Mr. Tonomy is unaware that the accounting firm has established an "echo capture system" that records all incoming and outgoing messages as redundant protection against loss. In reviewing the external e-mail traffic the following week, the head of computer security will find Mr. Tonomy's message and call it to the senior partner's attention. There is nothing illegal about doing so.

In this situation, Dr. Transmitter could not provide a detailed warning about this limitation on privacy or confidentiality because he had no knowledge about the system from which the message came.

Although the idea of bringing psychotherapy consultation swiftly and efficiently to people who might not find their way to a therapist's office is appealing, a headlong rush into new technological approaches without thoughtful and accountable professionalism invites disaster. Psychotherapy presents many challenges when a client presents him- or herself in your office. In addition to the lack of nonverbal communication typical of a telephone conversation, e-mail services also remove voice, pitch, tone, and other verbal cues as clinical data. This can only increase the potential for errors and problems. As real-time videophone technology becomes increasingly available and licensing issues are clarified, some of these difficulties may improve. However, for the moment we have significant concerns about the total lack of consumer-oriented regulation (Koocher & Morray, 2000).

UNTESTED OR FRINGE THERAPIES

From time to time, ethics complaints will develop in response to a new or unusual form of psychotherapy or supposedly psychotherapeutic technique. Often, these so-called treatments are of questionable merit or frankly dangerous. Notwithstanding the importance of evidence-based practice, as discussed at the beginning of this chapter, there must be room for appropriate innovation and the development of new treatment strategies in any scientific field. However, rigorous standards must be applied to avoid misleading, or actually harming, potential clients. No program of psychotherapy should be undertaken without a firm theoretical foundation and scientific basis for anticipating client benefits. New approaches to psychotherapy should be labeled as experimental with appropriate informed consent when that is the case and should be discontinued at the first indication that any harm is accruing to the clients.

This Is Therapy?

Jacobson and his colleagues provided a number of excellent and detailed illustrations in their book on controversial therapies for developmental disabilities (Jacobson et al., 2005). These include so-called emotional freedom techniques (EFTs), thought field therapy (TFT), neuro linguistic programming (NLP), and the visual/kinesthetic dissociation (v/k-d) technique. These have attracted some attention as posttraumatic therapies (Lohr et al., 2003). A Delphi poll of experts has also called attention to mental health theories (e.g., Bettleheim's 1967 assertions that emotionally detached "refrigerator mothers" caused childhood autism) and treatments or techniques once in popular use but now deemed discredited (Norcross et al., 2006). Examples of such treatments and techniques include angel therapy, the use of crystals to promote mental health, and Reich's use of orgone energy accumulators or orgone boxes (Reich, 1948a, 1948b). Some specific case examples follow.

Case 6–22: Millard Brute, Ph.D., prepared an audiotape for experimental use in implosive desensitization of child abusers. The tape described with vivid imagery the successively escalating physical assault on a child, culminating in the dismemberment and cannibalization of the corpse. The tape was played for a professional audience, and one outraged participant filed an ethics complaint.

Dr. Brute informed the ethics committee that the tape did not constitute an actual treatment tool but rather an experimental project he used for illustrative purposes with audiences exclusively composed of professionals. Nonetheless, the committee noted the sensitive nature of the tape and advised Dr. Brute to give more consideration to his audiences' sensitivities in the future. Certainly, the intense nature of the implosive therapy regimen would require thorough discussion with any client prior to implementation. Some might question whether adequate data exist on which to predicate such treatment.

Case 6–23: Renee Roper, M.S.W., is a proponent of "harassment therapy." This sometimes involves extended verbal attacks on particular clients and in other situations involves tying clients up and forcing them to struggle to get loose. When an ethics complaint was filed, Dr. Roper explained her belief that it was necessary to be "harsh" on "the whimpering dependent types."

Case 6–24: Gwendolyn Strange, Ed.D., required her individual therapy clients to participate in group therapy sessions at her home on a biweekly basis. They were required to sit in a circle on floor pillows, while Dr. Strange perched above them on a stool, clothed in a black leotard, and read to them from a book manuscript she was writing.

Case 6–25: Tanya Teton, L.M.H.C., is a proponent of "radical reparenting" therapy and strongly believes that she must help her clients to "recover from defective early nurturance" by fostering "regression and renurturing." Early in treatment, she asks her adult clients to sit in her lap and drink from a baby bottle. At times, clients are instructed to wear a diaper, and Dr. Teton powders their behinds. As treatment intensifies, she has occasionally invited these clients to nurse from her bare breast. One client complained to an ethics committee that the treatment seemed "way out of line."

The theoretical rationales of Ms. Roper and Dr. Strange are vague and questionable at best. It is difficult to imagine that either one has advised their clients of the potential risks involved in the so-called treatments. Have any of their clients received an objective description of more conventional and better proven, readily available treatments for their problems? Dr. Teton seemed surprised by the "empathic failure" of the client who complained about her to an ethics committee. The male client was experiencing confusing feelings of sexual arousal during the nursing experience, but Dr. Teton discounted this in her response to the ethics panel, noting that there was "nothing sexual about it" as far as she was concerned. Often, it is the most egocentric and least competent practitioners who come to the attention of ethics committees via this sort of complaint.

We have disguised the next case, but one can find a number of actual sites with similar offerings.

Case 6–26: One Web site describes "force intensity therapy" as "a methodology that integrates principles of human force psychology, mental control, and intensity therapy." The Web site also advertises a number of educational opportunities in the use of this technique, noting: "A previous background in intensity therapy is desirable but not required for training."

The Web site promoting force intensity therapy provides few scientific data, vague terminology and theoretical underpinnings, and considerable commercial advocacy. Sadly, many unlicensed practitioners lure members of the public with a mix of new age appeal and psychobabble.

Case 6–27: Flyers on community bulletin boards advertise the services Rhonda Rooter by explaining that she "begins with the premise that every physical symptom has a mental energy component." She uses her innovative psychotherapy, called central belief reinvention, to take on people with a wide range of physical ailments. These include high blood pressure, cancer, allergies, hypothyroidism, HIV, vaginismus, and sugar addiction. It seems that Rooter recognizes that the subconscious mind consists of a constellation of parts—each holding its own unique beliefs about the self and the universe. Conflicting beliefs, desires, and goals create confusion and stress. Rooter, in her own words, "ingeniously works to resolve such differences and reinvent essential collaboration between the subconscious and conscious mind, thus sidestepping psychological labeling and interpretation."

We have no clue about Rooter's credentials or the validity of her treatment techniques. Perhaps she actually helps some people, but aspects of her practice seem potentially scary. A number of the physical conditions she claims to treat have significant medical complexities. Her sales pitch makes no theoretical sense, leaving concern that people seeking her help may find themselves in worse condition after her intervention than before, possibly delaying needed medical treatment.

Sometimes things go terribly wrong. Applying a "new age" therapy technique, intended to bring Candace Newmaker closer to her adoptive mother by having the 10-year-old girl push her way out of a blanket to simulate birth, ended tragically. In a 70-minute videotape of an April 18, 2000, session, Candace begged for her life as she tried to escape the blanket meant to repre-

sent a womb. She died of asphyxiation the next day. Prosecutors charged two psychotherapists, Connell Watkins, a purported expert on children with reactive attachment disorder, and her colleague Julie Ponder with child abuse resulting in death. The video showed Candace struggling and gasping for breath as the therapists and two assistants pushed on either side of her in an effort to simulate her rebirth. On April 20, 2001, in Golden, Colorado, Watkins and Ponder were found guilty of reckless child abuse resulting in death. In addition, Watkins was convicted of a second felony, criminal impersonation, and of two misdemeanors—obtaining a signature by deception and unlawful practice of psychotherapy. They were each sentenced to 16 years in prison. On April 17, 2001, then Colorado Governor Bill Owens signed a bill into law (i.e., Candace's Law) that now specifically prohibits the use of "rebirthing" techniques by mental health professionals in Colorado (Colorado Revised Statutes Section 2, 12-43-222).

Proprietary Psychotherapy

From time to time, systems of psychotherapy have been developed and marketed as unique approaches to dealing with human problems. Any student of psychotherapy will think of Sigmund Freud as associated with psychoanalysis, Carl Rogers as linked to client-centered psychotherapy, and Albert Ellis as the founder of rational emotive therapy. As in the case of many systems and techniques of psychotherapy, research took place, books were written, lectures given, and students taught. In some cases, valuable brands resulted, and people earned a living catering to the brand. Some of these brands have developed significant proprietary aspects.

Characteristics of such systems usually include required specialized training, for which substantial fees are paid only to specifically designated instructors. The usual justification involves maintaining quality control or monitoring the purity of the intervention. As a result, there is often an aura of secrecy and lack of scientific scrutiny surrounding such approaches to treatment. Two modern examples that have become well known to professional communities and the public, but with very distinct differences in their scientific underpinnings and marketing, are Eye Movement Desensitization and Reprocessing (EMDR) and Erhard Seminars Training (est).

Eye Movement Desensitization and Reprocessing

The EMDR technique was developed by Francine Shapiro (Shapiro, 1995; Shapiro & Forrest, 2004) and is described as a comprehensive method for treating disturbing experiences such as trauma associated with sexual abuse, violence, combat, grief, or phobias. The treatment incorporates eight stages: taking the client's history and treatment planning, preparation, assessment, desensitization and reprocessing, installation of positive cognition, body scan, closure, and reevaluation (Chemtob et al., 2000). The treatment requires the client to describe aspects of traumatic memories, including images associated with the event, their emotional and physiological responses, the negative feelings of self inherent in the memories (induced by the traumatic experience in the case of posttraumatic stress disorder [PTSD]), and to describe an alternate, desired, more positive self-perception. This sequence of steps is repeated until the client's Subjective Units of Distress Scale (so-called SUDS rating) approaches zero.

Eye Movement Desensitization and Reprocessing has become among the fastest-growing interventions in the annals of psychotherapy, and its progression has many similarities with the history of mesmerism (McNally, 1999). EMDR as a treatment for PTSD has received widely divergent reactions from the scientific and professional community. Perkins and Rouanzoin (2002) noted that many points of confusion exist in the published literature on this technique, including its theoretical and historical foundation, placebo effects, exposure procedures, the eye movement component, treatment fidelity issues, and outcome studies. These authors described the scientific process and charges of "pseudoscience" surrounding EMDR and concluded that the confusion in the literature and the controversy seems linked to five factors: the

lack of an empirically validated model capable of convincingly explaining the effects of the technique; inaccurate or selective reporting of research; some poorly designed studies; inadequate treatment fidelity in some of the outcome studies; and multiple biased or inaccurate reviews by a relatively small group of authors.

One of the interesting questions about EMDR involves the inclusion of many elements of cognitive behavioral therapies along with the lateral eye movements, causing some to wonder whether what is effective about EMDR is actually new, and whether what is new about EMDR is actually effective (McNally, 1999). Francine Shapiro (comments on Reed and Johnson, personal communication to G. P. Koocher via e-mail, January 17, 2007) argued that EMDR actually integrates many components in addition to cognitive behavioral elements used in cognitive behavioral therapy, including those used in psychodynamic and experiential therapies. In one book (2002), she asked experts of the various orientations in experiential, cognitive, and psychodynamic treatment to identify the elements in EMDR that made it effective. Each one identified elements of their own orientation as the pivotal factors.

Various reviews of the related eye movement research have provided a range of conclusions. Some reviewers (Lohr, Lilienfeld, Tolin, & Herbert, 1999) stated that there is no compelling evidence that eye movements contribute to outcome in EMDR treatment, and the lack of unequivocal findings has led some reviewers to dismiss eye movements altogether (e.g., McNally, 1999). Other reviewers (e.g., Chemtob et al., 2000; Feske, 1998; Perkins & Rouanzoin, 2002) identified methodological failings (e.g., lack of statistical power, floor effects) and called for more rigorous study.

Nonetheless, many studies have demonstrated beneficial outcomes for some people using EMDR, and we cite a recent sampling here (Brown & Shapiro, 2006; Konuk et al., 2006; Raboni, Tufik, Suchecki, & Yehuda, 2006; Russell, 2006; G. Schneider, Nabavi, & Heuft, 2005; R. Shapiro, 2005; Tarrier, Liversidge, & Gregg, 2006). The Department of Veterans Affairs and Department of Defense (2004) have listed EMDR as a potentially effective treatment in their *Clinical Practice Guideline for the Management of Post-traumatic Stress*.

Although EMDR has clearly proved beneficial for some types of clients, the marketing, restrictions on teaching the technique, and aura of secretiveness that result have contributed to a sense of mystique and controversy at times. Shapiro has attempted to ensure a standard quality in the training in the technique (F. Shapiro, 1995; F. Shapiro & Forrest, 2004). A nonprofit professional organization named EMDR International Association (EMDRIA) was created as a forum "where practitioners and researchers seek the highest standards...by promoting training, research and the sharing of the latest clinical information...assuring that therapists are knowledgeable and skilled in the methodology" (according to its Web site at http://www.emdria.org/). Nonetheless, her work has spawned some very creative innovators that probably cause consternation to well-trained clinicians. Consider the following examples:

Case 6–28: The REMAP process utilizes the pathways and treatment points of the entire acupressure/acupuncture system to relieve emotional distress. It provides a complete map of this acupressure/acupuncture system, brain balancing eye movement techniques and other leading edge interventions. The synergetic effects of these treatments are used to alleviate mental, emotional, and energetic patterns of distress within the mind–body system. The goal of this approach is to eliminate trauma, stress and self-limiting patterns while promoting wholeness, inner harmony and higher levels of functioning. By revising our mental, emotional and energetic maps we seek to further emotional freedom and to better life's journey. The practitioner utilizes techniques that work closely with the client's subconscious, thus facilitating a process that honors the client's inner wisdom about where they need to go to foster healing. One of the best parts is that the process is so simple that you don't have to memorize any of the acupressure points. The REMAP process is an elegant standalone method that can also be combined with EFT, TFT, EMDR or other effective tools.

The text listed above was taken from the Web site of Steve B. Reed, L.P.C., L.M.S.W.,

L.M.F.T (http://www.psychotherapy-center.com) in November 2006. REMAP stands for Reed eye movement acupressure psychotherapy, as practiced by Mr. Reed. He has taken some elements of EMDR, added other components, and branded it with his own name. The key ethical question revolves around taking elements of different therapeutic approaches and then promoting the unresearched package as effective treatment. Readers will want to examine material offered by Mr. Reed's site and draw their own conclusions regarding the validity and efficacy of REMAP.

Case 6–29: Ranae N. Johnson, whose Web site for the Rapid Eye Institute describes her as the mother of 7 children, 22 grandchildren, and 4 great-grandchildren, also cites a Ph.D. in psychology from the unaccredited American Pacific University of Honolulu, Hawaii, and another doctorate in clinical hypnotherapy from the unaccredited American Institute of Hypnotherapy, Santa Ana, California. The site suggests that she attended three other colleges, but lists no degrees. She also reports graduating from the Institute of EMDR, Pacific Grove, California, with training in eye movement desensitization and reprocessing. Her Web site includes an animated demonstration of online rapid eye technology (http://www.rapideyetechnology.com/selfcare.htm).

Francine Shapiro (comments on Reed and Johnson, personal communication to G. P. Koocher via e-mail, January 17, 2007) reported that Ms. Johnson took the first part of the two-part program in 1991 under another licensed clinician's supervision. The requirements for attendance involved having either a mental health practice license or ability to provide mental health services under the supervision of a licensed clinician (e.g., in a licensing track). Ms. Johnson apparently started her rapid eye therapy based on that limited experience and never proceeded to licensure. At one time, Ms. Johnson tried to link her method to EMDR, claiming its research base supported her work, but she removed such claims from the Web site after being confronted about it (F. Shapiro, comments on Reed and Johnson, personal communication to G. P. Koocher via e-mail, January 17, 2007). Because Johnson calls her trainees "technicians," they may circumvent state laws aimed at regulating psychotherapy practice.

Erhard Seminars Training

Werner Erhard, the developer of est, was a skilled salesman with no professional training as a psychotherapist. His programs evolved to become the "Forum" seminars (Efran, Lukens, & Lukens, 1986; Finkelstein, Wenegrat, & Yalom, 1982; Wistow, 1986) and exist currently as the Landmark Education or the Forum, a genre of so-called large-group awareness programs. A recent Web search for critics for the current incarnation yielded more than 960,000 hits (e.g., Ross, 2005). The basic approach focused on challenging participants' sense of psychological identity or, as one commentator noted, systematic escalation and discounting of each participant's "adapted child," eventually forcing the participant into their "free child" state, thereby releasing a large amount of "bound energy" (Klein, 1983, p. 178). Other articles have described est as "brainwashing" (Moss & Hosford, 1983), and there was a report that a patient suffered a psychotic episode following his participation in an est program (Higgitt & Murray, 1983). One of the few careful attempts to study Erhard's techniques in a rigorous fashion showed no long-term treatment effects and concluded that claims of far-reaching effects for programs of the Forum were exaggerated (J. D. Fisher et al., 1989).

The ability of skilled salesmen, such as Erhard, to promote and morph their programs in the face of criticism by behavioral scientists is quite impressive. The central message from an ethical perspective is the obligation of therapists to have a sound scientific foundation for their psychotherapeutic work. Proof of efficacy should precede mass marketing of new techniques to the public or to colleagues.

SUMMARY GUIDELINES

1. When treating more than one person at a time, as in group or family therapy, take care to respect, protect, and balance the rights of all the clients.

2. Therapists should also remain sensitive to their own values with respect to the family or group and attempt to facilitate the growth of all concerned within the clients' value systems.

3. Clinicians conducting group treatment or educational programs should carefully define and articulate the goals, methods, and purposes of each group. This needs to be communicated in such a way that enables each potential client to make a fully informed choice about participation.

4. In the application of specialized therapeutic techniques that require dedicated training, including (but not limited to) sex therapy, behavior modification, hypnosis, and the use of medical and psychological devices, therapists assume ethical responsibility to ensure that their training adequately qualifies them to use the technique in question. Any mechanical or electrical devices (e.g., biofeedback equipment) must be free from defects that could harm a client and be appropriately sanitized. Therapists are also obliged to keep abreast of evolving standards and regulations governing the use of specialized techniques and devices.

5. When some symptoms or techniques raise special emotional or public policy questions, therapists should remain sensitive to the issues and discuss them and their implications with the client.

6. Coercion rarely becomes an appropriate component of a psychotherapeutic program. To the extent that subtle coercive pressures enter into a therapeutic relationship, therapists should attempt to ensure that these do not cause detriment to clients.

7. Only empirically validated or clinically proven approaches to treatment should be presented to clients as established treatment. Experimental procedures must be described to clients as such, and to minimize risk, extreme caution should be used in the development of new modalities of treatment.

8. When marketing or promoting psychotherapeutic techniques and products, mental health professionals must exercise appropriate caution and accuracy with respect to claims made and persons certified as competent to use the tool with clinical efficacy.

References

Ackerman, R. J., & Banks, M. E. (1990). Computers and ethical treatment for brain-injured patients. *Social Science Computer Review, 8,* 83–95.

Aguinis, H., & Handelsman, M. M. (1997). Ethical issues in the use of the bogus pipeline. *Journal of Applied Social Psychology, 27,* 557–573.

Aloni, R., & Katz, S. (2003). *Sexual difficulties after traumatic brain injury and ways to deal with it.* Springfield, IL: Thomas.

American Association of Sexuality Educators, Counselors, and Therapists. (2004). Code of ethics. Retrieved March 31, 2007, from http://www.aasect.org/codeofethics.asp

American Group Psychotherapy Association. (2002). *AGPA and NRCGP guidelines for ethics.* Retrieved March 31, 2007, from http://www.agpa.org/group/ethicalguide.html

American Psychiatric Association. (1998). *APA position statement on psychiatric treatment and sexual orientation: December 11, 1998.* Washington, DC: American Psychiatric Association.

American Psychiatric Association. (2000). Commission on Psychotherapy by Psychiatrists (COPP): Position statement on therapies focused on attempts to change sexual orientation (reparative or conversion therapies). *American Journal of Psychiatry, 157,* 1719–1721.

American Psychological Association. (1973). Guidelines for psychologists conducting growth groups. *American Psychologist, 28,* 933.

American Psychological Association. (1975). Report of the Task Force on Sex Bias and Sex Role Stereotyping in Psychotherapeutic Practice. *American Psychologist, 30,* 1169–1175.

American Psychological Association. (1981). *Task force report on psychologists' use of physical interventions.* Washington, DC: American Psychological Association.

American Psychological Association. (1998). Proceedings of the American Psychological Association, Incorporated, for the legislative year 1997. *American Psychologist, 53,* 934–935.

American Psychological Association. (2000). Guidelines for psychotherapy with lesbian, gay, and bisexual clients. *American Psychologist, 55,* 1440–1451.

American Psychological Association. (2002). Criteria for evaluating treatment guidelines. *American Psychologist, 57,* 1052–1059.

American Psychological Association Ethics Committee. (1997). *Statement on services by telephone, teleconferencing, and Internet.* Retrieved May 12, 2007. from http://www.apa.org/ethics/stmnt01.html

Ashton, A. K. (1999). Sildenafil treatment of paroxetine-induced anorgasmia in a woman. *American Journal of Psychiatry, 156,* 800.

Bailey, J. S., & Burch, M. R. (2006). *How to think like a behavior analyst: Understanding the science that can change your life.* Mahwah, NJ: Erlbaum.

Bailey, K. G. (1978). Psychotherapy or massage parlor technology? Comments on the Zeiss, Rosen, and Zeiss treatment procedure. *Journal of Consulting and Clinical Psychology, 46,* 1502–1506.

Balon, R. (2005). Sexual difficulties after traumatic brain injury and ways to deal with it. *Depression and Anxiety, 22,* 100–101.

Barlow, D. H. (2004). Psychological treatments. *American Psychologist, 59,* 869–878.

Barnett, J. E. (2005). Online counseling: New entity, new challenges. *Counseling Psychologist, 33,* 872–880.

Barnett, J. E., & Karin, S. (2003). Technological advances and telehealth: Ethics, law, and the practice of psychotherapy. *Psychotherapy: Theory, Research, Practice, Training, 40,* 86–93.

Bartlett, E. E. (1996). Protecting the confidentiality of children and adolescents. In *The Hatherleigh guide to child and adolescent therapy* (p. 275–290). New York: Hatherleigh Press.

Bass, B. A., & Quimby, J. L. (2006). Addressing secrets in couples counseling: An alternative approach to informed consent. *Family Journal: Counseling and Therapy for Couples and Families, 14,* 77–80.

Bastien, C. H., Morin, C. M., Ouellet, M., Blais, F. C., & Bouchard, S. (2004). Cognitive-behavioral therapy for insomnia: Comparison of individual therapy, group therapy, and telephone consultations. *Journal of Consulting and Clinical Psychology, 72,* 653–659.

Behr, H. (2006). Secrecy and confidentiality in groups. *Group Analysis, 39,* 356–365.

Bettleheim, B. (1967). *The empty fortress: Infantile autism and the birth of the self.* New York: Free Press.

Biaggio, M., Orchard, S., Larson, J., Petrino, K., & Mihara, R. (2003). Guidelines for gay/lesbian/bisexual-affirmative educational practices in graduate psychology programs. *Professional Psychology, 34,* 548–554.

Bohart, A. C. (2005). Evidence-based psychotherapy means evidence-informed, not evidence-driven. *Journal of Contemporary Psychotherapy, 35,* 39.

Bregman, J. D., Zager, D., Gerdtz, J., Volkmar, F. R., Paul, R., Klin, A., et al. (2005). Behavioral interventions. In *Handbook of autism and pervasive developmental disorders, Vol. 2: Assessment, interventions, and policy* (3rd ed., pp. 897–924). Hoboken, NJ: Wiley.

Brown, S., & Shapiro, F. (2006). EMDR in the treatment of borderline personality disorder. *Clinical Case Studies, 5,* 403–420.

Brown University. (2002) Sexual side effects of antidepressants common, but still seriously underestimated by physicians. *The Brown University Psychopharmacology Update, 13,* 6–9.

Candilis, P. J. (1998). Ethics, malingering, and a lie-detector at the bedside. *Journal of Forensic Sciences, 43,* 609–612.

Carpenter, L. L. (2006). Neurostimulation in resistant depression. *Journal of Psychopharmacology, 20,* 35–40.

Chemtob, C. M., Tolin, D. F., van der Kolk, B. A., Pitman, R. K., Foa, E. B., Keane, T. M., et al. (2000). Eye movement desensitization and reprocessing. In E. B. Foa, T. M. Keane, & M. J. Friedman (Eds.), *Effective treatments for PTSD: Practice guidelines from the International Society for Traumatic Stress Studies* (pp. 139–154). New York: Guilford Press.

Coleman, P. (2005). Privilege and confidentiality in 12-step self-help programs: Believing the promises could be hazardous to an addict's freedom. *Journal of Legal Medicine, 26,* 435–474.

Cook, S. W. (1975). Comments on ethical considerations in "Self-Control Techniques as an Alternative to Pain Medication." *Journal of Abnormal Psychology, 84,* 169–171.

Corey, G., Williams, G. T., & Moline, M. E. (1995). Ethical and legal issues in group counseling. *Ethics & Behavior, 5,* 161–183.

Davidson, G. C., & Stuart, R. B. (1975). Behavior therapy and civil liberties. *American Psychologist, 30,* 755–763.

Department of Veterans Affairs & Department of Defense. (2004). *Clinical practice guideline for the management of post-traumatic stress.* Washington, DC: Veterans Health Administration, Department of Veterans Affairs and Health Affairs, Department of Defense. Office of Quality and Performance publication 10Q-CPG/PTSD-04.

Dishion, T. J., & Stormshak, E. A. (2007). Ethical and professional standards in child and family interventions. In T. J. Dishion & E. A. Stormshak (Eds.), *Intervening in children's lives: An ecological, family-centered approach to mental health care* (pp. 241–264). Washington, DC: American Psychological Association.

Dolliver, R. H. (1971). Concerning the potential parallels between psychotherapy and brainwashing. *Psychotherapy: Theory, Research & Practice, 8,* 170–174.

Drescher, J. (2002). Ethical issues in treating gay and lesbian patients. *Psychiatric Clinics of North America, 25,* 605–621.

Dukakis, K., & Tye, L. (2006). *Shock: The healing power of electroconvulsive therapy.* New York: Avery/Penguin.

Efran, J. S., Lukens, M. D., & Lukens, R. J. (1986). It's all done with mirrors. *Family Therapy Networker, 10,* 41–49.

Farmer, R. F., & Nelson-Gray, R. O. (2005). *Personality-guided behavior therapy.* Washington, DC: American Psychological Association.

Feske, U. (1998). Eye movement desensitization and reprocessing treatment for posttraumatic stress disorder. *Clinical Psychology: Science and Practice, 5,* 171–181.

Finkelstein, P., Wenegrat, B., & Yalom, I. (1982). Large group awareness training. *Annual Review of Psychology, 33,* 515–539.

Fisher, C. B., & Fried, A. L. (2003). Internet-mediated psychological services and the American Psychological Association ethics code. *Psychotherapy: Theory, Research, Practice, Training, 40,* 103–111.

Fisher, J. D., Silver, R. C., Chinsky, J. M., Goff, B., Klar, Y., & Zagieboylo, C. (1989). Psychological effects of participation in a large group awareness training. *Journal of Consulting and Clinical Psychology, 57,* 747–755.

Fitzgerald, P. B. (2006). A review of developments in brain stimulation and the treatment of psychiatric disorders. *Current Psychiatry Reviews*, 2, 199–205.

Fromm, E. (1980). Values in hypnotherapy. *Psychotherapy: Theory, Research & Practice, 17*, 425–430.

Gaylin, W. (1974). On the borders of persuasion: A psychoanalytic look at coercion. *Psychiatry: Journal for the Study of Interpersonal Processes, 37*, 1–9.

Gianotten, W. L. (1997). Sexual bodywork as an adjunct to sex therapy? *Nordisk Sexologi, 15*, 20–36.

Gladding, S. T., & Coombs, R. H. (2005). Ethical and legal issues in family therapy. In R. H. Coombs (Ed.), *Family therapy review: Preparing for comprehensive and licensing examinations* (pp. 531–547). Mahwah, NJ: Erlbaum.

Glannon, W. (2006). Neuroethics. *Bioethics, 20*, 37–52.

Goodstein, L. D. (1975). Self-control and therapist-control: The medical model in behavioral clothing. *Journal of Abnormal Psychology, 84*, 178–180.

Greene, B. (2007). Delivering ethical psychological services to lesbian, gay, and bisexual clients. In K. J. Bieschke, R. M. Perez, & K. A. DeBord (Eds.), *Handbook of counseling and psychotherapy with lesbian, gay, bisexual, and transgender clients* (2nd ed., pp. 181–199). Washington, DC: American Psychological Association.

Grisso, T. J., & Vierling, L. (1978). Minors' consent to treatment: A developmental perspective. *Professional Psychology, 9*, 412–427.

Haldeman, D. E. (1991). Sexual orientation conversion therapy for gay men and lesbians: A scientific examination. In J. C. Gonsiorek & J. D. Weinrich (Eds.), *Homosexuality: Research implications for public policy* (pp. 149–160). Newbury Park, CA: Sage.

Haldeman, D. E. (1994). The practice and ethics of sexual orientation conversion therapy. Special section: Mental health of lesbians and gay men. *Journal of Consulting and Clinical Psychology, 62*, 221–227.

Hare-Mustin, R. T. (1979). Family therapy and sex role stereotypes. *Counseling Psychologist, 8*, 31–32.

Hare-Mustin, R. T. (1980). Family therapy may be dangerous for your health. *Professional Psychology, 11*, 935–938.

Hawkins, D. M., & Schermer, V. L. (2005). All for one and one for some? In L. Motherwell & J. J. Shay (Eds.), *Complex dilemmas in group therapy: Pathways to resolution* (pp. 29–37). New York: Brunner-Routledge.

Heckman, T. G., Anderson, E. S., Sikkema, K. J., Kochman, A., Kalichman, S. C., & Anderson, T. (2004). Emotional distress in nonmetropolitan persons living with HIV disease enrolled in a telephone-delivered, coping improvement group intervention. *Health Psychology, 23*, 94–100.

Higgitt, A. C., & Murray, R. M. (1983). A psychotic episode following Erhard Seminars Training. *Acta Psychiatrica Scandinavica, 67*, 436–439.

Hines, P. M., & Hare-Mustin, R. T. (1978). Ethical concerns in family therapy. *Professional Psychology, 9*, 165–171.

Hines, P. M., & Hare-Mustin, R. T. (1980). Ethical concerns in family therapy. *Advances in Family Psychiatry, 2*, 65–71.

Hurvitz, N. (1973). Psychotherapy as a means of social control. *Journal of Consulting and Clinical Psychology, 40*, 232–239.

Institute of Medicine. (2001). *Crossing the quality chasm: A new health system for the 21st century*. Washington, DC: National Academy Press.

Jacobs, M., Thompson, L. A., & Truxaw, P. (1975). The use of sexual surrogates in counseling. *Counseling Psychologist, 5*, 73–76.

Jacobson, J. W., Foxx, R. M., & Mulick, J. A. (Eds.). (2005). *Controversial therapies for developmental disabilities: Fad, fashion, and science in professional practice*. Mahwah, NJ: Erlbaum.

Jardin, X. (2005, August 19). Virtual reality therapy for combat stress. *National Public Radio*. Retrieved May 12, 2007, from http://www.npr.org/templates/story/story.php?storyId=4806921

Jerome, L. W., & Zaylor, C. (2000). Cyberspace: Creating a therapeutic environment for telehealth applications. *Professional Psychology, 31*, 478–483.

Karoly, P. (1975). Ethical considerations in the application of self-control techniques. *Journal of Abnormal Psychology, 84*, 175–177.

Klein, M. (1983). How EST works. *Transactional Analysis Journal, 13*, 178–180.

Kline, M. (1976). Dangerous aspects of the practice of hypnosis and the need for legislative regulation. *Clinical Psychologist, 29*, 3–6.

Klontz, B. T. (2004). Ethical practice of group experiential psychotherapy. *Psychotherapy: Theory, Research, Practice, Training, 41,* 172–179.

Konuk, E., Knipe, J., Eke, I., Yuksek, H., Yurtsever, A., & Ostep, S. (2006). The effects of eye movement desensitization and reprocessing (EMDR) therapy on posttraumatic stress disorder in survivors of the 1999 Marmara, Turkey, earthquake. *International Journal of Stress Management, 13,* 291–308.

Koocher, G. P. (Ed.). (1976). *Children's rights and the mental health professions.* New York: Wiley-Interscience.

Koocher, G. P. (1983). Consent to psychotherapy. In G. B. Melton, G. P. Koocher, & M. Saks (Eds.), *Children's competence to consent* (pp. 78–93). New York: Plenum.

Koocher, G. P. (2003). Ethical issues in psychotherapy with adolescents. *Journal of Clinical Psychology, 59,* 1247–1256.

Koocher, G. P. (2007). Twenty-first century ethical challenges for psychology. *American Psychologist, 62,* 375–384.

Koocher, G. P., & Keith-Spiegel, P. (1990). *Children, ethics, and the law: Professional issues and cases.* Lincoln: University of Nebraska Press.

Koocher, G. P., & Morray, E. (2000). Regulation of telepsychology: A survey of state attorneys general. *Professional Psychology, 31,* 503–508.

Kuriansky, J.B., Sharpe, L., & O'Connor, D. (1982). The treatment of anorgasmia: Long-term effectiveness of a short-term behavioral group therapy. *Journal of Sex and Marital Therapy, 8,* 29–43.

Lakin, M. (1994). Morality in group and family therapies: Multiperson therapies and the 1992 ethics code. *Professional Psychology, 25,* 344–348.

Lasky, G. B., & Riva, M. T. (2006). Confidentiality and privileged communication in group psychotherapy. *International Journal of Group Psychotherapy, 56,* 455–476.

Lasser, J. S., & Gottlieb, M. C. (2004) Treating patients distressed regarding their sexual orientation: clinical and ethical alternatives. *Professional Psychology, 35,* 194–200.

Leiblum, S. R., & Rosen, R. C. (Eds.). (2000). *Principles and practice of sex therapy.* New York: Guilford.

Levendusky, P., & Pankratz, L. (1975). Self-control techniques as an alternative to pain medication. *Journal of Abnormal Psychology, 84,* 165–168.

Lohr, J. M., Hooke, W., Gist, R., & Tolin, D. F. (2003). Novel and controversial treatments for trauma-related stress disorders. In S. O. Lilienfeld, S. J. Lynn, & J. M. Lohr (Eds.), *Science and pseudoscience in clinical psychology* (pp. 243–272). New York: Guilford Press.

Lohr, J. M., Lilienfeld, S. O., Tolin, D. F., & Herbert, J. D. (1999). Eye Movement Desensitization and Reprocessing: An analysis of specific versus nonspecific treatment factors. *Journal of Anxiety Disorders, 13,* 185–207.

LoPiccolo, J. (2002). Postmodern sex therapy. In F. Kaslow (Ed.), *Comprehensive handbook of psychotherapy* (Vol. 4, pp. 41–43.). New York: Wiley.

LoPiccolo, J., & Van Male, L. M. (2005a). Assessing and treating female sexual dysfunction. In G. Koocher, J. C. Norcross, & S. S. Hill (Eds.), *Psychologists' desk reference* (2nd ed., pp. 286–290). New York: Oxford University Press.

LoPiccolo, J., & Van Male, L. M. (2005b). Assessing and treating male sexual dysfunction. In G. Koocher, J. C. Norcross, & S. S. Hill (Eds.), *Psychologists' desk reference* (2nd ed., pp. 282–286). New York: Oxford University Press.

Lowery, T. S., & Lowery, T. P. (1975). Ethical considerations in sex therapy. *Journal of Marriage and Family Counseling, 1,* 229–236.

Maheu, M. M. (2003). The online clinical practice management model. *Psychotherapy Theory, Research, Practice, Training, 40,* 20–32.

Maheu, M. M., & Gordon, B. L. (2000). Counseling and therapy on the Internet. *Professional Psychology, 31,* 484–489.

Maheu, M. M., Whitten, P., & Allen, A. (2001). *E-health, telehealth, and telemedicine: A guide to start-up and success.* San Francisco: Jossey-Bass.

Margolin, G. (1982). Ethical and legal considerations in marital and family therapy. *American Psychologist, 37,* 788–801.

Margolin, G., Chien, D., Duman, S. E., Fauchier, A., Gordis, E. B., Oliver, P. H., et al. (2005). Ethical issues in couple and family research. *Journal of Family Psychology, 19,* 157–167.

Martin, G. L., & Pear, J. (1996). *Behavior modification: What it is and how to do it..* Upper Saddle River, NJ: Prentice-Hall.

Masters, W. H., & Johnson, V. E. (1976). Principles of the new sex therapy. *American Journal of Psychiatry, 133,* 548–554.

McKay, J. R., Lynch, K. G., Shepard, D. S., Ratichek, S., Morrison, R., Koppenhaver, J., et al. (2004). The effectiveness of telephone-based continuing care in the clinical management of alcohol and cocaine use disorders: 12-month outcomes. *Journal of Consulting and Clinical Psychology, 72,* 967–979.

McNally, R. J. (1999). EMDR and mesmerism: A comparative historical analysis. *Journal of Anxiety Disorders, 13,* 225–236.

Melton, G. B., Koocher, G. P., & Saks, M. J. (1983). *Children's competence to consent.* New York: Plenum Press.

Mercer, J. (2003). Radio and television programs approve of coercive restraint therapies. *The Scientific Review of Mental Health Practice, 2,* 163–164.

Mermelstein, R., Hedeker, D., & Wong, S. C. (2003). Extended telephone counseling for smoking cessation: Does content matter? *Journal of Consulting and Clinical Psychology, 71,* 656–574.

Messer, S. B. (2004). Evidence-based practice: Beyond empirically supported treatments. *Professional Psychology, 35,* 580–588.

Miller, S. D., & Hubble, M. A. (2004). Further archeological and ethnological findings on the obscure, late 20th century, quasi-religious earth group known as "the therapists" (a fantasy about the future of psychotherapy). *Journal of Psychotherapy Integration, 14,* 38–65.

Moberly, E. (1983). *Homosexuality: A new Christian ethic.* Greenwood, SC: Attic Press.

Morrow, S. L. (2000). First do no harm: Therapist issues in psychotherapy with lesbian, gay, and bisexual clients. In R. P. Perez, K. A. DeBord, & K. J. Bieschke (Eds.), *Handbook of counseling and psychotherapy with lesbian, gay, and bisexual clients* (pp. 137–156). Washington, DC: American Psychological Association.

Moss, C. S., & Hosford, R. E. (1983). Reflections on EST training from the viewpoint of two correctional psychologists. *Journal of Integrative and Eclectic Psychotherapy, 2,* 18–39.

Murphy, T. (1992). Redirecting sexual orientation: Techniques and justifications. *Journal of Sex Research, 29,* 501–523.

Nagy, T. F. (2005). Therapy. In T. F. Nagy (Ed.), *Ethics in plain English: An illustrative casebook for psychologists* (2nd ed., pp. 291–327). Washington, DC: American Psychological Association.

Nathan, P. E., & Gorman, J. M. (1998). *A guide to treatments that work.* New York: Oxford University Press.

Nathan, P. E., & Gorman, J. M. (2007). *A guide to treatments that work* (3rd ed.). New York: Oxford University Press.

National Association of Social Workers. (2000). *"Reparative" or "conversion" therapies for lesbian and gay men.* Washington, DC: National Association of Social Workers National Committee on Lesbian, Gay, and Bisexual Issues.

Newman, M. G. (2004). Technology in psychotherapy: An introduction. *Journal of Clinical Psychology, 60,* 141–145.

Nickelson, D. W. (1998). Telehealth and the evolving health care system: Strategic opportunities for professional psychology. *Professional Psychology, 29,* 527–535.

Norcross, J. C., Beutler, L. E., & Levant, R. F. (Eds.). (2005). *Evidence-based practices in mental health: Debate and dialogue on the fundamental questions.* Washington, DC: American Psychological Association.

Norcross, J. C., Koocher, G. P., & Garofalo, A. (2006). Discredited psychological treatments and tests: A Delphi poll. *Professional Psychology, 37,* 515–522.

Page, B. J. (2004). Online group counseling. In J. L. DeLucia-Waack, D. A. Gerrity, C. R. Kalodner, & M. T. Riva (Eds.), *Handbook of group counseling and psychotherapy* (pp. 609–620). Thousand Oaks, CA: Sage.

Parker, R. S. (1976). Ethical and professional considerations concerning high risk groups. *Journal of Clinical Issues in Psychology, 7,* 4–19.

Paul, P., Cassisi, J. E., & Larson, P. (1996). Ethical and practice considerations for biofeedback therapists in the treatment of urinary incontinence. *Biofeedback and Self-Regulation, 21,* 229–240.

Percival, G., & Striefel, S. (1994). Ethical beliefs and practices of AAPB members. *Biofeedback and Self-Regulation, 19,* 67–93.

Perkins, B. R., & Rouanzoin, C. C. (2002). A critical evaluation of current views regarding Eye

Movement Desensitization and Reprocessing (EMDR): Clarifying points of confusion. *Journal of Clinical Psychology, 58,* 77–97.

Poelzl, L. (2001). Bisexual issues in sex therapy: A bisexual surrogate partner relates her experiences from the field. *Journal of Bisexuality, 1,* 121–142.

Presidential Task Force on Evidence-Based Practice. (2006). Evidence-based practice in psychology. *American Psychologist, 61,* 271–285.

Raboni, M. R., Tufik, S., & Suchecki, D. (2006). Treatment of PTSD by Eye Movement Desensitization Reprocessing (EMDR) improves sleep quality, quality of life, and perception of stress. In R. Yehuda (Ed.), *Psychobiology of posttraumatic stress disorders: A decade of progress* (Vol. 1071, pp. 508–513). Malden, MA: Blackwell.

Ragusea, A. S., & VandeCreek, L. (2003). Suggestions for the ethical practice of online psychotherapy. *Psychotherapy Theory, Research, Practice, Training, 40,* 94–102.

Reamer, F. G. (2006). Nontraditional and unorthodox interventions in social work: Ethical and legal implications. *Families in Society, 87,* 191–197.

Rees, C. S., & Stone, S. (2005). Therapeutic alliance in face-to-face versus videoconferenced psychotherapy. *Professional Psychology, 36,* 649–653.

Reich, W. (1948a). *The discovery of the orgone; the cancer biopathy.* Vol. 2. New York: Orgone Institute Press.

Reich, W. (1948b). *The function of the orgasm* (T. P. Wolfe, Trans.) (2nd ed., Vol. 1). New York: Orgone Institute Press.

Rizzo, A. A., Strickland, D., & Bouchard, S. P. (2004). The challenge of using virtual reality in telerehabilitation. *Telemedicine Journal and e-Health, 10,* 184–195.

Rogers, C. (1970). *Carl Rogers on encounter groups.* New York: Harper & Row.

Rosen, R. C., & Leiblum, S. R. (1995a). Treatment of sexual disorders in the 1990s: An integrated approach. *Journal of Consulting and Clinical Psychology, 63,* 877–890.

Rosen, R. C., & Leiblum, S. R. (Eds.). (1995b). *Case studies in sex therapy.* New York: Guilford.

Rosenhan, D. (1973). On being sane in insane places. *Science, 179,* 250–258.

Ross, R. (2005, December 22). Landmark Education suffers humiliating legal defeat in New Jersey Federal Court. CultNews.com. Retrieved June 22, 2007, from http://www.cultnews.com/archives/000830.html

Russell, M. C. (2006). Treating combat-related stress disorders: A multiple case study utilizing Eye Movement Desensitization and Reprocessing (EMDR) with battlefield casualties from the Iraqi War. *Military Psychology, 18,* 1–18.

Safren, S. A. (2005). Affirmative, evidence-based, and ethically sound psychotherapy with lesbian, gay, and bisexual clients. *Clinical Psychology: Science and Practice, 12,* 29–32.

Sampson, J. P. (1983). An integrated approach to computer applications in counseling psychology. *Counseling Psychologist, 11,* 65–74.

Sandgren, A. K., & McCaul, K. D. (2003). Short-term effects of telephone therapy for breast cancer patients. *Health Psychology, 22,* 310–315.

Schneider, G., Nabavi, D., & Heuft, G. (2005). Eye movement desensitization and reprocessing in the treatment of posttraumatic stress disorder in a patient with comorbid epilepsy. *Epilepsy & Behavior, 7,* 715–718.

Schneider, M. S., Brown, L. S., & Glassgold, J. M. (2002). Implementing the resolution on appropriate therapeutic responses to sexual orientation: A guide for the perplexed. *Professional Psychology, 33,* 265–276.

Schopp, R. F. (2003). "Even a dog ... ": Culpability, condemnation, and respect for persons. In B. J. Winick & J. Q. La Fond (Eds.), *Protecting society from sexually dangerous offenders: Law, justice, and therapy* (pp. 183–195). Washington, DC: American Psychological Association.

Schultz, W. C. (1971). *Here comes everybody.* New York: Harper & Row.

Shapiro, F. (1995). *Eye movement desensitization and reprocessing: Basic principles, protocols, and procedures.* New York: Guilford.

Shapiro, F. (Ed.). (2002). *EMDR as an integrative psychotherapy approach: Experts of diverse orientations explore the paradigm prism.* Washington, DC: American Psychological Association.

Shapiro, F., & Forrest, M. S. (2004). *EMDR: The breakthrough therapy for overcoming anxiety, stress, and trauma.* New York: Basic Books.

Shapiro, R. (2005). *EMDR solutions: Pathways to healing.* New York: Norton.

Shidlo, A., & Schroeder, M. (2002). Changing sexual orientation: A consumers' report. *Professional Psychology, 33,* 249–259.

Sidman, M. (1999). Coercion in educational settings. *Behaviour Change, 16,* 79–88.

Slovenko, R. (1977). Group psychotherapy: Privileged communication and confidentiality. *Journal of Psychiatry and the Law, 5,* 405–466.

Snyder, D. K., & Doss, B. D. (2005). Treating infidelity: Clinical and ethical directions. *Journal of Clinical Psychology, 61,*1453–1465.

Southern, S. (1999). Facilitating sexual health: Intimacy enhancement techniques for sexual dysfunction. *Journal of Mental Health Counseling, 21,* 15–32.

Southern, S. (2006). Ethical code for the international association of marriage and family counseling. *Family Journal: Counseling and Therapy for Couples and Families, 14,* 92–98.

Southern, S., Smith, R. L., & Oliver, M. (2005). Marriage and family counseling: Ethics in context. *Family Journal: Counseling and Therapy for Couples and Families, 13,* 459–466.

Spiegel, A. (2002) Eighty-one words. *The America project: Radio documentaries.* Retrieved April 13, 2007, from http://www.theamericaproject.org/?doc=eightyone_words

Spirito, A., & Kazak, A. E. (2006). *Effective and emerging treatments in pediatric psychology.* New York: Oxford University Press.

Stolz, S. B. (1977). Why no guidelines for behavior modification? *Journal of Applied Behavior Analysis, 10,* 541–547.

Stolz, S. B. (1978). Ethics of social and educational interventions: Historical context and behavioral analysis. In A. C. Catania & T. A. Brigham (Eds.), *Handbook of applied behavior analysis* (pp. 278–292). New York: Irvington.

Tarrier, N., Liversidge, T., & Gregg, L. (2006). The acceptability and preference for the psychological treatment of PTSD. *Behaviour Research and Therapy, 44,* 1643–1656.

Thaw, J., Thorne, G. D., & Benjamin, E. M. (1978). Human rights, behavior modification, and the development of state policy. *Administration in Mental Health, 5,* 112–119.

Tkachuk, G. A., & Martin, G. L. (1999). Exercise therapy for patients with psychiatric disorders

research and clinical implications. *Professional Psychology, 30,* 275–282.

Turkat, I. D., & Forehand, R. (1980). Critical issues in behavior therapy. *Behavior Modification, 4,* 445–464.

VandenBos, G. R., & Williams, S. (2000). The Internet versus the telephone: What is telehealth anyway? *Professional Psychology, 31,* 490–492.

Vinogradov, S., & Yalom, I. D. (1994). Group therapy. In R. E. Hales, S. C. Yudofsky, & J. A. Talbott (Eds.), *The American Psychiatric Press textbook of psychiatry* (2nd ed., pp. 1143–1175). Washington, DC: American Psychiatric Association.

Wagner, N. N. (1978). Is masturbation still wrong? Comments on Bailey's comments. *Journal of Consulting and Clinical Psychology, 46,* 1507–1509.

Wiederhold, B. K., & Wiederhold, M. D. (2005). Ethical considerations. In B. K. Wiederhold & M. D. Wiederhold (Eds.), *Virtual reality therapy for anxiety disorders: Advances in evaluation and treatment* (pp. 87–92). Washington, DC: American Psychological Association.

Wilson, G. T. (1978). Ethical and professional issues in sex therapy: Comments on Bailey's "Psychotherapy of massage parlor technology?" *Journal of Consulting and Clinical Psychology, 46,* 1510–1514.

Wistow, F. (1986). Being there. *Family Therapy Networker, 10,* 20–29, 77–80.

Wong, S. E., & Wong, S. T. (2003). Behavior therapy in correctional settings: Fertile ground or quicksand? *Behavior Therapist, 25,* 308–309.

Wood, J. A. V., Miller, T. W., & Hargrove, D. S. (2005). Clinical supervision in rural settings: A telehealth model. *Professional Psychology, 36,* 173–179.

Wylie, K. R., Crowe, M. J., & Boddington, D. (1995). How can the therapist deal with a couple with male demands for anal sex? *Sexual and Marital Therapy, 10,* 95–98.

Yalom, I. D. (1995). *The theory and practice of group psychotherapy* (4th ed.). New York: Basic Books.

Zeiss, A. M., Rosen, G. M., & Zeiss, R. A. (1977). Orgasm during intercourse: A treatment strategy for women. *Journal of Consulting and Clinical Psychology, 45,* 891–895.

7

The Mental Health Business
Money and Managed Care

When it is a question of money, everyone is of the
same religion.

Voltaire

Contents

If you have just picked up this book and are reading this chapter first, most likely you are (or aspire to be) in independent practice. Perhaps you worry about whether such work will prove financially rewarding or even viable in the current marketplace. To make independent or institutional practice fiscally successful, one must pay careful attention to a variety of details not generally discussed in graduate school or training programs. Because we think of ourselves as members of the helping professions, discussing money may seem crass or pecuniary (DiBella, 1980), some sort of "dirty business" (Gabbard, 2005), or heavily laden with unconscious issues (Lanza, 2001). We live in a society more open to conversation about sex than money (Birnbach, 1999). Some have gone so far as to make an analogy between psychotherapy and prostitution (Holmes, 1998). Such attitudes overlook the fact that helpers also have bills to pay.

When finances are discussed in the course of a mental health professional's formal training, specific discussion of actual practices involving billing, collection, and third-party reimbursement are rarely mentioned (Lovinger, 1978; Totton, 2006; Waska, 1999). Perhaps this is one reason why client complaints and ethical difficulties frequently arise in connection with charges for psychotherapy services. Often, the problems arise from miscommunications, procedural ignorance, or naïveté rather than greed or malice (Zuckerman, 2003). Depending on the nature of the training program, such discussions (when they do occur) may range from viewing payment for services as a simple business transaction to ascribing profound relational or psychodynamic meanings (Holmes, 1998; Monger, 1998; Shapiro & Ginzberg, 2006; Tudor, 1998; Valentine, 1999; Waska, 1999).

Interestingly, factors that influence fee setting can differ as a function of the psychotherapist's gender (Buck, 1999). A single-county study surveyed fee-setting practices and found that psychologists considered education and training, business experience, and local competition in setting their fees. The genders valued their services equally, but women in the sample weighed local competition as having a greater influence than men. The authors opined that this finding might flow from greater numbers of nondoctoral female therapists in the community (Newlin, Adolph, & Kreber, 2004). Men have generally reported higher median full-time salaries than women (Stetell, Pingitore, Scheffler, Schwalm, & Haley, 2001) and charge self-pay clients more than women do (Finances, 2000). In addition, another study reported that developmental and sociocultural expectations may keep female patients and female therapists from addressing financial issues openly in group psychotherapy (Motherwell, 2002).

If you attended graduate school much before 1990, it is likely that you never even heard of financial aspects of psychotherapeutic practice or the term *managed care* discussed in the classroom (Hixson, 2004). The notion that therapists might have to account to third parties (i.e., the client and therapist as the first and second parties) for their therapeutic decisions or second parties) for their therapeutic decisions or prepare treatment plans for external review would have seemed remote and unreasonable. Few newly licensed mental health professionals prior to 1990 worried about their ability to secure a listing on overcrowded rolls of approved insurance program providers. Today and for the foreseeable future, any therapist who hopes to build a financially viable practice must prepare to work with managed care in some form (Fasone, 2002; Hixson, 2004).

WHAT TO CHARGE?

Determining the customary charges for one's services is a complicated task that mixes issues of economics, business, self-esteem, and a variety of cultural and professional taboos. When it comes to mental health services, the task is complicated by a host of both subtle and obvious psychological and ethical values (Auld, Hyman, & Rudzinski, 2005; Gabbard, 2005; Lanza, 2001; Motherwell, 2002; West, Wilk, Rae, Narrow, & Regier, 2003). Comparison of fees is further complicated by differences in procedures, length of sessions, and other variables. For example, rates can differ depending on whether the service provided involves psychotherapy, psychopharmacology, forensic services, neuropsychological assessment, or group therapy. In its periodic fee surveys, *Psychotherapy Finances* (http://www.psyfin.com/) has noted that the fee for a single therapy session might vary by more than 100% over the range of practitioners in a given region. Variation occurs by region, practice site, professional degree, experience, and specialty, among other variables (Norcross, 2005).

Psychiatrists have traditionally commanded the highest fees, although fewer and fewer of them practice psychotherapy as opposed to medication prescribing (Gabbard, 2005; Koocher, 2007). Since 1979, *Psychotherapy Finances* has conducted periodic fee surveys, publishing data from their 12th survey in three issues during 2006 (*Psychotherapy Finances*, 2006a, 2006b, 2006c). *Psychotherapy Finances* reported that, since their prior survey in 2000, managed care fees have generally remained flat, and professional incomes failed to keep pace with the relatively low inflation rates. Psychologists' incomes rose 16% between 2000 and 2006, but inflation totaled 17% during the same period. Marriage and family therapists (MFTs) posted a modest 4.5% income gain, licensed professional counselors' (LPCs) incomes stayed flat, and clinical social workers (CSWs) reported lower professional incomes even before taking inflation into account. Because of insufficient data, the survey could not reach definite conclusions regarding psychiatrists' incomes, but noted anecdotal data suggesting that they could command modest increases from managed care organizations (MCOs) by virtue of their relative scarcity. Actual fee data from the 2006 survey are summarized by profession in Table 7–1.

The *Psychotherapy Finances* survey used five regions to analyze self-pay fee data. A summary regional breakdown for 2006 appears in Table 7–2.

Psychological testing fees for 2 hours administering a Weschler IQ test averaged $210 for self-pay clients, with $150 paid by MCOs. A Minnesota Multiphasic Personality Inventory (MMPI) 2 or MMPI-A rated at 1 hour of professional time averaged $131 for self-pay clients and $105 when paid by MCOs. A Rorschach inkblot administration with Exner scoring rated at 2 hours of professional time averaged $219 for self-pay clients and $150 when paid by MCOs. These data and the material excerpted in Tables 7–1 and 7–2 represent a small slice of

the substantial survey data collected by *Psychotherapy Finances*. We present these few excerpts for illustrative purposes only and recommend that interested readers go to the original source for complete details.

In considering fees, matters are further complicated by the issue of what constitutes a "therapy hour." A session could range from an 8- to 10-minute medication check by a psychiatrist or psychiatric nurse to 120-minute or longer for a family or marathon group session. Some practitioners offer their clients 60-minute hours, whereas for most others a treatment session will more often occupy 50, 45, or even fewer minutes. Likewise, group or family therapy sessions might extend 90 minutes or more, making clear direct fee comparisons across modalities and practitioners difficult.

Shortening the session may seem a way to increase cash flow by degrees; however, the practice more often results from an effort to catch up on the hidden demands on the therapist's time. Paperwork requirements for filing health insurance reimbursement claims, detailing treatment plans, and making telephone contacts related to cases have increased significantly over the past few years. In many circumstances, therapists may spend 50 minutes meeting with the client, only to spend another 50 minutes completing therapy notes or other documentation necessary to seek third-party approval for addition sessions.

Some practitioners may offer a sliding fee scale for clients who can not afford to pay a

Table 7–1 Most Frequent Fees Paid

	Direct Pay	Managed Care
For Individual Therapy		
Marriage and family therapists	$100	$60
Licensed professional counselors	$90	$63
Psychologists	$120	$75
Social workers	$90	$60
For Group Therapy		
Marriage and family therapists	$46	$40
Licensed professional counselors	$40	$28
Psychologists	$50	$40
Social workers	$45	$33

Table 7–2 Self-Pay Individual Psychotherapy Fees by Region

	East	South	Midwest	West	Pacific[a]
Marriage and family therapists	$100	$100	$95	$100	$100
Licensed professional counselors	$90	$90	$87	$93	$85
Psychologists	$115	$125	$110	$120	$125
Social workers	$90	$98	$90	$83	$90

[a]Pacific states in this survey border the ocean; West states include the inland Rocky Mountain region.

customary charge, while others maintain a high "usual and customary rate" and provide an assortment of discounts. For example, a client who has remained in treatment for an extended period of time may pay a lower rate than a new client. Or, an individual whose treatment program necessitates 3 hours per week of professional time may have a lower hourly rate than a person seen once per week. From an ethical standpoint, the actual fee charged for services rendered is not as important as the manner in which it is set, communicated, managed, and collected. By definition, however, many of a therapist's clients may be regarded as somewhat vulnerable to potential abuse because of emotional dependency, social naïveté, psychosis, or other psychopathological conditions. It behooves the therapist not to take advantage of these factors.

Case 7–1: Arnold Avarice, Ph.D., was contacted by Sally Sibyl for treatment of her emotional problems. He diagnosed her as having a multiple personality disorder. During the first 2 months of treatment, Dr. Avarice claimed to have treated Ms. Sibyl an average of 3 hours per day (some days as many as 5 to 6 hours) at a rate of $175 per hour. Ms. Sibyl's wealthy family was billed more than $30,000 for services during this time. When Ms. Sibyl's family questioned the bill, Dr. Avarice justified the frequency of his work with the client by noting, "I often had sessions with two or three different personalities the same day. She is a very disturbed woman requiring intensive work."

Most psychotherapists, including those expert in treating people with a multiple personality disorder (also known as dissociative identity disorder), would question the necessity and appropriateness of Dr. Avarice's intervention. When called before an ethics committee, Dr. Avarice could not provide a treatment plan or detailed case notes for the many hours of treatment he claimed to have provided. Ms. Sibyl showed little improvement and could not remember when or how often she had seen Dr. Avarice.

From the outset of a relationship with a new client, the therapist should take care to explain the nature of services offered, the fees charged, the mode of payment used, and other financial arrangements that might reasonably be expected to influence the potential client's decision. If the therapist has reason to question the ability of the client to make a responsible decision, then this also must be considered in deciding to accept the client or make some specialized referral elsewhere. Of course, parents or legal guardians may grant permission for treatment of minors or adults over whom they have guardianship. Providing informed consent should be regarded as a process rather than a single event. The flow of information and mutual discussion of the treatment process—including costs—should be ongoing as needed throughout the professional relationship. If therapists provide an estimate of charges, they must honor such estimates unless unforeseen circumstances arise. In the last situation, any changes should be discussed with and agreed to by the client. If it seems that financial difficulties may become an issue, they should be dealt with openly at the very outset of the relationship.

Occasionally, clients complain to ethics committees about pressure to enter treatment at a higher fee than they can afford. Such practices include both "soft-sell" and "hard-sell" pitches by therapists. An example of the low-pressure pitch might involve explaining, "If you really want to get better, you will find a way to finance good therapy. It's an investment in yourself." A more pressured or aggressive pitch might sound like, "You can't afford not to see me. I have been very successful in solving your sort of problem. Things will only get worse if you don't take care of them now." Aside from the implication of special skill explicit in both these pitches, they subject clients to unethical pressure by playing on their insecurities.

More appropriate ways to address the issue of the client who can not afford the usual charges for services exist. Many mental health professionals offer a flexible fee schedule that varies as a function of client income. Most professional associations also encourage their members to offer at least some pro bono services (i.e., professional activity undertaken at no charge in the public interest). For example, under its aspirational ethical principles the American Psychological Association (APA) states, "Psychologists strive to contribute a portion of their professional time for little or no compensation or personal advantage" (APA 02: Principle B). A variety of surveys have yielded self-reports that suggest most psychologists do provide at least some services at little or no cost.

Many psychotherapists will offer a financially troubled client the opportunity to extend payment over a long period of time, but this practice will not prove helpful if the charges incurred remain beyond the reasonable means of the client. Some therapists tack on interest or "billing charges" to unpaid bills. This practice may also involve substantial administrative difficulties because state and federal laws generally require a special disclosure statement informing clients about such fees and obtaining their agreement in advance.

It is critical that the therapist consider these issues very early in the professional relationship and raise them openly with the client in a realistic, yet supportive, fashion. If a prospective client seems unable to reasonably afford the services of the practitioner in question, the therapist should be prepared to make a sensitive and appropriate referral. In this vein, it is important for all mental health practitioners to keep abreast of hospitals, clinics, community mental health centers, training programs, and other resources that might offer more affordable services for those with financial difficulties.

Along these lines, therapists must consider their obligations to the client and local agencies in terms of treatment continuity and limited financial resources in the community. A practice known as "creaming and dumping" illustrates this point.

Case 7–2: Roberta Poore consulted Phil T. Lucre, M.S.W., for treatment of long-standing difficulties with her parents and coworkers. After only one session, it was clear to Mr. Lucre that Poore would, at minimum, require several months of weekly psychotherapy to begin addressing her relationship problems effectively. Mr. Lucre's usual hourly rate was $100, and he did not have a policy of reducing his fee for clients who could not afford it. Poore had health insurance coverage that provided up to $500 per year in outpatient mental health benefits. Her salary was low, and she could not afford more than $50 per week to pay out of pocket for psychotherapy. Mr. Lucre saw her for five sessions. As soon as her insurance coverage was exhausted, he referred her to the local community health center, where she could receive treatment at a reduced fee.

In this case, Mr. Lucre skimmed the "cream" (insurance benefits due to the client) and then "dumped" her in the lap of a community agency. This constitutes a disservice to the client, who faces a disruption in her therapeutic care, as well as a disservice to the community agency, which would have benefited from the insurance payments while also providing continuity of care after the coverage was exhausted. When the possibility of service needs in excess of coverage becomes evident, the therapist should not take on the case but rather should make an appropriate referral immediately. If the therapist considers the treatment or evaluation plan early and discusses it with the client, including all relevant financial aspects, then the client would be in a position to express a preference considering the continuity issue as well.

The case of Mr. Lucre and Ms. Poore represents one type of abandonment of a client by the therapist, but what of the more general situation when a client can not pay for services rendered? Should the therapist terminate services in midcourse of treatment, or does that represent abandonment of the client as well? The ethical therapist will attempt to avoid abandoning clients for financial reasons with two specific strategies. The first is never to contract for services without first clarifying the costs to the client and reaching an agreement on affordability. The second is not to mislead the client into thinking that insurance or other such coverage will bear the full cost of services when it seems reasonably clear that benefits may become exhausted before the client's need for service. When a client becomes unemployed or otherwise can no longer pay for continued services during the course of therapy, the therapist should remain especially sensitive to the client's needs. If a client can not realistically be helped under existing reimbursement restrictions and the resulting process might be too disruptive, it is best simply to explain the problem and not take on the prospective client. While it may be necessary to terminate care or transfer the client's care elsewhere over the long term, this should never occur abruptly or in the midst of a crisis period in the client's life.

Increasing fees in the course of service delivery can also pose ethical dilemmas. Commitments made to provide consultation or to conduct an assessment for a given fee should be honored. Likewise, a client who enters psychotherapy at an agreed-on fee has a reasonable expectation that the fee will not increase excessively. Once service has begun, the provider must consider the obligations for continuity of care due to the client. Aside from financial hardship issues, therapists must not abuse the special influence they have with their clients.

Case 7–3: Chuck Gelt began psychotherapy with Helen Takem, M.D., expecting to pay $85 per session. After several weeks of treatment, Mr. Gelt shared some intense and painful concerns with Dr. Takem. These emotional issues included mixed feelings over relationships with Gelt's deceased parents, from whom he had just inherited substantial wealth. Dr. Takem pressed Gelt to contract with her for a minimum of 100 sessions at a cost of $190 per session. She argued that, for this partic-

ular affluent client, the fee needed to be high or else he would not perceive the therapy as "valuable." The minimum contract for 100 sessions was needed, Takem reasoned, because Gelt was "ambivalent and tended to lack commitment."

Dr. Takem's proposed contract is clearly unethical as it requires new terms independent of demonstrated client need and without meaningful client participation in the decision-making process. In addition, the client's mixed feelings may inhibit his ability to see or raise a complaint about the inappropriateness of the dramatic boost in fees. At the same time, the client may feel reluctant to go through the emotional pain of sharing his concerns all over again with a new therapist. The emotional investment made by the client during the first few sessions may contribute to making him less able to act as an informed, reasoning consumer.

When a client has participated in psychotherapy for an extended period of time (i.e., 6 months to a year or more) and inflation or other costs of conducting a professional practice have risen, it is not unreasonable to adjust fees upward accordingly. This should, however, be done thoughtfully, reasonably, and with due consideration for each client's economic status and treatment needs (Pepper, 2004). Some practitioners, for example, will raise fees for new clients while maintaining ongoing clients at their preexisting rate. The ethical point to consider is that mental health professionals incur added responsibility because of the influential roles they occupy relative to clients (Buck, 1999). Raising the fee exponentially or without a meaningful economic rationale, however, is seldom, if ever, therapeutically defensible.

Similar issues are discussed in Chapter 14 with respect to promotional offers of "free sessions" or "special bonus offers" used in advertisements to attract clients. Clients may not realize the subtle emotional pressures that may accompany an initial consultation or "free visit." While there is certainly nothing wrong with not charging a client under some circumstances, this should never become a lure to initiate a professional relationship through advertising media.

Some practitioners require clients to pay certain fees in advance of rendering services as a kind of retainer. This constitutes unusual practice in psychotherapy but is not unethical as long as the contingencies are by mutual agreement. The most common uses of such advance payments or retainers involve relationships in which the practitioner is asked to hold time available on short notice for some reasons (as in certain types of corporate consulting) or when certain types of time-consuming assessments or litigation are involved (see a discussion in Chapter 17). A specific example might occur when a therapist agrees to undertake a child custody evaluation, and the two hostile contesting parties (such as the Bicker family in Case 7–11) each agree to pay half of the fee in advance. In such cases, at least one of the parties will very likely become unhappy with the outcome, and in such circumstances the unhappy party may refuse to pay for the services rendered because of displeasure with the findings. Another example might involve a family requesting a private neuropsychological assessment of their child in the hope of securing changes in the child's special education IEP (Individualized Educational Plan). Such an evaluation may well require the neuropsychologist to invest 5 to 10 hours or more of data collection, plus similar amounts of time in preparing a report. In such situations, it is not unusual for the practitioner to request a retainer or escrow payment prior to commencing work.

Payment for missed appointments is another source of occasional inquiries to ethics committees. It is not unethical to charge a client for an appointment that is not kept or that is canceled on short notice (Auld et al., 2005; Birnbach, 1999; Napoli, 1999; Ritt, 2000; Sommers, 1999). Again, the key issue involves giving proper advance information about this practice to the client (APA 02: 6.04). No one wants to have their schedule disrupted or lose time that they might have reallocated for other useful purposes. In addition, if a practitioner has a waiting list and could well use the vacant appointment time, it is frustrating and costly to have a client cancel on short notice or simply fail to show up for the appointment. If the practitioner intends to charge the client in such

instances, however, it is necessary to advise the client of this at the start of the relationship and to make the conditions explicit, preferably in written form initialed by the client. When informing clients about such charges, it is important to advise them that insurance companies generally will not pay for missed appointments, as we discuss later in this chapter. In actual practice, it appears that few therapists charge clients for a missed appointment unless the behavior becomes a recurrent pattern.

Case 7–4: Skippy Session saw Harry Biller, L.M.H.C., for psychotherapy on a weekly basis for 6 weeks. During the first session, Mr. Biller explained his policy of charging clients for appointments canceled less than 24 hours in advance, and Mr. Session accepted those terms. A few hours before the scheduled seventh appointment, Session's father was killed in an automobile accident. Session telephoned Mr. Biller that he would be unable to keep the appointment and would call to reschedule. Mr. Biller did not charge Mr. Session for the canceled appointment out of deference to the unusual circumstances. Several months later, Mr. Session neglected to keep a scheduled appointment with Mr. Biller. When the therapist charged him for that missed appointment, Mr. Session complained, "That's unethical! After all, you never charged me the last time I missed one."

There may be many different reasons that Mr. Session missed his most recent appointment, ranging from "unconscious acting out" (Sommers, 1999; Valentine, 1999) to simple forgetting. He was informed about and did agree to, Mr. Biller's terms at the start of therapy. Mr. Biller's compassionate waiving of his fee the day Mr. Session's father died may have been misinterpreted by Session. Mr. Biller is ethically entitled to charge for the second missed session; however, in the interest of maintaining the therapeutic alliance and for risk management purposes (see Chapter 17), it probably would prove wiser to discuss both the misunderstanding and the meaning of "forgetting" the appointment, postponing the implementation of the missed session fee until the next occurrence.

Fees certainly do have substantial psychological impact on a number of levels and may often become a therapeutic issue (Hixson, 2004; Newlin et al., 2004; Newman, 2005; Sommers, 1999; Valentine, 1999). Lovinger noted that the fee is all that the client has to give, aside from coming to the clinician's office (Lovinger, 1978). The client does not owe the practitioner gratitude, respect, consensus, or anything other than a fee for services rendered. The fee may, in that sense, develop some special meaning via transference (Rogoff, 2006; Shapiro & Ginzberg, 2006; Totton, 2006; Waska, 1999). This means that the client may react to a fee change in the same manner as some duty owed in relationship with another significant person in his or her life. It may become a means of addressing the anger held in relation to a demanding parent or represent a penance to atone for some imagined wrong to a spouse. Lovinger, like Freud (who, he reported, viewed fees as a frank matter of the therapist's livelihood for matter-of-fact discussions with his patients) suggested that a direct and candid approach is the best means to begin a client–psychotherapist relationship.

FEE SPLITTING

Fee splitting, often termed a *kickback*, refers to a general practice under which part of a sum received for a product or service is returned or paid out because of some prearranged agreement or coercion. As practiced in medicine and the mental health professions, the client usually remains unaware of the arrangement. Traditionally, nearly universal agreement existed among medical and mental health professionals that such practices are unethical, chiefly because they may preclude a truly appropriate referral in the client's best interests, result in delivery of unneeded services, lead to increased costs of services, and generally exploit the relative ignorance of the client. Unfortunately, fee splitting may exist in rather complex and subtle forms that tend to mask the fact that it is occurring.

There is a continuum of types of fee-splitting or sharing agreements that range from reasonable and ethical to clearly inappropriate. At one end of the continuum we find employer–

employee relationships in which one party hires another to perform services; at the other end, we find arrangements in which the person making the referral gets money solely for sending business to another. The employer–employee relationship provides an ethically clear context (i.e., I pay you a salary, and I collect fees for the work you do as an employee). Unethical fee splitting occurs in the case of making payment or kickback simply for referring a new client. In between these two extremes one can find a range of business practices with varying incentives that raise ethical questions. In addition, actions by the Federal Trade Commission (FTC), as discussed in Chapter 14, have legitimized some practices previously prohibited by professional associations' ethics codes.

Case 7–5: Irving Slynapse, M.D., a prominent neurologist, agrees to refer substantial numbers of his patients to Ester Choline, Psy.D., for neuropsychological assessment. Dr. Choline bills the client or insurance company and pays Slynapse 10% of all the money collected on clients he refers to her. Slynapse characterizes that 10% as a continuing charge for medical coverage and consultation; however, there are no regular appointments scheduled for consultation, and Choline never avails herself of that service.

Case 7–6: Nick Proffit, M.D., P.C., has a large professional practice; he supervises several master's-level psychotherapists and rents office space to other doctoral-level mental health practitioners. His secretary bills all of the clients at a rate of $100 per session. The supervisees are paid 25% of the fees collected, and the renters are paid 40% of the fees collected. The clients remain unaware of this distribution plan.

Case 7–7: G. Ima Helper, M.S.W., is well known for her many self-help books and media appearances. Her public visibility results in many self-referrals by clients in the community. Ms. Helper refers such clients to Helper's Haven, her private clinic, where they are seen for $90 per session by master's-level therapists who are paid $35 per session. The clients are led to believe that their therapists are supervised or receive consultation from Dr. Helper. Actually, they are not even employees (i.e., salaried) but simply earn a fee for each session held and have no contact with Dr. Helper, who has little direct involvement with the clinic.

Each of the cases cited has a number of unethical features in common. To begin, the clients are generally unaware of the proprietary relationship between the service provider and the person making the referral. It is therefore unlikely that the clients would realize that the referrals originated because of motives other than their own best interests. In each of the cases, one party is also being paid for services not rendered. That is, Dr. Slynapse, Dr. Proffit, and Ms. Helper receive a commission in a manner concealed from, and to the detriment of, the clients. Clients may assume that referrals to therapists were based on the therapists' special abilities or competence rather than chiefly for profit. The more responsibility and liability the referrer has for the case, the more reasonable it is to pay that person a fee. None of these therapists has objectively weighed the needs of the individual client and considered these in making the referral. A key point is the matter of professional responsibility. Some clients may actually end up referred and charged for services that they do not need.

Dr. Proffit's situation is potentially more appropriate than those of Drs. Slynapse and Helper. If Proffit has a long-term contract with the therapists who rent space from him and provides supervision, consultation, or case oversight, he may be legitimately entitled to a percentage of fees collected. On the other hand, if he has no professional relationship with the therapists and no clear responsibility for their clients' welfare, he is not entitled to a fee. The key issue in determining appropriateness of such fees is the rendering of legitimate, reasonably priced services.

The case of Ms. Helper also raises the basic question of what one must disclose to a client about arrangements among practitioners. Helper may also be exploiting the other therapists in her clinic. The issue in the current context is that clients should be told any aspects of the arrangement that might reasonably be expected to influence their decision about whether to use the services. They have a right to know that Ms. Helper will not participate in

their treatment in any way. In all of the cases in which a commission is paid to someone not rendering services, the client should also be advised. By commission, we mean any payment made simply for a referral, as opposed to a payment made for some services rendered in a joint practice or professional collaboration.

Group Practice

Many mental health providers work in group practices or collaborative arrangements by sharing certain costs such as rent, secretarial services, utilities, and answering services. Many other therapists also have, or work as, assistants to other more senior clinicians and earn less than the full rate billed to the client. Although these types of arrangements may pass legal muster, we feel troubled when compensation is paid to some party simply for referring clients or when percentages of gross income are charged against a clinician automatically rather than for services legitimately provided. In such instances, the clients' welfare is too easily ignored.

In the group practice described above, for example, each therapist might be asked to make a monthly payment, based on actual or reasonably estimated costs and their use of the services, for office expenses. This charge should be calculated independently of the gross income or the number of clients seen and based instead on an actual usage paradigm. In the case of the assistant, it may prove more appropriate to pay the individual a salary or to base compensation on actual gross income less actual costs. Costs might include a reasonable charge for supervision (when allowed by law), administration, marketing, consultation, or office services, but these must be based on a mutually agreed-on set of actual expenses and be open to renegotiation as time-demand shifts occur. In all cases, the therapists must be free to make referrals outside the practice when this seems in their clients' best interests. No financial rewards or penalties should accrue to any party as the result of an inside versus outside referral.

One of the subtle difficulties involved in group practice arrangements or the use of assistants is the fair determination of costs and service use. Considerable opportunity for inflation of expenses or other manipulations exists. This is especially true when one of the mental health practitioners is in a position of power over others by virtue of being the senior party, owner of the practice, or a licensed clinician employing individuals in training or unable to obtain independent licensure. In such situations, it behooves the practitioner to avoid even the appearance of abuse and to be fully open with his or her colleagues.

Case 7–8: Debbie Doubter, Psy.D., has been invited to join a thriving group practice started 20 years ago by Wally Wealthy, Ph.D. She has been offered 40% of the fees collected for her services during her first year and 50% of the fees every year thereafter. Dr. Wealthy explains that he will provide close supervision and some training for her in the first year. In addition, he notes that 50% of the fees collected are his best estimate of the costs of rent, utilities, billing service, answering service, and coverage of her clients while she is on vacation. By joining the practice, Dr. Doubter will automatically qualify as a provider on several managed care preferred provider panels. Finally, Dr. Wealthy notes that his percentage includes some allowance for "return on investment." That is to say, he feels entitled to recover some money based on the years he has invested in building the practice.

In this case, Dr. Doubter must decide for herself whether she is comfortable with Dr. Wealthy's offer. It is not inappropriate on its face because Dr. Wealthy will indeed provide the stated services and will retain a significant degree of professional and clinical responsibility. Given the difficulties many young therapists face starting practices in today's economic climate, the 50% cut sought by Dr. Wealthy may seem acceptable to some.

Another subtle difficulty involves the tendency to refer clients to therapists one knows well. This can be a very appropriate and responsible practice, as one tries to help each client obtain the most fitting services for her or his needs. It is critical, however, that the person making the referral do so without any anticipation of financial benefit or gain as the result of the referral. If it happens that the most suitable referral may well be to a colleague or employee

and some indirect benefit might be a result (e.g., overhead costs in a group practice kept lower by virtue of more patients being seen), this would not cause the same type of ethical conflict. The client should be informed, however, of the fact that a relationship exists between the practitioners and the reasons why a referral is being made to that specific practitioner. Another alternative would be to offer the client a choice among practitioners that includes at least one with no linkage to the referring party.

Case 7–9: Finda Dockta, M.B.A., founded a psychotherapy referral service, Shrinks-R-Us, to "guide wise consumers to competent, effective, reasonably priced therapists." Psychotherapists pay Ms. Dockta a registration fee, provide proof that they are licensed, carry liability insurance, and supply three letters of reference. The therapists provide her database with details on their experience, languages spoken, office location, and other relevant data. They also agree to pay her a 5% royalty on all net fees collected from clients she refers to them. Ms. Dockta markets the service heavily. Clients are not charged a fee and are informed that all costs of the service are paid by the practitioners based on their collections.

Some might say that Ms. Dockta's program involves fee splitting, although the FTC would have no difficulty with it. Yes, she is getting a percentage of the fees (potentially for years to come, depending on the signed agreement with the therapists), but she is also legitimately earning those fees by providing useful referral information to consumers. The fact that providers pay for the service is not concealed. Although a state legislature may have authority to prohibit such activities within its borders (thus avoiding the FTC's interstate commerce oversight), practitioners participating in such a service would not be subject to disciplinary action by national professional organizations or their state affiliates. (For a discussion of other ethical issues related to client referrals, see Chapter 13.)

Special Business Agreements

Although technically not fee splitting, a variety of special business agreements common in the commercial world would be considered potentially unethical in mental health or medical practice for reasons similar to the issues raised thus far in this chapter. These agreements would include so-called covenants not to compete or contracts with liquidated damages clauses.

Case 7–10: Lester Workman, M.D., spent 10 years building a favorable professional reputation and busy private practice in a suburban community. He began to attract more referrals than he could handle, but he was not sure whether the volume would be sufficient to warrant the addition of a colleague as a full-time employee in the practice. Instead, he hired Peter Partner, L.M.F.T., as a half-time employee at a salary agreeable to both for a 1-year contract. By the end of the year, Mr. Partner, who was young and energetic, began to build his own strong reputation in the community and wondered if he ought to consider going into practice independently.

In an ideal world, Workman and Partner will sit down and attempt to sort matters out in their clients' best interests. If they are indeed to have separate practices in the same community, the choice of whom to consult should belong to the client. Clients in midtreatment with Mr. Partner, for example, should reasonably expect to continue their relationship with him. Unfortunately, however, such splits often result in considerable acrimony between the practitioners, with clients caught in between. It would have been preferable for Workman to consider this potential outcome as a possibility from the outset should they terminate working together and include some reasonable professional plan in the agreement with Partner to meet clients' needs. This agreement could include some fair allowance for the effort Workman put into building the practice.

Two types of advance agreement for the termination of such relationships cause serious ethical problems. In the first type, Dr. Workman might have attempted to sign Mr. Partner to a contract that included a "covenant not to compete." Under such a clause, Partner would agree, for example, not to set up an independent practice or work for any other practitioner

within a 50-mile radius of Workman's office for a period of time after leaving the practice. Whereas this might meet Workman's needs, it would deny clients their freedom to choose and is, therefore, clearly unethical. In some jurisdictions, state laws make such agreements among health care professionals illegal. The usual legal standard is "reasonableness." Although there are obviously many different perspectives on what is reasonable, the paramount ethical perspective would focus on the well-being of the clients. Clear differences exist between the obligations to a client who is psychologically vulnerable and the more usual circumstances in business and industry, in which such covenants are more appropriately used to protect trade secrets.

The second type of problematic contractual element Workman might have considered would be a liquidated damages clause. Such a clause might have asked that Mr. Partner pay Workman financial "damages" for each client he takes with him, either at a flat fee per client rate or as a percentage of future revenues. Paying a flat fee for each client who leaves with Dr. Partner might prove ethically acceptable as long as the cost of this fee is not passed to the client. Paying a percentage of future earnings or a royalty from the fees of the transferred clients is more clearly a fee-splitting situation and could be legally unenforceable in some states, even if Mr. Partner had agreed to it initially.

The message inherent in this discussion has three aspects. First, such issues require discussion and clarification prior to beginning the professional association. Second, the choice of a therapist should ultimately rest with the client. Finally, professional colleagues must exercise great care and at times suffer potential economic disadvantage so they do not abuse the relative position of power and influence they have over the clients they serve. Psychotherapists should not profit unfairly at the expense of either clients or colleagues.

Selling a professional practice is another kind of special business agreement that raises ethical questions. Suppose Dr. Workman wanted to retire after 30 years in solo private practice. Can he sell his practice? What does the practice include? Furniture, an office, some aging psychological test equipment, the name of the practice or clinic, and a group of clients make up a practice. One can indeed sell the furniture, real estate, and equipment. But, selling the clients, their files, and access to this information raises many significant ethical issues (Koocher, 2003; Manosevitz & Hays, 2003). Practitioners can not ethically transfer clinical responsibility for clients or confidential client records in a private practice without the clients' consent. Clients have the right to choose practitioners. In addition to freedom-of-choice (FOC) issues, the seller's clients may feel heavily influenced by the seller's recommendation that they continue to obtain services from the buyer. The seller is in a complex role with respect to these clients. That is, the clients are in some respects a commodity when they are referred en masse to the buyer. They have the right to expect that the referral to a new practitioner is based on careful professional judgment of their individual needs (Pope & Keith-Spiegel, 1986). Principles for valuing a practice, including ethical issues related to client lists and records were described by Woody (1997).

If Dr. Workman wanted to maximize his ability to transfer a thriving practice to another professional, the most ethical and effective way to accomplish this feat would be to spread it out over a period of years in what has been termed an "extended transition model" (Myers & Brezler, 1992). Ideally, Dr. Workman could attract a potential partner and forge an agreement (e.g., a legal entity, partnership, or professional corporation) that included a buyout of the practice over time. As Workman's retirement drew near, he could offer clients the opportunity to transfer to his partner or elsewhere in the community. The agreement could call for the partner to maintain and administer the practice's records for the legally mandated interval (see Chapter 8) and might even include a continuing consulting role for Workman on an as-needed basis should special issues with former clients arise. In this way, the selling of the practice actually becomes an evolutionary transfer that allows time, choice, and continuity options for the clients.

THIRD-PARTY RELATIONSHIPS

Clients typically pay for mental health services in one of three ways:

1. Directly out of pocket with no reimbursement.
2. In whole or in part by a health insurance plan, health maintenance organization (HMO), preferred provider organization (PPO) plan.
3. Some other employee assistance benefit plan or public funds (e.g., through a school system, Medicare, or Medicaid).

Whenever some company, agency, or organization other than the practitioner and client becomes involved in payment, we have a fiscal third-party relationship. There is no doubt that these third parties, their reimbursement policies, and the regulations that govern these policies have historically had a direct and powerful influence on practice and client care (Bachman, Pincus, Houtsinger, & Untzer, 2006; Gittelman, 1998; Harrison, Moran, Albrecht, Fitzpatrick, & Scrimshaw, 2000; Sperling, Sack, & Field, 2000; Sturm, 2004; Weisgerber, 1999). Although some well-established practitioners refuse to accept third-party payments (M. I. Bennett & Lazarus, 2005), it is unrealistic for most mental health practitioners to expect that they will be able to earn a living without substantial interactions with such third-party payment entities. Although many therapists will have no difficulties in their relationships with these entities, very few will consider them an unmitigated blessing.

In historical context, insurance coverage for mental health services has attracted a range of interesting critiques. Some asserted that including psychotherapy benefits in health insurance coverage represented inequitable service to different income groups (Albee, 1977a, 1977b). Others raised threats to clients' confidentiality (Alleman, 2001; Austad, Hunter, & Morgan, 1998), concern about accountability and review criteria grew (Acuff et al., 1999; Alleman, 2001; Austad et al., 1998; Bersoff, 2003), and some even cited expensive litigation as a disincentive to coverage (Kiesler & Pallak, 1980). Access to such coverage has also led to many intra- and interprofessional squabbles about who ought to qualify to bill third parties for what services. We discussed professional competence in Chapter 4 and confidentiality problems in Chapter 8, so we now defer to a discussion of what we deem chiefly *political* issues in insurance reimbursement in favor of a focus on the ethical problems such third-party relationships raise. Next, the topics of so-called FOC options and billing for services not covered are discussed as a lead in to a major discussion of fraud and the MCOs.

Freedom of Choice

The freedom of choice (FOC) issue refers to legislation and regulations that permit clients to choose their provider of services. As used in discussions of mental health services, FOC generally refers to whether the mental health practitioner is authorized to bill a third party directly for services rendered to a client or whether that therapist must first obtain the approval or referral of a psychiatrist. At least that was the historical battle. More recently, mental health benefits have come to be administered along with other specialty services so that a primary care physician (e.g., internist or pediatrician) must authorize a referral, whether to a mental health practitioner, allergist, or proctologist.

Psychologists pressed the FOC concept as a right of the client throughout the 1960s and 1970s, in an era when psychiatrists seemed in control of such matters. Psychologists argued that many of them had excellent qualifications to function as independent health service providers. Other arguments included the claim that the availability of psychologists improves consumer access to qualified care and increases competition among professional provider groups, with resulting cost benefits to consumers. Failure to recognize licensed psychologists as independent providers had been viewed by some as an unreasonable restraint of trade. As states granted licensing status to social workers, mental health counselors, marriage and family counselors, these professions soon began to clamor for so-called direct recognition laws. Some authors have articulately addressed the

unintended consequences of requiring a license to help (Crespi & Steir, 1997; Danish & Smyer, 1981; Hogan, 1977).

More recent developments of concern to mental health professionals involve limitations to access on closed provider panels and declining reimbursement rates. Managed care organizations frequently create a limited roster of practitioners approved to serve their policyholders. At times, categories of practitioners find themselves excluded or underrepresented on such panels. At other times, medical and mental health care providers have been abruptly dropped from the listing or denied entry for reasons that are unclear or seem unfair to one or another party. Access to membership on such provider panels remains a major professional concern, although not necessarily an ethical issue. Sometimes, however, practitioners find themselves ethically challenged when they fear that doing what is best for a client may compromise their provider status, as we discuss in a separate section.

Complaints may also come from specific providers or provider groups against their colleagues in kindred professions. When social workers, family counselors, psychiatric nurses, or unlicensed psychologists have sought entitlement to become independent vendors for third-party payments, they have generally cited the very same arguments advanced years earlier by psychologists (i.e., consumer's right to choose, lower fees based on increased competition, etc.). In general, the entitled practitioner groups tend to oppose direct reimbursement of unentitled groups for a variety of economic and political reasons. Quality-of-care issues and cost containment are oft-cited reasons for limiting the size of the practitioner pool to doctoral-level clinicians. Others occasionally argue that these reasons are merely covers for the desire to reduce competition for a limited supply of clients or to avoid fee reductions. This may indeed present some moral or ethical issues, but assigning an ethical infraction to a specific individual in this context will prove difficult. One can not usually identify specific individuals' malevolence or misconduct in contrast with their rights to free speech and attempts to influence the political process. Such concerns seem best addressed as professional standards problems.

Billing for Services Not Covered

A common third-party problem with major ethical and legal implications relates to billing for services not covered under the third party's contractual obligations. Most third-party payers limit their health coverage to treatments for illness or health-related problems, usually defined in terms of medical necessity. One must invariably assign a diagnosis to the client to secure payment. Many services provided by mental health professionals are not, strictly speaking, health or mental health services. For example, relationship counseling, educational testing, school consultation, vocational guidance, child custody evaluations, executive coaching, and a whole variety of forensic functions may not be considered health services. As such, these would not normally be covered by health insurance.

Some insurance carriers also specify certain types of diagnostic or therapeutic procedures as uncovered services. Such treatments or services might be considered ancillary, experimental, unproven, or simply health promoting (e.g., weight control and smoking cessation in the absence of a medical diagnosis), but not treatment for a specific illness. Attempts to conceal the actual nature of the service rendered, or otherwise attempt to obtain compensation in the face of such restrictions, may constitute fraud. (In the first section of this chapter, we discussed the practice of billing clients for missed appointments. Because such billing results from services that have not been rendered, virtually no third-party payer will cover such charges.)

Exactly which services are covered under any given insurance policy is a matter of the specific contract language. Some therapists have found themselves in the position of negotiating one fee if the client receives reimbursement by their insurer and a different fee if the service is not covered. This practice can lead to client resentment and put the therapist in clear violation of certain contracts between providers and insurance companies. One strategy offered by some therapists involves offering a reduced rate that represents a cash discount for clients who no longer use third-party coverage. A legally acceptable rationale would be passing on savings realized when the therapist no longer has to submit claims forms and case reports to the third party.

Case 7–11: Becky and Barney Bicker have been separated for 3 months and have filed for divorce. They are contesting for the custody of their two children. Their respective attorneys suggest a psychological consultation to prepare a forensic report for the courts on the best interests of the children. They are referred to Bill Lesser, Ph.D. Dr. Lesser assures the Bickers that their health insurance policy will cover his fee and proceeds with the evaluation. He subsequently files an insurance claim for his services without noting that it was conducted primarily for resolution of a custody dispute. He assigns the diagnosis "childhood adjustment reaction" to the Bicker children for billing purposes.

Case 7–12: Sven Gully, L.M.H.C., is trained in the use of hypnosis and relaxation techniques. He offers a smoking cessation program that regularly attracts clients. Potential clients often ask about costs and whether Gully will accept health insurance coverage for payment of his services. Gully knows that many companies will not cover hypnosis or will not pay for health-promoting programs in the absence of actual illness. He completes billing forms and lists his services simply as "psychotherapy" and assigns "adjustment reaction" diagnoses to his clients.

Both of the therapists described above may be competent and caring professionals, but both have engaged in unethical conduct and flirted with fraud charges. Perhaps neither has carefully inquired of the third parties in question regarding whether the services are indeed covered and are simply trying to expedite claim processing. On the other hand, each should recognize that the specific services rendered in both cases may not be considered mental health related or treatment of an illness. What appears expedient and helpful to the client (i.e., making services less expensive to the client in question) may constitute illegal practices and tend to increase insurance costs for other policyholders. The more appropriate behavior would be, when in doubt, to check with the third party for explicit advice and to inform clients accurately early in the relationship about whether their coverage applies. Drs. Lesser and Gully may believe that they have helped their clients, but they technically engaged in a "white-collar" ethical violation that costs all consumers money. If Dr. Lesser has concerns that health insurance will not cover his services and worries that the Bickers might squabble over paying for his time, he may reasonably consider requesting a retainer before initiating services.

MANAGED CARE

Managed care organizations (MCOs) take many forms. Some may be actual health care delivery organizations, such as a free-standing health maintenance organization (HMO) with its own physical facilities and employees serving as health care providers. Others may be networks of independent providers (so-called independent practice associations or IPA models). Still others may be HMOs that act as insurance companies and contract with a group of professionals organized as preferred provider organizations (PPOs) that agree to certain rules and reduced rates of reimbursement in exchange for patient referrals. Some large businesses and municipalities are self-insured. That is, these entities act as their own insurance company with the help of a program of claims and risk management, often run by an insurance company or MCO in exchange for a management fee.

In most models, the MCO manages a full spectrum of health care benefits. In other models, a state Medicaid agency or insurance company may "carve out" mental health benefits from overall health insurance packages and assign management of these particular benefits to an MCO organized chiefly as a benefits manager. A brief lesson on the microeconomics of health insurance can be useful in understanding the forces at work here (Harrison & Moran, 2000).

The goal of the various MCOs is essentially the same: to control the increasing costs of health care. When health insurance is provided on an indemnity basis (i.e., costs of covered services are paid for or reimbursed up to policy limits regardless of the provider), few controls or incentives exist to limit spending. In such circumstances, economists would say that the moral hazards of insurance are not well controlled.

The Moral Hazards of Insurance

Suppose we were to offer you "individual pregnancy insurance" at a very low price: complete coverage from prenatal care through delivery at a cost of $1 per month or $9 total per covered individual. Would you buy it? If your answer is, "Yes, where do I sign?" you are most likely a female who is considering becoming pregnant at some point within the span of coverage. If we decided that the policy would be available only to men, prepubertal girls, and postmenopausal women, do you think we would have many buyers? Likewise, would you buy automobile insurance if you did not own a car or hold a driver's license? These brief examples illustrate a basic moral hazard of insurance: Rational people are unlikely to buy it unless they think there is a chance they will need to use it (Hemenway, 1993). If your chance of becoming pregnant is near zero, you are unlikely to buy the insurance regardless of how low the cost. Similarly, a rational person with no access to a motor vehicle is unlikely to purchase automobile insurance regardless of cost. Pregnancy insurance is indeed available, but it is bundled together in family rate health insurance policies that take into account the fact that some members of some families will need the benefit, whereas others will not.

People who have insurance behave differently from people without it. This is another moral hazard that can be considered on an ex ante and ex post basis. The ex ante model refers to behavior prior to making an insurance claim. Simply stated, it means that people will be less careful in avoiding insured perils than they would without insurance coverage. Using the pregnancy model, a rational person who is capable of becoming pregnant will generally be less careful about contraception than she would be without any access to health insurance to cover pregnancy. In addition, an automobile owner whose insurance has expired might keep the car in the garage to avoid risk of damage until a new policy was in force.

The ex post model refers to behavior following the insured event. People with insurance will demand (i.e., consume) more and higher quality services than would an uninsured person. If your automobile's fender is dented but the car is drivable and you are uninsured, you might choose to drive the damaged car rather than pay for the repair out of pocket. If fully insured, on the other hand, the rational person would most likely seek complete repair from the best body shop in town. If your health insurance provides full pregnancy coverage, you will be more likely to use all of the prenatal care available to you rather than skipping some services to save money.

Insurance companies traditionally attempt to reduce the adverse effects of such moral hazards by devising ways to have policyholders share in the risk. Required deductibles, copayments, and variable coverage limits are examples of these strategies. Although the use of such techniques appears to be effective in the case of automobile and home owner's insurance, health insurance costs have not historically been well controlled in this manner. One reason is that health needs often must be dealt with as survival issues. One may choose not to rush to repair a dented fender or leaky roof or even to live with the damage rather than bear the expense of repair. Cost sharing reduces inappropriate utilization, but appropriate use is also reduced. However, it is not wise to postpone surgery for an inflamed appendix, ignore treatment for diabetes, or prematurely suspend cancer chemotherapy for economic reasons as the resulting harm may be irreparable later. In addition, our relationships with health care providers must be based on trust, confidence, and professionalism at a level of intimacy that is not usually expected from those we hire to patch a leak in our roof or fix a dented automobile fender.

It is in this context and amid demands from large group insurance purchasers (i.e., employers) that MCOs have evolved. In addition to policy limits, deductibles, and copayments, MCOs introduced case reviews, requirements

for prior approval, and other steps intended to reduce unnecessary, redundant, or ineffective (but costly) medical care. By doing so, insurance plans can theoretically reduce the cost of coverage and thereby offer less-expensive benefit packages. In reality, the individual consumer has little impact on the system, and the large employers, major purchasers of coverage, often make decisions with bottom-line cost as the prime directive.

Paramount Ethical Dilemmas

The central ethical threat in managed care involves conflicting loyalties. Mental health professionals working under managed care must balance the needs and best interests of their clients with an array of rewards, sanctions, and other inducements issued by the company. In its most common form, this conflict results in providing practitioners with financial incentives to alter or limit care. The limits on care proposed may prove efficient and appropriate and promote reasonable economies. On the other hand, limits curtail the freedom of both clients and service providers. In the worst circumstances, decisions that are adverse from a client's perspective may be orchestrated without the client's knowledge, input, or consent (Braun & Cox, 2005; Cohen, Marecek, & Gillham, 2006; Council on Ethical and Judicial Affairs, 1995; Inglehart, 1996; Kielbasa, Pomerantz, Krohn, & Sullivan, 2004; Mikalac, 2005; Moffic, 2004; A. M. Pomerantz & Segrist, 2006).

Sicker and Quicker

Many health and mental health practitioners have railed against MCOs, claiming that patients are turned out of hospitals "sicker and quicker" than in the past. Shore and Beigel (1996) noted that infringements on professional autonomy also have been a key point of antagonism between MCOs and service providers. The issue is an emotional one that often is not well understood by mental health practitioners. Karon (1995) observed that, although managed care programs are essentially vehicles intended to save money by eliminating unnecessary services, it is easier to save by simply cutting services. He worried that these are short-term approaches, with little interest in preventive mental health services. It is true that case review can potentially eliminate unnecessary psychiatric hospital admissions or psychotherapy in the same way second opinions can reduce unnecessary surgeries. However, review and decision making in the arena of mental health care are not often as clear-cut as problems in physical medicine (DeAngelis, 2006). Regulation of MCOs has become a significant public policy issue.

In this context, it is worthwhile to consider the case of *Wickline v. State of California* (1987).

Case 7–13: Ms. Wickline was a California Medicaid recipient who needed surgery for arteriosclerosis. When postsurgical complications arose, her physician requested an 8-day extension to the 10-day admission originally preauthorized. The reviewer authorized only a 4-day extension, and because the physician did not object and request additional time again, Ms. Wickline was discharged after a total hospitalization of only 14 days. She subsequently developed a blood clot that ultimately required amputation of her right leg. She sued, alleging that failure to grant the extra 4 days of hospital care requested caused her injuries. The trial court found the reviewer negligent and awarded $500,000 in damages. On appeal, however, the decision was reversed on two bases. First, Ms. Wickline's physician had not protested the lack of a full 8-day extension. Second, the court concluded that the blood clot and resulting amputation would have occurred even if she had remained in the hospital.

This case is worth reviewing carefully because the court also went on to state that third-party payers could be held legally accountable if appeals made on behalf of the patient by the care provider were "arbitrarily ignored or unreasonably disregarded or overridden" (*Wickline v. State of California*, 1987, p. 1645). The message in this case is that third-party payers can be held liable for negligently designed or implemented cost-containment strategies. Mental health professionals should actively call that point to the attention of case managers when they believe an inappropriate and potentially

harmful denial of service decision has been made.

In the case of *Muse v. Charter Hospital of Winston-Salem, Incorporated* (1995), a North Carolina appeals court held that a hospital was liable for punitive damages because of "wanton and willful" conduct. The hospital discharged a suicidal adolescent, against the advice of the treating physician, when the teenager's insurance coverage expired. The severely depressed 16-year-old committed suicide a few days following the discharge.

More recently, a unanimous U.S. Supreme Court decision blocked lawsuits in state courts for wrongful denial of coverage against employer-sponsored health plans (*Aetna Health Inc. v. Davila*, 2004). In that case, two beneficiaries of health care plans covered by the Employee Retirement Income Security Act of 1974 (ERISA, 29 USCS §§ 1001 et seq.) brought separate Texas state court suits, claiming that HMOs administering their employer's plans had wrongly refused to cover certain medical services in violation of a Texas health care statute, and that those refusals had caused damages. Two justices noted that Congress and the Supreme Court ought to revisit what they regarded as an unjust and increasingly tangled set of ERISA rulings. However, the decision voided statutes in 10 states that expressly allowed such suits (i.e., in state courts). For practitioners and hospitals, the main result of managed care's renewed immunity may translate to higher liability risk. Caregivers who prescribe treatment but do not provide it because health plans deny coverage may be forced to bear the full cost of liability if something goes wrong (Bloche, 2004). Although the *Aetna* case did not involve mental health issues, it may well apply to such cases.

Becoming a Provider and Staying on the Panel: Between a Rock and a Hard Place

The MCOs have many bases for failing to admit applicant providers to their service pools. They may already have enough practitioners in a limited area, or the applicant may have an ethics complaint, licensing board action, or major malpractice claim on his or her record.

In most cases, practitioners not admitted to or dropped from MCO provider panels have no clear grounds to appeal. As a result, many providers fear that if they "rock the boat" by raising active objections to decisions they believe are adverse to their clients or by speaking out against MCO policies, they may be terminated from the provider panel. Some MCO contracting strategies do little to reassure providers.

Case 7–14: On June 1, Psychotron Mental Services (PMS) mailed renewal contracts to 2,000 practitioners in three states and caused major symptoms of professional distress. Most recipients received the mailing on June 7 and were told that renewal contracts must be returned no later than June 15. The lengthy contracts included a "hold-harmless" clause and a "gag rule." Some providers, fearing economic losses, rushed to sign and return the contracts without seeking legal advice or raising objection.

So-called hold-harmless clauses specify that the practitioner will not hold the MCO responsible for actions it may take that may result in harm to the practitioner as a result of decisions they make regarding services to a client. For example, if the MCO denies services and the therapist continues treating the client without coverage to avoid abandonment, that therapist would not be able to attempt to recover damages from the MCO. As another example, suppose the MCO denies services, and as a result, the client commits suicide; the client's family files a wrongful death suit against the psychotherapist. Such clauses may be legally invalid as being against public policy. Therapists should refuse to sign such contractual conditions from the outset.

The so-called no disparagement or gag rule prohibits the provider from making "critical, adverse, or negative" statements about the MCO to clients or in any public forum. Such policies make sense in traditional business practices, but they are out of place when applied to health care. Aside from the blatant abrogation of practitioners' rights to free speech, such a rule might be deemed a limit on client advocacy and an attempt at intimidation. Such restrictions can interfere with the therapist's ethical obligation to provide patients with information about benefits, risks, and costs of various interventions. Nonetheless, many providers felt they had little choice but to sign, especially in the face of the time deadline. Fortunately, many states have now banned such contract provisions outright.

Some MCOs have been highly aggressive and heavy handed in contract offers. Among the problems reported in contracts offered to providers by MCOs are clauses stating that the provider will be solely responsible in any legal actions undertaken by any party; take no legal action against the MCO under any circumstances; deal exclusively with the MCO; agree to abide by all of the MCO's utilization review processes and decisions; agree not to bill clients for noncovered services without advance written consent; agree not to bill clients for covered services except for copayment and deductibles; agree to provide services when benefits are exhausted; and even agree to abide by future contract provisions that the therapist has not yet seen. Although many such provisions are unenforceable, no sane person would want to be the "test case."

Signing a contract with provisions of this sort does a disservice to clients and service providers alike. In particular, agreeing to such clauses may void coverage in related cases by the therapists' professional liability insurance and may compromise their ability to defend themselves in the case of a suit. It also represents an effort to shift unreasonable responsibility for MCO actions to the shoulders of unwitting or coerced providers. When you receive such a contract, have it reviewed by an attorney familiar with mental health practice. Often, state professional associations will be able to suggest such lawyers or refer you to clinicians in your locale familiar with that MCO's contracts. If you are pressed to sign a contract in haste, be wary.

Practical Considerations

Some illustrative examples may help the reader understand the nature of the struggles health and mental health practitioners must increasingly address on a daily basis.

Case 7–15: Ralph Downer is significantly depressed. His child died of leukemia a few months ago, he is experiencing tension in his marriage, and he has just learned that the company he works for is headed for a "major downsizing." Based on a careful intake evaluation, Opti Mum, Psy.D., has formulated a plan for individual and couples therapy over the next few weeks. Dr. Mum knows that antidepressant medication may also be useful, but he first wants to gauge the client's response to treatment without seeking a medication consult. When Mum contacts the case manager overseeing Mr. Downer's benefits, Mum is thanked for his assessment and is told to refer the client to a specific psychiatrist for a medication consultation. The manager explains that it is company policy to try treatment with generic antidepressant medication before authorizing any verbal psychotherapy because "a lot of patients get better with just a little medicine."

Case 7–16: Polly Substance, age 13, was brought to the office of Toomuch Thinkin, M.S.W. Her mother was concerned that Polly had been caught smoking pot at school. Her father has a history of problems with alcohol and has allegedly been physically threatening to his wife. Polly also has a history of learning disabilities and depression. Ms. Thinkin recommended family therapy at least once per week to begin addressing the multiple problems in the family. Comprehensive Regional Associated Programs (CRAP, corporate motto: "You're not sick until we say you're sick"), the managed care entity overseeing the family's benefits, will allow only four visits each for the mother and child during a 3-month period and insists on putting both on antidepressant drugs.

In both of these cases, the therapist's best clinical planning has been brushed aside by case managers with another agenda, presumably formulated by management with the intent of reducing costs. The preference of some managed care companies to prescribe medication instead of therapy is well known (Protos, 1996). In both cases, the ideal ethical conduct of the therapist would be similar. First, firmly but respectfully explain the reasons for the recommended treatment plan. Cite supportive research and other factual data whenever possible. If the case manager does not agree, respectfully ask about the appeals process or to speak with a supervisor. Again, make the case in a thoughtful, rational manner, stressing the potential adverse consequences of not following it (e.g., failure to address the significant family relationship problems will undermine the chances for permanent change and may result in need for hospitalization or more extensive and costly interventions later). If there is still no favorable resolution, therapists should meet with their clients and present both their recommendations and the response of the benefits management company. Clients should also be told of their own recourse (e.g., complaints directly to the management company, complaints to their employer, or contacts with regulatory agencies) if they wish to pursue such options. The three principles involved are holding the best interests of the client paramount, advocating for the client in a professional manner, and involving the client in the decision-making process.

Having stated the "ideal," it is important to recognize the constraints many psychotherapists feel. It is not unrealistic to fear that getting a reputation as a therapist who persistently appeals decisions or encourages clients to do so may result in a "no-cause termination." That is, the MCO may exercise a standard contract option to drop a provider without giving a specific reason. In addition, when a company is self-insured, employees may be reluctant to pursue legitimate benefits assertively out of fear of retaliation, even when this fear is unjustified. As noted, some MCOs occasionally attempt to secure contractual provisions intended to prevent practitioners from speaking critically of company practices or advocating too vigorously for clients. There are also significant financial pressures.

Case 7–17: Tom Swift, Psy.D., was very successful in doing focal short-term therapy. Pleased with his work, Giant Health Organization (GHO) sent him many referrals. A few months later, in a letter to all of its providers, GHO informed Dr. Swift that it planned to narrow its provider pool to those who could provide up to 30 hours of service per week. Soon, GHO subscribers became the major portion of Dr. Swift's practice. Then, GHO began to offer special incentives, including cash bonuses at the end of each calendar quarter, for meeting a certain quota of cases "successfully terminated in fewer than eight sessions."

In this example, Dr. Swift has become the victim of an insidious seduction. He has become increasingly dependent on GHO as a source of income and is then propositioned with a bonus plan that places corporate profit goals ahead of client welfare. Even if Dr. Swift is a therapist of the highest ethical integrity, he will be sorely tempted by the new plan. One must also wonder how vigorous an advocate he might be for a client who needed more services or wished to appeal a GHO decision. After all, Dr. Swift could be obliquely threatened with a no-cause termination. We do not wish to infer that all or even the majority of MCOs would engage in such conduct; however, we do advise our colleagues to be prepared and forewarned of such strategies and the resulting risks.

Two of the most common worrisome ethical questions raised by therapists who practice in MCOs are (1) If I go along with a managed care philosophy that only provides coverage for short-term therapy, can my client charge me with incorrect or inappropriate treatment? and (2) If the company decides that the treatment I am providing is not medically necessary, it can stop providing payment with little notice. If my client is unwilling to pay out of pocket, am I at risk for abandonment charges?

The answer to both questions has a similar focus: professional responsibility, competence, and planning. Under no circumstances should a therapist allow his or her care of a client to be dictated by a third-party payer. If an MCO dictates a "one-size-fits-all" (or even "one-size-fits-most") formula for psychotherapy, a therapist who agrees to that policy is headed for trouble. The policy implies that treatment is framed independent of a careful diagnostic assessment or plan matched to the client's needs. The nature of the treatment contract (see Chapter 5) highlights the importance of helping the client to understand and agree to the treatment plan and costs from the outset of the profes-

sional relationship. This includes helping clients to find out what mental health coverage their insurance provides, and that may include a recognition that out-of-pocket costs are likely at some point.

One can certainly advocate for a client whose need for services is questioned, and it is easiest to do this when clear, competent treatment plans and records are produced. If a third party refuses payment and a client can not or does not wish to pay out of pocket, the therapist should attempt a resolution consistent with the client's needs (e.g., offering a reduced fee or making a referral to an agency offering more affordable fees). There is no obligation to continue treating such clients indefinitely, although some reasonable interim coverage should be provided. No client should ever be abandoned in the middle of a crisis situation.

Emotional Outrage

Unfortunately, the net result of marketplace changes and occasional MCO horror stories is considerable emotional distress within the mental health community. The resulting behavior is not always rationally driven.

So intense are the emotions of mental health providers regarding managed care that one author, with some positive comments about managed care, felt the need to do so anonymously out of fear of reprisals from colleagues (Anonymous, 1995). It is unclear whether the article was intended as serious scholarly comment or a mischievous lampoon. Nonetheless, the editors agreed to publish it. The anonymous author cited four "hidden benefits of managed care: (1) technical assistance and education; (2) opportunities for socializing; (3) the promotion of interdisciplinary collaboration; and (4) free supervision"(p. 235). The author noted an improvement in personal technical skills that focused on having to learn the American Psychiatric Association's Global Assessment of Functioning (GAF) scale. Feeling lonely in the relative isolation of private practice, the anonymous clinician found the "built-in opportunity to chat" with managed care reviewers "refreshing" (p. 235). Citing the enigmatic processes of history, the author expressed the belief that managed care is having a unifying effect on the mental health professions that transcends "professional parochialism" (p. 236). Finally, the author noted that beneficent free supervision is provided by "knowledgeable and helpful colleagues" who are managed care case reviewers.

Although written in sincere (tongue-in-cheek?) tones, Anonymous' claims are rather shallow. For example, the GAF is widely regarded as a measure of dubious reliability and clinical validity. Its scores are easily manipulated to suit the needs of the clinician or care manager. Praising the technical assistance needed to help a doctoral-level clinician to master the GAF is comparable to lauding a school child's ability to hop on one leg while chewing gum.

In addition, the paperwork and other communication requirements involved in managed care can be quite significant. Completion of special treatment plans, approval forms, and other documents are time consuming. The need to schedule and participate in telephone case reviews takes additional time. It is not unusual to spend as much time engaged in paperwork and telephone work on a particular case as one spends in face-to-face contact with the client. There is no evidence that this additional effort improves the quality of client care.

Although the anonymous author is accurate in noting that the mental health professions have discovered common cause in their annoyance and frustration with aspects of managed care, the interdisciplinary alliance is an uneasy one. Some managed care plans differentially include or exclude specific professions or profession-linked services (e.g., psychological testing). There should be no illusions regarding the solidarity of these new alliances should managed care entities begin to offer incentives that offer differential benefits to one or another profession.

Finally, the anonymous author's delight in the free supervision is seriously misplaced. Citing professional ethics as a rationale for seeking expert assistance and guidance is indeed appropriate. However, the value of such advice and guidance evaporates rapidly when the "advisor" may have personal or corporate interests in cost savings at the patients' potential expense. It is true that many managed care reviewers are competent mental health professionals dedicated to giving high-quality clinical input. The case manager's obligation to the patient, however, is different and of a more diluted quality than the obligations of the primary clinician. Even the most competent and ethically sensitive case manager must balance accountability to the company with the patients' needs. To the extent that the relationship is based on a capitated model (i.e., in capitation models, the vendor is paid a set fee for covering a number of lives, regardless of actual service delivery), the ethical tension is even more acute. Free supervision in this context is worth exactly what the anonymous author pays for it.

There are indeed some benefits to society in managed care. These include reductions in the cost of services and insurance, lessening the so-called moral hazards of insurance (from the insurance company perspective) and putting new pressures on practitioners to think carefully regarding all aspects of their treatment planning. None of these potential benefits are hidden. At the same time, there are great risks inherent in a system of health care delivery that potentially provides systematic incentives to withhold care (as in the case of capitation models, in which a set fee is paid to cover all the mental health needs of a set number of insured people regardless of how much service is provided) or raises unreasonable barriers to reasonable care. Ironically, managed care and capitation models introduce a new kind of moral hazard by creating an incentive to provide less service.

Who actually saves money under managed care? Both nonprofit and for-profit MCOs exist. According to a survey commissioned by Blue Cross Blue Shield of America (BCBSA) in 2001, on average, 85.7% of commercial premiums for all health plans went to pay medical claims, while 11.6% went to administrative costs, and 2.7% went to profits (Gale Group, 2003). Some mental health professionals believe that the for-profit MCO data are quite different. For example, a former president of the American Psychiatric Association has asserted that some MCOs take 40% to 70% of the health care dollar for overhead, profit, and huge chief executive officer and other executive salaries, leaving the actual amounts spent on direct care for the mentally ill in the range of 2% to 4% of the health care dollar (Eist, 1998).

Some disputes against for-profit MCOs have led the APA and its state affiliates to seek remedies in the courts. Recent litigation against Humana in Florida, alleging conspiracy to reduce, delay, and deny provider payments, led to a $3.5 million settlement (Monitor on Psychology, 2006). In a settlement with CIGNA, more than 4,000 psychologists received nearly $2.2 million (Monitor on Psychology, 2005). Such litigation may chasten MCOs to behave more appropriately, but only time will tell.

Key Ethical Problems in Dealing With Managed Care Organizations

Managed care evolved as a function of changes in the economic realities of the health care marketplace. At the same time, managed care raises a number of stressful concerns for mental health professionals and consumers (Kremer & Gesten, 2003); these concerns range from "autonomy" (i.e., infringements on the tradition of a professional's independent judgment) to "zeal" (i.e., the energy with which some care managers have attempted to cut costs). Managed care came about in response to dramatically escalating costs of health care services, lack of meaningful economic controls on prices, demand by employers who contract for employee health insurance, and legislators who oversee payment under state and federal insurance plans. Not all of the concerns about managed care are ethical issues in the sense that they directly compromise one's ability to conform to professional ethics codes. Similarly, not all MCOs are sinister or malevolent. Many do a good job of controlling costs with reasonable peer review. When buying health care services, employers and subscribers must recognize that you get what you paid for. A low-cost plan will have more limited coverage and possibly less-professional management when it comes to case review decision making. In the end, the quality of services provided is dependent on the competence and integrity of the service providers. One should, however, always pay attention to the key ethical problems listed in Box 7–1.

FRAUD

As a legal concept, *fraud* refers to an act of intentional deception that results in harm or in-

---

Box 7–1 Ethical Challenges to Monitor When Dealing With Managed Care Entities

1. With primary emphasis on cost containment, the needs of specific clients may be compromised. Providers may find themselves placed in conflicting roles when they try to offer what the client needs versus what is covered.
2. Increasingly, providers (as individuals or groups) may feel pressure by third-party payers to agree to capitation schemes. Under such plans, clear financial incentives exist to reduce the amount of care provided, somewhat akin to the agricultural practice of paying some farmers to let land lie fallow. Such schemes will ultimately erode patients' trust, even when practitioners are justified in saying "no" to requests for incremental services.
3. The reduction in clients' free choice under managed care is significant. Clients may be forced to accept a provider from a particular pool, requiring them to work with someone who has a previously negotiated arrangement with the MCO to which the patient was not a party.
4. The same closed provider pools may lead to the creation of panels that are short on diversity (e.g., do not adequately include therapists skilled in working with ethnic minorities, people with sensory impairments, etc.).
5. Confidentiality concerns are potentiated because of demands for detailed case data by MCO reviewers (see Chapter 8).
6. Restrictive covenants, such as gag rules and hold-harmless clauses, can have far-reaching liability consequences for practitioners.

jury to another. There are four basic elements to a fraudulent act:

1. One party makes representations to another, either knowing the claims are false or ignorant of their truth. This may be done by misrepresentation, deception, concealment, or simply nondisclosure of some key fact.
2. The misrepresenter's intent is that another will rely on the false representation.
3. The recipient of the information is unaware of the intended deception.
4. The recipient of the information is justified in relying on or expecting the truth from the communicator. The resulting injury may include financial, physical, or emotional harm.

A variety of unethical acts might be considered fraudulent, including deception in some research paradigms or educational settings, lies about one's training or qualifications, or some types of promotional advertising. In this chapter, however, we focus on fraud as a financial matter. Cases 7–11, 7–12, 7–18, and 7–19 all highlight one aspect of the problem in the sense that the "victim" is a third-party corporate payer, not a person as more often occurs in scam situations. Because the fraud frequently takes place in paper transactions, some offenders tend to regard themselves as less-than-serious violators.

Case 7–18: Carla Dingle, M.D., was indicted for fraud by a grand jury and asked to answer for her conduct to an ethics panel. She explained that she consulted at a private proprietary hospital on a fee-for-service basis by which part of each charge went to her and part to the hospital for administrative costs. To "simplify" the billing process, Dr. Dingle signed several dozen blank claim forms and left them for the billing office secretary to complete. She simply had not noticed that insurance companies were paying her for services not rendered. She claimed that hospital administrators must have improperly added extra appointments to the billing sheets to inflate their income.

Case 7–19: Ernest Churchman, Ph.D., worked as a consulting psychologist for a nursing home run by a religious group. He offered his services free to the facility as an act of religious devotion and submitted bills for his services to a government agency, turning over all monies collected to the home. He was indicted for fraud when an audit disclosed that he had been paid for several thousand dollars worth of services not rendered. Churchman had simply added two to five extra visits to the billing for each of the clients he was asked to evaluate. He was apologetic when confronted but noted that the home was in need of funds, and the money did not come out of the pocket of any patients, all of whom had government-sponsored insurance plans.

Neither Dr. Dingle's poor judgment nor Dr. Churchman's well-intentioned diversion of federal funds is ethically defensible. Dingle should not have provided signed blank forms and remains fully responsible for any acts she delegated to others. Her carelessness and failure to monitor her accounts accurately raises serious questions about her competence and awareness of professional practices. Dr. Churchman was clearly guilty of defrauding the government despite his perceived harmless intentions and rationalized sense of economic necessity. Perhaps neither seems as culpable as the greedy individual who deliberately swindles an anxious or depressed senior citizen out of his or her life savings, but the financial impact of fraud on third-party payers and those who underwrite their services is substantial.

It is wise to retain duplicate copies or electronic records of all insurance claims completed. Such a practice will go far to prevent problems that result from alterations made on the forms after they leave the therapists' hands. In some cases, clients have been known to inflate listed charges, especially when insurance company procedures require the client (rather than the practitioner) to turn in claim forms, and the insurer reimburses the client directly.

Most third parties insist on signing a contract with providers before agreeing to pay for their services. Blue Shield is an example of such a provider in many states. In the typical contract, a provider agrees to accept the company's usual and customary payment as specified in the contract in full satisfaction for the service rendered to the subscriber or client. The provider also promises not to charge a policyholder more for any given service than would be charged to another client. In other words, the provider agrees to accept, from time to time, certain set fees determined by the company and agrees not to treat policyholders differently from non-policyholders. In this way, the company attempts to provide good, inexpensive coverage while attempting to prevent its policyholders from being overcharged or treated in a discriminatory manner. Ideally, the therapist gains access to a client population, timely payment for services, and the ability to treat covered clients at less expense to them.

Despite prior agreements between practitioners and MCOs, contractual violations occasionally form the basis of complaints. Intentionally violating contractual obligations generally constitutes illegal and unethical conduct. Three typical types of such contractual violations include the practices of ignoring the copayment, balance billing, and attempting to "boost your profile," as illustrated in the following cases.

Case 7–20: Some insurance coverage provides that the client must pay a small set portion of the mental health professional's fee, known as a copayment. Nell Sweetheart, M.S.W., often does not bother to collect $10 copayments from her clients. She believes she is doing them a favor and that "no one will mind." She does not realize that she may be accused of fraud.

Dr. Sweetheart's failure to make a reasonable effort to collect the copayments has the net effect of misrepresenting her fee to the insurer. Assume, for example, that she bills the third party $90 for a session and is paid $80 on the assumption that she will collect $10 from the client as a copayment. If she does not make a good faith effort to collect the $10, she has effectively lowered her fee to $80 while continuing to tell the insurer that it is $90. This practice might be interpreted as fraudulent misrepresentation. Dr. Sweetheart may choose not to press collection of the fee against indigent patients for whom this is a hardship, but she must be prepared to demonstrate that she made good faith efforts to collect it.

Case 7–21: Sam More, Ph.D., is treating a client whose Blue Mace/Blue Helmet health insurance policy provides payment of up to $500 per year for outpatient psychotherapy. His usual charge is $100 per hour, but his contract obliges him to accept a $75 payment from the company as full compensation for each session. Once the company pays out the $500 benefit, and the client no longer has coverage, the contract allows Dr. More to bill the client his usual $100 fee. Dr. Moore bills his client for the $25 net balance between the Blue Mace/Blue Helmet payment and his usual fee for each session, even though his contract prohibits this practice until the first $500 is reached.

Mr. More's behavior constitutes "balance billing," a clear contract violation and thus an unethical act. Some practitioners have been known to attempt to get around this issue by sending a bill marked "optional" or by telling the client, "You don't have to pay the difference, but I want you to know some of my clients do so voluntarily." Such pressure may constitute a subtle contract violation per se and does seem an abuse of the therapist's relative power position with respect to the client. Other therapists similar to Dr. More have been known to accept the $75 payment until the coverage is exhausted and then increase their charge to $125 (i.e., the fee plus net difference) for a like number of sessions to recoup their "loss." Such behavior would also constitute a contract violation because it treats the policyholder differently from uninsured people or those covered by different contracts. It is clearly of questionable ethical propriety both in terms of contract violation and in terms of a significant fee increase in midtreatment.

Case 7–22: I. B. Hire, L.M.H.C., knows that he will only be paid $75 per session by Blue Mace/Blue Helmet, and he abides by his obligation not to balance bill or otherwise subvert the client's coverage. He also knows that no matter what fee he lists on the insurance claim form, $75, $90, or $150, he will still be paid only $75 rather than the $90 per hour he usually charges clients who pay out of pocket. Hire also knows that, according to his contract, future increases in reimbursement by the company are based on his "billing profile," his usual charges filled in on claim forms for similar services. He knows that his future rates will be linked to this profile. As a result, he reports his usual hourly rate as $150 per hour on all the claim forms, reasoning that he will eventually get a fairer rate than if he lets the company know his usual fee is actually only $90.

Hire's behavior presents a more subtle form of contract violation. In some ways, it is actually fraud because he deliberately lies to the company in hopes of some future gain. Mr. Hire would probably rationalize that he is hurting no one because he will never bill the client more than his usual $90 when coverage is exhausted. He is, however, lying to the company and violating his agreement to provide them with honest data.

If Dr. More and Mr. Hire do not like the insurance contract offered by the company, they have the option not to sign it. They might lose out on some income or clients because they do not belong to the company's network, but professional disagreements over fee contracts do not lend themselves to individualized attempts at remedies as described above. The acts of Moore and Hire are both illegal and unethical given the contracts they agreed to sign.

BILL COLLECTING

Fee disputes frequently lead to legal complaints against mental health clinicians (B. E. Bennett et al., 2007; Faustman, 1982; Woody, 1988, 2000), and this is also true in instances of client-initiated ethical complaints. The creditor and debtor relationships are just as much a part of the therapist–client relationship as in most other purchases of service. Inevitably, some clients will fall behind in paying for services or fail to pay for them at all. Because of the nature of clients' reasons for consulting mental health professionals and the nature of the relationships we establish, however, we have some special obligations to consider in formulating debt collection strategies.

When a client remains in active treatment while incurring a debt, the matter should be dealt with frankly, including a discussion of the impact of the debt on treatment. In most cases,

however, the problems that arise occur after formal service delivery has terminated.

Case 7–23: Cindy Late complained to an ethics committee that her former therapist, Lucy Tort, Ed.D., had taken her to small claims court over $400 in unpaid bills. Ms. Late reported that she had been emotionally stressed and publicly embarrassed by having to appear in court to acknowledge that she had been treated by a psychologist. Dr. Tort advised the committee that Ms. Late had not responded to her bills or offers to work out an extended payment plan, noting that no confidential information was released; the court was only informed that Ms. Late had been a client and owed the money for services rendered.

Some psychotherapists have argued that disclosure of client status to the court violates a client's right to confidentiality unless specific informed consent is first obtained (Faustman, 1982). While that is an ethically considerate and conservative view, it probably is not unethical to initiate small claims actions in instances such as Dr. Tort's situation. An unpaid bill constitutes a broken contract between the client and therapist. The APA recognizes that such a breach of confidentiality to "obtain payment for services from a client/patient, in which instance disclosure is limited to the minimum that is necessary to achieve the purpose" (APA 02: 4.05b.4). Even such minimal disclosure might prove distressing to some clients because the court action is public and may even be reported in the community newspaper. Ideally, one should give the client ample notice that court action is being considered before it is actually initiated and include this as a limitation on confidentiality in the HIPAA (Health Insurance Portability and Accountability Act) notice given all clients (see Chapter 8).

Collection agencies represent quite a different matter from the small claims court, however, because the collection agent acts as an agent of the psychotherapist. This mechanism of resolving a debt is more private than using small claims court but has its own intrinsic hazards. In such instances, the therapist would retain responsibility for the behavior of the collector and would need to execute a HIPAA business associate confidentiality agreement with the collector. While most states regulate the nature and frequency of contacts by collection agencies, the mental health professional retains a degree of responsibility for any improper, abusive, invasive, or otherwise noxious collection activities initiated in their name. Debt collection practices may also trigger client complaints (see Chapter 17).

Psychotherapists stand in a unique position to cause clients emotional pain and should never take advantage of their professional status or power relationship to collect a debt. While "ethics" does not constitute an excuse to deprive therapists of their legal rights, we should use caution in exercising those rights vis-à-vis clients.

Case 7–24: Sara Caustic, L.M.F.C., was annoyed with Nellie Angst, who had terminated treatment and left a bill unpaid for several months. Dr. Caustic continued to bill Ms. Angst monthly and began adding handwritten notes to the statements, such as, "Don't hold me responsible for the resentment you have toward your mother."

In this instance, Ms. Caustic inappropriately expressed her anger through the pointed use of sensitive material gained in her professional capacity. While it would not necessarily be inappropriate to give a client factual warning that some collection agency or court action might follow if a bill remains unpaid, threats of this sort are unprofessional and not often effective. If emotional damage results from collection practices, a malpractice suit may follow. In this sense, a psychotherapist may have an obligation to assess the clinical risks associated with different debt collection strategies. As in any situation for which therapists employ other people to work in their practices, a degree of vicarious liability exists with bill collection activities. Debt collection should be businesslike and totally void of any psychological or clinical content.

Another way in which a psychotherapist may occasionally attempt to abuse a professional relationship to collect a debt involves the withholding of information.

Case 7–25: Nellie Angst was so distraught by the notes from Ms. Caustic (Case 7–24) that she sought treatment again, but from a new therapist. She signed a release of information, and the new therapist contacted Ms. Caustic to obtain data on the prior treatment. Caustic told the new therapist that she would not discuss the case or provide copies of any reports she had prepared until Angst paid her bill.

In this situation, Ms. Caustic continues to exercise her professional leverage irresponsibly. If she were asked to undertake new work on behalf of Ms. Angst, she certainly would have the right to decline. On the other hand, she may not ethically withhold materials already prepared or refuse to communicate with a colleague about a vulnerable client solely because of her own financial dispute with the client. In this instance, she is actually potentiating the harm to the client and compounding her own unethical behavior.

Practitioners seeking to avoid such problems should routinely discuss any payment issues with clients as they arise. In addition, we should take care that legitimate efforts to collect fees never compromise our professional obligations to clients.

SUMMARY GUIDELINES

1. Clients should be informed about fees, billing, collection practices, and other financial contingencies as a routine part of initiating the professional relationship. This information should also be repeated later in the relationship if necessary.
2. Mental health service providers should carefully consider the client's overall ability to afford services early in the relationship and should help the client to make a plan for obtaining services that will be both clinically appropriate and financially feasible. Encouraging clients to incur significant debt is not psychotherapeutic. In that regard, therapists should be aware of referral sources in the community.
3. Therapists ideally perform some services at little or no fee as a pro bono service to the public as a routine part of their practice.

4. Relationships involving kickbacks, fee splitting, or payment of commissions for client referrals may be illegal and unethical. Careful attention to the particular circumstances and state laws will be important before agreeing to such arrangements.

5. It is important for therapists to pay careful attention to all contractual obligations, understand them, and abide by them. Similarly, therapists should not sign contracts with stipulations that might subsequently place them in ethical jeopardy.

6. Therapists may be held responsible for financial misrepresentations effected in their name by an employee or agent they have designated (including billing and collection agents). They must therefore choose their employees and representatives with care and supervise them closely.

7. In dealing with MCOs, mental health providers should adhere to the same standards of competence, professionalism, and integrity as in other contexts. Heightened sensitivity should focus on the potential ethical problems inherent in such service delivery systems in which profit may trump client welfare.

8. Third-party payers will put pressures on practitioners to meet their needs in ways that do not necessarily hold the rights of individual clients paramount. In such instances, ethical clinicians will act in the best interests of their clients.

9. In all debt collection situations, therapists must be aware of the laws that apply in their jurisdiction and make every effort to behave in a cautious, businesslike fashion. They must avoid using their special position or information gained through their professional role to collect debts from clients.

References

Acuff, C., Bennett, B. E., Bricklin, P. M., Canter, M. B., Knapp, S. J., Moldawsky, S., et al. (1999). Considerations for ethical practice in managed care. *Professional Psychology, 30,* 563–575.

Aetna Health Inc. v. Davila (124 S.Ct. 2488 2004).

Ainsworth, M. (2002). My life as an E-patient. In R. A. Hsiung (Ed.), *e-Therapy: Case studies, guiding principles, and the clinical potential of the Internet* (pp. 194–215). New York: Norton.

Albee, G. W. (1977a). Does including psychotherapy in health insurance represent a subsidy to the rich from the poor? *American Psychologist, 32,* 719–721.

Albee, G. W. (1977b). Problems in living are not sicknesses: Psychotherapy should not be covered under national health insurance. *Clinical Psychologist, 30,* 3, 5–6.

Alleman, J. R. (2001). Personal, practical, and professional issues in providing managed mental health care: A discussion for new psychotherapists. *Ethics & Behavior, 11,* 413–429.

Anonymous. (1995). Hidden benefits of managed care. *Professional Psychology, 26,* 235–237.

Auld, F., Hyman, M., & Rudzinski, D. (2005). Structure of the therapy: Practical arrangements. In F. Auld, M. Hyman, & D. Rudzinski (Eds.), *Resolution of inner conflict: An introduction to psychoanalytic therapy* (2nd ed., pp. 65–85). Washington, DC: American Psychological Association.

Austad, C. S., Hunter, R. D. A., & Morgan, T. C. (1998). Managed health care, ethics, and psychotherapy. *Clinical Psychology: Science and Practice, 5,* 67–76.

Bachman, J., Pincus, H. A., Houtsinger, J. K., & Unützer, J. R. (2006). Funding mechanisms for depression care management: Opportunities and challenges. *General Hospital Psychiatry, 28,* 278–288.

Bennett, B. E., Bricklin, P. M., Harris, E. A., Knapp, S., VandeCreek, L., & Younggren, J. N. (2007). *Assessing and managing risk in psychological practice: An individualized approach.* Rockville, MD: American Psychological Association Insurance Trust.

Bennett, M. I. (2005). Obtaining reimbursement for outpatient services from managed and unmanaged insurance: Principles and procedures. In J. A. Lazarus (Ed.), *Entering private practice: A handbook for psychiatrists* (pp. 77–101). Washington, DC: American Psychiatric.

Bersoff, D. N. (2003). *Ethical conflicts in psychology* (3rd ed.). Washington, DC: American Psychological Association.

Birnbach, L. (1999). Funny money: The therapeutic fee and the patients' and analysts' relationship to money in psychotherapy. *Issues in Psycho-analytic Psychology*, 21, 21–31.

Bloche, M. G. (2004). Back to the '90s—The Supreme Court immunizes managed care. *New England Journal of Medicine*, 351, 1277–1279.

Braun, S. A., & Cox, J. A. (2005). Managed mental health care: Intentional misdiagnosis of mental disorders. *Journal of Counseling and Development*, 83, 425–433.

Buck, S. (1999). The function of the frame and the role of fee in the therapeutic situation. *Women & Therapy*, 22, 37–50.

Cohen, J., Marecek, J., & Gillham, J. (2006). Is three a crowd? Clients, clinicians, and managed care. *American Journal of Orthopsychiatry*, 76, 251–259.

Council on Ethical and Judicial Affairs, American Medical Association. (1995). Ethical issues in managed care. *Journal of the American Medical Association*, 273, 330–335.

Crespi, T. D., & Steir, M. E. (1997). Professional licensing and clinical practice: Credentialing electives for master's degree practitioners. *Psychotherapy in Private Practice*, 16, 35–51.

Danish, S. J., & Smyer, M. A. (1981). Unintended consequences of requiring a license to help. *American Psychologist*, 36, 13–21.

DeAngelis, C. D. (2006). The influence of money on medical science. *Journal of the American Medical Association*, 296, 996–998.

DiBella, G. A. (1980). Mastering money issues that complicate treatment: The last taboo. *American Journal of Psychotherapy*, 34, 510–522.

Eist, H. (1998). Treatment for major depression in managed care and fee-for-service systems. *American Journal of Psychiatry*, 155, 859–860.

Fasone, J. M. (2002). Everyone's health insurance crisis. *Annals of the American Psychotherapy Association*, 5, 5–6.

Faustman, W. O. (1982). Legal and ethical issues in debt collection strategies of professional psychologists. *Professional Psychology*, 13, 208–214.

Gabbard, G. O. (2005). How not to teach psychotherapy. *Academic Psychiatry*, 29, 332–338.

Gale Group. (2003). BCBSA reports how premium dollars are spent—Industry Watch—Brief Article. *Health Care Financial Management*, April 2003. Retrieved March 25, 2007, from http://findarticles.com/p/articles/mi_m3257/is_4_57/ai_100074894.

Gittelman, M. (1998). Public and private managed care. *International Journal of Mental Health*, 27, 3–17.

Harrison, S., Moran, M. (2000). Resources and rationing: Managing supply and demand in health care. In G. L. Albrecht, R. Fitzpatrick, & S. C. Scrimshaw (Eds.), *The handbook of social studies in health and medicine* (pp. 493–508). Thousand Oaks, CA: Sage.

Hemenway, D. (1993). *Prices and choices: Microeconomic vignettes* (3rd ed.). Lanham, MD: University Press of America.

Hixson, R. R. (2004). The business of therapy. *Annals of the American Psychotherapy Association*, 7, 16–21.

Hogan, D. B. (1977). *The regulation of psychotherapists* (Vols. 1–4). Cambridge, MA: Ballinger.

Holmes, J. (1998). Money and psychotherapy: Object, metaphor or dream. *International Journal of Psychotherapy*, 3, 123–133.

Inglehart, J. K. (1996). Managed mental health care. *New England Journal of Medicine*, 334, 131–135.

Karon, B. P. (1995). Provision of psychotherapy under managed care: A growing crisis and national nightmare. *Professional Psychology*, 26, 5–9.

Kielbasa, A. M., Pomerantz, A. M., Krohn, E. J., & Sullivan, B. F. (2004). How does clients' method of payment influence psychologists' diagnostic decisions? *Ethics & Behavior*, 14, 187–195.

Kiesler, C. A., & Pallak, M. S. (1980). The Virginia Blues. *American Psychologist*, 35, 953–954.

Koocher, G. P. (2003). Ethical and legal issues in professional practice transitions. *Professional Psychology*, 34, 383–387.

Koocher, G. P. (2007). Twenty-first century ethical challenges for psychology. *American Psychologist*, 62, 375–384.

Kremer, T. G., & Gesten, E. L. (2003). Managed mental health care: The client's perspective. *Professional Psychology*, 34, 187–196.

Lanza, M. L. (2001). Setting fees: The conscious and unconscious meanings of money. *Perspectives in Psychiatric Care*, 37, 69–72.

Lovinger, R. J. (1978). Obstacles in psychotherapy: Setting a fee in the initial contact. *Professional Psychology*, 9, 350–352.

Manosevitz, M., & Hays, K. F. (2003). Relocating your psychotherapy practice: Packing and unpacking. *Professional Psychology*, 34, 376–382.

Mikalac, C. M. (2005). *Money and outpatient psychiatry: Practical guidelines from accounting to ethics.* New York: Norton.

Moffic, H. S. (2004). Managed behavioral healthcare poses multiple ethical challenges for clinicians. *Psychiatric Annals*, 34, 98–104.

Monger, J. (1998). The gap between theory and practice: A consideration of the fee. *Psychodynamic Counseling*, 4, 93–106.

Monitor on Psychology. (2005). Psychologists receive $2.2 million payout in CIGNA settlement; VACP case appeal concludes. *Monitor on Psychology*, 36, 23.

Monitor on Psychology. (2006). Eligible psychologists may file claims for Humana settlement funds. *Monitor on Psychology*, 37, 12.

Motherwell, L. (2002). Women, money, and psychodynamic group psychotherapy. *International Journal of Group Psychotherapy*, 52, 49–66.

Muse v. Charter Hospital of Winston Salem, Inc., 452 S.E. 2d 589 (N.C. Ct. App. 1995).

Myers, W., & Brezler, M. F. 1992. Selling or buying a practice. *The Independent Practitioner*, 12, 92–93.

Napoli, M. (1999). Issues for pregnant therapists: Missed appointments and fee payments. *British Journal of Psychotherapy*, 15, 355–367.

Newlin, C. M., Adolph, J. L., & Kreber, L. A. (2004). Factors that influence fee setting by male and female psychologists. *Professional Psychology*, 35, 548–552.

Newman, S. S. (2005). Considering fees in psychodynamic psychotherapy: Opportunities for residents. *Academic Psychiatry*, 29, 21–28.

Norcross, J. C. (2005). Psychotherapists' fees and incomes. In G. P. Koocher, J. C. Norcross, & S. S. Hill (Eds.), *Psychologists' desk reference* (2nd ed., pp. 662–666). New York: Oxford University Press.

Pepper, R. (2004). Raising fees in group therapy: Some ethical and clinical implications. *Journal of Contemporary Psychotherapy*, 34, 141–152.

Pomerantz, A. M., & Segrist, D. J. (2006). The influence of payment method on psychologists' diagnostic decisions regarding minimally impaired clients. *Ethics & Behavior*, 16, 253–263.

Pope, K. S., & Keith-Spiegel, P. (1986). Is selling a practice malpractice? *APA Monitor, 4*, 40.

Protos, J. (1996). Ten things your HMO won't tell you. *Smart Money*, 134–144.

Psychotherapy Finances. (2000). Fee, practice, and managed care survey. *Psychotherapy Finances*, 26, 1–12.

Psychotherapy Finances. (2006a). Survey part I. *Psychotherapy Finances*, 32, 1–6.

Psychotherapy Finances. (2006b). Survey part II. *Psychotherapy Finances*, 32, 1–6.

Psychotherapy Finances. (2006c). Survey part III. *Psychotherapy Finances*, 32, 6–8.

Ritt, L. G. (2000). Pre-authorization forms and policies for increasing fee collections. In L. VandeCreek & T. L. Jackson (Eds.), *Innovations in clinical practice* (Vol. 18, pp. 297–300). Sarasota, FL: Professional Resource Press.

Rogoff, J. (2006). Money and outpatient psychiatry: Practice guidelines from accounting to ethics. *Psychiatric Services*, 57, 1051.

Shapiro, E. L., & Ginzberg, R. (2006). Buried treasure: Money, ethics, and countertransference in group therapy. *International Journal of Group Psychotherapy*, 56, 477–494.

Shore, M. F., & Beigel, A. (1996). The challenges posed by managed behavioral health care. *New England Journal of Medicine*, 334, 116–118.

Sommers, E. (1999). Payment for missed sessions: Policy, countertransference and other challenges. *Women & Therapy*, 22, 51–68.

Sperling, M. B., Sack, A., & Field, C. L. (2000). *Psychodynamic practice in a managed care environment: A strategic guide for clinicians.* New York: Guilford Press.

Stetell, T., Pingitore, D., Scheffler, R., Schwalm, D., & Haley, M. (2001). Gender differences in practice patterns and income among psychologists in professional practice. *Professional Psychology*, 32, 607–617.

Sturm, B. A. (2004). Ethics and care: An ethnographic study of psychiatric community health nursing practice. *Archives of Psychiatric Nursing*, 18, 106–115.

Totton, N. (2006). Psychotherapy and counseling: A professional business. *Psychodynamic Practice: Individuals, Groups and Organizations, 12*, 227–228.

Tudor, K. (1998). Value for money? Issues of fees in counseling and psychotherapy. *British Journal of Guidance and Counseling, 25,* 477–493.

Valentine, M. (1999). The cash nexus: Or how the therapeutic fee is a form of communication. *British Journal of Psychotherapy, 15,* 346–354.

Waska, R. T. (1999). Psychoanalytic perspectives concerning the impact of managed care on psychotherapy. *Psychoanalytic Social Work, 6,* 61–77.

Weisgerber, K. (1999). *The traumatic bond between the psychotherapist and managed care.* Lanham, MD: Aronson.

West, J. C., Wilk, J. E., Rae, D. S., Narrow, W. E., & Regier, D. A. (2003). Financial disincentives for the provision of psychotherapy. *Psychiatric Services, 54,* 1582–1583.

Wickline v. State of California, 239 Cal. Rptr. 805, 741 P. 2d 613 (1987).

Woody, R. H. (1988). *Protecting your mental health practice: How to minimize legal and financial risk.* San Francisco: Jossey-Bass.

Woody, R. H. (1997). Valuing a psychological practice. *Professional Psychology, 28,* 77–80.

Woody, R. H. (2000). Professional ethics, regulatory licensing, and malpractice complaints. In F. W. Kaslow (Ed.), *Handbook of couple and family forensics: A sourcebook for mental health and legal professionals.* New York: Wiley.

Zuckerman, E. L. (2003). *The paper office: Forms, guidelines, and resources to make your practice work ethically, legally, and profitably* (3rd ed.). New York: Guilford Press.

8

Privacy, Confidentiality, and Record Keeping

Three may keep a secret, if two of them are dead.

Benjamin Franklin

Contents

What do you know, and who will you tell? The confidential relationship between mental health professionals and their clients has long stood as a cornerstone of the helping relationship. The trust conveyed through assurance of confidentiality seems so critical that some have gone so far as to argue that therapy might lack all effectiveness without it (Epstein, Steingarten, Weinstein, & Nashel, 1977). In the words of Justice Stevens, citing the amicus briefs of the American Psychological and Psychiatric Associations:

> Effective psychotherapy...depends upon an atmosphere of confidence and trust in which the patient is willing to make a frank and complete disclosure of facts, emotions, memories, and fears. Because of the sensitive nature of the problems for which individuals consult psychotherapists, disclosure of confidential communications made during counseling sessions may cause embarrassment or disgrace. For this reason, the mere possibility of disclosure may impede development of the confidential relationship necessary for successful treatment. (*Jaffe v. Redmond*, 1996)

The changing nature of societal demands and information technologies have led many to express concerns about the traditional meaning of confidentiality in mental health practice and even whether true privacy exists any more.

HISTORICAL CONTEXT

American history provides ample public examples of how breaches in confidentiality of mental health data have had major implications for both the clients and society. Thomas Eagleton, a U.S. Senator from Missouri, was dropped as George McGovern's vice presidential running mate in 1968 when it was disclosed that he had previously been hospitalized for the treatment of depression (Post, 2004). Dr. Lewis J. Fielding, better known as "Daniel Ellsberg's psychiatrist," certainly did not suspect that the break-in at his office by Federal Bureau of Investigation (FBI) agents on September 3, 1971, might ultimately lead to the conviction of several high officials in the Nixon White House and contribute to the only resignation of an American president (Morganthau, Lindsay, Michael, & Gi-

vens, 1982; G. R. Stone, 2004). Disclosures of confidential information received by therapists also played prominently in the press during the well-publicized murder trials of the Menendez brothers (Scott, 2005) and O. J. Simpson (Hunt, 1999). In the Menendez case, threats made by one brother to the other's psychotherapist, Dr. Jerome Oziel, contributed to their conviction. In the Simpson case, a psychotherapist who had briefly treated the late Nicole Simpson drew national attention when the she felt the need to "go public" shortly after the homicide, revealing content from the therapy sessions.

Secrets of Dead People

Should a mental health professional's duty of confidentiality end when a client dies? Consider the following actual cases:

Case 8–1: After the deaths of Nicole Brown Simpson and Ron Goldman (see Hunt, 1999), Susan J. Forward, a clinical social worker who had held two sessions with Ms. Simpson in 1992, made unsolicited disclosures regarding her deceased former client. Ms. Forward commented in public that Ms. Simpson had allegedly reported experiencing abuse at the hands of O. J. Simpson.

The California Board of Behavioral Science Examiners subsequently barred Ms. Forward from seeing patients for 90 days and placed her on 3 years probation. In announcing the decision, Deputy Attorney General Anne L. Mendoza, who represented the board, commented, "Therapy is based on privacy and secrecy, and a breach of confidentiality destroys the therapeutic relationship" (Associated Press, 1995). Ms. Mendoza also noted that Ms. Forward had falsely represented herself as a psychologist in television interviews. Ms. Forward later asserted that she had not violated patient confidentiality because the patient was dead but had agreed not to appeal the board's decision to avoid a costly legal fight.

Case 8–2: On July 20, 1993, Vincent Walker Foster Jr. was found dead in Fort Marcy Park, near Virginia's George Washington Parkway. Mr. Foster served as a deputy White House counsel during

President Clinton's first term. He had also been a law partner and personal acquaintance of Hillary Clinton. Foster had struggled with depression and had a prescription for trazodone, authorized by his physician over the telephone just a few days earlier. His body was found with a gun in his hand, and gunshot residue was on that hand. An autopsy determined that he died as the result of a shot in the mouth. A draft of a resignation letter, torn into 27 pieces, lay in his briefcase. Part of the note read, "I was not meant for the job or the spotlight of public life in Washington. Here ruining people is considered sport" (Apple, 1993). Following investigations conducted by the U.S. Park Police, the U.S. Congress, and independent counsels Robert B. Fiske and Kenneth Starr, his death was ruled a suicide.

Shortly before his death, Mr. Foster had met with James Hamilton, his personal attorney. Kenneth D. Starr, the special prosecutor investigating the Clinton administration, sought grand jury testimony from Foster's lawyer. Foster's family refused to waive the deceased man's legal privilege, and Hamilton declined to testify. The case quickly reached the Supreme Court, which deemed by a 6 to 3 vote that communications between a client and a lawyer were protected by attorney–client privilege even after the client's death. The majority opinion by Chief Justice Rehnquist noted that, "A great body of case law and weighty reasons support the position that attorney–client privilege survives a client's death, even in connection with criminal cases" (*Swidler & Berlin and James Hamilton v. United States*, 1998).

Case 8–3: Author Diane Middlebrook set out to write a biography of then-deceased Pulitzer Prize-winning poet Anne Sexton with the permission of Sexton's family (Middlebrook, 1991). Martin Orne, M.D., Ph.D., served as Sexton's psychotherapist for the last years of her life. At Sexton's request, Dr. Orne had tape-recorded the sessions so that Sexton, who had a history of alcohol abuse and memory problems, could listen to them as she wished. Dr. Orne had not destroyed the tapes, and Ms. Middlebrook sought access to them to assist in her writing. Linda Gray Sexton, the poet's daughter and executrix of her literary estate, granted permission, and Dr. Orne released the tapes as requested.

Dr. Orne's release of the audiotapes caused considerable debate within the profession despite authorized release (Burke, 1995; Chodoff, 1992; Goldstein, 1992; Joseph, 1992; Rosenbaum, 1994). Unlike the Simpson and Foster cases, the Sexton case involved approval of release of the audio records by a family member with full legal authority to grant permission. In some circumstances, courts may order opening a deceased person's mental health records. Examples might include assisting an inquest seeking to rule on suicide as a cause of death or to determine the competence of a person to make a will should heirs dispute the document at probate. All of the cases described here involved situations with clear legal authority; however, very often mental health professionals will encounter circumstances in which the solution must rely on ethical principles as well as legal standards (Werth, Burke, & Bardash, 2002). For example, in some situations the legal standard may allow disclosure, whereas clinical issues or the mental health of others may lead to an ethical decision in favor of nondisclosure. Consider the following case:

Case 8–4: Sam Saddest had cystic fibrosis with very severe lung disease. In his mid-20s, Sam no longer had enough energy and financial resources to live independently, although his illness did not seem likely to prove fatal for at least 2 to 3 more years. His medical condition forced him to give up his own apartment and move in with his divorced father, who had plans to marry again, this time to a woman with two children, all of whom Sam did not like. Sam discussed with his therapist, Michael Muted, M.D., his sadness about his mortality, unhappiness about the impending living situation, and resulting thoughts about suicide Despite excellent clinical care and suicide precautions, Sam killed himself without reporting increased suicidal ideation or giving a hint of warning to anyone. Sam's father subsequently met with Dr. Muted in an effort to understand Sam's death. Dr. Muted discussed Sam's frustration with his terminal illness and inability to continue living independently, knowing that the father understood those issues well. However, Dr. Muted never disclosed Sam's distress about the father's planned remarriage or unhappiness with the soon-to-be blended family situation.

In this case, the therapist made efforts to assist the survivor of a family member's suicide to cope. The father readily understood and had known about these issues through discussions with his son over the prior months. Sam had not discussed his feelings about his father's remarriage openly as he did not want to hurt his father or stir up a sense of guilt. Dr. Muted's decision to keep Sam's confidence postdeath respected Sam's preferences and avoided causing incremental distress to the surviving family members. The key to resolving such issues will involve remembering that clients do have some rights to confidentiality that survive them and giving due consideration to the welfare of the survivors.

Espionage

More recently, following the attack on the World Trade Center, the Foreign Intelligence Surveillance Act (FISA) and Section 215 of the USA PATRIOT Act (i.e., officially known as "Uniting and Strengthening America by Providing Appropriate Tools Required to Intercept and Obstruct Terrorism Act of 2001) have made it clear that the illegal break-in to Dr. Fielding's office in 1971 could conceivably become a routinely legal practice just three decades later (Morganthau et al., 1982; G. R. Stone, 2004). Although we know of no instance in which a mental health professional has faced secret searches of client records based on national security, the well-documented case of Theresa Squillacote illustrates the potential intrusion of security agencies into the realm of psychotherapy.

Case 8–5: Theresa Marie Squillacote (also known as Tina, Mary Teresa Miller, The Swan, Margaret, Margit, Lisa Martin), and her husband, Kurt Stand, were convicted of espionage. Squillacote earned a law degree and worked for the Department of Defense in a position requiring security clearance. In 1996, the FBI obtained a warrant to conduct clandestine electronic surveillance, including the monitoring of all conversations in Squillacote's home, calls made to and from the home, and Squillacote's office. Based on the monitored conversations, including Squillacote's conversations with her psychotherapists, a Behavioral Analysis Program team (BAP) at the FBI prepared a report of her personality for use in furthering the investigation. The BAP report noted that she suffered from depression, took antidepressant medications, and had "a cluster of personality characteristics often loosely referred to as 'emotional and dramatic.'" The BAP team recommended taking advantage of Squillacote's "emotional vulnerability" by describing the type of person with whom she might develop a relationship and pass on classified materials. Ultimately, she did transmit national defense secrets to a government officer who posed as a foreign agent and used strategies provided by the BAP team (*United States v. Squillacote*, 2000).

We address ethical issues involved in use of mental health professionals and behavioral scientists in law enforcement and national security activities in Chapter 18 (work settings). In addition, privacy problems related to modern technologies are addressed in Chapter 6 (psychotherapy techniques).

Sensitivity to Technological Developments

We can not ignore the special sensitivity of information gleaned by both clinicians and behavioral scientists in their work, whether assessment, psychotherapy, consultation, or research. Unfortunately, the complexity of the issues related to the general theme of confidentiality often defy easy analysis. Bersoff (1995) wrote of confidentiality that, "No ethical duty [is] more misunderstood or honored by its breach rather than by its fulfillment" (p. 143). Modern telecommunications and computers have substantially complicated matters. Massive electronic databases of sensitive personal information can easily be created, searched, cross tabulated, and transmitted around the world at the speed of light. Even prior to the Internet and the World Wide Web, mental health professionals expressed concerns about the threats posed to individual privacy and confidentiality by computerized data systems (Sawyer & Schechter, 1968).

Lax fax practices provide but one example of ways that technology can lead to unintended or inadvertent betrayal of confidentiality.

Case 8–6: Edgar Fudd, Ph.D., decided to send the third billing notice to a slow-to-pay client to the fax machine in her office. However, the client was not in the office that day. The bill labeled "psychological services rendered" with the client's name and "Third Notice—OVERDUE!!" handwritten with a wide marker sat in the open-access mail pickup tray of the busy office all day.

Fudd's behavior was obviously improper, and he should have known better. Even if he was angry at the client for ignoring his bill, he should have figured that others in a place of business likely had access to the fax machine. Obviously, no private or sensitive material should be sent by fax unless it is known for sure that the recipient is the only one with access to it or a telephone call verifies that the intended party is standing by the machine, ready to retrieve it. In addition, as described in Chapter 7, Fudd's creditor message sent to the client's workplace may violate debt collection laws.

Another danger is the possibility of transmitting confidential information in error. Scores of detailed, confidential medical records are reported to have been faxed to an accountant's office with a telephone number very similar to that of the intended recipient. Despite the accountant's numerous attempts to inform the sender so that the situation could be remedied, confidential records continued to arrive at her office (Stanley & Palosky, 1997). (See Case 8–32 for an example of Internet transmission errors.)

Mental health professionals have both ethical and legal obligations to keep records of various sorts (e.g., interactions with clients and research participants, test scores, research data, and even patient account information) and must safeguard these files. Increasingly, people seek all types of medical and psychological information about others and about themselves. This leads to an entirely new subset of problems on the matter of records: What is in them? Who should keep them? How long should they be kept? Who has access? Is this a legal matter or a professional standard? How do these policies have an impact on the ethical principle of confidentiality? What about the rights of our students and research subjects? We attempt to address all such matters in this chapter.

A PROBLEM OF DEFINITIONS

Confusion about three commonly used terms—privacy, confidentiality, and privilege—often complicates discussions of ethical problems in this arena. At least part of the confusion flows from the fact that, in particular situations, these terms may have narrow legal meanings quite distinct from broader traditional meanings attached by mental health practitioners. Many difficulties link to a failure on the part of professionals to discriminate among the different terms and meanings. Still other difficulties grow out of the fact, discussed in Chapter 1, that legal obligations do not always align with ethical responsibilities.

Privacy

Although the word *privacy* does not occur in the U.S. Constitution, many consider the concept of individuals' rights to avoid government's intrusions into their affairs as granted in various contexts under the language of the Third, Fourth, Fifth, and Fifteenth Amendments. Privacy involves the basic entitlement of people to decide how much of their property, thoughts, feelings, or personal data to share with others. In this sense, privacy has seems essential to ensure human dignity and freedom of self-determination.

The concepts of both confidentiality and privilege grow out of the broader concept of an individual's right to privacy. Concern about electronic surveillance, the use of lie detectors, and a variety of other observational or data-gathering activities fall under the heading of privacy issues. The issues involved in public policy decisions regarding the violation of privacy rights parallel concerns expressed by therapists regarding confidentiality violations (Smith-Bell & Winslade, 1994). In general, mental health professionals' privacy rights may fall subject to violation when their behavior seriously violates the norms of society or somehow endangers others. An example would be the issuance of a search warrant based on "probable cause" that a crime has taken place or may soon occur. We discuss these principles from the psychological perspective in greater detail in this chapter. However, mental health professionals must also give consideration to the concept of privacy as a basic human right due all people and not simply limited to their clients.

We readily acknowledge that some societies, particularly in Africa and Asia, do not place the same value on individual, as opposed to community, rights as do most Western societies. Therapists must remain sensitive and respectful to cultural differences in this regard. At the same time, we must also obey the laws of the jurisdictions in which we practice. At times, this may create tensions that require helping people from other cultures to understand applicable laws and regulations that apply in the immediate circumstances at hand.

Case 8–7: Shana Shalom, an orthodox Jewish émigré from Israel, sought counseling regarding her unhappy marriage from Hebrew-speaking therapist Tanya Talmud, M.S.W. Ms. Shalom later complained to the state licensing board that Ms. Talmud had discussed matters she disclosed in therapy to the family rabbi without her knowledge or consent. The rabbi in turn communicated some of the content to Ms. Sahlom's spouse. Ms. Talmud replied to the licensing board that in Israel's orthodox Jewish communities, soliciting the aid from a couple's rabbi often proves a useful way to address marital problems.

The licensing board censured Ms. Talmud, reminding her that she treated Ms. Shalom in her capacity as a licensed social worker in the United States, not Israel. In addition, basic ethical principles of autonomy and human dignity entitled Ms. Shalom to have a voice in any decision about disclosing material offered in confidence.

Confidentiality

Confidentiality refers to a general standard of professional conduct that obliges a professional not to discuss information about a client with anyone. Confidentiality may also originate in statutes (i.e., laws enacted by legislatures), administrative law (i.e., regulations promulgated to implement legislation), or case law (i.e., interpretations of laws by courts). But, when cited as

an ethical principle, confidentiality implies an explicit contract or promise not to reveal anything about a client except under certain circumstances agreed to by both parties. Although the roots of the concept are in professional ethics rather than in law, the nature of the relationship between client and therapist does have substantial legal recognition (see, e.g., http://jaffee-redmond.org/). One can imagine, for example, that clients who believe that their confidences were violated could sue their psychotherapists in a civil action for breach of confidentiality and possibly seek criminal penalties if available under state law. For instance, a New York appeals court ruled that a patient may bring a tort action against a psychiatrist who allegedly disclosed confidential information to the patient's spouse, allowing the patient to seek damages for mental distress, loss of employment, and the deterioration of his marriage ("Disclosure of Confidential Information," 1982; *MacDonald v. Clinger*, 1982).

The degree to which one should, if ever, violate a client's confidentiality remains a matter of some historical controversy (see, e.g., Siegel, 1979), despite uniform agreement on one point: All clients have a right to know the limits on confidentiality in a professional relationship from the outset. The initial interview with any client (individual or organizational) should include a direct and candid discussion of limits that may exist with respect to any confidences communicated in the relationship (APA 02: 4.02). State and federal laws require providing such information in both health care (e.g., Public Law 104-191, Health Insurance Portability and Accountability Act of 1996 [HIPAA]) and forensic contexts (e.g., *Commonwealth v. Lamb*, 1974). Not only will failure to provide such information early on constitute unethical behavior, and possibly behavior illegal in health care settings, but such omissions may also lead to clinical problems later. In some contexts, conveying such information orally may suffice, but documenting the conversation becomes critical. Health care providers will need to provide a formal written HIPAA notice, and those who provide non-health-related services may want to do likewise or possibly provide "new client information" in a pamphlet or other written statement. Every therapist should give sufficient thought to this matter and formulate a policy for his or her practice that complies with applicable law, ethical standards, and personal conviction, integrated as meaningfully as possible given the legal precedents and case examples discussed in the following pages.

Privilege

The concepts of privilege and confidentiality often become confused, and the distinction between them has critical implications for understanding a variety of ethical problems. The concept of *privilege* (or privileged communication) describes certain specific types of relationships that enjoy protection from disclosure in legal proceedings. Designation of privilege originates in statute or case law and belongs to the client in the relationship. Normal court rules provide that anything relative and material to the issue at hand can and should be admitted as evidence. When privilege exists, however, the client has a degree of protection against having the covered communications revealed without explicit permission. If the client waives this privilege, the clinician must testify on the nature and specifics of the material discussed. The client can not usually permit a selective or partial waiver. In most courts, once a waiver is given, it covers all of the relevant privileged material.

Traditionally, such privilege extended to attorney–client, husband–wife, physician–patient, and certain clergy relationships. Some jurisdictions now extend privilege to the relationships between clients and mental health practitioners, but the actual laws vary widely, and each clinician has an ethical obligation to learn the statutes or case law in force for his or her practice jurisdiction. Prior to 1996, many states addressed the primary mental health professions (i.e., psychologists, psychiatrists, and social workers) while omitting mention of psychiatric nurses, counselors, or generic psychotherapists (DeKraai & Sales, 1982). The same authors also noted that no federally created privileges existed for any mental health profession, and that the federal courts generally looked to applicable state laws. All that changed in 1996 when the U.S. Supreme Court took up the issue based in part on conflicting rulings in different federal appellate court districts (*Jaffe v. Redmond*, 1996).

Case 8–8: Mary Lu Redmond was a police officer in Hoffman Estates, Illinois, a suburb of Chicago. On June 27, 1991, while responding to a "fight-in-progress" call, she fired her weapon and killed Ricky Allen Sr. as he pursued, rapidly gained ground on, and stood poised to stab another man with a butcher knife. After the shooting, Officer Redmond sought counseling from a licensed clinical social worker. Later, Carrie Jaffe, acting as administrator of Mr. Allen's estate, sued Redmond, citing alleged U.S. civil rights statutes and Illinois tort law. Jaffe wanted access to the social worker's notes and sought to compel the therapist to give oral testimony about the therapy. Redmond and her therapist, Karen Beyer refused. The trial judge instructed the jury that refusing to provide such information could be held against Officer Redmond. The jury awarded $545,000 damages based on both the federal civil rights and state laws.

On June 13, 1996, the Supreme Court overturned the lower court decision by a vote of 7–2, upholding the existence of a privilege under Federal Rules of Evidence to patients of licensed psychotherapists. In a decision written by Justice John Paul Stevens, the Court noted that this privilege is "rooted in the imperative need for confidence and trust," and that "the mere possibility of disclosure may impede development of the confidential relationship necessary for successful treatment" (*Jaffe v. Redmond*, 1996, 4492–4493). Writing for himself and Chief Justice Renquist, Justice Scalia dissented, arguing that psychotherapy should not be protected by judicially created privilege, and that social workers were not clearly expert in psychotherapy and did not warrant such a privilege (Smith, 1996). Nonetheless, this case has set a new national standard that affords privilege protections across jurisdictions, generally implying that a federal privilege extends to licensed mental health professionals.

LIMITATIONS AND EXCEPTIONS

Almost all of the statutes addressing confidentiality or providing privileges expressly require licensing, certification, or registration of mental health professionals under state law, although some states extend privilege when the client reasonably believes the alleged therapist to be licensed (DeKraai & Sales, 1982). Clients of students (including psychology interns, unlicensed postdoctoral fellows, or supervisees) may not specifically have coverage under privilege statutes. In some circumstances, trainees' clients may have privilege accorded to communication with a licensed supervisor, but state laws vary widely, and practitioners should not take this for granted.

Some jurisdictions permit a judge's discretion to overrule privilege between clinician and client on determination that the interests of justice outweigh the interests of confidentiality. Some jurisdictions limit privilege exclusively to civil actions, whereas others may include criminal proceedings, except in homicide cases. In many circumstances, designated practitioners have a legally mandated obligation to breach confidentiality and report certain information to authorities. Just as some physicians must under some state laws report gunshot wounds or certain infectious diseases, mental health practitioners may have an obligation to report certain cases, such as those involving child abuse, to state authorities. These restrictions could certainly affect a therapeutic relationship adversely, but the client has a right to know any limitations in advance, and the clinician has the responsibility both to know the relevant facts and to inform the client as indicated (APA 02: 3.10 and 4.02).

Other circumstances, such as a suit alleging malpractice, may constitute a waiver of privilege and confidentiality. In some circumstances, a client may waive some confidentiality or privilege rights without fully realizing the extent of potential risk. In certain dramatic circumstances, a therapist may also face the dilemma of violating a confidence to prevent some imminent harm or danger from occurring. These matters are not without controversy, but it is important for mental health professionals to be aware of the issues and think prospectively about how one ought to handle such problems.

When law and ethical standards diverge (e.g., when a confidential communication does not qualify as privileged in the eyes of the law), the situation becomes extremely complex, but one can not ethically fault a therapist for divulging confidential material if ordered to do so by a court of competent authority. On the other hand, one might reasonably question the appropriateness of violating the law if one believes that doing so has become necessary to behave ethically. Consider, for example, the clinician required by state law or court order to disclose some information learned about a client during the course of a professional relationship. If the practitioner claims that the law and ethical principles conflict, then by definition the ethical principles in question would seem illegal. The therapist may choose civil disobedience as one course of action but does so at personal peril in terms of the legal consequences. The APA ethics code advises psychologists to attempt to resolve such conflicts, but also provides that when such conflicts seem irresolvable, psychologists may ethically adhere to the requirements of the law, regulations, or other governing legal authority (APA 02: 1.02).

Students of ethical philosophy will immediately recognize a modern psychological version of the controversy developed in the writings of Immanuel Kant and John Stuart Mill. Which matters more: the intention of the actor or solely the final outcome of the behavior? For example, if competent therapists, intending to help their clients, initiate interventions that cause unanticipated harm, have they behaved ethically (because they had good intentions) or unethically (because harm resulted)? Clearly, we do not have the answer. Each situation presents different fact patterns, but the most appropriate approach to evaluate a case would involve considering the potential impact of each alternative course of action and choosing with regard to the outcomes one might reasonably expect. Perhaps the best guidepost we can offer involves a kind of balancing test in which the clinician attempts to weigh the relative risks and vulnerabilities of the parties involved. Several of the cases discussed in this chapter highlight such difficult decisions.

Statutory Obligations

As noted, in some circumstances the law specifically dictates a duty to notify certain public authorities of information that might be acquired in the context of a therapist–client relationship. The general rationale on which such laws are predicated holds that certain individual rights must give way to the greater good of society or to the rights of a more vulnerable individual (e.g., in child abuse or child custody cases; see Kalichman, 1993). Statutes in some states address the waiver of privilege in cases of clients exposed to criminal activity either as the perpetrator, victim, or third party. One might presume that violation of a confidence by obeying one's legal duty to report such matters (in the states where such duties exists) could certainly hinder the therapist–client relationship, yet the data on this point seem mixed (DeKraai & Sales, 1982; Kalichman, Brosig, & Kalichman, 1994; Nowell & Sprull, 1993; Woods & McNamara, 1980). Some commentators have argued that the therapeutic relationship can survive a mandated breach in confidentiality as long as a measure of trust is maintained (Brosig & Kalichman, 1992; Watson & Levine, 1989).

At times, state laws can be confusing and complicated:

Case 8–9: Euthan Asia was full of remorse when he came to his initial appointment with Oliver Oops, Ph.D. After asking and receiving assurance that their conversations would be confidential, Mr. Asia disclosed that, 2 months earlier, he had murdered his wife of 50 years out of compassion for her discomfort. Mrs. Asia was 73 years old and suffered from advanced Alzheimer's disease. Mr. Asia could not stand to see the woman he loved in such a state, so he gave his wife sleeping pills and staged a bathtub drowning that resulted in a ruling of accidental death by the medical examiner.

In some jurisdictions, Dr. Oops would be obligated to respect Mr. Asia's confidentiality because those states do not mandate reporting of past felonies that do not involve child abuse.

If the conversation took place in Massachusetts, however, Dr. Oops would be required by law to report Mr. Asia twice. First, Dr. Oops would have to notify the Department of Elder Affairs that Mr. Asia had caused the death of a person he was caring for over the age of 60. Next, he would be obligated to report to another state agency that Mr. Asia had caused the death of a handicapped person. Although every American state and Canadian province has mandatory child abuse reporting laws (Kalichman, 1993), not all have statutes mandating reporting of issues involving so-called dependent persons. As a result, mental health professionals have an affirmative ethical obligation to know all applicable exceptions for the jurisdiction in which they practice and provide full information on these limits to their clients at the outset of the professional relationship (APA 02: 4.02b).

Therapists worry about the potential obligation to disclose a client's stated intent to commit a crime at some future date. Shah (1969) argued that in most cases such disclosures of intent essentially constitute help-seeking behavior rather than an actual intent to commit a crime. Siegel (1979) also argued that interventions short of violating a confidence will invariably prove possible and more desirable, although he acknowledged that one must obey any applicable laws. No jurisdictions currently mandate mental health professionals to disclose such information. The prime exception to treating statements of intent to commit crimes confidentially involves the special context when particular clients pose a danger to themselves or others, discussed below as the "duty to warn or protect."

Malpractice and Waivers

Although not all states have specifically enacted laws making malpractice actions an exception to privilege, one must allow defendant therapists to defend themselves by revealing otherwise confidential material about their work together. Likewise, no licensing board or professional association ethics committee could investigate a claim against a mental health practitioner unless the complainant waives any duty of confidentiality that the clinician might owe.

In such instances, the waiver by the client of the therapist's duty of confidentiality or any legal privilege constitutes a prerequisite for full discussion of the case. While some might fear that the threat to reveal an embarrassing confidence would deter clients from reporting or seeking redress from offending clinicians, procedural steps can allay this concern. Ethics committees, for example, generally conduct all proceedings in confidential sessions and may offer assurances of privacy to complainants. In malpractice cases, judges can order spectators excluded from the courtroom and place records related to sensitive testimony under seal from the public's view.

In some circumstances, a therapist may want to advise an otherwise willing client not to waive privilege or confidentiality.

Case 8–10: Barbara Bash, age 23, suffered a concussion in an automobile accident, with resulting memory loss and a variety of neurological sequelae. Her condition improved gradually, although she developed symptoms of depression and anxiety as she worried about whether she would fully recover. She sought a consultation from Martha Muzzle, Ph.D., to assess her cognitive and emotional state, subsequently entering psychotherapy with Dr. Muzzle to deal with her emotional symptoms. During the course of her treatment, Ms. Bash informed Dr. Muzzle that she had previously sought psychotherapy at age 18 to assist her in overcoming anxiety and depression linked to a variety of family problems. Some 10 months after the accident, Bash had continued treatment and made much progress. A lawsuit remains pending against the other driver in the accident, and Bash's attorney wonders whether to call Dr. Muzzle as an expert witness at the trial to document the emotional pain Ms. Bash suffered, thus securing a better financial settlement.

If consulted, the therapist should remind Ms. Bash's attorney and inform Ms. Bash that, if called to testify on Ms. Bash's behalf, she would have to waive her privilege rights. Under cross-examination, the therapist might have to respond to questions about preexisting emotional problems, prior treatment, and a variety of other personal matters that Ms. Bash might prefer not to have brought out in court. In this case, the legal strategy involved documenting Bash's damages, with the intent of forcing an out-of-court settlement. But, the client ought to know the risks of disclosure should her attorney call the therapist as a witness.

Employers, schools, clinics, or other agencies may also apply pressure for clients to sign waivers of privilege or confidentiality. Often, the client may actually not wish to sign the form but may feel obligated to comply with the wishes of an authority figure or feel fearful that requested help would otherwise be turned down (Rosen, 1977). If a mental health professional has doubts about the wisdom or validity of a client's waiver in such circumstances, the best course of action would call for consulting with the client about any reservations prior to supplying the requested information.

The Duty to Warn or Protect Third Parties From Harm

No complete discussion of confidentiality in the mental health arena can take place without reference to the *Tarasoff* case (*Tarasoff v. Board of Regents of the University of California*, 1976) and a family of so-called progeny cases that have followed in its wake (Quattrocchi & Schopp, 2005; VandeCreek & Knapp, 2001). Detailed historical analyses of the legal case have evolved in the literature (Everstine et al., 1980; Quattrocchi & Schopp, 2005; A. A. Stone, 1976), but a brief summary follows for those unfamiliar with the facts.

Case 8–11: In the fall of 1969, Prosenjit Poddar, a citizen of India and naval architecture student at the University of California's Berkeley campus, shot and stabbed to death Tatiana Tarasoff, a young woman who had spurned his affections. Poddar had sought psychotherapy from Dr. Moore, a psychologist at the university's student health facility, and Dr. Moore had concluded that Poddar posed a significant danger. This conclusion stemmed from an assessment of Poddar's pathological attachment to Tarasoff and evidence that he intended to purchase a gun. After consultation with appropriate colleagues at the student health facility, Dr. Moore notified police both orally and in writing that he feared Poddar posed a danger to Tarasoff.

He requested that the police take Poddar to a facility for hospitalization and an evaluation under California's civil commitment statutes. The police allegedly interrogated Poddar and found him rational. They concluded that he did not really pose a danger and secured a promise that he would stay away from Ms. Tarasoff. After his release by the police, Poddar understandably never returned for further psychotherapy, and 2 months later stabbed Tarasoff to death.

Subsequently, Ms. Tarasoff's parents sued the regents of the University of California, the student health center staff members involved, and the police. Both trial and appeals courts initially dismissed the complaint, holding that, despite the tragedy, no legal basis for the claim existed under California law. The Tarasoff family appealed to the Supreme Court of California, asserting that the defendants had a duty to warn Ms. Tarasoff or her family of the danger, and that they should have persisted to ultimately ensure his confinement. In a 1974 ruling, the court held that the therapists, indeed, had a duty to warn Ms. Tarasoff. When the defendants and several amici (i.e., organizations trying to advise the court by filing amicus curiae, or "friend of the court," briefs) petitioned for a rehearing, the court took the unusual step of granting one. In their second ruling (*Tarasoff v. Board of Regents*, 1976), the court released the police from liability without explanation and more broadly formulated the obligations of therapists, imposing a duty to use reasonable care to protect third parties against dangers posed by a patient.

Although the influence of the decision outside California was not immediately clear, the issue of whether mental health professionals must be police or protectors or otherwise have a "duty to protect" rapidly became a national concern (see, e.g., Bersoff, 1976; Leonard, 1977; Paul, 1977; Quattrocchi & Schopp, 2005; VandeCreek & Knapp, 2001). A former president of the APA (Siegel, 1979) even argued that, if Poddar's psychologist had accepted the absolute and inviolate confidentiality position, Poddar could have remained in psychotherapy and never harmed Tatiana Tarasoff. Siegel believed the therapist "betrayed" his client, as-

serting that, if the psychologist had not considered Poddar "dangerous," no liability for "failure to warn" would have developed. This claim may have some validity; however, many therapists would argue the need to protect the public welfare via direct action. From both legal and ethical perspectives, a key test of responsibility remains whether therapists knew or should have known (in a professional capacity) of the client's dangerousness. No single ethically correct answer will apply in all such cases, but the therapists must also consider their potential obligations.

Perhaps the ultimate irony of the *Tarasoff* case in terms of outcome involves what happened to Mr. Poddar. His original conviction for second-degree murder was reversed because the judge had failed to give adequate instructions to the jury concerning the defense of "diminished capacity" (*People v. Poddar*, 1974). He was convicted of voluntary manslaughter and confined to the Vacaville medical facility in California, subsequently won release, went back to India, and claims to be happily married (A. A. Stone, 1976).

A variety of decisions by courts outside California and since *Tarasoff* have dealt with the duty of therapists to warn or protect potential victims of violence at the hands of their patients (Knapp & VandeCreek, 2000; Truscott, 1993; VandeCreek & Knapp, 1993, 2001; Weisner, 2006; Yufik, 2005). The cases are both fascinating and troubling from the ethical standpoint.

We have not disguised or synthesized examples in the next several cases but rather drew from public legal records that form a portion of the continually growing case law on the duty to warn. The cases themselves do not necessarily bespeak ethical misconduct. Rather, we cite them here to guide readers regarding legal cases that interface with the general principle of confidentiality.

Case 8–12: Dr. Shaw, a dentist, participated in a therapy group with Mr. and Mrs. Moe Billian. Shaw became romantically involved with Mrs. Billian, only to be discovered one morning at 2:00 A.M. in bed with her by Mr. Billian, who had broken into Shaw's apartment. On finding his wife in bed nude with Dr. Shaw, Mr. Billian shot at Shaw five times but did not kill him.

Dr. Shaw sued the psychiatric team in charge of the group therapy program because of the team's alleged negligence in not warning him that Mr. Billian's "unstable and violent condition" presented a "foreseeable and immediate danger" to him (*Shaw v. Glickman*, 1980). In this case, the Maryland courts held that, although the therapists knew Mr. Billian carried a handgun, they could not necessarily have inferred that Billian might have had a propensity to invoke the "old Solon law" (i.e., a law stating that shooting the wife's lover could constitute justifiable homicide) and may not even have known that Billian harbored any animosity toward Dr. Shaw. The court also noted, however, that even if the team had this information, they would have violated Maryland law had they disclosed it.

Case 8–13: Lee Morgenstein, age 15, had received psychotherapy from a New Jersey psychiatrist, Dr. Milano, for 2 years. Morgenstein used illicit drugs and discussed fantasies of using a knife to threaten people. He also told Dr. Milano of sexual experiences and an emotional involvement with Kimberly McIntosch, a neighbor 5 years his senior. Morgenstein frequently expressed anxiety and jealousy about Ms. McIntosch's dating other men, and he reported to Dr. Milano that he once fired a BB gun at a car in which she was riding. One day, Morgenstein stole a prescription blank from Dr. Milano, forged his signature, and attempted to purchase 30 Seconal tablets. The pharmacist became suspicious and called Dr. Milano, who advised the pharmacist to send the boy home. Morgenstein obtained a gun after leaving the pharmacy and later that day shot Kimberly McIntosch to death.

Dr. Milano had reportedly tried to reach his client by phone to talk about the stolen prescription blank but intervened too late to prevent the shooting. Ms. McIntosch's father, a physician who had read about the *Tarasoff* decision, and his wife ultimately filed a civil damage suit against Dr. Milano for the wrongful death of their daughter, asserting that Milano

should have warned Kimberly McIntosch or taken reasonable steps to protect her.

Dr. Milano sought to dismiss the suit claiming that the *Tarasoff* principle should not apply in New Jersey for four reasons. First, to do so would impose an unworkable duty because the prediction of dangerousness is unreliable. Second, violating the client's confidentiality would have interfered with effective treatment. Third, assertion of the *Tarasoff* principle could deter therapists from treating potentially violent patients. Finally, Milano claimed that all of this might lead to an increase in unnecessary commitments to institutions. The court rejected each of these arguments and denied the motion to dismiss the case (*McIntosch v. Milano*, 1979). The court noted the duty to warn as a valid concept under New Jersey law, and despite the fact that therapists can not be 100% accurate in predictions, they have the ability to weigh the relationships of the parties. The court drew an analogy comparing the situation with warning communities and individuals about carriers of a contagious disease and stated that confidentiality must yield to the greater welfare of the community, especially in the case of imminent danger. Ultimately, a jury did not find Milano liable for damages, but the *Tarasoff* principle had moved East.

Case 8–14: James, a juvenile offender, was incarcerated for 18 months at a county facility. During the course of his confinement, James threatened that he would probably "off some kid" (i.e., murder a child) in the neighborhood if released, although he did not mention any particular individual. James obtained parole and did indeed kill a child shortly thereafter.

In the litigation that resulted from this case (*Thompson v. County of Alameda*, 1980), the chief concern focused on whether the county had a duty to warn the local police, neighborhood parents, or James' mother of his threats. While recognizing the duty of the county to protect its citizens, the California Supreme Court declined to extend the Tarasoff doctrine it had created a few years earlier to this case, noting that doing so would prove impractical and negate rehabilitative efforts by giving out general public warnings of nonspecific threats for each person paroled. The court also deemed warning the custodial parent futile because one would not expect her to provide constant supervision ("Tarasoff Duty," 1980).

After many years of state court decisions clarifying the *Tarasoff* doctrines, a 1991 Florida decision (*Boynton v. Burglass*, 1991) complicated matters still further:

Case 8–15: The Florida state appeals court declined to adopt a duty to warn and held that a psychiatrist who knew or should have known that a patient presented a threat of violence did not have a duty to warn the intended victim. The case was brought against Dr. Burglass, a psychiatrist who had treated Lawrence Blaylock. Mr. Blaylock shot and killed Wayne Boynton, and Boynton's parents alleged that Burglass should have known about the danger to their son and should have warned him. The trial court dismissed the case for failure to state a cause of action. The appeals court declined to follow the *Tarasoff* case, ruling that such a duty seemed "neither reasonable nor workable and is potentially fatal to effective patient–therapist relationships." The court cited the inexact nature of psychiatry and considered it virtually impossible to foresee a patient's dangerousness. The court also noted a common law rule that one person has no duty to control the conduct of another. Although a "special circumstance" may create such an obligation in some cases, this did not seem true in Blaylock's case because the treatment occurred with Blaylock as a voluntary outpatient.

The bottom line for psychotherapists is this: Consult a lawyer familiar with the standards that apply in your particular jurisdiction. Such consultation proved very helpful to the two practitioners who treated Billy Gene Viviano:

Case 8–16: In March 1985, a jury awarded Billy Gene Viviano $1 million for injuries he had received at work. Much to Mr. Viviano's dismay, Judge Veronica Wicker overturned the verdict and ordered a new trial. During the next several months, Mr. Viviano became depressed and sought treatment from psychiatrist Dudley Stewart and psychologist Charles Moan. During the course of his treatment, Mr. Viviano voiced threats toward

Judge Wicker and other people connected with his lawsuit. Drs. Stewart and Moan informed the judge of these threats, and Mr. Viviano was arrested, pleaded guilty to contempt of court, and agreed to a voluntary psychiatric hospitalization. Viviano and his family sued the two doctors for negligence, malpractice, and invasion of privacy, but the jury found that the doctors had acted appropriately. Viviano appealed, but lost again (*In re Viviano*, 1994).

In ruling for Drs. Stewart and Moan, the Louisiana Court of Appeals cited the *Tarasoff* case, noted that Dr. Stewart repeatedly consulted an attorney prior to disclosing the threats, and cited testimony by both doctors that Mr. Viviano's threats had become increasingly intense to the point at which both believed he would attempt to carry them out. After weighing these factors, the appellate court reasoned the therapists had followed applicable standard of care in warning third parties.

What should therapists do if a threat comes to their attention from a family member rather than the patient? Recently, the California courts have broken new ground in the confidentiality and duty to protect arena, again emphasizing the need to obtain current legal advice when challenging cases, such as the matter of *Ewing v. Goldstein* (2004), come along.

Case 8–17: David Goldstein, Ph.D., a licensed marriage and family therapist, had treated Geno Colello, a former Los Angeles police officer for 3 years. Treatment focused on work-related injuries and the breakup of Colello's 17-year relationship with a woman named Diana Williams, who had begun dating Keith Ewing. Dr. Goldstein talked to Mr. Colello by telephone on June 21, 2001. Colello allegedly told Goldstein that he did not feel blatantly suicidal but did admit to thinking about it. Dr. Goldstein recommended hospitalization and asked permission to talk with the patient's father, Victor Colello. Victor reportedly told Goldstein that his son was very depressed and seemed to have lost his desire to live. The father went on to report that Geno could not cope with seeing Diana date another man, and that Geno had considered harming the young man. Geno later signed himself in as a voluntary patient at

Northridge Hospital Medical Center on the evening of June 21, 2001. The next morning, Dr. Goldstein received a call from Victor Colello, advising that the hospital would soon release Geno. Dr. Goldstein telephoned the admitting psychiatrist and urged him to keep Geno under observation for the weekend. The psychiatrist declined and discharged Geno, who had no further contact with Dr. Goldstein. On June 23, 2001, Geno Colello shot Keith Ewing to death and then killed himself with the same handgun.

Ewing's parents filed a wrongful death suit naming Goldstein as one of the defendants (*Ewing v. Goldstein*, 2004), alleging he had a duty to warn their son of the risk posed by Geno Colello. A judge granted summary dismissal of the case against Goldstein, who asserted that his patient never actually disclosed a threat directly to him. The California Court of Appeals, however, reinstated the case, noting, "When the communication of a serious threat of physical violence is received by the therapist from the patient's immediate family, and is shared for the purpose of facilitating and furthering the patient's treatment, the fact that the family member is not technically a 'patient,' is not crucial." The court noted that psychotherapy does not occur in a vacuum, and that therapists must learn contextual aspects of a patient's history and personal relationships to be successful. The court opined that communications from patients' family members in this context constitute a "patient communication."

With respect to actual risk to public safety, little hard data exist to demonstrate that warnings effectively prevent harm, although reasonable indirect evidence does suggest that treatment can prevent violence. Obviously, ethical principles precluded direct empirical validation of management strategies that may or may not prevent people at a high risk from doing harm to others (Douglas & Kropp, 2002; Litwack, 2001; Otto, 2000). In addition, violent behavior does not constitute an illness or mental disorder per se. We can not treat the violent behavior, but we can treat a number of clinical variables associated with elevated risks of violence, including depression, substance abuse, and un-

moderated anger (Douglas & Kropp, 2002; Otto, 2000).

HIV and AIDS

Therapists should remain current regarding medical data, treatments, transmission risks, interventions, and state laws regarding professional interactions with HIV (human immunodeficiency virus) patients. Therapists should speak openly and directly with clients about dangers of high-risk behaviors. Individuals who are putting others at risk typically have emotional conflicts about this behavior and may ultimately feel grateful for a therapist's attention to the difficult issue (Anderson & Barret, 2001; Stein, Freedberg, & Sullivan, 1998; Vande-Creek & Knapp, 2001). If the client continues to resist informing partners or using safe practices, clinical judgment becomes a key issue in assessing the duty to protect (Hook & Cleveland, 1999; Palma & Iannelli, 2002). After exhausting other options, the therapist may have to breach confidentiality to warn identified partners; however, one should first notify the client, explain the decision, and seek permission. The client may agree to go along with the notification. Once again, such case patterns constitute an occasion to consult colleagues and attorneys and to make certain that prejudices do not drive the decision.

Psychotherapists who work with clients infected with HIV or who have developed acquired immunodeficiency syndrome (AIDS) must consider additional issues with respect to confidentiality and reporting obligations (Parry & Mauthner, 2004; VandeCreek & Knapp, 2001). McGuire, Nieri, Abbott, Sheridan, and Fisher (1995) studied the relationship between therapist's beliefs and ethical decision making when working with HIV-positive clients who refuse to warn sexual partners or use safe sex practices. The study focused on psychologists licensed in Florida because of a state law mandating HIV–AIDS education. Although homophobia rated low among psychologists sampled, increases in homophobia were linked significantly to the likelihood of breaching confidentiality in AIDS-related cases. This finding suggests that some degree of prejudice may drive behavior in these circumstances.

Imminent Danger and Confidentiality

At one time, the APA's "Ethical Principles of Psychologists" (APA, 1981) authorized the disclosure of confidential material without the client's consent only "in those unusual circumstances in which not to do so would result in clear danger to the person or others." As a reflection of the legal developments reported here, the current APA ethics code notes:

> Psychologists disclose confidential information without the consent of the individual only as mandated by law, or where permitted by law for a valid purpose such as to (1) provide needed professional services; (2) obtain appropriate professional consultations; (3) protect the client/patient, psychologist, or others from harm; or (4) obtain payment for services from a client/patient, in which instance disclosure is limited to the minimum that is necessary to achieve the purpose" (APA 02: 4.05b).

Consider these case examples:

Case 8–18: Bernard Bizzie, L.M.H.C., was about to leave for the weekend when he received an emergency call from a client, who claimed to have taken a number of pills in an attempt to kill herself. Bizzie told her to contact her physician and to come in to see him at 9:00 A.M. on Monday morning. He made no other attempt to intervene, reasoning that contacting others on her behalf would breach confidentiality. The client died later that evening without making any other calls for assistance.

Dr. Bizzie clearly behaved in an unethical and negligent manner by not attending more directly to his client's needs. Even those rare mental health professionals who once asserted that one should never disclose confidential information without the consent of the client in the early post-*Tarasoff* era (e.g., Dubey, 1974; Siegel, 1979) or those who still advocate "absolute" confidentiality (Karon & Widen, 1998) would not likely counsel inaction in the face of such a risk. There are many steps Bizzie could

have taken short of violating the client's confidentiality. Most obviously, he should have attempted (at the very least) to learn her location and assure himself that help would reach her if he could not. Although suicidal threats or gestures may prove manipulative, rather than representing a genuine risk at times, only a foolish and insensitive colleague would ignore them or attempt to pass them off glibly to another.

Case 8–19: Mitchell Morose, age 21, received therapy from Ned Novice, a psychology intern at a university counseling center. Morose had felt increasingly depressed and anxious about academic failure and dependency issues with respect to his family. During one session, Morose told Novice that he had contemplated suicide, had formulated a plan to carry it out, and was working on a note that he would leave "to teach my parents a lesson." Novice attempted to convince Morose to enter a psychiatric hospital for treatment in view of these feelings, but Morose accused Novice of "acting like my parents" and left the office. Novice immediately called George Graybeard, Psy.D., his supervisor, for advice. Graybeard agreed with Novice about the risk of suicide, and acting under a provision of their state's commitment law, they contacted Morose's parents, who could legally seek an emergency involuntary hospitalization as his next of kin. Novice told the parents only that he had treated their son who experienced suicidal ideation, and that he had refused hospitalization. The parents then assisted in having their son committed for treatment. Following discharge, Morose filed an ethical complaint against Novice and Graybeard for violating his confidentiality, especially by communicating with his parents.

Mr. Novice certainly had reason for concern and discussed the matter with his supervisor. (As an aside, we must assume that, early in their work together, Novice had explained his "intern" status to Morose, including the fact that he would routinely discuss the case with his supervisor.) Novice had attempted to ensure the safety of his client through voluntary hospitalization, but the client declined. Because the state laws, well known to Dr. Graybeard, provided a mechanism that called for the involvement of next of kin, the decision to contact the parents was not inappropriate, despite going against the client's wishes. Morose had provided ample reason for Novice to consider him at risk, and the responsible parties disclosed only those matters deemed absolutely necessary to ensure his safety (i.e., that he seemed at risk for suicide and refused hospitalization). The therapist did not give the parents details or other confidential material. In the end, Morose's confidence was indeed violated, and he felt angry. Under the circumstances, however, Novice and Graybeard behaved in an ethically appropriate fashion. Also, in the next section we address specific federal legislation intended to protect the privacy of health care records (i.e., HIPAA). However, even the most protective of these regulations permits limited breaches of confidentiality necessary to provide appropriate treatment.

The best approach to avoid such problems in one's practice involves three separate issues. First, each practitioner should clearly advise every client at the start of their professional relationship of limits on confidentiality. Second, clinicians should think through and come to terms with the circumstances under which they will breach confidentiality or privilege. Consultation with an attorney about the law in the relevant practice jurisdiction will prove crucial because of diverse case law decisions and variable statutes. Finally, should an actual circumstance arise bearing on these issues, consultation with colleagues (while protecting the client's identity) can help sort out alternatives that may not come to mind initially.

ACCESS TO RECORDS AND PERSONAL HEALTH INFORMATION

Mental health practitioners keep records of their work and clients for a variety of reasons — legal obligation, reluctance to rely on memory, communication to other professionals, ready availability of important data, and documentation of services provided, to name a few. By definition, such records will often contain confidential material, and as long as they exist, someone other than the therapist who collected the material may seek access to them. In ad-dressing this issue, we must first consider the process of securing a client's informed consent for the release of information. We must then consider the claims and circumstances under which various parties might seek access, as well as the nature of the information sought. Finally, we consider the use of client records for teaching or research purposes, including the use of recordings and photographic materials.

Congress enacted Public Law 104-191, better known as the Health Insurance Portability and Accountability Act or HIPAA, on August 21, 1996. Regulations and implementation took several years, and many related resources now abound (see U.S. Department of Health and Human Services, 2003, 2006). Congress intended that HIPAA would do exactly what its name implies: protect the portability of health insurance and the privacy of personal health information (PHI). Among its provisions, HIPAA specifies notices that health care providers must give their patients about the confidentiality of records, lays out standards for authorizing the release of PHI, and addresses the security in electronic transmission of PHI. The privacy protections afforded by HIPAA preempt state laws unless those laws provide a higher standard of protection. We address many aspects of HIPAA in this section. Interestingly, the APA ethics code already addressed most of the key the principles mandated under HIPAA, albeit with less specificity (e.g., the need to alert clients about limits of confidentiality at the outset of the professional relationship, releasing information to third parties only with a client's consent, and taking pains to protect client privacy when transmitting insurance claims or other health information).

Consent for the Release of Records

The existence of transferable records can be of great assistance or substantial detriment to clients, depending on the contents and uses. Often, the process of consent getting occurs so hurriedly or perfunctorily that clients may not fully understand what they have authorized or why. Some may even sign release forms against their wishes because of a variety of subtle and obvious pressures or because no alternatives seem available (Damschroder et al., 2007; McSherry,

2004; Rosen, 1977). The practitioner has an important role in educating and helping to safeguard the client's interests in such cases (Clemens, 2006; Rogers, 2006).

A consent or release-of-information form should contain several key elements, including the following:

- the name of the person to whom the records are to be released
- which specific records are to be sent (including a distinction between general medical records and psychotherapy notes)
- the purpose or intended use
- the date the form was signed
- an expiration date
- any limitations on the data to be provided
- the name and signature of the person authorizing the release
- that person's relationship to the client (if not the client) and the signature of a witness (if signed outside the practitioner's presence)

If you receive a release or request for information that does not seem valid or might present some hazard to the client, it would be wise to consider contacting the client directly to seek confirmation prior to releasing any material.

Whenever signing a consent form, the client should receive a copy, and the therapist should make the original a part of that client's files. The practitioner should also keep a record of which materials were sent, to whom, and when. Clinical records should bear a confidential designation, and the recipient should remain aware of any limitations on their use. One should also exercise caution to see that only material appropriate to the need is sent. Consider this example:

Case 8–20: Kurt Files, Psy.D., had evaluated 8-year-old Sheldon Sputter at his family's request because of school problems. The evaluation included taking a developmental and family history, meeting with both parents, reviewing school progress reports, and administering cognitive and personality tests. Dr. Files discovered that Sheldon had a mild perceptual learning disability and was also coping poorly with a variety of family stresses, including his mother's reaction to paternal infidelity, his father's recent discovery that Sheldon

was not his child, and a host of other family secrets that had recently come to light. He recommended appropriate psychotherapeutic intervention, and the family followed through. Several weeks later, Dr. Files received a signed release form from the school Sheldon attended asking for "any" information he had on Sheldon's problem. Files responded with a letter describing the cognitive test results and referring in general terms to "emotional stresses in the family that are being attended to."

In this situation, the psychologist recognized the school's valid need to know information that could help better serve Sheldon. At the same time, Dr. Files recognized that some of the material bore no relevance to the school's role, and he made the appropriate discrimination despite the vague and broad request for any information. The current APA code, for example, notes that when discussing a case, one can "disclose information only to the extent necessary to achieve the purposes of the consultation" [APA 02: 4.06(2)].

Client Access to Records

Clients' access to their mental health records has historically been a matter of some controversy, although the issues have varied somewhat as a function of the precise type of records involved. In the past, patients did not always have access to their own medical and mental health records. This trend began to erode in the 1980s and died with HIPAA, which specifies patients' access rights to their health and mental health files. Therapists should generally assume that any patient may someday ask to see his or her records, and that all who persist will ultimately be able to obtain copies, whether the therapist agrees this is a good idea or not. Some portions of therapist's office records might include material that ought to be safeguarded from disclosure to nonprofessionals (e.g., copies of intelligence test protocols or other such test materials that could compromise test security by their release). Disclosure of psychological test data and materials raises special issues as discussed in Chapter 9. Generally, however, the category of records we have termed *working notes* causes the most concern.

In consideration of HIPAA, clinicians will want to recognize four special categories of records: (1) medical records, (2) psychotherapy notes, (3) forensic reports, and (4) working notes. HIPAA and patients' rights of access apply chiefly to records considered to be health information.

Medical records include the general office or institutional records that chronicle appointments kept, diagnoses, prescriptions, insurance claims, procedures, and the like as part of the PHI. In this context the term *medical record* includes the records kept by nonphysician mental health clinicians as well as the records of psychiatrists.

Psychotherapy notes have special status under HIPAA. Such notes include observations that therapists wish to record for their own use and could include details of the content and process of psychotherapy beyond the more standard documentation typically included in general medical records. Under the provisions of HIPAA, disclosure of psychotherapy notes requires special designation in the release or waiver form signed by the patient. In other words, a signed waiver authorizing the release of medical records does not include psychotherapy notes unless specific mention is made of that category.

Forensic reports involve data collected and reports written specifically for use in legal contexts and may not fall under the penumbra of HIPAA. Such reports for the courts might, for example, include information on competency to stand trial, criminal responsibility, or child custody evaluations. Although such reports may occasionally include health information, their purpose and utility focus on the legal system and may be governed by court rules or orders. Forensic practice standards typically ensure that the client has reasonably informed consent regarding the purpose of the interviews and the parties who will have access to the data, even though unenthusiastically given (Connell & Koocher, 2003). At times, a patient may also agree in advance not to have access to some data or reports prepared by mental health professionals, as in the case of some preemployment or independent medical evaluation examinations.

Working notes refer to those impressions, hypotheses, and half-formed ideas that a mental health professional or trainee may jot down to assist in formulating more comprehensive reports or recommendations later. Often, these notes are reworked into psychotherapy notes or a report, used for discussion with a supervisor, or simply discarded as new data come to light. Because of the speculative and impressionistic nature of such working notes, they may not have meaning or utility to anyone except the person who made them. Such notes are definitely not the sort of material a therapist would want released to anyone. They should be temporary documents, subsequently reworked into more formal office or institutional records, and subsequently destroyed. Mental health professionals should remain aware that at least some risk always exists that any written materials might someday come to light in public through a court proceeding. Clinicians who keep working notes should regularly review and consolidate detailed working notes into less sensitive summaries for all cases. This avoids the danger of an accusation the clinician has selectively edited a case file in anticipation of a client request for records or a court action. The reasons for this suggestion will become clear in the following pages.

One fact should remain uppermost in the reader's mind as the discussion of record access continues. The records do not belong to the client but rather are the property of the institution or private practitioner as their creator and keeper, depending on the setting involved. While clients may have a right to copies of or access to their records, and certainly an interest in them, the records themselves do not belong to the client unless expressly transferred to the client for some reason. Clients may from time to time assert the claim to a record "because I paid for that report" or "those therapy sessions." In fact, the client paid for services rendered, or perhaps a copy of a report, but not for the actual original records (e.g., case notes, process notes, or test protocols) unless specified as part of the agreement with the therapist or agency for some unusual reason.

Opponents of free client access to records generally make two types of claims. First, they assert that the therapist must feel free to speculate and jot down any thought or comments. Some of these will invariably seem erroneous or misleading if taken out of context. Second, opponents of open access claim that harm may follow release of technical professional information to clients who are not equipped to understand or deal with it (Strassburger, 1975). Consider the case of *Godkin v. Miller* (1975):

Case 8–21: On several occasions between 1962 and 1970, Janet Godkin had undergone treatment as a voluntary mental patient at three different New York hospitals. She and her husband decided to write a book about her experiences and sought access to her records, wishing to verify some of the material. The requests were refused, which led to a lawsuit against the New York State Commissioner of Mental Hygiene and the directors of the hospitals involved ("Doctor and the Law," 1975).

The judge in the case agreed with the refusal to provide the records when the hospitals expressed a preference for releasing the records to another professional rather than to the client herself. The rationales presented by hospital staff included that the records would be unintelligible to the layperson; certain of the information might prove detrimental to the individual's current well-being; and the records could contain references to other individuals, who might be harmed by disclosure (Roth, Wolford, & Meisel, 1980). The judge also noted that records are the property of the practitioner or the hospital, and that a client consults the practitioner for services, not for records ("Doctor and the Law," 1975). Some years later, the New York Supreme Court granted Matthew C. Fox, a former patient of the Binghamton Psychiatric Center, full access to his medical records despite the center's contention that such access would be antitherapeutic (*Fox v. Namani*, 1994). Fox was suing the center for malpractice and acting as his own attorney. HIPAA has now trumped all such reasoning in favor of granting clients access.

We generally favor full client access to their mental health records. However, there may be circumstances, such as notes on group therapy sessions or records collected on behalf of a corporate client regarding many individuals, when full access to records could violate the privacy and confidentiality of another party. Rare instances also exist when access to some recorded data might cause substantial and concrete detriment to an individual client.

Case 8–22: During an acute psychotic episode, Tyrone Propper penned a series of bizarre, sexually explicit notes to his psychotherapist. Because the notes seemed clinically relevant at the time, they remained in the therapist's private case files. Mr. Propper later recovered fully and returned to his job as a bank officer. He visited the therapist for a follow-up session and asked to review the case file to help gain perspective on what had happened to him. Propper had few memories from the psychotic period.

Case 8–23: Barry Icarus had been raised by his aunt and uncle because his parents died before his second birthday. He had suffered a reactive depression since his uncle's death from a heart attack on his 16th birthday. Six months of psychotherapy had helped him to deal with the loss successfully and go on to college away from home. A few years later, Barry's aunt died, and he returned to have a few sessions with the same psychotherapist who had helped him earlier. Barry expressed some interest in reviewing his records with respect to his prior treatment. The psychotherapist's file still contained a developmental history given by the aunt years earlier. This included the fact, still unknown to Barry, that his mother had been shot to death by his father, who later committed suicide.

In these cases, it might be appropriate for the practitioners in question to omit material (e.g., the sexually explicit notes and the circumstances of the parents' deaths) from the files prior to reviewing them with the clients. The notes could prove embarrassing to the recovered client. Revelation of them would serve no useful purpose and might possibly increase emotional distress. The information on Barry's parents seems irrelevant to his reason for seeking treatment now but constituted part of a thorough developmental history needed at the time. Providing him with this material now could add stress without an immediate constructive purpose.

When situations of this sort occur, it should be possible to supply the client with the sought-after information minus those sections that might violate the rights of others. In the case of the detrimental material, the residual content could be shared directly with the client. A decision about the actual degree of detriment, however, first ought to be made by a professional in a position to offer an unbiased consultation on the matter. However, if either client asked for their full medical record, HIPAA grants them access to the contents.

Therapists who make records available to clients should give serious consideration to the manner in which this occurs. Do you insist on being present? Do you charge for your time, or consider this part of your services? Do you make your policy on such matters clear to clients before therapy (or other service delivery) starts? We believe that it is desirable to let clients know such policies early in the course of the professional relationship. We also believe that it is important for the therapist to be present during the record review to offer elaboration, explain technical terms, or deal with the client's feelings related to the material. If this would require a significant amount of time, charging a fee for this service may be warranted; however, this should be tempered with an understanding of the client's financial situation, balanced with his or her needs and rights of access in a particular situation. The client who has terminated treatment for lack of funds, for example, should not be barred from a file review for inability to pay, and HIPAA requires release of records even when a client does not wish to review them with the therapist.

Access by Family Members

Occasionally, a concerned family member will seek access to a client's records. When the client is a child or deemed legally incompetent, parents or guardians have full legal entitlement to record access. Therapists should recognize the unique problems that arise when working with minors or families and should remain sensitive to each individual's right to privacy and confidentiality in such circumstances. From the outset of any such relationship, all parties should receive information about the specific nature of the confidential relationship. A discussion about what sorts of information might be shared and with whom should be raised early. This is not a difficult or burdensome process when done as a routine practice.

Case 8–24: Cynthia Childs, Psy.D., has treated 7-year-old Max Bashem for about a month. Max was referred for treatment because of secondary enuresis and acting-out behaviors of recent onset. The birth of a new sibling in the Bashem family several weeks ago seems to have contributed to the problem. Near the end of the fifth therapy session, Max expresses some anger about his new sibling and tells Dr. Childs, "Tonight after my parents go to bed, I'm gonna kill that little weasel!"

Case 8–25: Donna Rhea, age 14, also sees Dr. Childs regularly in psychotherapy. Donna feels alienated from her parents and is sexually active. Her parents discovered that she has contracted genital herpes, and, in a moment of emotional distress after they learn this fact, she accused them of not being as "understanding as Dr. Childs." The parents feel furious that the psychotherapist knew their daughter was sexually active and did not tell them. They demanded a full briefing from Dr. Childs, threatening to pull their daughter out of treatment. They also threatened to file an ethics complaint.

These two cases illustrate some difficult, but not insoluble, problems (Koocher & Keith-Spiegel, 1990; Taylor & Adelman, 1989). In the case of Max, Dr. Childs must consider several factors, not the least of which concerns the seriousness of Max's threat. Does Max have a history of violence toward others? Has he exaggerated his anger in the context of therapy for emphasis? Certainly, Dr. Childs will want to explore this issue with Max before ending the session, but suppose she does feel that he poses some risk to the sibling? Suppose that Max cannot commit himself to leave the baby unharmed in the coming week between sessions. Childs could express her concern and discuss with Max the need to help keep him from doing something he might later regret. She could talk with him about alternatives and explore a variety of them, one involving a family conference in which Max could be encouraged to share some of his angry feelings more directly. If all else fails and Childs believes that she can not otherwise stop Max from hurting his sibling, she must discuss the matter with his parents as a duty to protect issue. Not to do so would constitute malpractice. While such a circumstance would be rare indeed, Childs should certainly discuss the need to violate the confidence for his ultimate benefit.

Donna's situation poses a more complex problem. Dr. Childs almost certainly would have lost the trust of her client had she chosen to violate Donna's confidence. At the same time, providing a value-free climate in psychotherapy may have the net result of unintentionally condoning Donna's sexual behavior (Baumrind, 1990). The parents may feel jealous of the trust and respect their daughter seems to have in the psychotherapist, while feeling angry and disappointed at her sexual activity and resulting infection. A conference does not seem inappropriate but would probably best succeed as a family meeting with Donna present. Dr. Childs could attempt to retain a supportive and therapeutic stance in such a session without necessarily breaking confidence. The sort of information the parents expect seems unclear. A preventive step might have included a pretreatment family conference with a discussion of the psychotherapy relationship and any attendant limitations. An outright refusal to meet with the parents in this circumstance would not serve the interests of any of the parties. Many state laws do permit minors to obtain treatment for sexually transmitted diseases or birth control information without parental consent and in confidence. Dr. Childs' behavior does not seem unethical per se.

Access to records sought by family members of an adult should generally be denied unless some special reason justifies considering the request. Special reasons might include the imminent danger test or the legally adjudicated incapacity of the client.

Case 8–26: Marla Noma lived with cancer for many years, and during that period she occasionally consulted Michael Tact, M.S.W., about her

fears and concerns related to the illness. During a surgical procedure, Marla became comatose and remained alive on life support equipment, although with little chance of any recovery. Members of her family planned to seek court authorization to discontinue mechanical life-support equipment and wondered whether any of Tact's records or conversations with Marla might provide some guidance to them and the court about her wishes.

In such a case, when the client can not speak for herself, it probably would not be unethical for Tact to respond openly to a duly authorized request for information from the next of kin. The surviving line of consent generally recognized by courts is as follows. First in line to grant consent is the spouse (even if living apart from the client, as long as they are not divorced). Second are the children of legal age, with each such child having an equal voice. Next are parents or grandparents, followed by siblings, each also having equal voice. If none of the above survive, courts will occasionally designate the next nearest relative or closest friend.

Court Access to Records

The concept of privileged communication discussed in this chapter has a very narrow focus on protecting certain material from disclosure in court. Despite privilege, however, some courts or litigants may still seek access to privileged information as well as other confidential material. While mental health professionals must certainly respect appropriate requests emanating from the courts, they must also reasonably safeguard material from inappropriate release. Some practitioners assume that their working notes fall outside the realm of materials subject to disclosure in court, feel stunned when a subpoena duces tecum arrives, demanding that they appear in court bringing with them "any and all, files, documents, reports, papers, photographs, recordings, and notes in whatever form they exist" regarding the case in question.

In such instances, understanding the differences between a subpoena and a court order becomes critically important. A subpoena simply compels a response, and in some jurisdictions an attorney can obtain one simply by asking the court clerk. The response need not provide what the subpoena document demands. If the papers seek documents or testimony protected by privilege, the therapist should seek clarification from the client's attorney or the court. A court order, on the other hand, typically flows from a hearing before a judge and compels a disclosure unless appealed to a higher court. In the end, the court must decide what qualifies as protected or not.

If a subpoena or request for documents arrives from a client's own attorney and without a release form, check with your client, not the attorney, before releasing the documents. If a signed release form does accompany the request but the therapist believes that release of the material might cause clinical or legal damage, discuss it with the client. Practitioners concerned about releasing actual raw notes can offer to prepare a prompt report or summary. In a technical sense, a request from a client's attorney has the same force as a request from the client; however, it is not unreasonable for the therapist to personally confirm the client's wishes, especially if the records include sensitive content.

On occasion, a subpoena generated by an attorney opposing the therapist's client or representing another person may arrive at a therapist's office. Under such circumstances, it is reasonable to contact the attorney who issued the subpoena and say, "I can not disclose whether the person noted in the subpoena is now or ever was my client. If the person were my client, I could not provide any information without a signed release from that individual or a valid court order." Next, contact your client, explain the situation, and ask for permission to talk with his or her attorney. Ask the patient's attorney to work out privilege issues with the opposing attorney or move to quash the subpoena. These steps will ensure that the person to whom you owe prime obligations (i.e., your client) remains protected to the full extent allowed by law. When in doubt, consult your own attorney for advice, but never simply ignore a subpoena. Readers will find discussion of subpoenas intended to compel testimony and other forensic issues covered in Chapter 17.

Case 8–27: Clinical psychologist Polly Rost learned the hard way about the importance of consulting an attorney in response to a subpoena for records. The Pennsylvania Board of Psychology issued a formal reprimand to Rost for failing to seek legal advice in dealing with a subpoena. The parents of a child client sued the York Jewish Community Center because their child suffered headaches after a fall there. Rost released the records of the child to the parents' attorney, and later to the Community Center's attorney, in response to an attorney-issued subpoena. After receiving a complaint from the parents, the Pennsylvania licensing board ruled that Rost should have sought the advice of counsel before releasing records in response to the subpoena, and the courts upheld that ruling (*Rost v. Pennsylvania Board of Psychology*, 1995).

When appropriate to release original materials from your case files, offer an authenticated notarized copy rather than the originals. If the court specifies that you must provide the originals, be certain to retain a notarized copy of the records for yourself or have your attorney do so. Important documents can easily become lost or misplaced as they travel through the legal system.

Case 8–28: Arnold and Anita Abuser were being treated in marital therapy by Samuel Silent, Ph.D., when their child died, apparently of inflicted injuries. Prosecutors subpoenaed Dr. Silent to appear before a grand jury investigating the child's death and questioned him about the content of his sessions with the Abusers as the district attorney sought incriminating evidence about the couple. Dr. Silent asked for a judicial determination on privilege. He noted that, as a legally mandated reporter of suspected child abuse, he would have made an official report had he suspected anything. A judge ruled that the prosecutors should have adequate latitude to investigate, and because the case involved alleged child abuse, he would order the therapist to testify or face jail for contempt of court. Mr. and Mrs. Abuser did not wish Dr. Silent to discuss any material from their sessions before the grand jury.

Dr. Silent felt caught in a particularly difficult situation. If he bowed to the court order and testified, he would violate his clients' confidentiality. If the Abusers are guilty and the therapist's silence precludes prosecution, he may protect his clients to the detriment of the victim and society as a whole. In addition, if the Abusers had given Dr. Silent reason to suspect abuse, and he did not report it, he could face prosecution.

If Dr. Silent does not comply with a judge's order to testify, he faces fines or jail for contempt of court and may thereby stand accused of breaking the law. This situation is a prime example of a point at which ethical behavior may at times seem at variance with legal requirements. If Dr. Silent believes he should not testify, the best advice would involve resisting disclosure of confidential material using all legitimate legal avenues. If such avenues become exhausted or fail, Dr. Silent's colleagues would not likely sustain an ethical infraction against him for ultimately disclosing the confidential material (APA 02: 4.05). When conflicts between its ethics code and the law occur, the APA advises psychologists to attempt a responsible resolution, but note that, "If the conflict is irresolvable via such means, psychologists may adhere to the requirements of the law, regulations, or other governing authority in keeping with basic principles of human rights" (APA 02: Introduction).

If Silent knew of abuse and chose to disclose details from the outset under mandated reporting laws, he would also have behaved ethically. If Silent had known of abuse and had failed to report it, he could possibly decline to testify, citing his Fifth Amendment right under the U.S. Constitution against self-incrimination, although such a claim affords no protection from the ethical impropriety of not reporting the abuse.

Case 8–29: John Spleen, L.M.F.T., filed for divorce from his wife Sandra under less-than-amicable circumstances. John practices privately as a licensed marriage and family therapist, and Sandra believed that he lied about his income in the process of reaching a negotiated financial settlement. She sought a court order for her spouse to disclose the names, addresses, and billing records of his clients so that she and her attorney could verify the actual annual income from his practice.

Dr. Spleen stands in a difficult position, even assuming that he has nothing to hide in his personal financial affairs. Disclosing the names and addresses of his clients could certainly prove embarrassing and stressful to the clients. Perhaps he could arrange for an independent audit of his records in confidence by a bonded professional, without the need to contact clients individually or otherwise disclose their names. In any event, the Spleens' dispute involves a civil matter, and courts will be less likely to pursue disclosure for civil matters than for a criminal case. In a similar case, a California appellate court protected the confidentiality of the therapist's records from the spouse, noting that public disclosure of client status itself might prove harmful to a client.

Case 8–30: Cindy Weisbeck was treated by James Hess, Ph.D., from November 1986 until June 1987 at South Dakota's Mountain Plains Counseling Center. In September 1987, he hired her as a part-time secretary at the center, of which he was the sole owner. Some 20 months after he stopped counseling Ms. Weisbeck, Dr. Hess allegedly initiated a sexual relationship with her. Cindy's husband, James Weisbeck, sued. In seeking to show that Hess had a history of taking advantage of vulnerable female clients, Mr. Weisbeck sought access to a list of Hess's patients going back 7 years and the right to depose Hess's personal therapist, a social worker named Tom Terry (*Weisbeck v. Hess*, 1994).

In the case involving Dr. Hess, the South Dakota Supreme Court denied the request for access to client records and the right to depose Hess's therapist, although the court did not cite privacy of the clients as the primary rationale. Rather, the court noted that the APA ethics code in force at that time did not establish Hess's behavior as a "harmful act."

Computer Records and Cyberconfidentiality

The tremendous increase in the use of computers to store, retrieve, and transmit text and other data (including patient records) raises many new types of confidentiality concerns. Vast amounts of information can now be stored in small electronic, magnetic, or optical packages that can often be easily transported, misused, stolen, or misplaced. Use of the Internet for communications provides great convenience as well as considerable unresolved confusion and controversy related to rights and obligations of users (see, e.g., Barnett & Scheetz, 2003; Fisher & Fried, 2003; Hsiung, 2002; Kanani & Regehr, 2003; Rosenoer, 1995; U.S. Department of Health and Human Services, 2006). Mental health professionals making use of new technology must remain thoughtful and cautious about the hazards to confidentiality that result.

Case 8–31: Lydia Laptop, Psy.D., industriously caught up on her record keeping, typing on her portable computer as she flew home from a professional meeting. She had nearly finished the treatment summary on a new client when a familiar message came over the public address system: "In preparation for landing, please return your seatbacks to the full upright position, turn off any electrical equipment, and stow any items you removed for use during the flight." Dr. Laptop saved the file to her hard disk, carefully backed it up on a removable flash memory chip, and placed the stick in the seat back pocket as she packed up her computer. The aircraft experienced a bit of turbulence as she zipped up the travel bag and slipped it under the seat. She lost her train of thought for a moment. Dr. Laptop walked off the plane 10 minutes later, leaving the memory chip full of confidential client information in the seat back pocket. As soon as she got home, she realized what had happened and called the airline. Airline personnel never recovered the chip.

Case 8–32: Hugh-Jim Bissel, M.S.W., received a faxed HIPAA-compliant release of information form from a therapist in another city. One of Bissel's former clients had relocated and sought treatment in his new locale. The new therapist in turn sought information on the previous therapy. Bissel noted an e-mail address listed on the new therapist's letterhead and went on line to transmit the requested files. Unfortunately, Bissel became distracted by a phone call as he attempted this task, and he lapsed into an oft-repeated pattern of keystrokes, accidentally posting the confidential

material to 3,500 subscribers on the International Poodle Fanciers list server.

With a bit of luck Dr. Laptop clients' privacy may have remained intact if the memory chip ended up in the trash as the airline cleaning crew went through the cabin. Dr. Bissel and his client did not fare as well. Only our imaginations limit the extent of these and other horror stories on "virtual" privacy violations. Any practitioner planning to make use of new technology should carefully consider confidentiality issues in the implementation process. If Dr. Laptop had used commonly available encryption technology for her confidential files, the loss of the chip could mean only lost work because any curious finder of her diskette would have not had easy access to its contents. Before transmitting any confidential material by e-mail, fax, or other electronic means, Dr. Bissel should have ascertained the security and accuracy of the intended recipient address. Technology will continue to evolve, but the ethical principles remain constant: Therapists are ultimately responsible for safeguarding the privacy of material entrusted to them in confidence. If you do not feel confident that a particular new technology will adequately protect client privacy, stick with safer modes of communication to protect the client's welfare. (See material also related to cybertherapy in Chapter 6.)

Third-Party Access: Insurers and Managed Care

We address the ethics involved in dealing with so-called third-party payers from the business and financial perspective Chapter 7. We mention them here because clients may sometimes authorize the release of information to third parties without fully understanding the implications. When clients decide to submit a claim for mental health benefits to an insurance company (or authorize a clinician to do so on their behalf), they may not realize that, in so doing, the provider of services will share certain information (e.g., diagnosis, type of service offered, dates services took place, duration of treatment, etc.). In some circumstances, insurers or companies designated to manage mental health benefits may have authorization to seek detailed information from case files, including a client's current symptom status, details of a treatment plan, or other sensitive material. The HIPAA legislation addresses many of these concerns, but once information leaves a practitioner's office, it lies beyond the practitioner's control, and insurance companies may not exercise the same caution and responsibility as the individual practitioner. Some insurance companies, for example, participate in rating bureaus or similar reporting services that may become accessible to other companies at some future date. One public account described the case of a business executive denied an individual disability insurance policy because he had sought psychotherapy for family and work-related stresses. Disability underwriters described this denial as a nearly universal practice, and some insurers may use a history of therapy as an exclusionary criterion for individual health or life insurance policies (Bass, 1995).

Despite HIPAA-mandated notices and restrictions (U.S. Department of Health and Human Services, 2006), clients do not always read or understand the forms put in front of them to sign. This yields an interesting problem when it comes to informing clients about the implications of their using insurance coverage to pay for therapy and counseling services.

Case 8–33: In addition to the standard HIPAA notice, Victor Vigilant, Ph.D., routinely informs his clients about the issue of disclosure to insurance companies in the following manner: He tells clients who have coverage, "If you choose to use your coverage, I shall have to file a form with the company telling them when our appointments were and what services I performed (i.e., psychotherapy, consultation, or evaluation). I will also have to formulate a diagnosis and advise the company of that. The company claims to keep this information confidential, although I have no control over the information once it leaves this office. If you have questions about this, you may wish to check with the company providing the coverage.

You may certainly choose to pay for my services out of pocket and avoid the use of insurance altogether, if you wish."

Dr. Vigilant seems a bit sarcastic and ominous, but most clients have little choice. Refusing to authorize release of information will result in the insurer refusing to pay the claim. Some clients may not care about the issue. A parent whose child is being seen for an assessment of perceptually based learning disabilities, for example, may feel unconcerned. On the other hand, clients holding a sensitive public office or position might very well wish to avoid informing any third party that they sought mental health services. In some cases, the matter becomes further complicated by the fact that some employers use self-insurance programs that occasionally send claims forms or data back through company headquarters in a manner that might become accessible to management. This may not constitute a significant threat in a post-HIPAA era, but for certain clients and some diagnoses, it might prove best to avoid any type of disclosure without first checking on the channels through which the information will flow.

Case 8–34: In the spring of 2007, Blue Cross and Blue Shield of Massachusetts (BCBSMA) announced plans to introduce an outcomes measurement program using the BHL TOP (Behavioral Health Laboratories Treatment Outcomes Package, see http://www.bhealthlabs.com/products/) for voluntary use with all of their subscribers seeking mental health services. Clients would be asked by their therapists to voluntarily complete the form at the start of treatment and periodically thereafter. The forms would then be transmitted electronically to BHL for scoring and data storage, with feedback reports to the therapist and to BCBSMA. Promises of data security were made, and therapists were informed that they would receive higher reimbursement rates if significant numbers of their clients completed the voluntary forms. Questions on the forms asked, among other things, sexual orientation, family income, religion, and detailed usage patterns for alcohol, cocaine, crack, PCP (phencyclidine), heroin, and other illegal substances. Other questions asked about arrest and incarceration histories.

Several professional organizations raised significant ethical questions. Therapists would find themselves in the uncomfortable position of asking clients to voluntarily compromise their privacy by completing the forms, while the therapists faced a financial incentive to secure the data. Clients' data would ultimately be stored in electronic databases with no clear parameters on its future use for their benefit or detriment. Despite claims of data storage security, major breaches by private institutions and federal agencies in recent years (see, e.g., http://www.privacyrights.org/ and http://www.epic.org/privacy/) also raise legitimate concerns. Given the sensitive and personal nature of the data collection plan, including requests to delineate illegal behaviors, the BCBSMA plan seemed to pose serious potential risks to clients. The forms would become a part of therapists' records, leaving the content open to discovery under some legal proceedings. BCBSMA initially did not plan to provide any warnings or cautions about such hazards to their subscribers and provided each practitioner sample text of a very self-serving nature. The Massachusetts Psychological Association (MPA) assisted colleagues by suggesting more objective text for informing clients about the questionnaires, including an emphasis on the voluntary nature of the program and a clear statement that the practitioner has no control over the data once transmitted to BCBSMA. MPA also recommended that practitioners inform their clients about the financial incentive offered, while reassuring them that declining to complete the form would not affect their care. In the face of professional criticism, BCBSMA has made a series of modifications in their public information, while never acknowledging ethical missteps. Exactly how BCBSMA will make use of the data they collect going forward remains uncertain.

Peer review groups, such as professional association ethics committees, constitute a different type of third party with which the matter of disclosing confidential material occasionally becomes an issue. Members of professional associations must respond to inquiries from such

duly constituted bodies, although they must also observe the basic principle of confidentiality. When asked by an ethics committee to respond, the therapist should first determine whether the complaining party has signed an appropriate waiver of duty of confidentiality due them. No ethics committee can press an inquiry about a client unless it first obtains a signed release from the client regarding the therapist's obligation of confidentiality. The same holds true of complaints to licensing boards or other regulatory bodies. The therapist can not defend his or her case unless there is the freedom to discuss the content of the relationship in question openly.

Case 8–35: Roger Control filed an ethics complaint against a psychotherapist who allegedly "made my problems worse instead of better." Mr. Control complained about one session in particular that "caused me strong mental anguish and insomnia for several weeks." Mr. Control asserted that the dozen prior sessions with the therapist were irrelevant and would only agree to allow the therapist to talk about the one "traumatic session" he had cited.

The ethics committee, noting that this limitation would not permit a sufficient response by the therapist to their inquiry, declined to investigate the case without a broader authorization, which Roger did not accept. (We discuss suggestions for how to deal with licensing board and ethics committee complaints in greater detail in Chapter 3.)

TAKING ADVANTAGE OF CONFIDENTIAL INFORMATION

Occasionally, psychotherapists have an opportunity to gain personally as a result of information received in confidence. One such case involved Manhattan psychiatrist, Robert Willis.

Case 8–36: Robert Willis, M.D., treated Mrs. Joan Weill, wife of the board chair of Primerica Corporation. In the course of treatment, Willis learned of business events in the life of his client and her spouse that seemed likely to affect the value of Primerica stock. The information Mrs. Weill communicated during treatment was not public knowledge. Dr. Willis made strategic investment decisions based on the information and earned more than $27,000 as a result. In a widely reported turn of events, Dr. Willis was caught, prosecuted, and fined by the Securities and Exchange Commission for "insider trading" (Rosenbaum, 1994).

It is impossible to know how often psychotherapists may benefit in some way from information they receive in the course of work with clients. The use of such information does not intrinsically constitute ethical misconduct. For example, a client who reports distress about an unreliable automobile mechanic may lead the therapist to avoid using that business. However, that same sort of information is generally available to many people by word of mouth and would not lead to personal gain at the expense of others, as in the case of Dr. Willis.

CONFIDENTIAL MATERIAL IN THE CLASSROOM AND LABORATORY

We address ethical issues related to the classroom and social/behavioral research laboratories in Chapters 16 and 19; however, some noteworthy special issues relate to the use of confidential material in such settings. The first point involves confidential materials adapted for teaching purposes, and the second focuses on confidentiality problems involving research data.

Classroom Materials and Public Lectures

Ideally, any materials prepared for teaching that use sensitive or confidential material involve the full informed consent of the client. When adapting videotapes or audiotapes, detailed summaries of case material, or other accounts of psychological material not otherwise in the public domain, the client or client's legal guardian should have consented to the use of the material for teaching purposes. This becomes especially important when the nature of the material (e.g., visual reproductions or recognizable facts) might make it possible to identify the client. Formal consent may not be necessary if disguising the material makes identification of the client impossible. Below, we present some appropriate examples. Some of the cases cited in this book involve actual legal decisions in the public domain and are cited as such, but we have disguised others or synthesized versions of actual situations or case material, as in the cases that follow. Although the actual people involved might recognize themselves or think that they do (see, e.g., Case 19–9), this breaches no one's confidentiality.

Case 8–37: Emily Barrassed entered psychotherapy with Will U. Tell, Psy.D., and was seen several times per week for nearly 2 years. During the course of these sessions, Ms. Barrassed shared a number of intimate and sensitive fantasies and life events with Dr. Tell. At the end of their work together, both felt that she had made impressive progress. Dr. Tell asked whether Ms. Barrassed might permit him to mention some details of their work together in a book he planned to write, provided he disguised the material so that she could not be recognized. She agreed and signed a release form he had prepared. Several years later, Dr. Tell's book became a best seller, and Ms. Barrassed discovered, to her shock, that she was easily recognized in the book by those who knew her. Dr. Tell had changed some details, such as the name, city, and so on, but described her family, upbringing, occupation, and red-haired, one-eyed, amputee spouse without disguise.

We can not be certain whether Dr. Tell's inadequate efforts to disguise the client's identity resulted from carelessness or naïveté, but he might have prevented the problem by inviting his former client to preview the text. The best-disguised cases retain only the essential attributes of the original case, while changing several other potentially identifying variables.

Case 8–38: Barbara Binjer, M.S.W., has written several books on the treatment of eating disorders and often gives public talks on the topic to community groups. At one such presentation, she described a client as having been on a "see food diet," commenting that, "Whenever she sees food she eats it." The line got a laugh from the audience, and Ms. Binjer then described how just 2 weeks earlier one of her clients ate a whole plate of pastries while setting up for a church picnic, explaining how unhappy family relationships contributed to that behavior. Several people in the audience attended the same church event and recognized the identity of the client. One of them also attended a Calorie Counters group with the client and told her of the "funny story."

Ms. Binjer should have considered the possibility that people in the audience might know her local client or might even be her clients. She may have complicated her professional life significantly, both by hurting her client and by conveying a message to other potential clients that she can not be trusted to keep a confidence.

Case 8–39: Irwin Klunk, Ed.D., shared the test data obtained in an evaluation of a disturbed child with his graduate psychology class. He passed around copies of drawings, test protocols, and interpretations. All of the sheets bore the child's full name and other identifying information. One of the students in the class, a friend of the boy's mother, told her about the incident. The mother filed an ethics complaint against the professor for violating her son's confidentiality. The professor responded that, because the of the child's age and because the students studied at a graduate level, he had not believed it necessary to remove identifying data.

Professor Klunk may rely on the professionalism of his graduate students and hold them accountable to treat the material appropriately; however, that does not excuse him from removing unnecessary identifying data. As he sadly discovered, we live in a small world, and his lack of consideration caused a loss of privacy and emotional distress to a client.

The chances of having a relative, friend, acquaintance, or colleague of a client in the audience is not as small as one might imagine, and the consequences of revealing a confidence or sharing intimate details of a client's personal life in recognizable fashion may have devastating effects. There are times when this becomes unlikely, such as a classroom discussion of a response to the Rorschach inkblots in which the identifying data includes only age and sex or the use of a thoroughly blinded case history. Actual individual consent may prove unnecessary for such material. When in doubt, however, we

suggest reviewing the material with a colleague to ensure that some identifying facts have not inadvertently escaped attention. Likewise, one should delete any superfluous facts that might help to identify the client while not adding meaningful detail to the example.

Research Data

We address the confidentiality of research data in Chapter 19, but sometimes research in particularly sensitive topic areas creates special problems. Perhaps the best example of the difficulties resulting with respect to confidential research data involves the case of Samuel Popkin.

Case 8–40: On November 21, 1972, Samuel L. Popkin, an assistant professor of government at Harvard University, found himself imprisoned under a U.S. district court order for refusing to answer several questions before a federal grand jury investigating the publication of the "Pentagon Papers." Popkin asserted a First Amendment right to refuse to provide the information collected as part of his scholarly research on Vietnam and the United States involvement in that country. For failing to testify, the court ordered him confined for the duration of the grand jury's service. He won release from jail after 7 days when the grand jury's term ended. The U.S. Supreme Court later refused to review the order that led to his confinement (Carroll, 1973).

Popkin taught as a political scientist, but he might just as easily have had a background in another social/behavioral science, researching the personality structure of paramilitary groups or urban street gangs. Despite the fact that such research can not usually take place without some pledge of confidentiality to respondents, "national security interests" led the courts to overrule any claim of privilege or assertion of confidentiality.

On some occasions, even naturalistic study data can put people at risk. Consider the case that follows:

Case 8–41: Seb Terfuge, Ph.D., conducted a field study of homosexual encounters in a public men's lavatory. Using a set of unobtrusive timing devices and a periscopic videotape apparatus, Dr. Terfuge concealed himself in a toilet stall and recorded a variety of casual homosexual encounters over a period of several months. When he published an account of his findings in a professional journal, the local district attorney attempted to subpoena his videotapes to prosecute the men Terfuge had observed by using a state law against "unnatural acts."

Dr. Terfuge should have anticipated such difficulties, given the sensitive nature of the matters he studied, and attempted to determine whether he might collect the data in any other fashion. Assuming that alternatives proved ineffective, and assuming that the potential hazards to the people under study did not warrant cancellation of the project, he should have taken steps to protect their anonymity, including seeking a federal confidentiality certificate (Hoagwood, 1994). Dr. Terfuge did not simply conduct a field study, but rather actually put his intended research participants at some risk to themselves without their knowledge or consent. One could argue that a police officer present on the scene where the behavior took place might have made arrests, but Terfuge was not a police officer and had an obligation to consider the welfare of those he studied in the course of his research. There are additional problems with such research, such as the dubious benefits and privacy invasion. (See Chapter 19 for additional discussion.)

Not all confidential data become so threatening, and in fact, at times the revelation of sensitive or confidential research data provides enormous social benefit (Gordis & Gold, 1980). Epidemiological research presents a good example. The studies of diethylstilbestrol (DES) and its association with vaginal cancers a generation later, studies of occupational cancers with long dormancy intervals, and late-effects studies of long-term use of contraceptive or arthritis medications are but three examples. In each type of study cited here, it would become necessary to locate and track an identifiable individual over time to establish data of meaningful long-term risk to clients as individuals and society as a whole (Gordis & Gold, 1980). Sometimes, unexpected findings hold legitimate interest to research participants but may not come to light until long after they had en-

rolled in a study with a promise of confidentiality. Safeguards are indeed needed, but one must remain prepared to seek advice and consultation from institutional review boards (IRBs) or other appropriate bodies when conducting such studies. Knerr (1982) and Boruch, Dennis, and Cecil (1996) offered considerable information and advice on what to do if one's data are ever subpoenaed. An attorney should also be consulted regarding the impact of laws such as the Freedom of Information Act. Above all, the rights of the individual participants in the research must be considered.

RECORD CONTENT RETENTION AND DISPOSITION

Content of Records

What should clinicians include in clinical case records? The APA first adopted basic advisory guidelines for psychologists in 1993 and updated them in 2007 (APA, 1993, 2007). They cover a wide range of topics related to keeping and managing records, but we believe that some detailed recommendations regarding the prototype mental health record content will prove useful to readers. A high-quality clinical record provides the best way to document rendering of appropriate care. A jury or ethics committee might regard poor-quality notes or inadequate history taking as sloppy practice in a malpractice suit or complaint hearing, respectively. In a legal sense, if it was not written down, it did not happen. A suggested model for a clinical case record appears in Box 8–1.

Record Retention

How long should one keep records? The difficulty in answering this question arises because the number and type of records kept by mental health professionals, clinics, and other agencies vary widely in both content and purpose. The answer to this question will vary as a function of the type of record, nature of the client's need for documentation of prior services, probability of need for future services, validity of the data in the records, and the applicable

Box 8–1 Suggested Contents of Mental Health Records

CONTENT ISSUES

- Name, record or file number (if any), address, telephone number, sex, birth date, marital status, next of kin (or parent/guardian), school or employment status, billing and financial information.
- Date of initial client contact and referral source.
- Documentation that client has received notice related to privacy and other practice information (e.g., access to emergency coverage, fees, limits of confidentiality) required under federal (i.e., HIPAA) and state laws.
- Relevant history and risk factors, including a detailed social, medical, educational, and vocational history. This need not necessarily be done in the very first session and need not be exhaustive. The more serious the problem, the more history you should take. Get enough information to formulate a diagnosis and an initial treatment plan.
- Collect information on the client's medical status (i.e., When was his or her last physical exam? Does the client have a personal physician? Are there any pending medical problems or conditions?). This is especially important if the client has physical complaints or psychological problems that might be attributable to organic pathology.
- Collect information on all medications or drugs used, past and present, including licit (e.g., prescribed medications, alcohol, tobacco, and over-the-counter drugs) and illicit substances. Also note any consideration, recommendation, or referral for medication made by you or others over the course of your work with the client.
- Why is the client in your office? Include a full description of the nature of the client's condition, including the reason for referral and presenting symptoms or problem. Be sure to ask clients what brought them for help at this point in time and record the reasons.
- Include a current comprehensive functional assessment (including a mental status examination) and note any changes or alterations that occur over the course of treatment.
- Include a clinical impression and diagnostic formulation using the most current American Psychiatric Associations *Diagnostic and Statistical Manual* (*DSM*) or the *International Classification of Diseases* (*ICD*) model. Do not underdiagnose to protect the patient. If you believe it is absolutely necessary to use a "nonstigmatizing" diagnosis as opposed to some other label, use the R/O (rule-out) model by listing diagnoses with the notation "R/O," indicating that you will rule each "in" or "out" based on data that emerge over the subsequent sessions. The diagnosis must also be consistent with the case history and facts (e.g., do not use "adjustment reaction" to describe a paranoid hallucinating client with a history of prior psychiatric hospital admissions).
- Develop a treatment plan with long- and short-term goals and a proposed schedule of therapeutic activities. This should be updated every 4 to 6 months and modified as needed.
- Note progress toward achievement of therapeutic goals. Use clear, precise, observable facts (e.g., I observed patient . . . ; patient agreed that . . .). Avoid theoretical speculation, reports of unconscious content, attempts at humor, or sarcasm. If you must keep theoretical or speculative notes, use a separate working notes format, but recognize that these records may be subject to subpoena in legal proceedings.
- Include documentation of each visit, noting the client's response to treatment. In hospitals or large agencies, each entry should be dated and signed or initialed by the therapist with the name printed or typed in legible form. It is not necessary to sign each entry in one's private (i.e., noninstitutional) case files.

Box 8–1 Continued

- Include documentation of follow-up for referrals or missed appointment, especially with clients who may be dangerous or seriously ill. Retain copies of all reminders, notices, or correspondence sent to clients and note substantive telephone conversations in the record.
- Include copies of consent forms for any information released to other parties.
- Include a discharge or termination summary note for all clients. In cases of planned termination, be certain that case notes prior to the end of care reflect planning and progress toward this end.

NONCONTENT ISSUES

- Mental health professionals should maintain (in their own practice) or support (in institutional practice) a system that protects the confidentiality of records. Clear procedures should be in place to preserve client confidentiality and to release records only with proper consent. The media used (e.g., paper, magnetic) is not especially important as long as utility, confidentiality, and durability are ensured.
- In multiple-client therapies (e.g., family or group treatment), records should be kept in a manner that allows for the preservation of each individual's confidentiality should the records of one party be released.
- Mental health professionals are responsible for construction and control of their records and those of people they supervise.
- Therapists must be aware of and observe all federal and state laws that govern record retention. In the absence of clear regulatory guidance under law, the APA (1993) recommends maintaining complete records for 3 years after the last client contact and summaries for an additional 12 years.
- If the client is a child, some records should be maintained until at least 3 to 5 years beyond the date at which the child attains the age of majority.
- All records, active or inactive, should be stored in a safe manner, with limited access appropriate to the practice or institution.
- Outdated, obsolete, or invalid data should be managed in a way that ensures no adverse effects will result from its release. Records may be culled regularly as long as this is consistent with legal obligations. Records to be disposed should be handled in a confidential and appropriate manner.
- Therapists need to make arrangements for proper management or disposal of clinical records in the event of their death or incapacity.

state or federal regulations. In any given legal jurisdiction, for example, the responsibilities of a mental health professional might vary widely, depending on whether the records in question qualify as business files, medical records, school records, or research data. The two key factors a therapist should consider in making a decision about retention or disposition of records are applicable legal obligations and client welfare.

Consulting with an attorney familiar with the statutes that apply to one's practice will usually provide the best guidance. Dramatic differences exist from location to location. Considering only hospital records, Massachusetts permits the destruction of records 30 years following the discharge or final treatment of the patient. California requires retention of such hospital records for 7 years postdischarge or until the patient reaches age 21, but never less than 7 years. New York's statute is similar to the California requirement except that the time frame is 6 years. In Texas, the law specifies 10 years for general retention, whereas Pennsylvania specifies keeping the record itself for 15 years and keeping a permanent care file on each patient. Some states, such as South Dakota, specify keeping hospital records permanently.

Laws dealing with individual practitioners, as opposed to institutions or agencies, often give less specific retention times or require shorter retention spans for client files. Many state laws do not specifically mention mental health professionals in laws governing case records, although licensing boards may have applicable regulations. In general, the best recommendation we can offer has two prongs. First, check your legal obligations based on state law with respect to any statute of limitations on business and medical records. Second, we note that the APA (2007) recommended a minimum of 7 years' retention for the full record and keeping some summary of the record much longer. The APA also recommended that when the client is a minor, the time frame should be extended until at least 3 years past the age of majority. We recommend the APA standard as a minimum, even if your state permits shorter periods. The retention clock should start ticking at the end of the final professional service to the client.

The U.S. Internal Revenue Service (IRS) imposes yet another type of obligation on virtually all professionals with its 7-year record-keeping requirement. Although these obligations refer to business and financial records, one would obviously need some ability to access client names and payments made. A client facing an IRS audit might have to seek confirmation of payments made to the therapist, or the practitioner might have to document certain financial data regarding his or her practice to the IRS.

Client welfare concerns come up with respect to the matter of record retention in two ways. First, you must consider the client's need and the benefit to the client of such records. Second, you must consider the risks and hazards of such records to clients, especially when they contain obsolete or potentially harmful data and may pass beyond the originating mental health professional's control. Records benefit the client in a variety of ways, including their potential to assist in the continuity of care across providers and over time. Even long after

a client has improved and left the therapist's care, a need might arise to document a period of treatment or that a disability had occurred. Records do, after all, have the potential to recall events better than, and even outlive, the provider who prepared them. This last fact contributes to a potential hazard with respect to disposition of records, discussed in a separate section.

Potential problems with records, aside from the access issues mentioned in this chapter, often arise as the result of invalid or obsolete information. Determining a definition of *obsolete* can pose a problem, however. Resist the temptation, inherent in research training, to save any potentially analyzable data indefinitely. Attempt to balance this urge with an understanding of the reliability and validity of old data.

Case 8–42: A state agency serving children maintained its clinical files, including psychological test data, indefinitely. A request for information, validly executed, was received from a government agency, requesting copies of reports for purposes of security clearance on Warren Peace, a now 40-year-old job applicant, who had been seen at the agency 30 years earlier. The request raises the question of whether the IQ and other test or psychological information has current validity.

In the face of a valid waiver form, the agency must release the information on Mr. Peace requested under the circumstances cited above because the files exist, and the former client has agreed. On the other hand, one should legitimately question the appropriateness of keeping full test data and detailed notes this long, thus rendering them available for such requests. The IQ data obtained at age 10 will have no bearing on Mr. Peace's current employability, and any treatment or personality test data from that era also retain questionable likely validity. If the agency had destroyed obsolete information or purged its files of data no longer of any clinical value, little danger would exist to the former client that such information could return from the past and prove embarrassing or harmful. Likewise, facts of interest to treatment team members may rate as mere gossip years later (e.g., "paternal aunt suffered from melancholia," "intense sibling rivalry is present," "parents have difficulty with sexual intimacy'").

Disposition

When disposing of records or obsolete contents culled from them, their confidential nature demands respect and precautions. With paper records, therapists can shred, incinerate, recycle, or take other destructive action themselves or contract for such services. Actual responsibility for the proper destruction rests with the practitioner or agency head in charge of the material.

Case 8–43: Eurippides Upp, the administrator of a mental health agency planned to dispose of many outdated clinical records. He ordered the files piled into plastic trash bags, tied up, and inserted in an outdoor dumpster to await trash pickup. Neighborhood dogs, in quest of food scraps, tore several bags open, and the wind blew out many

---

Box 8–2 Suggestions for Managing Electronic Records

- Use encryption software to protect data transmission; protect stored data with complex passwords (i.e., letters, numerals, symbols, and upper- and lowercase mixes) and Internet firewalls.
- Discuss and develop security measures with professional and support personnel when storing files via a common server or backing them up on an institutional system or hub.
- Advise both trainees and supervisors on appropriate procedures to protect client/patient confidentiality when using the Internet for supervisory purposes.
- Keep removable data storage media in secure locations or use complex passwords to encrypt them.
- If using audio or visual records of client interactions for teaching purposes, consider distorting the client's voice or masking faces.
- Destroy recordings when no longer needed as long as their destruction does not conflict with other ethical or legal obligations to maintain scientific or professional records.
- Do not share passwords with others and do change them often.
- Remain mindful of security hazards of wireless devices and alert clients to this when using such devices.
- Avoid use of confidential information in e-mail or instant messaging unless you use encryption.
- Take extra measures to protect physical security of portable devices (e.g., laptop or smaller computers, personal digital assistants, and smart phones) used to work with client data, whether used in the office or at home.
- Use privacy screens to shield monitors or other types of screens from viewing by others.
- Update virus protection software and other security measures frequently for both personal and workspace computing devices on which PHI is kept.
- Remove all data when disposing or recycling old computers. This may require assistance from technical experts because even after erasing files or reformatting disks, traces of data may remain.

Source: Adapted from ideas suggested by Fisher and Fried (2003).

reports and notes bearing client names and other identifying material. Many of the clients whose records flew around in the streets still resided in the same community.

Case 8–44: Giga Byte purchased a dozen upgraded desktop computers for the clinic she managed and donated the older office computers to a local community center. She took care to delete all of the word processing and billing files she could locate before handing over the old equipment.

Mr. Upp evidently took little care to see to the proper disposal of sensitive records. He should have had the material shredded or stored securely until pickup by a responsible disposal agent. Ms. Byte may or may not have done an adequate job of protecting records stored in the computer. Simply deleting files on a hard drive does not permanently remove the data. In some cases, even reformatting a drive may not prevent recovery of some data. We recommend obtaining consultation from experts before disposing of computer equipment used to store client data. A special set of recommendations regarding electronic records and confidentiality issues appears in Box 8–2.

The death of a mental health practitioner can also raise a complex set of problems with respect to individual client records. In some cases, a surviving spouse or executor has simply destroyed records. In other cases, they have retained records but made no arrangements for the orderly processing and screening of requests to access information from them. Although we know of no complaints or litigation against the estates of dead mental health professionals for record-keeping infractions, failure to safeguard records following the death of a clinician could conceivably lead to filing suit against a therapist's estate. For this reason, as well as client welfare, we stress the importance of creating a will or other instructions addressing record disposition. One alternative could involve an arrangement with a professionally responsible colleague for the care and management of the records. Other alternatives would be to instruct one's spouse or executor on how to seek advice from others on record management or to ask a professional association to assist in managing the files for a period of time after the death.

SUMMARY GUIDELINES

1. Mental health practitioners should understand the distinctions between confidentiality (an ethical principle) and privilege (a legal concept) as they apply in their practice jurisdiction.
2. Therapists should remain mindful of any exceptions and limitations, such as the so-called duty to warn, obligations to report child abuse, collection of bills, or other special conditions bearing on confidentiality. Exceptions should be discussed with clients at the outset of the professional relationship, documenting this with a HIPAA-compliant notice form.
3. Prior to the release of any records, therapists should secure written informed consent from the client and attempt to alert the client regarding any reasonably foreseeable hazards to the release.
4. Therapists should recognize the different types of formal and informal records that exist, consider the prototype record we suggest in collecting data, and attempt to ensure that the contents remain factual, appropriate, and current.
5. The increasing trend toward freer client access to records should be kept in mind when reports are prepared and files are maintained. Always write with the assumption that the record will ultimately be seen by the client.
6. When properly releasing confidential material, therapists should carefully consider the need-to-know status of the intended recipient and the likely uses of the information.
7. Give extra consideration to the special rights and vulnerabilities of minors and legally incompetent individuals when considering requests for access to therapy files about them.
8. Remain informed about the proper response to subpoenas and other requests for records from courts or other third parties.
9. When using case materials for teaching or public lecture purposes, take care to secure

proper permission and to disguise material sufficiently to protect the client.

10. In the conduct of research, carefully consider the welfare of those under study with respect to confidentiality.

11. Take proper steps to ensure that the retention and disposition of records in whatever form takes place within the context of clients' best interests.

References

American Psychological Association. (1981). Ethical principles of psychologists. *American Psychologist*, 36, 633–638.

American Psychological Association. (1993). Record keeping guidelines. *American Psychologist*, 48, 984–986.

American Psychological Association. (2007). *Record keeping guidelines*. Washington, DC: American Psychological Association.

Anderson, J. R., & R. L. Barret (Eds.). (2001). *Ethics in HIV-related psychotherapy: Clinical decision making in complex cases*. Washington, DC: American Psychological Association.

Apple, R. W., Jr. (1993, August 11). Note left by White House aide: Accusation, anger and despair. *New York Times*. Retrieved March 15, 2007, from http://query.nytimes.com/gst/fullpage.html?sec=health&res=9F0CE7DC1E3AF932A2575BC0A965958260

Associated Press. (1995, November 24). Account of therapy for Nicole Simpson brings suspension. Retrieved March 15, 2007, from http://query.nytimes.com/gst/fullpage.html?sec=health&res=9805EED71339F937A15752C1A963958260

Bass, A. (1995, April 13). Insurers spurn anyone in therapy. *Boston Globe*, pp. 25, 29.

Barnett, J. E., & Scheetz, K. (2003). Technological advances and telehealth: Ethics, law, and the practice of psychotherapy. *Psychotherapy*, 40, 86–93.

Baumrind, D. (1990). Doing good well. In C. B. Fisher & W. W. Tryon (Eds.), *Ethics in applied developmental psychology: Emerging issues in an emerging field* (pp. 232–256). Norwood, NJ: Ablex.

Bersoff, D. N. (1976). Therapists as protectors and policemen: New roles as a result of *Tarasoff*. *Professional Psychology*, 7, 267–273.

Bersoff, D. N. (1995). *Ethical conflicts in psychology*. Washington, DC: American Psychological Association.

Boruch, R. F., Dennis, M., & Cecil, J. S. (1996). Fifty years of empirical research on privacy and confidentiality in research settings. In B. H. Stanley, J. E. Sieber, & G. B. Melton (Eds.), *Research ethics: A psychological approach* (pp. 129–173). Lincoln, NE: University of Nebraska Press.

Boynton v. Burglass, 590 So. 2d 466 (Fla. D. Ct. A.P. 1991).

Brosig, C. L., & Kalichman, S. C. (1992). Child abuse reporting decisions: Effects of statutory wording of reporting requirements. *Professional Psychology*, 23, 486–492.

Burke, C. A. (1995). Until death do us part: An exploration into confidentiality following the death of a client. *Professional Psychology*, 26, 278–280.

Carroll, J. D. (1973). Confidentiality of social science research sources and data: The Popkin case. *Political Science*, 6, unnumbered.

Chodoff, P. (1992). The Anne Sexton biography: The limits of confidentiality. *Journal of the American Academy of Psychoanalysis*, 20, 639–643.

Clemens, N. A. (2006). Putting your medical record on the line. *Journal of Psychiatric Practice*, 12, 250–252.

Commonwealth v. Lamb, 311 N.E.2d 47, 365 (Mass. 265 1974).

Connell, M., & Koocher, G. P. (2003). Expert opinion: HIPPA and forensic practice. *American Psychology Law Society News*, 13, 16–19.

Damschroder, L. J., Pritts, J. L., Neblo, M. A., Kalarickal, R. J., Creswell, J. W., & Hayward, R. A. (2007). Patients, privacy and trust: Patients' willingness to allow researchers to access their medical records. *Social Science & Medicine*, 64, 223–235.

DeKraai, M. B., & Sales, B. D. (1982). Privileged communications of psychologists. *Professional Psychology*, 13, 372–388.

Disclosure of confidential information gives rise to tort action against psychiatrist. (1982). *Mental Disability Law Reporter*, 6, 79.

Doctor and the law: On patient's right to read own medical records. (1975, February 10). *Medical World News*.

Douglas, K. S. and P. R. Kropp (2002). A prevention-based paradigm for violence risk assessment:

Clinical and research applications. *Criminal Justice and Behavior. 29*, 617–658.

Dubey, J. (1974). Confidentiality as a requirement of the therapist: Technical necessities for absolute privilege in psychotherapy. *American Journal of Psychiatry, 131*, 1093–1096.

Epstein, G. N., Steingarten, J., Weinstein, H. D., & Nashel, H. M. (1977). Panel report: Impact of law on the practice of psychotherapy. *Journal of Psychiatry and Law, 5*, 7–40.

Everstine, L., Everstine, D. S., Heymann, G. M., True, R. H., Frey, D. H., Johnson, H. G., et al. (1980). Privacy and confidentiality in psychotherapy. *American Psychologist, 35*, 828–840.

Ewing v. Goldstein, 120 Cal. App. 4th 807 (15 Cal. Rptr. 3rd 864, 867, 2004).

Fisher, C. B., & Fried, A. L. (2003). Internet-mediated psychological services and the American Psychological Association Ethics Code. *Psychotherapy: Theory, Research, Practice, Training, 40*, 103–111.

Fox v. Namani, 622 N.Y.S.2d 842 (N.Y. Sup. Ct. 1994).

Godkin v. Miller, 379 F Supp. 859 (ED N.Y. 1974), aff'd, 514 F 2d 123 (2d Cir. 1975).

Goldstein, R. L. (1992). Psychiatric poetic license? Post-mortem disclosure of confidential information in the Anne Sexton case. *Psychiatric Annals, 22*, 341–348.

Gordis, L., & Gold, E. (1980, January 11). Privacy, confidentiality, and the use of medical records in research. *Science, 207*, 153–156.

Hoagwood, K. (1994). The certificate of confidentiality at the National Institute of Mental Health: Discretionary considerations in its applicability in research on child and adolescent mental disorders. *Ethics & Behavior, 4*, 123–131.

Hook, M. K., & Cleveland, J. L. (1999). To tell or not to tell: Breaching confidentiality with clients with HIV and AIDS. *Ethics & Behavior, 9*, 365–381.

Hsiung, R. C. (2002). Suggested principles of professional ethics for E-therapy. In R. C. Hsiung, *e-Therapy: Case studies, guiding principles, and the clinical potential of the Internet* (pp. 150–165). New York: Norton.

Hunt, D. M. (1999). *O. J. Simpson: Facts and fictions.* Cambridge, UK: Cambridge University Press.

In re Viviano, 645 So. 2d 1301 (La. Ct. A.P. 1994).

Jaffe v. Redmond, 116 S.Ct. 95-266, 64L.W. 4490 (June 13, 1996).

Joseph, D. I. (1992). Discussion: Anne Sexton and the ethics of psychotherapy. *Journal of the American Academy of Psychoanalysis, 20*, 665–669.

Kalichman, S. C. (1993). *Mandated reporting of suspected child abuse: Ethics, law, and policy.* Washington, DC: American Psychological Association.

Kalichman, S. C., Brosig, C. L., & Kalichman, M. O. (1994). Mandatory child abuse reporting laws: Issues and implications for treating offenders. *Journal of Offender Rehabilitation, 21*, 27–43.

Kanani, K. R., & Regehr, C. (2003). Clinical, ethical, and legal issues in e-therapy. *Families in Society, 84*, 155–162.

Karon, B. P., & Widen, A. J. (1998) Repressed memories: The real story. *Professional Psychology, 29*, 482–487.

Knapp, S., & VandeCreek, L. (2000). Real-life vignettes involving the duty to protect. *Journal of Psychotherapy in Independent Practice, 1*, 83–88.

Knerr, C. R. (1982). What to do before and after a subpoena of data arrives. In J. E. Sieber (Ed.), *The ethics of social research. Surveys and experiments* (pp. 158–177). New York: Springer-Verlag.

Koocher, G. P., & Keith-Spiegel, P. C. (1990). *Children, ethics, and the law: Professional issues and cases.* Lincoln, NE: University of Nebraska Press.

Leonard, J. B. (1977). A therapist's duty to warn potential victims: A nonthreatening view of *Tarasoff. Law and Human Behavior, 1*, 309–318.

Litwack, T. R. (2001). Actuarial versus clinical assessment of dangerousness. *Psychology, Public Policy, and Law, 7*, 409–443.

MacDonald v. Clinger, No. 991/1981 (N.Y. A.P. Div., January 22, 1982).

McGuire, J., Nieri, D., Abbott, D., Sheridan, K., & Fisher, R. (1995). Do *Tarasoff* principles apply in AIDS-related psychotherapy? Ethical decision making and the role of therapist homophobia and perceived client dangerousness. *Professional Psychology, 26*, 608–611.

McIntosch v. Milano, 403 A. 2d 500 (N.J. Super. Ct. 1979).

McSherry, B. (2004). Third party access to shared electronic mental health records: Ethical issues. *Psychiatry, Psychology and Law, 11*, 53–62.

Middlebrook, D. W. (1991). *Anne Sexton: A biography.* New York: Vintage Books.

Morganthau, T., Lindsay, J. J., Michael, R., & Givens, R. (1982). The unanswered questions. *Newsweek, 99*, 40.

Nowell, D., & Sprull, J. (1993). If it's not absolutely confidential, will information be disclosed? *Professional Psychology, 24,* 367–369.

Otto, R. K. (2000). Assessing and managing violence risk in outpatient settings. *Journal of Clinical Psychology, 56,* 1239–1262.

Palma, T. V., & Iannelli, R. J. (2002). Therapeutic reactivity to confidentiality with HIV positive clients: Bias or epidemiology? *Ethics & Behavior, 12,* 353–370.

Parry, O., & Mauthner, N. S. (2004). Whose data are they anyway? Practical, legal and ethical issues in archiving qualitative research data. *Sociology, 38,* 139–152.

Paul, R. E. (1977). *Tarasoff* and the duty to warn: Toward a standard of conduct that balances the rights of client against the rights of third parties. *Professional Psychology, 8,* 125–128.

People v. Poddar, 10 Ca. 3d 750, 518, P.2d 342, 111 Cal. Rptr. 910 (1974).

Post, J. M. (2004). *Leaders and Their Followers in a Dangerous World: The psychology of political behavior.* Ithaca, NY: Cornell University Press.

Public Law 104-191, Health Insurance Portability and Accountability Act of 1996, August 21, 1996. Retrieved March 25, 2007, from http:// aspe.hhs.gov/admnsimp/pl104191.htm

Quattrocchi, M. R., & Schopp, R. F. (2005). Tarasaurus Rex: A standard of care that could not adapt. *Psychology, Public Policy, and Law, 11,* 109–137.

Rogers, W. A. (2006). *Pressures on confidentiality. Lancet, 367,* 553–554.

Rosen, C. E. (1977). Why clients relinquish their rights to privacy under sign-away pressures. *Professional Psychology, 8,* 17–24.

Rosenbaum, M. (1994). The travails of Martin Orne: On privacy, public disclosure, and confidentiality in psychotherapy. *Journal of Contemporary Psychotherapy, 24,* 159–167.

Rosenoer, J. (1995). Problems on the Internet: A lawyer's perspective. *Ethics & Behavior, 5,* 107–110.

Rost v. Pennsylvania Board of Psychology, 659 A.2d 626 (Pa. Commonwealth Ct. 1995).

Roth, L. H., Wolford, J., & Meisel, A. (1980). Patient access to records: Tonic or toxin? *American Journal of Psychiatry, 137,* 592–596.

Sawyer, J., & Schechter, H. (1968). Computers, privacy, and the national data center: The responsibility of social scientists. *American Psychologist, 23,* 810–818.

Scott, G. G. (2005). *Homicide by the rich and famous: A century of prominent killers.* Westport, CT: Praeger.

Shah, S. (1969). Privileged communications, confidentiality, and privacy: Privileged communications. *Professional Psychology, 1,* 56–59.

Shaw v. Glickman, 415A. 2d 625 (Md. Ct. Spec. A.P. 1980).

Siegel, M. (1979). Privacy, ethics, and confidentiality. *Professional Psychology, 10,* 249–258.

Smith, S. R. (1996). U.S. Supreme Court adopts psychotherapist–patient privilege. *Bulletin of the American Academy of Forensic Psychology, 17,* 1–15.

Smith-Bell, M., & Winslade, W. J. (1994). Privacy, confidentiality, and privilege in psychotherapeutic relationships. *American Journal of Orthopsychiatry, 64,* 180–193.

Stanley, D., & Palosky, C. S. (1997, February 28). Fax drops records in her lap. *Tampa Tribune,* p. B1.

Stein, M. D., Freedberg, K. A., & Sullivan, L. M. (1998). Sexual ethics. Disclosure of HIV-positive status to partners [comment]. *Archives of Internal Medicine, 158,* 253–257.

Stone, A. A. (1976). The *Tarasoff* decisions: Suing psychotherapists to safeguard society. *Harvard Law Review, 90,* 358–378.

Stone, G. R. (2004). *Perilous times: Free speech in wartime from the Sedition Act of 1798 to the war on terrorism.* New York: Norton.

Strassburger, F. (1975). Problems surrounding "informed voluntary consent" and patient access to records. *Psychiatric Opinion, 12,* 30–34.

Swidler & Berlin and James Hamilton v. United States, 524 U.S. 399 (1998).

Tarasoff duty to warn discussed in three cases; no such duty found in Maryland. (1980). *Mental Disability Law Reporter, 4,* 313–315.

Tarasoff v. Board of Regents of the University of California, 551 P. 2d 334 (Cal. Sup. Ct. 1976).

Taylor, L., & Adelman, H. S. (1989). Reframing the confidentiality dilemma to work in children's best interests. *Professional Psychology, 20,* 79–83.

Thompson v. County of Alameda, 614 P. 2d 728 (Cal. Sup. Ct. 1980).

Truscott, D. (1993). The psychotherapist's duty to protect: An annotated bibliography. *Journal of Psychiatry and Law, 21,* 221–244.

United States of America v. Theresa Marie Squilla-cote, 221 F.3d 542 (2000).

U.S. Department of Health and Human Services. (2003). *Protecting personal health information in research: Understanding the HIPAA Privacy Rule.* NIH Publication No. 03-5388. Retrieved September 25, 2003, from http://privacyruleand research.nih.gov/pr_02.asp

U.S. Department of Health and Human Services. (2006). Medical privacy—National standards to protect the privacy of personal health information. Retrieved January 15, 2006, from http://www.hhs.gov/ocr/hipaa/

VandeCreek, L., & Knapp, S. (1993). *Tarasoff and beyond: Legal and clinical considerations in the treatment of life-endangering patients* (Rev. ed.). Sarasota, FL: Professional Resource Exchange.

VandeCreek, L., & Knapp, S. (2001). *Tarasoff and beyond: Legal and clinical considerations in the treatment of life-endangering patients* (3rd ed.). Sarasota, FL: Professional Resource Press.

Watson, H., & Levine, M. (1989). Psychotherapy and mandated reporting of child abuse. *American Journal of Orthopsychiatry, 59,* 246–256.

Weisbeck v. Hess, 524 N.W. 2d 363 (S.D. Sup. Ct. 1994).

Weisner, D. A. (2006). From *Tarasoff* to *Ewing*: Expansion of the duty to warn. *American Journal of Forensic Psychology, 24,* 45–55.

Werth, J. L., Burke, C., & Bardash, R. J. (2002). Confidentiality in end-of-life and after-death situations. *Ethics & Behavior, 12,* 205–222.

Woods, K. M., & McNamara, J. R. (1980). Confidentiality: Its effect on interviewee behavior. *Professional Psychology, 1,* 714–721.

Yufik, A. (2005). Revisiting the Tarasoff decision: Risk assessment and liability in clinical and forensic practice. *American Journal of Forensic Psychology, 23,* 5–21.

9

Psychological Assessment
Testing Tribulations

One gets the impression that the major purpose...
was not to beat a dead horse but to administer
massive doses of statistics in the effort to bring the
unfortunate animal back to life.

Ann Anastasi

Contents

Imagine these headlines in your morning newspaper or podcast:

"Psychologist Devises a 'Toss and Catch the Child' Test for Use in Making Post-divorce Custody Decisions"

"Firefighter Applicant Challenges Use of Inkblot Test as a Measure Fitness to Fight Fires"

"Confidential Tests Available for Sale to the Highest Bidder on E-Bay"

"High School Students Sue the Educational Testing Service for Failing to Correct Errors in their Scholastic Aptitude Test Scores"

Psychological tests and psychodiagnostic assessments can have powerful effects, both good and bad, on peoples' lives. Those who plan to use such instruments with ethical integrity will need a thorough background in psychometrics, along with training in test administration and interpretation. Those most likely to receive such education and training include clinical, counseling, and school psychologists. Even among those specialty groups, however, the depth and breadth of assessment skills will vary widely.

Many professions have studied human behavior and capabilities, but in the realm of psychodiagnostic assessment or testing, the contributions of psychology remain unique. The use of small samples of human behavior, collected in standardized fashion and scientifically evaluated to categorize, diagnose, evaluate, or predict behavior, certainly stands as one of the most noteworthy accomplishments of behavioral scientists. Such tests provide powerful tools for advancing human welfare. Occasionally, great concern about the real, imagined, or potential misuses of tests have become key public policy issues. At other times, misunderstanding of technical subtleties, such as those critiqued by Anastasi (1975, p. 356) in the opening quotation for this chapter, give the false impression that the ability to quantify human behavior imparts some sort of intrinsic truth or merit.

One of the earliest and most striking public commentaries reflective of such misconceptions came from a the 24-year-old journalist named Walter Lippman in a series of six articles on "The Mental Age of Americans" and "Mr.

Binet's Test," published between October 25 and November 29, 1922, in *The New Republic*. Lippman stressed the potential misunderstanding and "great mischief" that might follow if parents and school authorities became confused about the nature and validity of the assessment techniques devised by Binet in France and later revised by Terman in the United States. He noted (1922):

> If, for example, the impression takes root that these tests really measure intelligence, that they constitute a sort of last judgment on the child's capacity, that they reveal "scientifically" his predestined ability, then it would be a thousand times better if all the intelligence testers and all their questionnaires were sunk without warning in the Sargasso Sea. (p. 297)

One can not underestimate the political and social significance that psychological testing has come to have in America and around the world and the converse impact of public attitudes on the field of psychometrics. Haney (1981) traced debates over the meaning of IQ, the social functions that tests serve, and the appropriate use of personality tests beginning with Terman's development of the Stanford-Binet scales in 1916 and the Army Alpha test during World War I. He provided a strong illustrative case demonstrating how social attitudes and values affect even professional writings on testing and affect issues that appear to be strictly technical on the surface. In the same vein, Laosa (1984) and others (Ridley, Hill, & Wiese, 2001) have documented the historic misuse of psychological assessment in forging social policies against immigrants and people of color.

The ethical problems growing out of the use and potential misuse of psychological tests and assessment techniques remain as varied as the many different types of instruments, users of them, purposes for which people use them, and consequences to those tested. For purposes of general definition, we consider a *psychological test* to be any questionnaire, examination, or similar sample of behavior collected in a prescribed or standardized fashion for the purposes of describing, classifying, diagnosing, evaluating, or predicting behavior. We must add the caveat that we refer only to those techniques devised and routinely employed by psychologists and other qualified mental health professionals in the course of their professional work. We intend to exclude, for example, scientific anthropological or sociological survey and measurement techniques, as well as astral charts, tea leaf readings, biorhythms, or fondling the viscera of certain animals as a means to predict future events.

JOINT TECHNICAL STANDARDS

Psychological assessment involves both art and science. The empirical foundations of testing remain critical for producing reliable and valid data. The ability to integrate these data with individual case factors to yield competent assessment, however, involves the art of clinical interpretation in addition to psychometric science (Cates, 1999).

In an effort to clearly articulate the fundamentals of the assessment science, the three major professional organizations involved developed *The Standards for Educational and Psychological Testing*, referred to as the *Joint Technical Standards* in earlier iterations (American Educational Research Association [AERA], American Psychological Association, & National Council on Measurement in Education [NCME], 1999). First published more than 50 years ago and updated regularly, it contains a comprehensive set of standards addressing test development, test use, special issues related to linguistic and cultural differences, testing the disabled, testing the aged, and computerized assessment. The standards address expectations regarding validity, reliability, errors of measurement, scales, norms, development and revision criteria, and required supporting documents. They also explain fundamentals of fair testing, the rights and responsibilities of both users and takers of tests, and assessing individuals with disabilities and diverse language backgrounds. The standards also address assessment for employment and credentialing, as well as legal and public policy issues. In so doing, the document provides the consensual foundation of ethical psychological and educational assessment.

VARIETIES OF TESTS

One can classify test instruments across a number of dimensions, including the purpose for designing them, the population used to standardize them, the nature of their administration, the mode of interpretation, and their psychometric properties. Types of tests according to intended use are listed below. Within each of these general categories, one can specify still more specific types of tests by intended function.

- personnel selection, promotion, or classification
- professional licensure or certification
- educational admission and placement
- certification testing in elementary and secondary schools
- ability and achievement testing in schools
- special education testing (including instruments designed for use with the blind, hearing impaired, and other people with disabilities)
- clinical assessment (including cognitive, neuropsychological, and personality testing)
- counseling and guidance (including vocational interest inventories)
- specialized instruments designed for program evaluation and programmatic decision making
- research instruments intended to draw inferences about the true or absolute standing of a group or individual on some hypothetical or investigative psychological dimension

In terms of standardization samples, some tests are designed only for use with literate, English-speaking adults. Others may focus on children under the age of 7 or individuals with advanced typing skills. Without specific knowledge of the intended subject population or group used to establish norms, test scores become meaningless. This assumes, of course, that the test does have norms available, and that it has undergone proper validation, as we discuss in this chapter.

Test administration may occur in large groups of test takers or individually, with one examiner assessing one client. The format may employ timed or untimed items; involve paper-and-pencil, oral, or computer-based administration; and require forced-choice or open-ended responses. Some tests require a skilled administrator, whereas others use self-administration methods monitored by a person without psychological training. Many tests are administered, scored, and partially interpreted solely based on the client's interaction with a computer terminal.

Similarly, test interpretation or data use may also vary widely. Some tests may be administered, scored, and interpreted quite simply by a person with little or no formal training (e.g., tests of typing speed and accuracy). Other tests may not require skilled administrators but demand sophisticated clinical training for proper interpretation (e.g., paper-and-pencil inventories, card-sort tasks, or computer-assisted tools.). Still other tests may require high levels of psychological skill and detailed knowledge of scoring complex systems for proper administration and interpretation (e.g., some neuropsychological assessment tools or projective personality assessment techniques such as the Rorschach inkblots).

KEY CONCEPTS IN TESTS AND MEASUREMENTS

Many important technical concepts necessarily come into play when attempting to understand the proper use of psychological tests for the purpose of psychological assessment (Betz, Watkins, & Campbell, 2000; Cone, Dalenberg, & Maruish, 2004; Hersen, 2004; Matarazzo, 1990). While we do not intend this chapter as a substitute for formal course work in test construction and measurement statistics, we summarize here the key terms important for understanding ethical test use. Portions of this chapter may seem rather basic to some readers, especially those who have a thorough familiarity with concepts related to tests and measurements. Unfortunately, however, such basics too often lie at the heart of ethical complaints related to testing or assessment. These include the concepts of reliability, validity, sources of error, and standard error of measurement.

Reliability

Reliability refers to the property of repeatable results. Will the test dependably measure whatever it measures over time and across pop-

ulations? Tests of relatively stable phenomena, for example, should have high test–retest reliability. If a person earns a certain score on a mathematics achievement test on Monday, that same person should earn a similar score on readministration of the same test several days later, assuming no special studying or additional teaching occurred during the interval. Likewise, the test should yield similar scores for people of relatively equal ability when these people take the test under similar conditions, whether or not they differ on the basis of other extraneous characteristics (e.g., age, sex, race, etc.). If the test does not measure something reliably, it becomes useless because we would never know whether differences in scores resulted from changes in the skill or trait measured or from the unreliability of the instrument.

Validity

The term *validity* refers to the concept of whether a reliable test actually measures what its proponents claim that it measures. A test can not possibly constitute a valid measure of anything unless it has good reliability. At the same time, a test may yield reliable scores yet not be a valid indicator of what it purports to measure. Test developers have an ethical responsibility to demonstrate that their tests have appropriate validity for any recommended applications.

Content and construct validity refer to whether the test samples behavior representative of the skill, trait, or other characteristic we want to measure. Content validity indicates the degree to which the items in the test come from the domain of behavior of interest. This addresses the question: Do the test questions or tasks relate to the performance ability we wish to gauge? The degree to which test scores may help us to infer how well any given construct describes individual differences is the key factor in construct validity (Cureton, Cronbach, Meehl, Ebel, & Ward, 1996; Green, 1981; Guion, 1974; Maher & Gottesman, 2005; McKelvie, 2005; Reckase, 1998; Waller & Meehl, 2002).

Cronbach (1980) claimed, "All validation is one, and in a sense all is construct validation" (p. 99), and the joint technical standards (AERA et al., 1999) stress the centrality of construct validation. The existence or operational definitions of many hypothetical constructs (e.g., ego-strength, happiness, or even intelligence) may prove controversial, with the result that tests predicated on these constructs become open to question. For example, a test predicated on psychoanalytic concepts (e.g., the Blacky test, in which prints depicting a dog named Blacky acting out or witnessing scenes depicting various Freudian concepts such as oral gratification, anal rage, or castration anxiety) would doubtless lead to ridicule from a behaviorally inclined clinician whose theoretical perspective focuses on directly observable behaviors rather than constructs familiar to the psychoanalytic community. Similarly, an operant behaviorist who argues that nonobservable intrapsychic events do not exist or lack clinical significance would likely seem naive to most experienced clinicians. The responsibility for establishing whether the test measures the construct or reflects the content of interest becomes the ethical burden of both the test developers and the test publishers.

Criterion-related validity addresses whether a given test's outcome relates to other criteria in predictive or concurrent fashion. For example, graduate departments have a long-standing interest in which data will best predict success in graduate school. Admissions offices collect test scores, undergraduate grades, reference letters, and other data to predict (and thereby select) those applicants who have the highest likelihood to do well in, and successfully complete, the degree program. Adequate demonstration of this type of relationship also becomes the responsibility of the test developers and publishers. Individual test users also have a responsibility to use test data in ways that reflect well-established predictive or criterion-related relationships or to sample a particular content domain.

Sources of error constitute a critical consideration when evaluating test scores. A person may feel more motivated to perform on one occasion than another. Another person may have a better ability to make educated guesses relative to peers. Still a third might feel ill, hungry, or anxious or have greater familiarity with specific test items on one particular form of a test instrument. The importance of any particular source of error depends on the spe-

cific use of the test in the context of the specific individual who took it. The goal of reliability studies focuses on establishing estimates of the magnitude of the errors of measurement from assorted sources. Any given test has many types of standard errors. The test user has responsibility for becoming familiar with these and for making appropriate selections depending on the comparisons they wish to make. A *standard error of measurement* is a score interval that, given certain assumptions, has a given probability of including any individual's true score.

Consider some cases related to these concepts as ethical issues:

Case 9–1: Norma Skew, Ph.D., developed a detailed interview schedule that one can score in an objective fashion, yielding a set of numbers she describes as a "leadership quotient," a "motivation index," and a "likelihood-of-success rating." She selected the items from a variety of existing personality assessment tools and questionnaires. Dr. Skew proceeded to advertise this instrument for use in "selecting executive talent," although as yet she has collected no validity data and simply presumes reliability "because the items are all based on questions asked in other reliable instruments."

Psychologists sophisticated in testing standards or who have familiarity with assessment and measurement theory will no doubt wince at the prospect that any practitioner could behave in this manner, but these types of problems prove all too common. Dr. Skew may have demonstrated "creative innovation" in designing her assessment instrument, but she has not bothered to validate it. We give her the benefit of one doubt and assume that she has secured permission to use any copyrighted material. The fact that she has used items of known validity related to other instruments, however, does not mean that these items will prove valid for the uses she ascribes to them in this new context. On the other hand, unless she has specific validity data to show that her items measure the constructs of leadership, motivation, and likelihood of success and that the scores her instruments yield predict some meaningful criterion of success in selecting talented executives, she has misused psychological tests.

Case 9–2: Marge N. O'Vera, Psy.D., retested a child who had taken the Wechsler Intelligence Scale for Children–Fourth Edition (WISC-IV) administered by another examiner a few months earlier. The youngster, described as mildly mentally retarded, earned IQ scores 3 to 5 points higher when O'Vera tested him. O'Vera then told the child's parents, "This shows that he could have intellectual progress potential."

Dr. O'Vera represents one of the most frightening kinds of practitioners because she has offered illusory grains of hope to the family of a child with a disability, perhaps with the result of promoting unfortunate expectations. The "new scores" fall within the standard error of the differences for each, as described in detail in the WISC-IV test manual. This means that the upward shift most likely relates to some chance variable or other trivial factor rather than a sign of intellectual gain. O'Vera's naïveté about mental retardation and the proper use of the test manual data also hints strongly at incompetence.

Case 9–3: Tanya Shallow, Ed.D., worked as a school psychologist charged with selecting a few dozen intellectually talented youngsters from the Plainville Regional School District to receive access to a special summer enrichment program. She decided that the simplest way to select candidates would be to group administer a standardized paper-and-pencil IQ test and select students from among the high scorers.

Dr. Shallow's choice of a group-administered paper-and-pencil measure of intelligence as the sole selection criterion constitutes a significant error in fairness. To begin, many intellectually talented youngsters may not score well on such tests. One child, for example, may have become distracted by spitballs dispatched by a classmate, another might feel preoccupied by family stresses, and still another might have an insufficient grasp of written English to do well on the test. Still others may have impressive abilities that are not reflected in the test items. Instead of using multiple criteria suited to the nature of the program and the type of students sought (Sternberg, 2004), Dr. Shallow appears to have sought a solution requiring the least effort on her part. She

has used an instrument designed chiefly for another purpose and ignored potential drawbacks of the instrument as a valid indicator of the one variable she is actually measuring (i.e., the ability to do well on a group-administered paper-and-pencil task). At the very least, she should not rely on a single data source.

PRIMARY REFERENCE SOURCES

The definitive reference sources for anyone with a substantial interest in the proper use of psychological tests include the Buros *Mental Measurements Yearbook* (Gutkin, 2000; Viswesvaran, 2005) and *Tests: A Comprehensive Reference for Assessments in Psychology, Education, and Business* (Maddox, 2003). The Buros Institute at the University of Nebraska provides online search capabilities (http://www.unl.edu/buros/). The most recent *Mental Measurements Yearbook* (15th edition) contains information on 2,200 tests, with detailed reviews of tests and books on testing.

The American Psychological Association (APA) also offers a plethora of useful information on testing at its public information (http://www.apa.org/pubinfo/testing.html) and Science Directorate Web sites. We particularly recommend the "Rights and Responsibilities of Test Takers: Guidelines and Expectations" (http://www.apa.org/science/ttrr.html), the Testing Information Clearinghouse (http://www.apa.org/science/testclearinghs.html), and the section on how to locate detailed information on psychological tests (http://www.apa.org/science/faq-findtests.html). The APA's casebook, *Responsible Test Use* (Eyde et al., 1993) also provides an excellent supplement, including 78 case studies carefully indexed by topics and fully cross-referenced.

Additional reference works that will interest many readers include the special issue of the *American Psychologist*, "Testing: Concepts, Policy, Practice, and Research" (October 1981). It contains 20 invited articles, including overviews and discussion of then-current controversies, and represents an excellent collection of basic concepts, historical information, and opinions from psychologists with expertise in assessment. Although somewhat dated, most of the articles have significant conceptual and historic value.

TEST ADEQUACY

Most readers will recognize by now that the question of whether any given psychological assessment instrument constitutes a "good test" or a "bad test" is quite complex. A test characterized as reliable, valid, and quite useful for one purpose may prove useless or inappropriate for another. An instrument adequate for its intended use in the hands of a trained examiner could be subject to substantial misuse in the hands of less qualified users. This section of the chapter focuses solely on the adequacy of particular instruments themselves and the factors that contribute to, or detract from, the appropriateness of the test.

Before moving ahead, however, it is important to note that techniques used in some forms of clinical assessment at times come to masquerade as psychological tests. The best example of this phenomenon involves the use of anatomically detailed dolls (occasionally referred to inaccurately as "anatomically correct dolls") in the assessment of children thought to be victims of sexual abuse. In a comprehensive overview of the scientific basis for using such dolls, Koocher and his colleagues (Koocher et al., 1995) noted that the assumption that such dolls constitute some form of psychological test (i.e., a formal instrument with demonstrated potential for detecting child sexual abuse or for stating with a degree of certainty that sexual abuse occurred) is unfounded and dangerous.

As noted, psychological tests provide standardized procedures for the presentation of common stimuli, rules for recording responses, and rules for then assigning quantitative features (i.e., a score) to the elicited responses. The range of anatomically detailed dolls offered in the marketplace does not meet any of these requirements. Such dolls appear in many shapes, sizes, and colors, even with varying genital and related characteristics that may affect a child's precepts and responses. No uniform set of questions to elicit responses, method of presentation,

or quantifiable means of evaluating responses exists. Although a number of suggested protocols for use of anatomically detailed dolls have appeared in print, many have not undergone validation studies or rigorous peer review (see, e.g., Boat & Everson, 1986; Friedemann & Morgan, 1985; Levy, Kalinowski, Markovic, Pittman, & Ahart, 1991). Sadly, some may assume that such dolls are appropriately labeled if called a "projective test" or "projective instrument." However, even projective techniques have a standard set of stimulus materials and specific rules of inquiry, and most have a set of scoring criteria. Anatomically detailed dolls have none of these attributes and do not properly fit any validated projective hypotheses.

If not a test, what should we call anatomically detailed dolls? Koocher and his colleagues (1995) noted that such dolls are best considered a diverse set of stimuli that can function as communication and memory aids to children and other individuals who have immature language, cognitive, or emotional development or who have impaired communication skills. They are simply intended to assist in the communication process, allowing children and others to demonstrate acts for which they have limited verbal descriptions, with which they have limited familiarity in life, or about which they are too embarrassed to speak. Other commentators have supported selective use of such dolls as communication aids (Faller, 2005), with caveats that individuals who use them bear the burden of proving that dolls constitute the best alternative for eliciting information about personally experienced events from children (Dickinson, Poole, & Bruck, 2005).

Unfortunately, police, child protective service workers, and even some therapists who do not understand the appropriate use or limitations can readily purchase such dolls. In fact, significant ethical complaints have grown out of evaluations conducted with such dolls. In some cases, for example, clinicians have too quickly assigned diagnoses of PTSD (posttraumatic stress disorder), "validating" child sexual abuse on the basis of observing repetitive anatomical doll play. Such presumed indications of PTSD may actually result from repeated investigatory interviews by law enforcement or child protection investigators (Fisher, 1996). Others have criticized the minimal generalizability of existing research to actual forensic practice (Everson & Boat, 1997). The problems described here illustrate how an evaluative approach with apparent content or face validity but no reliable measurement system and no predictive validity can take on the aura of a psychological test. More dangerous still, some tools of this sort often become readily available for misuse by individuals with no sophistication in psychometrics.

Test Manual

Each psychological assessment instrument should have a test manual that contains detailed information for potential users, including the following:

- the development and purpose of the test
- information on the standard administration conditions and scoring
- data on the sample population used to standardize the test
- information on its reliability and measurement error
- documentation of its validation
- any other information needed to enable a qualified user or reviewer to evaluate its appropriateness and adequacy for its intended use

The manual may have supplemental sections addressing particular issues or audiences (e.g., a technical measurement section or a section written in lay terms to help test takers understand the meaning of their scores). Optional versus mandatory components of a test manual will vary as a function of the intended applications of the tool. The manual must include sufficient detail to permit the user to determine the test's appropriateness for a specific population and assessment goal. The manual should also include references for all relevant published research on the instrument. Publication or distribution of a test without making such documentation available would constitute an ethical breach, as doing so omits critical information, violates accepted professional standards, and invites misuse.

Test manuals should also include data on potential biases, along with cautions to users regarding improper or unvalidated test applications. In advertising the test to professional or public audiences, the publisher must take care to avoid any suggestion that the instrument has greater utility or validity than the existing research base warrants. Implying that any given test satisfies federal guidelines or requirements without qualification, for example, would raise ethical concerns because even tests that have earned some type of official recognition or approval are limited to certain specific contexts (Bersoff, 1981; Novick, 1981). The following three cases involve tests that may have utility or validity, although presented or dealt with in a potentially unethical fashion.

Case 9–4: Guy Grand, Ed.D., developed a personnel selection instrument that proved to have some validity for selecting middle-level managers of a large consumer goods manufacturing company. In that context, the use of the test later won recognition as appropriate by the Equal Employment Opportunity Commission and the U.S. Department of Labor. Dr. Grand subsequently touted the ruling in advertising for the test sent to personnel officers of several other large corporations.

Dr. Grand's advertising may lead to unwarranted generalization regarding the meaning of "governmental approval" of the test. The most likely recipients of his announcements (e.g., corporate executives or human resource officers) will typically not have sufficient knowledge of tests and measurements to conceptualize the issues needed to evaluate his claims intelligently or to discriminate between the "recognized" and potential unrecognized uses of the test.

Case 9–5: The manual for the Omnibus Achievement Test gives the numbers, grade levels, and ages of the schoolchildren in the standardization sample. It fails to mention, however, primary language, ethnic/racial composition, geographic diversity, socioeconomic status, or similar demographic variables of the sample population.

The Omnibus Achievement Test severely handicaps any potential user by omitting crucial demographic data on the basic population sampled. This omission effectively undercuts any potential application of the test, valid and reliable though it might be, because the users have no basis to conclude that the population to be tested resembles the population for which norms exist. By omitting such critical data from the manual, users of this test would employ it at their peril because they could not draw generalizable conclusions. Marketing such a test with an incomplete manual would constitute a shared unethical act because it might lead an unsophisticated potential user to think that it has some appropriate application. We describe this as a shared violation because qualified test users should know better than to rely on defective instruments.

Case 9–6: Joyce Nerd, Ph.D., is the primary author of the National Nonsequitor Personality Inventory-3 (NNPI-3), which has won wide acceptance for personality screening. In revising the test manual, Dr. Nerd omits references to several articles published in peer-reviewed journals that criticize the NNPI-3's stated uses and validity studies. She reasons that the "overwhelming body of data over many years" documents the utility of the test, whereas the "few polemic studies" critical of the test are not worthy of mention.

Dr. Nerd may be letting her personal bias and investment in her work cloud her competence. She should not intentionally delete questions about the instrument raised in scholarly publications. Citing all relevant research, including critiques, allows the informed test user to make an independent decision. Dr. Nerd can certainly attempt to rebut such citations in her manual, but the conscious omission of this information represents an act of deception and misrepresentation regardless of Nerd's rationalization.

Test Administration

One of the important scientific values of a psychological assessment technique grows from the fact that it provides a means for assessing a standard slice of human behavior. This implies a specific test ecology, adherence to administration rules, and specific scoring criteria.

Consider these examples of variations in administration of certain tests.

Case 9–7: Erika, age 6, seemed to have become bored in first grade. Her parents called Mr. Blitz, the school principal, to request a conference regarding their daughter's progress and possible promotion. In a hurry to get some data before the parent conference, Mr. Blitz had Erika sent to a third-grade classroom one morning, without prior notice, to take paper-and-pencil intelligence and achievement tests scheduled for administration to the third graders. When comparing her scores to first-grade norms, they seem low, so Blitz concludes that the data prove her basic abilities are limited.

When Mr. Blitz removed Erika without warning from her first-grade class and put her in with a strange group of older children to take a test that was not explained to her, he put her at a substantial emotional disadvantage. Even if we assume that the tests have validity for the intended purpose, one can not base a conclusion about the child's ability solely on paper-and-pencil tests without considering such other factors as teacher reports, individual stresses on the child, and so on. The chief difficulty in this case, however, is the error of altering the child's ecology during the sampling of her behavior while not making any effort to assist her adjustment. It would have been much more appropriate to provide the child with an explanation and to schedule testing with a group of peers or with an individual examiner who could establish rapport with Erika and make individual observations of her work during the test.

Case 9–8: Sidney Mute is a deaf, nonverbal adult arrested as a suspect in a crime. Because of questions about his mental competence, Alice Stanine, Ph.D., was asked to undertake a psychological assessment. She discovered that Mr. Mute can read and write at an elementary school level, so she administered a test battery using intelligence and personality tests intended for hearing/speaking clients by providing Mr. Mute with cards she had specially prepared containing the test questions or instructions. Her behavioral observations noted that "Mr. Mute engaged in considerable hand-waving and finger-twitching ticlike behaviors suggestive of Tourette syndrome."

Dr. Stanine certainly attempted a creative approach in her evaluation of Mr. Mute. However, in so doing she deviated significantly from the test administration conditions prescribed in the manual. To be ethical, she must make note of that in any report of results. More importantly, she has used a test on an individual for whom it had not been validated. Some of the data she collects may prove useful, although clearly not in the same fashion as if the client had the ability to hear and speak. More troubling, however, is the fact that Dr. Stanine did not attempt to use one or more of the specific tests designed for use with the hearing impaired (e.g., the Hiskey-Nebraska Test of Learning Aptitude) or refer the case to an examiner familiar with assessment of deaf clients. She apparently did not consult anyone knowledgeable about assessing deaf clients and seems to have overlooked attempts by Mr. Mute to use sign language, misinterpreting these as suggestive of psychopathology. While this case has major implications regarding Dr. Stanine's competence, it also illustrates the problem of applying a standardized test instrument in a nonstandard fashion and of failure to recognize one's own lack of competence in a specific domain of expertise.

Case 9–9: A psychology state licensing board scheduled a nationally administered, multiple-choice licensing examination. Candidates were told to arrive promptly at 8:00 A.M.; however, disorganized operations at the testing site resulted in delays of 2.5 to 3 hours before people were seated for the test. Administration took place in a roped-off section of corridor in the lobby of a large state office building. During the course of the examination period, considerable pedestrian traffic passed through the lobby and corridor; people waited for elevators, the bells of which rang when the doors opened, and food aromas permeated the air from a cafeteria 100 feet from the roped-off area. When complaints were filed against the psychologist-members of the state licensing board, the board replied that a different branch of state

government over which they had no control assigned the testing sites.

The state licensing board ignored important aspects of test ecology and their own professional responsibility for ensuring an appropriate context for evaluation. The examination site and conditions could reasonably be expected to hinder concentration and amplify the stress on the candidates taking the test. Since the board retains legal responsibility for the licensing process, members can not absolve themselves of the duty to ensure satisfactory testing conditions by deferring responsibility. If board members can not ensure reasonable administration circumstances (e.g., timely registration and a quiet, reasonably comfortable setting without extraneous distractions), they should postpone or defer testing until proper facilities can be arranged. To do otherwise is a violation of proper test administration requirements and hence is unethical.

Another ethical concern regarding test administration involves the issue of supervising clients taking multiple-choice instruments. In April 1993, the APA Ethics Committee issued a policy statement in response to an inquiry about whether it is a per se ethics violation to send a Minnesota Multiphasic Personality Inventory (MMPI) home with a client for completion (APA Ethics Committee, 1993). The committee noted the importance of considering each such circumstance on a case-by-case basis and would involve any similar types of assessment, not simply the MMPI. Concerns focused on violations of test security, failure to supervise the testing adequately (with resulting potential validity problems), and impairment of client welfare. Debate ensued regarding whether there are ever any appropriate circumstances for which it might be reasonable and appropriate to allow administration of such a test away from a professional setting. In such cases, the psychologist would bear the burden of justifying why the client's welfare or other extenuating circumstances necessitated unmonitored administration. The psychologist would need to ensure that test security was maintained, and that the correct person completed the test. In addition, any reports resulting from data collected in a nonstandard manner should address that issue in terms of reliability and validity of the results under nonstandard conditions.

Finally, checking to confirm scoring accuracy constitutes a critical professional obligation, even when using the clear-cut scoring criteria or so-called objective test instruments. In one study, for example, scoring errors were detected in 53% of personality inventories that had been hand scored by trained clinic personnel at an "unnamed metropolitan outpatient mental health clinic" (Allard, Butler, Faust, & Shea, 1995). Fully 19% of the hand-scored test protocols in question contained errors sufficient to alter clinical diagnoses. The same tests scored by computer program were free of errors.

Test Bias

The problem of test bias has received intense scientific and public scrutiny over the years, generating considerable scholarly and public debate (Flaugher, 1978; Frederiksen, 1984; Helms, 2006; Koocher, 1993). Even the definition of the term *test bias* consists of many quite disparate facets (Flaugher, 1978). Bias may manifest itself as a function of the skill or trait tested, as a statistical phenomenon, as a selection model, as test content problems, as an overinterpretation issue, as in the use of wrong criteria, or even as test atmosphere or test ecology issues (APA 02: 9.06). When discussing ethical problems related to the matter of test bias, it therefore becomes critical to consider what sort of definition and which cluster of issues one has in mind.

Fredericksen (1984) noted increasing evidence that economical multiple-choice tests in academic settings have driven other testing procedures out of school evaluation programs, to the detriment of students. He argued that such testing has led to teacher and student behavior changes less conducive to practice with feedback and the development of higher-level cognitive skills. He termed the adverse influence of testing itself on teaching and learning the "real bias" in psychological testing programs.

Cole (1981) presented an excellent historical overview of research on test bias and included analyses of subtle differences in the content of

test items to which individuals react differently. She argued that the basic issue regarding test bias should more properly focus on validity. She made a careful distinction between whether a test has validity for some potential use and whether it should be used (even if valid). For example, a single test may predict success in a particular educational setting for some groups but not others. In such a situation, that test should not constitute the single selection criterion because it does not recognize the "others" who have the ability to succeed, despite a low score on that test. She noted that tests have often served as a kind of lightning rod or focal point of anger related to difficult social policy questions that seldom lend themselves to solution by test data (Laosa, 1984).

Cole (1981) cited several examples of social policy problems. In selecting for employment or promotion, for example, how can we best meet current employer needs while compensating for past wrongs and current individual rights? What role should selective admissions play in higher education, and how should broad opportunities be provided? What form should education for children with disabilities take? How should we deal with people for whom English is not a native language? We agree with Cole's assertion that the bias issues fundamentally boil down to questions of validity. The ethical problems are more clearly linked to the test developers and test users, who hold ultimate responsibility for remaining sensitive to the proper and improper application of the instruments they devise and employ, respectively. Mental health professionals should certainly speak out on major public policy issues, both as individual citizens and as scientists who may have data to assist in resolving problems beneficially, but the solution to complex social policy problems will rarely be found through a psychological test.

Case 9–10: Sara Slava, orphaned in Bosnia and relocated in the United States where she was adopted at age 16 by an American couple, found herself referred for psychological evaluation as she prepared to enroll in an American high school. Sara spoke passable English and the examiner tested her using, among other instruments, the current version of the Wechsler Adult Intelligence Scale (WAIS) and the Rorschach inkblots. On the basis of IQ scores in the 60 to 70 range and un-elaborated "explosion" or "fire" responses on the Rorschach, the psychologist described Sara as "most likely mildly retarded and prone to violent acting out."

Again, the issue is not clear-cut in terms of testing problems. One could argue, as in the case of Dr. Stanine (Case 9–8), that this seems a user competence problem. However, it is also evident that a test standardized on and designed for adult, native English-speaking Americans is not the ideal instrument to use for ability testing of a recent immigrant with limited English language experience. In fact, Sara proved to be a very bright youngster whose receptive and expressive language skills were limited in English. She believed she must not complain or question authorities and should behave in a compliant manner. As a result, she did not ask for clarification or protest her lack of understanding of instructions and test questions. All of Sara's family had been killed during an attack on their village, and she still suffered nightmares of that episode. In that context, her "explosion" responses to the Rorschach seem less subject to the usual interpretation. If the psychologist who saw Sara had given careful thought to these issues, or at least had included adequate cautionary statements in discussing the test data, the use of the tests might have been at least partially justified. In the context of Sara's situation, the evaluation and tests certainly created cultural and linguistic bias.

The importance of both linguistic and cultural sensitivity in testing are critical. For example, the English word *peach* (i.e., a fruit) has two common translations in Spanish. *Durazno* is the word children from Mexico would use to name the fruit, whereas children from Puerto Rico would call it *melocoton*. A vocabulary test in Spanish would have significant flaws unless both uses score as correct. Similarly, in teaching reading comprehension, programs in the United States stress the concept of the main idea. Schools in Israel, on the other hand, often stress the moral lesson of a given story. It is easy to see how tests keyed with one emphasis or the other

could seriously underrate a person from a different cultural or linguistic background (APA, 1990).

Subgroup Norming

During the 1980s, the U.S. Employment Service (USES) determined that an aptitude test used for referring job applicants to employers was having an adverse impact on the candidacy of members of ethnic minority groups, especially African Americans and Hispanics (Brown, 1994). In an effort to reduce the unfavorable impact of such testing on these groups, the USES made a decision to use within-group scoring, also known as subgroup norming. This practice resulted in percentile scores based on ethnic group membership. The practice has remained controversial among psychologists, civil rights activists, and legislators. In the context of so-called reverse discrimination, matters culminated with passage of the Civil Rights Act of 1991, by which the 102nd Congress banned any form of score adjustment predicated on race, color, religion, sex, or national origin (Public Law 102-166, Section 106).

A special section of the *American Psychologist* focused on this issue (Brown, 1994; Gottfredson, 1994; Sackett & Wilk, 1994). The articles trace the agony of behavioral scientists and psychometricians who find themselves drawn into public policy debates that alternately cast them as social advocates and as threats to the compromise of personnel selection science. From our perspective, however, this debate is not a matter of test bias so much as an attempt to use psychological assessment methods to resolve social and political problems. Some would argue that testing contributed to the origin of the problem, but one need look only to Matarazzo's (1990) distinction between psychological *testing* and psychological *assessment* to understand that the problem is not the tests. Rather, the difficulty lies with users who focus on easily gathered test scores instead of comprehensive assessments. As is too often the case, society would like inexpensive and easy solutions to complex assessment problems and will find those willing to deliver services that fit the demand.

Classic Test Case Litigation

Since major litigation has revolved about the issue of test bias, it seems reasonable to summarize some of the key cases here. We focus on two major cases in which issues of test bias were raised.

Griggs v. Duke Power Company

The case of *Griggs v. Duke Power Company* (1971) became the first major challenge to employment tests (Bersoff, 1981) and grew out of an objection to the legality of using general ability tests to hire and promote employees in a private company. Employees of African-American ancestry cited the 1964 Civil Rights Act, claiming that the practice of test usage constituted a form of racial discrimination. While the employer acknowledged that few people of color were employed or promoted and that the test may have had a prejudicial impact, the company claimed no intent to discriminate. A unanimous Supreme Court decision held that discriminatory practices were actionable regardless of whether the form is fair as long as the result is discriminatory. When statistical data were produced showing the disproportionate impact on Black workers, the court faulted the company for using broad and general testing devices (Bersoff, 1981). The court introduced the concept of "job relatedness" as critical to the valid use of personnel testing. That is, the human attributes measured by the test must be clearly relevant to the duties performed in the particular job.

Larry P. v. Riles

In the class action lawsuit *Larry P. v. Riles* (1979), the federal courts prohibited the use of standardized intelligence tests as a means of identifying educable mentally retarded (EMR) Black children or for placing such children in EMR classes. This case began because Black children had become disproportionately over-represented in such classes, and the primary basis for such placement in California (at that time) focused on such tests (Lambert, 1981; Powers, Hagans-Murillo, & Restori, 2004). At-torneys for the children argued that the test items originated from White, middle-class culture, that Whites had more advantages and opportunities than children of color, and that language used by Black or Latino children may not correspond to that used in the test. In addition, they noted that the motivation of some ethnic minority children to perform on the tests may have been adversely influenced by the race of the examiners, who were mostly White, and that the number of children of color in the standardization sample was very low.

The type of problem demonstrated in the *Larry P.* case is essentially a validity issue. That is, the test was being used for making a type of discrimination or judgment for which it was neither intended nor validated. Use of a single psychometric instrument as the sole or primary criterion in making critical educational or other life decisions fails to consider each individual as a whole being in a specific life context. Such lack of comprehensive assessment is a frequent type of test misuse (Moreland, Eyde, Robertson, Primoff, & Most, 1995).

PASE v. Hannon

In the case of *PASE v. Hannon* (1980), a federal court in Illinois reached the opposite decision from its West Coast counterpart in the *Larry P.* case. The court permitted continued use of psychological tests in special education placement decision making. This contrast is of interest because many of the same psychological experts testified in both cases, both cases were under active judicial review simultaneously, and the outcomes were quite different. One might be tempted to read these cases as a contrast or contradiction in the legal system. We believe the contrasting opinions are best viewed as context specific. That is, the court was most likely convinced that use of the psychometric tools in Illinois was more appropriate to the context than was the use of the same instruments by the psychologists in the San Francisco school district. The fact that two different judges and sets of facts were involved, however, makes a definitive conclusion on the legal merits impossible. The point is that the clinician who becomes involved in testing to be used for critical decision making bears an especially heavy ethical burden to ensure the data are applied in an appropriate scientific context that does not unfairly discriminate against any individual being assessed. (As an aside, it is somewhat ironic that the judge in the *PASE* case permitted the standard questions and keyed answers to the intelligence tests used to become a part of the public record of the trial. The court clearly had little concern for the matter of test security.)

The use of psychological tests for the educational classification and tracking of children in cases such as these was unethical in our judgment for three reasons: (1) The tests were not well suited for the sort of fair differentiation needed; (2) scores were being used inappropriately as paramount criteria for complex decisions affecting the lives of people; and (3) psychologists were not sufficiently sensitive to the flaws in their instruments and the manner in which these flaws could adversely affect the lives of others. There was little recognition of the tests' contribution to broader repressive social policies. It is incumbent on the psychometrician who uses intelligence tests to be sensitive to these issues and to take steps to ensure that the assessment is not used to the detriment of the person tested.

Atkins v. Virginia

Around midnight on August 16, 1996, Daryl Renard Atkins and William Jones abducted Eric Nesbitt. They took his money and drove him to an automated teller machine in his pickup truck; cameras recorded them withdrawing additional cash. They then took him to an isolated location where he was shot eight times and killed (*Atkins v. Virginia*, 2002).

After trial and conviction for capital murder, the defense relied on one witness during the penalty phase of the trial, Evan Nelson, Ph.D., a forensic psychologist. Dr. Nelson had evaluated Atkins before trial and concluded that he was "mildly mentally retarded." Dr. Nelson based his conclusion on interviews with people who knew Atkins, a review of school and court records, and the scores from a Weschler intelligence test indicating that Atkins had a full-scale IQ of 59.

The jury sentenced Atkins to death, but the Virginia Supreme Court ordered a second sentencing hearing because the trial court had used a misleading verdict form. At the resentencing, Dr. Nelson testified again. The state presented an expert rebuttal witness, Stanton Samenow, Ph.D., who expressed the opinion that Atkins was not mentally retarded but rather had "average intelligence, at least," and he offered a diagnosis of antisocial personality disorder. Samenow noted that Atkins's vocabulary, general knowledge, and behavior suggested that he possessed at least average intelligence. As a result, the jury again sentenced Atkins to death and the Virginia Supreme Court upheld the sentence.

In a 6-to-3 decision, the U.S. Supreme Court overturned the decision, noting two reasons consistent with the general legislative consensus that mentally retarded persons should be categorically excluded from execution. The court noted that the primary justifications for imposing the death penalty remain retribution and deterrence of capital crimes by prospective offenders. The Court found that executing the mentally retarded violates the Eighth Amendment's ban on cruel and unusual punishments. The APA had filed an amicus brief with the Court (see http://www.apa.org/psyclaw/atkins-v-va.html) addressing a range of issues, including established procedures for evaluating the presence of mental retardation and the attributes of such conditions that relate to criminal sentencing.

Ironically, although Atkins's case and ruling may have saved other mentally retarded inmates from the death penalty, a jury in Virginia subsequently decided in July, 2005, that he was intelligent enough to be executed because the constant contact he had with his lawyers had intellectually stimulated him and raised his IQ above 70, making him competent for execution under Virginia law. The prosecution had argued that the cause of his poor school performance originated with his use of alcohol and drugs, and that his lower scores in earlier IQ tests were not accurate representations of his true ability. His execution date was set for December 2, 2005, but the Virginia Supreme Court ultimately reversed his death sentence again on procedural grounds. On the one hand, this case raises significant ethical issues by placing psychological test data at the core of a life-or-death decision (Brodsky & Galloway, 2003; Koocher, 2003). On the other hand, the case raises the more ironic question about whether interacting with one's attorney can increase a person's IQ.

USER COMPETENCE

Although we have thus far focused chiefly on basic concepts in testing and issues in test adequacy, many of the examples we have cited raise issues of test user competency or, more accurately, incompetence on the part of some test users. Clearly, appropriate utilization of psychological tests involves much more than simply recording responses and totaling the score. Moreland and his colleagues (1995) described 86 test user competencies and seven factors accounting for most test misuse. Examples of the 86 competencies include the following:

- avoiding errors in scoring
- keeping scoring keys and test materials secure
- making certain that examinees follow directions
- refraining from coaching or training individuals on test items
- establishing rapport with examinees to obtain accurate scores
- using settings that allow for optimum test performance

The seven most common misuse factors noted by Moreland and his colleagues (1995) were the following:

1. Lack of a comprehensive assessment.
2. Improper test use.
3. Lack of psychometric knowledge.
4. Failure to maintain integrity of test results.
5. Inaccurate scoring.
6. Inappropriate use of norms.
7. Inadequate interpretive feedback.

The APA has also weighed in on the issue with a comprehensive report on test user qualifications (Turner, DeMers, Fox, & Reed, 2001). The competence issues, discussed in Chapter 4, are generally related to this point; however, testing also involves a special subset of competence problems. Many standardized psychological instruments seem deceptively easy to administer and score, requiring little or no formal training. However, the accurate interpretation and application of these instruments, as well as placing the test data in the context of the individual's life, become a much more complex matter entirely. In addition to training issues, we next raise a number of special ethical problems related to diagnosis, test security, and sale of tests to unqualified users.

Training Issues

How much and what types of training should the profession require as a prerequisite for designation as a "qualified" user of psychological tests (Bartram, 2001; Ekstrom, Elmore, & Schafer, 1997; Koene, 1997; Rupert, Kozlowski, Hoffman, Daniels, & Piette, 1999; Turner et al., 2001)? At times, individuals who do not meet APA's standards as qualified users have asserted claims of their ability to offer assessment services to the public (Clawson, 1997). The APA and state psychological associations have historically supported legislation that would allow only licensed psychologists to use most psychological tests (APA 02: 9.07).

The answer to the qualified user question becomes complicated when one considers the type of test, the use to which it is put, and the setting in which it is applied. For example, at present psychologists can successfully complete an APA-approved doctoral program in clinical psychology without ever having administered a projective personality assessment technique (e.g., the Rorschach inkblots or Thematic Apperception Test). Some would argue that mandatory course work in statistics, individual differences, personality theory, abnormal psychology, and cognitive processes should precede undertaking comprehensive psychological assessments. If the evaluator intends to practice in organizational or industrial settings, course work in organizational behavior, personnel law, and similar fields might be necessary prerequisites. If a school setting is to be the primary workplace, a psychologist may need additional course work in curriculum planning and educational theory prior to undertaking assessments. Few standards currently exist to specify the minimum competence needed to perform each assessment task adequately, and psychologists are generally left to address this matter on the basis of their own awareness of their competencies and limitations. Sometimes, this is an effective means of control, but at other times it is not.

Case 9–11: Dinah Saur, Psy.D., hired Mary Smurf to work in her private practice. Ms. Smurf had a B.A. degree in psychology, and Dr. Saur gave her a few hours training in the administration of the Wechsler tests, Thematic Apperception Test, and Rorschach inkblots. Dr. Saur would interview referred clients for about 10 minutes and then send them to Ms. Smurf, who would administer the tests she prescribed. Dr. Saur would then prepare and sign evaluation reports based on the data Smurf collected.

Dr. Saur has provided only minimal supervision and training to her relatively unqualified assistant. She then bases her reports on a superficial interview and data collected by a person not sufficiently trained to administer complex tests or to note the subtler aspects of meaningful variations in test behavior. The reactions of the client to certain test stimuli may go unrecorded. The nuance of a response, which may tend to suggest one meaning or interpretation over another, could be lost. Furthermore, Dr Saur seems to make no effort to ensure quality control of the process. In some ways, Dr. Saur is actually offering an impersonal service and giving the impression that she has conducted an evaluation when she has actually had only minimal direct contact with the client.

Case 9–12: Dexter Dendrite, Psy.D., had a busy neuropsychology assessment practice. He hired Sandra Synapse, M.Ed., who had worked for many years as a school psychologist, to assist him. In addition to her master's degree in education, Ms. Synapse had taken many continuing professional education courses to learn new assessment tools, and Dr. Dendrite trained and observed her in the administration of several neuropsychological instruments. Dendrite would meet with each client, review the client's history, speak with the referral source, and develop an assessment plan with Ms. Synapse. She would then administer the tests, score them, and provide her clinical observations. Dr. Dendrite would check the scoring and integrate the test data and other information into a single report that both he and Ms. Synapse would sign.

Some psychologists have questioned the use of individuals without a psychology license to administer psychological tests. The controversy has become fodder for discussion among clinicians, professional organizations, state and provincial boards of psychology, state governments, departments of education, and third-party health care insurers (Hall, Howerton, & Bolin, 2005). Unlike Dr. Saur in Case 9–11, Dr. Dendrite has taken a number of steps to ensure the quality of his work by hiring a skilled assistant, staying closely involved with her training, carefully monitoring her work, and jointly owning responsibility for the final product.

Case 9–13: Sandra Toddler, Ph.D., had specialized in clinical child psychology, although her course work and practica had always involved school-age children and their families. When she began to receive referrals for assessment of developmentally delayed infants and children under age 4, she ordered copies of several developmental instruments (e.g., Bayley Scales of Infant Development, etc.), read the manuals, and began using them in her practice.

Dr. Toddler may be bright and sensitive enough to learn the administration of new instruments from their manuals rather quickly. Is she qualified, however, to assess the meaning of the data and integrate it with other information to produce a valid and useful assessment? We really can not tell from the information provided. If Toddler were more attentive to her ethical responsibilities, she probably would have sought some consultation, supervision, training, or any combination of these from a colleague with expertise in infant assessment. Toddler could then, with a meaningful basis of comparison, be able to gauge her own competence and weakness on the tasks at hand.

Case 9–14: Norris Nemo, Ed.D., earned his degree in counseling psychology, and his doctoral program included supervised course work in the use of intelligence, personality, and vocational guidance assessment tools. He approached several large companies to offer "placement and exit counseling" services to their personnel offices.

Dr. Nemo seems rather naive. We can not know with certainty what he means by placement and exit counseling, and we do not know whether he has any background in personnel assessment or organizational consultation. He may not even recognize that he may well lack the typical qualifications expected of practitioners offering such services. On the other hand, he may indeed have the competence to offer the services he proposes, but these might not align with the needs of potential client–companies. Perhaps Nemo mistakenly assumes that vocational preference and IQ are the most important factors in successful job functioning. All we know for certain is that Nemo seems to have reached out to offer assessment in areas for which his training has not adequately prepared him.

Each of the last four cases cited demonstrates a need for awareness of adequate or necessary training across a variety of assessment activities. Although we would like to believe that there are few grounds for concern of this sort in day-to-day practice, a study by Smith and Dumont (1995) provides little reassurance. They found a group of psychologists all too willing to offer interpretive statements based on casual use of a poorly validated instrument for which they had little or no training. The clinicians tended to use the data at hand to find support for initial diagnoses (i.e., confirmatory bias) with an embarrassing lack of scientific rigor.

Diagnosis

Assigning a diagnostic label can have very serious consequences for a client. We address this issue in our discussion of confidentiality (Chapter 8), but the point is well illustrated in Hobbs's (1975) source books on issues in the classification of children, in which issues such as the adverse consequences of labeling and self-fulfilling prophecies are discussed. Classic works by Szasz (1970) and Goffman (1961) highlight the labeling problem for mentally ill adults, whereas Mercer (1973) documented similar adverse consequences for those labeled mentally retarded. Since psychological test data at least occasionally become the basis for applying diagnostic labels, it seems critical that those using tests for that purpose remain appropriately cautious and sensitive to potential alternatives.

Case 9–15: Kevin Bartley, age 15, arrived at a psychiatric facility accompanied by his mother, who demanded hospitalization for him. She felt overwhelmed by her life situation, including a divorce in progress and other young children at home. Kevin's truancy and problem behavior at home had become too much for her. Because Kevin was a minor, the psychiatrist on duty admitted Kevin despite the boy's objections and in the process assigned a psychiatric diagnosis. Several months later, the courts ordered Kevin's discharge (*Bartley v. Kremens*, 1975). Some time after his 18th birthday, Kevin was denied a municipal job because of his "history of psychiatric illness."

The case of Kevin Bartley has particular significance because his hospitalization arose as much because of his family situation as out of any psychopathology he may have had. He was "diagnosed," and that diagnosis had very real adverse consequences for him when he later sought employment. This occurred in spite of a federal court decision, which suggested that he ought not to have been hospitalized in the first place.

Case 9–16: Carla Split sought the services of Jack Label, Ph.D., to assist her in coping more effectively with a variety of emotional issues. Dr. Label asked her to complete some paper-and-pencil personality inventories and then offered her his diagnostic impression. Ms. Split, according to Dr. Label, was "a psychopath from the waist down and schizoid from the waist up." Ms. Split felt very upset by these rather unusual diagnoses. She had never heard of them, could not find reference to them in books she consulted, and began to believe that she had a major mental illness in view of the "serious diagnoses."

Dr. Label seems a proponent of the creative school of diagnostic psychopathology. It appears that he offered a rather rapid diagnosis of Ms. Split but failed to explain it adequately. In addition, he used an idiosyncratic, jargon-laden term that struck the client as more frightening than helpful. Even when a diagnosis based on valid data and a legitimate classification system properly applies, the terms should not be tossed off lightly to clients. In Dr. Label's case, one wonders how much thought he gave to the actual assessment, as well as to the capricious and demeaning terminology.

Case 9–17: Ivan Meek, age 7, transferred to the Rocky Coast School when his family moved to town from another part of the country. Ivan, shy and socially withdrawn, could not establish much rapport with Helen Brash, Ed.D., the school psychologist asked to assist in placing him in the proper class. Dr. Brash, very busy with the start of the new school year, recommended placing Ivan in a special education class on the basis of a 15-minute interview, during which she administered some "screening tests." Ivan spent 3 years in classes with mildly to moderately retarded youngsters before a full evaluation revealed him to have average intellectual ability. During the 3 years, the school system made no effort to assess his potential or to investigate the emotional issues that contributed to his shyness and withdrawal because most of the personnel simply assumed mental retardation by virtue of the placement Dr. Brash had suggested.

The situation in the case of Ivan Meek and Dr. Brash illustrates two major problems with labels and diagnoses. One can acquire either easily or by inference, and they may stick for a long time, much to the client's detriment. If we assume that Dr. Brash felt overworked, we might excuse some initial haste and misjudgment. Apparently, however, she forgot about Ivan, failed to check with his prior school, did not order any follow-up evaluation, and did not apply any of a number of standardized assessment tools that might have proved more accurate than her quick judgment. Teachers and

parents will often defer to professional judgment, and in Ivan's case it took 3 years for meaningful recognition of his needs and correction of the initial misclassification.

Cases 9–7, 9–8, and 9–10 provide additional examples of the risks of misdiagnosis based on psychological test data. Discussion of actuarial prediction and automated test scoring programs illustrate an extension of this hazard. This type of problem seems most likely to occur when assessment fails to consider all relevant evidence, including nontest data, such as data learned in history taking or with other interview techniques. Certainly, any psychologist who intends to use psychological test instruments for psychodiagnostic purposes should have completed formal studies related to these issues.

Strange as it may seem, in some circumstances a diagnostic label may become desirable or even sought by a particular client. For example, a diagnosis of learning disabilities might result in the ability to obtain special educational services or unique consideration at college examination time. In some court-related circumstances (*Atkins v. Virginia*, 2002; Brodsky & Galloway, 2003), certain diagnoses may suggest a lack of criminal responsibility or mitigating factors, leading to a reduced sentence. Some diagnoses might result in the ability to obtain disability insurance payments, while other diagnoses would not. Regardless of the client's preference, a psychologist should never offer a diagnostic assessment without adequate supporting data. The value of psychological assessment arises from the examiners' integrity as well as from their clinical skills.

Test Security

Well-conceptualized and carefully standardized assessment tools require considerable development effort and expense. The validity and utility of many such instruments could suffer serious compromise if their security were violated (APA 02: 9.11). Some tests also have substantial potential for abuse in the hands of untrained individuals, and publishers therefore restrict access to individuals trained in their use and application. Such security is not always easy to maintain, and any persistent person can obtain substantial "secure" test information by accessing journals, textbooks in major university libraries, or Internet sources (LoBello & Zachar, 2007; Ruiz, Drake, Glass, Marcotte, & van Gorp, 2002). Ample proof exists to show that as far back as the 1970s a moderately clever nonprofessional could easily obtain copies of secure test materials (Oles & Davis, 1977). So-called truth-in-testing statutes enacted during the 1980s in some states mandated public access to certain types of group-administered educational placement, achievement, and admissions tests (e.g., Scholastic Aptitude Tests [SATs] and Graduate Record Examinations [GREs]), along with the correct answers. Consider some cases for which the security of specialized clinical instruments was violated.

Case 9–18: A reporter working on a story about IQ testing sought an interview with Harlan Simp, Ph.D. During the course of the interview, Dr. Simp showed the reporter a test manual and many items from the WAIS-III. Subsequently, the reporter wrote an article for a national magazine, "How to Score High on IQ Tests." In the article, the reporter revealed 70% to 80% of the verbal questions on the test, along with practice hints and other clues linked to the items he had seen.

Dr. Simp felt outraged and embarrassed when he saw the reporter's article, but there was little he could do. In attempting to be "open and candid with a member of the press," he had inappropriately shared material he should have treated as confidential. The impact of the article in terms of inflated and invalid scores is obviously unknown.

Case 9–19: Adolph Snitler, Psy.D., wrote a book popular with the public about notorious criminals. The book included reduced black-and-white reproductions of the Rorschach inkblots, along with lists of common responses to the same stimuli.

For his book on notorious criminals, Dr. Snitler had sought and been granted permission by the publisher to reprint copies of the Rorschach plates in achromatic reduced-size format. Many clinicians would assert that doing so and listing common responses represent a serious unethical act. Others would note that one could easily find more detailed Rorschach textbooks available in public areas of many university libraries and suggest that the impact of reading such a book on potential test takers' subsequent performance is questionable. While a psychologically well-adjusted individual of sophisticated ability might have the ability to fake a disturbed Rorschach protocol, it seems most unlikely that a troubled client could muster the psychological resources to simulate a psychologically sound protocol no matter what information was available in the public domain. Again, the impact of this disclosure remains unknown, although the author certainly used questionable professional judgment.

Case 9–20: An executive of a large corporation qualified as one of a group of candidates for promotion to a major position in that organization. The company required all candidates to take some psychological tests administered by a psychologist as part of the selection process. The executive arranged a confidential consultation with Seb Vert, Ph.D., a psychologist with training in personnel selection, to help him prepare for the tests. Dr. Vert discussed a number of the potential test instruments and even suggested response styles that might help the executive to seem most appealing in the final assessment.

Dr. Vert regards himself as helpful to his client, the executive. Consulting on the general matter of how to "look good" in a specific type of interview situation does not necessarily constitute ethical misconduct. However, Vert's apparent willingness to reveal suggested responses to confidential test items to the client crosses the ethical threshold. In so doing, Vert may invalidate an instrument in secret, with the intent of undermining the objective ethical work of any colleagues who subsequently attempt to assess the candidate, unaware of his coaching.

Wetter and Corrigan (1995) surveyed a group of lawyers and law students and found nearly half of attorneys and fully a third of law students believed that clients referred for testing should be informed about the existence of validity scales for some psychological tests. Some lawyers also believed that it is appropriate to coach clients prior to such testing. Cooperation with such coaching by a psychologist would clearly be unethical as such conduct would undermine the validity of the instrument. At the same time, it is not inappropriate for a psychologist to advise an assessment client that some test scales may reveal atypical responses, unusual defensiveness, or other such response styles.

One can help prepare people for assessment and reduce anxiety by giving information that will not compromise the integrity of the assessment. Consider the following case:

Case 9–21: Tran Quility, Psy.D., routinely takes time to establish rapport with clients prior to beginning data collection during psychological assessment. This includes asking clients whether they have undergone testing previously and they understand the purpose of the assessment. When administering the MMPI-II, Dr. Quility explains that psychologists use the instrument with a wide range of people, including those with serious mental illness and normal folks. He notes that, as a result of the range of personality factors covered, some questions may seem odd or unrelated to the client. He urges them to simply respond as honestly as possible and not to feel rushed.

Dr. Quility's comments and attitude will go a long way to put many clients at ease, while not betraying any confidential data or engaging in coaching.

A related area of conflict in professional opinion involves the question of whether third parties (e.g., a child client's parents or a client's attorney) should be allowed to sit in on testing sessions (National Academy of Neuropsychology, 2000b). In general, we do not recommend permitting the presence of third parties as this could compromise test security and potentially lead to some response bias. However, we recognize that some forensic circumstances or situations involving clients with communication difficulties may necessitate the involvement of third parties.

High-Stakes Testing

The term *high-stakes tests* refers to cognitively loaded instruments designed to assess knowledge, skill, and ability with the intent of making employment, academic admission, graduation, or licensing decisions. For a number of public policy and political reasons, these testing programs face considerable scrutiny and criticism (Haney, Madaus, & Lyons, 1993; Sackett, Schmitt, Ellingson, & Kabin, 2001). Such testing includes the SAT, GRE, state examinations that establish graduation requirements, and professional or job entry examinations. Such tests can prove very useful but are also subject to misuse and a degree of tyranny in the sense that individuals' rights and welfare are easily lost in the face of corporate advantage and political struggles about accountability in education.

In May 2001, the APA issued a statement on such testing: "Appropriate Use of High Stakes Testing in Our Nation's Schools" (see: http://www.apa.org/pubinfo/testing.html). The statement noted that the measurement of learning and achievement are important, and that tests, when used properly, are among the most sound and objective ways to measure student performance. However, when test results are used inappropriately, they can have highly damaging unintended consequences. High-stakes decisions such as high school graduation or college admissions should not be made on the basis of a single set of test scores that only provide a "snapshot" of student achievement. Such scores may not accurately reflect a student's progress and achievement and do not provide much insight into other critical components of future success, such as motivation and character. The APA statement recommends that any decision about a student's continued education, retention in grade, tracking, or graduation should *not* be based on the results of a single test.

The APA statement noted:

- When test results substantially contribute to decisions made about student promotion or graduation, there should be evidence that the test addresses only the specific or generalized content and skills that students have had an opportunity to learn.
- When a school district, state, or some other authority mandates a test, the ways in which the test results are intended to be used should be clearly described. It is also the responsibility of those who mandate the test to mon-

itor its impact, particularly on racial and ethnic minority students or students of lower socioeconomic status, and to identify and minimize potential negative consequences of such testing.

- In some cases, special accommodations for students with limited English proficiency may be necessary to obtain valid test scores. If students with limited English skills are to be tested in English, their test scores should be interpreted in light of their limited English skills. For example, when a student lacks proficiency in the language in which the test is given (students for whom English is a second language, for example), the test could become a measure of their ability to communicate in English rather than a measure of other skills.
- Likewise, special accommodations may be needed to ensure that test scores are valid for students with disabilities. Not enough is currently known about how particular test modifications may affect the test scores of students with disabilities; more research is needed. As a first step, test developers should include students with disabilities in field testing of pilot tests and document the impact of particular modifications (if any) for test users.
- Test results should also be reported by sex, race/ethnicity, income level, disability status, and degree of English proficiency for evaluation purposes.

One adverse consequence of high-stakes testing is that some schools will almost certainly focus primarily on "teaching to the test" skills acquisition. Students prepared in this way may do well on the test but find it difficult to generalize their learning beyond that context and may find themselves unprepared for critical and analytic thinking in their subsequent learning environments. Some testing companies, such as the Educational Testing Service, developers of the SAT, at one time claimed that coaching or teaching to the test would have little meaningful impact and still publicly attempt to minimize the potential effect of coaching or teaching to the test. Amusingly, while maintaining that stance in public statements, ETS simultaneously offered and continues to market test preparation books for sale at a profit.

Perhaps the best rebuttal to such assertions is the career of Stanley H. Kaplan. An article in *The New Yorker* (Gladwell, 2001) documented not only Kaplan's long career as an entrepreneurial educator but also the fragility of "test security" and the ability to teach strategies to significantly improve test scores in exactly the way the industry claimed was impossible. When Kaplan began coaching students on the SAT in the 1950s and holding posttest pizza parties to debrief the students and learn about what was being asked, he was considered a kind of subverter of the system. Because the designers of the SAT viewed their work as developing a measure of enduring abilities (such as IQ), they assumed that coaching would do little to alter scores. Test designers seem to have given little thought to the notion that people are affected by what they learn, and that what they learn is affected by what they are taught (Gladwell, 2001). In addition, school curricula undergo change because of pressures from educators and parents. They typically respond to high-stakes testing by supporting curricula and teaching aimed at yielding higher scores. Kaplan's methods have helped many students to improve their test scores, notwithstanding the cautions of the test developers.

THE TESTING INDUSTRY

As the discussion of high-stakes testing illustrates, psychological testing has become big business. Apart from publishers who develop and revise test kits and computerized assessment tools, many large and small corporations develop and market assessment tools for mass testing markets. In fact, because many managed mental health benefit programs require special approval before agreeing to pay for individualized testing, psychologists are doing less of it, and the profitability of some expensive test kits palls by comparison with the profit margins of entities conducting large group testing programs. Finding accurate numbers regarding corporate revenues related to the testing industry has become complicated because of corporate buyouts and consolidated revenue reports. One account from the 1970s (Kohn, 1975) noted that American school systems spent in excess of $24 million annually in the early 1970s on testing secondary and elementary school children. Inflation alone would have grown that number to over a $ 1 billion annually by 2007.

Despite secretiveness about income related directly to their testing services, Haney and his colleagues (1993) estimated gross revenues of several major testing companies for 1987–1988 as follows (numbers in parentheses convert the 1998 dollars to their 2006 equivalent, corrected for inflation): ETS, $226 million ($387million); National Computer Systems, $242 million ($414 million); The Psychological Corporation (a division of Harcourt General), $50 million to $55 million ($86 million to $94 million); and the American College Testing Program, $53 million ($91 million). The actual revenues most likely reach much higher numbers, given the increased number of people taking the tests and the increased number of testing instruments for sale, particularly following the significant increase in high-stakes testing mandated under recent changes in state and federal law.

The spread of consumerism in America has seen increasing assaults on the testing industry and well-reasoned papers on test ethics from within the industry itself (Eyde et al., 1993; Haney et al., 1993; Kaplan, 1982; Messick, 1980; Reckase, 1998). Most of the ethical complaints leveled at the larger companies fall into the categories of marketing, sales to unauthorized users (Dattilio, Tresco, & Siegel, in press; Lo-Bello & Zachar, 2007), and the problem of so-called impersonal services. Publishers claim that they do make good-faith efforts to police sales so that only qualified users obtain tests. They note that they can not control the behavior of individuals in institutions to which tests are sent, and one could argue that documented episodes of improper sales involved at least a modicum of deception (Oles & Davis, 1977). Since test publishers must advertise in the media provided by organized psychology to influence their prime market, most major firms are also especially responsive to letters of concern from psychologists and committees of the APA. The use of automated testing services, however, raised a number of potential ethical issues that lead to frequent inquiries (Dattilio et al., in press).

Automated Testing Services

The advent of the computer age made possible the bulk scoring and analysis of test data, creation of new profile systems, and generation by computer of reports that spring from the printer untouched by human hands or comment. As this period dawned, psychologists argued about the advantages of clinical versus actuarial prediction (Dawes, Faust, & Meehl, 2002; Garb, 2005; Holt, 1970; Meehl, 1954, 1997). That is, can a computer-generated, statistically driven, actuarial diagnosis or prediction be more accurate and useful than predictions by clinicians in practice? We do not take sides in that debate, but simply note more recent developments (APA 02: 9.09).

Automated testing services and software can be a major boon to psychologists' practices and significantly enhance the accuracy and sophistication of diagnostic decision making, but there are important caveats to observe. Those who offer assessment or scoring services to other professionals should accurately describe the purpose, norms, validity, reliability, and applications of the procedures and any special qualifications applicable to their use. Those who use such scoring and interpretation services should select them based on evidence of the validity of the program and analytic procedures. In every case, ethical practitioners retain responsibility for the appropriate application, interpretation, and use of assessment instruments, whether they score and interpret such tests themselves or use automated or other services (APA 02: 9.09).

Computerization clearly presents a wide assortment of clinical and ethical challenges for those conducting clinical assessments. Several large testing corporations offer test scoring services to mental health professionals and provide nearly instant results based on a scanned or faxed score sheet or on responses entered by a client from an office-based computer terminal. Other software products enable local installation of sophisticated assessment software on a range of desktop, laptop, or handheld devices. Users may have the ability to obtain test scores or interpretive report services. In the latter circumstance, the computer can generate narrative paragraphs or simple statements describing the client diagnostically in terms of personality traits, vocational interests, or any of a number of other declarative or predictive ways.

Such applications have significant ethical implications for clinicians, client/responders, and those who construct or administer assessment systems. A lack of sophistication regarding hardware- or software-related issues may undermine clinicians' ability to ethically perform computerized psychological assessments. Both graduate students and practicing clinicians need exposure to ethical concerns, potential judgment errors, and pitfalls in evaluating computer-generated reports (Schulenberg & Yutrzenka, 2004). For example, the effects of computerization on item response theory, test designs, and emerging new item types on assessment practices demand attention (Hambleton, 2006). A comprehensive set of international guidelines on computer-based and Internet-delivered testing exists, but remains mostly unknown to American practitioners and graduate students (Lievens, 2006). Special ethical concerns also come into play around computer-based testing for professional licensing (Melnick & Clauser, 2006) and school-based use of computerized psychological assessment measures (Knauss, 2001).

Although one can expect that computer programs will become increasingly important for psychological assessment, many automated assessment programs and statistical prediction rules offer limited value. For example, validity may not be clearly established for many automated assessment programs. Statistical-prediction rules may have limited value because they typically originate with sample populations or models that flow from limited information without significant statistical power. Garb (2000) offered significant recommendations for ethically building, evaluating, and applying new computerized assessment programs.

Many assessment instruments originally developed for research have increasingly found their way into clinical practice as outcome measures or assessment tools. It seems reasonable to expect that innovative clinicians will increasingly seek to adapt such tools for computerized administration and interpretation. Garb (2007) attempted to assist psychologists in deciding on

the appropriateness of adapting interviews and rating scales for routine administration using computers. He focused on comparison of structured and unstructured assessment instruments, advantages and disadvantages of computer administration, and the validity and utility of computer-administered instruments.

One particular difficulty in the use of automated testing is the aura of validity conveyed by the adjective "computerized" and its synonyms. Aside from the long-standing debate within psychology about the merits of actuarial versus clinical prediction noted above, some people display a kind of magical faith that numbers and graphs generated by a computer program somehow equate with increased validity of some sort. Too often, skilled clinicians do not fully educate themselves about the underpinnings of various analytic models. Even when a clinician is so inclined, the copyright holders of the analytic program may be reluctant to share too much information lest they compromise their property rights.

In the end, the most reasonable approach involves recognizing that automated scoring and interpretive services comprise but one component of an evaluation and to carefully probe any apparently discrepant findings. This suggestion will not surprise most competent psychologists, but unfortunately they are not the only ones using these tools. Many users of such tests are nonpsychologists with little understanding of the interpretive subtleties. Some will take the computer-generated reports as valid on their face without considering important factors that make a client unique. A few users are simply looking for a quick-and-dirty source of data to help them make or justify a decision in the absence of clinical acumen. Other users inflate the actual cost of the tests and scoring services to enhance their own billings. When making use of such tools, psychologists should have a well-reasoned strategy for incorporating them in the assessment and interpret them with well-informed caution.

One obvious hazard involves lazy or incompetent practitioners, psychologists and non-psychologists alike, who rely on artificial intelligence and programmers' skills. One mailing brought us news of a new office system available to psychologists who wish to find "improved patient care, increased interaction time, and cost efficiency" by administering and interpreting some 20 different scales, indices, checklists, surveys, inventories, and schedules. Areas covered include intelligence, child development, personality, vocational preference, somatic problems, symptoms, and a measure of "depression and hopelessness." Can a commercial enterprise ignore a marketplace expansion opportunity for the sake of ethics, even if it is unregulated by government? Consider the following cases:

Case 9–22: A firm providing computer-generated MMPI-II interpretive reports ran an advertisement in the *APA Monitor* promoting a "sample kit" and everything one needs to use their service for a $50 trial offer. The coupon stated that one must be a qualified user but did not specify what this means and sought no evidence from responders. Subsequently, the same company solicited psychiatrists in a direct-mail invitation to use the service.

Case 9–23: Ann O. Vation, M.S.W., licensed social worker, makes use of computer-generated vocational guidance interest reports to offer career counseling to her clients in an effort to expand her practice.

Both of these cases illustrate the reach of the automated testing services to professionals outside psychology, as well as an emphasis on attracting new clients with little attention to the nuance of qualifications. The companies would argue that this is a clinician-to-clinician service, and the practitioner holds responsibility for use of the material. Representatives of such companies would also note that their interpretive reports are replete with cautions and warnings about the use of data. They might also argue that psychiatrists (or other physicians), social workers, marriage and family counselors, and other licensed mental health professionals have a right to such services. On the other hand, given that so many psychologists lack training to use certain complex psychometric tools, we must wonder how many nonpsychologist mental health service providers understand the complexities and proper use of these instruments. Such sales represent a serious ethical problem.

Case 9–24: An urban police department planned a civil service examination for new recruits and recognized the need to screen out psychologically troubled individuals. Because they could not afford to provide individual in-depth interviews for several hundred candidates, the department decided to use a computer-scored personality inventory as a sieve. Those candidates with deviant scores were selected for personal screening interviews to rule out serious psychopathology.

This case represents a fairly appropriate use of the instrument, but something interesting happened. A substantial portion of the applicants obtained "grossly deviant" scores. It seems that the hundreds of true/false items on the personality inventory came at the end of a day-long exam. Many of the candidates felt exhausted and found the items "silly" or "stupid." The purpose of the test was not explained by the civil service clerks administering the examination, so many candidates left most of the items blank, responded randomly, or "checked off the weird answers to gross out the administrators of the program."

Tyranny in the Marketplace

When a commercial testing company dominates a niche of the marketplace, a degree of tyranny can occasionally lead to abuses of the consumer. The fact that the companies involved were founded and are managed by psychologists may offer little reassurance. The following case examples use the actual names of the testing companies involved:

Case 9–25: A high school student took the SAT on two separate occasions. The student's scores improved significantly between the two administrations, but the ETS, which owns and administers the SAT, refused to release the newer, higher score to colleges to which the student had applied. The ETS personnel expressed the belief that the student cheated, citing mysterious statistical analyses they declined to make public. When the student threatened litigation and produced expert psychometric support, ETS offered a substantial settlement without admitting wrongdoing and requiring the student to keep the terms of the settlement confidential (Haney, 1993a, 1993b; Haney et al., 1993).

Case 9–26: The Professional Examination Service (PES) in collaboration with the Association of State and Provincial Psychology Boards (ASPPB) produce and administer the Examination for the Professional Practice of Psychology (EPPP), a multiple-choice examination used nationally in the licensing of psychologists. When state licensing board members previewed a draft copy of the EPPP, they discovered errors on several questions and notified PES. The testing company declined to make appropriate corrections and included three erroneous items in the next version of the EPPP administered nationally. The members of the state licensing board, who knew of the errors, granted licenses to three candidates who had "failed" the exam by virtue of making an "error" on one or more of the faulty questions, and one member of the licensing board wrote a journal article describing the entire incident. When leaders of PES and ASPPB were offered the opportunity to reply to the manuscript, they attempted unsuccessfully to block publication and ceased allowing state licensing boards to preview the draft examinations from that date forward. Representatives of ASPPB subsequently wrote a response that ignored the key issues and avoided mentioning their attempt to stifle publication of the information (Koocher, 1989a, 1989b; Rosen, Reaves, & Hill, 1989).

These cases illustrate that professional ethical codes do not necessarily ensure that psychologically sophisticated testing companies and the psychologists who manage them will act in the best interests of individual consumers, especially when the company holds a complete monopoly (as in the case of PES and ASPPB with respect to psychologists' licensing examinations) or dominates the marketplace (as ETS does with respect to college admissions testing).

Some have suggested that "testing police" should monitor, arbitrate, and enforce the use, administration, and interpretation of all types of psychological testing (Azar, 1994). Such recommendations grow from a sense that those individuals who feel wronged by testing, testers,

or test results have little recourse. The existing standards developed to clarify proper usage lack any enforcement component (AERA et al., 1999), and the standard-setting organizations (i.e., AERA, APA, and NCME) lack the resources or will to become testing police according to senior APA staff (Azar, 1994).

USE OF TEST RESULTS

From the discussion, it is evident that a good test may be ill used, either by inappropriate application or by misuses of the resulting scores. In this section, we raise special questions about access to test results and the potential use or misuse that can result.

Problems of Consent

The issue of informed consent is discussed several times in this book as it is important in all decision-making behavior by clients of mental health professionals. Insofar as assessment is concerned, clients have a right to know the purpose of the evaluation and the use that will be made of the results. They are also entitled to know who will likely have access to the information they provide to the evaluator. Such use and consent problems often arise when the individual who conducts the assessment does so as an agent of an institution or organization. Chapter 18 includes a detailed discussion of ethical dilemmas in special work settings, such as prisons, schools, and industry. Consent as an issue is also discussed in the chapters on psychotherapy, confidentiality, and research (Chapters 5, 6, 8, and 19, respectively). We raise it here to illustrate some of the special consent problems associated with psychological testing.

Consent implies three separate aspects: knowledge, voluntariness, and capacity. Regarding *knowledge*, the person seeking the consent must disclose sufficient information for the person granting consent to understand fully what is being asked. It is not necessary to disclose every potential aspect of the situation, only those facts a reasonable person might need to formulate a decision. *Voluntariness* refers to the absence of coercion, duress, misrepresenta-tion, or undue inducement. *Capacity* refers to legal competence to give consent. All adults are deemed competent to grant consent unless they are found to be incompetent in a court pro-ceeding. (Children are presumed to be incom-petent to grant consent under the law.)

Case 9–27: Sean Battery, Ed.D., was hired to consult with the Central City Fire Department. He put together a series of tests, including the MMPI, Rorschach inkblots, Thematic Apperception Test, Draw-a-Person, and a sentence completion series (i.e., all personality assessment tools) for admin-istration to potential firefighters along with the standard civil service examination. Several of the firefighters protested that such tests constituted an invasion of their privacy.

A complaint by the prospective firefighters seems quite appropriate. Requests that job ap-plicants reveal personal information that is not clearly relevant to the job in question consti-tutes an invasion of privacy (Lefkowitz, 2003; Lowman, 2006). Unless Dr. Battery has some basis for documenting the validity of the per-sonality assessment techniques as firefighter se-lection tools, he appears to have committed an ethics violation.

Case 9–28: Patricia Popquiz, Psy.D., works as a school psychologist for the Central City School Department. She scheduled and supervised the administration of standardized achievement test-ing and IQ testing for all students in Grades 3, 5, 7, and 9, as has routinely occurred over the years. Much to her surprise, several parents complain that their children have been tested without their consent. She responds by saying, "But it was only routine testing!"

Dr. Popquiz sees no problem in continuing what has been the routine practice of the school system for many years. The fact that no one has complained previously does not immunize Popquiz from her responsibility to solicit ap-propriate consent and to remove from the rou-tine testing program any child whose parents or guardians refuse to give consent. Permission

may not be required for some system or state-wide testing related to specific school curricula and given with advance notice, but it certainly is required for intelligence testing. Even rou-tinely collected intelligence test data can have a lasting impact on a child's education and life (Hobbs, 1975). If parents do not know that their child has been tested, they might never know that the scores exist. Inappropriate or erroneous data could not be challenged. While courts have ruled that the right of parents to veto testing is not absolute (Pryzwansky & Bersoff, 1978), fail-ing to notify them at all is unquestionably un-ethical. Seeking cooperative consent is certainly good psychological practice, even if inconve-nient. (We invite readers to skip ahead to Case 17–16 and see how the same principle applied to James P. Grigson, M.D., when he conducted a psychiatric assessment without adequate no-tice in a capital murder case.)

Obsolete Scores

Psychologists can not ethically base their as-sessments, intervention decisions, or recom-mendations on outdated data or test results. We also do not base decisions or recommendations on obsolete tests and measures and those not useful for the current purpose (APA 02: 9.08). Determining the precise definition of obsoles-cence can sometimes prove a challenge.

Case 9–29: Helen Duration began working for General Tool and Power Company 8 years ago. She had taken some paper-and-pencil general ability tests during the hiring period. She has re-cently applied for a higher-level opening within the company, but the personnel department is not seriously considering her because the test scores of 8 years earlier fall below those required for the new position.

The case of Helen Duration illustrates the problem of obsolescence. Test scores should be maintained in a client's file only as long as they serve a valid and useful purpose and continue to reflect the status of that client. Occasionally, some instruments do yield data that may be valid predictors some 8 or more years after they were collected, but that is a rare exception. The consulting psychologist who supervised the testing program at General Tool and Power Company should have cautioned the personnel department that Ms. Duration's scores should not form a basis for promotion decisions years later. In fact, efforts to ensure removal of obsolete test data from all employee files should occur as a matter of routine.

One survey of professional psychologists (Berndt, 1984) provided a "good news–bad news story." The good news: Most of the psychologists responding seemed to manage their testing practices in keeping with established ethical principles. They also seemed willing to give appropriate feedback on test results to clients. The bad news: Few of those surveyed had taken any steps to deal with the problem of obsolete data. The results also suggested that 76% expressed a willingness to release old test information to agencies with the consent of the client. This implied little recognition that such old records could be inaccurate or harmful.

It is difficult to formulate firm rules regarding when a given set of data is no longer useful; however, the APA *Record Keeping Guidelines* (APA, 2007) offer general guidance, and the *Standards for Educational and Psychological Testing* (AERA et al., 1999) give some helpful examples. Broad test scores used for initial employment screening have little usefulness if more detailed evaluation follows and are certainly of no value after a year or more of employment. Likewise, college placement test scores have little value after the college course work is completed. Retention of such data (particularly low scores) could have a long-term stigmatizing effect on test takers. It is certainly possible to code data for use in long-term archival research, when indicated, while removing all traces of the same data from individual files.

Access to Test Data

Fairly uniform agreement among professionals holds that clients have the right of access to information about themselves, and that parents have similar access to information about their minor children. The specific nature of the information, however, has sometimes been raised as a question. While this topic is addressed in Chapter 8, test data present some special difficulties because they seldom stand alone for interpretation. The test scores themselves may well prove meaningless or be misinterpreted by a layperson. One way of handling this is to frame reports in plain language, keeping in mind that the reports are likely to be read by the people about whom they are written. Likewise, psychologists who work with children must frame their reports with the parents' right of access in mind. At the same time, the Health Insurance Portability and Accountability Act (HIPAA) and state laws (as described in Chapter 8) clearly do consider test data (APA 02:9.04) as medical records, accessible to the client (or parents of a child client).

Psychologists who conduct assessments of individuals involved in litigation must expect that they will have to provide raw data (i.e., scores, observations, and client responses to test stimuli) to nonexperts in response to court orders or releases signed by the client (Committee on Legal Issues of the APA, 2006). Although ethics codes have traditionally discouraged release of raw data to unqualified persons, in response to a client release we must clearly provide such data to the client/patient or others identified in the release (APA 02: 9.04). We may seek to refrain from releasing test data to protect a client or others from substantial harm, misuse, or misrepresentation, but we must also recognize and obey the law (APA 02: 9.04).

In general, the best strategy in such circumstances is preventive (see Chapter 8 for a discussion of responding to subpoenas). Records should be kept with the understanding that they may ultimately be released to the client or to a court. We should write test reports with a directness and clarity that makes it possible to give copies of the report to the client. Ideally, the psychologist will review the report together with the client and address any questions that come up. If asked for test manuals, printed record forms, or other copyrighted test materials, the psychologist may decline to provide them and refer those making the request to the published source (APA 02: 9.11). Actually, a considerable amount of test material is readily available in the public domain.

Case 9–30: As part of a diagnostic evaluation, Dr. Ira Median administered intellectual and personality assessment tools to Victor Vector, age 8. Victor's parents felt dissatisfied with Dr. Median's evaluation and recommendation that Victor needed psychotherapy. They demanded a copy of all the tests and the answers that Victor gave, along with a copy of Dr. Median's report, as they prepared to seek a second opinion.

If Victor Vector's test protocols, for example, include themes of "murderous rage," "Oedipal anger," or similar psychodynamic concepts, one would hope that Dr. Median will deal with the meaning or basic issues, as opposed to something like, "Victor told stories in which a murderous boy kills evil father figures." Rather, Dr. Median might write: "Victor's test data suggest that he has difficulty dealing with angry feelings, especially in his relationship with his father." This sort of writing can convey all of the appropriate meaning, while avoiding jargon, which may be misunderstood or upsetting to the client.

Case 9–31: The Detroit Edison Company posted notice of six vacancies for the job classification "Instrument Man B" at a new power plant. All 10 employees who applied for the openings failed to achieve the acceptable cutoff score the company had set on a battery of psychological aptitude tests, so the vacancies were filled by promoting employees with less seniority who had scored at or above the recommended cutoffs. A union grievance was filed, and the union sought copies of the tests, employees' answer sheets, scores, and other related data, claiming that this was essential for arbitration (Eberlein, 1980).

The case involving Detroit Edison went to the Supreme Court, with the APA filing an amicus brief in support of withholding the requested information (*Detroit Edison Company v. National Labor Relations Board*, 1979). By a vote of 5 to 4, the Court agreed that the "undisputed and important interests in test secrecy" justified refusing to turn over the tests and answer sheets directly to the union. The court

noted that retaining test security represented a greater benefit to the public than would open disclosure of the test contents. By a 6-to-3 vote, the Court also ruled that the union's need for information was not so great as to require breaching the promise of confidentiality to the examinees or breaching the psychologists' code of ethics and resulting potential embarrassment to the examinees.

Teaching Psychological Testing

Psychologists who teach assessment have a unique opportunity to shape their students' professionalism and approach to ethics by modeling the active integration of professional ethics into the practice of assessment (Yalof & Brabender, 2001). Ethical standards in the areas of education and training are relevant: "Psychologists responsible for education and training programs must ensure that the programs offered will provide the appropriate knowledge and proper experiences, and meet the requirements for licensure, certification, or other goals for claimed by the program" (APA 02: 7.01). A primary responsibility involves ensuring competence in assessment practice by providing the requisite education and training.

We must continually ask ourselves whether our educational programs provide adequate breadth and depth of assessment experience using a competence-based approach. One review of studies evaluating the competence of graduate students and practicing psychologists in administration and scoring of cognitive tests demonstrated that errors occur frequently and at all levels of training (Alfonso & Pratt, 1997). The review also noted that relying only on practice assessments as a teaching methodology does not ensure competent practice. The authors concluded that teaching programs that include behavioral objectives and focus on evaluating specific competencies are generally more effective.

Multiple role problems also frequently complicate courses in psychological assessment. One example involves the common practice of using children of friends or relatives and students' classmates as "practice" subjects in psychological testing courses (Rupert et al., 1999). Imagine the complications when testing the child of a friend, and the outcome does not yield "good results," whatever that means to them or their family. The potential for violations of privacy can prove significant when graduate students are required to take personality tests or "practice" assessing their peers. Yalof and Brabender (2001) argued that students' introduction to ethical decision making in personality assessment occurs in assessment courses with practice components. They recommended that instructors demonstrate, highlight, and explore ethical principles with their students. The focus was on four particular concerns: students' role in procuring personal experience with personality testing, identification of participants for practice, development of informed consent procedures for assessment participants, and classroom presentations. Their discussion offered good illustrations of the relevant ethical principles.

One interesting solution involves asking students to role-play test subjects with different cognitive or emotional issues. By assigning client roles with details about particular styles and personalities, the student can both follow the assigned script and attempt improvisation based on their own research into the problems being assessed and instruments to be used.

DO-IT-YOURSELF TESTS

Executing a Google search on psychological testing in April 2007 yielded more than 1 million hits. When addressing psychological testing on the Internet, most members of the psychological community will think first about matters of data integrity, validity, security, or similar professional issues (Barak & English, 2002; Naglieri et al., 2004; Rapp, 2006). Others have expressed worries about test security after finding sales of obsolete and unwanted test materials on Internet auctions (LoBello & Zachar, 2007). During one 3-month interval of monitoring eBay, Lobello and Zachar found 82 tests or partial tests for sale.

Members of the public have increasingly become fascinated with do-it-yourself (DIY) tests available online. As noted in Chapter 15, many such self-care products confuse perceptions of

the public face of the mental health profession. Tests have circulated on the Internet for years, purporting to assess physical conditions (e.g., risk for assorted diseases). Increasingly, one can find psychological mass-screening tools (e.g., for attention deficit disorder, early Alzheimer's disease, depression) or actual versions of IQ and personality assessments. Often, the tests appear on Web sites associated with the advertisement of services for the problem purporting to be assessed. The ethical issues regarding DIY tests mirror criticisms of some self-help books. These include insufficient regulation or professional oversight of test validity, potential for misuse and errors in interpretation, and absence of in-person support counseling (Kier & Molinari, 2004).

Some of the online instruments seemed grounded in meaningful research, while others present more ambiguous constructs. For example, one site apparently based at the University of Pennsylvania under the auspices of a former APA president purports to assist participants in determining whether they have authentic happiness, leading to the question of whether inauthentic happiness represents delusional thinking. That site requires a personalized log on and appears intended for data collection and marketing related to other authentic happiness products. Another site with no clear expert connections offers a wide range of online testing opportunities. One fascinating site offers a personality assessment based on color preferences and describes the task as follows:

> ColorQuiz [www.colorquiz.com] is a free five minute personality test based on decades of research by color psychologists around the world. There are no complicated questions to answer, you simply choose colors with a click of the mouse! Your test results are completely confidential and we do not keep the results. Take the test now.
>
> This test is based on the work of Dr. Max Lüscher and is used worldwide, most notably in Europe, by psychologists, doctors, government agencies, and universities to screen their candidates. Since the 1950's the test has been given to hundreds of thousands of people.

Sadly, the site neglects to provide any specifics related to validity, although later text essentially acknowledges no reliability, because "human moods change." Americans are also warned that they may not fully grasp the concept of the test because of its European origins. This is an inappropriate excuse for an unreliable "quiz."

While most such tests may prove analogous to self-help books, one seems particularly noteworthy because of its potential to inflict distress. The Implicit Association Test (IAT) is a cognitive task that ostensibly helps diagnose implicit preferences the test taker possesses but does not consciously recognize. According to information on the Web site, more than three-fourths of the people who take a given test discover that they demonstrate implicit preferences for Whites over Blacks or for the young over older adults or that they subtly endorse gender stereotypes about relative abilities of men and women (Blanton & Jaccard, 2006; Blanton, Jaccard, Gonzales, & Christie, 2006). Of course, feedback of this sort can be disconcerting and distressing to people who believed, prior to taking the IAT, that they did not have such prejudices. The Web site offers advice for these individuals (Blanton & Jaccard, 2006; Blanton et al., 2006).

A Web site funded by the National Science Foundation and National Institute of Mental Health presents the public with an opportunity to take the IAT, and thousands have done so, often at the recommendations of people in the corporate world who promote or sell "diversity training" of various sorts. Blanton and his colleagues (Blanton & Jaccard, 2006; Blanton et al., 2006) cited the IAT as a prime example of inappropriate use of arbitrary metrics in psychology. They noted that many psychological tests have arbitrary metrics but remain appropriate for testing psychological theories. Metric arbitrariness becomes a much more significant concern when researchers wish to draw inferences about the true, absolute standing of a group or individual on the psychological dimension being measured. In the IAT, this ostensibly happens based on the milliseconds required to alternate between keystrokes at a computer keyboard in response to photographs or words flashed on the terminal screen.

The social psychologists who designed and promoted (or continue to promote) the IAT do so with many good intentions and clinically unsophisticated caveats to those who stumble onto or are directed to the site. Sadly, those directing others to the site often have little understanding of the underlying problems intrinsic to the whole exercise. To the extent that people sitting alone at a computer terminal taking the IAT depart feeling somehow diminished by the experience, the developers have inflicted harm. Have they done so with informed consent? Possibly. Have they done so with scientific rigor, accuracy, and concern for the welfare of those who feel hurt? Absolutely not.

SUMMARY GUIDELINES

1. Although many different varieties of tests exist, all must meet the *Standards for Educational and Psychological Testing* (AERA et al., 1999) insofar as they present facts through a user's manual. Psychologists should also adhere to these standards when making use of tests.

2. Different types of technical test data exist, including reliability and validity findings. Any test user should become familiar with these data for any instrument used and should understand limitations of the appropriate use of the instrument.

3. Test users should exercise great caution in the selection and interpretation of assessment techniques to ensure that each is valid for the intended purpose and specific situation in question.

4. Those developing new instruments bear a heavy scientific responsibility to ensure that potential users have the information necessary to use the test properly.

5. Those administering psychological tests are responsible for ensuring that the tests are given and scored according to standardized instructions.

6. Test users should also be aware of potential test bias or client characteristics that might reduce the validity of the instrument for that client in that context. Specific cautions should be reported along with test data in any situations in which bias or other problems with validity are suspected.

7. No test user is competent to use every standardized assessment tool. It is important to be self-critical and not attempt to

use instruments without proper training. One also should not employ assistants to administer tests unless the assistants are appropriately trained and supervised with those instruments.

8. The validity and confidence of test results often rely on the security of certain test information or items. This secure information should be protected carefully.

9. Automated testing services create a hazard to the extent that they may generate inaccurate data or produce valid results that are subsequently misused by individuals not fully knowledgeable regarding the instruments in use. Test users operating or using such services should observe the same stringent safeguards required with manually administered testing.

10. A client who is to be tested should be informed in understandable terms of the purpose and intended use of the tests and test data.

11. A client has a right to know the results of an evaluation and a right to have test data kept confidential within the limits promised when consent is obtained.

12. Clients to be tested (or their parents or legal guardians) must be given full informed consent about the nature of the evaluation, payment for services, access to results, and other relevant data prior to initiating the evaluation.

References

Alfonso, V. C., & Pratt, S. I. (1997). Issues and suggestions for training professionals in assessing intelligence. In D. P. Flanagan, J. L. Genshaft, & P. L. Harrison (Eds.), *Contemporary intellectual assessment: Theories, tests, and issues* (pp. 326–344). New York: Guilford Press.

Allard, G., Butler, J., Faust, D., & Shea, M. T. (1995). Errors in hand scoring objective personality tests: The case of the Personality Diagnostic Questionnaire Revised (PDQ R). *Professional Psychology, 26,* 304–308.

American Educational Research Association, American Psychological Association, & National Council on Measurement in Education. (1999). *Standards for educational and psycho-* logical testing. Washington, DC: AERA Publication Sales.

American Psychological Association. (1990). Guidelines for providers of psychological services to ethnic, linguistic, and culturally diverse populations. *American Psychologist, 48,* 45–48.

American Psychological Association. (2007). *Record keeping guidelines.* Washington, DC: American Psychological Association.

American Psychological Association Ethics Committee. (1993). *Policy statement of the APA Ethics Committee regarding "take home" tests.* Washington, DC: American Psychological Association.

Anastasi, A. (1975). Harassing a dead horse (review of D. R. Green, Ed., *The aptitude achievement distinction: Proceedings of the Second CTB/McGraw Hill Conference on Issues in Educational Measurement*). *Review of Education, 1,* 356–362.

Atkins v. Virginia, (00–8452) 536 U.S. 304; (2002) 260 Va. 375, 534 S. E. 2d 312, reversed.

Azar, B. (1994). Could "policing" test use improve assessments? *APA Monitor, 25,* 16.

Barak, A., & English, N. (2002). Prospects and limitations of psychological testing on the Internet. *Journal of Technology in Human Services, 19,* 65–89.

Bartley v. Kremens, 402 1039 (E.D. Pa. 1975).

Bartram, D. (2001). International guidelines for test use. *International Journal of Testing, 1,* 93–114.

Berndt, D. J. (1984). Ethical and professional considerations in psychological assessment. *Professional Psychology, 14,* 580–587.

Bersoff, D. N. (1981). Testing and the law. *American Psychologist, 36,* 1047–1056.

Betz, N. E., Watkins, C. E., Jr., & Campbell, V. L. (2000). Contemporary issues in testing use. In *Testing and assessment in counseling practice* (2nd ed., pp. 481–516). Mahwah, NJ: Erlbaum.

Blanton, H., & Jaccard, J. (2006). Arbitrary metrics in psychology. *American Psychologist, 61,* 27–41.

Blanton, H., Jaccard, J., Gonzales, P. M., & Christie, C. (2006). Decoding the implicit association test: Implications for criterion prediction. *Journal of Experimental Social Psychology 42,* 192–212.

Boat, B. W., & Everson, M. (1986). *Using anatomical dolls: Guidelines for interviewing young children in sexual abuse investigations.* Chapel Hill: University of North Carolina.

Brodsky, S. L., & Galloway, V. A. (2003). Ethical and professional demands for forensic mental health professionals in the post-*Atkins* era. *Ethics & Behavior, 13,* 3–9.

Brown, D. C. (1994). Subgroup norming: Legitimate testing practice or reverse discrimination? *American Psychologist, 49,* 927–928.

Cates, J. A. (1999). The art of assessment in psychology: Ethics, expertise, and validity. *Journal of Clinical Psychology, 55,* 631–641.

Clawson, T. W. (1997). Control of psychological testing: The threat and a response. *Journal of Counseling and Development, 76,* 90–93.

Cole, N. S. (1981). Bias in testing. *American Psychologist, 36,* 1067–1077.

Committee on Legal Issues of the American Psychological Association. (2006). Strategies for private practitioners coping with subpoenas or compelled testimony for client records or test data. *Professional Psychology, 37,* 215–222.

Cone, J. D., Dalenberg, C. J., & Maruish, M. E. (2004). Ethics concerns in outcomes assessment. In *The use of psychological testing for treatment planning and outcomes assessment: Volume 1: General considerations* (3rd ed., pp. 335–365). Mahwah, NJ: Erlbaum.

Cronbach, L. (1980). Validity on parole: How can we go straight? In W. Schrader (Ed.), *New directions for testing and measurement: Measuring achievement progress over a decade* (Vol. 5). San Francisco: Jossey-Bass.

Cureton, E. E., Cronbach, L. J., Meehl, P. E., Ebel, R. L., & Ward, A. W. (1996). Validity. In A. W. Ward, H. W. Stoker, & M. Murray-Ward (Eds.), *Educational measurement: Origins, theories, and explications, Vol. 1: Basic concepts and theories* (pp. 125–243). Lanham, MD: University Press of America.

Dattilio, F., Tresco, K., & Siegel, A. (in press) An empirical survey on psychological testing and the use of the term psychological: Turf battles or clinical necessity? *Professional Psychology.*

Dawes, R. M., Faust, D., & Meehl, P. E. (2002). Clinical versus actuarial judgment. In T. Gilovich, D. Griffin, & D. Kahneman (Eds.), *Heuristics and biases: The psychology of intuitive judgment* (pp. 716–729). New York: Cambridge University Press.

Detroit Edison Company v. National Labor Relations Board, 99 S. Ct. 1123, 1132 (1979).

Dickinson, J. J., Poole, D. A., & Bruck, M. (2005). Back to the future: A comment on the use of anatomical dolls in forensic interviews. *Journal of Forensic Psychology Practice, 5,* 63–74.

Eberlein, L. (1980). Confidentiality of industrial psychological tests. *Professional Psychology, 11,* 749–754.

Ekstrom, R. B., Elmore, P. B., & Schafer, W. D. (1997). Standards for educational and psychological tests and testing professionals. In R. F. Dillon (Ed.), *Handbook on testing* (pp. 39–64). Westport, CT: Greenwood Press/Greenwood Publishing Group.

Everson, M., & Boat, B. W. (1997). Anatomical dolls in child sexual abuse assessments: A call for forensically relevant research. *Applied Cognitive Psychology, 11* (special issue), S55–S74.

Eyde, L. D., Robertson, G. J., Krug, S. E., Moreland, K. L., Robertson, A. G., Shewan, C. M., et al. (1993). *Responsible test use: Case studies for assessing human behavior.* Washington, DC: American Psychological Association.

Faller, K. C. (2005). Anatomical dolls: Their use in assessment of children who may have been sexually abused. *Journal of Child Sexual Abuse, 14,* 1–21.

Fisher, C. B. (1996). The (mis)use of posttraumatic stress disorder to validate child sexual abuse. *Register Report—Newsletter of the National Register of Health Service Providers in Psychology, 22,* 8–10.

Flaugher, R. L. (1978). The many definitions of test bias. *American Psychologist, 33,* 671–679.

Frederiksen, N. (1984). The real test bias: Influences of testing on teaching and learning. *American Psychologist, 39,* 193–202.

Friedemann, V., & Morgan, M. (1985). *Interviewing sexual abuse victims using anatomical dolls: The professional's guidebook.* Eugene, OR: Shamrock Press.

Garb, H. N. (2000). Computers will become increasingly important for psychological assessment: Not that there's anything wrong with that! *Psychological Assessment, 12,* 31–39.

Garb, H. N. (2005). Clinical judgment and decision making. *Annual Review of Clinical Psychology, 1,* 67–89.

Garb, H. N. (2007). Computer-administered interviews and rating scales. *Psychological Assessment, 19,* 4–13.

Gladwell, M. (2001, December 17). What Stanley Kaplan taught us about the SAT. *The New*

Yorker. Retrieved March 15, 2007, from http://www.gladwell.com/2001/ 2001_12_17_a_kaplan.htm

Goffman, E. (1961). *Asylums*. Garden City, NY: Anchor Books.

Gottfredson, L. S. (1994). The science and politics of race-norming. *American Psychologist, 49*, 955–963.

Green, R. M. (1981). A primer of testing. *American Psychologist, 36*, 1001–1011.

Griggs v. Duke Power Company, 401 U.S. 424 (1971).

Guion, R. M. (1974). Open a new window: Validities and values in psychological measurement. *American Psychologist, 28*, 287–296.

Gutkin, T. B. (2000). Buros *Mental measurements yearbook*. In A. E. Kazdin (Ed.), *Encyclopedia of psychology, Vol. 1* (pp. 489– 491). Washington, DC: American Psychological Association.

Hall, J. D., Howerton, D. L., & Bolin, A. U. (2005). The use of testing technicians: Critical issues for professional psychology. *International Journal of Testing, 5*, 357–375.

Hambleton, R. K. (2006). Psychometric models, test designs and item types for the next generation of educational and psychological tests. In D. Bartram & R. Hambleton (Eds.), *Computer-based testing and the Internet: Issues and advances* (pp. 77–89). New York: Wiley.

Haney, W. (1981). Validity, vaudeville, and values: A short history of social concerns over standardized testing. *American Psychologist., 36*, 1021–1034.

Haney, W. (1993a). *Cheating and escheating on standardized tests*. Atlanta: American Educational Research Association.

Haney, W. (1993b, April 15). Preventing cheating on standardized tests. *Chronicle of Higher Education*, B3.

Haney, W. M., Madaus, G. F., & Lyons, R. (1993). *The fractured marketplace for standardized testing*. Norwell, MA: Kluwer Academic.

Helms, J. E. (2006). Fairness is not validity or cultural bias in racial-group assessment: A quantitative perspective. *American Psychologist, 61*, 845–859.

Hersen, M. (2004). *Psychological assessment in clinical practice: A pragmatic guide*. New York: Brunner-Routledge.

Hobbs, N. (Ed.). (1975). *Issues in the classification of children*. San Francisco: Jossey-Bass.

Holt, R. R. (1970). Yet another look at clinical and statistical prediction: Or, is clinical psychology worthwhile? *American Psychologist, 25*, 337–349.

Kaplan, R. M. (1982). Nader's raid on the testing industry: Is it in the best interests of the consumers? *American Psychologist, 37*, 15–23.

Kier, F. J., & Molinari, V. (2004). Do-it-yourself testing for mental illness: Ethical issues, concerns, and recommendations. *Professional Psychology, 35*, 261–267.

Knauss, L. K. (2001). Ethical issues in psychological assessment in school settings. *Journal of Personality Assessment, 77*, 231–241.

Koene, C. J. (1997). Tests and professional ethics and values in European psychologists. *European Journal of Psychological Assessment, 13*, 219–228.

Kohn, S. D. (1975). The numbers game: How the testing industry operates. *National Elementary Principal, 55*, 11–23.

Koocher, G. P. (1989a). Confirming content validity in the dark. *Professional Psychology, 20*, 275.

Koocher, G. P. (1989b). Screening licensing examinations for accuracy. *Professional Psychology, 20*, 269–271.

Koocher, G. P. (1993). Ethical issues in the psychological assessment of children. In T. H. Ollendick & M. Hersen (Eds.), *Handbook of child and adolescent assessment* (pp. 51–61). Needham Heights, MA: Allyn & Bacon.

Koocher, G. P. (2003). IQ testing: A matter of life or death. *Ethics & Behavior, 13*, 1–2.

Koocher, G. P., Goodman, G. S., White, C. S., Friedrich, W. N., Sivan, A. B., & Reynolds, C. R. (1995). Psychological science and the use of anatomically detailed dolls in child sexual-abuse assessments. *Psychological Bulletin, 118*, 199–222.

Lambert, N. M. (1981). Psychological evidence in *Larry P. v. Wilson Riles*: An evaluation by a witness for the defense. *American Psychologist, 36*, 937–952.

Laosa, L. (1984). Social policies toward children of diverse ethnic, racial, and language groups in the United States. In H. W. Stevenson & A. E. Siegel (Eds.), *Child development research and social policy* (Vol. 1, pp. 1–109.). Chicago: University of Chicago Press.

Larry P. v. Riles, 343 F. Supp. 1306 (N.D. Cal. 1972) (preliminary injunction), affirmed, 502 F. 2d

963 (9th Cir. 1974), opinion issued No. C 71 2270 RFP (N.D. Cal. October 16, 1979).

Lefkowitz, J. (2003). *Ethics and values in industrial–organizational psychology.* Mahwah, NJ: Erlbaum.

Levy, H., Kalinowski, N., Markovic, J., Pittman, M., & Ahart, S. (1991). *Victim sensitive interviewing in child sexual abuse: A developmental approach to interviewing and consideration of the use of anatomically detailed dolls.* Chicago: Mount Sinai Hospital Medical Center.

Lievens, F. (2006). The ITC guidelines on computer-based and Internet-delivered testing: Where do we go from here? *International Journal of Testing, 6,* 189–194.

Lippman, W. (1922). The abuse of tests. *The New Republic, 32,* 9, 10, 213–215, 246–248, 275–277, 297–298, 328–330.

LoBello, S. G., & Zachar, P. (2007). Psychological test sales and Internet auctions: Ethical considerations for dealing with obsolete or unwanted test materials. *Professional Psychology, 38,* 68–70.

Lowman, R. L. (2006). *The ethical practice of psychology in organizations* (2nd ed.). Washington, DC: American Psychological Association.

Maddox, T. (2003). *Tests: A comprehensive reference for assessments in psychology, education, and business* (5th ed.). Austin, TX: Pro-Ed.

Maher, B. A., & Gottesman, I. I. (2005). Deconstructing, reconstructing, preserving Paul E. Meehl's legacy of construct validity. *Psychological Assessment, 17,* 415–422.

Matarazzo, J. D. (1990). Psychological assessment versus psychological testing: Validation from Bitnet to the school, clinic, and courtroom. *American Psychologist, 45,* 999–1016.

McKelvie, S. J. (2005). Psychological testing: A practical approach to design and evaluation. *Canadian Psychology, 46,* 258–260.

Meehl, P. E. (1954). *Clinical versus statistical prediction.* Minneapolis: University of Minnesota Press.

Meehl, P. E. (1997). Credentialed persons, credentialed knowledge. *Clinical Psychology: Science and Practice, 4,* 91–98.

Melnick, D. E., & Clauser, B. E. (2006). Computer-based testing for professional licensing and certification of health professionals. In D. Bartram & R. K. Hambleton (Eds.), *Computer-based testing and the Internet: Issues and advances* (pp. 163–186). New York: Wiley.

Mercer, J. R. (1973). *Labeling the mentally retarded: Clinical and social system perspective on mental retardation.* Berkeley: University of California Press.

Messick, S. (1980). Test validity and the ethics of assessment. *American Psychologist, 35,* 1012–1027.

Moreland, K. L., Eyde, L. D., Robertson, G. J., Primoff, E. S., & Most, R. B. (1995). Assessment of test user qualifications: A research-based measurement procedure. *American Psychologist, 50,* 14–23.

Naglieri, J. A., Drasgow, F., Schmit, M., Handler, L., Prifitera, A., Margolis, A., et al. (2004). Psychological testing on the Internet: New problems, old issues. *American Psychologist, 59,* 150–162.

National Academy of Neuropsychology (NAN). (2000b). Presence of third party observers during neuropsychological testing. *Archives of Clinical Neuropsychology, 15,* 379–380.

Novick, M. R. (1981). Federal guidelines and professional standards. *American Psychologist, 36,* 1035–1046.

Oles, H. J., & Davis, G. D. (1977). Publishers violate APA standards on test distribution. *Psychological Reports, 41,* 713–714.

PASE v. Hannon, 506 F. Supp. 831 (N.D. Ill. 1980).

Powers, K. M., Hagans-Murillo, K. S., & Restori, A. F. (2004). Twenty-five years after *Larry P.:* The California response to overrepresentation of African Americans in special education. *California School Psychologist, 9,* 145–158.

Pryzwansky, W. B., & Bersoff, D. N. (1978). Parental consent for psychological evaluations: Legal, ethical, and practical consideration. *Journal of School Psychology, 16,* 274–281.

Rapp, J. (2006). Computer-based testing and the Internet: Issues and advances. *International Journal of Testing, 6,* 195–200.

Reckase, M. D. (1998). Consequential validity from the test developer's perspective. *Educational Measurement: Issues and Practice, 17,* 13–16.

Ridley, C. R., Hill, C. L., & Wiese, D. L. (2001). Ethics in multicultural assessment: A model of reasoned application. In L. A. Suzuki & J. G. Ponterotto (Eds.), *Handbook of multicultural assessment: Clinical, psychological, and educational applications* (2nd ed., pp. 29–45). San Francisco: Jossey-Bass.

Rosen, G. A., Reaves, R. P., & Hill, D. S. (1989). Reliability and validity of psychology licensing examinations: Multiple roles and redundant systems in development and screening. *Professional Psychology, 20,* 272–274.

Ruiz, M. A., Drake, E. B., Glass, A., Marcotte, D., & van Gorp, W. G. (2002). Trying to beat the system: Misuse of the Internet to assist in avoiding the detection of psychological symptom dissimulation. *Professional Psychology, 33,* 294–299.

Rupert, P. A., Kozlowski, N. F., Hoffman, L. A., Daniels, D. D., & Piette, J. M. (1999). Practical and ethical issues in teaching psychological testing. *Professional Psychology, 30,* 209–214.

Sackett, P. R., Schmitt, N., Ellingson, J. E., & Kabin, M. B. (2001). High-stakes testing in employment, credentialing, and higher education: Prospects in a post-affirmative action world. *American Psychologist, 56,* 302–318.

Sackett, P. R., & Wilk, S. L. (1994). Within-group norming and other forms of score adjustment in pre-employment testing. *American Psychologist, 49,* 929–954.

Schulenberg, S. E., & Yutrzenka, B. A. (2004). Ethical issues in the use of computerized assessment. *Computers in Human Behavior, 20,* 477–490.

Smith, D., & Dumont, F. (1995). A cautionary study: Unwarranted interpretations of the Draw a Person test. *Professional Psychology, 26,* 298–303.

Sternberg, R. J. (2004). Lies we live by: Misapplication of tests in identifying the gifted. In J. S. Renzulli (Ed.), *Identification of students for gifted and talented programs* (pp. 53–62). Thousand Oaks, CA: Corwin Press.

Szasz, T. (1970). *The manufacture of madness.* New York: Harper & Row.

Turner, S. M., DeMers, S. T., Fox, H. R., & Reed, G. (2001). APA's guidelines for test user qualifications: An executive summary. *American Psychologist, 56,* 1099–1113.

Viswesvaran, C. (2005). The *15th mental measurements yearbook. Personnel Psychology, 58,* 273–276.

Waller, N. G., & Meehl, P. E. (2002). Risky tests, verisimilitude, and path analysis. *Psychological Methods, 7,* 323–337.

Wetter, M. W., & Corrigan, S. K. (1995). Providing information to clients about psychological tests: A survey of attorneys' and law students' attitudes. *Professional Psychology, 26,* 474–477.

Yalof, J., & Brabender, V. (2001). Ethical dilemmas in personality assessment courses: Using the classroom for in vivo training. *Journal of Personality Assessment, 77,* 203–213.

10

Multiple-Role Relationships I
Boundaries, Risks, and Doing Business

The worst deluded are the self-deluded.

Christian Nestell Bovee

Contents

How curious that well-trained mental health professionals, presumably possessing enhanced self-awareness, can be astonished to find themselves entangled in messy role conflicts. Whenever personal needs take precedence, rationalizations can inhibit sound professional judgment. These can too easily lead to unanticipated consequences for clients as well as the precipitous downfall of therapists' careers. This is the reason we devote three chapters to professional role issues.

In a revealing article describing his own intense struggle to maintain a professional role with a particular client, Arthur Kovacs (1974) offered an overarching and thought-provoking rationale regarding why therapists may experience a pull toward complicated and complicating relationships with those with whom they work:

> The style of the calling of a psychotherapist cannot be separated from the great themes of his own existence. We delude ourselves often that our task consists of our merely executing a set of well learned techniques in the service of our patients' needs. I now know that this information is nonsense. What we do with our patients—whether we do so deviously and cunningly or overtly and brashly—is to affirm our own identities in the struggle with their struggles. (p. 376)

The American Psychological Association (APA) defines multiple-role relationships as occurring when a therapist is already in a professional role with a person *and*

- is also in another role with the same person,
- is also in a relationship with someone closely associated with or related to the person with whom the therapist has the professional relationship, or
- makes promises to enter into another relationship in the future with the person or a person closely associated with or related to the person. (APA 02: 3.05a)

To qualify under APA's definition, the initial relationship typically requires an established connectedness between the parties. The primary role relationship is usually with an ongoing therapy client. However, the primary role could be of another significant nature (such as a therapist's family member or employee) with the contemplated additional role being that of therapy client. Limited or inconsequential contacts that grow out of chance encounters with clients would not normally fall under the definition or cause any ethical concerns.

Multiple-role relationship may be active, as when a therapist hires a client to be a housekeeper in the family home. Or, it occurs as a proposal for the future, as when a therapist and a client plan to go into business together on termination of the therapy. Creating plans for the future alter the dynamics of the ongoing professional relationship in ways that may not be in the client's best interests. Nonsexual consecu-

tive role relationships with *ex*-clients do not fall under any specific prohibitions in the 2002 APA code. However, based on posttherapy incidents described in this chapter, we advise caution even after a natural termination of the professional role.

In the first edition of this book (Keith-Spiegel & Koocher, 1985), we included cautionary advice about nonsexual dual-role relationships despite the fact that we had no data-based references beyond one of our own student's unpublished work (Tallman, 1981). However, we saw the sometimes catastrophic consequences of blurred relationships during our services on ethics committees. Much more has since been learned, and it is currently widely recognized that certain types of complex therapist–client interactions can prove harmful (Bennett, Bricklin, & VandeCreek, 1994; Smith & Fitzpatrick, 1995).

We acknowledge up front that not all boundary crossings are unethical, and some may at times benefit clients. We provide examples of the ethically acceptable relaxing of boundaries in this and the next chapter.

THE BATTLE OVER BOUNDARIES

Boundaries between therapist and client come in many forms—from crisp to fuzzy—and can exist in various influential contexts (Gutheil & Gabbard, 1993). Mental health professionals continue to hold differing perceptions of role mingling that range from conscious efforts to sustain objectivity by avoiding any interaction or discourse outside of therapeutic issues to extremely lax policies by which the differences between therapist and best buddy become obliterated. However, even those who would stretch roles into other domains would condemn the psychiatrist accused of inviting her clients to move in with her in return for cooking her meals, helping her dress in the morning, cleaning her home, and serving her sexual needs. Conspicuous exploitation of clients, then, is *not* at issue in the professional disagreements over where best to draw boundary lines.

Some mental health professionals decry the concept of professional boundaries, asserting that they promote the conduct of psychotherapy as a mechanical technique rather than relating to clients as unique human beings. Such rigid, cold, and aloof "cookbook therapy," the critics of strict boundaries say, harms the formation of empathy and the natural process of psychotherapy. Instead, acting as a fully human therapist will provide the most constructive way to enhance personal connectedness and honesty in therapeutic relationships (Hedges, 1993) and may actually improve professional judgment (Tomm, 1993). Lazarus (1994) put it bluntly: "Practitioners who hide behind rigid boundaries, whose sense of ethics is uncompromising, will, in my opinion, fail to really help many of the clients who are unfortunate enough to consult them" (p. 253). Critics also contend that boundary violations have been improperly inserted into ethics codes, training programs, and licensing and malpractice litigation (Lazarus & Zur, 2002).

Those who criticize the drawing of firm professional boundaries further contend that role complexities are inevitable, and attempting to control them by invoking authority (e.g., ethics codes) oversimplifies the complexities inherent in the psychotherapy process and creates the practice of defensive therapy (Bogrand, 1993; Clarkson, 1994; Ryder & Hepworth, 1990). The answer, they say, involves educating both clients and therapists about how to deal with unavoidable breaks and disruptions in boundaries and to educate therapists that exploitation is always unethical, regardless of boundary issues.

Kovacs's revelation at the beginning of this chapter reminds us that human beings do not operate as a collection of isolated functions. The work of mental health professionals is conducive to leaky role boundaries because so much of it occurs in the context of relating, very often about intimate matters that the client has not spoken of to anyone else. The therapist, however, retains ultimate responsibility for keeping the process focused. As Gabbard (1994) concluded, "Because the needs of the psychotherapist often get in the way of the therapy, the mental health professionals have established guidelines . . . that are designed to minimize the opportunity for therapists to use their patients for their own gratification" (p. 283).

We view the therapy relationship as rich and complex in its own right and see no reason why clear boundaries need to have an impact on a therapist's warmth, empathy, and compassion. The correct task is to match therapy style and technique to a given client's needs (Bennett et al., 1994). This requires a clear vision, unencumbered by the therapist's personal agendas. Furthermore, we are convinced that lax professional boundaries are often a precursor of exploitation, confusion, and loss of professional objectivity.

We fully recognize that one can not possibly avoid all nonprofessional contact with one's clients. However, we also agree with Pope's (1991) contention that, "the professional therapeutic relationship is secured within a reliable set of boundaries on which both therapist and patient can depend" (p. 23). Conflicts, which are more likely to arise as boundaries blur, compromise the disinterest (as opposed to lack of interest) prerequisite for sound professional judgment. Clear and consistent boundaries provide a structured arena, and this may constitute a curative factor in itself (Borys, 1994). In short, the therapy relationship should remain a sanctuary in which clients can focus on themselves and their needs while receiving clear, clean feedback and guidance.

While reviewing the cases in this chapter, the reader will note the pervasive incidence of harm caused by therapists who were, themselves, completely out of touch with the effects that their judgments and decisions had on those with whom they worked. Ethics charges based on role blurring account for the majority of ethics complaints and licensing board actions (Bader, 1994; Montgomery & Cupit, 1999; Neukrug, Milliken, & Walden, 2001; Sonne, 1994). Legal suits and the cost of defending licensing board complaints cause professional liability insurance rates to rise, thus harming all therapists (Bennett et al., 1994).

EVALUATING MULTIPLE-ROLE RELATIONSHIPS

The APA ethics code admonishes psychologists to refrain from entering a multiple relationship if the psychologists' objectivity, competence, or effectiveness in performing their professional functions could become impaired or if a risk of exploitation might result (APA 02: 3.05). Other professional mental health organizations echo the same theme in their ethics codes. However, according to APA's current code, not all multiple-role relationships with clients are necessarily unethical as long as no exploitation or risk of harm can be reasonably expected (APA 02: 3.05a).

Here, mental health professionals are empowered to make judgments based on the likelihood that problems reasonably might or might not occur. Although we agree that careful consideration should occur prior to softening the boundaries of any professional role, we remain unconvinced that accurate outcome predictions of relationships involve a simple exercise in judgment. If that were so, therapists would have the lowest divorce rate of any professional group, yet there is no evidence of this. Indeed, the life of a psychotherapist carries its own risks for burnout and stress that have a negative impact on family relationships (Epstein & Bower, 2005). One prospective study found that psychiatrists (and surgeons) have a *greater* risk of divorce than physicians in other specialties. ("Physician divorces," 1997).

For therapists already predisposed to blend roles, rationalization processes are probably well under way, thus subverting the accuracy of any personal risk assessment. We also contend that there is never a justification for entering into some types of multiple-role relationships with persons in an active treatment. Sexual and business relationships, for example, pose inherent risk regardless of who is involved. Neither can be defended as reasonable dimensions to impose on a therapy relationship.

RISK ASSESSMENT

Kitchener (1988) suggested assessing the appropriateness of boundaries by using three guidelines to predict the amount of damage that role blending might create. Roles conflict, says Kitchener, when expectations in one role involve actions or behavior incompatible with another role. First, as the expectations of professionals and those they serve become more incompatible, the potential for harm increases. Second, as obligations associated with the roles become increasingly divergent, the risks of loss of objectivity and divided loyalties rise. Third, to the extent that the power and prestige of the psychotherapist exceeds that of the client, the potential for exploitation is heightened.

Gottlieb's oft-cited (1993) model for avoiding exploitative multiple relations tracks the level of the therapist's power (i.e., from interventions where little or no personal relationship was established with a client to clear power differential with profound influence) with the duration (or expected duration) of the professional relationship and the clarity of termination (i.e., defined as the level of mutual satisfaction with the conclusion of therapy and the likelihood that the client will have further professional contact). Thus, if after 2 years of intense therapy and a tenuous termination by which the client may need to return at any time, no additional roles should be contemplated. However, after a Saturday afternoon "growth workshop" that resulted in a mutually agreeable one-time experience, the risk if the therapist enters into another role with an attendee seems minimal, and the success (or failure) of this new role relationship would be more about what the parties do as individuals as opposed to the brief professional experience. That is, the therapist and the workshop attendee may go out together only to find that they have nothing in common and even grate on each other's nerves. However, the prior role is barely at issue.

Brown (1994) adds two additional factors that, if present, heighten risks of harm. First, objectification can occur, with the therapist using the client as an "it" for the purpose of providing entertainment or convenience. Second, boundary violations usually arise from impulse, rather than from careful, reasoned consideration of any therapeutic indications. Thus, hugging a client is not unethical per se, but an assessment of any negative indicators should precede such an act.

Risky Therapists

All therapists face some risk for inappropriate role blending. Those with underdeveloped competencies or poor training may be more prone to improperly blend roles with clients. However, even those with excellent training and high levels of competence may relate unacceptably with those with whom they work because their own boundaries are not firm, or they feel a need for adoration, power, or social connection. We must face the unfortunate reality that psychotherapy provides an almost ideal climate, a "perfect storm" if you will, for emotionally or morally precarious mental health professionals to seek to gratify their personal needs. The settings are private and intimate. The authority falls on the side of the therapist. And, if things turn sour, the therapist can simply eliminate the relationship by unilaterally terminating the therapy relationship.

Self-Disclosing Therapists

Most psychotherapists have engaged in some measure of self-disclosure with their clients (Pope, Tabachnick, & Keith-Spiegel, 1987), and many studies have examined the role played by self-disclosure in the process of therapy (e.g., Davis, 2002; Farber, Berano, & Capobianco, 2004; Kim et al., 2003; Peterson, 2002). However, those who engage in considerable and revealing self-disclosure with clients stand at greater risk for forming problematic relationships with them. Whereas well-considered illustrations from the therapist's life may help make a point or signal empathy, the decision to use personal data as an intervention comes down to a matter of clinical judgment. Absorbing therapy time with extended renditions of one's own personal history and family issues is not typically justifiable. We are reminded of a student's comment, who said of a therapist she consulted briefly, "All I could think about as he went on and on about his own college days was, 'This is costing me a dollar a minute.' " Furthermore, Gutheil (1994) noted, and our experience with ethics cases confirms, that excessive self-disclosure of personal information to clients

is a common antecedent to sexual misconduct with them.

Of course, clients may instigate inquiries about their therapists' personal lives. It seems reasonable to expect that they would want to know as much as possible about the person in whom they are placing so much trust. So, we agree with Lazarus's (1994) contention that it feels demeaning to have a question dismissed and then answered by another question: "Do you have children, Dr. Shell?" "Why do you ask me that, Maurice?" But, not all clients' questions should be answered, and it may prove wise to explore the intent of a client who is too inquisitive. The skillful therapist can respond without demeaning the client in the process.

Professional Isolation

Professional or personal isolation can conspire to cloud therapists' judgments. The first case involves an indignant response to a fading career, compounded by an absence of close ties with family or friends. Dr. Grandiose might elicit some sympathy were it not for her ill-conceived approach to solving her own personal problems:

Case 10–1: A well-known and outspoken therapist, Panacea Grandiose, Ph.D., alienated the professional community over the last several years with her ruthless personal attacks, especially when anyone referred to the theoretical foundation of the therapy orientation she pioneered in the 1970s as outmoded. Grandiose, a widow, continued to maintain a successful practice in her upscale condominium, and her clients became the focus of her life. She hosted frequent social events in her home and invited herself along on clients' vacations. Colleagues in the community became concerned that Grandiose had developed a cult of sorts, made up of high-paying, perennial clients who also provided her with adoration, loyalty, and "family."

During an APA Ethics Committee meeting in the early 1980s, we noted that the majority of cases involving boundary blurring (including sexual ones) occurred among therapists who maintained solo practices, often in isolated offices away from other mental health professionals. It seemed clear enough, way back then, that something about therapists either choosing to work in isolation or the isolating conditions themselves fostered the potential clouding of professional standards of care. Or, perhaps some therapists have experienced rejection by their colleagues, as with Dr. Grandiose, and turn to inappropriate substitutes for support and validation. Regardless of the reason, an insular practice with no provisions for ongoing professional contact diffuses professional identity.

If a therapist has no one with whom to bounce off ideas and consult about predicaments, the chances of making errors in judgment and using clients for the purpose of fulfilling personal needs appear to be substantially elevated. Therapists can gain collegial support in many ways, including peer supervision groups, consultation, participation in professional associations, and continuing professional education.

Therapeutic Orientation and Specialty Practices

Some therapists practicing according to certain types of therapeutic orientations are probably vulnerable to charges of boundary violations. For example, Williams (1998) noted that humanistic therapy and encounter group philosophies depend heavily on tearing down interpersonal boundaries. Such therapists often disclose a great deal about themselves, hug their clients, and insist on the use of first names. These therapists also become, according to Williams, vulnerable to ethics charges even though they simply practice according to their training.

Some therapists who specialize with a particular clientele or in certain settings may need to exercise extra vigilance because the nature of the services or service settings are conducive to (or even require) relaxed boundaries. Sports psychologists, for example, often travel, eat, and "hang out" with a team and may be called on to fill water bottles and help out with whatever else needs doing (M. B. Anderson, Van Raalte, & Brewer, 2001). An even more complex relationship exists for mental health professionals embedded in military units where quarters are close,

and unlike embedded journalists, they are expected to tend to the unit's needs and even engage in combat (Johnson, Ralph, & Johnson, 2005). In such instances, very fuzzy edges may be inherent in the nature of practice rather than inappropriate, but a firm boundary marker requiring vigilance does exist somewhere along the line.

Pastoral counseling, by which the therapist may also function as the client's religious guide, presents a sensitive preexisting dual role.

Case 10–2: Mildred Devine requested counseling for what she called a "spiritual crisis" from her minister, Luther Pew, who also held a license in marriage and family counseling. Ms. Devine experienced deep sadness and hopelessness and questioned her faith. At that time, Pew was dealing with his own troubles and struggling to manage his large congregation. His adult son living in another state seemed constantly in scrapes with the law, and his wife had become so intensely involved with her artist group that she no longer had much interest in church functions. When Ms. Devine relayed her feelings, blaming God for having forsaken her, Rev. Pew responded by pouring out details of his own family problems, including the particulars of a drinking problem in his youth. Pew hoped this one intense session would prove helpful, figuring that Devine would gain confidence from knowing that even he had to face and overcome hardships. Devine, however, became upset by these revelations, passed them along to other parishioners, and left the church. Several weeks later, she made a serious suicide attempt and required hospitalization for several months.

Reverend Pew appears to have seriously mismanaged his parishioner's clinical depression by failing to recognize its intensity and his own lack of competence to treat it. He also interjected too much of his own life while failing to recognize that Ms. Devine had asked him for spiritual guidance. Pew should have stuck to his role as a pastor and referred Ms. Devine to someone competent to treat her depression.

When a therapist agrees to be an expert witness in the client's behalf or enters into some other legal matter or institutional policy, a thorny dual role presents itself with very different forms of alliance and definitions of truth (Strasburger, Gutheil, & Brodsky, 1997; see also Chapter 17). The APA ethics code recognizes such situations and admonishes psychologists to clarify role expectations and how confidentiality with the client may be affected as a result (APA 02: 3.05c).

Finally, as job prospects become tighter, out of necessity psychotherapists have invented new marketplace niches for themselves. "Personal coaching," "psychologically based" home organization services, "authentic happiness" workshops, and "pet therapy" are but a few examples. Training standards for these offshoots of psychotherapy are virtually nonexistent, expectations on the part of clients are high, and boundaries seem more likely to become confusing for both clients and therapists.

Risky Career Periods

Therapists who engage in inappropriate role blending are often relatively inexperienced. Many have come from graduate programs in which students developed complex relationships with their educators and supervisors. Similarly, the internship or residency period often involves role blending, including social, evaluative, and business-related activities (Slimp & Burian, 1994; see also Chapters 11 and 16). It may be that many therapists, new to functioning independently, have insufficient opportunity to observe professionals who have put appropriate boundaries in place. Further, some therapists experienced appalling supervisory models, involving sexual advances and other improper behaviors, when they were students (Glaser & Thorpe, 1986; Pope, Levenson, & Schover, 1980).

The midcareer period can be risky for those therapists whose profession or life in general has not panned out according to their youthful goals. Divorce or other family-based stresses involving their teenage or young adult children, onset of a chronic illness, and apprehension about aging are among other midcareer difficulties that can impair professional judgment. Research findings reveal that the majority of therapists who engage in sexual relationships with their clients are middle-aged (see Chapter 12).

Another elevated risk period can occur at the far end of the career cycle. Sometimes, older therapists have, perhaps without full awareness, come to see themselves as having evolved beyond questioning or having earned some sort of "senior pass" bequeathing the freedom to do whatever they please. Pepper (1990) discussed the psychodynamics of charismatic, grandiose, authoritarian senior therapists who may harm clients by encouraging complicated multiple relationships. We know of ethics cases involving therapists who have practiced for 40 or more years who illustrate this phenomenon.

Case 10–3: Gloria Vast, Ph.D., refers to herself as the "grand dame of psychology." For many years, she has run large encounter groups based on her long-standing best-selling book, *Touch Yourself, Touch the Universe*. Now in her late 60s, she pays several of her current clients minimum wage to assist her. If her client–workers become disaffected, she berates them and sometimes banishes them. One client expelled from the circle successfully pressed charges of exploitation with the state licensing board.

Case 10–4: Alan Groupie, Ph.D., went into business with a famous movie star who suffered from severe depression and eventually became his manager. Groupie moved in with the star and personally monitored all of his activities, charging his usual fee of $150 per hour, 24 hours a day, 7 days a week. This arrangement lasted for more than a year until the star's legal counsel stepped in and filed extortion charges against Dr. Groupie.

Risky Clients

Not every client can tolerate boundary crossings. Even Lazarus (1994), who favored flexible boundaries, allowed that:

> With some clients, anything other than a formal and clearly delineated doctor–patient relationship is inadvisable and is likely to prove counterproductive. It is usually inadvisable to disregard strict boundary limits in the presence of severe psychopathology; involving passive–aggressive,

histrionic, or manipulative behaviors; borderline personality features; or manifestations of suspiciousness and undue hostility. (p. 257)

Trust issues often lie at the heart of the matter. Clients seen at social service and other outpatient community agencies may become disenfranchised due to deficits in cognition, judgment, self-care, and self-protection, as well as holding little social status and power. Such clients are at greater risk for exploitation (Walker & Clark, 1999). Clients who have experienced victimization through violent attacks or abuse because of difficulties with trust or ambivalence surrounding their caretakers also benefit from clear boundary setting, despite their frequent testing of such boundaries (Borys, 1994). Clients with self-esteem or individuation problems often depend on the constant approval of others for confirmation. Therapists who weaken boundaries by reassuring such clients that they are "special" by taking them to lunch, giving them gifts, or disclosing excessive detail from their own lives may unwittingly collude with this pattern, thereby reinforcing the pathology (Borys, 1994).

Those clients who have suffered early deprivations and have not fully mourned the finality of the past may still seek to meet their residual needs by earning favor with those who were physically or emotionally unavailable. Developing a therapeutic relationship often mobilizes high hopes that the therapist will be able to replace or supply what was lost. If the therapist responds as a rescuer, a totally inappropriate cycle becomes established, and the client will again experience the loss because a therapist never can (and never intended to) replace a parent or the past (Borys, 1994). In this context, we gain considerable insight into the psychodynamics behind the many charges of "abandonment" brought by clients involved in multiple-role relationships with their therapists.

The technique of positive limit setting should be mastered by all psychotherapists. It involves placing restrictions when responding to the client's request while reframing the response in a way that meets a legitimate underlying need. Essentially, this requires therapists to ask themselves how their potential comments or interventions will likely benefit their client. The next two cases provide examples of positive limit setting.

Case 10–5: Timmy Vulnerable, age 10, was enrolled in psychotherapy with Carla Carefull, Psy.D., by a state welfare agency and the foster parents with whom Timmy had been placed following a significant physical beating by his substance-abusing mother. After several months, the agency began to plan for a reunification with the mother, who would soon graduate from a drug rehabilitation program. During a session, Timmy asked Dr. Carefull, "Where do you live?" When she inquired why he wanted to know, Timmy replied, "I thought maybe if my mom started hitting me again, I could come over to your place." She told Timmy, "You're right! You do need a plan for what to do if things get bad at home. I'm not always home, so it will be better if we figure ways that you could get help any time." Dr. Carefull then informed Timmy of emergency resources and how to reach them.

Dr. Carefull was deeply moved by Timmy's situation and his poignant analysis of her as a helper in times of crisis. She also appropriately recognized, however, that she could not meet these needs in the way the child was asking.

Case 10–6: Rita Repeata sought psychotherapy with Hy Pedestal, Ph.D., following a breakup with the man she had been dating for 2 months. She described a series of relationships with three different men in the past 12 months. All followed the same pattern: casual social contacts leading to sexual intimacies by the second date and a breakup within a few weeks. Each time Rita said she "felt like ending it all." She began her second therapy session with Dr. Pedestal by telling him how helpful the first session had been and what an exceptional therapist he was. She then got out of her chair and sat on the floor at his feet, looking up at him adoringly. When Pedestal asked what she was doing, Rita replied, "I feel more comfortable like this."

Dr. Pedestal acknowledged Rita's feelings, but noted that sitting on the floor in that manner would do little to help her break out of the pattern for which she was seeking help. Politely, but firmly, Dr. Pedestal asked her to sit in one of the office chairs and initiated a discussion of the importance of focusing on the issues that brought her into therapy.

Making Blending Decisions

Table 10–1 is designed to help decide whether blending roles should even be considered. We have adapted it from the work of S. K. Anderson and Kitchener (1998), Brown (1994), Gottlieb (1993), Kitchener (1988), and Younggren and Gottleib (2004) and added our own observations and research. Of course, each situation that arises has its own idiosyncrasies that require reflection before acting. Furthermore, most risks can be contemplated along a continuum as opposed to the dichotomous scheme we present here. However, if an honest reflection results in

Table 10–1 Evaluating Additional Roles With Psychotherapy Clients

Considerations Regarding Added Role Dimensions	More Risky	Less Risky
Relevant therapeutic issues or sociocultural factors (e.g., diagnosis, client's religion and traditions, family situation and dynamics)	Unclear whether an added role would be wise	Clear indications favoring an added role
Therapist/client power differential	High	Low
Therapist and client expectations	Incongruent	Congruent
Therapist and client obligations in the contemplated relationship	Disparate	Similar
Duration (or expected duration) of therapy	Longer term	Short term
Termination (or expected termination)	Conflicted/no time specifiable	Mutual/satisfactory
Prospects that client requires follow-up later	Very likely	Unlikely
Extent to which therapist's personal needs would be gratified more than those of the client	Considerable	Very small; negligible
Impulsivity of the therapist	High	Low
Degree of client pathology or past abuse	High	Low
Firmness of client's personal boundaries	Loose	Solid
Degree of client's autonomy	Low/needy	High/self-confident
Duration of therapist's professional experience	Beginning practitioner	At least 1 year of active, independent practice
Extent to which confidentiality can be indefinitely maintained	Not likely	Very likely
Therapist's access to collegial interaction and support	Little/isolated	Considerable
Extent of client's understanding of, and informed consent to, the contemplated added relationship	Minimal	Full
The worst-case outcome scenario of the contemplated relationship is still relatively benign	No	Yes
A consultation with a colleague about the contemplated relationship has taken or will take place before going forward	No	Yes

any feature of a contemplated new role tending toward the "more risky" column, we advise *considerable* caution.

The problem is that many people are so adept at not seeing what they don't want to see, especially if their own need satisfaction is at issue, that they do not accurately predict what problems could arise. The next section lists cautionary signals in more concrete terms, making a decision somewhat less vulnerable to excuses.

Red Flag Alerts

Mental health professionals can be helpful, caring, empathic human beings and maintain professional parameters within which they effectively relate to their clients. And, we again acknowledge the impossibility of setting firm boundaries appropriate for every client under every circumstance. We remain concerned, however, that inappropriate crossings are often rationalized as benevolent or therapeutic. As Brown (1994) stated:

> In the many cases in which I have testified as an expert witness regarding abuses in psychotherapy and the standards of care, it is a very common experience for me to hear the accused therapist pleading the cause of greater humanity, and even love, as the rationale for having had sex with, breast fed, slow-danced with, gone into business with, moved in with, and so on with the complaining client. (p. 276)

Rationalizations even include blaming the client for untoward consequences. A senior psychologist was successfully sued in a highly publicized case when it was verified that her personal life and that of a young male client became completely intertwined. She told a news reporter, "Look what happened to me. I went out of my way to help him become a better person and he paid me back by destroying my career. I should have known. Once a snake, always a snake."

Here, we offer another personal assessment in the form of some early warning signs of non-sexual boundary crossings that could cause confusion and disadvantage clients. These signals, some of which are adapted from work by Ep-stein and Simon (1990) and Walker and Clark (1999), include the following:

- actively seeking opportunities to spend time with a client outside a professional setting
- anticipating, with excitement, a certain client's appointment
- expecting that a client should volunteer to do favors for you (e.g., getting you a better deal from his or her business)
- viewing a client as in a position to advance your own position and fantasizing regarding how that would play out
- wishing that a client were not a client and, instead, in some other type of relationship with you (e.g., your best friend or business partner)
- disclosing considerable detail about your own life to a client and expecting interest or nurturing in return
- trying to influence a client's hobbies, political or religious views, or other personal choices that have no direct therapeutic relevance
- allowing a client to take undue advantage without confronting him or her (e.g., allowing many missed appointments without calling to cancel)
- relying on a client's presence or praise to boost how you feel about yourself
- giving in to a client's requests and perspectives on issues from fear that he or she will otherwise leave therapy
- feeling entitled to *all* of the credit when a client improves, especially if a marked achievement is attained while under your care
- viewing one or more clients as among the central people in your life
- greatly resisting terminating a client despite indicators that termination is appropriate
- believing that you are the only person who can help a particular client
- noticing that the pattern of interactions with a client is becoming increasingly irrelevant to the therapeutic goals
- feeling jealous or envious of a clients' other close relationships
- frequently allowing the therapy session to go overtime
- instigating communications with a client in between sessions for reasons that are contrived or irrelevant to the therapy issues

- finding yourself trying to impress a client about yourself and your achievements
- experiencing a feeling of dread on sensing that a client may decide to leave therapy
- feeling uncomfortable discussing the "red flags" that pertain to you with a trusted colleague because you are concerned that the colleague would be critical of your thinking or behavior

Perhaps the most difficult message for us to convey in writing is how *right* it might feel at the time to slip into a more complex role with those receiving our services. Our brief case stories summarize situations that often take weeks and months to unfold. As a result, we may have failed to convey sufficiently the perceptions and rationalizations that are so often involved. So, perhaps the brightest red flags of all should pop up any time you say to yourself, "This person will be different," or "This particular circumstance doesn't qualify as a role conflict."

If you begin to sense the professional role stretching into any area unrelated to the purpose of the professional relationship, pause immediately to evaluate the situation. Imagine the worst-case scenario in terms of outcome should the present course continue and seek consultation with a peer (Canter, Bennett, Jones, & Nagy, 1994). This makes good sense considering that we can seldom fully predict harmful outcomes in advance.

Before presenting some specific types of multiple-role relationships in the remainder of this chapter and the next two chapters, and the peculiar challenges of each, remember that not all boundary crossings constitute ethical violations. Our primary goal is to sensitize readers to the possible conflicts and potential damage of one's actions so that reasoned, professional judgment may be exercised prior to risking any blending of roles. As Brown (1994) wisely stated: "The goal of an ethical decision is not to avoid any and all violations of boundaries, for this is impossible. Instead, the goal is to remain on the more innocuous end of the continuum, in the position where the abuse and exploitation of the power of the therapist are minimized" (p. 279).

ENTERING INTO BUSINESS RELATIONSHIPS WITH CLIENTS

Any business partnership is vulnerable to interpersonal conflict and financial loss. In the context of that obvious certainty it seems astonishing that therapists have willfully undertaken such risky associations with their ongoing clients. There is no such thing as "strictly business" when one of the partners has a fiduciary duty to uphold the trust and ensure the personal welfare of the other. Such ventures that have gone awry illustrate the damage done to both therapists and their clients.

Case 10–7: C. D. Rom had been a client of Teki Grabbit, Psy.D., for almost 2 years. Dr. Grabbit was in awe of Rom's astounding computer skills. When Rom announced his intent to start a software company and invited Dr. Grabbit to become an investor, she jumped at the chance. The company was formed, but things moved very slowly. Rom quit therapy because, as he later stated in his complaint to a state licensing board, "During our sessions, Dr. Grabbit focused almost exclusively on the company, demanded that I make certain changes in the business plan, and ignored the personal issues that I still needed to deal with. When I told her that I resented having to pay her to talk about the business, she yelled, 'You owe it to me.' "

Case 10–8: "You and I would make a great team," declared cosmetic surgeon Marcel Sculpt, M.D., to his counselor Barbie Dip, L.M.H.C. "My patients often need counseling, and some of your clients may be interested in my services. We could share an office suite and call ourselves something like, 'Beautiful Inside and Out.' I can get you lots of clients." Ms. Dip, whose client caseload was flagging, thought the idea a bit wacky. But, the more she considered the potential benefits, the more attracted she became. Dip did insist that Sculpt continue his therapy with someone else, figuring this would defuse any mixed-role dilemmas. However, the expected clientele did not materialize, and Ms. Dip's share of the lavish office expenses proved to be far more than she could afford. Her relationship with Sculpt soured, and when they argued, she brought up content from his past counseling sessions to use against him. The partnership was dissolved, leaving Ms. Dip deeply in debt. Dip blamed Sculpt for cajoling her into such a ridiculous venture and is considering suing him.

No one goes into business unless they want to profit financially, which puts immediate and complicating expectations and pressures on clients. Greed played a large role in both Grabbit's and Dip's cases, even though neither would likely admit it. As a result, they became entangled in business dealings to the detriment of their responsibilities to their clients needs and ultimately to their own welfare. Both should have recognized from the outset that these deals could reasonably impair their objectivity and judgment. Grabbit ultimately did lose her entire investment, more than $50,000, and was further admonished by her state licensing board. Ms. Dip believed that because Sculpt instigated the partnership and because she terminated the therapy with him, she had no responsibility for what then transpired. On the contrary, the responsibility rested exclusively with her because her training should have enabled her to foresee the potential hitch in the plan. Terminating a client for the purpose of going into business constitutes unacceptable professional practice, even if Dip did assist Sculpt in finding a new therapist. If Dip goes ahead with her lawsuit, she will be in for a surprise when the tables turn on her.

Whereas the APA places a time passage provision on having sexual relationships with ex-clients (see Chapter 12), no such waiting period is proscribed for entering into business or other deals with clients after they have been terminated. It appears, however, that engaging in business relationships with those one used to treat is not uncommon (Lamb et al. 1994; Pope et al., 1987). Unfortunately, these surveys did not probe how well these ventures fared.

ENTERING INTO PROFESSIONAL RELATIONSHIPS WITH EMPLOYEES

Some degree of relational overlapping occurs naturally in most work settings. Workers and their supervisors are often friendly, care about each other's welfare, and attend some of the same social events. The workplace can also be rife with land mines—gossip, conflicts, competition for promotions and resources, and disliked coworkers—all of which contribute to the potential for volatility. Therefore, this ever-changing environment should never be further complicated by willfully appending yet another professional role to it. Employees almost always have reasonable alternatives for any needed psychotherapy services.

Case 10–9: Jan Typer worked as a records clerk for a community mental health agency. Helmut Honcho, Ph.D., supervised her work. When Ms. Typer experienced some personal problems, she asked Dr. Honcho if he would treat her. He agreed. Ms. Typer later brought an ethics complaint against Honcho, charging him with blocking her promotion based on assessments of her as a client instead of on her performance as an employee.

It may prove impossible to unravel the true basis for any job-related decision in such situations. Whether valid or not, Ms. Typer can always interpret any unpleasant reactions to what happens on the job as linked to the therapy or vice-versa. When a client also works as an employee, the consequences of a multiple-role relationship gone awry can be especially devastating because of the potentially adverse career and economical ramifications. Dr. Honcho should have known better than to take on Ms. Typer as a client. Because of the clear foreseeable risk of harm, he clearly violated ethical standards.

Case 10–10: Renega Lease, L.S.W., owned an apartment building managed by William Wrench, who collected the rent and performed routine repairs. Wrench and his wife asked Lease to see them for couples counseling. During the second session, Lease learned from the wife that Wrench habitually drank heavily. She fired him, thus forcing him and his wife to leave their home.

Information shared in one sector of a relationship influences the entire relationship.

Whereas Lease can not be faulted for wanting sober management of her apartment complex, she unethically used information shared in confidence to the detriment of her client.

EMPLOYING CLIENTS

Working with people who have a variety of skills will inevitably lead to some degree of temptation to consider what these clients might have to offer therapists. Moreover, clients are often financially strapped. Offering to employ them may seem like doing a good deed. However, as with business relationships, such alliances are fraught with risk that can obliterate the professional relationship and disperse additional emotional and financial debris in its wake.

Case 10–11: Oscar Scatterbill, Ph.D., hired client Thomas Clerk as his personal secretary and bookkeeper. The relationship seemed to work well until Clerk asked for a raise. Dr. Scatterbill refused, saying that he was already paying Clerk a good hourly wage. Clerk countered by reciting Scatterbill's monthly income and comparing it to his own. Dr. Scatterbill allegedly laughed as he responded that a comparison between the two was hardly meaningful. An insulted Clerk quit his job as well as his therapy and wrote to an ethics committee claiming that Dr. Scatterbill had "ruined his whole life."

Dr. Scatterbill should have known better than to employ an ongoing client, especially for such a sensitive position that gave the client access to confidential information. Different roles call for different protocols, and the roles of "therapist" and "boss'" require markedly disparate and often-conflicting styles of relating.

Case 10–12: Snap Shudder needed additional work to make overdue payments on a new car. When Snap offered to photograph the upcoming wedding of his counselor at half price, Melvin Groom, L.M.F.T., agreed. However, the bride found the photographs unacceptable and argued against paying Shudder. In the meantime, Shudder increased the agreed-on price because the bride proved very demanding, causing him extra work and expense. The matter escalated into mayhem. Shudder quit therapy, told everyone in the small town that Groom had married a witch who had total control over him, and successfully sued Groom in small claims court.

That Shudder bought a car he could not afford was not Groom's problem to solve. Groom might have politely refused Shudder's offer, noting that all wedding plans had been finalized. Thus, even if the job is specific and time limited, competent judgment must supersede caving in to what appears on the surface to be "a good deal." In the meantime, Groom's reputation in the community as a competent person to consult for marriage counseling suffered.

Even financial dealings with clients motivated by genuine kindness can backfire. By becoming directly involved in a client's personal misfortune, the therapist in the next case unwittingly withdrew from his role as a safe, neutral haven.

Case 10–13: Barney Bigheart, Ph.D., felt sympathetic when his client Bart Busted faced foreclosure on his home. Bigheart offered to loan Busted several thousand dollars to stave off the lender. Busted gratefully accepted and signed an unsecured note with a generously low interest rate. Busted's financial situation did not improve, however, and he failed to make his loan payments to Bigheart. Even though Bigheart exerted no pressure regarding the late payments, Busted expressed considerable guilt over "letting down the only person who ever gave a damn about me." Busted's depression deepened, and he required hospitalization.

We can hardly question Bigheart's compassion, but we can fault his professional judgment. By attempting to solve his client's problem, he destroyed Busted's psychotherapeutic refuge. Simply remaining available as Busted's caring therapist, and perhaps substantially reducing the fee or seeing him at no cost, would have far better served the client's emotional well-being.

BARTERING ARRANGEMENTS WITH CLIENTS

The APA ethics code had long discouraged exchanging anything other than money for therapeutic services. However, APA has nearly reversed itself in recent years. The 1992 APA ethics code allowed for bartering but also included a strongly worded caution against such arrangements, citing the potential for taking advantage of clients and distortion of the professional relationship. The current code has dropped the introductory cautionary statement, leaving only the admonition that professional judgment be used regarding clinical contraindications and potential for exploitation before entering into a barter agreement with a client (APA 02: 6.05).

Why has bartering for psychological services transformed from a forbidden practice to a nearly incidental ethical matter? In the late 1980s, the vast majority of psychologists, according to a large national survey, had never accepted a service or product payment for therapy, and those who had did so only rarely (Borys & Pope, 1989). However, insurance coverage for mental health services has since decreased. Thus, more people seeking psychotherapy may lack the ability to afford it, but they may possess skills or objects to trade (Hill, 1999).

On the surface, allowing bartering in hard economic times may seem like a win–win situation for clients who want therapy and therapists who want clients. We acknowledge that entering into bartering agreements with clients appears reasonable and even a humanitarian practice toward those who require mental health services but are uninsured and strapped for cash. We also acknowledge that many bartering arrangements proved satisfactory to both parties. Here are a few examples that have come to our attention:

- A marriage and family therapist in a small farming community agreed to take fresh produce as payment for three sessions with a couple who needed professional advice regarding the management of an elderly parent.

- A counselor in a small town agreed to see a proud but poverty-stricken client who was mourning the loss of his spouse in return for the client's carpentry work on a charitable home restoration project organized by a group that the counselor actively supported.
- A psychologist performed a child assessment in exchange for five small trees from the parent, who was owner of a struggling nursery service.

In each of these situations, community mental health resources were limited, as were the clients' assets, and exploitation was not at issue. The services were of limited duration, the economic value of the exchanges was not excessive, and the clients' needs were specific and circumscribed and did not involve complex transference issues or open-ended demands. The chances of untoward results were minimal in all three cases, although the marriage and family counselor accepting the fresh produce did confide to us that "being practically knee deep in 150 pounds of corn presented a small logistical challenge."

Exchanging Services

Let us now compare the above examples to another that also appears also to be going very well. That is, for now.

Case 10–14: A gifted seamstress agreed to make clothes in exchange for counseling. The client was satisfied with the agreement because she needed counseling and had plenty of time available to sew. The therapist's elation was summarized by her giddy remark at a cocktail party, "I am most assuredly the best-dressed shrink in town."

This case illustrates the potential darker side of barter arrangements. Because the therapist openly acknowledged, with delight, her dual relationship at a social gathering, she apparently never considered the inherent risks of exploitation. What will happen when an outfit does not fit properly or does not meet the therapist's requirements? What if the client becomes displeased with the therapy and begins to feel like a one-woman sweatshop? What if the therapist remains so satisfied with this relationship that she creates within the client an unnecessary dependency to match her own? These "what ifs" are not idle speculation when one considers incidents of bartering that have already gone awry.

Case 10–15: Kurt Court, Esq., and Leonard Dump, Ph.D., met at a mutual friend's home. Mr. Court's law practice was suffering because of what he described as "mild depression." Dr. Dump was about to embark on what promised to be a bitter divorce. They hit on the idea of swapping professional services. Dr. Dump would see Mr. Court as a psychotherapy client, and Mr. Court would represent Dr. Dump in his divorce. Mr. Court proved to be far more depressed than Dr. Dump anticipated. Furthermore, Court's representation of Dump was erratic, and the likelihood of a favorable outcome looked bleak. Yet, it was Mr. Court who brought ethics charges against Dr. Dump. Court charged that the therapy he received was inferior, and that Dump spent most of the time blaming him for not getting better faster.

Case 10–16: Decora Shod, D.S.W., was treating a client who owned a furniture manufacturing outlet. Dr. Shod mentioned that she was in the process of redecorating her home. The client offered to let Shod select furniture from his warehouse at his cost if Shod would see him at a greatly reduced rate. The client reasoned that they would both benefit because Shod would be receiving more for far less than she could in retail outlets, and the client could also save money. Shod agreed to the proposal. In therapy, Shod increasingly confronted the client in areas in which she felt the client behaved in a self-destructive and defensive manner. The client reacted negatively and contacted an ethics committee, charging Shod with attempting to lock him in to unnecessary treatment until her home was completely refurnished.

These cases illustrate not only the destructive results that can occur when the follow-through phase of bartering results in unhappy clients, but also the vulnerable position in which the therapists placed themselves. Court's impatience and Shod's confrontations may have been appropriate under simpler circumstances. But, because of the intertwining of nonprofessional issues in each situation, Dr. Dump was perceived as being retaliatory and Dr. Shod as self-serving.

Charges of exploitation are heightened when the value placed on the therapist's time and skills are set at a higher rate than those of the clients. And, because the therapist's hourly rate is more likely to exceed that of what one would pay a client, this risk is probably present in most exchange agreements.

Case 10–17: Elmo Brush agreed to paint the rooms in the home of Paul Peelpaint, Ph.D., in exchange for counseling Brush's teenage daughter. Dr. Peelpaint saw the girl for six sessions and terminated the counseling. Brush complained that his end of the bargain would have brought $1,200 in a conventional deal. Thus, it was as though he paid $200 a session for services for which Peelpaint's other full-paying clients paid $100. Dr. Peelpaint argued that he had satisfactorily resolved the daughter's problems, and the arrangement was valid because task was traded for task, not dollar value for dollar value.

Trading a one-shot service with a known cost estimate, based on Brush's own professional experience, with a service that can not be cost estimated in advance spells trouble from the beginning. Brush's daughter might have required 50 sessions, valued at $5,000, if Dr. Peelpaint was willing to conduct as many sessions as therapeutically necessary and had been collecting his usual fees. Dr. Peelpaint's attitude also reveals little regard for fairness toward Brush. Some of the ethical complexities of Dr. Peelpaint's case might have been avoided had he hired Brush outright, leaving Brush free to make an independent decision about engaging Peelpaint as his daughter's therapist after the painting job was finished.

Case 10–18: X. Ploit, Ph.D., offered an unemployed landscaper, Sod Flower, the opportunity to design and redo his grounds in return for psychotherapy. Dr. Ploit charged $100 an hour and credited Flower at a rate of $15 an hour, which meant that Flower worked over 6 hours for every therapy session received. Flower complained to Dr. Ploit that the amount of time he was spending on the yard prevented him from entering into full-time employment. Dr. Ploit responded that Flower could choose to terminate therapy and return when he could afford to pay the full fee.

Dr. Ploit's case is even more complicated and bothersome. Ploit figured the amount due for an ongoing service considerably below the going rate for a skilled landscape artist. The bartering contract most likely did contribute substantially to the client's difficulties. When the landscaper–client complained, the therapist interrupted the agreement and abandoned the client. In the actual incident, the client eventually successfully sued the therapist for considerable damages.

Case 10–19: Notta Rembrandt proposed that she paint a portrait of Gig Grump, Psy.D., in exchange for psychotherapy. Dr. Grump posed, and Rembrandt received therapy on an hour-for-hour basis. On the 11th session, Grump viewed the almost-completed portrait for the first time and expressed dissatisfaction, calling it "hideous." An insulted Rembrandt insisted that the portrait was superb and "captured Grump's soul." The conversation escalated into a fervent argument. Rembrandt grabbed her canvas, stomped out, and did not return. Dr. Grump sent Rembrandt a bill for 10 sessions. Rembrandt filed an ethics charge. Grump responded that the whole arrangement was the client's idea, and he was not responsible for the outcome.

Possible transference and countertransference issues notwithstanding, the arrangement between Rembrandt and Grump was shaky given the wide variability in artistic tastes. Rembrandt prevailed in her ethics complaint. Grump's attempt to fault the client was not a persuasive defense, although he did offer to withdraw his bill.

Exchanging Services for Goods

So far we have discussed exchanging a service for a service. Here, we explore more fully the exchange of professional services for tangible objects. It has been suggested that this form of bartering is less problematic because a fair market price can be established by an outside, objective source (Canter et al., 1994). However, the value of goods depends almost entirely on what buyers are willing to pay for them. This means that determining the true value of some items will prove challenging, and charges of exploitation could easily arise. We know of numerous instances of service-for-item bargaining that turned out poorly. Therefore, we urge considerable caution when an object is traded for professional services and even when purchasing an item outright from a client.

Case 10–20: When Manifold Benz, Ph.D., learned that his financially strapped client planned to sell his classic automobiles to pay outstanding therapy and other bills, Benz expressed an interest in one of the cars. Dr. Benz said that he had seen the same model at an auto show for $19,000, and that he would be willing to credit the client with 200 hours of therapy in exchange for the car. The client stood 100 hours in arrears at the time.

Benz is exploiting his client by committing him to a specific number of future therapy sessions that the client may not need. Further, we do not know if the price Benz suggested represents fair market value, and this may be difficult to determine precisely because the item is rare, possibly unique. (The fact that Benz allowed a client to fall 100 hours in arrears creates another ethical issue, as discussed in Chapter 7.)

Case 10–21: Flip Channel, Ph.D., allowed Penny Pinched to pay her past due therapy bill with a television set that Penny described as "near new." However, when Dr. Channel set it up in his home, the colors were faded, and the picture flickered. He told Penny that the television was not as she represented it, and that she would have to take it back and figure some other method of payment. Penny angrily retorted that Dr. Channel must have broken it because it was fine when she brought it to him. When Channel insisted that the TV was defective, Penny terminated therapy and contacted an ethics committee. She charged that he broke both a valid contractual agreement and her television set.

Dr. Channel found himself in a no-win situation as a result of the television fiasco. A therapeutic relationship was also destroyed in the process. Channel could have avoided a confrontation and perhaps saved the relationship by junking the TV without mentioning it to Ms. Pinched. But, the therapeutic alliance might have suffered anyway due to lingering resentment that might leak out toward his client.

Case 10–22: When Gemmy Sparkle wanted to buy a house, she decided to start selling her mother's antique jewelry. She brought an exceptionally nice piece to show her therapist, Marilyn Buyit, M.S.W. Buyit asked how much Sparkle wanted for it, and Sparkle quoted her a price that seemed quite reasonable given the size of the rubies. Buyit bought the piece outright for the quoted price, paying cash. Over a year later, and after the therapy relationship had successfully terminated, Sparkle learned that the piece was worth far more than Buyit paid for it. Sparkle called Buyit, asking for an additional $2,000. A stunned Ms. Buyit refused.

In the actual case, the client took the therapist to small claims court and told everyone that the therapist had "taken her for a ride." The client did not prevail, but the local paper of the small town carried a brief article about the case. The therapist's client base fell substantially, and the residual effects had not gone away even 2 years later. Thus, even though the therapist did not elicit the sale and paid the full asking price, the ex-client's distress took a toll on the therapist's practice.

The important point to recognize is that when clients have something of true value to sell, there will rarely be any reason why their therapists should be the ones to purchase them. Today, especially, many ready markets exist, and objects can easily be offered for sale through Internet sites, reaching thousands of potential buyers at little or no cost to sellers.

Final Considerations Regarding Bartering

Because therapeutic services typically involve a combination of trust, sensitive evaluations, social influence, and the creation of some measure of dependency, the potential for untoward conse-

quences always exists with bartering agreements. We contend that it is impossible to confidently ascertain which clients will be well suited to a nontraditional, negotiated payment system and which should be turned down, especially near the outset of the therapeutic relationship. By definition, bartering involves a negotiation process. Is a client in distress and in need of professional services in a position to barter on an equal footing with the therapist? Furthermore, even therapists are attracted to a good deal. How does this pervasive human motive play itself out in a bartering situation with clients?

When a bartering arrangement is suggested by a client, a therapist without a clearly understood "no-barter policy" can be placed in any of three situations that could cause discomfort for all concerned. First, if a therapist is known to barter, which is especially probable in small communities, turning down an unwanted proposal could well be experienced as a rejection, which could hamper some clients' mental status. Zur (2003), who revealed that he barters on occasion, tells the story of a woman who was very unhappy with his decision to reject exchanging body massages for psychotherapy. Second, must a therapist accept something unneeded or unwanted? Can you say to a client, "Well, I sometimes accept goods for services, but I'm allergic to potatoes, and I don't need a llama rug"? Third, how does a therapist react when one client with whom you have a bartering arrangement refers someone who also wants to barter, but the referral clearly is not clinically suited to such an arrangement? These are some of the predicaments that may not end up on ethics committee tables but remain sticky nonetheless, with the potential to cause the kinds of hassles that therapists certainly would prefer to avoid.

A rarely discussed and serious bartering complication is that most professional liability insurance policies specifically *exclude* coverage involving business relationships with clients (Canter et al., 1994; Bennett et al., 2007). Liability insurance carriers may interpret bartering arrangements as business relationships and decline to defend covered therapists when bartering schemes go awry. To obscure matters even further, the fair market monetary value of bartered goods or services must be reported as income on the recipient's income tax returns. Failure to do so constitutes tax evasion. To fully meet legal requirements (and thereby behave in a fully honest and ethical manner) requires detailed documentation, creating another type of interaction with the client. The therapist who declared that there was nothing illegal about doing therapy for free and nothing illegal about that client agreeing to work in the therapist's dress shop for free has set up both for charges of income tax fraud and, for the therapist, labor law violations.

Those who advise against bartering arrangements as ways of protecting both clients and therapists have been accused of giving only lip service to serving the poor (Zur, 2003) and focusing primarily on protecting themselves rather than caring about clients. However, given the potential for glitches, actual exploitation of clients and the appearance of it, and unsatisfactory outcomes for both parties, we recommend that practitioners use bartering sparingly if at all. We advise using other special arrangements (as discussed in Chapter 7) for clients who can not afford psychotherapy.

If one still decides to undertake a bartering arrangement, we recommend preparation of a written contract that judiciously protects the client's welfare (Woody, 1998), one that the client *clearly* finds agreeable. A colleague told us of a client who needed money and offered the therapist the opportunity to purchase the client's rare antique carved Chinese screen. The client had even gone to the trouble of researching its fair market value at the local museum. However, there were clear indications that parting with this possession would be extremely emotionally painful for the client, and it was also very likely that the client would never again be financially capable of getting it back should he ever have that opportunity. As much as our colleague admired the screen, she explained that she could not purchase it and referred the client to a financial counselor to search for alternative solutions to his financial crisis.

We further recommend that therapists avoid *instigating* a bartering relationship. To the extent that the client sees the therapist as the more authoritative individual in the relationship or feels dependent on the therapist for emotional support, it may prove very difficult for a client to refuse the therapist's proposal.

Finally, bartering organizations capable of providing arm's length relationships between clients and therapists do exist. The use of such resources can defuse most of the ethical risks we have discussed. However, new concerns about client confidentiality, screening clients for appropriateness, and the integrity of the bartering organization remain as potentially sticky issues.

VIRTUAL MULTIPLE ROLES

It used to be difficult to obtain information about people. Today, the Internet provides multiple and ever-increasing ways to track individuals but without any assurance that the information is valid. Creating peculiar multiple-role relationships on the Internet is easy because people can easily misrepresent themselves. Modern technology can be abused in diabolical ways.

Case 10–23: Virtual Grifter, L.M.H.C., joined a number of online chat rooms in the persona of a woman who portrayed herself as having received excellent counseling from Grifter. "She" gave contact details, and Grifter successfully gained a number of new clients.

In a note of irony, the true story on which this case was loosely adapted is years old but can be accessed on the Internet, including the therapist's actual identity, for all time to come. (For more information about ethical issues pertaining to therapy on the Internet, see Chapter 6.)

SUMMARY GUIDELINES

1. While not all role blending is unethical and may occasionally be helpful, therapists should avoid most multiple-role relationships and conflict-of-interest situations with clients. The professional role is so often characterized by attributed power, trust, influence, and knowledge of the intimate details of client lives that objectivity is required. Role confusion is likely when roles

are superimposed, which reduces the therapist's position as a steady and grounded haven in the client's life.

2. Therapists should remain aware of the harm multiple-role relationships may cause to themselves as well as their clients. Therapists have sometimes faced public and professional disapproval for even the appearance of conflict.

3. Therapists must carefully monitor their own tendencies to use rationalizations when faced with multiple-role conflicts and should seek another opinion before mixing roles with clients. We strongly advise careful assessment of the potential risks.

4. Avoid entering into business relationships with clients, including employing them. The goals of therapy and business arrangements differ so significantly that they invite harm to one or both parties.

5. Accepting employees as psychotherapy clients, especially when the employee is directly supervised by the therapist or if the therapist has an evaluative role in the client's job performance, should be avoided. The potential for conflict is exceptionally high. Employers may certainly assist clients in finding appropriate professional help.

6. Even though most professional ethics codes do not rule out bartering goods or services with clients, bartering remains a risky activity. Bartering requires a careful assessment prior to taking on such arrangements, including how to report such transactions to the Internal Revenue Service and state tax boards.

References

American Psychological Association. (1992). Ethical principles of psychologists and code of conduct. *American Psychologist, 47,* 1597–1611.

Anderson, M. B., Van Raalte, J. L., & Brewer, B. W. (2001). Sport psychology service delivery: Staying ethical while keeping loose. *Professional Psychology: Research and Practice, 32,* 12–18.

Anderson, S. K., & Kitchener, K. S. (1998). Nonsexual post therapy relationships: A conceptual framework to assess ethical risks. *Professional Psychology: Research and Practice, 29,* 91–99.

Bader, E. (1994) Dual relationships: Legal and ethical trends. *Transactional Analysis Journal, 24,* 64–66.

Bennett, B. E., Bricklin, P. M., Harris, E. A., Knapp, S., VandeCreek, L., & Younggren, J. N. (2007). *Assessing and managing risk in psychological practice: An individualized approach.* Rockville, MD: American Psychological Association Insurance Trust.

Bennett, B. E., Bricklin, P. M., & VandeCreek, L. (1994). Response to Lazarus's "How certain boundaries and ethics diminish therapeutic effectiveness." *Ethics & Behavior, 4,* 263–266.

Bogrand, M. (1993, January–February). The duel over dual relationships. *The California Therapist,* 7–10, 12, 14, 16.

Borys, D. S. (1994). Maintaining therapeutic boundaries: The motive is therapeutic effectiveness, not defensive practice. *Ethics & Behavior, 4,* 267–273.

Borys, D. S., & Pope, K. S. (1989). Dual relationships between therapist and client: A national study of psychologists, psychiatrists, and social workers. *Professional Psychology: Research and Practice, 20,* 283–293.

Brown, L. S. (1994). Concrete boundaries and the problem of literal-mindedness: A response to Lazarus. *Ethics & Behavior, 4,* 275–281.

Canter, M. B., Bennett, B. E., Jones, S. E., & Nagy, T. F. (1994). *Ethics for psychologists: A commentary on the APA ethics code.* Washington, DC: American Psychological Association.

Clarkson, P. (1994). In recognition of dual relationships. *Transactional Analysis Journal, 24,* 32–38.

Davis, J. T. (2002). Countertransference temptation and the use of self of self-disclosure by psychotherapists in training: A discussion for beginning psychotherapists and their supervisors. *Psychoanalytic Psychology, 19,* 435–454.

Epstein, R., & Bower, T. (2005). Why shrinks have problems. *Psychology Today.* Retrieved October 17, 2006, from http://www.psychologytoday.com/articles/pto-19970701-000045.html

Epstein, R. S., & Simon, R. L. (1990). The exploitation index: An early warning indicator of boundary violations in psychotherapy. *Bulletin of the Menninger Clinic, 54,* 450–465.

Farber, B. A., Berano, K. C., & Capobianco, J. A. (2004). Clients' perceptions of the process and consequences of self-disclosure in psychotherapy. *Journal of Counseling Psychology, 51,* 340–346.

Gabbard, G. O. (1994). Teetering on the precipice: A commentary on Lazarus's "How certain boundaries and ethics diminish therapeutic effectiveness." *Ethics & Behavior, 4,* 283–286.

Glaser, R. D., & Thorpe, J. S. (1986). Unethical intimacy: A survey of sexual contact and advances between psychology educators and female graduate students. *American Psychologist, 41,* 43–51.

Gottlieb, M. C. (1993). Avoiding exploitive dual relationships: A decision-making model. *Psychotherapy, 30,* 41–48.

Gutheil, T. G. (1994). Discussion of Lazarus's "How certain boundaries and ethics diminish therapeutic effectiveness." *Ethics & Behavior, 4,* 295–298.

Gutheil, T. G., & Gabbard, G. O. (1993). The concept of boundaries in clinical practice: Theoretical and risk-management dimensions. *American Journal of Psychiatry, 150,* 188–196.

Hedges, L. E. (1993, May–June). In praise of the dual relationship. *The California Therapist,* 46–49.

Hill, M. (1999). Barter: Ethical issues in psychotherapy. *Women & Therapy, 22,* 81–91.

Johnson, W. B., Ralph, J., & Johnson, S. J. (2005). Managing multiple roles in embedded environments: The case of aircraft carrier psychology. *Professional Psychology, 36,* 73–81.

Keith-Spiegel, P., & Koocher, G. P. (1985). *Ethics in psychology: Standards and cases.* New York: Random House.

Kim, B. S. K., Hill, C. E., Gelso, C. J., Goates, M. K., Asay, P. A., & Harbin, J. M. (2003). Counselor self-disclosure, East Asian American client adherence to Asian cultural values, and counseling process. *Journal of Counseling Psychology, 50,* 324–332.

Kitchener, K. S. (1988). Dual role relationships: What makes them so problematic? *Journal of Counseling and Development, 67,* 217–221.

Kovacs, A. L. (1974). The valley of the shadow. *Psychotherapy: Theory, Research and Practice, 11,* 376–382.

Lamb, D. H., Strand, K. K., Woodburn, J. R., Buchko, K. J., Lewis, J. T., & Kang, J. R. (1994). Sexual and business relationships between therapists and former clients, *Psychotherapy, 31,* 270–278.

Lazarus, A. A. (1994). How certain boundaries and ethics diminish therapeutic effectiveness. *Ethics & Behavior, 4,* 253–261.

Lazarus, A. A., & Zur, O. (Eds.). (2002). *Dual relationships in psychotherapy.* New York: Springer.

Montgomery, L. M., & Cupit, B. E. (1999). Complaints, malpractice, and risk management: Professional issues and personal experiences. *Professional Psychology, 30,* 402–410.

Neukrug, E., Milliken, T., & Walden, S. (2001). Ethical complaints made against credentialed counselors: An updated survey of state licensing boards. *Counselor Education and Supervision, 41,* 57–70.

Pepper, R. S. (1990). When transference isn't transference: Iatrogenesis of multiple role relations between practicing therapists. *Journal of Contemporary Psychotherapy, 20,* 141–153.

Peterson, Z. D. (2002). More than a mirror: The ethics of therapist self-disclosure. *Psychotherapy: Theory, Research, Practice, Training, 39,* 21–31.

Physician divorces linked to specialties. (1997). *The Gazette: The Newspaper of the John's Hopkins University.* Retrieved December 16, 2006, from http://www.jhu.edu/gazette/janmar97/mar1797/briefs.html

Pope, K. S. (1991). Dual relationships in psychotherapy. *Ethics & Behavior, 1,* 21–34.

Pope, K. S., Levenson, H., & Schover, L. R. (1980). Sexual behavior between clinical supervisors and trainees: Implications for professional standards. *Professional Psychology: Research, Theory and Practice, 11,* 157–162.

Pope, K. S., Tabachnick, B. G., & Keith-Spiegel, P. (1987). Ethics of practice: The beliefs and behaviors of psychologists as therapists. *American Psychologist, 42,* 993–1006.

Ryder, R., & Hepworth, J. (1990). AAMFT ethical code: Dual relationships. *Journal of Marital and Family Therapy, 16,* 127–132.

Slimp, P. A. O., & Burian, B. K. (1994). Multiple role relationships during internship. Consequences and recommendations. *Professional Psychology: Research and Practice, 25,* 39–45.

Smith, D., & Fitzpatrick, M. (1995). Patient–therapist boundary issues: An integrative review of theory and research. *Professional Psychology: Research and Practice, 26,* 499–506.

Sonne, J. L. (1994). Multiple relationships: Does the new ethics code answer the right questions?

Professional Psychology: Research and Practice, 25, 336–343.

Strasburger, L. H., Gutheil, T. G., & Brodsky, A. (1997). On wearing two hats: Role conflict in serving as both psychotherapist and expert witness. *American Journal of Psychiatry, 154,* 448–456.

Tallman, G. (1981). *Therapist–client social relationships.* Unpublished manuscript, California State University, Northridge.

Tomm, K. (1993, January–February). The ethics of dual relationships. *The California Therapist, 7,* 9, 11, 13–14.

Walker, R., & Clark, J. J. (1999). Heading off boundary problems: Clinical supervision as risk management. *Psychiatric Services, 50,* 1435–1439.

Williams, M. H. (1998). Boundary violations: Do some contended standards fail to encompass commonplace procedures of humanistic, behavioral, and eclectic psychotherapies? *Psychotherapy, 34,* 238–249.

Woody, R. H. (1998). Bartering for psychological services. *Professional Psychology: Research and Practice, 29,* 174–178.

Younggren, J. N., & Gottleib, M. C. (2004). Managing risk when contemplating multiple relationships. *Professional Psychology: Research and Practice, 35,* 255–260.

Zur, O. (2003). Bartering in psychotherapy and counseling: Complexities, case studies and guidelines. Retrieved December 6, 2004, from http://www.drozur.com/bartertherapy.html

11

Multiple-Role Relationships II
Close Encounters

Good habits result from resisting temptation.

Ancient proverb

Contents

This chapter continues the presentation and illustration of specific multiple-role relationships that could likely prove problematic to psychotherapy clients and to those we are entrusted to teach. Risks and how to evaluate multiple roles are covered in Chapter 10.

MULTIPLE RELATIONSHIPS WITH THOSE ONE ALREADY KNOWS

Delivery of Services to Close Friends and Family Members

Mental health professionals come to expect frequent requests for advice from friends and family members. Queries range from how to handle a child's acting out against other children to how to convince a proud grandmother with short-term memory loss to move into an assisted living facility. When more than factual information or casual advice is indicated, a temptation may arise to enter into professional or quasi-professional relationships with good friends or family members. Therapists may reason that they are capable of providing especially good counsel because trust already exists. Furthermore, therapists may express a willingness to see these "clients" at bargain rates or at no cost whatsoever.

Despite the seeming advantages of offering formalized counseling to friends or family members, sustained therapy relationships with them should be avoided. Although close relations and psychotherapy exist in the context of intimacy, striking differences exist between the function and process of the two.

Successful personal relationships are free and aim for

- satisfaction of mutual needs
- open, evolving agendas that are not necessarily goal directed
- longevity

Professional relationships, on the other hand, normally involve payment to the therapist and aim for

- serving only the emotional needs of the client
- focusing on specific therapeutic goals
- achieving therapeutic goals followed by a termination of the relationship

When these two types of relationships are superimposed, the potential for adverse consequences to all concerned increases substantially. Notice how the differences are actually oppositional, meaning that expectations can clash, and trust can become easily broken.

Because a preexisting relationship exists, the American Psychological Association (APA) ethics code cautions us not to undertake a professional relationship if impairment of objectivity or effectiveness might result (APA 02: 3.05). Because we can not remain objective when it comes to dealing with close relationships given that the human equation invariably includes our own emotional needs, we should avoid accepting those with close preexisting relationships into a professional relationship.

Short-term support in times of crisis may qualify as an exception. Responding to a frantic call from a friend in the middle of the night is something friends do for each other. Should the friend require more than temporary comforting, offer a referral. Otherwise, as the following cases illustrate, unexpected entanglements can occur, even when therapists have benevolent intentions.

Case 11–1: Weight-reduction specialist Stella Stern, L.M.H.C., agreed, after many requests, to work on a professional basis with her good friend Zoftig Bluto. Progress was slow, and most of Bluto's weight returned shortly after it was lost. Dr. Stern became impatient because Bluto did not seem to be taking the program seriously. Bluto became annoyed with Dr. Stern's irritation as well as the lack of progress. Bluto expressed disappointment in Dr. Stern, whom she believed would be able to help her lose weight quickly and effortlessly.

Case 11–2: An intellectual assessment of 9-year-old Freddy was recommended by the boy's school. Freddy's father, Paul Proud, asked his brother, Peter Proud, Ph.D., to perform it. The results revealed some low-performance areas and a full-scale IQ score of 93. Paul was very upset with his psychologist–brother for "not making the boy look good to the school."

Case 11–3: Murray X. Plode, Psy.D., accepted his sister's 17-year-old daughter as a client. During the course of therapy, his niece revealed that she had been sexually abused by her father, the therapist's brother-in-law. Dr. Plode stormed over to the parents' home, threatened police action in front of the entire family, and demanded that his brother-in-law pack his things and leave the family home immediately. The father, who denied ever sexually molesting his daughter, complained to an ethics committee that Dr. Plode had violated his rights and destroyed his family. Plode responded that this was a personal matter and therefore nobody's business but his own.

Faulty expectations, mixed allegiances, role confusion, and misinterpretations of motives can lead to disappointment, anger, and sometimes a total collapse of relationships. Dr. Stern's friend could not commit to the obligations of the professional alliance but expected results anyway. Dr. Proud's brother assumed that a close family member would willingly cheat. Dr. Plode could not separate his role as an upset uncle from that of a counselor upholding professional decorum and utilizing established legal recourse.

Therapists are, by definition, emotionally involved with those with whom they have preexisting relationships. They may not even fully recognize extreme misuse of their own professional skills, as the next case well illustrates.

Case 11–4: Misty Resistant, the girlfriend of Lester Lovesick, L.M.H.C., rejected Dr. Lovesick's proposal of marriage. Ms. Resistant was badly hurt in a previous marriage. Lovesick was confident that if she could work out her issues that her attitude toward remarriage would change. He convinced her to put aside an hour every other day for "formal counseling" with him.

Mr. Lovesick tried desperately to manipulate his romantic interest into committing to him. Whereas Ms. Resistant did not receive competent, objective counseling, she may not have fully recognized Lovesick's self-serving ploy. In his role as a romantic suitor, Mr. Lovesick's concern about Resistant's lack of reciprocity does not, in itself, constitute unethical behavior. However, the appropriate step for Lovesick would be to suggest that they both enter counseling on an equal footing and with another

qualified professional, which is exactly what he finally did, which is how we came to know of this incident.

In summary, therapists are free to be completely human in their friendship and family interactions and to experience all of the attendant joys and heartaches. Their skills might prove helpful by offering emotional support, information, or suggestions. When the problems become more serious, however, the prudent course of action is always to assist in finding competent referrals.

Accepting Acquaintances as Clients

Another ready source of potential client contacts flows through therapists' circles of acquaintances. A member of the same athletic club or church congregation may request professional services. Disallowing casual acquaintances as potential clients would, in general, be unacceptable to consumers as well as to therapists. This section illustrates cautions that should be considered, however, before taking on clients who base their request for your services on the fact that they know you slightly from another context.

Case 11–5: Felina Breed, Ph.D., also raised pedigree cats. Many of her therapy clients were the "cat people" she met at shows. The small talk before and after treatment sessions was usually about cats. Clients also occasionally expressed interest in purchasing kittens from Dr. Breed. She agreed to sell them to her clients, which eventually came back to haunt her. When the therapy process was not proceeding as one client wished, he accused Dr. Breed of using him as a way to sell high-priced kittens. Another client became upset because Dr. Breed sold her a cat that never won a single prize. This client assumed that if the therapist raised "loser cats," the trustworthiness of her therapy skills should be questioned as well.

Dr. Breed did not adequately meet her responsibility to suppress her acquaintance role while engaging in a professional role. This disconnection can usually occur without untoward consequences if the continuation of the former acquaintance role does not require more than minimal energy or contact and avoids any conflicts of interest. The risks and contingency plans for likely incidental contact with clients should be discussed during the initial session. In Dr. Breed's case, that would have meant refraining from extended discussions of cats before or after the therapy session and abstaining from selling cats to any ongoing therapy client.

So what differences exist between a friend, who should *not* be accepted as a therapy client, and an acquaintance, who may appropriately become one? Making the distinction is not clear-cut because sociability patterns among therapists themselves vary considerably. Contextual issues, such as the potential for frequent interactions with the acquaintance in other settings, also demand consideration. Nevertheless, this simple exercise might prove useful, with PC standing for the potential client whose status requires consideration.

If your answer is "yes" to any of the below, the potential client is probably a friend:

- You would consider calling PC when you become upset and need to talk.
- If PC was injured in an accident, you would visit him or her in the hospital.
- You and PC have shared intimate social events, such as small dinner engagements.
- You are going to invite 15 people (who are not family members) to your birthday party. PC would be one of the people you would invite.
- You would trust PC with sensitive information about your private life.

If your answer to any of the below is "yes," the potential client is probably an acquaintance:

- If you and PC met in a hallway or on the street, you would acknowledge him or her and may even pause for a moment of idle chatter, but no detailed personal disclosures would transpire.
- If PC were seriously ill, you might call or send a card but would not visit him or her.
- If PC gave a small party, it is unlikely that you would be invited to it.
- If your father passed away, it is unlikely that PC would learn about it, at least not anytime soon.

- You know PC only well enough to recognize him or her on sight.

A twist on the acquaintance peril involves dealing appropriately with solicitations for services by someone who also holds some influence or advantage over you. Examples include a request from the head of admissions of the local college to which your daughter has applied to work with his troubled son. Or, a call for an appointment for marriage counseling from the advisor who manages your financial portfolio. Unless alternative services are unavailable, we encourage therapists placed in this awkward position to explain the dilemma to prospective clients and offer to help find alternative resources.

ENTERING INTO FRIENDSHIP RELATIONSHIPS WITH CLIENTS

Socializing With Current Clients

Commentators on the nature of psychotherapy have referred to it as, among other things, "the purchase of friendship" (Schofield, 1964). We contend that it is precisely the *differences* between psychotherapy and friendship that account for its potential effectiveness. Friendships should ideally begin on an equal footing, with each party capable of voluntarily agreeing to the relationship. However, as Bogrand (1993) has put it, "When the therapist or teacher offers the client or student friendship, it is an offer that cannot be refused" (p. 10). Here, we explore the ethical issues that emerge when therapists socialize outside professional settings with ongoing clients.

In the first empirically based inquiry into the practices of socialization with psychotherapy clients, Tallman (1981) reported that about one third of the respondents stated that they had occasionally formed social relationships with selected clients, usually including their respective spouses. Interestingly, the socializing respondents were all male, even though half of the sample was female, revealing a sex difference that has since been replicated (e.g., Borys, 1988). Tallman's respondents justified role blending on various therapeutic grounds, such as providing additional support and facilitating rapport.

Some therapists offered no justification, indicating simply that socializing occurred with clients whose company they enjoyed. In more than half of these instances, the friendships persisted after the therapy terminated.

Another third of Tallman's sample, mostly women, indicated that they occasionally attended special events in clients' lives, such as graduation ceremonies, musical recitals, or art show openings. They noted that these were single and isolated episodes, attended for the purpose of their presence and support to the client rather than as a vehicle for two-way socializing. A subsequent survey indicated that most therapists do not see an ethical problem with this type of socializing, although few have actually done it (Borys & Pope, 1989). We advise that when not otherwise contraindicated (e.g., transference issues), attending the symbolic portion of a client's special event (e.g., wedding or a bar mitzvah) is acceptable. In such circumstances, sending the client a card is also both acceptable and sufficient. A gift is not required.

The final third of Tallman's sample held to a strict policy of no client contact outside professional settings. This group believed that potential risks, including ethical hazards, were too likely. For example, new sets of needs may develop for both therapists and clients, and these may contaminate the therapy process. Clients could become unsure of where the new boundaries lie and experience anxiety or confusion. Some expressed concern that the therapists' capacity to remain objective might deteriorate, and that any dependencies on the part of clients might be reinforced.

The various complications that can arise when clients become friends are illustrated in the following cases. Do take note of the therapists' delayed awareness that anything was amiss; this is a common phenomenon that creates an unwelcome surprise.

Case 11–6: Soon after Patty Pal began counseling with Richard Chum, L.M.F.T., Patty asked Dr. Chum and his wife to spend the weekend at their beach house. The outing was enjoyable for all. During the next few sessions, however, Ms. Pal became increasingly reluctant to talk about her problems, insisting that things were going quite well. Dr. Chum confronted Ms. Pal with his impression that things were not moving forward. She broke down and admitted that she had been experiencing considerable distress but feared that if she revealed more about her problem areas Chum might choose to no longer socialize with her and her husband.

Patty Pal found herself in a double bind. As Peterson (1992) observed about boundary violations in general, the client is always faced with a conflict of interest. No matter what they do, they risk losing something.

Case 11–7: Jack Ace, D.S.W., and his client, King Draw, shared an affinity for poker. Ace accepted Draw's invitations to play with Draw's other friends on Wednesday nights. One evening, Dr. Ace was the big winner, and Draw was the big loser. After that evening, Draw began to cancel appointments as well as invitations to the games. A puzzled Dr. Ace confronted Draw, who then admitted the therapy no longer felt quite right. He could not be specific but did admit that after he lost several hundred dollars, Ace now seemed dangerous rather than someone he could depend on for support.

The above examples did not involve clients who pressed formal ethics charges against the therapists, but such cases do exist. In these instances, the clients felt exploited or duped and abandoned.

Case 11–8: Will Crony, Ph.D., had treated Buddy Flash for 2 years. They had also invited each other to their homes. Flash gave especially elegant parties, often attended by many influential community leaders. During one such event, Flash and Dr. Crony argued over what, to Crony, seemed to be a trivial matter. However, Flash terminated therapy and wrote to an ethics committee, complaining that Dr. Crony had kept him as a client for the sole purpose of capitalizing on his social status.

Case 11–9: Raphael Baroque, professional artist, complained to an ethics committee that Janis Face, Ph.D., did not follow through with her promises. Baroque had been Dr. Face's client for more than a year, during which time she praised his art work, accompanied him to art shows, and promised to introduce him to her gallery contacts. Baroque began to feel so self-assured that he terminated therapy, fully expecting that their mutual interest in his career would continue. However, Dr. Face did not return his calls. Baroque became frantic. When contacted by an ethics committee, Dr. Face explained that she always unconditionally supported her clients. But, because Baroque was no longer a client, she had no further obligations to him.

Ethics committees found in favor of both Flash and Baroque. The therapists had intertwined their lives in ways that confused the clients. Baroque, especially, experienced harm as a result of Dr. Face's failure to fully grasp the potential consequences of the significant dependency she had nurtured in her client.

Becoming Friends With Clients After Therapy Ends

When can more intimate social friendships be formed with former clients without the danger of multiple-role complications? Conservative critics say, "Never." An ex-client may need to reenter therapy, and a clear pathway — including the beneficial effects of continuing transference — should remain open for them.

The APA ethics code does not specify prohibitions against nonsexual posttermination friendships. However, if the friendship disappoints or turns sour, elements of issues that came up during therapy may resurface, raising new doubts in the client. The therapist that a client believed he or she knew so well may not completely resemble their professional personas in a nonprofessional context.

Case 11–10: Sue Nami, Ph.D., and her ex-client Marsha Nullify fully expected that they would get along exceptionally well because the therapy experience was extremely positive for both of them. However, Nullify found Dr. Nami overbearing and controlling in casual social situations, and Nullify's other friends intensely disliked Nami's strident manner. Nullify began to doubt Nami's overall competence and distanced herself from the

posttherapy friendship. She also began to suspect that the previous therapy was probably inept. She felt exploited and lost and sought the counsel of another therapist, who encouraged her to press ethics charges against Nami.

Nullify's charges against Dr. Nami came before an ethics committee, but not on the basis of the allegations that Nullify brought forward. Incompetence could not be conclusively proven, but what became clear to both a surprised respondent and the complainant was the finding of a multiple-role relationship violation. The investigation revealed that while Nullify was still in active therapy, Nami had clearly planned their evolving friendship and its longer-term continuation. Ironically, Nami herself provided these facts as a defense against Nullify's charges. This scenario also illustrates how one can never count on a new role working out as well as the first one. Nami's authoritative personality worked well with this client in therapy but played out poorly outside of the office.

So, can therapists ever safely establish friendships with former clients? The findings in a critical incident survey by Anderson and Kitchener (1996) suggest that nonsexual, nonromantic relationships occur with some regularity among therapists and their previous clients, but the judgments of the ethics of such relationships reveal little consensus. The view that friendships with clients are always off limits might deny opportunities for what could become productive, satisfying, long-term relationships. Gottlieb (1993, 1994), a strong supporter of maintaining clear professional boundaries, also believed that social relationships with some types of ex-clients may be acceptable. The next case provides one such example.

Case 11–11: Mountain bike enthusiast Wilber Wheel consulted Spike Speedo, Ph.D., whom he had casually met at a biking exhibition. The therapeutic relationship went well and terminated after 16 sessions. The two men found themselves in the same race a few months later and realized that they enjoyed knowing each other on a different basis. A close friendship endured for 25 years, and Wheel delivered the eulogy at Speedo's funeral.

Whether this account represents a likely outcome holds less relevance than the necessary precautions whenever contemplating a friendship with a person who was once a client. Recall that any attempt to deflect a role blending with current clients by promising or even hinting at the possibility of altering the roles after therapy termination instantly alters the nature of the current relationship.

ACCEPTING CLIENTS' REFERRALS OF THEIR CLOSE RELATIONS

In times of declining reimbursement for the delivery of psychotherapy service, it may feel tempting to relax the criteria used for accepting clients and, in the process, compromise ethical obligations (Shapiro & Ginzberg, 2003). Word of mouth from colleagues and current or previous clients is how many referrals are generated. However, care must be taken when satisfied clients recommend you to their own close friends or close relations. The potential for conflict of interest, unauthorized passing of information shared in confidence, and compromises in the quality of professional judgment constitute ever-present risks.

Case 11–12: Dum Tweedle felt pleased with his individual therapy progress and asked Rip Divide, Ph.D., to also counsel his fiancé Dee in individual therapy. Dum eventually pressed ethics charges against Dr. Divide for contributing to a breakup, a process that began, Dum said, at the time Dee entered therapy. He contended that Dr. Divide encouraged Dee to change in ways that were detrimental to him and to their relationship. Dr. Divide contended that it was his responsibility to facilitate growth in each party as individuals, a responsibility he felt she had upheld.

Case 11–13: Tuff Juggle, Psy.D., accepted Jane Amiga as a client with full knowledge that she and Sandy Comrade, an ongoing client, were best friends, and that aspects of the friendship were serious treatment issues for Sandy. He reasoned that he could compartmentalize them sufficiently, and that the women would benefit from the fact that he knew them both. One day, he slipped and shared with Sandy something that Jane had told him during a private session. Jane brought ethics charges against Juggle for breach of confidentiality.

Dr. Divide ignored the invisible "third client," namely, the relationship between the engaged couple—and attempted the improbable task of treating a duo as if they were unconnected entities. Although Dr. Juggle's situation involved a less engrossing relationship between two clients, that the friendship was an emotional issue should have provided a sufficient front-end warning. Juggle's slip of the tongue to the wrong party is an example of an ever-present pitfall when consulting people who know each other well enough to share some of the same material during their individual sessions. Even the sharpest of memories may fail under such circumstances (see also Chapter 8).

Problems can arise, even when a referral is not specifically made by an ongoing client. This is exactly what happened in the next case.

Case 11–14: Chance Encounter, M.D., ran into Possessia Grip, a particularly difficult and acute client, and her friend at a bakery. Dr. Encounter pretended not to see them, but Grip came over to greet him. The friend had followed, so Grip introduced them. The friend asked Encounter what he did for a living, and Encounter divulged his occupation without revealing his relationship with Ms. Grip. Encounter quickly paid for his bread and exited the situation. The friend called Dr. Encounter 2 days later to make an appointment for therapy. When Grip arrived for her next appointment, she was furious. "How could you do this?" she screamed. "You are my therapist, and I don't want you to see her. Either that, or I am quitting. What is it going to be?"

Ms. Grip illustrates the type of client who feels a sense of ownership of his or her therapist. These issues require attention in their own right. Nonetheless, Dr. Encounter has found himself in a bind not entirely of his making. He does not even know if the friend understands that Grip is his client, and he can not tell her. However, Encounter may have been wise to have referred Grip's friend to a colleague.

Sometimes there are warnings, even if somewhat offhanded, that the unwary therapist might miss. The next case, loosely adapted from a scenario provided by Shapiro and Ginzberg (2003), illustrates the situation.

Case 11–15: Paris Jug told her therapist, Ed Ipus, M.S.W., that she was recommending him to her mother for counseling. Ipus was elated because these were self-paying clients, and he needed the income. So, when Paris then giggled and said, "You will see how much more loveable I am than her," he failed to recognize the subtle warning. Therapy with the mother was difficult because her main complaints were about Paris, and Paris spent much of her time attempting to manipulate Ipus into saying that she was a much better person than her mother. He decided to make things simpler by terminating the mother, who then pressed ethics charges for abandonment and emotional harm.

Mr. Ipus was highly remiss in taking on the referral in the first place, knowing the intense issues between his ongoing client and her mother. He obviously should have told Paris at the onset that he could not ethically treat her mother as a separate client.

We are not suggesting here that accepting referrals from current clients is always inappropriate. Therapists must, however, assess as thoroughly as possible the relationship between the potential client and the referral source, the potential client and the context in which the established client and the referral know each other, and the motivations of the client to make the referral (Shapiro & Ginzberg, 2003). If things have any potential to become sticky, we advise referring the potential client to a suitable colleague.

RURAL SETTINGS AND OTHER SMALL-WORLD HAZARDS

Role clashes become impossible to avoid for mental health professionals working in small, isolated communities. As anyone who has lived in a rural town can readily attest, face-to-face contacts with clients outside the office inevitably occur, sometimes on a daily basis. One psychologist, who was the only mental health provider within in a 60-mile radius, relayed to us the special care taken to ensure that he and his client, the only sixth-grade teacher in town, could avoid difficulties that might arise due to the presence of the psychologist's rebellious 12-year-old son in her class. Another small-town marriage counselor shared the burden of scheduling neighbors to avoid unwelcome face-to-face meetings in the waiting room. Yet another therapist requested guidance from an ethics committee when a client's alcoholic and abusive husband yelled profanities at him at every opportunity—in the barbershop, bowling alley, restaurant, market, and even as they passed each other in their cars.

It is estimated that almost 25% of the 62 million people living in small towns and rural areas suffer from some sort of mental or emotional problem (Roberts, Battaglia, & Epstein, 1999). Unfortunately, demand for services often exceeds resources in these locales (Benson, 2003; Schank & Skovholt, 2006). The few therapists in town will know many of their clients in other contexts, and the townspeople will also know a great deal about the therapists and their families. Therefore, in small rural areas, boundary guidelines demand consideration in relation to the sociocultural contexts of the community (Roberts et al., 1999).

Attributes of small communities further complicate ethical dilemmas in the context of delivering therapy services. Information passes quickly, and standards of confidentiality among professionals and community service agencies may become relaxed to the point at which information, originally shared in confidence, becomes widely known (Hargrove, 1986; Solomon, Heisberger, & Winer, 1981). In smaller, isolated communities gossip can be rampant, making it even more difficult to ensure client confidentiality (Sleek, 1994).

A colleague of ours who moved from a large city to a smaller Midwestern town relayed an incident that disturbed him greatly as he waited to speak to a counselor about renting some space in her office suite. A boy about 10 years old came into the waiting room and calmly checked the phone messages at the reception table. Our colleague and two other adults could hear several clients attempting to schedule or cancel appointments, leaving complete identifying information and, in one case, additional information about an abusive boyfriend. The boy then yelled, "He didn't call Mom." "Thank you, Alex" came a voice from inside a closed office. "Mom" turned out to be the counselor with whom our colleague had the appointment. A couple of years later, our colleague reported that he still viewed the incident as improper, but that confidentiality had little meaning in this town. Most residents did not seem to expect it, and our colleague's clients even expressed surprise on learning that his wife was unaware of the details of their personal problems, assuming that our colleague would have shared these with her.

Residents of small communities are often more hesitant to seek professional counseling and are not quick to trust outsiders, preferring to rely on their kinship ties, friends, and clergy for emotional support. Because those who do seek therapy prefer someone known as a contributing member in the community, it may not be possible simply to commute from a neighboring town and expect to have much business. Ironically, then, earning acceptance and trust means putting oneself in the position of increasing complicated relationships (Campbell & Cordon, 2003; Stockman, 1990). Consider, for example, what might happen when a client also works as a salesperson at the local car dealership. When the therapist buys a new car—and everyone will know of the purchase, what make and model, and where it was purchased—the client may be deeply offended if the therapist purchased it from someone else. Yet, would the therapist have the same latitude to negotiate the price? Or, would the client feel obligated to give the therapist a better deal than anyone else would receive? And, what if the car turns out to be a lemon? This is the kind of dilemma that small-town therapists must routinely juggle, and good answers are not always obvious.

Just because it is unlikely that mental health professionals in smaller communities can separate their lives entirely from those of their clients does not mean that professional boundaries become irrelevant. On the contrary, therapists

must make constant and deliberate efforts to minimize the confusion. For example, no matter how small the community, a therapist and a client should never need to socialize *only* with each other, such as meeting for dinner. Potentially risky acts over which therapists always have complete control regardless of community size, such as giving gifts to clients, can still be easily avoided. The therapist can maintain confidentiality and refrain from chiming in during gossip sessions taking place outside the office. The therapist's family may also need instruction on how to interact in certain situations, while minimizing the details regarding why.

The therapist in the next case failed to attend to more than one ethical requirement, despite the more accepted practice of bartering in rural communities.

Case 11–16: Due to stresses caused by economic hardships, the Peeps required more marriage counseling sessions than originally estimated. The Peeps's chicken farm income had become insufficient to pay the regular bills, let alone therapy. Ronald Rooster, M.S.W., proposed that he would accept 2,000 chicks to continue counseling, provided the therapy did not last beyond a year. Dr. Rooster's wife had long wanted to start a chicken farm, so this deal would also fulfill one of the therapist's needs. The Peeps reluctantly agreed. Soon thereafter, a lethal virus dangerous to humans and believed to be carried by poultry resulted in the destruction of millions of chickens in Canada, driving up the price of chickens from their non-flu area. The Roosters made a huge profit and, at the same time, were also in business competition with the Peeps. The Peeps were locked into a therapy situation with which they felt very uncomfortable and successfully sued Dr. Rooster.

This case, adapted from Roberts et al. (1999), reveals the highly unethical role blending that can still occur in rural settings where roles are often already blended. Taking an exchange in advance for services that may not be needed is only the tip of the iceberg. Bartering a vulnerable client's assets to start a business that then competes with the client was unconscionable.

Small communities do not necessarily exist only in rural areas or geographical isolation. Close-knit military, religious, cultural, or ethnic communities existing within a much larger community can pose similar dilemmas. Therapists working in huge metropolitan settings can experience what amounts to small-world hazards, and the same need to view role conflicts in a sociocultural context pertains. The primary advantage of working in a heavily populated area is the availability of more alternatives. Still, even when one cohesive population is embedded in a large city, complications similar to those faced by rural therapists can arise. Gay, bisexual, and transgender communities provide one example (Kessler & Wachler, 2005).

Case 11–17: Lisa Lorne, Ph.D., specialized in counseling lesbian women. She accepted a client new to the city into her therapy group, and during the second session the new woman announced that she had just met someone named Sandra Split, and that they were going to be seeing each other. Dr. Lorne was still devastated by Sandra Split's recent breakup with her after 16 years together.

If Dr. Lorne's own issues would make it impossible to work with a specific client, arranging for some alternative that keeps the client's best interests in mind is well advised. Furthermore, the new client is very likely to learn of Split's relationship with Lorne sooner rather than later. Other less-dramatic ways that may cause complex interactions that require vigilance for gay, lesbian, bisexual, or transgendered therapists involve frequent socialization venues, both private and public.

Small-world hazards often occur in totally unexpected ways. A therapist might learn that his client is his wife's best friend's secret lover or that a client is his daughter's new boss. Such information is unlikely to be known in advance, as it would likely be in a small town. Discoveries that may emerge during the course of psychotherapy can often be handled by staunchly maintaining the professional role without regard for the coincidences that link the therapist and client in other ways. Things can, however, become more complicated, as illustrated in the next case.

Case 11–18: Sid Fifer consulted Ron Wrung, Ph.D., after Fifer's offensive and antisocial behavior caused increasing trouble in his family and at work. Early in therapy, it was casually revealed that Fifer and the therapist's wife worked for the same large company, although in different locations and different departments. Several weeks later, Fifer was fired. He charged that Dr. Wrung must have told his wife about what he talked about in therapy, which she in turn shared with the company boss. Wrung vehemently denied sharing material about Fifer or any other client with his wife or anyone else.

Dr. Wrung was a casualty of the type of circumstances that could be neither easily predicted nor prevented. Therapists are more likely to be judged culpable when a small-world hazard was perceived in advance and alternatives were clearly available. Here, other treatment options existed, but Wrung assumed that the remote connection between the client and his wife would preclude any conflict.

The future will likely see an increase in the use of electronically based distance forms of therapy. These may ease the shortage of resources and relieve some of the ethical problems inherent in rural communities and other small-world situations when appropriate options are scarce (Bischoff, Hollist, & Smith, 2004; Farrell & McKinnon, 2003). Of course, with teletherapy, other ethical challenges pertain, as described in Chapter 6.

EXCHANGING GIFTS AND FAVORS

Accepting Clients' Gifts and Asking Clients for Favors

Mental health professionals often receive expressions of appreciation from their clients. Sometimes expressions of gratitude extend beyond a verbal or written thank you. Holiday periods and the termination session are the most likely times that some clients will bestow gifts (Amos & Margison, 2006).

Accepting small material tokens, such as homemade cookies or an inexpensive item, typically poses no ethical problem. Some therapists with whom we have talked refuse any gift as a matter of principle, but most believe turning down small gifts would constitute rejection or an insult to the detriment of the client. Only a tiny minority of respondents in Borys's (Borys & Pope, 1989) large, national sample of psychologists believed that accepting gifts worth under $10 (about $18 today, controlled for inflation) was unethical, and the majority of respondents had done it. Pope, Tabachnick, and Keith-Spiegel (1987) found that most therapists would accept a gift worth under $5 (about $9 today), and almost none would accept a gift worth over $50 (around $90 today). There will be times, however, when accepting certain types of gifts (e.g., a nude calendar, boxer shorts, a condom, or any other highly personal or emotionally laden item) would be inappropriate and even require exploration regarding the client's meaning and motives. At other times, the wise practitioner might want to consider what meaning even small gifts had to the client based on the individual circumstances (e.g., purchased flowers, costume jewelry, a doll, or any item that has been in the client's family for years).

Gifts can, as we all know, be bestowed for reasons that have nothing to do with appreciation, and special dangers lurk here. Gifts have the power to control, manipulate, or symbolize far more than the recipient may fully understand. Some clients may even attempt to equalize power within the relationship by bestowing a gift (Knox, Hess, Williams, & Hill, 2003). When a gift is no longer a gesture of gratitude, or when even a small gift raises a therapeutic issue or potential manipulation, problems of ethics and competent professional judgment arise. Several ethics cases demonstrate that lines can be crossed, and ethical or other adverse consequences can ensue.

Case 11–19: Wealthy Rich Porsche gave his recently licensed therapist, Grad Freshly, Ph.D., a new car for Christmas, accompanied by a card stating, "To the only man who ever helped me." Dr. Freshly was flattered and excited. He convinced himself that his services were worth the bonus because Porsche had churned through many previous therapists with disappointing results. As a more seasoned therapist might have predicted, Rich soon began to find fault with Dr.

Freshly and sued him for manipulating him into giving an expensive gift.

Case 11–20: Phatel Attraction brought Newton Callow, L.M.H.C., suggestive little gifts almost every session from the beginning of their counseling relationship. These gifts included handkerchiefs hand embroidered with tiny women in bikinis, a T-shirt imprinted "Therapists Do It in Groups," erotic poems, and a fancy bottle with a label "Chemical That Makes Therapists Irresistible to Clients." Ms. Attraction ultimately pressed ethics charges against Callow for abruptly terminating and abandoning her after promising that he would "be there to make her better." During an ethics committee inquiry, Callow stated that he initially found Ms. Attraction to be a "fun client" who he thought needed massive support to help boost her self-confidence. As therapy progressed, however, he became increasingly uneasy with her flirtations. What seemed at first amusing and flattering turned demanding and a little scary. She soon became more than he felt he could handle. When Callow suggested referring her to another therapist, she became livid and stalked out of the session, allegedly threatening him with reprisal for leading her on.

These two cases illustrate naïveté and inexperience, which are fairly common denominators among therapists who accept gifts and favors beyond the realm of small one-time or appropriate special occasion tokens. Regardless of any other dynamics or considerations, a very valuable gift should be refused. A person in a vulnerable situation, such as a client or student, can always charge exploitation later, and such a charge may well have substance despite the recipient's rationalizations. Freshly's case may be unique, but it illustrates how blindly satisfying one's own interests can lead to trouble later. Callow was naive and probably coping with some unfulfilled needs of his own, which blurred his professional judgment. A strong professional identity appears to be the key ingredient in dealing appropriately with offers of gifts and favors and the probable motivation behind them on a case-by-case basis. Until one reaches a level of professional comfort, a conservative course of action may be in everyone's best interests.

Gifts and (usually) favors should never, of course, be requested *from* clients or those we are entrusted to teach or supervise. Unfortunately, cases involving direct solicitations have come to our attention. One therapist asked a client who owned a small beauty salon to do her nails every week at no cost in addition to paying the regular therapy fee. Another asked to borrow significant sums of money from his clients. Then, he went bankrupt, leaving them all unpaid.

When small, situational-based favors or requests are involved, the picture grays a little. A therapist might reasonably request that a client change a regular appointment time to accommodate his or her own special need on occasion. However, the most prudent course of action is to avail oneself of alternatives whenever possible and to remain vigilant to cues that draw the line between reasonable and unreasonable. Therapists must remember that a client may feel that he or she has no choice but to comply with any request.

Even when no contraindications exist in a specific case, any favor requiring more than a trivial inconvenience to a client should not be requested except in rare emergencies. The therapist who had a heart attack in the presence of his client in an otherwise-deserted office complex, requiring the client to assume rather major responsibilities for a short time, is an example of the exceptional case.

Giving Gifts to Clients

Many clients coming into therapy feel ignored, abandoned, violated, or uncared for and may more easily misinterpret the motivation of therapists who give them gifts. Besides the potential complications and misunderstandings, there is an ever-present possibility that the therapists' own motives of benevolence are unconscious rationalizations for self-serving intentions. We advise that it is almost always prudent to refrain from bestowing gifts on clients.

Case 11–21: Benny Nowalls, Ph.D., often gave many of his clients little trinkets he thought they would enjoy. The gifts included decorative key chains, figurines, and stuffed animals. He also sent them cards when he was on vacation, hugged

them often, worked out alongside them at the gym, and met them for lunch. Eventually, several clients complained about Dr. Nowalls for a variety of reasons, most dealing with abandonment issues.

Dr. Nowalls was stunned that those to whom he had been, in his own mind, so kind and giving, turned on him. He could never grasp how the multiple intrusions of his personal essence into his clients' lives initiated dependencies he could never ultimately satisfy. From another perspective, seeking gratification by attempting to please clients presents a serious problem, whereas helping clients to manage their feelings toward the therapist, both positive and negative, can prove beneficial. The question arises regarding whether clients can feel free to address negative feelings with a therapist who gives them gifts (Gabbard, 1994).

The therapists' motives for gift-giving are not necessarily unconscious or rationalized. The next case illustrates a therapist who knew exactly what he was doing.

Case 11–22: Herman Hustle, Ph.D., gave all of his clients, current and past, expensive cheese baskets at Christmas time. He confided to a colleague, "I want them to think about me as this terrific guy and then pass my name along to their friends."

Dr. Hustle wants to drum up business and is attempting to enlist clients as his sales force. Such a tactic is simply unprofessional.

So, can therapists ever give their clients gifts or do favors for them? We say yes, on occasion and after careful consideration. A book may be offered to a client when therapeutically indicated, especially if the client is on a limited budget. Therapists may also go out of their way to help clients locate other needed resources relevant to improving their overall life situation. Small favors based on a situational need and common sense, such as giving a client a quarter for the parking meter, would not raise concerns. In these acceptable cases, no ulterior motives pertain, and the scope is either related to the therapy or of a very specific and limited nature. A special situation can arise when the client is a child. Here, at times, it may be appropriate to give a small gift attending to the symbolic meaning that would advance the therapeutic function. For example, an anxious child about to leave for 3 weeks of summer camp might be soothed and emboldened by the gift of a flashlight.

Finally, it is worth a mention that the generous therapist who agrees to see a financially strapped client at no cost may set up a gift-giving dilemma, at least in the client's view. If a client no longer has the ability to pay, and the therapist believes that continuation is important to the client's well-being, we suggest reducing the fee to a point at which it becomes affordable. This also deflects the negative impact on the proud client who would not welcome charity.

NONTRADITIONAL THERAPY SETTINGS

Therapeutic goals can sometimes be better achieved outside a professional office-style setting. Delivering therapy in clients' residences may forestall the need for hospitalization or alleviate difficulties for clients who are physically frail or do not drive (Knapp & Slattery, 2004). Action-oriented therapies, including crisis modalities, may involve ecological involvements with clients. For example, a therapist might accompany his "fear-of-flying group" on a flight from Los Angeles to San Diego and back. A stress-reduction group might hold a special weekend at a serene lakeside lodge. A mental health professional, as part of an established eating disorder clinic program, may go out to eat pizza or other "real food" with a client to assist in addressing anxiety about eating in a realistic context.

Excursions beyond traditional professional settings require careful forethought to preclude subsequent charges of exploitation because of multiple-role or conflict-of-interest overtones, confusion, or impairment of the therapists' objectivity. When employing an atypical setting or technique, it becomes critical to clarify the therapeutic context and the activity.

Case 11–23: Homa Cloister feared crowds. Her therapist, Rip Vivo, Ph.D., suggested that they go out to dinner at busy, fancy restaurants after therapy sessions as a way of conditioning her to feel more comfortable around people. He did not charge an additional fee for the after-hour activity but did require her to pay the dinner bill. The treatment proved ineffective and uncomfortable for this client. Homa later charged that Dr. Vivo exploited her by disguising a free meal ticket as psychotherapy.

Case 11–24: Several encounter group members charged that the counselor associated with the Touchit Clinic conducted weekend retreats at a local hotel in a way that facilitated coercive and promiscuous behavior among the participants. They believed that various exercises encouraged and stimulated some members to become obnoxious and to pressure others into sexual activity after the formal evening activities concluded.

Case 11–25: Jake Sprint, Psy.D., suggested that he and Hal Jogger conduct their counseling sessions every Monday and Wednesday morning as they ran in the park. Later, Jogger complained to an ethics committee that he was not getting better because it was hard to concentrate, hear what his therapist was saying, respond, and run at the same time. Jogger believed that he was simply paying for Dr. Sprint's personal exercise regime.

Case 11–26: Lynn Bones broke both legs skiing and would not be able to drive for 6 weeks. Bud Visit, L.M.H.C., agreed to see Bones in her apartment until she could arrange transportation to his office. On arriving, he found that Bones had prepared lunch for the two of them, including a glass of wine. They chatted about politics and the weather while eating. After three such sessions in Bones's apartment, the therapy sessions shifted in that Bones began to treat Mr. Visit as a friend rather than as a therapist. Six week later when sessions resumed in the office, Visit attempted to get things back on track in his professional setting. An affronted Bones decided to find another therapist.

Vivo's technique with his claustrophobic client may have an appropriate therapeutic rationale, but he included the trappings of a social event and structured the financial aspects poorly. The Touchit Clinic staff did an insufficient job of setting ground rules and monitoring compliance. Sprint's motives may not have been as Jogger perceived, but attempting to perform therapy while running is difficult to justify. Mr. Visit settled too comfortably into the temporary therapy setting, and the relationship shifted just enough to compromise it. Those who make home-based visits or offer community-based treatment of those with serious mental problems must remember that boundaries are challenged in ways that do not ordinarily present themselves in professional office or hospital settings (Knapp & Slattery, 2004; Perkins, Hudson, Gray, & Stewart, 1998). Mr. Visit should have anticipated the dynamics of a home-based setting and prepared his client with the ground rules, which would not have included meal service and alcohol.

Earning a living without leaving home is more than ever before an option. The increasing popularity of working out of one's home is understandable, both from convenience and financial standpoints. While not inherently inappropriate, we do not advise conducting therapy in one's home. If one must conduct therapy in a private home, the room should be furnished along the lines of a typical therapy office and ideally have its own entrance. Some clients, however, may find receiving therapy anywhere in the therapist's home (even in a dedicated home office) confusing, and their emotional status could become compromised by connotations attached to the setting.

The therapist who practices out of his or her own living quarters also risks professional isolation unless colleagues are actively sought out in other venues. As we discussed in Chapter 10, isolated therapists may be more likely to look to clients to fulfill their own needs. Other clients could potentially become burdens on the family, as amusingly portrayed by actor Bill Murray in the movie *What About Bob?* More seriously, a client could act out in frightening ways. Unless the home-office therapist has another location available to screen new clients for suitability, one can not know in advance who will walk through the door. The next case describes an actual horrifying incident.

Case 11–27: Kevin Homebody, L.M.H.C., held counseling sessions in the den of his home. Rose Snow, a quiet and refined woman, sought assistance in dealing with her problems, including a cocaine-addicted daughter. Snow brought her daughter along to several sessions. One night while the Homebody family was watching TV, several young men brandishing knives broke into Homebody's house. They terrorized the family for several hours as they gathered up valuables. It was later learned that Snow's daughter had told her drug dealer about the "nice stuff" in Homebody's house and provided him with a map of how to get there.

The potential for adverse results, even if not as serious as the Homebody case, reveals that decisions to venture away from a strictly professional setting must be based on the following:

- A treatment plan for individual clients should clearly justify the arrangement as a more effective setting for facilitating specific therapeutic goals as opposed to mere convenience.
- There must be assurance that the client understands the proposed experience and gives fully informed consent.
- Assurance of enforcement of appropriate client and staff behavior for group experiences must be present.
- Preparation of the clients for the actual experience, as necessary, should occur.

UNANTICIPATED ENCOUNTERS WITH CLIENTS

Every mental health professional is at the mercy of coincidence, and a totally unexpected compounding of roles may occur by chance. Although the appropriate response may be difficult to discern, therapists must actively attempt to ameliorate the situation as best they can, trying to avoid devaluing or diminishing anyone in the process (Canter, Bennett, Jones, & Nagy, 1994). The APA code states that therapists who find themselves in a possibly harmful multiple-role relationship due to factors that could not be foreseen must take reasonable steps to resolve it in the most ethical manner possible (APA 02: 3.05). A therapist's response, which must often be made quickly, will depend on several factors. Confidentiality issues usually pertain. Unless the therapist and client have discussed how to handle situations when they encounter each by chance, the therapist will not know how to take the client's preferred option into account. The urgency of the situation is also a factor. Sometimes, problems can be deflected, if there is time.

When dealing with unforeseen factors, most of the time no *lasting* multiple-role relationship actually develops. The nature of the encounter itself determines, in large measure, the impact of the unanticipated encounter. Seeing each other in line at the post office is one thing, naked in the gym shower is quite another. Most therapists who have had unintended encounters with ongoing clients express surprise, uncertainly about what to do, discomfort, anxiety, and embarrassment. Most are also concerned about confidentiality and boundary complications (Sharkin & Birky, 1992).

Whereas fluke crossings are more likely to occur in smaller communities, unexpected situations can arise anywhere. In fact, three of the four incidents described in the next cases occurred in large metropolitan areas.

Case 11–28: Mildred Suit, a client of Gina Squeezed, Ph.D., announced that she is suing a lawyer for rendering incompetent services during her child custody hearing. Suit informed Dr. Squeezed that she will be subpoenaed to testify about the mental anguish she suffered during that period. Suit also, for the first time, reveals the name of the lawyer she is suing. It is Orin Trial, another client of Dr. Squeezed. (Case adapted from Leslie, 1994.)

Dr. Squeezed may be able to extricate herself from the case by discouraging Suit from calling her to testify, but only if she sincerely believes that she has nothing useful to offer the court. In addition, Ms. Suit's attorney may concur because opening a discussion into her mental state could lead to far-ranging inquiries that might ultimately hurt her case. If Ms. Suit still plans to call Dr. Squeezed as a witness, her other client, Attorney Trial, will soon know of the relationship. Dr. Squeezed will be on a list of potential witnesses, and Trial's own lawyer will most likely depose her. Ms. Suit, on the other hand, will not know of Dr. Squeezed's relationship to Mr. Trial unless he chooses to

reveal it. In the deposition, Dr. Squeezed will most likely have to testify about Ms. Suit's psychological life under oath in front of both clients. In a technical sense, Dr. Squeezed could testify or prepare an affidavit (i.e., a sworn written statement) regarding Ms. Suit's mental suffering without reference to Mr. Trial or even an acknowledgment of his status as a client. Obviously, he will have some feelings about this, as will Ms. Suit if she ever learns details after the fact. In addition, matters could become quite complicated if Mr. Trial's defense involved an attack on Dr. Squeezed's credibility or expertise.

The best advice to Dr. Squeezed would be to consult her attorney and, in the interim, avoid breaching the confidentiality of either client. Her attorney can ask Ms. Suit's lawyer whether and when Squeezed will be named on a potential witness list. When that occurs, she can discuss the fact of this listing (but no details of Suit's case) with Mr. Trial and discuss the implications for their continued work together. It may be that all parties will eventually permit the facts of her difficult conflict to be shared.

Case 11–29: Gilla Social gleefully announced to her psychotherapist husband that artist Pablo Miroklee agreed to speak at her monthly art guild meeting. She wants to volunteer her home for the event and to entertain Miroklee for a quiet dinner afterward. The artist, who is extremely depressed and emotionally volatile, has been a long-term client of Social's husband.

At first blush, the Socials' problem seems easy enough to solve. If the client already knows about the art guild arrangement, Dr. Social should consider discussing the quandary with his client, if that seems appropriate, and some agreement could be reached. But, what does Dr. Social tell his wife? Spouses, after all, are not exempt from confidentiality mandates. We suggest that all therapists reach an understanding with their partners and older children about the multiple-role problems that might impinge on their lives on occasion. Close relations can be told that the nature of their profession may require changes in plans, possibly abrupt ones. Like many health service providers, sacrifices that also touch others may have to be made. Therapists must ensure that their family members understand that no details can be given and no questions can be answered. Ms. Social's husband, if he has already reached an understanding with her, may simply say, "I'm sorry, the art guild meeting cannot take place here." She may be disappointed, but she would know that there is a good reason even if she will never know exactly what it is.

Case 11–30: During a New Year's Eve event at a fashionable restaurant with some friends, Eva Close, M.S.W., spots one of her clients at a table across the room. This client is particularly sensitive about therapy and constantly worries about anyone finding out that she even knows a psychotherapist. Mrs. Close and her husband had planned this evening for weeks and paid $200 in advance. Mrs. Close thinks she may be able to stay in her corner of the dining area, but as people begin to drink they also move around the room to chat with others and make new friends. Mrs. Close's husband and friends are also urging her to "get out there and dance."

Mrs. Close may have to figure out how to keep a low profile at the New Year's Eve event. She should not become intoxicated. Given the client's intense feelings, it would not have been inappropriate for Close to have earlier attempted to ensure that important events do not overlap with those of her client. In small communities, clients with such intense concerns about discovery might better be referred to someone in an adjacent city, or they may be suited for telephone or Web-based counseling.

Case 11–31: Fortuna Yikes, Psy.D., agreed to have dinner with friends and a blind date that her friends had arranged for her. When she arrived at the restaurant and peeked inside, she recognized the man sitting with her friends as one of her clients.

In the real story, the therapist was able to leave the restaurant before being seen. She paged her friends in the restaurant from her cell phone, telling them that she had fallen ill. Because such twists of fate do actually happen and quick exits may not be an option, we encourage

therapists to actively attempt to know in advance the identities of people with whom they will be interacting in any intimate social situation.

We also strongly encourage mental health professionals to raise the issue early on about chance meetings with their clients outside therapy. Some clients will prefer to pretend that the two do not know each other. Others may favor acting as though they are acquaintances and want to exchange brief greetings.

We suggest that therapists *not* be the ones to take the lead during such chance encounters, and that the clients understand in advance that the decision to interact with or ignore each other rests entirely with them. Clients should be assured that the therapists will be comfortable either way. Our plan is recommended for application to *all* clients. That way, the therapist does not have to remember which reaction each client prefers (and even these could vary, depending on the circumstance). There is no risk of being perceived as rejecting because the client will know always to take the lead when the two notice each other outside the office setting. With a preapproved plan well in place, common situations involving clients, such as finding oneself in the same line at the bank, can be handled somewhat gracefully and without incurring more than minimal discomfort. Pulakos (1994) surveyed clients who had already experienced outside encounters with their therapists and found that 54% of clients expressed wanting a brief acknowledgment, 33% would want a conversation, and only a small number would want to be ignored. Twenty-one percent would want a different response from the one they actually received. These results clearly verify that no one size fits all.

It must be noted before concluding this section that conflicts and role complications can occur in situations that are not face to face. An employer may call for a recommendation of an individual you know in the community who is (or was) also a client and about whom you would have reservations based on what transpired in therapy. In an actual case, a prominent psychologist was contacted by a state psychological association to approach a politician who had considerable power to affect the outcome of pending legislation favorable to psychologists. What the organization did not and could never know was that the psychologist had worked with the politician's family some years previously in regard to a sensitive problem of the sort that could ruin the politician's career. The psychologist felt torn between agreeing to set up some kind of meeting (even though he would not to be present) and alienating his professional organization by refusing to do it. He decided to tell the association's staff that "family problems" precluded his involvement, leaving the staff to infer that the family to which he was referring was his own.

WHEN THE THERAPIST IS SQUEEZED IN THE MIDDLE

We have focused on multiple-role relationships in which the mental health professionals directly occupied one of the roles. However, situations can arise that pinch therapists between two or more other forces. For example, demands of the agencies employing therapists may conflict with the needs and welfare of the agencies' clients. This dilemma is increasing as managed care takes over privately contracted services between a therapist and a client (Smith & Fitzpatrick, 1995).

Case 11–32: Paul Plastique, Ph.D., provides psychotherapeutic care to children with chronic medical conditions at a Megahealth Memorial Hospital. For 3 years he has worked with 8-year-old Zachary Mug through several stressful craniofacial surgical procedures to deal with malformations caused by Crouzon syndrome. Zack has experienced self-esteem and peer problems, school disruption, and painful recoveries, but Zack and his parents feel that Dr. Plastique understands him and his life experiences very well. The Mug family is covered by Monolith Insurance through Mr. Mug's employer Monolith recently "carved out" their mental health benefits and subcontracted these to CFI Care Services. Contract talks between CFI Care and Megaville Memorial Hospital on a new contract for mental health services have broken down. While Zack will still get medical and surgical care through Megahealth Memorial covered by Monolith, Dr. Plastique's psychotherapeutic services will

no longer be covered. CFI Care has referred Zack and his family to a counselor in the community who has no familiarity with Crouzon syndrome or children with craniofacial surgical abnormalities.

The issues confronted by Dr. Plastique and the Mug family have become all too common as third-party payers continually strive for economic advantage through the use of carved-out contracts and competitive pricing agreements. Coordinated continuous care in a single setting by therapists with the most relevant training and experience have become increasingly difficult to maintain. Perhaps Dr. Plastique and the Mug family can make a special circumstances plea to CFI Care or Monolith Insurance. Perhaps Megahealth Memorial will offer some reduced fee to the Mug family in the absence of coverage. Perhaps Dr. Plastique's practice is such that he can continue to treat Zack outside the Megahealth/Monolith system. More likely than not, however, Dr. Plastique and his client will find themselves trapped in an arcane world of contractual and fiscal constraints that allows little latitude to consider the best interests of individual patients. (See also Chapter 7.)

Government policy, legal requirements, or the welfare and safety of society in general may sometimes clash with therapists' judgments regarding what might be in the best interests of individuals with whom they are working. The identification of priorities and loyalties can cause acute stress and conflict-of-interest dilemmas. The APA ethics code specifies that psychologists should refrain from accepting a professional role when personal, scientific, professional, legal, financial, or other interests or relationships could reasonably be expected to impair their objectivity, competence, or effectiveness or expose an individual or an organization to any harm or exploitation (APA 02: 3.06). Often, therapists are not in an objective position when acting under such conditions because the more powerful of the conflict sources, such as the legal system or the employer, may issue sanctions if the therapist's actions do not comport with the position of the more powerful party. (See also Chapter 7.)

COMPLEX RELATIONSHIPS
WITH STUDENTS

Many mental health professionals also teach full or part time or occasionally. Complicated and ultimately destructive relationships can involve those we teach unless we remain sensitive to indications that inappropriate relationships are forming.

Appropriate boundaries with students and educators can be more difficult to discern than with therapy clients. Whereas therapists and their clients must actively and willfully make specific arrangements to alter a professional relationship, professors and students often do not. Indeed, encouragement to attend simultaneously many activities (e.g., sports events, festivals, and receptions) outside the classroom is commonplace. Because professor–student relationships typically do not involve quite the same level of trust or possess the same emotional closeness characteristic of psychotherapy relationships, mixing the contexts in which one interacts with students on a casual basis does not typically raise concerns. Nonetheless, responsibilities toward students and the power of educators to influence them and their life opportunities are forceful enough to warrant considerable caution.

Case 11–33: Marsha Scholar, Ph.D., was popular among students and socialized with many of them. She was shocked when grievance was brought against her. A student claimed Scholar had given her a low grade because the student's husband had disagreed with Professor Scholar's husband about the effectiveness of psychotherapy during another student's party. Scholar responded that her husband never mentioned any such incident, and that she had graded the student objectively and fairly.

Case 11–34: Several students complained to the department chair that Gregarious Bud, Ph.D., was nice to the students he liked and froze out the students he disliked. Professor Bud responded that he may have seemed friendlier to some students than to others because he socialized with the more assertive students who sought out his company.

Professors Scholar and Bud are apparently casualties of misperception. Educators are probably wise to limit their outside social contacts with classroom students to events associated with the institution (such as departmental social events) until the students graduate. Professors who wish to form closer relationships with current students should carefully assess the risks and be aware of the misunderstandings that might arise, including what meaning other students might place when observing a professor and one other student off by themselves. Educators must also remember that students are extremely sensitive to issues of equity and believe that those who operate (or appear to operate) on a tilted playing field are extremely unethical (Keith-Spiegel, Tabachnick, & Allen, 1992) but are inclined to be more accepting if student–educator relationships are perceived as strictly professional (Holmes, Rupert, Ross, & Shapera, 1999).

The next case involved an example of a professor who puts her own inappropriate needs first.

Case 11–35: Ginger Nailbrain, the daughter of the divorced boyfriend of Linda Pleasemore, D.S.W., was encouraged to enroll in Dr. Pleasemore's section of an introductory social work course. Pleasemore thought this experience would help solidify the relationship with the father. Halfway through the semester, however, the relationship between Pleasemore and Nailbrain's father dissolved. Nailbrain's final course grade was a D. Nailbrain and her father filed complaints with the university and a state ethics committee charging that Dr. Pleasemore was seeking vengeance by assigning the daughter a poor grade.

Pleasemore's professional judgment was faulty on several grounds. She not only instigated a multiple-role relationship up front, but also used a professional relationship as a vehicle for advancing a personal agenda. Even if the relationship had worked and the daughter had received a high mark, the ethical issues would remain unchanged, although they would not likely be contested.

Educators can become embroiled in gift-giving and favor situations similar to those of therapists. Small gifts are occasionally offered by students to their favorite teachers and sometimes for other, more suspect reasons.

Case 11–36: On the last day of class, a student gave Bic Smoke, Ph.D., a silver lighter engraved with his initials. When the student got a C in the course, she became irate and complained to the professor. Smoke shared his grading procedure with her, but she remained dissatisfied and went to the department chair and the dean. Smoke wrote an ethics committee, describing what he now saw as a bribe attempt, and asked for guidance regarding how to mount a defense. He noted that he was uncomfortable with the gift from the beginning, but because it was already engraved he did not know what else to do but to accept it.

Dr. Smoke's touchy situation, given the fact that the lighter was engraved and therefore inappropriate to give to someone else and unacceptable for a refund, might have been handled by asking the student to keep it until after she graduated. She could then give it to him if she still wanted to do so.

Another delicate peril involves therapists employed by colleges or universities who deliver private practice services to students in the same institution. Here, an acquaintance role involves contact that may actively continue, and its nature could conceivably include evaluations and other responsibilities that extend a powerful influence on the students. In short, both facets of the dual role relationship are (or could be) intense, and the potential dangers of role blurring could ensue. For example, the student, as a paying client, might expect special favors on campus, such as help getting into a needed class, a letter of recommendation, or some intervention on his or her behalf. Or, the therapist may view and evaluate the student's academic performance differently based on what is learned about the student during therapy sessions.

This dilemma can be greatly diminished by limiting student therapy clients to those who are not and are never likely to be in one's academic department and by discussing ground rules in advance. Some college and university departments have policies on this matter and allow mental health professionals who are also faculty members to see students in their private practices off campus but require a stipulation between the two that the educator will not serve the student in any academic evaluation capacity for the duration of the student's tenure at the institution. Although this policy defuses the potential for dual-role conflicts, students may be disadvantaged by the restriction. We recommend the conservative course of action in the spirit of protection for all concerned: Refer students to the nonteaching institution's counseling center staff or to other practitioners in the community.

Off-Campus Behavior

Professors need to monitor their behavior whenever and wherever students are around, even when not on campus. Professors are readily recognized by students, and they discuss among themselves what they see. Professor Plaster in our next case no doubt wished he had followed our advice.

Case 11–37: The team won the game, and the victory party at the local pub was raucous. Plenty of beer was consumed, and Professor Plaster downed several. When a student vocally disagreed with Plaster's choice of the team's best player, he tossed a glass of beer in her face.

The actual case from which our beer-tossing case is adapted (University suspends writer, 1995) was widely publicized in the popular press. The professor (not a mental health professional) was suspended for a semester.

A more common situation is more difficult to evaluate, perhaps because it usually satisfies everyone's needs.

Case 11–38: Professor Henry Hire lives in a small university town. Students often seek part-time employment, and he regularly hires them to do yard work, house repairs, and dog sitting

Ethical issues are virtually defused altogether if student employees are not in the same departmental unit. However, the practice of hiring students one knows is so prevalent that the attendant ethical issues are rarely considered. But, what if the student accidentally cuts down the wrong tree or loses the family pet? There are three precautions to take for the sake of students as well as one's own professional standing that will make dealing with any untoward occurrences cleaner.

- Students currently enrolled in one's classes should not be employed to do nonprofessionally related work because of the active dual role in effect. The student's performance in class may affect the performance (or lack thereof) on the job.
- Student employees should be selected for their competence and trustworthiness and paid a fair wage. These are smart ways to preclude complaints or entanglements.
- Expectations and agreements should be well formulated in advance, including provisions for termination that are predicated on respect for the needs and welfare of students.

The next case illustrates a poor match to the ultimate detriment of the all.

Case 11–39: To bring in extra income, Whatta Dump, Ph.D., and her husband fixed up their basement and rented it to a graduate student in Dump's department. Within a few weeks, the student complained that the basement stank, and that she was lonely and wanted to live in student housing. Dr. Dump reminded her that she had a lease and would have to pay in full. The student went to the dean of students and the campus newspaper, sharing other details about the household, including the content of the late night shouting matches between the Dumps.

The student prevailed with her complaints and received a release from her obligation. The Dumps became quite notorious along the campus grapevine and did not attempt to find a new renter.

The question arises also regarding whether a student who is simultaneously being evaluated by an educator can turn down *any* request, even if pay is involved. For example, a bilingual dissertation advisee is asked to translate an article by her advisor. Dare she tell him that she is already so overwhelmed with her own workload that she is not getting enough sleep (Canter et al., 1994)?

Relationships With Former Students

Social relationships with students after graduation pose a somewhat different set of dynamics than with therapy clients after termination. Once students leave, the primary student–professor role is terminated forever. Some students eventually become colleagues with whom educators will regularly interact at professional meetings or in other professional capacities. Continuing scholarly collaboration among educators and those who were once their students is not uncommon. Professors often form extremely close relationships with those they are mentoring, usually graduate students collaborating in some way that is deeply absorbing for both parties. Relationships occurring toward the end of the training period can last a lifetime.

The main risk of forming close relationships with an advanced student or an ex-student is that things could go awry, in which case the student could lose a valuable resource forever. In that case, an employer may wonder why a thesis chair, supervisor, or the program director was not listed as a reference. Both ex-students and their professors can cause each other continuing grief if their relationships disintegrate but they remain in the same circles (e.g., each can complain about how the other was as a student or as a professor). But, this issue becomes more a problem of interprofessional relationships than a conflict of roles and is discussed more fully in Chapter 13. Additional discussions about relationships with students, including sexual liaisons, appear in Chapters 12 and 16.

A FINAL WORD ABOUT NONSEXUAL MULTIPLE-ROLE RELATIONSHIPS

Zur (2003) and others have claimed that those of us who are cautious about role blending care only about protecting ourselves from any risk. We hope that in this and Chapter 10 we have made a valid case that role crossings should be undertaken *solely* for the benefit of the client.

Ironically, the more recent APA ethical codes, with their seemingly looser restrictions on nonsexual multiple roles as compared to three decades or so ago, might actually place the unaware therapist at far greater risk than earlier, stricter ethics codes. Why? Because fewer specific prohibitions beyond avoiding "exploitation" and "harm" remain. These are very general terms, somewhat vague, and open to interpretation. Therefore, any client who claims to have been "exploited" or "harmed" when roles became complicated would be difficult to challenge and refute, and unpredictable ethics committees and juries will make those findings on a case-by-case basis. Decisions should be documented should it ever become necessary to defend a venture into another role with a client (Younggren & Gottlieb, 2004).

Finally, complicated roles may lead to an increased risk of engaging in sexual relationships with clients. Critics of this slippery slope argument suggest that this thinking is a holdover from rigid psychoanalytic theory that sexualized any role crossing. However, data confirm that therapists with blurry role margins do not necessarily stop with gift giving, conducting sessions in the park, inviting clients out to dinner, or a kiss on the cheek. Surveys have established a relationship between nonsexual and sexual boundary crossing (Borys, 1988; Borys & Pope, 1989; Lamb & Catanzaro, 1998). This association should not come as any surprise because many forms of nonsexual multiple-role behaviors are those also routinely associated with dating and courtship rituals. Male therapists are more likely to mix roles than female therapists, and male therapists are also far more likely to engage in sexual relationships with their clients. The next chapter is devoted entirely to a discussion of romantic and sexual relationships with therapy clients and students.

SUMMARY GUIDELINES

1. The dynamics and functions of family and close friend relationship are markedly different from those of a professional therapy relationship. When approached by family members or close friends with requests for help with personal problems, it is appropriate to offer informational assistance.

However, refer them to appropriate professionals when longer-term professional services are indicated.

2. In cases involving an emergency, it is appropriate to provide therapeutic services to close relations until the crisis passes or until other resources can be arranged.

3. Before accepting people you know slightly in another context as therapy clients, actively suppress the basis of the acquaintance role as much as possible until the professional relationship is properly terminated.

4. Establishing friendships with ongoing clients may cause conflicts and confusion for clients and cause therapists to lose objectivity. Social interactions, if appropriate, should be restricted to attending the *formal* phase of a significant event in the client's life (e.g., wedding or graduation ceremony, funeral of spouse).

5. Friendships with previous clients pose less risk of harm but should be entered into with caution, especially if it is possible that the client may need additional services in the future.

6. Carefully evaluate the risks of accepting ongoing clients' referrals of their friends or family. Consider whether accepting them as individual clients will interfere with the needs or welfare of a current client. Pass the referral along if conflicts seem likely.

7. Sometimes, multiple-role relationships prove difficult or impossible to avoid, especially for therapists serving small communities. When alternatives are limited, therapists should be especially sensitive to possible complications and make every attempt to minimize them.

8. Therapists should avoid accepting gifts and favors from clients unless these are small and appropriate gestures of appreciation, which by not accepting would be construed as offensive or countertherapeutic. Requests for gifts or favors from clients are almost always inappropriate. Giving gifts to clients may occasionally be appropriate if therapeutically indicated.

9. When venturing outside a traditional office setting to undertake an assessment or to deliver psychotherapeutic services, the plan should be conscientiously conceived,

taking the needs and welfare of the client into consideration. The event should also be clearly defined and understood by the client as a professional as opposed to a social contact.

10. When unintended encounters with clients occur (e.g., on the golf course or in line at the bank), clients should take the lead regarding whether to acknowledge or disregard their therapists' presence. If chance encounters are likely to occur, we recommend discussing a protocol during an early session.

11. Relationships with students can more easily become complex because encounters outside the classroom are bound to occur, and attendance at school-sanctioned events is often encouraged. Educators and academic counseling center therapists must remain vigilant to ensure that misunderstandings do not arise, and that relationships that could harm students are avoided.

12. Maintaining professional boundaries while remaining a caring therapist is possible and, as the literature and case histories attest, the way to ensure that clients' needs always come first and remain the focal point of the client–therapist relationship.

References

Amos, T., & Margison, F. (2006). Fetters or freedom: Dual relationships in counseling. *International Journal for the Advancement of Counseling, 28,* 57–69.

Anderson, S. K., & Kitchener, K. S. (1996). Nonromantic, nonsexual post therapy relationships between psychologists and former clients: An exploratory study of critical incidents. *Professional Psychology, 27,* 59–66.

Benson, E. (2003, June). Beyond urbancentricism. *Monitor on Psychology, 54–55.*

Bischoff, R. J., Hollist, C. S., & Smith, C. W. (2004). Addressing the mental health needs of the rural underserved: Findings from a multiple case study of a behavioral telehealth project. *Contemporary Family Therapy: An International Journal, 26,* 179–198.

Bogrand, M. (1993, January–February). The duel over dual relationships. *The California Therapist, 7–10,* 12, 14, 16.

Borys, D. S. (1988). *Dual relationships between therapist and client: A national survey of clinicians' attitudes and practices.* Unpublished doctoral dissertation, University of California, Los Angeles.

Borys, D. S., & Pope, K. S. (1989). Dual relationships between therapist and client: A national study of psychologists, psychiatrists, and social workers. *Professional Psychology, 20,* 283–293.

Campbell, C. D., & Gordon, M. C. (2003). Acknowledging the inevitable: Understanding multiple relationships in rural practice. *Professional Psychology, 34,* 430–434.

Canter, M. B., Bennett, B. E., Jones, S. E., & Nagy, T. F. (1994). *Ethics for psychologists: A commentary on the APA ethics code.* Washington, DC: American Psychological Association.

Farrell, S. P., & McKinnon, C. (2003). Technology and rural mental health. *Archives of Psychiatric Nursing, 17,* 20–26.

Gabbard, G. O. (1994). Teetering on the precipice: A commentary on Lazarus's "How certain boundaries and ethics diminish therapeutic effectiveness." *Ethics & Behavior, 4,* 283–286.

Gottlieb, M. C. (1993). Avoiding exploitive dual relationships: A decision-making model. *Psychotherapy, 30,* 41–48.

Gottlieb, M. C. (1994). Ethical decision-making, boundaries, and treatment effectiveness: A reprise. *Ethics & Behavior, 4,* 287–293.

Hargrove, D. S. (1986). Ethical issues in rural mental health practice. *Professional Psychology, 17,* 20–23.

Holmes, D. L., Rupert, P. A., Ross, S. A., & Shapera, W. E. (1999). Student perceptions of dual relationships between faculty and students. Ethics & Behavior, 9, 70–107.

Keith-Spiegel, P., Tabachnick, B. G., & Allen, M. (1992). Ethics in academia: Students' views of professors' actions. *Ethics & Behavior, 3,* 149–162.

Kessler, L. E., & Wachler, C. A. (2005). Addressing multiple relationships between clients and therapists in lesbian, gay, bisexual, and transgender communities. *Professional Psychology, 36,* 66–72.

Knapp, S., & Slattery, J. M. (2004). Professional boundaries in nontraditional settings. *Professional Psychology, 35,* 553–558.

Knox, S., Hess, S. A., Williams, E. N., & Hill, C. E. (2003). "Here's a little something for you": How therapists respond to client gifts. *Journal of Counseling Psychology, 50,* 199–210.

Lamb, D. H., & Catanzaro, S. J. (1998). Sexual and nonsexual boundary violations involving psychologists, clients, supervisees, and students: Implications for professional practice. *Professional Psychology: Research and Practice. 29,* 498–503.

Leslie, R. S. (1994, November–December). The unavoidable conflict. *The California Therapist,* 24–26.

University suspends writer after incident. (1995, April 7). *New York Times.* Retrieved November 11, 2006, from http://query.nytimes.com/gst/fullpage.html?res=990CE7DB1731F934A35757C0A963958260.

Perkins, D. V., Husdon, B. I., Gray, D. M., & Stewart, M. (1998). Decisions and justifications by community mental health providers about hypothetical ethical dilemmas. *Psychiatric Services, 49,* 1317–1322.

Peterson, M. R. (1992). *At personal risk: Boundary violations in professional–client relationships.* New York: Norton.

Pope, K. S., Tabachnick, B. G., & Keith-Spiegel, P. (1987). Ethics of practice: The beliefs and behaviors of psychologists as therapists. *American Psychologist, 42,* 993–1006.

Pulakos, J. (1994). Encounters between therapists and clients: The client's perspectives. *Professional Psychology: Research and Practice, 25,* 300–303.

Roberts, L. W., Battaglia, J., & Epstein, R. S. (1999). Frontier ethics: Mental health care needs an ethical dilemmas in rural communities. *Psychiatric Services, 50,* 497–503.

Schank, J. A., & Skovholt, T. A. (2006). *Ethical practice in small communities: Challenges and rewards for psychologists.* Washington DC: American Psychological Association.

Schofield, W. (1964). *Psychotherapy: The purchase of friendship.* Englewood Cliffs, NJ: Prentice-Hall.

Shapiro, E. L., & Ginzberg, R. (2003). To accept or not to accept: Referrals and the maintenance of boundaries. *Professional Psychology, 34,* 258–263.

Sharkin, B. S., & Birky, I. (1992). Incidental encounters between therapists and their clients. *Professional Psychology, 23,* 326–328.

Sleek, S. (1994, May–June). Ethical dilemmas plague rural practice. *APA Monitor, 25,* 26.

Smith, D., & Fitzpatrick, M. (1995). Patient–therapist boundary issues: An integrative review of theory and research. *Professional Psychology, 26,* 499–506.

Solomon, G., Heisberger, J., & Winer, J. (1981). Confidentiality issues in rural community mental health. *Journal of Rural Community Psychology, 2,* 17–31.

Stockman, A. F. (1990). Dual relationships in rural mental health practice: An ethical dilemma. *Journal of Rural Community Psychology, 11,* 31–45.

Tallman, G. (1981). *Therapist–client social relationships.* Unpublished manuscript, California State University, Northridge.

Younggren, J. N., & Gottlieb, M. C. (2004). Managing risk when contemplating multiple relationships. *Professional Psychology, 35,* 255–260.

Zur, O. (2003). Bartering in psychotherapy and counseling: Complexities, case studies and guidelines. Retrieved December 6, 2004, from http://www.drozur.com/bartertherapy.html

12

Multiple-Role Relationships III

Attraction, Romance, and Sexual Intimacies

> Whatever houses I may visit, I will come for the benefit of the sick, remaining free of all intentional injustice, of all mischief, and in particular of sexual relations with both female and male persons, be they free or slaves.
>
> Hippocratic Oath (ca. 400 B.C.)

Contents

Psychotherapeutic alliances have peculiar and significant features that require firm professional resolve. Twemlow and Gabbard (1989) put it bluntly; "Every psychotherapist struggles with the temptation to seek personal gratification from the therapeutic situation" (p. 71). Student–teacher and supervisee–supervisor relationships may have fewer inherent complications, but they are hardly immune from becoming emotionally involving. Passionate feelings can, at times, overwhelm a person's commitment to professional standards.

This chapter is the longest in the book. However, we did not increase the length because of the natural human fascination with the subject matter. Instead, we believe that the most damage to both clients and therapists occurs when a professional relationship turns into a sexual affair. Furthermore, sexual transgressions with clients appear to be the most frequent specific cause for disciplinary action (Kirkland, Kirkland, & Reaves, 2004). Hence, we have chosen to be especially thorough.

Based on surveys conducted over past quarter century, we feel confident in predicting that every therapist and educator will face at some point in his or her career erotized stirrings in the context of conducting professional responsibilities. The emergence of such feelings is a function of human nature. However, the way we manage those feelings lies at the heart of ethical professionalism.

As with most typical human courtship rituals, sexual relationships between therapists and their clients often reveal similar progressive phases: feelings of attraction, mild flirtation, some friendly touching on "safe" body areas, a cup of coffee at the café across the street from the therapist's office, a switch in the client's schedule to the last appointment of the day, hanging around afterward to talk about things in general, and hugging good-bye. An overt sexual act is often the culmination of a process occurring over a period of time, starting with vague, uneasy feelings of excitement, but progressing in tidy, rationalized steps toward sexual contact.

SEXUAL ATTRACTION

Attraction to Clients

Feelings of sexual attraction require neither physical expression nor disclosure. They can remain one's own little secret and, most of the time, cause no real harm. To have fleeting erotic feelings toward other people is normal. So perhaps it surprised no one when the first published survey on sexual attraction in psychotherapy reported that therapists who claimed that they had *never* felt attracted to any of their clients fell into a distinct minority (Pope, Keith-Spiegel, & Tabachnick, 1986). However, of the 95% of the male therapists and 76% of the female therapists who admitted to having feelings of attraction to at least one client, the majority felt guilty, anxious, or confused about it. Older female therapists were less likely to report ever being attracted to a client, whereas the attraction rate for younger female therapists approached that of male therapists. (As the "younger respondents" of the 1980s would today be "older respondents," things may well have evened out between the sexes by now.) Despite the high rates of attraction, however, a much lower percentage of therapists (9.4% of the men and 2.5% of the women) reportedly allowed the attraction to escalate into sexual liaisons with their clients.

Another survey (Rodolfa et al., 1994) found that only 12% of their large sample of American Psychological Association (APA) members reported *never* having felt attracted to a client, only a few had ever acted on these feelings, just less than half reported negative consequences, and over half sought consultation. Pope and Tabachnick (1993) reported that almost half of the therapists responding to their national survey had experienced sexual arousal during a therapy session. About a third believed that their clients had, on occasion, become sexually aroused while with them.

So, to whom do therapists become attracted? Based on the Pope et al. (1986) survey, the overwhelming characteristic was, not surprisingly, "physical attractiveness." "Positive mental/cognitive traits" (e.g., intelligent, well educated, articulate) and "sexuality" were next followed by "vulnerability" attributes (e.g., needy, child-like, sensitive, fragile) and "good personality." Smaller percentages of respondents indicated attraction based on clients who fulfilled their needs (e.g., boosted the therapist's image, alleviated the therapist's loneliness or pressures at home) or based their attraction on the perception that the clients seemed attracted to them or the clients reminded them of someone else. A small number admitted feeling attraction to clients with serious psychopathology. We may debate whether some reasons seem more acceptable or at least more understandable than others. Nevertheless, a few therapists have obviously used their attraction to meet personal, nonprofessional needs and, in doing so, could have placed their most vulnerable clients at additional risk. For example, we know of a therapist who admitted to having had sexual relationships with very young, seriously ill anorexic clients while they were hospitalized.

Under what conditions should feelings of attraction become a cause for concern? How should one handle such feelings? If a therapist finds attraction occurring often, should outside consultation be sought? In an interview study with postdoctoral interns, most participants admitted to behaving in a more invested and attentive manner to those clients to whom they felt attracted, but that the attraction also caused them to become more easily distracted and less objective (Ladany et al., 1997). Because the therapy process may be compromised, it is regrettable that only half of the sample in this study reported disclosing their feelings to their supervisors.

When therapists can not bring their feelings well under control or sense that their feelings are having an adverse impact on how they treat their clients, and when consultation was sought but ineffective, we recommend a sensitive termination and referral as a way to protect all parties from complications, confusion, and harm. The therapist might say something like, "I would recommend that you work with someone more skilled than I in addressing the issues of concern to you." In our first case, the therapist got it only half right.

Case 12–1: Lovitt Firstsight, L.M.H.C., knew after only a few minutes into the initial session with Venus Exquisite that he could not be her therapist. He felt like a schoolboy again, had trouble focusing on what Venus was saying, and became sexually aroused. He had difficulty finding his "therapist voice," and after 10 minutes, he gently interrupted her to tell her that he was not the right therapist for her. Firstsight spoke honestly with her about why and offered to help her find another therapist.

At least Mr. Firstsight became immediately and consciously aware that his initial intense feelings may not subside and had already begun to reduce his abilities to perform competently. He also rightly recognized that the less information the client disclosed to him under the circumstances, the better. Unfortunately, in the actual incident, the therapist did not maintain a cautious stance. He married the woman within a matter of months, only to have the relationship dissolve shortly thereafter. The flattered "almost client" and the spellbound "almost therapist" realized that once the sparkle wore off, they had little in common and many areas of conflict.

Some might argue that Firstsight did not behave unethically because the woman was not, strictly speaking, a "former client." Ten minutes hardly seems enough time to have established a therapist–client relationship. If the woman were defined as an ex-client, Dr. Firstsight would have committed an ethical infraction. Why? Because even if the two had remained happily married forever after, he did not heed the required moratorium period (discussed in the section on posttermination sexual relationships with clients). Regardless, the fleeting therapeutic relationship involved sufficient emotional intensity to have warranted far more caution than Dr. Firstsight ultimately exercised.

Most instances of sexual attraction between clients and therapists do not strike with such an immediate, mighty force. More likely, a recognition that this person is pleasant to look at or intriguing in some way flickers and soon dissipates or remains at a safe level as the therapist focuses on the demands of a working professional relationship. Of course, attraction feelings can also escalate, and that is when things can begin to unravel.

When a therapist senses even a small attraction toward a client, we strongly recommend against ignoring it. We offer a dozen alerts, any of which would indicate that the attraction feelings may tend to put therapists at risk for loss of objectivity and thereby reduced competence.

- thinking often about the client outside of that client's sessions
- having recurring sexual thoughts or fantasies about the client, in or out of session
- dressing or grooming in an uncustomary or self-conscious fashion on the client's appointment day
- looking forward to sessions with that client above all others
- attempting to elicit information from the client to satisfy personal curiosities as opposed to that required to achieve therapeutic goals
- daydreaming about seeing the client socially
- becoming mildly flirtatious or eliciting discussions of sexual material during sessions when not therapeutically relevant
- indulging in rescue fantasies or seeing yourself as the only person who can heal this person
- believing that you can make up for all of the past deficits, sadness, or disappointments in this client's life
- becoming sexually aroused in the client's presence
- wanting to touch the client
- having trouble focusing during the therapeutic session

Therapists may experience surprise, even shock, to recognize that they have sexual feelings toward a client (Pope, Sonne, & Holroyd, 1993). Should one discuss such feelings the client? The answer used to be debated. But, after considering the available evidence, it is currently not recommended (Fisher, 2004). Why? First, the client may not be able to deal with a frank admission of the therapist's attraction and is likely to become confused, uncomfortable, and unclear about how to respond. Second, such disclosure injects the therapist's own issues into the client's life, which constitutes poor professional practice. Third, if unwelcome, a client might perceive such revela-

tions as harassing or repulsive. Finally, the intrigued client may readily interpret the revelation as an invitation to follow the therapist's lead outside the office, which may not (and should not) be the therapist's intent. The next case illustrates how overt expressions of attraction, even if they are not actually felt, can be problematic.

Case 12–2: A young Asian client saw herself as homely and unlikable. Letme Fixit, Ph.D., asserted that he was only trying to boost her self-esteem when he told her she had beautiful eyes, and that he could imagine her having a close relationship with a "White man" like him, even though it could not be him as much as he would like that. His attempts to exonerate himself on the grounds that he went overboard trying to convince the client that she was attractive were not persuasive to a licensing board.

Dr. Fixit may have meant well in his own mind; however, his actions illustrate insensitivity to sexual misunderstanding and racial bias. He has focused on physical attributes of the client he finds personally attractive and has clearly asserted White privilege with an implication that attractiveness to other people of Asian ancestry holds less value. Most therapists would not attempt to alter a client's self-perceptions without first attempting to understand the basis for the feelings. If some supportive comment seemed therapeutically indicated, Dr. Fixit might have said, "I think you are being too critical of yourself."

We do strongly advise that the therapist should discuss lingering attraction feelings toward a client with someone, preferably another therapist, an experienced and trusted colleague, or an approachable supervisor. When professional vision becomes distorted, excuses seem to flow all too easily. A fresh perspective will often prove helpful in clarifying the risk, neutralizing rationalizations, and offering advice on how to proceed from here on out.

Client Attraction to Therapists

That clients sometimes feel sexual attraction toward their therapists comes as no surprise given the emotionally intimate nature of psychotherapy. Rather than use the term *transference*, Parish and Eagle (2003) prefer the term *attachment*, which manifests itself in clients perceiving therapists as emotionally responsive, admirable, a secure base, unique, and irreplaceable. Such powerful feelings can readily be experienced as love or something like it. In a national survey of female psychologists, almost half reported potentially sexualized behavior emanating from their male and, less often, female clients. The younger the therapist, the more likely the sexualized behavior directed toward them (deMayo, 1997).

How should a therapist respond to a client's declarations of attraction? If a client openly and directly expresses erotic feelings, it is important to deal with these impulses in a way that both preserves professional boundaries and protects the client's self-esteem. Leaping into interpretations of unconscious issues may feel like the safe way to go but could be experienced as humiliating by the sincere client who has just mustered up the courage to disclose his or her innermost feelings. A therapist's too-fast declaration that acting on any such feelings would be unethical and unprofessional may come across as an anxious overreaction. And, therapists must remember that when a client directly expresses erotic feelings, it does not necessarily mean that the client expects them to be acted on. What the therapist interprets as seductive behavior could instead be signs of dependency (Gregory & Gilbert, 1992). The better course of action is further exploration of the client's feelings.

What if the therapist also harbors unspoken feelings of attraction toward the client who openly discloses attraction to the therapist? In an attempt to better understand such a situation, Goodyear and Shumate (1996) simulated therapy sessions portraying a client disclosing a sexual interest in a therapist. These were rated by groups of therapists. The portrayal of the therapist who disclosed reciprocal attraction (followed by an indication that it would not be acted on) was rated as less therapeutic for the client and less skillful than was a condition in which the therapist remained noncommittal.

We suggest that whenever a client makes any request or disclosure for which reciprocation would be inappropriate, first ask that client how they see the fulfillment of the request as helpful to them. Then, follow with a discussion about why granting the request would actually not be in the client's best interests. This way, the focus remains solely on a caretaking orientation. If a client becomes aggressively seductive, Gutheil and Gabbard (1992) suggested a more unyielding approach: Tell the client that therapy is a "talking relationship" and discuss why the client's behavior is inappropriate.

Rarely, a patient's acting out of exceptionally strong sexual or romantic interests may be uncontainable. This drastically limits the kinds of available interventions (Ogden, 1999). In such circumstances, the best course of action is to refer the client to another therapist.

Case 12–3: Edie Persistent's therapy with Tyler Engulfed, Ph.D., proceeded without incident for the first few sessions. But soon Ms. Persistent became belligerent, demanding that Engulfed hold her hand throughout the sessions and then wanting to sit on his lap during the entire therapy hour. She cried and flailed about uncontrollably whenever Engulfed attempted to get her back into a chair. The demands accelerated and became more bizarre, including insisting that Engulfed watch her masturbate, and that he have sex with her to simulate a rape that she allegedly endured as a child.

Although the actual therapist on which we base this case never engaged in sexual relations with his client, he endured a highly publicized licensing hearing resulting in sanctions for continuing to treat a client whose pathology fell well beyond his level of therapeutic competence. An expert witness in this case noted that borderline patients can "sneak up on you" because they can seem so ordinary at first. Such clients, according to Blatchford (2004) also often inspire empathy and a desire to rescue the client from their pathology.

TOUCHING CLIENTS

Touch is an intensely intimate, complex mode of communication that can convey support, consolation, empathy, caring, and sincere concern.

Yet, touch has several faces. It can also signal sexuality, anxiety, aggression, and even fear. The relationship between the "toucher" and the "touchee," and how and where each party is experiencing being touched by the other specifically or others generally, can create complicated ethical dilemmas for therapists.

Historically, the "laying on of hands" has been an integral part of the healing process. Modern-day science has repeatedly demonstrated the calming and attendant physical benefits of supportive stroking during such procedures as childbirth (Kertay & Reviere, 1993), healthy physical and emotional development in infancy (e.g., Harlow, 1958), and massage for relief from a wide variety of physical ailments and emotional disorders (Field, 1998). It would seem, then, that touching *should* be an integral procedure in mainstream psychotherapy. Despite vigorous protests (e.g., Zur & Nordmarken, 2004), however, any physical contact with psychotherapy clients should be approached with considerable caution.

Nonerotic Touching

When therapists do touch clients, the circumstances most frequently mentioned as appropriate include expressions of emotional support and reassurance or during initial greeting or closing of sessions. The emotionally or socially immature (e.g., children or schizophrenics) and the distressed or depressed were most frequently mentioned as the types of clients who might particularly benefit from receiving nonerotic touches (Holroyd & Brodsky, 1977). Very brief nonerotic touching on the hand, back, and shoulders are the safest areas of touch and can still convey a caring, supportive message (Wilson, 1982).

Early surveys revealed that the majority of psychologists and psychiatrists never or rarely engaged in nonerotic touching (Holroyd & Brodsky, 1977; Kardener, Fuller, & Mensh, 1973). Approximately half of the therapists responding to the Holroyd and Brodsky (1977) survey thought that nonerotic contact (such as hugging, kissing, or affectionate touching) could benefit both male and female clients under certain conditions, but only 27% reported ever actually doing so. Subsequent surveys suggest that nonerotic touching of clients began to increase. Stake and Oliver (1991) reported reasonably high rates of touching of the shoulder, arm, and hand and hugging by both male and female therapists with both male and female clients. Average rates were highest for women therapists and their female clients, and these touching behaviors were rarely viewed by the survey respondents as constituting misconduct. Similarly, the majority of respondents in the survey conducted by Pope, Tabachnick, and Keith-Spiegel (1987) reported "sometimes" or "often" hugging clients or shaking their hands. The prevailing attitude was that both of these behaviors were ethical under most circumstances. Kissing clients on the lips or cheek was reported as occurring less often and was more likely to be viewed as unethical.

Recent work suggests a return to more caution regarding touching clients. Stenzel and Rupert (2004) found that 90% of their national survey sample never or only rarely touched clients. A handshake on entering or exiting the session was the most common tactile event. It is possible that successful legal suits against therapists for charges of sexually motivated touching and sexual harassment resulted in chilling any form of touching beyond the most traditional of formalities.

Clients may initiate touching because of a desire to be physically close to their therapists, and a therapist's decision to touch or not to touch must often be made very quickly. Consider a dilemma that most therapists will face at some point:

Case 12–4: Ivy Holdme, a divorced mother with custody of two very challenging children experiencing serious troubles at school, had her car stolen the previous day with her purse and wallet inside. At the close of a dreary session, the mother said to the therapist, "I really need a great big hug."

Although the nature of the already-established relationship will play a large role in the therapist's response, several questions will still come to mind. Should I do it? Would it affect our therapeutic relationship? What kind of a hug should it be: short, long, tight, limp? According to Holub and Lee (1990), "The decision to touch or not to touch clients may involve more than its effectiveness or the positive light that it casts on the therapist. The decision must also include deliberation over the correctness, perceptions, motives, and interpretations of the touch" (p. 115). The therapist's own level of comfort with touching and being touched will also come into play (Kertay & Reviere, 1993). For therapists who have already recognized their own physical attraction toward a client, extra caution must be exercised. If the client has already indicated clear signs of sexual attraction toward the therapist, engaging in any physical contact becomes extremely risky.

In their risk-management approach to touching, Bennett, Bryant, VandenBos, and Greenwood (1990) admonished therapists to consider first how they think the client would react. The intent of the initiator may not come through clearly to the recipient. The following case illustrates how differing perceptions of touch can lead to ethical charges:

Case 12–5: Janet Demure complained to an ethics committee that her therapist, Patten Stroke, Psy.D., behaved in a sexually provocative manner, which caused her considerable stress and embarrassment. He allegedly put his arm around her often, massaged her back and shoulders, and leered at her. Dr. Stroke was shocked on learning of the charges and vehemently denied any improper intentions. He claimed that he often put his hand briefly on his clients' backs and patted or moved his hand with the intention of communicating warmth and acceptance. His customary constant eye contact was his way to communicate that clients had his full attention. He admitted that Demure seemed uneasy but expected this would quickly pass as it did with others who were not used to expressions of caring.

Dr. Stroke's training as a humanistically oriented practitioner disposed him to considerable nonerotic touching of clients (Durana, 1998; Holroyd & Brodsky, 1977; Zur & Nordmarken, 2004). Regardless of therapeutic orientation, it is necessary to remain aware of individual clients and their special needs and issues, a sensitivity that may well require an alteration in one's usual demeanor.

Because such issues may catch therapists completely off guard, wise practitioners will carefully consider these eventualities in advance. Not wanting to appear rejecting may overtake the moment, but a knee-jerk compliance with the request could, even if for only a small percentage of clients, have negative consequences. The next case illustrates the point.

Case 12–6: Sarah Needy felt very alone in a new, large city. On entering the fifth session with Tim Startled, L.M.H.C., she embraced and held onto him tightly and did not let go. The astonished therapist put his arms lightly around her and nervously patted her on the back. Unfortunately, Needy interpreted Startled's willingness to be held for an extended period as a nonverbal admission that their relationship had progressed beyond that of therapist and client. When, after several minutes, Mr. Startled moved away and continued with the usual mode of therapy, Needy became confused and angry. She walked out and later pressed ethics charges for "sexual misconduct."

Mr. Startled would have been wiser to proactively shorten Needy's unwelcome surprise embrace. Even if he had to take his client's arms and set them gently aside, he could maintain a stance of caring and concern without allowing prolonged physical contact. He should have also promptly addressed her affect, noting that her embrace surprised him and wondering whether they ought to discuss what she was feeling that triggered her wish for a hug. For some clients, touching can be inappropriate in *any* form and under *any* circumstances.

Case 12–7: Connie Sole, Ph.D., and Jason Mourner had a long-standing therapy relationship that never involved physical touching. On learning that Jason's father fell unexpectedly ill and died suddenly, Dr. Sole reached for Jason to give him a hug. Jason's body went rigid, and he did not return the gesture.

In an attempt at consolation, Dr. Sole misjudged her client. She may not choose to discuss the ill-fated gesture during that particular session (allowing her to consider how she will approach it with this client). Dr. Sole should, however, openly address it as soon as feasible, if only to apologize for unintentionally causing her client discomfort.

Case 12–8: Ava Batter, who suffered recent physical abuse at the hand of her husband, began to cry and shake uncontrollably after recounting her torment during her initial session with Holden Pity, M.S.W. Mr. Pity's words could not console her. He went to her chair, knelt down, and put his arms around her while rocking gently. Mrs. Batter did not return for a second session.

Ethically, this challenging situation pitted compassion against good professional practice. Because it occurred during the first session, Mr. Pity did not know his client well enough to have an awareness of her physical boundaries. He should have exercised more caution given his knowledge that she had experienced physical abuse.

Finally, we acknowledge that a "no touching policy" will *not* guide every situation, and we do not propose a ban on nonerotic touching. For example, it might seem that holding a patient's hand throughout an initial session would be exceptionally inappropriate. However, consider the next case:

Case 12–9: Irving Flexible, Ph.D., was called to consult on the case of a 23-year-old woman with advanced lung disease secondary to cystic fibrosis. After introducing himself to the patient and sitting in the chair at her bedside, the psychologist asked how he could be helpful. The young woman, who was having great difficulty breathing despite wearing an oxygen mask, gripped his hand tightly and said, "Don't let go." Between attempts to catch her breath, she spoke of her terror at sensations of suffocation and the thought of dying alone.

Occasionally, significant variations from the usual rules constitute the highest standard of care. Deviations, however, should only occur when the following question can be answered in the affirmative: "If my behavior was known to my colleagues, would they very likely agree that I served *only* the needs of my client?" Dr. Flexible easily passes that test.

Erotic Touching

The general definition of erotic contact offered by Holroyd and Brodsky (1977, 1980) includes behavior primarily intended to arouse or satisfy sexual desires. Using this definition, such touching (excluding intercourse) was reported by 9% of male and 1% of female therapists sampled in their 1977 survey. The advantage of a definition that focuses not on the act but on the intent is that touching *any* part of the person is unethical if the intent is sexual gratification. An obvious drawback is that accused therapists can always deny their intent, which may or may not be truthful.

Another way to define inappropriate contact focuses on exactly which body parts are touched. For example, improper touch has been defined as coming into contact with the bare skin or through clothing of the breast of a female or the sexual organ, anus, groin, or buttocks of either sex (California Business and Professions Code, Section 728.2) and is punishable by a fine or jail time (California Penal Code, Section 243.4). So, should therapists memorize the list of what not to touch? An advantage of such a list is that intent need not be proven. It also implicitly allows other forms of touching that should not normally raise concerns, such as shaking hands or a reassuring pat on the back. But, the list approach is problematic because humans can experience sensations as sexual just about everywhere on their bodies. The way one is touched is almost as telling as what is touched. Therefore, if a forbidden touch site is not specifically noted, one might assume that touching it is acceptable. But, is it really okay to massage a man's breasts or nibble on clients' ears?

Kissing and Beyond

A fascinating letter written by Sigmund Freud in 1931 to his disciple, Sandor Ferenczi, reveals that the issue of sexual innuendo in therapy was brewing over three quarters of a century ago. Ferenczi suggested that showing physical affection to patients might assist neutralizing early emotional deprivation. Freud responded:

You have not made a secret of the fact that you kiss your patients and let them kiss you. . . . Now I am assuredly not one of those who from prudishness or from consideration of bourgeois convention would condemn little erotic gratifications of this kind. . . . But that does not alter the fact . . . that with us a kiss signifies a certain erotic intimacy. . . . Now picture what will be the result of publishing your technique. . . . A number of independent thinkers will say to themselves: Why stop at a kiss? Certainly one gets further when one adopts "pawing" as well, which after all doesn't make a baby. And then bolder ones will come along who will go further, to peeping and showing—and soon we shall have accepted in the technique of analysis the whole repertoire of demiviergerie and petting parties, resulting in an enormous interest in psychoanalysis among both analysts and patients. (Jones, 1957, pp. 163–164, cited in Marmor, 1972)

Are therapists who touch and kiss clients also more likely to have sexual relationships with them? A slippery slope does appear to exist, which should astonish no one. Sexual activities usually start out slowly as intimate relationships progress. Holroyd and Brodsky (1980) found that those therapists who admitted having sexual relationships with their clients also advocated and engaged in more nonerotic touching of opposite-sex, but not same-sex, clients. These authors concluded that nonerotic touching is predictive only when the therapist is selective about the gender touched. Other surveys have found a relationship between nonsexual multiple-role relationships and sexual boundary crossing (Borys & Pope, 1989; Lamb & Catanzaro, 1998).

ROMANCING AND CASUALLY DATING CLIENTS

Giving a client a dozen red roses, taking a client to dinner or for a drink at happy hour, or staying after hours in the office to chat while listening to music are not classified as "sexual intimacies." We saw in Chapter 11, however, that such activities would involve the superimposition of inappropriate activities on to a therapeutic relationship. Casual social excursions outside the office become especially risky because they typically involve more self-disclosure on the part of the therapist and other behaviors that could easily be perceived by clients or students as courtship/dating rituals. Even therapists with no motivations beyond platonic pleasantries are likely to confuse and possibly harm their clients (Simon, 1991).

Case 12–10: Norman Forlorn, L.M.F.T., felt lonely after many of his friends moved away or passed away. He missed his adult children, who had since scattered around the country. He began to single out several male and female clients on whom to shower extra attention, alternating among them for one-on-one experiences. Sometimes, he would sit and talk for up to 3 hours after a session. He often took them out to lunch or dinner. Forlorn was shocked when one of the women complained to a licensing board that he "wined and then two-timed her."

Whereas we may sympathize with Mr. Forlorn's personal circumstances, he exercised poor judgment in using his clients as surrogate children. One's client base should never serve as a population of convenient intimacy. The next case reveals a much more common scenario.

Case 12–11: Simon Inchworm, Ph.D., was attracted to Selma Receptive, his client of several months. Selma readily accepted what Dr. Inchworm believed, at the time, to be a professionally appropriate invitation to attend a lecture on eating disorders, given that Selma's sister had a history of anorexia nervosa. The lecture concluded at 5 P.M., so Dr. Inchworm invited Ms. Receptive to stop for a bite at a nearby bistro. The next week, Inchworm accepted Receptive's gift of a book written by the speaker they had heard the previous week. The following week, Inchworm agreed to a reciprocal dinner at Receptive's apartment. Afterward, while enjoying a third glass of wine, they looked into each other's eyes, embraced, kissed for a while, and retreated into the bedroom.

It does not take a clairvoyant to predict such an outcome. Yet, it continually amazes us how highly educated male and female therapists have allowed themselves to put their clients and themselves in such precarious situations, which often eventually causes great harm to both. In this actual case, an affair persisted for a few weeks. In the meantime, Dr. Inchworm met someone else of more interest to him and terminated the affair. When Ms. Receptive became upset, he also terminated the therapy relationship. The client sought and won a large damage award through a civil malpractice complaint.

SEXUALLY INTIMATE BEHAVIOR WITH CLIENTS

Psychotherapists usually hold an advantage of power (or at least perceived power) because they become privy to intimate secrets. Clients new to therapy do not know what to expect, and they trust their therapists to act in their best interests. Consumers of mental health services also assume that their therapists exercise wise judgment and have considerable experience and highly specialized skills. In addition, clients usually come into therapy with vulnerabilities, struggling with their own problems for which they have come seeking assistance. They often feel in a "one-down" position as they walk through the door. The personal power of therapists can be so strong that it interferes significantly with clients' capacity to make decisions that, under a different set of circumstances, would be relatively easy. Occasionally, clients may not be so innocent, purposely seeking to seduce or manipulate their therapists. Yet, as we shall see, there is no excuse for other than a professional, self-controlled response.

Although data collection lacks the rigor demanded by traditional scientific methods, available evidence confirms that sexual activity with clients is likely to be exploitative and harmful due to abuse of power, mishandling of the transference relationship, role confusion, and other factors. Ironically, therapists can suffer major harm as well if a charge of misconduct is sustained. The extent of the devastation—which has often included loss of a job, license, spouse and family, financial security, and reputation— is typically far more pervasive and devastating than the fallout from committing other types of ethical transgressions.

The APA did not adopt the express prohibition against sexual intimacies in the 2,500-year-old Hippocratic Oath until 1977. The psychotherapy literature previously acknowledged that transference (i.e., feelings representational of earlier relationships manifesting themselves during psychotherapy) could be very strong in both clients and therapists. Sexual *contact* between clients and therapists, however, received little attention. Yet, even prior to 1977, sex with clients was viewed as poor professional practice, a dual-role relationship, and likely to be exploitative. But, without an express prohibition, complaints were more difficult to adjudicate and were not always taken seriously. Feminism, consumerism, and a growing admission and realization by therapists that such contact does occur with unacceptable frequency were among the factors leading to a swell of concern about those who would take sexual advantage of their clients (APA 02: 10.05).

Incidence

It is difficult to estimate accurately the frequency of sexual intimacies between psychotherapists and their clients. It is clear from self-report surveys, even if we assume that none of those who did not return their survey forms had been sexually intimate with their clients, that far more therapists engage in sexual behavior than is reported to ethics committees and state licensing boards (e.g., Parsons & Wincze, 1995).

Forer's (1981) classic survey conducted in California in 1968 reported that 17% of his sample of male private practice therapists admitted having had sexual relationships with clients. No similar frequency of sexual experience was reported by female private practice therapists or male therapists working in institutional settings. His work was so controversial that it was suppressed by his professional association, and no one would publish it at the time. Somewhat later survey data indicated that an average of about 10% of male and 2% of female therapists acknowledged having engaged in sexual intimacies with their clients, with no significant differences across psychiatry, social work, and psychology in the rates of self-reported sexual relationships (Borys & Pope,

1989). Some more recent self-report surveys offered signs that fewer therapists are engaging in such behavior with clients, students, and supervisees (Lamb & Catanzaro, 1998; Lamb, Catanzaro, & Moorman, 2003; Pope, 1993, 2001), although the rate may still reach an unacceptable 5% to 6%.

We can hope that the downward trend in self-report studies over the past decade reflects a true shift and mirrors the influence of the absolute condemnation of sexual misconduct by the helping professionals. However, that same impact may also result in underreporting on surveys. Consumer complaints have increased (Gottlieb, Sell, & Schoenfeld, 1988), perhaps causing therapists to fear detection and resulting litigation. Earlier, while the professional community mostly ignored the problem, clients may have felt too powerless to protest. Or, if they did complain, they were discounted as delusional, subject to fantasy, and in a struggle with their transference neuroses (Barnhouse, 1978; Schwendinger & Schwendinger, 1974). We remain hopeful that the steadily decreasing numbers indicate a continual reduction in the sexual exploitation of clients.

Who Is Responsible?

Some clients, students, and supervisees may actively and knowingly contribute to the creation of a sexually tempting atmosphere. Those with borderline or histrionic personality disorders have been especially singled out as potentially seductive (Gutheil, 1989; Notman & Nadelson, 1994). In interviews by Somer and Saadon (1999), almost one fourth of clients who admitted to having sexual relations with their therapists also admitted that they initiated the first embrace. Therapists, however, bear the responsibility to resist acting on their feelings of reciprocal attraction. Ethics committees and other hearing panels are not impressed when therapists whine that they are the ones who were lured and snared, the defenseless victims of beguiling clients.

Case 12–12: Hap Bowlover, Ph.D., wrote a letter in response to an ethics committee inquiry, insisting that he was systematically "worn down by a client who showed up for therapy sessions wearing dresses with the neckline and the hem almost meeting and started flirting with me the minute she walked into my office." He declared that she set a trap for him, and that he was being used as a symbol for "all the men who had messed her up in the past." He likened the client to a black widow spider and claimed to have contacted a lawyer for the purposes of suing her.

Such excuses surface more frequently than you might think. Some commentators seem sympathetic toward therapists, who, as Wright (1985) contended, are enticed into lustful moments by unscrupulous clients seeking to exploit the vulnerability of therapists to their own economic advantage. Clients who appear to encourage a sexual relationship with their therapists, however, may be repeating eroticized behaviors that are remnants of sexual abuse in their childhoods. Such clients are subject to revictimization because they are not like others who may find the therapist sexy or develop an erotic transference (Kluft, 1989, p. 485). Some clients may overwhelm the therapist incapable of managing erotic transference effectively, falling into what Gabbard and Lester (1995) labeled the "masochistic surrender" type. Here, the therapist may be attracted to difficult and demanding clients, pursuing humiliation and victimization in their personal and professional lives. The complex interactions with clients may lead them to accede to clients' demands, particularly those clients who are sadistic or psychopathic. Nevertheless, the bottom line is that shifting blame or responsibility to the client—even if the client is adeptly manipulative or seductive—is never an excuse for incompetent and unprofessional behavior. The obligation to uphold ethical, legal, and professional standards is not a duty that can be evaded or assigned to the client.

Harms to Clients

When sex enters into therapy, a helping environment has been shattered (Kluft, 1989). Even very early surveys of psychologists (Holroyd & Brodsky, 1977) and psychiatrists (Kardener et al., 1973) revealed that the majority of practitioners do not believe that erotic contact or sexual intercourse with clients could be beneficial and compared such acts to rape or incest (Barnhouse, 1978; Masters & Johnson, 1976). Indeed, one of the most unsettling research findings to date is that adult survivors of familial incest are at especially high risk for subsequent sexual abuse by their therapists (Armsworth, 1990; Broden & Agresti, 1998).

The available data on harm to clients do not represent *all* client–therapist sexual liaisons because they consist primarily of accounts by those who brought complaints against their therapists, who sought additional therapy and divulged their experience to their new therapists, or who responded to advertisements requesting information from those who had experienced sexual contact with their therapists. The majority of clients assessed from these populations reported sex with therapists as damaging (e.g., Bates & Brodsky, 1989; Bouhoutsos, Holroyd, Lerman, Forer, & Greenburg, 1983; Feldman-Summers, 1989; Kluft, 1989; Pope, 1990b, 2001; Pope & Vetter, 1991; Taylor & Wagner, 1976). Several poignant and absorbing personal accounts attest to the harm caused by sexualized therapy relationships (e.g., Bates & Brodsky, 1989; Freeman & Roy, 1976; Noel & Watterson, 1992; Plasil, 1985; Walker & Young, 1986).

Pope (1989a, 1994) described a cluster of symptoms seen in some clients who have had sexual relationships with their therapists. These include ambivalence about the therapist, akin to that of incest victims who hold both love and negative feelings toward the offending family member; feelings of guilt, as if the client were to blame for what happened; feelings of isolation and emptiness; cognitive dysfunction, particularly in the areas of attention and concentration; identity and boundary disturbances; difficulties in trusting others as well as themselves; confusion about their sexuality; lability of mood and feeling out of control; suppressed rage; and increased risk for suicide or other self-destructive reactions.

Some clients may view sexual relationships with therapists as pleasurable at the time but come to view it as exploitative later (Somer & Saadon, 1999). We saw, while serving on ethics committees, the manifestations of such feelings.

The complainants typically expressed outrage over what was done to them; described other relationships in their lives that were destroyed; expressed feelings of abandonment, exploitation, and hopelessness; questioned whether they could possibly trust another therapist again; and often stated that their reason for pressing charges was to make sure that what happened to them would never happen to anyone else. Ambivalence and guilt were often evident as well. Complainants often made it clear that they did not want anything bad to happen to their therapists. They just wanted them to stop hurting others.

Perhaps because of the especially serious professional, personal, and legal consequences that accompany sustained charges of sexual misconduct, the research on incidence and harmful impact on clients has been singled out for heavy criticism (e.g., Williams, 1992). Sampling, response, and experimenter biases are among the common criticisms of such research. Others have objected to the assumption that harm automatically accrues as a result of having sex with a client, or that an adult client is incapable of consenting to having sex with whomever he or she chooses (Slovenko, 1991). Although we may quibble about the quality of research and the generalizability of the findings, such debates obscure the basic point: Sex with clients is unethical and lies far outside accepted standards of care.

WHICH TYPES OF THERAPISTS ENGAGE IN SEXUAL RELATIONS WITH CLIENTS?

General Offender Characteristics

Sexually exploitative therapists as often portrayed in the movies appear as dashing, debonair, and self-assured. These depictions hardly reflect the portrait emerging from the available information about *real* therapists who engage in sexual activity with their clients.

Mental health professionals themselves may puzzle over how intelligent, educated men and women living in a world full of carnal opportunity could be so stupid as to engage in behaviors that are blatantly unprofessional and dangerous. One may also assume that therapists found guilty of sexual intimacies with clients consist chiefly of the poorly trained, obtuse, or psychopathic. Amazingly, actual cases from our personal knowledge include a past president of a state psychological association, current and former members of state licensing boards, a professor at a major university who authored an article on professional ethics, a chair of a state psychological association ethics committee, and even an author of an article condemning sex with clients! Indeed, although one can identify high-risk types of therapists and situations, no one seems immune from temptation or the potential to be exploitative.

Although data can not be collected with the scientific rigor of a controlled experiment, available reports suggest that therapists who engage in sexual intimacies with clients have one or more personal issues (Butler & Zelen, 1977; Dahlberg, 1970; Gabbard & Lester, 1995; Hetherington, 2000; Lamb et al., 2003; Marmor, 1972; Olarte, 1991; Pope, 1990a; Solursh & Solursh, 1993).

These include:

- general feelings of vulnerability
- fear of intimacy
- crises in their own personal sex, love, or family relationships
- feelings of failure as professionals or as individuals
- high needs for love or affection, positive regard, or power
- poor impulse control
- social isolation
- overvaluation of their abilities to heal
- isolation from peer support
- sexual identity and other unresolved conflicts
- depressive or bipolar disorders
- and narcissistic, sadistic, and other character or predatory psychopathologies

Offending therapists also tend to have strong denial or rationalization defenses in place (Celenza, 1998) and work alone (Somer & Saadon, 1999). They often deny to themselves that their behavior has any adverse impact on clients (Holroyd & Bouhoutsos, 1985) and are deficient in their ability to empathize (Regehr & Glancy, 2001). Most relationships apparently do not last long, and about half the time they are judged in retrospect as not worth having (Lamb et al., 2003).

The most common offender remains a male in his 40s or 50s (Brodsky, 1989; Butler & Zelen, 1977; Notman & Nadelson, 1994; Sonne & Pope, 1991). The middle-aged therapist going through a divorce or having other problems in a primary relationship should remain alert because the risk of overinvolvement with clients is especially high (Twemlow & Gabbard, 1989). Some abusing male therapists may have themselves experienced sexual abuse as children (Jackson & Nuttall, 2001).

Clients exploited by their therapists are mostly younger women. Perhaps as many as 5% are minors at the time of the sexual activity, and almost a third have been victims of incest or physical abuse as children (Pope & Vetter, 1991). A homosexual client of either sex with the same-sex therapist appears to be the next most frequent category, although a distant second (Brodsky, 1989).

Female therapists have a lower rate of engaging in sex with clients than do male therapists. Why women appear to be less likely to engage in sexual intimacies with clients has been debated in the absence of solid data. Perhaps female sex roles have allowed women to learn and practice a spectrum of techniques that do not involve sexuality for communicating love and nurturance. Maybe traditional cultural conditioning of women to refrain from taking the sexual initiative has also taught them better control of sexual impulses, as well as techniques for resisting sexual advances (Marmor, 1972).

When female therapists are respondents in ethics hearings or civil suits, the complainants will likely be lesbian clients or the wives, partners, or family members of the men with whom the therapist is having an alleged sexual relationship. The next case is illustrative.

Case 12–13: Maria Skeptic was so suspicious of her husband's claim that he was in therapy every Thursday night that she drove to the office just to make sure his car was parked in the office lot. She arrived just in time to observe her husband pressing the therapist up against his car for a passionate full-body embrace.

We do not hear much about single men complaining about sexual involvement with their therapists. The following incident, although bizarre, is a rare exception in terms of the dynamics.

Case 12–14: A convicted murderer escaped from a medium-security prison. It was later discovered that Helpya Flyout, L.M.H.C., a prison counselor, had helped create and execute the elaborate plan involving a helicopter picking up the prisoner at a preordained time on the prison grounds. Letters in Flyout's home detailed their sexual affair, and a photo of Flyout, wearing only black panties and a bra, was found on the wall of the inmate's cell.

We had no cases of a male client bringing an ethics charge of sexual exploitation against his female therapist to offer in the first edition of our book (Keith-Spiegel & Koocher, 1985) because none had ever come to our attention. Over three decades later, complaints against females remain rare but are no longer anomalies (Pope, 2001).

Case 12–15: Lura Bird, Ph.D., attempted to desensitize sexually repressed Alvin Stifle by reciting sexual fantasies she had about him. Mr. Stifle appeared unmoved. Frustrated by his nonresponsiveness, Dr. Bird decided to ratchet up her approach and, in one session, removed her clothing and embraced Stifle as he walked in the room. They fumbled around for a while before Stifle contained himself and left, never to return. He contacted an ethics committee complaining that his therapist was "a scary maniac."

Most cases are hardly this weird. We actually know little about how male clients are affected by sexual experiences with their female therapists. Slovenko (1991) suggested that it never occurs to the male client, even in litigious times, to sue a woman for having had sex with him. It has even been suggested that men would welcome such advances by their female therapists and perceive them as esteem building. However, a colleague who has treated several male clients in the aftermath of harm caused by engaging in sexual relations with previous female therapists told us that men do not make formal complaints because they fear a response of ridicule rather than of compassion and concern.

Uncommon Offender Scenarios

Only the rare case appears driven by a therapist's mean-spirited, premeditated attempt to exploit, such as the counselor who hypnotized clients for the purpose of getting them to masturbate in his presence or the psychologist who had sexual relationships with three of the most intriguing of his dissociative client's 16 personalities. Coerced sex is condemned in most societies, and thankfully such acts involving therapists and those with whom they have a professional relationship are also apparently exceedingly infrequent. Few complaints have alleged an attack, without provocation or warning, by their therapists.

Case 12–16: A client testified that during her second therapy session, Mel Sprint, Psy.D., bolted from his chair and started ripping at her clothing.

Sprint's behavior constituted assault, battery, and attempted rape, and he was tried in a court of law and jailed for 6 months. He lost his license to practice.

A more frequent but equally abhorrent scenario is an attempt by the therapist to either consciously manipulate or rationalize sexuality as a legitimate feature of the therapy. Therapists in this category manage actually to convince themselves that they are genuinely charitable by giving clients something special that will alleviate their problems. Rescue fantasies are also common in this group (Notman & Nadelson, 1994). Again, such therapists often have little insight into the self-serving nature of their actions

Case 12–17: Flash Johnson, Ph.D., admitted in court that he stripped in front of his female clients to prove that there is no shame in nudity.

Case 12–18: John Bestman, M.S.W., convinced Marcia Willing that a therapist was the perfect person with whom to have a sexual affair because no one else could better understand her needs or be as trusted. Marcia found Bestman a mediocre lover, and the therapy became confusing and somewhat repulsive. She contacted an ethics committee.

We know of cases in which the therapists invented techniques built around sexual exploitation. Again, these cases are rare but highly visible because they attract media exposure.

Case 12–19: As part of "reparenting therapy," Gloria Kanz, Ph.D., has her clients of both sexes "nurse" at her breast while she coos loving messages of devotion. One of her clients, Jeb Startle, became more "melancholy and strange" according to his friends, who insisted that he see another therapist for a consultation. Jeb's subsequent therapist assisted in pressing an ethics charge against Kanz.

Case 12–20: Ben Strippem, Psy.D., asked his young, female client to remove her clothes so he could measure her "vitals." He claimed that this procedure constituted an essential component of his smoking cessation program.

Case 12–21: Sparky Watt, L.M.H.C., also developed a behavior modification program to help people stop smoking. It involved having them look at a photo of a cigarette and then delivering a painful electric shock through electrodes attached to his clients' genitals.

Case 12–22: Blunt Force, M.D., performed his "Soma Release Therapy" on scores of women before his license was suspended. He claimed that having his client wear flimsy robes while he put extreme pressure on their genitals and breasts would release suppressed emotions.

These rare and creepy perversions of psychotherapy appear to represent attempts to satisfy the therapist's own peculiar proclivities without regard for the clients who came seeking help. The actual therapist involved in the incident from which the Dr. Kanz case was adapted lost her license and paid a large damage award. The real Mr. Strippem attempted to explain the theory behind a connection between smoking and taking measurements of nude clients to an ethics committee, but his machinations involved little more than twisted psychobabble. In the meantime, he had retired from practicing. The therapist on which the case of Dr. Watt is based

defended his technique by asserting that it was based on solid behavioral science techniques; instead, he was convicted of assault. Dr. Force also attempted a convoluted justification for his Soma Release Therapy but lost his license.

Another infrequent scenario is the therapist who uses drugs or alcohol to enhance the treatment–seduction process.

Case 12–23: Snow White, who had been rescheduled to the last appointment of the evening by Cokie Snort, Ph.D., agreed to start staying a while later at the end of her sessions to help Dr. Snort "relax" after a long day of doing therapy. Snort began by serving wine only. Then, one evening Snort produced cocaine. Sex and drugs soon became an integral part of an after-hour ritual.

This therapist, whose actions were adapted from a high-profile case, had lost any concept of boundaries in his practice. He was eventually sued by several parties and lost his license to practice. Another high-profile lawsuit, from which we adapted the next case, reveals an even more wicked use of drugs.

Case 12–24: Maxwell Comatose, M.D., treated over 200 women presenting sexual problems by drugging them with a potentially dangerous relaxant and then encouraging them to become sexually aroused in his presence. Sometimes, he would touch them on their breast or genitals to stimulate them before commencing a guided imagery exercise during which his patients simulated sexual interaction.

The psychiatrist in the actual case was tried for indecent assault based on 11 complaints but won acquittal based on his claim of having their informed consent. His license was briefly suspended, but amazingly he was then allowed to resume practicing as long as he did not use this particular technique.

Although not a frequent complaint, therapists have manipulated clients' dependencies by using sex as a tool to extend the length of therapy.

Case 12–25: Sam Trap, Psy.D., was Sandra Mayhem's rock in a sea of turmoil. She saw him as her only source of stability and became increasingly isolated except for her sessions with him. When Trap suggested that they have an affair, it did not occur to her that she had a choice. She would do anything he asked of her. She was his paying client and mistress for over 10 years. It was only many years later that she was able to discuss this painful and lonely period of her life.

Unfortunately, it is likely that many clients who succumb to therapists like Dr. Trap would not be assertive enough to complain, making it difficult to ascertain the prevalence of this pattern.

More Common Offender Scenarios

Although hardly an excuse, most often therapists who engage in sex with clients are facing regrets, calamities, or deficits in their own lives. Dr. Sorry is typical.

Case 12–26: Samuel Sorry, Ed.D., a counselor in his late 40s, explained to an ethics committee that his sexual relationship with a 26-year-old client was prompted primarily by a series of rapidly accelerating crises in his personal life. His wife of 25 years left him for another woman, and his father recently died. He was feeling lost and saw himself as a failure. His young client was trusting and complimentary, and in his exact words, "She was the only thing [sic] in my life that I looked forward to."

That most clients who become involved in sexual intimacies with male therapists tend to be younger females suggests that sexually exploitative male therapists may view such women as easy sources of "as if" intimacy or as a means to recapture waning youth and virility. However, the next case illustrates how sex may occur almost as a side effect of the therapist's more urgent needs.

Case 12–27: Lily Fading, Ph.D., was becoming more physically frail and increasingly isolated after her husband of 35 years passed away. Her children were grown and living in another state. A middle-aged male client willingly complied with requests by Dr. Fading for favors, which at first were small, helpful acts such as walking with her to her car after dark. Requests and enthusiastic compliance escalated, and soon the man was living in her

home, and they were speaking of marriage. Without a full understanding of the professional aspect of their relationship and its possible legal ramifications, Fading's children brought civil charges against the client for extortion. The charges were dismissed when it was discovered that the man was also their mother's client.

Very commonly, offending therapists fail to appropriately and respectfully monitor the intense emotional closeness that can accompany psychotherapy. The sexualization of therapy relationships typically starts tentatively and involves some back-and-forth attraction signals in the form of nonerotic hugging, mildly flirtatious remarks, or suggestive joking that slowly accelerated and then got out of hand (Pope & Bouhoutsos, 1986). Disengagement may be more difficult, as many therapists have discovered.

The first sign of deterioration after the relationship becomes more actively sexualized often occurs when the client expresses to the therapist a wish to extend the relationship and deepen the commitment between the two of them. At this point, most therapists (especially those who are married or in another committed relationship) react with some form of distancing. Whether a response to fear, guilt, delayed moralistic stirrings, disinterest, or a belated recognition that serious therapeutic errors have been committed, such withdrawal is often experienced by the clients as rejection and abandonment. The now-angry clients may seek redress.

Case 12–28: Willa Nip, Psy.D., realized too late that her outwardly affectionate and sometimes erotic kissing and touching of a client similarly attracted to her was not acceptable professional behavior. However, when she discontinued the behavior, the client felt that she no longer cared about him. Nip tried to assure him that this was not so, but the client contacted an ethics committee, charging that Dr. Nip's rejection and cold manner had worsened his mental state.

Case 12–29: Jack Scare, Ph.D., became concerned when a client, with whom he had intercourse on several occasions, started calling him at home "just to say hello." He had not predicted the increasing familiarity and did not welcome it. He suggested to his client that they should terminate therapy. She asked if that meant that they would then be "just lovers." When he responded that this also was not to be, the rejected client contacted a state licensing board.

A fair number of offenders appear to believe that transference-like feelings are not a result of the therapy dynamics but rather emanate from clients' genuine attraction to them as persons. They convince themselves that the clients would have the same reaction to them had they met casually in another setting under a different set of circumstance. Often complicating this profile is the rescue fantasy some therapists attach to their clients' idealization of them (Folman, 1991). Here, a perilous "fairy tale" dimension is interjected, with the therapists seeing themselves as heroes who will create "happily ever-after" endings.

Case 12–30: Iam Allthat, Ph.D., came to believe that he was an extraordinary therapist because, as a colleague put it, "He would often tell us during case conferences that he never had any problems to put on the table because his clients were always complimentary and grateful." He started writing his memoirs, tentatively titled, "Secrets From the #1 Headshrinker." His colleagues thought him rather arrogant but were surprised when two of the clinic's clients brought charges against him for sexual misconduct. Dr. Allthat vigorously defended himself by saying that they were crazy about him, and both had been trying to seduce him for a long time. The only reason they got upset, he claimed, is because he refused to commit to a long-term relationship with either of them.

Another fairly common offender profile involves inappropriate reactions to the needy or sad client who expresses implicitly or explicitly the need for physical comfort. This client can too readily be exploited by a therapist who too easily melts down professional boundaries.

Case 12–31: Adam Octopus, Ph.D., had always found the delicate and petite Wilma Wilt fetching. Wilt would fall into his arms and sob every time they discussed her drug-addicted 14-year-old daughter. Octopus began to massage and fondle her during these episodes, eventually making sexual moves to which she did not object at the time. Ms. Wilt soon realized, however, that what she needed and what she was getting were hardly one and the same. She told a subsequent therapist about Octopus's behavior, and the new therapist encouraged Wilt to press charges.

Finally, therapists who enter sexually intimate relationships with clients may attempt to excuse their sexual involvement because it is based on what they experience as heartfelt love. Gartrell, Herman, Olarte, Feldstein, and Localio (1986, 1989) reported that 65% of offenders stated that they were in love with the patients they bedded.

Case 12–32: Elmer Smitten, M.S.W., was attracted to Luna Fond from the first therapy session. He recalled wanting to reach out and hold her, to take care of her. He thought about Ms. Fond constantly and anxiously anticipated the sessions with her. If Fond canceled an appointment, he was disappointed for the rest of the day. The first social meeting occurred under conditions similar to the type that lovesick adolescents contrive. He would call to ask if she would mind changing her 10:00 A.M. appointment to 11:00 A.M. At the end of the session, he would then mention that he had not eaten all day and would casually ask Fond to join him at the deli across the street. He noted that he should have realized the pending danger when he found himself mentally rehearsing the invitation many times. They had lunch. There were more lunches, then dinners, and finally sexual activity. Smitten maintained that if he were free, he would have committed himself fully to this woman. Soon, the guilt about having an affair with a married man began to gnaw at Fond. Mr. Smitten began to feel pressured, and frequent spats occurred. Fond terminated both the therapy and the personal relationship, consulted another therapist, and contacted an ethics committee. Amazingly, Smitten continued writing her love letters, even after an ethics committee investigation had begun.

Compared with the other offender profiles, this one may evoke some degree of sympathy. Loving a client, however, does not excuse a therapist from professional responsibility. Twemlow and Gabbard (1989) and Gabbard and Lester (1995) described the lovesick therapist unsympathetically as a narcissistic, emotionally dependent individual who enters an altered state of conscience when in the presence of the special client, which then impairs judgment in that case, but not for others. The state of lovesickness may reduce guilt because the therapist becomes convinced that he or she can provide quality therapy and that the motives are honorable. Such therapists lack insight into the potentially destructive nature of their behavior.

In conclusion, we note that many cases do not fit neatly into any one of our profiles. Most situations are probably combinations of two or more scenarios, such as the lonely therapist who encourages personal closeness in his needy clients and believes that, because the clients need and care about him as an individual, they also help him feel cared about.

RISKS TO THERAPISTS

Whereas consequences to clients as the result of engaging in sexual intimacies with their therapists can be shattering, many therapists have not fared any better. In fact, we contend that having sex with a client constitutes the most unintelligent thing any mental health professional could possibly do. So, many perpetrators have lost their jobs, licenses, families, and reputations. Angry clients (or their significant others) become motivated to expose and sue. We know of only a few therapists who entered into relationships with their clients that lasted for more than a few months before collapsing. There are no doubt a few long-lasting marriages, although we can not help but note that Susan Polk, married to her previous therapist for many years, ended up brutally stabbing him to death. How their relationship came to be was a focal issue in her (unsuccessful) defense (Morrison, 2006).

He Said, She Said

Some people erroneously assume that therapists who engage in sexual intimacies with clients are risking very little because sessions are conducted in the absence of any witnesses. If a client complains, the accusation can be denied. Therapists can cite "fantasy," "delusion," or "transference" as the basis for the charges. Does this work? Sometimes it does. A substantial minority of the sexual intimacy cases result in "client said, therapist said" because neither party's story can be substantiated. But, damaging fallout often occurs anyway because others usually know of the charges, including confidants, wives, and employers. In addition, media accounts of the allegations attract wide public notice, sometimes prior to any actual adjudication.

Ethics committees usually can not sustain a violation when the therapist denies the charges, and no corroborating evidence exists. But, the therapists are not exonerated by default. Cases closed on account of lack of evidence about a single complaint can be reopened if a subsequent charge against the same individual suggests a pattern of offending.

Most malpractice insurance policies have a cap or limit on damages relating to sexual intimacies; these caps range from zero to about $25,000. If the therapist claims innocence, the policy will cover a defense but refuse to pay any damages above the cap if the therapist is found liable. This means that defendants may ultimately bear the total cost of any damages, and these can be substantial. For this reason, it is rare that a therapist is sued solely for sexual misbehavior. Typically, the grounds are some form of improper treatment, making a case for incremental non-sex-based damages. For example, the family in a high-profile case involving the seduction of a suicidal client settled a wrongful death charge with the psychiatrist's insurance carrier for $1 million.

Clients have increasing support in addition to ethics committees, although these differ among the states. Other sources of redress include criminal law statutes, civil suits and tort actions (including malpractice), mandated reporting statutes, injunctive relief, and licensing boards (Haspel, Jorgenson, Wincze, & Parsons, 1997). In some states, clients are also protected against unlicensed therapists who do not fall under the authority of ethics committees and licensing boards. Still other resources include the availability of expert witnesses, subsequent therapists who are prepared to testify regarding the damage that the previous sexual activity caused, clinics specializing in treating sexual abuse by professionals, and the ethics codes of all helping professional associations that are often brought out as favorite "witnesses" for the prosecution. Finally, recent scandals involving pastors, priests, and even U. S. congressmen have further raised the public awareness about the potential for betrayal by those to whom the ultimate trust has been assigned. That no bright professional would "do such a thing" is not an argument the public will ever again buy.

Modern technology and forensic science have been brought to bear in some cases. An undercover agent wore a radio transmitter to substantiate that a psychologist sexually preyed on his attractive female clients. In another high-profile case that saturated the media, a psychiatrist was found innocent of having relations with the more lustfully assertive of his client's multiple personalities. Her DNA evidence of his semen on her underwear did not sway a jury, who exonerated the psychiatrist, believing the defense attorney's contention that the woman was fanaticizing and transferred his semen to her own panties after stealing underwear from the psychiatrist's trash bin. Subsequent DNA tests run by CBS's *48 Hours* indicated, however, that the patterning and large amount of semen on the client's panties could not have resulted from such a transfer (CBS News, 2002).

Is punishing offenders as criminals a wise idea? Such penalties might be the only hook that can influence the behavior of therapists whose perceptions of less serious consequences are apparently insufficiently threatening or whose passions or pathology can not easily be brought under control. However, criminalization can be a double-edged sword with unintended repercussions. Why? When punishments are draconian, clients and colleagues may become less inclined to report offenders or to accept responsibility for putting another person in jail. Any motivation for sexually exploitative therapists to confess evaporates. Clients who have suffered and could benefit from an award of damages in a civil procedure are not afforded that advantage in a criminal proceeding. And, finally, the statutes also assume that psychother-

apy clients are incapable of voluntary consent, an assumption that infantilizes and stigmatizes adult clients who complain (see Deaton, Illingworth, & Bursztajn, 1992; Strasburger, Jorgenson, & Randles, 1991).

A few states have mandatory reporting statutes by which all licensed health providers are required to relate any instance of sexual misconduct that comes to their attention, even if the information is disclosed in a confidential relationship with a previously abused client or if there is reason to even believe that a colleague has been sexually involved with a client (Gartrell, Herman, Olarte, Feldstein, & Localio, 1988; Haspel et al., 1997). Although future exploitation by the previous therapist may be averted by a requirement to report strong suspicions, there remains a concern that mandatory reporting may have a negative effect on the current therapy relationship (Strasburger, et al., 1991). (Note: Therapists may be exempted from mandatory reporting when their client is a therapist who has engaged in sexual misconduct.)

One would think that enforceable ethics codes, licensing regulations, civil law, mandatory reporting, and other legal reforms should be sufficient to deter even the most recalcitrant offenders. Although the rate of sexual exploitation has appeared to decrease every decade (Pope, 2001), complaints continue, even in those states where sexual misconduct with clients constitutes a criminal offense.

The False Allegation

Some therapists are fearful that they may have to deal with a bogus charge by a client who misunderstood what was said or done. Some clients, as we have already seen, are sensitive to a fault. Gutheil and Gabbard (1993) describe a client who brought charges against a psychologist for conducting therapy with the top two buttons of his shirt undone. The next case also reveals how misunderstandings can result.

Case 12–33: Prudence Pureheart sought treatment with Carl Quizitor, Psy.D., for a severe anxiety disorder. During the course of taking a diagnostic history, Quizitor asked Ms. Pureheart about situations that made her anxious. She mentioned "pressures" from her husband and quickly changed the subject. Dr. Quizitor asked for additional details. Ms. Pureheart haltingly reported sexual acts demanded by her husband that she considered "dirty." Dr. Quizitor asked a few clarifying questions intended to assist in developing intervention strategies. Ms. Pureheart subsequently complained to a licensing board that he had needlessly embarrassed her by forcing her to discuss such upsetting matters.

Some clients who press bogus ethics charges may be angry, vengeful, antisocial, or severely narcissistic. It is difficult to acknowledge that anyone would unjustly risk destroying someone's professional and personal life with a false accusation of sexual contact, but it has happened in an estimated small percentage of cases (Pope & Vetter, 1991; Schoener, Milgrom, Gonsiorek, Leupker, & Conroe, 1989). How can therapists protect themselves against unwarranted claims of sexual impropriety and still act like a human being? The following precautions might be considered:

- Before engaging in any form of nonerotic touching or paying a compliment that could be interpreted as flirtatious or suggestive, make certain that you thoroughly understand your client's psychological functioning and history. As noted, some clients may remain unsuited to such comments or touching for the duration of therapy.
- If uneasy feelings involving sexual attraction are perceived as emanating from a client, consult a trusted, sensitive, and preferably experienced therapist or colleague to help you work through the proper course of action.
- Boundary violations of a nonsexual nature (such as taking a client to lunch, giving a client a gift, writing an "affectionate" note) are often taken by professional ethics committees and state licensing boards as presumptive evidence to corroborate allegations of sexual misconduct (Gutheil & Gabbard, 1992). Thus, it is recommended that any act that could conceivably be misconstrued at some later point be entered into the client's notes (e.g., "sent flowers for husband's funeral," "drove client to her workplace be-

cause her car wouldn't start and had to be towed").
- Unless part of the demands of the job, such as evaluative home visits to treat an incapacitated client, avoid offering therapy sessions or seeing clients in other than a professional setting. An office complex in which other professionals or a receptionist are in the general area most of the time is the most preferable.
- Avoid a solo practice in favor of locations where a receptionist or other practitioners work nearby, if at all possible. We offer this suggestion not only because such practice settings are often secluded, but also because informal evidence indicates that mental health professionals in practice by themselves will more likely feel emotionally isolated and may more easily relax professional boundaries. (See also the list of "red flags" in Chapter 10.)

The reader may experience a sense of frustration at this point. How can one be a caring, helping professional and also avoid any behavior that could be misconstrued or interpreted by someone else as unprofessional or unethical? Slovenko (1991) suggested that one of the consequences of the current climate is a "depersonalization" of therapy, with the therapist sitting defensively behind a desk and no longer coming across as a fellow human being. We believe, however, that competence, sensitivity, and a habit of regularly monitoring every client's treatment needs as well as one's own responses to each client will preclude problems from erupting and still allow numerous avenues of expression for caring and compassion.

PREVENTION, EDUCATION, AND DEALING WITH OFFENDERS

Educating the Public

The public has been more consistently advised in recent years that the seductive practitioner is not to be tolerated, and that sexualization of psychotherapy runs counter to their own best interests. Fortunately, people can become quickly knowledgeable after reading an informational brochure (Thorn, Shealy, & Briggs,

1993). The APA distributes a downloadable pamphlet, "If Sex Enters Into the Therapy Relationship" (http://www.apa.org/pi/therapy.html). Readers are informed about what they can do if they feel uncomfortable or if they want to report their therapist for violating sexual boundaries. Such materials, when displayed in the waiting room area, offers an easy and convenient way not only to educate clients, but also to set their expectations.

Some practitioners enter into written contracts with their new clients (see also Chapter 5). A section on clients' rights might read, "Clients have the right to a therapeutic experience that is free from sexual harassment or sexual behavior of any kind." Whereas it would be awkward and perhaps even alarming to discuss this topic during an initial session, putting it in writing along with a number of other matters makes the expectations of both parties clear from the onset.

Educating Students in Training and Already Practicing Therapists

The first line of prevention for sexual activity with clients is sensitive and competent training. Graduate programs in the helping professions have been slow to incorporate the full range of sexually oriented issues into their curricula. Whereas most contemporary students receive the clear message that sex with clients constitutes a serious ethical violation and a therapeutic error, instruction about sex bias in therapy, touching, sex with students and supervisees, and ways to understand and manage one's own erotic feelings and attractions toward clients continue to require more attention. In addition, supervisees need to be made to feel more comfortable discussing their feelings frankly with supervisors (Anderson, 1986; Berkman, Turner, Cooper, Polnerow, & Swartz, 2000; Blanchard & Lichtenberg, 1998; Borys & Pope, 1989; Hall, 1987; Hamilton & Spruill, 1999; Housman & Stake, 1999; Lamb et al., 2003; Mittendorf, 2000; Paxton, Lovett, & Riggs, 2001; Pope & Tabachnick, 1993; Strasburger, Jorgenson, & Sutherland, 1992). Problems occur when the trainers are uncomfortable or uninformed about the issues. Worse yet, some educators and supervisors provide appalling models to their students because they, themselves, are sexual predators (Glaser & Thorpe, 1986; Pope, Levenson, & Schover, 1979).

Because many practicing therapists have not had adequate training in the array of sexualized dilemmas and approaches for managing them, continuing education lectures and workshops should be made available by professional associations and educational institutions. Facilities employing therapists can be held liable (under the legal theory of respondeat superior, for negligent hiring, supervision, and retention). It therefore behooves hospitals, clinics, and other mental health organizations to ensure that education about sexual misconduct is offered in-house (Knapp & VandeCreek, 1997; Strasburger et al., 1992).

Rehabilitation and Sanctions

Intervention programs present a thorny dilemma because a substantial proportion of sexually abusing therapists go on to take advantage of multiple victims (Bates & Brodsky, 1989; Strasburger, Jorgenson, & Randles, 1990). But, should rehabilitation programs for therapists, who either enter counseling voluntarily or are mandated to do so, be made readily available? Opinions differ regarding whether offenders should ever be allowed to practice again, if counseling for this population is even effective, and if investing public resources in this population is a worthy priority (see Gartrell et al., 1988; Gonsiorek, 1997; Pope, 1987, 1989b, 1994; Schoener et al., 1989). In the absence of adequately validated rehabilitation interventions, clients of sexually exploitative therapists could still unknowingly be put at higher risk from therapists who have completed some ineffective rehabilitative procedure.

Rehabilitation potential is probably strongly related to the type of offender. Those who suffer from antisocial or psychopathic personality disorders are not likely to be successful candidates. Those who become aware of a one-time impropriety, experience sincere remorse, demonstrate a willingness to cease their sexual acting out, and show a desire to explore their motives are more likely to be amenable to change.

However, Butler and Zelen (1977) reported discouraging data. Despite the fears, conflicts, and guilt reported by 95% of their sample of offending therapists, most continued their sexual acting out. Psychotherapy was sought by only 40% of their sample. These data, however, were collected before the APA ethics code was revised to explicitly condemn sexual intimacies with clients. Raised consciousness and pressure from within the profession may have increased the motivation to rehabilitate.

Mandating therapy for offenders is an obvious idea to consider, but the efficacy of such treatment remains in question. As mental health professionals know, clients do better when therapy is voluntary. And, although comparing sexually offending therapists with sexual offenders is perilous for several reasons, the potential for rehabilitation remains in question (Layman & McNamara, 1997).

The APA Ethics Committee sometimes includes supervision or referral for therapy among the sanctions sexual offenders receive. The penalty often includes expulsion from the APA or a forced resignation, with the stipulation that membership may be reinstated (usually after 5 years) if the psychologist can give evidence of rehabilitation. The downside of kicking sexual offenders out of professional organizations and stripping them of their licenses is that they become totally afloat. Some may set up practices using their earned degree (which a professional organization can not remove) and an unprotected title (e.g., "Phoenix Hoodwink, Ph.D., Personal Coach"). In such cases, it may prove more cumbersome for any subsequent victims to find redress.

We conclude this section with an odd quandary. Once an offending therapist is dealt with, the client/victims are ignored despite the fact that they may still be in pain. L. Brown (1997) argued that helping professions should view making amends to the victims as part of their rehabilitation process. An apology may constitute an admission of guilt, which would seal the outcome for the therapist. But, apologies might go a long way toward healing victims. We know that apologies can often eliminate emotional turmoil in all parties, especially when they are accepted. We know of several complainants who have asked that their ethics cases be dismissed after receiving apologies from the respondents, and sometimes, a sincere apology acknowledging wrongdoing and remorse was all that the complainant ever wanted.

POSTTERMINATION SEXUAL RELATIONSHIPS WITH CLIENTS

Should a therapist and a client be "ethically free" to commence a sexual relationship when therapy has concluded? Are not consenting adults in our democratic society accorded the right to decide with whom they wish to consort? Was not client autonomy a primary goal of the therapy? As Bersoff (1994) contended, "Society in general and our professional association in particular should be committed to . . . respecting each individual's right to choose his or her own fate, even if the choices the individual makes do not serve . . . what the majority would consider to be in the individual's best interest" (p. 382). Or, could it be that other potential perils lurk for an indefinite period after termination of the professional relationship?

The Backdrop

Therapists who enter into sexual and even marital relationships with former clients are not uncommon. Taken together, available survey data indicate that between 3% and 10% of the respondents have sex with former clients (e.g., Borys & Pope, 1989; Lamb et al., 2003; Lamb et al., 1994; Pope et al., 1987, as cited in Pope, 1993). Fewer than half of the psychologists in Akamatsu's (1988) survey judged sex with ex-clients as a serious ethical problem.

Before 1992, the APA ethics code was silent on the question of sex with clients after the conclusion of therapy, as were most state boards and ethics committees (Sell, Gottlieb, & Schoenfeld, 1986). Ethics committees could pursue charges prior to 1992 when a complainant made a compelling argument that therapy was terminated irresponsibly and some form of harm resulted. However, substantiating or denying botched terminations "by committee" was difficult at best.

The next two cases are among those that ethics committees did accept for adjudication, even before mention of posttermination sex with clients appeared in the code.

Case 12–34: Tom Anxious, Ph.D., was sexually attracted to his client Sam Reciprocale. The vibes indicated that Sam felt the same way toward him. Although Sam's treatment issues were far from resolved, Dr. Anxious terminated him without recommending further treatment. Their sexual relationship began shortly after termination. It was brief, contentious, and unsatisfying.

Case 12–35: John Trick, Psy.D., provided counseling services for 7 months to Ashley Swinger, a high-priced call girl. Two weeks after he told Ms. Swinger that she needed no further therapy, he showed up at her door asking to now become one of her clients.

Both clients brought ethics charges against their ex-therapists. Mr. Reciprocale charged that Anxious maneuvered him into a sexual liaison and then abandoned him when their relationship did not meet his expectations, leaving Reciprocale considerably more troubled than he had ever been. Ms. Swinger argued that she felt pressured to quit therapy and was already upset about that. Then, when Dr. Trick wanted to reverse their roles by becoming her client, the issues of self-worth that brought her into therapy in the first place resurfaced more intensely than ever.

Case 12–36: A psychiatric resident, after treating a patient for alcohol and drug abuse, initiated a posttreatment relationship with the patient. They smoked marijuana and drank alcohol together, and their sexual activity resulted in the ex-patient's becoming pregnant.

The court found that the resident's behavior constituted malpractice and intentional infliction of emotional distress because the client's specific vulnerabilities were exploited (*Noto v. St. Vincent's' Hospital and Medical Center of New York*, described in Appelbaum & Jorgenson, 1991).

In 1992, the APA ethics code revision team confronted for the first time the issue of post-termination sex with clients. After lengthy debate about how to frame a prohibition, a 2-year posttermination moratorium clause was created, thus placing clear limitations in the short run but opening the opportunity for sexual relations between ex-therapists and ex-clients without professional repercussion at some point in the future. While the 1992 APA code was under development, a revision task force argued strongly in favor of prohibiting sex with ex-clients altogether, noting that sometimes sacrifices were necessary to uphold the highest standards of the profession (Vasquez, 1991). Although the APA Council of Representatives failed to issue a lifelong ban on sexual intimacies with former clients, the code did not unconditionally condone eventual liaisons with clients. Additional provisions warned psychologists that sexual intimacies with former clients were likely to be harmful and undermine public confidence in the profession. Thus, the psychologist who enters into a sexual relationship with a former client after 2 years would also bear the burden of demonstrating that there was no exploitation.

The 1992 APA code also listed considerations that should be carefully weighed before embarking on a sexual relationship with an ex-client. Time passage since termination was to be the primary consideration, with a presumption that the longer the delay the lower the ethical risk. Other considerations included the client's current mental status and degree of autonomy, type of therapy, how termination was handled, and what risks may still present themselves were a sexual relationship to commence (APA, 1992). Thus, the complaint in the next case would be heard by an ethics committee despite the fact that the minimum time frame of 2 years had passed before sexual activity occurred.

Case 12–37: On termination of 4 years of psychotherapy, Mattie Stringalong, Ph.D., suggested that she and Lenny Endure keep in touch. They started exchanging cards and letters, spoke on the phone almost every week, and occasionally met for lunch. After 20 months, Dr. Stringalong informed Endure that their relationship could become sexually involved soon if he were still interested.

They eventually married. Endure asked for a divorce a year later, also complaining to a state licensing board that Dr. Stringalong had been "laying in wait" so that she could get her hands on his substantial income.

Here, the sexual activity occurred in the "correct" time frame, but the therapist kept an uninterrupted relationship afloat. Even if Dr. Stringalong were not guilty of plotting to gain financially, her active perpetuation of an emotionally charged relationship commencing on termination was unethical. The 1992 APA code also defined as unethical any statements or actions on the part of the therapist while therapy was active that suggested or invited the possibility of an eventual relationship with a client. Had this code been in effect earlier, both Drs. Anxious and Trick (Cases 12–34 and 12–35) would have been guilty of an ethics violation prima facie, without the necessity of forcing complainants to convince anyone that the termination was improper.

The next case illustrates a therapist's comment just after termination that would also constitute an ethics violation.

Case 12–38: When Geraldo Futura, Psy.D., and his client Cecelia Sanguine tentatively acknowledged a mutual attraction, Futura allegedly told her that, because of professional ethics, they would not start an affair because he would get into "big trouble." However, during the last session, Dr. Futura winked and whispered to Cecelia, "Give me a call in a couple of years."

An ethics committee would not view this sort of termination as appropriate. Futura's parting shot set up an expectation that significantly altered how the therapeutic experience will be remembered by the client. So, what kind of posttermination relationship *might* be ethically acceptable? The next case, revealing a chance meeting years later, would likely cause an ethics committee no concern.

Case 12–39: Vasti Shamoo signed up with Slim Downe, Ph.D., for a weight reduction program that used behavioral techniques. Ms. Shamoo lost her goal of 17 pounds in 6 weeks, and the sessions were terminated by preagreement. Three years later, Shamoo and Dr. Downe found themselves face to face at a party. Shamoo had to remind Downe who she was. They talked for a while, learned that each was free to date, and started seeing each other regularly.

When it came time to revise the APA ethics code in the late 1990s, concerns were raised about the 2-year moratorium provision. An ethics code task force again proposed that the prohibition of sex with clients should exist in perpetuity (Martin, 1999). However, the 2002 revision is almost identical to the 1992 version (APA 02: 10.08), and an additional section discussing proper termination was added (APA 02: 10.10). But, questions remain unanswered. Does knowledge, on the part of the psychologist or the client, that a posttermination sexual involvement is possible, affect the service provided? Under which circumstances do posttermination sexual relationships result in harm? Are individuals able to exercise a truly autonomous choice to enter into sexual involvement with a former treating therapist? (Behnke, 2004). These questions have yet to be definitively answered.

The Case for Perpetuity

We have concerns about condoning posttermination sexual relationships, even with stated conditions. Anyone who has felt extremely attracted to another person knows that passions can not be effectively masked for very long. Data suggest that well over half of the posttermination sexual liaisons between therapists and their clients began quickly, within the first 6 months (Gartrell et al., 1986). If being together is not possible, however, both parties would typically go their own way and find other sources to satisfy their needs. In fact, taking human nature into account, those strictly following the provisions of the APA ethics code are unlikely to ever consummate another kind of relationship with ex-clients, making it tantamount to a lifetime ban in most instances.

Our main concern is that the APA stand on posttermination sex may alter the therapy relationship from the onset (Gabbard, 1994;

Gabbard & Pope, 1989). If clients feel attracted to their therapists (a common occurrence) or therapists feel attracted to their clients (also very common) and aspire to a different kind of relationship down the line, how likely are either to do or say anything that will put them in an unbecoming light during active therapy? Would what was said during sessions constitute psychotherapy or primarily a long-term investment in a potential future relationship? Vasquez (1991) puts it quite plainly, "The verbal disclosures, behaviors, attitudes, and feelings with a potential lover are quite different from those with a therapist who is clearly and solely a therapist" (p. 48). The therapist's ability to remain objective with a client toward whom a strong attraction is felt coupled with the knowledge that the two could possibly be "ethically together" eventually is also compromised.

Although transference began as a psychoanalytic construct, even therapists using cognitive, behavioral, or other approaches to treatment often agree that the therapist becomes imbued by the client with special attributes that convey a kind of emotional authority or influence. Such feelings do not simply evaporate once clients are no longer in active therapy (L. S. Brown, 1988). If after many years you ran into Sam Mendez, the high school teacher you respected above all others, would you say "Hey Sam?" or "Hello Mr. Mendez"? From a psychodynamic perspective, an "internalized therapist" continues to assist a client in coping and integrating processes (Gabbard, 1994; Vasquez, 1991) and in facilitating responses to new situations (Appelbaum & Jorgenson, 1991). Strong attachments to the therapist, not as a sexual being but as a secure base and a source of confidence even if only as a mental representation, can last indefinitely (Parish & Eagle, 2003). Thus, such dynamics may harm clients should they become, even years later, their previous therapists' lovers.

We must also note that a therapist's professional responsibilities do not conclude at termination. Continuing client rights to privacy, confidentiality, and privilege remain unaffected by therapy termination. The possibility of a subpoena of records and resulting court appearances also exists (Gabbard & Pope, 1989). As a result, clients could be severely disadvan-

taged should they have need of professional services from a therapist who is also a lover (or ex-lover), and if the sexual liaison ended badly.

Case 12–40: Donald Reprisal, Ph.D., and his ex-client, Alka Hollick, were married two and a half years after therapy was terminated. They had a child the next year and were divorced a year after that. During a bitter custody battle, Mr. Reprisal brought up his wife's previous alcohol abuse, her sexual escapades prior to their marriage, and her bizarre fantasies.

Case 12–41: Lola Snub and Milton Castoff, Ph.D., her therapist of several years, ran into each other 2 years later at a singles bar. They had a joyful reunion that culminated in a sexual act. When Grateful called for a follow-up date, Ms. Snub declined. Dr. Castoff's subsequent attempts to see his former client were rebuffed. When Ms. Snub contacted him months later to obtain financial billing records needed for a tax audit, he told her to get lost.

Therapists need to remain responsible for any continuing duties and carry them out free from any conflict and role confusion that a sexual relationship imposes. Dr. Reprisal used knowledge originally gained in confidence to the disadvantage of his former client. Dr. Castoff's refusal to comply with his previous client's request is unprofessional at best.

Perhaps the most controversial aspect of APA's 2-year moratorium provision is the impression communicated to the public that sex with one's therapist remains a viable possibility. The American Psychiatric Association, on the other hand, issued a clear message to the public, voting in 1992 to declare sex with former patients as always unethical (American Psychiatric Association, 2006).

Finally, we would note that should a client claim harm, even when the provision for a 2-year moratorium was satisfied, a therapist will have a difficult time defending him- or herself because so many factors could be submitted to substantiate any charge of exploitation. Furthermore, it is impossible to predict exactly how an ethics committee would respond to any charge of posttermination sex, even after 2 years have passed. For example, a diagnosis of borderline personality, previously abused, currently depressed, or any other circumstance indicating vulnerability could be considered by an ethics committee as sufficiently bad judgment to sustain an ethics charge. Furthermore, evidence suggests that one can not know how an ethics committee is going to react when an allegation or unsubstantiated evidence is up for interpretation, as it would almost always be in such cases. Members of the cohort of the APA Council of Representatives, the group responsible for approving the 1992 2-year moratorium on sex with former clients, themselves held widely divergent opinions about the appropriateness of eventual sexual liaisons. A few respondents even found the fairly innocuous situation described in Case 12–39 as unacceptable (Keith-Spiegel & Lett, 1997).

In summary, we strongly recommend seeking romantic and sexual satisfaction from among the huge number of human beings on the planet who have never been one's therapy clients.

DELIVERING THERAPY SERVICES TO FORMER LOVERS

In what seems like a no-brainer, delivering therapy to former lovers occurs often enough to earn an admonition in ethics codes (APA 02: 10.07). Such a prohibition reflects common sense given the probable inability to remain objective in treating an individual with whom one has also slept. However, we know little, save for a smattering of individual cases, about the incidence of accepting former lovers as psychotherapy clients.

Case 12–42: Sonja Ex, Psy.D., agreed to see Dennis Didit as a client, even though 4 years previously they had an intense romantic relationship that lasted for several months. Despite Ms. Ex's revelation that she was happily married, Didit started recalling lustful moments from their past and making suggestive remarks to her during the therapy sessions. Ms. Ex terminated Didit because, as she told him, "You are not taking therapy seriously." Didit wrote to an ethics committee, com-

plaining that Ms. Ex "took me for $450 before tossing me out as revenge for having dumped her 4 years ago."

Dr. Ex declared that she only agreed to see Didit because he seemed so miserable and claimed that he had nowhere else to turn. She vigorously denied any interest in revenge. Accepting him as a client in the first place, however, was an imprudent error in professional judgment. A sexually intimate background is never a foundation on which an objective therapeutic alliance can be built. Ms. Ex could have assisted Didit by making an appropriate referral.

SEXUAL RELATIONSHIPS WITH CLIENTS' SIGNIFICANT OTHERS

Little has been written specifically about sexual involvement with the sisters, brothers, guardians, adult children, parents, or very close friends of current psychotherapy clients. The APA ethics code disallows entering into therapy with such known persons and forbids using termination of therapy as a way of circumventing compliance (APA 02: 10.06). Nevertheless, these types of cases are seen in movie plots (e.g., *The Prince of Tides*, 1991) and in real life.

Case 12–43: A client abruptly terminated therapy and complained to the state licensing board on learning that Rob Cradle, Psy.D., has "slept with my baby girl." Although the daughter was 25 years old, the parent-client felt betrayed by Cradle. The client assumed that Cradle had shared everything she had said in therapy with her daughter and maybe they even shared laughs at her expense after they made love.

In this case, the therapist knew in advance that he was seeing his client's daughter. He erroneously reasoned that because the daughter did not have client status, and because the two were consenting adults, no ethical obligation pertained. However, it should have been obvious to Dr. Cradle that the ethic admonishing therapists to refrain from entering into any relationship if it appears that it could impair objectivity or interfere with effective therapy performance clearly applied in this situation.

Case 12–44: Wadyo Wannado, Ph.D., a clinical child psychologist, treated Bobby Boyster on an outpatient basis. Bobby, age 7, was showing signs of an adjustment disorder in reaction to his parents' deteriorating marriage. Dr. Wannado saw Bobby individually on a weekly basis for several months and met jointly and individually with his parents on three or four occasions to help them deal with Bobby's problems. Soon after Bobby's therapy was terminated, the relationship with Bobby's mother became sexually intimate. The father filed an ethics complaint against Dr. Wannado, who responded that he was doing nothing wrong because he was no longer seeing Bobby and the mother was never a client.

When the client is a child, it becomes therapeutically and ethically critical to consider the family as the unit of treatment. Although Dr. Wannado's clinical attention had focused on Bobby, the parents had legally contracted with him for professional services. In addition, meeting with the parents in any professional capacity constitutes a therapist–client relationship. Dr. Wannado owes ethical obligations to Bobby and both parents equally. The fact that Dr. Wannado had ended treatment with Bobby does not end his professional obligations to the boy. Even after divorce, children harbor fantasies of parental reunion. Most likely, Bobby will feel ambivalent, if not outright betrayed, by the invasion of the therapist into the relationship between his parents. Dr. Wannado's conduct is particularly reprehensible as it intrudes adversely into the relationships of three people undergoing a difficult transition, all of whom were owed duties of care.

TREATING SEXUAL ABUSE BY PREVIOUS THERAPISTS

Harm that befalls clients who have experienced sexual exploitation by previous therapists involves the possibility that they may never receive competent help. When one member of an occupational class breaks trust, all other members

become suspect. Even though victims recognize the need for counseling, they often do not trust their own ability to make to make wise decisions and may fear revictimization (Wohlberg, 1999).

One estimate suggests that a practicing therapists' chances of encountering at least one client who claims abuse by a previous therapist approximates 50%, and that only a small percentage will be false allegations (Pope, 1994; Pope & Vetter, 1991). Clients reporting sexual contact with previous therapists were reported by 43.6% of a sample of Missouri therapists (Stake & Oliver, 1991). In a survey of Rhode Island therapists, a quarter of the sample reported evaluating at least one client who had engaged in some form of sexual involvement with a previous therapist. Virtually all agreed that the previous experience had caused harm, and 15% of the perpetrators were female therapists (Parsons & Wincze, 1995).

Sonne and Pope (1991) presented an array of reactions that therapists may experience when treating clients who report a history of sexual exploitation by previous therapists. These included disbelief and denial that a well-trained colleague could have done such a thing, a suspicion that this "disturbed" client could be exaggerating or even lying, and a tendency to minimize the amount of harm done, perhaps as a reaction to denial or as a way of protecting a member of one's profession. Consider the next case.

Case 12–45: Mary Wary, an emotionally fragile, highly anxious young woman, sought therapy with Kantbe So, Ph.D., claiming that her previous therapist had raped her. Ms. Wary had developed some agoraphobic-like symptoms and seemed preoccupied with personal safety concerns. The accused therapist, well known in the community and active in the local psychological association, seemed pleasant and happily married with several small children.

Put yourself in Dr. So's place, and you will readily empathize with his difficult position. It may help if Dr. So keeps in mind that the acts of the previous therapist, if true, represent a serious ethical violation regardless of who committed them. Dr. So has an obligation to work with this client, although he should not attempt to take on a complaint process on his own. Dr. So can certainly refer the client to an attorney or licensing board for consultation and can provide emotional support for her during any proceedings. Depending on where Dr. So practices, he may have a legal mandate to report the incident to some state agency. As for the therapy itself, Wohlberg (1999) advised that therapists must recognize and accept the victims' difficulty in trusting, ambivalence toward the abuser, and setting the appropriate boundaries as critical factors determining successful treatment.

SEXUAL AFFAIRS WITH STUDENTS AND SUPERVISEES

Stories of college professors engaging in sexual liaisons with their young, nubile female students persist as durable an academic stereotype as ivy, football, tower clocks, caps and gowns, and founder statues in the quad. Aristides (1975) described the allure of the professor as "the man with the most knowledge in the room where knowledge is the only business of the hour, a figure of authority, confidence, intellectual grace—an object, if he does his work even half-well—of love" (p. 361). Some may even appreciate the professor at a prestigious university who told a magazine reporter that he was the appropriate one to help a female student who had "unusually prolonged her virginity" (O'Donnell & Friday, 1993).

Given the trappings of an academic environment, some students and some professors will confront the temptation to enter into romantic relationships based on a variety of motivations that run the gambit from gaining some future advantage to consummating true love. Indeed, most of us know professors who eventually married one of their own students. However, times have changed, and institutions of higher education have taken more vigorous stands to discourage educators from dating students. This stems neither from prudishness nor pressure from feminists. Rather, the increase in sexual harassment charges against professors, sometimes resulting in lawsuits (and sometimes countersuits by the accused professors) have

created an economic motivation to deter such relationships. (For a further discussion of sexual harassment, not necessarily involving sexual intimacies, see Chapter 13.)

The ethical issues regarding sex between student and educator revolve around the abuse of power and conflicts of interest more than about sex per se. Whereas policies across the country may fall short of an outright ban on all student–instructor dating, most campuses have rules that prohibit, restrict, or dissuade instructors from dating students over whom they have the direct evaluative authority, such as the students currently in one's class, advisees for theses or dissertations, and supervisees. Although male educators and female students remain the prevalent pairing, as more women enter academia as educators, as more older people return to the classroom as students, and as scattered cases of gay and lesbian student–faculty relationships surface, a discussion of dating students can no longer be exclusively confined to male professors and their 18- to 22-year-old female students.

Whereas opponents of the ethical ban on sexual relationships with psychotherapy clients are no longer to be found—at least not out in the open—critics of bans on romantic and sexual relationships among faculty and students remain vocal. A group called Consenting Academics for Sexual Equity argued that prohibitions against student–professor sex infantilizes students and creates an atmosphere of paranoia that will cause professors to make themselves less accessible to students (Gibbs, 1995). Others have declared that those who have reached their 18th birthdays can be intimate with whomever they please on their own time. We must note, however, that restrictions designed to prevent conflicts of interest in the workplace may legitimately extend to higher education settings and thereby not infringe on constitutionally guaranteed privacy rights (Mooney, 1993).

Regardless of the debate, we doubt that anyone would openly approve of clearly coerced sexual activity, such as the next case illustrates.

Case 12–46: Cloris Push, Psy.D., made numerous suggestive remarks to her student, Sam Shun, and implied that the closer their personal relationship, the more likely Shun's path to successful completion of his degree program. Shun was not particularly attracted to Professor Push, but he believed that rejecting her advances would endanger his academic status.

The question has been raised regarding whether students can give meaningful consent to persons who have, or are believed to have, authority, evaluative, or other power over them. Because of the unequal status, coupled with the potential for negative consequences should the more powerful educator decide to exercise it, completely voluntary consent becomes problematic (Quatrella & Wentworth, 1995; Zalk, Paludi, & Dederick, 1990).

A now-classic nationwide survey of psychologists (Pope et al., 1979) revealed that 10% of the respondents reported having had sexual contact, as students, with their educators, and 13% reported entering into sexual relationships, as educators, with their students. Gender differences were significant, mirroring both a traditional academic image and the difference trends in client–therapist sexual encounters (i.e., 16.5% of the women and 3% of the men reported sexual contact with their educators when they were students, and 19% of the men, compared with 8% of the women, reported sexual contact with their students). Moreover, when these students became psychotherapists, 12% of the males and 3% of the females reported sexual contact with their clients, which results in a slightly higher percentage for both sexes than revealed from other surveys of therapists taken during that era. In addition, student–educator sexual relationships seemed on the increase. Of the recent female graduates, 25% reported having had sexual contact with their educators, compared with 5% of those who had earned their degrees more than 21 years before the survey was conducted.

Other research has replicated both the extent of sexual relationships with psychologist educators or supervisors, as well as the later judgment that such involvement proved detrimental to them. In Robinson and Reid's (1985) survey, 96% of their female respondents who had experienced sexual contact or sexual harassment

as students believed that the relationship caused harm to one or both parties. Glaser and Thorpe (1986) found that 17% of their respondents had sexual contact with their educators as students, a little over a third of these with clinical supervisors. Interestingly, only 28% of the respondents felt coerced at the time, but overall attitudes about the relationships became far more negative in retrospect. The survey by Hammel, Olkin, and Taube (1996) indicated that the situation was not improving. Fifteen percent of female graduate students and 2% of male graduate students had experienced sexual contact with their educators. The modal pairing was a single female second-year graduate student with a 40-year-old married male educator. Again, in retrospect, most found the experience to be coercive and a hindrance to their working relationship.

Prohibitions against sexual encounters between professors and supervisors and their students or trainees were not explicitly included in the APA ethics code until 1992 and remain in effect. Psychologists may not engage in sexual relationships with students or supervisees in their department, agency, or training center or over whom they now or are likely in the future to have evaluative power (APA 02: 7.07). We would note that, technically speaking, educators and supervisors may have evaluative power for many years, given that the student or supervisee may require job recommendations or references for years after earning their degrees.

Risks to Students and Supervisees

How serious are the ramifications of consensual sexual relationships between educators and their students or supervisees? On the surface, it may appear that paternalistic moralists have intruded in matters that are simply none of their business. On the other hand, we must recognize that students and educators may not be in touch with their own highly vulnerable positions when their relationship turns sexual. When the affairs of students and their educators go askew, the effects must be reckoned with in both the private and professional realms. Emotional fallout can include grief, embarrassment, fear, bitterness, and a desire for vengeance. When these feelings become superimposed on the academic role, serious consequences for students, professors, or both can ensue. In the extreme, professors who see themselves as perpetually powerful and entitled to enjoying students in whatever way they find satisfying can, almost overnight, find themselves reduced to the target of snide gossip and administrative or legal sanctions.

Professors are far more vulnerable than therapists in the sense that psychotherapy clients usually lack access to other clients' identities and have trouble corroborating the offender's behavior pattern. Students, on the other hand, have ready access to each other, leaving the serial exploitative educator open to coalitions of accusers with a considerably greater probability for exposure and ultimate censure. Also, students do not have to deal with off-campus licensing boards or ethics committees. Mechanisms for redress are readily available within walking distance on campus. Other resources also remain available if the student does not find the campus response satisfying.

Case 12–47: After an affair between Gary Goferit, Ph.D., and Paula Jettison had ended, Jettison filed charges against Goferit for sexual harassment and exploitation. She also contacted the local newspapers, which ran the story. She was joined by several other students, who claimed that they, too, had experienced harassment and exploitation by Goferit. Ultimately, Dr. Goferit lost his wife and his job.

The contemporary popular press relishes stories like this, and even sophisticated academic publications, such as the *Chronicle of Higher Education*, feature them regularly. We collected dozens of articles from the popular press, several involving mental health and social science educators, from which to adapt our cases.

Students also have greater vulnerability than they may appreciate. At the time, some may see their relationship with professors as exciting, possibly even putting them on the fast rungs up the career ladder, only to later find themselves discarded and frozen out.

Case 12–48: Dexter Jerky, Ph.D., had frequent sexual liaisons with one of his graduate assistants, Jane Switch, for almost a year. Then, Switch met a young man she wished to date exclusively. When she told Professor Jerky that their affair was over, he allegedly became furious and expressed his intention to punish her. She abruptly lost her research assistantship. She heard rumors that Dr. Jerky had told other faculty members that she was fired due to gross incompetence and was not "graduate school material." When Switch confronted Jerky, he allegedly told her that he had only just begun to teach her a lesson, that he had status and clout, and that she should think twice about a career in the field.

Students may perceive professors as wise and sufficiently mature such that vicious retaliation would not be in their repertoire. However, Dr. Jerky is not an isolated case. Scorned lovers, regardless of their intellect or position, may respond with every means at their disposal. Although a therapist might cause emotional harm to a psychotherapy client, the client's career would rarely also be at stake. The next case illustrates another unfortunate pattern.

Case 12–49: Selma Long, a serious graduate student with high professional aspirations, greatly admired Professor Irving Idol. She took every advantage of opportunities to interact with him. Although she did not aspire to having an affair at first, he began to insist on cozy meeting places. As a sexual relationship evolved, Long fell in love with Dr. Idol. She envisioned a life with him as coworker and life partner. When she verbalized her fantasies, Dr. Idol turned cold. He told her that she had misunderstood his motives, and he had no long-range intentions. He suggested that, due to their mismatched needs, they should no longer work together. Long felt so abashed that she could not face him on campus. She dropped out of the degree program.

Ms. Long represents a potentially larger group of students about whom we know very little. It takes a certain assertiveness that Ms. Long lacked to make a formal complaint, and she simply disappeared. She certainly bore some responsibility in that she had options, but a prized student who was of no sexual interest to Dr. Idol would never have to face such a conflict. Ms. Long's story has similarities to several that have come to our attention over the years. In the actual case, "Dr. Idol" quickly moved on to his next student collaborator, unaware of his student's deeply disrupted life. Even had Idol been fully aware of Ms. Long's despair, it is not clear that he would have cared.

Sexual relationships also compromise the process of assigning unbiased and valid evaluations. Thus, sexual intimacies with students undermine the obligation to evaluate students fairly and accurately (Blevins-Knabe, 1992; Keith-Spiegel, Tabachnick, & Allen, 1993; Pope, Schover, & Levenson, 1980; Slimp & Burian, 1994). Further, students may alter their academic behavior in ways that inhibit or distort their learning. For example, a supervisee may not feel free to discuss sexual feelings toward clients for fear that a supervisor will interpret that line of discussion as flirting (Bartell & Rubin, 1990; Pope et al., 1986).

In conclusion, academia provides the environment in which the faculty and supervisors are paid to facilitate the intellectual, career, ethical, and personal development of students and supervisees. Mentoring students and the feelings that accompany passing along of the best one has to offer as a teacher can be emotionally intimate and exhilarating (Plaut, 1993). The intrusion of sexuality—always potentially volatile—into these fundamentally vital educational functions is diametrically opposed to the mission of higher education and professional training. It undermines the fiduciary duty we have to our students. Even when relationships work out better (or end more gently) than those we have presented above, serious concerns persist. We must ask the question, "What are these students learning?" It seems to us that they may learn it is acceptable to gratify needs under whatever circumstances they choose, with minimal regard for maintaining objectivity and clarity in professional relationships with those over whom they have substantial power, influence, and responsibility.

Graduate Students, Teaching Assistants, and Ex-Students

We have often heard the remark that undergraduate students should be off limits for dating and sexual relationships, but graduate students are acceptable and fair game. Survey data reveal that professor and graduate student liaisons are perceived as more ethically acceptable (Quatrella & Wentworth, 1995; Skinner et al., 1995). Such beliefs are likely based on the higher presumed maturity level of graduate students. The fact is, however, that graduate students are at *greater* risk than are undergraduates. Undergraduate students, even if exploited and scorned, have the option of moving to a new campus for graduate training. Undergraduates may have lost a good reference if an affair goes bad, but letters from other professors could make up for that. Graduate students do not have that many options. Because advanced programs typically have fewer teaching faculty in a given graduate specialty area, a highly desirable reference letter for jobs or continued training, funding decisions, and research opportunities (which are necessary to compete for jobs in academia) could be unavailable should the relationship go stale or end badly. Even if the relationship persists, the animosity other students might feel could have longer-term implications. For example, peers in graduate school often become valuable contacts later on, although not for resented classmates. Finally, in the worst-case scenario, if the sexual liaison involves the student's major professor, there would be no place to turn should the relationship sour.

What about the awkward status of the graduate teaching assistant (GTA)? When still a student, and yet also an instructor, what rules apply? Can the GTA date fellow students? Can the GTA date colleagues? Or, is the GTA off limits to both populations? Again, casual observation reveals that GTAs often date individuals from both groups. However, because many of the problems we have presented thus far apply to graduate assistants, we urge that, as an employee of an institution, GTAs follow the same policy expected of faculty: to refrain from dating anyone over whom they have evaluative authority or who has authority over them, thus defusing even an appearance of favoritism or conflict of interest.

Finally, what about entering into sexual relationships with ex-students? Nothing in any ethics code addresses such concerns, and we do know of many relationships (some leading to long-term, happy marriages) between educators and their former students (Pichaske, 1995). We also know of affairs and marriages that ended very badly, adding discomfort when both have similar, well-established careers in the same geographical locale. One academic couple essentially ended each other's private practice by bad-mouthing the other around town. Love and sex remain intricate and potentially knotty enough under less complicated conditions, confirming research findings suggesting considerable caution given that the long-term risk outweighs short-term pleasure (e.g., Hammel et al., 1996).

slope" is not always perceived until it is too late. On reviewing the record of sexual violators, fissures in professional boundaries are *almost always* revealed prior to engaging in any sexual activity. Coupled with areas of dissatisfaction in one's own life and rationalizations that excuse engaging in exceptions to what the violator usually knows to be competent practice, even therapists who have solid track records of exemplary work end up losing everything they had ever strived hard to attain.

Some may perceive our conservative stance as advocating a moralistic, humorless, inconsiderate approach to psychotherapy. We respond as follows: Most people do not have sexual relationships with most of the people they know and yet have no problem being warm and caring toward them. Nothing in our recommendations precludes kindly human expression, empathy, or compassion.

A FINAL WORD

Many mental health professionals involved in sexual improprieties reveal numerous additional conflicts and complex interactions with clients besides simply having sex with them. The more extreme cases, such as the one below, suggest that some therapists have no boundaries in any direction.

Case 12–50: Messum Allup, Ph.D., finally lost his license after going into business with some clients, having other clients live with him for days and weeks at a time, hiring some to work for him, sharing highly sensitive information about his clients with other clients, and having sexual relationships with clients and his clients' partners. Accounts of the devastatingly worsened condition of some of his clients revealed that they no longer trusted anyone, making it difficult to place them with new therapists.

Unlike Dr. Allup, most mental health professionals are capable of sustaining professional boundaries. However, we must end our trio of chapters dealing with multiple relationships by reminding readers that sliding down a "slippery

SUMMARY GUIDELINES

1. Whereas experiencing a sexual attraction to some clients appears to be quite common, professional and ethical responsibilities require careful assessment and restraint from acting on such attractions.
2. Therapists should remain aware of their vulnerabilities when it comes to sexual attraction. They should strive to recognize when these feelings manifest themselves in a professional relationship and seek consultation to ensure that objectivity and client welfare are not being compromised.
3. The kindness, passivity, adoration, and vulnerability of clients must never be exploited for personal gratification. Similarly, the common phenomena of transference (or therapist idealization or attachment) should be recognized and never manipulated to fulfill the therapist's personal needs for power, love, or respect.
4. Nonerotic touching of clients is not necessarily unethical and may even prove beneficial in some circumstances. However, therapists must carefully assess the appropriateness of touching clients, recognizing that considerable differences exist across

individuals along with varying perceptions about the meaning of touching and being touched. Some clients may remain unsuited for touching under any circumstance.

5. Touching intended for erotic gratification of the client or therapist is unethical.

6. Arranging to see clients to whom a therapist is attracted under less formal circumstances is a temptation that should be vigorously resisted.

7. Sexual intercourse and other sexually intimate acts with ongoing clients are unprofessional and constitute a very serious ethical, and possibly legal, violation.

8. Just because a client (or student or supervisee) initiated a romantic or sexual element into the professional relationship does not in any way absolve the therapist (or teacher or supervisor) from maintaining professional standards.

9. Therapists who are experiencing disappointments or loneliness in their personal lives must remain especially vigilant to temptations to develop compensating relationships with their clients.

10. Sexual relationships with former clients have such a high potential for a number of risks that we strongly discourage them, despite the 2-year time-lapse option included in the APA ethics code.

11. Therapists who treat clients with a history of sexual exploitation by previous therapists should fully understand the dynamics and reactions that will likely arise and focus on keeping the client's best interests paramount.

12. Therapists should never deliver psychotherapeutic services to their ex-lovers because objectivity is compromised from the outset.

13. Sexual intimacies with students and supervisees over whom one has (or may have) evaluative responsibilities are unethical. Unsuccessful relationship outcomes are likely and have resulted in longer-term consequences for students and supervisees as well as for their educators.

14. Professors and supervisors should ensure that the students receive sufficient course work in the areas of sexual attraction and sexual intimacies with clients. Attraction

feelings should not be interpreted as a therapeutic error, thus chilling the climate for discussing these feelings during supervision.

References

Akamatsu, T. J. (1988). Intimate relationships with former clients: National survey of attitudes and behavior among practitioners. *Professional Psychology, 19,* 454–458.

American Psychiatric Association. (1992, December 4). Assembly takes strong stance on patient–doctor sex. *Psychiatric News, 1,* 20.

American Psychiatric Association. (2006) *The principles of medical ethics with annotations especially applicable to psychiatry.* Washington DC: Author.

American Psychological Association. (1992). Ethical principles of psychologists and code of conduct. *American Psychologist, 47,* 1597–1611.

Anderson, W. (1986). Stages of comfort with sexual concerns of clients. *Professional Psychology, 17,* 352–356.

Appelbaum, P. S., & Jorgenson, J. D. (1991). Psychotherapist–patient sexual contact after termination of treatment: An analysis and a proposal. *American Journal of Psychiatry, 148,* 1466–1473.

Aristides. (1975). Life and letters: Sex and the professors. *American Scholar, 44,* 357–363.

Armsworth, M. W. (1990). A qualitative analysis of adult incest survivors' responses to sexual involvement with therapists. *Child Abuse & Neglect, 14,* 541–554.

Barnhouse, R. T. (1978). Sex between patient and therapist. *Journal of the American Academy of Psychoanalysis, 6,* 533–546.

Bartell, P. A., & Rubin, L. J. (1990). Dangerous liaisons: Sexual intimacies in supervision. *Professional Psychology, 21,* 442–450.

Bates, C. M., & Brodsky, A. M. (1989). *Sex in the therapy hour: A case of professional incest.* New York: Guilford.

Behnke, S. (2004, December). Sexual involvements with former clients: A delicate balance of core values. *Monitor on Psychology,* 76–77.

Bennett, B. E., Bryant, B. K., Vandenbos, G. R., & Greenwood, A. (1990). *Professional liability and risk management.* Washington, DC: American Psychological Association.

Berkman, C. S., Turner, S. G., Cooper, S. G., Polnerow, D., & Swartz, M. (2000). Sexual contact with clients: Assessment of social worker's attitudes and educational preparation. *Social Work, 45,* 223–235.

Bersoff, D. N. (1994). Explicit ambiguity: The 1992 ethics code as an oxymoron. *Professional Psychology, 25,* 382–387.

Blanchard, C. A., & Lichtenberg, J. W. (1998). Counseling psychologists' training to deal with their sexual feelings in therapy. *Counseling Psychologist, 26,* 624–639.

Blatchford, C. (2004, January 7). Psychotherapist tells his side of bizarre story. *Globe & Mail,* A8.

Blevins-Knabe, B. (1992). The ethics of dual relationships in higher education. *Ethics & Behavior, 2,* 151–163.

Borys, D., & Pope, K. S. (1989). Dual relationships between therapist and client: A national study of psychologists, psychiatry, and social workers. *Professional Psychology, 20,* 283–293.

Bouhoutsos, J., Holroyd, J., Lerman, H., Forer, B., & Greenburg, M. (1983). Sexual intimacy between psychotherapists and patients. *Professional Psychology, 14,* 185–196.

Broden, M. S., & Agresti, A. A. (1998). Responding to therapists' sexual abuse of adult incest survivors: Ethical and legal considerations. *Psychotherapy, 35,* 96–104.

Brodsky, A. M. (1989). Sex between patient and therapist: Psychology's data and response. In G. O. Gabbard (Ed.), *Sexual exploitation in professional relationships* (pp. 15–25). Washington, DC: American Psychiatric Press.

Brown, L. (1997). Remediation, Amends, or Denial? *Professional Psychology, 28,* 297–299.

Brown, L. S. (1988). Harmful effects of post-termination sexual and romantic relationships between therapists and their former clients. *Psychotherapy, 25,* 249–255.

Butler, S., & Zelen, S. L. (1977). Sexual intimacies between therapists and patients. *Psychotherapy, 14,* 139–145.

CBS News. (2002). A crime of the mind III. Retrieved December 17, 2004, from http://www.cbsnews.com/stories/2002/09/26/48hours/main523391.shtml

Celenza, A. (1998). Precursors to therapist sexual misconduct: Preliminary findings. *Psychoanalytic Psychology, 15,* 378–395.

Dahlberg, C. C. (1970). Sexual contact between patient and therapist. *Contemporary Psychoanalysis, 6,* 107–124.

Deaton, R. J., Illingworth, P. M., & Bursztajn, H. J. (1992). Unanswered questions about the criminalization of therapist–patient sex. *American Journal of Psychotherapy, 46,* 526–531.

deMayo, R. A. (1997). Patient sexual behavior and sexual harassment: A national survey of female psychologists. *Professional Psychology, 28,* 58–62.

Durana, C. (1998). The use of touch in psychotherapy: Ethical and clinical guidelines. *Psychotherapy, 35,* 269–280.

Feldman-Summers, S. (1989). Sexual contact in fiduciary relationships. In G. O. Gabbard (Ed.), *Sexual exploitation in professional relationships* (pp. 193–209). Washington, DC: American Psychiatric Press.

Field, T. M. (1998). Massage therapy effects. *American Psychologist, 53,* 1270–1281.

Fisher, C. D. (2004). Ethical issues in therapy: Therapist self-disclosure of sexual feelings. Ethics & Behavior, *14,* 105–121.

Folman, R. Z. (1991). Therapist–patient sex: Attraction and boundary problems. *Psychotherapy, 28,* 168–185.

Forer, B. R. (1981, August). *Sources of distortion in the therapeutic relationship.* Paper presented at the annual meeting of the American Psychological Association, Los Angeles.

Freeman, L., & Roy, J. (1976). *Betrayal.* New York: Stein & Day.

Gabbard, G. O. (1994). Reconsidering the American Psychological Association's policy on sex with former patients: Is it justifiable? *Professional Psychology, 25,* 329–335.

Gabbard, G. O., & Lester, E. P. (1995). *Boundaries and boundary violations in psychoanalysis.* New York: Basic Books.

Gabbard, G. O., & Pope, K. S. (1989). Sexual intimacies after termination: clinical, ethical, and legal aspects. In G. O. Gabbard (Ed.), *Sexual exploitation in professional relationships* (pp. 116–127). Washington, DC: American Psychiatric Press.

Gartrell, N., Herman, J., Olarte, S., Feldstein, M., & Localio, R. (1986). Psychiatrist–patient sexual contact: Results of a national survey, I: prevalence. *American Journal of Psychiatry, 143,* 1126–1130.

Gartrell, N., Herman, J., Olarte, S., Feldstein, M., & Localio, R. (1988). Management and rehabilitation of sexually exploitive therapists. *Hospital and Community Psychiatry, 39,* 1070–1074.

Gartrell, N., Herman, J., Olarte, S., Feldstein, M., & Localio, R. (1989). Prevalence of psychiatrist-patient sexual contact. In G. O. Gabbard (Ed.), *Sexual exploitation in professional relationships* (pp. 4–13). Washington, DC: American Psychiatric Press.

Gibbs, N. (1995, April 3). Romancing the student. *Time,* 58–59.

Glaser, R. D., & Thorpe, J. S. (1986). Unethical intimacy: A survey of sexual contact and advances between psychology educators and female graduate students. *American Psychologist, 41,* 43–51.

Gonsiorek, J. C. (1997). Suggested remediations to "remediation." *Professional Psychology, 28,* 300–303.

Goodyear, R. K., & Shumate, J. L. (1996). Perceived effects of therapist self-disclosure of attraction to clients. *Professional Psychology, 27,* 613–616.

Gottlieb, M., Sell, J. M., & Schoenfeld, L. S. (1988). Social/romantic relationships with present and former clients: State licensing board actions. *Professional Psychology, 19,* 459–462.

Gregory, B. A., & Gilbert, L. A. (1992). The relationship between dependency behavior in female clients and psychologists' perceptions of seductiveness. *Professional Psychology, 23,* 390–396.

Gutheil, T. G. (1989). Borderline personality disorder, boundary violations, and patient–therapist sex: Medicolegal pitfalls. *American Journal of Psychiatry, 146,* 597–602.

Gutheil, T. G., & Gabbard, G. O. (1992). Obstacles to the dynamic understanding of therapist-patient sexual relations. *American Journal of Psychotherapy, 46,* 515–525.

Gutheil, T. C., & Gabbard, G. O. (1993). The concept of boundaries in clinical practice: Theoretical and risk-management dimensions. *American Journal of Psychiatry, 150,* 188–196.

Hall, J. E. (1987). Gender-related ethical dilemmas and ethics education. *Professional Psychology, 18,* 573–579.

Hamilton, J. C., & Spruill, J. (1999). Identifying and reducing risk factors related to trainee-client sexual misconduct. *Professional Psychology, 30,* 318–327.

Hammel, G. A., Olkin, R., & Taube, D. O. (1996). Student-educator sex in clinical and counseling psychology doctoral training, *Professional Psychology, 27,* 93–97.

Harlow, H. F. (1958). The nature of love. *American Psychologist, 13,* 673–685.

Haspel, K. C., Jorgenson, L. M., Wincze, J. P., & Parsons, J. P. (1997). Legislative intervention regarding therapist sexual misconduct: An overview. *Professional Psychology, 28,* 63–72.

Hetherington, A. (2000). A psychodynamic profile of therapists who sexually exploit their clients. *British Journal of Psychotherapy, 16,* 274–286.

Holroyd, J., & Bouhoutsos, J. C. (1985). Biased reporting of therapist–patient sexual intimacy. *Professional Psychology, 16,* 701–709.

Holroyd, J. C., & Brodsky, A. M. (1977). Psychologists' attitudes and practices regarding erotic and nonerotic physical contact with patients. *American Psychologist, 32,* 843–849.

Holroyd, J. C., & Brodsky, A. M. (1980). Does touching patients lead to sexual intercourse? *Professional Psychology, 11,* 807–811.

Holub, E. A., & Lee, S. S. (1990). Therapists' use of nonerotic physical contact: Ethical concerns. *Professional Psychology, 21,* 115–117.

Housman, L. M., & Stake, J. E. (1999). The current state of sexual ethics training in clinical psychology: Issues of quantity, quality, and effectiveness. *Professional Psychology, 30,* 302–311.

Jackson, H., & Nuttall, R. L. (2001). A relationship between childhood sexual abuse and professional sexual misconduct. *Professional Psychology, 32,* 200–204.

Jones, E. (1957). *Life and work of Sigmund Freud* (Vol. 3). New York: Basic Books.

Kardener, S. H., Fuller, M., & Mensh, I. (1973). A survey of physicians' attitudes and practices regarding erotic and nonerotic contact with patients. *American Journal of Psychiatry, 130,* 1077–1081.

Keith-Spiegel, P., & Koocher, G. P. (1985). *Ethics in psychology: Standards and cases.* New York: Random House.

Keith-Spiegel, P., & Lett, R. (1997). *The 2-year moratorium on sex with ex-clients: How do the psychologists who adopted it interpret it?* Unpublished manuscript, Ball State University, Muncie, IN.

Keith-Spiegel, P., Tabachnick, B. G., & Allen, M. (1993). Ethics in academia: Students views of professors' actions. *Ethics & Behavior, 3*, 149–162.

Kertay, L., & Reviere, S. L. (1993). The use of touch in psychotherapy: Theoretical and ethical considerations. *Psychotherapy, 30*, 32–40.

Kirkland, K., Kirkland, K. L., & Reaves, R. P. (2004). On the professional use of disciplinary action. *Professional Psychology, 35*, 179–184.

Kluft, R. P. (1989). Treating the patient who has been sexually exploited by a previous therapist. *Psychiatric Clinics of North America, 12*, 483–499.

Knapp, S., & VandeCreek, L. (1997). Ethical and legal aspects in clinical supervision. In C. E. Watkins (Ed.), *Handbook of psychotherapy supervision* (pp. 589–599). New York: Wiley.

Ladany, N., O'Brien, K. M., Hill, C. E., Melincoff, D. S., Knox, S., & Petersen, D. A. (1997). Sexual attraction toward clients, use of supervision, and prior training: A qualitative study of predoctoral psychology interns, *Journal of Community Psychology, 44*, 413–424.

Lamb, D. H., & Catanzaro, S. L. (1998). Sexual and nonsexual boundary violations involving psychologists, clients, supervisees, and students: Implications for professional practice. *Professional Psychology, 29*, 498–503.

Lamb, D. H., Catanzaro, S. J., & Moorman, A. S. (2003). Psychologists reflect on their sexual relationships with clients, supervisees, and students: Occurrence, impact, rationales and collegial intervention. *Professional Psychology, 34*, 102–107.

Lamb, D. H., Strand, K. K., Woodburn, J. R., Buchko, K. J., Lewis, J. T., & Kang, J. R. (1994). Sexual and business relationships between therapists and former clients. *Psychotherapy, 31*, 270–278.

Layman, M. J., & McNamara, J. R. (1997). Remediation for ethics violations: Focus on psychotherapists' sexual contact with clients. *Professional Psychology, 28*, 281–292.

Marmor, J. (1972). Sexual acting-out in psychotherapy. *American Journal of Psychoanalysis, 22*, 3–8.

Martin, S. (1999, July–August). Revision of ethics code calls for stronger former client sex rule. *Monitor Online, 30*. Retrieved July 19, 2003, from http://www.apa.org/monitor/julaug99/as1.html

Masters, W. H., & Johnson, V. E. (1976). Principles of the new sex therapy. *American Journal of Psychiatry, 110*, 3370–3373.

Mittendorf, S. C. (2000). Sexual contact with clients. *Social Work, 45.* 473.

Mooney, C. J. (1993, April 14). U. of Virginia eyes formally banning student–faculty sex. *Chronicle of Higher Education*, A21.

Morrison, K. (2006). Why did Susan Polk kill her husband? Retrieved June 16, 2006, from http://www.msnbc.msn.com/id/9698604/

Noel, B., & Watterson, K. (1992). *You must be dreaming.* New York: Poseidon.

Notman, M. T., & Nadelson, C. C. (1994). Psychotherapy with patients who have had sexual relations with a previous therapist. *Journal of Psychotherapy Practice and Research, 3*, 185–193.

O'Donnell, P. O., & Friday, C. (1993, October 11). The professor of desire. *Newsweek*, 69.

Ogden, J. K. (1999). Love and sex in 45 minutes: Transference love as self- and mutual regulation. *Psychoanalytic Psychology, 16*, 588–604.

Olarte, S. W. (1991). Characteristics of therapists who become involved in sexual boundary violations. *Psychiatric Annals, 21*, 657–660.

Parish, M., & Eagle, M. N. (2003). Attachment to the therapist. *Psychoanalytic Psychology, 20*, 271–286.

Parsons, J. P., & Wincze, J. P. (1995). A survey of client–therapist sexual involvement in Rhode Island as reported by subsequent treating therapists. *Professional Psychology, 26*, 171–175.

Paxton, C., Lovett, J., & Riggs, M. L. (2001). The nature of professional training and perceptions of adequacy in dealing with sexual feelings in psychotherapy: Experiences of clinical faculty. Ethics & Behavior, *11*, 175–189.

Pichaske, D. R. (1995, February 24). When students make sexual advances. *Chronicle of Higher Education*, B1–B2.

Plasil, E. (1985). *Therapist.* New York: St. Martin's/Marek.

Plaut, S. M. (1993). Boundary issues in teacher–student relationships. *Journal of Sex & Marital Therapy, 19*, 210–219.

Pope, K. S. (1987). Preventing therapist–patient sexual intimacy: Therapy for a therapist at risk. *Professional Psychology, 18*, 624–628.

Pope, K. S. (1989a). Therapist–patient sex syndrome: A guide for attorneys and subsequent therapists to assessing damage. In G. Gabbard (Ed.), *Sexual exploitation in professional relationships* (pp. 39–55). Washington, DC: American Psychiatric Press.

Pope, K. S. (1989b). Therapists who become sexually intimate with a patient: Classifications, dynamics, recidivism and rehabilitation. *Independent Practitioner*, 9, 28–34.

Pope, K. S. (1990a). Therapist–patient sex as sex abuse: Six scientific, professional, and practical dilemmas in addressing victimization and rehabilitation. *Professional Psychology*, 21, 227–239.

Pope, K. S. (1990b). Therapist–patient sexual involvement: A review of the research. *Clinical Psychology Review*, 10, 477–490.

Pope, K. S. (1993). Licensing disciplinary actions for psychologists who have been sexually involved with a client: Some information about offenders. *Professional Psychology*, 24, 374–377.

Pope, K. S. (1994). *Sexual involvement with therapists: Patient assessment, subsequent therapy, forensics*. Washington, DC: American Psychological Association.

Pope, K. S. (2001). Sex between therapist and client. In J. Worell (Ed.), *Encyclopedia of women and gender: Sex similarities and the impact on society and gender* (Vol. 2, pp. 955–962). New York: Academic Press.

Pope, K. S., & Bouhoutsos, J. C. (1986). *Sexual intimacy between therapists and patients*. New York: Praeger.

Pope, K. S., Keith-Spiegel, P., & Tabachnick, B. G. (1986). Sexual attraction to clients: The human therapist and the (sometimes) inhuman training system. *American Psychologist*, 34, 682–689.

Pope, K. S., Levenson, H., & Schover, L. R. (1979). Sexual intimacy in psychology training. *American Psychologist*, 34, 682–689.

Pope, K. S., Schover, L. R., & Levenson, H. (1980). Sexual behavior between clinical supervisors and trainees: Implications for professional standards. *Professional Psychology*, 11, 157–162.

Pope, K. S., Sonne, J. L., & Holroyd, J. (1993). *Sexual feelings in psychotherapy*. Washington, DC: American Psychological Association.

Pope, K. S., & Tabachnick, B. G. (1993). Therapists' anger, hate, fear, and sexual feelings: National survey of therapist responses, client characteristics, critical events, formal complaints, and training. *Professional Psychology*, 24, 142–152.

Pope, K. S., Tabachnick, B. G., & Keith-Spiegel, P. (1987). Ethics of practice: The beliefs and behaviors of psychologists as therapists. *American Psychologist*, 42, 993–1006.

Pope, K. S., & Vetter, V. A. (1991). Prior therapist–patient sexual involvement among patients seen by psychologists. *Psychotherapy*, 28, 429–437.

Quatrella, L. A., & Wentworth, K. (1995). Student's perceptions of unequal status dating relationships in academia. *Ethics & Behavior*, 5, 249–258.

Regehr, C., & Glancy, G. (2001). Empathy and its influence on sexual misconduct. *Trauma Violence & Abuse*, 2, 142–154.

Robinson, W. L., & Reid, P. T. (1985). Sexual intimacies in psychology revisited. *Professional Psychology*, 16, 512–520.

Rodolfa, E., Hall, T., Holms, V., Davena, A., Komatz, D., Malu, A., et al. (1994). The management of sexual feelings in therapy. *Professional Psychology*, 25, 169–172.

Schoener, G. R., Milgrom, J. H., Gonsiorek, J. C., Leupker, E. T., & Conroe, R. M. (Eds.). (1989). *Psychotherapists' sexual involvement with clients: Intervention and prevention*. Minneapolis, MN: Walk-In Counseling Center.

Schwendinger, J. R., & Schwendinger, H. (1974). Rape myths in legal, theoretical, and everyday practice. *Crime and Social Justice*, 1, 18–26.

Sell, J. M., Gottlieb, M. C., & Schoenfeld, L. (1986). Ethical considerations of social/romantic relationships with present and former clients. *Professional Psychology*, 17, 504–508.

Simon, R. I. (1991). Psychological injury caused by boundary violation precursors to therapist–patient sex. *Contemporary Psychiatry*, 21, 614–619.

Skinner, L. J., Giles, M. K., Griffith, S. E., Sontag, M. E., Berry, K., & Beck, R. (1995). Academic sexual intimacy violations: Ethicality and occurrence reports from undergraduates. *The Journal of Sex Research*, 32, 131–143.

Slimp, A. O., & Burian, B. K. (1994). Multiple role relationships during internship: Consequences and recommendations. *Professional Psychology*, 25, 39–45.

Slovenko, R. (1991). Undue familiarity or undue damages? *Psychiatric Annals*, 21, 598–610.

Solursh, D. S., & Solursh, L. P. (1993). Patient–therapist sex: "Just say no" isn't enough. *Medicine and Law*, 12, 431–438.

Somer, E., & Saadon, M. (1999). Therapist–client sex: Clients' retrospective reports. *Professional Psychology, 30,* 504–509.

Sonne, J. L., & Pope, K. S. (1991). Treating victims of therapist–patient sexual involvement. *Psychotherapy, 28,* 174–187.

Stake, J. E., & Oliver, J. (1991). Sexual contact and touching between therapist and client: A survey of psychologists' attitudes and behavior. *Professional Psychology, 22,* 297–307.

Strasburger, L. H., Jorgenson, L., & Randles, R. (1990). Mandatory reporting of sexually exploitative psychotherapists. *Bulletin of the American Academy of Psychiatry and the Law, 18,* 379–384.

Strasburger, L. H., Jorgenson, L., & Randles, R. (1991). Criminalization of psychotherapist–patient sex. *American Journal of Psychiatry, 148,* 859–863.

Strasburger, L. H., Jorgenson, L., & Sutherland, P. (1992). The prevention of psychotherapist sexual misconduct: Avoiding the slippery slope. *American Journal of Psychotherapy, 46,* 544–555.

Stenzel, C. L., & Rupert, P. A. (2004). Psychologists' use of touch in individual psychotherapy. *Psychotherapy, 41,* 332–345.

Taylor, B. J., & Wagner, N. N. (1976). Sex between therapist and clients: A review and analysis. *Professional Psychology, 7,* 593–601.

Thorn, B. E., Shealy, R. C., & Briggs, S. D. (1993). Sexual misconduct in psychotherapy: Reactions to a consumer–oriented brochure. *Professional Psychology, 24,* 75–82.

Twemlow, S. W., & Gabbard, G. O. (1989). The lovesick therapist. In G. O. Gabbard (Ed.), *Sexual exploitation in professional relationships* (pp. 71–87). Washington, DC: American Psychiatric Press.

Vasquez, M. J. T. (1991). Sexual intimacies with clients after termination: Should a prohibition be explicit? *Ethics & Behavior, 1,* 45–61.

Walker, E., & Young, P. D. (1986). *A killing cure.* New York: Holt, Rinehart & Winston.

Williams, M. H. (1992). Exploitation and inference: Mapping the damage from therapist-patient sexual involvement. *American Psychologist, 47,* 412–421.

Wilson, J. M. (1982). The value of touch in psychotherapy. *American Journal of Orthopsychiatry, 52,* 65–72.

Wohlberg, J. W. (1999). Treatment subsequent to abuse by a mental health professional: The victim's perspective of what works and what doesn't. *Journal of Sex Education and Therapy 24,* 252–261.

Wright, R. H. (1985). Who needs enemies? *Psychotherapy in Private Practice, 3,* 111–118.

Zalk, S., Paludi, M., & Dederick, J. (1990). Women students' assessment of consensual relationships with their professors: Ivory power reconsidered. In E. Cole (Ed.), *Sexual harassment on campus* (pp. 103–133). Washington, DC: National Association of College and University Attorneys.

Zur, O., & Nordmarken, N. (2004). To touch or not to touch: Rethinking the prohibition on touch in psychotherapy and counseling Retrieved August 16, 2005, from http://www.drozur/touchintherapy.html

13

Relationships With Colleagues, Students, Supervisees, and Employees

> In quarrelling, the truth is almost always lost.
>
> Publilius Syrus

Contents

Can mental health professionals get along better with others because of their special understanding of the complexities of human relationships? From our vantage point, any relative advantage we might muster in some situations can disintegrate in others. Professionals are people first, some of whom function with difficulty under heavy stress or become overly focused on their own needs to the detriment of the welfare of others. Some have firmly established personal styles that make the work environment unpleasant for those around them. Warring colleagues can wreak havoc on everyone in the vicinity. Unfortunately, innocents on the sidelines can become victims of interprofessional disputes.

INTERPROFESSIONAL
AND PEER RELATIONSHIPS

Who Complains About Their Own and Why?

Many ethics complaints against mental health professionals, educators, and social/behavioral researchers are lodged by their own colleagues. This should not come as a surprise. Colleagues are the very people most likely to be aware of ethical standards and to observe unethical behavior directly. The truly intriguing feature of such complaints is the intensity—and occasionally bitter vindictiveness—with which such individuals sometimes pursue their grievances.

Conflicts involving performance or credential evaluations spawn many conflicts. The person being assessed is usually under considerable personal stress. The evaluator's failure to recognize and respond sensitively presents a serious hazard. Such edgy situations include doctoral examinations, tenure decisions, supervisory sessions, grievance hearings, annual salary reviews, or even the receipt of an exam or term project grade. Other hazardous situations that spawn disputes include poor communications among professionals and their students and supervisees, risky individuals, and a lack of procedures when conflicts arise.

The potential for uncollegial behavior also increases when any of the following conditions pervade the work setting:

- competitiveness
- limited resources
- few opportunities for advancement
- low morale
- extremely heavy workload
- inadequate or unpleasant working conditions (e.g., noisy, crowded, lack of privacy)
- incompetent or ambiguous management styles
- real or perceived inequities

Disputes become especially likely if the perception of bias appears to occur in any relevant decision-making process. Failure to live up to obligations made to one's peers also constitutes a potential risk for complaints. Unfortunately, these unstable conditions can exist in any institution and agency, including those where mental health professionals are employed.

Relationships with colleagues should ideally embody a climate of cooperation and mutual respect. The American Psychological Association's (APA) ethics code encourages cooperation with other professionals and consultation with colleagues (APA 02: 3.09). And, whereas the recognition of valid competencies and consumer interests should prevail in interprofessional relationships, this does not always happen. For example, the professional interests of psychologists clash with those of psychiatrists and marriage and family counselors on some issues. Despite a common focus on human behavior and the resolution of emotional problems, interprofessional relations will often manifest themselves as political, economic, and territorial disputes.

Case 13–1: Horace Pill, Ph.D., has nationally recognized expertise in psychopharmacology. When he began advocating laws that authorize prescription privileges for psychologists, he became the object of blistering attacks by psychiatrists. Editorials that criticized him in pejorative terms appeared in the *National Psychiatric News*, and officers of the Amalgamated Psychiatric Society wrote angry letters about Dr. Pill to his employer. Pill was invited to deliver a lecture at Urban Medical School. During the course of the talk, Pill made critical comments about the Amalgamated Psychiatric Society. Many psychologists in the interdisciplinary audience became distressed about the remarks, believing that they complicated relationships with their psychiatrist colleagues at the medical school.

Even *within* each profession, the goals and views of some members can clash with those of others. Deeply held differences in theoretical, practical, and methodological approaches abound. Such disputes can create conditions that sometimes erupt beyond the bounds of stimulating debate. We do not propose that professional disagreements must always follow the etiquette expected at an afternoon tea party. Whenever one earnestly believes that others have suffered harm at the hands of colleagues—ideally, after confirming that perception with others—putting on a show of respect for the offender can even be inappropriate. But, in virtually every circumstance, maintaining a professional demeanor will likely create the best climate for a reasonable outcome. (See Chapter 2 for recommended techniques for confronting an unethical colleague.)

Too often, we find that once-reasonable people sink into an extended cycle, and the abuse hurled by one elevates the mistreatment perpetrated by the other.

Case 13–2: Drs. Rosemary Spat and Dameon Tiff can not stand each other. No one at the clinic can recall when it all started. Both Spat and Tiff have created a litany of complaints against the other that range from misappropriation of a single postage stamp to maltreating clients. Each routinely stalks and spies on the other. The head of the agency has moved their offices to opposite ends of the building and even had to impose a gag order on the one not scheduled to present during group case management discussions.

Everyone working in the agency, including the unaware clientele, has become disadvantaged by this unfit dynamic duo. No excuse exists for such unprofessional misbehavior, yet such entrenched, angry relationships occur far more often than they should. If the combative parties can not reach a level of professional maturity, they should at least keep their feud out of the work setting. Certainly, colleagues should have the freedom to criticize or disagree with each other, even in a public forum. However, framing an argument in well-reasoned and respectful ways constitutes the best way to solve problems.

The next case illustrates how a conflict can be handled in a professional and ethical manner.

Case 13–3: Clarence Farrow, a young attorney, contacts Jack Forensic, Ph.D., for some advice regarding another psychologist. The psychologist in question, Marvin Turkey, Ph.D., was appearing as an expert witness against one of Farrow's clients and made some statements under oath that Farrow had reason to question. Dr. Forensic researched Dr. Turkey's credentials, using a professional directory, and learned that they did not appear to include the sort of experiences usually associated

with the type of expertise claimed. He suggested some questions Farrow could ask Turkey to establish or challenge his credibility. Forensic also provided Farrow with some publications that tended to refute the claims asserted by Turkey in his testimony. Dr. Turkey later telephoned Dr. Forensic and angrily claimed that Farrow had embarrassed him in public by using the information Forensic had supplied.

Forensic was asked for consultative advice by a third party, Attorney Farrow, and provided him with factual material (e.g., articles and readily available public information). If the material supplied to Farrow was used to embarrass Dr. Turkey, this was likely justified. If Turkey were as competent as he claimed, he should not have felt upset about answering direct questions about his credentials or about responding to questions raised in the published scientific literature. These are standard procedures used to establish the qualifications of expert witnesses. If Forensic offered gossip or a biased presentation of facts, an ethical infraction might exist; however, he owed no duty of protection to Turkey.

Cooperation With Other Professionals

Helping professionals are usually very busy people who can not be expected to drop everything and attend to a colleague's immediate need. Often, the correct response can be a simple, prompt response indicating when or if the request can be filled. Timeliness can become an ethical issue, however, when a colleague or professional in training feels completely ignored for an extended period of time. Sometimes, passive–aggressive behavior can create unnecessary lags. Whatever the reason, extended delays can prove harmful. The next cases imply a measure of passivity and lack of prompt cooperation.

Case 13–4: Gloria Seeker, M.S.W., proposed a research project to be carried out at a state psychiatric facility near her university. The project first required approval by the facility's institutional review board, headed by Tyrone Plod, Ph.D. Seeker eventually filed an ethics complaint alleging that

Plod had procrastinated for 10 months in the consideration of her study, despite the fact that it posed no substantial risk to the patients. She accused Plod of professional jealousy. Dr. Plod replied that he was kept very busy by his duties as chief psychologist and could not give high priority to the request from a colleague who was employed elsewhere.

While it is not clear whether Dr. Plod was intentionally thwarting Ms. Seeker's project, her request was obviously very low on his list. At the very least, Seeker deserved to know approximately when a decision would be forthcoming and what position the committee might take given its official policies and research practices. If Dr. Plod were truly unable to expeditiously perform his assigned review duties, he should have stepped down from that position in favor of someone who could. If evidence existed to confirm that Plod treated Seeker unfairly, given institutional policy or relative favoritism to others, his behavior would qualify as unethical.

Case 13–5: Rodney Freeman terminated counseling with Stefan Witholden, L.M.H.C., over a year ago. Mr. Freeman decided to begin counseling anew with another practitioner and signed a Health Insurance Portability and Accountability Act (HIPAA) compliant release-of-information form that authorized sending all medical records and psychotherapy notes to the new therapist. When no report or records were forthcoming, and after several unsuccessful attempts to contact Witholden, Freeman was finally told, "I don't have any materials that would be useful to you."

Witholden's behavior is not uncommon. At times, a former therapist may be angry at a client's decision to see another therapist, even after an appropriate termination. Witholden's reluctance to share information with the new therapist at the client's request constitutes potential harm to the client and violates federal law (i.e., HIPPA). The APA ethics code and several state statutes specify that records can not be withheld because a client still owes money (APA 02: 6.03). In this case, payment is not

at issue, making Witholden's behavior even more indefensible.

Case 13–6: Susan Predoc's thesis draft sat among the piles of papers and books on Professor Sloth's desk for 4 months. When Ms. Predoc politely inquired about it, noting that she was anxious to finish her degree and move her family to another city, Sloth said he would get to it as soon as possible. Three more months passed, and still no feedback was forthcoming.

Ms. Predoc's dilemma is particularly troublesome because Sloth retains considerable power over her future prospects, and she does not have professional clout or potential allies to assist her. How hard should she push? Should she enlist the assistance of one of Sloth's colleagues? If she angers her thesis chair, he may exact additional and less passive penalties, such as finding fault with any work she submits. The APA ethics code addresses such unresponsive behavior by requiring appropriate feedback processes for students (APA 02: 7.06a).

With all sorts of alternative medical practices gaining popularity in the mainstream, such dilemmas as the one in the next case will also occur more frequently.

Case 13–7: A client decided to drop Philip Customary, Ph.D., in favor of consulting Spaci Carrot, an individual with no discernible credentials who claimed skill as a "psychic, vegan healer able to channel with Ormont on Venus." The client requested that a copy of all treatment notes and assessment scores be sent to his new "therapist." Dr. Customary reasoned that it would be improper to send records to someone he believes incompetent and unlikely to help this client.

One may empathize with Customary's position, but it is one that may well make him vulnerable. Mental health practitioners can offer to provide treatment summaries but are also required to release records at the request of a client. As an alternative, Dr. Customary could provide the records to the client, expressing concern about the qualifications of the new practitioner but allowing the client to decide what to share with Ms. Carrot.

Interference With Ongoing Relationships

What about taking on a client while that person is still in an ongoing relationship with another therapist? The two most common concerns raised in this context are (1) agreeing to work with clients or others who initiate the contact but are currently involved in a relationship with another professional in a similar role and (2) active soliciting ("pirating") of psychotherapy clients in treatment elsewhere.

Accepting clients currently under the care of another professional is not necessarily unethical (APA 02: 3.07, 10.04) as long as the therapist minimizes the risk of confusion and conflict and focuses exclusively on the client's welfare. For example, an individual might well benefit from participating in group or family therapy with one professional while pursuing individual treatment with another. In such cases, both therapists should ideally know of the other's involvement. We suggest considerable reflection before agreeing to do multiple-therapist arrangements to ensure that the "what ifs" are well managed, There may be more to the story than you know.

Case 13–8: Sidney Switch was still in active treatment with a psychiatrist when he sought an appointment with Roberto Resque, Ph.D. Switch tells Dr. Resque that he believes his current therapist is not helping him. He would like to start seeing Resque instead.

What are Resque's obligations and duties? We acknowledge that Switch certainly has the right to choose his service provider. In our view, however, it would be inappropriate and possibly foolhardy for Dr. Resque simply to begin treating Switch, ignoring the other active professional relationship. Ideally, Resque would recognize that negative transference or misunderstandings can potentially complicate therapy and would suggest that Mr. Switch discuss his dissatisfaction directly with his current therapist. If Switch is unwilling to do that for some reason, Resque should seek his authorization to contact the therapist himself to confer about the case. If Switch refuses to permit this, it would be wisest for Resque to decline to offer him services. It could be that Switch intends to conceal some issues or is simply acting out in some way against his current therapist. Resque might soon find himself embroiled in an uncomfortable situation with a troubled and vulnerable client.

Uninvited in-person solicitations, disallowed in previous codes, appear to be implicitly allowed in the current APA code (APA 02: 10.04). We continue to advise, however, that direct solicitation of clients receiving services from another mental health professional should be undertaken only when it seems clear that a client is in harm's way as a result of the current treatment the client is receiving. The sole focus should be on the client's individual needs and best interests, and these may not always be immediately apparent.

Case 13–9: Sonia Victim sought psychotherapy with Anita Rule, Ph.D. Ms. Victim told Dr. Rule that she had recently decided to terminate her "psychotherapeutic" relationship with Peter Grossout, L.M.F.T., who had convinced her that she should engage in a variety of sexual activities with him as a means to "overcome the adverse psychological influence of her father in her life." Ms. Victim told Dr. Rule that she was feeling increasingly depressed and worthless in the wake of her encounters with Mr. Grossout. Rule inquired regarding whether Ms. Victim might wish to pursue a formal complaint against Grossout. The client responded that she wanted only to "forget those repulsive events" and go into treatment with Dr. Rule to work through other concerns.

Ms. Victim's situation constitutes an exception to the generally preferred way of accepting new clients. Estimates suggest that about half of all therapists will encounter at least one client who reports experiencing abuse by a previous therapist (Pope & Vetter, 1991). Dr. Rule would doubtless like to see Mr. Grossout called to account for the allegations made by Ms. Victim. If Victim's accusations are true, then Grossout's future clients may be at risk for sexual predation. On the other hand, Victim's disclosures were offered in confidence and cannot be disclosed without the client's consent (see Chapter 8). The client's relative vulnerability and the emotional cost of pursuing a complaint against Grossout may well be too high a price, and the choice must be hers.

Dr. Rule can and should provide her new client with the facts that the behavior she has described was unethical, unprofessional, and possibly illegal (depending on state law). The client should also be informed of avenues for pressing formal ethics or legal complaints available to her. Dr. Rule should not, however, attempt to pressure her client to pursue a formal complaint. Rule's client may ultimately develop sufficient personal resources to pursue the matter at a later time.

Not all ongoing relationships that pose interference issues involve psychotherapy. Other types of professional alliances can also yield troubling dilemmas.

Case 13–10: Tanya Trainee is an intern at a community mental health center where Lorna Doone, M.S.W., supervises her cases. Ms. Trainee disagrees with some of Doone's recommendations, so she approaches her testing supervisor, Mucho Nicer, Ph.D., for his suggestions.

Ms. Trainee appears to be splitting off aspects of her relationship with Ms. Doone that seem unsatisfactory to her. Dr. Nicer must recognize that the matters Ms. Trainee has approached him about fall under the authority of another supervisor. He should point this out to Ms. Trainee and suggest that she discuss differences directly with her designated supervisor or with the person directing the training program. For Dr. Nicer to offer supervisory consultation without the knowledge of Ms. Doone would create a potential for substantially more serious collegial anger, even if that was not Ms. Trainee's intent. If Trainee has serious questions regarding the nature of Ms. Doone's supervision or competence, and if Doone is unresponsive to a direct discussion with her, she could then reasonably consult with Doone's other colleagues in the setting for advice on how to proceed.

What about a request for consultation that turns into something more? Consider the following case examples:

Case 13–11: Fritz Couch, M.D., is a psychoanalyst who has been treating Hester Prynn in analysis for 3 years. Prynn has been blocking her free associations for several weeks, and Dr. Couch wonders about the possibility of an impending thought disturbance. He refers Ms. Prynn to Ursula Norms, Ph.D., for psychodiagnostic testing. During the course of the psychological assessment, Ms. Prynn tells Dr. Norms that she feels increasingly frustrated with the lack of progress in her treatment with Dr. Couch and asks whether Norms would take her on as a therapy client.

Case 13–12: Gladys Prudent, L.M.H.C., has significant concerns about Hedda Downward's persistent depressed mood. She refers Ms. Downward to Ingrid Meds, M.D., for a medication consultation. Ms. Downward is impressed when Dr. Meds expresses the belief that medication should offer her relief and asks Meds to begin managing her case completely, expressing a willingness to terminate with Prudent.

The cases of Ms. Prynn and Ms. Downward illustrate a not uncommon circumstance, and one can easily understand why. Clients have the right to free choice, even if the choice might run counter to their best interests as seen by their current therapists. Such consultants, however, may become idealized by virtue of a therapeutic transference situation or a simple transitory contrast effect. Often enough, ethical therapists recognize the potential limitations in their ability to adequately diagnose or treat a specific problem and seek specific consultations from qualified colleagues (APA 02: 4.08). Clients often have problems that may make them feel frustrated, depressed, or troubled. When both situations collide, the consultants can become imbued with a positive aura by the clients, who then ask the consultants to take over their care.

In both cases presented, the correct course of action would be similar. The consultants should refer the clients back to their therapists with the recommendation that they discuss the issue directly. In Ms. Prynn's situation, this might mean working through a negative transference, whereas for Ms. Downward it might mean discussing the frustrations of a prolonged depressive reaction. Ultimately, the clients may choose to terminate treatment with the therapists and seek treatment from the consultants or elsewhere. But, the consultants should not encourage this, recognizing the unusual nature of their limited relationships with the clients. Assuming the clients have authorized the consultants to communicate with the referring therapists, it might also be wise for Norms and Meds to inform Couch and Prudent, respectively, of their clients' concerns. That, after all, could be considered a part of the consultation that was originally sought, and these concerns may be impeding the progress of treatment.

Making a Referral

What about the client who seeks a referral for a friend in a neighboring state or the colleague who asks for a suggestion for a specialized type of consultant? The person asking for the referral has the right to expect that the mental health professional making it will offer the best recommendation available, regardless of his or her personal or financial interests.

Cases presented in Chapter 7 illustrate inappropriate referrals with respect to fee-splitting arrangements. This is not to say that therapists should never make referrals to colleagues with whom they are very familiar or have close working relationships. The key factor involves the anticipated best interests of the client, including geographic location, finances, and other relevant considerations.

Case 13–13: Eugene Defer, Psy.D., works in a group practice with several other mental health professionals. He conducts an intake interview with a new female client in her mid-30s who requests a female therapist. Two women work with Dr. Defer in the group practice. He describes both women in terms of age and special clinical interests, suggesting that the client might choose to have an appointment with one of them.

Case 13–14: A client calls Ronda Refer, Ph.D., to help locate a therapist to evaluate a relative in a distant state. Dr. Refer does not know anyone in that geographic area but consults a professional

directory to provide the client with the names and addresses of some appropriately licensed practitioners in that general vicinity.

Both of the therapists described above have behaved in an ethically appropriate manner. Dr. Defer has no specific financial interest in his referral to another member of the same practice group. While he may derive some diffuse benefit by keeping the client within the group, the client did, after all, approach that group in the first place. Presumably, the client also understands that Dr. Defer and his female colleagues work as part of a group in close association. Defer has also shown himself responsive to the client's stated preference for a female therapist and has presented some additional data regarding options within the group, giving the client an additional measure of informed choice.

Dr. Refer is not familiar with anyone in the distant geographical area and knows relatively little about the client's specific needs. By using a professional directory to locate licensed or board-certified therapists, she reasonably ensures at least minimal confidence in the practitioners' competence. One must presume that the practitioners receiving such a referral will have the ethical sensitivity to make additional local referrals should the client need services they are not equipped to offer. Dr. Refer, however, should offer appropriate caveats to her client, such as, "Please tell your cousin that I do not know these practitioners personally; however, they are listed as fully licensed." Whenever a therapist does not feel comfortable making such a referral, the inquirer might then be directed to a community agency.

Alas, despite good and pure intentions, a referral can go askance, as the next two cases reveal.

Case 13–15: A counselor in Maine called Dr. Assist, a friend in California, requesting a referral for a client moving to the Los Angeles area. Dr. Assist asked a few questions about the client's situation and suggested Dr. Mismatch, an acquaintance with a good reputation in the Los Angeles community. The client acted on the referral and was very displeased with Dr. Mismatch. The counselor in Maine contacted Dr. Assist to complain that the former client had called to express anger toward her for passing on a faulty suggestion; in the client's words, Mismatch was "a dreadful therapist." The counselor in Maine also seemed irritated with Dr. Assist, implying that Dr. Assist's referral was ill-conceived.

Case 13–16: A student whose behavior revealed a high level of agitation asked a Professor Will Helpout, D.S.W., for a referral to a therapist in the community. Dr. Helpout offered the student several names, specifically noting that the last one was also a very close friend. The student returned several weeks later and accused Dr. Helpout of "setting her up so that she could get a financial cut from the friend out of the referral." The student then recited a list of complaints about Dr. Helpout's friend/therapist before slamming the office door behind her.

Dr. Assist did her best, but it did not work out. Dr. Helpout was trying to be especially open by revealing the nature of her relationship with one of the referral options, but this time such candor backfired. Both therapists who related these true stories to us have also vowed never again to make referrals. This is an unfortunate decision, considering the valuable service to consumers that conscientious referrals can provide.

To help allay the potential for fallout when referrals do not pan out, therapists should always remember to convey what may be too obvious at the time: Even when the referral is personally known, professional services turn on personal rapport. No one can guarantee that a professional relationship will work out satisfactorily. Because part of any therapist's reputation and professional responsibility are carried in any referral made, appropriate caveats should be offered as thoughtfully as the referral itself (Leigh, 1998; Shapiro & Ginzberg, 2003).

Should all referrals coming in be accepted? Not necessarily (Cheston, 1991)—whenever one feels the fit is not right, for whatever reason, it is best to either decline the opportunity or pass on a better suggestion.

Finally, hundreds of sites offer mental health referral services to consumers in every state, and Google (http://www.google.com) or other search engines pull them up in less than a second. However, as we surfed for various types of services, we noticed that some so-called referral sites primarily funnel potential clients to individual therapists' private practices. If the Internet is utilized to help someone with a referral, we advise taking the time to view sites rather than sending potential clients off to do it on their own and sticking to recommending a few sites associated with legitimate professional or state mental health associations.

Professional Etiquette

Colleagues in all specialties deserve to be treated with outward respect and equanimity and in accordance with professional etiquette, even when one has reason to be annoyed with them. Tossing impolite barbs can result in an escalating professional feud. Ethics complaints occasionally arise out of issues that should have been resolved informally and early in the dispute.

Case 13–17: Horace Night, Ph.D., was asked by a journal editor to review a manuscript by Lester Day, Ph.D., with whom Night has long had substantial theoretical disagreements. Night drafted a scathing review of the paper based chiefly on theoretical disagreements, including such comments as, "Dr. Day continues to cling to obsolete ideas in a narrow-minded and idiotic fashion." Dr. Night also teaches a course at a local university. During the semester, he frequently attacks the work of Dr. Day, describing it as trivial, ill-conceived, and useless.

Certainly, personal motives—including anger, jealousy, competitiveness, and inflated views of one's importance—may contribute to anger toward colleagues. One should not express such passions in an unprofessional manner. In the case of Dr. Night, it appears that the theoretical disagreements with Dr. Day have become inappropriately personalized. If Night is not prepared to offer a critique in a rational and dispassionate manner, he should consider telling the editor that he feels too personally put off by Dr. Day to give this paper a fair reading.

The adjectives "narrow-minded" and "idiotic" have no place in an ethically formulated scholarly review.

Dr. Night's classroom attacks are also inappropriate. Such public statements are not in keeping with scientific foundations. Ideally, Night could outline Day's concepts and then contrast them to his own in a scholarly manner. In the case of legitimate scholarly or professional differences, the most fitting means of presenting the dispute is through articles and comments in peer-reviewed professional publications in which full citation and documentation of claims occurs under the critical eye of scholarly peers. Night's attacks on Day were, again, too personalized and lacked the appropriate validation necessary for presentation in an educational forum (APA 02: 7.03b). (See Chapter 16 for an additional discussion of classroom presentations.)

Case 13–18: Manfred Potz, Ph.D., and his colleague Stefan Blitz, Ph.D., have known each other personally and professionally for many years. After an unfortunate personal dispute leads to a dissolution of their friendship, Potz complains to an ethics committee that Blitz has spread untrue rumors to a mutual acquaintance that Potz is a terrorist sympathizer and is having an affair with a woman one third his age.

The type of dispute between Potz and Blitz unfortunately occurs more often than it should, especially in group or institutional settings. Colleagues usually have no way of assessing the validity of such personal criticisms with respect to professional competence, let alone the veracity of Blitz's verbal assault. If Blitz has some factual basis for criticizing Potz, then he should bring this evidence to appropriate authorities. Gossip and rumors, however, violate the obligations of a professional role.

The Vindictive Colleague

Some additional mention must be made of colleagues who become so angered by real or perceived wrongs that they either act out in a clearly unethical manner or seek redress through ethics committees for problems that are not, strictly speaking, ethical in nature. The vindictive colleague sincerely believes that he or she has been wronged by another and responds with either an impulsive reaction or (in rare cases) carefully plotted retaliation. These actions may eventually lead to feelings of remorse. In the meantime, considerable injury has taken place. The acts themselves often have an immature quality to them, with the angry colleague viewing an ethics committee as a parent figure who will swiftly redress the perceived wrong. Unfortunately, because the players are adults acting in a professional venue, the consequences of their actions can not be easily dismissed as mere immaturity.

Case 13–19: Rea Venge, Ph.D., gathered strong circumstantial evidence that her colleague and professional rival at Saltine University had stolen the sole disk containing her unprocessed research data. Dr. Venge was later seen releasing her colleague's laboratory rats in the university's botanical garden.

Case 13–20: Ralph Romeo, M.S., and Jane Juliet, Ph.D., both served as faculty members at the Hazyday Counseling Institute. They developed a sexual relationship from which Romeo contracted genital herpes. He filed an ethics complaint against Juliet, asserting that he had asked specifically whether she had any sexually transmitted diseases prior to their sexual intimacy and had received assurances from her that she did not.

Case 13–21: When Charlene Newer, Ph.D., was recruited to Chaos State University as head of a disorganized counseling psychology training program, she undertook a major overhaul. As a result, Abe Oldster, Ph.D., was reassigned from teaching an elective graduate seminar to a less desirable supervisory role. Insulted and angry, Oldster monitored Newer closely and discovered that she had made a critical comment about his attitude to another staff member. Dr. Oldster sent a detailed complaint of alleged unprofessional conduct by Dr. Newer to the APA. He filed the same complaint 6 weeks later with the university grievance board. Because each group investigates complaints independently, Dr. Newer had to defend herself serially in each forum. Although all complaints were ultimately dismissed, Dr. Newer, much to Dr. Oldster's delight, spent considerable time and energy defending herself.

Case 13–22: Drs. Katz and Dawgs were colleagues with markedly different political views on several sensitive issues. Their loud and furious arguments took place with little regard for their surroundings. Those overhearing the two battle it out worried about the form any escalation might take. On a subsequent Saturday night, the police arrested an inebriated Dr. Dawgs for firing a gunshot into the front window of the Katz family home.

In the case of Dr. Venge, we see that a possible but unproven ethical breach by a colleague provoked Venge to commit a clear violation in retaliation. While one can understand her ire, the resulting act of scattering her colleague's rodents into the bush is unethical (and will no doubt carry other consequences) and substantially compounds the situation.

The case of Drs. Romeo and Juliet is instructive from several standpoints. First, it illustrates a host of subsurface emotional issues that can not be resolved through an ethics inquiry but that may underlie a complaint by one colleague about another. Second, it illustrates the problem of attempting to address personal or interpersonal difficulties in the context of an ethics complaint. The ethics committee contacted Romeo, acknowledged his distress at contracting a disease, but noted that their infectious relationship did not constitute a professional one and hence fell beyond the purview of the committee.

It seems apparent that Oldster's primary goal was to complicate Dr. Newer's life, and he did not care what resources he burdened in the process. The APA code specifically warns against filing what the APA considers frivolous or nonsensical complaints motivated to harass (APA 02: 1.07).

Little comment is necessary regarding Katz and Dawgs except to affirm to our readers that this is a true story. Fortunately, such acted-out animosity is extremely uncommon. Yet, in a world in which interpersonal problems often impulsively escalate into violence, we worry that this phenomenon may become less unusual.

(See further discussion of impaired professionals in Chapter 4.)

Online Wars

Netiquette is roughly defined as the capacity to remain civil and the ability to maintain some measure of dignity and decorum while communicating over computer networks. Modern mass communication has created forms of professional relating that some do not handle well. People who have never met face to face can trash each other online in ways that appear far more vitriolic than most face-to-face professional disagreements.

The odd situational context may largely account for blunted inhibition. Because communicators are actually alone at their desks in their private space interacting with an inanimate computer, an illusion of privacy and safety exists. Passion and fury in the absence of seeming danger may blur the fact that hundreds, even thousands, of others may witness the cyberspace carnage. Practical restraints, such as mustering the courage to go directly to an offending colleague or to the bother of writing and mailing a letter, no longer stand guard. Instantaneous communication affords no reconsideration or cooling of feelings that the passage of time and thoughtful reflection might otherwise invite. Everything happens so quickly: Slam the send button, and the hostile message has left the building. (We discuss related issues in Chapter 15.)

Here, we offer examples of personal attacks on colleagues and an intimate faux pas picked up on the Internet.

Case 13–23: A therapist in an electronic discussion group disagreed with the assertion of Negate Recall, Psy.D., that repressed memory was merely a "cash cow for therapists and that no such phenomenon actually exists." Dr. Recall sent a message describing the psychologist who spoke out against him as being "witless, dangerous, impertinent, and dense." A number of other subscribers came to the defense of the disagreeing therapist, suggesting that the topic of repressed memories would profit from a two-sided, but restrained and scholarly, debate. Dr. Recall then blasted the entire group of subscribers for their stupidity and wrong-headedness and announced he was "unsubscribing immediately." The remaining subscribers gossiped about Dr. Recall for months afterward. Recall's tirade was also forwarded to scores of other lists.

Dr. Recall's outbursts provided prolonged entertainment for his colleagues, probably without his awareness. His reputation likely suffered as a result of the incident. Angry outbursts get noticed, but the impact is rarely favorable.

Case 13–24: Uri Knock, Ph.D., asked members of his online psychotherapy list if they had heard that Hefty Target, Ph.D., a very well-known and well-regarded clinical psychologist and not a member of the list, regularly abused alcohol. Knock said that he thought someone told him this a while back.

We have personally witnessed this kind of unsubstantiated gossip many times on special interest Internet lists. It was most unfair and unprofessional for Dr. Knock to post this question to hundreds of people. Even though Knock himself is unsure of the veracity of the story, the accusation and the name have been linked in people's minds, and many of those may have passed the story along. Furthermore, unless someone informs Dr. Target of the charge, he can not defend himself. When such slurs are publicly posted, we believe that the gossiper should be held accountable online, and if the charge is serious, the target should be located and informed.

Case 13–25: Lilly Whoops, L.M.F.T., noticed that a past lover posted a message in a newsgroup. She was so excited to see his name that she fired off a passionate note, declaring that he was "always better than my husband," and asking, "Am I still better than your wife?" Unfortunately, Dr. Whoops used the reply command instead of sending the message to her one-time lover's private e-mail address. The message is known to have reached more than 1,000 recipients.

Although most such mistakes may not be embarrassing and consequential, it is wise to take special care to ensure that the name in the "To" bar is what you intended. We also highly recommend making an agreement with yourself never to send online messages when feeling angry, intense, or impulsive. The expression of flaming feelings may well come home to haunt. When the anger subsides, the discussion of the issues can occur in ways that maintain professional decorum, with some discussions perhaps better done over the phone or in an old-fashioned letter. In addition, mental health professionals should remind themselves every time they send a message that it is "format ready" to instantly spread around to whomever any recipient pleases.

Finally, there is no absolute freedom of speech in cyberspace. Defamation pertains when false and unprivileged data are published and result in economic damages, imply that that a person is a criminal or has a stigmatizing disease, or injure an individual with respect to his or her profession or business. Thus, if someone can prove that the perpetrator damaged a reputation or good name by knowingly or recklessly spreading false information, the victim can sue for defamation. Having solid proof to verify any negative public statement about someone provides protection, as does, although to a lesser extent, clearly presenting a statement as an opinion rather than fact. Defamation and invasion-of-privacy legal actions based on Internet communications have already been won (Branscum, 1995) and will no doubt continue as casual use of the Internet mushrooms.

Journal Editors and Reviewers

The publication of scholarly papers is critical to the growth of a discipline, and depending on one's position, essential to one's professional status and advancement in the field. Those teaching in most traditional academic settings will not be retained or promoted unless they publish regularly in reputable, refereed journals. Even for positions that do not require publications, research and writing serves a variety of other needs. Therefore, it comes as no surprise that scholarly journals receive high volumes of manuscripts, yet only a small percentage ultimately win acceptance for publication. Competition for space in the most esteemed journals is especially keen, meaning that fairness in the journal review process is imperative given the critical importance of the acceptance/rejection decision-making process to the careers of many professionals. The ethics of the journal review process has elicited little attention in proportion to the far-ranging consequences (Rogers, 1992).

In this section, we focus on interprofessional relationship issues. Manuscripts are accepted or rejected by one's peers. And, as might be expected, criticisms abound concerning the treatment and negative decisions by journal editors and manuscript reviewers. Indeed, the number of complaints colleagues pass along to us has skyrocketed in recent years.

A common criticism by authors involves excessively editorial lag, long delays in providing feedback. Because the ethics of scholarly publishing require submission of articles to only one journal at a time, extended dwell time is wasteful, especially if the topic is timely.

Case 13–26: Editor Leonard Lag, D.S.W., rejected a 10-page manuscript about mental health emergency responses to the aftermath of a highly publicized natural disaster submitted by Margaret Moment, M.S.W., 9 months earlier. Moment immediately sent her manuscript to another journal and received a prompt response this time, indicating that the article would not have sufficient interest given the publication lag. Three other journal editors arrived at the same decision.

Journal reviewing is typically done by professionals in the field who volunteer their time to read and comment on manuscripts. Unless they are on the paid staff of professional organizations, editors typically receive only small stipends. Therefore, it is understandable that weeks would pass before reviewers find time in their schedules and for the editor to gather and distill the reviews and inform the author of the decision. Nine months, however, is too long, and Ms. Moment suffered harm as a result of Lag's lack of responsiveness. Editors often complain that they find it difficult to attract good reviewers (Finke, 1990), and that it takes only one to hold up the process. But, in the meantime, colleagues awaiting reviews face a serious disadvantage. Editors should drop re-

viewers from their roster who consistently fail to meet deadlines (Epstein, 1995).

Charges of bias against unknown authors or those affiliated with less prestigious institutions have also been leveled against editors (Bornstein, 1990), as has the practice of preselecting reviewers to ensure acceptance or rejection (Franzini, 1987). Journal editors and reviewers have also earned criticism for exhibiting favoritism and prejudices toward specific authors, harboring biases against certain topics or theoretical approaches or findings that are not statistically significant. Finke (1990) contended that original research representing new advances often faces rejection simply because the reviewers are uninformed.

Shoddy, deficient, or mean-spirited evaluations also rank high in frequency among the complaints we have heard about.

Case 13–27: Yu Flattenmi, Ph.D., received a response from an editor informing him that his manuscript had been rejected. It was accompanied by three (blinded) reviewer notes, two of which were mildly positive and one that was decidedly negative and unconstructive. The negative letter was derisive and insulting, concluding with a statement that Flattenmi was not qualified to do research if this paper was any indication of his competence.

Such treatment by an anonymous colleague certainly violates the spirit of professional ethics that call on colleagues to treat those with whom they work with respect and dignity (Hadjistavropoulos & Beiling, 2000; Sternberg, 2002, 2003). Flattenmi might appeal to the journal editor, pointing out that two reviewers rated the paper positively and that the other reviewer showed sufficient incivility as to warrant replacement. We know of at least one instance when this approach worked out well for the author.

That the peer review process is hardly an exact science was well proven in the now classic and still controversial article by Peters and Ceci (1982). These authors assessed the capriciousness of the reviewing process of 12 prestigious psychology journals by resubmitting cosmetically altered (author and affiliation changes), *previously published* articles to each respective journal again. Surprisingly, only three articles were detected as resubmissions, and eight of the nine remaining articles were rejected for publication by the same journals that had earlier published them! The authors confirmed that the rejection rates and editorial policies of the journals had not substantially changed in the interim.

We would note that *formal* ethics complaints against those who serve as publishing gatekeepers arrive only rarely, possibly because disgruntled or would-be published authors realize that ethics committees lack the authority to referee disputes of this nature or to dictate what ultimately gets published. Or, perhaps as a colleague whose manuscript was just rejected put it, "If I protest, it will be interpreted as whining."

Another interprofessional ethical issue related to publishing scholarly work involves improper use of materials under review. Reviewers should treat manuscripts sent to them as confidential. The proprietary rights of the authors demand respect (APA 02: 8.15).

Case 13–28: Eileen Pilfer, Ph.D., agreed to review a manuscript in her area of expertise. She wrote a critical review, concluding that the piece not be published. A year later, the author of the rejected manuscript was shocked to see much of the material from his submitted article appearing in a published report by Pilfer.

Cases of improper acquisition of material, compounded by the apparently intentional blocking of competing work, are rare. However, the trustworthiness of reviewers is critical because of the temptation to misappropriate ideas or materials from works under review. However, because authors and reviewers are working in the same area, acquisition of the work of others may not always be premeditated. As Douglas (1992) admitted:

> I have had my ideas stolen many times, at least twice by people who added insult to injury by ridiculing the ideas before stealing them. Yet when I have met these people at later times they have failed to act appropriately guilty. I honestly believe that they do not realize where their ideas

have come from, because I have similarly stolen ideas without being aware of doing so. (p. 407)

Epstein (1995) outlined several suggestions for ensuring that authors receive appropriate respect and attention from their peers. These include

- adherence to a reasonable decision-making timetable
- stating criticisms in a constructive manner and avoiding ad hominem comments
- recognizing the positive features in a submission as well as the negative
- distinguishing between correctable and uncorrectable limitations
- keeping one's own biases in check, allowing authors to recommend possible reviewers
- providing authors a meaningful appeals process
- providing forms for authors to provide feedback about the reviewers

Whether to allow authors to know the identity of the reviewer is more controversial. On the one hand, if reviewers have to stand behind their identifiable review, criticisms of nasty and poorly done reviewers may substantially decrease. On the other hand, unidentifiable reviewers may be more even-handed (Hartley, 1987), and anonymity reduces the chances of reprisals and allows reviewers to be more candid.

RELATIONSHIPS WITH SUPERVISEES AND EMPLOYEES

Educating supervisees probably constitutes the strongest weapon we have against ethical and professional misconduct (Vasquez, 1992). When the supervisees or trainees are paraprofessionals who may not have had prior ethics education, the need is even greater. As models of conduct in actual professional settings, supervisors can act either as exemplars or agents of poor professional socialization.

Relationships with supervisees and employees carry similar ethical duties and responsibilities as those due to therapy clients (e.g., APA 02: 3.03, 3.04, 3.08) as well as additional activities specific to supervision (e.g., APA 02: 2.05, 7.06, 7.07). The supervisor or employer is almost always the more powerful person in the relationship and must recognize the accompanying obligations. Supervisees and employees have the general rights to privacy, respect, dignity, courtesy, and due process.

Delegating Supervisee Tasks

Whenever supervisors delegate work to their supervisees, a number of ethical responsibilities pertain (APA 02: 2.05). They must attempt to ensure that supervisees are not assigned any duties that would involve multiple relationships that could lead to exploitation or lack of objectivity. Supervisors should only authorize responsibilities commensurate with the supervisees' attained level of competence. And, of course, supervisees require careful monitoring to ensure that they perform their services or other assigned tasks capably. The next two cases reveal lax supervision.

Case 13–29: Bucky Newbie told his supervisor that the student he saw for the first time in the university counseling center seemed "rather down." The supervisor responded, "All students are somewhat depressed around finals time. Don't worry about it." Three days later, the client made a serious suicide attempt.

Bucky, beginning his first year of supervised training, may not have adequately perceived or described the significant nature of the client's condition to the supervisor. Bucky seems obviously unprepared to work with a suicidal client or any client presenting with severe symptoms, and brushing off his concerns constituted improper supervision.

Case 13–30: Noah Vale had taken a course on cognitive assessment but had never administered the Ultra Sophisticated Learning and Education Scoring System (USLESS) before. He felt uneasy when his supervisor insisted that he administer that tool to a client scheduled for assessment 2 days later. Vale explained that he lacked familiarity with administration, scoring, and interpre-

tation of the USLESS. His supervisor told him, "Don't worry. Just take it home tonight and practice on your roommate."

Vale's supervisor's suggestions raise serious ethical problems. First, the supervisor has not paid sufficient attention to his trainee's reservations. By failing to heed Vale's concerns, the supervisor abdicated an important educational responsibility. By suggesting a superficial practice option, the supervisor puts the client at risk of facing an incompetent assessment by an unqualified and admittedly unprepared examiner. The supervisor has also conveyed a casual and inappropriate attitude toward the ethical principles of psychological assessment (see Chapter 9).

Therapy Supervision

Every licensed therapist began as a trainee once upon a time and most likely experienced formative influence from supervisors in important ways—for better and for worse—during that critical period of professional development (Pope & Vasquez, 1991). Alonzo (1985) characterized supervisors as "professional parents" and, like traditional parents, noted that they perform their duties with varying degrees of competence and sensitivity. Supervisors' characteristics and training responsibilities fall into three broad areas (Johnson, 2003; Vasquez, 1992):

- ethical knowledge and behavior,
- skill competencies,
- and personal functioning.

Each has relevance to the quality of the interpersonal relationship between supervisor and supervisee. Supervisory relationships are far more delicate and complicated than the typical educator–student relationship. The supervisor performs multiple roles that include teacher, mentor, evaluator, and facilitator of self-awareness and exploration, all of which contain elements of a psychotherapeutic relationship (Kurpius, Gibson, Lewis, & Corbet, 1991). In addition, supervisors will, of necessity, routinely address the feelings and emotional lives of their trainees as part of discussing their interactions with clients. In no other occupation do supervisors so routinely probe the inner lives of the people whose work they oversee. These inherent roles do not always integrate smoothly, such as the need to sometimes be critical while evaluating a supervisee's therapeutic blunder and listening empathically when the supervisee describes feeling stressed about a personal matter (Whiston & Emerson, 1989). Further, these roles include third parties—the supervisee's clients—making responsible, ethical management even more imperative. Finally, because supervisors often have access to information about the emotional lives of their supervisees, a special duty of care applies.

Students from cultures different from the supervisor or client population have unique supervisory needs. International students who report feeling less acculturated (defined as the level of acceptance of and by the culture and English proficiency) report weaker supervisory alliances. These findings suggest that international students become especially dependent on their supervisors for advice, support, personal validation, and discussions of cultural issues and differences (Nilsson & Anderson, 2004).

What do supervisees want? Surveys of supervisees (Allen, Szollos, & Williams, 1986; McCarthy, Kulakowski, & Kenfield, 1994) reported that expertise and facilitative characteristics (trustworthiness, empathy, and genuineness) were the most favored supervisor characteristics. Many supervisees also welcomed assistance with personal growth issues more than the teaching of technical skills. Communication of expectations and clear feedback also ranked high, whereas sexist or authoritarian treatment, unavailability, and interpersonal conflicts were seen as especially detrimental to the quality of supervision.

Negative experiences with supervisors can have profound and adverse impacts on future career goals, suggesting that the consequences of bad supervision experiences are global and long lasting (Ramos-Sanchez et al., 2002). It is also disheartening to note that more than half of the trainees surveyed in one sample perceived ethical breaches by their supervisors in the course of training; these acts included inadequate performance evaluation, session boundary issues, and disrespectful treatment (Ladany, Lehrman-Waterman, Molinaro, & Wolgast, 1999).

Case 13–31: Supervisee Jimbo Tryhard felt dissatisfied with the progress of his clients and experienced considerable self-doubt. Tryhard's supervisor, Dr. Twosides, always reacted in a critical tone whenever Tryhard attempted to disclose his therapeutic errors. Because Dr. Twosides would have a direct impact on his success in the program and his chances of obtaining a job after graduation, Tryhard switched to playing out the supervisory sessions by reporting only positive aspects of his sessions and relaying whatever he thought would please Twosides.

Tryhard may have reacted in an overly sensitive manner to Dr. Twosides' criticisms, but the supervisor also failed to establish a valid and beneficial relationship with his supervisee. Although a challenge to accomplish, supervisors must seek to create alliances that allow supervisees to admit mistakes without fear. The ultimate competence levels reached by supervisees and the welfare of future clients depend heavily on the success of this pivotal phase of training (Bosk, 1979).

Supervisors sometimes forget whose needs are being served, as the next two cases illustrate.

Case 13–32: Jane Dumpee eagerly anticipated her upcoming supervision by Queenie Topdog, Ph.D., a highly respected clinician known for tireless dedication to her profession. At first, Dumpee enjoyed hearing about Topdog's work, even though such discussions took up almost half of the supervisory hour. However, as Topdog's self-revelations became more personal, Dumpee became concerned because her own needs for case review went unmet.

Case 13–33: The minute Melanie Chic arrived for her clinical supervisory session, Leery Fox, M.S.W., commented on her appearance (e.g., "That color doesn't do anything for you," or "That sweater is absolutely gorgeous"). He often lost track or interrupted the flow of her attempts to focus on her clients' issues with remarks such as, "Speaking of drinking too much, have you been to the new jazz bar on 4th Street?"

Supervisors who use their status and power for their own gratification or entertainment exploit those who have entrusted their professional development to them. Even though neither of the above cases may have apparently involved intentional abuse, both supervisors have abdicated professional roles in favor of their personal agendas. Although we can not be sure about Dr. Fox's motives, his behavior may border on sexual harassment.

Case 13–34: Urlee Abused revealed her struggles with alcoholic parents to her clinical supervisor, Dee Cipher, Ph.D. Thereafter, every time Urlee reported difficulties with a client or the program, Dr. Cipher told Urlee that her current concerns and shortcomings seemed linked to her childhood trauma.

The supervisory relationship appears badly contaminated by Dr. Cipher's focus on and lack of sensitivity about Urlee's disclosure. While mental health professionals may at times react to clients based on emotional events in their lives, Dr. Cipher's interpretations appear to undermine the supervisee's confidence and create tension in the supervisory relationship. If Dr. Cipher believes that Urlee's own issues frequently get in the way of treatment, she should recommend that Urlee seek treatment.

Unfortunately, supervisees who feel devalued, humiliated, ignored, or criticized in a nonconstructive way will not likely protest, especially if the supervisor is otherwise well liked and respected in the work setting. This compounds their disadvantage in advocating for themselves should the boundaries of the relationship further collapse (Jacobs, 1991).

Just as teaching supervisees about inappropriate role crossings with their clients constitutes a critical curricular component of their training, the supervisor–supervisee role also becomes vulnerable to blurring boundaries (Burian & Slimp, 2000; Walker & Clark, 1999) It is disturbing to note that data from anonymous surveys revealed that sexual contact between clinical supervisees and supervisors occurs fairly frequently (Glaser & Thorpe, 1986; Pope, Levenson, & Schover, 1979). These surveys were conducted before 1992 when the APA ethics code first expressly disallowed sexual relations with supervisees in training (APA 02: 7.07), but

unfortunately such activity persists (Koenig & Spano, 2003; Lamb & Catanzaro, 1998), and overtures often enough appear to be invited or initiated by the supervisees (Lamb, Catanzaro, & Moorman, 2004). (For an additional discussion of sexual relations with supervisees and resulting harms, see Chapter 12.)

Performance Evaluations

Timely feedback, or lack thereof, lies at the root of many ethical complaints that grow out of supervisory relationships. This becomes especially common when supervisees abruptly receive notification of a likely unfavorable rating or termination.

Case 13–35: Near the end of a 12-month clinical internship, Sheldon Lout was stunned by an evaluation from his supervisor describing him as insensitive and rude in his relationships with colleagues. He was fearful that these comments would hurt his chances to find employment and asserted that this critical evaluation was unethical because he had heard nothing of such concerns earlier.

Routine feedback sessions and written evaluations should be built into all supervisory relationships (APA 02: 7.06a). When discussing serious criticisms with supervisees, one should invariably offer these in writing, followed or accompanied by a dialogue about expected changes with a remedial plan (Harrar, VandeCreek, & Knapp, 1990). One could argue that if Mr. Lout were truly insensitive, he might not have heeded supervisory criticism. Nonetheless, he was certainly entitled to feedback and would be justified in asserting the inappropriateness of saying nothing about shortcomings until the final evaluation. Such behavior, if true, afforded Lout no opportunity to attempt remediation of his defects and denied him due process.

Case 13–36: Bertram Bizzy, Ph.D., served as clinical supervisor for Suzie Slipper, a graduate student placed at Bizzy's community agency 2 days a week for practicum training. Bizzy also juggled a thriving multioffice practice that involved frequent out-of-town consultations. Ms. Slipper appeared very independent and believed she functioned "just fine" without supervision. One month, Bizzy had to cancel one supervision hour because of professional travel and a second hour when he was out with the flu. Then, Ms. Slipper missed supervision the third week to attend a funeral. Slipper's schedule seemed to preclude make-up sessions, which was just as well as far as the preoccupied Dr. Bizzy was concerned. When they finally met after a hiatus of nearly 6 weeks, Dr. Bizzy discovered that Ms. Slipper had made some potentially serious errors in managing a case. He submitted a highly unflattering entry into her evaluation record.

Neophyte professionals often have more self-confidence about their competence than is actually warranted. Close supervision mitigates against this. Dr. Bizzy bears the brunt of the responsibility for Ms. Slipper's errors. Agency guidelines making backup supervision policies clear might have prevented this problem.

Case 13–37: Lennie Carnal, in the final stages of completing his doctorate, approached Marcus Glide, Ph.D., to arrange for private supervision. Carnal wanted to see a few private clients at his home office and contracted with Dr. Glide to supervise him. Glide agreed and was paid by Carnal for several hours of supervision time. Some months later, several women complained that they were sexually molested by Carnal in the guise of therapy. Carnal fled the state, and a malpractice lawsuit subsequently named Dr. Glide as a defendant for inadequately supervising Carnal. Dr. Glide defended himself by testifying that Carnal never told him about the sexual activities, the names of the clients involved, or even that he was practicing in his own home.

It seems that Dr. Glide extended far more trust than warranted to Mr. Carnal when agreeing to provide off-site supervision for private clients. While it is possible that Carnal lied or selectively reported material to his supervisor, Glide failed to monitor Carnal's work in adequate detail. Under the legal principle of *respondeat superior*, it was argued that Dr. Glide

knew or should have known of activities under his supervision and was therefore also liable for negligence. Dr. Glide's defense became complicated by the fact he had signed as supervisor on insurance claim forms for Mr. Carnal indicating that he had been "present on site when the services were rendered." This put Dr. Glide in the uncomfortable position of explaining whether he lied about knowing what Carnal was doing or lied on the insurance claim form.

The Client's Right to Know

When a client receives services from a therapist who is, in turn, supervised or otherwise in training, the client has the right to know this as well as the name of the supervisor (APA 02: 10.01c). Similarly, the supervisor should know the names, addresses, and other basic information about clients whose cases they supervise. The client should also be told explicitly that aspects of the case will be shared with the supervisor. Indeed, many clients would be pleased to know that their therapist will have ongoing consultation about their cases with a senior colleague. This should not come to a client's attention as a surprise at a sensitive moment, however, and is best presented factually as a part of the initial contract between client and therapists in training.

Case 13–38: Amy Shy arrived at the mental health center for her usual weekly appointment with a psychology intern and was met by Solomon Foot, Ph.D., the intern's supervisor. Dr. Foot explained that the intern had broken her leg skiing the weekend before and would not be back at the clinic for 4 to 6 weeks. He offered to provide interim services for Ms. Shy because he was familiar with her case through his supervision of the intern. Ms. Shy felt embarrassed that this person had such intimate knowledge of her personal problems.

Dr. Foot appeared to have Amy Shy's best interests at heart, although she clearly felt distressed by his awareness of the details of her case. We do not know whether the intern failed to inform Ms. Shy that a supervisor oversaw her case or whether Dr. Foot's introduction was a bit too abrupt for her to tolerate. Foot's behavior was not unethical, but it reveals the difficulty a sensitive client may face if supervisory relationships are not carefully articulated.

Terminating Impaired or Otherwise Unfit Supervisees

Intellectual prowess alone does not make a good psychotherapist. Not every student capable of passing the academic course work has the interpersonal and emotional strengths necessary to function effectively as a mental health professional. Not until the supervised practice phase of training begins do personality style, character issues, temperament, and personal psychopathology come into full consideration in trainee evaluations. Even then, this becomes a difficult ethical dilemma, requiring well-documented evidence of both the trainee's deficiencies and efforts of appropriate intervention or remediation. Only when sensitive attempts to resolve the problems have failed, when no biases or unfair discrimination exist, and when institutional policies regarding termination from the program have been scrupulously followed should the trainee be dismissed.

In a survey of graduate students, almost all (95%) reported awareness of peers with impairments in professional functioning, and half knew of ethical improprieties by their peers (Mearns & Allen, 1991). Next is one example.

Case 13–39: Several trainees in Tim Quicktrip's group were unimpressed when Tim confessed to them that he cut client sessions 15 minutes shorter than what appeared in his reports, and that when a clients did not attend, he created therapy notes as if they had.

Trainees whose ethical and professional slips may create an ongoing pattern, especially if they are reinforced in some way, need the earliest possible intervention. Tim Quicktrip's "reward" was more discretionary time. This is the time when socialization into a profession occurs, and if it is not successful, the profession and the public may suffer in the longer term.

Supervision Models

To help diffuse some of the inherent role entanglements and abuses in supervision, models other than "one on one" have been proposed. These include group supervision, vertical supervision, and the use of multiple supervisors (Minnes, 1987). A concern, however, is that a diffusion in responsibility may also occur if trainees are fanned out among several sources of supervision. Vertical- and multiple-supervision models may also be too burdensome on the resources in many settings.

Group supervision may lessen the resource drain and provide opportunities to hear diverse views. However, a reduction of individual attention may also result. Supervisees may be less willing to disclose their difficulties or perceived errors in the presence of their peers, and intragroup conflicts could hinder the supervisory process (Enyedy et al., 2003). Some combination of models, however, may help mitigate the deficiencies and risks inherent in the one-on-one model of supervision.

Technological advances offer the potential for online supervision via chat rooms, e-mail, and videoconferencing. A distinct advantage is that distance no longer stands as a barrier, allowing coverage of certain kinds of issues and cases where no local expert or sufficient supervisory services exist. Potential licensure issues can complicate matters (e.g., the supervisor may not hold a license in the state where the patient or trainee sits), and the considerable advantages of personal, face-to-face interaction between supervisors and supervisees are missing (Kanz, 2001).

Clear understandings of the contract between supervisees and supervisors regarding the nature of their relationship, mutual expectations, frequency of contact, feedback format and intervals, and other contingencies, including legal ones, remain essential regardless of the supervision model adopted (Sutter, McPherson, & Geeseman, 2002). While these arrangements need not take the form of formal written contracts, they should be explicit and thoughtfully articulated. Such arrangements not only obligate the supervisor, but also are much desired by supervisees (Nelson, 1978;

Scofield & Scofield, 1978). We wholeheartedly agree with Sherry's (1991) conclusion that, because supervision has elements similar to therapy and requires multiple roles of its participants, it should be conceived as an intervention highly vulnerable to ethical infractions.

Research Supervision

Some research experience is critical if graduate students are to become competitive applicants for employment in many settings. Graduate students in institutions where faculty do research usually have the opportunity to become involved with their educators' work, often as a paid assistant. Even research experience as an undergraduate is highly desirable for applicants for advanced training in many kinds of programs, including most traditional clinical psychology programs (Keith-Spiegel, 1991).

Students and their research supervisors are locked into a symbiotic relationship. Each must depend on the other, and the stakes are high. Researchers not only need help with various facets of their projects but also appreciate having others around with whom they can talk about their work. After all, their students may constitute the primary source of interest in the investigator's work. Students need the experience as well as the financial assistance that often attends these positions. When a project goes well, everyone is advantaged. If one or the other falls down on agreed-on responsibilities or engages in some form of scientific misconduct, everybody loses, including the scientific community should any ill-generated data seep into the research record.

In some ways, supervising research can feel less engrossing than supervising therapy because the conduct of research often does not typically involve discussions of feelings or personal disclosures. However, with the focus on the competence, integrity, and mutual trust, ethical problems can easily arise. These include abandonment, unfair authorship practices, incompetent and inadequate supervision, inappropriate boundary blurring, and abusive or unfair behavior on the part of supervisors (Goodyear, Crego, & Johnston, 1992; Johnson & Nelson, 1999; Sullivan & Ogloff, 1998).

Case 13–40: Simi Gradbound enthusiastically agreed to collaborate on a research project with Professor Desert because she needed to list research experience on her résumé. Dr. Desert also indicated that they could present the paper at a regional professional meeting, which would prove even more helpful to her. Gradbound collected and analyzed the data and turned the material over to Dr. Desert, who, by prior agreement, would draft a manuscript. In the meantime, Dr. Desert received a large grant and was elected chair of the university personnel committee. Each time Gradbound would drop by to ask how things were going, Desert would apologize profusely and promise to get around to the project as soon as he could. The deadline for the regional meeting passed, and Gradbound graduated without any further work completed on the project.

Gradbound is perhaps a too common type of victim of a mentor's busy schedule. Suffering neglect by one's mentor is one of the most frequently cited sources of student discontent (Johnson & Huwe, 2002). The project was obviously of low priority on Desert's list, but to Gradbound it was of primary significance. Gradbound rightly feels abandoned and may blame Desert for any difficulties she experienced in gaining admission to a graduate program. Desert should not have taken Gradbound on as a supervisee unless he felt relatively confident of his ability to keep his word. Even after becoming aware of the complications in his own schedule, he should have followed through anyway or at least facilitated the completion of the project in some other way.

Case 13–41: Professor Frawd encouraged his research supervisee, Lionel Twist, to eliminate any outlier cases because they would elevate the error term. "If we don't get a significant finding, we won't be able to publish this article. Extremes don't tell us much about the phenomenon anyway. And besides, everybody does it."

Mr. Twist finds himself in a terrible position and may be professionally corrupted. Frawd's attempt to rationalize away misconduct may well persuade an admiring supervisee who also needs a publication to advance his own future in a similar manner. Mentors are often drawn to protégés who remind them of themselves and who they can groom to pursue a career very much like their own (Johnson, 2003). However, some research mentors may have more interest in creating clones of themselves than in fulfilling their professional obligation to help students find their own scholarly voice. (See Chapters 16 and 19 for more information about collaborative relationships with students and scientific misconduct.)

Employee Supervision

Mental health professionals have responsibilities for training and monitoring the behavior of their employees with respect to any duties delegated to them. Employees who handle grade books, confidential records, data sets, or billing, for example, must understand the ethical requirements that attend their duties and behave in a trustworthy manner. Often, they must also be prepared to deal with other situations that might not arise in more traditional work settings.

Case 13–42: An anonymous caller to a marriage and family counselors' office reached the bookkeeper, explaining that she feels afraid that she is about to abuse her child. The caller refused to give her name but wanted to talk to someone. The therapist was not available.

If the anonymous caller does not get some professional help, a tragedy could result. Therapists should prepare all their office staff to refer such callers to the local child abuse hotline (if one exists) or to another agency or hospital emergency room at which trained personnel might be available. In some work settings, or for some therapists specializing in crisis management, crisis hotline training for the nonprofessional staff may be indicated.

Case 13–43: After beginning work as an administrative assistant to a group of therapists, a young man discovered that several of his acquaintances from the same small town are clients of therapists in the group. His work routinely involved typing reports and billing people he knows personally.

While it is possible to respect the privacy and confidences of personal acquaintances in many situations, employers should assess the ability and sensitivity of all potential staff members prior to hiring. This becomes especially important in communities where social circles will likely overlap, such as university towns, distinct cultural communities, or rural settings. The new assistant may have the capability to adequately handle the situation, but the counselors hiring him hold ultimate responsibility for his behavior and should take special precautions to protect clients' privacy. For example, safeguards might include placing sensitive files in secure locations unavailable to the staff.

Both situations demonstrate the care and training that must go into the selection and hiring of employees. We have chosen two examples typical of mental health practices. They hold equally well for academic, research, or business settings in terms of the needs to safeguard confidential materials and to deal with others appropriately.

There are times when it may simply be inappropriate for mental health professionals to delegate clerical or other nonpsychological tasks to others, as the next case illustrates.

Case 13–44: Teeneyville is in turmoil. Allegations of raids on the city treasury by several top officials have created headlines in the town's newspaper for weeks. The mayor's wife has entered counseling with Dr. Sanctuary because, she alleges, her husband has taken to drinking and has made threats to kill himself. He has refused therapy, but his wife calls frequently, asking to speak to Dr. Sanctuary immediately.

This explosive small-town crisis requires taking special measures regarding how messages from this particular party are received, who transcribes the records, and who has access to these sensitive materials. Similar situations can arise for any high-profile clients and their families.

Letters of Reference

Practitioners and educators are often called on to write letters evaluating the qualifications of colleagues, supervisees, students, and employees. Such letters have a very influential role in the applicant selection process, giving the letter writer considerable power over the future of those about whom they agree to write (Purdy, Reinehr, & Swartz, 1989; Templer & Thacker, 1988; Williams, 2004). On the other hand, serving as a referee—especially if any negative commentary will be offered—has become increasingly risky (Taylor, Pajo, Cheung, & Stringfield, 2004; Weiss, 2004). Referees might even have to defend themselves from charges of defamation or negligence for what they had considered an innocuous remark (Peshiera, 2003). Complicating matters further, the recipient may consider suing the referee if a significant shortcoming known to the referee remained unmentioned and led to damages perpetrated by the hire at the new job site.

Letter writers feel squeezed in the middle of a multidimensional dilemma. Students and employees expect a positive letter that will assist in fulfilling their goals, whereas graduate schools and employers want an honest appraisal of the effectiveness of individuals, enabling them to make an informed decision. Applicants expect to know what is said about them, whereas graduate school program staff and employers believe that confidential letters will prove more candid and valid. Finally, applicants will feel upset if the outcome is unfavorable, and the recipients will be upset if they accept an applicant who does not live up to what is described in the contents of the letter (Williams, 2004).

Letter Content

An ethically appropriate letter states verifiable facts, positive or negative, that have relevance to the position the applicant seeks. Writing a factual letter will also constitute the best protection against liability from an unhappy applicant or recipient. An ethically accurate—and legally safer—letter should not be motivated by malice or retaliation (Taylor et al., 2004).

Legal cases have confirmed that a reference must not leave a misleading impression, although it does not always have to contain full and comprehensive data (Couzins, 2004). The most credible letters contain specific performance and other relevant examples as opposed to vague generalities (Templer & Thacker, 1988). The writer should also remain aware of the biases that could affect how a letter is received. For example, those with positive dispositions write more positive letters (Judge & Higgins, 1998), which could perhaps unfairly favor some applicants. When writing letters of reference, one ought to assume that the person about whom it is written will eventually view or learn the contents. Services are now available to those seeking new employment that will call ex-employers and pose as a prospective employer to learn how the ex-employer is evaluating them (Taylor et al., 2004). Some letters arrive accompanied by a confidentiality waiver, but the writer can never be assured of this after dropping the letter in the mail.

Research on the reference letter process has revealed some odd circumstances that work against referees who want to provide complete candor. Unless a referee views the candidate in a highly positive light, truthfulness carries the risk that the candidate will face a summary rejection (Keith-Spiegel, 1991). Studies have demonstrated that a negative comment, even if couched in a letter predominantly positive in tone, will likely to result in the candidate's rejection. Why? Because most letters are completely positive, creating a sort of "letter inflation" (Hardin, Craddick, & Ellis, 1991; Miller & Van Rybroek, 1988; Siskind, 1966). Therefore, it seems probable that a less-than-enthusiastic letter damns the candidate by dint of faint praise, and a minor criticism stands out like a glazed ham at a Bar Mitzvah party.

Obviously, one should always approach those from whom a reference is being sought prior to using their names. Asking whether the potential referees feel they could write a helpful letter of reference in relation to a given position is a fair question. If the reaction hints at hesitancy or reluctance on the part of a potential referee, the option of asking someone else remains open and probably should be taken.

Many referees have some reservations. How can one most reasonably present the negative material? Consider the following four letters:

Case 13–45: Professor Snuff wrote the following single-sentence letter regarding a student seeking graduate training: "Save yourself a headache and burn Ms. Bonk's application. This woman should not be allowed to breed."

Case 13–46: Dr. Slapdown's letter regarding Rose Clueless contained general references to problems, such as, "Ms. Clueless has shown disrespect toward me," and, "A colleague told me that he thinks she regularly smokes pot."

Case 13–47: Dr. Golightly wrote a generally positive letter but also described clear examples of Mike Breezebrain's absentmindedness and the trouble it caused other supervisees in the clinic. Once, for example, he misplaced the group appointment book and could not recall where he put it. It surfaced a day later on the bottom shelf of the coffee room refrigerator. Another time, Breezebrain did not show up for his morning appointments, thinking they were for the following day. Dr. Golightly concluded his letter with, "Mike is a nice guy, but he couldn't find his rear end with both hands and a full-length mirror."

Case 13–48: Dr. Fact carefully detailed a number of events that strongly suggested that Fred Firestarter probably had an antisocial personality disorder, although Fact never used an actual diagnostic term in the letter. Each entry stressed the applicant's behavior and was anchored in verifiable facts should such documentation ever become necessary. For example, Fact and others had witnessed Firestarter's verbal outbursts, and an administrative record existed of an investigation of improper use of university stationery to perpetrate a fraud.

These four letters form a hierarchy from totally unacceptable to an appropriate way of relaying negative evaluations in a reference letter. Dr. Snuff provides no basis for his terse and lethal assessments. Was Ms. Bonk truly without merit, or might Snuff be the one with a problem? The letter's recipients may never know, but Ms. Bonk will not likely survive such a paper bomb in her application file. It was unethical (and defamatory) for Snuff to write such a letter because it does not offer the evaluators any factual or interpretable information. An ex-employer who told a "job detective" that the ex-employee was only suited to work in a brothel or strip joint was sued for $82 million (Cadrain, 2004).

Dr. Slapdown's letter is almost as bad in that we do not know the basis of the disrespect or if the secondhand report about marijuana use is accurate. Nevertheless, Ms. Slapdown will likely be written off as a result of this letter. Dr. Golightly's letter was fine, grounding his concerns in behavioral examples, until the last sentence. Although perhaps intended as a cute wrap-up, he stated a probable untruth and violated professional decorum. Dr. Fact, however, acted correctly in presenting clear and supportable data, which allowed the recipients of the letter to reach their own decisions about Mr. Firestarter.

Generally, one never has an obligation to write a letter of recommendation (Couzins, 2004) and therein lies one way to avoid the liability of writing a negative letter. Concern about applicants who abuse alcohol or drugs, who have exhibited unethical behavior, who lack motivation, or who demonstrate irresponsibility comprise the major cluster of people for whom referees refuse to write letters (Grote, Robiner, & Haut, 2001).

Should one ever agree to write a letter without indicating to the requester that it will contain fault-finding content? This question leads us to the complex issue of loyalties. In Mebane's (1983) survey of professors in a position to recommend students to graduate clinical programs, approximately half of the sample expressed a primary allegiance to the student. The rest of the sample aligned with the graduate school enrolling the applicant, to the profession, and to society at large. These data suggest that perhaps as many as half of those who serve as referees believe that it is their duty to signal potential problems to the recipients of their letters, and that informing the applicant in advance is a matter of discretion. However, Grote and his colleagues found that negative characteristics (such as alcohol abuse and unethical behavior) were rarely described according to survey respondents who had recently read submitted letters. When negative characteristics were disclosed, they were more likely to be about inadequate interpersonal or academic skills (Grote et al., 2001).

Case 13–49: When Max Gluteus asked Selma Mire, Ed.D., to write a letter supporting his application to a counseling program, she felt torn. Gluteus had a fairly good record as a student but behaved unkindly to others, acted brashly, and seemed interested only in making money. He once announced in class that rich, crazy people would be his ticket to the good life. Mire felt an obligation to warn the graduate programs.

One can hope that students like Gluteus do not find their way into the helping professions, and the argument can be made that their educators have an obligation to help ensure that. Hardin et al. (1991) advised that a decision must be made regarding whether colleagues should be alerted or whether a more neutral letter will give the student a chance to continue training and possibly improve. Regardless of the referee's final decision, keep mindful that it is absolutely critical to keep unfavorable remarks well grounded in fact and concrete, observed, and verifiable behaviors as opposed to relating suspicions and innuendo. It appears that Dr. Mire would have sufficient corroboration should she clearly describe Bummer's bad attitude.

A glowing letter should never be used as a means to rid oneself or one's institution of an incompetent or corrupt employee or a difficult student. This is unfair to the hapless employer or graduate program selection committee who trusted in the veracity of the letter's content. The recipients of endorsed, but clearly unfit, candidates could have legal recourse if they act or perform in inappropriate ways clearly known in advance to the referral sources.

Case 13–50: Wally Weasel came highly recommended with a positive endorsement from a medical practice across town, so the partners at Zenith Psychotherapy Associates had no hesitation about hiring him as their office manager. Six months later, after their auditor discovered that Mr. Weasel had skimmed copayment money, they

fired him and notified the local police. Only then did they learn that his previous employers had made a similar complaint but dropped the charges when Weasel made a restitution payment.

In one high-profile case, an employee was fired for bringing a gun to work. However, this incident was not mentioned in the employee's reference letter. The employee subsequently killed three supervisors at his new job, and the estates of the slain successfully sued the previous employer for fraud and misrepresentation (Cadrain, 2004). Finally, one should never word a statement cleverly so that the true meaning could not be discerned, as this unfairly misleads the recipient. For example, for a student or employee who rarely shows up for appointments, it would be grossly misleading to write, "It would be hard to find an applicant like this."

What if one receives a telephone call requesting an assessment of a student or colleague? Can one safely give a completely honest report over the telephone?

Case 13–51: Chuck Chum, Ph.D., called his old friend Bernie Pal, M.S.W., for a spontaneous assessment of one of Pal's colleagues, who has applied for a position in Chum's department. Pal gave a generally positive appraisal but also divulged some detail about the colleague's odd wife, slight limp, and funny-looking mustache.

Dr. Pal should have stuck to a job-related discussion despite the fact that he was talking to an old friend. Pal's colleague may have been unfairly disadvantaged by off-handed remarks that were totally unrelated to the purpose at hand. We also caution that it is unwise to say anything in private that might ultimately be repeated to the candidate unless one is willing to have the candidate learn about it. Finally, some have issued a warning against agreeing to refer anyone on the phone because one can not reconstruct the conversation should it ever be challenged. Others note, however, that an unrecorded phone conversation would make defamation more difficult to substantiate. Finally, we note that for many higher-level jobs (e.g., recruiting a dean, provost, or college president), only oral evaluations are elicited. In addition, second- and third-level contacts are made. That is to say, the search firms ("headhunters") call the references named by the candidates, and when getting the oral reference statements, they also ask for the names of others who know the candidate.

Fulfilling the Commitment

An ethical abuse that occurs too commonly involves the agreed-on reference letter that never materializes. The referee who promised to supply a letter never gets around to doing it. Even the somewhat better intentioned referee who sends off a letter 2 weeks late may still ensure the candidate's rejection. Job, postdoctoral, or graduate school applicants may not discover such omissions until decisions have already been made, or they may never know that their bids were unsuccessful because their incomplete files were never reviewed. Keith-Spiegel (1991) surveyed doctoral program directors' secretaries, who reported that about 20% of reference letters, on the average, came in well after the deadline. It was not unusual for these candidates to remain unconsidered.

The unwritten or past due letter constitutes a particularly merciless act, even when that was not an intent. Whereas a dilatory referee may have been too busy to fulfill a pledge to support an applicant, the would-be recipients may interpret the silence as a lack of enthusiasm (or worse) for the candidate. An initial agreement to be supportive, then, becomes an act of betrayal instead. This is one reason some programs ask applicants to collect letters of reference in signed, sealed envelopes and mail all together with their application.

Sexual and Gender Harassment

Not so very long ago Western society expected women to passively endure uninvited expressions of sexual interest and suggestive remarks made by the men who occupied positions of power in the workplace. Recipients who took poorly to such remarks or behavior risked sanctions that ranged from ostracism to dismissal. Early complaints under Title VII of the Civil Rights Act of 1964, which prohibited employment discrimination on the basis of sex, were often dismissed simply as inharmonious relationships between the sexes, an unfortunate social experience, or a mere consequence of attraction between the sexes (Koen, 1989).

Current law protects both men and women from a sexually harassing workplace environment, and the victim does not have to be of the opposite sex. However, 85% of all incidents reported come from women (Equal Employment Opportunity Commission, 2004). As women increasingly achieve positions of authority, however, they are also finding that their own behavior may make them vulnerable to charges of harassment. Still, most incidents of sexual harassment probably go unreported (Rubin & Borgers, 1990), perhaps partially due to the grievance procedure itself (Riger, 1991). Sexual harassment places recipients in a potential no-win situation by forcing them to keep quiet or enter into an arduous process that could end up costing them their jobs and reputation. Management tends to deny or minimize the events through denial ("It didn't happen"), minimization ("It wasn't intentional," or "She misunderstood"), or blaming the victim ("She came on to me"). Nevertheless, as legal sanctions and grievance procedures become more formalized and available, they are increasingly being used.

Definitions

Clearly agreed-on specifications of what constitutes sexual or gender harassment and the tipping point at which harm becomes inflicted are difficult to specify. Except for the more extreme vituperations or lewd acts, perspectives on behaviors vary depending on the motivations of the perpetrator, the interpretation of the recipient, the nature of the relationship between the parties involved, and the context in which the incident occurred.

Men and women have substantially different attitudes toward the acceptability of sexually oriented behavior (Rubin & Borgers, 1990), and men seem more tolerant of behavior seen as harassing (Kearney, Rochlen, & King, 2004; Reilly, Lott, & Gallogly, 1986). Some forms of sexual harassment may have an ostensibly benevolent intent, taking protective and affectionate actions toward those who hold to traditional women's roles. Others arise from hostility, to dominate and to show antipathy toward women who appear to usurp men's power (Glick & Fiske, 1997). Even the attractiveness of the perpetrators and victims may constitute a complicating factor in judging harassment (Wuensch & Moore, 2004). Most acts of sexual harassment take place in private, so credibility becomes an additional murky factor (Binder, 1992; Feldman-Schorrig & McDonald, 1992). Exceptionally vulnerable or damaged victims may come across as hysterical and unreliable, and smooth perpetrators may be convincing.

In 1980, the Equal Employment Opportunity Commission (EEOC) defined sexual harassment and issued guidelines for employers. Sexual harassment consisted of the following:

- unwelcome sexual advances
- requests for sexual favors and other verbal or physical conduct of a sexual nature that force submission as an explicit or implicit condition of employment or academic standing
- statements or conduct that interfere with an individual's work or academic performance and create an intimidating, hostile, or offensive work or learning environment

The plaintiff does not have the burden of proving tangible economic detriment. However, the plaintiff must demonstrate that the harassment was sufficiently severe or pervasive to create an abusive working environment. Cases have also applied and defined the "reasonable woman standard" as a way of attempting to determine a representative woman's response to assist the court in deciding whether a claim is frivolous or trivial (Thacker & Gohmann, 1993). This standard shields employers from having to accommodate the idiosyncratic concerns of the hypersensitive woman (Feldman-Schorrig & McDonald, 1992). The reasonable woman standard also provides a means of precluding any trauma that could be caused by a thorough psychological examination of a plaintiff to determine the merits of her allegations (Thacker & Gohmann, 1993). Other changes in federal and state laws allow victims to receive compensatory and punitive damages for substantiated claims of sexual harassment.

The Supreme Court, in its first sexual harassment case (*Meritor Savings Bank v. Vinson*, 1986), ruled that an offensive, hostile environment constitutes illegal sexual harassment as long as it is sufficiently severe and pervasive and causes an abusive working environment because it was unwelcome (Binder, 1992). *Vinson* specified two types of sexual harassment, both of which can also be found in the EEOC definitions (1980a, 1980b): *quid pro quo* (explicit or implicit trades of sexual favors, either in exchange for some job benefit such as a promotion or raise or as a way of preventing some job detriment such as demotion or termination) and *hostile working environment*. The current APA code reflects the EEOC definition and reasonable woman standards (APA 02: 3.02, 3.03). The victim is usually subordinate to the accused, which means that reporting can be risky (Bergman, Langhout, Palmiere, Cortina, & Fitzgerald, 2002). The APA code specifies that anyone found to penalize those coming forward with an ethics complaint has also committed an ethics violation (APA 02: 1.08)

Sexual and Gender Harassment on the Job and in the Classroom

The first set of cases illustrates the pervasive hostile environment. (Sexually intimate behavior with psychotherapy clients, students, and trainees was discussed in detail in Chapter 12.)

Case 13–52: Professor Jerry Built, Ph.D., often told his technical equipment supervisee, Dyna Graph, that he would dole out the supplies issued as a vital part of her work responsibilities only if she were "nice to him." When the supplies were not forthcoming, he would say that they would be made available when she treated him better. According to Ms. Graph, "being nice" meant complimenting Dr. Built on his appearance and being flirtatious. She resented feeling forced to perform in this manner as a prerequisite to performing her job.

Case 13–53: Sherman Tactile, Ph.D., habitually rested his hand on his clinical supervisee's lower back for a prolonged period of time. When she tried to turn her body or stand farther away,

Dr. Tactile would either alter his position so that he could resume his touching or would say, "Come back here so I can explain this to you," or "Why are you such a distant and unfriendly person? Cold people don't make good therapists." The supervisee complained to Tactile's superior after completing her traineeship.

Case 13–54: Dexter Swinish, D.S.W., was known for making suggestive remarks to his female supervisees. When he approached Sandra Firm with, "Want to get it on this weekend?," Ms. Firm replied, "Go sit on your thumb." Swinish reportedly avoided her after that and, at the end of the term, entered unflattering and undocumented criticisms into her evaluation file.

These cases illustrate how demands for sexual favors, and reprisals for rejecting them, can interfere with job and academic status. The ongoing behavior of all three supervisors described above violates both ethical standards and the law.

The next case is loosely adapted and, believe it or not, very much toned down from an actual series of bizarre incidents (Wilson, 1995). This case shows how an entire working unit can be ripped apart by an instigating incident that was apparently intended just for laughs.

Case 13–55: Professor Crude circulated a memo in his department suggesting that extra office space be outfitted to accommodate innovative student–professor conferences. His suggested furnishings included a water bed and an inflatable Madonna doll. The memo also stated that such a room would be especially useful when a student is unhappy with her grade. Although the memo's author claimed it was obviously a joke, other professors objected and complained to Professor Anita Affront, the university appointee to handle sexual harassment cases. Finding the memo offensive, Affront issued a letter to the faculty stating that Crude's memo was vulgar and violated sexual harassment laws. Crude wrote and distributed a letter stating that whereas Affront used to be a "fat, funny, nobody," she was now a "nasty bitch." Affront has sued Crude.

Intimidations can also occur in a more diffuse manner than those presented thus far, as illustrated by the next case. *Gender harassment* is defined as comments or behavior directed at one sex but not the other (Fuller, 1979).

Case 13–56: Professor Tim Traditional, Ph.D., announced to his classes that he is admittedly "old school who likes to flirt with the ladies." He then noted that if anyone found his small pleasure a burden, they had better just put up with it or drop his course because he was "unwilling to keep up with this feminist nonsense."

Here, women students were placed in a separate category and put on notice. The net effect was to categorize them as potential targets and to deliver the message that they were unworthy of the contemporary mores that favor equality and respect between the sexes. Dr. Traditional's stance contains the elements of gender harassment (covered under APA 02: 3.03) that need not involve direct references to sexuality.

Not all gender-related behavior can be reasonably defined as harassing, but it does result when the behavior causes discomfort or humiliation (e.g., referring to all men as "stud muffins" or "beefcakes") or is used as a means of power containment (e.g., only inviting male students to collaborate on research projects). To those who would declare that Dr. Traditional's behavior is simply the residua of an earlier generation and therefore quite harmless, we would ask the following questions: If a woman asked Dr. Traditional to write a letter of recommendation, how powerful do you think it would be? Or, do you think Traditional would nominate a woman for an outstanding student award?

Below are two cases that illustrate other variations of gender harassment.

Case 13–57: When Zena Freeman asked Macho Mann, Ph.D., for assistance with problems she was having understanding certain concepts in her organizational psychology class, he commented that women did not belong in the course because they were not suited to the field. He refused to respond to her specific questions. Instead, he continued to refer to the general unsuitability of women for work in the business world and cited her difficulties in comprehension as evidence.

Case 13–58: Flora Bloom complained that Wag Rogue, Ph.D., made jokes at her expense during class. She alleged that he would tease her about such things as her colorful clothing, black fingernail polish, close-cropped hair, and oversize purse. Professor Rogue was surprised by her formal complaint. He thought her customary shy, giggling responses were indications that she enjoyed his "gentle chiding."

These two cases do not involve direct sexual references or touching, but the effect was to keep the women in a subordinate position through exclusion or ridicule. The women's work or academic experiences became uncomfortable for them, which in turn had implications for their ability to perform their primary roles as students. Gender-biased remarks used to be commonplace and passively endured by women. But times have drastically changed, as Larry Summers, a past president of Harvard University, learned the hard way when his comment that innate differences between the sexes might help explain why relatively few women become scientists or engineers was made public and set off an international furor (Tolson, 2005).

The next two cases illustrate how important it is for people to maintain an ethical sensitivity to professional interactions in the workplace regardless of how one defines and interprets sexual or gender harassment. The first incident came to our attention from a middle-aged supervisor, who concluded ultimately that her trainee must be gay, never recognizing that her own behavior might well be unwelcome to any young man.

Case 13–59: Thelma Flitty, Ph.D., was very fond of her supervisee, Jack Frost. She always gave him a big hug when he arrived for supervisory sessions, winked at him when he made funny comments, took his hand when he seemed unsure of his therapy decisions, and hugged him again when he left. "You are cute as a button," she told him, "I could just eat you up!" Dr. Flitty was taken aback when, during one of their sessions, Jack said, "I feel very uncomfortable with the way you behave toward me."

It is difficult to tell whether Dr. Flitty was interested in Mr. Frost sexually or acting like a doting mother. Either way, Flitty did treat him differently from her other supervisees, and she remained oblivious about how she came across, as evidenced by her reasoning that Jack had overreacted. Women are not used to being perceived of as bothersome when they are showing interest in a man. This response is similar to how men used to discount their own harassing behavior.

In a somewhat similar vein, the next case illustrates how behavior that might have been meant as a gesture of friendly familiarity could disadvantage the recipient.

Case 13–60: A slightly nervous Lina Luckout, Ph.D., was called into the executive board meeting of a large mental health organization to present her proposal for a high school drug awareness program. Jerome Foreclose, Ph.D., a man Luckout had met on several occasions, was in charge of the meeting. When she entered the room, Foreclose exclaimed, "Hi there, pretty little lady. Whatcha got for us today?" Dr. Luckout had prepared a very formal presentation and was rattled by the tone of the introduction. She stumbled often, and her bid to implement the program was denied.

Dr. Luckout was, perhaps unintentionally, infantilized before she had a chance to make her own first impression. We have no way of knowing for sure whether a more professionally respectful greeting might have altered the quality of Luckout's presentation, the way she was perceived, or the outcome of her proposal. Because the incident involved the use of a fleeting term of endearment, it would not come close to meeting any legal definition of sexual harassment. Because of the "severe and pervasive" criteria, an even more offensive single incident than this one would not qualify (Perry, 1993). But, first impressions count, and the board probably did not get an initial perception of Dr. Luckout as a mature professional.

Finally, although rarely discussed as such, we note that sexual harassment can occur in psychotherapy sessions. Its expression often has an interface with competency deficiency or, as the next case illustrates, lack of impulse control on the part of the therapist.

Case 13–61: Sheldon Blurt, Ph.D., had met with Mr. and Mrs. Wobble for several sessions of marital therapy. Increasingly frustrated by what he regarded as an alternating pattern of seductive and aversive behavior by Mrs. Wobble toward her spouse, Dr. Blurt bellowed, during a joint session, "Well, aren't you a world class cockteaser."

Therapists must often respond to what they are witnessing on the spot, which puts them at some risk of crossing over a line. Sarcasm and hostility should be avoided. Hurtful comments do not help clients, even if such comments might be well deserved under a different set of relationship circumstances.

DEALING WITH RISKY INDIVIDUALS

We conclude this chapter with a focus on the student, employee, or colleague whose behaviors or interpersonal styles are troublesome, although not necessarily in violation of specific ethical standards. By recognizing and dealing with hazardous individuals, particularly as they may have an interface with risky situations, ethical problems can often be avoided. (The troublesome client is discussed in Chapter 5 as a special problem. Ideas for confronting colleagues who may have committed an ethical infraction are presented in Chapter 2.)

Some people are worrisome or hard to get along with simply by virtue of their personalities. Such people, however, may be perfectly happy with themselves, making conflict resolution especially difficult. Individuals who are emotionally labile or unstable certainly present some risk. Arrogance, narcissism, or critical personality styles also contribute to such problems. We could create a long list of unwholesome personality traits—procrastination, impulsivity, hostility, and so on—but the point is clear. Given the basics of human nature, every risky situation often includes one or more difficult individuals.

Case 13–62: Bernice Dweezel, Ph.D., is a distinguished psychologist whose research is world renowned. Unfortunately, she is also rude, egotistical, and demanding. Students willing to endure criticism and pontification often benefit from working with her, but not everyone can tolerate her presence. The faculty respects her scholarly work and appreciates the way her professional reputation enhances the status of their department, although few would choose to socialize with her.

Dr. Dweezel may be an obnoxious individual by many standards and may border on behaving unethically when inconsiderate to her students and colleagues. Unfortunately, she may have little insight into the nature of how she is perceived and have no motivation to attempt to alter how she comes across to others. In any event, an ethics complaint would not likely evoke a positive change given her ingrained characterological attributes. The more serious danger will occur if or when Dr. Dweezel encounters a hostile student or colleague more inclined to act out than back off. One might caution others about the hazards of working with her or suggest avoiding her entirely. Anyone whose opinion Dr. Dweezel admires might attempt some collegial consultation, with gentle references to a need for personal change. Regrettably, however, there will always be "Dr. Dweezels" in the environment, and ethics codes and committees are of little help in dealing with them.

Rules and due process procedures, known to all and applied consistently and without bias (creating what is called *procedural justice*), comprise the most powerful tools available to deal with the difficult associate in a risky situation. Having an explicit set of guidelines and standards can provide a giant step toward avoiding conflict and reducing stress for all concerned. The use of formal procedures not only enhances communication, but also cools passions by drawing out a decision in a deliberate fashion (Clark, 1974).

While one can not restructure personality to suit circumstances, it is possible to minimize risk in a volatile situation by imposing structure and enhancing communication. Evaluations, for example, should always be presented thoughtfully and emphatically, with the evaluator listening as well as informing. At the same time, it is often advisable to offer the same evaluative material in writing because oral communications may be forgotten or tempered by intervening variables.

These suggestions may seem contrary to the concept of attempting to resolve disputes informally by mutual agreement. Indeed, an informal mechanism is always preferable when a situation is well suited to it; however, if communication is already complicated or difficult or one or more of the players is problematic, a more formal approach may be required. The irony is that the ethics complaints that result from such circumstances are rarely true ethics matters.

Case 13–63: William Cheapo, M.D., Frank Fussy, M.S.W., and Mildred Decibel, Ph.D., worked together in a group practice arrangement. They shared the cost of office space, utilities, and a receptionist's salary. As time went on, it became clear that each engaged in behavior that annoyed the other two. Dr. Cheapo demanded that he should pay less because he used fewer utilities and little receptionist time. Mr. Fussy complained about everything that seemed out of place, such as leaving a dirty cup in the coffee room sink. Dr. Decibel played her office radio so loudly that it could be heard throughout the whole complex, and efforts to tone down the noise resulted in only temporary compliance.

How can three highly educated individuals get themselves into such a predicament? They thought of themselves as compatible, so they never considered drafting contractual contingencies for handling disputes. Each has a strong will, and now they are threatening each other with ethics charges and legal action. This sort of problem happens frequently enough for us to suggest that any business arrangement among colleagues should include formal contracts—a professional prenuptial agreement, if you will—that deal with both operational contingencies and details of dispute resolution (e.g., an agreement to use binding arbitration). Even if all parties have had close friendships for years,

sufficient informal evidence reveals the wisdom of planning for untoward future developments.

When the difficult associate is a superior or supervisor rather than a peer or subordinate, similar fundamental principles apply in terms of the ideal course of action. Unfortunately, management tends to support itself without a full examination of the issues. Raising an objection, however valid, may be regarded as "rocking the boat" or exhibiting disloyalty. Formal written grievance procedures can be helpful, if they exist; however, one must be sensitive to the potential hazards. Less powerful colleagues in an organizational work setting are advised to scout out difficult associates in advance and chart their courses accordingly. If they are snared into a confrontation, they may seek alliances with more powerful colleagues known for their willingness to take a moral stand.

In conclusion, mental health professionals, educators, and researchers are just as human as any other group of people, and ethics complaints can not serve as a means to overhaul irritable personalities, reform the prejudiced, or enforce social agreements between consenting adult colleagues. Still, it behooves us to tolerate our colleagues with as much professionalism as can be mustered.

SUMMARY GUIDELINES

1. Colleagues should always do their best to cooperate with other professionals when the best interests of clients, supervisees, or students are at stake.
2. Although the ultimate choice of with whom to seek therapy or advice belongs to the client, services should not be provided in a manner that causes confusion or conflicts with a client's preexisting or ongoing relationships with other professionals.
3. A display of courtesy while relating to other professionals is usually the most appropriate demeanor, even when one has reason to be annoyed with them. In those instances when professional disagreements require a candid airing, the forum should be an appropriate one, and the goal should be focused on upholding professional in-

tegrity rather than on getting even. Displays of personal animosity should be kept away from the professional arena.

4. Colleagues should try to resolve disputes informally whenever possible and appropriate and should attempt to prevent disputes by clarifying mutual expectations at the outset of any collaborative arrangement.

5. Supervisees, employees, and students are at an inherent disadvantage in any disagreement or conflict with their educators, supervisors, and employers, respectively. This fact should be recognized with respect to the obligation to treat these individuals with courtesy, fairness, and dignity.

6. Therapists should exercise caution and diligence in training and monitoring the behavior of employees and supervisees to ensure their conformity with ethical practice.

7. When preparing letters of reference, it is wise to be honest and direct, grounding evaluations in behavioral indicators and objective, verifiable evidence rather than opinion and innuendo. The sort of letter one can write in good conscience should, in most cases, also be discussed in advance with the candidate.

8. Both male and female mental health professionals must familiarize themselves with the subtle and more obvious forms of sexual and gender harassment and avoid engaging in such acts.

9. When placed in a decision-making role with respect to a supervisee, colleague, or student (e.g., regarding grades, promotion, or tenure), mental health professionals should recognize the stress on these individuals and afford appropriate consideration and due process.

10. In dealing with an especially difficult or troubling student, employee, or colleague, it is generally best to use formal rules and procedures while attempting to avoid being caught up in an angry emotional response.

References

Allen, G. J., Szollos, S. J., & Williams, B. E. (1986). Doctoral students' comparative evaluations of best and worst psychotherapy supervision. *Professional Psychology, 17*, 91–99.

Alonzo, A. (1985). *The quiet profession: Supervisors of psychotherapy.* New York: Macmillan.

Bergman, M. E., Langhout, R. D., Palmieri, P. A., Cortina, L. M., & Fitzgerald, L. F. (2002). The (un)reasonableness of reporting: Antecedents and consequences of reporting sexual harassment. *Journal of Applied Psychology, 87*, 230–242.

Binder, R. L. (1992). Sexual harassment: Issues for forensic psychiatrists. *Bulletin of the Academy of Psychiatry Law, 20*, 409–418.

Bornstein, R. F. (1990). Manuscript review in psychology: An alternative model. *American Psychologist, 46*, 672–673.

Bosk, C. L. (1979). *Forgive and remember.* Chicago: University of Chicago Press.

Branscum, D. (1995, May). Cyberspace lawsuits. *MacWorld*, 149–150.

Burian, B. K., & Slimp, A. O. (2000). Social dual-role relationships during internship: A decision-making model. *Professional Psychology, 31*, 332–338.

Cadrain, D. (2004). Job detectives dig deep for defamation. *HR News, 49*, 34, 36.

Cheston, S. E. (1991). *Making effective referrals: The therapeutic process.* New York: Gardner Press.

Civil Rights Act of 1964. Title VII, 42 U.S.C. 2000e-2(a) (1982).

Clark, R. D. (1974). Tenure and the moderation of conflict. In R. H. Peairs (Ed.), *Avoiding conflict in faculty personnel practices* (pp. 17–40). San Francisco: Jossey-Bass.

Couzins, M. (2004, October 26). Legal Q & A employee references. *Personnel Today*, 19.

Douglas, R. J. (1992). How to write a highly cited article without even trying. *Psychological Bulletin, 112*, 405–408.

Enyedy, K. C., Arcinue, A., Puri, N. N., Carter, J., Goodyear, R., & Getzelman, M. A. (2003). Hindering phenomena in group supervision: Implications for practice. *Professional Psychology, 34*, 312–317.

Epstein, S. (1995). What can be done to improve the journal review process? *American Psychologist, 50*, 883–885.

Equal Employment Opportunity Commission. (1980a). Guidelines and discrimination because of sex (Sec. 1604.11). *Federal Register, 45*, 74676–74677.

Equal Employment Opportunity Commission. (1980b). Sex discrimination harassment. *Federal Register, 45*, 25024–25025.

Equal Employment Opportunity Commission. (2004). Retrieved May 16, 2006, from http://www.eeoc.gov/stats/harass.html

Feldman-Schorrig, S. P., & McDonald, J. J. (1992). The role of forensic psychiatry in the defense of sexual harassment cases. *Journal of Psychology and the Law, 20*, 5–33.

Finke, R. A. (1990). Recommendations for contemporary editorial practices. *American Psychologist, 45*, 669–670.

Franzini, L. R. (1987). Editors are not blind. *American Psychologist, 42*, 104.

Fuller, M. M. (1979). *Sexual harassment—how to recognize and deal with it.* Annapolis, MD: Eastport Litho.

Glaser, R. D., & Thorpe, J. S. (1986). Unethical intimacy: A survey of sexual contact and advances between psychology educators and female graduate students. *American Psychologist, 41*, 43–51.

Glick, P., & Fiske, S. T. (1997). Hostile and benevolent sexism: Measuring ambivalent sexist attitudes toward women. *Psychology of Women Quarterly, 21*, 119–135.

Goodyear, R. K., Crego, C. A., & Johnston, M. W. (1992). Ethical issues in the supervision of students' research: A study of critical incidents. *Professional Psychology, 23*, 203–210.

Grote, C. L., Robiner, W. M., & Haut, A. (2001). Disclosure of negative information in letters of recommendation: Writers' intentions and readers' experiences. *Professional Psychology, 32*, 655–661.

Hadjistavropoulos, T., & Beiling, P. J. (2000). When reviews attack: Ethics, free speech, and the peer review process. *Canadian Psychology, 41*, 152–159.

Hardin, K. N., Craddick, R., & Ellis, J. B. (1991). Letters of recommendation: Perspectives, recommendations, and ethics. *Professional Psychology, 22*, 389–392.

Harrar, W. R., VandeCreek, L., & Knapp, S. (1990). Ethical and legal aspects of clinical supervision. *Professional Psychology, 21*, 37–41.

Hartley, J. (1987). A code of practice for refereeing journal articles. *American Psychologist, 42*, 959.

Jacobs, C. (1991). Violations of the supervisory relationship: An ethical and educational blind spot. *Social Work, 36*, 130–135.

Johnson, W. B. (2003). A framework for conceptualizing competence to mentor. Ethics & Behavior, *13*, 127–151.

Johnson, W. B., & Huwe, J. M. (2002). Toward a typology of mentorship dysfunction in graduate school. *Psychotherapy, 39*, 44–55.

Johnson, W. B., & Nelson, N. (1999). Mentor-protégé relationships in graduate training: Some ethical concerns. *Ethics & Behavior, 9*, 189–210.

Judge, T., & Higgins, C. A. (1998). Affective disposition and the letter of reference. *Organizational Behavior & Human Decision Processes, 75*, 207–221.

Kanz, J. E. (2001). Clinical-supervision.com: Issues in the provisions of online supervision. *Professional Psychology, 32*, 415–420.

Keith-Spiegel, P. (1991). *The complete guide to graduate school admission.* Hillsdale, NJ: Erlbaum.

Kearney, L. K., Rochlen, A. B., & King, E. B. (2004). *Psychology of Men and Masculinity, 5*, 72–82.

Koen, C. M. (1989). Sexual harassment: Criteria for defining hostile environment. *Employee Responsibilities and Rights Journal, 2*, 289–301.

Koenig, T. L., & Spano, R. N. (2003). Sex, supervision, and boundary violations: Pressing challenges and possible solutions. *Clinical Supervisor, 22*, 1–19.

Kurpius, D., Gibson, G., Lewis, J., & Corbet, M. (1991). Ethical issues in supervising counseling practitioners. *Counselor Education and Supervision, 31*, 48–57.

Ladany, N., Lehrman-Waterman, Molinaro, M., & Wolgast, B. (1999). Psychotherapy supervisor ethical practices: Adherence to guidelines, the supervisory working alliance, and supervisee satisfaction. *Counseling Psychologist, 27*, 443–475.

Lamb, D. H., & Catanzaro, S. J. (1998). Sexual and nonsexual boundary violations involving psychologists, clients, supervisees, and students: Implications for professional practice. *Professional Psychology, 29*, 498–503.

Lamb, D. H., Catanzaro, S. J., & Moorman, A. S. (2004). A preliminary look at how psychologists identify, evaluate, and proceed when faced with possible multiple relationship dilemmas, *Professional Psychology, 35*, 248–254.

Leigh, A. (1998). *Referral and termination issues for counselors*. London, England: Sage.

McCarthy, P., Kulakowski, D., & Kenfield, J. A. (1994). Clinical supervision practices of licensed psychologists. *Professional Psychology, 25*, 177–181.

Mearns, J, & Allen, G. J. (1991). Graduate students' experiences in dealing with impaired peers, compared with faculty predictions. Ethics & Behavior, *1*, 191–202.

Mebane, D. L. (1983, April). *Ethical issues in writing recommendation letters*. Paper presented at the annual meeting of the Western Psychological Association, San Francisco.

Meritor Savings Bank, FSB v. Vinson et al., 477 U.S. 57 (1986).

Miller, R. K., & Van Rybroek, G. J. (1988). Internship letters of recommendation: Where are the other 90%? *Professional Psychology, 19*, 115–117.

Minnes, P. M. (1987). Ethical issues in supervision. *Canadian Psychology, 28*, 285–290.

Nelson, G. L. (1978). Psychotherapy supervision from the trainee's point of view: A survey of preferences. *Professional Psychology, 9*, 539–550.

Nilsson, J. E., & Anderson, M. Z. (2004). Supervising international students: The role of acculturation, role ambiguity, and multicultural discussions. *Professional Psychology, 35*, 306–312.

Perry, N. W. (1993). Sexual harassment on campus: Are your actions actionable? *Journal of College Student Development, 34*, 406–410.

Peshiera, R. (2003). References become a legal minefield. *Director, 56*, 40.

Peters, D. P., & Ceci, S. J. (1982). Peer review practices of psychological journals: The fate of published articles, submitted again. *The Behavioral and Brain Sciences, 5*, 187–195.

Pope, K. S., Levenson, H., & Schover, L. R. (1979). Sexual intimacy in psychology training: Results and implications of a national survey. *American Psychologist, 42*, 993–689.

Pope, K. S., & Vasquez, M. J. T. (1991). *Ethics in psychotherapy and counseling*. San Francisco: Jossey-Bass.

Pope, K. S., & Vetter, V. A. (1991). Prior therapist–patient sexual involvement among patients seen by psychologists. *Psychotherapy, 28*, 429–438.

Purdy, J. E., Reinehr, R. C., & Swartz, J. D. (1989). Graduate admissions criteria of leading psychol-

ogy departments. *American Psychologist, 44*, 960–961.

Ramos-Sanchez, L., Esnil, E., Riggs, S., Wright, L. K., Goodwin, A., Touster, L. O., et al., &. (2002). Negative supervisory events: Effects on supervision satisfaction and supervisory alliance. *Professional Psychology. 33*, 197–202.

Reilly, M. E., Lott, B., & Gallogly, S. M. (1986). Sexual harassment of university students. *Sex Roles, 15*, 333–358.

Riger, S. (1991). Gender dilemmas in sexual harassment: Policies and procedures. *American Psychologist, 46*, 497–505.

Rogers, R. (1992). Investigating psychology's taboo: The ethics of editing. *Ethics & Behavior, 2*, 253–261.

Rubin, L. J., & Borgers, S. B. (1990). Sexual harassment in universities during the 1980s. *Sex Roles, 23*, 397–411.

Scofield, M. E., & Scofield, B. J. (1978). Ethical concerns in clinical practice supervision. *Journal of Applied Rehabilitation Counseling, 9*, 27–29.

Shapiro, E. L., & Ginzberg, R, (2003). To accept or not to accept: Referrals and the maintenance of boundaries. *Professional Psychology, 34*, 258–263.

Sherry, P. (1991). Ethical issues in the conduct of supervision. *Counseling Psychologist, 19*, 566–584.

Siskind, G. (1966). Mine eyes have seen a host of angels. *American Psychologist, 21*, 804–806.

Sternberg, R. J. (2002). On civility in reviewing. *APS Observer, 15*, 3, 34.

Sternberg, R. J. (2003, July–August). To be civil. *Monitor on Psychology*, 5.

Sullivan, L. E., & Ogloff, J. R. P. (1998). Appropriate supervisor–graduate student relationships. *Ethics & Behavior, 8*, 229–248.

Sutter, E., McPherson, R. H., & Geeseman, R. (2002). Contracting for supervision. *Professional Psychology, 33*, 495–498.

Taylor, P, J., Pajo, K, Cheung, C. W., & Stringfield, P. (2004). Dimensionality and validity of a structured telephone reference check procedure. *Personnel Psychology, 57*, 745–772.

Templer, A. J., & Thacker, J. W. (1988). Credible letters of reference: How you read them is important. *Journal of Managerial Psychology, 3*, 22–26.

Thacker, R. A., & Gohmann, S. A. (1993). Male/female differences in perceptions and effects of hostile environment sexual harassment: "reasonable" assumptions? *Public Personnel Management, 22*, 461–472.

Third International Congress on Biomedical Peer Review and Global Communications. (1997). Retrieved May 17, 2006, from http://www.ama-assn.org/public/peer/session.htm

Tolson, J. (2005, March 7). Lessons: What colleges can learn from the Brouhaha at Harvard. *U.S. News & World Report*, pp. 31–36.

Vasquez, M. J. T. (1992). Psychologist as clinical supervisor: Promoting ethical practice. *Professional Psychology: Research and Practice, 23*, 196–202.

Walker, R., & Clark, J. J. (1999). Heading off boundary problems: Clinical supervision as risk management. *Psychiatric Services, 50*, 1435–1439.

Weiss, G. (2004). Should you give references? *Medical Economics, 81*, 46–50.

Whiston, S. C., & Emerson, S. (1989). Ethical implications for supervisors in counseling of trainees. *Counselor Education and Supervision, 28*, 318–325.

Williams, A. (2004, December) Opening Pandora's box: Appraising the tortuous liability of employers in respect to employment references. *Business Law Review*, 308–316.

Wilson, R. (1995, January 3). A fractured department. *Chronicle of Higher Education*, A, 15–16.

Wuensch, K. L., & Moore, C. H. (2004). Effects of physical attractiveness on evaluations of a male employee's allegation of sexual harassment by his female employer. *Journal of Social Psychology, 144*, 207–217.

14

Marketing Professional Services

Advertising may be described as the science of arresting the human intelligence long enough to get money from it.

Stephen Butler Leacock

Contents

How do you feel about these statements adapted from actual advertisements by mental health professionals?

- "Suffer no more from depression or low self-esteem. I am the one to help you. Call me now!"
- "I have discovered a new unique therapy technique to cure anxiety. No drugs. No hassle."
- "Dr. LeTrain is your one-stop station for improved mental health."
- "High-quality therapy for any emotional problem at rock bottom rates. Ask about our bring-a-friend two-for-one special."

The manner in which mental health professionals offer their services to the public has important ethical implications on a variety of fronts. Certainly, some forms of marketing or calling attention to one's services or products constitute appropriate ways to educate and inform potential consumers. However, some psychotherapists have occasionally used confusing, anxiety-provoking, or frankly deceptive practices in presenting themselves to the public. In addition, by their very nature mental health services do not easily lend themselves to comparison across vendors in the same manner as breakfast cereals, life insurance, or used cars. Almost by definition, some of our potential clients suffer from cognitive or emotional impairments and possibly financial disadvantage that may put them in more vulnerable positions than the average member of the consuming public.

Inappropriate commercial public statements by psychotherapists range from the factual to the bizarre, and one can not easily identify specific clients as "victims" of such infractions. It often becomes evident, however, that certain public behaviors reflect quite unfavorably on mental health professions as a whole. Because our profession has commercial or business aspects, and because professional regulatory bodies are arms of state government or professional organizations (e.g., the American Counseling Association, American Psychological Association [APA], American Psychiatric Association, or National Association of Social Workers), a tension between maintaining appropriate conduct and avoiding restraint of trade may also exist. We

begin with a review of the evolution of today's advertising patterns and attitudes among the professions and among mental health care providers in particular.

HISTORICAL ISSUES

Historically, the professions considered advertising of services or direct solicitation of clients as déclassé at the very least. The professions have traditionally liked to think of themselves as self-regulating and rejected the notion that advertising constituted a meaningful distinction of value to their clients. The first American Medical Association (AMA) Code of Ethics in 1847 unambiguously forbade it (Tomycz, 2006). The usual point cited as justification for this view holds that an advertisement can not reflect true skill or competence, and one should instead rely on the referral of a presumably informed and knowing colleague. Many people considered certain types of advertising distasteful or even misleading because they traded on public fears or ignorance related to the services offered.

Medicine and psychology provide good illustrative examples of the progression in advertising among mental health practitioners. From the time of psychology's emergence as an autonomous profession following World War II, practitioners emulated existing practices in medicine (i.e., psychiatry), the prime professional competitor of the era. Advertising had to qualify as "professional in tone," which generally meant discrete, formal, terse, and narrow in scope. The preferred format was more an announcement of availability than an active effort to recruit clients. The imitated model originated with physicians and attorneys, but we focus on psychology for the next few pages because we have well-documented knowledge of how these issues evolved in that field.

A set of guidelines for telephone directory listings published by the APA (1969) nearly four decades ago provides a typical example of the attitudes held at the time. The guidelines enjoined psychologists to list only names, highest relevant degree, and some narrow indication of specialization if desired (e.g., "practice limited to children" or "psychological consultant to management"). Psychologists were advised that the size and typeface should be uniform, and boldface fonts should be avoided. Listing of multiple specializations was considered "a form of self-aggrandizement and...unwarranted." So-called box ads were to be avoided, as was listing in directories outside the area where one maintained a bona fide office.

A psychologist, psychiatrist, or other practitioner opening a new practice might reasonably insert a tasteful box notice in the local newspaper, such as

Ronald J. MacDonald, Ph.D., announces the opening of his office for the practice of clinical psychology at
555 Main Street
Anytown, U.S.A.
Office hours by appointment.
Call 333–555–7777.

Professional custom dictated that the psychotherapist could not repeat such announcements more than once or twice without exceeding the bounds of good taste. One might reasonably send a printed notice by mail to fellow professional colleagues in the community as a way of encouraging them to refer clients. At least these were the views that held sway within medicine, law, psychology and many other professions until the Federal Trade Commission (FTC) became involved.

Federal Trade Commission Actions Against Professional Associations

The FTC sits as an independent agency within the federal government. Founded in 1914, it consists of two main branches. The Bureau of Competition focuses on antitrust issues, while the Bureau of Consumer Protection investigates charges of false or deceptive advertising. Stimulated by the work of Ralph Nader and other consumer advocates as well as publicized class action lawsuits against major corporations, a wave of consumer activism became prominent in America during the 1960s and 1970s. This climate became an important factor in the decision of the FTC and the U.S. Department of Justice to bring about changes in the ways professional associations attempted to regulate their members (Koocher, 1977, 1994a, 1994b).

By the early 1970s, the Bureau of Competition began approaching professional organizations with concerns about association practices that barred the presentation of useful consumer information through advertising. From the perspective of the FTC's Bureau of Competition, three prime directives seemed to apply. We can best summarize these as:

1. Truthful advertising is good.
2. False or deceptive advertising is bad.
3. Attempting to block truthful advertising is as bad as false and misleading advertising.

In 1972, the FTC and the Antitrust Division of the Justice Department initiated complaints against a variety of professional associations, including the American Institute of Architects, the American Institute of Certified Public Accountants, and the National Society of Professional Engineers. On June 6, 1975, the U.S. Supreme Court unanimously struck down the publication of fee schedules by bar associations, effectively terminating attempts to enforce a minimum fee schedule for lawyers (*Goldfarb v. Virginia State Bar*, 1975). The *Goldfarb* ruling (1975) and a similar case (*Bates et al. v. State Bar of Arizona*, 1977) made it clear that professions do not enjoy some special form of antitrust exemption. In addition, at least some rules of professional associations that directly reduced or eliminated competition may constitute unlawful behavior per se. The FTC actions specifically concerned professional ethical codes that prohibited soliciting business by advertising, engaging in price competition, and otherwise engaging in competitive practices. In the case of medical societies, enforcing the existing medical ethics code (AMA, 1971) was deemed to create de facto price interference and frustrate the consumer's right to choose services in an unrestrained fashion (Koocher, 1977).

As early as 1976, the APA Ethics Committee decided to act prospectively rather than awaiting a call from the FTC (Koocher, 1977). At about the same time, the APA had begun work on the third major revision of the its ethics code (APA, 1981) and declined to take action on any advertising complaints as long as the advertisements seemed accurate and provided information important or relevant to consumers. The revised code (APA, 1981), which remained in force until 1989, directed that advertising in general would remain ethically acceptable as long as certain basic tenets were followed. These included avoiding misleading claims, eschewing testimonials, and avoiding anxiety-inducing advertisements (Winters, 2000). The principal goal of these sections of the code focused on protecting potential consumers of psychological services from being taken advantage of by virtue of their cognitive or emotional vulnerabilities.

Psychology also mounted strong political support for consumer interests within the FTC. When members of Congress introduced bills during the Reagan administration to exempt the professions (including psychology) from regulation by the FTC, political action groups associated with the APA actively opposed the legislation (Association for the Advancement of Psychology, 1982). The APA won wide praise as a leader among the professions in the consumer protection community for striving to become a good citizen and pro-consumer.

Formal investigation of the APA by the FTC began shortly after adoption of the 1981 ethics code, much later than many other professional and scientific associations. According to Attorney Steven Osnowitz,[1] who represented the FTC in parts of the APA case, this timing occurred because the APA was "not the most offensive" and because the FTC was "fine tuning" its enforcement via its actions against other professions with practices regarding advertising by members that seemed more troubling. Osnowitz also noted that APA staff had allegedly given advice to state psychological associations and licensing boards on the interpretation of the code. As a result, some psychologists reportedly became subject to local enforcement actions by state psychological association ethics committees or licensing boards that reportedly relied

on the APA's advice. These individuals later complained about the APA, and the FTC staff became concerned about the appearance of inappropriate consultation and improper influence by a tax exempt national professional association.

Our recollections of APA Ethics Office operations in the late 1970s and early 1980s (while they served as members of the APA Ethics Committee) aligns with Onsowitz's comments. For example, it was not uncommon for the APA Ethics Office to direct callers with questions to members of the Ethics Committee in their geographic area for advice on interpretation of general aspects of the code. In addition, a period of considerable staff turnover in the APA Ethics Office occurred during this time, and we recall specific instances when inappropriate advice was given out. For example, a complaint came in regarding an APA member whose name and photograph (identifying him as a psychologist) appeared in a nationally published magazine advertisement endorsing a particular brand of Scotch whiskey. The APA Ethics Committee began an investigation, but closed the case with considerable embarrassment when the psychologist reported that he had requested a prior opinion from the then APA ethics officer, who told him that such an endorsement would not violate the existing code. The staff member in question admitted giving the advice without consulting any members of the APA Ethics Committee.

Although the APA code's provisions regarding advertising restrictions were not the most outrageous and had not been enforced egregiously, the FTC deemed APA's flat ban on the use of client testimonials as "inherently suspect." Similarly, the FTC opposed APA's prohibitions against making claims of "uniqueness" because these might conceivably be true in some cases. One nonpsychologist who also complained to the FTC ran a referral service in the state of Maryland. In a manner akin to

1. The comments reported here were made in two telephone interviews the author had with Attorney Osnowitz during July 1993. The material within quotation marks are verbatim comments transcribed during the conversation. Readers will want to be mindful that the memories and interpretations made by one party to a series of events may differ from the recollections of other parties.

some urban dating services in the pre-Internet era, prospective clients could browse at their leisure through a set of videotapes made by psychotherapists listed with the referral service. The Maryland Psychological Association ethics committee began to investigate psychologists who affiliated with this service. According to Attorney Osnowitz, some members of the APA Ethics Committee "went berserk over the videos." Asked for clarification, Osnowitz explained that the reactions of some psychologists serving on the ethics panel addressing these investigations seemed overly zealous in their sense of outrage.

American Psychological Association's 1989 "Emergency Actions"

On June 2, 1989, the APA Board of Directors declared an emergency and amended the "Ethical Principles of Psychologists" with no advance notice to members. Although the few hundred members of the APA active in governance received an explanatory memo, this information did not circulate widely. Alert members might have noticed a few brief mentions of the ongoing APA–FTC dialogue in the *APA Monitor* (see March 1988 and January 1990 issues) or embedded in occasional committee reports published in the *American Psychologist*. However, the newly truncated version of the code first widely published in the *American Psychologist* (APA, 1990) contained no explanations regarding the changes made or the nature of the emergency. Many members of the APA felt confused, thinking somehow that the entire ethics code had undergone revision since the publication did not note the specific modifications.

The emergency changes made in 1990 to the 1981 version of the code *removed* prohibitions against using testimonials from patients; claims of unusual, unique, or one-of-a-kind abilities; appeals to clients' fears if services are not obtained; claims of the comparative desirability of one service over another; or direct solicitation of individual clients. In addition, a sentence that had previously barred psychologists from "giving or receiving any remuneration for referring clients for professional services" vanished. Even though this principle, intended

to prevent fee-splitting or kickback arrangements (see Chapter 7), the FTC interpreted it as having the potential to prohibit participation in legitimate referral service businesses and some managed care operations (Koocher, 1994b).

Another sentence also disappeared in the 1990 ethics code. It had read, "If a person is receiving similar services from another professional, psychologists do not offer their services to such a person." The APA intended this sentence as a kind of noninterference clause to prevent piracy of clients already receiving services elsewhere. In addition, it reflected a belief that clients simultaneously receiving services from different practitioners might receive compromised care as the result of conflicting advice. The FTC viewed the sentence as creating a barrier to free choice of the consumer.

The reason for the emergency nature of the changes involved a pending consent agreement between the APA and the FTC. Prior to the emergency declaration, considerable lobbying within the APA governance structure had focused on retaining prohibitions of unfair/deceptive advertising, use of testimonials, and advertising that appealed to fear if services are not obtained. Several divisions, APA committees, and the Board of Social and Ethical Responsibility for Psychology adopted resolutions asking the board of directors to pursue these issues in negotiations or even litigation with the FTC. However, the APA board did not wish to raise any red flags that might have compromised its tax-exempt status as a scientific organization. The FTC has routinely been invited to review and comment on all subsequent changes in the APA's code prior to adoption.

Interestingly, one of the FTC commissioners wrote a partial dissent to the FTC decision that tended to corroborate APA's original position. Commissioner Mary L. Azcuenaga (1990) expressed support of the APA's ban on advertising that appeals to clients' fears. We discuss this issue in more detail below; however, she observed, "as often happens in cases of this nature, the respondent has substantial financial incentives to accept the settlement rather than litigate" (p. 2).

THE NATURE OF GOVERNMENT RESTRICTIONS ON ADVERTISEMENTS

If the general goals of the FTC focus on making useful information available to the general public, then one can understand how clinging to vestiges of sameness in public statements solely to maintain a sense of professionalism would not survive. However, some limits on advertising do serve legitimate public interests. This is especially true in professions, such as psychology, that may unduly influence consumers because of the consumers' compromised cognitive or emotional status.

State's Interest Doctrine

The FTC has not focused on state licensing boards and would not likely act against state boards that take well-reasoned steps to enforce greater restrictions than are allowed professional associations as a matter of a "state's interests." In the case of *Virginia State Board of Pharmacy et al. v. Virginia Citizens Consumer Council, Inc., et al.* (1975), the Supreme Court ruled in part that, "The State is free to require whatever professional standards it wishes of its pharmacists, and may subsidize them or protect them from competition in other ways, but it may not do so by keeping the public in ignorance of the lawful terms that competing pharmacists are offering" (pp. 766–770). The decision struck down a Virginia law that specified a pharmacist licensed in Virginia could be guilty of unprofessional conduct if he or she "published or advertised any prices, discounts, or rebates in any manner whatsoever for prescription drugs."

At the same time, the court carved out the state's interest exception by noting, "If there is a kind of commercial speech that lacks all First Amendment protection ... it must be distinguished by its content" (*Virginia State Board of Pharmacy*, 1975, p. 761). For example, in the *Bates* decision (*Bates et al. v. State Bar of Arizona*, 1977), the court noted "peculiar problems associated with advertising claims relating to *quality* of legal services," noting one advertising can not precisely measure such quality and "under some circumstances, might well be deceptive or misleading to the public, or even false"

(p. 366). The bottom line appears to involve whether the state can document a legitimate governmental interest in protecting its citizens.

It appears likely that state professional licensing boards, which unlike the ethics committees of professional associations, originate from statutory actions of a legislature, would have authority to implement more restrictive limitations on advertising than specified in the associations' professional codes. For example, a statutory licensing authority might specifically define a state's interest in proscribing "appeals to fear" or testimonial advertising by mental health professionals. In such cases, the FTC would not likely object and could even lack authority to take action since intrastate regulation lies outside the FTC's interstate commerce mandate. National professional associations, however, would be specifically prevented from cooperating with state agencies in the development of such regulations.

Is Commercial Speech Free Speech, Too?

Do restraints imposed by professional association restrictions on advertising violate commercial free speech? While not the same as political free speech in the constitutional sense, the concept remains highly relevant and has often come up as an issue in efforts to limit advertising by lawyers. Commercial speech stands protected under the First and Fourteenth Amendments similar to political speech (*Virginia State Board of Pharmacy*, 1975); however, the courts have ruled that authorities can reasonably demand substantiation in the face of alleged false or deceptive advertising. The FTC's thrust has focused on expanding access to truthful information in the marketplace although allowing some exceptions, such as "in-your-face" solicitations.

One good example of the commercial free speech argument involved an enterprising attorney named Shapero.

Case 14–1: The U.S. Supreme Court dealt with a case involving a young Kentucky lawyer named Shapero (*Shapero v. Kentucky Bar Association*, 1988), who wanted to solicit business by sending truthful, nondeceptive letters to potential clients known to be confronting certain legal problems, such as property foreclosures. The letter in question was to go to potential clients who had a foreclosure suit filed against them; it advised, "You may be about to lose your home," and that "Federal law may allow you to ... ORDER your creditor to STOP." Potential clients were invited by Mr. Shapero to "call my office for FREE information ... It may surprise you what I may be able to do for you" (p. 1919).

Mr. Shapero had the foresight to ask the Kentucky state bar for an advisory opinion regarding whether they deemed his proposed letter to people facing foreclosure as acceptable. Although the state bar commissioners ruled that the letter was not misleading, they told Shapero not to use the letter, citing a then-existing Kentucky Supreme Court rule prohibiting the direct solicitation of individuals (i.e., as opposed to members of the general public) as a direct result of some specific event. Shapero appealed to the U.S. Supreme Court and won. The key point in the decision noted the content of his notice was not false or deceptive and held genuine potential interest for the intended recipients, which they could then choose to act on or ignore.

In-Your-Face Solicitation

What if the nature of the commercial exercise of free speech involves a more intense approach than Shapero's letter or takes advantage of a client in a vulnerable position? Existing case law suggests that so-called in-your-face solicitations, especially with vulnerable clients, can result in professional discipline.

Consider the case of an enterprising lawyer named Ohralik from Montville, Ohio (*Ohralik v. Ohio State Bar Association*, 1978).

Case 14–2: On February 13, 1974, attorney Ohralik was picking up his mail at the Montville Post Office and learned in casual conversation with the postmaster's brother that 18-year-old Carol McClintock had been injured in an automobile accident a week and a half earlier. Attorney Ohralik decided to pay a call on Carol's parents. While at the McClintock home, he learned that Carol and her passenger, Wanda Lou Holbert, were riding together in the McClintock family car when they were struck by an uninsured motorist. Both girls required hospitalization. Since Carol was 18 and no longer a minor, attorney Ohralik immediately set out for the hospital, where he found Carol lying in traction. He attempted to sign her up as a client in the hospital room, but she demurred to seek parental advice. He then went to find Wanda Lou Holbert, but she had just been released by the hospital. On his way back to the McClintock home, attorney Ohralik stopped to take photos of the accident scene and concealed a tape recorder under his raincoat in an apparent effort to document oral permission to hire him. He reviewed the family insurance policy and discovered that both Carol and Wanda Lou could recover up to $12,500 each under an uninsured motorist clause. Ohralik made a variety of different misrepresentations to the girls, who initially were swayed by his arguments but soon sought to discharge him from representing them in this matter. He then sued both of them for breach of contract, using excerpts from the surreptitiously made tape recordings in an effort to prove that an oral contract existed.

Both girls complained to the county bar association, which passed the action on to the state bar. Attorney Ohralik was found to have violated the Ohio Code of Professional Responsibility, despite his claim of First and Fourteenth Amendment protections. In particular, the Ohio Supreme Court found that this direct solicitation of business was inconsistent with the profession's ideal of the attorney–client relationship. Ohralik had claimed that his solicitation was no different from that of the *Bates* (*Bates et al v. State Bar of Arizona*, 1977) case, but the U.S. Supreme Court disagreed and ruled that Ohralik's conduct posed "dangers that the state has a right to prevent" (*Ohralik v. Ohio State Bar Association*, 1978, p. 449), noting that the "appellant not only foisted himself upon these clients; he acted in gross disregard for their privacy" (p. 469). This approach was bolstered in another Supreme Court ruling (*Florida Bar v. Went For It, Inc.*, et al., 1995). That ruling supported the Florida Bar, which had prohibited personal injury lawyers from sending targeted direct mail solicitations to victims and their relatives for 30 days following an accident or disaster. The decision found that the prohibition did not violate the lawyers' First and Fourteenth Amendment rights.

In general, we advise against direct solicitation of individual clients by mental health professionals, even when not as obnoxious as attorney Ohralik. The central issue involves the potential vulnerability of the client relative to the psychotherapist. Vulnerability may include client insecurities, emotional problems, naïveté, lack of information, or simply awe of the professional. The therapist's special expertise and knowledge are generally accorded a degree of respect or deference that may predispose clients to follow their advice and recommendations, even if this means changing long-standing patterns of behavior. Therapists must recognize this social influence or power and consider its use carefully. Advice must be presented with due respect to the limitations of our scientific knowledge and the recognition of a client's freedom to choose a lifestyle or course of action. Recommendations must always be tailored to an understanding of the client and his or her unique life situation.

A personal solicitation of the in-your-face variety may pit the expert's advantage directly against the potential client's insecurities and fears. It may capitalize on a client's ignorance or social naïveté. While there is nothing wrong with a therapist's announcing general availability to the community through advertising, the direct solicitation of individual clients has considerable potential for abuse and distress to the object of the pitch.

Case 14–3: Max Pusher, M.D., a psychiatrist well known for his syndicated newspaper column, was invited to teach an extension course at Thunder State University dealing with the topics anxiety, tension, and depression. A huge audience was attracted by his name and reputation. Dr. Pusher was accompanied by several assistants wearing colored armbands, who passed out brochures about Dr. Pusher's private clinic and other private workshops he offered. In addition, some of the assistants approached selected students, saying, "You look troubled. Perhaps you could use an appointment or two."

This approach clearly upset many of the students approached and certainly would play on the insecurities of others. This seems little more than an appeal to fear as a means to recruit clients in the guise of a public lecture.

As in the case of testimonials, discussed in the next section, there are some tolerable exceptions to the general prohibition on solicitation of individual clients. These generally apply when the client is not an individual, but an agency, business firm, or other organizational entity. Consider the following examples:

Case 14–4: Effie Casey, Ph.D., an industrial and organizational psychologist, has developed a well-validated practice assessment program to evaluate pharmacists. He prepares a factually accurate descriptive brochure and mails it to potential employers of pharmacists and colleges of pharmacy, offering his consultative and evaluative services.

Case 14–5: Karen Kinder, M.Ed., is trained as an early childhood educator and school psychologist. She has developed a kindergarten screening instrument with good reliability and predictive validity. She has appropriate information printed in pamphlet form and mails these with cover letters offering to conduct training workshops to superintendents of schools and directors of special education in school systems throughout her locale.

While the clients approached by Dr. Casey and Ms. Kinder are indeed contacted as individuals, they are not in the same relative position of vulnerability as an "unaffiliated" individual in emotional distress. Employers, schools, or other organizations will generally stand in a better position to know their needs for such services, and the nature of the services offered is quite different from individual offers of psychotherapy. (For the sake of illustration, we are assuming that the programs and instruments used by Ms. Kinder and Dr. Casey are properly validated and reasonably useful. Issues related to assessment in general are discussed in Chapter 9.) In some circumstances, therapeutic services might also be offered in this manner.

Case 14–6: Ethyl Fluid, L.M.H.C., plans to approach a variety of large corporations to encourage their purchase of alcoholism counseling services for their employees using an EAP (employee assistance program) model. She will offer to provide a team of properly trained clinicians to staff an inhouse clinic at each company's plant. Employees would be seen on a self-referral basis, with appropriate confidentiality safeguards for counseling. Dr. Fluid cites that the advantages of the program include convenience for employees and improved conditions of employment, with a possible reduction in alcohol-related work problems and absenteeism. She presents this plan in letters to presidents and personnel directors of the companies.

Assuming that Dr. Fluid observes other ethical obligations related to providing the treatment she proposes, this type of solicitation presents no problem. No outrageous claims are made, and each company is clearly free to evaluate its own need for the program as well as other alternatives. Client freedom is ensured, and no one is pressured individually.

Testimonials

The use of testimonials by "satisfied users" has a kind of inherent "face validity" that appealed to the FTC. Unfortunately, like many forms of face validity, the true predictive potential of a testimonial endorsement becomes far more complex with regard to mental health services. If psychotherapy research has taught us anything, it is that any given psychotherapist will not have equal success in treating all potential clients.

The FTC did allow the APA to bar the use of testimonials from "current psychotherapy patients" or from "persons who because of their particular circumstances are vulnerable to undue influence" (APA, 1990). However, psychotherapists know very well that their influence in the life of their clients does not end at the close of the last treatment session. Apparently, the FTC does not regard the lingering influence of the transference relationship and its potential consequences as an automatic barrier to testimonial advertising (e.g., potentially unfair and deceptive endorsements provided in the afterglow of a positive transference).

Although most psychotherapists know that satisfied clients and the people who referred those clients do become their best sources of future referrals, few data exist to suggest that the public will rely on commercially advertised testimonials in selecting medical or psychological care providers. Among all the professions, one notable exception in the merits of testimonial advertising may be among plastic and cosmetic surgeons, for whom the concept of face validity takes on a unique meaning.

It can certainly feel gratifying when a client values services or has praise for professional efforts, but there are many reasons not to cite such laudatory comments in advertisements for professional services. Such statements may be taken out of context or reflect value judgments from which the public can not reasonably draw valid generalizations. In addition, testimonials or public endorsements may compromise a client's confidentially or later prove embarrassing in ways that may not be anticipated when initially agreeing to the quotation. Although most professional ethics code, revised under pressure from the FTC as described in this chapter, permit the use of testimonials from former clients, we strongly advise our colleagues not to use them in advertising services.

One type of advertising testimonials that have traditionally proved acceptable involves promotions of books or other products aimed at professionals. The rationale for permitting specific use of testimonials in this exceptional circumstance links to the potential consumer and the presumption that the mental health practitioner who permits the use of a quotable endorsement will do so fairly. Unlike the potential client who seeks the help of a therapist during a period of emotional distress, we assume that the scholarly review of a book or assessment tool occurs in a relatively thoughtful and dispassionate manner. In addition, one can assume that the professional evaluating the book has some competence to do so critically. The reader of such endorsements will more likely evaluate such testimonials from a critical standpoint than would the emotionally troubled client. The fact that client testimonials are tolerated places an extra burden on those who use them. Users of testimonial advertising must take assiduous care not to use the comments out of context or in a misleading fashion.

Case 14–7: Cherry Picker, Psy.D., created an advertisement for her book, Master of My Mind, citing words from a review that appeared in a professional journal. She claimed that the reviewer described her work as "unique" and "fascinating" In fact, the reviewer had written, "Dr. Picker has shown a unique ability to take a fascinating topic, the human mind, and make it mundane and superficial."

Such ill-used quotations will likely be discovered because the use will sooner or later come to the attention of its originator. In fact, permission should be sought prior to the use of such quotations in promoting one's authored works.

Case 14–8: Fred Furniture asked several psychoanalysts to endorse his new line of analytic couches with water-filled mattresses. When his efforts to obtain an endorsement failed, he scanned the Internet for people with the surname "Freud" and found one willing to give a testimonial in exchange for a fee. Fred then advertised that he sold the only couches endorsed by the Freud family.

Most psychotherapists would purchase furniture based on utility, comfort, and cost factors. Few would find the endorsement by someone named Freud an important distinguishing factor, but Fred's marketing ploy just might net him a few sales.

Appeals to Fear

Many psychotherapists might wonder why the FTC would object to a professional association's ban of advertising that appeals to potential clients' fears. After all, some of our clients have emotional insecurities and may have greater vulnerability to inappropriate duress than Carol McClintock and Wanda Lou Holbert (Case 14–2). From the FTC's perspective, global bans on advertising that appeals to fear if services are not obtained seemed simply unacceptable on general principles. A lot of effective advertising appeals to emotions and fears at some level (e.g., fear of tooth decay if you do not

brush, fears of accidental injury or death if you ride in a car without seat belts and air bags, or fears of AIDS as a result of not practicing "safe sex"). In fact, social psychology has taught us that an "appeal to fear" coupled with a designated course of action proves highly effective in evoking attitude change.

How might an ethics committee have become involved in such complaints? In one instance, actual complaints were filed when consumers objected to advertising by psychologists who ran programs to help people quit smoking. The advertisements powerfully articulated the potentially fatal consequences of smoking-induced lung cancer and other pulmonary diseases (Miller, 2000; O'Sullivan & Murphy, 1998). A more troubling example is the coupling of an appeal to fear with so-called in your face solicitation, such as the case in the *Ohralik* decision. Imagine the following scenario:

Case 14–9: Dinah Saur, L.M.F.C., arrives unsolicited at the home of a child who witnessed a playground shooting, urging the parents to subscribe to a course of therapy to prevent "inevitable posttraumatic stress syndrome" in their as-yet-asymptomatic child.

As noted in the section on the APA's emergency actions, FTC Commissioner Azcuenaga (1990) disagreed with her colleagues on this point. She supported the APA's wish to continue a ban on scare advertising, noting that the justification for banning such advertising by psychologists was plausible, and that the FTC ought not to substitute its judgment on the matter without having a sound basis to do so. She cited the FTC's lack of expertise concerning psychotherapy and noted that, "Nothing, even hypothetically, suggests that the [APA's] justification is either implausible or invalid" (p. 2). She was outvoted.

Fee Splitting

Providing bribes or kickbacks (fee splitting) in exchange for referrals never qualified as an acceptable practice, but from the FTC's perspective, some ethics panels or licensing boards had interpreted prohibitions on this point as forbidding psychotherapists' participation in health maintenance organizations (HMOs), preferred provider organizations (PPOs), or referral services during the 1980s. The FTC regards referral services as procompetitive, and barring participation in them per se posed a significant competition problem. Unfortunately, what constitutes a bribe, as opposed to a legitimate fee reduction or membership payment, remains open to a wide range of opinion. The FTC (1993) consent order does permit the professional associations to issue "reasonable" principles that require disclosures to consumers regarding fees paid to referral services or similar entities. In Case 7–9 we gave an example of a referral service that collected 5% of net revenues on cases referred, without specifying an end date or maximum. What would happen if the referral service charged fees of 10%, 25%, or 50% of fees collected simply for making a referral to the therapist? The key to discriminating between reasonable and inappropriate payment will have to depend on the rationale for the charges or fee reductions and the openness of information on these arrangements to the consumers of the services.

CURRENT PRACTICES

The FTC did not intend that mental health practitioners or other professions should necessarily adopt the market tactics of miraculous weight loss pills and carnival barkers but rather focused on universal advertising prohibitions. Potential harm that could result from hucksterism and advertising abuses remains a valid focus of specific tailored restrictions by professional associations. However, claims to "professional dignity" and the imagined need for "uniformity" would no longer constitute a legitimate basis for limiting advertising by professionals.

For the reader interested in reviewing the relevant sections of the current version of the APA ethics code (Appendix A), the matters most directly covered by the FTC mandated changes include the following:

- We must avoid making false or deceptive public statements, including any related to one's practice, research, or professional credentials (APA 02: 5.01).
- We must maintain the integrity of statements made by others on our behalf (APA 02: 5.02). In so doing advertisements must be identified as such, and we retain responsibility for those we engage to promote our work.
- We do not compensate those in the media for publicity in news items.
- We must uphold the accuracy of any workshops or nondegree educational programs we offer (APA 02: 5.03).
- When we offer public advice (including broadcast and Internet communications), we must clarify the scientific basis of the advice and make any professional roles with respect to the advice recipients clear (APA 02: 5.04).
- We do not solicit testimonials from current therapy clients or other persons whose particular circumstances make them vulnerable to undue influence (APA 02: 5.05).
- We do not personally or through agents attempt uninvited in-person solicitation of business from actual or potential clients whose particular circumstances make them vulnerable to undue influence (APA 02: 5.06).

Nothing in this section of the APA code should preclude meeting with collateral contacts of current clients. For example, ethics codes do not consider a child therapist's request for parents to attend a family session a prohibited solicitation. Similarly, an adult's therapist's invitation for a spouse or significant other to a session with the client's permission would also be appropriate in many circumstances. It is also very acceptable to offer to provide disaster relief and community outreach services.

Did the FTC–APA interaction lead to an improved ethics code? We believe that some improvements resulted from directing the APA and other professional associations concerned with advertising to focus on substance rather than style. On the other hand, we also believe that the FTC failed to fully accept the principle that the relationships between mental health professionals and their clients are qualitatively different from those that exist in many other professions.

The result will be a greater reluctance on the part of ethics enforcement groups in psychology to tackle complaints in this arena. Readers interested in an international perspective on these issues may find the discussion by Shead and Dobson and Koocher of interest (Koocher, 2004; Shead & Dobson, 2004a, 2004b).

ELEMENTS ALLOWED IN ADVERTISING

Over the years, an expanded array of ethical permissible advertising or marketing has bloomed. Along with the growth in such advertising, some new opportunities for missteps have developed (Perrott, 1998).

Citation of Organizational Membership Status

For many years, the APA prohibited mention in advertising of a psychologist's membership status. The original rationale cast the APA as a scientific and professional organization with membership practices that do not include evaluation of individual credentials. As such, mention of APA membership status might inappropriately imply APA approval of the psychologist in question. Others argued from time to time that association memberships do represent credentials of sorts. Since members of the APA and other professional associations have an obligation to follow the associations' ethics codes, and since many organizations hold their members accountable to such standards, membership may indeed represent a special qualification that merits public attention.

In recognition of the last viewpoint, the APA Ethics Committee voted in October 1978 to recommend that, should they wish, members are permitted to list their APA membership status in public advertising. The recommendation was adopted as official policy by the APA Council of Representatives in January 1979. The manner of listing must not, however, suggest that APA membership status implies sponsorship of the psychologist's activities, competence, or specialized qualifications. When in doubt, members of a particular profession should consult the organization's ethics office before listing membership status in advertising.

Mention of Other Credentials

A variety of other credentials exist in the mental health professions, including membership in certain organizations that have special entry requirements, a diploma from a postgraduate accrediting or certification body (e.g., specialty board certification status), listing in the professional registers of various sorts, and honorary degrees or other titles. Some controversy exists regarding whether membership or receipt of such recognition constitutes a meaningful credential to potential consumers since the recipient may have acquired it via some grandparenting process or based solely on recognition of other more valid indicators of professional accomplishment (Koocher, 1979). In general, one should advertise only those credentials that could reasonably be deemed meaningful to the consumer population (e.g., state licensure, earned degrees, and valid specialty certifications). Honorary degrees and degrees earned in fields other than health or mental health practice should not form a basis for advertising one's offering of mental health services.

Diplomate or board certification status presents a problem because of the proliferation of so-called vanity boards within different fields (Dattilio, 2002; Dattilio, Sadoff, & Gutheil, 2003; Foxhall, 2000; Packard & Simon, 2006). Legitimate professional certification groups, such as the American Board of Professional Psychology (ABPP), the Academy of Certified Social Workers (ACSW), National Board for Certified Counselors (NBCC), and the American Board of Medical Specialties (ABMS) and its subsidiary American Board of Psychiatry and Neurology (ABPN) all have several important features in common. These include close affiliations with recognized professional associations, nonprofit status, and respected professionals serving on their governing boards (Dattilio, 2002). All require an advanced degree, several years of postgraduate experience, submission of a work sample or a formal examination to earn the diploma. The well-recognized credentials will often qualify for listing in professional association directories.

Other frankly disreputable organizations have sprung up to grant diplomas in so-called specialty or subspecialty fields not generally recognized by mainstream professional associations. Such vanity boards may offer their credentials chiefly based on personal attestations of the candidates and payment of a fee. Others have extensive grandparenting periods during which diplomas are awarded following minimal review of credentials and questionable examinations, if any. An article, "Expertise to Go," in the *ABA Journal* described and dissected the antics of one such entity, the American College of Forensic Examiners (ACFE) (Hansen, 2000). For example, the article described the ACFE's founder as a man with a Ph.D. in philosophy who worked as a small-town policeman, a juvenile probation officer, and a children's counselor before beginning teaching criminal justice full time. The university reportedly fired him over allegations of plagiarism. He decided to form an association of handwriting experts because he had a personal interest in handwriting analysis but no formal training in the field. Soon, he was awarding expert credentials to others.

The public may have no ability to separate the wheat from the chaff when such diplomas or board certifications appear in advertising. However, we believe that competent ethical mental health professionals should only cite credentials recognized by national professional associations independent of the credential's grantor. An important clue to such recognition will be listing of the certification in professional associations' membership directories or in the regulations of state licensing boards.

Citing One's Degrees

The most correct way to indicate an earned degree from an accredited educational institution would be to use initials following the holder's name (i.e., John Jones, Ph.D., or Mary Smith, M.D.). Simply using the title "Doctor" invites confusion since the doctorate may be in psychology, divinity, social work, law, nursing, or even medicine. In fact, many mental health professionals do hold graduate degrees in fields unrelated to their clinical or research work. In some professions, a licensing designation such as L.I.C.S.W. (Licensed Independent Clinical

Social Worker), L.M.H.C. (Licensed Mental Health Counselor), or L.M.F.T. (Licensed Marital and Family Therapist) may be the preferred mode of listing since the simply alphabetical designation of the master's degree tells the consumer little. In any case, one should list only the designations one has earned as completed academic degrees or professional licenses and that have relevance for the services advertised (Gooding, 2004).

Case 14–10: Donnatella Nobody, L.M.F.T., Ph.D., holds a master's degree in family counseling and a Ph.D. in history. She advertises her family therapy practice using both degrees.

Dr. Nobody does indeed have an earned Ph.D. and deserves to take pride in that accomplishment. However, use of that degree to advertise her services as a mental health practitioner will likely mislead the public to conclude that her doctorate falls in a field relevant to her practice. Such ambiguous listing with significant potential for misrepresentation is unethical.

Case 14–11: Anne Ticipatory, has an M.A. in psychology and has begun work on a doctoral dissertation as the last requirement for a Ph.D. in that field. While working at a practicum site she signs her case notes and reports as "Ann Ticipatory, Ph.D. (c)" or "Ann Ticipatory, Ph.D. (cand)."

Ms. Ticipatory takes pride in her academic accomplishments and can see the light at the end of the long academic tunnel leading to her doctorate. Her university may even have formally declared her a Ph.D. candidate, thus authorizing her to begin dissertation research. Still, she has not yet earned the Ph.D. and the use of "Ph.D. (c)," "Ph.D. Cand.," or "A.B.D." (as in "all but dissertation") might imply some type of earned credential that she does not hold. This type of listing is deceptive and is considered ethically inappropriate because only earned degrees may be listed. Neither "admission to candidacy" nor "all but ..." references relate to an earned degree. One certainly should explain the precise nature of professional training and credentials directly to clients, but abbreviations that falsely imply actual degrees should never be used. It is hoped her supervisor will notice Ms. Ticipatory's listing and suggest correction.

Similarly, one must strive for factual accuracy in mentioning any professional licenses. Most states have so-called generic licensing laws, but a few states have different levels of licensure. In a state with generic laws, psychological practitioners are licensed as psychologists. It is therefore inappropriate to list oneself as a licensed clinical psychologist or licensed school psychologist in such states. Some states license social workers at three or more levels (e.g., Licensed Social Worker, Licensed Clinical Social Worker, or Licensed Independent Clinical Social Worker). No state licenses anyone as a psychiatrist; rather, psychiatrists are licensed physicians who go on to specialize in psychiatry. Thus, one might qualify as a "board-certified psychiatrist" but not as a "licensed psychiatrist." The best guide in determining how to advertise one's services involves looking carefully at the certificate or license itself and using only the specific title authorized. Other accurate elaborations are possible. Someone may handle such a situation by a listing "Mary Roe, Psy.D., Licensed Psychologist, practice limited to clinical psychology." This would be both factually accurate (i.e., official state-granted title) and ethically appropriate (i.e., accurately descriptive of specialty functioning).

Clinical psychology has grown to acquire a degree of status as a specialization within psychology. Many licensed practitioners, whose doctoral degrees were awarded in counseling psychology, school psychology, or other fields, have taken to identifying themselves as "clinical psychologists" in dealings with the public. The stated rationale of such individuals often focuses on licensing by their state to deliver so-called clinical services (by which most seem to mean health services), or they assert that their education and training are similar or equivalent to that obtained in clinical psychology doctoral programs. Some such psychologists attempt to distinguish between Clinical Psychology (as a proper noun) and clinical psychology, much as one would between Kleenex brand and generic facial tissue. Such reasoning places the clinician on a very slippery slope. It is always most appropriate to list oneself only by the proper titles of credentials actually earned rather than those acquired by idiosyncratic or wishful interpretation.

Listing Affiliations

Many mental health professionals work in more than one agency or practice relationship. For example, it is not uncommon for a therapist to hold full-time employment at a clinic or hospital while also conducting a part-time practice or consultation business. Many mental health practitioners also serve on boards and committees of corporations, professional organizations, and private agencies. When presenting this information to others, however, it is important that such affiliations do not wrongly suggest sponsorship by or approval of that organization or agency. Clients must also clearly understand whether the organization mentioned has any role in their relationship with the practitioner. Consider the case of the "all-purpose" psychologist:

Case 14–12: Robert Hartley received a letter from a psychology ethics committee after a neighbor complained of a 6-foot-high sign he had erected on his lawn that announced in 4-inch letters his practice of psychology. He replied to the committee on stationery even more interesting than the sign. The stationery was headed: "Dr. Robert Hartley, Ph.D., Consulting Clinical Psychologist and Sexologist." Three-color printing and assorted institutional logos ran down the side of the page and listed the services Hartley offered. These included

- Psychotherapy with Adults, Adolescents, and Children
- Individuals and Group Counseling
- Hypnosis
- Lay Analysis
- Psychological Testing
- Neuropsychological Evaluation
- Personality Assessment
- Intellectual Evaluation
- Diagnostic Evaluation

- Vocational Evaluation
- Counseling
- Sex and Divorce
- Marriage Enrichment Courses
- Management Consulting
- Executive Leadership, Development, and Assessment
- Personnel Evaluations

Across the bottom of the page, the following institutions were listed: Mid-America Hypnosis Clinic, XYZ Learning Disabilities Center, Sex Counseling Institute, Affective Education Foundation, and Plainville Marriage Enrichment Center.

To begin, for Hartley to list himself with the prefix "Dr." and the suffix "Ph.D." is redundant and simply in poor taste. The 6-foot sign and the three-color stationery were equally inappropriate. The double doctorate, sign, and stationery design, while tacky, are not unethical per se. On investigation, however, the ethics panel learned that Hartley's Ph.D. was earned in sociology and from a university not regionally accredited. He did hold a valid master's degree in psychology, but the context in which he listed his doctorate was inappropriate. The organizations listed across the stationery turned out to have two things in common: They were all headquartered in his office, and he was the sole employee of each. When asked about his training relative to the services listed, Hartley proudly cited a long chain of briefly held jobs and brief workshops he had attended, which covered virtually all of the services mentioned. Suffice it to say that the training was actually rather shallow in most of the areas mentioned, creating a very substantial competence question (discussed in detail in Chapter 4). Although Hartley's presentation of self seemed rather cloddish and he appeared truly ignorant of his infractions, the potential for public deception in his self portrayal is obvious.

Case 14–13: Roger Snob, M.D., was in full-time private practice but volunteered a few hours a week to supervise a resident at the university hospital. In exchange for his time, Dr. Snob was given a largely symbolic appointment as an adjunct

professor at the university. He promptly had new stationery printed that included his new title with the university seal and used it for all his professional correspondence.

Case 14–14: C. U. Infer, M.S.W., worked at the Northeast Mental Health Institute, a prestigious nationally known facility, on a research project that was to last for 2 years. He was a licensed social worker and was permitted to see private clients in his office at the institute during hours when he was technically off duty from the project. Many clients assumed that they were being treated by a clinical staff member of the institute under its auspices. When Infer moved away at the end of the project, several of his former clients were surprised to find that the institute had no records of their treatment and could not easily provide continuity of care for them.

Dr. Snob's misrepresentation is one of pride and possibly ignorance. While he has not demonstrably harmed any individual, he is clearly attempting to trade on the reputation of the university to enhance his own status. In reality, his relationship to the university is rather limited and remote and does not have actual relevance to much of his professional work. Mr. Infer, on the other hand, may have mislead clients, to their ultimate detriment. He also is trading on the reputation of an agency in which his actual affiliation is quite different from what the clients may be led to believe. Some clients may have chosen to use his services in part because of the presumed coverage, backup, or expertise represented by the institute. It is inappropriate for Mr. Infer simply to remain silent. Rather, he has an obligation to disabuse others of incorrect impressions or conclusions they may draw.

Product Endorsements

Endorsements by mental health professionals of products intended for sale to the general public are not generally considered appropriate, particularly when the therapist earns rewards or compensation in some way for providing the endorsement. The rationale is twofold. First, if the product is psychological in nature (e.g., a relaxation tape, biofeedback apparatus, assessment technique, etc.), its merit should stand on a foundation of empirical research rather than personal testimony. Second, if the product is not psychological in nature (e.g., a brand of toothpaste, pet food, or soft drink), the therapist is using his or her professional stature in an irrelevant realm to endorse a product in a way that may be deceptive and misleading to the public. If a therapist were to have a dual career, performing psychotherapy by day and announcing television commercials in the evening, the circumstances might theoretically be ethically appropriate as long as the therapist's role (i.e., by day) was not mentioned or otherwise employed as a means of influencing the public to buy products in the evening.

Endorsements may be appropriate in the marketing of products of a professional nature to colleagues. These products might include testing equipment, computer software, or other items sold chiefly to qualified professionals. The key point, again, is that the endorsement should be fair and accurate and should not depend on personal or financial gain. As noted, this principle especially holds true when the mental health professional has played a major role in the development of a particular device, book, or other product. Often, one may be blind to difficulties of this sort when personal involvement is substantial. Nonetheless, every effort should be made to ensure that commercial products offered for public sale are presented in a professional, scientifically acceptable, and factually informative manner. The use of due caution and scientific modesty and the avoidance of sensationalism or undocumented claims will go far in preventing careless ethical infractions of this sort. Many illustrations of problems in this realm are also found in Chapter 15 in the discussion of "self-help" books.

Tackiness

Occasionally, mental health professionals will engage in advertising practices that, while not clearly unethical, hold their profession up to ridicule or are otherwise in poor taste. Certainly, Dr. Hartley (Case 14–12) showed such tenden-

cies with his tricolor stationery and lawn billboard, but other and more bizarre examples abound.

Case 14–15: In anticipation of a lecture and workshop program by two psychologists who had written a self-help book for mass consumption, their publisher took out a full-page ad in a large metropolitan newspaper. The ad described the psychologists as the "Butch Cassidy and Sundance Kid of Psychology" and included a detailed cartoon depicting the two in cowboy outfits, with guns drawn, charging over the "boot hill" of psychology with grave markers inscribed "Freud," "Adler," and "Jung." It is unclear whether the goal of the ad was to portray them as "straight shooters" or psychological "outlaws."

The psychologists were reportedly embarrassed by the ads, claiming that they had not been consulted. On the other hand, they had certainly not exercised much care in monitoring how their names were being used.

Case 14–16: Consider the following newspaper advertisement:

> The Name's Doc Lame
> Psychotherapy's the game
> Call for appointment:
> Jack Lame, Ph.D.
> 555-1212

or this new business card:

> Roger A. Droit, Ph.D. (c), MAT, C.Ht.
> Health Psychology
> 111-5555

Although the names have been changed, the examples are genuine. While not unethical per se, Dr. Lame's advertisement is certainly not doing much to maintain a professional image or demonstrate a sense of responsibility that would reassure clients and colleagues. Such advertisements are likely to imply a lack of sensitivity and awareness of public reaction. Whether the author of such an ad could also be sensitive to the emotions and problems of others remains an open question.

When asked to explain the abbreviations on his business card, Mr. Droit noted that Ph.D. (c) meant that he was a "Ph.D. candidate" (albeit from an unaccredited program in "psychology and transpsychology"), the MAT was a Master of Arts in Teaching, and C. Ht. stood for Clinical Hypnotist (a credential based on a correspondence course).

Case 14–17: The epitome of mixing tackiness with slippery product endorsement can be found in the April 1995 issue of *Playboy* magazine. Barbara Keesling, Ph.D., who "earned a doctorate in psychology" from an unnamed university appears nude on several pages while posing with her three "self-help" books titled *Sexual Healing, Sexual Pleasure,* and *How to Make Love All Night (and Drive a Woman Wild).* Citations for these texts are not provided in the article, which describes how Dr. Keesling found her way into psychology through work as a sex surrogate involved in doing "hands on counseling" (pp. 68–70).

We know of three female psychologists who have posed nude in *Playboy* (October 1994, April 1995, and October 1997 for those readers who wish to undertake original source research). To the best of our knowledge, none are APA members. We are not aware of any psychiatrists, social workers, or male psychologists who have posed nude for national magazines (while citing their profession or otherwise). We regard citing ones' profession while posing nude in such contexts as tacky but not intrinsically unethical. However, Dr. Keesling's nude marketing of her books causes us to wonder whether she has an empirical basis to document the claim inherent in the titles of her books.

Contents of Acceptable Advertisements

In general, it is appropriate to advertise in the print and broadcast media as long as the tone and content of the advertisement are appropriate. Specific examples of unethical and inappropriate public statements and advertisements are also discussed in this chapter, but here are some samples of the acceptable statements.

Case 14–18: The following notice appeared weekly in a metropolitan newspaper:

Harry Childs, L.M.F.T.

- Licensed Marriage and Family Therapist
- M.A., granted by Western State University, 2003
- Specializing in the treatment of parent–child problems
- Convenient office hours
- Sliding fee scale
- Hablo español
- Health insurance accepted
- Family therapy available
- 24-hour answering service
- Call 777-555-6666

Case 14–19: The following is the text of a radio announcement aired in a major metropolitan area: "Mary Okay, Ph.D., is a clinical psychologist specializing in marital therapy. She is opening her practice in Centerville at the Glenwood Mall, with ample free parking and convenient evening office hours. If you are having marital problems, she may be able to help. Call 333-555-2211 for an appointment."

Assuming that the facts are accurate and truthful and that Mr. Childs and Dr. Okay are indeed qualified to perform the services they list, there is nothing wrong with these notices. Any information that might be of interest to a consumer, including facility in speaking a foreign language, application of special techniques (e.g., behavioral treatment of obesity, relaxation training, parent consultation, or hypnosis for habit control), convenience of office location, availability of evening hours, or other facts would be permissible. One must be careful not to mix facts that may be misleading, however. In Chapter 7, for example, we noted that some psychological services (e.g., child custody evaluations or other forensic services) may not be covered by health insurance. Therefore, if Mr. Childs were to note that his practice involves only child custody work, he should not simultaneously mention that he accepts health insurance without caveats about coverage. To do so might mislead readers into thinking that his services will be covered by insurance. Likewise, if Mr. Childs has no more room for low-fee clients in his practice, then he should drop the reference to a sliding fee scale. It is true that such matters can be dealt with in a first session or telephone consultation, but to leave a false impression in the advertisement is inappropriate even if the situation is later remedied with no harm to the client.

If a psychotherapist does intend to advertise in any way, we recommend several precautionary steps.

- Consult with colleagues regarding the plan to obtain informal opinions about the nature and content of your plan, as well as for a sense of community standards.
- Do not delegate the details of the advertising to others, especially those with aggressive marketing strategies and little understanding of psychological ethics.
- Proofread or carefully monitor the final product before distribution or broadcast.
- Retain a copy of the advertisement, whether in print, film, magnetic, or optical media. In that way, you will have documentation of exactly what was communicated should questions come up later. This can be especially important if the broadcast media are used.

We know of instances when clinicians, anxious to take advantage of liberalized advertising policies, hired public relations firms. All were unhappy with the flashy packages created for them but had to pay the high fees anyway.

From Yellow Pages to the Web

A decade or more ago, listing oneself in the classified (yellow) pages of the telephone directory seemed an important way to attract clients. Some problems emanated from the fact that the directory publishers have an interest in selling space and remain relatively unconcerned about the ethics of professions. Little is known by way of scientific data about whether telephone directory advertising generates client referrals. After all, if one were searching for a skilled surgeon or trial lawyer and relied solely on a colorful, cutely illustrated box ad in the telephone directory, the consequences might indeed be unfortunate. Still, telephone directories were highly visible and attracted the attention—and occasionally the ire—of colleagues, if not clients.

With the era of the Internet and ubiquity of the Web-enabled cell phone, paper directories have become less valuable resources. Businesses focus more attention on Internet-based marketing and finding ways bring consumers to Web sites. In February 2007, searching Google (http://www.google.com) under the term "find a therapist" yielded 3,450,000 hits. Web sites of well-trained mental health professionals, con artists, and everything in between exist on the Internet, and consumers must beware (Heinlen, Welfel, Richmond, & O'Donnell, 2003).

When ethical psychotherapists plan to advertise their availability, whether in paper directories, online directories, or their own Web sites some common elements apply.

- Any public listing should accurately list the practitioner's credentials and licenses, as discussed in earlier examples.
- Clinicians should have the requisite competence to perform the services listed.
- A published directory may have a relatively long shelf life, so practitioners must stand prepared to honor promises made in any advertisement (e.g., specific fees) for an extended period.
- If one maintains a Web site for marketing purposes, an obligation to keep it current with respect to services, fees, and other relevant data of interest to potential consumers applies.

UNACCEPTABLE ADVERTISING

Although the professional associations are now largely blocked from addressing advertising complaints, state licensing boards do have the authority to do so under the state's interest doctrine, as discussed in a separate section of this chapter. We provide the following illustrations of what many state licensing boards might consider unacceptable, including misrepresentation, guarantee or promise of favorable outcome, appeals to client fears or vulnerability, claims of unique or one-of-a-kind services, statements critical of competitive providers, and direct solicitation of vulnerable individual clients. The next three cases have a common element that might best be termed lack of a professional perspective, poor taste, or simply gross insensitivity. Each also has some rather distinctive and difficult aspects.

Case 14–20: Martha Newby, Psy.D., a recently licensed psychologist, in an attempt to get her private practice off to a brisk start, took out a full-page ad in the local newspaper to announce an "office open house," complete with a visit from "Psycho, the Crazy Clown," free balloons imprinted with her address and phone number, a "first session free" certificate, and a door prize of "20 free sessions for you or the significant other of your choice."

Dr. Newby is a relatively inexperienced psychologist in a big hurry and is making ethical blunders out of an impulsive effort to get her practice off and running. Fortunately, such colleagues are generally amenable to constructive, educative approaches to their ethical misconduct. Psycho, the Crazy Clown, certainly does little to enhance the image of the profession, while tending to making a mockery of people with emotional problems. In addition, the offer of free treatment sessions via a door prize drawing tends to belie the careful assessment and planning that should accompany any course of competently delivered psychotherapeutic services. Finally, the first session free coupons create a problem akin to the bait-and-switch routines used by unscrupulous salespeople. In the *bait-and-switch* scam (see case examples in Chapters 1, 3, and 5), the potential client is drawn to the store or potential sale by an attractive offer but on showing interest is encouraged to switch to an item or service more profitable to the seller. In psychotherapeutic service delivery, a first interview is often critical to the formation of a working rapport between therapist and client. Often, the client will share emotion-laden material and form an attachment to the therapist, which may predispose the client to continue the relationship. In this sense, the offer of a free first session represents a type of bait, with implications the client will seldom

recognize. There is nothing wrong with offering to waive the fee for a session. Many therapists will do this if they find it unlikely that they will be able to work with a client after the first session; however, this is quite different from advertising that there is no fee for the first session as bait to bring in clients.

Case 14–21: The New Wave Underground Milita kidnapped a bus full of schoolchildren and held them at gunpoint for several hours before the police were able to negotiate the children's release. Tym Lee Buck, M.D., drove to a shopping center parking lot where the children were to be reunited with their parents. He passed out handbills describing himself as an expert on trauma therapy. The material included the following: "It is a well-known fact that hostages can suffer serious emotional delayed reactions. Preventive psychotherapy for your child is a must." His address and phone number were also listed.

Dr. Buck's behavior is much more obnoxious than Dr. Newby because he is trading on the fears and vulnerabilities of people. He may be correct in anticipating psychological problems among the hostage children, but his presumption that virtually all will need so-called preventive psychotherapy is out of line, and his style is offensive. He is also soliciting individual clients directly and personally, which is unethical even when appeals to emotionalism are not used. His behavior and the circumstances under which he approached the families actually seems to create a potential for increasing the emotional stress on the already-strained families.

Case 14–22: The advertisement read:

"You'll just have to live with it!"
Is that what you've been told? It's not true!
New techniques available at the
Southside Psychological Development Center
will help you master your chronic problems,
whatever they may be: bad habits,
chronic pain, or relationship problems.
Don't delay, call today! 666-555-9999.

The advertisement from the Southside Psychological Development Center seems folksy and well meaning, but it also appears to promise or ensure the likelihood of a favorable outcome. Aside from the inherent misleading quality of its tone, the ad implies success with recalcitrant problems and suggests the application of some novel or unique technique not available elsewhere. In fact, the center turned out to be a group practice of well-intentioned, but overzealous, psychologists trained in behavioral techniques. The comparative desirability of their services and the new techniques were more representative of their hopes than of documented scientific claims. The ad has an additional flaw in that it does not name the individuals responsible for the operation. It is desirable that qualified therapists not hide behind a corporate or group practice title, and it would be preferable (and, in some states, legally required) to have the names of the therapists listed along with the name of the center. The final problem with this ad is the implication that effective treatment will be available at the Southside Center for virtually any problem. This is the same sort of problem evident in Dr. Hartley's situation (Case 14–12). It is likely that the range of effective services to be offered at the center is actually more narrow than the public would be led to believe.

What Potential Clients Think

Little research has been done to document the impact of psychologists' advertising on potential clients, but the results of one creative study on what potential clients think provide an interesting perspective (Keith-Spiegel, Seegar, & Tomison, 1978). Keith-Spiegel and her colleagues surveyed 164 California college students who had already completed at least one psychology course. The students were presented with 13 sets of five brief ads each and asked to imagine that they had a need for psychological services for themselves or someone close to them. They were told to imagine that they were to consult a telephone directory and find the sets of ads in question. Within each set, they were to indicate the rank order of their choices of whom to call first, after reading all five ads in the set. Within each set of ads, a variety of factors were varied. For example, in some the psychologist was lis-

ted as Dr. Jones, instead of J. Jones, Ph.D. Some listed professional affiliations (e.g., APA member); others listed all earned degrees (e.g., B.A., M.A., Ph.D.); still others included slogans (e.g., "the psychologist who cares") or offers (e.g., "no charge for first appointment").

In formulating the study, the investigators had been concerned that flashy, hard-sell, or gimmicky ads might be highly rated in contrast to more simple, professionally dignified ones. While the data and analyses are by no means conclusive, the trends were both interesting and somewhat reassuring. Degrees definitely made a difference in the rankings; the ads that used Ph.D. ranked higher than those ads without it, although the suffix M.A. was rated more impressive than the appellation "Dr." The dual listing of M.A. and Ph.D. was most favored, suggesting that the public believes the more degrees the better and may not realize that most doctoral-level mental health professionals also have master's degrees or their equivalent.

Certification, licensure, and memberships in professional associations also tended to enhance selection potential. Interestingly, personalized "grabber" lines (e.g., the psychologist who cares) did not do well. Some particular demographic variables also seem influential. The sex, ethnicity of the name, and even the oddness of the psychologist's name were varied. For example, participants identifying themselves as Jewish on the questionnaire seemed more likely to choose a psychologist named Cohen or Goldstein than one named Caldwell or Thomas. Women participants generally ranked women psychologists higher, and an odd-sounding name (e.g., Fabian Tuna) tended to reduce the likelihood of a high ranking.

When fees were specified, a Ph.D. psychologist with a low fee was chosen most often, and an M.A. psychotherapist with a low fee was chosen over a Ph.D. with a very high fee. On the other hand, a doctoral-level therapist was generally chosen over a master's-level therapist when the M.A. person's fee was only slightly lower. Lowest ranking of all was the person listed with no degree, even though the fee was modest. Ads with additional descriptive or factual information tended to be selected over less detailed ads or those ads that seemed to have an emotional appeal line. In general, a conservative ad listing degree, license, specialty, and the phrase "reasonable rates" seemed to do best. Come-on lines such as "money-back guarantee" rated very low.

Ads offering a free consultation were extremely popular but would be unethical, as explained earlier in this chapter. The ethical issue is not the free service per se, but the promise of free service as an inducement to a professional relationship. Appeals to informality, such as "Hang-ups are my business," did not go over well, and visual illustrations or promises of effective results were also not very impressive to the college student sample.

Except for the preference for the "free session" ads, the students seemed to select in favor of ethical appropriateness, even though these standards were not presented to the students. Factual detail and informational material had the most striking impact. Interestingly, diplomate status, as mentioned in the section on mention of credentials, did have a favorable impact when listed. However, no student queried had any idea what diplomate status entailed, but most thought that it "sounded good." It seems as though this segment of the general public has expectations regarding professionals' behavior in the marketplace that are consistent with ethical decorum.

Growth Groups and Educational Programs

One type of counseling service that has often skirted the border between ethical and clearly unethical behavior in terms of marketing issues is the so-called growth or enrichment seminars and workshops. When does a course or workshop become psychotherapy? Is there a difference between a seminar that has a psychotherapeutic impact on an individual and psychotherapy conducted in the form of a seminar? While psychotherapy and related ethical matters are covered chiefly in Chapters 5 and 6, it is clear that one is not permitted to solicit clients for therapy. May one then solicit clients for a psychotherapeutic course? Consider these examples of more than semantic interest:

Case 14–23: The Happy Karma Institute, under the direction of Harry Creeshna, M. Div., frequently advertises seminars in "personal power and creative change" and "relaxation systems." Clients are solicited by direct mail advertising and told that the seminars teach "increasing harmony in interpersonal relationships, self-analysis, Sullivanian analysis, biofeedback, autogenics, deep muscle relaxation, and guided fantasy." Mr. Creeshna is described in the mailings as having been trained in psychological techniques and esoteric disciplines.

Case 14–24: Communication Associates, LLP, advertises a seminar entitled, "Introduction to Personal Growth." The format is described as lecture and experiential group participation, including "psychodrama, confrontation, gestalt, assertive, encounter transactional analysis, and training" techniques. The ad appears weekly in a metropolitan newspaper.

Case 14–25: Psycho-Tron Laboratory Learning Systems, Incorporated, directed by Lester Clone, Ph.D., uses a business card with an optical illusion imprinted on it. Instructions on the card explain that viewing the illusion in a certain way is a sign of an inflexible problem-solving style in need of "cogno-effective reprogramming," which can be obtained through an individualized course at Psycho-Tron.

While it is one thing to give didactic or explanatory lectures about therapeutic techniques, it is another thing entirely to apply techniques intended to have some psychotherapeutic outcome in the context of a course or seminar. To begin, certain therapeutic techniques, such as group confrontation, can have a harmful impact on some individuals. On other occasions, individuals with serious somatic problems might seek out psychologically based treatments such as relaxation training instead of first obtaining proper medical care. Without appropriate screening and follow-up, the sampling of seminar topics seems more like random indiscriminant episodes of play with therapy techniques. This may be educational, but it is also potentially harmful if targeted at the lay public in a commercial venture. In addition, the promises or claims alluded to, especially in the ads from the Karma Institute and Psycho-Tron Laboratory, are at best inane and at worst blatant misrepresentation. One can hardly be taught the work of Harry Stack Sullivan in a few weeks of a group seminar, and cogno-effective reprogramming seems a term conjured up by an Orwellian psychotherapist. Communication Associates mentions training in their ad, but they target it to the lay public. Who do they intend to train to train and for what?

Those psychotherapists oriented toward group enhancement of the human potential must fully explore their goals. If these are therapeutic in nature, they should use appropriate professional cautions. If their goals are educative, then the didactic nature of the course or seminar must be stressed, and it must be clear to all concerned that the program is not intended as therapy or therapeutic training.

Referral Services

In some parts of the country, professional associations operate a service by which callers can specify a needed type of psychological consultation or intervention and be given the names of potential providers. In some cases, similar services are offered by for-profit entities, private practitioners, community agencies, or clinics. The three referral services listed below all have one feature in common: They provide clients with the names of psychotherapists. Presumably, they also advertise their services in telephone directories, the media, or elsewhere. Certainly, the same advertising obligations that bind therapists as individual or group practitioners should also bind the operators of such referral services.

Case 14–26: The Northeast State Psychological Association offers a referral service to its members for the benefit of the public. It was developed in response to frequent telephone inquiries from the public. Any members of the association who are licensed, carry professional liability insurance, and have no ethical complaints pending against them may be listed. A file containing provider information, including the availability of a sliding fee scale, foreign language skills, specialty train-

ing, and the like is maintained. When a person calls seeking a referral, a message is taken and referred to a doctoral-level psychologist hired as the coordinator of the service. The coordinator contacts the caller to establish the nature of the request and provides three names of psychologists whose skills, location, and availability fit the client's needs. No fees are charged either party, and the service is paid for out of general membership dues. Often, the calls are requests for speakers or general information rather than for referral to a practitioner.

The service run by the state psychological association does not charge any fees and is intended as a public service. Clients are advised that the service is not endorsing any particular provider but rather is giving a list of qualified practitioners who seem to meet the client's stated needs. The rationale for listing only members may be supported on the basis that the organization can only enforce consumer ethical complaints about members. Clients unable to pay normal practitioner fees are referred to those who offer a sliding fee scale or to community clinics. The service is paid for out of general association funds for public benefit.

Case 14–27: Psychotherapy Assistance is a psychotherapist-finding service run by three therapists in a large metropolitan area. They attempt to match potential clients with therapists on the basis of many factors, including fees charged, areas of specialization, treatment style, and so forth. Therapists who wish to receive referrals are interviewed by the service operators regarding their practice. All must be appropriately licensed and carry liability insurance. Clients who call the service are given a diagnostic interview and charged the usual and customary rate for that service. They are then given the names of two or more therapists recommended by the service, assuming that psychotherapy is a recommendation. The only fees are those paid by the client.

Psychotherapy Assistance represents a fee-for-service matching program. A clinical service is rendered in the form of an evaluation, and referral is then made to practitioners presumably known to the referrer. Supposedly, the matching is more individualized and based on clinical judgments of psychologists, which are not possible under the more limited state association system. No fees are charged to the providers, an appropriate model lest the specter of fee splitting (see Chapter 7) come up. Care should be taken, however, to be certain that any advertising or promotion activity undertaken is appropriate and responsible.

Case 14–28: Nadia Nerk is an unemployed real estate agent who has opened a storefront service known as "Shrink Finders." Clients pay Nerk a fee and are offered access to a set of videotaped interviews with psychotherapists, recorded in their offices. Clients may look through as many tapes as they wish and will then be given the names and addresses of any therapists whose tapes impress them. The therapists have paid Nerk $100 for making their tape and an additional $10 per session for each client visit based on a referral from her service.

The Shrink Finders service seems questionable on several fronts. The effort at a "catchy" name for the services and the video interviews raise the potential for some anxiety that superficial data are being promulgated as the basis for important decisions. There seems to be no efforts to tailor the service to client needs or otherwise introduce professional judgment or advice. While no advertising has been presented for the service, one must wonder what form it would take and how appropriate it might be. Most troubling, however, are the financial arrangements. Because the providers pay a commission to Ms. Nerk, this may pose an ethical problem for the therapists if the financial arrangement is concealed from clients.

While referral services can be helpful to clients and the public at large, their modus operandi determines their ethical propriety. Advertising and financial aspects of the operations may singly or together raise ethical problems. Any therapist considering involvement with such a service should be quite careful about exploring all of these issues prior to signing on. The legitimate economic needs of the practitioner should never take precedence over client needs.

Other Public Statements

Mental health professionals will often have the opportunity to be heard in public. Advertising is only one such avenue; another is the media, as addressed in Chapter 15. Other opportunities to influence the public occur while teaching, as discussed in Chapter 16, or while giving public lectures. Potential opportunities for misrepresentation, striving for personal gain, causing distress, or embarrassing the profession and one's colleagues abound. It is important to consider the impact of any public pronouncements made in the role of psychotherapist before presenting them.

Case 14–29: Hokey Line is a clever journalist who majored in psychology as an undergraduate. He is very adept at translating research findings into readable newsy tidbits that would make great filler items for community newspapers. He is marketing two products to mental health professionals. The first is a set of such articles that he is willing to sell and permit the buyers to send to local newspapers under their own names. That is, the therapist-buyers could send the articles to their local newspapers for possible publication in a weekly professional column. Of course, the newspaper would note that the therapist is a practitioner in the vicinity, and the column (actually written by Line) could serve as a subtle advertisement. Line's second product is a "newsletter" full of such material. He will sell copies of the newsletter imprinted with the practitioner's name and office address so that the buyer can do bulk mailings to the community to give out the free information, along with the impression that the buyer actually wrote it.

In April 1993, the APA Ethics Committee issued a policy statement dealing with so-called canned columns or preauthored newsletters. The statement notes that it is unethical to identify oneself as the author of such a publication using the term "by." Associating oneself with such a column can be false and deceptive, violate publication credit standards, and permit others to make deceptive statements on one's behalf.

Presentation of Self

The manner in which people present themselves to others often represents a form of marketing or self-promotion. It is always a heady feeling to be flattered or to hear one's expertise celebrated in public, but it is also important to be represented accurately and objectively. Mental health practitioners are trained as professionals with a scientific base of knowledge. It is just as important to be honest and objective about the limitations of one's knowledge as about one's credentials. If introduced incorrectly or in a misleading manner, even if well intentioned, the therapist has a duty to correct the misinformation promptly.

Case 14–30: Hank Puffery, M.D., held an adjunct academic appointment as an assistant professor in a large medical school. Several documents, including a lecture program and a grant application, listed his academic rank as associate professor or professor. His failure to correct these inaccurate listings over several months ultimately led to the loss of his academic appointment on the basis of professional misrepresentation.

We do not know for certain whether Dr. Puffery's inaccurate listings were intentional or inadvertent, but it was clear to his superiors at the medical school that he did not correct the errors despite many opportunities to do so. Many other examples of presentation-of-self problems with respect to the public appear in Chapter 15, but encounters with problems may also occur between therapist and client when alone.

Case 14–31: After an evaluation by Roger Fallic, Ph.D., a competently trained sex therapist, the client was informed that he could probably be helped by a treatment plan involving at least 6 months of office visits. This prediction, Fallic said, was based on the normative patterns documented in his treatment of clients with similar problems. When the client balked at the $200-per-hour fee, Dr. Fallic commented, "You really ought to come up with it somehow since I'm the only one who can really help you in your current situation."

Perhaps Fallic did have a good treatment plan, which was well validated and potentially quite effective, for his client. The implication that no one else could provide effective treatment, however, is most likely false. The high fee charged and apparent unwillingness of Fallic to reduce it are not unethical per se, but the statement, with its grandiose implications, and Fallic's apparent unwillingness to make a less-costly referral represent serious problems.

Embarrassing Others

Just as self-promotion represents a form of marketing, some professionals denigrate the abilities of competitors to enhance their own public image. It is not unethical to be a fool or an abrasive lout, but such behavior becomes embarrassing to the profession when the perpetrator is identified as a mental health professional. At the same time, public comments presented in a sarcastic or offensive manner can easily exceed the bounds of ethical propriety. Chapter 13 deals with these issues vis-à-vis individual colleagues, but consider more globally expressed remarks, such as these comments overhead in public lectures or meetings:

> "Psychoanalysis really never helps anyone do anything except enhance their own narcissism."

> "Social workers really aren't trained to do deep therapy and ought to be supervised by psychologists or psychiatrists for most direct service work."

The following is a remark to a group of students in an abnormal psychology class: "Okay, what crazies did we read about this week? Any nominations for psychotic of the week based on people you know on campus?"

These overgeneralizations, offensive comments, casual demeaning of people with problems, and similar remarks tend to hurt the entire profession. The following chapter (Chapter 15) pursues these matters in more detail, using the print and broadcast media as context. It is important to remember that other public forums are important as well. When lecturing, testifying before a legislative or judicial body, or making any statement for public consumption, one must consider the impact of one's words and style carefully, especially when the public is looking at a person identified as a mental health professional.

SUMMARY GUIDELINES

1. Advertising by mental health professionals is clearly acceptable and can not be banned, although the content of advertisements should ideally focus on facts of meaningful interest to the potential consumer.
2. One must take great care when listing affiliations, degrees, and other data to ensure that the public is not misled, confused, or otherwise deceived. Both intentional deception and inadvertent errors that are not corrected raise ethical issues.
3. Once completely prohibited, soliciting testimonials or quotations from "satisfied users" is now permissible as long as they are not solicited from current psychotherapy clients or others subject to undue influence. The effectiveness of such advertising is unknown.
4. The uninvited, direct, in-your-face solicitation, as opposed to mass solicitation through media advertising, of individuals as clients is also prohibited to the extent it subjects the potential client to undue influence. However, this does not include barriers to inviting the significant others of current clients for collateral treatment.
5. Mental health professionals who serve organizational or industrial clients are entitled to broader latitude than those who serve individuals (e.g., current organizational clients could be solicited for endorsements), lay groups, and families; however, they also must observe factual, validity-based criteria and avoid deception in their advertising claims.
6. Fees may be mentioned in advertisements but must also be honored for the reasonable life of the announcement.
7. Referral services may ethically charge a fee to clients, therapists, or both, although this should not be secret from the client, and the fee should not be the primary basis for making the specific referral. When portions of fees are paid to other parties, such fees should be in payment for services actually rendered (e.g., referral service, consultation, supervision, office space rental, etc.).
8. Although there is no longer any prohibition to offer treatment to a client who is receiving services from another professional, specific discussions with the client of the potential risks and conflicts is now required. It would also be wise to seek authorization from the client to contact the other professional and to consult with that person.
9. Therapists must consider their style of presentation of self and public statements carefully in any public context, whether or not advertising per se is involved.
10. States may impose more stringent restrictions on professional advertising than professional associations as long as a legitimate state's interest is documented and as that state's interest does not violate a consumer's access to useful information.

References

American Medical Association. (1971). *Principles of medical ethics.* Chicago: Author.

American Psychological Association. (1969). Guidelines for telephone directory listings. *American Psychologist, 24,* 20–71.

American Psychological Association. (1981). Ethical principles of psychologists. *American Psychologist, 36,* 633–638.

American Psychological Association. (1990). Ethical principles of psychologists (amended June 2, 1989). *American Psychologist, 45,* 390–395.

American Psychological Association Ethics Committee. (1993). *Advertisement and canned columns, revised statement.* Washington, DC: American Psychological Association.

Association for the Advancement of Psychology. (1982). FTC's jurisdiction over professions threatened. *Advance, 8,* 5

Azcuenaga, M. L. (1990). *Separate statement of Commissioner Mary L. Azcuenaga concurring in part and dissenting in part in American Psychological Association.* Washington, DC: Federal Trade Commission.

Bates et al. v. State Bar of Arizona, 443 U.S. 350 (1977).

Dattilio, F. M. (2002). Board certification in psychology: Is it really necessary? *Professional Psychology, 33,* 54–57.

Dattilio, F. M., Sadoff, R. L., & Gutheil, T. G. (2003). Board certification in forensic psychiatry and psychology: Separating the chaff from the wheat. *Journal of Psychiatry and Law, 31,* 5–19.

Federal Trade Commission. (1993, March). FTC consent order text is published in its entirety. *APA Monitor, 8,* 8.

Florida Bar v. Went For It, Inc., et al., 63 *United States Law Week* 4644 (1995).

Foxhall, K. (2000). What's behind that credential? When it comes to credentialing, caveat emptor. *APA Monitor, 31,* 39.

Goldfarb v. Virginia State Bar, 421 U.S. 773 (1975).

Gooding, A. D. (2004). Basic requirements for psychotherapists transitioning into coaching (Part II). *Annals of the American Psychotherapy Association, 7,* 38.

Hansen, M. (2000). Expertise to go. Retrieved September 30, 2007, from http://www.truthinjustice.org/02fpert.htm

Heinlen, K. T., Welfel, E. R., Richmond, E. N., & O'Donnell, M. S. (2003). The nature, scope, and ethics of psychologists' e-therapy Web sites: What consumers find when surfing the Web. *Psychotherapy: Theory, Research, Practice, Training, 40,* 112–124.

Keith-Spiegel, P., Seegar, P., & Tomison, G. (1978, August). *What potential clients think of various modes of advertising.* Paper presented at 88th Annual Meeting of the American Psychological Association, Toronto.

Koocher, G. P. (1977). Advertising for psychologists: Pride and prejudice or sense and sensibility? *Professional Psychology, 8,* 149–160.

Koocher, G. P. (1979). Credentialing in psychology: Close encounters with competence? *American Psychologist, 34,* 696–702.

Koocher, G. P. (1994a). APA and the FTC: New adventures in consumer protection. *American Psychologist, 49,* 322–328.

Koocher, G. P. (1994b). The commerce of professional psychology and the new ethics code. *Professional Psychology, 25,* 355–361.

Koocher, G. P. (2004). Ethics and the advertising of professional services: Blame Canada. *Canadian Psychology, 45,* 137–138.

Miller, W. R. (2000). Professional ethics and marketing of treatment. *Addiction, 95,* 1764–1765.

Ohralik v. Ohio State Bar Association, 436 U.S. 447 (1978).

O'Sullivan, P., & Murphy, P. (1998). Ambush marketing: The ethical issues. *Psychology and Marketing, 15,* 349–366.

Packard, T., & Simon, N. P. (2006). Board certification by the American Board of Professional Psychology. In T. J. Vaughn (Ed.), *Psychology licensure and certification: What students need to know* (pp. 117–126). Washington, DC: American Psychological Association.

Perrott, L. A. (1998). When will it be coming to the large discount chain stores? Psychotherapy as commodity. *Professional Psychology, 29,* 168–173.

Shapero v. Kentucky Bar Association, 486 U.S. 466 (1988).

Shead, N. W., & Dobson, K. S. (2004a). Psychology for sale: The ethics of advertising professional services. *Canadian Psychology, 45,* 125–136.

Shead, N. W., & Dobson, K. S. (2004b). Towards more assertive advertising practices: An evolutionary, not revolutionary, step forward. *Canadian Psychology, 45,* 139–140.

Tomycz, N. D. (2006). A profession selling out: Lamenting the paradigm shift in physician advertising. *Journal of Medical Ethics, 32,* 26–28.

Virginia State Board of Pharmacy et al. v. Virginia Citizens Consumer Council, Inc., et al., 425 U.S. 747 (1975).

Winters, K. (2000). Warning label: This treatment approach may cause claims of a magic cure. *Addiction, 95,* 1770.

15

The Public Face of Mental Health Professionals

We live in an age of journalism: An age of skimmed surfaces, of facile confidence that reality is whatever can be seen and taped and reported.

George F. Will

Contents

FRACTURED PUBLIC IMAGES

The public's image of mental health services and those who deliver them remains incomplete, splintered, confused, and often enough downright erroneous. The quality of information about emotional well-being and mental

illness available to the public is often inferior, sensationalized, and distorted. A dizzying array of traditional and fringe psychotherapies contributes to misunderstandings. Most people can not differentiate accurately among clinical psychologists, experimental psychologists, psychiatrists, social workers, marriage and family counselors, or those using the generic title "psy-chotherapist." The media parade an array of "experts" appearing to function as psychother-apists, sporting titles such as "aggression spe-cialist," "grief worker," "life coach," "crisis in-tervener," and "divorce consultant." Only rarely do we learn of the training (if any) and experi-ence held by many such media mavens.

Legitimate mental health providers also have to compete with astrologers, Tarot card readers, spiritual guides, and a host of other self-proclaimed mental healers. Whereas some ther-apists decry the foolishness of those who would entrust their emotional well-being to such per-sons, it can also be said that mental health professionals have not done their job in edu-cating the public about why their services are more valid (Salzinger, 2003). Interactive media and computer networks have led to rapid evo-lution in the way people disperse and absorb the knowledge that shapes what and how they think, and the impact of these more recent in-novations on mental health professions is also profound. Ethical risks and pitfalls lurk close by, with many as-yet-to-be fully conceptualized consequences.

We differentiate the best that mental health professionals have to contribute—information derived from a research or strong practice base—from the clichés and psychobabble that permeate much of what the public absorbs as fact. We do not intend to suggest that any media or other public forums be designated ethically off limits to mental health professionals. How-ever, risks are present whenever we accept op-portunities to present ourselves and our ideas and research to the public. The challenge is not *whether* but *how* we involve ourselves with the media that raises ethical questions about social responsibility, competence, conflict of interest, and the public image of the helping professions and social/behavioral research.

MEDIA PORTRAYALS OF HELPING PROFESSIONALS, EDUCATORS, AND RESEARCHERS

Every day, mass media punctuate the awareness of us all. Intricate stories or complex issues are usually stripped bare to fit within narrow time and space constraints. Broadcast media person-alities routinely cut off those they are inter-viewing if the answers to their questions exceed 30 seconds, regardless of the scope and neces-sary complexity of satisfactory answers. Believ-ing what one sees in print or hears espoused by self-proclaimed experts has become a pervasive human failing.

Mental health professionals face a signifi-cant quandary with respect to the media. On the one hand, society clearly benefits when practitioners, educators, and social/behavioral researchers actively disseminate relevant infor-mation. We can help people gain sensible per-spectives of societies and the people who pop-ulate them. We can better understand ourselves and gain insights into how to live more mean-ingful lives. Yet, unfortunately, some within our ranks may fail to inform or may even misinform. Misguidance can occur unwittingly, as when journalists or producers edit an interview with a blunt hatchet or interject their own, often er-roneous, take on what data mean. Misinfor-mation can be transmitted purposefully, as when authors who are also mental health pro-fessionals and their publishers want to sell more books than a sober and reasoned presentation of the facts would warrant.

In the 1980s, the American Psychological Association (APA) placed specific expectations on its members with respect to public state-ments. Psychologists were specifically admon-ished to avoid sensationalism, exaggeration, and superficiality when making any public pro-nouncements. The 2002 APA code no longer mandates a watchful eye with regard to a glitter factor but does require avoiding false, fraudu-lent, or deceptive statements in any venue (in-cluding electronic ones) to which the public has access (APA 02: 5.01, 5.04).

Case 15–1: Maggie Showoff, Ph.D., took out a full-page ad in the town's paper inviting the whole community to the grand opening of her counseling office. The affair featured live music from a local rock band and offered appetizer trays with little printed labels, such as Freud Fritters, Chocolate Addictions, and Depressed Duck Pate. Copies of her résumé were passed out that included her educational status, intern sites, and specialties, including "eating disorders." However, Dr. Showoff had no formal education or training in that specialty, noting that she had spent 1 month as a summer intern in an eating disorders clinic.

In years gone by, all helping professions would have considered Dr. Showoff's advertisement and splashy event tacky and unprofessional. However, following the FTC actions described in Chapter 14, the APA can only express concerns with the single misleading item on her résumé: Dr. Showoff's brief experience with eating disorders, which is insufficient to qualify her as anywhere near competent to independently treat eating disordered clients.

In the preamble (aspirational, but unenforceable) of the 2002 APA code, psychologists are urged to commit to increasing scientific and professional knowledge about behavior and people and to use such information to improve individuals, organizations, and society as a whole. This would seem to apply to public statements. In another aspirational section of the APA code, seeking to promote accuracy, honesty, and truthfulness is encouraged in science, teaching, and practice activities, but public statements are not explicitly included. An enforceable code item (APA 02: 2.04) admonishes psychologists to base their work on established scientific and professional knowledge, but the item concerns the foundations for scientific and professional judgments, not public statements. However, it would not be a long leap to assume that similar standards should apply when one puts oneself "out there." Yet, unless another specific principle of the code is violated, such as disclosing information shared in confidence in a public forum, it would currently prove difficult to sustain an ethics charge against an APA member, leaving the integrity of the public image of psychology resting heavily on each member's willingness to remain as truthful and dignified as possible.

When it comes to matters other than accurately presenting oneself and one's credentials, pinning down what constitutes problematical public statements becomes more difficult. "Fraud," "deception," and "misleading" may be tricky because mental health professionals hold many conflicting and inconsistent theories. Research findings are also often unclear, contradictory, or incomplete. One professional's life passion may well constitute another's pet peeve. For example, the existence of repressed memories remains an area of hot debate, or whether expressing anger releases it or builds it up has adherents both ways.

Distortions of Psychotherapeutic, Diagnostic, and Research Concepts

Television characters who would qualify for diagnoses as homicidal dissociative personality disorders—often erroneously referred to as schizophrenics—populate the airwaves with a frequency that suggests to uninformed viewers that such frightening people could be behind them in the supermarket line or living next door. Indeed, television portrayals of people with a mental illness are estimated as 10 times more violent than other television characters generally, and at least 10 times more violent than the mentally ill in the general population (Diefenbach, 1997). The mentally ill are also often stereotyped by the media as victimized, unemployed, and leading failed lives (Signorielli, 1989).

Jokes and casual use of medical terms also frequently directed toward the mentally disabled include name-calling through the use of diagnostic labels or their archaic or popularized derivatives, such as "moron," "lunatic," "cretin," and "schizo." Other overrepresented, and usually inaccurately presented, mental conditions in the media include amnesia, homicidal mania, hysterical paralysis, and phobic disorders (Schneider, 1987). More recently, obsessive–compulsive disorder (OCD) became the "diagnosis du jour," with a popular TV show featuring a detective with OCD who solves crimes in between his fussy antics played for laughs. There are exceptions to such extreme portrayals, but they are rare. For example, *The Rain Man* and *As Good as It Gets* are among the more sympathetic portrayals of people with mental problems. Also, *Shine* and *A Beautiful Mind* illustrate how individuals with serious mental disorders can be talented and make significant contributions to society (Wedding, 2005).

A media portrayal of a psychotherapy session is usually boiled down to a few exchanges between "client" and "therapist," often concluding with a remarkable moment in which a lifelong search for just the right insight occurs. Most portrayals of successful therapy focus on trauma or dramatic emotional breakthroughs in a way that greatly misrepresents the actual process of psychotherapy (Gordon, 1994). The psychiatrists taking center stage on the classic and long-running series *Frasier* were mostly viewed as endearing, despite the quirky frolics of the Crane brothers. More often, depictions of psychotherapists are portrayed as uncaring exploiters, rogues with no sense of professional role boundaries, or riddled with their own serious pathologies. In the movie *The Jacket*, for example, a soldier in the first Gulf War is sent to a menacing-looking mental hospital where a creepy doctor orders him restrained, drugged, and put into what appears to be a large file cabinet drawer. A made-for-TV movie, *Cheaters Club*, revealed a therapist who discloses her sexual problems with her own husband and encourages the unhappily married women in her group therapy to have affairs. Any who do not cheat are reprimanded because they have nothing to share. Other examples abound.

Schneider (1987) reviewed 207 American films depicting psychiatrists (excluding the exploitative horror genre). Of these, 35% fit his "Dr. Dippy" type, the psychiatrist who is crazier than the patients; 22% were classified as "Dr. Wonderfuls," the type that skillfully maneuvers or interprets at precisely the correct moment, resulting in a total cure; and 22% were classified as "Dr. Evils," who dabble in forbidden, coercive experimentation for personal profit or self-gratification. In a survey of 99 films with mental health professional characters, women characters were more likely to be sexualized, and male characters were more likely to be portrayed as inept (Bischoff & Reiter, 1999). In a survey of 45 films, over half of the mental health practitioners engaged in some form of unethical behavior (Lipsitz, Rand, Cornett, Sassler, & White, 2000). A fourth of them killed another character, with self-defense accounting for only one case. Others had sex with their patients or their patients' close relations, and some suffered

from serious pathology or were abysmal partners and parents. For example, in *Final Analysis*, a psychologist, played by Richard Gere, sleeps with his client's sister. Extreme involvement in clients' lives seemed the overriding theme, which could raise false public expectations about what mental health professionals do for and with their clients.

These depictions of extreme boundary violations are further complicated in that they are often accompanied by the inference that such intrusions are helpful and curative. Robin Williams, portraying the therapist in *Good Will Hunting*, for example, was portrayed as making significant inroads into his client's (Matt Damon's) problems, but in the process he divulged his own intimate issues and threatened to physically harm his client (Sleek, 1998). The more professional and cautious portrayals on the *Law and Order* series offer a welcome exception. "Dr. Melfi," Tony Soprano's psychiatrist on the popular cable series *The Sopranos*, came across as rather stiff and distant but not as an embarrassment to the profession until she abruptly decided to terminate Tony's treatment after her character and colleagues inaccurately interpret an actual published journal articles.

The public's lack of understanding of science and the widespread belief in pseudoscience has been well documented, with the blame often placed on media misrepresentation (Hall, 2003). Social and behavioral scientists are largely absent from dramatic media fare. Occasionally, there are weird portrayals of social scientists as power-hungry mind controllers who seduce unsuspecting victims into their gadget- and drug-stocked laboratories, or ancient, eccentric scholars who dabble in the supernatural. Philip Zimbardo was rightfully disturbed by the German movie adaptation of his classic "Stanford prison experiment" (Haney, Banks, & Zimbardo, 1973). *Das Experiment* portrayed beatings, rapes, torture, and murder, acts that never occurred in the actual experiment (Murray, 2002).

Actual research findings, when cited at all, often seem selected on the basis of curiosity or controversy rather than scientific quality. Isolated or minor findings, if intriguing, may reach public attention in a way that gives the impression that far more was discovered than the actual data warrant. For example, an early-stage study of a vaccine for Alzheimer's disease made a vigorous media splash, falsely raising hopes that a cure was imminent (Kolata, 2000). Correlational data are consistently presented as discoveries of a cause. For example, there was a report that kids who are in the school band are also better-than-average students. The unsupported conclusion was that playing a musical instrument enhances educational achievement.

Typically, compact conclusions are presented with no effort to describe the qualifications and cautions that should reasonably attend an evaluation of almost any social/behavioral science research study. Overblown and misleading research findings also circulate quickly, with the next commentator using the previously stated erroneous conclusions, possibly altering them just a tad more to fit the media's immediate agenda. Support for social/behavioral research itself suffers as a result of misinformation because policymakers often rely on the media as a source of data on which to base their decisions. It is not unusual to hear politicians report a flawed media version of a scientific finding as the basis for their stands on policies that have implications for human welfare.

Display of Sullied Linen

It is unfortunate that exemplary and socially responsible mental health professionals do not seem to attract much media interest. Instead, news items usually display flagrant violations of professional responsibilities or the commission of malicious, reprehensible, and bizarre acts. Although the cases presented next involve serious ethical or legal violations ripped from the headlines and could fit elsewhere in this book, these actual cases, using bogus names, attracted considerable media attention.

Case 15–2: Hy Kick, L.M.F.T., owned a clinic serving abused children. The press discovered that he listed individuals as members of his board of directors who had never heard of him. A mental health agency then terminated its contracts with his clinic when a young girl, covered with bedsores, died of neglect while under his care. He

then lost his state certification after being convicted of punching and kicking his girlfriend. In the meantime, criminal investigations are underway related to the death of the little girl.

Case 15–3: Sik Imposter, Ph.D., trained as a social psychologist, used the name and qualifications of a psychiatrist from another state and accepted a position as a staff psychiatrist in a state mental hospital. When Imposter became suspicious that his true identity was on the verge of discovery, he traveled across the country to the office of the psychiatrist whose identity he had stolen and attempted to kill the authentic psychiatrist as he exited a taxicab.

Case 15–4: While bathing her daughter shortly after a therapy session, a mother noticed that the child's genitals were reddened. When questioned, the girl replied that it happened during the "secret game" that she always played with her therapist, Phil Pedo, M.D. Dr. Pedo would take off the girl's panties and have her sit on his face. The mother called the police.

Case 15–5: Fearful that a wealthy client with whom he was having an affair was going to report him to the authorities, Ben Berserk, M.S.W., broke into her home and attempted to strangle her as she slept.

These cases create an alarming image of those who deliver mental health services. Psychologists, psychiatrists, counselors, and social workers are, after all, not exempt from the range of pathology and deviance that affects humankind as a whole. To the extent that the public generalizes its attitudes about those who deliver mental health services from these high-profile accounts, they would stereotype the members of our professions as potentially fraudulent, exploitative, perverted, and violent.

In the past, considerable debate has focused on whether ethics committees should investigate crimes or other highly questionable acts *unrelated* to one's professional identification and duties, as discussed in Chapter 3. The 2002 APA code, it will be recalled, limits actionable offenses to scientific, educational, or professional roles. Private conduct unrelated to crimes or professional competence is explicitly excluded from the code's purview. Regardless, the public image of all mental health professionals clearly suffers when actions *unrelated* to professional activities become publicized, as illustrated by the following news accounts, using bogus names:

Case 15–6: A young boy was seriously injured by a hit-and-run driver, Hooch Boozer, M.S.W. A heavily intoxicated Boozer was quickly apprehended. Newspaper accounts highlighted Boozer's three previous arrests for drunk driving and mentioned that he was a counselor at the local university.

Case 15–7: School psychologist, Picki Pocket, Ed.D., gambled away thousands of dollars in a state-run casino. She was arrested for credit card theft and larceny after being caught red-handed stealing from teachers' wallets left in the faculty lounges of the schools where she worked.

Case 15–8: When the neighbors sensed a foul odor coming from the apartment where Bates Poe, Ph.D., and his mother lived, they called the police. They found the mother's dead body sitting up on the living room sofa and Bates asleep in his bed. The mother had been dead for at least a week. Although the coroner found that the mother died of natural causes, the son, identified in the paper as a therapist at a local clinic, had no explanation regarding why he let her just sit there for so long.

Case 15–9: An eight-page story in a major news magazine detailed the bizarre plot of a woman and her lover to kill her husband. The detailed story of the crime and murder convictions noted the woman's profession as a practicing psychologist and a dabbler in witchcraft.

Whether Boozer's irresponsible drinking and driving behavior compromised his ability to counsel students is not known. However, along with Boozer himself, his institution and the discipline of social work likely suffered some loss in reputation. Dr. Pocket may have been a competent school psychologist, but her pilfering shattered the trust of the community as well as her job and her freedom. One can safely bet that from now on the teachers in Dr. Pocket's district will keep a better eye on their purses when her replacement shows up. And, Mr. Poe

may have performed adequately in the clinic, but his personal problems clearly exceed that of "mama's boy." As for the psychologist-witch-murderess, this juicy story had very long media legs, much to the chagrin of others in the profession (see Pound, 2005).

Breaking the law and engaging in bizarre behavior are not the only necessary ingredients to a decline in public trust in the mental health professions. As the next case illustrates, publicized acts may not violate any legal statutes, but they nevertheless smear the image of mental health practitioners. The next case is an example of how character deficits can smear a profession's reputation.

Case 15–10: Fast Buck, Ph.D., was treating Persona Aplenty for a dissociative disorder. Dr. Buck discovered more than 60 "personalities" within Miss Galore. She signed over exclusive book and movie rights to her story at his urging. Some time later after a falling out between the two, Galore contacted the media to tell her story of how Dr. Buck exploited her condition and trust by holding a contract that allows him all of the book and movie royalties.

The contract may be valid, and Dr. Buck may well have more skill than Ms. Aplenty when it comes to writing a salable book. Nevertheless, the media found the dissolution of their agreement intriguing and allowed Ms. Aplenty time to denigrate Dr. Buck in the hopes that their prodding questions would result in various personalities popping out.

Unfortunately, the public trust in mental health professionals may suffer even when no ethical wrongdoing occurred, as the next two cases illustrate.

Case 15–11: Edna Scholarly, Ph.D., a prominent research psychologist, wrote to an ethics committee expressing concern about an incident brought to her attention. She had received a letter from a distraught mother blaming Dr. Scholarly for having lost her child in a custody dispute. Further inquiry revealed that the father's attorney had used Dr. Scholarly's article on the effects of working mothers on child development as the basis of his argument that the mother was a bad parent and that certain comments taken out of context and embellished inappropriately may have influenced the court's decision. Dr. Scholarly believed that citation of her work in this manner constituted misconduct and sought counsel for possible redress.

Case 15–12: Journalist Quick Whip advocated the use of physical punishment for children's wrongdoings. He cited a number of sources to bolster his argument that corporal punishment, including use of electric shock devices, constitutes an effective means of eliminating unwanted behaviors. The cited research had focused solely on institutionalized, severely self-injurious, autistic children. The psychologists credited by Whip were appalled by his alleged promotion of a technique never intended for use with children with minor behavior problems. Even though these psychologists wrote a stern letter to the journalist and the newspaper editor, they were never acknowledged, and a retraction never appeared.

"Unringing the bell" is rarely an option. Unfortunately, a misuse of one's work is usually not discovered until it is already publicized, and the damage is done. Even so, the APA ethics code specifies that if psychologists learn of the misuse of their work, they attempt to take whatever corrective action they reasonably can (APA 02: 1.01). So, when mental health professionals find that their work has been misused, a letter should be written to the editor or other parties involved. Or, a retraction or corrective action can be requested. Such action may or may not be effective, but it is expected that one will try.

MENTAL HEALTH PROFESSIONALS AND MEDIA RELATIONSHIPS

Public Statements Based on Interviews With Journalists

Journalists have total control over what actually gets through to the public. Inevitable alterations occur in the form of small selected segments that fit media needs. Although many fine journalists select interview elements well, one must take as a matter of faith that the portions finally aired will not violate the integrity of the interview. Journalists rarely afford the opportunity to review their final copy and seldom honor requests to do so. Unforgiving deadlines can also preclude journalists from doing thorough and fully accurate work.

We would expect trained science news journalists to do the best job. However, these journalists typically have less interest in the social and behavioral sciences than in the so-called harder sciences (Dunwoody, 1980). Journalists who do write about psychological and mental health topics apparently think they know a lot more about these subjects than they actually do (McCall, 1988). For this reason, those who agree to interact under circumstances of minimal editorial control are advised to proceed with caution to ensure that their names and their work will be treated fairly.

Encounters With the Media: Horror Stories

It is natural to feel flattered when a reporter, writer, or associate producer calls to express interest in your work. The outcome of resulting publicity can offer benefits to all. Your work is disseminated to an audience, and your influence, popularity, and demand for your expertise might increase as a result (Fox & Levin, 1993). However, not all such alliances prove satisfying. During informal discussions with colleagues, we have consistently observed that those who have interfaced often with the media have at least one foul experience to share. Mental health professionals have complained that journalists have usurped credit for the meaty material while crediting the interviewees with trivial comments, misquoting or quoting them out of context, or greatly altering the intended meaning. Other complaints include the misrepresentation of affiliations, the setting up of interviewees for harsh criticism by writing in a provocative style, and a promise to send copies of the story that then never arrive. Sometimes, the result is amusing, as when a colleague agreed to talk to a freelance reporter only to be told 3 weeks later by the colleague's mother that he had been quoted in an infamous tabloid right next to a story claiming that an 8-year-old girl gave birth to four turtles. At other times, the results prove more disturbing.

Case 15–13: Burt Trapped, Psy.D., was thrilled to be invited to appear on a major network magazine show. But, during the filming it became painfully clear that the host was biased against Trapped's work. He felt blindsided and forced to defend himself throughout the entire interrogation. He considered walking out but realized that would make him look cowardly, antisocial, and guilty. He stayed, and, as he put it, "just looked pathetic instead."

Occasionally, a piece written by a journalist has come to the attention of an ethics committee. In the majority of such instances, blame for the problem ultimately fell on the irresponsible or incompetent journalists. This is not to say that one can not be held accountable for inappropriate disclosures to journalists, as seen in the next two cases.

Case 15–14: Groupie Squeal, L.M.H.C., was interviewed about his celebrity clients in a popular movie magazine. He identified his clients by name and offered additional personal and interpretive comments. His response to an ethics committee inquiry was that his clients would welcome the free publicity.

Case 15–15: Tim Uppie, Ph.D., was so convinced that a commonly used antidepressant medication was essential to mental well-being that he suggested to a reporter 15 minutes into an interview that she looked depressed and should try it. He then invited her to become his client.

An ethics committee found Mr. Squeal professionally irresponsible and strongly admonished him to leave the promotion of his celebrity clients to their publicists. Whether Dr. Uppie's enthusiasm for a particular psychoactive drug is warranted is not the issue here, but his quick diagnosis and verbal prescription raises questions about competence and ability to render professional judgments. Uppie should have realized that a reporter would surely report this twist in their interview, and that the result would be damaging to the more respectful image of psychologists as discrete professionals

who function within legally mandated limits. Furthermore, it was inappropriate for Uppie to make an uninvited solicitation of a client (APA 02: 5.06).

Sometimes, as the next case reveals, professionals can be faulted for trusting too much.

Case 15–16: Jethrow Relaxed, Ph.D., and his colleague Kelia Kasual, M D., met with a reporter at a local coffee shop to discuss some of the problems facing the state's new governor. The reporter treated them to lunch, and everyone exchanged amusing stories. The discussion slowly moved to the topic at hand. The therapists were, by then, so comfortable with the reporter that they made an offhanded joke about the governor's possible early toilet training experiences as evidenced by his "rigid personality." When lunch was over and the interview appeared to be formally under way, serious, professional opinions about the problems facing the governor were offered. The next day, the newspaper article included the therapists' speculations about the governor's probable stressful potty training.

All of us have made casual remarks about others, especially when the company is sociable, that would result in considerable distress if made public. It is especially important to maintain a keen awareness of the situation and the people present when acting in a professional role. The mental health professionals in this case faced considerable unflattering publicity from the public and from their colleagues. In the actual incident on which this case was adapted, the governor's campaign staff threatened defamation charges and reported the therapists to the state licensing board.

Minimizing the Risk

We offer some hints for ensuring a successful journey between your mouth and the public's ear and eye. First, try to learn the purpose of the story, including the journalist's approach to it, and details about any unfamiliar media outlet. If the story or media outlet seems exploitative, sensational, or superficial, consider waiting for a better opportunity to share your expertise. Remember that scholarly publishing and the mass media have very different purposes. The first strictly informs, and the second often entertains and draws in paying sponsors. Keeping these differences in mind may assist in a decision to participate as well as an understanding why the final outcome is the way it is.

If you do decide to give an interview, you can improve how the results are reported by providing tight, clearly stated summaries for the journalist. Such written material often yields direct quotations that highlight the points you deem most significant, thus greatly reducing error in the final product.

If you are contacted to comment on a topic about which you have insufficient knowledge or experience, we strongly advise that you politely refuse the interview or refer the reporter to a better resource. Although the 2002 APA ethics code does not speak directly to competence when making comments unrelated to giving personal advice, the general spirit enjoins us to remain within our competence boundaries. Journalists may press hard because an imminent deadline renders nearly any professional's views acceptable. Never allow a pushy journalist under pressure to overpower your personal integrity.

Avoid getting too comfortable with the interviewer. Remember, members of the press work to fulfill their own agenda and view you as a means to that end. They usually seem very pleasant and are skilled in the art of opening people up. We certainly are not suggesting that every journalist conceals his or her true plan, but the frequent use of hidden cameras, snares, and bait-and-switch tactics of "investigative reporting" prompt us to encourage caution. Also, remember that any bad joke, side comment, or gesture (including groans, sighs, and facial expressions) are fair game. A colleague told us that he blew his nose during an interview, and this was reported in print!

Always keep in mind that you can not speak for the entire profession or for your professional organization unless authorized to do so (APA 02: 5.01 a, b). The next case is illustrative.

Case 15–17: In his testimony to the members of a state senate committee, Kidman Brash, Ph.D., made the following statement regarding the effi-

cacy of the treatment of pedophiles: "The American Psychological Association would support my contention that it is impossible to render any pedophile safe enough to be let out in public." When questioned about this statement, which was sent to an ethics committee by another witness holding a differing view, Dr. Brash noted that such a review appeared in an APA-sponsored journal that, he felt, legitimized his stance.

Unless an organization officially issues a policy or legal brief that takes a specific position, it is misleading and irresponsible to invoke one's professional organization in an effort to bolster one's argument, even if that argument has merit. Dr. Brash's justification for declaring the support of an entire professional organization was flawed. Embarrassment and ethics complaints can be avoided by refraining from making generalizations that imply some unanimous endorsement or agreement unless hard data exist to verify such a statement. As a citizen, you can always offer your own opinions.

You may find yourself contacted to comment about such topics as psychological/emotional ramifications of national disasters, hostage crises, repressed memories, the effects of emotional well-being on physical health, prisoner abuse, or what parents should do when a young child discovers that Santa Claus does not exist. Whenever no solid data on which to base a definitive comment exists, be modest by suggesting possibilities clearly labeled as tentative. As Cardinal (1994) put it after reviewing his own ordeal with journalists, "Representatives of the news media do not appear to understand that disagreement almost always exists in journals in the social sciences on any given research question.... Yet the media frequently want a simple answer, demanding consensus where it doesn't exist" (p. B3).

Sometimes, journalists are interested in "psychological evaluations" of a specific newsworthy individual that the mental health professional has never met. Commentary in such instances would likely be irresponsible and probably inaccurate and should therefore be avoided. Or, reporters may seek quotations from experts to bolster an already established slant or point of view. Several Boston psychologists faced criticism following the 1988 presidential campaign when they appeared to offer gratuitous analyses of why Kitty Dukakis, wife of the Democratic contender for the presidency of the United States, abused prescription drugs and alcohol. Their analyses included slightly unflattering speculations about her husband's personality and style. When challenged, the psychologists later claimed that their comments were misapplied and taken out of context by the reporter, who already seemed to have made up her mind.

If you have had professional contact with newsworthy individuals (including deceased persons), confidentiality becomes a critical issue and should not be compromised (see Chapter 8). Even if a notable individual consents or invites you to make public statements, professional judgment may dictate against sharing such information. A clinical social worker drew considerable criticism for discussing the content of her brief number of counseling sessions with the murdered Nicole Brown Simpson. The social worker made numerous television appearances and later defended her actions as a kind of a public service by raising awareness of domestic abuse. She further justified disclosing the content of a confidential relationship because the victim had told others about the same matters, thus rendering the information no longer "privileged." This inaccurate interpretation might have discouraged more people from seeking help from therapists (who they could assume might later talk about what was said in a private session on national television) than could possibly be offset by her spate of remarks assailing domestic violence.

Although you may not be able to review how your contribution will be disseminated to the public, you can make sure that the journalist is keenly aware of the importance you place on the story's accuracy. Invite the journalist to call you back if any questions arise. If you feel embarrassed or dissatisfied with the final product, let the journalist know about it. Because recipients can easily dismiss angry messages, frame your remarks in a constructive way that may help educate the journalist.

Finally, we do not wish readers to conclude from the troubling incidents we have shared

that the best course of action is to refrain from speaking to journalists and reporters altogether. A well-done story can provide a genuine contribution to public understanding. We do, however, encourage careful preparation and due caution because even journalists themselves are torn between commerce and ethics (Gardener, Csikszentmihalyi, & Damon, 2001).

Guest Appearances on Radio and Television

Mental health professionals are often interviewed live on radio or television. This format can produce frustrations, such as getting cut off before the point was fully made, fielding stupid or inappropriate questions, or being repeatedly referred to incorrectly (e.g., as a psychiatrist when one is a psychologist). Sometimes, however, full responsibility lies with the guest, as the following case illustrates:

Case 15–18: Flamba Gambit, M.A., made occasional appearances on local radio programs to discuss relationship issues. Her authoritative manner and choice of words could be easily interpreted as implying knowledge based on scientific findings, although this was rarely the case. One of several complaints concerned her assertion that women who were raped unconsciously wanted it, and that her research indicated that this was due to "a childhood fantasy of being simultaneously loved and punished by Daddy for being both a good and bad little girl."

Gambit's highly misleading and irresponsible statements may have caused some listeners psychological harm. A marriage and family counselor listening to the show complained to an ethics committee. On inquiry, the "research" Gambit cited consisted of no more than her opinion based on interactions with several of her clients who had been raped.

Some media hosts call on therapists to comment on the problems of other guests on the show, ostensibly to provide intervention and educate the public. After the guests with the problems are opened up and wrung dry, an expert is brought on stage to solve the complex quandaries that have usually been steeping for years.

This late-in-the-show maneuver, often made as few as 10 minutes before the program ends, serves as a quick-and-easy attempt to lend an air of legitimacy and redeeming social value to otherwise morally dubious entertainment. Often, the experts turn out to be mere window dressing, fading behind the psychobabbling hosts who retain tight control of the analysis and advice. Typically, the host asks the helping professional to make a quick, quasi diagnosis of the problem, get the guests to talk to (or yell at) each other for a couple more minutes, and then offer commentary. The advice is usually simplistic. Although most guests may not suffer incremental harm from the therapists' brief remarks, and some guests or audience members may even pick up a useful idea or perspective, there are certainly exceptions, as illustrated in the next cases.

Case 15–19: On a national television talk show, a father who repeatedly physically and sexually abused his wife and 12 children joined the family by satellite. The now-adult children aggressively confronted the father, and the host skillfully drew out harrowing details of their grotesque childhoods. A social psychologist was introduced for the purpose of "starting the healing process." She first attempted to sweetly cajole the father into opening up, but he was rightly suspicious of her motivations and clammed up. The by-now-frustrated psychologist loudly referred to the man as "a monster" and added, "He has what seems to me to be, and I have not diagnosed him, but he seems to be what we call a borderline personality." Although the children were now grown and out of the house, she fiercely assailed the mother, an obviously distraught and cognitively limited woman, for not protecting her children: "Why did you stay with this man? Was he great in bed?" (Multimedia Entertainment, Inc., 1994).

The father, hardly a sympathetic character, elicited predictable negative responses from his children. However, the guest professional seemed little more than the mob leader. This approach created an unfortunate lost opportunity because earlier the father had admitted to some of the accusations, and the family members and audience alike might have acquired some degree of enlightenment had the psychologist employed a more professional approach. The public diagnosis was also inappropriate (especially coming from a psychologist without clinical training). And, although the mother's behavior represented a curious and destructive form of marital loyalty, such patterns occur commonly enough to have already generated considerable discussion in the scholarly literature. To boorishly attack the mother with a crude question hardly reflects what we expect of competent and responsible mental health professionals.

Case 15–20: A psychiatrist complained to an ethics committee that counselor Nanna Nosey, M.S.W., a guest on a radio show inviting listeners' questions, had done irreparable harm to the therapeutic alliance established between himself and a client. The client had called in to the show and complained that her psychiatrist was unresponsive to her needs and constantly gave her a hard time. The counselor allegedly replied, "Get a new shrink. It sounds like you have a cold fish who isn't helping you at all." The psychiatrist explained in his complaint that his borderline client was in a very critical phase of therapy, and that this incident damaged progress that had taken many months to achieve.

It turns out that Nosey was invited to talk about careers in mental health, but took on the off-task caller anyway. This one-sided take on the caller's rant against her therapist was short-sighted and unprofessional, especially when considering the patterns and shifts that can occur in long-term psychotherapy. Even though no formal client–therapist relationship had been established between the caller and Nosey, inappropriate interference in the treatment relationship occurred.

Sometimes, the therapist simply should have known better. Common sense, rather than professional ethics, may be at issue.

Case 15–21: An educational psychologist agreed to a taped interview on a very popular comedy "news" show. As any regular viewer knows, the singular goal is laughs. Perhaps the psychologist did answer the comedian-interviewer's questions appropriately, but the tape was sliced in such as way that it portrayed the psychologist as a fool.

Since the last edition of this book, legitimate mental health providers are somewhat less prominent on the remaining shows that routinely display and exploit guests who appear highly dysfunctional or embroiled in pitiful life circumstances. Today, "reality TV" has taken over as a modern coliseum where people, apparently willingly, expose themselves to being embarrassed, harassed, disgraced, and shamed. (We do wonder what the high ratings these programs often enjoy say about the viewing public.)

Advice Programs With Therapists as Hosts

A number of mental health professionals have become media celebrities, interacting with real people who present their personal problems for commentary by the host. The picture has changed in the last two decades, replacing dozens of radio and television therapists with a few minor ones, two mega-enterprises, and hundreds of Internet sites.

Media Therapy Programs in Historical Context

Mental health professionals who host live radio and TV shows featuring people calling in their problems were far more prevalent in the 1980s and early 90s than now. In their heyday, about three dozen therapists populated the airwaves and took calls from distraught listeners. The ethical dimensions of "radio therapy" became hotly debated. Some believed that this airborne mode of advice giving did more good for psychotherapists than any previous movement because the public received an inkling of what therapy, and those who conduct it, are really like. People who may have felt isolated or uniquely troubled or attached a stigma to seeking help might have benefited by learning that others have similar conflicts and concerns.

Critics, however, decried radio therapists as "fast food shrinks," embarrassing to the professions and possibly even harmful to the "quasi clients" or passive listeners. Despite the potential for educating the public, critics claimed that media advice givers were hired not for their clinical competence or expertise as educators and scholars, but rather for qualities aligned with media business criteria such as voice, verbal facility, physical appearance, and engaging or charismatic personalities. Show business standards pertained in the forms of maintaining a quick turnover of calls, fast-paced and upbeat dialogue, and high interest or entertainment value achieved largely through encouraging the callers to share sordid details followed by the therapist's snappy commentary. Critics also noted that callers and listeners alike received drastic misperceptions about the psychotherapeutic process. The advice was viewed as suspicious because it was based on minimal information offered by a stranger. Harm could result, particularly for vulnerable or emotionally brittle people with no other ongoing support systems, those advised to make some major life changes, those hit with an interpretation they were not prepared to handle, or those who acted on the advice and found that it failed to ameliorate the problem. Audience members and participants may be led to believe that quick answers can solve even serious emotional or interpersonal problems.

Despite the many criticisms and concerns about potential harm to callers as well as the listening audience and the image of the profession, ethics committees seldom received complaints against media therapists. Thus, the once-thunderous debate about dispensing advice over the radio softened to a hush by the mid-1990s. This is not because the ethical issues themselves were resolved. Research simply has not substantiated widespread discontent among listeners (e.g., Levy, 1989; Raviv, Yunovitz, & Raviv, 1989). Evidence proving harm has not materialized, save for a few seemingly isolated cases. Anyone who may have experienced problems rarely complained, or if they did, complained to the broadcast stations but not to an ethics committee or licensing board. We think that a major reason for the virtual disappearance of the media therapist debate is that the listening audience turned instead to the influx of call-in programs hosted by loud, brash, and sometimes outrageous nonpsychologist radio personalities.

The APA ethics code admonishes psychologists to base their public comments and advice on their professional knowledge, training, and experience. Psychologists should refrain from indicating that a professional relationship exists with the recipient of the communication and violate no other provisions of the code (APA 02: 5.04). Thus, advice giving is currently allowed in a public forum as long as the person is deemed competent to give the advice offered. Advice that significantly deviates from, or is inconsistent with, established practice and scientific literature would constitute a violation of the APA code (Fisher, 2003). Whereas such restrictions help curb foolish and irresponsible commentary, they may sometimes inhibit the expression of otherwise sensible, innovative ideas. And, whereas earlier versions of the code specifically prohibited assigning a diagnosis in a public forum, no explicit prohibition against it appears in the 2002 APA code, despite the fact that we and others who have analyzed and interpreted the code (e.g., Fisher, 2003) view public assignments of diagnostic labels as unethical and unprofessional.

The Survivors

A handful of mainstream media therapists are left standing today, and two of them are especially noteworthy. The more controversial of the two, Dr. Laura Schlessinger, holds a Ph.D. in physiology and later attained a Marriage, Family, and Child Counseling license in California through a certificate program. Schlessinger's advice flows from an ultraconservative moral stance, and she admonishes her callers in blunt and no uncertain terms. She has run afoul of several groups, most noticeably gays and lesbians. Epstein (2001), the editor-in-chief of *Psychology Today*, summarized his staff's analysis of "Physiologist Laura." He reports being sickened and saddened by her expressed attitudes about gays and her intolerance, hatefulness, and abusiveness. Epstein chided her advice as divisive and more likely to lead to clashes within families than to heal them. He noted hypocrisy in that Dr. Laura touts the value of honoring family but was estranged from close members of her own family.

Schlessinger's flashy Web page touts herself and her program. Books, tapes, and other merchandise from the "Dr. Laura Collection" are offered for sale. Items, when we accessed the page, included T-shirts, expensive costume jewelry, and her own sailboat. Several Web sites devoted exclusively to criticizing her and requesting boycotts of her sponsors also exist. Regardless of the criticisms and the hype, Dr. Laura continues to be among the top-rated daytime radio shows.

The second surviving media therapist, Dr. Phil McGraw, is a psychologist who linked up with Oprah Winfrey in Texas by becoming her consultant during Winfrey's renowned "mad cow disease" defamation trial. Oprah prevailed and credited Dr. McGraw with her victory. He began as an occasional guest on Oprah's television show, and the rest is history. Dr. Phil's affable personality coupled with no-nonsense advice has made him a household name. He has a top-rated TV show and several best-selling books. Although a large man himself, he promoted a weight loss program through his books and Web site. His Web site also features, on the day we visited, plenty of advice tidbits, a message board on which visitors can comment on the shows and the people who appear on them, and an array of merchandise, including Dr. Phil T-shirts, photo frames engraved with the "I love Dr. Phil" logo, embroidered caps, scrubs, and a mug. Visitors can also apply online to appear on the TV show if they fit into the list of upcoming topics, such as "Jealousy eating away at you?" and "Do you have an unforgivable past?"

Despite the creation of an almost circuslike empire, public criticism of Dr. Phil is minimal. Invited to discuss his career and work at the 2006 convention of the APA in New Orleans, McGraw described screening and follow-up elements of his program. He told the psychologists in attendance that he makes no pretense of doing "10-minute psychotherapy" but rather attempts to get both his guests and people watching the broadcast to "wake up and do something about their problems." He reported that he will not take on guests who are in therapy without first clearing the appropriateness with their therapist. He also has established a network of community-based practitioners to whom he refers some guests in need of follow-up care. He has also funded a charitable foundation.

Dr. Phil did endure flak for his commentary in a 2004 prime time special about families. Video clips showed family households in out-of-control situations. One 9-year-old boy was especially sadistic and hostile. Dr. Phil commented that the boy exhibited 9 of the 14 characteristics common to serial killers, whereas Jeffrey Dahmer (a serial killer whose methods were exceedingly gruesome) had only 7. What that "inflicted insight" did for the tenor of the household one can only imagine. McGraw placed blamed on the family and outlined requirements for "reparenting" the boy. Critics charged that McGraw's failure to consider a biologically based brain disorder was irresponsible, and that viewers may withhold proper assessments of their troubled children by taking instead Dr. Phil's advice to just try to be better parents.

Dr. Phil's licensing of his name to vitamin nutritional products also met with disapproval, largely because people view him not as a celebrity spokesman but as an expert "doctor," despite having no medical training. The weight management supplements were very expensive, and the claims were highly suspect. No research substantiated that the supplements actually promote weight loss, and none of the individual ingredients are associated with losing weight (Schardt, 2004). Ultimately, dissatisfied consumers filed a class action suit and reached a $10 million settlement (see http://www.msnbc.msn .com/id/15014778/).

Individual Web Pages

Although the number of paid media therapists has dwindled, the irony is that *anyone* can be an advice giver to whoever on the planet can find them. Domain names and hosting services are inexpensive, and Web pages are easy to create. As a result, hundreds of sites at any point in time are put up by people who claim mental health expertise. These sites often dispense advice, usually associated with advertising fee-based services, although perhaps as many as a third do not appear to have any professional training or credentials (Heinlen, Welfel, Richmond, & Rak, 2003). Troubling ethical questions exist regarding the services offered (Heinlen, Welfel, Richmond, & O'Donnell, 2003). (See also Chapter 6.)

Web sites range from those offering simple referral information and links to reputable resources, to those with sound and animated graphics. At one site, a counselor (no credentials offered, although she refers to herself as "Dr.") offers some general advice for those suffering loss and promises all of the answers if you sign up for her workshops. An elaborate marriage counselor's site features a dozen video clips on such topics as stress, overeating, and depression, along with how to contact him for his various fee-based services. Another asks the reader a series of questions and promises to help if any answers are "yes," through for-fee counseling by Webcam, e-mail, or telephone. A radio therapist operating a small geographical niche market uses her Web page to attract face-to-face paying clients. A dating service founder (listing himself as a certified psychoanalyst) claims to use an extensive research-based system to match people. The most complicated page we found features wild bird images squawking and flapping their wings, music blaring, and an array of brightly colored buttons linked to all sorts of offers, mostly self-promoting. Some sites publish considerable information about psychodiagnostic and other assessment techniques that pose threats to test security (Ruiz, Drake, Glass, Marcotte, & van Gorp, 2002).

More solid resources and information are offered by the federal government, professional organizations, and nonprofit agencies. The APA (http://www.APA.org.), for example, offers numerous educational articles on a variety of topics of interest to the public. (Chapter 6 covers teletherapy in more detail. Chapter 14 offers additional material about how the Internet has drastically changed the advertising of professional services.)

Popular Works Written by Mental Health Professionals

Books and articles written for the trade or mass markets (as opposed to self-help books, considered in this chapter, and scholarly writing, considered in Chapter 19) pose few ethical concerns when done conscientiously and objectively. Many of these are excellent contributions that reveal a talent for making complicated psychological concepts and research findings accessible, interesting, and intelligible to the public. Occasionally, ethically perplexing cases arise.

Case 15–22: Gustav Slammen, Ph.D., wrote a popular article for a women's magazine on the psychological effects of being mugged and robbed in the streets. Based on his literature review and interviews with victims, he asserted that people who resist their attackers have a better chance of foiling the robbery attempts, recover more quickly from the emotional impact, and maintain more self-esteem compared to those who do not resist. He concluded by encouraging readers to resist assaults vigorously should they ever be placed in such an unfortunate situation.

A research psychologist charged Dr. Slammen with irresponsible scholarship. The complainant did not dispute the facts as far as they went. She noted, however, that research also supports the fact that victims who resist run a far greater risk of being hurt or killed than do nonresisters, and that readers should have been made aware of this peril. The researcher claimed that Dr. Slammen was well aware of this fact because her work was cited in his article.

Another controversial example is the best-selling *Bush on the Couch*, by Justin A. Frank, M.D. (2004), professor of psychiatry at George Washington University. Although Frank never interviewed or treated George W. Bush, he researched public records, starting from Bush's childhood. Using a psychoanalytic framework, he concluded that Bush, who was running for reelection as president of the United States at the time the book was released, was a seriously disturbed man resulting largely from a scarred childhood and untreated alcoholism. Critics, of course, cried foul. Is it ethical to publish a medical opinion about a person one has never treated? Is it ethical to use one's professional status to further a political agenda? Should Bush have sued for libel? Or, is this kind of

scrutiny simply a downside of being a public figure? Although these questions were bantered about on Internet blogs and newsgroups, as far as we can tell nothing much happened in the wake of this publication.

What about public lectures of a nonpsychological nature and other forms of published expression, such as letters to the editor? Helping professionals, like all citizens, have a right to free speech, even if it is offensive or embarrassing to others. However, as noted, it is ethically inappropriate to saddle the entire profession or a professional organization with implied condoning of messages that clearly constitute the individual's personally held opinions. The next case is illustrative.

Case 15–23: Adolf Hitter, Ph.D., launched a vigorous and insolent attack against Jews and a Jewish civil rights lawyer in an "open letter" appearing in a nationally distributed newsletter. The letter was signed by the psychologist, followed by "Diplomate in Clinical Psychology, American Board of Professional Psychology."

Several psychologists sent this article to the APA Ethics Committee; the committee agreed that, aside from the offensive intolerant assault permitted as free speech, the psychologist brought undeserved shame on his colleagues by using his affiliation in a way that might enhance his credibility and possibly suggest American Board of Professional Psychology sponsorship of the contents in his letter or his reasoning.

Case 15–24: Peppy Wonderbody appeared as the nude centerfold in a popular men's magazine as, she stated, "a form of self-expression." Her credentials as a postdoctoral psychology fellow were also described.

Although professions limit the scope of their ethical codes to professionally relevant activities, some conduct, although perfectly legal, causes us to wince. Public image is important to every mental health professional, and such decisions on the part of only one may alter that image in unwelcome directions. One might also question Dr. Wonderbody's level of professional identity and commitment.

Advice to Individuals Offered in Writing

When offering written advice, a number of the same ethical issues raised regarding media appearances apply here. Some ethical dilemmas, however, are diminished by this format. The author can take time to respond thoughtfully and to consult relevant literature or others with specialized expertise. The author can focus on educating the readers. Confidentiality can more easily be guaranteed. Occasionally, however, complaints have been leveled specifically at this format, as the next case illustrates.

Case 15–25: A counselor at a women's center complained that the advice column in a local paper by Tacky Crass, Ph.D., was used to entertain readers at the expense of a distressed correspondent. An elderly woman expressed how frustrating it was to have sexual desires but no sex partner. Dr. Crass suggested that she hang around a senior citizen's center after bingo, attend funerals whether she knew the dearly departed or not, or plant a cucumber patch.

An ethics committee responded unsympathetically to Dr. Crass's brand of humor. His response was not based on professional knowledge in accord with appropriate literature (APA 02: 5.04), and his behavior demeaned someone to whom he was responding in his role as a mental health provider (APA 02: 3.03).

SELF-ADMINISTERED THERAPEUTIC PROGRAMS

Among the long-standing favorite forms of "mass psychology" are self-help books, audiotapes, and various paraphernalia and contraptions that purport to assist with emotional and physical healing. Stressful living conditions, little spare time, tight budgets, concern about the future, attraction to the promise of quick-and-painless solutions, and the desire for self-reliance perpetuate the considerable success of the self-help industry. Mahoney (1988)

described the allure of therapeutic self-care products as a near-universal search for simple, guaranteed solutions to life's problems and challenges. And, although the underlying motivations to develop products for this huge consumer market certainly vary, the potential for fame, fortune, and increased clientele are surely among them.

Self-care materials range from the diffuse "feel good" to very specific advice regarding narrowly focused conditions. Three common categories of subjects matter are

1. How to improve (e.g., self-concept, self-confidence, social assertiveness, parenting skills, physical fitness, sexual functioning, memory, and life satisfaction)
2. How to control (e.g., smoking, weight, stress, phobias, anger)
3. How to cope (e.g., with depression, guilt, fears and phobias, shyness, insomnia, anxiety, problem children, loss of love, caring for elderly parents, and divorce)

Many of these works, including some that have had great success in the marketplace, are written by people with no discernible qualifications as experts in the subject. Readers may assume the most popular authors hold legitimate professional credentials because of their seeming comfort with psychological terminology in concert with their "Ph.D. degrees," often issued by diploma mills or correspondence schools. However, many genuine mental health professionals, including some exceptionally prominent ones, have entered the do-it-yourself therapy market.

Creators of Self-Care Products

We restrict our discussion here to books and other media products, such as audiotapes, created by legitimately trained mental health providers and totally self-administered by the consumer. Even though the self-help market is gorged with vacuous potboilers and filled to the brim with cleverly named but contrived syndromes, well-trained and experienced mental health professionals are capable of creating self-administered programs that may prove beneficial for some purposes at a fraction of the cost of long-term, professional care. Experts in a given field can offer their knowledge and insights to those with no prospect for direct access to them. All of the time and effort required to create products of the highest possible quality can and should be expended. Professional experts are capable of offering the public sound, economical, effective programs that do not require extensive professional intervention. Although ethical concerns surround the creation of self-care programs, even by professionals, it is acknowledged that positive potential exists (e.g., Ellis, 1993; Rosen, 1993; Starker, 1988a, 1988b).

Despite the unquestionable potential for good, however, a number of ethical questions have arisen about what actually happens. Consumers are often given instructions on how to solve difficult problems or manage their lives but without a support system necessary to sustain them through the process, to correct errors, to clarify misunderstood statements or directions, to caution against particular individual contraindications, or to alleviate any negative consequences that result from following (or failing to follow) the program. It should also come as no surprise that publishers accept and advertise books based largely on their sales potential. The result, from a scientific perspective, is often inappropriate flamboyance, superficiality, and conclusions not warranted by available evidence.

Case 15–26: The promotional advertisement and content of a do-it-yourself psychotherapy book promised to save the reader thousands of dollars because it would make it "unnecessary to consult paid advisors." The book also pledged "relief within 2 weeks from guilt, anxiety, and depression" and claimed that anyone can follow the easy-to-understand program. No data are presented to support any of the benefits guaranteed to the readers.

Extravagant claims that may cause unrealistic expectations of favorable results are often promoted in the title, text, or promotional materials supplied by the publishers or their agents. The situation becomes even further exacerbated when the text or promotional materials actually discourage obtaining in vivo professional services, suggesting that they are unnecessary or a waste of money. This tactic could preclude consumers for whom the product was not sufficiently beneficial from seeking more appropriate alternatives.

Self-care products often profess innovation and uniqueness, promising the reader something brand new. Although claims of newness or uniqueness are tried-and-true marketing techniques, most self-help books involve variations on simple behavioral, relaxation, imagery, and self-suggestion principles that have existed in one form or another for a very long time. Again, the primary ethical issue for mental health professionals is simple honesty. Work should not be labeled as a "breakthrough" when they know (or should know) better.

Observers of the self-help industry have expressed concern that creators of these products leave diagnoses up to the consumers (Rosen, 1987, 1993). By purchasing self-care products, consumers have at least tentatively diagnosed themselves as needing a particular kind of assistance. Products typically require either a general self-diagnosed problem, such as "social inadequacy" or "dissatisfaction with life," or more specific self-diagnoses, such as phobic, depressed, shy, or sexually inadequate. Few self-help products acknowledge or attempt to caution the consumer regarding the dangers of misdiagnosis.

Readers may misapply the program or label themselves as failures when the advice does not work and give up altogether. Because the book was written by someone they believe to be an expert, consumers may more likely fault themselves than a defective product. Or, consumers may have a different problem for which a self-help program or any psychological approach is ineffective or even contraindicated (Barrera, Rosen, & Glasgow, 1981). Consider the next case:

Case 15–27: Wanda Weary was told by her best friend that a brief new book on psychic energy, written by a "real doctor," could help restore her vigor. Weary, who had been feeling exceptionally sluggish for several weeks, was willing to try it. She practiced the breathing and imaging techniques for several more weeks but continued to feel drained. Weary finally consulted a physician, who quickly diagnosed hypothyroidism and prescribed appropriate hormone replacement.

Ms. Weary was lucky. Other physical conditions or psychopathologies can cause more permanent damage if left to linger.

Ideally, before selling instructions to people about how to deal with general or specific life problems, a responsible author would gather evidence that his or her program or advice has, in fact, beneficial effects. An adequate evaluation requires the consideration of many variables, such as expectancy for improvement, format and program length, levels of task difficulty, involvement and role of significant others, reading level, long-term gains, and so on (Glasgow & Rosen, 1978, 1979). The feel-good self-care books would prove difficult to evaluate for any long-term gains and should therefore never make any promises.

In reality, most totally self-administered materials, including those by legitimate mental health professionals, have not been subjected to any systematic evaluation prior to publication and marketing (Rosen, 1993). On occasion, programs have been evaluated after their publication and have been found to be useless or even to have produced additional negative consequences. In their evaluation of the now-classic *Toilet Training in Less Than a Day* (Azrin & Foxx, 1974), Matson and Ollendick (1977) found that only one of the five mothers in the self-administration (book-only) group successfully trained her child in the manner prescribed. In addition, those mothers who were unsuccessful reported increased behavior problems in their children and tension in the mother–child relationship.

We recommend that, *at the very least,* those who create untested self-care products include a disclaimer placed so that readers can not help but notice. It might go something like this: *"Fighting Naysayer Noise in Your Head* is based on the author's ideas and experiences with her psychotherapy clients over the past 22 years." We have seen a few products that outline steps readers might consider if the advice proves

unhelpful or if they have more severe symptoms than those their advice is intended to alleviate. Such disclaimers certainly earn kudos compared to their promise-blaring companions on the bookstore shelves.

The frustrating bottom line is that honesty could hurt sales (Holtje, 1988). One author (Mahoney, 1988) believed that his book sold poorly compared to its competitors because he honestly stated that long-term weight control is a difficult and time consuming and with no guarantees of success. The great majority of publishers may be more interested promoting a lousy product that will sell than in a top-rate product that is unlikely to sell (Ellis, 1993).

Do-it-yourself (DIY) tests, many of which have been around for a while to assess physical conditions (e.g., blood pressure, blood sugar level, pregnancy, HIV), are now appearing for psychological screening (e.g., attention-deficit disorder, early Alzheimer's disease, depression). Many can be found on the Internet, often associated with the advertisement of services for the problem purporting to be assessed. Ethical issues regarding DIY tests include insufficient regulation or professional oversight of test validity, potential for misuse and errors in interpretation, and absence of in-person support counseling (Kier & Molinari, 2004). (See also Chapter 9.)

Prescribing Self-Care Products

Not every consumer who reads a self-help book found it while browsing in bookstores. According to Starker's (1988a) survey, the majority of respondents prescribed self-help books as supplementary treatments for their clients. Of these, almost half did so frequently. Virtually all respondents believed that the books were at least somewhat helpful, and reports of harmfulness were virtually nonexistent. Starker concluded that the prescription of self-help books is common, that the mood is optimistic about their efficacy, and that little concern exists regarding their potential for harm (Starker, 1988c). Extensive surveys of clinical and counseling psychologists by Norcross and his colleagues have resulted in helpful lists of highly rated self-help books (Norcross et al., 2003; Norcross & Simansky, 2005).

Indeed, bibliotherapy—which is not necessarily confined to assigning self-help books written by mental health professionals—is increasing in popularity. Books are usually prescribed as an adjunct to ongoing face-to-face therapy or when services are limited or unavailable (Adams, 2000; den Boer, Wiersma, & Van Den Bosch, 2004; Mains & Scogin, 2003; Richards, 2004). Evaluation research generally supports some measure of effectiveness for a variety of emotional, social, and developmental disorders (Joshua & DiMenna, 2000; Pardeck & Pardeck, 1998b). Examples of program areas include depression, panic attacks, disenfranchised grievers, smoking cessation, insomnia, at-risk alcoholism, children's respect for diversity, transcultural counseling, and fear of flying (Apodaca & Miller, 2003; Berns, 2003; Curry, Ludman, & McClure, 2003; Floyd, Scogin, McKendree-Smith, Floyd, & Rokke, 2004; Hames & Pedreira, 2003; Lidren et al. 1994; McFadden & Banich, 2003; Mimeault & Morin, 1999; Palmer, Bor, & Josse, 2000; Pardeck & Pardeck, 1998a; Smith, Floyd, Scogin, & Jamison, 1997).

Psychotherapists do need to approach the assignment of books with professional objectivity and should read the books carefully themselves first (Starker, 1988c). Works that are clearly gimmicky (e.g., those suggesting that men and women originated on different planets, coupled with unsubstantiated generalizations about sex differences) are unlikely to prove helpful in the long run. Even for more substantial self-help books, therapists should inform their clients about possible shortcomings and encourage them to discuss anything that troubles them or seems difficult to understand. Therapists can also issue cautions, even if the authors do not, about how the books came to be. They might tell a client, "This book is not created from a research base, but I think the author has some good ideas that might prove helpful for you to consider." Or, "This book is not a tested therapeutic tool, but I find the prose is inspirational, and it may make you feel better as you cope with your loss."

Although "cinema therapy" has not been sufficiently evaluated using a research paradigm, assigning clients films to watch has gained considerable popularity in recent years (Gabbard & Gabbard, 1999; Hesley, 1998; Paquette, 2003; Schulenberg, 2003; Sharp, 2002). Some movies can probably motivate people to find new ways of looking at themselves and their circumstance. And, even though films are rarely intended to reflect the absolute, research-based truth, viewers already know that. Compliance is rarely a problem because most people are willing to go to the theater or rent a recommended movie. Although, as already discussed, some films grossly misrepresent psychotherapists and the therapy process, many other films may be enlightening or supportive (Hill, 1993; Wedding & Niemiec, 2003). Therapists should remember, however, that when they prescribe a movie, the client will take the viewing experience far more seriously than had they selected it on their own. Therefore, therapists should view a film prior to prescribing it, evaluate its appropriateness for a specific client, and prepare for a follow-up discussion with the client afterward. The next case illustrates the consequences of not adequately assessing the film's suitability.

Case 15–28: Peter Prudish complained to a licensing board that Bee Hinda Greendoor, Psy.D., insisted that he view a video that he found extremely disturbing. He abruptly terminated therapy and called Dr. Greendoor "a panderer in filthy smut."

Dr. Greendoor felt stunned by her client's strong response. She insisted that she meant no harm and had suggested only that the film might be an enjoyable and a safe way to desensitize Prudish's sexual anxiety. She had not actually seen the film, but a friend told her that it was a "delightful romp."

PUBLIC STATEMENTS OVER THE INTERNET

Electronic communication via the Internet is, at once, a window to the world from the comfort of one's home or office, a pathway to communicate with one or thousands of others simultaneously by a issuing a simple send command, and a potential trapdoor leading to serious trouble.

Case 15–29: Web Strew, claiming to hold a Ph.D. degree in psychology, figured that he could tell the world about his practice at virtually no cost. He typed out a lengthy and glowing advertisement, declaring that, among other things, he could help make important decisions and ease psychic pain. He sent this message to every newsgroup he could join along with all the individuals whose e-mail addresses crossed his desk.

Dr. Strew's behavior constitutes spamming, an irritating practice that has proven difficult to eradicate. Some worry that spammers will increasingly clog the system with unwanted and junky material, and the vigilantes may not always know the difference between eliminating electronic litter and censorship (Wilson, 1995). Dr. Strew may find himself in violation of the Federal CAN-SPAM Act of 2003 (Controlling the Assault of Non-Solicited Pornography and Marketing Act, 2003).

Other online behaviors seem likely to cause far more harm. A problem that comes with the capacity to disseminate information instantly from one's office desk to hundreds of people via the use of a few keystrokes is the lack of time for thoughtful reflection. Once the message is sent, it can travel indefinitely as others pass it along. Anyone who surfs the net on a regular basis can not help but notice the mean-spirited insults ("flaming") on blogs, electronic groups and bulletin boards, or chat rooms. Among mental health professionals, online debates about the existence of repressed memories, mental health professional's role in the courts, or the efficacy of various therapeutic modalities provide ready examples.

Case 15–30: When Bulah Blowout, Ph.D., read a message on a discussion group that was mildly critical of the academic program from which she received her degree, she ripped off a response that raked the critic's graduate department: "It is a 10th-rate program in an ugly building populated with old, white guys and their white rats." Over 700 people read her impulsive and ill-conceived message, and the response was not positive.

Perhaps little harm resulted except to Dr. Blowout's professional image. But, it would not take too much more to approach a legal definition of defamation.

Case 15–31: In response to a posted message in an open forum for anyone interested in current events, a marriage and family counselor referred to a female colleague who had agreed to testify in a high-profile murder case as "a whore." That message and numerous others reflecting both support and outrage spread rapidly. Therapists who were active frequenters of the Internet reported receiving the same message many times from different sources, which indicated that this particular exchange was widely disseminated. One counselor wanted to press ethics charges against the name caller. Another intended to press charges against the person defending the maligned counselor for defaming the name caller.

One can not help but wonder if the originator might have expressed himself a little differently had he known how his message would be received. As O'Neil (1995) stated, "Electronic communication does seem to inspire excess, hyperbole, and incivility among users to a degree seldom found in print" (p. A68).

Defamation lawsuits have succeeded. As one example, a former professor at the Emory School of Medicine was awarded $675,000 based on a false, anonymous Internet message placed on a Yahoo group. The perpetrator claimed the professor had taken kickbacks and was forced to resign his university position. With some clever sleuthing, the perpetrator was identified as a competitor of the former professor's private business (Ackman, 2000). As people spend more time on the Internet, the risk of erroneous or malicious gossip increases dramatically, and many more such suits seem likely.

Other problems can arise and come back to haunt Internet users who are sloppy or not yet proficient at negotiating cyberspace.

Case 15–32: Hana Hurried, L.M.H.C., wanted a quick consultation about a suicidal client from a colleague who also belonged to the same moderated Internet discussion group. She included identifying information and a detailed account of the client's personal circumstances. However, she accidentally sent the message to the listserv rather than to the colleague's private e-mail address.

This mistake is one of many that are easy to make courtesy of the convenient "reply" (and "reply all") function. We strongly recommend that all identifying information be removed when sending confidential material, even when one feels assured that the message will be received by only the recipient. Even when communicating with a specific individual on the Internet, privacy is not guaranteed and readily available to those who know how to assess it. With more and more public citizens surfing the Internet, it is important to recognize that every time we contribute our thoughts and identify our profession online, we may be making a statement to a large public audience even though we are completely alone in our office or a room at home.

Finally, just because "confidential" is included in the subject line does not guarantee that recipients are going to honor it, especially if the message is sent to a large number of recipients. We are reminded of a message marked "highly confidential," sent to a large list, detailing highly sensitive information about a famous colleague who was not a member of the list. This electronic information circulated at the speed of light and went far beyond the members of the list to the continued detriment of the hapless victim.

PAYING FOR PUBLICITY

Attracting publicity serves many needs, ranging from personal desire for acknowledgment and validation to a practical way to acquire clientele. However, it is considered unethical to compensate the media in exchange for publicity that readers would assume is news rather than an advertisement (APA 02: 5.02.b).

Case 15–33: Rosemary Oregano, Ph.D., asked an acquaintance who was a writer for a regional agricultural magazine to do a story on the workshops she conducted on the grounds of her 2-acre herb garden in exchange for a fresh supply of herbs for a year.

Dr. Oregano is in violation of the APA code even though no cash changed hands. A more common form of the violation involves paying a media outlet for what appears to the reader as a newsworthy column or article written about or by the therapist. This activity would currently be acceptable only if the column or article is readily identifiable or clearly labeled as an advertisement (APA 02: 5.02.c).

Nothing in an ethics code precludes a therapist, educator, or researcher from attempting to attract publicity for his or her work through issuing a news release or making a personal contact that informs the media of a story. Sometimes, the media are interested in a therapy technique, research or book project, or an intriguing personality who just happens to be a helping professional. But, it is up to the media to make the decision without temptation by remuneration from the source of the story.

SOCIALLY RESPONSIBLE PUBLIC ACTS

Public Disclosure at a Risk to Oneself

"Going public" for reasons involving the highest sense of integrity is, regrettably, very risky. We refer to whistle-blowing (or "ethical resisters," as some prefer) and present a discussion here because the act often involves informing the public as well as perhaps gaining the attention of (or seeking support from) the media.

The overall spirit of the APA ethics code inspires integrity and holds as paramount maintaining the well-being of consumers. And, there is certainly nothing in the code that would condemn "ethical resistance." But, there is also little support for bucking the system. Psychologists are required to make their commitment to the ethics code known whenever conflicts arise with the law, regulations, government agencies, or organizations but may then backpedal if their expressed concerns are ignored or have no impact (APA 02: 1.02) or if they can not themselves resolve the ethical conflict (APA 02: 1.03). However, if an intractable individual *causing* the harm also holds APA membership, a formal ethics complaint can be lodged (APA 02: 1.05).

The APA ethics code actually places psychologists in an acute ethical dilemma because they are asked to first raise the issue directly with the appropriate parties within the organization. Employers can always try to find a way to get rid of an employee who makes unwanted waves.

Case 15–34: Chester Valid, Ph.D., complained to his supervisor when he was instructed to use assessment techniques he considered to be extremely inappropriate because they resulted in the misclassification of hundreds of job applicants. His supervisor told him that this was not his decision to make. He subsequently attempted again to explain how this test was unfair to job applicants. Two weeks later, Valid found himself "laid off," ostensibly because of budget cuts.

Should Dr. Valid have retreated after the first confrontation with his supervisor? How far should be have gone? Was the decision to push the issue again worth it? Did he make a difference? These are agonizing questions that ethically courageous people must ask themselves.

In its typical and better-known form, whistle-blowing occurs among those who hold a position as an insider (often of some authority) in a government, agency, business, or institution. Unethical, illegal, or socially deleterious practices within the work setting became cause for concern because of the whistle-blower's conviction that harm has been or will be caused to others or to the environment. The whistle-blower has usually attempted to remediate the situation through established channels within the organization but was ignored (Faugier & Woolnough, 2002). The employer's stonewalling, delays, excuses, or unresponsiveness eventually lead to sharing information with an outside source in the hope of eliminating the practice by external pressure (Glazer & Glazer, 1989; Miceli & Near, 1992, 2002; Nader, Petkas, & Blackwell, 1972).

Incidents of whistle-blowing rarely come to the attention of the public unless the stakes are high. One of the few cases involving a research psychologist gained media attention. Dr. Robert L. Sprague, a colleague of psychologist Stephen Breuning, who conducted research on drug treatment of retarded children and adults, became suspicious when Breuning was producing more uniform data than seemed probable. Sprague investigated on his own until he became convinced that the research contained serious flaws suggestive of fraud. He then contacted his program officer at the National Institute of Mental Health (NIMH). Breuning eventually admitted wrongdoing, but what Sprague thought would amount to making the painful decision to turn in his colleague became a 3-year ordeal. Sprague himself was called into question, and he endured threats by an official of Breuning's university. And, although cause and effect have never been proven, he had his long-standing NIMH funding cut by 75% (Committee on Government Operations, 1990; Sprague, 1993).

In an analysis of 10 cases in higher education settings, most whistle-blowers experienced retaliation by their universities (Weiss, 1991). Those who were untenured or were being paid by "soft" grant funds usually lost their jobs. Yet, even tenured full professors have suffered indignities, ranging from slurs directed at them through their children to having an academic office relocated to an isolated site over a grocery store (Ernhart, Scarr, & Geneson, 1993; Sprague, 1993). Many have had to obtain their own legal counsel, sometimes because of having their behavior called into question despite no evidence of impropriety. The time spent and anxiety endured can be extensive. Most disconcerting is the possibility that the action itself may ultimately amount to an exercise in futility if the information shared is ignored by the outside contact, suspended indefinitely in bureaucratic red tape, or if the accused are found innocent of wrongdoing. Even when the accused has been found guilty, the penalties can be paltry.

Successful whistle-blowers who have garnered notoriety typically have irrefutable proof that society, or some large segment of it, faces immediate danger and stand willing to risk everything. Under these circumstances, the level of journalistic and public support available may allow a whistle-blower to survive and perhaps earn accolades as a national hero (Johnson, 2003). Most incidents coming to our attention about mental health professionals do not involve matters of national or scientific significance. This also means that the risks are higher because the potential for exposure and public outcry is low or absent altogether. History has demonstrated that higher retaliation occurs when whistle-blowers do not have public support (Parmerlee, 1982).

In the more typical case involving mental health professionals, the rights or welfare of some people were believed to be jeopardized, and guidance was requested regarding how to expose the dubious practices. The incidents were confined to a local organization or agency and not of national significance.

Case 15–35: A psychologist protested that confidential client records were available for viewing by anyone, including other clients, because they were stored openly on shelves in the busy reception area of a mental health clinic. When he objected to his supervisor, he was told that there was no other space available, and that he would be better off spending his time paying attention to what he was being paid to do.

Case 15–36: A staff psychiatrist noticed that the death of a mental hospital patient went unreported, and that the deceased was instead listed as "AWOL." When he questioned the administrator of the facility, he was simply told that he was mistaken and was challenged to find a body.

Case 15–37: A social work faculty member opposed the hiring practices at his university, which he claimed were blatantly sexist and racist, as evidenced by remarks made during closed recruitment meetings. After he complained to the dean, a colleague told him to keep quiet or he would end up as "roadkill on the tenure track."

Case 15–38: A psychologist at a Veterans Affairs hospital protested that his patients should not be summarily dumped onto the streets as the medical director ordered after the building where the psychologist worked was found to be unsafe. His patients called the local newspaper in support of the psychologist. A front-page story ran that was critical of the medical director, and the psychologist was fired for "insubordination," only to regain his position after an arduous 2-year appeal process.

Case 15–39: A psychologist working for a managed care organization (MCO) became distraught when treatment she deemed necessary for the welfare of her clients were repeatedly denied. She became increasingly vocal about her concerns within the organization. Her services were promptly terminated under a "no cause" contract provision. The psychologist wrote an article published in the local paper that condemned the ethics of the MCO.

Not every practitioner represented in the above examples went public, but all agonized over how to respond. The inherent risks in even these less publicized opportunities to blow the whistle are numerous and include loss of employment or, failing that, demotion or transfer to some undesirable location or position. If the individual remains within the organization, he or she is often frozen out, even by those thought to be close friends. Those known to be potential informants may have difficulty finding other employment, or they may be accused of acting out of vindictiveness or revenge. Ironically, withholding the sharing of acts known to be illegal or immoral are more likely to be rewarded by the organization, creating an ethical ambivalence in those considering blowing the whistle (Alford, 2001; Jansen & von Glinow, 1985). We expect this ambivalence to increase as more and more therapists are involved with profit-driven MCOs (Acuff et al., 1999).

So, why would anyone put him- or herself at such risk? The main reasons are a strong belief in individual responsibility and a feeling of obligation to the community (Glazer & Glazer, 1989). Unfortunately, there is no surefire source of support for those who upset a powerful organization in the course of upholding professional standards, although whistle-blower protection statutes are emerging at the state and national levels. Yet, one must still expect the worst. Even though federal rules forbid universities from punishing whistle-blowers, witnesses have testified that these rules have been ignored (Burd, 1994).

Below is a list of assessments that the would-be whistle-blower should make prior to acting. Some of the items are adapted from Nader et al. (1972), and others are based on colleagues' and our own challenging experiences as ethical resistors.

Before making the decision to become a whistle-blower, we suggest the following:

- Determine the accuracy, strength, and completeness of your knowledge and evidence. Keep a detailed log of every relevant event. If other parties are central to the case as witnesses, evaluate any assurances that they will stand by you.
- Determine which persons or public interest would be harmed should the matter remain unchallenged.
- Assess the climate of the organization in terms of how likely it is to be responsive to your concerns and then decide how far up in the organization you can likely go to evoke a favorable outcome.
- Assess any confidentiality issues. If you will be violating any rules or confidential information by contacting outside parties, the risk increases, requiring a particularly serious assessment of the consequences for both yourself and others.
- If your planned action will violate any laws or ethical duties by *not* contacting external parties, factor this into your decision. (Remember, if you are forced to break a law or violate an ethics code as a condition of employment, the fact that you brought the problem to the attention of the organization would not, in itself, exempt you from also being charged.)
- Evaluate the interest, commitment, and fair consideration you can expect from outside the organization.
- Assess whether alternatives to whistle-blowing exist that might prove more effective and less risky.
- Carefully, informally, and confidentially (if possible) discuss your plan with highly trusted colleagues to get their assessment of the matter.

- Ask yourself if you are ready to risk your career status and compare that risk to how you would feel if you did nothing and others were harmed. Would you be forever haunted by your inaction?

After making the decision,

- Determine the best way to proceed. Is anonymity an option? Should you resign your position before speaking out?
- Be clear about what you expect will be achieved by whistle-blowing in this particular situation.
- Seek out one or more support groups.
- Stay on your best behavior. You do not want to provide ammunition for discounting you as a disgruntled employee or a crackpot.
- Develop a hierarchy of authority or interested parties in a position to act on the information and consider where in the sequence your "whistle" will be most effectively heard and heeded.
- Disclose facts and avoid to the extent possible pointing to an individual. Let the facts lead to the parties who created them.

As long as whistle-blowers remain the heroes who are shunned and ignored, our society remains in harm's way. Whistle-blowing requires a personal constitution and sense of ethics, backed by considerable courage that few of us possess. And yet, to maintain the health of our society, we desperately need whistle-blowers. As Rothchild and Miethe (1999) stated:

> Because of low public visibility, technical complexity, and explicit cover-ups of much misconduct that goes on in organizations, we would have little chance of learning about organizational wrongdoings were it not for conscientious employees who are in the best position to observe the wrongdoings firsthand.... Without their aid in bringing to light abuses of law or public trust, we would have little hope of learning or controlling what goes on inside most work organizations. (p. 126)

Finally, do things *always* turn out badly for the whistle-blower? Gunsalus (1998b) and Sieber (1999) claimed that successful whistle-blowers are the ones we never hear about. Almost a third of the whistle-blowers surveyed by

Lubalin and Matheson (1999) reported no permanent negative consequences resulting from their actions. Advice about how to increase the chances of a successful outcome includes taking precautions, and much depends on the skill and sensitivity with which the organization handles allegations of wrongdoing (Gunsalus, 1998a, 1998b).

Advocating for Consumers in a Public Forum

Possessing information, accidentally or through a process of deliberate discovery, that forces us to confront our moral courage is not an everyday occurrence. However, another opportunity to correct the record occurs regularly and is far less taxing. It is simply advocating for the consumers of mental health services in a public forum. Unfortunately, mental health professionals are not known for doing as much client advocacy as they should.

We began this chapter by noting the proliferation of incorrect stereotypes and labeling about the helping profession's realm of expertise. One can not go very far into a week without hearing someone say something about human behavior that is not only outlandish but is likely to degrade or stigmatize some group of people in the process. As part of the general ethic to promote human welfare, we believe that taking opportunities to educate others—both informally and formally—about the current status of psychological knowledge is a primary social responsibility.

People with mental disabilities face significant discrimination barriers. The gains made by other reference groups are immense in comparison. People with a psychiatric history, particularly if they were ever hospitalized, are still met with fear and mistrust (Corrigan, 2005; Mayer & Barry, 1992). The Department of Health and Human Services surgeon general's report on mental health (1999) summarizes the burdens that people with mental problems face.

> [Stigma] is manifested by bias, distrust, stereotyping, fear, embarrassment, anger, and/or avoidance. Stigma leads others to avoid living, socializing or working with, renting to, or employing people with mental disorders, especially severe

disorders such as schizophrenia. It reduces patients' access to resources and opportunities (e.g., housing, jobs) and leads to low self-esteem, isolation, and hopelessness. It deters the public from seeking, and wanting to pay for, care. In its most overt and egregious form, stigma results in outright discrimination and abuse. More tragically, it deprives people of their dignity and interferes with their full participation in society. (p. 6)

Public education requires more than one-shot corrections. A simple disclaimer (e.g., "Violence is not characteristic of mentally ill people") at the end of a film portraying a psychotic serial killer does not measurably alter the impact of the film on viewers' attitudes (Wahl & Lefkowits, 1989). The helping professions are in a legitimate position to replace misinformation with useful, solid data, including promoting portrayals that disconfirm inaccurate stereotypes that plague those who suffer from mental illness (Reinke, Corrigan, Leonhard, Lundin, & Kubiak, 2004).

Educational programs can start with the very young (e.g., Rickwood, Cavanagh, Curtis, & Sakrouge, 2004; Shaw, 2004). We can increase collaboration with public education and patient advocacy groups and help monitor negative portrayals of the mentally disabled (Corrigan & Penn, 1999; Estroff, Penn, & Toporek, 2004; Hyler, Gabbard, & Schneider, 1991). It takes a little courage and commitment to speak up, but it is our collective responsibility as mental health professionals to do so.

Professionals who work with the mentally ill do, as one would expect, express more positive attitudes about the mentally ill than do members of the general public. However, mental health professionals may not differ from the public's view regarding the amount of social distance they place between themselves and those types of clients with whom they work (Lauber, Anthony, Ajdacic-Gross, & Rossler, 2004; Phokeo, Sproule, & Raman-Wilms, 2004). Stigmatization of the mentally ill comes full circle by substantially reducing the willingness among those who need it to seek professional help (Cooper, Corrigan, & Watson, 2003; Corrigan, 2004; Mann & Himelein, 2004). Ironically, in the end, mental health professionals forgo their own interests as a result of the stigma heaped on those whose career choice is to help them.

SUMMARY GUIDELINES

1. While committing themselves to assisting the public in understanding relevant knowledge, ethical mental health professionals attempt to ensure accuracy, maintain due caution and modesty, avoid the exploitation of others, and exhibit a high level of professional responsibility. This may mean that some invitations to participate in media activities or other public forums might best be refused.

2. Exaggeration, superficiality, and sensationalism should be avoided to the greatest extent possible when making public statements in any media forum. When signing contracts for commercial books or other products, it is wise to seek prior approval or at least consultation on all advertising copy.

3. Mental health practitioners, educators, and researchers must acknowledge and accept responsibility to a public who may readily accept their statements by virtue of presumed expertise.

4. Recognizing the limits of one's knowledge and experience is especially critical in media activities because large numbers of people can be misled or misinformed by incorrect statements made public.

5. When offering public advice intended to ameliorate particular problems, considerable caution must be exercised. Such advice should, ideally, have a strong practice or research base. In any event, commentary should not be presented as factual unless a reasonable database exists. Opinions or personal experiences should be clearly identified as such.

6. Public statements that purport to speak for one's entire profession should be avoided.

7. It is important to keep in mind that the goals and purposes of those who report, produce, or distribute media are likely to differ from those of the interviewee. Such awareness may help to detect instances requiring caution.

8. Public statements should never be made for entertainment or self-gratification purposes at the expense of others or of the mental health professions.

9. Generally, one should not publicly comment on the emotional or psychological status of identified others.

10. With the ready availability of electronic distribution channels, such as e-mail, blogs, chat rooms, or listservs, consider carefully the ethical dilemmas that could follow before posting messages relating to professional matters or colleagues.

11. Whistle-blowers often act on the basis of their moral courage and are to be admired. One can not, however, be faulted for thinking through the consequences to oneself. Seeking consultation prior to taking action is recommended.

12. Opportunities should be taken to correct the public statements of others that depict the mentally ill and others in unfair, untrue, stereotypical ways.

References

Ackman, D. (2000). Net libel. Retrieved January 26, 2005, from http://www.forbes.com/2000/12/29/1229netlibel.html

Acuff, C., Bennett, B. E., Bricklin, P. M., Canter, M. B, Knapp, S. J., Moldawsky, S., et al. (1999). Considerations for ethical practice in managed care. *Professional Psychology: Research and Practice, 30,* 563–575.

Adams, S. J. (2000). Who uses bibliotherapy and why? A survey from an underserved area. *Canadian Journal of Psychology, 45,* 645–649.

Alford, C. F. (2001) *Whistleblowers: Broken lives and organizational power.* Ithaca, NY: Cornell University Press.

Apodaca, T. R., & Miller, W. R. (2003). A meta-analysis of the effectiveness of bibliotherapy for alcohol problems. *Journal of Clinical Psychology, 59,* 289–304.

Azrin, N. H., & Foxx, R. M. (1974). *Toilet training in less than a day.* New York: Simon & Schuster.

Barrera, M., Rosen, G. M., & Glasgow, R. E. (1981). "Rights," risks and responsibilities in the use of self help psychotherapy. In G. T. Hannah, W. P. Christian, & H. B. Clark (Eds.), *Preservation of client rights* (pp. 204–220). New York: McMillan Free Press.

Berns, C. F. (2003), Bibliotherapy: Using books to help bereaved children. *Omega, 48,* 321–336.

Bischoff, R. J., & Reiter, A. D. (1999). The role of gender in the presentation of mental health clinicians in the movies: Implications for clinical practice. *Psychotherapy: Theory, Research, Practice, and Training, 36,* 180–189.

Burd, T. (1994, December 14). Federal panel weighs a whistle blower's bill of rights. *The Chronicle of Higher Education,* A30.

Cardinal, D. (1994, October 12). Researchers and the press: A cautionary tale. *The Chronicle of Higher Education,* B3.

Committee on Government Operations. (1990, September 10). *Are scientific misconduct and conflict of interest hazardous to our health?* Washington, DC: U.S. Government Printing Office.

Controlling the Assault of Non-Solicited Pornography and Marketing Act, Pub. L. 108-187, codified as 15 U.S.C. 7701–7713 and 18 U.S.C. 1037 (2003).

Cooper, A. E., Corrigan, P. W., & Watson, A. C. (2003). Mental illness stigma and care seeking. *Journal of Nervous and Mental Disease, 191,* 339–341.

Corrigan, P. (2004). How stigma interfered with mental health care. *American Psychologist, 59,* 614–625.

Corrigan, P. (2005). *On the stigma of mental illness: Practical strategies for research and social change.* Washington, DC: American Psychological Association.

Corrigan, P. W., & Penn, D. L. (1999). Lessons from social psychology on discrediting psychiatric stigma. *American Psychologist, 54,* 765–776.

Curry, S. J., Ludman, E. J., & McClure, J. (2003). Self-administered treatment for smoking cessation. *Journal of Clinical Psychology, 59,* 305–319.

den Boer, P. C., Wiersma, D., & Van Den Bosch, R. J. (2004). Why is self-help neglected in the treatment of emotional disorders? A meta-analysis. *Psychological Medicine, 34,* 959–971.

Department of Health and Human Services. (1999). *Mental health: A report of the surgeon general.* Rockville, MD: U.S. Department of Health and Human Services.

Diefenbach, D. L. (1997). The portrayal of mental illness on prime-time television. *Journal of Community Psychology, 25,* 289–302.

Dunwoody, S. (1980). The science writing inner club: A communication link between science and the lay public. *Science, Technology and Human Values, 5,* 14–22.

Ellis, A. (1993). The advantages and disadvantages of self-help therapy materials. *Professional Psychology: Research and Practice, 24,* 335–339.

Epstein, R. (2001). Physiologist Laura. Retrieved August 5, 2007, from http://psychologytoday.com/articles/pto-20010701-000001.html

Ernhart, C. B., Scarr, S., & Geneson, D. F. (1993). On being a whistleblower: The Needleman case. *Ethics & Behavior, 3,* 73–93.

Estroff, S. E., Penn, D. L., & Toporek, J. R. (2004). *Schizophrenia Bulletin, 30,* 493–509.

Faugier, J., & Woolnough, H. (2002). Valuing voices from below. *Journal of Nursing Management, 20,* 315–320.

Fisher, C. (2003). *Decoding the ethics code: A practical guide for psychologists.* Thousand Oaks, CA: Sage.

Floyd, M., Scogin, F., McKendree-Smith, N. L., Floyd, D. L., & Rokke, P. D. (2004). Cognitive therapy for depression: A comparison of individual psychotherapy and bibliotherapy for depressed older adults. *Behavior Modification, 28,* 297–318.

Fox, J. A., & Levin, J. (1993). *How to work with the media.* Newbury Park, CA: Sage.

Frank, J. A. (2004). *Bush on the couch: Inside the mind of the president.* New York: Regan Books.

Gabbard, G. O., & Gabbard, K. (1999). *Psychiatry and the cinema.* Washington, DC: American Psychiatric Association.

Gardener, H., Csikszentmihalyi, M., & Damon, W. (2001). *Good work: When excellence and ethics meet.* New York: Basic Books.

Glasgow, R. E., & Rosen, G. M. (1978). Behavioral bibliotherapy: A review of self-help behavior therapy manuals. *Psychological Bulletin, 85,* 1–23.

Glasgow, R. E., & Rosen, G. M. (1979). Self help behavior therapy manuals: Recent developments and clinical usage. *Clinical Behavior Therapy Review, 1,* 1–20.

Glazer, M. P., & Glazer, P. M. (1989). *The whistleblowers.* New York: Basic Books.

Gordon, P. (1994). The celluloid couch: Representations of psychotherapy in recent cinema. *British Journal of Psychotherapy, 11,* 142–145.

Gunsalus, C. K. (1998a). How to blow the whistle and still have a career afterwards. *Science and Engineering Ethics, 4,* 51–64.

Gunsalus, C. K. (1998b). Preventing the need for whistleblowing: Practical advice for university administrators. *Science and Engineering Ethics, 4,* 75–94.

Hall, J. (2003). Science versus pseudoscience: Educating the public via Bookstore Project. *APS Observer, 16,* 19.

Hames, C. C., & Pedreira, D. (2003). Children with parents in prison: Disenfranchised grievers who benefit from bibliotherapy. *Illness, Crisis, and Loss, 11,* 377–386.

Haney, C., Banks, W. C., and Zimbardo, P. G. (1973). *Study of prisoners and guards in a simulated prison* [Naval Research Reviews 9 (1–17)]. Washington, DC: Office of Naval Research.

Heinlen, K. T., Welfel, E. R., Richmond, E. N., & O'Donnell, M. S. (2003). The nature, scope, and ethics of psychologist's E-therapy Web sites: What consumers find when surfing the Web. *Psychotherapy, 40,* 112–124.

Heinlen, K. T., Welfel, E. R., Richmond, E. N., & Rak, C. F. (2003). The scope of Web counseling: A survey of services and compliance with NBCC's guidelines for Internet counseling. *Journal of Counseling and Development, 81,* 61–69.

Hesley, J. W. (1998). *Rent two films and let's talk in the morning: Using popular movies in psychotherapy.* New York: Wiley.

Hill, G. (1993, March–April). Movies as therapy. *The California Therapist, 51.*

Holtje, H. F. (1988). Comment on Rosen. *American Psychologist, 43,* 600.

Hyler, S. E., Gabbard, G. O., & Schneider, I. (1991). Homicidal maniacs and narcissistic parasites: Stigmatization of mentally ill persons in the movies. *Hospital and Community Psychiatry, 42,* 1044–1148.

Jansen, E., & von Glinow, M. A. (1985). Ethical ambivalence and organizational reward systems. *Academy of Management Review, 10,* 814–822.

Johnson, R. A. (2003). *Whistleblowing: When it works—and why.* Boulder, CO: Lynne Rienner.

Joshua, J. M., & DiMenna, D. (2000). *Read two books and let's talk next week: Using bibliotherapy in clinical practice.* New York: Wiley.

Kier, F. J., & Molinari, V. (2004). Do-it-yourself testing for mental illness: Ethical issues, con-

cerns, and recommendations. *Professional Psychology, 35,* 261–267.

Kolata, G. (2000, July 18). Separating research from news. *New York Times.* Retrieved May 3, 2005, from   http://query.nytimes.com/gst/fullpage .html?sec= health&res=9E03E2DF133BF93B A25754C0A9669C8B63

Lauber, C., Anthony, M., Ajdacic-Gross, V., & Rossler, W. (2004). What about psychiatrists' attitude to mentally ill people? *European Psychiatry, 19,* 423–427.

Levy, D. A. (1989). Social support and the media: Analysis of responses by radio psychology talk shows. *Professional Psychology: Research and Practice, 20,* 73–78.

Lidren, D. M., Watkins, P. L., Gould, R. A., Clum, G. A., Asterino, M., & Tulloch, H. L. (1994). A comparison of bibliotherapy and group therapy in the treatment of panic disorder. *Journal of Consulting and Clinical Psychology, 62,* 865–869.

Lipsitz, A., Rand, K., Cornett, J., Sassler, M., & White, A. (2000, August). *Out of focus: The image of psychology in current cinema.* Paper presented at the annual meeting of the American Psychological Society, Miami Beach.

Lubalin, J., & Matheson, J. (1999). The fallout: What happens to whistleblowers and those accused but exonerated of scientific misconduct? *Science and Engineering Ethics, 5,* 229–250.

Mahoney, M. J. (1988). Beyond self-help polemics. *American Psychologist, 43,* 598–599.

Mains, J. A., & Scogin, F. R. (2003). The effectiveness of self-administered treatments: A practice-friendly review of the research. *Journal of Clinical Psychology, 59,* 237–246.

Mann, C. E., & Himelein, M. J. (2004). Factors associated with stigmatization of persons with mental illness. *Psychiatric Services, 55,* 185–187.

Matson, J. L., & Ollendick, T. H. (1977). Issues in toilet training normal children. *Behavior Therapy, 8,* 549–553.

Mayer, A., & Barry, D. D. (1992). Working with the media to destigmatize mental illness. *Hospital and Community Psychiatry, 43,* 77–78.

McCall, R. B. (1988). Science and the press: Like oil and water? *American Psychologist, 43,* 87–94.

McFadden, J., & Banich, M. (2003). Using bibliotherapy in transcultural counseling. In F. D. Harper (Ed.), *Culture and counseling: New approaches* (pp. 285–295). Needham Heights, MA: Allyn & Bacon.

Miceli, M. P., & Near, J. P. (1992). *Blowing the whistle*. New York: Lexington.

Miceli, M. P., & Near, J. P. (2002). What makes whistle-blowers effective? Three field studies. *Human Relations, 55*, 455–479.

Mimeault, V., & Morin, C. M. (1999). Self-help treatment for insomnia: Bibliotherapy with and without professional guidance. *Journal of Consulting and Clinical Psychology, 67*, 511–519.

Multimedia Entertainment, Inc. (1994, May 2). *Sally*. New York: Author.

Murray, B. (2002). Film criticized as irresponsible. *Monitor on Psychology*. Retrieved June 15, 2004, from http://www.apa.org/monitor/mar02/film critic.html

Nader, R., Petkas, P., & Blackwell, K. (Eds.). (1972). *Whistle blowing*. New York: Bantam.

Norcross, J. C., Santrock, J. W., Campbell, L. E., Smith, T. P., Sommer, R., & Zuckerman, E. L. (2003). *Authoritative guide to self-help resources in mental health* (2nd ed.). New York: Guilford Press.

Norcross, J. C., & Simansky, J. A. (2005). Highly rated self-help books and autobiographies. In G. P. Koocher, J. C. Norcross, & S. S. Hill (Eds.). *Psychologists' desk reference* (2nd ed., pp. 494–497). New York: Oxford University Press.

O'Neil, R. M. (1995, November 3). Free speech on the electronic frontier. *Chronicle of Higher Education*, A68.

Palmer, S., Bor, R., & Josse, J. (2000). A self-help tool kit for conquering fears and anxieties about flying. *Counseling Psychology Review, 15*, 18–29.

Paquette, M. (2003). Real life and real films. *Perspectives in Psychiatric Care, 39*, 47–48.

Pardeck, J. T., & Pardeck, J, A. (1998a). An exploration of the uses of children's books as an approach for enhancing cultural diversity. *Early Child Development and Care, 147*, 25–31.

Pardeck, J. T., & Pardeck, J. T. (1998b). *Using books in clinical social work practice: A guide to bibliotherapy*. Binghamton, NY: Haworth Press.

Parmerlee, M. A. (1982). Correlates of whistleblowers' perceptions of organizational retaliation. *U.S.: Administrative Science Quarterly, 27*, 17–34.

Phokeo, V., Sproule, B., & Raman-Wilms, L. (2004). Community pharmacists' attitudes toward professional interactions with users of psychiatric medication. *Psychiatric Services, 55*, 1434–1436.

Pound, E. T. (2005, December 19). Desperate housewife. *U.S. News and World Report*, 46–58.

Raviv, A., Yunovitz, R., & Raviv, A. (1989). Radio psychology and psychotherapy: Comparison of client attitudes and expectations. *Professional Psychology, 20*, 67–72.

Reinke, R. R., Corrigan, P. W., Leonhard, C., Lundin, R. K., & Kubiak, M. A. (2004). Examining two aspects of contact on the stigma of mental illness. *Journal of Social and Clinical Psychology, 23*, 377–389.

Richards, D. (2004). Self-help: Empowering service users or aiding cash strapped mental health services? *Journal of Mental Health, 13*, 117–123.

Rickwood, D., Cavanagh, S., Curtis, L., & Sakrouge, R. (2004). Educating young people about mental health and mental illness: Evaluating a school-based programme. *International Journal of Mental Health Promotion, 6*, 23–32.

Rosen, G. M. (1987). Self-help treatment books and the commercialization of psychotherapy. *American Psychologist, 42*, 46–51.

Rosen, G. M. (1993). Self-help or hype? Comments on psychology's failure to advance self-care. *Professional Psychology, 24*, 340–345.

Rothchild, J., & Miethe, T. D. (1999). Whistleblower disclosures and management retaliation. *Work and Occupation, 26*, 107–128.

Ruiz, M. A., Drake, E. B., Glass, A., Marcotte, D., & van Gorp, W. G. (2002). Trying to beat the system: Misuse of the Internet to assist in avoiding the detection of psychological symptom Dissimulation. *Professional Psychology, 33*, 294–299.

Salzinger, K. (2003, February). Foolish behavior. *Monitor on Psychology*, 63.

Schardt, D. (2004, January–February). Dr. Phil's pills. *Nutrition Action Newsletter*, 5.

Schneider, I. (1987). The theory and practice of movie psychiatry. *American Journal of Psychiatry, 144*, 996–1002.

Schulenberg, S. E. (2003). Psychotherapy and movies. On using films in clinical practice. *Journal of Contemporary Psychotherapy, 33*, 35–48.

Sharp, C. (2002). Cinematherapy: Metaphorically promoting therapeutic change. *Counseling Psychology Quarterly, 15*, 269–276.

Shaw, N. (2004). Changing minds at the earliest opportunity. *Psychiatric Bulletin, 28*, 213–215.

Schulenberg, S. E. (2003). Psychotherapy and movies: On using films in clinical practice. *Journal of Contemporary Psychotherapy, 33*, 35–48.

Sieber, J. E. (1999). Why fallout from whistleblowing is hard to avoid. *Science Engineering Ethics, 5*, 255–260.

Signorielli, N. (1989). The stigma of mental illness on television. *Journal of Broadcasting and Electronic Media, 33*, 325–331.

Sleek, S. (1998). How are psychologists portrayed on screen? *Monitor on Psychology, 29*, 11. Retrieved November 11, 2006, from http:www.apa.org/monitor/nov98/film.html

Smith, N. M., Floyd, M, R., Scogin, F., & Jamison, C. S. (1997). Three-year follow-up of bibliotherapy for depression. *Journal of Consulting and Clinical Psychology, 65*, 324–327.

Sprague, R. L. (1993). Whistleblowing: A very unpleasant avocation. *Ethics & Behavior, 3*, 103–133.

Starker, S. (1988a). Do-it-yourself therapy: The prescription of self-help books by psychologists, *Psychotherapy, 25*, 142–146.

Starker, S. (1988b). *Oracle at the supermarket*. New Brunswick, NJ: Transaction.

Starker, S. (1988c). Self-help treatment books: The rest of the story. *American Psychologist, 43*, 599–600.

Wahl, O. F., & Lefkowits, J. Y. (1989). Impact of a television film on attitudes towards mental illness. *American Journal of Community Psychology, 17*, 521–528.

Wedding, D. (2005). Popular films portraying mental disorders. In G. P. Koocher, J. C. Norcross, & S. S. Hill (Eds.), *Psychologists' desk reference* (pp. 497–501). New York: Oxford University Press.

Wedding, D., & Niemiec, R. M. (2003). The clinical use of films in psychotherapy. *Journal of Clinical Psychology, 59*, 207–215.

Weiss, T. (1991, June 26). Too many scientists who "blow the whistle" end up losing their jobs and careers. *The Chronicle of Higher Education*, A36.

Will, G. F. (1982, July 19). *Newsweek*, p. 76.

Wilson, D. L. (1995, January 13). Vigilantes gain quiet approval on networks. *The Chronicle of Higher Education*, A17–A19.

16

Ethical Dilemmas in Academic Settings

To educate a person in mind and not in morals is
to educate a menace to society.

Theodore Roosevelt

Contents

The role of educators extends well beyond transmitting information to others. Whether they realize it, mental health professionals who teach also serve as powerful role models. The values and actions of educators matter because they will be passed along, for better or for worse, to the next generation of professionals.

THE DARKER SIDE OF
THE ACADEMIC CULTURE

Colleges and universities traditionally honor and encourage productivity, creativity, and critical thinking. How the young are educated largely determines a nation's fitness and status in the world community. Unfortunately, the negatives receive far more attention in the mainstream media than do the considerable positive contributions made by students and their educators. Yet, unacceptable numbers of incidents involving racism, sexual harassment, and academic dishonesty continue to smear the reputations of our institutions of higher learning. Huge, impersonal lecture classes and overreliance on multiple-choice examinations and teaching assistants cause the public to wonder what really goes on behind those impressive-looking pillars. Once sacred grounds for freedom of expression, colleges and universities must now wrestle with what can and can not be uttered in a public forum or even in a private conversation. Some schools have issued speech guidelines, hailed by some as promoting civility and decried by others as imposing thought control (Bartlett, 2002). Campus scandals range from illegal perks for athletes to misconduct committed by research faculty.

Hard economic times coupled with stagnant or declining enrollments have led to funding cutbacks for most academic institutions. Shrinking resources invariably lead to increased competition among faculty for equipment, travel funds, laboratory space, and promotions. Shortages often lead to tension, which may reveal itself in low morale and explosive bickering and dissension among faculty members. Academics who find it difficult, for whatever reason, to conduct research and publish it in scholarly journals often put their job status in jeopardy.

The ironic result finds energy diverted from teaching students while churning uninspired, shoddy, or trivial work into the knowledge stockpile.

Forms of academic freedom assumed to be enjoyed by the faculty may, in fact, be illusive. The next case reveals how asserting assumed autonomy and authority can backfire.

Case 16–1: A senior, tenured psychology professor assigned a failing grade to a student (after checking to make sure the student did not have a medical or other compelling excuse) who attended only three sessions of the class and never completed any of the basic course work. The professor was ordered to change the grade to an "incomplete" by the university president but refused to do so. The professor was suspended. The professor wrote a critical review of the president and was eventually fired.

In the actual case, the professor sued the president and other university officials for dismissing him in retaliation for his refusal to change a student's grade and for violating his rights to free academic expression and rights under the First and Fourteenth Amendments to the U.S. Constitution. He did not prevail in a U.S. Circuit Court of Appeals (Ewing, 2001).

Academic communities have no immunity from the growing tendency to eschew personal responsibility and to blame others for real or perceived shortcomings. More typical lawsuits brought by students against faculty members or the institution seek to challenge grades or lack of due process regarding charges of misconduct (Mosier, 1989; Whitley & Keith-Spiegel, 2002). A few of the more unusual cases, snatched from headlines, appear below.

Case 16–2: Two students sought monetary damages because a course proved too difficult. The judge in small claims court ruled that the professor was guilty of educational malpractice for making an entry-level course too demanding (Shea, 1994).

Case 16–3: While "mooning" those below by pressing his bare backside against a window, an undergraduate student fell through and hurtled 30 feet to the ground. He attempted to sue the university for close to a million dollars for his minor injuries, that included "deeply bruised buttocks" and "trauma." The student alleged that the university was at fault for failing to specifically warn students about the dangers of upper-story windows (Gose, 1994).

Case 16–4: A client, who had already successfully sued her therapist and the clinic employing the therapist, attempted to take legal action against the institution where the therapist had trained for failing to ensure the competence of its graduates (Custer, 1994).

Case 16–5: A theater student sued five professors, claiming that she was forced to leave her academic program when the faculty refused to allow her to replace profane words in copyrighted play scripts with "nicer" words ("Acting on Faith," 2000).

It is ironic that the complex academic environment with conditions posing profound ethical ramifications is discussed *less* often in the ethics literature than the topic of any other chapter topic in this book. Whereas writings may mention ethical issues involved in the teaching of students, the coverage tends toward the superficial or narrowly focused. (Examples of the relatively small body of literature that attempts to tackle an array of the ethics of teaching include Braxton & Bayer, 1999; Fisch, 1996; Forsyth, 2003; Hogan & Kimmel, 1992; Keith-Spiegel, Whitley, Balogh, Perkins, & Wittig, 2002; Kitchener, 1992; Long, 1992; Strike & Moss, 1997; and Whicker & Kronenfeld, 1994.) A presumption that ethical improprieties are best handled within the institution probably accounts for the relatively modest interest in supporting external sources to establish guidelines for secondary and postgraduate educators. A faculty member's conduct, however, typically must involve an egregious violation before any formal action occurs within the institution. Even when institutional channels function in ways that allow for fair hearings and due process, only the most assertive aggrieved students appear to use them. Many students may feel relatively powerless, which in turn discourages them from seeking formal redress.

We can not do justice to the full array of ethical dilemmas that invade the academy in a single chapter and instead focus on a handful of topics that cut across the spectrum. Some of the cases presented in this chapter are adapted from *The Ethics of Teaching: A Casebook* (Keith-Spiegel et al., 2002). Related issues are also discussed in other sections of this book; for instance, more about confidential case material in the classroom is found in Chapter 8, social and other multiple-role relationships between educators and students in Chapters 11 and 12, ethical issues in writing letters of recommendation in Chapter 13, competent institutions in Chapter 4, and research collaboration with students in Chapter 19.

COMPETENCY ISSUES IN TEACHING

When criticism is solicited, college and university students offer up lots of complaints about their educators. Among the main student gripes are inferior course planning, weak lecturing skills (e.g., monotonic, too stiff, too long-winded), annoying mannerisms, making poor use of class time, arrogance, unapproachability, confusing grading criteria, and even faculty attire (Perlman & McCann, 1998). Not all of these complaints are ethical matters, but notice that not one of them questions the professors' mastery of the subject matter, probably because students are not usually in a position to judge.

At the very least, educators should present accurate information and stay within the boundaries of their competence, based on such indicators as education and supervised experiences (APA 02: 7.03.b; APA 02: 2.01) However, we believe that proficiency requirements extend well beyond mastery of the subject matter being taught. A number of other matters that require competent pedagogic judgments and adept management skills seem relevant, such as maintaining classroom decorum, teaching style effectiveness, the quality of assignments, and the handling of sensitive topics.

Teaching Skills and Course Preparation

The knowledge base of the helping professions evolves continually, creating major implications for those who teach. Keeping up with specialty areas ensures offering students the best education to prepare them for their life's work. Mental health professionals who teach, for example, are mandated to maintain ongoing competence (APA 02: 2.03.). This may include taking courses or self-directed reading, collegial discussions, mentoring, and attendance at professional meetings and teaching conferences. (See also Chapter 4.)

Most students do not realize that ill-prepared instructors or those who exclusively cite older work and theories when more recently recognized work and updated theories are readily available have failed to fulfill the ethical requirements of their profession. Student consumers can not easily assess the accuracy, objectivity, and completeness of the information taught. Whereas the grumbles about educators most often focus on disputed performance evaluations and offensive interpersonal styles, occasional complaints about teaching skills have come to our attention.

Case 16–6: Professor Daze Fluster was charged with incompetence by an angry student who doubted the quality of education he was receiving from Fluster and was upset by the department's apparent unwillingness to remedy the situation. The student claimed that Professor Fluster always arrived late, spent most of the time flipping through a tangled mass of papers in his briefcase, had no apparent agenda for each class session, and rambled in an unconnected fashion. The student asserted that his time and tuition were not being well served.

Assuming validity of the student's account of the course, we can not tell for sure if Professor Fluster has competence in his field but lacks skill as a lecturer, or if he has some more serious underlying problem. If Fluster appears ill prepared for class on a regular basis, regardless of the reason, he fulfills neither his professional nor his ethical responsibilities.

Teaching Courses Without Formal Training

Graduate school training does not necessarily represent the skills and interest areas that will endure across an entire career. Sometimes, by choice, instructors seek proficiency to teach in an area for which they have received no or insufficient formal training. Often enough, and especially at small colleges, instructors may find themselves assigned several courses, including some for which they possess only a rudimentary background.

Case 16–7: Professor Mutate received no graduate-level training in industrial psychology but wanted to teach the undergraduate course, "Psychology and Business." He spent a summer reading relevant textbooks and a number of primary sources. He interviewed an industrial psychologist for several hours.

Instructors can often arrange a course of study that will enable them to teach competently some classes for which they received no graduate training. The nature of an adequate plan can vary from self-directed reading to undertaking additional course work or obtaining supervised experiences. The time and effort required is based on such factors as the course level (e.g., lower-division survey vs. specialized upper division or graduate) and type (e.g., text knowledge vs. technique application). It is less likely that preparing to teach an advanced techniques course can be accomplished informally by someone with no relevant formal background.

Whether Professor Mutate has put together a sufficient undergraduate course is not entirely clear, but there are ways he can reassure himself. Consultation with colleagues who are fully capable of teaching the course should be sought. Locating a colleague who will supervise course progress (i.e., content, exams, and assignments) during the time the course is first taught is also highly desirable.

Maintaining Classroom Decorum

Not all students share equal enthusiasm about a course. Late-arriving, sleeping, whispering, and "eye-rolling" students disrupt the learning environment for everyone. Not all students appreciate the demands of the teaching performance and the despair instructors feel when carefully crafted lectures appear to fall on indifferent ears. However, overly rigid or uncharitable classroom decorum policies can create ethical concerns.

Case 16–8: Professor Harsh deducts grade points from exam scores when students talk in class or engage in other behaviors he deems disruptive. He defends his practice on the grounds that one can reasonably expect mature behavior from college-level students.

Professor Harsh's stance illustrates the risky business of subtracting points earned for academic performances in response to undesirable classroom behavior. Whereas Professor Harsh most certainly has the right and the obligation to maintain a classroom environment conducive to learning, legitimately earned academic credit should remain intact.

Humiliating students can swiftly control unwanted classroom behaviors, but such techniques also raise ethical questions.

Case 16–9: Professor Bringem Down shouts at students who engage in any behaviors she finds annoying and chides them if questions strike her as off target or ill conceived. For example, she told one student who asked what she perceived to be an unintelligent question to leave the room and return only if he could locate his brain.

Professor Down may have whipped her class into her notion of proper deportment, but we have no idea what else her students have learned. Students are very sensitive to humiliation or ridicule. According to the findings of a large survey of undergraduate students, 80% of the respondents rated insulting or ridiculing students or telling a student during a class discussion their input was stupid as "extremely unethical" (Keith-Spiegel, Tabachnick, & Allen, 1993). We believe that shaming tactics undermine the respect that should define relationships between students and their educators. Sometimes, however, strong measures seem necessary, as the next case illustrates.

Case 16–10: Beanie Blowout made loud "raspberry" sounds when the instructor turned to the chalkboard, smirked as he asked questions that were purposely irrelevant or inane (e.g., "Was the hippocampus named after a school for large animals?"), and constantly dropped his pen and pencil. The instructor felt at her wits end and sought to have Blowout removed from the class.

Assuming that the instructor attempted unsuccessfully to convince Blowout, in private, that his behavior made it impossible for her to do her job and for other students to learn, and that the instructor had consulted with the department chair or dean, who proved unable to help, we cannot fault the instructor for instituting Blowout's permanent dismissal from the classroom. Most campuses have policies and procedures related to difficult students that allow due process while preserving a climate for learning (Pavela, 1985).

Unfortunately, the rate of student insubordination and intimidation in the classroom appears on the rise, creating trying dilemmas for faculties. Schneider (1998) used the extreme descriptor "classroom terrorists" to describe a no-longer-uncommon phenomenon and offered examples that live up to the term. Educators have experienced verbal abuse and even challenges to engage in a fight. The reasons usually involve unwelcome grades, but often enough arise from matters most of us would consider relatively minor. One student, for example, left a hateful message containing excessively foul language on a professor's message machine because her textbook was not eligible to resell as a new edition had come out in the meantime. How to deal with such incidents in a way that allows the faculty to remain stable and respond with integrity presents a challenge, requiring strong administrative support.

Impaired Instructors

Even mental health professionals who teach can themselves be impaired, ranging from mild to debilitating. First, we consider the more common types of personal difficulties that plague almost everybody, including instructors, at least on occasion. A national survey revealed that 92% of a large sample of psychology professors admitted to being unprepared for class on occasion, and 66% have taught classes at times when they felt too distressed to teach effectively (Tabachnick, Keith-Spiegel, & Pope, 1991).

Case 16–11: The refrigerator broke down, a friend needed to spill out the problems she was having with her boss, and the dog vomited on the brand new carpet. So much for the evening that Professor Addie Lib was planning to spend preparing tomorrow morning's lecture.

Case 16–12: Professor Wo Izmee had a terrible fight with his girlfriend, and his son from a previous marriage was just arrested for possession of cocaine. When the alarm went off the next morning, he felt so agitated that he called in sick and arranged for a film to be shown instead.

Professors Adlib and Izmee (adapted from Keith-Spiegel et al., 2002) will most likely rebound fully. In the meantime, can they deal with their misfortune in a way that protects students while still fulfilling their professional responsibilities? Professor Adlib could have "pulled an all-nighter" just as students force themselves to do sometimes and put together an adequate presentation. Or, she could have facilitated a useful discussion among the students. Because unanticipated events occur so commonly, such anecdotes serve as reminders that early preparation is always preferable.

Professor Izmee's stressors seem most acute, and he may not have the ability to perform adequately that day. Arranging to show films instead, or even canceling classes if no other options existed, are ethically acceptable because his extreme mental anguish is probably as debilitating as an acute physical illness might be. Otherwise, something like the unfortunate scene in the next case could happen.

Case 16–13: Professor Iva Lostit smashed her car into a tree and did not have funds to cover the insurance deductible to have it repaired. She became enraged when her father refused to loan her the money. On entering the departmental office in a huff after having to take a taxi to work, she threw a book at the receptionist, who, noting her intensity, asked in jest, "Did you just eat a firecracker?" She then went to her class and angrily announced to the students that not one of them had what it takes to ever make it into graduate school.

Professor Lostit would have spared everyone, most of all herself, had she taken sufficient time

out to calm down. Should a distressed state prove other than transient, instructors are responsible for seeking professional help and to refrain from teaching altogether when they can not function competently (APA 02: 2.06b).

Case 16–14: Once a vibrant and active member of the department, Professor Downhill has steadily backed away from contributions to the college. He has become withdrawn, assigns minimal work, and often tells colleagues that "nothing much matters anymore." He leaves campus as soon as he can to go home and watch TV or nap.

Professor Downhill seems burned out (and most likely clinically depressed) and appears disinterested in or unable to seek assistance. Although Downhill may have other problems, his students and commitment to the university and its mission have certainly eroded significantly.

More rarely, instructors can also experience severe disturbance, at least temporarily.

Case 16–15: Professor Spurn had recently been divorced by his wife. When he discovered that he and a graduate student working in his lab were both dating the same woman, he terminated the student's access to lab equipment. Professor Spurn became increasingly paranoid and subsequently accused the student of turning poisonous spiders loose in his office, although no such spiders were ever found.

Psychotherapy clients can be hurt by vengeful or troubled therapists, but clients have greater freedom to "fire" the therapist at any time and seek help elsewhere. Students, however, can not extricate themselves so easily from a relationship that is inseparable from their academic program, thus running the risk of a poor grade assignment or worse. In some situations, the faculty member might even cause students longer-range career problems. For example, if Professor Spurn was the only instructor teaching in the student's specialty areas, the student's professional future could be endangered. In this actual episode, Spurn's student fortunately found academic shelter in the laboratory of a sympathetic colleague.

Case 16–16: Professor Gloom, spoke in great detail in his abnormal psychology class about his hospitalized wife's condition. She was diagnosed as schizophrenic and believed herself to be an Amazon warrior queen. Whenever Gloom went to see her, she ordered him executed. The class heard a rundown on her condition after each of his visits. Finally, a class representative approached Gloom and expressed considerable sympathy but firmly communicated that Gloom's disclosures provided far more detail about his wife's illness and their marital relationship than the students felt comfortable in knowing.

Gloom is an example of a more piteous figure and surely requires considerable support. But, his students are not the appropriate source of it. (For more information about impaired mental health professionals, see Chapter 4.)

Some difficult instructors fall short of having clear signs of mental illness but sport rather nasty temperaments much of the time and may even take pleasure in exerting power over students. They appear to feel entitled to treat students with disrespect at the slightest provocation.

Instructors with combative interpersonal styles rarely have insight into the harm that they cause students and the institution. Unfortunately, institutions of higher education have not proven effective in managing perpetually grumpy, mean-spirited, or irksome faculty members once they achieve tenure.

PERSONAL STYLES AND CLASSROOM ACTIVITY

Lecturing on Sensitive or Controversial Topics

It is impossible for teachers to be totally objective and value free. With today's widely diverse student population and the inherently delicate and controversial nature of many mental health and psychological topics, remaining both sensitive and evenhanded becomes somewhat of a challenge. Here, we use the terms *controversial* and *sensitive* to refer to topics or theories about which strong enough differences in opinion

exist or the potential for distressing reactions warrants caution. Instructors should remain aware of their own biases and students' sensitivities. This can prove trying, despite their best efforts.

Case 16–17: Chip Straight complained that Professor Open offended him by discussing homosexuality in class and showing a film that depicted people of the same sex embracing. He believed such matters should be "confined to the gutter and not discussed in an institution of higher learning."

This case illustrates how an instructor might offend a particularly sensitive student. During an inquiry, Professor Open produced materials indicating that the topic of homosexuality had relevance to the course content and was based on scholarly writings. He said he showed balance in terms of varying views people have about the topic. The movie was an educational film, owned by the university library.

It is possible to lower the incidence of offensiveness to some students without compromising the rights of instructors to express themselves. Students should be informed from the onset if sensitive or controversial material will be covered. Such up-front disclosures allow students to make a voluntary, informed decision about whether to remain in the class. If exceptionally sensitive material will be covered on a particular day, the instructor might consider informing the students during the prior meeting and at the very beginning of the class session. Offering other points of view, in as objective a fashion as possible, is encouraged.

It is best to stick as close as possible to a scientific database (if one exists) when discussing sensitive or controversial topics. If the information base originates only in opinion or controversial studies, the full range should be presented rather than only one side. An instructor can always state why he or she personally disagrees with other opinions. Students should be allowed an opportunity to express their own views respectfully without penalty, censure, or ridicule and be given opportunities to discuss in private any feelings they might have about the sensitive or controversial material presented in class.

As long as class presentations can be justified on pedagogical grounds and related directly to the course, disapproval is less likely to occur and attempts to censure less likely to succeed. Sometimes, criticism arises because the material was added for "effect" or "shock value." The American Association of University Professors' Principles on Academic Freedom and Tenure (1984) warned against persistently interjecting into the classroom controversial matter that has no relation to the subject at hand.

Arguable Classroom Demonstrations

Issues associated with arguable classroom demonstrations, including films, align closely with lectures on controversial topics. No bright line demarcates creative and innovative teaching techniques from those that would qualify as inappropriate or ethically questionable. Sometimes, instructors find themselves taken off guard, and at other times they are insensitive to their students' values.

Case 16–18: Professor Ablation showed a movie in his undergraduate neuropsychology class; the movie demonstrated vivid depictions of brain surgery techniques on a dog and a cat. Two students fled the room in tears, and many others became visibly distressed. When one student asked Professor Ablation why he had not given them some warning, he replied, "That's not a requirement. You're supposed to attend every class. This is a course about the brain, after all."

Images evoke powerful emotions. Having sat through multiple previous showings, instructors may lose touch with the reactions some people have to seeing a film for the first time. Contemporary students seem to be either more squeamish or more open than students from previous decades in expressing distress when shown films or demonstrations that involve animal experimentation (Herzog, 1990). We recommend remaining alert to what kinds of film experiences may prove too intense for some students and excuse them or provide alternative assignments if at all possible. In areas that predictably upset many or most undergraduate students, such as animal experimen-

tation using primates or companion animals, the instructor might consider available alternatives.

Unusual classroom demonstrations can range from exciting and memorable to questionable or inappropriate learning experiences. The next case is illustrative.

Case 16–19: Professor Wily Sly came to class a little early, left his briefcase on the desk, and walked out of the room. While students were still filing in, a young man snatched the briefcase and ran from the room. When Sly returned, he looked confused, then worried, and then boomed out, "Has anyone seen my briefcase? I left it here just a minute ago."

Professor Sly is attempting to bring his about-to-be-delivered lecture on eyewitness testimony to life. As long as the students do not feel embarrassed or upset by such demonstrations in which they become unwitting participants, no ethical issues pertain. However, a number of students indicated that they would be upset by demonstrations that had been published by APA as suggested classroom activities (Harcum & Friedman, 1991). Potentially controversial demonstrations might be checked out with a focus group because regional and cultural differences may lead to varying degrees of acceptability. This procedure would help to ensure that the intended lesson is received without untoward side effects, such as the student who informed on the "thief" who stole Professor Wily's briefcase later being scorned as a "snitch." In any event, students should never be deceived for long, and any staged demonstration should be easily defensible as educationally sound.

Case 16–20: At 2 days after the shootings at Virginia Tech, during which several students and faculty were shot by a troubled student, a part-time faculty member at a small college walked around the classroom pointing his finger at various students and shouting, "Bang, you're dead." Several students later complained, and the instructor defended himself by both claiming academic freedom and arguing that he had simply demonstrated the fragility of life.

The college dismissed the instructor within a few days, noting that he had made several students in his class anxious and uncomfortable. Spontaneity and classroom demonstrations can have pedagogical value but require thoughtful consideration of others' sensitivities.

Case 16–21: Professor Bobtail stunned his students when he showed stills of male and female genitalia in his human sexuality class and then announced that the last slide of the series was a photograph of his own penis.

Professor Bobtail used terrible judgment and skidded way past the bounds of propriety. In the actual case, it eventually cost him his job. We do not imply, however, that all forms of personal disclosure fall out of bounds. Instructors in psychology, social work, and related fields, especially, find that what has occurred in their personal or professional lives often closely parallels what they are teaching. Students enjoy stories with a personal touch, especially if the stories are also amusing. But, it is wise to think twice before getting into intimately personal areas.

Unconventional Teaching Styles and Assignments

Unconventional or nontraditional teaching styles and assignments may raise questions of an ethical nature. Many instructors are deeply involved with innovations geared to motivate students' involvement in the learning process. It is, indeed, a daunting task to try to second-guess all possible sensibilities in an increasingly pluralistic culture. While we neither desire nor intend to regiment teaching style or stunt originality, it is worthwhile to note how ethical controversy can arise. In each of the next three cases, the instructors argued that their methods were used to "focus attention" or to "bring a sense of reality to the learning process." However, questions about pedagogical justification arose in each instance.

Case 16–22: John Nicetalk complained about the teaching style of Professor Flam Boyant. Nicetalk felt offended by Boyant's frequent use of four-letter words to describe nearly everything he lectured

about in the classroom. He found such language not only unprofessional, but also as providing a poor role model for other students as well as trivializing the knowledge imparted.

Just as some comedians have become known for their ability to be funny *without* resorting to a barrage of the "F word," so should instructors strive to teach effectively without using language offensive to others. Instructors may use off-color language because they think all students will enjoy it. The available data suggest that this is untrue. A national survey revealed that, although the majority of students did not view the use of profanity in lectures as an ethical problem, about 27% rated the use of profanity as unethical under "most" or "virtually all" circumstances, indicating that over one in four students may have strong negative reactions. Students presented far more concern with off-color stories or jokes, as opposed to words, with more than half of the students regarding the telling of such material during class as unethical under "many" or "virtually all" circumstances. Only 12% viewed off-color stories as ethically acceptable in the classroom (Keith-Spiegel et al., 1993). At least one professor has experienced a suspension for "creating a hostile learning environment" due to his colorful expressions uttered in the classroom (Southwick, 2001).

What about unusual out-of-class assignments? Instructors must discriminate between the acceptably nontraditional and the problematical.

Case 16–23: Professor Blatant faced university sanctions when students complained about required assignments for a course on contemporary lifestyles. These included visiting swinging singles clubs, gay bars, group living compounds such as nudist camps and religious cults, massage parlors and bathhouses, militant political group meetings, and sexual paraphernalia shops.

It would appear that Professor Blatant's assignments did mirror the course topic. However, a number of the students objected to having to do "such strange things" off campus. Blatant might have escaped some of the criticism had he included other options that did not demand such intense experiences. But, he did not seem to realize that by requiring his students to engage in off-campus experiences that could put them at some risk of emotional and possibly even physical harm, he could also place the university at legal risk.

Educational Experiences Requiring Student Disclosure

The experiential group seminar, in which students are encouraged to explore and share their own feelings and conflicts, can pose risks to students (Grauerholz & Copenhaver, 1994). It may prove valuable to expose students to experiences that could assist them in interacting with people about delicate topics, especially for those aspiring to become mental health service providers. Those who plan someday to do group process work may also benefit from participating in this course model. Judging from the paucity of ethics complaints received about them, it seems probable that such experiences usually run satisfactorily.

However, concern has been expressed about the ethical risks of blending elements of therapeutic treatment with academic course work. When complaints do arise, they typically involve intense feelings, and the inherent dual role (i.e., student/quasi client and instructor/quasi therapist) usually constitutes the root of the dissatisfaction.

Case 16–24: Lettit Hangout always spoke up during her sensitivity training class. She revealed many areas of personal discontent and assumed that by doing so she acting as a "good student." She soon began to notice, however, that the instructor became increasingly distant toward her. The other students began to withdraw from her as well. Her advising professor began making vague suggestions that she select another major. Hangout eventually instituted grievance procedures against the instructor for explicitly encouraging her to reveal personal problems, resulting in considerable gossip and endangerment of her academic reputation and alienation from her peers.

Case 16–25: Tim Orous complained against Professor Tellall on receiving a D in Group Experience 463, a required class in his degree pro-

gram. His grade reflected his silence throughout the quarter, although he told the professor early in the term that he did not feel comfortable participating in the discussions. Orous asserted that it was inappropriate to require students to reveal personal, nonacademic information and then jeopardize their academic status for noncompliance.

The instructor should have pulled Ms. Hangout aside the moment it became clear that her vision of achieving success in the course seemed inappropriate. Even if Ms. Hangout had significant psychopathology and seemed potentially unfit to deliver mental health services, this particular forum was not the appropriate one to expose her lack of suitability. Tim Orous, illustrating the other end of the participatory pole, was punished academically for refusing to disclose strictly personal information. We particularly question the wisdom of requiring this type of class of undergraduates. Some students are simply unsuited for this type of experience (APA 02: 7.04).

A variation on the self-disclosure theme involves written assignments, sometimes in the form of a journal, requiring students to record their personal feelings and share private recollections. This type of assignment has also been under ethical scrutiny, with claims that it often requires inappropriate self-revelation (e.g., Berman, 2001; Hanley, 2004). An assignment to write about a childhood trauma, for example, may exacerbate feelings of powerlessness and deference to authority figures (Swartzlander, Pace, & Stamler, 1993). Confidentiality and privacy issues also apply.

Instructors may never become aware of any harmful, longer-term effects of highly personal disclosures. We suggest considering this type of assignment risky and therefore subject to special scrutiny regarding appropriateness. Precautions that may preclude untoward consequences for "affective" learning experiences, particularly for courses required as part of a degree or training program, include

- informing students in published course descriptions and at the beginning of the course of exactly what will be expected of them, coupled with a candid revelation of some of the possible negative effects

- offering a choice of course assignments, at least one of which does not demand highly personal disclosure
- making time for a private discussion with any student who is experiencing difficulties with the class or its assignments
- grading on bases other than the nature of the students' problems or willingness to share them

The APA has taken a detailed stand on the issue of requiring self-disclosure by listing specific topics in the ethics code (APA 02: 7.04) that psychologists may *not* require students to recount. These include sexual and abuse history, psychological treatment, and relationships with parents, peers, spouses, or significant others. There are two exceptions. The first is clear-cut; if the admissions or program at a training facility requires such information and clearly identifies such expectations in their program and application materials, then requesting such disclosures does not violate the code. The second exception is tricky. Requiring such information is *not* unethical if it seems necessary to evaluate and obtain assistance for students who are not competently performing their training or professionally related activities due to personal problems or because they may pose a risk to others. Fisher (2003) gave the example of a student who the supervisor suspects may be seeing clients socially. When confronted, the student replies in the affirmative. At this point, the supervisor asks if the relationship is romantic. Thus, during the advanced stage of training, more intrusive measures may be necessary to ensure that the individual is fit to practice as a mental health provider.

Some programs allow (or require) students to enter individual psychotherapy for academic credit or as part of an advanced training program. We do not recommend using faculty members who regularly teach courses in the program to provide clinical services, even if the students do not pay extra fees for the services.

Case 16–26: Ned Fears revealed to his therapist that he has a panic attack whenever he encounters a four-legged animal or a human under 3 feet tall.

He described the many ingenious ways he attempts to avoid these beings. The therapist also served as a faculty member at Fears's university and could not be avoided as the only instructor in an advanced personality theory seminar. Fears began to feel so self-conscious in class that he dropped out of the graduate program.

Mr. Fears required professional services, but they should not have been delivered by someone who has become his classroom instructor. It would have been better if the two could have figured out how Mr. Fears could continue his course work with another instructor while being treated for his phobia.

Creating a separation from the ongoing training pipeline greatly softens any dual-role conflicts that might be experienced by both students and regular, ongoing faculty (APA 02. 7.05b). One exception might be psychoanalytic training, in which faculty members may serve as both instructors and training analysts for the candidates. In this instance, the training model is generally well described by the analytic institute and well understood by the candidates.

DISHONESTY IN ACADEMIA

Oral Plagiarism

A rarely discussed ethical issue involves the overuse of the work and words of others to create verbal presentations. Whereas it is obvious that instructors usually craft their lectures with a reliance on the already produced work of others, how does one acknowledge those sources? Is acknowledgment always necessary? After all, as opposed to the printed word, lectures leave no visible tracks. Besides, even if it were possible to credit every source of every point made, it would take up valuable class time and probably contribute little of educational or lasting use to the students. Consider the following two cases:

Case 16–27: Professor Copycat duplicates sections from various textbooks that competed with the one she assigned to her students, pasted them together, and reads them to her students. Students find her lecture style dull and unappealing and yet also mistakenly assume that she created the material herself.

Case 16–28: Professor Goodcredit created a lecture on memory loss that drew heavily from two articles. At the beginning of the lecture, Professor Goodcredit announced, "Most of my lecture material is based on two articles, one by Dexter Noengram and another by Webster Blankbrain. I can give you the full references after class if any of you would like to delve further into their work."

Professor Copycat is a lazy oral plagiarist (APA 02: 8.11). She lacks inspiration and is stealing others' intellectual property. For lecture development, the question to ask oneself is, "Did you find your own voice in interpreting published information?" Professor Copycat did not.

Professor Goodcredit's technique is sound. Because he focused heavily on the work of two authors, it was proper for him to credit them briefly. Spending great amounts of class time reading lecture references is not necessary. Goodcredit's acknowledgments took less than 20 seconds. Being generous to those who created material that provides information or inspiration by acknowledging their efforts is always both commendable and appropriate. (For a discussion of written plagiarism, see Chapter 19.)

Dealing With Dishonest Students

Unethical students pose ethical dilemmas for their teachers. Sadly, it appears that too many students are more interested in getting a degree by following a course of least resistance than in acquiring a genuine education. It is widely acknowledged that the rate of cheating in our nation's colleges and universities is occurring at unacceptably high rates (Davis & Ludvigson, 1995; McCabe & Bowers, 1994; McCabe & Trevino, 1993; McCabe, Trevino, & Butterfield, 2001; Whitley & Keith-Spiegel, 2002). We also know that many instructors will likely ignore cheating, and that administrators do too little to address academic dishonesty (Correnti, 1986; Kibler, 1992; Whitley & Keith-Spiegel, 2001). Intriguingly, however, students themselves overwhelmingly believe that it is unethical for professors to ignore strong evidence of cheating (Keith-Spiegel et al., 1993).

Case 16–29: Professor Hesitant suspected that Peeka Boo was looking at her neighbor's test paper but was not sure. Boo's term paper also had a "familiar look" and exceeded, in both style and content, the level expected of an undergraduate student. The mere thought of confronting and dealing with the matter made Hesitant nauseous. Professor Hesitant figured that he could never prove that Boo cheated and instead resolved not to give her any benefit of a doubt when he assigned the final grade. If, for example, her grade was to fall between a C and a B, he would assign the lower grade as his way of dealing with the matter.

Professor Hesitant's "solution" to handling a student suspected of cheating is probably widespread. In a survey of teaching psychologists, 77% agreed that dealing with a cheating student was among the most distasteful aspects of the profession. When asked why they thought that many instructors ignored strong evidence of cheating, the inability to prove the case conclusively was the major reason given. Other frequently selected reasons included stress, anxiety on contemplating a formal hearing, insufficient time to track down the evidence, lack of courage, and a concern about how the conflict would escalate if the student denied the charges (Keith-Spiegel, Tabachnick, Whitley, & Washburn, 1998).

Despite the burden of establishing proof and the noxiousness of confronting dishonest students, cheating must be managed effectively if the mission of higher education is to remain valid. Ignoring cheating positively reinforces dishonest behavior and gives a message to students that actual accomplishment is unimportant. As for Ms. Boo, if she were innocent, she could be potentially disadvantaged without an opportunity to explain herself. If Boo is guilty, then her dishonest method of handling the rigors of a college education has been fortified. As unsettling as it may be, Professor Hesitant should call Boo in for a private talk. Preventive tactics can make this process easier, such as telling students in advance (and in the syllabus) that they may be asked to discuss their papers or exams with the instructor, and that academic dishonesty will not be tolerated. Unfortunately, many preventive techniques, while they do discourage cheating, are labor intensive and not feasible for use in very large classes.

The task of having to retype plagiarized material has all but disappeared thanks to scanners and "cut and paste." The Internet poses a special challenge as it provides students with an untold wealth of information that can easily be downloaded and woven into a paper to hand in as their own. Surveys reveal that students do directly use material they find online (e.g., Szabo & Underwood, 2004). However, it is also increasingly easier to detect cybercheats thanks to services set up for that purpose. Faculty members can often find the original sources themselves by using the right keywords and phrases as search engines become increasingly sophisticated. Few faculty members, however, have the time or inclination to engage in such chases unless serious suspicions are raised.

Whereas solving the problem of students' plagiarism by dropping a requirement for written assignments has a surface appeal, we remain concerned. The next generation of citizens needs to be able to communicate effectively through writing. Eliminating writing assignments in school does not serve society. Perhaps the best deterrent to plagiarism is to let students know that they may be asked to answer questions about their written assignments (e.g., "You say, 'Direct observation of children remains the best way to assess behavior despite the many limitations.' What limitations were you referring to?") Those who did not work with the material will be unlikely to answer questions that those who created a paper themselves can. Instructors may require a meeting with students during the process of creating their papers so that they confirm that the papers are valid.

EVALUATING STUDENT PERFORMANCE

Grading Students' Performances

Most professional ethics codes contain a mandate to do no harm to those with whom they work. Educators are in a unique position in that, at times, they have a *duty* to inflict harm, to issue a failing (or unwanted) grade or to terminate a student from a program. Of course, the instructor or program director must be able to substantiate that such actions were taken fairly and according to school policy should they be challenged.

Ethics committees are not typically the appropriate forum for resolving grading disputes, even if the assignment could be proven to be unjustified.

Case 16–30: Brittany Brilliant was upset because she received a C in her counseling class, and it was the only C on her record. She wrote to the ethics committee, claiming that Professor Washout's exams were unfair, and that his term assignment was not carefully explained.

Such cases are virtually always returned to the student with the suggestion to use the grievance procedure within the institution. Only on rare occasions, when a student has documented negligent or prejudicial evaluations, have ethics committees intervened. In many instances, the student typically has support from other faculty members and institutional officials, who corroborate the student's position. It is common to also find departments that are embroiled in bitter factional disputes or controversies. The grievance mechanisms have broken down, and the student appears to have received insufficient due process. (See Chapter 4 for relevant cases.)

Case 16–31: Sookey Judge received a negative evaluation from her clinical supervisor, Professor Dilatory, during the last term of her academic program. She complained that the supervisor could have warned her of any perceived shortcomings and given her an opportunity to remedy them. She also asserted that her attempts to meet with Professor Dilatory about some of the problems she was experiencing with her internship assignment were met with excuses such as, "I am too busy today; maybe next week."

Professor Dilatory responded that he had refrained from issuing early evaluations of substandard performance and from meeting with the student because, "It looked like Ms. Judge was improving at the time." However, to withhold feedback for 7 months in areas in which improvement was required was unfair to Ms. Judge and did not fulfill Dilatory's ethical obligation to facilitate the development of professionals in training (APA 02: 7.06).

The fact that professional association ethics committees do not address, except under unusual and extreme circumstances, grading and evaluation disputes does not mean that profound ethical issues are not inherent in the evaluation of students. Indeed, academic performance ratings are assumed to differentiate among bright, average, and poor students. Given the significance of such labels in our culture, these blessings and stigmas have major implications for admission to advanced educational programs and future employment. In this context, academics must hold themselves accountable for their judgments. To assess students using hastily developed test questions or biased evaluation criteria constitutes infliction of harm and is therefore unethical.

Ironically, grade inflation is an insidious issue that we can not fail to mention. Skewing grades toward the upper end of the curve has plagued the academy for many years now and shows no signs of abating, even at the nation's top colleges and universities (Goldman, 1985; Gose, 1997; Mansfield, 2001; Pederson, 1997; Young, 2003). Grade inflation may make more students feel happier and consequently lead to better course evaluation ratings for instructors. However, the best students are disadvantaged because they can not be differentiated from those whose transcripts are bloated despite less stellar performances. Instead of complaining about Ds and Fs, today's students complain about (and have even sued over) a grade of C. It is not uncommon to find students dissatisfied with a B grade. Professors who try to hold the line and maintain high standards may risk being sued or even fired (Wilson, 2002). This is extremely demoralizing because faculty can no longer use grades to reward outstanding achievement (Kfir, Fresko, & Benjamin-Paul, 2002).

Course Exams

Case 16–32: Barney Bummed complained to the dean of students that Professor Bubblein based a semester's grade only on a single final exam, consisting of 50 multiple-choice questions that seemed vague and poorly written.

Psychological and diagnostic tests and assessments (see Chapter 9) emerge as more relevant for ethics committee scrutiny than do students' performances on course examinations. This is not because clinical assessments are more important but because the "rules" of their construction, administration, and interpretation have been formalized, making it easier to assess their validity. Academic course assessments are based on information and assignments unique to the educational experience that each instructor offers. These factors, however, do not excuse instructors from personal and ethical obligations to invest considerable effort in educating and evaluating students fairly, based on actual performance, and in a timely manner (APA 02: 7.06).

Biases in Evaluation

Regardless of the many issues associated with grading systems, we expect instructors to remain objective when evaluating students (APA 02: D). Students see the maintenance of a "level playing field" as a primary ethic of the professorate. The vast majority of students in a national survey rated "grading students based on how much the instructor liked them" as unethical under "most" or "virtually all" circumstances (Keith-Spiegel et al., 1993). Almost two thirds of instructors, however, admitted to allowing how much they like (or dislike) a student to influence the grades they assign, at least on occasion. However, most of these same respondents also agreed that such biased practices were ethically questionable (Tabachnick et al., 1991).

Case 16–33: From his men's room stall, Professor Uptite overheard his best student, Alfie Slip, refer to him as "an arrogant dork." Later, Uptite made a point of being particularly critical of Slip's next paper, assigning it a B minus. When Slip subsequently asked for a letter of reference, Uptite refused.

Professor Uptite has no obligation to write any student a letter of reference, and Mr. Slip's remark cost him dearly. It was unethical, however, for Uptite to bias his grading criteria in retaliation for the bathroom blunder. Professor Uptite might have better used the incident as a valuable teaching moment, confronting Slip directly about the consequences of how (and where) we characterize others.

Case 16–34: At the urging of his vocational rehabilitation counselor, Joe Fleet, a disabled Iraq war veteran, returned to school. Fleet had been volunteering as a counselor for a year at the local junior high school and had received outstanding evaluations. The school principal told Fleet that he would hire him for a full-time position once he had earned a master's degree. One of Fleet's instructors, Professor Wannahelp, also advocates for Fleet and his goal but has concerns because Fleet's grades are below average. Professor Wannahelp feels sure that Fleet has the capability to do better but had trouble motivating himself to do, as Fleet calls it, "this busy paper work." Professor Wannahelp assigns Fleet a B in the course even though, based on the class curve, he earned a low C.

Professor Wannahelp is trying to assist a student who needs a credential to enter a profession for which he already has demonstrated skill and suitability. However, Wannahelp acted unfairly to the other students who received no special consideration. Other options for advocacy—such as providing detailed letters of recommendation that focus on Fleet's strengths, arranging for some tutoring sessions, or attempting to alter Fleet's attitude about the basics of schoolwork—were appropriate and available options that Wannahelp should have considered instead.

If institutions of higher education and other training facilities are to provide valid credentials, fair and unbiased assessment of students is mandatory. Advanced courses, especially when the students are performing supervised services, may require evaluations of personality and suitability for delivering psychological services. However, even these judgments should be based on established behavioral criteria rather than idiosyncratic personal judgments that may say as much about the evaluator as about the student.

EXPLOITATION OF STUDENTS

When professors place their own needs above the welfare of their students, abuse can result. Because students often want to please their instructors, they may allow themselves to be mistreated. Or, because students can sometimes benefit from participating in activities that also fulfill their instructors' needs, they may not recognize the point at which a collaborative relationship leaks into exploitation. This section provides examples of instructors taking from students with little or nothing given in return. (Additional issues involving student exploitation that arise from multiple-role relationships are discussed in Chapters 11 and 12.)

Case 16–35: Clinton Clever's term paper contained a literature background and detailed design for an ingenious experiment. Professor Purloin fleshed it out a little more, collected data, and published it without reference to Clever's contribution. Clever complained to his advisor, who in turn confronted Purloin. Purloin's response was, "Clever expressed no intention of ever running the study. He is just an undergraduate student. If he had asked to be involved, I would have let him help with it. He could never have done it on his own."

Professor Purloin's attitude reflects a lack of sensitivity to students' rights. That Clever is "just an undergraduate student" is not relevant in and of itself. Further, it was not Clever's responsibility to initiate an intention to execute the study to maintain ownership of the design. It may well be true that Clever did not intend to run the study on his own. However, Professor Purloin should have at least consulted with the student. At that point, Clever could have declined the invitation to collaborate and given Purloin permission to go ahead independently. Even here, it would have been very appropriate for Purloin to credit Clever's contribution to the design in a footnote (APA 02: 8.12a &8.12b).

What if Clever's work had been less detailed, maybe in the form of a few sentences that suggested an idea for a study? We acknowledge that there certainly comes a point at which a student paper or a casual discussion provides a glimmer of an idea that stimulates the development of an executable project. In such instances, involving the others who may have jump-started an independent creation is not morally mandated, although we maintain that acknowledging the contributions of others never hurts anyone and can even enhance a positive reputation for mentoring.

Research collaboration with students (including undergraduate students) is popular because of the benefits that can accrue to everyone involved. Scholarly output remains the major factor in faculty promotion and retention decisions. Research experience is one of the primary determinants of graduate school admission for many academic programs (Keith-Spiegel, 1991; Keith-Spiegel, Tabachnick, & Spiegel, 1994). Instructors must be careful, however, to carefully prepare their students with a realistic picture of expectations.

Case 16–36: Professor Gallop's research fascinated Sid Sweat. Gallop warned Sweat that coming on board as a volunteer research assistant would be time consuming. Sweat assumed that he would be actively collecting data as part of a team. But, what started out as a boon for Sweat became a drab and tedious drain on his already busy schedule. Sweat's task was to enter data while sitting alone in a small cubicle for up to 15 hours a week. Sweat felt betrayed, did not always pay careful attention to what he was doing, and had to squelch urges to enter bogus numbers just to get away early.

Although a plan can not always be cast in stone, this case illustrates how feelings of exploitation might have been greatly diminished had the student fully understood and voluntarily agreed to all aspects of the commitment in advance. That Professor Gallop has unknowingly put her own work in serious jeopardy by insufficiently preparing her now-resentful helper illustrates how clear lines of communication are also in everyone's best interests. Inexperienced research assistants, in particular, should be monitored carefully, not only for the quality and accuracy of their work, but also for their satisfaction with the arrangement.

CONFIDENTIALITY ISSUES IN ACADEMIA

Telling Students' Stories in Class

Instructors in psychology, social work, counseling, and other mental health-related areas probably have more opportunities to learn intimate details of students' lives than instructors in other disciplines because the subject matters are so often conducive to discussion of personal issues. Furthermore, such instructors are likely viewed as having more expertise in dealing with personal problems. The openness of many students during private office hours, especially when they explain why they did not take an exam or meet a deadline, suggests that they believe that their personal disclosures will be held in strict confidence. That assumption is not well founded. A large, national survey revealed that, at least on occasion, 38% of the faculty sample passed along material shared in confidence, even though most of those who admitted doing so also thought it wrong (Tabachnick et al., 1991).

Student–teacher interactions are very different from the client–therapist relationship. Instructors and students are with each other in various contexts (e.g., as advisees, denizens of the hallways and canteen, and so on) making the lines of communication complex and sometimes gnarly. The integration of possibly identifiable information about psychotherapy clients into class lecture notes is discussed in Chapter 8, but the same concerns can be applied to what students divulge to their educators.

Case 16–37: A case of a sordid, abusive childhood was relayed in class by Professor Lucy Lips. Although no identities were shared, a current student recognized the story as one that a sorority sister had recently told her in the strictest of confidence and had mentioned that she told it to Professor Lips as well. The victim felt devastated on learning that her story had been openly relayed to others.

Students very much enjoy lectures heavily peppered with interesting case stories. Removing names and other identifying data, however, may not always be sufficient. Therefore, instructors must thoroughly disguise material before using someone's private life as a teaching tool (APA 02: 4.07).

Revealing Information About Students Outside Class

Another type of confidentiality dilemma arises when colleagues relax with each other and talk shop. Instructors behave just like everyone else with a job. Flushing out frustrations in the presence of sympathetic peers can facilitate release of work-related stress. However, if the sessions have a ritualistic or obsessive quality (e.g., a weekly contest to see who can tell the most outrageous student story), the appropriateness and constructiveness of this social tourney must be questioned (Keith-Spiegel et al., 2002).

Case 16–38: Six instructors in the psychology department enjoy meeting at the faculty club on Friday afternoons. The usual agenda focuses on divulging student behavior that was stupid, weird, or suspicious. Several students have become especially fair game because most of the instructors know them. "Guess what Nancy Noskull put as the answer to a quiz question this week?" typifies how such interactions start.

Students' behavior can be very amusing (even when not intended as such). Purposely disgracing students, however, is not an ethical way to release tension, and actual harm is more likely than may be evident in the lightness of the moment. In this case, Ms. Noskull has little chance of gaining serious support by other faculty because, by now, her reputation precedes her. Unflattering stories that identify the students by name or other means will likely influ-

ence the way future instructors will see them. To the extent that such discussion includes information about a student's academic records (e.g., grades), such casual discussion may violate federal law (i.e., see discussion of Family Educational Rights and Privacy Act [FERPA]).

We would note that naming students can not always be avoided in conversations with colleagues. An instructor who is having trouble dealing with a particular student may seek counsel from a colleague known to be wise in such matters or who has previously taught that student. Although such discussions approach the edge of confidentiality mandates (APA 02: 4.06), when such consultations take place they should occur in private and in a professional setting (e.g., campus office rather than the local pub). Addressing issues that will advance the student's welfare should be the sole intent of any such discussions.

Sometimes an emergency creates an unavoidable confidentiality dilemma for instructors.

Case 16–39: Bonnie Bruised told her instructor, Professor Disclose, that she feared for her life. Her boyfriend had beaten her badly when she broke up with him and was currently stalking her. Professor Disclose advised the student to contact the campus police and the counseling center immediately. The student adamantly refused to interact with either resource. Professor Disclose contacted them herself to warn them about the potential danger to her student.

Professor Disclose has been put in a terrible position and feels obligated to take some action to protect the student (APA 02: 4.05b). For a while, at least, Professor Disclose must become involved with a student's personal life and, simultaneously, risk alienating her student by divulging information presumably shared in confidence. It may be difficult to rebuild the student–instructor relationship with Ms. Bruised. Under emergency conditions, ethical guidelines are not always helpful. Instructors (and therapists) can minimize the risk of future censure, however, as long as their actions can later be viewed as attempts to protect others rather than to exploit or harm them. (See Chapter 8 for a discussion of the duty to protect.)

Futzing With the Family Educational Rights and Privacy Act

Many academics have never heard of the Family Educational Rights and Privacy Act (FERPA), a federal law (i.e., 20 U.S.C. § 1232g; 34 CFR Part 99) that applies to all schools that receive federal funds from programs administered by U.S. Department of Education and imposes firm limits on disclosing records of students. The law protects the privacy of student education records.

Specific rights are assigned to parents by FERPA, but it transfers these to the student at attaining the age of 18 or when attending a school beyond the high school level. The law calls students to whom the rights have transferred "eligible students." These rights include the ability to inspect and review any of the student's education records maintained by the school. Schools may not have to provide actual copies of records unless, for reasons such as great distance, it becomes impossible for parents or eligible students to review the records. Schools may charge a fee to produce copies. Parents or eligible students also have the right to request correction of records they believe to be inaccurate or misleading. If the school declines to amend the record, the parent or eligible student may seek a formal hearing. If, after a hearing, the school still does not amend the record, the parents or eligible students have the right to place a statement in the record setting forth their views regarding the disputed information.

Generally, schools must have written permission from the parent or eligible student to release any information from a student's education record. However, FERPA does allow schools to disclose records, without consent, under certain circumstances (see 34 CFR § 99.31). Examples of such releases might include school officials with legitimate educational interests; other schools to which a student seeks to transfer; appropriate parties in connection with accreditation, audits, or financial aid; responses to a judicial order or lawful subpoena; appropriate officials in cases of health and safety emergencies; and state and local authorities, pursuant to specific state law.

Schools may disclose, without consent, directory information such as a student's name, address, telephone number, date and place of birth, honors and awards, and dates of attendance. However, schools must inform parents and eligible students about directory information and allow them a reasonable amount of time to request nondisclosure. Schools must notify parents and eligible students annually of their rights under FERPA, although the form of the notice (e.g., special letter, inclusion in a parent–teacher association bulletin, student handbook, or newspaper article) falls to the discretion of each school.

Case 16–40: Professor Sam Slippage has taught college students for nearly three decades. He routinely posts exam grades on his office door listing students by their initials. At the end of each semester he piles graded term papers in a box outside his office door so students can pick them up at their convenience.

Case 16–41: Noah Vale contacted the dean of students at Cookie University, seeking a progress report on his daughter, Flail, a 19-year-old sophomore. He explained that Flail had not done well during her freshman year due to homesickness and a breakup with her high school sweetheart. He wanted to "quietly check on how she's doing, without sensitizing her to the fact her parents have concerns."

Professor Slippage's practices clearly violate FERPA rules and could subject his university to regulatory enforcement actions. He should use identifiers clearly unrecognizable to others if he wishes to post students' grades. Similarly, he should find some other way of returning graded materials to students (e.g., inviting students to leave postage-paid envelopes for mailing or arranging with a support staff member to return the papers to each student during business hours). Along the same line of privacy protection, the dean will doubtless explain to Mr. Vale that she can not reveal information about Vale's adult daughter's academic progress without her permission.

ADVISING AND MENTORING TANGLES

When it comes to shared interests, faculty members have closer connections to their students than to each other. Colleagues' specialty areas typically differ markedly because a department's faculty must represent the fullest possible spectrum of the discipline. Students, on the other hand, can enter their educators' narrow circles, nurturing and embracing similar interests. Ethical problems can result from advising and mentoring. (Chapter 11 discusses purely social relationships with students.)

Case 16–42: Professors Angela Sturm and Portia Drang are intense rivals at Trenchant University. Drang filed an ethics complaint against Sturm, charging that she took on a graduate student and convinced the student to develop a dissertation aimed at discrediting Drang's research.

Students have the freedom to select their own advisors and dissertation sponsors. Once having done so, advisors usually have a heavy influence on their students. Whereas the freedom to pursue any area of valid scientific inquiry must always remain open, one should exercise special care to avoid pulling students into personal disputes. In this instance, it is not clear that Sturm behaved unethically in attempting to interest a student in a dissertation topic, but she may well have jeopardized that student's welfare by injecting him into her dispute with Drang. Research should seek scientific truths, and initiating studies primarily designed to embarrass individuals rather than to seek the truth lacks integrity.

Sometimes, the student, perhaps unwittingly, may start a troubling ball rolling.

Case 16–43: After taking a seminar from Professor Trance, an impressed graduate student decided to change his master's thesis topic to hypnosis. The student had already been working on a master's project for some time with Professor Drop, who had recruited the student the previous year. The student told Trance that he wanted to terminate his association with Professor Drop and start a new project with Professor Trance.

Professor Trance might reasonably send the student to Professor Drop to discuss the situation or prefer to approach Professor Drop himself, depending on what feels most comfortable and reasonable given the nature of the relationships. The two professors should communicate about the situation at some point to ensure that an equitable understanding occurs. Responses by major professors to students who express a desire to jump ship vary from acceptance (sometimes even relief) to feelings of resentment toward both the student and the new advisor. Sometimes, the original advisor already has a poor relationship with the potential new advisor, and the student's departure might feel like a humiliating mutiny.

How far the student's project had already progressed, the interdependence that had been created, and the level of the advisor's commitment to the student or the student's project constitute important factors that will have an impact on the original advisor's response.

In most instances, a wise potential advisor will remain cautious until the student and the original advisor have reached an understanding. Sometimes, simply refusing to take on a student already working for someone else will yield the best outcome. Perhaps noting that other opportunities to work together in the future might arise will satisfy all concerned. Switching advisors from the master's thesis to the doctoral dissertation occurs frequently, and Trance could suggest that the student discuss the possibility of working together later. Professor Trance may also want to remind the student that he had, after all, committed to work with Professor Drop. Just because the student's interests have changed does not automatically absolve a responsibility or erase a commitment.

Finally, when does student advisement go beyond acceptable boundaries? Instructors in a mental health field may find themselves sought after for free personal advice on matters that go well beyond a discussion of the literature, school- or class-related topics, and the student's future education or career.

Case 16–44: Virgil Vestal fidgeted in the chair, looking very disturbed. "What is it?" Professor Blunt asked. "I have a girlfriend," Virgil responds, "who wants to make love." "So, what's the problem?" asked Blunt. "I'm 22 and haven't ever had sex. I am really afraid of sex, and I wanted to ask you what I should do," replied Virgil. "Go for it," replied Professor Blunt with a big grin. "Seize the moment."

Matters relating to sex, family and relationship conflicts, personal fears, and complaints about almost anything constitute typical conversational staples for approachable instructors. However, Professor Blunt treated what may have been a very complex personal issue as one that he thought required only a little encouragement. His impulsive blessing could well have been contraindicated. Blunt would have served the student better had he indicated that, whereas this is an issue Mr. Vestal should talk over with somebody, he was not the right person. An offer to set up an appointment with the counseling center would be both caring and ethically acceptable.

We advise setting one's professional training and expertise aside when students seek highly personal advice. Instead, instructors should ask themselves, "Does this matter seem one that an instructor in another discipline might refer to the counseling center or some other type of mental health professional?" If the answer is even "probably," we suggest that such a referral be made.

DESIGN AND DESCRIPTIONS OF EDUCATION AND TRAINING PROGRAMS

Educational programs and course descriptions included in catalogs or other promotional materials constitute a type of service advertisement, although we usually do not think of them as such. However, students (including professionals seeking continuing education and nonprofessionals interested in nondegree educational experiences) will likely rely on the promotional materials when making decisions. Accuracy, then, becomes an ethical issue. (Discussions of contracts for therapy clients and advertising can be found in Chapters 5 and 14, respectively.)

Complaints about program and catalog entries rarely come to the attention of ethics committees, probably because they are an unlikely choice of redress should students become dissatisfied. Nevertheless, and perhaps because of the potential for misrepresentation, the most detailed coverage of teaching-related ethics in the APA's ethics code deals with program and course advertisements (APA 02: 7:01. and 7.02).

Program Descriptions

Those responsible for training programs should ensure that they include a suitable coverage of knowledge and required experiences to qualify for whatever claims the program makes, such as fulfilling requirements to obtain licensure or certification (APA 02: 7.01). They should also ensure that published materials accurately describe the program content, what stipends or benefits are available, and the requirements for successful completion of the program, including any mandated counseling or therapy, projects, or service to the community (APA 02: 7.02). Those responsible for promoting workshops and nondegree programs should also include accurate descriptions of the content and objectives, the presenters, the audience for whom the program is intended, and any fees (APA 02: 5.03).

Case 16–45: After Pam Sincere completed a semester of her master's-level counseling program at Minus College, she learned that the degree would not qualify her to sit for a professional licensing exam. When she confronted her advisor, he pointed out that the program did offer a legitimate academic degree in counseling but made no promises about qualifications to enter into a licensed profession. He advised her to complete the program and later try to transfer into a doctoral-level program. Sincere had not planned on committing to a doctoral program.

Case 16–46: Mark Skinnerman selected the M&M Institute for his doctoral training because of its strong behavioral orientation. However, soon after he enrolled it became clear that the program lacked substantial expertise in this area. Two of the senior behaviorist faculty members had retired the previous year, and a major transformation in program emphasis had begun.

One may feel tempted to fault the students for not asking enough questions. Certainly, were Ms. Sincere and Mr. Skinnerman more assertive in seeking information they might have saved themselves time, grief, and money. Students may easily assume, as Ms. Sincere did, that an advanced degree in counseling would lead to the opportunity to practice as a counselor without having to take additional course work. Minus College should have issued an appropriate caveat in its program description. Mr. Skinnerman's plight illustrates how failing to update program descriptions promptly, especially when a substantial change occurs, can disadvantage students. Program representatives must take whatever extra steps are necessary to ensure that applicants are informed of changes or circumstances that may affect their interest in entering a program.

Helping professionals who become involved with continuing education programs and workshops must realize that today's busy consumers on a budget (and that includes other helping professionals) expect to get value when spending both their time and money. Promotional materials should offer current and complete information, including realistic depictions of what to expect from the experience. We have heard complaints from workshop attendees that the participants added nothing new beyond presenting material from their already-published books that the attendees had already read.

Course Descriptions and Syllabi

Many students base their course selections on the catalog description, especially when signing up for an unfamiliar course or one outside their major field of study. When a significant course component is added, shifted, or eliminated, a correction should be made in the next catalog printing. In the meantime, any discrepancies should be communicated in other forums (e.g., e-mail and Web sites, bulletin boards, department newsletters) and, most certainly, specifically addressed on the first day of class.

Case 16–47: Doogie Stretch was eager to obtain more hands-on research experience. He enrolled in Psychology 314 because the catalog description stated that the course required the completion of an original research project. However, the syllabus handed out on the first day of classes included only required textbook readings and two brief review papers. When Doogie inquired about the research project, Professor Switcheroo replied, "Oh, we used to do that, but it got to be too much of a bother."

It appears that Switcheroo's department had known of the discrepancy for some time. That nothing was done about it was very unfair to students, especially those as serious as Mr. Stretch.

Educators would be wise to think of their syllabi as representing far more than "first-day handouts." Course syllabi provide the basis of a student's informed consent to commit to a course (Handelsman, Rosen, & Arguello, 1987). When a student recognizes that a catalog description is inconsistent with a syllabus, the student usually has the option of dropping the class. However, if the syllabus fails to reflect how the course will actually play itself out, students can be unfairly disadvantaged.

Circumstances beyond the instructor's control can arise that require deviations from the syllabus plan. For example, new knowledge or opportunities can arise during the course of a semester that could be to the students' advantage but require a syllabus modification in the process. Or, a genuine emergency can legitimately require a scheduling adjustment. In such instances, instructors should minimize any negative impact.

Syllabi are increasingly viewed as contracts with students and can even serve as legal exhibits when disputes arise.

Case 16–48: Les Miserables instigated a grievance procedure against Professor Crisplist. Miserables was graded down for poor class attendance and given a 25% deduction for a late paper. Miserables supplied the single-page syllabus for the course that made no mention of these penalties. Professor Crisplist retorted that he had made announcements about these matters several times in class, but Miserables was never there to hear them.

Although Mr. Miserables is hardly a paragon of responsibility, Professor Crisplist fell vulnerable to criticism because the rules that governed student evaluation did not exist in writing. To be an effective guide for students, as well as the best possible defense should complaints arise, syllabi should detail what will be covered in the course, learning objectives, required reading, details about assignments and deadlines, test formats and bases for performance evaluation, any penalties for nonattendance or late papers, and whatever else will help connect the student to the course (Rubin, 1985; APA 02: 7.03.a). We strongly suggest including a statement about expectations for honesty as this can, in and of itself, serve as a deterrent to cheating (Whitley & Keith-Spiegel, 2002). Students do not attend to everything in the syllabus (Becker & Calhoon, 2002), so it benefits both students and faculty to issue reminders.

Faculty Web pages provide another source of information that students find useful. Included on the page might be how to contact the instructor (e-mail address and phone number), office hours, syllabi of courses offered, advising information, and descriptions of research interests and background (Palmiter & Renjilian, 2003). Students seem more willing to seek outside-of-class support from their instructors when instructors explicitly include mention of their willingness to provide it in the syllabus (Perrine, Lisle, & Tucker, 1995).

SELF-SERVING INTERESTS

Textbook Adoption Practices

Instructors have the obligation to select required readings with care, and textbook adoption decisions should be based strictly on the merits of the content.

Case 16–49: Professor Miniracket told a book sales representative that she would adopt the company's text for her classes if the company agreed to a $1 kickback on each copy purchased by her students.

Case 16–50: Professor Snooker agreed to adopt a particular company's book after receiving an offer of $500 for providing the company with a three-page book review.

Unfortunately, as the textbook publishing industry becomes more competitive and sales representatives' jobs depend on how many adoptions they score, questionable adoption practices may accelerate (Bartlett, 2003). Faculty salaries are usually quite modest, and some may find such offers enticing, despite the strings attached. Nevertheless, Miniracket and Snooker exploited students for personal gain. They shortchanged their students, who trusted that instructors respect their learning interests by selecting resources based entirely on merit.

Moonlighting

Does working off campus during the active school year, in addition to holding a full-time teaching position, constitute an ethical issue? One can argue that it is unfair to students if an instructor is available minimally or only at odd hours or is often is too tired or distracted to attend to students' legitimate needs.

Case 16–51: Tillie Rushbutt holds a full-time university teaching position and sees 25 private practice clients per week. She also consults regularly to mental health clinics around the country, which causes her to miss classes several times a semester. Professor Rushbutt reasons that her outside employment provides excellent lecture material and keeps her current in her field, and that her national reputation brings status to the university.

The ethics of moonlighting are difficult to resolve at a macrolevel. From an ethical perspective, we can not establish a meaningful hour limit for off-campus employment. People have higher or lower energy levels, require more or less sleep, have no or many family obligations, require considerable or little effort to do their outside job, and so on. These factors affect the impact of outside employment on students as well as the quality of teaching, advising, and committee service to the institution. Regardless of an instructor's stamina and life circumstance, however, a tipping point is reached at which both the students and the institution are being shortchanged. Professor Rushbutt, for example, sees more clients than do most full-time private practitioners.

Some types of moonlighting are more self-serving than others. This is the most extreme case that has come to our attention.

Case 16–52: Buzi Agent, D.S.W., is a tenured professor with a real estate broker's license. He holds office hours from 6 to 7 A.M. and teaches his classes from 7 A.M. until noon three mornings a week. Students rarely come to his predawn office hours, and Agent uses this time to pull out his lecture notes and to create and grade multiple-choice exams. He leaves promptly at noon to go to his real estate office. He never comes to campus on Tuesdays or Thursdays.

Professor Agent contributes nothing to his campus community besides meeting the barest job requirements. It would be difficult to argue convincingly that his ongoing real estate career contributes anything of substance to teaching his neuropsychology courses. Many colleges and universities have disclosure policies that limit the extent of outside employment and restrict how many classes can be taught end to end. Regardless, it remains every instructors' personal responsibility to know when extracurricular activities—whether outside employment, an absorbing hobby, or even textbook writing—impair the quality of the services they have undertaken on behalf of the academic institution and its students.

SUMMARY GUIDELINES

1. Course materials should reflect careful preparation and should include recent, important work relevant to the topic and course.

2. Educators should teach only in those areas in which they have gained sufficient mastery relative to the level of the course.

3. Educators should not present their own values or opinions in ways that could be mistaken for established facts.

4. Educators need to monitor their own emotional status and take appropriate steps if personal problems interfere with their ability to teach or to fulfill responsibilities to the institution.

5. When lecturing on sensitive or controversial topics, educators should prepare the students in advance, present in as objective and well balanced a manner as is possible, and select pedagogically defensible content.

6. Outside assignments should be pedagogically defensible and not place students in harms way.

7. To maintain the quality and meaning of higher education, academic dishonesty must be dealt with in a proactive and direct manner.

8. When lecturing, educators should find their own voice when creating lecture presentations and should credit sources from which they adapt extensively.

9. Students must be graded fairly using criteria that apply equally to all students.

10. In interactions with students, educators should treat them with respect and maintain appropriate professional boundaries. Students should never be exploited.

11. Except under very unusual circumstances, student confidences must be respected. Any use of personal materials they supply that might be instructive during classroom presentations must be very carefully disguised.

12. Descriptions of academic courses or other educational programs should accurately reflect the experiences students will receive and the obligations they will incur.

13. Selection of assignments and textbooks should occur solely with their pedagogical appropriateness in mind.

14. Teaching must be balanced with other obligations to the institution and outside activities in a way that ensures that educators meet their responsibilities.

References

Acting on faith, spurning profanity. (2000, February 11). *Chronicle of Higher Education*, A12.

American Association of University Professors. (1984). *Statement on professional ethics. Policy documents and reports*. Washington, DC: Author.

Bartlett, T. (2002, September 27). Guidelines for discussion, or thought control. *Chronicle of Higher Education*, A10–A11.

Bartlett, T. (2003, June 27). Selling out: A textbook example. *Chronicle of Higher Education*, 49, A8

Becker, A. H., & Calhoon, S. K. (2002). What introductory psychology students attend to on a course syllabus. In R. A. Griggs (Ed.), *Handbook for teaching introductory psychology: Vol. 3: With an emphasis on assessment* (pp. 14–19). Mahwah, NJ: Erlbaum.

Berman, J. (2001). Sexual self-disclosures in an expository writing course. *Journal for the Psychoanalysis of Culture and Society, 6*, 181–194.

Braxton, J. M., & Bayer, A. E. (1999). *Faculty misconduct in collegiate teaching*. Baltimore, MD: Johns Hopkins University Press.

Correnti, R. (1986). Introduction. In D. Gehring, E. M. Nuss, & G. Pavela (Eds.), *Issues and perspectives on academic integrity* (p. A33). Columbus, OH: National Association of Student Personnel Administration.

Custer, G. (1994, November). Can universities be liable for incompetent grads? *APA Monitor*, 7.

Davis, S. F., & Ludvigson, H. W. (1995). Additional data on academic dishonesty and a proposal for remediation. *Teaching of Psychology, 22*, 119–121.

Ewing, C. P. (2001, July–August). Is academic freedom legally protected? *Monitor in Psychology*, 22.

FERPA Web site. http://www.ed.gov/policy/gen/guid/fpco/ferpa/index.html

Fisch, L. (Ed.). (1996). *Ethical dimensions of college and university teaching*. San Francisco: Jossey-Bass.

Fisher, C. B. (2003). *Decoding the ethics code: A practical guide for psychologists*. Thousand Oaks, CA: Sage.

Forsyth, D. (2003). *The professor's guide to teaching: Psychological principles and practices*. Washington, DC: American Psychological Association.

Goldman, L. (1985). The betrayal of the gatekeepers: Grade inflation. *Journal of General Education, 37*, 97–121.

Gose, B. (1994, April 17). Lawsuit "feeding frenzy." *Chronicle of Higher Education*, A27–A28.

Gose, B. (1997, July 25). Efforts to curb grade inflation get an F from many critics. *Chronicle of Higher Education*, A41–A42.

Grauerholz, E., & Copenhaver, S. (1994). When the personal becomes problematic: The ethics of using experiential teaching methods. *Teaching Sociology, 22*, 319–327.

Handelsman, M. M., Rosen, J., & Arguello, A. (1987). Informed consent of students: How much information is enough? *Teaching of Psychology, 14*, 107–109.

Hanley, M. R. (2004). Ethical dilemmas associated with self-disclosure in student writing. *Teaching of Psychology, 31*, 167–171.

Harcum, E. R., & Friedman, H. (1991). Student's ethics ratings of demonstrations in introductory psychology. *Teaching of Psychology, 19*, 215–218.

Herzog, H. A. (1990). Discussing animal rights and animal research in the classroom. *Teaching of Psychology, 17*, 90–94.

Hogan, P. M., & Kimmel, A. J. (1992). Ethical teaching of psychology: One department's attempts at self-regulation. *Teaching of Psychology, 19*, 205–210.

Keith-Spiegel, P. (1991). *The complete guide to graduate school admission*. Hillsdale, NJ: Erlbaum.

Keith-Spiegel, P., Tabachnick, B. G., & Allen, M. (1993). Ethics in academia: Students' views of professors' actions. *Ethics & Behavior, 3*, 149–162.

Keith-Spiegel, P., Tabachnick, B. G., & Spiegel, G. (1994). When demand exceeds supply: Second order criteria in graduate school selection criteria. *Teaching of Psychology, 21*, 79–85.

Keith-Spiegel, P., Tabachnick, B. G., Whitley, B. E., & Washburn, J. (1998). Why do professors ignore cheating? Opinions of a national sample of psychology instructors. *Ethics & Behavior, 8*, 215–227.

Keith-Spiegel, P., Whitley, B. E., Balogh, D. W., Perkins, D. V., & Wittig, A. F. (2002). *The ethics of teaching: A casebook* (2nd ed.). Mahwah, NJ: Erlbaum.

Kfir, D., Fresko, B., & Benjamin-Paul, I. (2002). Professional responsibility and grade inflation. *Megamot*, *42*, 296–313.

Kibler, W. L. (1992, November 11). Cheating—Institutions need a comprehensive plan for promoting academic integrity. *Chronicle of Higher Education*, B1–B2.

Kitchener, K. S. (1992). Psychologist as teacher and mentor: Affirming ethical values throughout the curriculum. *Professional Psychology*, *23*, 190–195.

Long, E., Jr. (1992). *Higher education as a moral enterprise*. Washington, DC: Georgetown University Press.

McCabe, D. L., & Bowers, W. J. (1994). Academic dishonesty among males in college: A 30 year perspective. *Journal of College Student Development*, *35*, 5–10.

McCabe, D., & Trevino, L. K. (1993). Faculty responses to academic dishonesty. *Research in Higher Education*, *34*, 647–658.

McCabe, D., Trevino, L. K., & Butterfield, K. D. (2001). Cheating in academic institutions: A decade of research. *Ethics & Behavior*, *11*, 219–232.

Mansfield, H. C. (April 6, 2001). Grade inflation: It's time to face the facts. *Chronicle of Higher Education*, B24.

Mosier, G. C. (1989). Why students sue. *AGB Reports*, *31*, 27–29.

Palmiter, D., & Renjilian, D. (2003). Improving your psychology faculty home page: Results of a student-faculty online survey. *Teaching of Psychology*, *30*, 163–166.

Pavela, G. (1985). *The dismissal of students with mental disorders: Legal issues, policy considerations and alternative responses*. Asheville, NC: College Administration.

Pederson, D. (1997, March 3). When A is average. *Newsweek*, 64.

Perlman, B., & McCann, L. I. (1998). Students' pet peeves about teaching. *Teaching of Psychology*, *25*, 201–203.

Perrine, R. M., Lisle, J., & Tucker, D. L. (1995). Effects of a syllabus offer of help, student age, and class size on college students' willingness to seek support from faculty. *Journal of Experimental Education*, *64*, 41–52.

Rubin, S. (1985, August 7). Professors, students, and the syllabus. *Chronicle of Higher Education*, 56.

Schneider, A. (1998, March 27). Insubordination and intimidation signal the end of decorum in many classrooms. *Chronicle of Higher Education*, A12–A14.

Shea, C. (1994, July 20). Two students at Pace U. win refund and damages over computer course they say was too hard. *Chronicle of Higher Education*, A28.

Southwick, R. (March 5, 2001) Professor's defense of his classroom profanity created "hostile" environment, appeals court rules. *Chronicle of Higher Education*, A4.

Strike, K. A., & Moss, P. A. (1997). *Ethics and college student life*. Boston: Allyn & Bacon.

Swartzlander, S., Pace, D., & Stamler, V. L. (1993, February 17). The ethics of requiring students to write about their personal lives. *Chronicle of Higher Education*, B1–B2.

Szabo, A., & Underwood, J. (2004). Cybercheats: Is information and communication technology fuelling academic dishonesty? *Active Learning in Higher Education*, *5*, 180–199.

Tabachnick, B. G., Keith-Spiegel, P., & Pope, K. S. (1991). The ethics of teaching: Beliefs and behaviors of psychologists as educators. *American Psychologist*, *46*, 506–515.

Whicker, M. L., & Kronenfeld, J. J. (1994). *Dealing with ethical dilemmas on campus*. Thousand Oaks, CA: Sage.

Whitley, B. E., & Keith-Spiegel, P. (2001). Academic integrity as an institutional issue. *Ethics & Behavior*, *11*, 325–342.

Whitley, B. E., & Keith-Spiegel, P. (2002). *Academic dishonesty: An educators guide*. Mahwah, NJ: Erlbaum.

Wilson, R. (2002, January 20). Citing "neglect of duty," Temple U. outs tenured professor [Electronic version]. *Chronicle of Higher Education*. Retrieved April 22, 2005, from http://chronicle.com/subscribe/login?url=/daily/2002/01/2002013005n.html

Young, J. R. (2003, January 30). Duke professor data on grade inflation in 34 colleges [Electronic version]. *Chronicle of Higher Education*. Retrieved April 22, 2005, from http://chronicle.com/free/2003/01/2003013007n.htm

17

Mental Health Practitioners in the Legal System

Tort and Retort

Whatever their other contributions to our society, lawyers could be an important source of protein.

Dick Guindon, cartoonist

Contents

Mental health and social/behavioral science professionals have increasingly found themselves involved with the legal system as both defendants and plaintiffs. They also play important roles as expert witnesses or consultants for many different types of legal matters. The professional and scientific literature has grown dramatically over the past few decades, including numerous books, handbooks, and a growing number of scholarly journals, such as the *Journal of Forensic Psychiatry, Journal of Forensic Social Work, Law and Human Behavior*, and *Psychology, Public Policy, and Law*. The legal arena also serves as a model of an especially challenging work setting, as described in Chapter 18, replete with ethical dilemmas for mental health practitioners (Adshead, 2003; Committee on the Revision of the Specialty

Guidelines for Forensic Psychology, 2006; Sakar & Adshead, 2003). The reasons for this phenomenon are many, but include the evolving nature of mental health practice, the increasing acceptance and utilization of behavioral science data in legal proceedings, and the heightened accountability to which mental health professionals are held when clients believe they have suffered damages as the result of therapists' behavior.

The evolution of behavioral science and practice in forensic roles links directly to the increasing popularity of forensic mental health as a specialty (Adshead, 2003; Bartol & Bartol, 2006; Drogin & Barrett, 2007; Taylor & Buchanan, 1998; Weiner & Hess, 2006; Wettstein, 2002). Practitioners have recognized that forensic services do not fall under the same constraints managed care has imposed on health care services. In addition, research on topics such as competency assessment, child custody outcomes, dangerousness prediction, jury selection, and other areas have had a direct impact on the utility and acceptance of psychological testimony. Sometimes, researchers are surprised to find their published work cited inaccurately in court without their knowledge. With regard to mental health practitioners as defendants, survey research and case reports have proven useful in documenting the damages that some clients suffer due to professional negligence. As a result, the ability of aggrieved clients to seek compensation through legal proceedings has shifted accordingly in the direction of increased litigation.

We do not address the role of the mental health professionals as plaintiffs in this volume. Except for special considerations when a therapist sues a client for nonpayment of professional fees, addressed in Chapter 7, mental health clinicians have no different standing than any other profession when bringing suit against another person. This chapter focuses instead on the role of the practitioner or behavioral scientist as an expert witness and the issues confronting such experts as defendants in legal actions. Both circumstances can evoke considerable anxiety for similar reasons. In either instance, the consequences of the mental health professional's behavior can have great significance in people's lives. In addition, the legal system, its procedures,

culture, and officialdom differ considerably from those to which such practitioners are usually accustomed. The ethical codes of mental health professionals and lawyers also differ greatly in focus and content, resulting in frequent misunderstandings.

THE CULTURE GAP BETWEEN MENTAL HEALTH PROFESSIONALS AND LAWYERS

Several key differences exist in training and culture between mental health practitioners and lawyers that contribute to confusion between the two professions. Our traditional training as behavioral scientists teaches us to believe that an individual who applies rigorous experimental methods can discover significant truths within ranges of statistical certainty. We seldom give simple dichotomous answers to questions, preferring to use probabilities, ranges, norms, and continua that reflect the complexity of individual differences. Lawyers train as advocates, taught to believe that the search for truth is best conducted in a vigorous adversarial cross-examination of the facts. They learn that seeking truth requires the "trying" or weighing the facts on the scales of justice, and that clear, precise, and unambiguous decisions must be the end result. A criminal defendant must be found guilty or innocent. A civil defendant is either liable or not liable for damages. When damages are assessed, a specific dollar value is determined, even for such complex concepts as the value of a human life. The law seeks black-and-white answers to resolve disputes and reject the shades of gray that behavioral scientists relish. One can not simultaneously act as a dispassionate scientist seeking to explain behavior in objective terms as well as a partisan advocate seeking to win the day for one's client.

Mental health practitioners and behavioral scientists must be especially wary when treading into the legal system as they are about to enter philosophically alien territory. They will experience frequent opportunities and enticements to compromise their scientific integrity, overlook their ethical obligations, or otherwise put themselves at risk. Consider the following case examples:

Case 17–1: Wellin Tentioned, M.D., is recruited to serve as an expert witness by Prima Facie, attorney-at-law. Ms. Facie is representing a client injured in an automobile accident. She hopes that Dr. Tentioned's research on the effects of alcohol ingestion on reaction time will bolster her client's lawsuit. Facie will portray her injured client in the most sympathetic light possible, pay Dr. Tentioned an hourly rate far in excess of his usual hourly psychotherapy rate, and press him hard to state his findings in the way that most strongly supports her case.

Case 17–2: Carl Cathexis, Psy.D., treated Phineas Bluster in psychoanalysis five times per week for nearly 2 years. Dr. Cathexis offered Mr. Bluster a clinical interpretation and was taken aback by the rageful transference reaction it precipitated. Bluster stormed out of the office saying, "You'll hear from my lawyer; I'm going to sue." Bluster did not return for further sessions. A few weeks later, Dr. Cathexis receives a letter from an attorney representing Mr. Bluster, accompanied by a release form asking for copies of all case records. Dr. Cathexis jots a note to himself, "Telephone Bluster and suggest he stop this acting out and return to treatment so that we can work through the transference."

In each of these cases, the clinician stands in a highly vulnerable position with a significant chance of slipping into ethical quicksand because of inexperience with the legal system. Dr. Tentioned risks becoming an unwitting partisan in attorney Facie's advocacy plan. If Tentioned agrees to consult as an expert witness, he must stand ready to assert and maintain his scholarly and professional integrity. He can certainly feel empathy for the client and accept reasonable compensation for his professional time but can not allow his professional judgment to be swayed by cajoling, sympathy, or monetary considerations. Dr. Cathexis risks allowing his potentially valid theoretical conceptualization of Mr. Bluster's behavior to cloud his judgment in what has clearly become a legal matter, regardless of whether Cathexis chooses to recognize it as such. His planned phone call will almost certainly exacerbate the situation and put him at still greater legal risk.

Many sources of potential curricula for forensic mental health practice exist (Bartol & Bartol, 2006; Bucky, Callan, & Stricker, 2005; Krauss & Sales, 2006; Lewis, 2004; Neighbors et al., 2002; Poythress, 1979; Schouten, 2001; Sparta & Koocher, 2006). Most agree that mental health professionals interested in forensic work should

- study topical introductions (e.g., philosophical issues, legal terminology, relevant case law, application of psychological skills to legal problems, and ethical issues)
- take seminars in practice specialties (e.g., criminal law, civil law, child/juvenile law)
- engage in supervised practica or field placements

Such formal training is obviously a necessity for those who plan to practice as forensic "experts." A special issue of the journal *Ethics & Behavior* (1993, Vol. 3, No. 3 & 4), highlighted the complexity and diversity of the content domain. In the discussion that follows, we review in detail the hazards of becoming a psychological or mental health expert or defendant. The key principle to keep in mind: When venturing into the legal arena, whether by choice or chance, specialized training or expert guidance is an *absolute* necessity. When in doubt, consult a skilled attorney who will represent only your interests.

THE FORENSIC EXPERT

As previously noted, the logic of jurisprudence assumes that truth may best be revealed when two parties confront each other with passionate debate on the merits of their respective cases. In contrast, the rules of science assume that a single party or same-side team employing rigorous scientific methods can test and eliminate erroneous conclusions (Anderten, Staulcup, & Grisso, 1980). Anderten and her colleagues also noted that the law requires us to base decisions on available evidence regardless of residual ambiguities. Science, and psychology in particular, does not require that all problems investigated reach clear conclusions. Scientists must endure ambiguity with nearly infinite patience to avoid conclusions based on inadequate data and can always design another experiment, while attorneys must bring cases to a timely end. These differences highlight key sources of potential ethical conflicts.

Foote and Shuman (2006) noted that litigants may arrive for mental health evaluation along at least three different routes. First, some are sent by their lawyers seeking an assessment of their mental or emotional state relevant to a potential claim or defense (e.g., an evaluation relative to a potential insanity defense). Second, some litigants may come for evaluation under a court order (e.g., to assess the defendant's competence to stand trial or in some child custody cases). Third, the parties may agree to have a litigant evaluated in the absence of a court order (e.g., in many civil and criminal cases, the parties understand that the opposing side has a right to an evaluation conducted by their own experts and informally agree to do so.) In some cases, the evaluation may have aspects that feel coercive to the person under evaluation. In every case, the litigant's approach to participation in the evaluation has important legal as well as psychological consequences and should follow full information regarding all conditions and options (Connell, 2006; Foote & Shuman, 2006; Knapp & VandeCreek, 2001).

Unlike so-called percipient witnesses, who testify about what they personally perceived (e.g., saw, heard, touched, smelled, or tasted), expert witnesses may give opinions to the court. Experts help the trier of fact (i.e., judge or jury) reach an opinion by providing specialized information not available to the layperson. Experts may report on specialized examinations they conduct, critique or interpret data provided by others, and respond to hypothetical situations or fact patterns proposed by lawyers. In this context, the word *expert* constitutes a legal term established under rules of evidence, not a psychological or medical term. Expert status becomes conferred by a judge's ruling after review of information on the training, education, and *voir dire* examination of the witness. Based on the old French term meaning to "speak the truth," the voir dire involves preliminary questioning of the expert under oath to establish qualifications. The legal system uses breadth, depth, and duration of experience and

education as part of qualifying or credentialing an expert witness. Judges and juries expect expert witnesses to act as unbiased educators who help them understand technical information necessary for their deliberations, despite the fact that one side pays for the service (Ackerman, 1995; Committee on the Revision, 2006). Clinicians must remain aware, however, that clinical experience alone does not ensure the accuracy of diagnostic judgments in the absence of data and the ability to apply it (Faust, 1994; Garb, 1989, 1992, 2005; Garb & Boyle, 2003).

In addition to the differences in perspectives between mental health professionals and lawyers described above, the courtroom setting can prove a disarmingly seductive place where an expert witness can too easily forget about professional rigor. Imagine a setting in which you are asked to play a role in assessing truth and justice, both central values of American society. Surrounded by the trappings of power (e.g., official buildings, flags, robed judges, and uniformed court officers), you stand at center stage in the witness box, acknowledged as an expert in the eyes of the court, and carefully questioned about your opinions (a luxury not extended to lay witnesses). All of those present hang on your every word, and a stenographer dutifully records it all for posterity.

You are asked about weighty matters, and the fate of others may well turn on what you have to say. Will the temptation to provide crisp answers and have your advice taken cause you to forget, even for a moment, the scientific underpinnings and caveats that necessarily accompany psychological "facts"? How can therapists or behavioral scientists most fairly and ethically apply their skills in the courtroom and other legal contexts? Should the expert act as a dispassionate educator about behavioral science or a fully partisan collaborator on the advocacy team? The questions are clearly rhetorical, but the ethical dilemmas remain quite serious. The trappings of expertise can not be allowed to cloud the judgment or analytical ability of the mental health professional. Rather, they should remain highly sobering and signal to the would-be expert a need for thoughtful, cautious, nondefensive, and scientifically rigorous testimony.

Specialty Guidelines for Forensic Psychologists

The American Psychology–Law Society, also known as Division 41 of the American Psychological Association (APA), developed a set of practice guidelines, and a revision is in progress under the direction of the division and the American Academy of Forensic Psychology (Committee on Ethical Guidelines for Forensic Psychologists, 1991; Committee on the Revision, 2006). Although never submitted to the APA Council of Representatives for adoption as official APA standards, these guidelines will provide an important model of practice to which all forensic psychologists should aspire and generalize well to other mental health professions. We stress that the nature of psycholegal work is exceptionally complicated when it comes to matters such as maintaining confidentiality and the rights of the client, avoidance of multiple-role conflicts, the requirement to remain objective in adversarial settings, appropriate structuring of fee agreements, and the need to be familiar with many aspects of law and the legal system, just to name a few. Elements of the guidelines crop up throughout this chapter; however, some aspects that bear on the differences between mental health professionals and lawyers deserve special mention here.

Contingent fee agreements provide a useful example of a practice commonly used by lawyers but very inappropriate for expert witnesses in forensic contexts. Lawyers will frequently take on cases in which the client pays a small percentage of the legal fees and agrees that the lawyer will be entitled to a percentage of any financial award if the case is won. Because the lawyer functions as an advocate for the client, such a contingency appropriately provides an incentive to vigorously pursue an outcome favoring the client. However, when a mental health practitioner offers expert testimony on which a judge or jury trying the facts of the case will rely, agreeing to a fee based on the trial outcome is ethically inappropriate.

Case 17–3: Slimy Grubber, Ph.D., was approached by an attorney representing Eben Fired in an employment discrimination case against Large Multinational Corporation (LMC). LMC has alleged that Mr. Fired had serious personality problems that compromised his work and led to his termination. The attorney believes Mr. Fired's assertion that he was inappropriately fired from his job at LMC for discriminatory reasons and tells Dr. Grubber that he anticipates a good chance of winning triple punitive damages to yield a financial award of $1.5 million or more. Mr. Fired's attorney would like Grubber to evaluate his client with an eye toward rebutting LMC's assertions. Unfortunately, Fired is unemployed and has no money to pay for evaluation service. The attorney offers Grubber 2% of the ultimate financial settlement in exchange for his services.

If Dr. Grubber agrees to these terms, he would be engaging in significant unethical conduct. To begin, Grubber would essentially have agreed to support the plaintiff's position before ever evaluating Mr. Fired. In addition, Dr. Grubber would have a significant incentive to cast Mr. Fired in a favorable light regardless of the actual facts of the case or psychological data. Even if Dr. Grubber had the ability to ignore his potential gain and testify objectively, his testimony would have the appearance of conflicting interests and would easily be discredited under cross-examination in court once the contingency arrangement became known.

Role conflicts also constitute a significant issue for forensic mental health professionals. In many situations, invitations to switch roles from therapist to an evaluator (or vice versa) will present themselves. The demands of conducting an ethical, objective, expert evaluation often conflict with those required to function as an effective therapist. It may be possible to shift from one role to another under some circumstances, with the full informed consent of the client, but such changes should be undertaken only with extreme caution.

Case 17–4: Dahlia Discord, M.S.W., has been treating Melissa Malfunction for anxiety and mild depression in the aftermath of an automobile accident. Ms. Malfunction has been out of work for 3 months and receives disability insurance payments. The insurer has scheduled her for a disability case review, and she has asked Ms. Discord to complete a disability evaluation form and possibly testify as an expert in support of her claim before an administrative law judge. Ms. Discord would like to support her psychotherapy client but is not certain that she can objectively support Ms. Malfunction's claim that she is totally unable to work at any job for emotional reasons.

Psychotherapists are often asked to write letters of various sorts in support of their clients but must take care not to compromise their professional integrity. Ms. Discord should not allow herself to be manipulated into making a recommendation or evaluative statement that she can not support. At the same time, she does not want to disrupt the rapport with her client. One possible solution would involve advising Ms. Malfunction that, although she cares deeply about her welfare, Ms. Discord can not take on the role of an independent evaluator to determine disability. Ms. Discord could also agree to write a letter, with the client's consent, documenting her work with Ms. Malfunction, the symptoms reported by the client, her diagnostic impressions, an estimate of the level of symptom severity, and other treatment information. However, the letter should include only accurate information and should avoid commenting specifically on Ms. Malfunction's ability to work or qualification for disability. Those recommendations should be left to other mental health experts who do not have preexisting or ongoing therapeutic relationships with her.

Case 17–5: Ben and Bettina Bombast felt so angry toward each other about their impending divorce that they could not seem to agree about anything. They certainly could not imagine agreeing on custody plans for their children, Barney and Bella. When Hugh Kidder, Psy.D., a private practitioner with extensive experience in child custody matters, was appointed to provide family mediation services through the court clinic, they reluctantly agreed to try. The Bombast's were amazed by Dr. Kidder's ability to establish rapport with each of them and with the children. He refocused the parents on the children's needs, and they ultimately agreed on a joint custody plan without judicial intervention. Dr. Kidder issued a report to the court in support of their joint decision. A few weeks after the divorce became final, the Bombasts both contacted Dr. Kidder at his private office. Barney was having some school adjustment problems, and both parents agreed that they would like Dr. Kidder to evaluate and counsel him. They expressed considerable mutual confidence in Dr. Kidder because of their previous experience with him.

Assuming that Dr. Kidder's arrangement with the court clinic does not preclude working with former court-referred clients in this way, the Bombasts' request may be a reasonable one. However, Dr. Kidder would first have to carefully consider and discuss with the Bombasts the nature of this role transition. Once he agrees to become the therapist for one member of the divorced family, he could not reasonably resume a mediator or evaluator role should the Bombasts again begin to bicker. His primary obligation would have become refocused on the best interests of their child. Assuming that all agree and that no other roadblocks exist, Dr. Kidder could ethically proceed in his new role.

Training Issues

Traditional graduate degree programs in psychology, medicine, social work, or counseling have not historically prepared graduates for participation in the forensic arena. Most mental health professionals and behavioral scientists lack familiarity with the adversary system and with legal terms and concepts such as levels of proof, competence to stand trial, criminal responsibility, or legal definitions of insanity. Well-trained mental health clinicians often confuse psychological concepts (e.g., psychosis) with legal ones (e.g., insanity). Even when the practitioner understands the legal concepts and questions asked by the court, usual graduate training in psychodiagnostic assessment or psychotherapy will often prove of little help in answering them (Bartol & Bartol, 2006; Drogin & Barrett, 2007; Knapp & VandeCreek, 2001; Lewis, 2004; Neighbors et al., 2002; Poythress, 1979; Schouten, 2001). Few of the standard instruments used in psychological test batteries have, for example, content or construct validity that bears on competence issues or the prediction of dangerousness (Archer, 2006; Weiner & Hess, 2006; Weisner, 2006).

Case 17–6: Hasty Injuria, Ph.D., was approached by an attorney to do a pretrial evaluation of his client who had been charged with assault and battery. Injuria administered the WAIS-IV (Wechsler Adult Intelligence Scale—IV), Thematic Apperception Test, Rorschach inkblots, Minnesota Multiphasic Personality Inventory 2 (MMPI-2), and the House-Tree-Person (HTP) drawing. When testifying on the witness stand, Dr. Injuria was asked about the defendant's propensity to commit violent acts against others and about his criminal responsibility at the time of the alleged assault. Although Injuria had no information regarding the defendant's history (which was devoid of violent acts) and was unfamiliar with the concept of criminal responsibility, he testified that the defendant had a diagnosis of schizophrenia and was therefore clearly both dangerous and not responsible.

Not only did Dr. Injuria misunderstand the legal concepts in question, he was also not in a position to address the questions on the basis of appropriate knowledge. He did not, for example, consider one of the most consistent predictors of dangerous behavior (i.e., prior dangerous behavior) and made the erroneous assumption that being schizophrenic per se absolves one of responsibility for one's acts and indicates dangerousness. In this case, the psychologist made the major mistake of falling back on an old and successful assessment behavior (i.e., his standard clinical test battery) without recognizing his involvement in a special setting with unique requirements and complexities he was not qualified to address (Archer, 2006; Archer, Buffington-Vollum, Stredny, & Handel, 2006; Committee on the Revision, 2006; Greene & Goldstein, 2007; Knapp & VandeCreek, 2001; Yufik, 2005; Zapf & Roesch, 2006). Dr. Injuria also overlooked other instruments specifically designed for use in the psychological assessment of dangerousness (Edens, Buffington-Vollum, Keilen, Roskamp, & Anthony, 2005; Krauss, Lieberman, Costanzo, Krauss, & Pezdek, 2007; Litwack, Zapf, Groscup, & Hart, 2006; Scott &

Resnick, 2006). In his ignorance, Injuria may well have caused serious problems for his client.

The Quality of Expertise: *Daubert* Revisited

A key example of the importance of understanding the legal context and rules of evidence regarding acceptable testimony flows from the *Daubert* decision of the U.S. Supreme Court (*Daubert v. Merrell Dow Pharmaceuticals, Inc.*, 1993; Youngstrom & Busch, 2000). The court held that experts may testify only within the scope of reasonable and accepted scientific knowledge. The *Daubert* decision identified four factors courts can use to assess validity when admitting scientific conclusions under the Federal Rules of Evidence (Grove & Barden, 1999; Mark, 1999; Slobogin, 1999): (1) falsifiability, (2) error rate, (3) peer review and publication, and (4) general acceptance. Using these standards, expert testimony on eyewitness identification would hold up well under scrutiny for scientific validity, whereas expert testimony regarding so-called repressed memories might not (Bruck, Ceci, & Hembrooke, 2002; Dalenberg, 2006; Loftus & Davis, 2006; London, Bruck, Ceci, & Shuman, 2005). Research results should be used in an impartial manner in the face of adversarial pulls of attorneys. It is not unethical to disagree with other experts about applications of knowledge, but it is unethical to relinquish the role of neutral expert in favor of highly selective gleaning of knowledge (Sales & Shuman, 2005). Do not deny existing information that contradicts your conclusions. Instead, freely and without defensiveness acknowledge and discuss any such information, pointing out any shortcomings if appropriate.

The applicable case law clearly indicates a need for mental health professionals to understand basic research methods, even if they never plan to conduct research themselves. One can often easily find a basis to criticize a study on methodological grounds, and when practicing in forensic contexts, being a smart consumer of research is important. For example, understanding the differences between correlation and causation or knowing how to compare one sample population to another will significantly enhance the effectiveness of an expert witness.

A more basic question that is often debated among mental health experts and attorneys involves what kinds of mental health opinions, if any, have sufficient reliability and validity to warrant admissibility in court (Adshead, 2003; Bank & Packer, 2007; Bush, Connell, & Denney, 2006; Garb, 2005; Garb & Boyle, 2003; Melton, Petrila, Poythress, & Slobogin, 1997). Beyond the question of whether courts should admit such opinions lies the issue of the limits that ethics must place on the expression of opinions. This becomes especially important when such experts are called to give "informed speculation" (Bonnie & Slobogin, 1980; Golding, 1990; McCloskey, Egeth, & McKenna, 1986) on matters defined in law rather than behavioral science. For example, it is clearly unethical to provide a so-called ultimate issue opinion without also giving the caveat that such opinions constitute legal judgments and have no basis in behavioral science expertise. In a legal case, the term *ultimate issue* refers to the question before the trier of fact (i.e., the judge or the jury charged with weighing the evidence).

Case 17–7: Barney Bezerk was to stand trial for the axe murder of his family of four. His attorney was planning to use an insanity defense and hired Cruddy O'Pinion, Psy.D., to conduct an expert psychological evaluation. The evaluation revealed that Mr. Bezerk had a major thought disorder, poor impulse control, considerable unmodulated anger, and frequently expressed paranoid ideation. In particular, Mr. Bezerk's auditory hallucinations had repeatedly warned him that alien beings had taken over the bodies of his family and were about to embark on the conquest of Earth. Dr. O'Pinion cited all these findings and concluded his report with the statement that Mr. Bezerk was clearly insane at the time of the offense.

The ultimate issue of whether a defendant was "insane" at the time of an offense does not fall within the valid realm of a psychological question because the concept of insanity is defined by law rather than by behavioral science. A bit of history reveals the complexity of the issue. In 1843 Daniel M'Naghten, a Scottish wood turner, attempted to assassinate the prime minister of England while suffering from stark paranoid delusions and killed a different man instead. The court found him not guilty because he clearly did not understand the nature or wrongfulness of his act. Public outrage after his acquittal prompted the creation of a formal legal definition of insanity that became known as the M'Naghten rule. In the 1950s, Monte Durham was convicted of housebreaking in the District of Columbia, and his only defense at trial asserted Durham was of unsound mind at the time of the offense (*Durham v. United States*, 1954). In that case, the U.S. Court of Appeals for the District of Columbia adopted a so-called product test under which legal insanity hinged on whether the person committed the criminal act because of a mental disease or defect. Considerable criticism followed because that standard gave mental health experts too much influence in a decision of insanity and not enough to jurors.

The next development, known as the Model Penal Code (MPC), published by the American Law Institute (ALI), provided a compromise standard for legal insanity, blending elements of the stricter M'Naghten rule and the more lenient Durham ruling. Under the MPC/ALI standard, insanity defenses hinged on whether at the time of the criminal conduct, as a result of mental disease or defect, the defendant lacked substantial capacity to appreciate the wrongfulness of the act or lacked the ability to behave in conformity with the requirements of the law. The MPC/ALI standard enjoyed popularity until 1981, when John Hinckley was found not guilty by reason of insanity under those guidelines after attempting to assassinate President Ronald Reagan. Public outrage at Hinckley's acquittal led federal lawmakers to pass legislation reverting reverted back to the stricter M'Naghten standard. Some states attempted to abolish the insanity defense altogether by offering juries a verdict of "guilty, but mentally ill," which allowed sentencing of people to terms of years in psychiatric facilities. Today's standard for proving legal insanity vary widely from state to state, requiring those offering expert testimony to focus their opinions on the elements of the particular statutes in question.

Dr. O'Pinion can appropriately describe the defendant's bizarre behavior, confirm his impulsivity and instability using test or interview data, explain how a lack of control might result, link these findings to the facts of the case, and provide other such expert commentary. Based on his knowledge of schizophrenia and his evaluation of Mr. Bezerk, Dr. O'Pinion may also testify about the probability that the symptoms observed most likely affected the defendant's behavior on the day of the crime. However, the judge or jury must weigh the evidence and decide whether the information presented proves beyond a reasonable doubt that Mr. Bezerk met the legal definition of insanity. Too frequently, mental health professionals will neglect such caution in their testimony and may even find themselves encouraged to comment on ultimate issues by some attorneys and judges (Melton et al., 1997; Sales & Shuman, 1993, 2005; Sales & Simon, 1993).

Sometimes, even experienced forensic mental health professionals have been caught making inappropriate assertions from the witness stand. Andrea Yates, the Texas woman convicted of drowning her children in a bathtub, was granted a new trial by an appeals court after an expert witness for the prosecution gave false testimony.

Case 17–8: Andrea Yates confessed to the police in 2001 that she had drowned her five children, ages 6 months to 7 years. A Houston jury subsequently convicted her of murder the next year for three of the deaths, rejecting her insanity defense. The case reignited national debate about mental illness, postpartum depression, and the legal definition of insanity. The court overturned the initial conviction because of false testimony by Park Dietz, M.D., a psychiatrist who testified as the prosecution's only mental health expert. Dr. Dietz, who charged $500 per hour, testified that Ms. Yates was psychotic at the time of the murders but knew right from wrong, meaning that she did not qualify as insane under the narrow legal definition in Texas. On cross-examination, Dr. Dietz was asked about his work as a consultant on *Law & Order*, a television program Ms. Yates was known to watch. Asked whether any of the episodes he had worked on concerned "postpartum depres-

sion or women's mental health," Dietz replied, "As a matter of fact," he answered, "There was a show of a woman with postpartum depression who drowned her children in the bathtub and was found insane, and it was aired shortly before the crime occurred" (Powell, 2005).

That statement by Dietz proved false. No such episode of the television show existed. The falsehood was discovered only after the jury convicted Ms. Yates. Dietz later claimed that he simply made an honest mistake (Powell, 2005). In this particular case, expensive and presumably high-quality expertise (see http://www .parkdietzassociates.com/index.htm) proved significantly flawed. Dietz did notify the prosecution of his mistake and submitted a letter to the judge stipulating to his error after the fact. He had apparently confused a similar episode of *L.A. Law* with *Law & Order*.

The Use of Research Data

A number of papers by experimental psychologists triggered a historic debate on the extent to which behavioral scientists called to testify as expert witnesses can ethically fall back on scientific research data (Loftus & Monahan, 1980; McCloskey et al., 1986; Tanke & Tanke, 1979). Since then, many others have weighed in on the issue (Connolly, Price, & Read, 2006; Fiske et al., 2000; Kovera & McAuliff, 2000; Krauss et al., 2007; Mark, 1999; Sales & Shuman, 2005; Shuman & Sales, 1998; Tolman & Mullendore, 2003; Weiss, 1999). Expert behavioral science testimony based on empirical data has been offered in cases that deal with jury size, eyewitness identification, prediction of dangerousness, adequacy of warning labels, and child custody, to name just a few topics. However, judges and juries are not always influenced by these presentations. Some interesting ethical questions have come up regarding the context in which such research is presented.

- Are the findings valid and generalizable to the situation in question?
- Are there legitimate differences in interpretation of the data, and if so, must the expert testifying present both sides?

- How should such testimony deal with the probabilistic nature of some research findings?
- What role should the expert's personal values play in the decision to testify or not in certain cases?

Case 17–9: Helena Scruples, Ph.D., has considerable knowledge regarding eyewitness identification. Her own research shows the frequent unreliability of such identifications. When asked to serve as an expert witness by the defense in a rape case, Dr. Scruples feels sympathetic to the female victim and knows that prosecution of alleged perpetrators is difficult. If she agrees to help the defense, she may reduce a guilty defendant's chance of conviction.

Case 17–10: Herman Beastly is accused of raping and murdering an adolescent babysitter. Evidence strongly indicates that he is guilty and may meet criteria for a death sentence based on a state law that permits capital punishment for criminals likely to commit repeated violent crimes of this sort. John Qualm, M.D., considered an expert on the prediction of dangerousness, has published reports that highlight the difficulty in making such predictions reliably. He is asked to testify by the defense in the hope that his opinions may save Beastly from execution.

Both of these cases illustrate major clashes in personal value systems. Both Scruples and Qualm may feel repulsed by their client's behavior. At the same time, each defendant is entitled to a vigorous legal defense. Although the defendant has a right to present the relevant scientific data, any given mental health professional has no specific ethical duty to testify in such a case simply because he or she is asked to do so. The expert's beliefs, preferences, and personal values certainly enter into any decision about testifying (Cunningham, 2006). In similar situations, Loftus reported reasoning that her testimony could help to prevent the conviction of an innocent person (Loftus & Monahan, 1980). Monahan reported testifying for the defense in a case similar to Dr. Qualm's because, although repulsed by the defendant, he feels morally opposed to the death penalty (Loftus & Monahan, 1980).

The extent to which an expert witness is obligated to present both sides when discussing psychological research or theory is also a very complex matter. Several experts (Rachlin, 1988; Rivlin, 1973; Wolfgang, 1974) have argued for the legitimacy of the expert scientist as an adversary. That is, they assert that a balanced objective presentation of research or theory is not needed in expert testimony. Loftus and Monahan (1980) pointed out, on the other hand, that an oath to "tell the whole truth and nothing but the truth" is violated if the "whole truth" is not told. They noted also that opposing counsel may always ask the witness: "Do you know of any studies which show the opposite result?" (p. 279). We would not argue in favor of universal discussion of all possible interpretations of a data set, but we strongly agree with the assertion that the whole truth remains a necessity for the behavioral science expert acting as an expert witness.

Hypnosis in the Courtroom

Hypnosis has been widely used in forensic settings by mental health practitioners and others (Scheflin, 2005) and presents an excellent prototypical example of how a technique widely used by clinicians can lead to special complications in forensic settings. Inappropriate applications of hypnotic techniques have occasionally led to significant compromise in the judicial process (Grove & Barden, 1999; Haber & Haber, 2000; Scoboria, Mazzoni, Kirsch, & Milling, 2002; Slobogin, 1999). An article published in *Science* (Kolata, 1980) nearly three decades ago summarized the problem succinctly: "Researchers fear misuse by police and warn that hypnotic state is no guarantor of truth" (p. 1443). While the intense concentration that characterizes hypnosis often enables individuals to recall events or details in striking fashion, many individuals may respond with embellishments to subtle suggestions of the examiners. Following a hypnotic session, some hypnotic subjects may "confabulate" or inject new elements into their reports of events. These confabulations may be based on conscious or unconscious motivations (Kolata, 1980).

Case 17–11: Theodore Trance, L.M.H.C., consulted with the police investigating a double homicide. He hypnotized and interrogated a woman who claimed to be an eyewitness to the murders but recalled little of what happened. During the hypnotic sessions, the woman emotionally recalled being forced by two male companions to shoot the two victims. Her testimony resulted in conviction of the two for murder. Subsequently, it became clear that the two were innocent, and that the woman had substantial motivation to wish them punished for reasons of her own.

It seems that Mr. Trance failed to investigate fully the background and motivation of the woman he was asked to hypnotize. At the time of the trial, there were also allegations that Mr. Trance may have conducted his questioning of the witness in a suggestive manner; however, recordings of his sessions with the woman had somehow been erased. No information was provided to the jury regarding the potential for confabulation by individuals using hypnotic techniques to "enhance" memory for purposes of testimony.

As a result of cases such as this, many jurisdictions now prohibit information uncovered through hypnosis from being admitted as evidence at a trial. Psychologists have long recognized the fact that hypnosis interacts significantly with suggestibility, and Dr. Trance's role in applying it with few caveats and cautions raises serious ethical problems (Annon, 1989; Knight, Meyer, & Goldstein, 2007; Scheflin, 2005).

Child Custody

Divorce may affect as many as 40% of children (Krauss & Sales, 2000) and 50% of first marriages (Wallerstein & Lewis, 2004), and parents agree on child custody and visitation 90% of the time (Melton et al., 1997), leaving no dispute for the court to decide. However, in the 10% of disputed cases mental health professionals have increasingly become involved as *guardians ad litem*, evaluators, mediators, and psychotherapists (APA, 1994; Sparta & Koocher, 2006). Therapists may also find themselves unwittingly involved in such cases when the marriage of one of their clients (or child client's parents) begins to dissolve.

What should we consider the prime standards in child custody evaluation? Most mental health professionals have historically agreed that matters of child custody should focus on the best interests of the child. Occasionally, that seems their only point of agreement. Some writers on the "nature" side of the fence (Boszhormenyi-Nagy & Spark, 1973) have asserted that "Family loyalty is ... [based] ... on biological hereditary kinship" (p. 42). Others, on the "nurture" side (Goldstein, Freud, & Solnit, 1979), argued that biological ties are far less important than psychological ones based on "a continuing, day-to-day basis ... [which] ... fulfills the child's psychological needs for a parent, as well as the child's physical needs" (p. 98). More recently, mental health experts have urged refocusing from the best interests of the child to a least detrimental alternative standard (Goldstein, Solnit, Goldstein, & Freud, 1996; Krauss & Sales, 2000, 2001).

Common criticisms of mental health professionals' work in child custody cases include

- deficiencies and abuses in professional practice
- inadequate familiarity with the legal system and applicable legal standards
- inappropriate application of psychological assessment techniques
- presentation of opinions based on partial or irrelevant data
- overreaching by exceeding the limits of psychological knowledge of expert testimony
- offering opinions on matters of law
- loss of objectivity through inappropriate engagement in the adversary process
- failure to recognize the boundaries and parameters of confidentiality in the custody context (Weithorn, 1987, 2006)

Predicting what will happen as a result of custody decisions remains a difficult challenge. Unfortunately, however, one can reliably predict that a contested custody situation will have an adverse effect on the children. Great stresses, both emotional and financial apply, along with prolonged periods of uncertainty and instability in the lives of such children. Too often, the children become pawns in the legal struggle between sets of angry combatants for custody. Into this void rides (or are tossed) too many unwary would-be psychological Solomons ready to share their wisdom with the courts to resolve these agonizing cases, despite the fact that little research exists on which to support many opinions about custody (Clingempeel & Reppucci, 1982; Clingempeel, Shuwall, & Heiss, 1988; Krauss & Sales, 2001; Melton et al., 1997; Sales & Shuman, 2005; Weithorn, 2006). Too often, mental health professionals agree to assist in performing child custody evaluations with little understanding of statutes that govern child custody, adversarial proceedings, data useful for making such decisions, or their own values and attitudes that might contribute to biased outcomes (Krauss & Sales, 2001; Melton et al., 1997; Weithorn, 2006). At times, these custodial struggles actually harm a child rather than attend to his or her best interests.

At times, however, testimony or participation by mental health experts, even short of actual courtroom appearances, can become highly relevant and constructive (Melton et al., 1997; Sales & Shuman, 2005). Ideally, the clinician should function as an advocate for the child or as a neutral expert, preferably appointed by the court to avoid being cast as the advocate of one contesting party or the other (Weithorn, 1987, 2006). This will not always work, however, and at times full adversarial proceedings, with experts on both sides, result. We do not seek to provide a "how-to-do-it" manual here (see, e.g., Connell, 2006; Melton et al., 1997; Oberlander, 1995) but rather to highlight some potential ethical problems that can arise and be detrimental to all concerned.

Case 17–12: Helen Tester, Ph.D., agreed to undertake a child custody evaluation. During the course of her assessment, she administered psychological tests, including the MMPI-2 and the Rorschach inkblots to both parents. The mother, who was a foreign national, had an elevated L-scale score on the MMPI-2 and was "evasive" on the Rorschach inquiry. As a result, Dr. Tester

concluded that she was a "highly defended pathological liar" and recommended against awarding her custody.

Dr. Tester made several serious errors. To begin, she seems to be basing her evaluation on two instruments never validated for predictive use in child custody work (i.e., the Rorschach and MMPI-2). Indeed, she seems to have misinterpreted the actual meaning of the L scale and interpreted one score out of context from the overall profile. Her reading of an MMPI-2 profile obtained from a foreign national, whose culture and language may differ from the standardization group, raises additional validity questions. Dr. Tester's conclusion, based on two isolated test findings that have many alternative explanations, seems highly suspect. One wonders if Dr. Tester ever bothered to do critically important interviews with the child or observe parent–child interactions.

Case 17–13: Jack Balance, M.D., undertook a child custody evaluation at the request of the attorney representing the child's father. The attorney advised Dr. Balance that both parents were interested in cooperating with the evaluation. Balance met with the father and the child for assessment purposes, but the mother subsequently declined to participate. At the trial, Dr. Balance testified only with respect to the child–father relationship, but the mother's attorney attempted to discredit him as an expert because he had not interviewed the child's mother.

Dr. Balance would have been better advised to confirm in advance the willingness of all parties to cooperate. He might have accomplished this through personal contact or by court order, if necessary. He certainly behaved ethically in commenting only on his actual contacts (i.e., the adequacy of the child–father relationship), while refraining from any comments about the parent who declined to participate. In addition, Dr. Balance had to pay special attention to note the limitations, based on incomplete data, of any recommendations he might make. The attempt to discredit his testimony is unfortunate but not a matter of the ethics of mental health professionals.

Case 17–14: Sam and Sylvia Splitter found themselves in the midst of a bitter divorce and child custody dispute. Each sought and identified a mental health professional willing to advocate on their behalf at the custody hearing. Both professionals testified in support of "their client" based on interviews with the one parent and children. Neither professional had sought contact with the other parent or the other professional prior to the hearing, and each testimony dramatically contradicted the other.

The Splitters have successfully "split" the clinicians they each hired and set up a so-called battle of the shrinks. Nothing does more to discredit the mental health professions in public than adversarial confrontations by experts with incomplete pieces of the data. While the Splitters may have set up this situation, both mental health professionals were foolish to agree to participate. Under ideal circumstances, the professionals would have insisted on functioning as nonpartisan experts, demanded access to all appropriate data, and sought the right to interview the other spouse as a prerequisite for agreeing to do the evaluation. One can not help but wonder whether their contradictory testimony grew out of information that their clients kept from them.

Case 17–15: Cynthia Oops, M.S.W., conducted a careful evaluation of both parents and two children involved in a custody dispute. One parent had recruited her, but the other had seemingly agreed to her participation. When Ms. Oops completed her report prior to the hearing, the parent who was not favored asserted her right of confidentiality and demanded that the report be kept out of court. Ms. Oops had not obtained a signed waiver from the parties.

Ms. Oops had the best of intentions, but she should have spelled out the parameters of her role from the outset (Connell, 2006). Her clients (i.e., the two parents and the children) should have been given a clear understanding of her obligations to each one of them, especially since their needs and wishes were mutually exclusive in some areas. In particular, she should have secured written waivers from all

concerned to share her findings with the court. Now, the status of one claim of privilege is unclear and will have to be resolved by the judge. It is not possible to predict the outcome based on the information presented, but the problem was easily avoidable. A summary of the key elements one might wish to incorporate in a custody consent process appear in Box 17–1.

While the case of Ms. Oops seems a routine confidentiality problem, a slight variation yields a rather commonly noted problem of a more complex nature. Suppose that Dr. Oops had provided marriage counseling to both parents prior to their decision to divorce and subsequently found herself subpoenaed by one to testify in a child custody dispute. In this situation, a legitimate duty of confidentiality to both parties might exist even if Oops believes that she has some basis on which to offer an opinion to the courts. Ideally, Ms. Oops should avoid such a role by discussing the potential problem early (if it appears a couple in treatment may divorce) or by suggesting that they obtain expert testimony from another mental health professional who does not have a preexisting relationship with them. All of these examples support the overarching premise that no substitute exists for specialized education and training, including acquiring appropriate sensitivity to special ethical issues inherent in forensic work (Bank & Packer, 2007; Benjamin & Gollan, 2003; Bucky et al., 2005; Ratner, 2002; Woody, 2000).

Conducting a Forensic Evaluation

In undertaking any sort of evaluation that is likely to come before the courts, a mental health expert should pay special attention to helping the person facing an evaluation understand the purpose of the activity and the people or agencies who will have access to the information (APA 02: 4.02). Even when the evaluation is court ordered or paid for by a governmental agency, the mental health practitioner must recognize that the individual under evaluation also holds client status.

Consent and confidentiality issues must be treated differently from traditional mental health practice when forensic issues are involved. Before undertaking any forensic evaluation, interviewees must have appropriate notification that any of their statements or findings of the evaluation may become a part of public court records. The APA ethics code (APA 02: 4.02a and b) requires that clients be notified of the limits of confidentiality from the outset of the professional relationship as well as whenever new circumstances warrant. In a forensic evaluation, many layers of clients often exist (e.g., the court, the attorney, and the person under evaluation). Rather than assuring confidentiality, forensic evaluators must fully inform the people they interview when no privilege exists.

These individuals should be cautioned to avoid saying anything that they prefer not be revealed. In many jurisdictions and circumstances, the written consent of the interviewee to such disclosures is not technically required because of the statutory wording or judicial orders. We recommend, however, that the practitioner always give notice of the limitations and seek evidence to confirm that the client understands this information. Ideally, this notice should be acknowledged by the client in writing or witnessed by an objective third party. In some criminal cases, expert testimony may be excluded from consideration if such notice was not given.

Box 17–1 Elements of Notification in a Custody Evaluation

Provide a statement of adult parties' legal rights with respect to the anticipated assessment:
    Give a clear statement regarding the purpose of the evaluation.
    Identify the requesting entity. (Who asked for the evaluation?)
    Describe the nature of anticipated services. (What procedures will you follow?)
    Explain the methods to be utilized. (What instruments and techniques will you use?)
    Specify whether the services are court ordered.

Delineate the parameters of confidentiality:
    Will anything be confidential from the court, the parties, or the public?
    Who will have access to the data and report?
    How will access be provided?

Provide information regarding:
    The evaluator's credentials.
    The responsibilities of evaluator and the parties.
    The potential disposition of data.
    The evaluator's fees and related policies.
    What information will be provided to the child, and by whom. (What will the child be told regarding the assessment purpose, nature, and confidentiality limits as developmentally appropriate?)
    Any prior relationships between evaluator and parties.
    Any potential examiner biases (e.g., presumptions regarding joint custody).

Consent documentation:
    Obtain formal consent to disclose material learned during evaluation in litigation.
    Obtain formal waiver of confidentiality from adult litigants or their legal representatives.
    Provide written documentation of consent.
    Obtain consent for recording, if applicable.

Source: Excerpted and adapted from Connell, 2006, p. 448.

Case 17–16: Mr. Smith was indicted for murder, and the prosecutor for the state of Texas announced that he would seek the death penalty. James P. Grigson, M.D., a psychiatrist who some later nicknamed "Dr. Death," was assigned to evaluate Smith's competence to stand trial. After a single 90-minute interview, Dr. Grigson determined that Smith was competent and so testified. Smith was tried and convicted. A separate penalty-phase proceeding was held for the jury to determine whether to impose the death penalty. One factor the jury had to consider was any propensity for Smith to commit similar acts again. Dr. Grigson was again called by the state to testify about any proclivity of Mr. Smith toward future violence. Based on the same 90-minute interview, Dr. Grigson opined that Smith would be a continuing danger to society. The jury sentenced Smith to death.

The facts summarized here are the essentials of *Estelle v. Smith* (1981), in which the Supreme Court overturned the death sentence. This case is fully discussed by Bersoff (2003), but the key issue can best be understood as one of consent. Mr. Smith was not advised that he had a right to remain mute when interviewed by Dr. Grigson, and Smith was not told that whatever he told Grigson might later be used in the death penalty phase of the case. The same principle applies to all forensic evaluations, both civil and criminal. The client has the right to know at the outset the full purpose of the evaluation and the parties who will have access to it. Even when an evaluation is not court ordered but may ultimately serve some forensic purpose, we recommend clarifying these issues. When conducting a child custody evaluation, for example, it is wise to obtain reciprocating waivers of confidentiality that cover all the contesting parties and their counsel. Many divorcing couples who seek consultation from a mental health professional on custody matters as they plan their custody agreement never intend to litigate the issue, but change their minds later (Coates, Deutsch, Starnes, Sullivan, & Sydlik, 2004; Koocher, 1999; Mahoney & Fine, 2006; Sales, Miller, & Hall, 2005; Weithorn, 2006).

Case 17–17: Bob and Harriet Splinter have decided to divorce and want to do what is best for their three young children. They seek therapeutic consultation with Connie Sensus, L.M.F.C., a family counselor in the community, about joint custody and visitation options. During their sessions together, Bob acknowledges that Harriet would be better as the custodial parent because he has a drinking problem and was involved in some unsavory delinquent conduct as a youth. They agree that the children will live with Harriet, and that Bob will have frequent visitation. Just before finalizing the full divorce agreement, Bob and Harriet have a falling out over financial issues, and Bob states his intent to seek sole custody of the children. Harriet wants to call Ms. Sensus as a witness and plans to use her testimony to get Bob's admitted character flaws on the record. Bob demands that Sensus keep confidential all that he told her.

One may not agree with either Bob's or Harriet's conduct, but Ms. Sensus's lack of forethought has created a problem. In some jurisdictions, any rights of confidentiality that Bob or Harriet might assert with respect to their own mental health records could potentially be set aside if deemed in the interests of the children by a judge. If Ms. Sensus had raised this issue at the outset and had obtained consensual waivers from Bob and Harriet, she would be free to testify about any elements of her work with the Splinters that is relevant to the court.

Record keeping and documentation are especially important in forensic cases. Practitioners should keep more precisely detailed records than might be necessary in more routine treatment or assessment work (Drogin et al., 2007; Greenberg et al., 2007; Knapp & VandeCreek, 2006; Otto, Slobogin, Greenberg, & Goldstein, 2007; Reid, 2006). Detailed information of dates, times, durations of appointments, phone calls, sources of information, reviews of records, examination of corroborating information (e.g., police reports), and other points that lead to an opinion should be recorded and cited in any forensic reports. Vagueness may become a source of vulnerability on the witness stand (Barone, 2004; Brodsky, 2004). Some practitioners take loose notes or make tentative observations and consolidate them into structured notes or reports, but once a formal report or official case note is written, it should not be altered. One can always write and date an addendum or supplementary information to notes, but altering completed reports creates a reasonable aura of suspicion. For similar reasons, we recommend keeping only one set of records.

Case 17–18: Melba Meticulous, Ed.D., undertook a court-ordered child custody investigation for the Fragmento family. She conducted nearly 20 hours of interviews with the parties, the children, and collateral sources. Much of the information she gathered was relevant to the matters before the court, but some was extraneous (e.g., Mr. Fragmento wore a poor-quality hairpiece; Mrs. Fragmento's great aunt Tillie died 6 years ago, and her husband had the temerity to tell jokes at the wake; Mrs. Fragmento is at least 30 pounds overweight; and the maternal grandmother recently underwent a facelift). The extraneous data made their way into Dr. Meticulous's files as she did not know which bits would be relevant as she heard them. She will now complete her report, citing all relevant factors, and either will not cite or will discard all extraneous material.

The procedures employed by Dr. Meticulous are entirely appropriate. If material she gathers proves relevant, it should become a part of the case file and her report. If any of the data collected prove to be irrelevant, they should not become a part of the permanent file.

Preparation for deposition and trial are important obligations of the forensic practitioner. It is important for forensic specialists to ensure that their knowledge remains current in psychological conceptualization, assessment practices, ethical standards, and other relevant professional issues (Barone, 2004; Brodsky, 2004; Brodsky & Galloway, 2003; Otto & Martindale, 2007). For example, if choosing to use psychological tests, one must be sure that the test is validated for the intended purpose (Borum & Grisso, 1995; Grisso & Vincent, 2005; Lipsitt & Goldstein, 2007; Otto & Martindale, 2007). Surprisingly little normative data for applying many psychological tests to forensic assessment

exist (Heilbrun, Marczyk, DeMatteo, Mack-Allen, & Goldstein, 2007), and some techniques commonly used by naive evaluators in forensic assessment (e.g., anatomically detailed dolls used to interview alleged child sexual abuse victims) do not even qualify as psychological tests (Koocher et al., 1995).

Depositions (i.e., questioning under oath outside court) are used by both sides for purposes of discovery. Depositions help each side to weigh evidence that may lead to settlement discussions. They also allow witnesses to learn lines of inquiry that may be pursued at trial. Practitioners should expect to have their clinical records reviewed and questioned during depositions. It is entirely appropriate for experts to meet with the attorney who has hired them to review testimony beforehand (Brodsky, 2004). If you do not know the answer to a question, simply say so. Do not speculate beyond your knowledge, competence, or findings (Brodsky & Galloway, 2003).

Mental health and behavioral science experts must take care to stay within the boundaries of our personal expertise. For example, special training beyond a generic terminal degree or professional license is often required prior to undertaking forensic assessments that involve children, geriatric patients, or individuals with neuropsychological injuries. Do not feel defensive about your credentials. Readily admit any and all nonaccomplishments in a matter-of-fact manner. Do not fear admitting ignorance or saying "I don't know" in response to questions posed by attorneys.

Case 17–19: Windy Fluffball, J.D., Ph.D., agreed to serve as an expert witness in a civil lawsuit that involved alleged wrongful termination of a clinical psychology graduate student from a doctoral program. Dr. Fluffball expounded on his years of teaching and membership on the National Psychological Society's Education and Training Oversight Committee. On cross-examination, Fluffball was forced to admit that his doctorate was in physiological psychology, that he never had clinical training, that he never worked or taught in a clinical psychology program, that he was not licensed as a psychologist, and although he had recently won appointment to the Education and Training Oversight Committee of his professional association, he had yet to attend a single meeting.

After the jury returned a verdict favoring the other side, the lawyers were allowed to poll the jurors and discovered that Dr. Fluffball's testimony was given very little weight. One must wonder whether the side for which he testified would have fared better using a witness who did less to inflate his qualifications.

MENTAL HEALTH PROFESSIONALS AS DEFENDANTS

Rather than simply focus on mental health malpractice, it seems more reasonable to think of the broader concept of professional liability as applying to all of one's professional service delivery activities. In a legal sense, there are four elements that must be present before a successful civil liability lawsuit is possible. Think of them as the four Ds: *duty, dereliction, direct causation*, and *damages*. First, the clinician must have a professional relationship with the party in question. That is, a practitioner–client relationship must have existed with a resulting duty to the client. Second, there must be some negligence or dereliction of that duty on the part of the therapist. Third, some harm must have accrued to the client as a direct result of the negligence or dereliction of the duty. Finally, a causal relationship between the negligence and the resulting damages must be shown (Bennett et al., 2007; Bucky et al., 2005; Caudill, 2006; Falender & Shafranske, 2004; Leesfield, 1987; Schouten, 2001). Needless to say, by this definition a successful prosecution for malpractice would necessarily mean that the clinician had behaved unethically by virtue of negligence. Read the next three cases with these standards in mind and see whether you can hazard a guess about the outcomes.

Case 17–20: Ima Hurtin sought the services of Anna Sthesia, Psy.D., in response to her newspaper announcement of a pain clinic Dr. Sthesia had recently opened. Ms. Hurtin gave a history of low

back pain that began several years earlier, and she expressed interest in the application of biofeedback techniques. Ms. Hurtin told Dr. Sthesia that she had "been to everyone, chiropractors, orthopedists, hypnotists, and even tried acupuncture and a herbalist." The psychologist initiated biofeedback training. Several weeks later, Ms. Hurtin collapsed at work and was taken to a hospital, where she was discovered to have a malignant tumor of the spine. The disease had metastasized widely and was too advanced for all but palliative care.

Case 17–21: Regina Yahoo met Sonia Specula, M.S.W., at a cocktail party. On learning that Specula was a psychotherapist who specialized in work with children, Ms. Yahoo began telling her about threats that her 15-year-old daughter was making to run away from home. Ms. Specula casually mentioned that "lots of teenagers say things like that to annoy their parents, but they never do it." Two days later, Ms. Yahoo's daughter ran away from home and was hit by a truck and killed while attempting to hitchhike out of town.

Case 17–22: Manual Kant felt very angry that, after 9 months in psychotherapy with Seymour Suregood, M.D., he still could not get women to date him again after the first date. Several of the women had told Mr. Kant: "You need a lot of help!" Dr. Suregood had agreed to work with Kant on this problem, but as far as Kant could tell, things had not changed much.

All three of these clients attempted to sue the therapist in question, but only one proved successful. If you guessed Ms. Hurtin, then you probably understand the basic concepts of malpractice liability. Hurtin clearly held client status with Dr. Sthesia, and the clinician clearly had an obligation to treat Hurtin reasonably. She neglected to check on her physical status or send for reports from the other professionals to whom Hurtin alluded, and she began to treat an important physical symptom (i.e., pain) without first ruling out a medical problem. By this negligent act, she contributed to a delay in forcing Ms. Hurtin to seek other treatment or proper evaluation, giving her cancer time to spread. While we do not know whether Ms.

Hurtin's life could have been saved with early treatment, the psychologist's behavior may have cost her the opportunity to find out.

Ms. Specula was not guilty of malpractice. Perhaps she should have exercised more caution in the willing way she gave advice, but it seems clear that Ms. Yahoo never held client status. The contact was casual because it took place at a social gathering rather than in an office, no fees were charged or paid, no clinical records were created, and the relationship between the alleged advice and the injury sustained remains unclear.

In the case of Dr. Suregood and Mr. Kant, a psychotherapist–client relationship did indeed exist. We have no evidence of negligence, however, and no evidence that the client sustained any harm. If Dr. Suregood had promised results within a certain time span and these did not occur, one might accuse him of misrepresentation or misleading the client. But, we have no evidence that any promises of hard results were made. It is also unclear whether the best psychotherapist in the world would have provided any greater help to Mr. Kant.

In some cases, causality becomes an important issue, as in the case of a psychologist named Carmichael, who practiced in Washington, DC.

Case 17–23: Frederica Saunders sought psychological treatment from Dr. Carmichael. During the course of counseling, Carmichael and Saunders engaged in sexual relations, and Dr. Carmichael convinced Saunders to divorce her husband. Carmichael and Saunders then married. Saunders later brought a malpractice action against her new husband after he sued for divorce. The trial court found Carmichael liable for malpractice and also granted the divorce. Carmichael appealed, claiming his wife did not prove harm. The appeals court found that Saunders did not present any expert testimony that showed a causal relationship between the malpractice and her injury. Her expert testified about the nature of transference and stated that initiating a sexual relationship during the course of a professional relationship was a fundamental betrayal of a patient's trust. This testimony could establish that Carmichael breached the applicable standard of care, and that Saunders' symptoms, which included depression, distress,

and suicidal feelings, were consistent with the effects of a doctor betraying a patient's trust. The witness did not testify "to a reasonable degree of medical certainty" that Carmichael's behavior played a substantial part in causing his wife's injuries. Moreover, the expert admitted under cross-examination that all of Saunders's symptoms could have existed when she first sought treatment from Carmichael (*Carmichael v. Carmichael,* 1991).

The ethical offensiveness of Dr. Carmichael's conduct is clear. Unfortunately for Mrs. Carmichael's (the former patient–wife) effort to recover financial damages, it was not possible to legally link his behavior as the cause of the damages she suffered. One message sent to District of Columbia therapists by this case may be as follows: If you plan to have sex with former clients, you may want to marry them.

Standards of Care and the "Good Enough Clinician"

Perfection is not the standard expected in professional practice. No one is perfect, and everyone makes mistakes or errors based on reasonable judgment calls. People can not avoid mistakes, but a mistake does not necessarily equal negligence.

One step beyond an error in the hierarchy of risk would be termed a deviation or departure from the standard of care provided by other well-trained clinicians in the community. The best test of your risk level is to compare yourself to others who are competent to perform the particular service or to treat the specific type of client in question. Perhaps you have the requisite skills but do some things in your practice that, while not unethical, others would not do. In such a case, you should give careful consideration to such practices. The far extreme of risk is gross negligence. This amounts to an extreme departure from usual professional conduct, and something most practitioners would not do. A plaintiff's lawyer will seek experts in your field in an effort to prove that your unusual practice amounts to negligence. By consulting nondefensively with colleagues who practice in the same specialty and geographic area, you can effectively assess new ideas or practice plans that others think may stretch the limits of reasonableness.

Common Precipitants of Suits Against Practitioners

Although at least 25 different types of suits (causes of action) against mental health practitioners have been conceptualized (Hogan, 1979), most are unlikely hazards for therapists in the sense that they are in the lower incident bases of complaints (e.g., breach of contract, undue influence, alienation of affection, failure to supervise properly, failure to treat, complaints linked to serving on licensing boards or ethics committees, abandonment, false arrest or false imprisonment, abuse of process, assault and battery, and misrepresentation). Interestingly, the greatest number of malpractice or professional liability insurance claims against mental health professionals arise from complaints about boundary violations of both sexual and nonsexual natures, client suicides, clients who commit homicide, finances or billing, or problematic forensic evaluations, including those associated with child custody and child sexual abuse evaluations. Such data underscore the need to develop significant expertise before venturing into such work (Bennett et al., 2007; Costanzo, Krauss, & Pezdek, 2007; Drogin & Barrett, 2007; Sparta & Koocher, 2006; Wettstein, 2002; Woody, 1988).

Retrospective review of claims against psychologists (Bennett et al., 2007) revealed some very clear triggers of suits against mental health clinicians: sex with clients, management of clients' dangerous behaviors, and disputes regarding fees for service. Allegations of sexual misconduct are predictable enough as sources of complaint, but it is also worth noting that suits are also frequently filed when a practitioner takes steps to collect a debt (i.e., engages a collection agency or files suit against the client; see Chapter 7). Several commentators offer useful suggestions about what therapists should do in the event of an actual or threatened lawsuit (Bennett et al., 2007; Koocher, 2005; Woody, 2005). Many of these suggestions are incorporated in recommendations we offer. The good news is that the cumulative risk of a

psychologist in the United States being sued is less than 0.5% (Bennett et al., 2007). The bad news is that defending such a suit is time consuming and costly in both financial and emotional terms.

Avoiding the Tort of Defamation

When false or misleading statements (or true statements that can not be proven in court) damage a person's reputation, a defamation lawsuit may result. Oral defamation or slander may occur whenever comments about clients are made aloud in public settings. It is wise to remain cautious in public statements regarding current or former clients, even when one has their consent. Exercise particular caution if you are inclined to use disguised clinical case materials in teaching or other oral public presentations. Written defamation or libel may occur when material in reports, letters, or other written media are deemed to have wrongly harmed another's reputation. Use care in record keeping, report writing, and the use of disguised case materials in books or other published materials.

Be especially careful of repeating information provided by angry spouses unless the source is clearly documented.

Case 17–24: I. B. Leaveder, L.M.H.C., had seen Kenya Trustme for only four psychotherapy sessions when Ms. Trustme asked him to write a letter on her behalf. She told Mr. Leavder that her sessions with him had given her new resolve. She told Leavder that her spouse had abused her for many years, and that she had finally decided to take action to protect herself and her children. She planned to move to a friend's house and go into court the next day with an ex parte request for a restraining order. She asked whether Mr. Leavder would write a supportive letter, and he did so, repeating all of the acts of abuse she had recounted to him.

Sadly, Ms. Trustme had lied to her therapist in an effort to extract an improved settlement in a divorce action she planned to file. Sadder still, Mr. Leavder's letter provided a narrative that seemed to support her claims as fact. Ms. Trustme made several copies of the letter and sent them to her spouse's employer, family, and teachers at their children's school. The spouse, who Mr. Leaveder had neither met nor spoken to filed both a licensing board complaint and a defamation suit. He might have avoided such problems had he qualified his report by incorporating notations that all of the content came solely from Ms. Trustme's self-report (i.e., "Ms. Trustme told, reported, or informed me that ...") rather than providing a report suggesting he had firsthand or confirmed knowledge of her claims.

Specific Prevention Strategies

Aside from being competent and applying sound professional practices, when devising specific prevention strategies it is important to know and respect both your limitations and those of your employees and supervisees. Be aware of your psychological issues and vulnerabilities, including transference and countertransference hazards. Avoid behaviors that might lead to sexual intimacies with clients (see Chapter 12). Seek treatment for any substance abuse or personal emotional problems you may have (see Chapter 4). Heed cautions from colleagues; if one of them dares to express concerns, there are probably several others who are thinking the same thing but are afraid to speak up. Avoid grandiose claims or outcome promises. Provide meaningful supervision to your support staff and to trainees whose work you oversee because you can be held responsible for their actions under the doctrine of respondeat superior.

The next case illustrates the consequences of failing to heed this advice.

Case 17–25: A woman known as Jane Doe sued the Samaritan Counseling Center as respondeat superior for the acts of one of its pastoral counselors; the counselor had sexual intercourse with her when she came to seek "emotional and spiritual therapy." During two of Doe's sessions at the agency, the counselor allegedly kissed and fondled her. Sexual intercourse followed outside the center after she had canceled her counseling sessions. A trial court initially dismissed the case, finding that the agency was not responsible for its

employee's acts; however, the state supreme court disagreed. The court ruled that the fact that sexual intercourse occurred after Doe canceled therapy did not bar employer liability because the counselor's conduct during the sessions constituted the initiation of a sexual relationship and negligence in handling transference issues (*Doe v. Samaritan Counseling Center,* 1990).

In this case, the supervising agency was held financially responsible for the unethical acts of one of its employees, even though much of the offensive behavior took place off site. Problems began while the therapist should have been under agency supervision.

Be especially sensitive when treating high-risk clients and in problematic practice areas. High-risk clients include any client you are not competent to treat, litigious clients, those with volatile psychopathology (e.g., borderline personality disorder, especially with histrionic or paranoid features), people with histories of dangerousness, and clients who develop a rapid or intense transference relationship. High-risk practice areas include child custody or other forensic or "high-scrutiny" arenas and work with some trauma victims (e.g., those seeking to recover memories of abuse). We certainly do not suggest that mental health professionals should avoid such clients or provide such services. Rather, we emphasize the importance of training and competence when dealing with these populations or providing services that carry an above-average risk component.

Take care to carry adequate professional liability insurance and understand your coverage. Know the differences between a "claims-made" policy and an "occurrence-based" policy (Bennett, 2005). Significant delays often occur between triggering adverse events and lawsuits. Only about half of the legal claims against therapists surface during the insurance policy year in which the incident occurred. As a result, it is important to maintain continuous coverage. A claims-made policy covers acts that occurred during the policy year only if a renewed policy is in force when the complaint is filed. Therapists who have such policies should buy "tail coverage" to cover any cases filed in subsequent years if they switch insurance companies or retire. The "tail" refers to the trailing off likelihood of claims being filed as years go by and the statute of limitations on filing passes.

An occurrence policy is more expensive because tail coverage is built into the price. Such policies provide coverage forever for any incidents that occurred during the policy year. Alternatively, if one switches insurance companies, it may be possible to purchase "nose coverage," technically known as *prior acts coverage*. Such policies will cover potential claims, as yet unknown to the therapist, that may have occurred under another company's policy. We believe that professional liability insurance is an ethical necessity because it provides a means for clients to recover damages, especially when the therapist has few financial resources, in the event of professional errors.

Use consultation. Pay for consultation when needed and treat it as a professional service (Bennett et al., 2007). Keep a list of potential consultants handy for use on short notice and have contingency plans for who to call if you must consider admitting a client to a hospital, provide a warning about a dangerous client, deal with a suicidal client, or have another risky clinical situation. Use your consultant as soon as you suspect any risky situation. Do not wait for a disastrous event or a lawsuit. Although not absolutely necessary, in many cases it may be best to go to the head of your agency or outside your immediate circle of colleagues. When you do consult, document it and include the date, details, and actions taken. Mental health professionals who act as consultants will also want to keep careful notes and beware of vicarious liability (i.e., when someone who consults you is sued, and you are also named as a defendant). Develop clear payment and collection policies and follow them. Inform clients of your billing and payment policies. Do not allow large or unexpected bills to accumulate. Keep "affect" (e.g., emotional outbursts) out of billing and collection letters (see Chapter 7).

When Prevention Fails: What to Do When an "Adverse Incident" Occurs

Professional liability cases and licensing board complaints take a heavy toll on practitioners (Thomas, 2005; Woody, 1988, 2000, 2005). Most clinicians who face board complaints or liability litigation experience significant personal and professional distress. They may become vulnerable to cognitive, emotional, and behavioral responses that in turn may compromise their clinical skills and even their ability to effectively defend themselves. But, remaining aware of the most common sources of distress associated with complaints can allow mental health professionals to take steps to minimize problematic behaviors and self-defeating responses (Thomas, 2005).

Should some significant difficulties or adverse events arise (e.g., a client is not benefiting from treatment, is not adhering to key aspects of a treatment program, has become too difficult to work with, threatens you, or harms a third party), consider the following series of steps, even if no filing or threat of a lawsuit has occurred.

- First, obtain a consultation from a colleague experienced with such clients or issues and take any appropriate actions recommended.
- Consider whether the circumstances suggest that you should initiate termination of the professional relationship.
- If you decide that it is appropriate to do so, notify the patient both orally and in writing, specifying the effective date for termination and providing a specific and appropriate reason for terminating the relationship.
- Agree to continue providing interim services for a reasonable period and recommend other care providers or means of locating them.
- Offer to provide records to new care providers on receipt of a signed authorization.
- Document all of these steps in your case records (see APA 02: 10.10).
- We recommend avoiding unilateral termination if the client is in the midst of a mental health crisis or emergency situation or if substitute services will be difficult for the client to obtain (e.g., in a rural area where other practitioners might not be readily available).
- It would also be unethical to seek to terminate a client if the basis for doing so is unreasonably discriminatory (e.g., terminating psychotherapy with a client after learning of his or her HIV status).

- If a high-risk client does not return for a scheduled appointment, follow up by telephone and in writing, documenting these steps in your records. Be especially prompt in doing so if the client seemed depressed or emotionally distressed in the last session.
- If a high-risk client complains to you about some aspect of your professional relationship, listen carefully and treat the complaint with serious professional concern. Investigate, if necessary, and respond in as sympathetic and tactful a manner as possible. Try not to be defensive. Apologize, if appropriate. Document in your record all steps taken.
- In the event of a client's death, express sincere compassion and sympathy to surviving relatives but do not discuss any personal feelings of guilt you may be experiencing. Save those feelings for your personal psychotherapist.

If you become aware of the possibility of a suit against you, do not wait for formal notice of the suit to arrive. Follow these steps:

- Notify your insurance carrier immediately so that they can open a case file and assign legal counsel, if needed.
- Never interact orally or in writing, "informally" or otherwise, with a client's lawyer once a case is threatened. Once a lawyer representing your client contacts you in any dispute that involves you and that client, get your own attorney or one hired by your liability insurance carrier involved. Cease all further personal contact with that client until you have consulted your attorney. Never try to settle matters yourself.
- Do not make incriminating statements or discuss the case with anyone other than representatives of the insurance carrier or your lawyer. Do not discuss details of the case with colleagues. These other parties may later become subject to subpoena and testimony about what you told them.
- Compile and organize all of your records, case materials, chronicles of events, and so on to assist in your defense. Do not throw away or destroy any documents, recordings, or other items linked to the case and do not show any of these to anyone except your attorney.

- When asked to provide information or documents to your legal counsel, send copies and safeguard the originals.
- In any malpractice or professional liability action, you may want to consult a personal attorney (in addition to the one assigned by the insurance carrier), especially if sued for damages in excess of the limits of the policy. Before agreeing to a settlement, consult an attorney whose only interest is you (rather than you *and* your insurer).
- Take steps to manage your own anxiety and stress level. Such cases can take a severe emotional toll and require several years to resolve, even though there may be no legitimate basis for the suit. Seeking support from friends and colleagues is a normal reaction; however, discussions of specific details should occur only in privileged contexts.

SUMMARY GUIDELINES

1. Recognize that forensic practice constitutes a specialty area that demands specific clinical skills and knowledge of the legal system. Do not venture into this arena without specialized training.
2. When mental health professionals find themselves drawn into a legal case inadvertently, they should seek consultation from a colleague with specialized forensic knowledge before responding to the legal proceeding.
3. Child custody disputes constitute a frequent basis for ethics complaints, particularly when the clinician makes a recommendation based on incomplete data or interviews with only one party. Therapists should exercise great caution and follow professional guidelines when undertaking such assignments.
4. Therapists should carefully clarify their roles and stay within agreed-on or court-defined parameters in all forensic cases.
5. Therapists must distinguish carefully between legal issues and mental health issues and, when serving as an expert witness, remain focused on the latter.
6. It is important to follow the specific preventive steps outlined in the final section of this chapter should an adverse event occur.

References

Ackerman, M. (1995). *Clinician's guide to child custody evaluations*. New York: Wiley.

Adshead, G. (2003). Commentary: Medical evidence based law? *Journal of the American Academy of Psychiatry and the Law 31*, 333–335.

American Psychological Association. (1994). Guidelines for child custody evaluations in divorce proceedings. *American Psychologist, 49*, 667–680.

Anderten, P., Staulcup, V., & Grisso, T. (1980). On being ethical in legal places. *Professional Psychology, 11*, 764–773.

Annon, J. S. (1989). Use of hypnosis in the forensic setting: A cautionary note. *American Journal of Forensic Psychology, 7*, 37–48.

Archer, R. P. (2006). *Forensic uses of clinical assessment instruments*. Mahwah, NJ: Erlbaum.

Archer, R. P., Buffington-Vollum, J. K., Stredny, R. V., & Handel, R. W. (2006). A survey of psychological test use patterns among forensic psychologists. *Journal of Personality Assessment, 87*, 84–94.

Bank, S. C., & Packer, I. K. (2007). Expert witness testimony: Law, ethics, and practice. In A. M. Goldstein (Ed.), *Forensic psychology: Emerging topics and expanding roles* (pp. 421–445). Hoboken, NJ: Wiley.

Barone, N. M. (2004). Coping with cross-examination and other pathways to effective testimony. *Journal of Psychiatry and Law, 32*, 403–404.

Bartol, C. R., & Bartol, A. M. (2006). History of forensic psychology. In L. B. Weiner & A. K. Hess (Eds.), *The handbook of forensic psychology* (3rd ed., pp. 3–27). Hoboken, NJ: Wiley.

Benjamin, G. A. H., & Gollan, J. K. (2003). Ethics, competence, and training. In G. A. H. Benjamin & J. K. Gollan (Eds.), *Family evaluation in custody litigation: Reducing risks of ethical infractions and malpractice* (pp. 29–35). Washington, DC: American Psychological Association.

Bennett, B. E. (2005). Essential features of professional liability insurance. In G. P. Koocher, J. C. Norcross, & S. S. Hill (Eds.), *Psychologists' desk reference* (2nd ed., pp. 625–634). New York: Oxford University Press.

Bennett, B. E., Bricklin, P. M., Harris, E. A., Knapp, S., VandeCreek, L., & Younggren, J. N. (2007). *Assessing and managing risk in psychological practice: An individualized approach*. Rockville, MD.

Bersoff, D. N. (2003). *Ethical conflicts in psychology* (3rd ed.). Washington, DC: American Psychological Association.

Bonnie, R., & Slobogin, C. (1980). The role of mental health professionals in the criminal process: The case for "informed speculation." *Virginia Law Review, 66*, 427–522.

Borum, R., & Grisso, T. (1995). Psychological test use in criminal forensic evaluations. *Professional Psychology: Research and Practice, 26*, 465–473.

Boszhormenyi-Nagy, I. B., & Spark, G. (1973). *Loyalties*. New York: Harper & Row.

Brodsky, S. L. (2004). *Coping with cross-examination and other pathways to effective testimony*. Washington, DC: American Psychological Association.

Brodsky, S. L., & Galloway, V. A. (2003). Ethical and professional demands for forensic mental health professionals in the post-Atkins era. *Ethics & Behavior, 13*, 3–9.

Bruck, M., Ceci, S. J., & Hembrooke, H. (2002). The nature of children's true and false narratives. *Developmental Review, 22*, 520–554.

Bucky, S. F., Callan, J. E., & Stricker, G. (2005). *Ethical and legal issues for mental health professionals: A comprehensive handbook of principles and standards*. Binghamton, NY: Haworth Maltreatment and Trauma Press/Haworth Press.

Bush, S. S., Connell, M. A., & Denney, R. L. (2006). *Ethical practice in forensic psychology: A systematic model for decision making*. Washington, DC: American Psychological Association.

Carmichael v. Carmichael, 597 A. 2d 1326 (D.C. Ct. App. 1991)

Caudill, O. B. (2006). Avoiding malpractice in child forensic assessment. In S. N. Sparta & G. P. Koocher (Eds.), *Forensic mental health assessment of children and adolescents* (pp. 74–87). New York: Oxford University Press.

Clingempeel, W. G., & Reppucci, N. D. (1982). Joint custody after divorce: Major issues and goals for research. *Psychological Bulletin, 91*, 102–127.

Clingempeel, W. G., Shuwall, M. A., & Heiss, E. (1988). Divorce and remarriage: Perspectives on the effects of custody arrangements on children. In S. A. Wolchik & R. Karoly (Eds.), *Children of divorce: Empirical perspectives on adjustment* (pp. 145–181). New York: Gardner Press.

Coates, C. A., Deutsch, R., Starnes, H. H., Sullivan, M. J., & Sydlik, B. (2004). Parenting coordination for high-conflict families. *Family Court Review, 42*, 246–262.

Committee on Ethical Guidelines for Forensic Psychologists. (1991). Specialty guidelines for forensic psychologists. *Law and Human Behavior, 15*, 655–665.

Committee on the Revision of the Specialty Guidelines for Forensic Psychology. (2006). *Specialty guidelines for forensic psychology—Second official draft.* Washington, DC: American Psychology-Law Society.

Connell, M. (2006). Notification of purpose in custody evaluation: Informing parities and their counsel. *Professional Psychology, 37*, 446–451.

Connolly, D. A., Price, H. L., & Read, J. D. (2006). Predicting expert social science testimony in criminal prosecutions of historic child sexual abuse. *Legal and Criminological Psychology, 11*, 55–74.

Costanzo, M., Krauss, D., & Pezdek, K. (2007). *Expert psychological testimony for the courts.* Mahwah, NJ: Erlbaum.

Cunningham, M. D. (2006). Informed consent in capital sentencing evaluations: Targets and content. *Professional Psychology, 37*, 452–459.

Dalenberg, C. (2006). Recovered memory and the *Daubert* criteria: Recovered memory as professionally tested, peer reviewed, and accepted in the relevant scientific community. *Trauma, Violence, & Abuse, 7*, 274–310.

Daubert v. Merrell Dow Pharmaceuticals, Inc., 509 579 (U.S. Supreme Court 1993).

Doe v. Samaritan Counseling Center, 791 P.2d 344 (Alaska, 1990).

Drogin, E. Y., & Barrett, C. L. (2007). Off the witness stand: The forensic psychologist as consultant. In A. M. Goldstein (Ed.), *Forensic psychology: Topics and expanding roles* (pp. 465–488). Hoboken, NJ: Wiley.

Durham v. United States, United States Court of Appeals District of Columbia Circuit 214 F.2d 862 (1954).

Edens, J. F., Buffington-Vollum, J. K., Keilen, A., Roskamp, P., & Anthony, C. (2005). Predictions of future dangerousness in capital murder trials: Is it time to "disinvent the wheel?" *Law and Human Behavior, 29*, 55–86.

Estelle v. Smith, 451 454 (U.S. 1981).

Falender, C. A., & Shafranske, E. P. (2004). Ethical and legal perspectives and risk management. In C. A. Falender & E. P. Shafranske (Eds.), *Clinical supervision: A competency-based approach* (pp. 151–194). Washington, DC: American Psychological Association.

Faust, D. (1994). Are there sufficient foundations for mental health experts to testify in court? In S. A. Kirk & S. D. Einbinder (Eds.), *Controversial issues in mental health* (pp. 288–306). Needham Heights, MA: Allyn & Bacon.

Fiske, S. T., Bersoff, D. N., Borgida, E., Deaux, K., Heilman, M. E., & Stangor, C. (2000). Social science research on trial: Use of sex stereotyping research in Price Waterhouse v. Hopkins. In *Stereotypes and prejudice: Essential readings* (pp. 338–352). New York: Psychology Press.

Foote, W. E., & Shuman, D. W. (2006). Consent, disclosure, and waiver for forensic psychological evaluation: Rethinking the roles for psychologist and lawyer. *Professional Psychology, 37*, 437–445.

Garb, H. N. (1989). Clinical judgment, clinical training, and professional experience. *Psychological Bulletin, 105*, 387–396.

Garb, H. N. (1992). The trained psychologist as expert witness. *Clinical Psychology Review, 12*, 451–467.

Garb, H. N. (2005). Clinical judgment and decision making. *Annual Review of Clinical Psychology, 1*, 67–89.

Garb, H. N., & Boyle, P. A. (2003). Understanding why some clinicians use pseudoscientific methods: Findings from research on clinical judgment. In S. O. Lilienfeld, S. J. Lynn, & J. M. Lohr (Eds.), *Science and pseudoscience in clinical psychology* (pp. 17–38). New York: Guilford Press.

Golding, S. L. (1990). Mental health professionals in the courts: The ethics of expertise. *International Journal of Law and Psychiatry, 13*, 281–307.

Goldstein, J., Freud, A., & Solnit, A. J. (1979). *Beyond the best interests of the child.* New York: Free Press.

Goldstein, J., Solnit, A. J., Goldstein, S., & Freud, A. (1996). *The best interests of the child: The least detrimental alternative.* New York: Free Press.

Greenberg, S. A., Shuman, D. W., Feldman, S. R., Middleton, C., Ewing, C. P., & Goldstein, A. M. (2007). Lessons for forensic practice drawn from the law of malpractice. In Goldstein, A. M. (Ed.), *Forensic psychology: Emerging topics and expanding roles* (pp. 446–461). Hoboken, NJ: Wiley.

Greene, R. L., & Goldstein, A. M. (2007). Forensic applications of the Minnesota Multiphasic Personality Inventory-2. In A. M. Goldstein (Ed.), *Forensic psychology: Emerging topics and expanding roles* (pp. 73–96). Hoboken, NJ: Wiley.

Grisso, T., & Vincent, G. (2005). The context for mental health screening and assessment. In T. Grisso, C. Vincent, & D. Seagrave (Eds.), *Mental health screening and assessment in juvenile justice* (pp. 44–70). New York: Guilford Press.

Grove, W. M., & Barden, R. C. (1999). Protecting the integrity of the legal system: The admissibility of testimony from mental health experts under *Daubert/Kumho* analyses. *Psychology, Public Policy, and Law, 5,* 224–242.

Haber, R. N., & Haber, L. (2000). Experiencing, remembering and reporting events. *Psychology, Public Policy, and Law, 6,* 1057–1097.

Heilbrun, K., Marczyk, G., DeMatteo, D., Mack-Allen, J., & Goldstein, A. M. (2007). A principles-based approach to forensic mental health assessment: Utility and update. In A. M. Goldstein (Ed.), *Forensic psychology: Emerging topics and expanding roles* (pp. 45–72). Hoboken, NJ: Wiley.

Hogan, D. B. (1979). *The regulation of psychotherapists* (Vols. 1–4). Cambridge, MA: Ballinger.

Knapp, S., & VandeCreek, L. (2001). Ethical issues in personality assessment in forensic psychology. *Journal of Personality Assessment, 77,* 242–254.

Knapp, S. J., & VandeCreek, L. D. (2006). Confidentiality, privileged communications, and record keeping. In S. J. Knapp & L. D. VandeCreek (Eds.), *Practical ethics for psychologists: A positive approach* (pp. 111–128). Washington, DC: American Psychological Association.

Knight, S. C., Meyer, R. G., & Goldstein, A. M. (2007). Forensic hypnosis. In A. M. Goldstein (Ed.), *Forensic psychology: Emerging topics and expanding roles* (pp. 734–763). Hoboken, NJ: Wiley.

Kolata, G. B. (1980). Forensic use of hypnosis on the increase. *Science, 208,* 1443–1444.

Koocher, G. P. (1999). Afterthoughts on child custody evaluations. *Clinical Psychology: Science and Practice, 6,* 332–334.

Koocher, G. P. (2005). Basic principles for dealing with legal liability risk situations. In G. P. Koocher, J. C., Norcross, & S. S. Hill (Eds.), *Psychologists' desk reference* (2nd ed., pp. 558–559). New York: Oxford University Press.

Koocher, G. P., Goodman, G. S., White, C. S., Friedrich, W. N., Sivan, A. B., & Reynolds, C. R. (1995). Psychological science and the use of anatomically detailed dolls in child sexual-abuse assessments. *Psychological Bulletin, 118,* 199–222.

Kovera, M. B., & McAuliff, B. D. (2000). The effects of peer review and evidence quality on judge evaluations of psychological science: Are judges effective gatekeepers? *Journal of Applied Psychology, 85,* 574–586.

Krauss, D., Lieberman, J., Costanzo, M., Krauss, D., & Pezdek, K. (2007). Expert testimony on risk and future dangerousness. In *Expert psychological testimony for the courts* (pp. 227–249). Mahwah, NJ: Erlbaum.

Krauss, D. A., & Sales, B. D. (2000). Legal standards, expertise, and experts in the resolution of contested child custody cases. *Psychology, Public Policy, and Law, 6,* 843–879.

Krauss, D. A., & Sales, B. D., (2001). The child custody standard: What do 20 years of research teach us? In S. O. White (Ed.), *Handbook of youth and justice* (pp. 411–435). Dordrecht, Netherlands: Kluwer Academic.

Krauss, D. A., & Sales, B. D. (2006). Training in forensic psychology: Training for what goal? In I. B. Weiner & A. K. Hess (Eds.), *The handbook of forensic psychology* (3rd ed., pp. 851–871). Hoboken, NJ: Wiley.

Leesfield, I. (1987). Negligence of mental health professionals. *Trial, 57,* 61.

Lewis, C. F. (2004). Teaching forensic psychiatry to general psychiatry residents. *Academic Psychiatry, 28,* 40–46.

Lipsitt, P. D., & Goldstein, A. M. (2007). Ethics and forensic psychological practice. In A. M. Goldstein (Ed.), *Forensic psychology: Emerging topics and expanding roles* (pp. 171–189). Hoboken, NJ: Wiley.

Litwack, T. R., Zapf, P. A., Groscup, J. L., & Hart, S. D. (2006). Violence risk assessment: Research, legal, and clinical considerations. In I. B. Weiner & A. K. Hess (Eds.), *The handbook of forensic psychology* (3rd ed., pp. 487–533). Hoboken, NJ: Wiley.

Loftus, E. F., & Davis, D. (2006). Recovered memories. *Annual Review of Clinical Psychology, 2,* 469–498.

Loftus, E. F., & Monahan, J. (1980). Trial by data: Psychological research as legal evidence. *American Psychologist, 35,* 270–283.

London, K., Bruck, M., Ceci, S. J., & Shuman, D. W. (2005). Disclosure of child sexual abuse: What does the research tell us about the ways that children tell? *Psychology, Public Policy, and Law, 11,* 194–226.

Mahoney, M. M., & Fine, M. A. (2006). The law of divorce and relationship dissolution. In J. H. Harvey (Ed.), *Handbook of divorce and relationship dissolution* (pp. 533–552). Mahwah, NJ: Erlbaum.

Mark, M. M. (1999). Social science evidence in the courtroom: *Daubert* and beyond? *Psychology, Public Policy, and Law, 5,* 175–193.

McCloskey, M., Egeth, H., & McKenna, J. (1986). The experimental psychologist in court: The ethics of expert testimony. *Law and Human Behavior, 10,* 1–13.

Melton, G. B., Petrila, J., Poythress, N. G., & Slobogin, C. (1997). *Psychological evaluations for the courts: A handbook for mental health professionals and lawyers* (2nd ed.). New York: Guilford.

Neighbors, I. A., Green-Faust, L., Beyer, K. v., Neighbors, I. A., Chambers, A., Levin, E., et al. (2002). Curricula development in forensic social work at the MSW and Post-MSW levels. In *Social work and the law: Proceedings of the National Organization of Forensic Social work, 2000* (pp. 1–11). New York: Haworth Press.

Oberlander, L. B. (1995). Ethical responsibilities in child custody evaluations: Implications for evaluation methodology. *Ethics & Behavior, 5,* 311–332.

Otto, R. K., & Martindale, D. A. (2007). The law, process, and science of child custody evaluation. In M. Costanzo, D. Krauss, & K. Pezdek (Eds.), *Expert psychological testimony for the courts* (pp. 251–275). Mahwah, NJ: Erlbaum.

Otto, R. K., Slobogin, C., Greenberg, S. A., & Goldstein, A. M. (2007). Legal and ethical issues in accessing and utilizing third-party information. In A. M. Goldstein (Ed.), *Forensic psychology: Emerging topics and expanding roles* (pp. 190–205). Hoboken, NJ: Wiley.

Powell, T. (2005, January 15). An honest mistake—The psychiatrist whose testimony led to an overturned conviction for Andrea Yates explains what happened [Electronic version]. *Newsweek.* Retrieved May 12, 2007, from http://www.msnbc.msn.com/id/6830050/site/newsweek

Poythress, N. G. (1979). A proposal for training in training in forensic psychology. *American Psychologist, 34,* 612–621.

Rachlin, S. (1988). From impartial expert to adversary in the wake of *Ake. Bulletin of the American Academy of Psychiatry and Law, 16,* 25–33.

Ratner, R. A. (2002). Ethics in child and adolescent forensic psychiatry. *Child and Adolescent Psychiatric Clinics of North America, 11,* 887–904.

Reid, W. H. (2006). Forensic practice: A day in the life. *Journal of Psychiatric Practice, 12,* 50–54.

Rivlin, A. (1973). Forensic social science. *Harvard Educational Review, 43,* 61–75.

Sales, B. D., Miller, M. O., & Hall, S. R. (2005). Marriage dissolution and child custody. In B. D. Sales, M. O. Miller, & S. R. Hall (Eds.), *Laws affecting clinical practice* (pp. 113–120). Washington, DC: American Psychological Association.

Sales, B. D., & Shuman, D. W. (1993). Reclaiming the integrity of science in expert witnessing. *Ethics & Behavior, 3,* 223–229.

Sales, B. D., & Shuman, D. W. (2005). *Experts in court: Reconciling law, science, and professional knowledge.* Washington, DC: American Psychological Association.

Sales, B. D., & Simon, L. (1993). Institutional constraints on the ethics of expert testimony. *Ethics & Behavior, 3,* 231–249.

Sarkar, S. P., & Adshead, G. (2003). Ethics in forensic psychiatry. *Current Opinion in Psychiatry, 15,* 527–531.

Scheflin, A. W. (2005). Forensic uses of hypnosis. In A. K. Hess & I. B. Weiner (Eds.), *The handbook of forensic psychology* (3rd ed.). New York: Wiley.

Scheflin, A. W., Weiner, I. B., & Hess, A. K. (2006). Forensic uses of hypnosis. In *The handbook of forensic psychology* (3rd ed., pp. 589–628). Hoboken, NJ: Wiley.

Schouten, R. (2001). Law and psychiatry: What should our residents learn? *Harvard Review of Psychiatry, 9,* 136–138.

Scoboria, A., Mazzoni, G., Kirsch, I., & Milling, L. S. (2002). Immediate and persisting effects of misleading questions and hypnosis on memory reports. *Journal of Experimental Psychology: Applied, 8,* 26–32.

Scott, C. L., & Resnick, P. J. (2006). Violence risk assessment in persons with mental illness. *Aggression and Violent Behavior, 11,* 598–611.

Shuman, D. W., & Sales, B. D. (1998). The admissibility of expert testimony based upon clinical judgment and scientific research. *Psychology, Public Policy, and Law, 4,* 1226–1252.

Slobogin, C. (1999). The admissibility of behavioral science information in criminal trials: From primitivism to Daubert to voice. *Psychology, Public Policy, and Law, 5,* 100–119.

Sparta, S. N., & Koocher, G. P. (Eds.). (2006). *Forensic mental health assessment of children and adolescents.* New York: Oxford University Press.

Tanke, E. D., & Tanke, T. J. (1979). Getting off a slippery slope: Social science in the judicial process. *American Psychologist, 34,* 1130–1138.

Taylor, R. W., & Buchanan, A. (1998). Ethical problems in forensic psychiatry. *Current Opinion in Psychiatry, 11,* 695–702.

Thomas, J. T. (2005). Licensing board complaints: Minimizing the impact on the psychologist's defense and clinical practice. *Professional Psychology, 36,* 426–433.

Tolman, A. O., & Mullendore, K. B. (2003). Risk evaluations for the courts: Is service quality a function of specialization? *Professional Psychology, 34,* 225–232.

Wallerstein, J. S., & Lewis, J. M. (2004). The unexpected legacy of divorce: Report of a 25-year study. *Psychoanalytic Psychology, 21,* 353–370.

Weiner, I. B., & Hess, A. K. (2006). *The handbook of forensic psychology* (3rd ed.). Hoboken, NJ: Wiley.

Weisner, D. A. (2006). From *Tarasoff* to *Ewing*: Expansion of the duty to warn. *American Journal of Forensic Psychology, 24,* 45–55.

Weiss, K. J. (1999). Psychiatric testimony and the "reasonable person" standard. *Journal of the American Academy of Psychiatry and the Law, 27,* 580–589.

Weithorn, L. A. (1987). *Psychology and child custody determinations: Knowledge, roles, and expertise.* Lincoln, NE: University of Nebraska Press.

Weithorn, L. A. (2006). The legal contexts of forensic assessment of children and families. In S. N. Sparta & G. P. Koocher (Eds.), *Forensic mental health assessment of children and adolescents* (pp. 11–29). New York: Oxford University Press.

Wettstein, R. M. (2002). Ethics and forensic psychiatry. *Psychiatric Clinics of North America, 25,* 623–633.

Wolfgang, M. E. (1974). The social scientist in court. *Journal of Criminal Law and Criminology, 65,* 239–247.

Woody, R. H. (1988). *Protecting your mental health practice: How to minimize legal and financial risk* San Francisco, CA: Jossey-Bass.

Woody, R. H. (2000). Professional ethics, regulatory licensing, and malpractice complaints. In F. W. Kaslow (Ed.), *Handbook of couple and family forensics: A sourcebook for mental health and legal professionals.* New York: Wiley.

Woody, R. H. (2005). Defending against legal complaints. In G. Koocher, J. C. Norcross, & S. S. Hill (Eds.), *Psychologists' desk reference* (2nd ed., pp. 560–565). New York: Oxford University Press

Youngstrom, E. A., & Busch, C. P. (2000). Expert testimony in psychology: Ramifications of Supreme Court decision in *Kumho Tire Co., Ltd. v. Carmichael. Ethics & Behavior, 10,* 185–193.

Yufik, A. (2005). Revisiting the *Tarasoff* decision: Risk assessment and liability in clinical and forensic practice. *American Journal of Forensic Psychology, 23,* 5–21.

Zapf, P. A., & Roesch, R. (2006). Competency to stand trial: A guide for evaluators. In I. B. Weiner & A. K. Hess (Eds.), *The handbook of forensic psychology* (3rd ed., pp. 305–331). Hoboken, NJ: Wiley.

18

Challenging Work Settings
Juggling Porcupines

Do the right thing.

Spike Lee

Contents

A psychologist evaluates children's reactions to prototypes of video games for a large computer media company.

A marriage and family therapist assists a dating service with procedures for matching its members.

A social scientist creates messaging that will attract investors for a financial investment firm.

A psychiatrist hired by a group of bounty hunters assists in better understanding personality and cultural factors that will assist them in tracking and catching fugitives.

A group of mental health professionals consults for a political campaign to formulate opposition research on the opposing candidate regarding the competitor's moral, cognitive, and emotional suitability for office.

A wide range of work settings that have traditionally employed mental health professionals usually adhere to common ethical values that cut across the professions. Increasingly, however, mental health practitioners and behavioral scientists have found interesting employment opportunities in nontraditional work settings. Ethical pressures or challenges within such workplaces may trigger reactions leading from subtle erosion of professional values to overwhelming emotional distress. Some settings seem especially likely to evoke ethical quandaries. For example, the mental health professionals described above will invariably run into specific ethical and moral dilemmas not well addressed by ethics codes. As video games become ultrarealistic and increasingly violent, will the psychologist become concerned about desensitizing players to violent acts? Will the marriage and family therapist balk on learning that the matching scheme is actually far more superficial than the "sophisticated scientific selection program" advertised to its members? Will the social scientist have moral stirrings when she realizes that the messaging is more hype than reality, and as a result, people may put their financial welfare at risk should they invest in the company's offering? How will the psychiatrist feel when he learns more about the actual tactics bounty hunters use to "catch their man"? Will the mental health professionals have qualms about offering professional advice for the sole purpose of tearing down someone's candidacy?

This chapter discusses the more common examples of work settings that present unusual ethical challenges such as the military, government security agencies, schools, medical centers, prisons, and even independent practice. In each of these work settings, therapists and behavioral scientists may find themselves expected to serve clients with specialized needs under unique constraints. At times, individual needs may actually become incongruent with other demands of the agency or institution, automatically placing the mental health professional in an ethical predicament. Independent practice also represents a unique type of work setting with its own special pressures, as do academic and social and behavioral research laboratories.

(The last two categories are also addressed in Chapters 16 and 19.)

In categorizing the sorts of difficulties linked to specialized work settings, consider three distinct areas of focus:

- the nature and demands of the agency, organization, or special context within which the professional renders services
- how the ethical issues relate to the particular nature of the clients and their problems
- the special skills or competencies (including ethical sensitivities) professionals should have to work in such settings.

BASIC CONSIDERATIONS

Who Is the Client?

The classic monograph, "Who Is the Client?" (Monahan, 1980) grew out of the work of the American Psychological Association's (APA's) Task Force on the Role of Psychology in the Criminal Justice System. Despite the "criminal justice" focus, the edited collection of papers has important and generic value for helping mental health professionals recognize the complex nature of different types of client relationships. Many of the issues that arise in the mental health treatment of incarcerated persons are either unique to or significantly different from the services offered to nonincarcerated persons (Walsh, 2003). In particular, we must always remain mindful of who we owe professional duties to and remain prepared to define carefully client relationships with respect to matters of confidentiality, responsibility, and other critical ethical issues.

Many employment situations involve serving varying categories of clients and distinct client need hierarchies. It is critical that therapists carefully think through and conceptualize these situations because the needs of the different components may often compete or be mutually exclusive. For example, mental health professionals employed by a government agency (e.g., the U.S. Justice Department, Bureau of Prisons) could provide services to an individual person (e.g., an inmate at a federal correctional center). In such circumstances, the practitioner owes certain professional duties to that individual (i.e., inmate), the employing agency (i.e., the Bureau of Prisons), and to society as a whole (i.e., the citizens, who may be taxpayers or the victims of crime), although the specific details and clarity of the lines of obligation will obviously have great potential variability. In such situations, the professional has an obligation to clarify the nature of the ethical duties due each party, to inform all concerned about the ethical constraints, if any, and to take any steps necessary to ensure appropriate respect for the rights of the person at the bottom of the client hierarchy.

What Skills Are Needed?

The issue of competence assessment and recognition of limitations by mental health professionals is addressed in Chapter 4, along with the difficulties inherent in evaluating competence, especially with respect to new or emerging areas of practice. In this chapter, we stress the importance of recognizing a more subtle issue in assessing one's skills: the ability to perform with appropriate sensitivity and expertise in unique contexts. For example, one may be highly competent at performing psychodiagnostic assessment and psychotherapy in general practice, but these talents will not necessarily transfer directly to providing psychotherapeutic treatment in a prison setting or conducting psychodiagnostic assessments to aid in the selection of a corporate executive.

In some circumstances enthusiasm, necessity, or poor judgment may propel a mental health professional into a new professional arena. The transfer or generalizability of training across situations or populations varies considerably, and those who fail to recognize and compensate for this fact may encounter serious ethical problems. Without a clear and thoughtful assessment of the situational demands, the risk of an ethical violation is substantially increased. A cautious approach affords the primary means of avoiding these sorts of problems, but the discussion that follows highlights some of the more subtle aspects of specialized skills needed at certain work sites.

Organizational Demands

As detailed in Chapter 3, most individual mental health professionals pledge accountability to a set of ethical standards or code of conduct when they seek professional licensure or join a professional association. Enforcement of such codes may take place through such associations or through investigations by statutory licensing bodies. However, people who do not join professional associations, who do not hold a specialized licensed, and organizations can not be held accountable in the same manner. There are times when clinician–employees may find themselves asked or ordered to behave in an ethically inappropriate manner as a function of the employing organization's needs. Monahan and his colleagues (1980) provided a cogent example by citing the case of a client of a psychologist in independent practice who reveals racist attitudes or behavior in the course of treatment. Such attitudes may or may not have relevance for the treatment program, but the content clearly constitutes a confidential matter between client and therapist. However, what if part of a therapist's work involves providing consultation to a law enforcement agency, and in the course of interviewing various employees, the clinician discovers a pattern of racist organizational policies or discrimination? The therapist might feel both repulsed and outraged but simultaneously under an ethical obligation to keep that finding confidential from the general public. However, cooperating in establishing, maintaining, or implementing such policies would constitute unethical conduct. Going public with insider information may violate organizational policy or legal standards in some situations. The mental health professional must balance an obligation to protect the individual and organizational client's confidentiality with the rights of the public or other parties not privy to the inner workings of the agency.

What if the mental health professional in the situation described chose to inform the agency's governing body (e.g., the legislative body or board of directors supervising the government agency or employer) about the racist policies? What if the mental health professional took the story to the press? As discussed in Chapter 8, limited breaches of confidentiality may be permissible to the extent needed to protect intended victims from clear and imminent danger or if otherwise mandated by law. However, racist behavior does not usually meet such imminent danger test or legal mandate tests. Certainly, in some circumstances "whistle-blowing" behavior does become appropriate ethical behavior, although the matter is not a simple one to sort out. As Monahan (1980) noted:

> We are not suggesting that psychologists should avoid serving in imperfect organizations, only that the perennial debate concerning whether it is better to work from inside to achieve gradual change or to leave the organization and apply pressure from the outside for reform … is common to all organizational structures. (p. 3)

The point to remember is that what is ethically appropriate for a practitioner's work with an individual client may not ideally suit the best interests of client organizations or employing agencies and vice versa. The differentiation of obligations and the linkage of these obligations to broader issues of human welfare constitute important ethical questions that require thoughtful analysis. Yet, clear answers are often lacking.

When Interventions Cause Harm

Public trust in behavioral science and mental health professionals has led to wide acceptance of our work in many areas of commerce and government service, as well as in both medical and mental health care. With such successes come new workplace-related ethical challenges, not the least of which involves identification of our ethical responsibilities both to individuals and to society at large. We must begin to conceptualize our professional obligations much like the leaves of an artichoke, all connected at the base by our ethical responsibilities and closely packed but still distinct and separable.

Beneficence and nonmaleficence lie at the core of most health professions' ethics codes, followed closely by concepts of fidelity and responsibility. We strive to benefit those with whom we work, while attempting to do no harm. We attempt to safeguard the welfare and rights of those with whom we interact professionally and with other affected persons. When we confront conflicts among our obligations or concerns, we seek to resolve them responsibly while seeking to avoid causing harm. Unfortunately, avoiding *all* harm becomes impossible at times, and we must instead seek to minimize harm resulting from our work. At the same time, we strive to establish relationships of trust with our clients, and we must remain mindful of our professional and scientific responsibilities to society and our communities (APA 02: Preamble).

At times, the medical tradition has recognized the necessity to favor the needs of one person over others (e.g., making a triage decision to provide immediate treatment for the patient who has suffered a respiratory arrest even though another person who arrived earlier must wait in acute pain with a compound fracture) or to coercively limit the freedom of individuals to advance the interests of society at large (e.g., quarantine of highly infectious patients or the use of restraints with a violent mentally ill patient). In the past half century, many mental health professionals have taken on the mantle of applying behavioral science for societal benefit apart from direct individual-focused contracts. These include services to multiple individuals delivered as a unit, services provided at the behest of a known third party, and professional activities undertaken on behalf of a third party unknown by or invisible to the individuals under treatment or study (Koocher, 2007).

The individual client offers the simplest case for observing principles of beneficence, nonmaleficence, fidelity, and responsibility. After all, with only one client the therapist's professional obligations seem well focused. However, history and law have long recognized the role of healers to assist in acting on behalf of the greater good of society. The doctrine of *parens patriae* (as descried in Chapter 8) provides an example of how government may mandate some types of medical or mental health intervention or usurp the rights of parents or legal guardians to act as the protector of a vulnerable person (e.g., a child whose parents are unable or unwilling to provide care or an incapacitated and dependent individual of any age).

Under this doctrine, legislative bodies have routinely enacted statutes mandating breaches of confidentiality and reporting by designated professionals to government authorities when a vulnerable person or society becomes threatened in defined ways. The most common examples affecting mental health practitioners in the United States include laws that command us to breach a patient's confidentiality to report suspicions that a child or an elderly or dependent person has suffered abuse. We may also face obligations to seek the hospitalization of people who pose a danger to themselves or to others, including an obligation to warn potential intended victims. Similarly, physicians and nurses may face requirements to report patients seeking treatment for gunshot wounds or highly infectious diseases to police or public health authorities, respectively. Obviously, some of the clients who come to us and disclose such behaviors or hazards would prefer that we keep silent and may find the consequences of our reporting and subsequent intervention by the state as nonbeneficent or harmful.

The couple, family, or group of clients seen together poses a more complex situation of conflicting interests. Suppose a couple seeks the services of a therapist to help improve their relationship. Now suppose that, over time, it becomes clear to the therapist that the best outcome for one member of the dyad would involve exiting the relationship, while the best outcome for the other would require maintaining the relationship. In such situations, one party may well suffer harm, while the other benefits. Does the fault lie with the therapist whose intervention triggered a decision-making insight by one partner, or does the decision rest on free will of one client?

Similarly, whenever groups of people enter treatment together, the best outcomes for all parties will seldom prove congruent. We constantly strive to do good, retain clients' trust, and minimize harm, even when we recognize that some parties may ultimately feel unhappy or harmed as a result of their participation. Our ethical obligation involves foreseeing potential difficulties, affording thoughtful informed consent or permission, and retaining our professional integrity as we strive to advance the common interests. Nonetheless, sometimes we must recognize that some parties to our interventions may well experience feelings of harm resulting from participation in multiple client interventions.

Conflicting interests also occur frequently when the authority or request for a practitioner's services originates with a known third party. In the most benign context, a third party such as an insurer or managed care company provides its customers with a panel of selected providers who have agreed to provide selected services for specified fees. Subtle conflicts may sometimes occur in such situations if a mental health professional feels dependent on or subject to pressure from the third party in a way that precludes acting in the client's best interest. In most circumstances, however, little reason exists to question the practitioner's goal of helping and not harming the client. In a number of other situations, however, therapists may ethically undertake intervention or evaluation at the behest of a third party that may lead a client to feel harmed. Examples include child custody, competency, or criminal responsibility evaluations and independent examinations to determine disability, fitness for duty, or suitability for employment. In such contexts, a third party (e.g., the courts, an employer, an insurance company, or a government agency) may have requested or ordered the evaluations.

Both the contracting party and the party undergoing evaluation hold a kind of client status in such cases. The process involves an appearance of mutual consent but conflicting interests and hence a degree of subtle coercion. The individual facing evaluation may decline to participate or to share the results of such an evaluation with the requesting party. However, such refusals will have predictable adverse consequences, such as loss of custody, loss of employment, or loss of disability coverage. We hope that a competent professional with a high degree of integrity will perform an excellent evaluation and provide accurate, useful data that benefit both the institutional client and the individual client. Society as a whole clearly gains by having significant decisions of this sort aided by valid behavioral science data. Still, one party may experience a degree of harm or fail to benefit from the otherwise entirely ethical and competent work of the behavioral science practitioner.

Case 18–1: Theodore John Kaczynski, Ph.D., also known as the Unabomber, sent mail bombs that killed 3 and wounded 23 people at several universities and airlines between the late 1970s and early 1990s. Federal agents arrested him on April 3, 1996, at a remote cabin outside Lincoln, Montana. On January 7, 1998, Kaczynski attempted to hang himself in jail. Two weeks later, he pleaded guilty to all the government's charges and received a sentence of life in prison without possibility of parole. The careful evaluation of Kaczynski in 1998 by Sally C. Johnson, M.D., chief psychiatrist and associate warden of health services for the Federal Correctional Institution in Butner, North Carolina, helped make the negotiated plea agreement possible.

Dr. Kaczynski has a very high IQ and a troubled psychological history with paranoid and other psychopathological symptoms. He resisted allowing discussion of his mental state in court and refused to permit use of an insanity defense by his attorneys. The thorough and careful court-ordered evaluation conducted by Dr. Johnson enabled both defense and prosecuting attorneys to reach a plea agreement with Kaczynski that spared him from the death penalty and avoided a potentially challenging criminal trial. This case illustrates a situation in which the clinician had ethical obligations to many parties. She owed professional duties to the court, counsel for both sides, and the defendant. By conducting a thorough and fair evaluation that delineated how Kaczynski's mental state interacted with the legal issues (e.g., intelligent, competent to stand trial, but highly paranoid and prone to decompensate or act out in court), she produced a report that facilitated a negotiated settlement in a highly contentious case.

The Invisible Practitioner

A more complex set of ethical issues arises when the authority or request for a mental health professional's services originates with a con-cealed or invisible third party. In such situations, therapists become invisible to the objects of their professional attention. For example, attorneys with cases that involve psychological issues or testimony by mental health experts will often hire their own experts to review and critique the work of the other side's experts, who will soon face cross-examination. Still other experts might help advise a lawyer on jury selection, run a jury simulation, use crime details to devise profiles of perpetrators to assist police investigators, help the Secret Service assess the seriousness of threats made against the president, help an employer strategize about interviewing applicants for a specific job, or develop a training program to assist investigators (pick the venue of your choice) with training or suggestions about interviewing or interrogation techniques. In such instances, the client owed the ethical duty may well not be the person on whom the mental health professional focuses attention but rather a third party seeking advice. The person under scrutiny may never know that they have been studied, profiled, critiqued, or subjected to behavioral observation as the expert's activities effectively take place invisibly behind the scenes. In addition, the people studied without their knowledge may experience harm as the result of the practitioner's work. Serial killers may find themselves identified and convicted based on psychological analysis of crime scene evidence. Candidates for executive positions may lose a job opportunity because of emotional or personality factors uncovered during a probing interview. Careless or incompetent alleged experts may find themselves embarrassed on the witness stand.

Consumers also become frequent objects of study by anonymous social science researchers in the employ of advertising agencies. One notorious example became public in the late 1980s when the R. J. Reynolds Tobacco Company planned to test market two new brands of cigarettes. One called Uptown contained menthol, and its marketing was aimed heavy toward African-American smokers. Marketing for the other brand, called Dakota, was aimed at young, poorly educated, white females, termed *virile females* (Cotton, 1990). The APA urged its members not to participate in helping to market "lethal and addictive" products, although some members objected, noting that the profession should not bar colleagues from working for purveyors of legal commercial entities. Still others argued that professional ethics should preclude assisting in the marketing of alcohol and firearms as well.

Hostage situations afford another example. Suppose that an angry and troubled teenager has brought a gun to school and taken a class captive. A special weapons and tactics (SWAT) team arrives and prepares to storm the classroom as snipers focus their laser sights on the armed teen. Now, suppose that a behavioral science expert working with the police interviews a parent of the hostage taker, who has since arrived on the scene. Based on information gleaned from the parent, the expert contacts the hostage taker via cell phone, attempts to establish rapport, asks questions, and engages him emotionally. Based on the intentional work of the behavioral science expert, the teen ultimately becomes tearful or distracted and momentarily lowers his weapon, allowing the SWAT team the seconds needed to rush in and disarm him. By using psychological skills and personal data in such situations, clinicians have saved lives while never incurring a therapeutic obligation or even disclosing professional identities to the people whose behavior they attempt to influence.

Yet another example involves concerns about mental health professionals consulting to interrogations associated with national security. Shameful behaviors by nonpsychologist military personnel dealing with detainees at the Abu Ghraib prison in Iraq (e.g., intimidation of detainees with dogs, sleep deprivation, infliction of physical discomforts, forced nudity, and other types of humiliation) have rightly attracted condemnation. The APA has clearly stated that psychologists who commit role violations (i.e., mixing health services delivery and interrogation support) or who participate in any way in torture or inhumane or degrading practices have violated the ethics code (Behnke, 2006; Presidential Task Force on Psychological Ethics and National Security [PENS], 2005). We discuss these issues in more detail later in this chapter.

Some mental health professionals occasionally argue against any concealed roles involving application of behavioral science to serve the needs of some third parties, usually by asserting a personal moral values position. Ethics codes have generally not attempted to prohibit such activities as long as the professionals in such roles perform their duties lawfully. As behavioral science advances, we must expect that private parties, governments, and corporations will continue to seek such consultation out of public view. Our ethics codes should compel attention to human welfare, integrity, appropriate role clarity, and obedience to law but not become a tool for advancing political or narrow social agendas.

Protection of the public and vulnerable members of society should remain a prime directive for mental health professionals. In many situations, we will face requests for services that involve multiple layers of clients, each with different positions in a hierarchy of control and vulnerability. We must remain mindful of these nuances and focus on retaining our professional integrity while providing high-quality service in the context of relative strengths and weaknesses of the parties involved.

WORK SETTINGS POSING SPECIAL ETHICAL CHALLENGES

Government Employment

The government employs mental health professionals on many levels and in all branches. These individuals serve at the municipal, state, and federal levels and have roles in the legislative, judicial, and executive branches. We specifically discuss some subsets of governmental agencies (i.e., the military, schools, community agencies, and the criminal justice system) in detail. First, however, it is worth considering government service as a whole. Working for the government involves upholding an important degree of public trust while potentially falling under high levels of political pressure. Functioning as a public servant–behavioral scientist/clinician can provide both rewards and frustrations, especially at the level of integrating professional judgment with policymaking (De-Leon, 2002, 2006; Sullivan, Groveman, Heldring, DeLeon, & Beauchamp, 1998).

The next three case vignettes illustrate the range and complexity of issues that may occur in government service.

Case 18–2: Sam Uncle, Ph.D., a psychologist working as a clinician at a federally operated hospital, was instructed to provide access to case records in a manner that seemed contrary to the APA ethics code. He expressed his reservations to his nonpsychologist supervisor, who replied, "Those ethical principles do not apply to federal employees at this facility."

Dr. Uncle's supervisor's claim that the agency employees' professional ethics codes do not apply to professionals working within that (or other) government agencies is simply untrue. The APA ethics code addresses such matters in the very first section of its code of conduct. Under the heading "Conflicts Between Ethics and Law, Regulations, or Other Governing Legal Authority," the code specifies that when "ethical responsibilities conflict with law, regulations, or other governing legal authority, psychologists make known their commitment to the Ethics Code and take steps to resolve the conflict. If the conflict cannot be resolved, psychologists may adhere to the requirements of the law, regulations, or other governing legal authority" (APA 02: 1.02). The following section, "Conflicts Between Ethics and Organizational Demands," notes, "If the demands of an organization with which psychologists are affiliated or for whom they are working conflict with this Ethics Code, psychologists clarify the nature of the conflict, make known their commitment to the Ethics Code, and to the extent feasible, resolve the conflict in a way that permits adherence to the Ethics Code" (APA 02: 1.03).

Members of mental health professional societies pledge to uphold their group's ethical standards when joining and are bound by the code in all contexts of their work. The supervisor in this particular case actually misinterpreted federal policy; however, situations may arise in which employers will demand that their employees behave contrary to the dictates of ethical standards. Each person must consider how best to handle individual situations as they occur, but the basic principles are not waived for any employer, government or otherwise. The APA code, as cited above, enjoins members to adhere as closely as possible to the code, while recognizing that some laws, regulatory procedures, or institutional rules may differ. By the use of this language, the APA intended to say, in essence, that when law prescribes a different course of action, obeying the law does not constitute ethical misconduct. However, the language also allows a member who may have a conscientious objection to a law or policy the option to decline to follow it. The context clearly asks members to work within the system by calling attention to the problem and attempting to resolve it within parameters allowed by the ethics code.

Case 18–3: Under the auspices of MK-Ultra, a secret mind control project undertaken by the U.S. government during the 1960s, unwitting individuals were administered doses of hallucinogenic drugs and were observed to study the resulting behavioral changes. At least one person who participated in the project reportedly committed suicide. Two psychologists, recruited to participate in the project by a clandestine government agency, cooperated in the execution of the project.

In the case of the covert administration of hallucinogenic drugs to uninformed individuals who had not consented to participate in an experiment of this sort, the psychologists clearly were guilty of unethical complicity. The actual events took place in the 1960s and came to the attention of the APA in complaints filed during the late 1970s. The psychologists' claims of a national security exemption and assertions they had not personally administered the drugs did not persuade the ethics panel that investigated the case. By actively participating in the project, the psychologists had condoned serious ethical misconduct. The ethics committee could legally take no action, however, because the time limit for filing complaints had long since passed. Many records describing MK-Ultra have become declassified and are readily available via Internet archives (see, e.g., http://michael-robinett.com/declass/c000.htm).

Case 18–4: A municipal government hired Maxine Datum, Ed.D., to explore the question of whether racist attitudes among certain officials influenced hiring practices. Datum's study and analysis of the personnel system confirmed the presence of active racial discrimination. The officials ordered Dr. Datum to keep these findings confidential and after several months had done nothing to alter the illegal personnel practices.

The case of the municipal personnel research adds a new wrinkle to the role of the mental health professional. Presumably, the city in question was the client, and the same government officials who hired Dr. Datum have a right to control the data collected on their behalf, much as an individual would have a right of confidentiality. One could argue that the public interest would best be served by making the data public, but would that produce the socially desirable change? Suppose the municipal officials say to Datum that they will use the information to "bring about appropriate change in our own way." Does Datum have a right or a duty to challenge this assertion? Can one draw an analogy to the racist client in therapy (see Ralph Redneck in Case 5–24), who listens to the therapist interpret the racist behavior but has no desire to change current attitudes? These questions are not easily answered, but they lead to an important issue in understanding appropriate ethical behavior. The consultant must assume the burden of articulating the nature and expectations of his or her professional role (APA 02: 3.11). When a mental health professional works for a government agency, it is no less important to explore these issues to assess the degrees of freedom and ethical comfort one may expect to enjoy in the job.

Next, we explore specific ethical issues related to particular components of government: the military, espionage and antiterrorist activities, schools (including both public and private schools), criminal justice settings, and community agencies. We then discuss special considerations that arise in psychologists' work in business and industry, medical institutions, independent practice, and pastoral counseling contexts.

The Armed Services

Given that mental health professionals and behavioral scientists dedicate themselves to advancing the cause of human welfare, should they work for the military, the Central Intelligence Agency, or similar governmental units? The question is not as simplistic as it might seem. Military and intelligence services are certainly necessary for national security, and the behavioral sciences have much to contribute to any other complex human organization (Allen, Chatelier, Clark, & Sorenson, 1982; W. B. Johnson, 1995; Lazarus & Zur, 2002; Russell, 2006; Staal & King, 2000). At the same time, many mental health professionals might feel concern about the contribution of their expertise to military activities.

An article on military psychology published during the Viet Nam era (Crawford, 1970) evoked a stinging response (Saks, 1970), which claimed that, "The chief goal of military psychology is the transformation of human beings into more efficient murder machines" (p. 876). This in turn brought forth a series of rebuttals (Kelley, 1971; Leuba, 1971) and considerable acrimony. While that debate may have been more a function of the political ethos of the times than of ethics issues, some would express similar concerns today on both sides of the issue. Current political controversy regarding the global war on terrorism and government practices involving secret prisons, allegations of torture, and the detention facilities established at Guantanamo Bay, Cuba, have reawakened questions about the role of behavioral scientists and mental health professionals during wartime (see e.g., Bobo et al., 2006; Bongar, Brown, Beutler, Breckenridge, & Zimbardo, 2007; Kimmel & Stout, 2006; Rose, 2006; Stephenson & Staal, 2007; Wilks, 2006; Williamson, 2006; Wilson, 2006). We discuss some specific related ethical issues in this chapter but must make an important observation at the outset harkening back to the Viet Nam era, to wit: Anger at government policies should not translate to a pervasive emotional indictment of those who serve. We should hold our colleagues accountable for ethical misconduct, but the standards of proof must remain the same for all, regardless of the political climate of the times.

For purposes of this chapter, we delineate two distinct aspects of military psychology. One is the work of the civilian employee or military personnel in research and consultation, and the other is the role of civilian employee or military personnel in the delivery of mental health services in military settings. Much of the ethical decision making is precisely analogous to that which goes into the work of the research or industrial–organizational psychologist or the clinician in general. But, special subtleties do exist, and there are matters of relative emphases that necessitate critical ethical review. A separate discussion of the role of behavioral scientists and mental health professionals in national security matters follows as these also involve both members of the military and civilians.

Allen et al. (1982) described a variety of roles behavioral scientists or professionals trained in mental health perform for the military in the nonclinical realm. These may include personnel functions (e.g., selection, assessment, classification, and retention of military personnel); training (e.g., leadership development, skill acquisition, teaching, and effectiveness enhancement); human performance research (e.g., human factors engineering, job design, information process, and decision-making studies); development of specialized training (e.g., simulators and assessment centers); and health-related research (e.g., sleep deprivation, fatigue, and physical fitness studies). While the goal of such research may involve enhancing the ability to destroy an enemy before being destroyed, any moral decision about whether to participate in such programs is chiefly a matter of personal conscience. The constraints on such research or training programs are essentially the same as those in nonmilitary settings (i.e., informed consent of participants, appropriate respect for the rights of the individual, etc.). It is evident that much of the research conducted on behalf of the military will have beneficial civilian applications, such as flight simulators designed for

the military that can also be adapted to train civilian pilots. Physical fitness research and treatment protocols for posttraumatic recovery done for the military may be generalized for the public at large.

When a military mental health professional functions as a provider of clinical or counseling services, some special ethical dilemmas do arise from time to time, as illustrated in the following situations:

Case 18–5: Captain Henry B. Trayed filed a complaint with an ethics committee against a military counselor at his base hospital. The counselor had informed Captain Trayed's superiors of his extreme depression and other psychopathological symptoms; this resulted in considerable career sanctions. Captain Trayed believed that the counselor had indicated that information received in the context of treatment would be held in confidence. The counselor responded to the committee's inquiry by noting that Captain Trayed knew the base hospital treatment setting operated different from those "on the outside."

It is not unethical to disclose confidential information without an individual's consent when the law demands it. However, practitioners must inform their clients of the limits of confidentiality at the outset of the professional relationship. The obligation to provide such information applies in both military and civilian settings. Federal law does allow officials of the U.S. Department of Defense (DoD) access to service members' health care records on a need-to-know basis; however, these circumstances are vaguely defined. Active duty military practitioners occupy multiple roles as therapist-clinicians and commissioned military officers. Frequently, simultaneous allegiance to professional ethics and military regulations becomes impossible. Ongoing collaboration between the APA and the DoD has focused on establishing appropriate criteria to manage the resulting difficulties (W. B. Johnson, 1995; W. B. Johnson, Ralph, & Johnson, 2005; Staal & King, 2000).

Case 18–6: Major Freddy Flakey, a skilled fighter pilot, appeared tense and interpersonally erratic in ways that his squadron commander could not precisely grasp. Flakey refused attempts to discuss these issues, so the commanding officer ordered him to the base hospital for an outpatient evaluation. After Major Flakey had met with a psychiatrist for several sessions, the commander went to the hospital and confiscated the patient's file for review without consulting the attending clinician.

Confidentiality issues are a key source of concern in mental health service delivery to military personnel by military personnel. On the one hand, individuals in sensitive defense-related positions could be especially dangerous when attempting to perform their duties in emotionally troubled states. At the same time, such individuals ought to have the same rights to privacy and confidentiality so important to effective general psychotherapeutic care. One way to deal with the issue, as noted, is to make certain that clients are informed from the outset of the professional relationship of all limitations placed on their confidentiality.

The military client will typically be informed in the first session that certain types of problems (e.g., those related to fitness for duty) must be reported. An individual with concerns about privacy might then have the option to seek treatment off base or from civilian personnel, if appropriate. Obviously, such referral is not possible on a ship or in a battle zone (W. B. Johnson et al., 2005; Staal & King, 2000). In addition, military personnel can be ordered to submit to evaluation or treatment against their personal wishes. Although it is easy to understand the concerns of Major Flakey's commander, confiscation of the records was inappropriate. The content of the records may not specifically address issues of concern (e.g., fitness for duty), which could be more specifically and comprehensively addressed by consulting the clinician who assessed and treated Major Flakey. Having given proper warning to Major Flakey, the clinician can reasonably release information in accord with military regulations.

Increasingly, mental health practitioners find themselves embedded with units at or near the front lines. How can a clinician deployed as an embedded member of a small team or military unit ethically manage pervasive and uncomfortable multiple-role relationships? Embedded practice often enhances the clinician's understanding of service members' needs and increases the likelihood of members to seek services. Yet, such proximity also ensures multiple roles with every member of the community and diminishes the clinician's ability to employ usual ethical strategies for minimizing multiple-relationship hazards.

The matter of whether sexual preference has any bearing on job performance in the military or elsewhere has been the subject of considerable litigation that led to a "don't ask, don't tell" policy by executive order of President Bill Clinton. A mental health practitioner may find him- or herself in the position of having to help enforce such criteria while having personal reservations about their validity. Because federal law prohibits gay, lesbian, and bisexual (GLB) persons from serving openly in the military, the 65,000 GLB men and women estimated to currently serve in the armed forces face unique occupational stressors and a heightened need for supportive services (W. B. Johnson & Buhrke, 2006). Mental health practitioners in military settings face numerous obstacles in efforts to provide ethical and efficacious clinical services to GLB service members. A detailed discussion of the most common clinical problems and referral issues for GLB persons in military settings, primary ethical and administrative problems for those who treat them, along with several recommendations for enhancing appropriate care while minimizing harm can be found in the W. B. Johnson and Buhrke (2006) article.

We adapted the following examples from W. B. Johnson and Buhrke:

Case 18–7: Following an episode of excessive intoxication, a 19-year-old Army soldier is referred for substance abuse evaluation. During routine screening, he appears depressed and reluctantly acknowledges some suicidal ideation. During the course of a subsequent inpatient admission, he cautiously discloses anxiety about "being gay" and being found out by both peers and family members. His family and conservative religious church hold strongly homonegative views. He insists on keeping his sexual orientation "secret" and refuses to disclose his concerns about being gay to anyone other than his clinician. He also fears this information will be used against him, resulting in his discharge from the Army.

Case 18–8: An Air Force psychologist does an intake on a new patient, a major who has just transferred to the base. Her health record indicates 2 years of psychoanalytically oriented therapy for depression. The former provider, an Air Force psychiatrist, noted only symptoms of depression in her records. She reports that most of her therapy addressed same-sex attraction, with significant emphasis on the connection between unmet needs from parents and her current sexual orientation. She denied ever engaging in a lesbian relationship and expressed interest in "overcoming" these feelings. Despite taking a selective serotonin reuptake inhibitor for more than a year, she reports continuing depression. She seems genuinely surprised when the clinician suggests that her sexual orientation might be neither an indication of pathology nor something easily or appropriately changed.

Case 18–9: A petty officer referred by one of the chaplains at a naval base reports anxiety, depression, and existential distress. He feels quite anxious about seeing a psychologist. He acknowledges that he had seen the chaplain for nearly 4 months to rid himself of sinful thoughts and impulses. Further inquiry reveals that these are homosexual in nature, and that the client has powerful internalized homonegative views. He had refused to disclose these feelings to anyone but his chaplain, knowing that such conversations hold full privilege in the military, with all information gathered during confession and pastoral counseling thoroughly protected from disclosure. It becomes clear that the chaplain had attempted some sort of "reparative" therapy to eliminate the homosexual feelings and attractions. The intervention had not proved effective, and the client had become increasingly despondent and hopeless about his chances for change (W. B. Johnson & Buhrke, 2006).

Readers are referred to W. B. Johnson and Buhrke's original 2006 writing for detailed ethical commentary, but the complexity of the issues seems evident. We must strive to do no harm, provide ongoing informed consent, conduct GLB-sensitive clinical assessments, attend to issues of GLB identity development, remain sensitive to contextual factors, collaboratively address harassment and victimization, exercise appropriate caution in record keeping, and attempt to strike a balance between a client's best interests and DoD regulations (Biaggio, Orchard, Larson, Petrino, & Mihara, 2003; Lasser & Gottlieb, 2004; Morrow, 2000).

The last two decades have seen increased attention to the ethical problems of mental health clinicians in the military. The DoD requires that practitioners in professions that qualify for licensing must maintain an active state license. Johnson and colleagues (W. B. Johnson, 1995; W. B. Johnson et al., 2005) noted that military psychologists strive to maintain a delicate balance between APA and DoD requirements. However, this can become particularly challenging in some unavoidable situations. W. B. Johnson and her colleagues also presented some fascinating examples related to confidentiality and multiple-role relationships while serving as warfare-qualified officers and psychologists on an aircraft carrier. The following three cases are adapted from that article (W. B. Johnson et al., 2005):

Case 18–10: Having treated an emotionally fragile dental technician for several months, the psychologist arrived at the onboard dental clinic for a teeth-cleaning appointment only to find the client assigned to the task. The psychologist became a captive audience, as the technician scraped, sprayed, and suctioned, along the way unloading a stream of personal material more appropriate for the psychotherapy office. The psychologist attempted to respond authentically despite having a mouth full of fingers and equipment. When the dental appointment ended, the psychologist wondered about the need to make a clinical note of this "session."

Case 18–11: As a warfare-qualified officer, the psychologist must stand regular watch on the bridge of the ship. While doing so during flight operations one evening, the helmsman fails to listen to a command issued by the psychologist, becomes flustered, and turns the ship in the wrong direction. Although quickly corrected, the error could have led to disaster had an aircraft been on final approach at that moment. The psychologist quietly had a few words with the helmsman, after which the captain called the psychologist over and half-jokingly remarked on the soft approach in responding to the helmsman's egregious error. He expected the psychologist to address the helmsman more forcefully. The psychologist quietly reminded the captain that he ordered this sailor to psychotherapy by the psychologist a few weeks earlier. The psychologist noted that a dual relationship with this particular helmsman exists, and that any screaming delivered now will become fodder for the next therapy session. The captain shakes his head and rolls his eyes as if to say, "Now I've heard everything."

Case 18–12: During a morning briefing, a female psychologist learns that her social security number has been randomly selected for the day's "operation golden flow," the term given to the random urine collection and drug-testing program. The rather demeaning process involves the master-at-arms personnel accompanying the person being tested into a bathroom and closely observing while the examinee urinates into a cup. Both then march back to the security office carrying the sample in plain view. When the psychologist reports for testing, only male observers are present, requiring a call for a qualified female observer. One of the psychologist's long-term patients walks through the door and gasps, visibly embarrassed to be in this position. Both do their best to make small talk and maintain some professional demeanor as the psychologist disrobes and urinates in front of her. Fortunately, they are able to look back and laugh at the incident during later sessions.

In an earlier paper, W. B. Johnson and Wilson (1993) presented examples of problems unique to psychology internships at military sites. Others have written of the difficulty of being "in service of two masters" (Jeffrey, Rankin, & Jeffrey, 1992) and presented two illustrative case studies on point. In one instance, a military psychologist was reportedly disciplined by the APA for failure to maintain the confidentiality of a service member's care records long after the psychologist had been transferred

to another post. In the second case, a psychologist was disciplined by his commanding officer for failure to reveal an alleged violation of the Uniform Code of Military Justice by a third party. Psychologists are not alone in confronting such dilemmas. Camp (1993) wrote of the "double-agent" status of psychiatrists serving the military in the Viet Nam era.

Medication in the Military

The role of psychologists in prescribing medication on military bases has drawn considerable attention because of the DoD's demonstration project, in which a specially selected cadre of psychologists received special training to qualify for that role. However, at least one ethics inquiry about psychologists prescribing medication pre-dated the DoD project, occurring in the early 1980s.

Case 18–13: During the mid-1980s a psychologist in the community became concerned when he learned that a female client, whose husband was a military officer, was taking psychoactive medication prescribed by another psychologist working at the base hospital. The community-based psychologist feared that the prescription had been fraudulently written and called this to the attention of a state licensing board.

The psychologist accused of prescribing medication without a medical degree had indeed done so, but not unethically. In addition to his psychology degree, this individual had trained as a physician's assistant and secured authorization under military regulations to prescribe medication, under specific circumstances, for military personnel and their dependents receiving treatment at military facilities. In this instance, the psychologist practiced within his sphere of competence in full compliance with military regulations appropriate to the care of the client in question. While this particular type of service was unusual for psychologists in the 1980s, the subsequent demonstration project undertaken by the DoD in the 1990s proved extremely successful in providing sufficient psychopharmacology training to enable psychologists to function successfully in such roles under military authorization. The DoD demonstration project also helped pave the way for state legislation allowing psychologists with specialized training and credentials to include psychopharmacology in their practices (Sammons, Paige, & Levant, 2003).

Espionage and Terrorism

Cases that involve the national intelligence or espionage will by definition not often come into the public view, but occasional cases have historically called attention to the work of mental health practitioners. Since the events of September 11, 2001, creation of detention facilities outside the United States, press accounts of abuse of detainees, and criticism of a number of other policies initiated in the name of national security have led to considerable reexamination of the roles played by behavioral scientists and mental health professionals in such activities.

One of the most thoughtful attempts to study the ethics of participating in national security activities began when then APA President Ronald F. Levant appointed a Presidential Task Force on PENS. The resulting report (Behnke, 2006; Presidential Task Force on PENS, 2005), vetted by the APA Ethics Committee and Board of Directors, underscored APA's long-standing objection to all forms of torture and explicitly stated that its members would be held ethically accountable for participating in any manner in torture or cruel, inhuman, or degrading treatment of others. At the same time, the report made clear that appropriate roles may exist for mental health professionals to assist in national security and other intelligence activities.

The next two case examples illustrate some historical roles of mental health experts in the context of espionage.

Case 18–14: Carl Covert, M.D., worked on the staff of a defense-related federal agency during the 1960s and was assigned to a project that drafted interrogation protocols for enemy prisoners. His job was to assist in applying principles likely to place emotional pressures to divulge information on the subjects of interrogation. In one "experiment," Covert was assigned to monitor the effectiveness of hallucinogenic drugs in breaking down

the resistance of an American soldier. Some years later, the soldier would charge that he had never knowingly volunteered for such an experiment and was harmed psychologically by his unwitting participation.

Case 18–15: Cassandra Troy, Ph.D., also works in a defense-related intelligence service. Her job is to study the behavior and writings of world leaders and to prepare personality profiles for secret use by other branches of government. She attempts to predict how the individuals may respond in different sets of circumstances and is often asked to provide confidential briefings to state and defense department negotiators prior to their meetings with these leaders.

Drs. Covert and Troy are in some sense responsible chiefly to their governmental client, although the immediate impact of their work certainly affects other people. One might argue that their work falls into a special category and is in the national interest. To the extent that Covert was truly involved in the experiment, as claimed by the soldier, he stands guilty of participating in the unethical abuse of a research participant (i.e., an unwilling one). If her work is accurately able to predict behavior, Dr. Troy may provide her employer some very useful data. Her work is not unethical per se, although she would certainly want to present appropriate scientific caveats regarding its predictive validity to those who may rely on the briefings to the exclusion of other factors.

Shortly after the terrorist attacks of September 11, 2001, several federal policy changes came into force. These included expanded military orders for the detention and trial of certain noncitizens thought to be involved in the global war on terror. Finkel (2006) wrote of moral monsters and patriot acts in attempting to describe the silence and rationalization of eroded civil rights occasioned by wartime. In addition, the policy changes expanded traditional roles of the military by establishing joint military and law enforcement intelligence tracking systems and by handing over some judicial, law enforcement, and correctional authority to the secretary of defense (Bobo et al., 2006). According to press accounts (Klaidman, Taylor, & Thomas,

2006), Attorney John Yoo at the Department of Justice drafted a memorandum supporting the alleged legality of torture short of maiming or killing a prisoner, not officially amended until December 2004.

Many mental health professionals have expressed considerable concern about allegations of involvement in torture by physicians, psychologists, and others (Miles, 2006). Some commentators have asserted that professional bodies adjusted or blurred ethical guidance, tilting toward endorsing malpractice, in support of continued involvement by their members (Wilks, 2006). Others offered a reasoned examination of steps taken by the U.S. government to detain, interrogate, and put on trial alleged terrorists in potential violation of international human rights standards (Rose, 2006; Williamson, 2006).

In some instances, critics of the Guantanamo Bay detention centers, the Abu Ghraib prison in Iraq, or the Bush administration's policies in general have reached the conclusion that any medical or mental health professional who works at such facilities or in intelligence-gathering activities must certainly have behaved in an unethical manner. We strongly agree that any participation in or condoning of torture or cruel, inhuman, or degrading treatment of another human being in *any* setting constitutes ethical misconduct for any health or mental health professional. At the same time, we agree with those who assert that some legitimate ethical roles do exist for behavioral scientists and mental health professionals in national security roles and legally authorized secure detention facilities.

Case 18–16: Ahmgonna Askhim, holds a Ph.D. in social psychology and studies in interpersonal influence, grew up in the Middle East and speaks fluent Arabic. He developed relationship- and rapport-based strategies for training interrogators of detainees. Elements of his curriculum involved teaching that people share information with others who appear empathic; elders and seniority are respected in Arab culture; learning about a subject's background can enhance cooperation; establishment of rapport is based on quid pro quo, commonalities, fairness, and mutual respect; a

detainee's narrative should be listed to carefully without interruption, then be gone back over; and detainees' sense of honor should be understood and acknowledged. He taught that recruitment would most likely occur through social networks, be based on collectivist values, and through wanting to be a part of a larger meaningful cause. He explained that, in traditional Arab culture, "Who I am is part of who I am with and who is in my network." In addition, he explained that the culture of learning Sharia (Islamic law) confers status based on memorization of the Koran, not by analysis of ambiguity or nuance, fostering a culture of obedience (Gelles, McFadden, Borum, & Vossekuil, 2006). He also taught interrogators that Arab culture focuses on relationships, oriented toward a larger collective, and on impression management. He noted that many Middle Eastern Arab males think associatively rather than in the more linear or goal-oriented manner of Western thinkers (Nydell, 2002).

Dr. Askhim's knowledge about Arab culture and social psychology provided valuable tools to interrogator trainees. The information helped both to establish rapport and to craft strategies to elicit information in a nonabusive manner. The trainees in Dr. Askhim's course learned how values, culture, and thought processes among detainees might differ significantly from American or European cultures. Armed with such information, interrogators could more skillfully elicit desired information. Using sociological and psychological data to assist interrogators in this manner does not constitute unethical behavior.

We encourage readers to become familiar with government policy changes brought about following the September 11 attacks (see, e.g., Bongar et al., 2007; Reams & Anglim, 2002; Rose, 2006) and to consider existence of legitimate and ethical roles for mental health professionals and behavioral scientists in support of national security. We take some solace in noting reports of mental health professionals who have spoken out against abuses witnessed at detention facilities (Miles, 2006). In addition, we strongly endorse ethical vigilance while relying on facts, as opposed to unconfirmed allegations, when attempting to reach conclusions about the actual behavior of the mental health and behavioral scientists involved. Many efforts to expand such dialogues have occurred, including a 16-hour "teach-in," "Ethics and Interrogations: Confronting the Challenge," at the APA's 2007 convention in San Francisco and development of a detailed commentary on the PENS report (Presidential Task Force on PENS, 2005) by the APA Ethics Committee.

School Systems

Schools come in all shapes and sizes: public and private, secular or religious, day or residential. Most American children are required by law to attend school and hence become subject to the powerful influence of the school as a socialization agent. Many psychologists, counselors, and other mental health professionals who practice in school settings hold master's degrees rather than doctorates. Some controversy in the practice of school psychology or counseling involves issues of competence, credentials, and professional control. We address questions of competence and qualifications in Chapter 4. We shall not rehash regulatory or professional disputes in school psychology here but instead focus on more specific types of ethical dilemmas in the schools that apply to all the mental health professionals working in school settings (Jacob & Hartshorne, 2003).

Many important issues of special ethical concern have come to light in school settings (Hansen, Green, & Kutner, 1989; Jacob & Hartshorne, 2003; Woody, 1989), including

- informed consent for assessment and intervention
- privacy and confidentiality (Kopels & Lindsey, 2006; A. Lewis & Porter, 2004; McDivitt, 2001; McGivern & Marquart, 2000; Nagy, 2005; Raines, 2004; Reamer, 2005)
- rights of children with disabilities (Jacob & Hartshorne, 2003; A. Lewis & Porter, 2004; Perrin, 1998)
- determination of classroom goals
- legitimacy of rewards and aversive controls in the classroom (Koocher, 1976)
- the use of the "time-out" as a potential type of abuse (Prilleltensky, 1991)

A survey of school psychology training directors suggests that the most common ethical violations among their students involve confidentiality, competence, and professional and academic honesty (Tryon, 2000). We also discuss the role of the school psychologist as "whistle-blower" (Bersoff, 2003).

Special problems for school-based mental health professionals also occur at the interface of ethics and the law. At times, laws bearing on mental health and educational issues may conflict (Jacob & Hartshorne, 2003). For example, FERPA (Family Educational Rights and Privacy Act, 1974), IDEA (Individuals With Disabilities Education Improvement Act of 2004, 2004), and related state laws give parents access to the relevant records as well as control over whether their child receives evaluations or special services. Suppose that the state also gives minors the right to independent access to drug counseling, sexually transmitted disease information, abortion advice, or psychotherapy? Which set of laws does the school psychologist obey? The next four cases raise, in a fashion somewhat exaggerated for emphasis, a sampling of the issues confronted regularly by school psychologists.

Case 18–17: International Psychometric Services was in the process of developing specialized norms for its high-school-level achievement tests for use in job classification assignments of new recruits by the military. They offered school systems the opportunity to have their senior classes evaluated on the instrument free of charge to establish an improved normative base. They also added some additional questions regarding "attitudes toward the military" to the instrument. These included some potentially sensitive questions, such as asking male students, "Have you registered with the selective service?" Schools were offered the service only if they would require all of their high school seniors to take the test. The director of psychological services at the Lakeville Unified School District accepted the offer.

This case illustrates the issues of informed consent and privacy with respect to testing. In particular, one wonders whether the answers to questions irrelevant to school functioning (i.e., draft registration information) would reach the military along with the student's name. If the school requires a student to take a test, compelling answers to such questions would constitute an invasion of privacy. It appears that the director of psychological services should carefully examine the intended uses of the test information before signing up for the program. In addition, the students should not be required to take the examination or otherwise provide personal data without appropriate informed consent relative to the nature of data to be collected, purpose of the program, and information regarding who will have access to it. We would assert that the school has no justification to waive these important personal rights of the students.

There is not much by way of actual case law on this type of situation, but at least one federal district court decision seems relevant. In the case of *Merriken v. Cressman* (1973), the American Civil Liberties Union represented the mother of a student who objected to an ill-conceived program intended to predict which junior high school students in Norristown, Pennsylvania might become drug or alcohol abusers. A "consent" form asking whether parents objected to the program was sent home. School authorities assumed that parental consent was granted if no objections were raised (Bersoff, 1983). Although the case raised many constitutional issues, the court specifically addressed the invasion of family privacy rights, finding in favor of Mrs. Merrikin acting on behalf of her son. The court noted, the children were "never given the opportunity to consent to the invasion of their privacy; only the opportunity to refuse consent by returning a blank questionnaire" (p. 919). The court also criticized the lack of "candor and honesty" on the part of the school system, comparing the so-called consent letter to a Book-of-the-Month Club solicitation (Bersoff, 1983). The question of the child's privacy rights above and beyond those asserted by his parent on his behalf were not clarified in this case; however, we would encourage colleagues to extend respect for privacy to child as well as adult clients.

Case 18–18: Jonathan Swift, M.Ed., gave a lecture on the use of time-out interventions to teachers and administrators at the Centerville Public

Schools, where he was employed as a school psychologist. Several weeks later, he discovered that a school principal had interpreted his talk as a license to lock misbehaving children in a darkened closet for up to an hour at a time.

When Mr. Swift gave his lecture on time-out practices, he never dreamed that it would result in misinterpretation and abuse. While the school principal was most directly responsible for the inappropriate intervention, Mr. Swift should have used warnings and cautions in an effort to avoid any misunderstanding. Ideally, Mr. Swift could have helped to formulate a school or systemwide policy on the use of time-out techniques and arranged for appropriate training or supervision of those authorized to use isolation strategies. As the expert presenting the information, Swift had the additional responsibility of presenting appropriate limitations or otherwise alerting the participants at the lecture on appropriate constraints.

Case 18–19: At the Farnsworth Elementary School, teachers have full access to a child's cumulative school record. Material of a personal nature entered in these records occasionally became a topic of conversation in the teacher's lounge. When school social worker Sylvia Caution, M.S.W., learned of this, she decided that she would no longer document any of her clinical observations in the record.

The case of the school record system highlights a variety of issues covered in Chapter 8 and well described specifically in the school confidentiality context by others (Bor, Ebner-Landy, Gill, & Brace, 2002; Glosoff & Pate, 2002; Jacob & Hartshorne, 2003; McDivitt, 2001; Moriya, 2006; Reamer, 2005). Sadly, Ms. Caution's response seems a bit overreactive. As discussed in Chapter 8, record entries must be considered with a balance of utility and the need to know. The teachers may not need to know that Johnny Smith was born prior to his parents' marriage, but it would clearly help Johnny if his teachers understood his tendency to withdraw socially when stressed. The circumstances of Johnny's birth add nothing to assist in the promotion of his educational progress, but information regarding a tendency toward social withdrawal might help a teacher reach out to him more effectively in the classroom. In any case, his parents have a right to know who within the school will have access to what information and have the option to give or withhold their consent. Ms. Caution should take some professional initiative in educating her colleagues about more appropriate treatment of confidential information, or she could take steps to limit access to records if necessary.

Case 18–20: Andrew Rigor, Ed.D., was frequently asked to assess "special needs children" in his role as a psychologist for the South Suburbia school system. When the special education budget began to show signs of strain, the superintendent instructed Dr. Rigor to administer shorter evaluations, produce briefer reports, and refrain from recommending additional services or evaluations for the children he assessed. The superintendent explained that these steps were needed to keep costs in line.

The case of Dr. Rigor applies increasingly to public school systems under pressure to control costs while also obligated under federal law (IDEA, 2004) to meet the needs of special students. It also applies to other nonschool institutions in which administrators without credentials in assessment may attempt to limit or modify professional standards as a way to meet institutional needs. In a case similar in some ways to Dr. Rigor's, although considerably more complex, the APA filed an amicus brief in support of a school psychologist attempting to cope with such pressures (APA, 1980).

Ideally, Dr. Rigor should vigorously resist any attempt to do less than a fully professional job on his assigned cases. He should stand willing to consider any reasonable administrative requests consistent with professional standards but should not compromise his integrity by providing less-than-adequate services (or violate legal obligations to report genuine student needs) to comply with administrative fiat. The difficulty, of course, falls to sorting out the appropriateness of each position and balancing one's integrity with threats of job loss or other retaliation (Glosoff & Pate, 2002; D. Lewis,

2006). In some circumstances, one may have to choose between a job and his or her conscience, but often a reasoned attempt at accommodation and a careful explanation of professional standards will bring less drastic formulas to bear on a solution.

The Criminal Justice System

We began this chapter with reference to the APA task force report on the ethics of psychological intervention in the criminal justice system (Monahan, 1980), and in Chapter 17 we discuss the role of mental health professionals in the courtroom. It seems appropriate, however, to dwell at least briefly on the broader role of mental health practitioners within the criminal justice system, including their work with criminal defendants, prison populations, and police agencies (Brodsky & Galloway, 2003; Dvoskin, Spiers, & Brodsky, 2007; Haag, 2006; Hartwig, Granhag, & Vrij, 2005; Porter, 2005; Walsh, 2003).

In each of these contexts, the critical route to successfully negotiating the complex ethical relationships involves carefully sorting out obligations to clients. This requires that the mental health professional give substantial forethought to the matter of duties owed different parties and spend sufficient time and energy clarifying the accompanying obligations, roles, expectations, and work conditions. When one can explicate ethical duties clearly in advance, a violation becomes much less likely, in part because the practitioner has anticipated potential problems and in part because the client has received appropriate cautions.

More than 2 million Americans sit incarcerated domestically, and except for the occasional exposé, their treatment remains hidden from most of society. Some have described the prevailing ideology of correctional administration as one that deemphasizes treatment or "corrections" and focuses attention on punishment, security, and custodial matters (Weinberger & Sreenivasan, 1994). Others noted that the choice of the word *corrections* implies the ability to change human behavior for the better in the punitive and sometimes rehabilitative institutions we call jails and prisons (Dvoskin, et al., 2007). Others asked whether we can truly instill a professional ethic for prison personnel given formal regulatory constraints and the nature of such institutions (Kipnis, 2001). The American Correctional Health Services Association (ACHSA) and the American Association for Correctional and Forensic Psychology (AACFP) have developed codes of ethics to provide mental health care professionals a clinician-derived guide for ethical clinical practice within correctional settings. These specialized codes complement existing general ethical principles in decision making for correctional mental health providers. The major foci of these codes include client welfare, informed consent, competence, dual relationships, confidentiality, and social responsibility (Bonner & Vande-Creek, 2006).

Mental health practitioners in correctional settings find themselves using their expertise to perform a wide range of duties. These might include evaluating and classifying inmates, conducting psychotherapy or crisis intervention, providing employee assistance, participating in the personnel selection process, and serving as consultants for institutional decisions and policies related to the correctional climate (Brandt, 2005; Lowman, 2006a). Similar concerns arise for correctional psychologists in Canada (Haag, 2006). Haag focused particular concerns from the Canadian Code of Ethics for Psychologists (Canadian Psychological Association, 2000), included in this volume as Appendix B, on the issues of who is the client, confidentiality, protection of psychological records, informed consent, assessment, corroboration, refusal of services, nondiscrimination, competence, knowledge of legal structure, accuracy and honesty, misuses of psychological information, and multiple relationships.

At the same time, research tells us that psychotherapy alone will not lower recidivism rates significantly (Ochipinti & Boston, 1987), leading some to assert that psychotherapists who work in correctional settings often serve only as "window dressing" (Weinberger & Sreenivasan, 1994, p. 166) and frequently do not provide meaningful clinical services. In support of their contention, Weinberger and Sreenivasan (1994) cited a Federal Bureau of Prisons' orientation program for new employees that focuses on correctional concepts, self-defense, and searching for contraband (among other topics). They cited case examples in which mental health professionals find themselves ordered to perform the duties of correctional officers during personnel shortages (i.e., contraband or pat-down searches in inmate cells), asked to undertake psychological testing with a specific goal of finding a reason to prolong incarceration, or asked to participate in disciplinary hearings. In addition, they described circumstances in which institutional staff with differing priorities and views may ignore or trivialize a clinician's legitimate therapeutic recommendations. They raised important and valid issues, but also appeared to paint all corrections systems with an overly broad brush. The common thread in the situations they described remains the difficulty faced by mental health specialists who work for departments of correction as opposed to those who work for administratively distinct mental health units.

The key ethical issues involve the degree to which a mental health professional's ethical standards and professional role become compromised by any given correctional setting. When working in such settings, practitioners do not become exempt from their ethical responsibilities. Prior to undertaking such employment, the wise mental health practitioner will carefully examine the expectations placed on them in the new job and raise any apparent conflicts with their superiors from the outset. To the extent that role expectations seem inconsistent with appropriate ethical standards, practitioners should make every effort to bring the role into conformity with their ethics code (APA 02: 1.02–1.03). If that is impossible, they should not agree to remain in the inappropriate role.

The next three cases represent classic ethical problems for the mental health professional in the criminal justice system. They are modified from material presented by Monahan (Monahan, 1980) and Vetter and Rieber (1980).

Case 18–21: Roberta Reason, Ph.D., often participates in the evaluation of criminal defendants as part of court-ordered determinations of their competence to stand trial. Defendants must usually

meet with her unaccompanied by their lawyers. When she begins to interview a woman
charged with the beating death of an infant, the
defendant complains, "If I don't talk to you, they'll
say I'm not cooperating, and I'll be in trouble. If I
do talk to you, I'll be losing my Fifth Amendment
rights."

The defendant who confronted Dr. Reason
quite accurately recognized the risks of her cooperation or noncooperation. We hope Dr.
Reason has thought through her role sufficiently
to guide the defendant. Dr. Reason might note,
"My job is to help determine whether you have
the ability to understand the charges against you
and their potential consequences, and that you
can cooperate in your own defense. You may
choose not to answer some of my questions if
you wish, but I shall try to focus them on matters
relative to your ability to assist your lawyer at the
trial. I do not want to discuss your guilt or innocence." Dr. Reason must clearly delineate for
herself and the defendant her role and responsibilities and must do her best to avoid an undue
invasion of privacy or placing her client at inappropriate legal risk.

Dr. Reason should also consult carefully
with the defense attorney and judge to ensure
issuance of proper protective orders that limit
access to her reports. Most courts that have
considered the problem have held that the Fifth
and Sixth Amendments prohibit admitting as
evidence information obtained during a competency evaluation. Some prosecutors might
seek to use such information as investigative
leads for delving further into or planning the
conduct of the case. Such use of Dr. Reason's
report would be ethically troubling.

Case 18–22: Andrew Penal, L.M.H.C., works at
the Stateville Prison Colony as a correctional
counselor. During an individual treatment session,
a new inmate reports that an escape attempt involving taking hostages will soon take place. Following this revelation, the client begs, "Please
don't tell anyone about this. If the other cons find
out I snitched, they'll kill me."

Mr. Penal now stands in a very difficult predicament. As noted in Chapter 8, a mental

health professional facing such a difficult decision might have an obligation to warn certain
potential victims, but Mr. Penal must also protect the rights and welfare of his client. Several
commentators reported a full range of conflicting views on what Mr. Penal should do (Brodsky,
1980; Brunswig & Parham, 2004; Dvoskin et al.,
2007), varying from upholding absolute confidentiality to the opinion that no such thing as
confidentiality exists in prison settings. In such
confinement, inmates/clients will often test the
therapist, particularly to determine whether they
can possibly trust the clinician. The reasons why
inmates seek treatment or consultation will vary
widely; these range from the traditional (e.g., "I
need psychological help") to the pragmatically
self-serving (e.g., "It will look good when I come
up for a parole hearing to have therapy on my
record here"). While we do not know enough
about the context to determine exactly which
options Mr. Penal has available, we can outline
the steps he should have considered prior to this
situation.

Mr. Penal should have clarified his legal and
professional obligations with prison authorities
relative to their expectations. If they expect him
to report all infractions of the rules, for example, he would need to evaluate his willingness
to work in that context. When beginning work
with inmates, Mr. Penal should also have clarified with each authority and inmate the limits
of his role and the nature of their relationship.
For example, will he honor every confidence?
Which confidences can he not respect? Do inmates have the right to ask that he not speak to
the parole board or that he clear with them in
advance what he would say? These few examples illustrate the questions that mental health
professionals should routinely raise. A mental
health practitioner should never surrender
professional integrity and standards to competing pressures of the work site. Each client has
the right to know the special constraints on, or
parameters of, the professional relationships
prior to entering it.

Case 18–23: George Cops, Psy.D., is a special
consultant to the Center City Police Department.
He is available on retainer to provide therapeutic
intervention to police officers under pressure from

job-related stress and especially to assist officers with their feelings following involvement in shootings resulting in a suspect's death. A newly appointed police chief has asked Dr. Cops to provide comments for the personnel files of the officers he has counseled.

Dr. Cops will hopefully advise the new chief of police that he must respect the confidentiality of the officers he is asked to treat as therapy clients, citing both professional standards and court rulings (*Jaffe v. Redmond*, 1996). If the chief wishes personnel selection advice, fitness for duty evaluations, or other consultation, that information should not come from the same person expected to provide an uncritical therapeutic role. In addition, the officers have the right to know in advance who will have access to and what use will be made of any data they provide (APA 02: 4.02). We have not raised the more complex situation regarding what Dr. Cops should do if an officer he counsels appears to be at some nonspecific but real risk for future behavior problems. The point at which Dr. Cops becomes responsible to report a "clear and immediate danger" becomes an important ethical problem he will have to address for himself. Ideally, we hope that Dr. Cops will have thought through and resolved these issues with the police department prior to accepting the job (Bartol & Bartol, 2006).

Community Agencies

A community agency, for purposes of this discussion, might include a government-funded community mental health center, a nonprofit community-run clinic, a municipal hospital, or some similar service delivery system. These facilities provide critically important community service resources but function in a politically reactive mode by their very nature (Backlar & Cutlar, 2002; Caldwell, Domahidy, Gilsinan, & Penick, 2000; Helbok, 2003; Melton, Levine, Koocher, Rosenthal, & Thompson, 1988; O'Neill, 2005; Riger, 1989; Serrano Garcia, 1994). They often depend on funding or regulatory support from local governments. Such agencies often have competing demands placed on them by various interests, and mental health

professionals working in these agencies are likewise subject to multiple demands that occasionally conflict (O'Neill, 1989, 2005). At times, these conflicts become significant ethical issues.

Joseph and Peele (1975) illustrated the particular problems presented by the fact that professionals in such settings serve both the community and their individual clients. The following two cases are adapted from their presentation:

Case 18–24: Tuff, a 14-year-old boy, found himself referred to a community agency by his mother and his school because of his unmanageable, hostile, and aggressive behavior. The assessment indicated that collateral treatment for both Tuff and his mother would provide the best chance for success. Although she initially agreed to the plan, Tuff's mother refused to keep appointments. She did not respond to information that the program would cease serving Tuff if she refused to participate. Ultimately, the program discharged Tuff because his mother would not cooperate in the treatment plan.

Case 18–25: The inpatient service of a community mental health center admitted Mrs. Morass for treatment of severe depression. Because she had abused her children, a protective services agency also became involved in her case. After a few weeks, her depression had improved sufficiently to warrant her discharge to outpatient treatment. Afraid that she would again harm her children, the protective service agency urged the mental health center to delay her discharge.

Joseph and Peele (1975) noted that the mental health professionals in both cases felt caught between two conflicting sets of duties. In Tuff's case, they had begun serving the young client but soon realized that their treatment plan could not work effectively without the support and involvement of his mother. Without maternal involvement, allowing Tuff to occupy a treatment slot might result in deprivation of services to some other client who might make more effective use of treatment. When Tuff's mother broke her initial participation contract, the clinic's obligation to Tuff was likewise ended.

In Mrs. Morass's case, a similar situation existed in terms of the allocation of scarce resources and effective cost control in community agencies. The mental health center had the obligation to provide the most effective and least restrictive treatment to their client, Mrs. Morass. Since she no longer required inpatient care, hospitalizing Mrs. Morass simply to serve the needs or convenience of another social agency, however laudable the goal, clearly violates professional ethics. The children's protective service agency had the obligation to provide necessary care for the children regardless of their mother's hospital status.

While other creative solutions might have existed in the cases of Tuff and Mrs. Morass, our attention focuses on how professionals may often find themselves caught between their appropriate concern for individual clients and concern for the community. Bureaucratic demands in such social welfare agencies can become overwhelming at times, and legislation intended to improve services may result in unrealistic expectations and frustrations. Sharfstein and Wolfe (1978) cited the example of a community mental health regulation that required centers to have a wide range of services operational within a limited amount of time if they hoped to obtain continued funding. The relatively inflexible rules did not take into consideration startup costs, redundant services in the community, components of desirable services, or adequacy of service levels.

Sometimes, mental health professionals at community agencies run into unusual issues as they attempt outreach work. One anecdote reported on an attempt to deliver home-based care services while a disabled client's dog barked and snarled, making the therapist quite anxious during the visit, as the client laughed (Knapp & Slattery, 2004). Other examples included requests for the therapist to babysit or assist with family chores.

Not surprisingly, some self-report studies of agency workers and administrators have suggested that the supremacy of agency needs over individual client needs may constitute the norm (Billingsley, 1984). As governmental budgets face cuts and as managed care constraints on private insurance and other revenue sources increase, clinics and mental health centers have come under continuing pressure to take direction from the bureaucracy regarding how to contain costs and serve clients. This will place substantial pressure on the value systems of practitioners working in community settings. Individual long-term psychotherapy will likely suffer as a service option in place of modes of treatment judged more cost-efficient. The only question is the degree to which clients' needs will be subordinated to their detriment (Backlar, 2002; Riger, 1989; Serrano Garcia, 1994). When the survival of the agency (or one's job) stands at stake, considerable intellectualization and rationalization becomes possible (O'Neill, 1989, 2005). Community mental health work and service in public social welfare agencies clearly forces mental health professionals in those settings to examine their values and motivations closely.

Business and Industry

Behavioral scientists and mental health professionals are often involved as participants in, or consultants to, businesses or industries. Their roles might include management consulting, personnel selection, organizational research, human factors applications, program evaluation, training, consumer psychology and advertising applications, public relations services, marketing studies, or even applying clinical skills to enhance the functioning of an organization and its executives. The ethical difficulties such professionals face in business settings derive both from the special demands of their particular role and from the fact that the ethics of mental health professionals and the ethics of business often seem incongruent.

We refocus on the basic question: Who is the client? This point forms a repeating theme in widely read books and articles on the ethics of the industrial or organizational practitioner (Brady & Hart, 2006; Fuqua & Newman, 2006; Ilgen & Bell, 2001; Jones, Felps, & Bigley, 2007; Lefkowitz, 2003; Lowman, 2006b; Newman & Fuqua, 2006). The notion of the consultant's seduction by the pressures of the industry or the marketplace, with resulting severe role conflicts, is hardly a new issue (APA Task Force on the Practice of Psychology in Industry, 1971). Most ethical complaints against mental health and behavioral science experts arising in business settings deal with a practitioner's responsibility to his or her client or assessment, advertising, or marketing issues. Often, one senses that the psychologist or other behavioral or mental health consultant in the business world who becomes the object of a complaint may have become a servant of economic power or may have lost some focus on human values compared to those of productivity and the company.

Case 18–26: Hardy Driver has been a member of the management team at Western Bolt and Wrench Corporation for the past 6 years. He has become lead candidate for promotion to the chief operating officer position in the company, and the human resources office has referred him to the company psychologist for an evaluation as part of the final selection process. Driver knows that he can refuse to participate in the evaluation but probably would lose the promotion in that case. He worries about what sort of personal information revealed in the evaluation might fall into the hands of others in the company.

The situation involving Mr. Driver occurs frequently. London and Bray (1980) discussed the issue of predicating a promotion on a psychological assessment in detail. Psychologists conducting such assessments (see Chapter 9) understand the problem well (Lefkowitz, 2003; Lowman, 2006b). The evaluator involved will hopefully recognize the vulnerability of Mr. Driver as well as the legitimate needs and rights of Western Bolt and Wrench. The company has a right to screen its applicants using reliable and valid assessment tools. Driver knows that he has the right to refuse participation, just as the company has the right to pass him over should he do so. One assumes that the evaluator will carefully discuss these issues with Driver, including the nature of the assessment, type of report planned, and the likely uses of the report, including access issues. Driver, for example, may fear that some personality inadequacy

come to light and become widely circulated in the company, when in fact the planned assessment does not include personality assessment tools. Driver also has a right to know in advance whether he will have access to the report, test data, debriefing, and so on. In summary, Mr. Driver has the right to fully informed consent regarding the nature of the planned evaluation before he decides to participate. The evaluator should recognize this and provide Driver with ample information to assist him in making his decision.

Case 18–27: Because of declining sales linked to an economic recession, the Paragon Electronics Corporation plans to lay off several hundred workers. The company wants to attempt a modification of its union contract and base the layoffs on employee productivity rather than seniority, as the union's contract specifies. They ask their corporate psychologist to prepare a detailed memorandum that cites research data to support their position. They have no interest in contrary data and in fact would prefer that the psychologist not mention any that might exist. Headquarters also wants a detailed plan for assessing the productivity of its workers to fit these needs.

The Paragon Electronics case raises the use of research as an influence strategy (Ilgen & Bell, 2001; Lefkowitz, 2003; Lowman, 2006b; Purcell et al., 1974) but does so in a manner that implies a one-sided bias. Many business executives firmly believe that corporate self-interest is inexorably involved in the well-being of the society or, as Charles Wilson put it long ago, "What's good for GM is good for the country" (Purcell et al., 1974, p. 441). Many businesses find nothing wrong in asserting their best interests using all legal means available; they rationalize that they ultimately help society and the economy. Economic success does not require intellectual or scientific honesty in many cases, and total scientific honesty might not help (or even harm) the business in some instances. Assuming that data exist to support the company's position, that valid assessment of productivity can occur, and that laying off employees who do not perform well is desirable, has the psychologist who found the data and conducted the assessment behaved ethically in applying it? The answer is probably yes, as long as in doing so the psychologist did not ignore or conceal meaningful contrary data.

Case 18–28: Bozo Pharmaceutical Industries sells over-the-counter "natural food" diet aids. They have developed a new diet, known as Kelp Power, based on seaweed extracts. The company approached a consumer psychologist to work as a consultant in devising a marketing survey and advertising plan. Bozo Industries offered a substantial fee plus a bonus based on the ultimate effectiveness of the program in boosting sales. When the consultant asks about data on the product to incorporate in the project, she discovers that no evidence exists to support claims that the product actually helps in dieting. While not harmful, the Kelp Power formula has shown no documented benefits.

How about the ethics of overlooking misleading public statements as long as the lies are benign? That question forms the heart of the Bozo Pharmaceutical case. Any marketing plan would, at the very least, focus on making the public believe that Kelp Power could help them lose weight. The consultant might reason that the product will not actually hurt anyone or that placebo effects might actually help some people. Does that constitute a sufficient ethical basis for assisting in the promotion of an ineffective product? We would argue that providing support for this product's marketing constitutes unethical behavior, although this would prove difficult to establish as an ethics case. As described earlier in this chapter, the psychologist in this consulting role would have little public visibility (Koocher, 2007), and an ethics complaint most likely would not occur as an idea to the parties who had firsthand knowledge of the otherwise invisible professional activity.

Case 18–29: Manny Jobs, Psy.D., works as an industrial psychologist assigned to a job-enrichment program aimed at improving the quality of life, and hence quality of work, among assembly line workers at Amalgamated Motors. After a careful job analysis, many hours of interviews, and considerable effort, Dr. Jobs produced a report

with many potentially useful suggestions. Management thanked him and shelved the report, which they regarded as "ahead of its time." Dr. Jobs felt frustrated that his efforts and the potential benefits he had conceptualized went ignored and toyed with the idea of leaking the report to union negotiators prior to the next round of contract talks.

The Amalgamated Motors case presents another set of complex and conflicting needs. Amalgamated Motors wanted information and ideas but was not necessarily prepared to act on them. Dr. Jobs feels angry that his hard work has seemingly been wasted, although Amalgamated Motors paid him paid, and his client, the company, seems satisfied. Does he have the right to violate his duty of confidentiality to the client corporation by revealing information to the unions? Dr. Jobs might argue "society's interests are at stake," but he has an obligation to respect the proprietary rights of his employer as long as it is possible to do so and still maintain standards of ethical practice (Ilgen & Bell, 2001; Lefkowitz, 2003; London & Bray, 1980; Lowman, 2006b).

Medical Settings

It will come as no surprise to the thousands of mental health professionals at work in medical settings that behavioral and medical care providers do not always speak the same language. A degree of mutual education and, implicitly, a willingness to learn are required for any mental health professional planning to work in such settings. One must, for example, acquire a new lexicon of terminology that may seem paradoxical (e.g., a "progressive disease" is one that gets worse and "positive findings" are a bad sign when discovered during a physical examination). Knowledge of physical illnesses, their symptoms, and treatments as well as an understanding of how medical hospitals (as distinct from mental hospitals, community mental health centers, or college counseling services) will prove very important.

Mental health practitioners in medical settings also must remain keenly aware of their expertise and its limitations. These include interdisciplinary collaboration in outpatient settings, maintaining competencies (Tovian, 2006), and attending to issues in hospital practice related to confidentiality (Robinson & Baker, 2006) and the Health Insurance Portability and Accountability Act (HIPAA) (Benefield, Ashkanazi, & Rozensky, 2006). Many medical conditions can present in ways that suggest psychopathology, and having a medical degree does not insure against diagnostic errors. Some physicians seem at times too willing to see physical complaints as psychological, and some mental health practitioners seem all too eager to go along with them. Although the following case is unusual, it provides an important illustration.

Case 18–30: Teri Slim found herself referred to a major pediatric teaching hospital for the treatment of anorexia nervosa. She had always been petite and slender, but seemed unusually thin to her father just prior to her 14th birthday. She underwent medical evaluation at a large hospital near her home, and the staff referred her to the specialized pediatric hospital for treatment. The admission team at the second hospital confirmed the diagnosis of anorexia and admitted Teri to their Psychosomatic Unit for treatment. The hospital staff easily identified family stressors that might account for Teri's emotional problems. Her parents had recently divorced; her father had lost his job as business executive; and her mother, who lived in another state, allegedly had a serious addiction problem. At the end of 2 months of treatment, Teri remained malnourished and had made "no progress" in treatment. The staff contemplated initiating intravenous feeding in the face of her progressive weight loss. They prepared to transfer Teri to the surgical ward for placement of a venous feeding line. Only then did a senior pediatrician sent to screen her for transfer ask, "Has anyone evaluated her for Crohn's disease?" Several weeks later, Teri went home from the hospital minus a segment of inflamed intestine and taking anti-inflammatory medication. She continued to do well in response to the treatment for Crohn's disease.

Teri Slim had twice been evaluated by physicians outstanding in their field, and her care took place under continual supervision by well-trained psychiatrists slow to diagnose her physical illness and quick to refer her to an inpatient psychiatric treatment program. Crohn's disease does present diagnostic challenges, but so do a host of other medical problems, ranging from neurological disorders to endocrine problems, that seem to manifest themselves chiefly through symptoms that might mistakenly be regarded as psychological (e.g., hallucinations, aberrant behavior, appetite loss, agitation, and mood swings). Successful diagnosis and treatment of such patients requires a close, collaborative, and collegial relationship that includes good integration of social, psychological, and medical care.

Typically, mental health professionals working in medical settings will be employed under the supervision of physicians (e.g., in departments of psychiatry or pediatrics). At other times, they may be administratively organized in a separate department (e.g., medical psychology, social work, or family services). Wherever they work, mental health professionals must take care not to surrender their professional integrity or standards.

Case 18–31: Bertram Botch, M.D., served as the chief of neurology at a pediatric hospital and often chaired interdisciplinary case conferences. Reporting on her assessment of a low-functioning mentally retarded child, Melissa Meek, Ph.D., presented her detailed findings in descriptive terms. Dr. Botch listened to her presentation and asked for the child's IQ. When Dr. Meek replied that the instruments used were developmental indices that did not yield IQ scores, Dr. Botch demanded that she compute a specific IQ score to use in his preferred report format.

Case 18–32: After sitting in on some lectures that Ralph Worthy, Psy.D., was giving to a group of medical students in regard to projective testing, the chief of medicine called him in to set up a workshop on the topic for medical residents. The chief told Worthy that he thought it would be a good idea to teach the residents how to use "those tests" and assumed that it could be done in "a half-dozen meetings or so."

We hope that Drs. Meek and Worthy will not yield to the pressures described. Meek could politely, but firmly, attempt to educate Dr. Botch with respect to the inappropriateness of attempting to produce an IQ score in the situation. She can perhaps help to identify estimated ranges of scores or find other terms useful and meaningfully appropriate for his report, but she should not feel coerced or bullied into contriving the digits Dr. Botch seems to want.

Likewise, we hope Dr. Worthy will attempt to educate his chief regarding the nature of personality assessment and the inappropriateness of thinking that six lectures will enable anyone to use such techniques competently. He might explain that knowledge of personality theory, abnormal behavior, psychotherapeutic interventions, and psychometrics all play integral roles in using use these tools effectively.

These situations may, of course, generalize to any context in which one's employer does not understand the applicable theory and practice or a cooperative team effort is required for effective and successful work. Mental health professionals must take the lead in defining the appropriate role for their services. They must also remain prepared to recognize and uphold appropriate professional standards.

Independent Practice

Over 30 years ago, Taylor (1978) presented the idealized portrayal of the independent practitioner as living a life of luxury and self-indulgence, working less than full time for $60 an hour treating only movie stars, the wives of corporate executives, and a few high-level bureaucrats. At least that was the fantasy or myth of the independent practitioner's lot prior to the advent of managed care (Appelbaum, 1992; Lewin, 1974; Taylor, 1978). Rumors still persist that such independent practitioners are out there, although we never seem to meet any of them.

The realities of independent practice are far less alluring today than the fantasies of the past might suggest. The $60 rate that seemed impressive in 1978 would translate to approximately $193 in 2006 dollars when corrected for inflation (see Chapter 7). Conversely, the typical reimbursement rate for an hour of psycho-

therapy paid by Blue Shield in Boston, Massachusetts, in 2007 (approximately $100) translates to a 1978 value of just over $31. The vicissitudes of dealing with managed care plans (e.g., gaining access to provider panels, incremental documentation of service needs, requests for additional sessions, reduced payments, etc.) have also made the small-business management of an independent practice far more demanding. In many ways, individual and small-group independent practices have become more taxing than the work of mental health professionals at larger agencies, clinics, or hospitals. True, the independent practitioner is his or her own boss, but that must be balanced with overhead costs, employee relations (e.g., with a receptionist, answering service, etc.), backup coverage, billing, advertising, and a host of other mundane, but necessary, chores. In addition, a kind of professional loneliness can afflict the independent practitioner, especially when isolated in a small office with no easy access to colleagues (Appelbaum, 1992).

Little has been written on the ethical problems faced by the independent practitioner, although a number of the examples cited throughout this volume certainly apply. The greatest problem in the ethical sense is probably related to the fact that the independent practitioner must be both a professional and an entrepreneur to survive, roles that are not always congruent (Appelbaum, 1992; Bennett, 2005; Hixson, 2004; Mikalac, 2005). In addition, the absence of peer collaborators may lead to less social comparison of a professional nature and a resulting failure to always think carefully about the manner in which one practices or manages cases.

The independent practitioner who may have an administrative assistant or other employees who require careful supervision generally does not have the luxury of paid vacations or sick days and is far more susceptible to the mundane case management headaches of working with emotionally troubled people (e.g., the client who does not pay bills or often fails to keep scheduled appointments). The material in this volume that deals with psychotherapy, managed care, advertising of services, higher risks for inappropriate role blending, and employee relations all applies directly to the independent practitioner. However, some unique ethical problems also come up from time to time.

Case 18–33: Napoleon Solo, M.S.W., practiced psychotherapy on his own in a private office. An automobile accident disabled him for a period of 3 months. During that time, no coverage was available for any of his clients.

We hope Mr. Solo had the foresight to take out adequate disability and office overhead insurance to cover his personal financial needs during the recovery period. He apparently did not consider any means of providing backup for his clients, however, and clearly had no ability to do so easily from his hospital bed. Depending on the clients' individual needs, this could present a serious ethical oversight.

In the next case, Dr. Taylor's account of his humorous experience (Taylor, 1978) illustrates that the independent practitioner never knows precisely what to expect when a prospective client comes through the door.

Case 18–34: A young woman appeared in the office of Robert Taylor, Ph.D. Dr. Taylor noted that she seemed to become increasingly uneasy with the surroundings and the direction of his questions. Finally, she interrupted and made the red-faced confession that she had thought she had made an appointment at a gynecologist's office.

The therapist must prepare to evaluate each client and recognize that he or she may not be the sort of person the client really seeks for or needs and must stand ready to make appropriate referrals as needed (Appelbaum, 1992).

Pastoral Counseling

Pastoral counseling presents some unique work-setting issues for several reasons; not the least of these is widely varying training. Some members of the clergy are trained as psychologists, psychiatrists, and social workers. Others receive minimal pastoral counseling training that integrates basic counseling skills with religious and moral philosophy content (Dueck, 1987; Erde, Pomerantz, Saccocci, Kramer-Feeley, &

Cavalieri, 2006; Foskett, 1992; Merrill & Trathen, 2003; Richards & Bergin, 2005) but no training in professional ethics for psychological or psychotherapeutic practice (Bleiberg & Skufca, 2005; Miller & Atkinson, 1988). Still others have little or no formal training in psychodiagnostics or psychotherapy and focus chiefly on a religious or spiritually based approach. The problem is well illustrated by a guidebook, intended for "Christian counselors of all sorts," *Counselor's Guide to the Brain and Its Disorders: Knowing the Difference Between Disease and Sin* (Welch, 1991). The volume attempts to explain the functions of the brain, organic and functional psychopathological disorders, and issues of moral responsibility from a framework that is "thoroughly biblical." One chapter discusses "The No. 1 Culprit: Licit and Illicit Drugs." Overall, the general standards and orientation of pastoral counseling, as a field, are far less rigorous than graduate training for psychotherapeutic practice (Bleiberg & Skufca, 2005; Erde et al., 2006; Richards & Bergin, 2005).

Some dilemmas follow: What options does a pastor have if a parishioner's right to confidentiality and self-determination conflict with the goals of their church? What happens if, during a counseling session, a married elder divulges having an affair with the organist? What if a board member reports alcoholism and spousal abuse? Merrill and Trathen thoughtfully addressed these and other multiple-role conflicts that confront pastoral counselors in church-based settings (2003).

Other issues arise when the client or counselor fails to clearly delineate roles between the pastoral function and more secular psychodiagnostic or psychotherapeutic needs (Craig, 1991; Miller & Atkinson, 1988). We agree with the viewpoint that clergy trained as psychotherapists should not attempt to function in both roles for the same clients.

Case 18–35: An ethics committee received a complaint from George Gothic, whose psychotherapist, Reverend Dan Damien, D.Min., was both an ordained minister and a licensed psychologist. Dr. Damien had recommended that Gothic undergo an exorcism to relieve his emotional distress. Gothic had taken offense and described Dr. Damien as "a quack in preacher's clothing." When approached for an explanation by the ethics committee, Dr. Damien explained that he knew Gothic needed such treatment because, "His face contorts in a gargoyle like tic whenever God is mentioned." When questioned further on the validity of his diagnosis, Damien denounced the members of the ethics committee as "a bunch of Godless heretics."

The ethics committee had serious questions about Dr. Damien's competence as a psychotherapist but could not pursue their investigation adequately when he ceased replying to their inquiries. As a result, he was expelled from the organization for not responding.

Case 18–36: Simon Shifty, L.M.F.T., found himself called before a licensing board for failure to report child abuse as mandated under state law. Dr. Shifty, who was also an ordained minister, had provided family therapy to a couple who regularly and severely beat their children with leather straps for perceived religious infractions. The case came to public attention when one of the badly beaten children collapsed at school. Dr. Shifty had known about the beatings and about the mandated reporter status of licensed marriage and family therapists in his state but explained to the licensing board that clergy were not covered by that statute because of the constitutional separation of church and state.

The licensing board was not impressed by Dr. Shifty's constitutional argument. The board noted that he was functioning as a licensed marriage and family therapist, not a member of the clergy, when performing family therapy, as evidenced by his clinical case notes and bills to the family's health insurer. The board noted that he could not be functioning simultaneously with one set of clients as both a spiritual counselor and licensed psychologist.

SUMMARY AND GUIDELINES

Each work setting has unique aspects, although those discussed here present special challenges for the mental health practitioner or behavioral scientist. The key issue common across settings involves the need to remain mindful of the ethical duties owed to differing categories and levels of clients. By focusing on the welfare of the most vulnerable parties in a client hierarchy, a practitioner should be able to determine the most appropriate ethical course of action.

Some other basic guidelines include the following:

1. When entering a new work setting for the first time, mental health professionals must familiarize themselves with the special needs and demands of the job. This includes consulting with colleagues about the ethical pressures and problems unique to that type of work setting.

2. In complex service delivery or consultation systems, the usual professional–client relationship may become blurred. Professionals should take the lead in defining their roles and obligations to each level of client served. In addition, the practitioner should clarify role expectations with all relevant parties from the outset of professional contact.

3. A mental health professional is never exempted from any portion of their association's ethics code by virtue of an employer's dictum.

4. The matter of whether to work for reform within an unethical institution or whether to "blow the whistle" in public often becomes a matter of personal judgment and one's conscience. A mental health professional should not, however, cooperate as a party to unethical behavior. In addition, we must carefully consider any duty of confidentiality owed to a client (including a client organization) before making public disclosures about that client.

5. When a special work setting demands special qualifications or competencies, mental health professionals should be exceptionally careful to meet these standards prior to beginning work in that context. Consultation with colleagues experienced in the specialized setting will often prove the best way to make that assessment.

6. When mental health professionals have trained in another profession (e.g., health

care provider and member of the clergy), they must clearly delineate for themselves and explain to their clients the professional capacity in which they are providing services.

References

Allen, J. P., Chatelier, P., Clark, H. J., & Sorenson, R. (1982). Behavioral science in the military: Research trends for the 80s. *Professional Psychology, 13,* 918–929.

American Psychological Association. (1980). *Amicus brief in Forrest v. Ambach.* Retrieved February 1, 2007, from http://www.apa.org/psyclaw/forrest.html

American Psychological Association Task Force on the Practice of Psychology in Industry. (1971). Effective practice of psychology in industry. *American Psychologist, 26,* 974–991.

Appelbaum, S. A. (1992). Evils in the private practice of psychotherapy. *Bulletin of the Menninger Clinic, 56,* 141–149.

Backlar, P., & Cutler, D. L. (Eds.). (2002). *Ethics in community mental health care: Commonplace concerns.* New York: Kluwer Academic/Plenum.

Bartol, C. R., & Bartol, A. M. (2006). History of forensic psychology. In I. B. Weiner & A. K. Hess (Eds.), *The handbook of forensic psychology,* (3rd ed., pp. 3–27). Hoboken, NJ: Wiley.

Behnke, S. (2006). Psychological ethics and national security: The position of the American Psychological Association. *European Psychologist, 11,* 153–155.

Benefield, H., Ashkanazi, G., & Rozensky, R. H. (2006). Communication and records: HIPPA issues when working in health care settings. *Professional Psychology, 37,* 273–277.

Bennett, M. I. (2005). Obtaining reimbursement for outpatient services from managed and unmanaged insurance: Principles and procedures. In J. A. Lazarus (Ed.), *Entering private practice: A handbook for psychiatrists* (pp. 77–101). Washington, DC: American Psychiatric.

Bersoff, D. N. (1983). Children as participants in psychoeducational assessment. In G. B. Melton, G. P. Koocher, & M. J. Saks (Eds.), *Children's competence to consent* (pp. 149–178.). New York: Plenum.

Bersoff, D. N. (2003). *Ethical conflicts in psychology* (3rd ed.). Washington, DC: American Psychological Association.

Biaggio, M., Orchard, S., Larson, J., Petrino, K., & Mihara, R. (2003). Guidelines for gay/lesbian/bisexual-affirmative educational practices in graduate psychology programs. *Professional Psychology, 34,* 548–554.

Billingsley, K. R. (1984). Critical decisions in survey/feedback designs. *Group and Organizational Studies, 1,* 448–453.

Bleiberg, J. R., & Skufca, L. (2005). Clergy dual relationships, boundaries, and attachment. *Pastoral Psychology, 54,* 3–22.

Bobo, W. V., Keller, R. T., Greenberg, N., Alfonzo, C. A., Pastor, L. H., Grieger, T. A., et al. (2006). Psychological responses to terrorism. In T. Britt, A. B. Adler, & C. A. Castro (Eds.), *Military life: The psychology of serving in peace and combat. Vol. 1: Military performance* (pp. 31–60). Westport, CT: Praeger Security International.

Bongar, B., Brown, L. M., Beutler, L. E., Breckenridge, J. N., & Zimnardo, P. G. (Eds.). (2007). *Psychology of terrorism.* New York: Oxford University Press.

Bonner, R., & Vandecreek, L. D. (2006). Ethical decision making for correctional mental health providers. *Criminal Justice and Behavior, 33,* 542–564.

Bor, R., Ebner-Landy, J., Gill, S., & Brace, C. (2002). *Counseling in schools.* Thousand Oaks, CA: Sage.

Brady, F. N., & Hart, D. W. (2006). An aesthetic theory of conflict in administrative ethics. *Administration & Society, 38,* 113–134.

Brandt, S. M. (2005). Correctional psychology: Looking beyond the bars. In R. D. Morgan, T. L. Kuther, & C. J. Habben (Eds.), *Life after graduate school in psychology: Insider's advice from new psychologists* (pp. 151–165). New York: Psychology Press.

Brodsky, S. L. (1980). Ethical issues for psychologists in corrections. In J. Monahan (Ed.), *Who is the client: The ethics of psychological intervention in the criminal justice system* (pp. 63–92). Washington, DC: American Psychological Association.

Brodsky, S. L., & Galloway, V. A. (2003). Ethical and professional demands for forensic mental health professionals in the post-Atkins era. *Ethics & Behavior, 13,* 3–9.

Brunswig, K. A., & Parham, R. W. (2004). Psychology in a secure setting. In W. T. O'Donohue & E. R. Levensky (Eds.), *Handbook of forensic psychology: Resource for mental health and legal professionals.* (pp. 851–871). New York: Elsevier Science.

Caldwell, K., Domahidy, M., Gilsinan, J. F., & Penick, M. (2000). Applied ethics for preparing interprofessional practitioners in community settings. *Ethics & Behavior, 10,* 257–269.

Camp, N. M. (1993). The Vietnam war and the ethics of combat psychiatry. *American Journal of Psychiatry, 150,* 1000–1010.

Canadian Psychological Association (Ed.). (2000). *Canadian code of ethics for psychologists* (3rd ed.). Ottawa, Ontario: Canadian Psychological Association.

Cotton, P. (1990). Tobacco foes attack ads that target women, minorities, teens and the poor. *Journal of the American Medical Association, 264,* 1505.

Craig, J. D. (1991). Preventing dual relationships in pastoral counseling. *Pastoral Psychology, 36,* 49–54.

Crawford, M. P. (1970). Military psychology and general psychology. *American Psychologist, 25,* 328–336.

DeLeon, P. H. (2002). Presidential reflections—Past and future. *American Psychologist, 57,* 425–430.

DeLeon, P. H. (2006). Involvement in shaping public policy. In G. D. Oster (Ed.), *Life as a psychologist: Career choices and insights* (pp. 46–47). Westport, CT: Praeger.

Dueck, A. (1987). Ethical contexts of healing: Peoplehood and righteousness. *Pastoral Psychology, 35,* 239–253.

Dvoskin, J. A., Spiers, E. M., & Brodsky, S. L. (2007). Correctional psychology: Law, ethics, and practice. In A. M. Goldstein (Ed.), *Forensic psychology: Emerging topics and expanding roles* (pp. 605–632). Hoboken, NJ: Wiley.

Erde, E., Pomerantz, S. C., Saccocci, M., Kramer-Feeley, V., & Cavalieri, T. A. (2006). Privacy and patient–clergy access: Perspectives of patients admitted to hospital. *Journal of Medical Ethics, 32,* 298–402.

Family Education Rights and Privacy Act, 34 C.F.R. Part 99 C.F.R. (1974).

Finkel, N. J. (2006). Moral monsters and patriot acts: Rights and duties in the worst of times. *Psychology, Public Policy, and Law, 12,* 242–277.

Foskett, J. (1992). Ethical issues in counseling and pastoral care. *British Journal of Guidance and Counseling, 20,* 39–50.

Fuqua, D. R., & Newman, J. L. (2006). Moral and ethical issues in human systems. *Consulting Psychology Journal: Practice and Research, 58,* 206–215.

Gelles, M. G., McFadden, R., Borum, R., & Vossekuil, B. (2006). Al-Qaeda-related subjects: A law enforcement perspective. In T. Williamson (Ed.), *Investigative interviewing: Rights, research, regulation* (pp. 23–41). Annandale, NSW, Australia: Federation Press.

Glosoff, H. L., & Pate, R. H. (2002). Privacy and confidentiality in school counseling. *Professional School Counseling, 6,* 20–27.

Haag, A. M. (2006). Ethical dilemmas faced by correctional psychologists in Canada. *Criminal Justice and Behavior, 33,* 93–109.

Hansen, J. C., Green, S., & Kutner, K. B. (1989). Ethical issues facing school psychologists working with families. Professional School Psychology. *Professional School Psychology, 4,* 245–255.

Hartwig, M., Granhag, P. R. A., & Vrij, A. (2005). Police interrogation from a social psychology perspective. *Policing & Society, 15,* 379–399.

Helbok, C. M. (2003). The practice of psychology in rural communities: Potential ethical dilemmas. *Ethics & Behavior, 13,* 367–384.

Hixson, R. R. (2004). The business of therapy. *Annals of the American Psychotherapy Association, 7,* 16–21.

Ilgen, D. R., & Bell, B. S. (2001). Conducting industrial and organizational psychological research: Institutional review of research in work organizations. *Ethics & Behavior, 11,* 395–412.

Individuals With Disabilities Education Improvement Act of 2004, Pub. L. 108-446 (2004).

Jacob, S., & Hartshorne, T. S. (2003). *Ethics and law for school psychologists* (4th ed.). New York: Wiley.

Jaffe v. Redmond, 116 95 266, 264L.W. 4490 (S. Ct. 1996).

Jeffrey, T. B., Rankin, R. J., & Jeffrey, L. K. (1992). In service of two masters: The ethical–legal dilemma faced by military psychologists. *Professional Psychology, 23,* 91–95.

Johnson, S. C. (1998). Forensic evaluation Name: KACZYNSKI, Theodore John, dated January 16, 1998. Retrieved June 2, 2007, from http://www.courttv.com/trials/unabomber/documents/psychological.html

Johnson, W. B. (1995). Perennial ethical quandaries in military psychology: Toward American Psychological Association–Department of Defense collaboration. *Professional Psychology, 26*, 281–287.

Johnson, W. B., & Buhrke, R. A. (2006). Service delivery in a "Don't ask, don't tell" world: Ethical care of gay, lesbian, and bisexual military personnel. *Professional Psychology, 37*, 91–98.

Johnson, W. B., Ralph, J., & Johnson, S. J. (2005). Managing multiple roles in embedded environments: The case of aircraft carrier psychology. *Professional Psychology, 36*, 73–81.

Johnson, W. B., & Wilson, K. (1993). The military internship: A retrospective analysis. *Professional Psychology, 24*, 312–318.

Jones, T. M., Felps, W., & Bigley, G. A. (2007). Ethical theory and stakeholder-related decisions: The role of stakeholder culture. *Academy of Management Review, 32*, 137–155.

Joseph, D. I., & Peele, R. (1975). Ethical issues in community psychiatry. *Hospital and Community Psychiatry, 26*, 295–299.

Kelley, C. R. (1971). In defense of military psychology. *American Psychologist, 26*, 541–515.

Kimmel, P. R., & Stout, C. E. (2006). *Collateral damage: The psychological consequences of America's war on terrorism.* Westport, CT: Praeger/Greenwood Publishing Group.

Kipnis, K. (2001). Health care in the correctional setting: An ethical analysis. In J. Kleinig & M. L. Smith (Eds.), *Discretion, community, and correctional ethics* (pp. 113–124). Lanham, MD: Rowman & Littlefield.

Klaidman, D., Taylor, S., & Thomas, E. (2006, February 6). Palace Revolt. *Newsweek*, 35–40.

Knapp, S., & Slattery, J. M. (2004). Professional boundaries in nontraditonal settings. *Professional Psychology, Research and Practice, 35*, 553–558.

Koocher, G. P. (1976). Civil liberties and aversive conditioning for children. *American Psychologist, 31*, 94–95.

Koocher, G. P. (2007). Twenty first century ethical challenges for psychology. *American Psychologist, 62*, 375–384.

Kopels, S., & Lindsey, B. C. (2006). The complexity of confidentiality in schools today: The school social worker context. *School Social Work Journal, 31* (Special Issue), 63–78.

Lasser, J. S., & Gottlieb, M. C. (2004). Treating patients distressed regarding their sexual orientation: Clinical and ethical alternatives. *Professional Psychology, 35*, 194–200.

Lazarus, A. A., & Zur, O. (2002). *Dual relationships and psychotherapy.* New York: Springer.

Lefkowitz, J. (2003). *Ethics and values in industrial–organizational psychology.* Mahwah, NJ: Erlbaum.

Leuba, C. (1971). Military are essential. *American Psychologist, 26*, 515.

Lewin, M. H. (1974). Diaries of the private practitioner: Secrets revealed. *Professional Psychology, 5*, 234–236.

Lewis, A., & Porter, J. (2004). Interviewing children and young people with learning disabilities: Guidelines for researchers and multi-professional practice. *British Journal of Learning Disabilities, 32*, 191–197.

Lewis, D. (2006). The contents of whistleblowing/confidential reporting procedures in the UK: Some lessons from empirical research. *Employee Relations, 28*, 76–86.

London, M., & Bray, D. W. (1980). Ethical issues in testing and evaluation for personnel decisions. *American Psychologist, 35*, 890–901.

Lowman, R. L. (2006a). Case 6. Personnel screening for emotional stability. In R. L. Lowman (Ed.), *The ethical practice of psychology in organizations* (2nd ed., pp. 23–26). Washington, DC: American Psychological Association.

Lowman, R. L. (Ed.). (2006b). *The ethical practice of psychology in organizations* (2nd ed.). Washington, DC: American Psychological Association.

McDivitt, K. L. (2001). Ethics in group work with children and adolescents. *Dissertation Abstracts International, 61* (12-A), 4673 (UMI No. AA19999874).

McGivern, J. E. M., & Marquart, A. M. (2000). Legal and ethical issues in child and adolescent assessment. In E. S. Shapiro & T. R. Kratochwill (Eds.), *Behavioral assessment in schools: Theory, research, and clinical foundations* (2nd ed., pp. 387–434). New York: Guilford Press.

Melton, G. B., Levine, R. J., Koocher, G. P., Rosenthal, R., & Thompson, W. C. (1988). Community consultation in socially sensitive research: Lessons from clinical trials of treatments for AIDS. *American Psychologist, 43*, 573–581.

Merriken v. Cressman, 913 E.D. Pa (1973), 364 913 (E.D. Pa. 1973).

Merrill, T. H., & Trathen, D. W. (2003). Dual role relationships: Toward a greater understanding in the church-based setting. *Marriage and Family: A Christian Journal, 6*, 69–77.

Mikalac, C. M. (2005). *Money and outpatient psychiatry: Practical guidelines from accounting to ethics*. New York: Norton.

Miles, S. (2006). *Oath betrayed: Torture, medical complicity, and the war on terror*. New York: Random House

Miller, H. M., & Atkinson, D. R. (1988). The clergy person as counselor: An inherent conflict of interest. *Counseling and Values, 32*, 116–123.

Monahan, J. (Ed.). (1980). *Who is the client? The ethics of psychological intervention in the criminal justice system*. Washington, DC: American Psychological Association.

Moriya, D. (2006). Ethical issues in school art therapy. *Art Therapy, 23*, 59–65.

Morrow, S. L. (2000). First do no harm: Therapist issues in psychotherapy with lesbian, gay, and bisexual clients. In R. P. Perez, K. A. DeBord, & K. J. Bieschke (Eds.), *Handbook of counseling and psychotherapy with lesbian, gay, and bisexual clients* (pp. 137–156). Washington, DC: American Psychological Association.

Nagy, T. F. (2005). Privacy and confidentiality. In T. F. Nagy (Ed.), *Ethics in plain English: An illustrative casebook for psychologists* (2nd ed., pp. 107–130). Washington, DC: American Psychological Association.

Newman, J. L., & Fuqua, D. R. (2006). What does it profit an organization if it gains the whole world and loses its own soul? *Consulting Psychology Journal: Practice and Research, 58*, 13–22.

Nydell, M. (2002). *Understanding Arabs: A guide for Westerners* (3rd ed.). Yarmouth, MA: Intercultural Press.

Ochipinti, L. A., & Boston, R. (1987). The new man at the top. *Corrections Today, 49*, 16–20.

O'Neill, P. T. (1989). Responsible to whom? Responsible to what? Some ethical issues in community intervention. *American Journal of Community Psychology, 17*, 323–341.

O'Neill, P. T. (2005). The ethics of problem definition. *Canadian Psychology, 46*, 13–20.

Perrin, E. C. (1998). Ethical questions about screening. *Journal of Developmental and Behavioral Pediatrics, 19*, 350–352.

Porter, L. E. (2005). Policing the police: Theoretical and practical contributions of psychologists to understanding and preventing corruption. In L. Alison (Ed.), *The forensic psychologist's casebook: Psychological profiling and criminal investigation* (pp. 143–169). Devon, U.K.: Willan.

Presidential Task Force on Psychological Ethics and National Security (PENS). (2005). *Report of the Presidential Task Force on Psychological Ethics and National Security*. Washington, DC: American Psychological Association.

Prilleltensky, I. (1991). The social ethics of school psychology: A priority for the 1990s. *School Psychology Quarterly, 6*, 200–222.

Purcell, T. V., Albright, L. E., Grant, D. L., Lockwood, H. C., Schein, V. E., & Friedlander, F. (1974). What are the social responsibilities for psychologists in industry? A symposium. *Professional Psychology, 9*, 68–70.

Raines, J. C. (2004). To tell or not to tell: Ethical issues regarding confidentiality. *School Social Work Journal, 28*, 61–78.

Reamer, F. G. (2005). Update on confidentiality issues in practice with children: Ethics risk management. *Children & Schools, 27*, 117–120.

Reams, B. D., & Anglim, C. (Eds.). (2002). *USA Patriot Act: A legislative history of the Uniting and Strengthening America by Providing Appropriate Tools Required to Intercept and Obstruct Terrorism Act*. Littleton, CO: Rothman.

Richards, P. S., & Bergin, A. E. (2005). Ethical and process issues and guidelines. In P. S. Richards & A. E. Bergin (Eds.), *A spiritual strategy for counseling and psychotherapy* (2nd ed., pp. 183–217). Washington, DC: American Psychological Association.

Riger, S. (1989). The politics of community intervention. *American Journal of Community Psychology, 17*, 379–383.

Robinson, J. D., & Baker, J. (2006). Psychological consultation and services in a general medical hospital. *Professional Psychology, 37*, 264–267.

Rose, D. (2006). American interrogation methods in the war on terror. In T. Williamson (Ed.),

Investigative interviewing: Rights, research, regulation (pp. 42–63). Devon, U.K.: Willan.

Russell, M. C. (2006). Treating combat-related stress disorders: A multiple case study utilizing eye movement desensitization and reprocessing (EMDR) with battlefield casualties from the Iraqi War. *Military Psychology, 18,* 1–18.

Saks, M. J. (1970). On Meredith Crawford's "Military Psychology." *American Psychologist, 25,* 876.

Sammons, M. T., Paige, R. U., & Levant, R. F. (Eds.). (2003). *Prescriptive authority for psychologists: A history and guide.* Washington, DC: American Psychological Association.

Serrano Garcia, I. (1994). The ethics of the powerful and the power of ethics. *American Journal of Community Psychology, 22,* 1–20.

Sharfstein, S. S., & Wolfe, J. C. (1978). The community mental health centers program: Expectations and realities. *Hospital & Community Psychiatry, 29,* 46–49.

Staal, M. A., & King, R. E. (2000). Managing a multiple relationship environment: The ethics of military psychology. *Professional Psychology, 31,* 698–705.

Stephenson, J. A., & Staal, M. A. (2007). An ethical decision making model for operational psychology. *Ethics & Behavior, 17,* 61–82.

Sullivan, M. J., Groveman, A. M., Heldring, M. B., DeLeon, P. H., & Beauchamp, B. (1998). Public policy leadership opportunities for psychologists. *Professional Psychology, 29,* 322–327.

Taylor, R. E. (1978). Demythologizing private practice. *Professional Psychology, 9,* 68–70.

Tovian, S. M. (2006). Interdisciplinary collaboration in outpatient practice. *Professional Psychology, 37,* 269–272.

Tryon, G. S. (2000). Ethical transgressions of school psychology graduate students: A critical incidents survey. *Ethics & Behavior, 10,* 271–279.

Vetter, H. J., & Rieber, R. W. (Eds.). (1980). *The psychological foundations of criminal justice* (Vol. 2). New York: John Jay Press.

Walsh, E. R. (2003). Legal and ethical issues related to the mental health treatment of incarcerated persons. In B. K. Schwartz (Ed.), *Correctional psychology: Practice, programming, and administration* (pp. 6-1–6-15). Kingston, NJ: Civic Research Institute.

Weinberger, L. E., & Sreenivasan, S. (1994). Ethical and professional conflicts in correctional psychology. *Professional Psychology, 25,* 161–167.

Welch, E. T. (1991). *Counselor's guide to the brain and its disorders: Knowing the difference between disease and sin.* Grand Rapids, MI: Zondervan.

Wilks, M. (2006). A stain on medical ethics. In R. Falk, I. Gendzier, & R. J. Lifton (Eds.), *Crimes of war: Iraq* (pp. 362–366). New York: Nation Books.

Williamson, T. (Ed.). (2006). *Investigative interviewing: Rights, research, regulation.* Annandale, NSW, Australia: Federation Press.

Wilson, S. (2006). Terrorist detainees—Psychiatry or morals? *Psychiatric Bulletin, 30,* 75.

Woody, R. H. (1989). Working with families: A school psychology training perspective. *Professional School Psychology, 4,* 257–260.

19

Scholarly Publication and the Responsible Conduct of Research

Your manuscript is both good and original, but the part that is good is not original, and the part that is original is not good.

Samuel Johnson

Contents

TRUST AND BETRAYAL

When Public Trust Is Betrayed

Scholarly writers and scientists have traditionally enjoyed the public's respect and trust. However, concerns about individual rights, scandals involving reports of plagiarism and scientific misconduct, conflicts of interest between scientists and big businesses, and a creeping reluctance to accept the pronouncements of those claiming expertise have fostered more public scrutiny in recent times. Stunning high-profile abuses that receive prime time media coverage further erode the public's confidence in science. Consider these examples:

- The now disgraced South Korean scientist Woo Suk Hwang gained notoriety when he falsely claimed to have successfully cloned

518

close to a dozen human embryos (Onishi, 2006). All of Hwang's previous accomplishments, including Snuppy the allegedly cloned Afghan hound, are now viewed with skepticism.

- Dr. Eric Poehlman became the first academic scientist in the United States to serve prison time for misconduct not involving fatalities and to receive a lifetime ban on receiving federal research funding. Poehlman published articles containing bogus data and submitted falsified grant applications that brought in almost $3 million in federal grant money ("Research Specialist Sentences," 2005).

- Dr. Paul Kornack was held responsible for criminally negligent homicide for falsely representing results of blood chemical analyses in a chemotherapy study. One participant who should have been excluded from the study perished. Kornack received a 71-month sentence in a federal prison and was ordered to pay over $600,000 restitution to two drug companies and the Department of Veterans Affairs. He is also barred for life from receiving federal funding for research ("Research Specialist Sentences," 2006).

When Researchers Are Betrayed

Researchers must not only contend with those among them who are dishonest and irresponsible but also endure two outside forces that work against them. First, attempts to suppress, misrepresent, or discount scientific findings for political gain have become more prevalent in recent years. Examples include ignoring evidence of global warming and environmental deterioration. Furthermore, Congress has approved legislation that would allow the revocation of funding for federally funded research, thus allowing those with political agendas but no scientific expertise to meddle with the peer review process (Winerman, 2005). Second, well-conducted, refereed research can produce findings that clash with reality as we want it to be and may be suppressed or unfairly criticized (Ricciuti, 2005).

Perhaps the best example of a political wildfire was set off by an article on the effects of child sexual abuse published in a journal owned by the American Psychological Association (APA).

The authors of "A Meta-analytic Examination of Assumed Properties of Child Sexual Abuse Using College Samples" (Rind, Tromovitch, & Bauserman, 1998) asserted, among other things, that not all victims of child sexual abuse suffer harm years later, and not all types of sexual activity with minors can reasonably be lumped under the rubric of "abuse." For example, the authors noted a significant difference between the rape of a 5-year-old and consensual sex between a 15- and 17-year-old (technically qualifying as statutory rape in many states). The authors did not intend for this article to cause major controversy, but they could not have been more mistaken. The North American Man/Boy Love Association (NAMBLA) cited the article as supportive of its pro-pedophile agenda. Conservative groups, pop radio personality Laura Schlessinger, and ultimately members of the U.S. Congress (including the now-infamous ex-congressman Tom Delay) got wind of this article and condemned the APA for allegedly promoting child abuse and condoning pedophilia. Anyone who actually reads this scholarly article carefully would find such accusations unfair. And, although the APA vigorously and publicly defended itself against charges of condoning sexual activity with children, it fumbled the more difficult issues regarding the protection of scientific freedom, the degree of autonomy accorded scholarly journal editors, and censure of controversial research. (For more on this complex and thorny series of events, see Albee, 2002; Garrison & Kobar, 2002; Lilienfeld, 2002; Ruark, 1999; Sher & Eisenberg, 2002; and Sternberg, 2002.)

Perhaps researchers can take some comfort in knowing the outside forces that plague them are not as severe as they could be. Six health care workers were sentenced to death by firing squad in Libya for allegedly infecting almost 400 children with the AIDS virus so that they could then attempt to discover a cure. Evidence suggests that the children were already infected due to unsanitary hospital conditions, perhaps as long as 3 years before the health workers arrived. But, the grim verdict was handed down anyway (Thayer, 2006). Fortunately for the medics, their repatriation was successfully negotiated, and they were freed in July 2007 after 8 years in prison.

SCHOLARLY PUBLISHING ISSUES AND ABUSES

Knowledge is shared and advanced through scholarly books and journals and, with increasing frequency, over the Internet. The primary purpose of scholarly publishing outlets is to disseminate useful discoveries as soon as practicable, sometimes as quickly as a few months following the completion of the study.

Despite what one might assume to be a sophisticated and collaborative process, scientific writing and research publication is, in fact, fraught with the potential for intense conflict and spiteful disputes. Why do smart people have such problems here? The main reason is that the stakes are very high for those who want to advance their careers. Publication credits are often required to gain entrance into graduate school or to land an attractive postdoctoral appointment, to obtain or retain a job, to earn a promotion, or to be awarded grant funding. Publications also elevate researchers' status among their peers. And, whereas publications used to carry no direct monetary gain, scientific findings can be the basis for profit-making partnerships with mainstream business ventures.

The competition to "get published" can interject unhealthy features into the scientific enterprise. A focus on quantity rather than quality may prompt some researchers to pursue projects that can be completed rapidly rather than tackling more noteworthy undertakings or studying a subject matter in more depth.

Unfortunately, the peer review process does not protect against unsound findings entering the scientific record. The Third International Congress on Biomedical Peer Review and Global Communications (1997) reported that papers containing errors (especially in statistical design and analysis), plagiarized papers, and even papers based on fraudulent data have been published in peer-reviewed journals. Other criticisms include the tendency for authors to inflate the importance of their work and failing to provide sufficient discussion of study limitations. In fairness, we would note that journal editors and reviewers are not in a position to make many of the discoveries without more information than can be revealed in a few pages

of manuscript. Authors are also cautioned to "write tightly," often feeling that they have to gloss over important information and discussion points because of manuscript length restrictions.

Publication Credits

The project is done. So, now it may seem like a relatively straightforward procedure to decide who deserves authorship credit and in what order to list multiple contributors, but this is not so. Research has become more specialized in recent years, often requiring teams composed of many people who have no or minimal overlapping skills. Occasionally a single article lists over 100 authors (McDonald, 1995). Because of the potential boost to one's career, bitter disputes over the assignment of publication credits have become increasingly common. Over a fourth of the respondents to a large survey believed that they had fallen victim to unfair or unethical authorship assignments (Sandler & Russell, 2005).

Senior (first listed) authorship ranks as the most coveted position. Why the fuss over whose name appears first? It turns out that the first listed individual is assumed to be the major contributor and the name by which the work will be indexed (Fine & Kurdek, 1993). "Junior" (second and later listed) authors have become upset when individuals—usually those with the power and authority over them—claim the senior authorship for themselves, even though they were minimally involved in the project (Holaday & Yost, 1995). Some contributors complain that they received footnote credit or no acknowledgment whatsoever when their involvement warranted a junior authorship.

Ethics committees have agreed that sometimes more powerful and sometimes exploitative researchers disadvantaged junior authors. But, at other times honest differences in opinion about the value placed on each other's contributions are at issue. We have seen cases of graduate students alleging that thesis and dissertation supervisors insisted on being listed as coauthors on any published version of the students' project. Whereas students appear to view their supervisors as fulfilling the obligation to facilitate their professional development, supervising professors may see their contributions as essential to acceptable publication quality. Ethics committees have agreed, however, that supervisors have sometimes taken unfair advantage of their students' work.

Case 19–1: Amy Shutout completed her master's thesis under the supervision of Jack Swallowup, Ph.D., within the framework of his programmatic line of inquiry. Dr. Swallowup provided office space and computer access. He also introduced Shutout to a colleague who could help her enlist people as participants in her survey. Swallowup approved the design and read drafts of the work as it progressed. After completion, Swallowup insisted that his name appear as the senior author. Shutout felt exasperated because she believed that Dr. Swallowup was primarily interested in getting himself another publication by using a student to do the grunt work and exploiting the thesis requirement. She asked an ethics committee for an opinion.

Misappropriation of authorship and exploitation of students by senior faculty, as illustrated in the case above, undermines the meaning and integrity of the authorship process (Wagena, 2005). Thesis advisors are expected to facilitate their student's projects in whatever ways they can. However, things are not always as they appear, as is illustrated in the next case.

Case 19–2: Hang Tight, D.S.W., agreed to work on a research project with an initially enthusiastic graduate student, Flashin Pan. Dr. Tight helped Pan strengthen the design and arrange for data collection. Dr. Tight also supervised the data analysis. But, Pan quit coming around. Tight intercepted Pan in the hallway to inquire about preparing the study for publication. Pan said he had been very busy but would drop by the next day. He never showed up. In the meantime, Pan graduated from the program and left town. Dr. Tight waited 6 months before deciding to write the article himself, giving Pan a footnote credit for early work on the project. When the article ultimately appeared in a respected journal, Pan complained to an ethics committee that Dr. Tight stole his project.

Almost every researcher we know has at least one story to tell about a student who abandoned what started out happily as a joint research venture. How aggressively the student should be sought out before proceeding independently is a matter of judgment. However, an ethics committee exonerated Dr. Tight, agreeing that Pan had not followed through in a timely manner. In a case with similar features, a student sued the university for over a million dollars, and won. However, when the record revealed that the student had greatly exaggerated her involvement in the project, the decision was reversed (Woolston, 2002).

Disagreements can arise when the amount of time devoted to a project is thrown into the mix.

Case 19–3: Job Tedious worked for 3 years at an agreed-on hourly rate for Elmo Plop, Ed.D. Tedious administered a structured interview to parents of premature babies and transcribed the sessions into a computer database. Tedious became upset because he was not listed as an author on the final manuscript submitted for publication in a prestigious journal. He argued that he had put in at least 10 times more hours than anyone else associated with the project and therefore deserved at least a junior authorship. Dr. Plop argued that a footnote credit was proper because Tedious was paid to perform supervised, routine procedures.

Dr. Plop did not act improperly in acknowledging Tedious in a footnote because of the nature of the work he performed. Mr. Tedious was carrying out an assigned, prescribed plan. He had no involvement in the formulation of the design, methods, analyses, or manuscript preparation, all of which comprise primary criteria for authorship credit. Time spent on a project per se is not a significant factor in determining authorship credits. Yet, although Plop was not acting unethically, he could have structured this arrangement better. This case illustrates the wisdom of reaching agreements about what each person can reasonably expect in terms of credit before the research or writing collaboration begins and addressing any need for modifications should changes in the project's status occur (Hopko, Hopko, & Morris, 1999).

We might note that errors in the opposite direction also have ethical implications. "Gift authorships," offered as a favor to enhance a student's application to graduate school or to advantage an untenured colleague, appear on the surface to be generous gestures. However, to the extent that the authorship was unearned, the research record has been corrupted, and others may be unfairly disadvantaged. For example, in a competitive employment situation, the applicant with an unearned authorship could unfairly prevail over others who were just as (or more) qualified. Assigning authorship to a senior researcher who had minimal involvement in the work for the purpose of possibly enhancing the potential for publication constitutes another form of gift authorship that is unacceptable.

Professional ethics codes do address these issues. The APA ethics code (APA 02: 8.12a and 8.02b) specifies that authorship credits are to be assigned in proportion to authors' actual contributions. Minor or routine professional contributions or extensive nonprofessional assistance (e.g., typing a complicated manuscript, coding data, or helpful ideas offered by a colleague) may be acknowledged in a footnote or in an introductory statement (APA 02: 8.02b). Publications arising from students' theses or doctoral dissertations should normally list the student as the senior author, even when advisors or others were heavily involved in the project (APA 02: 8.12c).

A trend that may catch on is the concept of "contributorship." The term *authorship* is actually somewhat misleading because the individual who delivered the most substance to a project may not have written a word of the manuscript. Increasingly, journal editors require that a description of each listed author's role appear in the manuscript on an accompanying cover letter. Such published listings would offer readers, and document in the research record, the most accurate description of how the project developed.

Plagiarism and Unfair Use

Plagiarism, the act of passing the work of someone else off as one's own, derives from the

Latin *plagiarus* meaning "kidnapper" (Hawley, 1984) and is specifically condemned in most ethics codes (e.g., APA 02: 8.11). In the strictest sense of the definition, plagiarism involves the intent to deceive others, although ignorance can play a role, such as when an attribution is inaccurate (Froese, Boswell, Garcia, Koehn, & Nelson, 1995). Plagiarism can range from careless paraphrasing (very common) to intentional copying of an entire work without citing the original source. If the copying is extensive or if economic disadvantage befalls the original author, legal issues pertain through federal copyright infringement statutes (LaFollette, 1992). "Who owns what" has become an even more significant concern as scientific and economic interests merge.

Some younger professionals may have become desensitized to the seriousness of plagiarism because, as students, they accessed information from the Internet and passed it on, basically unaltered, as part of their assignments (Whitley & Keith-Spiegel, 2002). However, even famous authors and academics who should have known better have been caught copying chunks of previously published works created by someone else. Sometimes, the practice is chronic, as the next case reveals.

Case 19–4: Rob Baggit, Ph.D., was finally exposed after a decade of translating articles by Argentinean scholars appearing in Spanish language journals and publishing them in English language journals under his own name.

Some might say that Dr. Baggit was a scoundrel, but that he did no real harm. After all, he only duplicated the research record in another language, thus broadening the audience that could partake of the information. However, the actual person we call Baggit gained employment and won promotions based on his bogus publication record, thus giving him an undeserved advantage over others.

Obvious instances of plagiarism, in which large amounts of material were copied verbatim, are easy for ethics boards to adjudicate because the evidence usually exists in overwhelming tangible form. Interestingly, the most common source of uncovering major acts of plagiarism is neither by the public nor by other seasoned scholars, but by students conducting literature reviews for their own research papers or theses.

Violation of "fair use" standards is related to plagiarism but is more likely to occur unintentionally. Scholars are allowed to use copyrighted material, attributed properly to its creators, in a reasonable manner without the consent of the copyright owners. Scholarly writings often quote short sections of properly cited works by others without explicit permission from the author or owner of the copyright. However, fair use can be exceeded, even when the material is meticulously attributed, as is illustrated in the next case.

Case 19–5: Armond Gatherup, L.M.H.C., self-published a small book on self-esteem. He quoted, with correct attribution, over 80% of the content from 30 other sources. One of the authors he cited sent a copy of the book to an ethics committee, complaining that Gatherup had used her work as well as that of many authors as a means of crediting himself with a book that others, in effect, actually wrote.

Less clear-cut cases that allege plagiarism or unfair use are based on brief or occasionally similar passages, heavy paraphrasing, or unattributed previously published ideas. These complaints are more difficult to uphold conclusively. The next case illustrates why.

Case 19–6: Tick Off, Ph.D., complained to an ethics committee that Kinda Like, M.D., used a number of his previously published ideas, including a few similar sentences, in Like's article on community alcohol abuse programs. Dr. Off claims he should have been cited. The committee noted the similarity in ideas and an occasional resemblance in wording. Dr. Like, however, adamantly denied using or even having read Off's work, provided the full text of other cited articles as her primary sources, and asserted that the occasional wording similarities were coincidental.

Writers or researchers working in the same specialty area may cull notions from each other and even adopt similar ways of expressing themselves. This can render cases based on related written material impossible to unravel. Although Dr. Like probably had access to Off's already-published work, it can not be proved that she ever read it. The basic ideas also appeared elsewhere, and these were properly cited by Like.

Plagiarism and unfair use can result from sloppy scholarship. Authors often use (or are inspired by) the work of others and keep notes consisting of direct quotations as well as their own original notes. Or, they hire students to take notes for them, again possibly blending actual quotes with original notations. What is original and what is not can easily become confused. However, the negative impact on a career can be substantial, as the popular historian Doris Kearns Goodwin discovered when she admitted slipping up (Gates, 2002).

Finally, just as the Internet has made it easier than ever to find and download material to claim as one's own, it has also never been easier to detect. Institutions can subscribe to anti-plagiarism software services, although just googling a few words can often locate an original source in a few seconds.

Publishing Case Studies

Public fascination about unusual people and the odd things they do as well as the emotional lives of more normal people has created a great market for writings about psychological histories. Therapists have a steady stream of material, and some choose to write and publish articles and books about their clients (Wharton, 2005). Other mental health professionals are intrigued by cases that explore symptoms and diagnoses, that offer treatments based on a successful outcome studies, or that illustrate and enliven theories (Patterson, 1999). Thus, cases stories find their way into many practice-oriented scholarly publications as well as more popular media.

Using material based on work with clients in published work is not intrinsically unethical, but serious issues regarding informed consent, confidentiality, and privacy invasion pertain. When therapists have clear agreements (ideally in writing) with their clients about the content to appear in print, ethical concerns are reduced. However, it can be argued that clients may not feel free to decline any request from their therapists. Although carefully disguising cases by removing all identifying information often provides a satisfactory solution, therapists who publish facts about their clients must remember that when writing about one person or one family, the risk of "outing" them is ever present.

Case 19–7: Nicki Brandywine was startled to read a review of a recently published book on self-mutilation authored by her therapist, Mark Potboiler, M.D. The book presented a graphic and detailed case of a young woman who cut herself every time she had too much to drink, which was most weekends. The book described her as having "a J.D. degree from a top ivy league law school" and "working as corporate in-house counsel for a major software company," descriptors that applied to Nicki. Potboiler had promised confidentiality, but now Nicki felt totally betrayed. She dreaded the idea of anyone finding out about what she referred to as "my repulsive secret."

Case 19–8: Stark Naked saw an article written by Bryan Sneaky, M.F.C.T., in a popular magazine describing a man who occasionally ran though the streets of Brooklyn wearing nothing but a pair of tennis shoes and an old Dodger's cap. The article went on to describe the dynamics of exhibitionism, using material from therapy notes with Mr. Naked. Naked abruptly quit therapy and contacted an ethics committee. The therapist produced in his defense the lengthy initial contract, signed by Naked. It contained two sentences that read, "Mr. Sneaky writes articles for magazines about various counseling issues. I agree to allow Mr. Sneaky to use information about my counseling sessions as long as my name is not revealed."

Perhaps in some cases no one other than the clients themselves could identify who the therapists had described. However, divulging too much unnecessary detail potentially compromised the clients' privacy in these instances. For example, Ms. Brandywine could have been simply described as someone who "earned an advanced degree from a highly regarded university and held a responsible job at a large corporation." Mr. Potboiler revealed more than was clinically necessary or ethically appropriate.

Seeking a current or former client's specific authorization of the actual content would prove a wiser course of action. Furthermore, even if extremely detailed descriptions, such as essentially a verbatim transcript of therapy notes, appear in highly disguised contexts, the courts could find in favor of the offended client. This pertains even when the ability of others to discern the client's identity remains unclear (Leland, 1978). Thus, Mr. Naked may have a basis to take legal action if he chose to do so.

Sometimes, an interesting reversal can occur by which clients feel harmed by seeing themselves in a description of another person.

Case 19–9: Seena Tall, Psy.D., had worked as a therapist with high-conflict divorcing families for 20 years before she wrote *Guide to Treating Category Five Divorces*. After reading the book, a former client, Itsa Mee, complained to a licensing board that her confidentiality had been violated. Dr. Tall described a pattern typical of cases in which one parent attempts to alienate the children from the other parent. Dr. Tall gave an example in which one parent continually criticized or denigrated the other using foul language in front of the children, sabotaged visitation while casting blame on the other parent, and telling the children that the other parent never wanted them. Dr. Tall explained that, "The pattern resulted from deeply rooted insecurities on the part of the alienating parent." As Ms. Mee told the licensing board, "That's exactly what I did, and everyone will recognize her criticism of me."

Although Ms. Mee did indeed recognize a description of her behaviors, the same holds true for a multitude of other people who behave in a similar manner. Dr. Tall violated no ethical obligation of confidentiality, although Ms. Mee felt injured by reading Dr. Tall's criticism of people who act in that manner.

Ignoring Older Work

Scholarly writers and researchers should remember an occasional and yet rarely discussed faulty practice that can occur when documenting previous work. Some make the mistake of overlooking work more than a few years old, perhaps because they make the faulty assumption that earlier work is not worthwhile or is out of date. And, with literature reviews so easy to do on the Internet, older material may fall at the end of the list or not appear at all. However, those who pass over earlier work may conclude that they discovered something fresh and innovative when in fact the same findings were published many years ago.

Such ignorance can evoke seriously critical responses by the authors of earlier work. A study conducted at Harvard, and published in the prestigious journal *Nature*, brought initial positive media attention to its young author. The author was later roundly criticized for failing to cite earlier equivalent work, thereby making his study appear to be completely original and far more important than it really was (Farley, 2003).

RESEARCH ON PEOPLE

A large body of literature on the responsible conduct of social and behavioral research has developed over the last several decades. Interest surged shortly after World War II when the Nazis' obscene interpretation of what constituted legitimate science and the criminal acts they committed in the name of science became known (Spitz, 2005). Concerns accelerated with revelations of questionable and risky procedures used on human beings without their voluntary and informed consent in other countries, including the United States. The federal government began creating research policies in the 1950s. Institutional review boards (IRBs) became established at each site anticipating or receiving federal funds to educate researchers and to ensure that research followed federal policy regarding the ethical treatment of participants.

Researchers must now adhere to high standards of care, many of which are similar to those of mental health service providers. However, clients in need of mental health care usually present themselves for services and fully understand that they are receiving assessment or psychotherapeutic services. Investigators must usually seek out research participants. Sometimes, those who participate in research do not always know or fully understand what is going

on or even know that they are under study. When offering therapeutic and assessment (i.e., clinical) services, meeting the *clients'* needs is the sole purpose of the activity. Data collection, on the other hand, is the means by which the *researcher's* goals are achieved. In general, then, the therapist holds the interests and welfare of each individual as primary, whereas the researcher contends with the motivation also to fulfill personal agendas that can, without constant self-monitoring, overshadow the rights and welfare of those they study. Herein lies another major reason why research participants deserve utmost respect and care. Whereas therapy clients pay us for our time so that we can help them, research participants typically volunteer their time so that they can help us.

Scientific Misconduct

The scientific enterprise is built on the premise that truth seeking is every researcher's principal motivation. Those who review submitted grants or papers for publication accept on faith that researchers subscribe to the highest standards of integrity (Grinnell, 1992). And, fortunately, researchers themselves value the ethical standards to which they are held (Roberts & McAuliffe, 2006). Unfortunately, other motives have prompted some researchers to cheat.

Recurring themes in unmasked data fraud involve perpetrators who were lax in the supervision of the data gathering and analysis and excessively ambitious with previous records of prolific writing. Usually present is an intense pressure to produce new findings. Researchers who publish first are credited with a "discovery," and showing good progress is essential to continued grant funding. In fact, one reason many researchers may jump ahead of their actual findings by reporting bogus or manipulated data is because they sincerely believe that they already know what factual findings will show. Their commitment to a theory or hypothesis may be so strong that it even diminishes fears of detection (Bridgstock, 1982).

Additional elements present within the scientific enterprise itself can tempt researchers to deceive. A project that fails to produce significant findings may not gain acceptance for publication due to a bias against publishing statistically insignificant findings. Or, legitimate data may never get reported because a financial interest in a particular outcome failed to materialize. The organizational culture in which researchers conduct their studies can also contaminate science. That is, when a researcher sees others behaving unethically as a way of getting ahead in a competitive environment, and those with the authority to take action turn a blind eye, undue moral pressure is exerted on those who would otherwise behave ethically (Keith-Spiegel, Koocher, & Tabachnick, 2006). Sometimes, those in authority behave in an overly restrictive, unresponsive, biased, unfair, or offensive manner that inhibits the ability to do sound research, thus inviting rule breaking.

Case 19–10: Nancy Icarus, Ph.D., had always prided herself on her commitment to conducting ethical research. However, the IRB at her university was unreasonable in its demands in a way that unduly restricted her ability to work in her specialty area. Furthermore, the memos the IRBs issued were arrogant and rude. In frustration, she went ahead and conducted her research without fully informing the IRB about what she was doing.

Ethical standards demand that when research requires approval by an institution, the information in the protocol must be accurate (APA 02: 8.01). Paradoxically, however, IRBs charged with upholding the responsible conduct of science may actually encourage deceit. We may have some sympathy for Dr. Icarus, who runs up against a wall and breaks the rules to get around it. In the meantime, however, such research is not being properly monitored as required by federal policy. Participants' rights could be ignored, but the institution would know nothing about it. Unfortunately, charges that IRBs are unreasonable, unresponsive, and incompetent are common (Cohen, 1999, Giles, 2005; Keith-Spiegel & Koocher, 2005).

Types of Misconduct

The two most serious and often discussed forms of scientific misconduct are *fabrication* and *falsification*. Fabrication is usually in the form of

"dry lab" data that are simply invented. Falsification can take several forms. Actual data can be "smoothed" or "cooked" to approach more closely the desired or expected outcome. Or, collected data points can be dropped ("trimmed") to delete unwanted information.

Similar to plagiarism, the purposeful creation of unsound data is considered among scientists and scholars as a grievous ethical violation (see APA 02: 8.10a). The consequences of making invalid data public is, however, far more serious than simply duplicating the work of others (i.e., plagiarism) because the spurious conclusions contaminate the research record. Conducting good science requires a process of building on previous work. Time and effort become wasted when unquestioning researchers pursue inquiries based on previously reported findings they do not realize are bogus. Application of findings based on tainted data can even cause harm. For example, if a researcher proposing an experimental therapy technique "trims" data, and the tainted findings appear in a reputable journal, the results may be applied by unsuspecting clinicians. By the time someone notices that clients are not improving (or their condition is worsening), serious setbacks could occur. Or, if a developer of a psychodiagnostic assessment "cooks" the validity data, once it is published and in use people could be misclassified using what is erroneously believed to be a well-founded instrument. To the extent that such test results are used to determine diagnoses or treatment approaches or to determine who should not be hired, serious errors are committed that have a deleterious impact on people's lives.

Several much less frequently discussed questionable acts can also distort the scientific record to the same degree as fabrication or falsification, such as setting up an experimental condition so that the collected data are more likely to confirm a hypothesis. For example, a researcher may purposely select those with only the *mildest* symptoms of a diagnostic category to bolster the chances of "proving" that a particular therapy works. Or, conversely, participants with the *most severe* symptoms may be purposely placed in the control group so that the experimental group will appear to fare more favorably by comparison. Biased reporting of results, such as presenting the findings in such a way that they appear far more significant than they actually are, misleads readers. Relying on secrecy to get ahead, refusing to share data, and withholding details in methodology or results run against the grain of scientific integrity because they make it more difficult or impossible for anyone else to successfully pursue that same line of inquiry (Grinnell, 1992; Martinson, Anderson, & de Vries, 2005; Sieber, 1991a, 1991b). "Data torturing" is another ignoble practice, involving analyzing the same data many different ways until one finds statistical significance (Whitley, 1995). These ethically questionable acts may be more likely to occur when the source of financial support has an interest in obtaining findings favorable to their predetermined desired outcome.

Sometimes, invalid data were not purposefully created. Incompetence may be at issue, resulting in inappropriate design, poor or biased sampling procedures, misused or wrongly applied statistical tests, inadequate record keeping, and just plain carelessness. Even though there may be no intent to deceive, inaccurate information can also seriously contaminate the research record.

One may be tempted to assume that such inaccuracies, purposeful or not, will be discovered, but we can not count on it. Whereas errors in alleged scientific advances are assumed to be eventually self-correcting through replication, funding sources typically do not support replication research. Furthermore, most scholarly journals do not normally publish replication studies. Thus, there is little incentive for researchers to repeat the work already reported by others.

Incidence

We want to believe that most professionals who conduct research are overwhelmingly honest. However, in a now-classic survey of doctoral candidates and faculty members from 99 departments, anonymous responses to questions about knowledge of instances of scientific misconduct revealed that over two thirds of the graduate students and about one half of the

faculty had direct knowledge of the commission of some form of scientific misconduct. Most did not confront or report it, usually from fear of reprisal (Swazey, Anderson, & Lewis, 1993). A more recent study suggested that the situation has not improved. Although very few of the several thousand scientists responding to an anonymous survey disclosed committing more serious research sins of fabrication or falsification, one of every three admitted to committing an act that could be labeled as questionable (Martinson et al., 2005). Thus, unfortunately, poor conduct may be neither rare nor ever adequately resolved.

Difficulties in Detection

Most of the highly publicized data scandals have occurred in biomedical research laboratories. No one knows for sure whether the incidence is higher in biomedical science than in social and behavioral science, or whether it is simply easier to detect fraud in biomedicine. Most social and behavioral research does not involve chemical analyses, tissue cultures, change in physical symptoms, invasive procedures, or similar "hard" documentation. Social science data, on the other hand, often take the form of numerical scores from questionnaires, psychological assessments, performance measures or qualitative data based on interviews or behavioral observations. The actual research participants have long since gone, taking their identities with them. Such data are relatively easy to generate, fudge, or trim. We can hope that social science researchers are motivated by the responsible quest for truth, but it is disquieting to note that the same publish-or-perish and grant-seeking pressures exist for social and behavioral scientists working in competitive settings, that fame is an ever-present allure for those in any field, and that the practice of fabricating data may start when researchers are students (e.g., Kimmel, 1996; Whitley & Keith-Spiegel, 2002).

Case 19–11: Hocum Bunk, Ph.D., was charged by a member of his academic department with presenting research results at a professional meeting based on experimental trials never actually conducted. The colleague based her suspicions on the fact that the student "subject pool" records did not reveal any use by Bunk during the last year, although he stated that data were collected during that period using undergraduate students. Furthermore, the research room shared by several faculty members showed no signs of use by Dr. Bunk. He never signed up for it and was never seen in it, and his experimental apparatus never changed position and was accumulating dust.

When challenged, Dr. Bunk responded that he did not use the student research pool because he conscripted students directly and ran them through a similar device he claimed to keep in his office. He could not produce original data, saying he threw the raw records out when he completed his analysis. Furthermore, Bunk claimed that the allegations against him constituted an act of revenge because he got a promotion, and the complainant did not. Although Bunk's defense was viewed as deficient, neither he nor an ethics committee could conclusively prove or disprove his story.

Case 19–12: Bart Rascal, a research assistant, turned in 50 interview schedules allegedly collected at a busy mall. His supervisor became suspicious because the exact same phrasing occurred repeatedly across many transcripts, and the "voices" all sounded alike. Many different opinions and styles of expression would normally be expected, as evidenced by the interview records of other assistants. When the supervisor gently confronted Rascal, he denied that he fabricated any records.

Mr. Rascal's supervisor made the decision not to include the student's interview records in his project. But, the evidence that Rascal cheated also proved sufficiently inconclusive to prompt a formal hearing.

Does actual harm result only from biomedical research fraud? This is not necessarily the case. Dishonest social and behavioral scientists can seriously disadvantage people as well. In a case that came to light in the late 1980s, the federally funded research of psychologist Stephen Breuning reported findings based on data

that were never collected. This case is especially disturbing because Breuning's findings became a basis for actual treatment decisions before his work was discredited. The fraudulent reports were also then used as a basis to determine drug therapy for institutionalized severely retarded persons, a treatment later proven detrimental based on the results of competent research conducted by others (Bell, 1992; Committee on Government Operations, 1990).

In the light of disturbing reports, what credibility should the public place on researchers' work? The public's generalized distrust, which is sure to ensue as the media prominently exposes cases of scientific intrigue, could have disastrous consequences for everyone. Scientists are as dependent on the public for continued support as society is on their valuable, legitimate contributions. Although part of the problem is a system of rewards that implicitly encourages dishonest and irresponsible scientific practices, researchers must remain true to the search for truth if the entire scientific enterprise is to remain stable and healthy. In response to a growing concern about scientific dishonesty, the Public Health Service established the Office of Research Integrity to direct activities focused on research integrity on behalf of the Department of Health and Human Services (with the exception of the Federal Drug Administration). This office creates policies and regulations with regard to preventing, detecting, and investigating scientific misconduct.

Competency to Conduct Research

The scientific merit of a research design has been widely acknowledged as a competence issue, and many mental health providers have not had extensive training in research design and data analysis. These techniques have become extremely sophisticated in the last few decades, largely made possible by the wide availability of high-speed computers. We strongly advise including someone with expertise in design and statistics on any research team, at least as a consultant. No meaningful information can possibly result from poorly formulated studies or improperly collected or analyzed data. The use of human beings or animals in research can not be justified on any grounds if the study design is flawed. At best, the participants' efforts are wasted, and, at worst, they could suffer harm.

The scientific record also becomes tarnished when poor-quality work is dumped into the scientific literature. Ideally, the editors of scholarly journals weed out most incompetent submissions. But, shoddy work slips by for a variety of reasons, such as inadequate or biased reviews. The more critical the topic (e.g., heart disease as opposed to heartburn), the more willing manuscript reviewers may be to overlook or underrate methodological flaws (Wilson, DePaulo, Mook, & Klaaren, 1993).

Even the most proficient researchers face many serious dilemmas. Quality science and ethical research practices typically provide the best results, but scientific merit and ethical considerations are sometimes at odds, requiring the sacrifice of some measure of one to comply with the requirements of the other. For example, fully informing the participants of the purpose of the study may weaken or distort scientific validity. The privacy of vulnerable people may be invaded in long-term follow-up studies designed to evaluate and improve treatment techniques from which they and others may eventually benefit. Balanced placebo designs may require misinforming participants to reduce the effects of expectancies. Participants in a control group could be denied a valuable experimental treatment, but without a control group that treatment could not conclusively be proven superior. Fortunately, many seeming conflicts between science and ethics can often be resolved or minimized by competent researchers after careful reflection and consultation (Sieber, 1993).

Consent to Participate

The basic obligation of the responsible researcher is to enter into a fair and clear agreement with research participants. Consent procedures were designed to preclude repetition of a grotesque period in world history when Nazi physicians forced horrific experiments on Jews, the mentally retarded, homosexuals, and other groups not meeting the criteria for membership in Adolf Hitler's "pure Aryan race."

The requirement of consent as a protection for participants first appeared in the Nuremburg code, published in the United States in the *Journal of the American Medical Association* in 1946. Adopted after the war crimes trials of 23 Nazi physicians indicted for crimes against humanity, the code includes the essential elements of consent. Consent to participate requires legal capacity to give it, freedom to decline participation without coercion, and sufficient knowledge about the nature of study to make an informed decision (Capron, 1989). Although never used as a legal precedent, the Nuremberg code is the basis from which subsequent codes and policies were developed (APA 02: 8.02; 8.03).

It is now well accepted that, with a few carefully proscribed exceptions, research participants must know the nature of their volunteering and agree freely to do it. The only consent issues that remain open at present or in flux focus on specific applications, such as how to deal with consent issues when conducting research online, when people may not have the ability to competently consent (e.g., as suicidal or delusional individuals), or when people can not consent for themselves (e.g., children) (Flewitt, 2005; Mishara & Weisstub, 2005; Rees & Hardy, 2003; Varnhagen et al., 2005).

Voluntariness

Because a person's decision to participate in a research project can be manipulated in both subtle and blatant ways, many complex factors make it difficult to ensure completely voluntary research participation. A researcher can exert influence without conscious intent. For example, solicitation by someone perceived as prestigious and an authority may itself be persuasive. Influence is especially likely if the researcher is enthusiastic and likable or if the potential participant is vulnerable, deferent, or in need of attention. People desperate for a solution to a personal matter that relates to the subject under investigation may overlook any risks. Groups such as inmates, students, or employees of the organization sponsoring the research may feel pressured to participate for fear of retribution, even when explicitly told that they are free to decline without penalty. Many of the people who are sought for participation in the social and behavioral sciences are troubled, in need of assistance or resources, or in a weaker bargaining position compared to the researchers.

The explicit offer of rewards, monetary or otherwise, is a sensitive matter that can affect a decision to participate in research. Offering to pay participants a small amount to offset inconvenience and transportation costs is unlikely to be considered coercive. Ethical issues arise when the reimbursements or rewards for participating are significant enough to influence consent decisions (APA 02: 8.06a, 8.06b).

Case 19–13: Edward Noharm, M.D., complained to a university IRB that a sponsored project involved excessively enticing tactics. To obtain a control group for a hospitalized experimental treatment group of infants, the researchers approached parents in a low-income neighborhood and offered them several hundred dollars if they would allow their babies to undergo periodic laboratory tests, some of which involved considerable discomfort. Dr. Noharm argued that the control group of healthy children could in no way benefit from the study, and that the offer to financially limited parents of such a large sum constituted a persuasion that could override concern for their babies' best interests.

Case 19–14: Mimi Dogood, Psy.D., complained to a state legislature that prisoners were being subjected to poorly designed, dangerous experiments in return for $10 a day. Ironically, the prisoners objected to her intervention, noting that the money kept them supplied with cigarettes, candy, and other small items that enhanced the quality of their otherwise routine and boring lives.

Both cases, based on true occurrences, illustrate how people of limited means or opportunity may accept attractive enticements that others with greater resources or freedoms would see as trivial.

Another form of subtle coercion involves appealing to the participants' altruism. Such requests can range from personal pleas for help

to suggestions that cooperation will advance science or benefit humankind. To the extent that researchers genuinely need participants and are sincere in their beliefs that they are doing worthy work, some level of altruistic appeal is probably unavoidable.

Case 19–15: When told that participating in an experiment would help keep starving children from dying by the thousands, 80% of school-aged children agreed to eat a bite of a baked mouse.

This actual result is found in a study by Keith-Spiegel and Maas (1981). No baked mouse was ever served to the children, of course, because the point of the sturdy was to evaluate altruistic appeals. But, the surprising level of effectiveness of a fervent altruistic appeal on a vulnerable population was clearly demonstrated. In the same study, a majority of the children would also agree to have their eye poked with a glass rod when the research was described as helping blind children see again.

Some participants may discount any potential risks in the hope of securing needed benefit. Or, they may believe that needed services are contingent on participation in research. Researchers must be careful not to engage in "hyperclaiming," that is, suggesting to potential participants that the study will reach goals that are, in fact, unlikely to be achieved (Rosenthal, 1994).

Researchers should never create guilt feelings in those who decline to participate in a research project. In its nastiest form, a researcher may actually hint that refusal to particulate suggests selfishness or lack of caring about others who could benefit from the "good people" who have agreed to be part of the study.

Can research participants withdraw their previous decision to participate? Despite the disappointments that researchers undoubtedly experience when participants change their minds midcourse (especially if this occurs well into a complicated or longitudinal study), the right to withdraw should be honored (APA 02: 8.02). This right to disengage from a study should be made explicit during the initial consent phase. Rare exceptions involve needed interventions available only in a research context.

Knowledge and Understanding

For research participants to understand what they are being asked to agree to do, they (or their surrogates) must have the capacity to comprehend and evaluate the information that is offered to them prior to actual participation. Gaining informed consent is a critical communication process during which an agreement is reached.

Case 19–16: Sue Dontgettit complained to the research office at her university that a study conducted by Hy Wordlevel, Ph.D., subjected her to an upsetting experience by asking embarrassing questions about her childhood relationships. Dr. Wordlevel produced Dontgettit's signed consent form as a defense. Dontgettit contended, however, that the wording of the form was confusing to her and included terms like "participatory negative junctions" that she did not understand.

Ms. Dontgettit might have asked questions (assuming she was invited to do so, as she should have been; see APA 02: 8.02) or declined to involve herself in something she did not understand. But, many participants may not have sufficient self-efficacy to admit that they do not comprehend something, especially if they do not feel in control of the situation. Researchers must recognize that a signed consent form is *not* synonymous with informed consent. If the individual did not fully grasp what he or she signed, informed consent has not occurred. Unfortunately, it has been documented that many legally competent adults had minimal understanding of what they agreed to do (e.g., Cassileth, 1980; Sieber & Levine, 2004; Taub, Baker, & Sturr, 1986).

Individuals who have trouble with the language, for whatever reason, require special consideration. Non-English-speaking participants have the right to appropriate translations. Individuals with poor reading skills should also receive special assistance. All participants should be made to feel comfortable asking questions to preclude attempts to "save face" by agreeing to participate in an activity that is not fully understood.

When participants lack the legal capability to give consent, permission (i.e., proxy consent) must be obtained from authorized others. Nevertheless, except for infants, nonverbal children, and seriously impaired uncommunicative individuals, participants should be offered some explanation of what they are being asked to do. In addition, if practical, their proactive assent should be sought. It is our position that even if permission has been obtained, an individual who expresses lack of desire or interest in participating should be excused unless there is a very compelling reason, such as a likelihood of direct therapeutic benefit, to override the participant's wishes (Koocher & Keith-Spiegel, 1990). After all, a fussy or begrudging person will not likely provide valid data.

Finally, it must be noted that consent forms protect researchers and their institutions, allowing for a "record of agreement" should the participant complain later (Sieber & Levine, 2004). However, we do note that formal informed consent procedures are not always required for some types of data collection methods, such as so-called minimal risk research when the project is highly unlikely to cause any harm or distress. Examples include anonymous questionnaires, naturalistic observations, and some types of archival research or review of data collected for nonresearch purposes with participant identities removed (APA 02: 8.05; Department of Health and Human Services, 2005). In addition, formal consent agreements are typically unnecessary for service and program evaluations in educational settings or for job or organizational effectiveness as long as there is no risk to employability, and confidentiality is protected. We suggest keeping a good record of how the research was conducted whenever written informed consent is not required just in case someone seeks clarification.

Deception

Some pretext in conducting research may occur unintentionally and unavoidably. Despite a researcher's plan to disclose all aspects of a study's purpose, some aspects will remain unexplained or not fully understood by every participant. It is the *purposeful* use of deceptive techniques that remains controversial, despite a decline since the heyday of deception studies in the 1970s (Nicks, Korn, & Mainieri, 1997).

Intentional deception techniques range widely from outright lies or concealment of risks to mild or ambiguous misrepresentations or omissions. Types of deceptions described by Gross and Flemming (1982), Kimmel (1996), and Sieber (1982a) include

- *misinforming participants* (e.g., offering inaccurate information during the consent phase that might have influenced the decision to participate)
- *concealing information* (e.g., leaving out relevant information during the consent phase that might have influenced the decision to participate)
- *enlisting confederates* (e.g., "stooges" pose or interact with the participants in some predetermined way)
- *making false guarantees* (e.g., failing to maintain confidentiality or not ultimately providing a promised prize or compensation)
- *misrepresenting one's identity* (e.g., referring to oneself falsely as a medical doctor or an actor)
- *creating false feedback* (e.g., giving participants inaccurate performance or untrue evaluations)
- *concealing observations or recordings*
- *not informing participants that they are being assessed or observed for research purposes*

Packing all of these deceptions in one brief case poses a challenge, but the next contrived case—the only one in this book—offers a far-fetched attempt.

Case 19–17: To test the hypothesis that women are less likely to engage in a mildly humiliating act for money than are men, a confederate of the researcher approaches male and female strangers in a public place. He says to the unsuspecting research participant, "See that guy over there? If you walk over to him and loudly oink like a pig, he will give you a $100 bill. See? I just got one" (and flashes a genuine C note). The confederate disappears, and the experimenter waits for takers. If anyone comes up and "oinks," he just looks at him or her in puzzlement and does whatever else

is necessary to convince the individual that he does not hand out $100 bills, and that they must have been accosted by a practical joker. He then records the sex of the "oinker."

Why is the use of deceptive techniques sometimes deemed necessary? Support for the use of deception usually involves protection of the validity of the data by intentionally manipulating the actual purpose of an experiment to avoid the participants' conscious reactions (Broder, 1998). For some types of research, participant knowledge of exactly what the researcher is studying would render the resulting data meaningless. Considerable useful and valid knowledge might never be accumulated if the participants had foreknowledge of the complete purpose of the study or its procedures (Broder, 1998; Taylor & Shepperd, 1996). Further, despite the potential for harm, participants apparently rarely feel harmed or upset by participating in deceptive social science research (Christensen, 1988; Sharpe, Adair, & Roese, 1992). Therefore, to lump deceptive techniques into a single pot, as if they all had a potential for harm, would be an error (Kimmel, 1998).

Critics of deception argue that it, by definition, compromises the consent agreement and that allowing it condones lying. Some fear that such research causes the public to regard social scientists as a manipulative, exploitative, suspicious group (Ortmann & Hertwig, 1997). Others allege that such techniques provide quick, noncreative, and undesirable shortcuts to more careful and creative experimentation. And, finally, degradation, embarrassment, anger, disillusionment, and other harms and wrongs can potentially occur when participants are duped.

The APA ethics code explicitly, although cautiously, allows the use of deception in research. The code admonishes researchers to ensure that a study using deception has scientific or applied value (in contrast to our fictional Case 19–17). Effective alternatives must have been considered but proven unfeasible (APA 02: 8.07a). Further, deceiving participants about aspects of the study that might otherwise alter their consent to participate (such as the potential for physical discomfort or risks or other unpleasant experiences) is disallowed (APA 02: 8.07b).

Very few complaints about deception come to the attention of ethics committees. We offer a couple of examples in which one or more participants objected.

Case 19–18: When volunteers arrived at Elmo Gotcha's laboratory, they were told that they would be asked to examine some objects carefully and would later be tested on what they saw. Items included a flashlight, several hand tools, a teddy bear, and a suitcase. When students opened the suitcase, they found a 2-foot-long energetic garden snake. Mr. Gotcha recorded each student's response. He wrote a paper that classified college students' reactions to "unexpected events," emphasizing that the snake was small and totally harmless.

Researchers probably differ in their judgments of the potential for emotional distress. In this case, the data suggested that many participants' responses to the snake were highly unfavorable. In the next case, we touch on an especially important factor when it comes to deciding whether deception was ethical.

Case 19–19: Tillie Testy was outraged about a study unwittingly conducted on her and her classmates by Henry Sneak, Ed.D. The students were told that they would be taking a multiple-choice test on a given day that would cover certain textbook readings. On exam day, the teaching assistant entered the room, explained that Dr. Sneak was ill and had been unable to prepare the test, and that an essay question would be substituted. The assistant wrote a question unrelated to the assigned readings on the board. After 10 minutes, Dr. Sneak entered the room and explained that he was doing a study on the effects of confusion and stress and asked the students to fill out a brief questionnaire. He then handed out the real exam and told the students to "carry on."

Ms. Testy was upset not only because she was tricked, but also because she was forced to take an actual exam immediately following what was, for her, an apprehensive 10 minutes. An ethics committee agreed that expecting students to perform on an exam that would count toward a course grade right after a manufactured, nerve-racking disruption was unfair. Further concerns were expressed by the ethics committee because the study was judged to be poorly conceived and unlikely to contribute useful, new scientific knowledge.

Researchers who utilize deception have an obligation to come clean with their participants in a timely fashion after data collection. They must also attempt to correct any misconceptions or supply any information purposely withheld. Telling the truth, however, does not necessarily mean that participants will automatically feel good about what was done to them. This process should occur in a sensitive and educational manner so that the participants can understand and accept the reasons offered, including why deception was necessary. Or, put another way, participants may have to be "disabused" and "dehoaxed" as well as informed (Holmes, 1976).

Any participant should be allowed to withdraw the data they contributed on learning that they were deceived, thus giving what might be described as a "post hoc consent" opportunity (APA 02: 8.07c; 8.08a). Ideally, all anxieties are alleviated. But, this is not always the case, as the next case illustrates.

Case 19–20: Tempty Snookered was horrified to learn that she had agreed to commit a dishonest act as part of a research study. A confederate of the researcher managed to convince Tempty to engage in a less-than-honest enterprise. She was to go around asking professors if they had any textbooks they did not want, explaining that she was trying to build her personal library, but then handing them over to a confederate who would then sell them and split the take with her. Tempty was later informed that this was only a study of effective persuasion techniques, and that the books were all donated to the library. She was so upset that she transferred to another college at the end of the term, fearing that others would know that she had been willing to lie to professors.

If researchers maintained confidentiality, as they are supposed to, Tempty probably had nothing to be concerned about. Some social influence techniques are known to be extremely persuasive, and the researcher likely forgot all about Tempty as a "known individual" as soon as the data were recorded. Nevertheless, this case illustrates again how research participants can remain upset even when they have no actual reason for concern. The last three cases also illustrate how participants can be debriefed but not disabused. In each case, the student participants may remain upset even though they had been given the additional information. In those very rare cases when scientific or humane reasons exist for delaying or withholding information altogether, researchers should minimize any possible risks (APA 02: 8.08b).

The use of deception with child participants raises especially difficult issues. Parents should be fully informed of exactly what their children will experience, and special precautions are essential to ensure that children leave the experimental session feeling at least as whole as they did when they started. This might require the need for special additional sessions, for example, adding a play session in which the "confederate" who purposely provoked the children's anger is able to repair the relationship (see Hubbard, 2005).

We believe that a research project must be significant to warrant misleading participants. Alternative methodologies should be explored before contemplating the use of a deceptive technique, especially if it is one that may cause participants distress when they learn the truth about the true purpose of the research.

Ethical Issues With Vulnerable Study Populations

Research ethics standards apply best to samples composed of competent adults with well-developed senses of autonomy, thus allowing them to make fully informed decisions on their own behalf. The researcher's role is to approach these people in good faith and, if they agree to participate, cause them no harm. Ironically, this may be the most difficult type of participant to procure because they are rarely readily available. They are not institutionalized or found in groups in which researchers typically have bargaining power. Ironically, advantaged people— with the exception of college students, organizational employees, and respondents to opinion polls and surveys—rarely become participants in social and behavioral research.

Fortunately, we have come a long way since the days when highly vulnerable people seemed ready fodder for the kind of studies that now offend our sensibilities. For example, to test the theory that stuttering results from psychological pressure, 22 orphan children were relentlessly belittled for a period of 6 months in an attempt to induce speech imperfections. Over 60 years later, some of the unwitting participants are attempting to sue the study's sponsoring university, claiming that they have suffered lifelong emotional problems (Dvorak, 2003).

Most research populations of interest and available to mental health professionals are restricted or vulnerable in ways that do not allow a full measure of self-determination. These populations include children, the institutionalized, those at high risk for some possibly preventable outcome, and those who are disadvantaged socially or economically. Some noninstitutionalized study populations pose additional vulnerabilities because of their mental or emotional condition, such as the chronically depressed (Stanton & New, 1988). Others are vulnerable because of physical illness. Issues of confidentiality and stigma can pertain, for example, with participants who are HIV positive or victims of spousal abuse.

When research populations are legally incompetent, permission to participate must be granted by appropriate persons (proxies). Persons with severe mental illnesses require special considerations. However, children comprise the population that receives the most attention with regard to proxy consent procedures. Legally, the researcher must obtain permission from the parents or legal guardians, but that procedure does not necessarily settle the ethical questions.

Case 19–21: Bernice and Benny Bubbly enthusiastically enrolled their 9-year-old son, Notso Bubbly, in a study on math readiness. As the researchers approached Notso, asking if he will be part of it, Notso says he wants to go home to watch his favorite TV show and does not want to take any tests.

How much the child's wishes to participate should be taken into account has been debated, eventually leading to the recommendation that the verbal child's assent be obtained along with parental permission for most types of research (Koocher & Keith-Spiegel, 1990). Notso Bubbly's reasoning might seem illogical or annoying to the researchers and his parents, but the quality of data gleaned from an unhappy little boy is probably not worth much either.

Other populations require special ethical sensitivities because they may be vulnerable to exploitation due to their restrictive, unstimulating environments. Mentally competent, but lonely or bored individuals residing in assisted living or convalescent homes may be willing to engage in almost any activity in return for some attention or a change of routine. Concerns have been raised about conducting research on prisoners, a group who can not be said to have freedom of choice. Attitudes toward prisoners may not be particularly compassionate and could translate into a justification for relaxing ethical standards observed for others (Kimmel, 1996).

Cultural and Demographic Issues in Research

Social and behavioral researchers often study those who differ in some substantial way from themselves, such as in age, race, age, religion, country of origin, sexual orientation, gender, social and economic status, and any number of cultural variables. Researchers ignorant about the characteristics and customs of the study group and who, in addition, hold biases or stereotypical attitudes are likely to design poor studies with results that not are only in error or misleading but also may cause social harm (sometimes referred to as *social injury*) to the population under study. When comparing one group to another, as in much cross-cultural research, the assumption that the data are equivalent is not always valid. Any measure, such as a personality test or an interview schedule, may be systematically biased.

Multicultural Considerations

Multicultural research is important despite the many ethics-related challenges, especially when it comes to the pressing need to better understand the mental health needs and service availability to racial and ethnic minority groups (Fisher et al., 2002). Yet, to the extent that researchers, most of whom in North America are middle class and Caucasian, see their study target population as "not like me," the (probably unintentional) potential for harm exists unless special sensitivities and competencies are cultivated and maintained. The researchers' responsibilities are made more complicated if the researcher does not speak the study population's language. That includes honoring preferred communication modes when the participants are deaf (Pollard, 1992).

When discussing research ethics, those from other cultures or subcultures used to be placed under the category of "vulnerable populations." This suggests the need for special safeguards and implies, as Pollard (1992) noted, "that prospective participants have cognitive or at least volitional limitations that undermine their ability to participate knowledgeably and freely in research" (p. 89). In a real sense, then, viewing people from groups different from one's own as vulnerable builds a bias of "less than" into the mental framing of one's work.

Just as therapists should attain cultural competencies to work with those who are significantly different from themselves, so must researchers do the same (see Chapter 5). According to S. Sue (1998) and D. W. Sue (1999), *cultural competency* describes the ability to work effectively with other cultural groups. The usually valued attributes of empathy and openness, for example, are not always culturally appropriate. One must take into account the history of the race relations and discrimination. It is not enough simply to learn facts and figures (Philogène, 2004). The next case illustrates that point.

Case 19–22: Wellie Cleaner, D.S.W., had been fascinated with a particular Native American tribe for years, having read many books written about it. She was concerned about a recently reported lack of adequate clean water and the impact on the tribe members' health. She wanted to do an actual research-based intervention in a sincere attempt to be helpful. She created a design and evaluation, expecting to be welcomed with open arms on confidently presenting her plan to a tribal representative. She was stunned when she was rebuffed.

Dr. Cleaner may have known everything books could tell her, but she was ignorant about how members feel about what was perceived as a cocky outsider blustering in to tell them what they are doing wrong. Cleaner failed to appreciate the problem and why it existed, how the tribe had been ignored by those who had already been approached on numerous occasions about a foul water source, as well as how one should properly introduce themselves and their agenda to the tribal governance.

Just as we tend to mistakenly assume that everyone else views the world like we do, another prevalent false belief assumes that people classified into a particular cultural or demographic group are all alike. Stuart refers to applying a single label to a diverse group as the "myth of uniformity." As a consequence, research designs may fail to allow for the study of important factors that differentiate among members *within* a particular population. Levine (1982), for example, discussed aging research and the ethical implications of ignoring social class, ethnicity, race, and sex as critical factors that contribute to the understanding of older people.

Case 19–23: Kid Youngdumb, Psy.D., designed a study to test his hypothesis that adults over 65 exhibit declines in knowledge of current events compared to individuals under 40 because older people have less awareness of what is going on around them. He received permission to administer a brief questionnaire in two nursing homes, a day care facility for elderly individuals diagnosed with early onset Alzheimer's disease, a bridge club, a Bible study group, and a senior dance club. He compared the merged results with a younger sample of continuing education students in business and English literature courses. He reported confirmation of his hypothesis.

Dr. Youngdumb has treated an age cohort (people over 65) as if all members are the same. Fortunately, no scholarly publication accepted the article, recognizing both the sampling errors

as well as the fact that other research already revealed that active, healthy older adults remain well aware of current events.

A blanket reference to race suffers from the same "uniformity" error. For example, Stuart (2004) pointed to the prevalent but misleading use of the term *African American*, which lumps people of African heritage into a single group: "It implies that 33.9 million people share certain salient characteristics because of their ties with some 797 million people in Africa who live in 50 different countries and speak more than 1,000 different languages, unless, of course, their forbearers came from the West Indies, South America, or New Zealand" (p. 2). Stuart made similar points about the terms *Native Americans* and *Hispanics*.

Experimental methodology (including tests and assessments) may simply be inappropriate for some groups or in some cultural settings, producing results that are misleading at best and at worst harmful. The next case illustrates the improper assignment of a dependent variable, likely resulting in the stigmatization of Black urban youth.

Case 19–24: Myron Myopic, M.S.W., wants to study differences in delinquent behavior between Anglo and Black teenage boys in poor urban neighborhoods, using arrest records as the measure of delinquency. In this same neighborhood, local activists were documenting biased arrest patterns, mostly targeting young Black men hanging out on street corners. The police mostly ignored young Anglos engaging in similar behavior.

The results of this study will appear to support a hypothesis that young Blacks have higher delinquent rates than Whites. Unless Mr. Myopic understands the way of life and police profiling in that community, he will miss the serious flaw in his work.

Finally, full collaboration (as opposed to pro forma engagement) with the community from the very start is essential if most multicultural and cross-cultural research is to be properly conducted. Researchers should try to identify beforehand which questions and issues are of importance to the population under study. Forming community partnerships will avoid misunderstandings about such concepts as privacy and risk, resistance to being studied, any cultural meaning to offering participants compensation, and identifying invalid measures or dependent variables. In addition, it is important to assess any benefits or possible stigmatization as a result of the group's participation (Carpenter, 2001). Lack of respect for the decisions made by local authorities was the main reason the Crees (hunting and trapping communities in northern Quebec) ejected seven of the eight researchers from their territory (Darous, Hum, & Kurtness, 1991). In addition, these authors noted how ensuring value to the community under study, remaining cautious and patient, maintaining flexibility, using qualitative and participative methods, and accepting and giving feedback are important features of successful cross-cultural and multicultural research (APA, 2003; APA 02: General Principles B, D, & E; 2.01).

Social Science's "Fruit Flies"

Students enrolled in college and university introductory social science courses deserve their own section in our book because they comprise a large percentage of the participants in social science research. This is despite the fact that these mostly young people hardly comprise a random sample of adults (Jaffe, 2005). Although this population is not normally thought of as vulnerable, the way students are conscripted can involve coercion. Students are often recruited through "subject pools" and may be offered academic credit in their introductory psychology courses, thereby creating a convenient, inexpensive study population (Korn & Bram, 1987; Sieber & Saks, 1989).

The use of college student recruits has been debated on grounds of methodological and other biases. For example, research requiring participants to be naive about the purpose of the research is likely to be contaminated because the information is passed around, even when participants are asked not to talk about what the experiment was like afterward (Klein & Cheuvront, 1990). Coercion and related forms of exploitation can occur if alternative ways of satisfying course requirements are not offered, if

alternatives are noxious or excessively time consuming, if students receive no worthwhile feedback or educational benefit, or if no readily accessible complaint resource is provided (Diener & Crandall, 1978).

Case 19–25: Professor Bully Compel, Ph.D., allows his students to choose between participating for 10 hours in research conducted by himself and other faculty or writing a 20-page term paper on difficult topics that he assigns individually. Every semester, 100% of his students select the research option.

Although students tend to find their research assignment satisfying (Bowman & Waite, 2003), the APA ethics code mandates that alternative assignments to research participation remain both available and equitable (APA 02: 8.04.b). In fact, although the majority of psychology departments apparently offer alternatives, students regard most as relatively unattractive (Sieber & Saks, 1989).

Offering incentives to students who volunteer to participate raises similar concerns. Students who earn extra points that will affect their grade are being coerced unless there are reasonable alternative ways of earning extra credit. The professor who gave students points for volunteering and then subtracted points already earned from students who refused is clearly unethical (Aragon & Laanan, 2001).

Balancing Benefits and Risks

Incidents of blatant disregard for the welfare of participants have led to closer scrutiny of potential risks before allowing a research project to go forward. A horrendous example involves the government-sponsored Tuskegee study in which poor, black, syphilitic men in Alabama were left largely untreated for the purpose of understanding how this ravaging disease progresses. As many as 400 men may have lingered and died from a curable disease (Jones, 1981). How such a study could have been publicly tolerated from 1932 until the early 1970s remains a matter of debate and consternation to this day.

As recently as the 1980s, over 100 unwary women with abnormal cervical smears were left untreated as a way to study the natural progression of this fatal disease. As a result, these women died of in situ carcinoma of the cervix at 25 times the rate of women who received treatment (Young, 2005). Other high-profile tragedies involve medical research at prestigious institutions in which the scientists' own assessment of risks or the information offered to prospective participants was ultimately deemed inadequate, resulting in deaths and serious disabilities in volunteers (e.g., Begley, 2001; Lemonick & Goldstein, 2002).

Risks in experimentation are complicated by the fact that commercial product developers are required to conduct research to ensure the safety of their products and to head off the possibility of future product liability lawsuits. The problem is that the experimentation to ensure safety may prove dangerous. For example, a seven-page consent form did not dissuade dozens of students from accepting a paid assignment by the Dow Chemical Company to take a pill containing the active ingredient in Raid Ant & Roach Killer (Rawe, 2002). Studies administering toxic substances to human beings have since been banned by the Environmental Protection Agency, but no one knows how many dangerous experiments are still taking place. Unless a project is funded by the federal government or approved by an IRB, no monitoring or oversight exists.

Arriving at a risk/benefit ratio is a necessary, important, but often elusive judgment call. In general, the level of acceptable risk can be greater if the project is judged to be significant and important work, especially if the participants themselves might profit from some form of intervention available only in the research context.

The two extremes—known low risk and high potential benefit and known high risk and low potential benefit—create little debate when it comes to deciding whether to conduct a study. Whenever risks are known to be low and considerable benefit may result, the research will very likely gain approval. When known risks are high and the likelihood of benefits are low or unknown, the research will not likely receive approval, except perhaps when individuals are in irreversible states, and no other prospects to help them are available anywhere. As one gets closer to the middle, moderate risk and moderate potential for benefit, the decision becomes more complex, and the requirement for consent forms that participants understand becomes more critical.

Assessing Benefits

The potential benefits accruing from research participation are often impossible to estimate accurately. By definition, an experimental procedure is conducted to provide answers to heretofore unanswered questions. If a procedure were already known to afford benefit, there would be no need to study it.

Benefit assessment for biomedical research is often easier to evaluate than for social and behavioral research, as, for example, when a study sample population is terminally ill and the experimental treatment holds even a remote prospect of helping. Even here, a profound dilemma occurs when a treatment appears to be helpful, but the assessment of risks has not been completed. Should the study continue (meaning that some participants will not have access to the apparently beneficial treatment), or should it be terminated early, allowing the treatment to be given to all participants even though any long-term effects will remain unknown? The ethical issues are even more intense when commercial profits may accompany early study termination so that the treatment can get to market faster (Iltis, 2005).

In social and behavioral research, benefit may often exist primarily in the eye of the beholder. For example, a researcher may study ways to enhance children's assertiveness, figuring that early training will provide young people with coping skills that will serve them well, increase independence, decrease vulnerability to manipulation, and elevate self-efficacy. A critic might argue that assertive children would be perceived by adults as bratty, selfish, demanding, and disrespectful. Therefore, some may say that to encourage youngsters to be assertive, given traditional expectations for appropriate child behavior, would actually put them at risk in their homes and in the traditional school system.

The benefit test has also been debated regarding who or what benefits. Some argue that the test should be applied strictly to the research participants themselves. That is, as a result of their participation, some benefit might reasonably be expected to accrue directly to them. Others say that it is not necessary to expect that benefits be experienced by the participants of a given investigation, but that some likelihood exists for the possibility that the results will be useful in directing future research that may eventually benefit others. Indeed, science is a continuous and evolving process, and important findings can often be traced to the end of a chain of studies, with some tributaries leading to dead ends. Finally, still others believe that the benefit test is inappropriate altogether because the process of knowledge accumulation is in itself valuable regardless of whether anyone benefits directly or indirectly.

Assessing Risks

Risk assessment is defined as the probability that unwanted harms will occur as a result of participating in a given study. Risks are evaluated according to what those harms could be and to whom, how serious they might be, and whether they could be reversed should they materialize. The National Research Council (2003) designated six types of potential risks in research with human participants:

1. physical,
2. psychological,
3. social,
4. economic,
5. legal, and
6. dignitary.

We see most of these risks portrayed in the first 2 minutes of the now-classic comedy film, *Ghostbusters*, in which a researcher, portrayed by actor Bill Murray, behaves very badly. He brutally coerces and mistreats his participants, uses electric shock dangerously, and attempts to coax a pretty female participant into a sexual liaison.

In reality, and thankfully, potential risks in social and behavioral research are nonexistent or trivial most of the time. It is unfortunate that many researchers have been unnecessarily burdened when they are reviewed using standards for high-risk research. Minor risks include

- boredom
- inconvenience
- performance anxiety
- confusion regarding how to interpret the experimenters' directions

Somewhat more serious risks that could materialize include:

- invasion of privacy
- breach of confidentiality
- longer-term stress and discomfort
- lowering of self-esteem
- upset reactions to being deceived or debriefed
- embarrassment
- negative effects from assignment to a no-treatment control group
- collective risks by which potential social consequences exist directly for the participants or for the class of individuals represented in the research (Sieber & Stanley 1988).

A complicating problem relative to risk assessment is that many contemplated techniques or study approaches have not been previously studied. Pretesting with animals or less vulnerable participants (i.e., competent adults) may not be feasible. Thus, the degree of risk may simply be unknown. So, whereas risk minimization should always be contemplated from the onset, prediction of risks is often difficult in social and behavioral sciences because of the seemingly infinite variety of ways people respond to psychological phenomena. What one may find frightening or stressful—such as being asked to touch a spider, view pornography, or answer very personal questions—another may experience as exciting, fun, or pleasurably novel.

Case 19–26: Privy Bod, an undergraduate student complained to the university research ethics committee that a sociology professor administered a survey asking questions about sexual practices. Ms. Bod was particularly upset because the desks were so close together that others could see her answers.

The complaint could have been easily avoided had the research assistant asked the participants to sit in alternating seats. Many risks in social and behavioral sciences can be minimized with a little empathy and forethought. However, there will always be people who are sensitive or biased in ways that can not be foretold in advance.

Case 19–27: Taken Aback, M.S.W., was flabbergasted when an interviewee in his study assessing a community daycare program jumped up from her chair, told Mr. Aback that he should be ashamed of himself, waved her fists at him, and stomped out of the office. Mr. Aback reviewed the questions on his interview schedule with colleagues. No one could ascertain what the trigger for the extreme reaction could have been. It was later discovered that Mr. Aback's appearance and mannerisms reminded the woman of her ex-husband, who she now detested.

Occasionally, there may be a risk in *not* taking a risk. For example, if the researcher senses that a participant is extremely depressed or scores as such on a depression inventory, is it right to simply ignore concerns because such intrusion is not part of the research protocol? Or, what about asking people to divulge their own dangerous behavior or dangerous behavior that has been perpetrated on them? Whereas ethical concerns about self-report research tends to center around the degree of allowable intrusiveness, perhaps such questions should be asked more often when researching child abuse because the costs of missed opportunities to intervene are so high (Beeker-Blease & Freyd, 2006).

Finally, we must always remember that science has much yet to offer, despite the highly publicized cases of tragic research outcomes for which serious risks materialized. There is some concern that the pendulum may be swinging too far in the direction of *overprotecting* human participants, which could substantially slow scientific progress (Gunsalus, 2002).

Research Conducted Outside Traditional Settings

The majority of discussions in this chapter apply most directly to research conducted inside the walls of academic institutions, hospitals, community agencies, or other facilities where participants come *to* the researchers. However, data of interest to mental health professionals are sometimes collected in schools, public places where "subjects of interest" gather, and even private homes. In these instances, some ethical requirements in structured settings do not translate well to these venues, and some new ethical dilemmas present themselves.

Field Research

Participants in field research may not always be aware that they are being observed, thus precluding any advance voluntary and informed consent contract. Sometimes, the participants are simply observed in naturalistic settings (e.g., a rock concert or rave) without any experimental manipulation. Sometimes, the context is contrived (e.g., observing people's reactions to an unusual object placed on the sidewalk). At other times, the participants are deceived, and their reactions are observed (e.g., a confederate of the experimenter poses as an obnoxious store customer, while another confederate records the salesperson's reaction). The ethical investigator will inform and reassure the unknowing participants afterward, if possible, especially if people were made to feel uncomfortable or distraught.

Confidentiality concerns are minimized if unobtrusive (no manipulations), naturalistic observations of public behavior are made in such a way that identifying information can not be linked to those being observed (APA 02: 8.05). However, technological advances that allow visual or audio recordings of people's behavior using portable and easily concealed equipment complicate the ethical issue because a permanent record is created, heightening the potential for recognition of unwitting participants (APA 02: 8.03). In such cases, it is necessary to disguise or remove the possibility of identification.

When the participants perceive themselves to be in a private or confidential setting, additional ethical issues pertain whenever experimenters intrude themselves surreptitiously. The next case is adapted from a study by Middlemist, Knowles, and Matter (1976).

Case 19–28: Unsuspecting male students attempting to urinate in a university lavatory were either crowded or not crowded by a confederate at a urinal. A researcher with a periscope and stopwatch sitting in one of the stalls recorded the latency and duration of students' micturation (i.e., urination) to test the hypothesis that crowding delayed starting and slowed finishing.

As Koocher's (1977) criticisms of this study pointed out, everyone who comes into a bathroom (public or not) has an expectation of total privacy and assumes that their "privates in action" are not being monitored. Humphreys' (1970) classic "tearoom trade" account of the author's observations while volunteering as a "watchqueen" (the individual ready to issue a warning if anyone might interrupt the acts of homosexual contacts in public restrooms) was also controversial (Sieber, 1982b; Warwick, 1973), as was West, Gunn, and Chernicky's (1975) "ubiquitous Watergate" study in which an attempt was made to induce participants to agree to commit burglary (Cook, 1975). Because it is usually impossible to assess whether harm befell any of the participants who disappear after being observed and whose actual identities may not be discernible, the ethical acceptability of such controversial techniques will continue to be debated.

Primary Prevention/Intervention Research

Research designed to minimize the manifestation of identified or suspected risks is often conducted outside traditional research settings. Primary prevention research is usually regarded as cost-effective and humanistic because it attempts to discover ways to minimize human suffering by intervening prior to evolvement of full-scale maladjustment or damage. Benefit to the participants in the "treatment" group is always the intent, and many well-designed projects have served as model programs that have helped many. Usually, individuals judged as susceptible to developing potential maladjustment are recruited to participate in a program designed to reduce their risk level so that the maladjustment will not ultimately manifest itself. Examples of at-risk populations include the children of schizophrenic parents, recently divorced people, preschoolers from disadvantaged homes, parents who fit patterns indicating

a susceptibility to abusing their children, and people functioning under high stress. Educational, psychotherapeutic, and coping and skill-building training are among the interventions frequently employed.

However, profound ethical issues lurk just below the surface. As Trickett (1992) so succinctly put it: "Primary prevention activities involve a value-driven, premeditated intrusion into the lives and settings of individuals and groups" (p. 94).

Case 19–29: A grant-funded study attempted to identify male children aged 3 to 4 who evidenced "female" interests, such as playing with baby dolls and other female gender-typed activities, while displaying an adversity to male gender-typed activities. An intervention used behavioral techniques to strengthen an interest in activities that little boys typically prefer. Punishment was administered when the boys acted like little girls in an attempt to "masculinize" them. The rationale was that boys who display feminine characteristics as youngsters are at high risk for ridicule and rejection.

The researchers were denounced as homophobic and intolerant of individual differences. Their response was that an unfortunate outcome was already known from previous case histories, and that they were not responsible for society's cruel prejudices. However, they might be able to help some boys avoid a sad life, being often rejected by other boys as well as girls. Regardless of your opinion on this matter, this study well illustrates how attitudes and values play a major role in the targets and goals of prevention research.

Because the participants in primary prevention research have not, by definition, presented diagnosable symptomatology relative to the purpose of the intervention, four additional potential ethical problems arise: (1) faulty risk predictions, (2) labeling, (3) privacy invasion, and (4) abandonment. First, risk-level assignment is an imprecise art, and the potential for harm is present whenever risk decisions are made inappropriately. For example, using the case above, a little boy might be interested in feminine activities because he has older sisters who will play with him only if he fulfils certain roles.

The boy may not harbor any intrinsic interest in female gender-stereotyped activities.

Following directly from risk-level assignment is the process of labeling participants as at risk for something not yet manifested. That label (such as "predelinquent" or "potential school dropout") may carry a stigma or other consequences that could limit participants' access to opportunity and growth. Others who know of the risk label may treat the individual differently than if had they not known. For example, how likely is a harried junior high school teacher, who wants to spend as much time as possible with students perceived as having considerable potential, to tend to the needs of a student who has been labeled as a future dropout?

And, finally, primary prevention and intervention programming research is more likely than most other types of research to create dependencies. Researchers must be careful not to dump the participants as soon as data are collected, leaving the participants resourceless (or even more exposed) than before. For example, if counseling is part of the intervention, terminating participants when the study is over without regard for where they are in the counseling process is ethically problematical, especially if the participants remain in crisis or can not afford to continue counseling on their own. These dilemmas must be considered and minimized to the greatest extent possible during the design phase of prevention research programs. The consent procedure of any intervention treatment must be especially clear with regard to what is and what is not included as a result of participation in the experimental program (APA 02:8.02.b).

Research and Multiple-Role Relationships

When research participants are also current or previous clients, additional ethical obligations arise. Is truly voluntary consent possible? That is, will the client feel coerced, and can participation be refused without feeling guilty? Most clients would go out of their way to avoid displeasing their therapists. However, their participation could jeopardize the therapeutic services being rendered. The next case is an example of causing a client to lose trust and feel exploited.

Case 19–30: Willy Limp had developed difficulties satisfying his wife sexually. His psychiatrist asked if he would participate in a drug trial for erectile dysfunction. Willy was wary of drugs and rarely took as much as an aspirin. However, he felt like he could not decline or else his psychiatrist would be put off just at the point where Willy had begun to feel confident that the therapy alone was beginning to help. Unbeknown to Willy, his psychiatrist received compensation for referring potential participants to the study.

Whether Mr. Limp was helped in the long run by participating in the drug study is not at issue here. In the situation on which this true story is based, the client felt so torn that he quit therapy as well as the drug trials. The therapeutic alliance had been broken by what the client perceived as an unwelcome intrusion into his safe therapeutic sanctuary. In addition, the notion of compensating physicians for identifying and referring patients who might benefit from a particular treatment creates an unethical conflict of interest.

Conducting research on those with whom a fiduciary relationship has already been established for another purpose, and that includes students and supervisees as well as clients, constitutes a dual-role relationship. We recommend against conscripting current and previous clients into research unless needed benefits are likely and not otherwise available. Even here, care should be taken to present the opportunity to decline in a compelling way. When the power differential between the researcher and potential participants is especially large, special safeguards, such as a participant advocate, should be introduced (APA 02:8.04a; Fisher, 2003).

Privacy and Confidentiality Issues in Research

Unless otherwise specified and agreed to by the research participants, data collected on human participants should be treated as confidential. Ensuring confidentiality also benefits the researchers because participants are more likely to be open and honest (Blanck, Bellack, Rosnow, Rotheram-Borus, & Schooler, 1992). When research involves disclosing an individual's health information, normally protected from disclosure under the Health Insurance Portability and Accountability Act (HIPAA; see Chapter 8), a specific authorization by the participant (or legal guardian) is usually required as part of the consent procedure. (See http://www.hhs.gov/ocr/hipaa/guidelines/research.pdf.)

Research participants would not normally discover a confidentiality breach. Someone other than a research participant is the usual complainant, as the next case illustrates.

Case 19–31: Tab Cross, M.S., works at a university counseling center and teaches two classes in the educational psychology department. He administered a large number of personality inventories to educational psychology students. Their names were required, but Dr. Cross promised that identities would be held in the strictest confidence and would be destroyed as soon as data were coded. Cross published an article on personality differences between those students who had sought counseling and those who had not. However, a counseling center employee contacted an ethics committee to express concern that Dr. Cross accessed the center's files to identify those who had sought counseling. The colleague argued that Cross entered confidential files for a purpose unrelated to the center's business, that students were not sufficiently informed of the study's purpose, and that consent was not obtained to access counseling center files.

Despite the fact that individual identities were not disclosed to anyone else, Dr. Cross committed an ethical violation by not obtaining consent from the students regarding his intent to ascertain whether they had ever sought counseling.

Protecting the privacy and maintaining the confidentiality of data are usually routine procedures in social and behavioral research. In most cases, the task of researchers is far simpler than that of mental health professionals because keeping actual identities on file is usually unnecessary. The interest is often on how groups perform or differ from each other. Even when data are not anonymous, the researcher can usually take simple precautions to ensure that no one has access to identifying information,

often by assigning code numbers and keeping identifying information safe and separate.

Nevertheless, complex problems with regard to confidentiality can arise in research. For example, a mental health professional may conduct a qualitative study on a very few individuals who share a common but unusual diagnosis. This approaches the same ethical issues as discussed regarding case studies. To the extent that information is shared about their personal lives and habits, care must be taken to ensure that readers can not discern identities. Or, if conducting research on abused persons, the dilemma of mandatory reporting can arise unless special arrangements are made, such as obtaining a federal confidentiality certificate (Haggerty & Hawkins, 2000).

Researchers may promise confidentiality without a full understanding of disclosures that could possibly occur later. For example, lists of research participants can sometimes be accessed by others, and unauthorized follow-up studies or analyses for purposes other than the original one consented to by the participants could be performed. Any limits to confidentiality should be made known to the participants in advance (APA 02: 8.02).

The Internet is an increasingly popular research tool because, after the cost of upfront programming, the size of the research population can be very large, and data can be automatically stored and made ready for analysis. Mail surveys, on the other hand, must often limit the number to be sent because of the high cost of mailing and data transfer. However, for most surveys, especially if the requested information is sensitive, special care must be taken to ensure that participants' anonymity is in fact ensured (Keller & Lee, 2003; Kraut et al., 2004; Mathy, Kerr, & Haydin, 2003). The participants must also *perceive* that anonymity is ensured, or the response rate will suffer. A Web-based survey (as opposed to an e-mail survey that allows respondents to be easily traced) reduces the possibility of tracking identities and is reassuring to respondents because no one can verify exactly who responded (Simsek & Veiga, 2001).

Computers and electronic transfer systems allow inexpensive, instant data sharing anywhere in the world that was never envisioned a few decades ago. Data sharing among scientists holds the potential for hastening the evolution of a line of inquiry, helps to ensure validity and error corrections, encourages collaborative ventures, and is generally encouraged when done responsibly (APA 02: 8.14). Even research participants receive an advantage in the sense that their contributions are maximized. However, concerns about privacy invasion have drastically increased as technological advances allow sophisticated surveillance as well as links and access among computer storage banks. Researchers should resist opportunities to contribute information to databanks if confidentiality can not be safeguarded (see also Chapter 8).

Finally, is it acceptable to share information without consent when it appears that participants are in danger to themselves or others? A research participant may disclose that he sells drugs to schoolchildren, intends to commit suicide, or wants to kills an ex-friend, even when the content of such disclosures are not integral features of the studies at hand. Many researchers have no mental health counseling training and may feel insecure about how to respond. As a result, some may lack familiarity with state laws that mandate reporting of abuse of children and other dependent persons (e.g., the elderly and disabled) or that require certain protective actions in response to revelation of planned harmful acts. As is discussed in Chapter 8, it is difficult enough to decide what to do when such situations arise in therapy settings. The obligations of researchers are even more complex (Jeffrey, Snaith, & Voss, 2005). Immediate consultation with a trusted expert is a must.

SUMMARY GUIDELINES

1. Publication credit should be given only for substantial contributions to the project.
2. Early discussions of authorship credit expectations and assignments are encouraged in collaborative research teams to reduce the possibility of later conflict.
3. In their publications, scholars and researchers take care to properly attribute material created by others.

4. Despite any pressures to publish, researchers must uphold the integrity of science and to the public trust by gathering and reporting data accurately.
5. When publishing a case study about an individual or conducting research on a small and unusual sample, care must be taken to protect the welfare and privacy of the participants.
6. Researchers must actively maintain their competencies, including methods of study design and analysis. They should seek expert consultation whenever they lack needed expertise.
7. Researchers must fully familiarize themselves with the laws, ethics codes, and institutional policies that govern research activity.
8. Researchers must assess the design, procedures, and experiences to which the participants will be subjected. Special attention must be paid to cultural or value biases that may have an impact on the participants' welfare, the meaningfulness of the data, and the interpretation of results.
9. Consent from participants should be voluntary and informed. In those cases for which participants can not give meaningful or legal consent, researchers are obligated to take special safeguards.
10. Deception should be used only if the study is significant enough to warrant temporarily misleading research participants. Participants should receive adequate debriefing in a timely manner and receive sufficient justification for the use of deceptive methods.
11. Explaining the freedom to withdraw from the research project at any time is an important feature of ethical research.
12. When participants remain unaware of being observed, data should be gathered and disseminated in a manner that maintains anonymity.
13. Concern for research participants' welfare is paramount. Whenever risks or harms to participants are possible, researchers have special obligations to search for alternative study methods.
14. If participants become upset during the course of collecting data or afterward, the

researcher has a responsibility to institute ameliorative procedures.

15. Avoid conflicts of interest and dual-role relationships in the conduct of research.

16. Means of ensuring confidentiality must be implemented. Researchers must remain aware of any potential access to participant identities or databases and inform participants of any such possibilities during the consent phase.

References

Albee, G. W. (2002). Exploring a controversy. *American Psychologist, 57,* 161–164.

American Psychological Association (2003). Guidelines on multicultural education, training, research, practice, and organizational change for psychologists. *American Psychologist, 58,* 377–402.

Aragon, S. R., & Laanan, F. S. (2001). Coercing participation in research: When an incentive is no longer an incentive. *Advances in Developing Human Resources, 3,* 41–43.

Beeker-Blease, K. A., & Freyd, J. J. (2006). Research participants telling the truth about their lives. *American Psychologist, 61,* 218–226.

Begley, S. (2001, July). Dying for science. *Newsweek,* 36.

Bell, R. (1992). *Impure science.* New York: Wiley.

Blanck, P. D., Bellack, A. S., Rosnow, R. L., Rotheram-Borus, M. J., & Schooler, N. R. (1992). *American Psychologist, 47,* 959–965.

Bowman, L. L., & Waite, B. M. (2003). Volunteering in research: Student satisfaction and educational benefits. *Teaching of Psychology, 30,* 102–106.

Bridgstock, M. (1982). A sociological approach to fraud in science. *Australian and New Zealand Journal of Statistics, 18,* 364–383.

Broder, A. (1998). Deception can be acceptable. *American Psychologist.* 53, 805–806

Capron, A. M. (1989). Human experimentation. In R. M. Veatch (Ed.), *Medical ethics* (pp. 125–172). Boston: Jones & Bartlett.

Carpenter, S. (October, 2001). Experts weigh ethical issues in research with ethnic minority-youth. *Monitor on Psychology,* 34–35.

Cassileth, B. R. (1980). Informed consent—why are its goals imperfectly realized? *New England Journal of Medicine, 302,* 896–900.

Christensen, L. (1988). Deception in psychological research: When it its use justifiable? *Personality and Social Psychology Bulletin, 14,* 664–675.

Cohen, J. (1999, November). The federal perspective on IRBs. *APS Observer, 5,* 19.

Committee on Government Operations. (1990). *Are scientific misconduct and conflicts of interest hazardous to our health?* (House Report 101-688). Washington, DC: Author.

Cook, S. W. (1975). A comment on the ethical issues involved in West, Gunn, and Chernicky's "Ubiquitous Watergate: An attributional analysis." *Journal of Personality and Social Psychology, 32,* 66–68.

Darous, W. G., Hum, A., & Kurtness, J. (1991). An investigation of the impact of psychosocial research on a native population. *Professional Psychology, 24,* 325–329.

Department of Health and Human Services. (2005). Code of Federal Regulation, Title 45, Part 46, Protection of Human Subjects. Retrieved January 23, 2006, from http://www.hhs.gov/ohrp/humansubjects/guidance/45cfr46.htm

Diener, E., & Crandall, R. (1978). *Ethics in social and behavioral research.* Chicago: University of Chicago Press.

Dvorak, T. (2003). 1939 stuttering study draws suit. *Laredo Morning Times,* June 23, 2005, A8.

Farley, P. (2003, January 21). Young scientist's paper gets him in hot water with colleagues. *Boston Globe.* Retrieved January 28, 2003, from http://search.boston.com/local/Search.do?s.sm.query=young+scientist%27s&s.author=farley&s.si%28simplesearchinput%29.sortBy=&docType=&date=&s.startDate=&s.endDate=&s.collections=bostonGlobe&x=17&y=7

Fine, M. A., & Kurdek, L. A. (1993). Reflections on determining authorship credit and authorship order on faculty–student collaborations. *American Psychologist, 18,* 1141–1147.

Fisher, C. B. (2003). *Decoding the ethics code: A practical guide for psychologists.* Thousand Oaks, CA: Sage.

Fisher, C. B., Hoagwood, K., Boyce, C., et al. (2002). Research ethics for mental health science involving ethnic minority children and youths. *American Psychologist, 57,* 1024–1040.

Flewitt, R. (2005). Conducting research with young children: Some ethical considerations. *Early Child Development and Care, 175,* 553–565.

Froese, A. D., Boswell, K. L., Garcia, E. D., Koehn, L. J., & Nelson, J. M. (1995). Citing secondary sources: Can we correct what students so not know? *Teaching of Psychology, 22,* 235–238.

Garrison, E. G., & Kobar, P. C. (2002). Weathering a political storm: A contextual perspective on a psychological research controversy. *American Psychologist, 57,* 165–175.

Gates, D. (2002, March 18). No ordinary crime. *Newsweek,* 46–47.

Giles, J. (2005). Researchers break the rules in frustration at review boards. *Nature, 438,* 136–137.

Grinnell, F. (1992). *The scientific attitude* (2nd ed.). New York: Guilford Press.

Gross, A. E., & Flemming, L. (1982). Twenty years of deception in social psychology. *Personality and Social Psychology Bulletin, 12,* 82–86.

Gunsalus, C. K. (2002, November 15). Rethinking protections for human subjects. *Chronicle of Higher Education,* B24.

Haggarty, L. A., & Hawkins, J. (2000). Informed consent and the limits of confidentiality. *Western Journal of Nursing Research, 22,* 508–514.

Hawley, C. S. (1984). The thieves of academe: Plagiarism in the university system. *Improving College and University Teaching, 32,* 35–39.

Holaday, M., & Yost, T. E. (1995). Authorship credit and ethical guidelines. *Counseling and Values, 40,* 24–31,

Holmes, D. S. (1976). Debriefing after psychological experiments. *American Psychologist, 31,* 858–875.

Hopko, D. R., Hopko, S. D., & Morris, T. L. (1999). The application of behavioral contracting to authorship status. *Behavior Therapist, 22,* 93–95.

Hubbard, J. A. (2005). Eliciting and measuring children's anger in the context of their peer interactions: Ethical considerations and practical guidelines. *Ethics & Behavior, 15,* 247–258.

Humphreys, L. (1970). *Tearoom trade: Impersonal sex in public places.* Chicago: Aldine.

Iltis, A. S. (2005). Stopping trials early for commercial reasons: The risk–benefit relationship as a moral compass. *Journal of Medical Ethics, 31,* 410– 414.

Jaffe, E. (2005). How random is that? *APS Observer, 18,* 20–30.

Jeffery, A., Snaith, R., & Voss, L. (2005). Ethical dilemmas: Feeding back results to members of a longitudinal cohort study. *Journal of Medical Ethics, 31,* 153.

Jones, J. (1981). *Bad blood.* New York: Free Press.

Keith-Spiegel, P., & Koocher, G. (2005). The IRB Paradox: Could the protectors also encourage deceit? *Ethics & Behavior, 14,* 339–349.

Keith-Spiegel, P. Koocher, G., & Tabachnick, B. (2006). What scientists want from their research ethics committees. *Journal of Empirical Research on Human Research Ethics, 1,* 67–81.

Keith-Spiegel, P., & Maas, T. (1981, August). *Consent to research: Are there developmental differences?* Paper presented at the annual meetings of the American Psychological Association, Los Angeles.

Keller, H. E., & Lee, S. (2003). Ethical issues surrounding human participants research using the Internet. *Ethics & Behavior, 13,* 211–219.

Kimmel, A. J. (1996). *Ethical issues in behavioral research.* Cambridge, MA: Blackwell.

Kimmel, A. J. (1998). In defense of deception. *American Psychologist, 53,* 803–805.

Klein, K., & Cheuvront, B. (1990). The subject–experimenter contract: A reexamination of subject pool contamination. *Teaching of Psychology, 17,* 166–169.

Koocher, G. P. (1977). Bathroom behavior and human dignity. *Journal of Personality and Social Psychology, 35,* 120–121.

Koocher, G. P., & Keith-Spiegel, P. (1990). *Children, ethics and the law.* Lincoln: University of Nebraska Press.

Korn, J. H., & Bram, D. R. (1987). What is missing in the method section of APA journal articles? *American Psychologist, 42,* 1091–1092.

Kraut, R., Olson, J., Banaji, M., Bruckman, A., Cohen, J., & Couper, M. (2004). Psychological research online. *American Psychologist, 59,* 105–117.

LaFollette, M. C. (1992). *Fraud, plagiarism, and misconduct in scientific publishing.* Berkeley: University of California Press.

Leland, C. R. (1978, April). Psychiatrist encounters perils in publication. *Legal Aspects of Medical Practice, 51,* 53.

Lemonick, M. D., & Goldstein, A. (2002, April 22). At your own risk. *Time,* 44–51.

Levine, E. K. (1982). Old people are not all alike: Social class, ethnicity/race, and sex are bases for important differences. In J. E. Sieber (Ed.), *The ethics of social research: Surveys and experiments* (pp. 127–143). New York: Springer–Verlag.

Lilienfeld, S. O. (2002). When worlds collide: Social science, politics, and the Rind et al. (1998) child sexual abuse meta-analysis. *American Psychologist, 57,* 176–188.

Martinson, B. C., Anderson, M. S., & de Vries, R. (2005). Scientists behaving badly. *Nature, 435,* 737–738.

Mathy, R. M., Kerr, D. L., & Haydin, B. M. (2003). Methodological rigor and ethical considerations in Internet-mediated research. *Psychotherapy, 40,* 77–85.

McDonald, K. A. (1995, April 28). Too many co-authors. *Chronicle of Higher Education,* A35.

Middlemist, R. D., Knowles, E. S., & Matter, C. F. (1976). Personal space invasions in the lavatory: Suggestive evidence for arousal. *Journal of Personality and Social Psychology, 33,* 541–546.

Mishara, B. L., & Weisstub, D. N. (2005). Ethical and legal issues in suicide research. *International Journal of Law and Psychiatry, 28,* 23– 41.

National Research Council. (2003). *Protecting participants and facilitating social and behavioral sciences research.* Washington DC: National Academies Press.

Nicks, S. D., Korn, J. H., & Mainieri, T. (1997). The rise and fall of deception in social psychology and personality research. *Ethics & Behavior, 7,* 69–77.

Office of Research Integrity. (2005). Retrieved August 19, 2006, from http://ori.dhhs.gov/misconduct/cases/press_release_poehlman.shtml

Onishi, N. (2006, January 22). In a country that craved respect, stem cell researcher rode a wave of Korean pride. Retrieved January 23, 2006, from http://www.nytimes.com/2006/01/22/science/22clone.html

Ortmann, A., & Hertwig, R. (1997). Is deception acceptable? *American Psychologist, 52,* 746–747.

Patterson, A. (1999). The publication of case studies and confidentiality—and ethical predicament. *Psychiatric Bulletin, 23,* 562–564.

Philogène, G. (Ed.). (2004). *Racial identity in context: The legacy of Kenneth B. Clark.* Washington, DC: American Psychological Association.

Pollard, R. Q. (1992). Cross-cultural ethics in the conduct of deafness research. *Rehabilitation Psychology, 37,* 87–101.

Rawe, J. (2002). Poisoning for dollars [Electronic version]. *Time Magazine.* Retrieved June 16, 2005, from http://www.time.com/time/covers/1101020422/poisons.html

Research specialist sentences to federal prison for almost 6 years. (2006, March). *Office of Research Integrity Newsletter,* p.2.

Rees, E., & Hardy, J. (2003). Novel consent process for research in dying patients unable to give consent. *British Medical Journal, 327,* 198–200.

Ricciuti, H. (2005). When research findings and social norms collide. *APS Observer, 18,* 20–23.

Rind, B., Tromovitch, P., & Bauserman, R. (1998). A meta-analytic examination of assumed properties of child sexual abuse using college samples. *Psychological Bulletin, 124,* 22–53.

Roberts, L. W., & McAuliffe, T. L. (2006). Investigators' affirmation of ethical, safeguard, and scientific commitments in human research. *Ethics & Behavior, 16,* 135–150.

Rosenthal, R. (1994). Science and ethics in conducting, analyzing, and reporting psychological research. *Psychological Science, 5,* 127–134.

Ruark, J. K. (1999, May 28). Conservative groups blast psychology journal over paper on sexual abuse. *Chronicle of Higher Education,* A18.

Sandler, J. C., & Russell, B. L. (2005). Faculty–student collaborations: Ethics and satisfaction in authorship credit. *Ethics & Behavior, 15,* 65–80.

Sharpe, D., Adair, J. G., & Roese, N. J. (1992). Twenty years of deception research: A decline in subject's trust? *Personality and Social Psychology Bulletin, 18,* 585–590.

Sher, K. J., & Eisenberg, N. (2002). Publication of Rind et al. (1998): The editor's perspective. *American Psychologist, 57,* 206–210.

Sieber, J. E. (1982a). Deception in social research I: Kinds of deception and the wrongs they may involve. *IRB: A Review of Human Subjects Research, 4,* 1–6.

Sieber, J. E. (1982b). *The ethics of social research: Surveys and experiments.* New York: Springer–Verlag.

Sieber, J. E. (1991a). Openness in the social sciences: Sharing data. *Ethics & Behavior, 1,* 69–86.

Sieber, J. E. (Ed.). (1991b). *Sharing social science data: Advantages and challenges.* Newbury Park, CA: Sage.

Sieber, J. E. (1993). Ethical considerations in planning and conducting research on human subjects. *Academic Medicine, 9,* 59–513.

Sieber, J. E., & Levine, R. J. (2004). Informed consent and consent forms for research participants. *APS Observer, 17,* 25–26.

Sieber, J. E., & Saks, M. J. (1989). A census of subject pool characteristics and policies. *American Psychologist, 44,* 1053–1061.

Sieber, J. E., & Stanley, B. (1988). Sharing scientific data I: New problems for IRBs. *IRB: A Review of Human Subjects Research, 11,* 4–7.

Simsek, Z., & Veiga, J. F. (2001). A primer on Internet organizational surveys. *Organizational Research Methods, 4,* 218–235.

Spitz, V. (2005). *Doctors from hell: The horrific account of Nazi experiments on humans.* Boulder, CO: Sentient.

Stanton, A. L., & New, M. J. (1988). Ethical responsibilities to depressed research participants. *Professional Psychology, 19,* 279–285.

Sternberg, R. J. (2002). Everything you need to know to understand the current controversies you learned from psychological research: A comment on the Rind and Lilienfeld controversies. *American Psychologist, 57,* 193–197.

Stuart, R. B. (2004). Twelve practical suggestions for achieving multicultural competence. *Professional Psychology, 35,* 3–9.

Sue, D. W. (1999). The diversification of psychology: A multicultural revolution. *American Psychologist, 54,* 1061–1069.

Sue, S. (1998). In search of cultural competence in psychotherapy and counseling. *American Psychologist, 53,* 440–448.

Swazey, J. P., Anderson, M. S., & Lewis, K. S. (1993). Ethical problems in academic research. *American Scientist, 81,* 542–553.

Taub, H. A., Baker, M., & Sturr, J. F. (1986). Informed consent for research: Effects of readability, patient age, and education. *Law and Public Policy, 34,* 601–606.

Taylor, K. M., & Shepperd, J. A. (1996). Probing suspicion among participants in deception research. *American Psychologist, 51,* 886–887.

Thayer, W. (2006, December 19). Libyan court condemns Bulgarian nurses. http://www.washingtonpost.com/wp-dyn/content/article/2006/12/19/AR2006121900906.html

Trickett, E. J. (1992). Prevention ethics: Explicating the context of prevention activities. *Ethics & Behavior, 2,* 91–100.

Varnhagen, C. K., Gushta, M., Daniels, J., Peters, T. C., Parmar, N., Law, D., et al. (2005). How informed is online informed consent? *Ethics & Behavior, 15,* 37–48.

Wagena, E. J. (2005). The scandal of unfair behaviour of senior faculty. *Journal of Medical Ethics, 31,* 308.

Warwick, D. P. (1973). Tearoom trade: Means and ends in social research. *Hastings Center Studies, 1,* 27–38.

West, S. G., Gunn, S. P., & Chernicky, P. (1975). Ubiquitous Watergate: An attributional analysis. *Journal of Personality and Social Psychology, 32,* 55–65.

Wharton, B. (2005). Ethical issues in the publication of clinical material. *Journal of Analytical Psychology, 50,* 83–89.

Whitley, B. E., Jr. (1995). *Principles of research in behavioral science.* Mountain View, CA: Mayfield.

Whitley, B. E., Jr., & Keith-Spiegel, P. (2002). *Academic dishonesty: An educator's guide.* Mahwah, NJ: Erlbaum.

Wilson, T. D., DePaulo, B. M., Mook, D. G., & Klaaren, K. J. (1993). Scientists' evaluations of research: The biasing effects of the importance of the topic. *Psychological Science, 4,* 322–325.

Winerman, L. (2005). A congressional attack on peer-reviewed behavioral research. *Monitor on Psychology, 36,* 22–23.

Woolston, C. (2002). When a mentor becomes a thief. *Science.* Retrieved June 19, 2005, from http://sciencecareers.sciencemag.org/career_development/previous_issues/articles/1470/when_a_mentor_becomes_a_thief/(parent)/158

Young, D. (2005). Will exercising informed consent stop "unfortunate experiments"? *Birth: Issues in Perinatal Care, 32,* 1–3.

Appendix A

American Psychological Association

Ethical Principles of Psychologists and Code of Conduct (2002)

INTRODUCTION AND APPLICABILITY

The American Psychological Association's (APA's) Ethical Principles of Psychologists and Code of Conduct (hereinafter referred to as the Ethics Code) consists of an Introduction, a Preamble, five General Principles (A–E), and specific Ethical Standards. The Introduction discusses the intent, organization, procedural considerations, and scope of application of the Ethics Code. The Preamble and General Principles are aspirational goals to guide psychologists toward the highest ideals of psychology. Although the Preamble and General Principles are not themselves enforceable rules, they should be considered by psychologists in arriving at an ethical course of action. The Ethical Standards set forth enforceable rules for conduct as psychologists. Most of the Ethical Standards are written broadly, in order to apply to psychologists in varied roles, although the application of an Ethical Standard may vary depending on the context. The Ethical Standards are not exhaustive. The fact that a given conduct is not specifically addressed by an Ethical Standard does not mean that it is necessarily either ethical or unethical.

This Ethics Code applies only to psychologists' activities that are part of their scientific, educational, or professional roles as psychologists. Areas covered include but are not limited to the clinical, counseling, and school practice of psychology; research; teaching; supervision of trainees; public service; policy development; social intervention; development of assessment instruments; conducting assessments; educational counseling; organizational consulting; forensic activities; program design and evaluation; and administration. This Ethics Code applies to these activities across a variety of contexts, such as in person, postal, telephone, internet, and other electronic transmissions. These activities shall be distinguished from the purely private conduct of psychologists, which is not within the purview of the Ethics Code.

Membership in the APA commits members and student affiliates to comply with the standards of the APA Ethics Code and to the rules and procedures used to enforce them. Lack of awareness or misunderstanding of an Ethical Standard is not itself a defense to a charge of unethical conduct.

The procedures for filing, investigating, and resolving complaints of unethical conduct are described in the current Rules and Procedures of the APA Ethics Committee. APA may impose sanctions on its members for violations of the standards of the Ethics Code, including termination of APA membership, and may notify other bodies and individuals of its actions. Actions that violate the standards of the Ethics Code may also lead to the imposition of sanctions on psychologists or students whether or not they are APA members by bodies other than APA, including state psychological associations, other professional groups, psychology boards, other state or federal agencies, and payors for health services. In addition, APA may take action against a member after his or her conviction of a felony, expulsion or suspension from an affiliated state psychological association, or suspension or loss of licensure. When the sanction to be imposed by APA is less than expulsion, the 2001 Rules and Procedures do not guarantee an opportunity for an in-person hearing, but generally provide that complaints will be resolved only on the basis of a submitted record.

The Ethics Code is intended to provide guidance for psychologists and standards of professional conduct that can be applied by the APA and by other bodies that choose to adopt them. The Ethics Code is not intended to be a basis of civil liability. Whether a psychologist has violated the Ethics Code standards does not by itself determine whether the psychologist is legally liable in a court action, whether a contract is enforceable, or whether other legal consequences occur.

The modifiers used in some of the standards of this Ethics Code (e.g., *reasonably, appropriate, potentially*) are included in the standards when they would (1) allow professional judgment on the part of psychologists, (2) eliminate injustice or inequality that would occur without the modifier, (3) ensure applicability across the broad range of activities conducted by psychologists, or (4) guard against a set of rigid rules that might be quickly outdated. As used in this Ethics Code, the term *reasonable* means the prevailing professional judgment of psychologists engaged in similar activities in similar circumstances, given the knowledge the psychologist had or should have had at the time.

In the process of making decisions regarding their professional behavior, psychologists must consider this Ethics Code in addition to applicable laws and psychology board regulations. In applying the Ethics Code to their professional work, psychologists may consider other materials and guidelines that have been adopted or endorsed by scientific and professional psychological organizations and the dictates of their own conscience, as well as consult with others within the field. If this Ethics Code establishes a higher standard of conduct than is required by law, psychologists must meet the higher ethical standard. If psychologists' ethical responsibilities conflict with law, regulations, or other governing legal authority, psychologists make known their commitment to this Ethics Code and take steps to resolve the conflict in a responsible manner. If the conflict is unresolvable via such means, psychologists may adhere to the requirements of the law, regulations, or other governing authority in keeping with basic principles of human rights.

PREAMBLE

Psychologists are committed to increasing scientific and professional knowledge of behavior and people's understanding of themselves and others and to the use of such knowledge to improve the condition of individuals, organizations, and society. Psychologists respect and protect civil and human rights and the central importance of freedom of inquiry and expression in research, teaching, and publication. They strive to help the public in developing informed judgments and choices concerning human behavior. In doing so, they perform many roles, such as researcher, educator, diagnostician, therapist, supervisor, consultant, administrator, social interventionist, and expert witness. This Ethics Code provides a common set of principles and standards upon which psychologists build their professional and scientific work.

This Ethics Code is intended to provide specific standards to cover most situations encountered by psychologists. It has as its goals the welfare and protection of the individuals and groups with whom psychologists work and the education of members, students, and the public regarding ethical standards of the discipline.

The development of a dynamic set of ethical standards for psychologists' work-related conduct requires a personal commitment and lifelong effort to act ethically; to encourage ethical behavior by students, supervisees, employees, and colleagues; and to consult with others concerning ethical problems.

GENERAL PRINCIPLES

This section consists of General Principles. General Principles, as opposed to Ethical Standards, are aspirational in nature. Their intent is to guide and inspire psychologists toward the very highest ethical ideals of the profession. General Principles, in contrast to Ethical Standards, do not represent obligations and should not form the basis for imposing sanctions. Relying upon General Principles for either of these reasons distorts both their meaning and purpose.

Principle A: Beneficence and Nonmaleficence

Psychologists strive to benefit those with whom they work and take care to do no harm. In their professional actions, psychologists seek to safeguard the welfare and rights of those with whom they interact professionally and other affected persons, and the welfare of animal subjects of research. When conflicts occur among psychologists' obligations or concerns, they attempt to resolve these conflicts in a responsible fashion that avoids or minimizes harm. Because psychologists' scientific and professional judgments and actions may affect the lives of others, they are alert to and guard against personal, financial, social, organizational, or political factors that might lead to misuse of their influence. Psychologists strive to be aware of the possible effect of their own physical and mental health on their ability to help those with whom they work.

Principle B: Fidelity and Responsibility

Psychologists establish relationships of trust with those with whom they work. They are aware of their professional and scientific responsibilities to society and to the specific communities in which they work. Psychologists uphold professional standards of conduct, clarify their professional roles and obligations, accept appropriate responsibility for their behavior, and seek to manage conflicts of interest that could lead to exploitation or harm. Psychologists consult with, refer to, or cooperate with other professionals and institutions to the extent needed to serve the best interests of those with whom they work. They are concerned about the ethical compliance of their colleagues' scientific and professional conduct. Psychologists strive to contribute a portion of their professional time for little or no compensation or personal advantage.

Principle C: Integrity

Psychologists seek to promote accuracy, honesty, and truthfulness in the science, teaching, and practice of psychology. In these activities psychologists do not steal, cheat, or engage in fraud, subterfuge, or intentional misrepresentation of fact. Psychologists strive to keep their promises and to avoid unwise or unclear commitments. In situations in which deception may be ethically justifiable to maximize benefits and minimize harm, psychologists have a serious obligation to consider the need for, the possible consequences of, and their responsibility to correct any resulting mistrust or other harmful effects that arise from the use of such techniques.

Principle D: Justice

Psychologists recognize that fairness and justice entitle all persons to access to and benefit from the contributions of psychology and to equal quality in the processes, procedures, and services being conducted by psychologists. Psychologists exercise reasonable judgment and take precautions to ensure that their potential biases, the boundaries of their competence, and the limitations of their expertise do not lead to or condone unjust practices.

Principle E: Respect for People's Rights and Dignity

Psychologists respect the dignity and worth of all people, and the rights of individuals to privacy, confidentiality, and self-determination. Psychologists are aware that special safeguards may be necessary to protect the rights and welfare of persons or communities whose vulnerabilities impair autonomous decision making. Psychologists are aware of and respect cultural, individual, and role differences, including those based on age, gender, gender identity, race, ethnicity, culture, national origin, religion, sexual orientation, disability, language, and socioeconomic status and consider these factors when working with members of such groups. Psychologists try to eliminate the effect on their work of biases based on those factors, and they do not knowingly participate in or condone activities of others based upon such prejudices.

ETHICAL STANDARDS

1. Resolving Ethical Issues

1.01 Misuse of Psychologists' Work

If psychologists learn of misuse or misrepresentation of their work, they take reasonable steps to correct or minimize the misuse or misrepresentation.

1.02 Conflicts Between Ethics and Law, Regulations, or Other Governing Legal Authority

If psychologists' ethical responsibilities conflict with law, regulations, or other governing legal authority, psychologists make known their commitment to the Ethics Code and take steps to resolve the conflict. If the conflict is unresolvable via such means, psychologists may adhere to the requirements of the law, regulations, or other governing legal authority.

1.03 Conflicts Between Ethics and Organizational Demands

If the demands of an organization with which psychologists are affiliated or for whom they are working conflict with this Ethics Code, psychologists clarify the nature of the conflict, make known their commitment to the Ethics Code, and to the extent feasible, resolve the conflict in a way that permits adherence to the Ethics Code.

1.04 Informal Resolution of Ethical Violations

When psychologists believe that there may have been an ethical violation by another psychologist, they attempt to resolve the issue by bringing it to the attention of that individual, if an informal resolution appears appropriate and the intervention does not violate any confidentiality rights that may be involved. (See also Standards 1.02, Conflicts Between Ethics and Law, Regulations, or Other Governing Legal Authority, and 1.03, Conflicts Between Ethics and Organizational Demands.)

1.05 Reporting Ethical Violations

If an apparent ethical violation has substantially harmed or is likely to substantially harm a person or organization and is not appropriate for informal resolution under Standard 1.04, Informal Resolution of Ethical Violations, or is not resolved properly in that fashion, psychologists take further action appropriate to the situation. Such action might include referral to state or national committees on professional ethics, to state licensing boards, or to the appropriate institutional authorities. This standard does not apply when an intervention would violate confidentiality rights or when psychologists have been retained to review the work of another psychologist whose professional conduct is in question. (See also Standard 1.02, Conflicts Between Ethics and Law, Regulations, or Other Governing Legal Authority.)

1.06 Cooperating With Ethics Committees

Psychologists cooperate in ethics investigations, proceedings, and resulting requirements of the APA or any affiliated state psychological association to which they belong. In doing so, they address any confidentiality issues. Failure to cooperate is itself an ethics violation. However, making a request for deferment of adjudication of an ethics complaint pending the outcome of litigation does not alone constitute noncooperation.

1.07 Improper Complaints

Psychologists do not file or encourage the filing of ethics complaints that are made with reckless disregard for or willful ignorance of facts that would disprove the allegation.

1.08 Unfair Discrimination Against Complainants and Respondents

Psychologists do not deny persons employment, advancement, admissions to academic or other programs, tenure, or promotion, based solely upon their having made or their being the subject of an ethics complaint. This does not preclude taking action based upon the outcome of such proceedings or considering other appropriate information.

2. Competence

2.01 Boundaries of Competence

(a) Psychologists provide services, teach, and conduct research with populations and in areas only within the boundaries of their competence, based on their education, training, supervised experience, consultation, study, or professional experience.

(b) Where scientific or professional knowledge in the discipline of psychology establishes that an understanding of factors associated with age, gender, gender identity, race, ethnicity, culture, national origin, religion, sexual orientation, disability, language, or socioeconomic status is essential for effective implementation of their services or research, psychologists have or obtain the training, experience, consultation, or supervision necessary to ensure the competence of their services, or they make appropriate referrals, except as provided in Standard 2.02, Providing Services in Emergencies.

(c) Psychologists planning to provide services, teach, or conduct research involving populations, areas, techniques, or technologies new to them undertake relevant education, training, supervised experience, consultation, or study.

(d) When psychologists are asked to provide services to individuals for whom appropriate mental health services are not available and for which psychologists have not obtained the competence necessary, psychologists with closely related prior training or experience may provide such services in order to ensure that services are not denied if they make a reasonable effort to obtain the competence required by using relevant research, training, consultation, or study.

(e) In those emerging areas in which generally recognized standards for preparatory training do not yet exist, psychologists nevertheless take reasonable steps to ensure the competence of their work and to protect clients/patients, students, supervisees, research participants, organizational clients, and others from harm.

(f) When assuming forensic roles, psychologists are or become reasonably familiar with the judicial or administrative rules governing their roles.

2.02 Providing Services in Emergencies

In emergencies, when psychologists provide services to individuals for whom other mental health services are not available and for which psychologists have not obtained the necessary training, psychologists may provide such services in order to ensure that services are not denied. The services are discontinued as soon as the emergency has ended or appropriate services are available.

2.03 Maintaining Competence

Psychologists undertake ongoing efforts to develop and maintain their competence.

2.04 Bases for Scientific and Professional Judgments

Psychologists' work is based upon established scientific and professional knowledge of the discipline. (See also Standards 2.01e, Boundaries of Competence, and 10.01b, Informed Consent to Therapy.)

2.05 Delegation of Work to Others

Psychologists who delegate work to employees, supervisees, or research or teaching assistants or who use the services of others, such as interpreters, take reasonable steps to (1) avoid delegating such work to persons who have a multiple relationship with those being served that would likely lead to exploitation or loss of objectivity; (2) authorize only those responsibilities that such persons can be expected to perform competently on the basis of their education, training, or experience, either independently or with the level of supervision being provided; and (3) see that such persons perform these services competently. (See also Standards 2.02, Providing Services in Emergencies; 3.05, Multiple Relationships; 4.01, Maintaining Confidentiality; 9.01, Bases for Assessments; 9.02, Use of Assessments; 9.03, Informed Consent in Assessments; and 9.07, Assessment by Unqualified Persons.)

2.06 Personal Problems and Conflicts

(a) Psychologists refrain from initiating an activity when they know or should know that there is a substantial likelihood that their personal problems will prevent them from performing their work-related activities in a competent manner.

(b) When psychologists become aware of personal problems that may interfere with their performing work-related duties adequately, they take appropriate measures, such as obtaining professional consultation or assistance, and determine whether they should limit, suspend, or terminate their work-related duties. (See also Standard 10.10, Terminating Therapy.)

3. Human Relations

3.01 Unfair Discrimination

In their work-related activities, psychologists do not engage in unfair discrimination based on age, gender, gender identity, race, ethnicity, culture, national origin, religion, sexual orientation, disability, socioeconomic status, or any basis proscribed by law.

3.02 Sexual Harassment

Psychologists do not engage in sexual harassment. Sexual harassment is sexual solicitation, physical advances, or verbal or nonverbal conduct that is sexual in nature, that occurs in connection with the psychologist's activities or roles as a psychologist, and that either (1) is unwelcome, is offensive, or creates a hostile workplace or educational environment, and the psychologist knows or is told this or (2) is sufficiently severe or intense to be abusive to a reasonable person in the context. Sexual harassment can consist of a single intense or severe act or of multiple persistent or pervasive acts. (See also Standard 1.08, Unfair Discrimination Against Complainants and Respondents.)

3.03 Other Harassment

Psychologists do not knowingly engage in behavior that is harassing or demeaning to persons with whom they interact in their work based on factors such as those persons' age, gender, gender identity, race, ethnicity, culture, national origin, religion, sexual orientation, disability, language, or socioeconomic status.

3.04 Avoiding Harm

Psychologists take reasonable steps to avoid harming their clients/patients, students, supervisees, research participants, organizational clients, and others with whom they work, and to minimize harm where it is foreseeable and unavoidable.

3.05 Multiple Relationships

(a) A multiple relationship occurs when a psychologist is in a professional role with a person and (1) at the same time is in another role with the same person, (2) at the same time is in a relationship with a person closely associated with or related to the person with whom the psychologist has the professional relationship, or (3) promises to enter into another relationship in the future with the person or a person closely associated with or related to the person.

A psychologist refrains from entering into a multiple relationship if the multiple relationship could reasonably be expected to impair the psychologist's objectivity, competence, or effectiveness in performing his or her functions as a psychologist, or otherwise risks exploitation or harm to the person with whom the professional relationship exists.

Multiple relationships that would not reasonably be expected to cause impairment or risk exploitation or harm are not unethical.

(b) If a psychologist finds that, due to unforeseen factors, a potentially harmful multiple relationship has arisen, the psychologist takes reasonable steps to resolve it with due regard for the best interests of the affected person and maximal compliance with the Ethics Code.

(c) When psychologists are required by law, institutional policy, or extraordinary circumstances to serve in more than one role in judicial or administrative proceedings, at the outset they clarify role expectations and the extent of confidentiality and thereafter as changes occur. (See also Standards 3.04, Avoiding Harm, and 3.07, Third-Party Requests for Services.)

3.06 Conflict of Interest

Psychologists refrain from taking on a professional role when personal, scientific, professional, legal, financial, or other interests or relationships could reasonably be expected to (1) impair their objectivity, competence, or effectiveness in performing their functions as psychologists or (2) expose the person or organization with whom the professional relationship exists to harm or exploitation.

3.07 Third-Party Requests for Services

When psychologists agree to provide services to a person or entity at the request of a third party, psychologists attempt to clarify at the outset of the service the nature of the relationship with all individuals or organizations involved. This clarification includes the role of the psychologist (e.g., therapist, consultant, diagnostician, or expert witness), an identification of who is the client, the probable uses of the services provided or the information obtained, and the fact that

there may be limits to confidentiality. (See also Standards 3.05, Multiple Relationships, and 4.02, Discussing the Limits of Confidentiality.)

3.08 Exploitative Relationships

Psychologists do not exploit persons over whom they have supervisory, evaluative, or other authority such as clients/patients, students, supervisees, research participants, and employees. (See also Standards 3.05, Multiple Relationships; 6.04, Fees and Financial Arrangements; 6.05, Barter With Clients/Patients; 7.07, Sexual Relationships With Students and Supervisees; 10.05, Sexual Intimacies With Current Therapy Clients/Patients; 10.06, Sexual Intimacies With Relatives or Significant Others of Current Therapy Clients/Patients; 10.07, Therapy With Former Sexual Partners; and 10.08, Sexual Intimacies With Former Therapy Clients/Patients.)

3.09 Cooperation With Other Professionals

When indicated and professionally appropriate, psychologists cooperate with other professionals in order to serve their clients/patients effectively and appropriately. (See also Standard 4.05, Disclosures.)

3.10 Informed Consent

(a) When psychologists conduct research or provide assessment, therapy, counseling, or consulting services in person or via electronic transmission or other forms of communication, they obtain the informed consent of the individual or individuals using language that is reasonably understandable to that person or persons except when conducting such activities without consent is mandated by law or governmental regulation or as otherwise provided in this Ethics Code. (See also Standards 8.02, Informed Consent to Research; 9.03, Informed Consent In Assessments; and 10.01, Informed Consent to Therapy.)

(b) For persons who are legally incapable of giving informed consent, psychologists nevertheless (1) provide an appropriate explanation, (2) seek the individual's assent, (3) consider such persons' preferences and best interests, and (4) obtain appropriate permission from a legally authorized person, if such substitute consent is permitted or required by law. When consent by a legally authorized person is not permitted or required by law, psychologists take reasonable steps to protect the individual's rights and welfare.

(c) When psychological services are court ordered or otherwise mandated, psychologists inform the individual of the nature of the anticipated services, including whether the services are court ordered or mandated and any limits of confidentiality, before proceeding.

(d) Psychologists appropriately document written or oral consent, permission, and assent. (See also Standards 8.02, Informed Consent to Research; 9.03, Informed Consent in Assessments; and 10.01, Informed Consent to Therapy.)

3.11 Psychological Services Delivered To or Through Organizations

(a) Psychologists delivering services to or through organizations provide information beforehand to clients and when appropriate those directly affected by the services about (1) the nature and objectives of the services, (2) the intended recipients, (3) which of the individuals are clients, (4) the relationship the psychologist will have with each person and the organization, (5) the probable uses of services provided and information obtained, (6) who will have access to the information, and (7) limits of confidentiality. As soon as feasible, they provide information about the results and conclusions of such services to appropriate persons.

(b) If psychologists will be precluded by law or by organizational roles from providing such information to particular individuals or groups, they so inform those individuals or groups at the outset of the service.

3.12 Interruption of Psychological Services

Unless otherwise covered by contract, psychologists make reasonable efforts to plan for facilitating services in the event that psychological services are interrupted by factors such as the psychologist's illness, death, unavailability, relocation, or retirement or by the client's/papatient's relocation or financial limitations. (See also Standard 6.02c, Maintenance, Dissemination, and Disposal of Confidential Records of Professional and Scientific Work.)

4. Privacy And Confidentiality

4.01 Maintaining Confidentiality

Psychologists have a primary obligation and take reasonable precautions to protect confidential information obtained through or stored in any medium, recognizing that the extent and limits of confidentiality may be regulated by law or established by institutional rules or professional or scientific relationship. (See also Standard 2.05, Delegation of Work to Others.)

4.02 Discussing the Limits of Confidentiality

(a) Psychologists discuss with persons (including, to the extent feasible, persons who are legally incapable of giving informed consent and their legal representatives) and organizations with whom they establish a scientific or professional relationship (1) the relevant limits of confidentiality and (2) the foreseeable uses of the information generated through their psychological activities. (See also Standard 3.10, Informed Consent.)

(b) Unless it is not feasible or is contraindicated, the discussion of confidentiality occurs at the outset of the relationship and thereafter as new circumstances may warrant.

(c) Psychologists who offer services, products, or information via electronic transmission inform clients/patients of the risks to privacy and limits of confidentiality.

4.03 Recording

Before recording the voices or images of individuals to whom they provide services, psychologists obtain permission from all such persons or their legal representatives. (See also Standards 8.03, Informed Consent for Recording Voices and Images in Research; 8.05, Dispensing With Informed Consent for Research; and 8.07, Deception in Research.)

4.04 Minimizing Intrusions on Privacy

(a) Psychologists include in written and oral reports and consultations, only information germane to the purpose for which the communication is made.

(b) Psychologists discuss confidential information obtained in their work only for appropriate scientific or professional purposes and only with persons clearly concerned with such matters.

4.05 Disclosures

(a) Psychologists may disclose confidential information with the appropriate consent of the organizational client, the individual client/patient, or another legally authorized person on behalf of the client/patient unless prohibited by law.

(b) Psychologists disclose confidential information without the consent of the individual only as mandated by law, or where permitted by law for a valid purpose such as to (1) provide needed professional services; (2) obtain appropriate professional consultations; (3) protect the client/patient, psychologist, or others from harm; or (4) obtain payment for services from a client/patient, in which instance disclosure is limited to the minimum that is necessary to achieve the purpose. (See also Standard 6.04e, Fees and Financial Arrangements.)

4.06 Consultations

When consulting with colleagues, (1) psychologists do not disclose confidential information that reasonably could lead to the identification of a client/patient, research participant, or other person or organization with whom they have a confidential relationship unless they have obtained the prior consent of the person or organization or the disclosure cannot be avoided, and (2) they disclose information only to the extent necessary to achieve the purposes of the consultation. (See also Standard 4.01, Maintaining Confidentiality.)

4.07 Use of Confidential Information for Didactic or Other Purposes

Psychologists do not disclose in their writings, lectures, or other public media, confidential, personally identifiable information concerning their clients/patients, students, research participants, organizational clients, or other recipients of their services that they obtained during the course of their work, unless (1) they take reasonable steps to disguise the person or organization, (2) the person or organization has consented in writing, or (3) there is legal authorization for doing so.

5. Advertising and Other Public Statements

5.01 Avoidance of False or Deceptive Statements

(a) Public statements include but are not limited to paid or unpaid advertising, product endorsements, grant applications, licensing applications, other credentialing applications, brochures, printed matter, directory listings, personal resumes or curricula vitae, or comments for use in media such as print or electronic transmission, statements in legal proceedings, lectures and public oral presentations, and published materials. Psychologists do not knowingly make public statements that are false, deceptive, or fraudulent concerning their research, practice, or other work activities or those of persons or organizations with which they are affiliated.

(b) Psychologists do not make false, deceptive, or fraudulent statements concerning (1) their training, experience, or competence; (2) their academic degrees; (3) their credentials; (4) their institutional or association affiliations; (5) their services; (6) the scientific or clinical basis for, or results or degree of success of, their services; (7) their fees; or (8) their publications or research findings.

(c) Psychologists claim degrees as credentials for their health services only if those degrees (1) were earned from a regionally accredited educational institution or (2) were the basis for psychology licensure by the state in which they practice.

5.02 Statements by Others

(a) Psychologists who engage others to create or place public statements that promote their professional practice, products, or activities retain professional responsibility for such statements.

(b) Psychologists do not compensate employees of press, radio, television, or other communication media in return for publicity in a news item. (See also Standard 1.01, Misuse of Psychologists' Work.)

(c) A paid advertisement relating to psychologists' activities must be identified or clearly recognizable as such.

5.03 Descriptions of Workshops and Non-Degree-Granting Educational Programs

To the degree to which they exercise control, psychologists responsible for announcements, catalogs, brochures, or advertisements describing workshops, seminars, or other non-degree-granting educational programs ensure that they accurately describe the audience for which the program is intended, the educational objectives, the presenters, and the fees involved.

5.04 Media Presentations

When psychologists provide public advice or comment via print, Internet, or other electronic transmission, they take precautions to ensure that statements (1) are based on their professional knowledge, training, or experience in accord with appropriate psychological literature and practice; (2) are otherwise consistent with this Ethics Code; and (3) do not indicate that a professional relationship has been established with the recipient. (See also Standard 2.04, Bases for Scientific and Professional Judgments.)

5.05 Testimonials

Psychologists do not solicit testimonials from current therapy clients/patients or other persons who because of their particular circumstances are vulnerable to undue influence.

5.06 In-Person Solicitation

Psychologists do not engage, directly or through agents, in uninvited in-person solicitation of business from actual or potential therapy clients/patients or other persons who because of their particular circumstances are vulnerable to undue influence. However, this prohibition does not preclude (1) attempting to implement appropriate collateral contacts for the purpose of benefiting an already engaged therapy client/patient or (2) providing disaster or community outreach services.

6. Record Keeping and Fees

6.01 Documentation of Professional and Scientific Work and Maintenance of Records

Psychologists create, and to the extent the records are under their control, maintain, disseminate, store, retain, and dispose of records and data relating to their professional and scientific work in order to (1) facilitate provision of services later by them or by other professionals, (2) allow for replication of research design and analyses, (3) meet institutional requirements, (4) ensure accuracy of billing and payments, and (5) ensure compliance with law. (See also Standard 4.01, Maintaining Confidentiality.)

6.02 Maintenance, Dissemination, and Disposal of Confidential Records of Professional and Scientific Work

(a) Psychologists maintain confidentiality in creating, storing, accessing, transferring, and disposing of records under their control, whether these are written, automated, or in any other medium. (See also Standards 4.01, Maintaining Confidentiality, and 6.01, Documentation of Professional and Scientific Work and Maintenance of Records.)

(b) If confidential information concerning recipients of psychological services is entered into databases or systems of records available to persons whose access has not been consented to by the recipient, psychologists use coding or other techniques to avoid the inclusion of personal identifiers.

(c) Psychologists make plans in advance to facilitate the appropriate transfer and to protect the confidentiality of records and data in the event of psychologists' withdrawal from positions or practice. (See also Standards 3.12, Interruption of Psychological Services, and 10.09, Interruption of Therapy.)

6.03 Withholding Records for Nonpayment

Psychologists may not withhold records under their control that are requested and needed for a client's/patient's emergency treatment solely because payment has not been received.

6.04 Fees and Financial Arrangements

(a) As early as is feasible in a professional or scientific relationship, psychologists and recipients of psychological services reach an agreement specifying compensation and billing arrangements.

(b) Psychologists' fee practices are consistent with law.

(c) Psychologists do not misrepresent their fees.

(d) If limitations to services can be anticipated because of limitations in financing, this is discussed with the recipient of services as early as is feasible. (See also Standards 10.09, Interruption of Therapy, and 10.10, Terminating Therapy.)

(e) If the recipient of services does not pay for services as agreed, and if psychologists intend to use collection agencies or legal measures to collect the fees, psychologists first inform the person that such measures will be taken and provide that person an opportunity to make prompt payment. (See also Standards 4.05, Disclosures; 6.03, Withholding Records for Nonpayment; and 10.01, Informed Consent to Therapy.)

6.05 Barter With Clients/Patients

Barter is the acceptance of goods, services, or other nonmonetary remuneration from clients/patients in return for psychological services. Psychologists may barter only if (1) it is not clinically contraindicated, and (2) the resulting arrangement is not exploitative. (See also Standards 3.05, Multiple Relationships, and 6.04, Fees and Financial Arrangements.)

6.06 Accuracy in Reports to Payors and Funding Sources

In their reports to payors for services or sources of research funding, psychologists take reasonable steps to ensure the accurate reporting of the nature of the service provided or research conducted, the fees, charges, or payments, and where applicable, the identity of the provider, the findings, and the diagnosis. (See also Standards 4.01, Maintaining Confidentiality; 4.04, Minimizing Intrusions on Privacy; and 4.05, Disclosures.)

6.07 Referrals and Fees

When psychologists pay, receive payment from, or divide fees with another professional, other than in an employer-employee relationship, the payment to each is based on the services provided (clinical, consultative, administrative, or other) and is not based on the referral itself. (See also Standard 3.09, Cooperation With Other Professionals.)

7. Education and Training

7.01 Design of Education and Training Programs

Psychologists responsible for education and training programs take reasonable steps to ensure that the programs are designed to provide the appropriate knowledge and proper experiences, and to meet the requirements for licensure, certification, or other goals for which claims are made by the program. (See also Standard 5.03, Descriptions of Workshops and Non-Degree-Granting Educational Programs.)

7.02 Descriptions of Education and Training Programs

Psychologists responsible for education and training programs take reasonable steps to ensure that there is a current and accurate description of the program content (including participation in required course- or program-related counseling, psychotherapy, experiential groups, consulting projects, or community service), training goals and objectives, stipends and benefits, and requirements that must be met for satisfactory completion of the program. This information must be made readily available to all interested parties.

7.03 Accuracy in Teaching

(a) Psychologists take reasonable steps to ensure that course syllabi are accurate regarding the subject matter to be covered, bases for evaluating progress, and the nature of course experiences. This standard does not preclude an instructor from modifying course content or requirements when the instructor considers it pedagogically necessary or desirable, so long as students are made aware of these modifications in a manner that enables them to fulfill course requirements. (See also Standard 5.01, Avoidance of False or Deceptive Statements.)

(b) When engaged in teaching or training, psychologists present psychological information accurately. (See also Standard 2.03, Maintaining Competence.)

7.04 Student Disclosure of Personal Information

Psychologists do not require students or supervisees to disclose personal information in course- or program-related activities, either orally or in writing, regarding sexual history, history of abuse and neglect, psychological treatment, and relationships with parents, peers, and spouses or significant others except if (1) the program or training facility has clearly identified this requirement in its admissions and program materials or (2) the information is necessary to evaluate or obtain assistance for students whose personal problems could reasonably be judged to be preventing them from performing their training- or professionally related activities in a competent manner or posing a threat to the students or others.

7.05 Mandatory Individual or Group Therapy

(a) When individual or group therapy is a program or course requirement, psychologists responsible for that program allow students in undergraduate and graduate programs the option of selecting such therapy from practitioners unaffiliated with the program. (See also Standard 7.02, Descriptions of Education and Training Programs.)

(b) Faculty who are or are likely to be responsible for evaluating students' academic performance do not themselves provide that therapy. (See also Standard 3.05, Multiple Relationships.)

7.06 Assessing Student and Supervisee Performance

(a) In academic and supervisory relationships, psychologists establish a timely and specific process for providing feedback to students and supervisees. Information regarding the process is provided to the student at the beginning of supervision.

(b) Psychologists evaluate students and supervisees on the basis of their actual performance on relevant and established program requirements.

7.07 Sexual Relationships With Students and Supervisees

Psychologists do not engage in sexual relationships with students or supervisees who are in their department, agency, or training center or over whom psychologists have or are likely to have evaluative authority. (See also Standard 3.05, Multiple Relationships.)

8. Research and Publication

8.01 Institutional Approval

When institutional approval is required, psychologists provide accurate information about their research proposals and obtain approval prior to conducting the research. They conduct the research in accordance with the approved research protocol.

8.02 Informed Consent to Research

(a) When obtaining informed consent as required in Standard 3.10, Informed Consent, psychologists inform participants about (1) the purpose of the research, expected duration, and procedures; (2) their right to decline to participate and to withdraw from the research once participation has begun; (3) the foreseeable consequences of declining or withdrawing; (4) reasonably foreseeable factors that may be expected to influence their willingness to participate such as potential risks, discomfort, or adverse effects; (5) any prospective research benefits; (6) limits of confidentiality; (7) incentives for participation; and (8) whom to contact for questions about the research and research participants' rights. They provide opportunity for the prospective participants to ask questions and receive answers. (See also Standards 8.03, Informed Consent for Recording Voices and Images in Research; 8.05, Dispensing With Informed Consent for Research; and 8.07, Deception in Research.)

(b) Psychologists conducting intervention research involving the use of experimental treatments clarify to participants at the outset of the research (1) the experimental nature of the treatment; (2) the services that will or will not be available to the control group(s) if appropriate; (3) the means by which assignment to treatment and control groups will be made; (4) available treatment alternatives if an individual does not wish to participate in the research or wishes to withdraw once a study has begun; and (5) compensation for or monetary costs of participating including, if appropriate, whether reimbursement from the participant or a third-party payor will be sought. (See also Standard 8.02a, Informed Consent to Research.)

8.03 Informed Consent for Recording Voices and Images in Research

Psychologists obtain informed consent from research participants prior to recording their voices or images for data collection unless (1) the research consists solely of naturalistic observations in public places, and it is not anticipated that the recording will be used in a manner that could cause personal identification or harm, or (2) the research design includes deception, and consent for the use of the recording is obtained during debriefing. (See also Standard 8.07, Deception in Research.)

8.04 Client/Patient, Student, and Subordinate Research Participants

(a) When psychologists conduct research with clients/patients, students, or subordinates as participants, psychologists take steps to protect the prospective participants from adverse consequences of declining or withdrawing from participation.

(b) When research participation is a course requirement or an opportunity for extra credit, the prospective participant is given the choice of equitable alternative activities.

8.05 Dispensing With Informed Consent for Research

Psychologists may dispense with informed consent only (1) where research would not reasonably be assumed to create distress or harm and involves (a) the study of normal educational practices, curricula, or classroom management methods conducted in educational settings; (b) only anonymous questionnaires, naturalistic observations, or archival research for which disclosure of responses would not place participants at risk of criminal or civil liability or damage their financial standing, employability, or reputation, and confidentiality is protected; or (c) the study of factors related to job or organization effectiveness conducted in organizational settings for which there is no risk to participants' employability, and confidentiality is protected or (2) where otherwise permitted by law or federal or institutional regulations.

8.06 Offering Inducements for Research Participation

(a) Psychologists make reasonable efforts to avoid offering excessive or inappropriate financial or other inducements for research participation when such inducements are likely to coerce participation.

(b) When offering professional services as an inducement for research participation, psychologists clarify the nature of the services, as well as the risks, obligations, and limitations. (See also Standard 6.05, Barter With Clients/Patients.)

8.07 Deception in Research

(a) Psychologists do not conduct a study involving deception unless they have determined that the use of deceptive techniques is justified by the study's significant prospective scientific, educational, or applied value and that effective nondeceptive alternative procedures are not feasible.

(b) Psychologists do not deceive prospective participants about research that is reasonably expected to cause physical pain or severe emotional distress.

(c) Psychologists explain any deception that is an integral feature of the design and conduct of an experiment to participants as early as is feasible, preferably at the conclusion of their participation, but no later than at the conclusion of the data collection, and permit participants to withdraw their data. (See also Standard 8.08, Debriefing.)

8.08 Debriefing

(a) Psychologists provide a prompt opportunity for participants to obtain appropriate information about the nature, results, and conclusions of the research, and they take reasonable steps to correct any misconceptions that participants may have of which the psychologists are aware.

(b) If scientific or humane values justify delaying or withholding this information, psychologists take reasonable measures to reduce the risk of harm.

(c) When psychologists become aware that research procedures have harmed a participant, they take reasonable steps to minimize the harm.

8.09 Humane Care and Use of Animals in Research

(a) Psychologists acquire, care for, use, and dispose of animals in compliance with current federal, state, and local laws and regulations, and with professional standards.

(b) Psychologists trained in research methods and experienced in the care of laboratory animals supervise all procedures involving animals and are responsible for ensuring appropriate consideration of their comfort, health, and humane treatment.

(c) Psychologists ensure that all individuals under their supervision who are using animals have received instruction in research methods and in the care, maintenance, and handling of the species being used, to the extent appropriate to their role. (See also Standard 2.05, Delegation of Work to Others.)

(d) Psychologists make reasonable efforts to minimize the discomfort, infection, illness, and pain of animal subjects.

(e) Psychologists use a procedure subjecting animals to pain, stress, or privation only when an alternative procedure is unavailable and the goal is justified by its prospective scientific, educational, or applied value.

(f) Psychologists perform surgical procedures under appropriate anesthesia and follow techniques to avoid infection and minimize pain during and after surgery.

(g) When it is appropriate that an animal's life be terminated, psychologists proceed rapidly, with an effort to minimize pain and in accordance with accepted procedures.

8.10 Reporting Research Results

(a) Psychologists do not fabricate data. (See also Standard 5.01a, Avoidance of False or Deceptive Statements.)

(b) If psychologists discover significant errors in their published data, they take reasonable steps to correct such errors in a correction, retraction, erratum, or other appropriate publication means.

8.11 Plagiarism

Psychologists do not present portions of another's work or data as their own, even if the other work or data source is cited occasionally.

8.12 Publication Credit

(a) Psychologists take responsibility and credit, including authorship credit, only for work they have actually performed or to which they have substantially contributed. (See also Standard 8.12b, Publication Credit.)

(b) Principal authorship and other publication credits accurately reflect the relative scientific or professional contributions of the individuals involved, regardless of their relative status. Mere possession of an institutional position, such as department chair, does not justify authorship credit. Minor contributions to the research or to the writing for publications are acknowledged appropriately, such as in footnotes or in an introductory statement.

(c) Except under exceptional circumstances, a student is listed as principal author on any multiple-authored article that is substantially based on the student's doctoral dissertation. Faculty advisors discuss publication credit with students as early as feasible and throughout the research and publication process as appropriate. (See also Standard 8.12b, Publication Credit.)

8.13 Duplicate Publication of Data

Psychologists do not publish, as original data, data that have been previously published. This does not preclude republishing data when they are accompanied by proper acknowledgment.

8.14 Sharing Research Data for Verification

(a) After research results are published, psychologists do not withhold the data on which their conclusions are based from other competent professionals who seek to verify the substantive claims through reanalysis and who intend to use such data only for that purpose, provided that the confidentiality of the participants can be protected and unless legal rights concerning proprietary data preclude their release. This does not preclude psychologists from requiring that such individuals or groups be responsible for costs associated with the provision of such information.

(b) Psychologists who request data from other psychologists to verify the substantive claims through reanalysis may use shared data only for the declared purpose. Requesting psychologists obtain prior written agreement for all other uses of the data.

8.15 Reviewers

Psychologists who review material submitted for presentation, publication, grant, or research proposal review respect the confidentiality of and the proprietary rights in such information of those who submitted it.

9. Assessment

9.01 Bases for Assessments

(a) Psychologists base the opinions contained in their recommendations, reports, and diagnostic or evaluative statements, including forensic testimony, on information and techniques sufficient to substantiate their findings. (See also Standard 2.04, Bases for Scientific and Professional Judgments.)

(b) Except as noted in 9.01c, psychologists provide opinions of the psychological characteristics of individuals only after they have conducted an examination of the individuals adequate to support their statements or conclusions. When, despite reasonable efforts, such an examination is not practical, psychologists document the efforts they made and the result of those efforts, clarify the probable impact of their limited information on the reliability and validity of their opinions, and appropriately limit the nature and extent of their conclusions or recommendations. (See also Standards 2.01, Boundaries of Competence, and 9.06, Interpreting Assessment Results.)

(c) When psychologists conduct a record review or provide consultation or supervision and an individual examination is not warranted or necessary for the opinion, psychologists explain this and the sources of information on which they based their conclusions and recommendations.

9.02 Use of Assessments

(a) Psychologists administer, adapt, score, interpret, or use assessment techniques, interviews, tests, or instruments in a manner and for purposes that are appropriate in light of the research on or evidence of the usefulness and proper application of the techniques.

(b) Psychologists use assessment instruments whose validity and reliability have been established for use with members of the population tested. When such validity or reliability has not been established, psychologists describe the strengths and limitations of test results and interpretation.

(c) Psychologists use assessment methods that are appropriate to an individual's language preference and competence, unless the use of an alternative language is relevant to the assessment issues.

9.03 Informed Consent in Assessments

(a) Psychologists obtain informed consent for assessments, evaluations, or diagnostic services, as described in Standard 3.10, Informed Consent, except when (1) testing is mandated by law or governmental regulations; (2) informed consent is implied because testing is conducted as a routine educational, institutional, or organizational activity (e.g., when participants voluntarily agree to assessment when applying for a job); or (3) one purpose of the testing is to evaluate decisional capacity. Informed consent includes an explanation of the nature and purpose of the assessment, fees, involvement of third parties, and limits of confidentiality and sufficient opportunity for the client/patient to ask questions and receive answers.

(b) Psychologists inform persons with questionable capacity to consent or for whom testing is mandated by law or governmental regulations about the nature and purpose of the proposed assessment services, using language that is reasonably understandable to the person being assessed.

(c) Psychologists using the services of an interpreter obtain informed consent from the client/patient to use that interpreter, ensure that confidentiality of test results and test security are maintained, and include in their recommendations, reports, and diagnostic or evaluative statements, including forensic testimony, discussion of any limitations on the data obtained. (See also Standards 2.05, Delegation of Work to Others; 4.01, Maintaining Confidentiality; 9.01, Bases for Assessments; 9.06, Interpreting As-

sessment Results; and 9.07, Assessment by Unqualified Persons.)

9.04 Release of Test Data

(a) The term *test data* refers to raw and scaled scores, client/patient responses to test questions or stimuli, and psychologists' notes and recordings concerning client/patient statements and behavior during an examination. Those portions of test materials that include client/patient responses are included in the definition of *test data*. Pursuant to a client/patient release, psychologists provide test data to the client/patient or other persons identified in the release. Psychologists may refrain from releasing test data to protect a client/patient or others from substantial harm or misuse or misrepresentation of the data or the test, recognizing that in many instances release of confidential information under these circumstances is regulated by law. (See also Standard 9.11, Maintaining Test Security.)

(b) In the absence of a client/patient release, psychologists provide test data only as required by law or court order.

9.05 Test Construction

Psychologists who develop tests and other assessment techniques use appropriate psychometric procedures and current scientific or professional knowledge for test design, standardization, validation, reduction or elimination of bias, and recommendations for use.

9.06 Interpreting Assessment Results

When interpreting assessment results, including automated interpretations, psychologists take into account the purpose of the assessment as well as the various test factors, test-taking abilities, and other characteristics of the person being assessed, such as situational, personal, linguistic, and cultural differences, that might affect psychologists' judgments or reduce the accuracy of their interpretations. They indicate any significant limitations of their interpretations. (See also Standards 2.01b and c, Boundaries of Competence, and 3.01, Unfair Discrimination.)

9.07 Assessment by Unqualified Persons

Psychologists do not promote the use of psychological assessment techniques by unqualified persons, except when such use is conducted for training purposes with appropriate supervision. (See also Standard 2.05, Delegation of Work to Others.)

9.08 Obsolete Tests and Outdated Test Results

(a) Psychologists do not base their assessment or intervention decisions or recommendations on data or test results that are outdated for the current purpose.

(b) Psychologists do not base such decisions or recommendations on tests and measures that are obsolete and not useful for the current purpose.

9.09 Test Scoring and Interpretation Services

(a) Psychologists who offer assessment or scoring services to other professionals accurately describe the purpose, norms, validity, reliability, and applications of the procedures and any special qualifications applicable to their use.

(b) Psychologists select scoring and interpretation services (including automated services) on the basis of evidence of the validity of the program and procedures as well as on other appropriate considerations. (See also Standard 2.01b and c, Boundaries of Competence.)

(c) Psychologists retain responsibility for the appropriate application, interpretation, and use of assessment instruments, whether they score and interpret such tests themselves or use automated or other services.

9.10 Explaining Assessment Results

Regardless of whether the scoring and interpretation are done by psychologists, by employees or assistants, or by automated or other outside services, psychologists take reasonable steps to ensure that explanations of results are given to the individual or designated representative unless the nature of the relationship precludes provision of an explanation of results (such as in some organizational consulting, preemployment or security screenings, and forensic evaluations), and this fact has been clearly explained to the person being assessed in advance.

9.11. Maintaining Test Security

The term *test materials* refers to manuals, instruments, protocols, and test questions or stimuli and does not include *test data* as defined in Standard 9.04, Release of Test Data. Psychologists make reasonable efforts to maintain the integrity and security of test materials and other assessment techniques consistent with law and contractual obligations, and in a manner that permits adherence to this Ethics Code.

10. Therapy

10.01 Informed Consent to Therapy

(a) When obtaining informed consent to therapy as required in Standard 3.10, Informed Consent, psychologists inform clients/patients as early as is feasible in the therapeutic relationship about the nature and anticipated course of therapy, fees, involvement of third parties, and limits of confidentiality and provide sufficient opportunity for the client/patient to ask questions and receive answers. (See also Standards 4.02, Discussing the Limits of Confidentiality, and 6.04, Fees and Financial Arrangements.)

(b) When obtaining informed consent for treatment for which generally recognized techniques and procedures have not been established, psychologists inform their clients/ patients of the developing nature of the treatment, the potential risks involved, alternative treatments that may be available, and the voluntary nature of their participation. (See also Standards 2.01e, Boundaries of Competence, and 3.10, Informed Consent.)

(c) When the therapist is a trainee and the legal responsibility for the treatment provided resides with the supervisor, the client/patient, as part of the informed consent procedure, is informed that the therapist is in training and is being supervised and is given the name of the supervisor.

10.02 Therapy Involving Couples or Families

(a) When psychologists agree to provide services to several persons who have a relationship (such as spouses, significant others, or parents and children), they take reasonable steps to clarify at the outset (1) which of the individuals are clients/patients and (2) the relationship the psychologist will have with each person. This clarification includes the psychologist's role and the probable uses of the services provided or the information obtained. (See also Standard 4.02, Discussing the Limits of Confidentiality.)

(b) If it becomes apparent that psychologists may be called on to perform potentially conflicting roles (such as family therapist and then witness for one party in divorce proceedings), psychologists take reasonable steps to clarify and modify, or withdraw from, roles appropriately. (See also Standard 3.05c, Multiple Relationships.)

10.03 Group Therapy

When psychologists provide services to several persons in a group setting, they describe at the outset the roles and responsibilities of all parties and the limits of confidentiality.

10.04 Providing Therapy to Those Served by Others

In deciding whether to offer or provide services to those already receiving mental health services elsewhere, psychologists carefully consider the treatment issues and the potential client's/patient's welfare. Psychologists discuss these issues with the client/patient or another legally authorized person on behalf of the client/patient in order to minimize the risk of confusion and conflict, consult with the other service providers when appropriate, and proceed with caution and sensitivity to the therapeutic issues.

10.05 Sexual Intimacies With Current Therapy Clients/Patients

Psychologists do not engage in sexual intimacies with current therapy clients/patients.

10.06 Sexual Intimacies With Relatives or Significant Others of Current Therapy Clients/Patients

Psychologists do not engage in sexual intimacies with individuals they know to be close relatives, guardians, or significant others of current clients/patients. Psychologists do not terminate therapy to circumvent this standard.

10.07 Therapy With Former Sexual Partners

Psychologists do not accept as therapy clients/patients persons with whom they have engaged in sexual intimacies.

10.08 Sexual Intimacies With Former Therapy Clients/Patients

(a) Psychologists do not engage in sexual intimacies with former clients/patients for at least two years after cessation or termination of therapy.

(b) Psychologists do not engage in sexual intimacies with former clients/patients even after a two-year interval except in the most unusual circumstances. Psychologists who engage in such activity after the two years following cessation or termination of therapy and of having no sexual contact with the former client/patient bear the burden of demonstrating that there has been no exploitation, in light of all relevant factors, including (1) the amount of time that has passed since therapy terminated; (2) the nature, duration, and intensity of the therapy; (3) the circumstances of termination; (4) the client's/patient's personal history; (5) the client's/patient's current mental status; (6) the likelihood of adverse impact on the client/patient; and (7) any statements or actions made by the therapist during the course of therapy suggesting or inviting the possibility of a post-termination sexual or romantic relationship with the client/patient. (See also Standard 3.05, Multiple Relationships.)

10.09 Interruption of Therapy

When entering into employment or contractual relationships, psychologists make reasonable efforts to provide for orderly and appropriate resolution of responsibility for client/patient care in the event that the employment or contractual relationship ends, with paramount consideration given to the welfare of the client/patient. (See also Standard 3.12, Interruption of Psychological Services.)

10.10 Terminating Therapy

(a) Psychologists terminate therapy when it becomes reasonably clear that the client/patient no longer needs the service, is not likely to benefit, or is being harmed by continued service.

(b) Psychologists may terminate therapy when threatened or otherwise endangered by the client/patient or another person with whom the client/patient has a relationship.

(c) Except where precluded by the actions of clients/patients or third-party payors, prior to termination psychologists provide pretermination counseling and suggest alternative service providers as appropriate.

HISTORY AND EFFECTIVE DATE

This version of the APA Ethics Code was adopted by the American Psychological Association's Council of Representatives during its meeting, August 21, 2002, and is effective beginning June 1, 2003. Inquiries concerning the substance or interpretation of the APA Ethics Code should be addressed to the Director, Office of Ethics, American Psychological Association, 750 First Street, NE, Washington, DC 20002-4242. The Ethics Code and information regarding the Code can be found on the APA web site, http://www.apa.org/ethics. The standards in this Ethics Code will be used to adjudicate complaints brought concerning alleged conduct occurring on or after the effective date. Complaints regarding conduct occurring prior to the effective date will be adjudicated on the basis of the version of the Ethics Code that was in effect at the time the conduct occurred.

Appendix B

Canadian Psychological Association

Canadian Code of Ethics
for Psychologists (2000)

INTRODUCTION

Every discipline that has relatively autonomous control over its entry requirements, training, development of knowledge, standards, methods, and practices does so only within the context of a contract with the society in which it functions. This social contract is based on attitudes of mutual respect and trust, with society granting support for the autonomy of a discipline in exchange for a commitment by the discipline to do everything it can to assure that its members act ethically in conducting the affairs of the discipline within society; in particular, a commitment to try to assure that each member will place the welfare of the society and individual members of that society above the welfare of the discipline and its own members. By virtue of this social contract, psychologists have a higher duty of care to members of society than the general duty of care that all members of society have to each other.

The Canadian Psychological Association recognizes its responsibility to help assure ethical behaviour and attitudes on the part of psychologists. Attempts to assure ethical behaviour and attitudes include articulating ethical principles, values, and standards; promoting those principles, values, and standards through education, peer modelling, and consultation; developing and implementing methods to help psychologists monitor the ethics of their behaviour and attitudes; adjudicating complaints of unethical behaviour; and, taking corrective action when warranted.

This Code articulates ethical principles, values, and standards to guide all members of the Canadian Psychological Association, whether scientists, practitioners, or scientist practitioners, or whether acting in a research, direct service, teaching, student, trainee, administrative, management, employer, employee, supervisory, consultative, peer review, editorial, expert witness, social policy, or any other role related to the discipline of psychology. [For more introductory material about the CPA code, its development, and intended use, see http://www.cpa.ca/cpasite/userfiles/Documents/Canadian%20Code%20of%20Ethics%20for%20Psycho.pdf]

PRINCIPLE I: RESPECT FOR THE DIGNITY OF PERSONS

Values Statement

In the course of their work as scientists, practitioners, or scientist-practitioners, psychologists come into contact with many different individuals and groups, including: research participants; clients seeking help with individual, family, organizational, industrial, or community issues; students; trainees; supervisees; employees; business partners; business competitors; colleagues; employers; third party payers; and, the general public.

In these contacts, psychologists accept as fundamental the principle of respect for the dignity of persons; that is, the belief that each person should be treated primarily as a person or an end in him/herself, not as an object or a means to an end. In so doing, psychologists acknowledge that all persons have a right to have their innate worth as human beings appreciated and that this worth is not dependent upon their culture, nationality, ethnicity, colour, race, religion, sex, gender, marital status, sexual orientation, physical or mental abilities, age, socioeconomic status, or any other preference or personal characteristic, condition, or status.

Although psychologists have a responsibility to respect the dignity of all persons with whom they come in contact in their role as psychologists, the nature of their contract with society demands that their greatest responsibility be to those persons in the most vulnerable position. Normally, persons directly receiving or involved in the psychologist's activities are in such a position (e.g., research participants, clients, students). This responsibility is almost always greater than their responsibility to those indirectly involved (e.g., employers, third party payers, the general public).

Adherence to the concept of moral rights is an essential component of respect for the dignity of persons. Rights to privacy, self-determination, personal liberty, and natural justice are of particular importance to psychologists, and they have a responsibility to protect and promote these rights in all of their activities. As such, psychologists have a responsibility to develop and follow procedures for informed consent, confidentiality, fair treatment, and due process that are consistent with those rights.

As individual rights exist within the context of the rights of others and of responsible caring (see Principle II), there might be circumstances in which the possibility of serious detrimental consequences to themselves or others, a diminished capacity to be autonomous, or a court order, would disallow some aspects of the rights to privacy, self-determination, and personal liberty. Indeed, such circumstances might be serious enough to create a duty to warn or protect others (see Standards I.45 and II.39). However, psychologists still have a responsibility to respect the rights of the person(s) involved to the greatest extent possible under the circumstances, and to do what is necessary and reasonable to reduce the need for future disallowances.

Psychologists recognize that, although all persons possess moral rights, the manner in which such rights are promoted, protected, and exercised varies across communities and cultures. For instance, definitions of what is considered private vary, as does the role of families and other community members in personal decision making. In their work, psychologists acknowledge and respect such differences, while guarding against clear violations of moral rights.

In addition, psychologists recognize that as individual, family, group, or community vulnerabilities increase, or as the power of persons to control their environment or their lives decreases, psychologists have an increasing responsibility to seek ethical advice and to establish safeguards to protect the rights of the persons involved. For this reason, psychologists consider it their responsibility to increase safeguards to protect and promote the rights of persons involved in their activities proportionate to the degree of dependency and the lack of voluntary initiation. For example, this would mean that there would be more safeguards to protect and promote the rights of fully dependent persons than partially dependent persons, and more safeguards for partially dependent than independent persons.

Respect for the dignity of persons also includes the concept of distributive justice. With respect to psychologists, this concept implies that all persons are entitled to benefit equally from the contributions of psychology and to equal quality in the processes, procedures, and services being conducted by psychologists, regardless of the person's characteristics, condition, or status. Although individual psychologists might specialize and direct their activities to particular populations, or might decline to engage in activities based on the limits of their competence or acknowledgment of problems in some relationships, psychologists must not exclude persons on a capricious or unjustly discriminatory basis.

By virtue of the social contract that the discipline has with society, psychologists have a higher duty of care to members of society than the general duty of care all members of society have to each other. However, psychologists are entitled to protect themselves from serious violations of their own moral rights (e.g., privacy, personal liberty) in carrying out their work as psychologists.

Ethical Standards

In adhering to the Principle of Respect for the Dignity of Persons, psychologists would:

General Respect

I.1 Demonstrate appropriate respect for the knowledge, insight, experience, and areas of expertise of others.

I.2 Not engage publicly (e.g., in public statements, presentations, research reports, or with clients) in degrading comments about others, including demeaning jokes based on such characteristics as culture, nationality, ethnicity, colour, race, religion, sex, gender, or sexual orientation.

I.3 Strive to use language that conveys respect for the dignity of persons as much as possible in all written or oral communication.

I.4 Abstain from all forms of harassment, including sexual harassment.

General Rights

I.5 Avoid or refuse to participate in practices disrespectful of the legal, civil, or moral rights of others.

I.6 Refuse to advise, train, or supply information to anyone who, in the psychologist's judgement, will use the knowledge or skills to infringe on human rights.

I.7 Make every reasonable effort to ensure that psychological knowledge is not misused, intentionally or unintentionally, to infringe on human rights.

I.8 Respect the right of research participants, clients, employees, supervisees, students, trainees, and others to safeguard their own dignity.

Non-discrimination

I.9 Not practice, condone, facilitate, or collaborate with any form of unjust discrimination.

I.10 Act to correct practices that are unjustly discriminatory.

I.11 Seek to design research, teaching, practice, and business activities in such a way that they contribute to the fair distribution of benefits to individuals and groups, and that they do not unfairly exclude those who are vulnerable or might be disadvantaged.

Fair Treatment/Due Process

I.12 Work and act in a spirit of fair treatment to others.

I.13 Help to establish and abide by due process or other natural justice procedures for employment, evaluation, adjudication, editorial, and peer review activities.

I.14 Compensate others fairly for the use of their time, energy, and knowledge, unless such compensation is refused in advance.

I.15 Establish fees that are fair in light of the time, energy, and knowledge of the psychologist and any associates or employees, and in light of the market value of the product or service. (Also see Standard IV.12.)

Informed Consent

I.16 Seek as full and active participation as possible from others in decisions that affect them, respecting and integrating as much as possible their opinions and wishes.

I.17 Recognize that informed consent is the result of a process of reaching an agreement to work collaboratively, rather than of simply having a consent form signed.

I.18 Respect the expressed wishes of persons to involve others (e.g., family members, community members) in their decision making regarding informed consent. This would include respect for written and clearly expressed unwritten advance directives.

I.19 Obtain informed consent from all independent and partially dependent persons for any psychological services provided to them except in circumstances of urgent need (e.g., disaster or other crisis). In urgent circumstances, psychologists would proceed with the assent of such persons, but fully informed consent would be obtained as soon as possible. (Also see Standard I.29.)

I.20 Obtain informed consent for all research activities that involve obtrusive measures, invasion of privacy, more than minimal risk of harm, or any attempt to change the behaviour of research participants.

I.21 Establish and use signed consent forms that specify the dimensions of informed consent or that acknowledge that such dimensions have been explained and are understood, if such forms are required by law or if such forms are desired by the psychologist, the person(s) giving consent, or the organization for whom the psychologist works.

I.22 Accept and document oral consent, in situations in which signed consent forms are not acceptable culturally or in which there are other good reasons for not using them.

I.23 Provide, in obtaining informed consent, as much information as reasonable or prudent persons would want to know before making a decision or consenting to the activity. The psychologist would relay this information in language that the persons understand (including providing translation into another language, if necessary) and would take whatever reasonable steps are needed to ensure that the information was, in fact, understood.

I.24 Ensure, in the process of obtaining informed consent, that at least the following points are understood: purpose and nature of the activity; mutual responsibilities; confidentiality protections and limitations; likely benefits and risks; alternatives; the likely consequences of non-action; the option to refuse or withdraw at any time, without prejudice; over what period of time the consent applies; and, how to rescind consent if desired. (Also see Standards III.23–30.)

I.25 Provide new information in a timely manner, whenever such information becomes available and is significant enough that it reasonably could be seen as relevant to the original or ongoing informed consent.

I.26 Clarify the nature of multiple relationships to all concerned parties before obtaining consent, if providing services to or conducting research at the request or for the use of third parties. This would include, but not be limited to: the purpose of the service or research; the reasonably anticipated use that will be made of

information collected; and, the limits on confidentiality. Third parties may include schools, courts, government agencies, insurance companies, police, and special funding bodies.

Freedom of Consent

I.27 Take all reasonable steps to ensure that consent is not given under conditions of coercion, undue pressure, or undue reward. (Also see Standard III.32.)

I.28 Not proceed with any research activity, if consent is given under any condition of coercion, undue pressure, or undue reward. (Also see Standard III.32.)

I.29 Take all reasonable steps to confirm or re-establish freedom of consent, if consent for service is given under conditions of duress or conditions of extreme need.

I.30 Respect the right of persons to discontinue participation or service at any time, and be responsive to non-verbal indications of a desire to discontinue if a person has difficulty with verbally communicating such a desire (e.g., young children, verbally disabled persons) or, due to culture, is unlikely to communicate such a desire orally.

Protections for Vulnerable Persons

I.31 Seek an independent and adequate ethical review of human rights issues and protections for any research involving members of vulnerable groups, including persons of diminished capacity to give informed consent, before making a decision to proceed.

I.32 Not use persons of diminished capacity to give informed consent in research studies, if the research involved may be carried out equally well with persons who have a fuller capacity to give informed consent.

I.33 Seek to use methods that maximize the understanding and ability to consent of persons of diminished capacity to give informed consent, and that reduce the need for a substitute decision maker.

I.34 Carry out informed consent processes with those persons who are legally responsible or appointed to give informed consent on behalf of persons not competent to consent on their own behalf, seeking to ensure respect for any previously expressed preferences of persons not competent to consent.

I.35 Seek willing and adequately informed participation from any person of diminished capacity to give informed consent, and proceed without this assent only if the service or research activity is considered to be of direct benefit to that person.

I.36 Be particularly cautious in establishing the freedom of consent of any person who is in a dependent relationship to the psychologist (e.g., student, employee). This may include, but is not limited to, offering that person an alternative activity to fulfill their educational or employment goals, or offering a range of research studies or experience opportunities from which the person can select, none of which is so onerous as to be coercive.

Privacy

I.37 Seek and collect only information that is germane to the purpose(s) for which consent has been obtained.

I.38 Take care not to infringe, in research, teaching, or service activities, on the personally, developmentally, or culturally defined private space of individuals or groups, unless clear permission is granted to do so.

I.39 Record only that private information necessary for the provision of continuous, coordinated service, or for the goals of the particular research study being conducted, or that is required or justified by law. (Also see Standards IV.17 and IV.18.)

I.40 Respect the right of research participants, employees, supervisees, students, and trainees to reasonable personal privacy.

I.41 Collect, store, handle, and transfer all private information, whether written or unwritten (e.g., communication during service provision, written records, e-mail or fax communication, computer files, video-tapes), in a way that attends to the needs for privacy and security. This would include having adequate plans for records in circumstances of one's own serious illness, termination of employment, or death.

I.42 Take all reasonable steps to ensure that records over which they have control remain personally identifiable only as long as necessary in the interests of those to whom they refer and/or to the research project for which they were collected, or as required or justified by law (e.g., the possible need to defend oneself against future allegations), and render anonymous or destroy any records under their control that no longer need to be personally identifiable. (Also see Standards IV.17 and IV.18.)

Confidentiality

I.43 Be careful not to relay information about colleagues, colleagues' clients, research participants, employees, supervisees, students, trainees, and members of organizations, gained in the process of their activities as psychologists, that the psychologist has reason to believe is considered confidential by those persons, except as required or justified by law. (Also see Standards IV.17 and IV.18.)

I.44 Clarify what measures will be taken to protect confidentiality, and what responsibilities family, group, and community members have for the protection of each other's confidentiality, when engaged in services to or research with individuals, families, groups, or communities.

I.45 Share confidential information with others only with the informed consent of those involved, or in a manner that the persons involved cannot be identified, except as required or justified by law, or in circumstances of actual or possible serious physical harm or death. (Also see Standards II.39, IV.17, and IV.18.)

Extended Responsibility

I.46 Encourage others, in a manner consistent with this Code, to respect the dignity of persons and to expect respect for their own dignity.

I.47 Assume overall responsibility for the scientific and professional activities of their assistants, employees, students, supervisees, and trainees with regard to Respect for the Dignity of Persons, all of whom, however, incur similar obligations.

PRINCIPLE II: RESPONSIBLE CARING

Values Statement

A basic ethical expectation of any discipline is that its activities will benefit members of society or, at least, do no harm. Therefore, psychologists demonstrate an active concern for the welfare of any individual, family, group, or community with whom they relate in their role as psychologists. This concern includes both those directly involved and those indirectly involved in their activities. However, as with Principle I, psychologists' greatest responsibility is to protect the welfare of those in the most vulnerable position. Normally, persons directly involved in their activities (e.g., research participants, clients, students) are in such a position. Psychologists' responsibility to those indirectly involved (e.g., employers, third party payers, the general public) normally is secondary.

As persons usually consider their own welfare in their personal decision making, obtaining informed consent (see Principle I) is one of the best methods for ensuring that their welfare will be protected. However, it is only when such consent is combined with the responsible caring of the psychologist that there is considerable ethical protection of the welfare of the person(s) involved.

Responsible caring leads psychologists to take care to discern the potential harm and benefits involved, to predict the likelihood of their occurrence, to proceed only if the potential benefits outweigh the potential harms, to develop and use methods that will minimize harms and maximize benefits, and to take responsibility for correcting clearly harmful effects that have occurred as a direct result of their research, teaching, practice, or business activities.

In order to carry out these steps, psychologists recognize the need for competence and self-knowledge. They consider incompetent action to be unethical per se, as it is unlikely to be of benefit and likely to be harmful. They engage only in those activities in which they have competence or for which they are receiving supervision, and they perform their activities as competently as possible. They acquire, contribute to, and use the existing knowledge most relevant to the best interests of those concerned. They also engage in self-reflection regarding how their own values, attitudes, experiences, and social context (e.g., culture, ethnicity, colour, religion, sex, gender, sexual orientation, physical and mental abilities, age, and socio-economic status) influence their actions, interpretations, choices, and recommendations. This is done with the intent of increasing the probability that their activities will benefit and not harm the individuals, families, groups, and communities to whom they relate in their role as psychologists. Psychologists define harm and benefit in terms of both physical and psychological dimensions. They are concerned about such factors as: social, family, and community relationships; personal and cultural identity; feelings of self-worth, fear, humiliation, interpersonal trust, and cynicism; self-knowledge and general knowledge; and, such factors as physical safety, comfort, pain, and injury. They are concerned about immediate, short-term, and long-term effects.

Responsible caring recognizes and respects (e.g., through obtaining informed consent) the ability of individuals, families, groups, and communities to make decisions for themselves and to care for themselves and each other. It does not replace or undermine such ability, nor does it substitute one person's opinion about what is in the best interests of another person for that other person's competent decision making. However, psychologists recognize that, as vulnerabilities increase or as power to control one's own life decreases, psychologists have an increasing responsibility to protect the well-being of the individual, family, group, or community involved. For this reason, as in Principle I, psychologists consider it their responsibility to increase safeguards proportionate to the degree of dependency and the lack of voluntary initiation on the part of the persons involved. However, for Principle II, the safeguards are for the well being of persons rather than for the rights of persons.

Psychologists' treatment and use of animals in their research and teaching activities are also a component of responsible caring. Although animals do not have the same moral rights as persons (e.g., privacy), they do have the right to be treated humanely and not to be exposed to unnecessary discomfort, pain, or disruption.

By virtue of the social contract that the discipline has with society, psychologists have a higher duty of care to members of society than the general duty of care all members of society have to each other. However, psychologists are entitled to protect their own basic well-being (e.g., physical safety, family relationships) in their work as psychologists.

Ethical Standards

In adhering to the Principle of Responsible Caring, psychologists would:

General Caring

II.1 Protect and promote the welfare of clients, research participants, employees, supervisees, students, trainees, colleagues, and others.

II.2 Avoid doing harm to clients, research participants, employees, supervisees, students, trainees, colleagues, and others.

II.3 Accept responsibility for the consequences of their actions.

II.4 Refuse to advise, train, or supply information to anyone who, in the psychologist's judgment, will use the knowledge or skills to harm others.

II.5 Make every reasonable effort to ensure that psychological knowledge is not misused, intentionally or unintentionally, to harm others.

Competence and Self-Knowledge

II.6 Offer or carry out (without supervision) only those activities for which they have established their competence to carry them out to the benefit of others.

II.7 Not delegate activities to persons not competent to carry them out to the benefit of others.

II.8 Take immediate steps to obtain consultation or to refer a client to a colleague or other appropriate professional, whichever is more likely to result in providing the client with competent service, if it becomes apparent that a client's problems are beyond their competence.

II.9 Keep themselves up to date with a broad range of relevant knowledge, research methods, and techniques, and their impact on persons and society, through the reading of relevant literature, peer consultation, and continuing education activities, in order that their service or research activities and conclusions will benefit and not harm others.

II.10 Evaluate how their own experiences, attitudes, culture, beliefs, values, social context, individual differences, specific training, and stresses influence their interactions with others, and integrate this awareness into all efforts to benefit and not harm others.

II.11 Seek appropriate help and/or discontinue scientific or professional activity for an appropriate period of time, if a physical or psychological condition reduces their ability to benefit and not harm others.

II.12 Engage in self-care activities that help to avoid conditions (e.g., burnout, addictions) that could result in impaired judgment and interfere with their ability to benefit and not harm others.

Risk/Benefit Analysis

II.13 Assess the individuals, families, groups, and communities involved in their activities adequately enough to ensure that they will be able to discern what will benefit and not harm the persons involved.

II.14 Be sufficiently sensitive to and knowledgeable about individual, group, community, and cultural differences and vulnerabilities to discern what will benefit and not harm persons involved in their activities.

II.15 Carry out pilot studies to determine the effects of all new procedures and techniques that might carry more than minimal risk, before considering their use on a broader scale.

II.16 Seek an independent and adequate ethical review of the balance of risks and potential benefits of all research and new interventions that involve procedures of unknown consequence, or where pain, discomfort, or harm are possible, before making a decision to proceed.

II.17 Not carry out any scientific or professional activity unless the probable benefit is proportionately greater than the risk involved.

Maximize Benefit

II.18 Provide services that are coordinated over time and with other service providers, in order to avoid duplication or working at cross purposes.

II.19 Create and maintain records relating to their activities that are sufficient to support continuity and appropriate coordination of their activities with the activities of others.

II.20 Make themselves aware of the knowledge and skills of other disciplines (e.g., law, medicine, business administration) and advise the use of such knowledge and skills, where relevant to the benefit of others.

II.21 Strive to provide and/or obtain the best possible service for those needing and seeking psychological service. This may include, but is not limited to: selecting interventions that are relevant to the needs and characteristics of the client and that have reasonable theoretical or empirically-supported efficacy in light of those needs and characteristics; consulting with, or including in service delivery, persons relevant to the culture or belief systems of those served; advocating on behalf of the client; and, recommending professionals other than psychologists when appropriate.

II.22 Monitor and evaluate the effect of their activities, record their findings, and communicate new knowledge to relevant others.

II.23 Debrief research participants in such a way that the participants' knowledge is enhanced and the participants have a sense of contribution to knowledge. (Also see Standards III.26 and III.27.)

II.24 Perform their teaching duties on the basis of careful preparation, so that their instruction is current and scholarly.

II.25 Facilitate the professional and scientific development of their employees, supervisees, students, and trainees by ensuring that these persons understand the values and ethical prescriptions of the discipline, and by providing or arranging for adequate working conditions, timely evaluations, and constructive consultation and experience opportunities.

II.26 Encourage and assist students in publication of worthy student papers.

Minimize Harm

II.27 Be acutely aware of the power relationship in therapy and, therefore, not encourage or engage in sexual intimacy with therapy clients, neither during therapy, nor for that period of time following therapy during which the power relationship reasonably could be expected to influence the client's personal decision making. (Also see Standard III.31.)

II.28 Not encourage or engage in sexual intimacy with students or trainees with whom the psychologist has an evaluative or other relationship of direct authority. (Also see Standard III.31.)

II.29 Be careful not to engage in activities in a way that could place incidentally involved persons at risk.

II.30 Be acutely aware of the need for discretion in the recording and communication of information, in order that the information not be misinterpreted or misused to the detriment of others. This includes, but is not limited to: not recording information that could lead to misinterpretation and misuse; avoiding conjecture; clearly labeling opinion; and, communicating information in language that can be understood clearly by the recipient of the information.

II.31 Give reasonable assistance to secure needed psychological services or activities, if personally unable to meet requests for needed psychological services or activities.

II.32 Provide a client, if appropriate and if desired by the client, with reasonable assistance to find a way to receive needed services in the event that third party payments are exhausted and the client cannot afford the fees involved.

II.33 Maintain appropriate contact, support, and responsibility for caring until a colleague or other professional begins service, if referring a client to a colleague or other professional.

II.34 Give reasonable notice and be reasonably assured that discontinuation will cause no harm to the client, before discontinuing services.

II.35 Screen appropriate research participants and select those least likely to be harmed, if more than minimal risk of harm to some research participants is possible.

II.36 Act to minimize the impact of their research activities on research participants' personalities, or on their physical or mental integrity.

Offset/Correct Harm

II.37 Terminate an activity when it is clear that the activity carries more than minimal risk of harm and is found to be more harmful than beneficial, or when the activity is no longer needed.

II.38 Refuse to help individuals, families, groups, or communities to carry out or submit to activities that, according to current knowledge, or legal or professional guidelines, would cause serious physical or psychological harm to themselves or others.

II.39 Do everything reasonably possible to stop or offset the consequences of actions by others when these actions are likely to cause serious physical harm or death. This may include reporting to appropriate authorities (e.g., the police), an intended victim, or a family member or other support person who can intervene, and would be done even when a confidential relationship is involved. (Also see Standard I.45.)

II.40 Act to stop or offset the consequences of seriously harmful activities being carried out by another psychologist or member of another discipline, when there is objective information about the activities and the harm, and when these activities have come to their attention outside of a confidential client relationship between themselves and the psychologist or member of another discipline. This may include reporting to the appropriate regulatory body, authority, or committee for action, depending on the psychologist's judgment about the person(s) or body(ies) best suited to stop or offset the harm, and depending upon regulatory requirements and definitions of misconduct.

II.41 Act also to stop or offset the consequences of harmful activities carried out by another psychologist or member of another discipline, when the harm is not serious or the activities appear to be primarily a lack of sensitivity, knowledge, or experience, and when the activities have come to their attention outside of a confidential client relationship between themselves and the psychologist or member of

another discipline. This may include talking informally with the psychologist or member of the other discipline, obtaining objective information and, if possible and relevant, the assurance that the harm will discontinue and be corrected. If in a vulnerable position (e.g., employee, trainee) with respect to the other psychologist or member of the other discipline, it may include asking persons in less vulnerable positions to participate in the meeting(s).

II.42 Be open to the concerns of others about perceptions of harm that they as a psychologist might be causing, stop activities that are causing harm, and not punish or seek punishment for those who raise such concerns in good faith.

II.43 Not place an individual, group, family, or community needing service at a serious disadvantage by offering them no service in order to fulfill the conditions of a research design, when a standard service is available.

II.44 Debrief research participants in such a way that any harm caused can be discerned, and act to correct any resultant harm. (Also see Standards III.26 and III.27.)

Care of Animals

II.45 Not use animals in their research unless there is a reasonable expectation that the research will increase understanding of the structures and processes underlying behaviour, or increase understanding of the particular animal species used in the study, or result eventually in benefits to the health and welfare of humans or other animals.

II.46 Use a procedure subjecting animals to pain, stress, or privation only if an alternative procedure is unavailable and the goal is justified by its prospective scientific, educational, or applied value.

II.47 Make every effort to minimize the discomfort, illness, and pain of animals. This would include performing surgical procedures only under appropriate anaesthesia, using techniques to avoid infection and minimize pain during and after surgery and, if disposing of experimental animals is carried out at the termination of the study, doing so in a humane way.

II.48 Use animals in classroom demonstrations only if the instructional objectives cannot be achieved through the use of video-tapes, films, or other methods, and if the type of demonstration is warranted by the anticipated instructional gain.

Extended Responsibility

II.49 Encourage others, in a manner consistent with this Code, to care responsibly.

II.50 Assume overall responsibility for the scientific and professional activities of their assistants, employees, supervisees, students, and trainees with regard to the Principle of Responsible Caring, all of whom, however, incur similar obligations.

PRINCIPLE III: INTEGRITY IN RELATIONSHIPS

Values Statement

The relationships formed by psychologists in the course of their work embody explicit and implicit mutual expectations of integrity that are vital to the advancement of scientific knowledge and to the maintenance of public confidence in the discipline of psychology. These expectations include: accuracy and honesty; straightforwardness and openness; the maximization of objectivity and minimization of bias; and, avoidance of conflicts of interest. Psychologists have a responsibility to meet these expectations and to encourage reciprocity.

In addition to accuracy, honesty, and the obvious prohibitions of fraud or misrepresentation, meeting expectations of integrity is enhanced by self-knowledge and the use of critical analysis. Although it can be argued that science is value-free and impartial, scientists are not. Personal values and self-interest can affect the questions psychologists ask, how they ask those questions, what assumptions they make, their selection of methods, what they observe and what they fail to observe, and how they interpret their data.

Psychologists are not expected to be value-free or totally without self-interest in conducting their activities. However, they are expected to understand how their backgrounds, personal needs, and values interact with their activities, to be open and honest about the influence of such factors, and to be as objective and unbiased as possible under the circumstances.

The values of openness and straightforwardness exist within the context of Respect for the Dignity of Persons (Principle I) and Responsible Caring (Principle II). As such, there will be circumstances in which openness and straightforwardness will need to be tempered. Fully open and straightforward disclosure might not be needed or desired by others and, in some circumstances, might be a risk to their dignity or well-being, or considered culturally inappropriate. In such circumstances, however, psychologists have a responsibility to ensure that their decision not to be fully open or straightforward is justified by higher-order values and does not invalidate any informed consent procedures.

Of special concern to psychologists is the provision of incomplete disclosure when obtaining informed consent for research participation, or temporarily leading research participants to believe that a research project has a purpose other than its actual purpose. These actions sometimes occur in research where full disclosure would be likely to influence the responses of the research participants and thus invalidate the results. Although research that uses such techniques can lead to knowledge that is beneficial, such benefits must be weighed against the research participant's right to self-determination and the importance of public and individual trust in psychology. Psychologists have a serious obligation to avoid as much as possible the use of such research procedures. They also have a serious obligation to consider the need for, the possible consequences of, and their responsibility to correct any resulting mistrust or other harmful effects from their use.

As public trust in the discipline of psychology includes trusting that psychologists will act in the best interests of members of the public, situations that present real or potential conflicts of interest are of concern to psychologists. Conflict-of-interest situations are those that can lead to distorted judgment and can motivate psychologists to act in ways that meet their own personal, political, financial, or business interests at the expense of the best interests of members of the public. Although avoidance of all conflicts of interest and potential exploitation of others is not possible, some are of such a high risk to protecting the interests of members of the public and to maintaining the trust of the public, that they are considered never acceptable (see Standard III.31). The risk level of other conflicts of interest (e.g., dual or multiple relationships) might be partially dependent on cultural factors and the specific type of professional relationship (e.g., long-term psychotherapy vs. community development activities). It is the responsibility of psychologists to avoid dual or multiple relationships and other conflicts of interest when appropriate and possible. When such situations cannot be avoided or are inappropriate to avoid, psychologists have a responsibility to declare that they have a conflict of interest, to seek advice, and to establish safeguards to ensure that the best interests of members of the public are protected.

Integrity in relationships implies that psychologists, as a matter of honesty, have a responsibility to maintain competence in any specialty area for which they declare competence, whether or not they are currently practising in that area. It also requires that psychologists, in as much as they present themselves as members and representatives of a specific discipline, have a responsibility to actively rely on and be guided by that discipline and its guidelines and requirements.

Ethical Standards

In adhering to the Principle of Integrity in Relationships, psychologists would:

Accuracy/Honesty

III.1 Not knowingly participate in, condone, or be associated with dishonesty, fraud, or misrepresentation.

III.2 Accurately represent their own and their colleagues' credentials, qualifications, education, experience, competence, and affiliations, in all spoken, written, or printed communications, being careful not to use descriptions or information that could be misinterpreted (e.g.,

citing membership in a voluntary association of psychologists as a testament of competence).

III.3 Carefully protect their own and their colleagues' credentials from being misrepresented by others, and act quickly to correct any such misrepresentation.

III.4 Maintain competence in their declared area(s) of psychological competence, as well as in their current area(s) of activity. (Also see Standard II.9.)

III.5 Accurately represent their own and their colleagues' activities, functions, contributions, and likely or actual outcomes of their activities (including research results) in all spoken, written, or printed communication. This includes, but is not limited to: advertisements of services or products; course and workshop descriptions; academic grading requirements; and, research reports.

III.6 Ensure that their own and their colleagues' activities, functions, contributions, and likely or actual outcomes of their activities (including research results) are not misrepresented by others, and act quickly to correct any such misrepresentation.

III.7 Take credit only for the work and ideas that they have actually done or generated, and give credit for work done or ideas contributed by others (including students), in proportion to their contribution.

III.8 Acknowledge the limitations of their own and their colleagues' knowledge, methods, findings, interventions, and views.

III 9. Not suppress disconfirming evidence of their own and their colleagues' findings and views, acknowledging alternative hypotheses and explanations.

Objectivity/Lack of Bias

III.10 Evaluate how their personal experiences, attitudes, values, social context, individual differences, stresses, and specific training influence their activities and thinking, integrating this awareness into all attempts to be objective and unbiased in their research, service, and other activities.

III.11 Take care to communicate as completely and objectively as possible, and to clearly differentiate facts, opinions, theories, hypotheses, and ideas, when communicating knowledge, findings, and views.

III.12 Present instructional information accurately, avoiding bias in the selection and presentation of information, and publicly acknowledge any personal values or bias that influence the selection and presentation of information.

III.13 Act quickly to clarify any distortion by a sponsor, client, agency (e.g., news media), or other persons, of the findings of their research.

Straightforwardness/Openness

III.14 Be clear and straightforward about all information needed to establish informed consent or any other valid written or unwritten agreement (for example: fees, including any limitations imposed by third-party payers; relevant business policies and practices; mutual concerns; mutual responsibilities; ethical responsibilities of psychologists; purpose and nature of the relationship, including research participation; alternatives; likely experiences; possible conflicts; possible outcomes; and, expectations for processing, using, and sharing any information generated).

III.15 Provide suitable information about the results of assessments, evaluations, or research findings to the persons involved, if appropriate and if asked. This information would be communicated in understandable language.

III.16 Fully explain reasons for their actions to persons who have been affected by their actions, if appropriate and if asked.

III.17 Honour all promises and commitments included in any written or verbal agreement, unless serious and unexpected circumstances (e.g., illness) intervene. If such circumstances occur, then the psychologist would make a full and honest explanation to other parties involved.

III.18 Make clear whether they are acting as private citizens, as members of specific organizations or groups, or as representatives of the discipline of psychology, when making statements or when involved in public activities.

III.19 Carry out, present, and discuss research in a way that is consistent with a commitment to honest, open inquiry, and to clear communication of any research aims, sponsorship, social context, personal values, or financial interests that might affect or appear to affect the research.

III.20 Submit their research, in some accurate form and within the limits of confidentiality, to persons with expertise in the research area, for their comments and evaluations, prior to publication or the preparation of any final report.

III.21 Encourage and not interfere with the free and open exchange of psychological knowledge and theory between themselves, their students, colleagues, and the public.

III.22 Make no attempt to conceal the status of a trainee and, if a trainee is providing direct client service, ensure that the client is informed of that fact.

Avoidance of Incomplete Disclosure

III.23 Not engage in incomplete disclosure, or in temporarily leading research participants to believe that a research project or some aspect of it has a different purpose, if there are alternative procedures available or if the negative effects cannot be predicted or offset.

III.24 Not engage in incomplete disclosure, or in temporarily leading research participants to believe that a research project or some aspect of it has a different purpose, if it would interfere with the person's understanding of facts that clearly might influence a decision to give adequately informed consent (e.g., withholding information about the level of risk, discomfort, or inconvenience).

III.25 Use the minimum necessary incomplete disclosure or temporary leading of research participants to believe that a research project or some aspect of it has a different purpose, when such research procedures are used.

III.26 Debrief research participants as soon as possible after the participants' involvement, if there has been incomplete disclosure or temporary leading of research participants to believe that a research project or some aspect of it has a different purpose.

III.27 Provide research participants, during such debriefing, with a clarification of the nature of the study, seek to remove any misconceptions that might have arisen, and seek to re-establish any trust that might have been lost, assuring the participants that the research procedures were neither arbitrary nor capricious, but necessary for scientifically valid findings. (Also see Standards II.23 and II.44.)

III.28 Act to re-establish with research participants any trust that might have been lost due to the use of incomplete disclosure or temporarily leading research participants to believe that the research project or some aspect of it had a different purpose.

III.29 Give a research participant the option of removing his or her data, if the research participant expresses concern during the debriefing about the incomplete disclosure or the temporary leading of the research participant to believe that the research project or some aspect of it had a different purpose, and if removal of the data will not compromise the validity of the research design and hence diminish the ethical value of the participation of the other research participants.

III.30 Seek an independent and adequate ethical review of the risks to public or individual trust and of safeguards to protect such trust for any research that plans to provide incomplete disclosure or temporarily lead research participants to believe that the research project or some aspect of it has a different purpose, before making a decision to proceed.

Avoidance of Conflict of Interest

III.31 Not exploit any relationship established as a psychologist to further personal, political, or business interests at the expense of the best interests of their clients, research participants, students, employers, or others. This includes, but is not limited to: soliciting clients of one's employing agency for private practice; taking advantage of trust or dependency to encourage or engage in sexual intimacies (e.g., with clients not included in Standard II.27, with clients' partners or relatives, with students or trainees not included in Standard II.28, or with research participants); taking advantage of trust or dependency to frighten clients into receiving services; misappropriating students' ideas, research or work; using the resources of one's employing institution for purposes not agreed to; giving or

receiving kickbacks or bonuses for referrals; seeking or accepting loans or investments from clients; and, prejudicing others against a colleague for reasons of personal gain.

III.32 Not offer rewards sufficient to motivate an individual or group to participate in an activity that has possible or known risks to themselves or others. (Also see Standards I.27, I.28, II.2, and II.49.)

III.33 Avoid dual or multiple relationships (e.g., with clients, research participants, employees, supervisees, students, or trainees) and other situations that might present a conflict of interest or that might reduce their ability to be objective and unbiased in their determinations of what might be in the best interests of others.

III.34 Manage dual or multiple relationships that are unavoidable due to cultural norms or other circumstances in such a manner that bias, lack of objectivity, and risk of exploitation are minimized. This might include obtaining ongoing supervision or consultation for the duration of the dual or multiple relationship, or involving a third party in obtaining consent (e.g., approaching a client or employee about becoming a research participant).

III.35 Inform all parties, if a real or potential conflict of interest arises, of the need to resolve the situation in a manner that is consistent with Respect for the Dignity of Persons (Principle I) and Responsible Caring (Principle II), and take all reasonable steps to resolve the issue in such a manner.

Reliance on the Discipline

III.36 Familiarize themselves with their discipline's rules and regulations, and abide by them, unless abiding by them would be seriously detrimental to the rights or welfare of others as demonstrated in the Principles of Respect for the Dignity of Persons or Responsible Caring. (See Standards IV.17 and IV.18 for guidelines regarding the resolution of such conflicts.)

III.37 Familiarize themselves with and demonstrate a commitment to maintaining the standards of their discipline.

III.38 Seek consultation from colleagues and/or appropriate groups and committees, and give due regard to their advice in arriving at a responsible decision, if faced with difficult situations.

Extended Responsibility

III.39 Encourage others, in a manner consistent with this Code, to relate with integrity.

III.40 Assume overall responsibility for the scientific and professional activities of their assistants, employees, supervisees, students, and trainees with regard to the Principle of Integrity in Relationships, all of whom, however, incur similar obligations.

PRINCIPLE IV: RESPONSIBILITY TO SOCIETY

Values Statement

Psychology functions as a discipline within the context of human society. Psychologists, both in their work and as private citizens, have responsibilities to the societies in which they live and work, such as the neighbourhood or city, and to the welfare of all human beings in those societies.

Two of the legitimate expectations of psychology as a science and a profession are that it will increase knowledge and that it will conduct its affairs in such ways that it will promote the welfare of all human beings.

Freedom of enquiry and debate (including scientific and academic freedom) is a foundation of psychological education, science, and practice. In the context of society, the above expectations imply that psychologists will exercise this freedom through the use of activities and methods that are consistent with ethical requirements.

The above expectations also imply that psychologists will do whatever they can to ensure that psychological knowledge, when used in the development of social structures and policies, will be used for beneficial purposes, and that the discipline's own structures and policies will support those beneficial purposes. Within the context of this document, social structures and policies that have beneficial purposes are defined as those that more readily support and

reflect respect for the dignity of persons, responsible caring, integrity in relationships, and responsibility to society. If psychological knowledge or structures are used against these purposes, psychologists have an ethical responsibility to try to draw attention to and correct the misuse. Although this is a collective responsibility, those psychologists having direct involvement in the structures of the discipline, in social development, or in the theoretical or research data base that is being used (e.g., through research, expert testimony, or policy advice) have the greatest responsibility to act. Other psychologists must decide for themselves the most appropriate and beneficial use of their time and talents to help meet this collective responsibility.

In carrying out their work, psychologists acknowledge that many social structures have evolved slowly over time in response to human need and are valued by the societies that have developed them. In such circumstances, psychologists convey respect for such social structures and avoid unwarranted or unnecessary disruption. Suggestions for and action toward changes or enhancement of such structures are carried out through processes that seek to achieve a consensus within those societies and/or through democratic means.

On the other hand, if structures or policies seriously ignore or oppose the principles of respect for the dignity of persons, responsible caring, integrity in relationships, or responsibility to society, psychologists involved have a responsibility to speak out in a manner consistent with the principles of this Code, and advocate for appropriate change to occur as quickly as possible.

In order to be responsible and accountable to society, and to contribute constructively to its ongoing development, psychologists need to be willing to work in partnership with others, be self-reflective, and be open to external suggestions and criticisms about the place of the discipline of psychology in society. They need to engage in even-tempered observation and interpretation of the effects of societal structures and policies, and their process of change, developing the ability of psychologists to increase the beneficial use of psychological knowledge and structures, and avoid their misuse. The discipline needs to be willing to set high standards for its members, to do what it can to assure that such standards are met, and to support its members in their attempts to maintain the standards. Once again, individual psychologists must decide for themselves the most appropriate and beneficial use of their time and talents in helping to meet these collective responsibilities.

Ethical Standards

In adhering to the Principle of Responsibility to Society, psychologists would:

Development of Knowledge

IV.1 Contribute to the discipline of psychology and of society's understanding of itself and human beings generally, through free enquiry and the acquisition, transmission, and expression of knowledge and ideas, unless such activities conflict with other basic ethical requirements.

IV.2 Not interfere with, or condone interference with, free enquiry and the acquisition, transmission, and expression of knowledge and ideas that do not conflict with other basic ethical requirements.

IV.3 Keep informed of progress in their area(s) of psychological activity, take this progress into account in their work, and try to make their own contributions to this progress.

Beneficial Activities

IV.4 Participate in and contribute to continuing education and the professional and scientific growth of self and colleagues.

IV.5 Assist in the development of those who enter the discipline of psychology by helping them to acquire a full understanding of their ethical responsibilities, and the needed competencies of their chosen area(s), including an understanding of critical analysis and of the variations, uses, and possible misuses of the scientific paradigm.

IV.6 Participate in the process of critical self-evaluation of the discipline's place in society, and in the development and implementation of structures and procedures that help the disci-

pline to contribute to beneficial societal functioning and changes.

IV.7 Provide and/or contribute to a work environment that supports the respectful expression of ethical concern or dissent, and the constructive resolution of such concern or dissent.

IV.8 Engage in regular monitoring, assessment, and reporting (e.g., through peer review, and in programme reviews, case management reviews, and reports of one's own research) of their ethical practices and safeguards.

IV.9 Help develop, promote, and participate in accountability processes and procedures related to their work.

IV.10 Uphold the discipline's responsibility to society by promoting and maintaining the highest standards of the discipline.

IV.11 Protect the skills, knowledge, and interpretations of psychology from being misused, used incompetently, or made useless (e.g., loss of security of assessment techniques) by others.

IV.12 Contribute to the general welfare of society (e.g., improving accessibility of services, regardless of ability to pay) and/or to the general welfare of their discipline, by offering a portion of their time to work for which they receive little or no financial return.

IV.13 Uphold the discipline's responsibility to society by bringing incompetent or unethical behaviour, including misuses of psychological knowledge and techniques, to the attention of appropriate authorities, committees, or regulatory bodies, in a manner consistent with the ethical principles of this Code, if informal resolution or correction of the situation is not appropriate or possible.

IV.14 Enter only into agreements or contracts that allow them to act in accordance with the ethical principles and standards of this Code.

Respect for Society

IV.15 Acquire an adequate knowledge of the culture, social structure, and customs of a community before beginning any major work there.

IV.16 Convey respect for and abide by prevailing community mores, social customs, and cultural expectations in their scientific and professional activities, provided that this does not contravene any of the ethical principles of this Code.

IV.17 Familiarize themselves with the laws and regulations of the societies in which they work, especially those that are related to their activities as psychologists, and abide by them. If those laws or regulations seriously conflict with the ethical principles contained herein, psychologists would do whatever they could to uphold the ethical principles. If upholding the ethical principles could result in serious personal consequences (e.g., jail or physical harm), decision for final action would be considered a matter of personal conscience.

IV.18 Consult with colleagues, if faced with an apparent conflict between abiding by a law or regulation and following an ethical principle, unless in an emergency, and seek consensus as to the most ethical course of action and the most responsible, knowledgeable, effective, and respectful way to carry it out.

Development of Society

IV.19 Act to change those aspects of the discipline of psychology that detract from beneficial societal changes, where appropriate and possible.

IV.20 Be sensitive to the needs, current issues, and problems of society, when determining research questions to be asked, services to be developed, content to be taught, information to be collected, or appropriate interpretation of results or findings.

IV.21 Be especially careful to keep well informed of social issues through relevant reading, peer consultation, and continuing education, if their work is related to societal issues.

IV.22 Speak out, in a manner consistent with the four principles of this Code, if they possess expert knowledge that bears on important societal issues being studied or discussed.

IV.23 Provide thorough discussion of the limits of their data with respect to social policy, if their work touches on social policy and structure.

IV.24 Consult, if feasible and appropriate, with groups, organizations, or communities being studied, in order to increase the accuracy of interpretation of results and to minimize risk of misinterpretation or misuse.

IV.25 Make themselves aware of the current social and political climate and of previous and possible future societal misuses of psychological knowledge, and exercise due discretion in communicating psychological information (e.g., research results, theoretical knowledge), in order to discourage any further misuse.

IV.26 Exercise particular care when reporting the results of any work regarding vulnerable groups, ensuring that results are not likely to be misinterpreted or misused in the development of social policy, attitudes, and practices (e.g., encouraging manipulation of vulnerable persons or reinforcing discrimination against any specific population).

IV.27 Not contribute to nor engage in research or any other activity that contravenes international humanitarian law, such as the development of methods intended for use in the torture of persons, the development of prohibited weapons, or destruction of the environment.

IV.28 Provide the public with any psychological knowledge relevant to the public's informed participation in the shaping of social policies and structures, if they possess expert knowledge that bears on the social policies and structures.

IV.29 Speak out and/or act, in a manner consistent with the four principles of this Code, if the policies, practices, laws, or regulations of the social structure within which they work seriously ignore or contradict any of the principles of this Code.

Extended Responsibility

IV.30 Encourage others, in a manner consistent with this Code, to exercise responsibility to society.

IV.31 Assume overall responsibility for the scientific and professional activities of their assistants, employees, supervisees, students, and trainees with regard to the Principle of Responsibility to Society, all of whom, however, incur similar obligations.

Appendix C

American Counseling Association
Code of Ethics (2005)

MISSION

The mission of the American Counseling Association is to enhance the quality of life in society by promoting the development of professional counselors, advancing the counseling profession, and using the profession and practice of counseling to promote respect for human dignity and diversity.

SECTION A: THE COUNSELING RELATIONSHIP

INTRODUCTION

Counselors encourage client growth and development in ways that foster the interest and welfare of clients and promote formation of healthy relationships. Counselors actively attempt to understand the diverse cultural backgrounds of the clients they serve. Counselors also explore their own cultural identities and how these affect their values and beliefs about the counseling process.

Counselors are encouraged to contribute to society by devoting a portion of their professional activity to services for which there is little or no financial return (pro bono publico).

A.1. Welfare of Those Served by Counselors

A.1.a. Primary Responsibility

The primary responsibility of counselors is to respect the dignity and to promote the welfare of clients.

A.1.b. Records

Counselors maintain records necessary for rendering professional services to their clients and as required by laws, regulations, or agency or institution procedures. Counselors include sufficient and timely documentation in their client records to facilitate the delivery and continuity of needed services. Counselors take reasonable steps to ensure that documentation in records accurately reflects client progress and services provided. If errors are made in client records, counselors take steps to properly note the correction of such errors according to agency or institutional policies. (See A.12.g.7., B.6., B.6.g., G.2.j.)

A.1.c. Counseling Plans

Counselors and their clients work jointly in devising integrated counseling plans that offer reasonable promise of success and are consistent with abilities and circumstances of clients. Counselors and clients regularly review counseling plans to assess their continued viability and effectiveness, respecting the freedom of choice of clients. (See A.2.a., A.2.d., A.12.g.)

A.1.d. Support Network Involvement

Counselors recognize that support networks hold various meanings in the lives of clients and consider enlisting the support, understanding, and involvement of others (e.g., religious/spiritual/community leaders, family members, friends) as positive resources, when appropriate, with client consent.

A.1.e. Employment Needs

Counselors work with their clients considering employment in jobs that are consistent with the overall abilities, vocational limitations, physical restrictions, general temperament, interest and aptitude patterns, social skills, education, general qualifications, and other relevant characteristics and needs of clients. When appropriate, counselors appropriately trained in career development will assist in the placement of clients in positions that are consistent with the interest, culture, and the welfare of clients, employers, and/or the public.

A.2. Informed Consent in the Counseling Relationship *(See A.12.g., B.5., B.6.b., E.3., E.13.b., F.1.c., G.2.a.)*

A.2.a. Informed Consent

Clients have the freedom to choose whether to enter into or remain in a counseling relationship and need adequate information about the counseling process and the counselor. Counselors have an obligation to review in writing and verbally with clients the rights and responsibilities of both the counselor and the client. Informed consent is an ongoing part of the counseling process, and counselors appropriately document discussions of informed consent throughout the counseling relationship.

A.2.b. Types of Information Needed

Counselors explicitly explain to clients the nature of all services provided. They inform clients about issues such as, but not limited to, the following: the purposes, goals, techniques, procedures, limitations, potential risks, and benefits of services; the counselor's qualifications, credentials, and relevant experience; continuation of services upon the incapacitation or death of a counselor; and other pertinent information. Counselors take steps to ensure that clients understand the implications of diagnosis, the intended use of tests and reports, fees, and billing arrangements. Clients have the right to confidentiality and to be provided with an explanation of its limitations (including how supervisors and/or treatment team professionals are involved); to obtain clear information about their records; to participate in the ongoing counseling plans; and to refuse any services or modality change and to be advised of the consequences of such refusal.

A.2.c. Developmental and Cultural Sensitivity

Counselors communicate information in ways that are both developmentally and culturally appropriate. Counselors use clear and understandable language when discussing issues related to informed consent. When clients have difficulty understanding the language used by counselors, they provide necessary services (e.g., arranging for a qualified interpreter or translator) to ensure comprehension by clients. In collaboration with clients, counselors consider cultural implications of informed consent procedures and, where possible, counselors adjust their practices accordingly.

A.2.d. Inability to Give Consent

When counseling minors or persons unable to give voluntary consent, counselors seek the assent of clients to services, and include them in decision making as appropriate. Counselors recognize the need to balance the ethical rights of clients to make choices, their capacity to give consent or assent to receive services, and parental or familial legal rights and responsibilities to protect these clients and make decisions on their behalf.

A.3. Clients Served by Others

When counselors learn that their clients are in a professional relationship with another mental health professional, they request release from clients to inform the other professionals and strive to establish positive and collaborative professional relationships.

A.4. Avoiding Harm and Imposing Values

A.4.a. Avoiding Harm

Counselors act to avoid harming their clients, trainees, and research participants and to minimize or to remedy unavoidable or unanticipated harm.

A.4.b. Personal Values

Counselors are aware of their own values, attitudes, beliefs, and behaviors and avoid imposing values that are inconsistent with counseling goals. Counselors respect the diversity of clients, trainees, and research participants.

A.5. Roles and Relationships With Clients
(See F.3., F.10., G.3.)

A.5.a. Current Clients

Sexual or romantic counselor–client interactions or relationships with current clients, their romantic partners, or their family members are prohibited.

A.5.b. Former Clients

Sexual or romantic counselor–client interactions or relationships with former clients, their romantic partners, or their family members are prohibited for a period of 5 years following the last professional contact. Counselors, before engaging in sexual or romantic interactions or relationships with clients, their romantic partners, or client family members after 5 years following the last professional contact, demonstrate forethought and document (in written form) whether the interactions or relationship can be viewed as exploitive in some way and/or whether there is still potential to harm the former client; in cases of potential exploitation and/or harm, the counselor avoids entering such an interaction or relationship.

A.5.c. Nonprofessional Interactions or Relationships (Other Than Sexual or Romantic Interactions or Relationships)

Counselor–client nonprofessional relationships with clients, former clients, their romantic partners, or their family members should be avoided, except when the interaction is potentially beneficial to the client. *(See A.5.d.)*

A.5.d. Potentially Beneficial Interactions

When a counselor–client nonprofessional interaction with a client or former client may be potentially beneficial to the client or former client, the counselor must document in case records, prior to the interaction (when feasible), the rationale for such an interaction, the potential benefit, and anticipated consequences for the client or former client and other individuals significantly involved with the client or former client. Such interactions should be initiated with appropriate client consent. Where unintentional harm occurs to the client or former client, or to an individual significantly involved with the client or former client, due to the nonprofessional interaction, the counselor must show evidence of an attempt to remedy such harm. Examples of potentially beneficial interactions include, but are not limited to, attending a formal ceremony (e.g., a wedding/commitment ceremony or graduation); purchasing a service or product provided by a client or former client (excepting unrestricted bartering); hospital visits to an ill family member; mutual membership in a professional association, organization, or community. *(See A.5.c.)*

A.5.e. Role Changes in the Professional Relationship

When a counselor changes a role from the original or most recent contracted relationship, he or she obtains informed consent from the client and explains the right of the client to refuse services related to the change.

Examples of role changes include

1. changing from individual to relationship or family counseling, or vice versa;
2. changing from a nonforensic evaluative role to a therapeutic role, or vice versa;
3. changing from a counselor to a researcher role (i.e., enlisting clients as research participants), or vice versa; and
4. changing from a counselor to a mediator role, or vice versa. Clients must be fully informed of any anticipated consequences (e.g., financial, legal, personal, or therapeutic) of counselor role changes.

A.6. Roles and Relationships at Individual, Group, Institutional, and Societal Levels

A.6.a. Advocacy

When appropriate, counselors advocate at individual, group, institutional, and societal levels to examine potential barriers and obstacles that inhibit access and/or the growth and development of clients.

A.6.b. Confidentiality and Advocacy

Counselors obtain client consent prior to engaging in advocacy efforts on behalf of an identifiable client to improve the provision of services and to work toward removal of systemic barriers or obstacles that inhibit client access, growth, and development.

A.7. Multiple Clients

When a counselor agrees to provide counseling services to two or more persons who have a relationship, the counselor clarifies at the outset which person or persons are clients and the nature of the relationships the counselor will have with each involved person. If it becomes apparent that the counselor may be called upon to perform potentially conflicting roles, the counselor will clarify, adjust, or withdraw from roles appropriately. (See A.8.a., B.4.)

A.8. Group Work (See B.4.a.)

A.8.a. Screening

Counselors screen prospective group counseling/therapy participants. To the extent possible, counselors select members whose needs and goals are compatible with goals of the group, who will not impede the group process, and whose well-being will not be jeopardized by the group experience.

A.8.b. Protecting Clients

In a group setting, counselors take reasonable precautions to protect clients from physical, emotional, or psychological trauma.

A.9. End-of-Life Care for Terminally Ill Clients

A.9.a. Quality of Care

Counselors strive to take measures that enable clients

1. to obtain high quality end-of-life care for their physical, emotional, social, and spiritual needs;
2. to exercise the highest degree of self-determination possible;
3. to be given every opportunity possible to engage in informed decision making regarding their end-of-life care; and
4. to receive complete and adequate assessment regarding their ability to make competent, rational decisions on their own behalf from a mental health professional who is experienced in end-of-life care practice.

A.9.b. Counselor Competence, Choice, and Referral

Recognizing the personal, moral, and competence issues related to end-of-life decisions, counselors may choose to work or not work with terminally ill clients who wish to explore their end-of-life options. Counselors provide appropriate referral information to ensure that clients receive the necessary help.

A.9.c. Confidentiality

Counselors who provide services to terminally ill individuals who are considering hastening their own deaths have the option of breaking or not breaking confidentiality, depending on applicable laws and the specific circumstances of the situation and after seeking consultation or supervision from appropriate professional and legal parties. (See B.5.c., B.7.c.)

A.10. Fees and Bartering

A.10.a. Accepting Fees From Agency Clients

Counselors refuse a private fee or other remuneration for rendering services to persons who are entitled to such services through the counselor's employing agency or institution. The policies of a particular agency may make explicit provisions for agency clients to receive counseling services from members of its staff in private practice. In such instances, the clients must be informed of other options open to them should they seek private counseling services.

A.10.b. Establishing Fees

In establishing fees for professional counseling services, counselors consider the financial status of clients and locality. In the event that the established fee structure is inappropriate for a client, counselors assist clients in attempting to find comparable services of acceptable cost.

A.10.c. Nonpayment of Fees

If counselors intend to use collection agencies or take legal measures to collect fees from clients who do not pay for services as agreed upon, they first inform clients of intended actions and offer clients the opportunity to make payment.

A.10.d. Bartering

Counselors may barter only if the relationship is not exploitive or harmful and does not place the counselor in an unfair advantage, if the client requests it, and if such arrangements are an accepted practice among professionals in the community. Counselors consider the cultural implications of bartering and discuss relevant concerns with clients and document such agreements in a clear written contract.

A.10.e. Receiving Gifts

Counselors understand the challenges of accepting gifts from clients and recognize that in some cultures, small gifts are a token of respect and showing gratitude. When determining whether or not to accept a gift from clients, counselors take into account the therapeutic relationship, the monetary value of the gift, a client's motivation for giving the gift, and the counselor's motivation for wanting or declining the gift.

A.11. Termination and Referral

A.11.a. Abandonment Prohibited

Counselors do not abandon or neglect clients in counseling. Counselors assist in making appropriate arrangements for the continuation of treatment, when necessary, during interruptions such as vacations, illness, and following termination.

A.11.b. Inability to Assist Clients

If counselors determine an inability to be of professional assistance to clients, they avoid entering or continuing counseling relationships. Counselors are knowledgeable about culturally and clinically appropriate referral resources and suggest these alternatives. If clients decline the suggested referrals, counselors should discontinue the relationship.

A.11.c. Appropriate Termination

Counselors terminate a counseling relationship when it becomes reasonably apparent that the client no longer needs assistance, is not likely to benefit, or is being harmed by continued counseling. Counselors may terminate counseling when in jeopardy of harm by the client, or another person with whom the client has a relationship, or when clients do not pay fees as agreed upon. Counselors provide pretermination counseling and recommend other service providers when necessary.

A.11.d. Appropriate Transfer of Services

When counselors transfer or refer clients to other practitioners, they ensure that appropriate clinical and administrative processes are completed and open communication is maintained with both clients and practitioners.

A.12. Technology Applications

A.12.a. Benefits and Limitations

Counselors inform clients of the benefits and limitations of using information technology applications in the counseling process and in business/billing procedures. Such technologies include but are not limited to computer hardware and software, telephones, the World Wide Web, the Internet, online assessment instruments and other communication devices.

A.12.b. Technology-Assisted Services

When providing technology-assisted distance counseling services, counselors determine that clients are intellectually, emotionally, and physically capable of using the application and that the application is appropriate for the needs of clients.

A.12.c. Inappropriate Services

When technology-assisted distance counseling services are deemed inappropriate by the counselor or client, counselors consider delivering services face to face.

A.12.d. Access

Counselors provide reasonable access to computer applications when providing technology assisted distance counseling services.

A.12.e. Laws and Statutes

Counselors ensure that the use of technology does not violate the laws of any local, state, national, or international entity and observe all relevant statutes.

A.12.f. Assistance

Counselors seek business, legal, and technical assistance when using technology applications, particularly when the use of such applications crosses state or national boundaries.

A.12.g. Technology and Informed Consent

As part of the process of establishing informed consent, counselors do the following:

1. Address issues related to the difficulty of maintaining the confidentiality of electronically transmitted communications.

2. Inform clients of all colleagues, supervisors, and employees, such as Informational Technology (IT) administrators, who might have authorized or unauthorized access to electronic transmissions.

3. Urge clients to be aware of all authorized or unauthorized users including family members and fellow employees who have access to any technology clients may use in the counseling process.

4. Inform clients of pertinent legal rights and limitations governing the practice of a profession over state lines or international boundaries.

5. Use encrypted Web sites and e-mail communications to help ensure confidentiality when possible.

6. When the use of encryption is not possible, counselors notify clients of this fact and limit electronic transmissions to general communications that are not client specific.

7. Inform clients if and for how long archival storage of transaction records are maintained.

8. Discuss the possibility of technology failure and alternate methods of service delivery.

9. Inform clients of emergency procedures, such as calling 911 or a local crisis hotline, when the counselor is not available.

10. Discuss time zone differences, local customs, and cultural or language differences that might impact service delivery.

11. Inform clients when technology assisted distance counseling services are not covered by insurance. (See A.2.)

A.12.h. Sites on the World Wide Web

Counselors maintaining sites on the World Wide Web (the Internet) do the following:

1. Regularly check that electronic links are working and professionally appropriate.

2. Establish ways clients can contact the counselor in case of technology failure.

3. Provide electronic links to relevant state licensure and professional certification boards to protect consumer rights and facilitate addressing ethical concerns.

4. Establish a method for verifying client identity.

5. Obtain the written consent of the legal guardian or other authorized legal representative

prior to rendering services in the event the client is a minor child, an adult who is legally incompetent, or an adult incapable of giving informed consent.

6. Strive to provide a site that is accessible to persons with disabilities.

SECTION B: CONFIDENTIALITY, PRIVILEGED COMMUNICATION, AND PRIVACY

INTRODUCTION

Counselors recognize that trust is a cornerstone of the counseling relationship. Counselors aspire to earn the trust of clients by creating an ongoing partnership, establishing and upholding appropriate boundaries, and maintaining confidentiality. Counselors communicate the parameters of confidentiality in a culturally competent manner.

B.1. Respecting Client Rights

B.1.a. Multicultural/Diversity Considerations

Counselors maintain awareness and sensitivity regarding cultural meanings of confidentiality and privacy. Counselors respect differing views toward disclosure of information. Counselors hold ongoing discussions with clients as to how, when, and with whom information is to be shared.

B.1.b. Respect for Privacy

Counselors respect client rights to privacy. Counselors solicit private information from clients only when it is beneficial to the counseling process.

B.1.c. Respect for Confidentiality

Counselors do not share confidential information without client consent or without sound legal or ethical justification.

B.1.d. Explanation of Limitations

At initiation and throughout the counseling process, counselors inform clients of the limi-
tations of confidentiality and seek to identify foreseeable situations in which confidentiality must be breached. (See A.2.b.)

B.2. Exceptions

B.2.a. Danger and Legal Requirements

The general requirement that counselors keep information confidential does not apply when disclosure is required to protect clients or identified others from serious and foreseeable harm or when legal requirements demand that confidential information must be revealed. Counselors consult with other professionals when in doubt as to the validity of an exception. Additional considerations apply when addressing end-of-life issues. (See A.9.c.)

B.2.b. Contagious, Life-Threatening Diseases

When clients disclose that they have a disease commonly known to be both communicable and life threatening, counselors may be justified in disclosing information to identifiable third parties, if they are known to be at demonstrable and high risk of contracting the disease. Prior to making a disclosure, counselors confirm that there is such a diagnosis and assess the intent of clients to inform the third parties about their disease or to engage in any behaviors that may be harmful to an identifiable third party.

B.2.c. Court-Ordered Disclosure

When subpoenaed to release confidential or privileged information without a client's permission, counselors obtain written, informed consent from the client or take steps to prohibit the disclosure or have it limited as narrowly as possible due to potential harm to the client or counseling relationship.

B.2.d. Minimal Disclosure

To the extent possible, clients are informed before confidential information is disclosed and are involved in the disclosure decision-making process. When circumstances require the disclosure of confidential information, only essential information is revealed.

B.3. Information Shared With Others

B.3.a. Subordinates

Counselors make every effort to ensure that privacy and confidentiality of clients are maintained by subordinates, including employees, supervisees, students, clerical assistants, and volunteers. *(See F.1.c.)*

B.3.b. Treatment Teams

When client treatment involves a continued review or participation by a treatment team, the client will be informed of the team's existence and composition, information being shared, and the purposes of sharing such information.

B.3.c. Confidential Settings

Counselors discuss confidential information only in settings in which they can reasonably ensure client privacy.

B.3.d. Third-Party Payers

Counselors disclose information to third-party payers only when clients have authorized such disclosure.

B.3.e. Transmitting Confidential Information

Counselors take precautions to ensure the confidentiality of information transmitted through the use of computers, electronic mail, facsimile machines, telephones, voicemail, answering machines, and other electronic or computer technology. *(See A.12.g.)*

B.3.f. Deceased Clients

Counselors protect the confidentiality of deceased clients, consistent with legal requirements and agency or setting policies.

B.4. Groups and Families

B.4.a. Group Work

In group work, counselors clearly explain the importance and parameters of confidentiality for the specific group being entered.

B.4.b. Couples and Family Counseling

In couples and family counseling, counselors clearly define who is considered "the client" and discuss expectations and limitations of confidentiality. Counselors seek agreement and document in writing such agreement among all involved parties having capacity to give consent concerning each individual's right to confidentiality and any obligation to preserve the confidentiality of information known.

B.5. Clients Lacking Capacity to Give Informed Consent

B.5.a. Responsibility to Clients

When counseling minor clients or adult clients who lack the capacity to give voluntary, informed consent, counselors protect the confidentiality of information received in the counseling relationship as specified by federal and state laws, written policies, and applicable ethical standards.

B.5.b. Responsibility to Parents and Legal Guardians

Counselors inform parents and legal guardians about the role of counselors and the confidential nature of the counseling relationship. Counselors are sensitive to the cultural diversity of families and respect the inherent rights and responsibilities of parents/guardians over the welfare of their children/charges according to law. Counselors work to establish, as appropriate, collaborative relationships with parents/guardians to best serve clients.

B.5.c. Release of Confidential Information

When counseling minor clients or adult clients who lack the capacity to give voluntary consent to release confidential information, counselors seek permission from an appropriate third party to disclose information. In such instances, counselors inform clients consistent with their level of understanding and take culturally appropriate measures to safeguard client confidentiality.

B.6. Records

B.6.a. Confidentiality of Records

Counselors ensure that records are kept in a secure location and that only authorized persons have access to records.

B.6.b. Permission to Record

Counselors obtain permission from clients prior to recording sessions through electronic or other means.

B.6.c. Permission to Observe

Counselors obtain permission from clients prior to observing counseling sessions, reviewing session transcripts, or viewing recordings of sessions with supervisors, faculty, peers, or others within the training environment.

B.6.d. Client Access

Counselors provide reasonable access to records and copies of records when requested by competent clients. Counselors limit the access of clients to their records, or portions of their records, only when there is compelling evidence that such access would cause harm to the client. Counselors document the request of clients and the rationale for withholding some or all of the record in the files of clients. In situations involving multiple clients, counselors provide individual clients with only those parts of records that related directly to them and do not include confidential information related to any other client.

B.6.e. Assistance With Records

When clients request access to their records, counselors provide assistance and consultation in interpreting counseling records.

B.6.f. Disclosure or Transfer

Unless exceptions to confidentiality exist, counselors obtain written permission from clients to disclose or transfer records to legitimate third parties. Steps are taken to ensure that receivers of counseling records are sensitive to their confidential nature. (See A.3., E.4.)

B.6.g. Storage and Disposal After Termination

Counselors store records following termination of services to ensure reasonable future access, maintain records in accordance with state and federal statutes governing records, and dispose of client records and other sensitive materials in a manner that protects client confidentiality. When records are of an artistic nature, counselors obtain client (or guardian) consent with regards to handling of such records or documents. (See A.1.b.)

B.6.h. Reasonable Precautions

Counselors take reasonable precautions to protect client confidentiality in the event of the counselor's termination of practice, incapacity, or death. (See C.2.h.)

B.7. Research and Training

B.7.a. Institutional Approval

When institutional approval is required, counselors provide accurate information about their research proposals and obtain approval prior to conducting their research. They conduct research in accordance with the approved research protocol.

B.7.b. Adherence to Guidelines

Counselors are responsible for understanding and adhering to state, federal, agency, or institutional policies or applicable guidelines regarding confidentiality in their research practices.

B.7.c. Confidentiality of Information Obtained in Research

Violations of participant privacy and confidentiality are risks of participation in research involving human participants. Investigators maintain all research records in a secure manner. They explain to participants the risks of violations of privacy and confidentiality and disclose to participants any limits of confidentiality that reasonably can be expected. Regardless of the degree to which confidentiality will be maintained, investigators must disclose to participants any limits of confidentiality that reasonably can be expected. *(See G.2.e.)*

B.7.d. Disclosure of Research Information

Counselors do not disclose confidential information that reasonably could lead to the identification of a research participant unless they have obtained the prior consent of the person. Use of data derived from counseling relationships for purposes of training, research, or publication is confined to content that is disguised to ensure the anonymity of the individuals involved. *(See G.2.a., G.2.d.)*

B.7.e. Agreement for Identification

Identification of clients, students, or supervisees in a presentation or publication is permissible only when they have reviewed the material and agreed to its presentation or publication. *(See G.4.d.)*

B.8. Consultation

B.8.a. Agreements

When acting as consultants, counselors seek agreements among all parties involved concerning each individual's rights to confidentiality, the obligation of each individual to preserve confidential information, and the limits of confidentiality of information shared by others.

B.8.b. Respect for Privacy

Information obtained in a consulting relationship is discussed for professional purposes only with persons directly involved with the case. Written and oral reports present only data germane to the purposes of the consultation, and every effort is made to protect client identity and to avoid undue invasion of privacy.

B.8.c. Disclosure of Confidential Information

When consulting with colleagues, counselors do not disclose confidential information that reasonably could lead to the identification of a client or other person or organization with whom they have a confidential relationship unless they have obtained the prior consent of the person or organization or the disclosure cannot be avoided. They disclose information only to the extent necessary to achieve the purposes of the consultation. *(See D.2.d)*

SECTION C: PROFESSIONAL RESPONSIBILITY

INTRODUCTION

Counselors aspire to open, honest, and accurate communication in dealing with the public and other professionals. They practice in a nondiscriminatory manner within the boundaries of professional and personal competence and have a responsibility to abide by the *ACA Code of Ethics*. Counselors actively participate in local, state, and national associations that foster the development and improvement of counseling. Counselors advocate to promote change at the individual, group, institutional, and societal levels that improve the quality of life for individuals and groups and remove potential barriers to the provision or access of appropriate services being offered. Counselors have a responsibility to the public to engage in counseling practices that are based on rigorous research methodologies. In addition, counselors engage in self-care activities to maintain and promote their emotional, physical, mental, and spiritual well-being to best meet their professional responsibilities.

C.1. Knowledge of Standards

Counselors have a responsibility to read, understand, and follow the ACA *Code of Ethics* and adhere to applicable laws and regulations.

C.2. Professional Competence

C.2.a. Boundaries of Competence

Counselors practice only within the boundaries of their competence, based on their education, training, supervised experience, state and national professional credentials, and appropriate professional experience. Counselors gain knowledge, personal awareness, sensitivity, and skills pertinent to working with a diverse client population. *(See A.9.b., C.4.e., E.2., F.2., F.11.b.)*

C.2.b. New Specialty Areas of Practice

Counselors practice in specialty areas new to them only after appropriate education, training, and supervised experience. While developing skills in new specialty areas, counselors take steps to ensure the competence of their work and to protect others from possible harm. *(See F.6.f.)*

C.2.c. Qualified for Employment

Counselors accept employment only for positions for which they are qualified by education, training, supervised experience, state and national professional credentials, and appropriate professional experience. Counselors hire for professional counseling positions only individuals who are qualified and competent for those positions.

C.2.d. Monitor Effectiveness

Counselors continually monitor their effectiveness as professionals and take steps to improve when necessary. Counselors in private practice take reasonable steps to seek peer supervision as needed to evaluate their efficacy as counselors.

C.2.e. Consultation on Ethical Obligations

Counselors take reasonable steps to consult with other counselors or related professionals when they have questions regarding their ethical obligations or professional practice.

C.2.f. Continuing Education

Counselors recognize the need for continuing education to acquire and maintain a reasonable level of awareness of current scientific and professional information in their fields of activity. They take steps to maintain competence in the skills they use, are open to new procedures, and keep current with the diverse populations and specific populations with whom they work.

C.2.g. Impairment

Counselors are alert to the signs of impairment from their own physical, mental, or emotional problems and refrain from offering or providing professional services when such impairment is likely to harm a client or others. They seek assistance for problems that reach the level of professional impairment, and, if necessary, they limit, suspend, or terminate their professional responsibilities until such time it is determined that they may safely resume their work. Counselors assist colleagues or supervisors in recognizing their own professional impairment and provide consultation and assistance when warranted with colleagues or supervisors showing signs of impairment and intervene as appropriate to prevent imminent harm to clients. *(See A.11.b, F.8.b.)*

C.2.h. Counselor Incapacitation or Termination of Practice

When counselors leave a practice, they follow a prepared plan for transfer of clients and files. Counselors prepare and disseminate to an identified colleague or "records custodian" a plan for the transfer of clients and files in the case of their incapacitation, death, or termination of practice.

C.3. Advertising and Soliciting Clients

C.3.a. Accurate Advertising

When advertising or otherwise representing their services to the public, counselors identify their credentials in an accurate manner that is not false, misleading, deceptive, or fraudulent.

C.3.b. Testimonials

Counselors who use testimonials do not solicit them from current clients nor former clients nor any other persons who may be vulnerable to undue influence.

C.3.c. Statements by Others

Counselors make reasonable efforts to ensure that statements made by others about them or the profession of counseling are accurate.

C.3.d. Recruiting Through Employment

Counselors do not use their places of employment or institutional affiliation to recruit or gain clients, supervisees, or consultees for their private practices.

C.3.e. Products and Training Advertisements

Counselors who develop products related to their profession or conduct workshops or training events ensure that the advertisements concerning these products or events are accurate and disclose adequate information for consumers to make informed choices. *(See C.6.d.)*

C.3.f. Promoting to Those Served

Counselors do not use counseling, teaching, training, or supervisory relationships to promote their products or training events in a manner that is deceptive or would exert undue influence on individuals who may be vulnerable. However, counselor educators may adopt textbooks they have authored for instructional purposes.

C.4. Professional Qualifications

C.4.a. Accurate Representation

Counselors claim or imply only professional qualifications actually completed and correct any known misrepresentations of their qualifi-

cations by others. Counselors truthfully represent the qualifications of their professional colleagues. Counselors clearly distinguish between paid and volunteer work experience and accurately describe their continuing education and specialized training. *(See C.2.a.)*

C.4.b. Credentials

Counselors claim only licenses or certifications that are current and in good standing.

C.4.c. Educational Degrees

Counselors clearly differentiate between earned and honorary degrees.

C.4.d. Implying Doctoral-Level Competence

Counselors clearly state their highest earned degree in counseling or closely related field. Counselors do not imply doctoral-level competence when only possessing a master's degree in counseling or a related field by referring to themselves as "Dr." in a counseling context when their doctorate is not in counseling or related field.

C.4.e. Program Accreditation Status

Counselors clearly state the accreditation status of their degree programs at the time the degree was earned.

C.4.f. Professional Membership

Counselors clearly differentiate between current, active memberships and former memberships in associations. Members of the American Counseling Association must clearly differentiate between professional membership, which implies the possession of at least a master's degree in counseling, and regular membership, which is open to individuals whose interests and activities are consistent with those of ACA but are not qualified for professional membership.

C.5. Nondiscrimination

Counselors do not condone or engage in discrimination based on age, culture, disability, ethnicity, race, religion/spirituality, gender, gender identity, sexual orientation, marital status/partnership, language preference, socioeconomic status, or any basis proscribed by law. Counselors do not discriminate against clients, students, employees, supervisees, or research participants in a manner that has a negative impact on these persons.

C.6.Public Responsibility

C.6.a. Sexual Harassment

Counselors do not engage in or condone sexual harassment. Sexual harassment is defined as sexual solicitation, physical advances, or verbal or nonverbal conduct that is sexual in nature, that occurs in connection with professional activities or roles, and that either

1. is unwelcome, is offensive, or creates a hostile workplace or learning environment, and counselors know or are told this; or
2. is sufficiently severe or intense to be perceived as harassment to a reasonable person in the context in which the behavior occurred. Sexual harassment can consist of a single intense or severe act or multiple persistent or pervasive acts.

C.6.b. Reports to Third Parties

Counselors are accurate, honest, and objective in reporting their professional activities and judgments to appropriate third parties, including courts, health insurance companies, those who are the recipients of evaluation reports, and others. *(See B.3., E.4.)*

C.6.c. Media Presentations

When counselors provide advice or comment by means of public lectures, demonstrations, radio or television programs, prerecorded tapes, technology-based applications, printed articles, mailed material, or other media, they take reasonable precautions to ensure that:

1. the statements are based on appropriate professional counseling literature and practice,

2. the statements are otherwise consistent with the ACA *Code of Ethics,* and
3. the recipients of the information are not encouraged to infer that a professional counseling relationship has been established.

C.6.d. Exploitation of Others

Counselors do not exploit others in their professional relationships. *(See C.3.e.)*

C.6.e. Scientific Bases for Treatment Modalities

Counselors use techniques/ procedures/momodalities that are grounded in theory and/ or have an empirical or scientific foundation. Counselors who do not must define the techniques/procedures as "unproven" or "developing" and explain the potential risks and ethical considerations of using such techniques/procedures and take steps to protect clients from possible harm. *(See A.4.a. E.5.c., E.5.d.)*

C.7. Responsibility to Other Professionals

C.7.a. Personal Public Statements

When making personal statements in a public context, counselors clarify that they are speaking from their personal perspectives and that they are not speaking on behalf of all counselors or the profession.

SECTION D: RELATIONSHIPS WITH OTHER PROFESSIONALS

INTRODUCTION

Professional counselors recognize that the quality of their interactions with colleagues can influence the quality of services provided to clients. They work to become knowledgeable about colleagues within and outside the field of counseling. Counselors develop positive working relationships and systems of communication with colleagues to enhance services to clients.

D.1. Relationships With Colleagues, Employers, and Employees

D.1.a. Different Approaches

Counselors are respectful of approaches to counseling services that differ from their own. Counselors are respectful of traditions and practices of other professional groups with which they work.

D.1.b. Forming Relationships

Counselors work to develop and strengthen interdisciplinary relations with colleagues from other disciplines to best serve clients.

D.1.c. Interdisciplinary Teamwork

Counselors who are members of interdisciplinary teams delivering multifaceted services to clients, keep the focus on how to best serve the clients. They participate in and contribute decisions that affect the well-being of clients by drawing on the perspectives, values, and experiences of the counseling profession and those of colleagues from other disciplines. *(See A.1.a.)*

D.1.d. Confidentiality

When counselors are required by law, institutional policy, or extraordinary circumstances to serve in more than one role in judicial or administrative proceedings, they clarify role expectations and the parameters of confidentiality with their colleagues. *(See B.1.c., B.1.d., B.2.c., B.2.d., B.3.b.)*

D.1.e. Establishing Professional and Ethical Obligations

Counselors who are members of interdisciplinary teams clarify professional and ethical obligations of the team as a whole and of its individual members. When a team decision raises ethical concerns, counselors first attempt to resolve the concern within the team. If they cannot reach resolution among team members, counselors pursue other avenues to address their concerns consistent with client well-being.

D.1.f. Personnel Selection and Assignment

Counselors select competent staff and assign responsibilities compatible with their skills and experiences.

D.1.g. Employer Policies

The acceptance of employment in an agency or institution implies that counselors are in agreement with its general policies and principles. Counselors strive to reach agreement with employers as to acceptable standards of conduct that allow for changes in institutional policy conducive to the growth and development of clients.

D.1.h. Negative Conditions

Counselors alert their employers of inappropriate policies and practices. They attempt to effect changes in such policies or procedures through constructive action within the organization. When such policies are potentially disruptive or damaging to clients or may limit the effectiveness of services provided and change cannot be effected, counselors take appropriate further action. Such action may include referral to appropriate certification, accreditation, or state licensure organizations, or voluntary termination of employment.

D.1.i. Protection From Punitive Action

Counselors take care not to harass or dismiss an employee who has acted in a responsible and ethical manner theory and/or have an empirical or scientific foundation. Counselors who do not must define the techniques/procedures as "unproven" or "developing" and explain the potential risks and ethical considerations of using such techniques/procedures and take steps to protect clients from possible harm. *(See A.4.a., E.5.c., E.5.d.)*

D.2. Consultation

D.2.a. Consultant Competency

Counselors take reasonable steps to ensure that they have the appropriate resources and competencies when providing consultation services. Counselors provide appropriate referral resources when requested or needed. *(See C.2.a.)*

D.2.b. Understanding Consultees

When providing consultation, counselors attempt to develop with their consultees a clear understanding of problem definition, goals for change, and predicted consequences of interventions selected.

D.2.c. Consultant Goals

The consulting relationship is one in which consultee adaptability and growth toward self-direction are consistently encouraged and cultivated.

D.2.d. Informed Consent in Consultation

When providing consultation, counselors have an obligation to review, in writing and verbally, the rights and responsibilities of both counselors and consultees. Counselors use clear and understandable language to inform all parties involved about the purpose of the services to be provided, relevant costs, potential risks and benefits, and the limits of confidentiality. Working in conjunction with the consultee, counselors attempt to develop a clear definition of the problem, goals for change, and predicted consequences of interventions that are culturally responsive and appropriate to the needs of consultees. *(See A.2.a., A.2.b.)*

SECTION E: EVALUATION, ASSESSMENT, AND INTERPRETATION

INTRODUCTION

Counselors use assessment instruments as one component of the counseling process, taking into account the client personal and cultural context. Counselors promote the well-being of individual clients or groups of clients by developing and using appropriate educational, psychological, and career assessment instruments.

E.1. General

E.1.a. Assessment

The primary purpose of educational, psychological, and career assessment is to provide measurements that are valid and reliable in either comparative or absolute terms. These include, but are not limited to, measurements of ability, personality, interest, intelligence, achievement, and performance. Counselors recognize the need to interpret the statements in this section as applying to both quantitative and qualitative assessments.

E.1.b. Client Welfare

Counselors do not misuse assessment results and interpretations, and they take reasonable steps to prevent others from misusing the information these techniques provide. They respect the client's right to know the results, the interpretations made, and the bases for counselors' conclusions and recommendations.

E.2. Competence to Use and Interpret Assessment Instruments

E.2.a. Limits of Competence

Counselors utilize only those testing and assessment services for which they have been trained and are competent. Counselors using technology assisted test interpretations are trained in the construct being measured and the specific instrument being used prior to using its technology based application. Counselors take reasonable measures to ensure the proper use of psychological and career assessment techniques by persons under their supervision. *(See A.12.)*

E.2.b. Appropriate Use

Counselors are responsible for the appropriate application, scoring, interpretation, and use of assessment instruments relevant to the needs of the client, whether they score and interpret such assessments themselves or use technology or other services.

E.2.c. Decisions Based on Results

Counselors responsible for decisions involving individuals or policies that are based on assessment results have a thorough understanding of educational, psychological, and career measurement, including validation criteria, assessment research, and guidelines for assessment development and use.

E.3. Informed Consent in Assessment

E.3.a. Explanation to Clients

Prior to assessment, counselors explain the nature and purposes of assessment and the specific use of results by potential recipients. The explanation will be given in the language of the client (or other legally authorized person on behalf of the client), unless an explicit exception has been agreed upon in advance. Counselors consider the client's personal or cultural context, the level of the client's understanding of the results, and the impact of the results on the client. *(See A.2., A.12.g., F.1.c.)*

E.3.b. Recipients of Results

Counselors consider the examinee's welfare, explicit understandings, and prior agreements in determining who receives the assessment results. Counselors include accurate and appropriate interpretations with any release of individual or group assessment results. *(See B.2.c., B.5.)*

E.4. Release of Data to Qualified Professionals

Counselors release assessment data in which the client is identified only with the consent of the client or the client's legal representative. Such data are released only to persons recognized by counselors as qualified to interpret the data. *(See B.1., B.3., B.6.b.)*

E.5. Diagnosis of Mental Disorders

E.5.a. Proper Diagnosis

Counselors take special care to provide proper diagnosis of mental disorders. Assessment tech-

niques (including personal interview) used to determine client care (e.g., locus of treatment, type of treatment, or recommended follow-up) are carefully selected and appropriately used.!

E.5.b. Cultural Sensitivity

Counselors recognize that culture affects the manner in which clients' problems are defined. Clients' socioeconomic and cultural experiences are considered when diagnosing mental disorders. *(See A.2.c.)*

E.5.c. Historical and Social Prejudices in the Diagnosis of Pathology

Counselors recognize historical and social prejudices in the misdiagnosis and pathologizing of certain individuals and groups and the role of mental health professionals in perpetuating these prejudices through diagnosis and treatment.

E.5.d. Refraining From Diagnosis

Counselors may refrain from making and/or reporting a diagnosis if they believe it would cause harm to the client or others.

E.6. Instrument Selection

F.6.a. Appropriateness of Instruments

Counselors carefully consider the validity, reliability, psychometric limitations, and appropriateness of instruments when selecting assessments.

E.6.b. Referral Information

If a client is referred to a third party for assessment, the counselor provides specific referral questions and sufficient objective data about the client to ensure that appropriate assessment instruments are utilized. *(See A.9.b., B.3.)*

E.6.c. Culturally Diverse Populations

Counselors are cautious when selecting assessments for culturally diverse populations to avoid the use of instruments that lack appropriate psychometric properties for the client population. *(See A.2.c., E.5.b.)*

E.7. Conditions of Assessment Administration *(See A.12.b., A.12.d.)*

E.7.a. Administration Conditions

Counselors administer assessments under the same conditions that were established in their standardization. When assessments are not administered under standard conditions, as may be necessary to accommodate clients with disabilities, or when unusual behavior or irregularities occur during the administration, those conditions are noted in interpretation, and the results may be designated as invalid or of questionable validity.

E.7.b. Technological Administration

Counselors ensure that administration programs function properly and provide clients with accurate results when technological or other electronic methods are used for assessment administration.

E.7.c. Unsupervised Assessments

Unless the assessment instrument is designed, intended, and validated for self-administration and/or scoring, counselors do not permit inadequately supervised use.

E.7.d. Disclosure of Favorable Conditions

Prior to administration of assessments, conditions that produce most favorable assessment results are made known to the examinee.

E.8. Multicultural Issues/ Diversity in Assessment

Counselors use with caution assessment techniques that were normed on populations other than that of the client. Counselors recognize the effects of age, color, culture, disability, ethnic group, gender, race, language preference, religion, spirituality, sexual orientation, and socioeconomic status on test administration and interpretation, and place test results in proper perspective with other relevant factors. *(See A.2.c., E.5.b.)*

E.9. Scoring and Interpretation of Assessments

E.9.a. Reporting

In reporting assessment results, counselors indicate reservations that exist regarding validity or reliability due to circumstances of the assessment or the inappropriateness of the norms for the person tested.

E.9.b. Research Instruments

Counselors exercise caution when interpreting the results of research instruments not having sufficient technical data to support respondent results. The specific purposes for the use of such instruments are stated explicitly to the examinee.

E.9.c. Assessment Services

Counselors who provide assessment scoring and interpretation services to support the assessment process confirm the validity of such interpretations. They accurately describe the purpose, norms, validity, reliability, and applications of the procedures and any special qualifications applicable to their use. The public offering of an automated test interpretations service is considered a professional-to-professional consultation. The formal responsibility of the consultant is to the consultee, but the ultimate and overriding responsibility is to the client. *(See D.2.)*

E.10. Assessment Security

Counselors maintain the integrity and security of tests and other assessment techniques consistent with legal and contractual obligations. Counselors do not appropriate, reproduce, or modify published assessments or parts thereof without acknowledgment and permission from the publisher.

E.11. Obsolete Assessments and Outdated Results

Counselors do not use data or results from assessments that are obsolete or outdated for the current purpose. Counselors make every effort to prevent the misuse of obsolete measures and assessment data by others.

E.12. Assessment Construction

Counselors use established scientific procedures, relevant standards, and current professional knowledge for assessment design in the development, publication, and utilization of educational and psychological assessment techniques.

E.13. Forensic Evaluation: Evaluation for Legal Proceedings

E.13.a. Primary Obligations

When providing forensic evaluations, the primary obligation of counselors is to produce objective findings that can be substantiated based on information and techniques appropriate to the evaluation, which may include examination of the individual and/ or review of records. Counselors are entitled to form professional opinions based on their professional knowledge and expertise that can be supported by the data gathered in evaluations. Counselors will define the limits of their reports or testimony, especially when an examination of the individual has not been conducted.

E.13.b. Consent for Evaluation

Individuals being evaluated are informed in writing that the relationship is for the purposes of an evaluation and is not counseling in nature, and entities or individuals who will receive the evaluation report are identified. Written consent to be evaluated is obtained from those being evaluated unless a court orders evaluations to be conducted without the written consent of individuals being evaluated. When children or vulnerable adults are being evaluated, informed written consent is obtained from a parent or guardian.

E.13.c. Client Evaluation Prohibited

Counselors do not evaluate individuals for forensic purposes they currently counsel or individuals they have counseled in the past. Counselors do not accept as counseling clients individuals they are evaluating or individuals they have evaluated in the past for forensic purposes.

E.13.d. Avoid Potentially Harmful Relationships

Counselors who provide forensic evaluations avoid potentially harmful professional or personal relationships with family members, romantic partners, and close friends of individuals they are evaluating or have evaluated in the past.

SECTION F: SUPERVISION, TRAINING, AND TEACHING

INTRODUCTION

Counselors aspire to foster meaningful and respectful professional relationships and to maintain appropriate boundaries with supervisees and students. Counselors have theoretical and pedagogical foundations for their work and aim to be fair, accurate, and honest in their assessments of counselors-in-training.

F.1. Counselor Supervision and Client Welfare

F.1.a. Client Welfare

A primary obligation of counseling supervisors is to monitor the services provided by other counselors or counselors-in-training. Counseling supervisors monitor client welfare and supervisee clinical performance and professional development. To fulfill these obligations, supervisors meet regularly with supervisees to review case notes, samples of clinical work, or live observations. Supervisees have a responsibility to understand and follow the ACA *Code of Ethics*.

F.1.b. Counselor Credentials

Counseling supervisors work to ensure that clients are aware of the qualifications of the supervisees who render services to the clients. *(See A.2.b.)*

F.1.c. Informed Consent and Client Rights

Supervisors make supervisees aware of client rights including the protection of client privacy and confidentiality in the counseling relationship. Supervisees provide clients with professional disclosure information and inform them of how the supervision process influences the limits of confidentiality. Supervisees make clients aware of who will have access to records of the counseling relationship and how these records will be used. *(See A.2.b., B.1.d.)*

F.2. Counselor Supervision Competence

F.2.a. Supervisor Preparation

Prior to offering clinical supervision services, counselors are trained in supervision methods and techniques. Counselors who offer clinical supervision services regularly pursue continuing education activities including both counseling and supervision topics and skills. *(See C.2.a., C.2.f.)*

F.2.b. Multicultural Issues/Diversity in Supervision

Counseling supervisors are aware of and address the role of multiculturalism/diversity in the supervisory relationship.

F.3. Supervisory Relationships

F.3.a. Relationship Boundaries With Supervisees

Counseling supervisors clearly define and maintain ethical professional, personal, and social relationships with their supervisees. Counseling supervisors avoid nonprofessional relationships with current supervisees. If supervisors must assume other professional roles (e.g., clinical and administrative supervisor, instructor) with supervisees, they work to minimize potential conflicts and explain to supervisees the expectations and responsibilities associated with each role. They do not engage in any form of nonprofessional interaction that may compromise the supervisory relationship.

F.3.b. Sexual Relationships

Sexual or romantic interactions or relationships with current supervisees are prohibited.

F.3.c. Sexual Harassment

Counseling supervisors do not condone or subject supervisees to sexual harassment. *(See C.6.a.)*

F.3.d. Close Relatives and Friends

Counseling supervisors avoid accepting close relatives, romantic partners, or friends as supervisees.

F.3.e. Potentially Beneficial Relationships

Counseling supervisors are aware of the power differential in their relationships with supervisees. If they believe nonprofessional relationships with a supervisee may be potentially beneficial to the supervisee, they take precautions similar to those taken by counselors when working with clients. Examples of potentially beneficial interactions or relationships include attending a formal ceremony; hospital visits; providing support during a stressful event; or mutual membership in a professional association, organization, or community. Counseling supervisors engage in open discussions with supervisees when they consider entering into relationships with them outside of their roles as clinical and/or administrative supervisors. Before engaging in nonprofessional relationships, supervisors discuss with supervisees and document the rationale for such interactions, potential benefits or drawbacks, and anticipated consequences for the supervisee. Supervisors clarify the specific nature and limitations of the additional role(s) they will have with the supervisee.

F.4. Supervisor Responsibilities

F.4.a. Informed Consent for Supervision

Supervisors are responsible for incorporating into their supervision the principles of informed consent and participation. Supervisors inform supervisees of the policies and procedures to which they are to adhere and the mechanisms for due process appeal of individual supervisory actions.

F.4.b. Emergencies and Absences

Supervisors establish and communicate to supervisees procedures for contacting them or, in their absence, alternative on-call supervisors to assist in handling crises.

F.4.c. Standards for Supervisees

Supervisors make their supervisees aware of professional and ethical standards and legal responsibilities. Supervisors of post degree counselors encourage these counselors to adhere to professional standards of practice. *(See C.1.)*

F.4.d. Termination of the Supervisory Relationship

Supervisors or supervisees have the right to terminate the supervisory relationship with adequate notice. Reasons for withdrawal are provided to the other party. When cultural, clinical, or professional issues are crucial to the viability of the supervisory relationship, both parties make efforts to resolve differences. When termination is warranted, supervisors make appropriate referrals to possible alternative supervisors.

F.5. Counseling Supervision Evaluation, Remediation, and Endorsement

F.5.a. Evaluation

Supervisors document and provide supervisees with ongoing performance appraisal and evaluation feedback and schedule periodic formal evaluative sessions throughout the supervisory relationship.

F.5.b. Limitations

Through ongoing evaluation and appraisal, supervisors are aware of the limitations of supervisees that might impede performance. Supervisors assist supervisees in securing remedial assistance when needed. They recommend dismissal from training programs, applied counseling settings, or state or voluntary professional credentialing processes when those supervisees are unable to provide competent professional services. Supervisors seek consultation and document their decisions to dismiss or refer supervisees for assistance. They ensure that supervisees are aware of options available to them to address such decisions. *(See C.2.g.)*

F.5.c. Counseling for Supervisees

If supervisees request counseling, supervisors provide them with acceptable referrals. Counselors do not provide counseling services to supervisees. Supervisors address interpersonal competencies in terms of the impact of these issues on clients, the supervisory relationship, and professional functioning. *(See F.3.a.)*

F.5.d. Endorsement

Supervisors endorse supervisees for certification, licensure, employment, or completion of an academic or training program only when they believe supervisees are qualified for the endorsement. Regardless of qualifications, supervisors do not endorse supervisees whom they believe to be impaired in any way that would interfere with the performance of the duties associated with the endorsement.

F.6. Responsibilities of Counselor Educators

F.6.a. Counselor Educators

Counselor educators who are responsible for developing, implementing, and supervising educational programs are skilled as teachers and practitioners. They are knowledgeable regarding the ethical, legal, and regulatory aspects of the profession, are skilled in applying that knowledge, and make students and supervisees aware of their responsibilities. Counselor educators conduct counselor education and training programs in an ethical manner and serve as role models for professional behavior. *(See C.1., C.2.a., C.2.c.)*

F.6.b. Infusing Multicultural Issues/Diversity

Counselor educators infuse material related to multiculturalism/diversity into all courses and workshops for the development of professional counselors.

F.6.c. Integration of Study and Practice

Counselor educators establish education and training programs that integrate academic study and supervised practice.

F.6.d. Teaching Ethics

Counselor educators make students and supervisees aware of the ethical responsibilities and standards of the profession and the ethical responsibilities of students to the profession. Counselor educators infuse ethical considerations throughout the curriculum. *(See C.1.)*

F.6.e. Peer Relationships

Counselor educators make every effort to ensure that the rights of peers are not compromised when students or supervisees lead counseling groups or provide clinical supervision. Counselor educators take steps to ensure that students and supervisees understand they have the same ethical obligations as counselor educators, trainers, and supervisors.

F.6.f. Innovative Theories and Techniques

When counselor educators teach counseling techniques/procedures that are innovative, without an empirical foundation, or without a well-grounded theoretical foundation, they define the counseling techniques/procedures as "unproven" or "developing" and explain to students the potential risks and ethical considerations of using such techniques/procedures.

F.6.g. Field Placements

Counselor educators develop clear policies within their training programs regarding field placement and other clinical experiences. Counselor educators provide clearly stated roles and responsibilities for the student or supervisee, the site supervisor, and the program supervisor. They confirm that site supervisors are qualified to provide supervision and inform site supervisors of their professional and ethical responsibilities in this role.

F.6.h. Professional Disclosure

Before initiating counseling services, counselors-in-training disclose their status as students and explain how this status affects the limits of confidentiality. Counselor educators ensure that the clients at field placements are aware of the services rendered and the qualifications of the students and supervisees rendering those services. Students and supervisees obtain client permission before they use any information concerning the counseling relationship in the training process. *(See A.2.b.)*

F.7. Student Welfare

F.7.a. Orientation

Counselor educators recognize that orientation is a developmental process that continues throughout the educational and clinical training of students. Counseling faculty provide prospective students with information about the counselor education program's expectations:

1. the type and level of skill and knowledge acquisition required for successful completion of the training;
2. program training goals, objectives, and mission, and subject matter to be covered;
3. bases for evaluation;
4. training components that encourage self-growth or self-disclosure as part of the training process;
5. the type of supervision settings and requirements of the sites for required clinical field experiences;

6. student and supervisee evaluation and dismissal policies and procedures; and
7. up-to-date employment prospects for graduates.

F.7.b. Self-Growth Experiences

Counselor education programs delineate requirements for self-disclosure or self-growth experiences in their admission and program materials. Counselor educators use professional judgment when designing training experiences they conduct that require student and supervisee self growth or self-disclosure. Students and supervisees are made aware of the ramifications their self-disclosure may have when counselors whose primary role as teacher, trainer, or supervisor requires acting on ethical obligations to the profession. Evaluative components of experiential training experiences explicitly delineate predetermined academic standards that are separate and do not depend on the student's level of self disclosure. Counselor educators may require trainees to seek professional help to address any personal concerns that may be affecting their competency.

F.8. Student Responsibilities

F.8.a. Standards for Students

Counselors-in-training have a responsibility to understand and follow the ACA *Code of Ethics* and adhere to applicable laws, regulatory policies, and rules and policies governing professional staff behavior at the agency or placement setting. Students have the same obligation to clients as those required of professional counselors. *(See C.1., H.1.)*

F.8.b. Impairment

Counselors-in-training refrain from offering or providing counseling services when their physical, mental, or emotional problems are likely to harm a client or others. They are alert to the signs of impairment, seek assistance for problems, and notify their program supervisors when they are aware that they are unable to effectively provide services. In addition, they seek appropriate professional services for themselves to

remediate the problems that are interfering with their ability to provide services to others. *(See A.1., C.2.d., C.2.g.)*

F.9. Evaluation and Remediation of Students

F.9.a. Evaluation

Counselors clearly state to students, prior to and throughout the training program, the levels of competency expected, appraisal methods, and timing of evaluations for both didactic and clinical competencies. Counselor educators provide students with ongoing performance appraisal and evaluation feedback throughout the training program.

F.9.b. Limitations

Counselor educators, throughout ongoing evaluation and appraisal, are aware of and address the inability of some students to achieve counseling competencies that might impede performance. Counselor educators

1. assist students in securing remedial assistance when needed,
2. seek professional consultation and document their decision to dismiss or refer students for assistance, and
3. ensure that students have recourse in a timely manner to address decisions to require them to seek assistance or to dismiss them and provide students with due process according to institutional policies and procedures.

(See C.2.g.)

F.9.c. Counseling for Students

If students request counseling or if counseling services are required as part of a remediation process, counselor educators provide acceptable referrals.

F. 10. Roles and Relationships Between Counselor Educators and Students

F.10.a. Sexual or Romantic Relationships

Sexual or romantic interactions or relationships with current students are prohibited.

F.10.b. Sexual Harassment

Counselor educators do not condone or subject students to sexual harassment. *(See C.6.a.)*

F.10.c. Relationships With Former Students

Counselor educators are aware of the power differential in the relationship between faculty and students. Faculty members foster open discussions with former students when considering engaging in a social, sexual, or other intimate relationship. Faculty members discuss with the former student how their former relationship may affect the change in relationship.

F.10.d. Nonprofessional Relationships

Counselor educators avoid nonprofessional or ongoing professional relationships with students in which there is a risk of potential harm to the student or that may compromise the training experience or grades assigned. In addition, counselor educators do not accept any form of professional services, fees, commissions, reimbursement, or remuneration from a site for student or supervisee placement.

F.10.e. Counseling Services

Counselor educators do not serve as counselors to current students unless this is a brief role associated with a training experience.

F.10.f. Potentially Beneficial Relationships

Counselor educators are aware of the power differential in the relationship between faculty and students. If they believe a nonprofessional relationship with a student may be potentially beneficial to the student, they take precautions similar to those taken by counselors when working with clients. Examples of potentially beneficial interactions or relationships include, but are not limited to, attending a formal ceremony; hospital visits; providing support during a stressful event; or mutual membership in a professional association, organization, or community. Counselor educators engage in open discussions with students when they consider entering into relationships with students outside

of their roles as teachers and supervisors. They discuss with students the rationale for such interactions, the potential benefits and drawbacks, and the anticipated consequences for the student. Educators clarify the specific nature and limitations of the additional role(s) they will have with the student prior to engaging in a nonprofessional relationship. Nonprofessional relationships with students should be time-limited and initiated with student consent.

F.11. Multicultural/Diversity Competence in Counselor Education and Training Programs

F.11.a. Faculty Diversity

Counselor educators are committed to recruiting and retaining a diverse faculty.

F.11.b. Student Diversity

Counselor educators actively attempt to recruit and retain a diverse student body. Counselor educators demonstrate commitment to multicultural/diversity competence by recognizing and valuing diverse cultures and types of abilities students bring to the training experience. Counselor educators provide appropriate accommodations that enhance and support diverse student well-being and academic performance.

F.11.c. Multicultural/Diversity Competence

Counselor educators actively infuse multicultural/diversity competency in their training and supervision practices. They actively train students to gain awareness, knowledge, and skills in the competencies of multicultural practice. Counselor educators include case examples, role-plays, discussion questions, and other classroom activities that promote and represent various cultural perspectives.

SECTION G: RESEARCH AND PUBLICATION

INTRODUCTION

Counselors who conduct research are encouraged to contribute to the knowledge base of the profession and promote a clearer understanding of the conditions that lead to a healthy and more just society. Counselors support efforts of researchers by participating fully and willingly whenever possible. Counselors minimize bias and respect diversity in designing and implementing research programs.

G.1. Research Responsibilities

G.1.a. Use of Human Research Participants

Counselors plan, design, conduct, and report research in a manner that is consistent with pertinent ethical principles, federal and state laws, host institutional regulations, and scientific standards governing research with human research participants.

G.1.b. Deviation From Standard Practice

Counselors seek consultation and observe stringent safeguards to protect the rights of research participants when a research problem suggests a deviation from standard or acceptable practices.

G.1.c. Independent Researchers

When independent researchers do not have access to an Institutional Review Board (IRB), they should consult with researchers who are familiar with IRB procedures to provide appropriate safeguards.

G.1.d. Precautions to Avoid Injury

Counselors who conduct research with human participants are responsible for the welfare of participants throughout the research process and should take reasonable precautions to avoid causing injurious psychological, emotional, physical, or social effects to participants.

G.1.e. Principal Researcher Responsibility

The ultimate responsibility for ethical research practice lies with the principal researcher. All others involved in the research activities share ethical obligations and responsibility for their own actions.

G.1.f. Minimal Interference

Counselors take reasonable precautions to avoid causing disruptions in the lives of research participants that could be caused by their involvement in research.

G.1.g. Multicultural/Diversity Considerations in Research

When appropriate to research goals, counselors are sensitive to incorporating research procedures that take into account cultural considerations. They seek consultation when appropriate.

G.2. Rights of Research Participants
(See A.2, A.7.)

G.2.a. Informed Consent in Research

Individuals have the right to consent to become research participants. In seeking consent, counselors use language that

1. accurately explains the purpose and procedures to be followed,
2. identifies any procedures that are experimental or relatively untried,
3. describes any attendant discomforts and risks,
4. describes any benefits or changes in individuals or organizations that might be reasonably expected,
5. discloses appropriate alternative procedures that would be advantageous for participants,
6. offers to answer any inquiries concerning the procedures,
7. describes any limitations on confidentiality,
8. describes the format and potential target audiences for the dissemination of research findings, and
9. instructs participants that they are free to withdraw their consent and to discontinue participation in the project at any time without penalty.

G.2.b. Deception

Counselors do not conduct research involving deception unless alternative procedures are not feasible and the prospective value of the research justifies the deception. If such deception has the potential to cause physical or emotional harm to research participants, the research is not conducted, regardless of prospective value. When the methodological requirements of a study necessitate concealment or deception, the investigator explains the reasons for this action as soon as possible during the debriefing.

G.2.c. Student/Supervisee Participation

Researchers who involve students or supervisees in research make clear to them that the decision regarding whether or not to participate in research activities does not affect one's academic standing or supervisory relationship. Students or supervisees who choose not to participate in educational research are provided with an appropriate alternative to fulfill their academic or clinical requirements.

G.2.d. Client Participation

Counselors conducting research involving clients make clear in the informed consent process that clients are free to choose whether or not to participate in research activities. Counselors take necessary precautions to protect clients from adverse consequences of declining or withdrawing from participation.

G.2.e. Confidentiality of Information

Information obtained about research participants during the course of an investigation is confidential. When the possibility exists that others may obtain access to such information, ethical research practice requires that the possibility, together with the plans for protecting confidentiality, be explained to participants as a part of the procedure for obtaining informed consent.

G.2.f. Persons Not Capable of Giving Informed Consent

When a person is not capable of giving informed consent, counselors provide an appropriate explanation to, obtain agreement for participation from, and obtain the appropriate consent of a legally authorized person.

G.2.g. Commitments to Participants

Counselors take reasonable measures to honor all commitments to research participants. *(See A.2.c.)*

G.2.h. Explanations After Data Collection

After data are collected, counselors provide participants with full clarification of the nature of the study to remove any misconceptions participants might have regarding the research. Where scientific or human values justify delaying or withholding information, counselors take reasonable measures to avoid causing harm.

G.2.i. Informing Sponsors

Counselors inform sponsors, institutions, and publication channels regarding research procedures and outcomes. Counselors ensure that appropriate bodies and authorities are given pertinent information and acknowledgement.

G.2.j. Disposal of Research Documents and Records

Within a reasonable period of time following the completion of a research project or study, counselors take steps to destroy records or documents (audio, video, digital, and written) containing confidential data or information that identifies research participants. When records are of an artistic nature, researchers obtain participant consent with regard to handling of such records or documents. *(See B.4.a, B.4.g.)*

G.3. Relationships With Research Participants (When Research Involves Intensive or Extended Interactions)

G.3.a. Nonprofessional Relationships

Nonprofessional relationships with research participants should be avoided.

G.3.b. Relationships With Research Participants

Sexual or romantic counselor–research participant interactions or relationships with current research participants are prohibited.

G.3.c. Sexual Harassment and Research Participants

Researchers do not condone or subject research participants to sexual harassment.

G.3.d. Potentially Beneficial Interactions

When a nonprofessional interaction between the researcher and the research participant may be potentially beneficial, the researcher must document, prior to the interaction (when feasible), the rationale for such an interaction, the potential benefit, and anticipated consequences for the research participant. Such interactions should be initiated with appropriate consent of the research participant. Where unintentional harm occurs to the research participant due to the nonprofessional interaction, the researcher must show evidence of an attempt to remedy such harm.

G.4. Reporting Results

G.4.a. Accurate Results

Counselors plan, conduct, and report research accurately. They provide thorough discussions of the limitations of their data and alternative hypotheses. Counselors do not engage in misleading or fraudulent research, distort data, misrepresent data, or deliberately bias their results. They explicitly mention all variables and conditions known to the investigator that may have affected the outcome of a study or the interpretation of data. They describe the extent to which results are applicable for diverse populations.

G.4.b. Obligation to Report Unfavorable Results

Counselors report the results of any research of professional value. Results that reflect unfavorably on institutions, programs, services, prevailing opinions, or vested interests are not withheld.

G.4.c. Reporting Errors

If counselors discover significant errors in their published research, they take reasonable steps to correct such errors in a correction erratum, or through other appropriate publication means.

G.4.d. Identity of Participants

Counselors who supply data, aid in the research of another person, report research results, or make original data available take due care to disguise the identity of respective participants in the absence of specific authorization from the participants to do otherwise. In situations where participants self-identify their involvement in research studies, researchers take active steps to ensure that data is adapted/changed to protect the identity and welfare of all parties and that discussion of results does not cause harm to participants.

G.4.e. Replication Studies

Counselors are obligated to make available sufficient original research data to qualified professionals who may wish to replicate the study.

G.5. Publication

G.5.a. Recognizing Contributions

When conducting and reporting research, counselors are familiar with and give recognition to previous work on the topic, observe copyright laws, and give full credit to those to whom credit is due.

G.5.b. Plagiarism

Counselors do not plagiarize, that is, they do not present another person's work as their own work.

G.5.c. Review/Republication of Data or Ideas

Counselors fully acknowledge and make editorial reviewers aware of prior publication of ideas or data where such ideas or data are submitted for review or publication.

G.5.d. Contributors

Counselors give credit through joint authorship, acknowledgment, footnote statements, or other appropriate means to those who have contributed significantly to research or concept development in accordance with such contributions. The principal contributor is listed first and minor technical or professional contributions are acknowledged in notes or introductory statements.

G.5.e. Agreement of Contributors

Counselors who conduct joint research with colleagues or students/ supervisees establish agreements in advance regarding allocation of tasks, publication credit, and types of acknowledgement that will be received.

G.5.f. Student Research

For articles that are substantially based on students course papers, projects, dissertations or theses, and on which students have been the primary contributors, they are listed as principal authors.

G.5.g. Duplicate Submission

Counselors submit manuscripts for consideration to only one journal at a time. Manuscripts that are published in whole or in substantial part in another journal or published work are not submitted for publication without acknowledgment and permission from the previous publication.

G.5.h. Professional Review

Counselors who review material submitted for publication, research, or other scholarly purposes respect the confidentiality and proprietary rights of those who submitted it. Counselors use care to make publication decisions based on valid and defensible standards. Counselors review article submissions in a timely manner and based on their scope and competency in research methodologies. Counselors who serve as reviewers at the request of editors or publishers make every effort to only review materials that are within their scope of competency and use care to avoid personal biases.

SECTION H: RESOLVING ETHICAL ISSUES

INTRODUCTION

Counselors behave in a legal, ethical, and moral manner in the conduct of their professional work. They are aware that client protection and trust in the profession depend on a high level of professional conduct. They hold other counselors to the same standards and are willing to take appropriate action to ensure that these standards are upheld. Counselors strive to resolve ethical dilemmas with direct and open communication among all parties involved and seek consultation with colleagues and supervisors when necessary. Counselors incorporate ethical practice into their daily professional work. They engage in ongoing professional development regarding current topics in ethical and legal issues in counseling.

H.1. Standards and the Law *(See F.9.a.)*

H.1.a. Knowledge

Counselors understand the ACA *Code of Ethics* and other applicable ethics codes from other professional organizations or from certification and licensure bodies of which they are members. Lack of knowledge or misunderstanding of an ethical responsibility is not a defense against a charge of unethical conduct.

H.1.b. Conflicts Between Ethics and Laws

If ethical responsibilities conflict with law, regulations, or other governing legal authority, counselors make known their commitment to the ACA *Code of Ethics* and take steps to resolve the conflict. If the conflict cannot be resolved by such means, counselors may adhere to the requirements of law, regulations, or other governing legal authority.

H.2. Suspected Violations

H.2.a. Ethical Behavior Expected

Counselors expect colleagues to adhere to the ACA *Code of Ethics*. When counselors possess knowledge that raises doubts as to whether another counselor is acting in an ethical manner, they take appropriate action. *(See H.2.b., H.2.c.)*

H.2.b. Informal Resolution

When counselors have reason to believe that another counselor is violating or has violated an ethical standard, they attempt first to resolve the issue informally with the other counselor if feasible, provided such action does not violate confidentiality rights that may be involved.

H.2.c. Reporting Ethical Violations

If an apparent violation has substantially harmed, or is likely to substantially harm a person or organization and is not appropriate for informal resolution or is not resolved properly, counselors take further action appropriate to the situation. Such action might include referral to state or national committees on professional ethics, voluntary national certification bodies, state licensing boards, or to the appropriate institutional authorities. This standard does not apply when an intervention would violate confidentiality rights or when counselors have been retained to review the work of another counselor whose professional conduct is in question.

H.2.d. Consultation

When uncertain as to whether a particular situation or course of action may be in violation of the *ACA Code of Ethics*, counselors consult with other counselors who are knowledgeable about ethics and the *ACA Code of Ethics*, with colleagues, or with appropriate authorities.

H.2.e. Organizational Conflicts

If the demands of an organization with which counselors are affiliated pose a conflict with the *ACA Code of Ethics*, counselors specify the nature of such conflicts and express to their supervisors or other responsible officials their commitment to the *ACA Code of Ethics*. When possible, counselors work toward change within the organization to allow full adherence to the *ACA Code of Ethics*. In doing so, they address any confidentiality issues.

H.2.f. Unwarranted Complaints

Counselors do not initiate, participate in, or encourage the filing of ethics complaints that are made with reckless disregard or willful ignorance of facts that would disprove the allegation.

H.2.g. Unfair Discrimination Against Complainants and Respondents

Counselors do not deny persons employment, advancement, admission to academic or other programs, tenure, or promotion based solely upon their having made or their being the subject of an ethics complaint. This does not preclude taking action based upon the outcome of such proceedings or considering other appropriate information.

H.3. Cooperation With Ethics Committees

Counselors assist in the process of enforcing the *ACA Code of Ethics*. Counselors cooperate with investigations, proceedings, and requirements of the ACA Ethics Committee or ethics committees of other duly constituted associations or boards having jurisdiction over those charged with a violation. Counselors are familiar with the *ACA Policy and Procedures for Processing Complains of Ethical Violations* and use it as a reference for assisting in the enforcement of the *ACA Code of Ethics*.

Appendix D

National Association of Social Workers

Code of Ethics (1999)

PREAMBLE

The primary mission of the social work profession is to enhance human well-being and help meet the basic human needs of all people, with particular attention to the needs and empowerment of people who are vulnerable, oppressed, and living in poverty. A historic and defining feature of social work is the profession's focus on individual well-being in a social context and the well-being of society. Fundamental to social work is attention to the environmental forces that create, contribute to, and address problems in living.

Social workers promote social justice and social change with and on behalf of clients. "Clients" is used inclusively to refer to individuals, families, groups, organizations, and communities. Social workers are sensitive to cultural and ethnic diversity and strive to end discrimination, oppression, poverty, and other forms of social injustice. These activities may be in the form of direct practice, community organizing, supervision, consultation, administration, advocacy, social and political action, policy development and implementation, education, and research and evaluation. Social workers seek to enhance the capacity of people to address their own needs. Social workers also seek to promote the responsiveness of organizations, communities, and other social institutions to individuals' needs and social problems.

The mission of the social work profession is rooted in a set of core values. These core values, embraced by social workers throughout the profession's history, are the foundation of social work's unique purpose and perspective:

- service
- social justice
- dignity and worth of the person
- importance of human relationships
- integrity
- competence.

This constellation of core values reflects what is unique to the social work profession. Core values, and the principles that flow from them, must be balanced within the context and complexity of the human experience.

PURPOSE OF THE NASW CODE OF ETHICS

Professional ethics are at the core of social work. The profession has an obligation to articulate its basic values, ethical principles, and ethical standards. The NASW Code of Ethics sets forth these values, principles, and standards to guide social workers' conduct. The Code is relevant to all social workers and social work students, regardless of their professional functions, the settings in which they work, or the populations they serve.

The NASW Code of Ethics serves six purposes:

1. The Code identifies core values on which social work's mission is based.
2. The Code summarizes broad ethical principles that reflect the profession's core values

and establishes a set of specific ethical standards that should be used to guide social work practice.

3. The Code is designed to help social workers identify relevant considerations when professional obligations conflict or ethical uncertainties arise.
4. The Code provides ethical standards to which the general public can hold the social work profession accountable.
5. The Code socializes practitioners new to the field to social work's mission, values, ethical principles, and ethical standards.
6. The Code articulates standards that the social work profession itself can use to assess whether social workers have engaged in unethical conduct. NASW has formal procedures to adjudicate ethics complaints filed against its members. In subscribing to this Code, social workers are required to cooperate in its implementation, participate in NASW adjudication proceedings, and abide by any NASW disciplinary rulings or sanctions based on it.

The Code offers a set of values, principles, and standards to guide decision making and conduct when ethical issues arise. It does not provide a set of rules that prescribe how social workers should act in all situations. Specific applications of the Code must take into account the context in which it is being considered and the possibility of conflicts among the Code's values, principles, and standards. Ethical responsibilities flow from all human relationships, from the personal and familial to the social and professional.

Further, the NASW Code of Ethics does not specify which values, principles, and standards are most important and ought to outweigh others in instances when they conflict. Reasonable differences of opinion can and do exist among social workers with respect to the ways in which values, ethical principles, and ethical standards should be rank ordered when they conflict. Ethical decision making in a given situation must apply the informed judgment of the individual social worker and should also consider how the issues would be judged in a peer review process where the ethical standards of the profession would be applied.

Ethical decision making is a process. There are many instances in social work where simple answers are not available to resolve complex ethical issues. Social workers should take into consideration all the values, principles, and standards in this Code that are relevant to any situation in which ethical judgment is warranted. Social workers' decisions and actions should be consistent with the spirit as well as the letter of this Code.

In addition to this Code, there are many other sources of information about ethical thinking that may be useful. Social workers should consider ethical theory and principles generally, social work theory and research, laws, regulations, agency policies, and other relevant codes of ethics, recognizing that among codes of ethics social workers should consider the NASW Code of Ethics as their primary source. Social workers also should be aware of the impact on ethical decision making of their clients' and their own personal values and cultural and religious beliefs and practices. They should be aware of any conflicts between personal and professional values and deal with them responsibly. For additional guidance social workers should consult the relevant literature on professional ethics and ethical decision making and seek appropriate consultation when faced with ethical dilemmas. This may involve consultation with an agency-based or social work organization's ethics committee, a regulatory body, knowledgeable colleagues, supervisors, or legal counsel.

Instances may arise when social workers' ethical obligations conflict with agency policies or relevant laws or regulations. When such conflicts occur, social workers must make a responsible effort to resolve the conflict in a manner that is consistent with the values, principles, and standards expressed in this Code. If a reasonable resolution of the conflict does not appear possible, social workers should seek proper consultation before making a decision.

The NASW Code of Ethics is to be used by NASW and by individuals, agencies, organizations, and bodies (such as licensing and regulatory boards, professional liability insurance providers, courts of law, agency boards of directors, government agencies, and other professional groups) that choose to adopt it or use it as a frame of reference. Violation of standards in this Code does not automatically imply legal liability or violation of the law. Such determination can only be made in the context of legal and judicial proceedings. Alleged violations of the Code would be subject to a peer review process. Such processes are generally separate from legal or administrative procedures and insulated from legal review or proceedings to allow the profession to counsel and discipline its own members.

A code of ethics cannot guarantee ethical behavior. Moreover, a code of ethics cannot resolve all ethical issues or disputes or capture the richness and complexity involved in striving to make responsible choices within a moral community. Rather, a code of ethics sets forth values, ethical principles, and ethical standards to which professionals aspire and by which their actions can be judged. Social workers' ethical behavior should result from their personal commitment to engage in ethical practice. The NASW Code of Ethics reflects the commitment of all social workers to uphold the profession's values and to act ethically. Principles and standards must be applied by individuals of good character who discern moral questions and, in good faith, seek to make reliable ethical judgments.

ETHICAL PRINCIPLES

The following broad ethical principles are based on social work's core values of service, social justice, dignity and worth of the person, importance of human relationships, integrity, and competence. These principles set forth ideals to which all social workers should aspire.

Value: *Service*

Ethical Principle: *Social workers' primary goal is to help people in need and to address social problems.*

Social workers elevate service to others above self-interest. Social workers draw on their knowledge, values, and skills to help people in need

and to address social problems. Social workers are encouraged to volunteer some portion of their professional skills with no expectation of significant financial return (pro bono service).

Value: *Social Justice*

Ethical Principle: *Social workers challenge social injustice.*

Social workers pursue social change, particularly with and on behalf of vulnerable and oppressed individuals and groups of people. Social workers' social change efforts are focused primarily on issues of poverty, unemployment, discrimination, and other forms of social injustice. These activities seek to promote sensitivity to and knowledge about oppression and cultural and ethnic diversity. Social workers strive to ensure access to needed information, services, and resources; equality of opportunity; and meaningful participation in decision making for all people.

Value: *Dignity and Worth of the Person*

Ethical Principle: *Social workers respect the inherent dignity and worth of the person.*

Social workers treat each person in a caring and respectful fashion, mindful of individual differences and cultural and ethnic diversity. Social workers promote clients' socially responsible self-determination. Social workers seek to enhance clients' capacity and opportunity to change and to address their own needs. Social workers are cognizant of their dual responsibility to clients and to the broader society. They seek to resolve conflicts between clients' interests and the broader society's interests in a socially responsible manner consistent with the values, ethical principles, and ethical standards of the profession.

Value: *Importance of Human Relationships*

Ethical Principle: *Social workers recognize the central importance of human relationships.*

Social workers understand that relationships between and among people are an important vehicle for change. Social workers engage people as partners in the helping process. Social workers seek to strengthen relationships among people in a purposeful effort to promote, restore, maintain, and enhance the well-being of individuals, families, social groups, organizations, and communities.

Value: *Integrity*

Ethical Principle: *Social workers behave in a trustworthy manner.*

Social workers are continually aware of the profession's mission, values, ethical principles, and ethical standards and practice in a manner consistent with them. Social workers act honestly and responsibly and promote ethical practices on the part of the organizations with which they are affiliated.

Value: *Competence*

Ethical Principle: *Social workers practice within their areas of competence and develop and enhance their professional expertise.*

Social workers continually strive to increase their professional knowledge and skills and to apply them in practice. Social workers should aspire to contribute to the knowledge base of the profession.

ETHICAL STANDARDS

The following ethical standards are relevant to the professional activities of all social workers. These standards concern (1) social workers' ethical responsibilities to clients, (2) social workers' ethical responsibilities to colleagues, (3) social workers' ethical responsibilities in practice settings, (4) social workers' ethical responsibilities as professionals, (5) social workers' ethical responsibilities to the social work profession, and (6) social workers' ethical responsibilities to the broader society.

Some of the standards that follow are enforceable guidelines for professional conduct, and some are aspirational. The extent to which each standard is enforceable is a matter of pro-fessional judgment to be exercised by those responsible for reviewing alleged violations of ethical standards.

1. Social Workers' Ethical Responsibilities to Clients

1.01 Commitment to Clients

Social workers' primary responsibility is to promote the well-being of clients. In general, clients' interests are primary. However, social workers' responsibility to the larger society or specific legal obligations may on limited occasions supersede the loyalty owed clients, and clients should be so advised. (Examples include when a social worker is required by law to report that a client has abused a child or has threatened to harm self or others.)

1.02 Self-Determination

Social workers respect and promote the right of clients to self-determination and assist clients in their efforts to identify and clarify their goals. Social workers may limit clients' right to self-determination when, in the social workers' professional judgment, clients' actions or potential actions pose a serious, foreseeable, and imminent risk to themselves or others.

1.03 Informed Consent

(a) Social workers should provide services to clients only in the context of a professional relationship based, when appropriate, on valid informed consent. Social workers should use clear and understandable language to inform clients of the purpose of the services, risks related to the services, limits to services because of the requirements of a third-party payer, relevant costs, reasonable alternatives, clients' right to refuse or withdraw consent, and the time frame covered by the consent. Social workers should provide clients with an opportunity to ask questions.

(b) In instances when clients are not literate or have difficulty understanding the primary language used in the practice setting, social workers should take steps to ensure clients' comprehension. This may include providing clients with a detailed verbal explanation or arranging for a qualified interpreter or translator whenever possible.

(c) In instances when clients lack the capacity to provide informed consent, social workers should protect clients' interests by seeking permission from an appropriate third party, informing clients consistent with the clients' level of understanding. In such instances social workers should seek to ensure that the third party acts in a manner consistent with clients' wishes and interests. Social workers should take reasonable steps to enhance such clients' ability to give informed consent.

(d) In instances when clients are receiving services involuntarily, social workers should provide information about the nature and extent of services and about the extent of clients' right to refuse service.

(e) Social workers who provide services via electronic media (such as computer, telephone, radio, and television) should inform recipients of the limitations and risks associated with such services.

(f) Social workers should obtain clients' informed consent before audiotaping or videotaping clients or permitting observation of services to clients by a third party.

1.04 Competence

(a) Social workers should provide services and represent themselves as competent only within the boundaries of their education, training, license, certification, consultation received, supervised experience, or other relevant professional experience.

(b) Social workers should provide services in substantive areas or use intervention techniques or approaches that are new to them only after engaging in appropriate study, training, consultation, and supervision from people who are competent in those interventions or techniques.

(c) When generally recognized standards do not exist with respect to an emerging area of practice, social workers should exercise careful judgment and take responsible steps (including appropriate education, research, training, consultation, and supervision) to ensure the competence of their work and to protect clients from harm.

1.05 Cultural Competence and Social Diversity

(a) Social workers should understand culture and its function in human behavior and society, recognizing the strengths that exist in all cultures.

(b) Social workers should have a knowledge base of their clients' cultures and be able to demonstrate competence in the provision of services that are sensitive to clients' cultures and to differences among people and cultural groups.

(c) Social workers should obtain education about and seek to understand the nature of social diversity and oppression with respect to race, ethnicity, national origin, color, sex, sexual orientation, age, marital status, political belief, religion, and mental or physical disability.

1.06 Conflicts of Interest

(a) Social workers should be alert to and avoid conflicts of interest that interfere with the exercise of professional discretion and impartial judgment. Social workers should inform clients when a real or potential conflict of interest arises and take reasonable steps to resolve the issue in a manner that makes the clients' interests primary and protects clients' interests to the greatest extent possible. In some cases, protecting clients' interests may require termination of the professional relationship with proper referral of the client.

(b) Social workers should not take unfair advantage of any professional relationship or exploit others to further their personal, religious, political, or business interests.

(c) Social workers should not engage in dual or multiple relationships with clients or former clients in which there is a risk of exploitation or potential harm to the client. In instances when dual or multiple relationships are unavoidable, social workers should take steps to protect clients and are responsible for setting clear, appropriate, and culturally sensitive boundaries. (Dual or multiple relationships occur when social workers relate to clients in more than one relationship, whether professional, social, or business. Dual or multiple relationships can occur simultaneously or consecutively.)

(d) When social workers provide services to two or more people who have a relationship with each other (for example, couples, family members), social workers should clarify with all parties which individuals will be considered clients and the nature of social workers' professional obligations to the various individuals who are receiving services. Social workers who anticipate a conflict of interest among the individuals receiving services or who anticipate having to perform in potentially conflicting roles (for example, when a social worker is asked to testify in a child custody dispute or divorce proceedings involving clients) should clarify their role with the parties involved and take appropriate action to minimize any conflict of interest.

1.07 Privacy and Confidentiality

(a) Social workers should respect clients' right to privacy. Social workers should not solicit private information from clients unless it is essential to providing services or conducting social work evaluation or research. Once private information is shared, standards of confidentiality apply.

(b) Social workers may disclose confidential information when appropriate with valid consent from a client or a person legally authorized to consent on behalf of a client.

(c) Social workers should protect the confidentiality of all information obtained in the course of professional service, except for compelling professional reasons. The general expectation that social workers will keep information confidential does not apply when disclosure is necessary to prevent serious, foreseeable, and imminent harm to a client or other identifiable person. In all instances, social workers should disclose the least amount of confidential information necessary to achieve the desired purpose; only information that is directly relevant to the purpose for which the disclosure is made should be revealed.

(d) Social workers should inform clients, to the extent possible, about the disclosure of confidential information and the potential consequences, when feasible before the disclosure is made. This applies whether social workers disclose confidential information on the basis of a legal requirement or client consent.

(e) Social workers should discuss with clients and other interested parties the nature of confidentiality and limitations of clients' right to confidentiality. Social workers should review with clients circumstances where confidential information may be requested and where disclosure of confidential information may be legally required. This discussion should occur as soon as possible in the social worker-client relationship and as needed throughout the course of the relationship.

(f) When social workers provide counseling services to families, couples, or groups, social workers should seek agreement among the parties involved concerning each individual's right to confidentiality and obligation to preserve the confidentiality of information shared by others. Social workers should inform participants in family, couples, or group counseling that social workers cannot guarantee that all participants will honor such agreements.

(g) Social workers should inform clients involved in family, couples, marital, or group counseling of the social worker's, employer's, and agency's policy concerning the social worker's disclosure of confidential information among the parties involved in the counseling.

(h) Social workers should not disclose confidential information to third-party payers unless clients have authorized such disclosure.

(i) Social workers should not discuss confidential information in any setting unless privacy can be ensured. Social workers should not discuss confidential information in public or semi-public areas such as hallways, waiting rooms, elevators, and restaurants.

(j) Social workers should protect the confidentiality of clients during legal proceedings to the extent permitted by law. When a court of law or other legally authorized body orders social workers to disclose confidential or privileged information without a client's consent and such disclosure could cause harm to the client, social workers should request that the court withdraw the order or limit the order as narrowly as possible or maintain the records under seal, unavailable for public inspection.

(k) Social workers should protect the confidentiality of clients when responding to requests from members of the media.

(l) Social workers should protect the confidentiality of clients' written and electronic records and other sensitive information. Social workers should take reasonable steps to ensure that clients' records are stored in a secure location and that clients' records are not available to others who are not authorized to have access.

(m) Social workers should take precautions to ensure and maintain the confidentiality of information transmitted to other parties through the use of computers, electronic mail, facsimile machines, telephones and telephone answering machines, and other electronic or computer technology. Disclosure of identifying information should be avoided whenever possible.

(n) Social workers should transfer or dispose of clients' records in a manner that protects clients' confidentiality and is consistent with state statutes governing records and social work licensure.

(o) Social workers should take reasonable precautions to protect client confidentiality in the event of the social worker's termination of practice, incapacitation, or death.

(p) Social workers should not disclose identifying information when discussing clients for teaching or training purposes unless the client has consented to disclosure of confidential information.

(q) Social workers should not disclose identifying information when discussing clients with consultants unless the client has consented to disclosure of confidential information or there is a compelling need for such disclosure.

(r) Social workers should protect the confidentiality of deceased clients consistent with the preceding standards.

1.08 Access to Records

(a) Social workers should provide clients with reasonable access to records concerning the clients. Social workers who are concerned that clients' access to their records could cause serious misunderstanding or harm to the client should provide assistance in interpreting the records and consultation with the client regarding the records. Social workers should limit clients' access to their records, or portions of their records, only in exceptional circumstances when there is compelling evidence that such access would cause serious harm to the client. Both clients' requests and the rationale for withholding some or all of the record should be documented in clients' files.

(b) When providing clients with access to their records, social workers should take steps to protect the confidentiality of other individuals identified or discussed in such records.

1.09 Sexual Relationships

(a) Social workers should under no circumstances engage in sexual activities or sexual contact with current clients, whether such contact is consensual or forced.

(b) Social workers should not engage in sexual activities or sexual contact with clients' relatives or other individuals with whom clients maintain a close personal relationship when there is a risk of exploitation or potential harm to the client. Sexual activity or sexual contact with clients' relatives or other individuals with whom clients maintain a personal relationship has the potential to be harmful to the client and may make it difficult for the social worker and client to maintain appropriate professional boundaries. Social workers–not their clients, their clients' relatives, or other individuals with whom the client maintains a personal relationship–assume the full burden for setting clear, appropriate, and culturally sensitive boundaries.

(c) Social workers should not engage in sexual activities or sexual contact with former clients because of the potential for harm to the client. If social workers engage in conduct contrary to this prohibition or claim that an exception to this prohibition is warranted because of extraordinary circumstances, it is social workers—not their clients—who assume the full burden of demonstrating that the former client has not been exploited, coerced, or manipulated, intentionally or unintentionally.

(d) Social workers should not provide clinical services to individuals with whom they have had a prior sexual relationship. Providing clinical services to a former sexual partner has the potential to be harmful to the individual and is likely to make it difficult for the social worker and individual to maintain appropriate professional boundaries.

1.10 Physical Contact

Social workers should not engage in physical contact with clients when there is a possibility of psychological harm to the client as a result of the contact (such as cradling or caressing clients). Social workers who engage in appropriate physical contact with clients are responsible for setting clear, appropriate, and culturally sensitive boundaries that govern such physical contact.

1.11 Sexual Harassment

Social workers should not sexually harass clients. Sexual harassment includes sexual advances, sexual solicitation, requests for sexual favors, and other verbal or physical conduct of a sexual nature.

1.12 Derogatory Language

Social workers should not use derogatory language in their written or verbal communications to or about clients. Social workers should use accurate and respectful language in all communications to and about clients.

1.13 Payment for Services

(a) When setting fees, social workers should ensure that the fees are fair, reasonable, and commensurate with the services performed. Consideration should be given to clients' ability to pay.

(b) Social workers should avoid accepting goods or services from clients as payment for professional services. Bartering arrangements, particularly involving services, create the potential for conflicts of interest, exploitation, and inappropriate boundaries in social workers' relationships with clients. Social workers should explore and may participate in bartering only in very limited circumstances when it can be demonstrated that such arrangements are an accepted practice among professionals in the local community, considered to be essential for the provision of services, negotiated without coercion, and entered into at the client's initiative and with the client's informed consent. Social workers who accept goods or services from clients as payment for professional services assume the full burden of demonstrating that this arrangement will not be detrimental to the client or the professional relationship.

(c) Social workers should not solicit a private fee or other remuneration for providing services to clients who are entitled to such available services through the social workers' employer or agency.

1.14 Clients Who Lack Decision-Making Capacity

When social workers act on behalf of clients who lack the capacity to make informed decisions, social workers should take reasonable steps to safeguard the interests and rights of those clients.

1.15 Interruption of Services

Social workers should make reasonable efforts to ensure continuity of services in the event that services are interrupted by factors such as unavailability, relocation, illness, disability, or death.

1.16 Termination of Services

(a) Social workers should terminate services to clients and professional relationships with them when such services and relationships are no longer required or no longer serve the clients' needs or interests.

(b) Social workers should take reasonable steps to avoid abandoning clients who are still in need of services. Social workers should withdraw services precipitously only under unusual circumstances, giving careful consideration to all factors in the situation and taking care to minimize possible adverse effects. Social workers should assist in making appropriate arrangements for continuation of services when necessary.

(c) Social workers in fee-for-service settings may terminate services to clients who are not paying an overdue balance if the financial contractual arrangements have been made clear to the client, if the client does not pose an imminent danger to self or others, and if the clinical and other consequences of the current nonpayment have been addressed and discussed with the client.

(d) Social workers should not terminate services to pursue a social, financial, or sexual relationship with a client.

(e) Social workers who anticipate the termination or interruption of services to clients should notify clients promptly and seek the transfer, referral, or continuation of services in relation to the clients' needs and preferences.

(f) Social workers who are leaving an employment setting should inform clients of appropriate options for the continuation of services and of the benefits and risks of the options.

2. Social Workers' Ethical Responsibilities to Colleagues

2.01 Respect

(a) Social workers should treat colleagues with respect and should represent accurately and fairly the qualifications, views, and obligations of colleagues.

(b) Social workers should avoid unwarranted negative criticism of colleagues in communications with clients or with other professionals. Unwarranted negative criticism may include demeaning comments that refer to colleagues' level of competence or to individuals' attributes such as race, ethnicity, national origin, color, sex, sexual orientation, age, marital status, political belief, religion, and mental or physical disability.

(c) Social workers should cooperate with social work colleagues and with colleagues of other professions when such cooperation serves the well-being of clients.

2.02 Confidentiality

Social workers should respect confidential information shared by colleagues in the course of

their professional relationships and transactions. Social workers should ensure that such colleagues understand social workers' obligation to respect confidentiality and any exceptions related to it.

2.03 Interdisciplinary Collaboration

(a) Social workers who are members of an interdisciplinary team should participate in and contribute to decisions that affect the well-being of clients by drawing on the perspectives, values, and experiences of the social work profession. Professional and ethical obligations of the interdisciplinary team as a whole and of its individual members should be clearly established.

(b) Social workers for whom a team decision raises ethical concerns should attempt to resolve the disagreement through appropriate channels. If the disagreement cannot be resolved, social workers should pursue other avenues to address their concerns consistent with client well-being.

2.04 Disputes Involving Colleagues

(a) Social workers should not take advantage of a dispute between a colleague and an employer to obtain a position or otherwise advance the social workers' own interests.

(b) Social workers should not exploit clients in disputes with colleagues or engage clients in any inappropriate discussion of conflicts between social workers and their colleagues.

2.05 Consultation

(a) Social workers should seek the advice and counsel of colleagues whenever such consultation is in the best interests of clients.

(b) Social workers should keep themselves informed about colleagues' areas of expertise and competencies. Social workers should seek consultation only from colleagues who have demonstrated knowledge, expertise, and competence related to the subject of the consultation.

(c) When consulting with colleagues about clients, social workers should disclose the least amount of information necessary to achieve the purposes of the consultation.

2.06 Referral for Services

(a) Social workers should refer clients to other professionals when the other professionals' specialized knowledge or expertise is needed to serve clients fully or when social workers believe that they are not being effective or making reasonable progress with clients and that additional service is required.

(b) Social workers who refer clients to other professionals should take appropriate steps to facilitate an orderly transfer of responsibility. Social workers who refer clients to other professionals should disclose, with clients' consent, all pertinent information to the new service providers.

(c) Social workers are prohibited from giving or receiving payment for a referral when no professional service is provided by the referring social worker.

2.07 Sexual Relationships

(a) Social workers who function as supervisors or educators should not engage in sexual activities or contact with supervisees, students, trainees, or other colleagues over whom they exercise professional authority.

(b) Social workers should avoid engaging in sexual relationships with colleagues when there is potential for a conflict of interest. Social workers who become involved in, or anticipate becoming involved in, a sexual relationship with a colleague have a duty to transfer professional responsibilities, when necessary, to avoid a conflict of interest.

2.08 Sexual Harassment

Social workers should not sexually harass supervisees, students, trainees, or colleagues. Sexual harassment includes sexual advances, sexual solicitation, requests for sexual favors, and other verbal or physical conduct of a sexual nature.

2.09 Impairment of Colleagues

(a) Social workers who have direct knowledge of a social work colleague's impairment that is due to personal problems, psychosocial distress, substance abuse, or mental health difficulties and that interferes with practice effectiveness should consult with that colleague when feasible and assist the colleague in taking remedial action.

(b) Social workers who believe that a social work colleague's impairment interferes with practice effectiveness and that the colleague has not taken adequate steps to address the impairment should take action through appropriate channels established by employers, agencies, NASW, licensing and regulatory bodies, and other professional organizations.

2.10 Incompetence of Colleagues

(a) Social workers who have direct knowledge of a social work colleague's incompetence should consult with that colleague when feasible and assist the colleague in taking remedial action.

(b) Social workers who believe that a social work colleague is incompetent and has not taken adequate steps to address the incompetence should take action through appropriate channels established by employers, agencies, NASW, licensing and regulatory bodies, and other professional organizations.

2.11 Unethical Conduct of Colleagues

(a) Social workers should take adequate measures to discourage, prevent, expose, and correct the unethical conduct of colleagues.

(b) Social workers should be knowledgeable about established policies and procedures for handling concerns about colleagues' unethical behavior. Social workers should be familiar with national, state, and local procedures for handling ethics complaints. These include policies and procedures created by NASW, licensing and regulatory bodies, employers, agencies, and other professional organizations.

(c) Social workers who believe that a colleague has acted unethically should seek resolution by discussing their concerns with the colleague when feasible and when such discussion is likely to be productive.

(d) When necessary, social workers who believe that a colleague has acted unethically should take action through appropriate formal channels (such as contacting a state licensing board or regulatory body, an NASW committee on inquiry, or other professional ethics committees).

(e) Social workers should defend and assist colleagues who are unjustly charged with unethical conduct.

3. Social Workers' Ethical Responsibilities in Practice Settings

3.01 Supervision and Consultation

(a) Social workers who provide supervision or consultation should have the necessary knowledge and skill to supervise or consult appropriately and should do so only within their areas of knowledge and competence.

(b) Social workers who provide supervision or consultation are responsible for setting clear, appropriate, and culturally sensitive boundaries.

(c) Social workers should not engage in any dual or multiple relationships with supervisees in which there is a risk of exploitation of or potential harm to the supervisee.

(d) Social workers who provide supervision should evaluate supervisees' performance in a manner that is fair and respectful.

3.02 Education and Training

(a) Social workers who function as educators, field instructors for students, or trainers should provide instruction only within their areas of knowledge and competence and should provide instruction based on the most current information and knowledge available in the profession.

(b) Social workers who function as educators or field instructors for students should evaluate students' performance in a manner that is fair and respectful.

(c) Social workers who function as educators or field instructors for students should take reasonable steps to ensure that clients are routinely informed when services are being provided by students.

(d) Social workers who function as educators or field instructors for students should not engage in any dual or multiple relationships with students in which there is a risk of exploitation or potential harm to the student. Social work educators and field instructors are responsible for setting clear, appropriate, and culturally sensitive boundaries.

3.03 Performance Evaluation

Social workers who have responsibility for evaluating the performance of others should fulfill such responsibility in a fair and considerate manner and on the basis of clearly stated criteria.

3.04 Client Records

(a) Social workers should take reasonable steps to ensure that documentation in records is accurate and reflects the services provided.

(b) Social workers should include sufficient and timely documentation in records to facilitate the delivery of services and to ensure continuity of services provided to clients in the future.

(c) Social workers' documentation should protect clients' privacy to the extent that is possible and appropriate and should include only information that is directly relevant to the delivery of services.

(d) Social workers should store records following the termination of services to ensure reasonable future access. Records should be maintained for the number of years required by state statutes or relevant contracts.

3.05 Billing

Social workers should establish and maintain billing practices that accurately reflect the nature and extent of services provided and that identify who provided the service in the practice setting.

3.06 Client Transfer

(a) When an individual who is receiving services from another agency or colleague contacts a social worker for services, the social worker should carefully consider the client's needs before agreeing to provide services. To minimize possible confusion and conflict, social workers should discuss with potential clients the nature of the clients' current relationship with other service providers and the implications, including possible benefits or risks, of entering into a relationship with a new service provider.

(b) If a new client has been served by another agency or colleague, social workers should discuss with the client whether consultation with the previous service provider is in the client's best interest.

3.07 Administration

(a) Social work administrators should advocate within and outside their agencies for adequate resources to meet clients' needs.

(b) Social workers should advocate for resource allocation procedures that are open and fair. When not all clients' needs can be met, an allocation procedure should be developed that is nondiscriminatory and based on appropriate and consistently applied principles.

(c) Social workers who are administrators should take reasonable steps to ensure that adequate agency or organizational resources are available to provide appropriate staff supervision.

(d) Social work administrators should take reasonable steps to ensure that the working environment for which they are responsible is consistent with and encourages compliance with the NASW Code of Ethics. Social work administrators should take reasonable steps to eliminate any conditions in their organizations that violate, interfere with, or discourage compliance with the Code.

3.08 Continuing Education and Staff Development

Social work administrators and supervisors should take reasonable steps to provide or arrange for continuing education and staff development for all staff for whom they are responsible. Continuing education and staff development should address current knowledge and emerging developments related to social work practice and ethics.

3.09 Commitments to Employers

(a) Social workers generally should adhere to commitments made to employers and employing organizations.

(b) Social workers should work to improve employing agencies' policies and procedures and the efficiency and effectiveness of their services.

(c) Social workers should take reasonable steps to ensure that employers are aware of social workers' ethical obligations as set forth in the NASW Code of Ethics and of the implications of those obligations for social work practice.

(d) Social workers should not allow an employing organization's policies, procedures, regulations, or administrative orders to interfere with their ethical practice of social work. Social workers should take reasonable steps to ensure that their employing organizations' practices are consistent with the NASW Code of Ethics.

(e) Social workers should act to prevent and eliminate discrimination in the employing organization's work assignments and in its employment policies and practices.

(f) Social workers should accept employment or arrange student field placements only in organizations that exercise fair personnel practices.

(g) Social workers should be diligent stewards of the resources of their employing organizations, wisely conserving funds where appropriate and never misappropriating funds or using them for unintended purposes.

3.10 Labor-Management Disputes

(a) Social workers may engage in organized action, including the formation of and participation in labor unions, to improve services to clients and working conditions.

(b) The actions of social workers who are involved in labor-management disputes, job actions, or labor strikes should be guided by the profession's values, ethical principles, and ethical standards. Reasonable differences of opinion exist among social workers concerning their primary obligation as professionals during an actual or threatened labor strike or job action. Social workers should carefully examine relevant issues and their possible impact on clients before deciding on a course of action.

4. Social Workers' Ethical Responsibilities as Professionals

4.01 Competence

(a) Social workers should accept responsibility or employment only on the basis of existing competence or the intention to acquire the necessary competence.

(b) Social workers should strive to become and remain proficient in professional practice and the performance of professional functions. Social workers should critically examine and keep current with emerging knowledge relevant to social work. Social workers should routinely review the professional literature and participate in continuing education relevant to social work practice and social work ethics.

(c) Social workers should base practice on recognized knowledge, including empirically based knowledge, relevant to social work and social work ethics.

4.02 Discrimination

Social workers should not practice, condone, facilitate, or collaborate with any form of discrimination on the basis of race, ethnicity, national origin, color, sex, sexual orientation, age, marital status, political belief, religion, or mental or physical disability.

4.03 Private Conduct

Social workers should not permit their private conduct to interfere with their ability to fulfill their professional responsibilities.

4.04 Dishonesty, Fraud, and Deception

Social workers should not participate in, condone, or be associated with dishonesty, fraud, or deception.

4.05 Impairment

(a) Social workers should not allow their own personal problems, psychosocial distress, legal problems, substance abuse, or mental health difficulties to interfere with their professional judgment and performance or to jeopardize the best interests of people for whom they have a professional responsibility.

(b) Social workers whose personal problems, psychosocial distress, legal problems, substance abuse, or mental health difficulties interfere with their professional judgment and performance should immediately seek consultation and take appropriate remedial action by seeking professional help, making adjustments in workload, terminating practice, or taking any other steps necessary to protect clients and others.

4.06 Misrepresentation

(a) Social workers should make clear distinctions between statements made and actions engaged in as a private individual and as a representative of the social work profession, a professional social work organization, or the social worker's employing agency.

(b) Social workers who speak on behalf of professional social work organizations should accurately represent the official and authorized positions of the organizations.

(c) Social workers should ensure that their representations to clients, agencies, and the public of professional qualifications, credentials, education, competence, affiliations, services provided, or results to be achieved are accurate. Social workers should claim only those relevant professional credentials they actually possess and take steps to correct any inaccuracies or misrepresentations of their credentials by others.

4.07 Solicitations

(a) Social workers should not engage in uninvited solicitation of potential clients who, because of their circumstances, are vulnerable to undue influence, manipulation, or coercion.

(b) Social workers should not engage in solicitation of testimonial endorsements (including solicitation of consent to use a client's prior statement as a testimonial endorsement) from current clients or from other people who, because of their particular circumstances, are vulnerable to undue influence.

4.08 Acknowledging Credit

(a) Social workers should take responsibility and credit, including authorship credit, only for work they have actually performed and to which they have contributed.

(b) Social workers should honestly acknowledge the work of and the contributions made by others.

5. Social Workers' Ethical Responsibilities to the Social Work Profession

5.01 Integrity of the Profession

(a) Social workers should work toward the maintenance and promotion of high standards of practice.

(b) Social workers should uphold and advance the values, ethics, knowledge, and mission of the profession. Social workers should protect, enhance, and improve the integrity of the profession through appropriate study and research, active discussion, and responsible criticism of the profession.

(c) Social workers should contribute time and professional expertise to activities that promote respect for the value, integrity, and competence of the social work profession. These activities may include teaching, research, consultation, service, legislative testimony, presentations in the community, and participation in their professional organizations.

(d) Social workers should contribute to the knowledge base of social work and share with colleagues their knowledge related to practice, research, and ethics. Social workers should seek to contribute to the profession's literature and to share their knowledge at professional meetings and conferences.

(e) Social workers should act to prevent the unauthorized and unqualified practice of social work.

5.02 Evaluation and Research

(a) Social workers should monitor and evaluate policies, the implementation of programs, and practice interventions.

(b) Social workers should promote and facilitate evaluation and research to contribute to the development of knowledge.

(c) Social workers should critically examine and keep current with emerging knowledge relevant to social work and fully use evaluation and research evidence in their professional practice.

(d) Social workers engaged in evaluation or research should carefully consider possible consequences and should follow guidelines developed for the protection of evaluation and research participants. Appropriate institutional review boards should be consulted.

(e) Social workers engaged in evaluation or research should obtain voluntary and written informed consent from participants, when appropriate, without any implied or actual deprivation or penalty for refusal to participate; without undue inducement to participate; and with due regard for participants' well-being, privacy, and dignity. Informed consent should include information about the nature, extent, and duration of the participation requested and disclosure of the risks and benefits of participation in the research.

(f) When evaluation or research participants are incapable of giving informed consent, social workers should provide an appropriate explanation to the participants, obtain the participants' assent to the extent they are able, and obtain written consent from an appropriate proxy.

(g) Social workers should never design or conduct evaluation or research that does not use consent procedures, such as certain forms of naturalistic observation and archival research, unless rigorous and responsible review of the research has found it to be justified because of its prospective scientific, educational, or applied value and unless equally effective alternative procedures that do not involve waiver of consent are not feasible.

(h) Social workers should inform participants of their right to withdraw from evaluation and research at any time without penalty.

(i) Social workers should take appropriate steps to ensure that participants in evaluation and research have access to appropriate supportive services.

(j) Social workers engaged in evaluation or research should protect participants from unwarranted physical or mental distress, harm, danger, or deprivation.

(k) Social workers engaged in the evaluation of services should discuss collected information only for professional purposes and only with people professionally concerned with this information.

(l) Social workers engaged in evaluation or research should ensure the anonymity or confidentiality of participants and of the data obtained from them. Social workers should inform participants of any limits of confidentiality, the measures that will be taken to ensure confidentiality, and when any records containing research data will be destroyed.

(m) Social workers who report evaluation and research results should protect participants' confidentiality by omitting identifying information unless proper consent has been obtained authorizing disclosure.

(n) Social workers should report evaluation and research findings accurately. They should not fabricate or falsify results and should take steps to correct any errors later found in published data using standard publication methods.

(o) Social workers engaged in evaluation or research should be alert to and avoid conflicts of interest and dual relationships with participants, should inform participants when a real or potential conflict of interest arises, and should take steps to resolve the issue in a manner that makes participants' interests primary.

(p) Social workers should educate themselves, their students, and their colleagues about responsible research practices.

6. Social Workers' Ethical Responsibilities to the Broader Society

6.01 Social Welfare

Social workers should promote the general welfare of society, from local to global levels, and the development of people, their communities, and their environments. Social workers should advocate for living conditions conducive to the fulfillment of basic human needs and should promote social, economic, political, and cultural values and institutions that are compatible with the realization of social justice.

6.02 Public Participation

Social workers should facilitate informed participation by the public in shaping social policies and institutions.

6.03 Public Emergencies

Social workers should provide appropriate professional services in public emergencies to the greatest extent possible.

6.04 Social and Political Action

(a) Social workers should engage in social and political action that seeks to ensure that all people have equal access to the resources, employment, services, and opportunities they require to meet their basic human needs and to develop fully. Social workers should be aware of the impact of the political arena on practice and should advocate for changes in policy and legislation to improve social conditions in order to meet basic human needs and promote social justice.

(b) Social workers should act to expand choice and opportunity for all people, with special regard for vulnerable, disadvantaged, oppressed, and exploited people and groups.

(c) Social workers should promote conditions that encourage respect for cultural and social diversity within the United States and globally. Social workers should promote policies and practices that demonstrate respect for difference, support the expansion of cultural knowledge and resources, advocate for programs and institutions that demonstrate cultural competence, and promote policies that safeguard the rights of and confirm equity and social justice for all people.

(d) Social workers should act to prevent and eliminate domination of, exploitation of, and discrimination against any person, group, or class on the basis of race, ethnicity, national origin, color, sex, sexual orientation, age, marital status, political belief, religion, or mental or physical disability.

Appendix E

American Association for Marriage and Family Therapy

Code of Ethics (2001)

PREAMBLE

The Board of Directors of the American Association for Marriage and Family Therapy (AAMFT) hereby promulgates, pursuant to Article 2, Section 2.013 of the Association's By-laws, the Revised AAMFT Code of Ethics, effective July 1, 2001.

The AAMFT strives to honor the public trust in marriage and family therapists by setting standards for ethical practice as described in this Code. The ethical standards define professional expectations and are enforced by the AAMFT Ethics Committee. The absence of an explicit reference to a specific behavior or situation in the Code does not mean that the behavior is ethical or unethical. The standards are not exhaustive. Marriage and family therapists who are uncertain about the ethics of a particular course of action are encouraged to seek counsel from consultants, attorneys, supervisors, colleagues, or other appropriate authorities.

Both law and ethics govern the practice of marriage and family therapy. When making decisions regarding professional behavior, marriage and family therapists must consider the AAMFT Code of Ethics and applicable laws and regulations. If the AAMFT Code of Ethics prescribes a standard higher than that required by law, marriage and family therapists must meet the higher standard of the AAMFT Code of Ethics. Marriage and family therapists comply with the mandates of law, but make known their commitment to the AAMFT Code of Ethics and

take steps to resolve the conflict in a responsible manner. The AAMFT supports legal mandates for reporting of alleged unethical conduct.

The AAMFT Code of Ethics is binding on Members of AAMFT in all membership categories, AAMFT-Approved Supervisors, and applicants for membership and the Approved Supervisor designation (hereafter, AAMFT Member). AAMFT members have an obligation to be familiar with the AAMFT Code of Ethics and its application to their professional services. Lack of awareness or misunderstanding of an ethical standard is not a defense to a charge of unethical conduct.

The process for filing, investigating, and resolving complaints of unethical conduct is described in the current Procedures for Handling Ethical Matters of the AAMFT Ethics Committee. Persons accused are considered innocent by the Ethics Committee until proven guilty, except as otherwise provided, and are entitled to due process. If an AAMFT Member resigns in anticipation of, or during the course of, an ethics investigation, the Ethics Committee will complete its investigation. Any publication of action taken by the Association will include the fact that the Member attempted to resign during the investigation.

PRINCIPLE I. RESPONSIBILITY TO CLIENTS

Marriage and family therapists advance the welfare of families and individuals. They respect

the rights of those persons seeking their assis-
tance, and make reasonable efforts to ensure that
their services are used appropriately.

1.1. Marriage and family therapists provide professional assistance to persons without discrimination on the basis of race, age, ethnicity, socioeconomic status, disability, gender, health status, religion, national origin, or sexual orientation.

1.2 Marriage and family therapists obtain appropriate informed consent to therapy or related procedures as early as feasible in the therapeutic relationship, and use language that is reasonably understandable to clients. The content of informed consent may vary depending upon the client and treatment plan; however, informed consent generally necessitates that the client: (a) has the capacity to consent; (b) has been adequately informed of significant information concerning treatment processes and procedures; (c) has been adequately informed of potential risks and benefits of treatments for which generally recognized standards do not yet exist; (d) has freely and without undue influence expressed consent; and (e) has provided consent that is appropriately documented. When persons, due to age or mental status, are legally incapable of giving informed consent, marriage and family therapists obtain informed permission from a legally authorized person, if such substitute consent is legally permissible.

1.3 Marriage and family therapists are aware of their influential positions with respect to clients, and they avoid exploiting the trust and dependency of such persons. Therapists, therefore, make every effort to avoid conditions and multiple relationships with clients that could impair professional judgment or increase the risk of exploitation. Such relationships include, but are not limited to, business or close personal relationships with a client or the client's immediate family. When the risk of impairment or exploitation exists due to conditions or multiple roles, therapists take appropriate precautions.

1.4 Sexual intimacy with clients is prohibited.

1.5 Sexual intimacy with former clients is likely to be harmful and is therefore prohibited for two years following the termination of therapy or last professional contact. In an effort to avoid exploiting the trust and dependency of clients, marriage and family therapists should not engage in sexual intimacy with former clients after the two years following termination or last professional contact. Should therapists engage in sexual intimacy with former clients following two years after termination or last professional contact, the burden shifts to the therapist to demonstrate that there has been no exploitation or injury to the former client or to the client's immediate family.

1.6 Marriage and family therapists comply with applicable laws regarding the reporting of alleged unethical conduct.

1.7 Marriage and family therapists do not use their professional relationships with clients to further their own interests.

1.8 Marriage and family therapists respect the rights of clients to make decisions and help them to understand the consequences of these decisions. Therapists clearly advise the clients that they have the responsibility to make decisions regarding relationships such as cohabitation, marriage, divorce, separation, reconciliation, custody, and visitation.

1.9 Marriage and family therapists continue therapeutic relationships only so long as it is reasonably clear that clients are benefiting from the relationship.

1.10 Marriage and family therapists assist persons in obtaining other therapeutic services if the therapist is unable or unwilling, for appropriate reasons, to provide professional help.

1.11 Marriage and family therapists do not abandon or neglect clients in treatment without making reasonable arrangements for the continuation of such treatment.

1.12 Marriage and family therapists obtain written informed consent from clients before videotaping, audio recording, or permitting third-party observation.

1.13 Marriage and family therapists, upon agreeing to provide services to a person or entity at the request of a third party, clarify, to the extent feasible and at the outset of the service, the nature of the relationship with each party and the limits of confidentiality.

PRINCIPLE II. CONFIDENTIALITY

Marriage and family therapists have unique confidentiality concerns because the client in a therapeutic relationship may be more than one person. Therapists respect and guard the confidences of each individual client.

2.1 Marriage and family therapists disclose to clients and other interested parties, as early as feasible in their professional contacts, the nature of confidentiality and possible limitations of the clients' right to confidentiality. Therapists review with clients the circumstances where confidential information may be requested and where disclosure of confidential information may be legally required. Circumstances may necessitate repeated disclosures.

2.2 Marriage and family therapists do not disclose client confidences except by written authorization or waiver, or where mandated or permitted by law. Verbal authorization will not be sufficient except in emergency situations, unless prohibited by law. When providing couple, family or group treatment, the therapist does not disclose information outside the treatment context without a written authorization from each individual competent to execute a waiver. In the context of couple, family or group treatment, the therapist may not reveal any individual's confidences to others in the client unit without the prior written permission of that individual.

2.3 Marriage and family therapists use client and/or clinical materials in teaching, writing, consulting, research, and public presentations only if a written waiver has been obtained in accordance with Subprinciple 2.2, or when appropriate steps have been taken to protect client identity and confidentiality.

2.4 Marriage and family therapists store, safeguard, and dispose of client records in ways that maintain confidentiality and in accord with applicable laws and professional standards.

2.5 Subsequent to the therapist moving from the area, closing the practice, or upon the death of the therapist, a marriage and family therapist arranges for the storage, transfer, or disposal of client records in ways that maintain confidentiality and safeguard the welfare of clients.

2.6 Marriage and family therapists, when consulting with colleagues or referral sources, do not share confidential information that could reasonably lead to the identification of a client, research participant, supervisee, or other person with whom they have a confidential relationship unless they have obtained the prior written consent of the client, research participant, supervisee, or other person with whom they have a confidential relationship. Information may be shared only to the extent necessary to achieve the purposes of the consultation.

PRINCIPLE III. PROFESSIONAL COMPETENCE AND INTEGRITY

Marriage and family therapists maintain high standards of professional competence and integrity.

3.1 Marriage and family therapists pursue knowledge of new developments and maintain competence in marriage and family therapy through education, training, or supervised experience.

3.2 Marriage and family therapists maintain adequate knowledge of and adhere to applicable laws, ethics, and professional standards.

3.3 Marriage and family therapists seek appropriate professional assistance for their personal problems or conflicts that may impair work performance or clinical judgment.

3.4 Marriage and family therapists do not provide services that create a conflict of interest that may impair work performance or clinical judgment.

3.5 Marriage and family therapists, as presenters, teachers, supervisors, consultants and researchers, are dedicated to high standards of scholarship, present accurate information, and disclose potential conflicts of interest.

3.6 Marriage and family therapists maintain accurate and adequate clinical and financial records.

3.7 While developing new skills in specialty areas, marriage and family therapists take steps to ensure the competence of their work and to protect clients from possible harm. Marriage and family therapists practice in specialty areas new to them only after appropriate education, training, or supervised experience.

3.8 Marriage and family therapists do not engage in sexual or other forms of harassment of clients, students, trainees, supervisees, employees, colleagues, or research subjects.

3.9 Marriage and family therapists do not engage in the exploitation of clients, students, trainees, supervisees, employees, colleagues, or research subjects.

3.10 Marriage and family therapists do not give to or receive from clients (a) gifts of substantial value or (b) gifts that impair the integrity or efficacy of the therapeutic relationship.

3.11 Marriage and family therapists do not diagnose, treat, or advise on problems outside the recognized boundaries of their competencies.

3.12 Marriage and family therapists make efforts to prevent the distortion or misuse of their clinical and research findings.

3.13 Marriage and family therapists, because of their ability to influence and alter the lives of others, exercise special care when making public their professional recommendations and opinions through testimony or other public statements.

3.14 To avoid a conflict of interests, marriage and family therapists who treat minors or adults involved in custody or visitation actions may not also perform forensic evaluations for custody, residence, or visitation of the minor. The marriage and family therapist who treats the minor may provide the court or mental health professional performing the evaluation with information about the minor from the marriage and family therapist's perspective as a treating marriage and family therapist, so long as the marriage and family therapist does not violate confidentiality.

3.15 Marriage and family therapists are in violation of this Code and subject to termination of membership or other appropriate action if they: (a) are convicted of any felony; (b) are convicted of a misdemeanor related to their qualifications or functions; (c) engage in conduct which could lead to conviction of a felony, or a misdemeanor related to their qualifications or functions; (d) are expelled from or disciplined by other professional organizations; (e) have their licenses or certificates suspended or revoked or are otherwise disciplined by regulatory bodies; (f) continue to practice marriage and family therapy while no longer competent to do so because they are impaired by physical or mental causes or the abuse of alcohol or other substances; or (g) fail to cooperate with the Association at any point from the inception of an ethical complaint through the completion of all proceedings regarding that complaint.

PRINCIPLE IV. RESPONSIBILITY TO STUDENTS AND SUPERVISEES

Marriage and family therapists do not exploit the trust and dependency of students and supervisees.

4.1 Marriage and family therapists are aware of their influential positions with respect to students and supervisees, and they avoid exploiting the trust and dependency of such persons. Therapists, therefore, make every effort to avoid conditions and multiple relationships that could impair professional objectivity or increase the risk of exploitation. When the risk of impairment or exploitation exists due to conditions or multiple roles, therapists take appropriate precautions.

4.2 Marriage and family therapists do not provide therapy to current students or supervisees.

4.3 Marriage and family therapists do not engage in sexual intimacy with students or supervisees during the evaluative or training relationship between the therapist and student or supervisee. Should a supervisor engage in sexual activity with a former supervisee, the burden of proof shifts to the supervisor to demonstrate that there has been no exploitation or injury to the supervisee.

4.4 Marriage and family therapists do not permit students or supervisees to perform or to hold themselves out as competent to perform professional services beyond their training, level of experience, and competence.

4.5 Marriage and family therapists take reasonable measures to ensure that services provided by supervisees are professional.

4.6 Marriage and family therapists avoid accepting as supervisees or students those individuals with whom a prior or existing relationship could compromise the therapist's objectivity. When such situations cannot be avoided, therapists take appropriate precautions to maintain objectivity. Examples of such relationships include, but are not limited to, those individuals with whom the therapist has a current or prior sexual, close personal, immediate familial, or therapeutic relationship.

4.7 Marriage and family therapists do not disclose supervisee confidences except by written authorization or waiver, or when mandated or permitted by law. In educational or training settings where there are multiple supervisors, disclosures are permitted only to other professional colleagues, administrators, or employers who share responsibility for training of the supervisee. Verbal authorization will not be sufficient except in emergency situations, unless prohibited by law.

PRINCIPLE V. RESPONSIBILITY TO RESEARCH PARTICIPANTS

Investigators respect the dignity and protect the welfare of research participants, and are aware of applicable laws and regulations and professional standards governing the conduct of research.

5.1 Investigators are responsible for making careful examinations of ethical acceptability in planning studies. To the extent that services to research participants may be compromised by participation in research, investigators seek the ethical advice of qualified professionals not directly involved in the investigation and observe safeguards to protect the rights of research participants.

5.2 Investigators requesting participant involvement in research inform participants of the aspects of the research that might reasonably be expected to influence willingness to participate. Investigators are especially sensitive to the possibility of diminished consent when participants are also receiving clinical services, or have impairments which limit understanding and/

or communication, or when participants are children.

5.3 Investigators respect each participant's freedom to decline participation in or to withdraw from a research study at any time. This obligation requires special thought and consideration when investigators or other members of the research team are in positions of authority or influence over participants. Marriage and family therapists, therefore, make every effort to avoid multiple relationships with research participants that could impair professional judgment or increase the risk of exploitation.

5.4 Information obtained about a research participant during the course of an investigation is confidential unless there is a waiver previously obtained in writing. When the possibility exists that others, including family members, may obtain access to such information, this possibility, together with the plan for protecting confidentiality, is explained as part of the procedure for obtaining informed consent.

PRINCIPLE VI. RESPONSIBILITY TO THE PROFESSION

Marriage and family therapists respect the rights and responsibilities of professional colleagues and participate in activities that advance the goals of the profession.

6.1 Marriage and family therapists remain accountable to the standards of the profession when acting as members or employees of organizations. If the mandates of an organization with which a marriage and family therapist is affiliated, through employment, contract or otherwise, conflict with the AAMFT Code of Ethics, marriage and family therapists make known to the organization their commitment to the AAMFT Code of Ethics and attempt to resolve the conflict in a way that allows the fullest adherence to the Code of Ethics.

6.2 Marriage and family therapists assign publication credit to those who have contributed to a publication in proportion to their contributions and in accordance with customary professional publication practices.

6.3 Marriage and family therapists do not accept or require authorship credit for a publication based on research from a student's program, unless the therapist made a substantial contribution beyond being a faculty advisor or research committee member. Coauthorship on a student thesis, dissertation, or project should be determined in accordance with principles of fairness and justice.

6.4 Marriage and family therapists who are the authors of books or other materials that are published or distributed do not plagiarize or fail to cite persons to whom credit for original ideas or work is due.

6.5 Marriage and family therapists who are the authors of books or other materials published or distributed by an organization take reasonable precautions to ensure that the organization promotes and advertises the materials accurately and factually.

6.6 Marriage and family therapists participate in activities that contribute to a better community and society, including devoting a portion of their professional activity to services for which there is little or no financial return.

6.7 Marriage and family therapists are concerned with developing laws and regulations pertaining to marriage and family therapy that serve the public interest, and with altering such laws and regulations that are not in the public interest.

6.8 Marriage and family therapists encourage public participation in the design and delivery of professional services and in the regulation of practitioners.

PRINCIPLE VII. FINANCIAL ARRANGEMENTS

Marriage and family therapists make financial arrangements with clients, third-party payors, and supervisees that are reasonably understandable and conform to accepted professional practices.

7.1 Marriage and family therapists do not offer or accept kickbacks, rebates, bonuses, or other remuneration for referrals; fee-for-service arrangements are not prohibited.

7.2 Prior to entering into the therapeutic or supervisory relationship, marriage and family therapists clearly disclose and explain to clients and supervisees: (a) all financial arrangements and fees related to professional services, including charges for canceled or missed appointments; (b) the use of collection agencies or legal measures for nonpayment; and (c) the procedure for obtaining payment from the client, to the extent allowed by law, if payment is denied by the third-party payor. Once services have begun, therapists provide reasonable notice of any changes in fees or other charges.

7.3 Marriage and family therapists give reasonable notice to clients with unpaid balances of their intent to seek collection by agency or legal recourse. When such action is taken, therapists will not disclose clinical information.

7.4 Marriage and family therapists represent facts truthfully to clients, third-party payors, and supervisees regarding services rendered.

7.5 Marriage and family therapists ordinarily refrain from accepting goods and services from clients in return for services rendered. Bartering for professional services may be conducted only if: (a) the supervisee or client requests it, (b) the relationship is not exploitative, (c) the professional relationship is not distorted, and (d) a clear written contract is established.

7.6 Marriage and family therapists may not withhold records under their immediate control that are requested and needed for a client's treatment solely because payment has not been received for past services, except as otherwise provided by law.

PRINCIPLE VIII. ADVERTISING

Marriage and family therapists engage in appropriate informational activities, including those that enable the public, referral sources, or others to choose professional services on an informed basis.

8.1 Marriage and family therapists accurately represent their competencies, education, training, and experience relevant to their practice of marriage and family therapy.

8.2 Marriage and family therapists ensure that advertisements and publications in any media (such as directories, announcements, business cards, newspapers, radio, television, Internet, and facsimiles) convey information that is necessary for the public to make an appropriate selection of professional services. Information could include: (a) office information, such as name, address, telephone number, credit card acceptability, fees, languages spoken, and office hours; (b) qualifying clinical degree (see subprinciple 8.5); (c) other earned degrees (see subprinciple 8.5) and state or provincial licensures and/or certifications; (d) AAMFT clinical member status; and (e) description of practice.

8.3 Marriage and family therapists do not use names that could mislead the public concerning the identity, responsibility, source, and status of those practicing under that name, and do not hold themselves out as being partners or associates of a firm if they are not.

8.4 Marriage and family therapists do not use any professional identification (such as a business card, office sign, letterhead, Internet, or telephone or association directory listing) if it includes a statement or claim that is false, fraudulent, misleading, or deceptive.

8.5 In representing their educational qualifications, marriage and family therapists list and claim as evidence only those earned degrees: (a) from institutions accredited by regional accreditation sources recognized by the United States Department of Education, (b) from institutions recognized by states or provinces that license or certify marriage and family therapists, or (c) from equivalent foreign institutions.

8.6 Marriage and family therapists correct, wherever possible, false, misleading, or inaccurate information and representations made by others concerning the therapist's qualifications, services, or products.

8.7 Marriage and family therapists make certain that the qualifications of their employees or supervisees are represented in a manner that is not false, misleading, or deceptive.

8.8 Marriage and family therapists do not represent themselves as providing specialized services unless they have the appropriate education, training, or supervised experience.

Appendix F

American Psychiatric Association

The Principles of Medical Ethics

With Annotations Especially Applicable to Psychiatry
2006 Edition

In 1973, the American Psychiatric Association (APA) published the first edition of *The Principles of Medical Ethics With Annotations Especially Applicable to Psychiatry*. Subsequently, revisions were published as the APA Board of Trustees and the APA Assembly approved additional annotations. In July of 1980, the American Medical Association (AMA) approved a new version of the *Principles of Medical Ethics* (the first revision since 1957), and the APA Ethics Committee incorporated many of its annotations into the new *Principles*, which resulted in the 1981 edition and subsequent revisions. This version includes changes to the *Principles* approved by the AMA in 2001.

FOREWORD

All physicians should practice in accordance with the medical code of ethics set forth in the *Principles of Medical Ethics* of the American Medical Association. An up-to-date expression and elaboration of these statements is found in the Opinions and Reports of the Council on Ethical and Judicial Affairs of the American Medical Association. Psychiatrists are strongly advised to be familiar with these documents.

However, these general guidelines have sometimes been difficult to interpret for psychiatry, so further annotations to the basic principles are offered in this document. While psychiatrists have the same goals as all physicians, there are special ethical problems in psychiatric practice that differ in coloring and degree from ethical problems in other branches of medical practice, even though the basic principles are the same. The annotations are not designed as absolutes and will be revised from time to time so as to be applicable to current practices and problems.

Following are the AMA *Principles of Medical Ethics*, printed in their entirety, and then each principle printed separately along with an annotation especially applicable to psychiatry.

PRINCIPLES OF MEDICAL ETHICS AMERICAN MEDICAL ASSOCIATION

Preamble

The medical profession has long subscribed to a body of ethical statements developed primarily for the benefit of the patient. As a member of this profession, a physician must recognize responsibility to patients first and foremost, as well as to society, to other health professionals, and to self. The following *Principles* adopted by the American Medical Association are not laws, but standards of conduct which define the essentials of honorable behavior for the physician.

Reprinted with permission of the American Psychiatric Association.

Section 1

A physician shall be dedicated to providing competent medical care, with compassion and respect for human dignity and rights.

Section 2

A physician shall uphold the standards of professionalism, be honest in all professional interactions, and strive to report physicians deficient in character or competence, or engaging in fraud or deception, to appropriate entities.

Section 3

A physician shall respect the law and also recognize a responsibility to seek changes in those requirements which are contrary to the best interests of the patient.

Section 4

A physician shall respect the rights of patients, colleagues, and other health professionals, and shall safeguard patient confidences and privacy within the constraints of the law.

Section 5

A physician shall continue to study, apply, and advance scientific knowledge, maintain a commitment to medical education, make relevant information available to patients, colleagues, and the public, obtain consultation, and use the talents of other health professionals when indicated.

Section 6

A physician shall, in the provision of appropriate patient care, except in emergencies, be free to choose whom to serve, with whom to associate, and the environment in which to provide medical care.

Section 7

A physician shall recognize a responsibility to participate in activities contributing to the improvement of the community and the betterment of public health.

Section 8

A physician shall, while caring for a patient, regard responsibility to the patient as paramount.

Section 9

A physician shall support access to medical care for all people.

PRINCIPLES WITH ANNOTATIONS

Following are each of the AMA *Principles of Medical Ethics* printed separately along with annotations especially applicable to psychiatry.

Preamble

The medical profession has long subscribed to a body of ethical statements developed primarily for the benefit of the patient. As a member of this profession, a physician must recognize responsibility to patients first and foremost, as well as to society, to other health professionals, and to self. The following Principles adopted by the American Medical Association are not laws, but standards of conduct which define the essentials of honorable behavior for the physician.

Section 1

A physician shall be dedicated to providing competent medical care with compassion and respect for human dignity and rights.

1. A psychiatrist shall not gratify his or her own needs by exploiting the patient. The psychiatrist shall be ever vigilant about the impact that his or her conduct has upon the boundaries of the doctor patient relationship, and thus upon the well-being of the patient. These requirements become particularly important because of the essentially private, highly personal, and sometimes intensely emotional nature of the relationship established with the psychiatrist.

2. A psychiatrist should not be a party to any type of policy that excludes, segregates, or demeans the dignity of any patient because of ethnic origin, race, sex, creed, age, socioeconomic status, or sexual orientation.

3. In accord with the requirements of law and accepted medical practice, it is ethical for a physician to submit his or her work to peer review and to the ultimate authority of the medical staff executive body and the hospital administration and its governing body. In case of dispute, the ethical psychiatrist has the following steps available:

a. Seek appeal from the medical staff decision to a joint conference committee, including members of the medical staff executive committee and the executive committee of the governing board. At this appeal, the ethical psychiatrist could request that outside opinions be considered.
b. Appeal to the governing body itself.
c. Appeal to state agencies regulating licensure of hospitals if, in the particular state, they concern themselves with matters of professional competency and quality of care.
d. Attempt to educate colleagues through development of research projects and data and presentations at professional meetings and in professional journals.
e. Seek redress in local courts, perhaps through an enjoining injunction against the governing body.
f. Public education as carried out by an ethical psychiatrist would not utilize appeals based solely upon emotion, but would be presented in a professional way and without any potential exploitation of patients through testimonials.

4. A psychiatrist should not be a participant in a legally authorized execution.

Section 2

A physician shall uphold the standards of professionalism, be honest in all professional interactions and strive to report physicians deficient in character or competence, or engaging in fraud or deception to appropriate entities.

1. The requirement that the physician conduct himself/herself with propriety in his or her profession and in all the actions of his or her life is especially important in the case of the psychiatrist because the patient tends to model his or her behavior after that of his or her psychiatrist by identification. Further, the necessary intensity of the treatment relationship may tend to activate sexual and other needs and fantasies on the part of both patient and psychiatrist, while weakening the objectivity necessary for control. Additionally, the inherent inequality in the doctor-patient relationship may lead to exploitation of the patient. Sexual activity with a current or former patient is unethical.

2. The psychiatrist should diligently guard against exploiting information furnished by the patient and should not use the unique position of power afforded him/her by the psychotherapeutic situation to influence the patient in any way not directly relevant to the treatment goals.

3. A psychiatrist who regularly practices outside his or her area of professional competence should be considered unethical. Determination of professional competence should be made by peer review boards or other appropriate bodies.

4. Special consideration should be given to those psychiatrists who, because of mental illness, jeopardize the welfare of their patients and their own reputations and practices. It is ethical, even encouraged, for another psychiatrist to intercede in such situations.

5. Psychiatric services, like all medical services, are dispensed in the context of a contractual arrangement between the patient and the physician. The provisions of the contractual arrangement, which are binding on the physician as well as on the patient, should be explicitly established.

6. It is ethical for the psychiatrist to make a charge for a missed appointment when this falls within the terms of the specific contractual agreement with the patient. Charging for a missed appointment or for one not canceled 24 hours in advance need not, in itself, be considered unethical if a patient is fully advised that the physician will make such a charge. The practice, however, should be resorted to infrequently and always with the utmost consider-

ation for the patient and his or her circumstances.

7. An arrangement in which a psychiatrist provides supervision or administration to other physicians or nonmedical persons for a percentage of their fees or gross income is not acceptable; this would constitute fee splitting. In a team of practitioners, or a multidisciplinary team, it is ethical for the psychiatrist to receive income for administration, research, education, or consultation. This should be based on a mutually agreed-upon and set fee or salary, open to renegotiation when a change in the time demand occurs. (See also Section 5, Annotations 2, 3, and 4.)

Section 3

A physician shall respect the law and also recognize a responsibility to seek changes in those requirements which are contrary to the best interests of the patient.

1. It would seem self-evident that a psychiatrist who is a law-breaker might be ethically unsuited to practice his or her profession. When such illegal activities bear directly upon his or her practice, this would obviously be the case. However, in other instances, illegal activities such as those concerning the right to protest social injustices might not bear on either the image of the psychiatrist or the ability of the specific psychiatrist to treat his or her patient ethically and well. While no committee or board could offer prior assurance that any illegal activity would not be considered unethical, it is conceivable that an individual could violate a law without being guilty of professionally unethical behavior. Physicians lose no right of citizenship on entry into the profession of medicine.

2. Where not specifically prohibited by local laws governing medical practice, the practice of acupuncture by a psychiatrist is not unethical per se. The psychiatrist should have professional competence in the use of acupuncture. Or, if he or she is supervising the use of acupuncture by nonmedical individuals, he or she should provide proper medical supervision. (See also Section 5, Annotations 3 and 4.)

Section 4

A physician shall respect the rights of patients, colleagues, and other health professionals, and shall safeguard patient confidences and privacy within the constraints of the law.

1. Psychiatric records, including even the identification of a person as a patient, must be protected with extreme care. Confidentiality is essential to psychiatric treatment. This is based in part on the special nature of psychiatric therapy as well as on the traditional ethical relationship between physician and patient. Growing concern regarding the civil rights of patients and the possible adverse effects of computerization, duplication equipment, and data banks makes the dissemination of confidential information an increasing hazard. Because of the sensitive and private nature of the information with which the psychiatrist deals, he or she must be circumspect in the information that he or she chooses to disclose to others about a patient. The welfare of the patient must be a continuing consideration.

2. A psychiatrist may release confidential information only with the authorization of the patient or under proper legal compulsion. The continuing duty of the psychiatrist to protect the patient includes fully apprising him/her of the connotations of waiving the privilege of privacy. This may become an issue when the patient is being investigated by a government agency, is applying for a position, or is involved in legal action. The same principles apply to the release of information concerning treatment to medical departments of government agencies, business organizations, labor unions, and insurance companies. Information gained in confidence about patients seen in student health services should not be released without the students' explicit permission.

3. Clinical and other materials used in teaching and writing must be adequately disguised in order to preserve the anonymity of the individuals involved.

4. The ethical responsibility of maintaining confidentiality holds equally for the consultations in which the patient may not have been

present and in which the consultee was not a physician. In such instances, the physician consultant should alert the consultee to his or her duty of confidentiality.

5. Ethically, the psychiatrist may disclose only that information which is relevant to a given situation. He or she should avoid offering speculation as fact. Sensitive information such as an individual's sexual orientation or fantasy material is usually unnecessary.

6. Psychiatrists are often asked to examine individuals for security purposes, to determine suitability for various jobs, and to determine legal competence. The psychiatrist must fully describe the nature and purpose and lack of confidentiality of the examination to the examinee at the beginning of the examination.

7. Careful judgment must be exercised by the psychiatrist in order to include, when appropriate, the parents or guardian in the treatment of a minor. At the same time, the psychiatrist must assure the minor proper confidentiality.

8. When, in the clinical judgment of the treating psychiatrist, the risk of danger is deemed to be significant, the psychiatrist may reveal confidential information disclosed by the patient.

9. When the psychiatrist is ordered by the court to reveal the confidences entrusted to him/her by patients, he or she may comply or he/she may ethically hold the right to dissent within the framework of the law. When the psychiatrist is in doubt, the right of the patient to confidentiality and, by extension, to unimpaired treatment should be given priority. The psychiatrist should reserve the right to raise the question of adequate need for disclosure. In the event that the necessity for legal disclosure is demonstrated by the court, the psychiatrist may request the right to disclosure of only that information which is relevant to the legal question at hand.

10. With regard for the person's dignity and privacy and with truly informed consent, it is ethical to present a patient to a scientific gathering if the confidentiality of the presentation is understood and accepted by the audience.

11. It is ethical to present a patient or former patient to a public gathering or to the news media only if the patient is fully informed of enduring loss of confidentiality, is competent, and consents in writing without coercion.

12. When involved in funded research, the ethical psychiatrist will advise human subjects of the funding source, retain his or her freedom to reveal data and results, and follow all appropriate and current guidelines relative to human subject protection.

13. Ethical considerations in medical practice preclude the psychiatric evaluation of any person charged with criminal acts prior to access to, or availability of, legal counsel. The only exception is the rendering of care to the person for the sole purpose of medical treatment.

14. Sexual involvement between a faculty member or supervisor and a trainee or student, in those situations in which an abuse of power can occur, often takes advantage of inequalities in the working relationship and may be unethical because:

a. Any treatment of a patient being supervised may be deleteriously affected.
b. It may damage the trust relationship between teacher and student.
c. Teachers are important professional role models for their trainees and affect their trainees' future professional behavior.

Section 5

A physician shall continue to study, apply, and advance scientific knowledge, maintain a commitment to medical education, make relevant information available to patients, colleagues, and the public, obtain consultation, and use the talents of other health professionals when indicated.

1. Psychiatrists are responsible for their own continuing education and should be mindful of the fact that theirs must be a lifetime of learning.

2. In the practice of his or her specialty, the psychiatrist consults, associates, collaborates, or integrates his or her work with that of many professionals, including psychologists, psychometricians, social workers, alcoholism counselors, marriage counselors, public health nurses, and the like. Furthermore, the nature of modern psychiatric practice extends his or her contacts to such people as teachers, juvenile and adult

probation officers, attorneys, welfare workers, agency volunteers, and neighborhood aides. In referring patients for treatment, counseling, or rehabilitation to any of these practitioners, the psychiatrist should ensure that the allied professional or paraprofessional with whom he or she is dealing is a recognized member of his or her own discipline and is competent to carry out the therapeutic task required. The psychiatrist should have the same attitude toward members of the medical profession to whom he or she refers patients. Whenever he or she has reason to doubt the training, skill, or ethical qualifications of the allied professional, the psychiatrist should not refer cases to him/her.

3. When the psychiatrist assumes a collaborative or supervisory role with another mental health worker, he or she must expend sufficient time to assure that proper care is given. It is contrary to the interests of the patient and to patient care if the psychiatrist allows himself/herself to be used as a figurehead.

4. In relationships between psychiatrists and practicing licensed psychologists, the physician should not delegate to the psychologist or, in fact, to any nonmedical person any matter requiring the exercise of professional medical judgment.

5. The psychiatrist should agree to the request of a patient for consultation or to such a request from the family of an incompetent or minor patient. The psychiatrist may suggest possible consultants, but the patient or family should be given free choice of the consultant. If the psychiatrist disapproves of the professional qualifications of the consultant or if there is a difference of opinion that the primary therapist cannot resolve, he or she may, after suitable notice, withdraw from the case. If this disagreement occurs within an institution or agency framework, the differences should be resolved by the mediation or arbitration of higher professional authority within the institution or agency.

Section 6

A physician shall, in the provision of appropriate patient care, except in emergencies, be free to choose whom to serve, with whom to associate, and the environment in which to provide medical care.

1. Physicians generally agree that the doctor-patient relationship is such a vital factor in effective treatment of the patient that preservation of optimal conditions for development of a sound working relationship between a doctor and his or her patient should take precedence over all other considerations. Professional courtesy may lead to poor psychiatric care for physicians and their families because of embarrassment over the lack of a complete give-and-take contract.

2. An ethical psychiatrist may refuse to provide psychiatric treatment to a person who, in the psychiatrist's opinion, cannot be diagnosed as having a mental illness amenable to psychiatric treatment.

Section 7

A physician shall recognize a responsibility to participate in activities contributing to the improvement of the community and the betterment of public health.

1. Psychiatrists should foster the cooperation of those legitimately concerned with the medical, psychological, social, and legal aspects of mental health and illness. Psychiatrists are encouraged to serve society by advising and consulting with the executive, legislative, and judiciary branches of the government. A psychiatrist should clarify whether he/she speaks as an individual or as a representative of an organization. Furthermore, psychiatrists should avoid cloaking their public statements with the authority of the profession (e.g., "Psychiatrists know that ...").

2. Psychiatrists may interpret and share with the public their expertise in the various psychosocial issues that may affect mental health and illness. Psychiatrists should always be mindful of their separate roles as dedicated citizens and as experts in psychological medicine.

3. On occasion psychiatrists are asked for an opinion about an individual who is in the light of public attention or who has disclosed information about himself/herself through public media. In such circumstances, a psychiatrist may share with the public his or her expertise about psychiatric issues in general. However, it is unethical for a psychiatrist to offer

a professional opinion unless he or she has conducted an examination and has been granted proper authorization for such a statement.

4. The psychiatrist may permit his or her certification to be used for the involuntary treatment of any person only following his or her personal examination of that person. To do so, he or she must find that the person, because of mental illness, cannot form a judgment as to what is in his/her own best interests and that, without such treatment, substantial impairment is likely to occur to the person or others.

5. Psychiatrists shall not participate in torture.

Section 8

A physician shall, while caring for a patient, regard responsibility to the patient as paramount.

New section recently adopted by the AMA.

Section 9

A physician shall support access to medical care for all people.

New section recently adopted by the AMA.

Index